About the author

Respected wine critic and vigneron James Halliday AM has a career that spans forty-five years, but he is most widely known for his witty and informative writing about wine. As one of the founders of Brokenwood in the Lower Hunter Valley, New South Wales, and thereafter of Coldstream Hills in the Yarra Valley, Victoria, James is an unmatched authority on every aspect of the wine industry, from the planting and pruning of vines through to the creation and marketing of the finished product. His winemaking has led him to sojourns in Bordeaux and Burgundy, and he has had a long career as a wine judge in Australia and overseas. In 1995 he received the wine industry's ultimate accolade, the Maurice O'Shea Award. In 2010 James was made a Member of the Order of Australia.

James has written or contributed to more than 70 books on wine since he began writing in 1979. His books have been translated into Japanese, French, German, Danish, Icelandic and Polish, and have been published in the United Kingdom and the United States, as well as in Australia. He is the author of *Varietal Wines*, *James Halliday's Wine Atlas of Australia* and *The Australian Wine Encyclopedia*.

Halliday
WINE COMPANION

ESTABLISHED 1986 – WINECOMPANION.COM.AU

The bestselling and
definitive guide to
Australian wine

2016

hardie grant books

Wine zones and regions of Australia

0 ———— 500 km

120°

INDIAN

20°

Tropic of Capricorn

OCEAN

30°

WEST
AUSTI

Perth •

NEW SOUTH WALES			
WINE ZONE		WINE REGION	
Big Rivers	(A)	Murray Darling	1
		Perricoota	2
		Riverina	3
		Swan Hill	4
Central Ranges	(B)	Cowra	5
		Mudgee	6
		Orange	7
Hunter Valley	(C)	Hunter	8
		Upper Hunter	9
Northern Rivers	(D)	Hastings River	10
Northern Slopes	(E)	New England	11
South Coast	(F)	Shoalhaven Coast	12
		Southern Highlands	13
Southern New South Wales	(G)	Canberra District	14
		Gundagai	15
		Hilltops	16
		Tumbarumba	17
Western Plains	(H)		

SOUTH AUSTRALIA			
WINE ZONE		WINE REGION	
Adelaide Super Zone includes Mount Lofty Ranges, Fleurieu and Barossa wine regions			
Barossa		Barossa Valley	18
		Eden Valley	19
Fleurieu	(J)	Currency Creek	20
		Kangaroo Island	21
		Langhorne Creek	22
		McLaren Vale	23
		Southern Fleurieu	24
Mount Lofty Ranges		Adelaide Hills	25
		Adelaide Plains	26
		Clare Valley	27
Far North	(K)	Southern Flinders Ranges	28
Limestone Coast	(L)	Coonawarra	29
		Mount Benson	30
		Mount Gambier	31
		Padthaway	32
		Robe	33
		Wrattonbully	34
Lower Murray	(M)	Riverland	35
The Peninsulas	(N)	Southern Eyre Peninsula*	36

VICTORIA			
WINE ZONE		WINE REGION	
Central Victoria	(P)	Bendigo	37
		Goulburn Valley	38
		Heathcote	39
		Strathbogie Ranges	40
Gippsland	(Q)	Upper Goulburn	41
		Alpine Valleys	42
North East Victoria	(R)	Beechworth	43
		Glenrowan	44
		King Valley	45
		Rutherglen	46
North West Victoria	(S)	Murray Darling	47
		Swan Hill	48
Port Phillip	(T)	Geelong	49
		Macedon Ranges	50
		Mornington Peninsula	51
		Sunbury	52
		Yarra Valley	53
Western Victoria	(U)	Ballarat*	54
		Grampians	55
		Henty	56
		Pyrenees	57

* For more information see page 48.

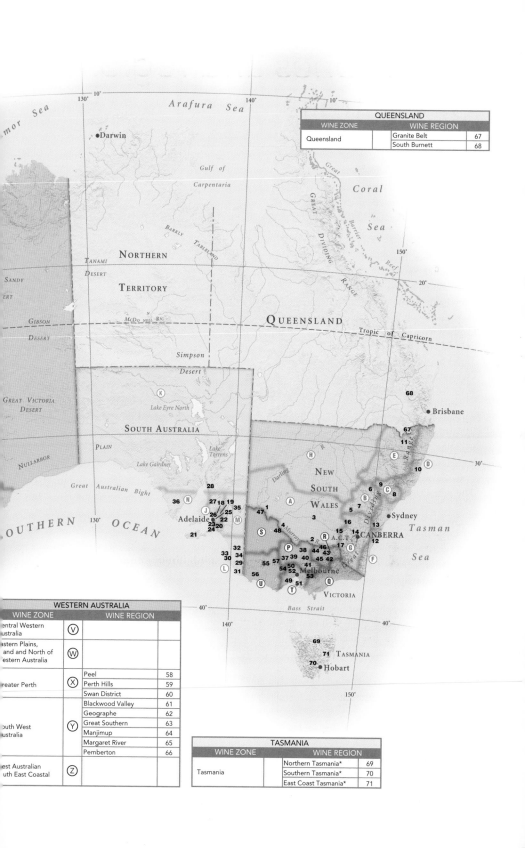

Published in 2015 by Hardie Grant Books

Hardie Grant Books (Australia)
Ground Floor, Building 1
658 Church Street
Richmond, Victoria 3121
www.hardiegrant.com.au

Hardie Grant Books (UK)
5th and 6th Floors
52–54 Southwark Street
London SE1 1UN
www.hardiegrant.co.uk

The *Australian Wine Companion* is a joint venture between James Halliday and
Explore Australia Pty Ltd.

The map in this publication incorporates data copyright © Commonwealth of Australia
(Geoscience Australia) 2004. Geoscience Australia has not evaluated the data as altered and
incorporated within this publication and therefore gives no warranty regarding accuracy,
completeness, currency or suitability for any particular purpose.

Australian wine zones and wine regions data copyright © Australian Wine and
Brandy Corporation, April 2005

ISBN 978 1 74379 004 5

Typeset by Megan Ellis
Cover design by Design by Pidgeon
Author photograph by Julian Kingma
Printed and bound in Australia by McPherson's Printing Group

Contents

Introduction

The world of wine is fermenting vigorously, streams flowing in all directions, some good, some not. Exports, domestic sales, taxes, climate change and health are all issues of everyday concern.

The news on exports is unambiguously good. On the moving annual total to March 31, 2015, exports increased by 3.9% to $1.85 billion. Even better was the increase in total exports to China by 20% to $242 million; within that total, wines in the $7.50 to $9.99 per litre FOB soared by 28% to 2.6 million litres, while the $10 and above category increased by 4% to 4.4 million litres, making China Australia's largest market for wines in the super-premium sector, with ongoing growth. The picture is similar throughout the rest of Asia, so it's strange language when people talk or write about 'the potential' of China.

The value of domestic wine sales through retail shops increased by 0.8% for the 12 months to February 1, 2015, with sales of beer, spirits and RTDs all declining. The volume decreased for all categories, wine suffering the least.

If present trends continue, the value of wine sales will exceed that of beer. The elephant in the room is the mooted change in the way wine is taxed, the outcome depending on the detail of the changes. The concern is that small and medium-sized wineries will be more affected than the large wineries by a change to a volumetric tax.

There is incessant chatter across radio, the internet and newsprint about the deadly consequences of global warming, and the need for immediate action inter alia by grapegrowers and winemakers. The inconvenient truth is that five of the last six vintages in eastern Australia, and all six in Western Australia, have enjoyed a series of stellar vintages.

The one exception was the cold and wet 2011 vintage, only the Hunter Valley escaping. So how can it be that, despite the apparent heat and early vintages, the quality has been so high, and in 2015 perfect acidity has been a feature? Dr John Gladstones (indirectly) provides the answer: if temperature and CO_2 rise together, yield will increase, the vines will have greater efficiency of water use, and the ripening process will be quicker, all without any loss of quality.

The health issue is not going to go away, despite the fact that consumption of alcohol has decreased steadily over the past six years. Yes, abuse of alcohol in the home, on the streets and in Indigenous communities has to be minimised. But the fact that wine is by far the category of alcohol least likely to be abused and trigger violence is deliberately ignored by the anti-alcohol lobby.

So, it would seem, is the beneficial effect of moderate wine consumption in combating cardiovascular disease, still the largest cause of death in the western world. Despite the epidemiological evidence from dozens of studies over the past 50 years establishing the benefits of moderate consumption of wine, health warnings about the possible dangers of even light consumption to pregnant women now appear on all wine labels. No one, it seems, has paused to think about the 1200-year consumption of wine in western Europe.

How to use this book

Wineries

Tahbilk

254 O'Neils Road, Tabilk, Vic 3608 **Region** Nagambie Lakes
T (03) 5794 2555 **www**.tahbilk.com.au **Open** Mon–Sat 9–5, Sun 11–5
Winemaker Alister Purbrick, Neil Larson, Alan George **Est.** 1860 **Dozens** 100 000
Vyds 221.5ha
A winery steeped in tradition (with National Trust classification), which should be visited at least once by every wine-conscious Australian, and which makes wines – particularly red wines – utterly in keeping with that tradition. The essence of that heritage comes in the form of the tiny quantities of Shiraz made from vines planted in 1860. Serendipitous, perhaps, but the current release wines are absolutely outstanding. A founding member of Australia's First Families of Wine. 2016 *Wine Companion* Winery of the Year. Exports to all major markets.

Winery name   Tahbilk

The name appearing on the front label as the producer is used throughout the book.

Winery rating ★★★★★

I look at the ratings for this and the previous two years; if the wines tasted this year justified a higher rating than last year, that higher rating has been given. If, on the other hand, the wines are of lesser quality, I take into account the track record over the past two years (or longer where the winery is well known) and make a judgement call on whether it should retain its ranking or be given a lesser one. In what I call the mercy rating, in most instances a demotion is no more than half a star. Where no wines were submitted by a well-rated winery with a track record of providing samples, I may use my discretion to roll over last year's rating.

While there are (only) 1317 wineries profiled in this edition, there are more than 2800 wineries to be found on www.winecompanion.com.au.

The percentage at the end of each rating below is that of the total number of wineries in the *Wine Companion* database at the time of going to print. Two caveats: first, I retain a discretionary right to depart from the normal criteria. Second, the basis of the rating will best be understood on the website, where all wine ratings appear.

Some may think my ratings are too generous, but less than half (46.8%) of the wineries in our database, believed, or known to be, active, are given ratings in this book, spread across the eight categories. Moreover, if I were to reduce the number of wineries in each category by (say) 50%, the relative ranking would not change, other than a massive increase in the NR category, providing no useful guidance for the reader.

★★★★★ Outstanding winery regularly producing wines of exemplary quality and typicity. Will have at least two wines rated at 95 points or above, and had a five-star rating for the previous two years. 282 wineries, 10%

Where the winery name itself is printed in red, it is a winery generally acknowledged to have a long track record of excellence in the context of its region – truly the best of the best. 102 wineries, 3.6%

★★★★★ Outstanding winery capable of producing wines of very high quality, and did so this year. Also will usually have at least two wines rated at 95 points or above. 204 wineries, 7.2%

★★★★☆ Excellent winery able to produce wines of high to very high quality, knocking on the door of a five-star rating. Will normally have one wine rated at 95 points or above, and two (or more) at 90 and above, others 87–89. 271 wineries, 9.6%

★★★★ Very good producer of wines with class and character. Will have two (or more) wines rated at 90 points and above (or possibly one at 95 and above). 311 wineries, 11%

★★★☆ A solid, usually reliable, maker of good, sometimes very good wines. Will have one wine at 90 points and above, others 86–89. 102 wineries, 3.6%

★★★ A typically good winery, but often has a few lesser wines. Will have wines at 86–89 points. 36 wineries, 1.3%

NR The NR rating mainly appears on www.winecompanion.com.au. The rating is given in a range of circumstances: where there have been no tastings in the 12-month period; where there have been tastings, but with no wines scoring more than 88 points; or where the tastings have, for one reason or another, proved not to fairly reflect the reputation of a winery with a track record of success. NR wineries in the book are generally new wineries with no wine entries. 4 wineries, 0.14%

Contact Details 254 O'Neils Road, Tabilk, Vic 3608 **T** (03) 5794 2555

The details are usually those of the winery and cellar door, but in a few instances may simply be a postal address; this occurs when the wine is made at another winery or wineries, and is sold only through the website and/or retail outlets.

Region Nagambie Lakes

A full list of Zones, Regions and Subregions appears on pages 48–51. Occasionally you will see 'Various' as the region. This means the wine is made from purchased grapes, from a number of regions – often a winery without a vineyard of its own.

www.tahbilk.com.au

An important reference point, normally containing material not found (for space reasons) in this book.

Open Mon–Sat 9–5, Sun 11–5

Although a winery might be listed as not open or only open on weekends, some may in fact be prepared to open by appointment. Many will, some won't; a telephone call will establish whether it is possible or not. For space reasons, we have simplified the opening hours listings, taking out 'or by appt' as superfluous; also, convoluted opening hours dictated by winter, summer or whatever, do not appear. The assumption is the details can be found via their website.

Winemaker Alister Purbrick, Neil Larson, Alan George

In all but the smallest producers, the winemaker is simply the head of a team; there may be many executive winemakers actually responsible for specific wines in the medium to large companies (80 000 dozens and upwards). Once again, space constraints mean usually only two or three winemakers are named, even if they are part of a larger team.

Est. 1860

Keep in mind that some makers consider the year in which they purchased the land to be the year of establishment, others the year in which they first planted grapes, others the year they first made wine, and so on. There may also be minor complications where there has been a change of ownership or a break in production.

Vyds 221.5ha

Shows the hectares of vineyard(s) owned by the winery.

Dozens 100 000

This figure (representing the number of 9-litre/12-bottle cases produced each year) is merely an indication of the size of the operation. Some winery entries do not feature a production figure; this is either because the winery (principally, but not exclusively, the large companies) regards this information as confidential.

Summary A winery steeped in tradition (with National Trust classification), which should be visited at least once by every wine-conscious Australian …

Surely self-explanatory, except that I have tried to vary the subjects I discuss in this part of the winery entry.

New wineries

 The vine leaf symbol indicates the 92 wineries that are new entries in this year's *Wine Companion*.

New feature: Ten of the best value wineries

In previous years, only one Best Value Winery was chosen. I have extended the choice to ten, but continue to award the top winery of this category.

Tasting notes

There has been a progressive adoption of the 100-point system in wine shows and in reviews by other commentators. The majority follow the system outlined below, which I used in precisely this form in the 2015 *Wine Companion*. Space means that only 3859 notes are printed in full in this book, with points, drink-to dates and prices for a further 2629 wines. Tasting notes for all wines receiving 84 points or above appear on www.winecompanion.com.au. See also page 20.

Ratings

Points	Medal	Glasses	Description
97–99	GOLD	🍷🍷🍷🍷🍷	**Exceptional.** Wines that have won a major trophy or trophies in important wine shows, or are of that standard.
95–96	GOLD	🍷🍷🍷🍷🍷	**Outstanding.** Wines of gold medal standard, usually with a great pedigree.
94	SILVER	🍷🍷🍷🍷🍷	Wines on the cusp of gold medal status, virtually indistinguishable from those wines receiving 95 points.
90–93	SILVER	🍷🍷🍷🍷🍷	**Highly Recommended.** Wines of silver medal standard; wines of great quality, style and character, and worthy of a place in any cellar.
89	BRONZE	🍷🍷🍷🍷	**Recommended.** Wines on the cusp of silver medal standard, the difference purely a judgement call.
86–88	BRONZE	🍷🍷🍷🍷	Wines of bronze medal standard; well-produced, flavoursome wines, usually not requiring cellaring.
		✪	**Special Value.** Wines considered to offer special value for money within the context of their glass symbol status.
84–85		🍷🍷🍷🍷	**Acceptable.** Wines of good commercial quality, free from significant fault.
80–83		🍷🍷🍷	**Over to You.** Everyday wines, without much character, and/or somewhat faulty.

🍷🍷🍷🍷🍷 **Museum Release The Creation Barossa Valley Shiraz 2009**
Has retained excellent hue; this is truly liquid history, as every one of the vines was planted in 1860, with no replants – just ever-increasing gaps where vines have died. This is a super-elegant, perfectly balanced, medium-bodied wine ... Screwcap. 12.5% alc. **Rating 98 To 2050 $290**

The tasting note opens with the vintage of the wine tasted. This tasting note will have been made within the 12 months prior to publication. Even that is a long time, and during the life of this book the wine will almost certainly change. More than this, remember the tasting is a highly subjective and imperfect art. The price of the wine is listed where information is available. Tasting notes for wines 95 points and above are printed in red.

The initials CM or TS appearing at the end of a tasting note signifies that Campbell Mattinson or Tyson Stelzer tasted the wine and provided the tasting note and rating.

To 2050

Rather than give a span of drinking years, I have simply provided a (conservative) 'drink-to' date. Modern winemaking is such that, even if a wine has 10 or 20 years' future during which it will gain greater complexity, it can be enjoyed at any time over the intervening months and years.

Screwcap

This is the closure used for this particular wine. The closures in use for the wines tasted are (in descending order): screwcap 90.7% (last year 91.7%), one-piece natural cork 5.5% (last year 4.6%), Diam 3.1% (last year 3%). The remaining 0.7% (in approximate order of importance) comprises ProCork, Twin Top, Crown Seal, Zork and Vino-Lok. I believe the percentage of screwcap-closed wines will continue to rise for red wines; 98.4% (last year 97.6%) of white wines tasted are screwcapped, leaving little room for any further increase.

12.5% alc

As with closures, I have endeavoured to always include this piece of information, which is in one sense self-explanatory. What is less obvious is the increasing concern of many Australian winemakers about rising alcohol levels, and much research and practical experimentation (picking earlier, higher fermentation temperatures in open fermenters, etc.) is occurring. Reverse osmosis and yeast selection are two of the options available to decrease higher than desirable alcohol levels. Recent changes to domestic and export labelling mean the stated alcohol must be within 0.5% of that obtained by analysis.

$290

I use the price provided by the winery. It should be regarded as a guide, particularly if wine is purchased retail.

Winery of the year

Tahbilk

When brooding about the selection of Winery of the Year, I recalled that in 1994 the Maurice O'Shea Award had been given to Jacob's Creek, and in 2002 to the Australian Wine Research Institute, both examples of lateral thinking that (in very different ways) made my choice of Tahbilk seem conventional. But prior awards for the *Companion's* Winery of the Year had been selected by currently available wines as the main criteria.

The liquid history of Tahbilk's wine portfolio is unique. Its 1860 Vines Shiraz is made from vines that were all planted in 1860, with no replacement vines to fill gaps created by vines dying through disease – or frost, as in 2007, when 40% of the vines were killed. The result is that in a good year, production will only be 150 dozen. After 18 months' maturation in French oak, the wine is bottled and held in the Tahbilk cellars for four years before release. It is exquisitely rare liquid history, and of great quality.

Then there is the block of marsanne planted in 1927, now kept separate from the major annual release, and held in bottle for a prodigious seven years before release, the longest maturation for any Australian table wine; it is arguably as remarkable as the 100 years for each new vintage of Seppeltsfield's Para.

The other two flagbearers are the twin Eric Stevens Purbrick Shiraz and Cabernet Sauvignon wines, the former largely from 80-year-old vines, the latter from vines with an average age of 40 years. Both these wines are held in bottle for four years, like the 1860 Vines, and released when six years old.

These wines are made in a winery that breathes history. The first underground cellar was constructed in 1860; the 'new' cellar in 1875, running at right angles to the first; and in 1882 the four-storey tower (still depicted on the labels of Tahbilk's commercial wines) was built, the first level used for winemaking until the 1940s.

The 227 hectares of estate vineyards with 16 varieties are planted on a 1214-hectare property that has a frontage of 11km to the Goulburn River and 8km of permanent backwaters and creeks. The spacious winery restaurant is perched above the river, and overlooks part of a 4km eco walking circuit of paths and boardwalks that wends its way through vegetation and trees full of birdlife, with the option of taking to electric-powered undercover boats for all (30 minutes) or part of the journey.

Alister Purbrick undertook a lead role in developing the First Families of Wine, which has been an unqualified success. He has served on wine industry boards and associations with clear-eyed intelligence, unafraid to express views different from the stance of some or all of his peers. Finally, he has guided Tahbilk through a decade of financial challenges impacting on every sector of the Australian wine industry. One aspect of this success has been the enhancement of what must be one of the most successful wine clubs, connecting Tahbilk with its thousands of loyal customers.

Previous Winery of the Year winners are Paringa Estate (2007), Balnaves of Coonawarra (2008), Brookland Valley (2009), Tyrrell's (2010), Larry Cherubino Wines (2011), Port Phillip Estate/ Kooyong (2012), Kilikanoon (2013), Penfolds (2014) and Hentley Farm Wines (2015).

Winemaker of the year

Peter Fraser

There is a strong thread of karma in following Pete Fraser's journey in life from a reserve infantry officer in the Australian Army to chief winemaker of Yangarra Estate Vineyard. It was in the officers' mess that he first tasted great old Australian red wines and diverted from ideas of a career in veterinary science or straight agriculture. Instead he enrolled in the Bachelor of Agricultural Science (Oenology) at the Roseworthy campus of the University of Adelaide in 1993, aged 19.

In September '97 he was appointed winemaker at Normans Clarendon Winery. The UK importer of Normans was so impressed with the wines he asked Fraser to consult on some projects in Spain including the vintage in 1999, and as a payback he was given a three-week study tour through Bordeaux, Burgundy and the Rhône Valley, which Fraser says 'really started to shape my winemaking'. In 2000 (aged 26) he was officially appointed chief winemaker of Normans, and this brought him into contact with the Californian Jackson Family Wine Group and its plans to invest in Australia.

At the beginning of 2001 he left Normans to work with Jackson Family as a full-time consultant, and later that year helped the family acquire from Normans what is now Yangarra Estate Vineyard.

From 2003 to 2008 he made Shiraz in California for Jackson Family, and each year worked at Yangarra with vineyard manager Michael Lane. They guided the vineyard through to organic and then Biodynamic 'A' Certification.

The vineyard is now wholly focused on the grapes of the Rhône Valley. Fraser and Lane are on a journey to evaluate cinsaut, carignan, graciano, counoise and muscardin, with picpoul noir, terret noir and vaccarese around the corner. While these red varieties are the most important, viognier and roussanne will be joined with grenache blanc, bourboulenc and picpoul blanc.

He has included philosophical and practical changes in his approach to winemaking; reducing alcohol levels to 14–14.5% is one facet of the new approach.

More striking has been his willingness to embrace partial or total whole-bunch and/or whole-berry fermentation of shiraz and grenache after choosing whether or not to employ cold-soak pre-fermentation in small open fermenters, an approach more frequently encountered in cooler regions.

His use of 675-litre ceramic eggs in 2013 for red wine fermentation is another thing altogether. 'My initial interest was driven by sourcing a vessel that would not impart barrel character but would not have the "plainness" of a stainless steel vessel,' he says. 'I looked into concrete, but I feel the chemicals used in making concrete are not very friendly. The ceramic eggs are not porous, but have similar thermal properties to concrete or clay vessels. A staunch biodynamic advocate would say the shape of the egg is very important, and say that the shape causes constant thermal movement. I understand the logic, but I have not seen evidence that the lees in fact move within the wine as some of the promotional literature suggests. Disregarding any of the hocus pocus of eggs, we have been extremely happy with the results.'

Wine of the year

2014 Serrat Yarra Valley Shiraz Viognier

As the ten-month gestation of the *Wine Companion* progresses, with a four-month daily grind of tasting 80 wines day in, day out, I become totally immersed in the fabric of current Australian wines and winemaking.

Obviously enough, somewhere in the back of my mind is the task of choosing one wine out of a starting field of the 6283 wines I will have personally tasted at the end of the process, and another 2497 tasted by Campbell Mattinson.

The field auto-selects the slice of 29 table wines scoring 98 points and above. I can't include fortified wines of Seppeltsfield, Rutherglen and Glenrowan, simply because they would monopolise the award year in, year out.

Last year and this year, a wine jumped out near the end of the tasting schedule with an x-factor that took hold of all my olfactory and cerebral senses. There was no expectation this would happen – indeed it is of the essence that I have no preconceived idea if this mode of selection is used.

Taking this rationale one step further, it's more likely that sooner or later Campbell and I will somehow come up with a shortlist, taste the wines together, and agree on one wine. Without boring you, the logistics of achieving this in the frantic weeks at the end of the *Wine Companion* tasting schedule is challenging.

This year Serrat's 2014 Yarra Valley Shiraz Viognier smote my senses to the point where I came to my conclusion in a millisecond. To be sure I wasn't deluding myself, I took the bottle up to my house and drank part of it that night, the remainder the following night. Those who know of Tom Carson's track record with Pinot Noir – winning an inordinate number of trophies for Yabby Lake's Pinots, including the long talked about, but never previously achieved, awarding of the Jimmy Watson Trophy to a Pinot – might have expected it would be for his and wife Nadege's micro, estate-grown Pinot Noir, not their Shiraz Viognier.

My tasting note shows a drink-to date 30 years hence, yet the wine already has a gossamer fragrance and a glorious palate that will surely mean that precious few bottles will be intact come 2044. Finally, its price of $40 contrasts with that of the other 99-point wine (Grange): $785.

Best value winery

West Cape Howe Wines

Although West Cape Howe didn't know it, it came perilously close to receiving this award in the 2015 *Wine Companion*. While the field of contenders this year had many wineries with seriously good portfolios, West Cape Howe was clearly the best.

The reason why it was (and doubtless will continue to be) able to street the field lies in the history of very astute acquisitions of an exceptional array of vineyards and a modern 7700-tonne winery; strategic sales of assets (both vineyards and a much smaller winery) have also shaped the West Cape Howe business of today.

It is owned by four Western Australian families, headed by viticulturist Rob Quenby, who has played a key role since 1997, and long-term regional winemaker Gavin Berry, with 27 vintages in the Great Southern region under his belt.

The estate vineyards are Langton (100ha, Mount Barker), with sauvignon blanc (22ha), shiraz (21ha), chardonnay (18ha), cabernet sauvignon (16ha), semillon (12ha) and riesling (11ha); Landsdale (60ha, Mount Barker); Jindawarra (39ha, Margaret River); and Russell Road (210ha, Frankland River).

These vineyards are managed with organic practices; in spring a mineral-based fertiliser that is microbially seeded is applied where needed, and liquid kelp for leaf health likewise applied in summer. Organically approved sulphurs and copper to prevent mildew damage are the backbone of the spray program.

It is a statement of the obvious to say that even with the majority of the grapes being sold to others (and/or being custom-made into wine for pre-committed sale to others, either in bottle or in bulk) the business has great flexibility and positive cashflow. The winery is also able to contract-make wine from external vineyard sources as far afield as Margaret River, Geographe, Pemberton and Manjimup.

The winemaking team of Gavin Berry, Andrew Vasey and Caitlin Gazey is matched by the viticultural team of Rob Quenby and Glen Harding. Thus the grapes being used by West Cape Howe are specifically grown for the end use of the business, the cost of production known before the first grape is crushed.

Thus every one of the 15 wines tasted for this edition received a value symbol (from a fixed, predetermined grid for every one of the 8951 wines tasted for this edition). The prices of the five wines receiving 95 or 96 points ranged between $19 and $30; two wines with 94 points were $22 and $17 respectively. The portfolio covers Riesling, Sauvignon Blanc, Sauvignon Blanc Semillon, Chardonnay, Shiraz, Cabernet Sauvignon, Cabernet Merlot and Tempranillo.

Finally, those who work in the West Cape Howe group do so because they love the business – and the unpolluted environment in which they live.

Best new winery

Bicknell fc

The flow of new wineries into the *Wine Companion* continues to be healthy: in the 2010 edition there were 148, and in the following years there were 111, 102, 66, 94 and 80, with 92 in this edition. There have, of course, been near-deaths and deaths along the way, but the number of wineries in the *Companion* database has increased over the period from 2010 to the present total of 2816.

Bicknell fc – Bicknell family company – is owned by David Bicknell, better known for his role as chief winemaker at Oakridge, and his viticulturist wife, Nicky Harris. Since grapes are the prerequisite of wine, her career comes first. After graduating from Roseworthy, she started at Henschke (what better place could there be?), then Seppelt with both its Great Western and Drumborg vineyards, thence Coldstream Hills between 1997 and 2001. Says David, 'Her full-time role for the past 14 years has been CEO of her [and his] family of three children in the Yarra Valley, which has greatly improved her palate.'

David Bicknell is a veteran of 23 Yarra vintages, first at De Bortoli and thereafter (since 2002) at Oakridge, where he has lifted the quality of the wines to take it into the upper echelon of the Valley's wineries. It is no desk job: his hands have wine stains every day of the year: on nights and weekends from Bicknell fc, the lion's share from Oakridge.

With one exception – a Pinot Noir sourced from Lucinda Estate at Leongatha in Gippsland in 2013 – the Bicknell fc grapes since the first vintage in 2011 have been sourced from Upper Yarra Valley vineyards. As from 2014 they have all come from a single 2.5ha close-planted vineyard established by Val Stewart in 1988. Bicknell fc has leased this vineyard long-term, and will be responsible for all aspects of growing the grapes, bringing Nicky out of retirement.

The quality of the wines in this year's *Companion* is quite simply enthralling. Three of the wines received 97 points, one 96 points, the only 'miss' being the 2011 Pinot Noir. The wet, cool vintage was perfect for chardonnay, nigh on impossible for pinot noir.

Quite apart from David Bicknell's disdain for any winemaker who says he has made the perfect wine, and won't be able to make a better one in the years ahead, there is also the unknowable improvement to come from their stewardship of the Stewart vineyard. Both David and Nicky believe squeezing that last few percentage points of quality primarily comes from the vineyard, not the winery.

David Bicknell has had a long-term preference for chardonnay and pinot noir from the Upper Yarra Valley, which he is convinced provides greater fragrance, finesse and length, the area particularly suited to his preference for chardonnay picked a little earlier than that of other wineries using these grapes. Thus the three Chardonnays have alcohol levels of 12.7%, 12.8% and 13.3% respectively. This in turn means development in bottle is slowed, and drives his desire to hold them as long as possible prior to release – great for quality, but not for cashflow.

Finally, the wines are all priced below $40, variously $32 and $39. What more is there to say?

ENJOY OUR AWARD WINNING
WINE LIST ON THE GROUND

qantasepiqure.com.au

Qantas
epiQure

Best of the best by variety

I make my usual disclaimer: while there are two periods of intense tasting activity in the 12 months during which the tasting notes for this edition were made, and while some wines are tasted more than once, an overarching comparative tasting of all the best wines is simply not possible, however desirable it might be.

So the points for the individual wines stand uncorrected by the wisdom of hindsight. Nonetheless, the link between variety and region (or, if you prefer, between variety and terroir) is in most instances strikingly evident. It is for this reason that I have shown the region for each of the best wines. Medium and longer term prosperity will depend on a sense of place, of regional identity. It is also the reason for the overview of the varietal/regional mosaic on page 52.

Riesling

The spoils of war were more widely spread than last year, with Henty (Vic) providing the best wine (98 points), and Canberra (ACT), Southern Highlands (NSW) and Tasmania all represented in the top echelon (97 points). It was then left to the Clare and Eden valleys (SA) with five wines and Great Southern (also five wines) to join Henty (with three wines) to complete the list on 97 points. The next tier (96 points) included all the above regions, plus Adelaide Hills (SA), Macedon Ranges (Vic), and Pemberton (WA).

RATING	WINE	REGION
98	2004 Crawford River Reserve	Henty
97	2014 Willoughby Park Kalgan Ironrock	Albany
97	2014 Mount Majura Vineyard	Canberra District
97	2014 Grosset Polish Hill	Clare Valley
97	2014 Pikes The Merle	Clare Valley
97	2014 Wines by KT Churinga Vineyard Watervale	Clare Valley
97	2014 Hardys HRB	Clare Valley/Tasmania
97	2010 Peter Lehmann Wigan	Eden Valley
97	2014 Alkoomi Black Label	Frankland River
97	2014 Frankland Estate Isolation Ridge Vineyard	Frankland River
97	2014 Crawford River	Henty
97	2014 Seppelt Drumborg Vineyard	Henty
97	2014 Forest Hill Vineyard Block 1	Mount Barker
97	2008 Abbey Creek Vineyard Museum Release	Porongurup
97	2014 Duke's Vineyard Magpie Hill Reserve	Porongurup
97	2013 Tertini Private Cellar Collection	Southern Highlands
97	2014 Pressing Matters R9 Coal River Valley	Tasmania
96	**Adelaide Hills** 2014 Henschke Green's Hill, **Canberra District** 2014 Capital Gundaroo Vineyard, **Clare Valley** 2014 Crabtree, 2014 Knappstein Slate Creek Vineyard, 2014 Leo Buring Leonay, 2014 O'Leary Walker Polish Hill River, 2010 Paulett Polish Hill River Aged Release, 2014 Petaluma Hanlin Hill, 2014 Rieslingfreak No. 2, 2014 Taylors St Andrews Single Vineyard Release, 2014 Wines by KT 5452, 2014 Wines by KT Peglidis Vineyard Watervale, **Eden Valley** 2014 Dandelion Vineyards Wonderland, 2009 Forbes & Forbes Cellar Matured, 2013 Handpicked Regional Selections, 2014 Thorn-Clarke Eden Trail, 2014 Two Hands The Boy, **Frankland River** 2014 Frankland Estate Poison Hill Vineyard,	

Grampians 2014 Clarnette & Ludvigsen, **Great Southern** 2010 Howard Park Museum Release, 2014 Kerrigan + Berry Mt Barker Great Southern, 2014 3 Drops, 2014 Trevelen Farm, **Henty** 2006 Crawford River Museum Release, 2014 Crawford River Young Vines, **Macedon Ranges** 2013 Granite Hills Knight, 2013 Granite Hills Tor, **Mount Barker** 2014 West Cape Howe, **Mudgee** 2012 Lowe Icon Nullo Mountain, **Pemberton** 2014 Bellarmine Dry, **Porongurup** 2014 Castle Rock Estate, 2014 Howard Park, **Tasmania** 2014 Bay of Fires, 2013 Eddystone Point, 2014 Leo Buring Leopold Tamar Valley, 2014 Moores Hill Estate, 2014 Pipers Brook Vineyard Estate, 2013 Waterton Vineyards, 2012 Waterton Vineyards.

Chardonnay

891 wines were tasted, 29 receiving 97 points plus one at 98, leading a massive field. Margaret River and the Yarra Valley, both with great wines, but in different styles, tied with eight wines each; the remainder came from Adelaide Hills, Beechworth, Macedon Ranges and Tasmania. Another six regions joined in on the second (96 point) tier.

RATING	WINE	REGION
98	2013 Deep Woods Estate Reserve	Margaret River
97	2012 Petaluma Tiers Piccadilly Valley	Adelaide Hills
97	2013 Fighting Gully Road	Beechworth
97	2013 Giaconda Estate	Beechworth
97	2013 Golden Ball là-bas	Beechworth
97	2013 Singlefile Family Reserve	Denmark
97	2014 Bress Le Grand Coq Noir Single Vineyard	Macedon Ranges
97	2012 Curly Flat The Curly	Macedon Ranges
97	2013 Cape Mentelle	Margaret River
97	2013 Evoi Reserve	Margaret River
97	2011 Flowstone Queen of the Earth	Margaret River
97	2012 Hamelin Bay Five Ashes Reserve	Margaret River
97	2012 Leeuwin Estate Art Series	Margaret River
97	2013 Vasse Felix Heytesbury	Margaret River
97	2013 Xanadu Reserve	Margaret River
97	2013 Garagiste Merricks	Mornington Peninsula
97	2013 Jones Road Nepean	Mornington Peninsula
97	2013 Ten Minutes by Tractor Judd Vineyard	Mornington Peninsula
97	2013 Yabby Lake Vineyard Single Block Release Block 6	Mornington Peninsula
97	2011 Stefano Lubiana Collina	Tasmania
97	2013 Tolpuddle Vineyard	Tasmania
97	2012 Penfolds Yattarna	Tasmania/Henty/ Adelaide Hills
97	2013 Bicknell fc	Yarra Valley
97	2011 Bicknell fc	Yarra Valley
97	2013 Hoddles Creek Estate 1er	Yarra Valley
97	2013 Innocent Bystander Giant Steps Tarraford Vineyard	Yarra Valley
97	2013 Mac Forbes Hoddles Creek	Yarra Valley
97	2013 Mac Forbes Woori Yallock	Yarra Valley
97	2013 Mount Mary	Yarra Valley
97	2013 Oakridge 864 Single Block Release Block A Lusatia Park Vineyard	Yarra Valley
96	**Adelaide Hills** 2012 Lofty Valley Lani's View Single Vineyard, 2014 Murdoch Hill The Tilbury Single Vineyard Piccadilly Valley, 2013 Petaluma Piccadilly Valley,	

2013 Scott, **Albany** 2013 Willoughby Park Kalgan Ironrock, **Ballarat** 2013 Eastern Peake Block P58, **Denmark** 2013 Castelli Estate Il Liris, 2013 Rockcliffe Single Site, 2013 Singlefile The Vivienne, **Geelong** 2012 Bannockburn Vineyards, 2011 Bannockburn Vineyards S.R.H., 2013 By Farr, **Gippsland** 2013 Lightfoot & Sons Single Block, **Great Southern** 2013 Harewood Estate, 2014 Marchand & Burch Villages, **Henty** 2013 Seppelt Drumborg Vineyard, **Hunter Valley** 2014 First Creek Winemaker's Reserve, 2014 Lake's Folly Hill Block, 2014 Silkman Reserve, 2011 Tyrrell's Vat 47, **Macedon Ranges** 2013 Curly Flat, 2013 Lane's End Vineyard, **Margaret River** 2013 Amelia Park, 2013 Chapman Grove Atticus Single Vineyard, 2014 Cherubino, 2014 Cloudburst, 2012 Cowaramup Reserve Limited Edition, 2013 Cullen Kevin John, 2012 Evans & Tate Redbrook, 2011 Flowstone, 2012 Flowstone Queen of the Earth, 2013 Flying Fish Cove Prize Catch, 2013 Hay Shed Hill Block 6, 2013 Moss Wood Margaret River, 2014 Robert Oatley Finisterre, 2012 Stella Bella Serie Luminosa, 2012 Streicker Ironstone Block Old Vine, 2013 Thompson Estate, 2013 Vasse Felix, 2012 Voyager Estate, 2012 Voyager Estate Project 95, 2013 Woodlands Chloe, 2013 Xanadu Stevens Road, **Margaret River/Mount Barker** 2013 Burch Family Howard Park Allingham, **Mornington Peninsula** 2013 Jones Road, 2013 Kooyong Single Vineyard Selection Farrago, 2013 Main Ridge Estate, 2013 Montalto Estate, 2013 Montalto Single Vineyard The Eleven, 2013 Moorooduc Estate The Moorooduc McIntyre, 2011 Scorpo, 2012 Stonier Jack's Ridge Vineyard, 2013 Stonier Thompson Vineyard, 2013 Ten Minutes by Tractor McCutcheon, 2013 Tuck's Ridge Buckle, 2013 Yabby Lake Vineyard Single Vineyard, **Orange** 2009 Patina, 2012 Printhie Super Duper, 2013 Swinging Bridge Reserve, **Porongurup** 2013 Marchand & Burch, **Tasmania** 2013 Bay of Fires, 2012 Bellwether Tamar Valley, 2013 Dawson & James, 2013 Holm Oak The Wizard, 2013 Ministry of Clouds, **Tasmania/Yarra Valley** 2013 Hardys Eileen Hardy, **Tumbarumba** 2013 Eden Road Maragle, 2014 Eden Road Maragle, **Yarra Valley** 2012 Bicknell fc Yarra Valley, 2011 Chandon Australia Barrel Selection, 2013 Coldstream Hills Reserve, 2013 Innocent Bystander Giant Steps Sexton Vineyard, 2012 Mandala The Compass, 2013 Oakridge 864 Single Block Release Drive Block Funder & Diamond Vineyard, 2013 Oakridge Local Vineyard Series Guerin Vineyard, 2013 Punch Lance's Vineyard, 2013 Rochford, 2014 Serrat, 2013 Seville Estate Reserve, 2014 Soumah Single Vineyard, 2013 Toolangi Vineyards Estate, 2013 YarraLoch Stephanie's Dream Single Vineyard, 2013 Yering Station Reserve, 2013 Yeringberg, Yarra Valley/Margaret River 2013 Truffle & Wine Co.

Semillon

Little needs to be said, except to repeat Bruce Tyrrell's comment on the impact of screwcaps: 'Hunter Valley is entering a golden age.' These wines are all screwcapped, and span 2005 (the first vintage) to 2014; I strongly suspect they will easily see out 20 years, the best, 50 years. The two outsiders from Shoalhaven were contract-made by Tyrrells, the climate having much in common with the Hunter Valley.

RATING	WINE	REGION
97	2009 Brokenwood ILR Reserve	Hunter Valley
97	2014 Cockfighter's Ghost Poole's Rock	Hunter Valley
97	2005 Meerea Park Aged Release Alexander Munro	Hunter Valley
97	2014 Mount Pleasant 1946 Vines Lovedale Vineyard	Hunter Valley
97	2007 Peter Drayton Peter Drayton TJD Reserve	Hunter Valley
97	2014 Thomas Braemore Individual Vineyard	Hunter Valley
97	2009 Thomas Cellar Reserve Braemore Individual Vineyard	Hunter Valley
97	2014 Tyrrell's Johnno's	Hunter Valley
97	2014 Tyrrell's Vat 1	Hunter Valley

96	2014 Audrey Wilkinson The Ridge	Hunter Valley
96	2014 Belford Block Eight Reserve	Hunter Valley
96	2011 Bimbadgen Signature	Hunter Valley
96	2009 Bimbadgen Signature Palmers Lane	Hunter Valley
96	2009 Brokenwood Maxwell Vineyard	Hunter Valley
96	2014 Keith Tulloch Field of Mars Block 2A	Hunter Valley
96	2014 McGuigan The Shortlist	Hunter Valley
96	2010 Meerea Park Alexander Munro	Hunter Valley
96	2009 Mount Pleasant Elizabeth	Hunter Valley
96	2010 Mount Pleasant Lovedale Single Vineyard	Hunter Valley
96	2014 Pepper Tree Single Vineyard Limited Release Rhodes	Hunter Valley
96	2014 Pepper Tree Single Vineyard Reserve Alluvius	Hunter Valley
96	2009 Pokolbin Estate Phil Swannell	Hunter Valley
96	2014 Silkman Reserve	Hunter Valley
96	2014 Thomas The O.C. Individual Vineyard	Hunter Valley
96	2014 Wills Domain Block 2	Margaret River
96	2005 Coolangatta Estate Aged Release Estate Grown	Shoalhaven Coast
96	2014 Coolangatta Estate Individual Vineyard Wollstonecraft	Shoalhaven Coast

Sauvignon Blanc

The net was cast far and wide with this select group; the common feature of the two top wines was the successful integration of texture and structure without compromising varietal character.

RATING	WINE	REGION
97	2012 Flowstone	Margaret River
97	2014 Terre à Terre Single Vineyard	Wrattonbully
96	2014 Geoff Weaver Lenswood	Adelaide Hills
96	2013 Flowstone	Margaret River
96	2014 Castelli Estate Empirica Fume Blanc	Pemberton
96	2014 Bress Silver Chook	Yarra Valley
95	**Adelaide Hills** 2014 Dandelion Vineyards Wishing Clock, 2013 Geoff Weaver Ferus Lenswood, 2013 Heirloom Vineyards, 2014 Penny's Hill The Agreement, 2013 Romney Park Fume Blanc, 2014 SC Pannell, 2014 Shaw + Smith, 2014 Tomich Woodside Vineyard, **Denmark** 2014 Apricus Hill Single Vineyard, **Frankland River**, 2014 Alkoomi Black Label, **Geelong** 2014 Bellbrae Estate Southside, 2014 Clyde Park Vineyard, 2013 Scotchmans Hill Cornelius Single Vineyard, **Geographe** 2013 Whicher Ridge, **Granite Belt** 2013 Witches Falls Wild Ferment Granite Belt, **Great Southern/Margaret River** 2014 Burch Family Howard Park, **Henty** 2013 Crawford River Cielo, **Margaret River** 2014 Flametree S.R.S. Karridale, 2014 Forester Estate, 2014 Redgate Reserve Oak Matured, 2014 Watershed Premium Senses, 2014 Windows Estate Single Vineyard, **Mornington Peninsula** 2013 Telera Fume, **Orange** 2014 Bimbadgen Art Series Fume Blanc, 2014 Brokenwood Forest Edge Vineyard, 2014 Ross Hill Pinnacle Series, 2014 Tamburlaine Reserve, **Pemberton** 2014 Cherubino, 2014 Houghton Wisdom, 2014 Larry Cherubino The Yard Channybearup Vineyard, 2014 Merum Estate Premium Reserve, 2014 Singlefile Fume Blanc, **Tasmania** 2013 Moorilla Estate Muse, 2014 Moorilla Estate Praxis, **Yarra Valley** 2013 Gembrook Hill, 2014 Out of Step Lone Star Creek.	

Sauvignon Blends

This is a distinctly Australian blend to which New Zealand sauvignon blanc has no answer. As in prior years, Margaret River dominates the field, much like the Hunter Valley does with semillon. The maritime climate replicates that of Bordeaux, the Old World home of the blend (the percentage of muscadelle is decreasing in Bordeaux).

RATING	WINE	REGION
97	2012 Cape Mentelle Wallcliffe	Margaret River
97	2013 Fraser Gallop Estate Parterre Semillon Sauvignon Blanc	Margaret River
96	2014 Grosset Semillon Sauvignon Blanc	Clare Valley/ Adelaide Hills
96	2014 Harewood Estate Reserve Semillon Sauvignon Blanc	Great Southern
96	2014 Pepper Tree Single Vineyard Limited Release Polly Fume	Hunter Valley/Orange
96	2013 Juniper Estate Aquitaine	Margaret River
96	2011 Stella Bella Suckfizzle Sauvignon Blanc Semillon	Margaret River
96	2012 Voyager Estate Tom Price Semillon Sauvignon Blanc	Margaret River
96	2012 Warner Glen Estate P.B.F. Sauvignon Blanc Semillon	Margaret River
96	2014 Windows Estate Single Vineyard Semillon Sauvignon Blanc	Margaret River
95	**Beechworth** 2013 Sorrenberg Sauvignon Blanc Semillon, **Denmark** 2014 The Lake House Premium Reserve Single Vineyard Semillon Sauvignon Blanc, **Geographe** 2014 Willow Bridge Estate Dragonfly Sauvignon Blanc Semillon, **Granite Belt** 2014 Golden Grove Estate Semillon Sauvignon Blanc, **Margaret River** 2014 Amelia Park Sauvignon Blanc Semillon, 2014 Chapman Grove Reserve Semillon Sauvignon Blanc, 2014 Cullen Vineyard Sauvignon Blanc Semillon, 2013 Domaine Naturaliste Sauvage Sauvignon Blanc Semillon, 2014 Forester Estate Semillon Sauvignon Blanc, 2014 Fraser Gallop Estate River Semillon Sauvignon Blanc, 2014 Grace Farm Sauvignon Blanc Semillon, 2014 Happs Sauvignon Blanc Semillon, 2013 Happs Three Hills Eva Marie, 2014 Hay Shed Hill Block 1 Semillon Sauvignon Blanc, 2014 Ibizan Semillon Sauvignon Blanc, 2014 Lenton Brae Semillon Sauvignon Blanc, 2012 Lenton Brae Wilyabrup Semillon Sauvignon Blanc, 2014 Marq Wild and Worked Sauvignon Blanc Semillon, 2014 Thompson Estate SSB Semillon Sauvignon Blanc, 2013 Warner Glen Estate P.B.F. Sauvignon Blanc Semillon, 2014 Xanadu DJL Sauvignon Blanc Semillon, **Yarra Valley** 2013 Oakridge Local Vineyard Series Guerin & Oakridge Fumare.	

Other White Wines and Blends

A disparate group of ten varieties, either alone or in blends, from 20 regions.

RATING	WINE	REGION
96	2014 Ochota Barrels Weird Berries in the Woods Gewurztraminer	Adelaide Hills
96	2013 Yalumba The Virgilius Viognier	Eden Valley
96	2013 Yangarra Estate Vineyard Roux Beaute Roussanne	McLaren Vale
96	2013 Montalto Estate Pinot Gris	Mornington Peninsula
96	2006 Tahbilk 1927 Vines Marsanne	Nagambie Lakes
96	2005 Tahbilk 1927 Vines Marsanne	Nagambie Lakes
96	2014 Pooley Pinot Grigio	Tasmania
95	**Adelaide Hills** 2013 CRFT K1 Vineyard Kuitpo Gruner Veltliner, 2013 Golding Cascara Savagnin, 2014 Pike & Joyce Separe Gruner Veltliner, 2014 Smidge The GruVe Gruner Veltliner, 2014 The Pawn Wine Co. The Austrian Attack Gruner Veltliner, **Alpine Valleys** 2014 Billy Button The Happy Gewurztraminer, **Barossa**	

Valley 2014 Gatt Accent Viognier, 2013 Turkey Flat The Last Straw, **Beechworth** 2013 Domenica Roussanne Marsanne, **Canberra District** 2014 Clonakilla Viognier, 2013 Collector Lamp Lit Marsanne, **Clare Valley** 2014 Grosset Apiana, **Eden Valley** 2013 Yalumba Roussanne, **Geelong** 2012 By Farr Viognier, 2013 Oakdene Ly Ly Single Vineyard Pinot Gris, **Granite Belt** 2014 Heritage Estate Fiano, 2013 Witches Falls Winery Wild Ferment Viognier, **Heathcote** 2014 Bress Silver Chook Limited Release Vermentino, 2013 Chalmers Fiano, **Henty** 2014 Di Sciascio Family D'Sas Pinot Gris, **Macedon Ranges** 2014 Lindenderry at Red Hill Pinot Gris, **Margaret River** 2012 Flowstone Gewurztraminer, **McLaren Vale** 2014 Yangarra Estate Vineyard Viognier, **Mornington Peninsula** 2014 Paradigm Hill Pinot Gris, 2014 Scorpo Pinot Gris, **Nagambie Lakes** 2013 McPherson Princess Butterfly Marsanne, 2009 Tahbilk Museum Release Marsanne, **Pemberton** 2014 Millbrook Arneis, **Sunbury** 2013 Craiglee Viognier, 2013 Galli Estate Adele Fiano, **Tasmania** 2013 Gala Estate Pinot Gris, 2014 Derwent Estate Pinot Gris, 2014 Pipers Brook Vineyard Estate Gewurztraminer, 2014 Sinapius Vineyard Tamar Valley Riesling et al, 2014 Tamar Ridge Pinot Gris, **Upper Goulburn** 2014 Delatite Pinot Gris, 2013 Delatite Pinot Gris, **Yarra Valley** 2013 Mount Mary Triolet, 2013 Pimpernel Vineyards Viognier, 2014 Punt Road Napoleone Vineyard Pinot Gris, 2014 St Huberts Roussanne, 2014 Warramunda Estate Marsanne, 2013 Yarra Yering Dry White No. 1, **Yarra Valley/Tasmania** 2013 Hardys HRB Pinot Gris.

Sparkling

The clear majority of the best sparkling wines are now solely sourced from Tasmania, the remainder coming from the coolest sites in the southern parts of the mainland, with altitude playing a major role. They are all fermented in the bottle, and the best have had extended lees contact prior to disgorgement, giving them great complexity.

White and rose

RATING	WINE	REGION
97	2004 Arras Blanc de Blancs	Tasmania
96	2010 Chandon Blanc de Blancs	Cool-climate blend
96	2008 Stonier Cuvee Rose	Mornington Peninsula
96	2005 Arras Rose	Tasmania
96	2008 Jansz Single Vineyard Vintage Chardonnay	Tasmania
95	2009 Deviation Road Beltana Blanc de Blancs	Adelaide Hills
95	2008 Willow Creek Brut	Mornington Peninsula
95	2010 Blue Pyrenees Estate Midnight Cuvee Chardonnay	Pyrenees
95	2005 Arras Blanc de Blancs	Tasmania
95	2010 Bangor Estate Vintage	Tasmania
95	NV Bay of Fires Cuvee Pinot Noir Chardonnay Brut	Tasmania
95	NV Bay of Fires Cuvee Pinot Noir Chardonnay Rose	Tasmania
95	2001 Clover Hill Blanc de Blancs Late Disgorged	Tasmania
95	2009 Jansz Single Vineyard Vintage Chardonnay	Tasmania
95	2010 Jansz Vineyard Rose	Tasmania
95	2004 Kreglinger Vintage Brut Rose	Tasmania
95	NV Pirie	Tasmania
95	2010 Chandon Vintage Collection Les Trois Rose	Tasmania/King Valley
95	2002 Courabyra 805 Late Disgorged Pinot Noir Chardonnay Pinot Meunier	Tumbarumba

Sparkling red

A tiny group of wines, eagerly sought by the small percentage of wine drinkers who understand the peculiarities of the style and who, better still, are prepared to cellar them for a year or more, the longer the better.

RATING	WINE	REGION
96	2008 Ashton Hills Sparkling Shiraz	Adelaide Hills
95	NV Hentley Farm Black Beauty Sparkling Shiraz	Barossa Valley
95	2010 Peter Lehmann Black Queen Sparkling Shiraz	Barossa Valley

Sweet

Two classes of Riesling have continued to evolve, and cannot be grouped together: off-dry (in Mosel Kabinett style) and fully sweet (Auslese in German terminology).

Off-dry Riesling

RATING	WINE	REGION
96	2014 Grosset Alea Riesling	Clare Valley
96	2014 Hay Shed Hill G40 Riesling	Mount Barker
96	2014 Bellarmine Riesling Half Dry	Pemberton
95	2014 Pewsey Vale Prima Single Vineyard Riesling	Eden Valley
95	2014 Mac Forbes RS33 Riesling	Strathbogie Ranges

Sweet Riesling

RATING	WINE	REGION
96	2014 Bellarmine Riesling Select	Pemberton
96	2013 Frogmore Creek Iced Riesling	Tasmania
95	2013 Lamont's Winery Dessert Riesling	Frankland River
95	2014 Singlefile Riesling	Mount Barker
95	2014 Frogmore Creek FGR Riesling	Tasmania
95	2013 Frogmore Creek FGR Riesling	Tasmania
95	2012 Gala Estate Late Harvest Riesling	Tasmania

... And others

It makes no sense to put these and the Rieslings into the same group. Altogether different dynamics are in play; these are barrel-fermented, highly botrytised wines with vanilla bean, peaches and cream, crème brulee, apricot or cumquat flavours – take your pick.

RATING	WINE	REGION
95	2013 Lerida Estate Lake George Botrytis Pinot Gris	Canberra District
95	2013 Chalmers Sagrantino Appassimento	Heathcote
95	2013 Woodstock Botrytis Semillon	McLaren Vale
95	2011 De Bortoli Noble One Botrytis Semillon	Riverina
95	2013 De Bortoli Noble One Botrytis Semillon	Riverina
95	2010 Home Hill Kelly's Reserve Late Harvest Sticky	Tasmania

Rose

The number of roses on the market may be approaching saturation point. There are no rules: they can be bone-dry or very sweet; they can be made from almost any red variety; they may be a convenient way of concentrating the red wine left after the rose is run off (bleeding or saignee) from the fermenter shortly after the grapes are crushed, or made from the ground up using grapes specifically chosen for the purpose. The vast majority fall in the former camp; those listed mainly come from the latter.

RATING	WINE	REGION
96	2013 Dandelion Vineyards Fairytale Rose	Barossa
96	2014 Charles Melton Rose of Virginia	Barossa Valley

95	2013 David Franz Survivor Vines Red Rose	Barossa Valley
95	2014 Turkey Flat Rose	Barossa Valley
95	2014 Woods Crampton Mataro Rose	Barossa Valley
95	2014 Fighting Gully Road Rose	Beechworth/ Alpine Valleys/ Heathcote
95	2014 Shadowfax Werribee Rose	Geelong
95	2014 Marq Serious Rose	Margaret River
95	2014 Montalto Pennon Hill Rose	Mornington Peninsula
95	2014 Willow Creek Rose	Mornington Peninsula

Pinot Noir

The three regions that produce most of Australia's best Pinot Noirs are (in alpha order) the Mornington Peninsula, Tasmania and the Yarra Valley. Adelaide Hills and Geelong come next, with a lesser number of wines but a similar high standard of quality.

RATING	WINE	REGION
98	2012 Bannockburn Vineyards De La Terre	Geelong
98	2013 Mount Mary	Yarra Valley
97	2013 Ashton Hills Estate	Adelaide Hills
97	2012 Ashton Hills Reserve	Adelaide Hills
97	2007 Ashton Hills Reserve	Adelaide Hills
97	2004 Ashton Hills Reserve	Adelaide Hills
97	2012 Bannockburn Vineyards Serre	Geelong
97	2012 Bannockburn Vineyards Stuart	Geelong
97	2013 Sangreal by Farr	Geelong
97	2013 Bicknell fc	Gippsland
97	2013 Garagiste Terre de Feu	Mornington Peninsula
97	2013 Handpicked Capella Vineyard	Mornington Peninsula
97	2013 Montalto Single Vineyard Main Ridge Block	Mornington Peninsula
97	2013 Moorooduc Estate The Moorooduc McIntyre	Mornington Peninsula
97	2013 Stonier W-WB	Mornington Peninsula
97	2013 Tuck's Ridge Buckle	Mornington Peninsula
97	2013 Yabby Lake Vineyard Single Block Release Block 1	Mornington Peninsula
97	2013 Yabby Lake Vineyard Single Block Release Block 2	Mornington Peninsula
97	2013 Dawson & James	Tasmania
97	2013 Freycinet	Tasmania
97	2013 Home Hill Kelly's Reserve	Tasmania
97	2012 Morningside Vineyard Pressings	Tasmania
97	2012 Stefano Lubiana Sasso	Tasmania
97	2013 Tolpuddle Vineyard	Tasmania
97	2013 Hillcrest Vineyard Premium	Yarra Valley
97	2013 Hoddles Creek Estate 1er	Yarra Valley
97	2013 Oakridge 864 Single Block Release Guerin Vineyard Block 4	Yarra Valley
97	2013 Punch Lance's Vineyard Close Planted	Yarra Valley
97	2013 Punch Lance's Vineyard	Yarra Valley
97	2013 Toolangi Vineyards Pauls Lane	Yarra Valley

| 97 | 2013 Yering Station Scarlett | Yarra Valley |

96   **Adelaide Hills** 2013 Ashton Hills Blend No. 2 Cemetery Block Piccadilly Valley, 2013 Ashton Hills Reserve, 2005 Ashton Hills Reserve, 2013 BK Remy Single Barrel Lenswood, **Ballarat** 2012 Eastern Peake Walsh Block Tres Ancienne, **Geelong** 2012 Austins & Co. Kyberd, 2012 Bannockburn Vineyards, 2013 Bannockburn Vineyards, 2012 Brown Magpie Paraparap Single Vineyard Reserve, 2013 Brown Magpie Paraparap Single Vineyard Reserve, 2014 Clyde Park Vineyard Block D, 2014 Clyde Park Vineyard Block F Geelong College, 2014 Clyde Park Vineyard, 2013 Farr Rising, 2013 Farrside by Farr, 2012 Tout Pres by Farr, 2012 Lethbridge Mietta, 2012 Scotchmans Hill Cornelius Single Vineyard, **Henty** 2013 Seppelt Drumborg Vineyard, **Macedon Ranges** 2012 Curly Flat, 2013 Lane's End Vineyard, 2013 Mons Rubra, **Mornington Peninsula** 2013 Shadowfax Waterson Road, 2013 Allies Main Ridge, 2013 Dexter, 2013 Eldridge Estate of Red Hill Clonal Blend, 2013 Foxeys Hangout Kentucky Road 777, 2013 Foxeys Hangout Scotsworth Farm, 2013 Foxeys Hangout White Gates Vineyard, 2013 Garagiste Merricks, 2013 Kooyong Single Vineyard Selection Ferrous, 2013 Kooyong Single Vineyard Selection Meres, 2013 Main Ridge Estate Half Acre, 2013 Montalto Single Vineyard Tuerong Block, 2013 Paradigm Hill L'ami Sage, 2013 Paringa Estate Estate, 2012 Paringa Estate The Paringa Single Vineyard, 2013 Scorpo, 2013 Stonier KBS Vineyard, 2013 Stonier Lyncroft Vineyard, 2012 Stonier Merron's Vineyard, 2013 Stonier Reserve, 2013 Stonier Family Vineyard, 2013 Ten Minutes by Tractor Wallis Vineyard, 2013 Willow Creek, 2013 Yabby Lake Single Vineyard, **Mount Barker** 2014 Byron & Harold The Partners, **Tasmania** 2013 Bay of Fires, 2012 Brook Eden Vineyard, 2012 Brown Brothers 125 Years Special Release Reserve, 2014 Chatto Isle, 2013 Dalrymple Single Site Bicheno, 2012 Freycinet, 2013 Handpicked Collection, 2013 Home Hill Estate, 2013 Moores Hill Estate, 2013 Sinapius Home Vineyard, 2013 Stoney Rise Holyman Project X, **Yarra Valley** 2013 Coldstream Hills Deer Farm Vineyard, 2013 Coldstream Hills Reserve, 2013 De Bortoli Estate Grown, 2014 De Bortoli Estate Grown, 2013 Hillcrest Village, 2013 Innocent Bystander Giant Steps Applejack Vineyard, 2013 Mac Forbes Woori Yallock, 2013 Mayer Granite, 2013 Oakridge Local Vineyard Series Guerin Vineyard, 2013 Pimpernel Three, 2014 Rochford L'Enfant Unique, 2014 Serrat, 2013 Trapeze, 2013 Yarra Yering Carrodus, 2013 Yering Station Reserve, **Yarra Valley/Tasmania** 2013 Hardys Eileen Hardy.

Shiraz

The number of wines that received 97 points or more (a total of 84) may seem extreme, but represents a major resurgence of the Barossa/Barossa Valley, the Eden Valley and McLaren Vale, courtesy of the 2012 and 2013 vintages. The Hunter Valley is next in importance numerically, and, strange though it may seem, shares the medium body and moderate alcohol of the cooler regions (in alpha order) of Adelaide Hills, Canberra District, Frankland River, Geelong, Grampians, Hilltops, Mornington Peninsula and Yarra Valley.

RATING	WINE	REGION
99	2010 Penfolds Grange	South Australia
98	2012 St Hallett Old Block	Barossa
98	2012 Langmeil Winery The Freedom 1843	Barossa
98	2012 Kaesler Old Bastard	Barossa Valley
98	2013 Kalleske Greenock Single Vineyard	Barossa Valley
98	2012 Penfolds RWT	Barossa Valley
98	2013 Wendouree	Clare Valley
98	2012 Henschke Mount Edelstone	Eden Valley
98	2012 Mount Langi Ghiran Vineyards Mast	Grampians
98	2013 Mount Pleasant 1946 Vines Rosehill Vineyard	Hunter Valley
98	2013 Mount Pleasant Maurice O'Shea	Hunter Valley
98	2011 Mount Pleasant Mountain D Full Bodied Dry Red	Hunter Valley

| 98 | 2012 Clarendon Hills Astralis | McLaren Vale |
| 98 | 2009 Tahbilk 1860 Vines | Nagambie Lakes |

97   **Adelaide Hills** 2012 Bird in Hand Nest Egg, 2013 SC Pannell Syrah, 2013 Shaw + Smith, 2013 Sidewood Estate Mappinga, **Adelaide Zone** 2012 Penfolds Magill Estate, **Barossa Zone** 2012 Elderton Command Single Vineyard, 2010 Jacob's Creek St Hugo Vetus Purum, 2012 Thorn-Clarke Ron Thorn, **Barossa Valley** 2012 Charles Melton Grains of Paradise, 2012 Charles Melton Voices of Angels, 2013 Final Cut Take Two, 2013 Head The Brunette Moppa, 2013 Hentley Farm Clos Otto, 2013 Hentley Farm H Block, 2010 Hentley Farm Museum Release The Beauty, 2013 Hentley Farm The Beauty, 2013 Hentley Farm The Creation, 2012 Kaesler Alte Reben, 2012 Kaesler The Bogan, 2012 Kellermeister Black Sash, 2012 Kilikanoon Crowhurst Reserve, 2012 Lanz Vineyards Limited Edition The Grand Reserve, 2012 Murray Street Vineyards Sophia, 2012 Peter Lehmann VSV Hongell, 2012 Rolf Binder Hanisch, 2010 Schild Estate Moorooroo Limited Release, 2012 Stonefish Icon, 2012 Trevor Jones Fine Belle-Terroir Sorciere Sauvage, **Barossa Valley/Heathcote** 2012 Glen Eldon Black Lady, 2012 Munari Black Lady, **Canberra District** 2014 Clonakilla O'Riada, 2013 Nick O'Leary Bolaro, **Clare Valley** 2012 Annie's Lane Copper Trail, 2010 Leasingham Classic Clare Provis Vineyard, 2012 Skillogalee Trevarrick Single Contour, **Coonawarra** 2012 Wynns Coonawarra Estate Michael Limited Release, **Eden Valley** 2013 Eden Hall Block 4, 2013 Eperosa Elevation, 2010 Henschke Hill Of Grace, 2013 St Hallett Single Vineyard Release Mattschoss, **Frankland River** 2012 Houghton Thomas Yule, 2012 Rockcliffe Single Site, **Geelong** 2010 Bannockburn Vineyards, 2013 Barrgowan Vineyard Simonsens, 2012 By Farr, 2012 Lethbridge Indra, 2013 Oakdene William Single Vineyard, **Glenrowan** 2013 Baileys of Glenrowan 1904 Block, **Grampians** 2013 Mount Langi Ghiran Mast, 2013 Seppelt St Peters, **Heathcote** 2012 La Pleiade, 2013 Paul Osicka Moormbool Reserve, 2013 Seppelt Mount Ida Heathcote, **Hilltops** 2013 Moppity Reserve, **Hunter Valley** 2013 Audrey Wilkinson The Lake, 2013 Brokenwood Graveyard Vineyard, 2013 Brokenwood Mistress Block Vineyard, 2013 De Iuliis Steven Vineyard, 2013 Leogate Estate The Basin Reserve, 2013 Mount Pleasant 1880 Vines Old Hill Vineyard, 2011 Mount Pleasant Mountain A Medium Bodied Dry Red, 2013 Mount Pleasant Old Paddock & Old Hill, 2013 Pepper Tree Single Vineyard Reserve Coquun, 2013 Thomas Kiss Limited Release, 2013 Tyrrell's Old Patch, **McLaren Vale** 2013 Bekkers Syrah, 2012 Ekhidna Rarefied, 2013 Fox Creek Old Vine, 2010 Hardys Eileen Hardy, 2012 Haselgrove The Cruth, 2013 Ministry of Clouds Single Vineyard Blewitt Springs, 2012 Mitolo The Furies, 2013 Patritti JPB Single Vineyard, 2012 Paxton Jones Block Single Vineyard, 2012 Reynella Basket Pressed, 2012 Serafino Terremoto Single Vineyard Syrah, 2013 Shingleback Unedited, 2012 Yangarra Estate Vineyard Ironheart, **Margaret River** 2011 Streicker Bridgeland Block Syrah, **Mornington Peninsula** 2013 Foxeys Hangout, 2013 Montalto Pennon Hill, **Nagambie Lakes** 2009 Tahbilk Eric Stevens Purbrick, **Pyrenees** 2013 Jamsheed Pyren Syrah, **Yarra Valley** 2013 Oakridge Local Vineyard Series Whitsend & Oakridge Vineyards.

Shiraz Viognier

Cool regions provide the majority of the best wines in this group, in which fragrance, spice and red fruits are the flavour cornerstones; the Hunter Valley and McLaren Vale are exceptions to prove the rule.

RATING	WINE	REGION
99	2014 Serrat	Yarra Valley
98	2013 Yering Station Reserve	Yarra Valley
96	2012 Turner's Crossing Vineyard	Bendigo
96	2013 Capital Kyeema Vineyard Reserve	Canberra District
96	2014 Clonakilla	Canberra District
95	2012 Hillbillé Signature James Brittain	Blackwood Valley
95	2013 Lerida Estate Lake George	Canberra District

95	2012 Alkoomi Black Label	Frankland River
95	2013 Boireann	Granite Belt
95	2013 Silver Spoon	Heathcote
95	2013 Bimbadgen Estate	Hunter Valley
95	2013 Tinklers Vineyard	Hunter Valley
95	2013 Hugh Hamilton Jekyll & Hyde	McLaren Vale
95	2012 Orange Mountain 1397	Orange
95	2012 Millbrook Estate	Perth Hills
95	2012 Yering Station	Yarra Valley

Cabernet Sauvignon

The affinity of cabernet sauvignon with a maritime climate is put beyond doubt by its home in Bordeaux's Medoc region. So it comes as no surprise to find that most (but not all) of Australia's top-quality Cabernets come from regions with climates similar to Bordeaux. The dominance of Margaret River (with 14 of the top-scoring wines) is likely to continue; not only is the climate ideally suited, but it is also far more consistent than that of any other Australian region.

RATING	WINE	REGION
98	2012 Penfolds Bin 707	South Australia
98	2013 Larry Cherubino Cherubino	Frankland River
98	2012 Cape Mentelle	Margaret River
98	2011 Devil's Lair 9th Chamber	Margaret River
98	2012 Domaine Naturaliste Rebus	Margaret River
98	2013 Flying Fish Cove Prize Catch	Margaret River
98	2012 Xanadu Reserve	Margaret River
97	2013 Elderton Ashmead Single Vineyard	Barossa
97	2013 Purple Hands Planta Circa Ancient Vine	Barossa Valley
97	2012 Rockford Rifle Range	Barossa Valley
97	2012 Hardys Thomas Hardy	Coonawarra/ Margaret River/ McLaren Vale
97	2012 Knappstein Block 5 Enterprise Vineyard Clare Valley	Clare Valley
97	2013 Wendouree	Clare Valley
97	2013 Balnaves of Coonawarra The Tally Reserve	Coonawarra
97	2012 Wynns Coonawarra Estate John Riddoch Limited Release	Coonawarra
97	2010 Henschke Cyril Henschke	Eden Valley
97	2012 Thorn-Clarke William Randell	Eden Valley
97	2012 Howard Park Scotsdale Great Southern	Great Southern
97	2013 Paul Osicka Old Vines Majors Creek Vineyard	Heathcote
97	2012 Bleasdale Vineyards The Iron Duke	Langhorne Creek
97	2013 Deep Woods Estate Reserve	Margaret River
97	2012 Deep Woods Wilyabrup	Margaret River
97	2011 Flowstone Queen of the Earth	Margaret River
97	2009 Heydon Estate W.G. Grace Single Vineyard	Margaret River
97	2012 Houghton Gladstones	Margaret River
97	2012 Mandoon Estate Reserve Research Station	Margaret River
97	2011 Stella Bella Serie Luminosa	Margaret River
97	2012 Woodlands Thomas	Margaret River

97	2012 Xanadu Stevens Road	Margaret River
97	2013 Wirra Wirra The Angelus	McLaren Vale
97	2013 Dalwhinnie Moonambel Cabernet	Pyrenees
97	2013 Yarra Yering Carrodus	Yarra Valley

96   **Adelaide Zone** 2012 Geoff Hardy Rifle & Hunt, **Adelaide Hills** 2013 Bird in Hand, 2012 Bird in Hand Nest Egg, 2013 Howard Vineyard Amos, **Barossa Valley** 2012 Peter Lehmann Mentor, **Clare Valley** 2012 Taylors The Visionary Exceptional Parcel Limited Release, **Coonawarra** 2013 Balnaves, 2012 Brand's Laira One Seven One, 2010 Jacob's Creek St Hugo Vetus Purum, 2013 Lindeman's St George Vineyard, 2012 Parker Estate 95 Block, 2012 Penley Estate Steyning, 2013 Pepper Tree Single Vineyard Reserve Calcare, 2013 Wynns Black Label, 2012 Wynns Childs Single Vineyard, 2010 Zema Estate Family Selection, **Eden Valley** 2013 Flaxman Reserve Cabernet, 2012 Poonawatta Sub-Regional Collection Single Vineyard Bob's Block, **Frankland River** 2013 Castelli Estate, 2013 Larry Cherubino The Yard Riversdale, 2013 Singlefile, 2012 Singlefile The Philip Adrian, **Geographe** 2011 Whicher Ridge Elevation, **Great Southern/Margaret River** 2012 Howard Park Abercrombie, **Heathcote** 2013 Paul Osicka Majors Creek Vineyard, **Hilltops** 2013 Moppity Single Vineyard, **Langhorne Creek** 2010 Bremerton Walter's Reserve, **Limestone Coast Zone** 2012 Tidswell Jennifer Limited Release, **Margaret River** 2012 Amato Vino Mantra, 2012 Brookland Valley Reserve, 2012 Cape Grace, 2012 Cloudburst, 2013 Cloudburst, 2013 Devil's Lair, 2012 Domaines & Vineyards Robert Bowen, 2013 Fermoy Estate Reserve, 2013 Flying Fish Cove The Wildberry Reserve, 2012 Forester Estate, 2012 Fraser Gallop Estate Parterre Wilyabrup, 2013 Grace Farm, 2013 Grace Farm Reserve, 2011 Juniper Estate, 2013 Mandoon Estate Reserve Research Station, 2012 McHenry Hohnen Rocky Road Vineyard, 2012 Robert Oatley Finisterre, 2012 Rosabrook Single Vineyard Estate, 2012 Stella Bella Serie Luminosa, 2010 Victory Point, 2012 Windows Estate Basket Pressed, 2012 Xanadu, 2013 Beresford Estate Blewitt Springs, 2012 Clarendon Hills Sandown, 2010 Shaw Family Vintners The Ballaster, 2012 Woodstock Collett Lane, **Mount Barker** 2012 West Cape Howe Book Ends, **Mount Benson** 2012 Dorrien Estate Black Wattle Vineyards Icon, **Pyrenees** 2013 Mitchell Harris, **Wrattonbully** 2013 Pepper Tree Single Vineyard Reserve Block 21A, 2013 Pepper Tree Single Vineyard Reserve Elderslee Road, 2013 Terre à Terre Single Vineyard, **Yarra Valley** 2013 Five Oaks Vineyard, 2013 Handpicked Highbrow Hill Vineyard, 2013 Helen & Joey Estate Alena Single Vineyard, 2012 Mandala Butterfly, 2012 Oakridge 864 Single Block Release Oakridge Vineyard Winery Block, 2013 St Huberts, 2013 Tokar Estate.

Cabernet and Family

A thoroughly diverse range of Bordeaux blends and varieties on the one hand, and the classic Australian blend of cabernet and shiraz on the other.

RATING	WINE	REGION
98	2013 Cullen Diana Madeline	Margaret River
98	2012 Yeringberg	Yarra Valley
97	2010 Hentley Farm Museum Release The Creation Shiraz Cabernet	Barossa Valley
97	2010 Kaesler WOMS Shiraz Cabernet	Barossa Valley
97	2012 Henschke Keyneton Euphonium	Barossa
97	2012 Castelli Estate Il Liris Rouge	Frankland River
97	2013 Jasper Hill Emily's Paddock Shiraz Cabernet Franc	Heathcote
97	2010 McGuigan The Philosophy	Hunter Valley
97	2012 Bleasdale Vineyards Double Take Malbec	Langhorne Creek
97	2010 Lake Breeze The Drake Shiraz Cabernet Sauvignon	Langhorne Creek
97	2012 Wolf Blass The Master Pasquin Vineyard Cabernet Shiraz	Langhorne Creek
97	2011 Flametree Jeremy John Cabernet Sauvignon Malbec	Margaret River
97	2012 Penfolds Bin 389 Cabernet Shiraz	South Australia

97	2010 Wolf Blass Black Label Cabernet Sauvignon Shiraz	South Australia
97	2012 Wolf Blass Black Label Cabernet Sauvignon Shiraz	South Australia
97	2013 Yarra Yering Dry Red No. 1	Yarra Valley

96   **Clare Valley** 2013 Eldredge The Reserve Malbec, 2013 Wendouree Cabernet Malbec, **Coonawarra** 2013 Lindeman's Limestone Ridge Vineyard Shiraz Cabernet, 2013 Lindeman's Pyrus Cabernet Sauvignon Cabernet Franc Malbec, **Frankland River** 2013 Larry Cherubino Ad Hoc Avant Gardening Cabernet Sauvignon Malbec, **Geelong** 2012 Lethbridge Hugo George, **Great Southern** 2012 Houghton CW Ferguson Cabernet Malbec, **Langhorne Creek** 2012 Lake Breeze Arthur's Reserve Cabernet Sauvignon Petit Verdot Malbec, **Manjimup** 2012 Rosenthal The Marker Southern Forest Cabernet Shiraz, **Margaret River** 2012 Brown Hill Estate Signature Range Bill Bailey Shiraz Cabernet, 2013 Churchview Estate St Johns Limited Release Cabernet Sauvignon Malbec Merlot, 2010 Flowstone Cabernet Sauvignon Touriga, 2012 Handpicked Collection Cabernet Merlot, 2013 House of Cards Limited Release Ace of Spades, 2012 McHenry Hohnen Rolling Stone, 2013 Mandoon Estate Cabernet Merlot, 2012 Moss Wood Ribbon Vale Vineyard Cabernet Sauvignon Merlot, 2012 Moss Wood Ribbon Vale Vineyard Merlot, 2011 Pierro Reserve Cabernet Sauvignon Merlot, 2013 Woodlands Margaret, **Nagambie Lakes** 2012 Tahbilk Old Vines Cabernet Shiraz, **Robe** 2013 Coates The Malbec, **Robe/ Mount Benson** 2012 Wolf Blass White Label Shiraz Cabernet, **Wrattonbully** 2013 Pepper Tree Single Vineyard Reserve 8R Merlot, 2012 Tapanappa Whalebone Vineyard Merlot Cabernet Franc, **Yarra Valley** 2013 Coombe Farm Tribute Series Armstrong Merlot, 2013 Giant Steps Sexton Vineyard Merlot, 2013 Giant Steps Harry's Monster, 2013 Helen & Joey Estate Alena Single Vineyard Cabernet Sauvignon Merlot, 2012 Levantine Hill Estate Samantha's Paddock Melange Traditionelle, 2012 Mac Forbes Hugh, 2013 Mount Mary Quintet.

Shiraz and Family

A South Australian stronghold, indeed stranglehold, mostly with some or all of shiraz, grenache and mourvedre. At least with this selection, grenache is on the march, especially that planted in McLaren Vale. I may be accused of bias, but I genuinely believe McLaren Vale Grenache and GMS blends to be of world standard.

RATING	WINE	REGION
97	2012 Yelland & Papps Divine Grenache	Barossa Valley
97	2013 Hungerford Hill Heavy Metal	Blend
97	2012 Golden Grove Estate Vintage Grand Reserve Mourvedre	Granite Belt
97	2012 d'Arenberg The Beautiful View Grenache	McLaren Vale
97	2012 d'Arenberg The Blewitt Sands Grenache	McLaren Vale
97	2012 Yangarra Estate Vineyard High Sands Grenache	McLaren Vale

96   **Adelaide Zone** 2012 Patritti Marion Vineyard Limited Release Grenache Shiraz, **Barossa Valley** 2012 Charles Melton Nine Popes, 2013 Eperosa Synthesis Mataro Grenache Shiraz, 2013 Hentley Farm The Quintessential Shiraz Cabernet, 2012 Hewitson Old Garden Mourvedre, **Barossa Zone** 2013 Tim Smith Mataro, **Clare Valley** 2013 Wendouree Shiraz Malbec, 2013 Wendouree Shiraz Mataro, **Eden Valley** 2013 Eperosa Stonegarden Grenache, 2013 Head Ancestor Vine Springton Grenache, **Hunter Valley** 2013 Briar Ridge Vineyard H.R.B Single Vineyard Shiraz Pinot Noir, 2013 Silkman Shiraz Pinot Noir, **Kangaroo Island** 2013 The Islander Estate Vineyards Old Rowley Shiraz Grenache, **King Valley** 2008 Brown Brothers 125 Years Special Release Shiraz Mondeuse Cabernet Sauvignon, **McLaren Vale** 2013 Angove Warboys Vineyard Grenache, 2013 BK Sparks Whole Bunch Blewitt Springs Grenache, 2012 Patritti Sitadela Shiraz Grenache, 2013 Two Hands Twelftree Schuller Blewitt Springs Grenache, 2013 Wirra Wirra The Absconder Grenache, 2013 Yangarra Estate Vineyard Small Pot Ceramic Egg Grenache, **Yarra Valley** 2013 Ben Haines B Minor Shiraz Marsanne, 2013 Pimpernel Vineyards GSM2, 2014 Serrat Grenache Noir, 2013 Yarra Yering Dry Red No. 2.

The Italians and Friends

With each year the quality (and quantity) of Sangiovese and Nebbiolo increases, with greater vine age and winemaking experience the drivers. Tempranillo is under-represented, but the two included are lovely, with others close behind.

RATING	WINE	REGION
97	2013 Mayford Porepunkah Tempranillo	Alpine Valleys
96	2013 Massena Vineyards Primitivo	Barossa Valley
96	2013 Jasper Hill Georgia's Paddock Nebbiolo	Heathcote
96	2013 Hugh Hamilton The Mongrel Sangiovese	McLaren Vale
96	2013 Kangarilla Road Vineyard Black St Peters Zinfandel	McLaren Vale
96	2012 Rudderless Sellicks Hill Graciano Malbec	McLaren Vale
96	2012 Valhalla Durif	Rutherglen
96	2013 Sedona Estate Yea Valley Sangiovese	Upper Goulburn
96	2013 Stefani Estate Boccalupo Sangiovese	Yarra Valley
96	2012 Tarrahill. Le Batard	Yarra Valley
96	2013 Tokar Estate The Aria Tempranillo	Yarra Valley

Fortified Wines

The points speak for themselves. These wines are unique to Australia in terms of their age, their complexity, their intensity and their varietal make-up. They arguably represent the best value of all Australian wines given the cost of production, notably in the amount of working capital tied up for decades.

RATING	WINE	REGION
100	1915 Seppeltsfield 100 Year Old Para Liqueur	Barossa Valley
99	NV Seppeltsfield Paramount Collection DP 273 Museum Reserve Rich Rare Apera	Barossa Valley
99	NV Seppeltsfield Paramount Collection DP 62 Museum Reserve Muscat	Barossa Valley
99	NV Seppeltsfield Paramount Collection DP 64 Museum Reserve Tokay	Barossa Valley
99	NV Chambers Rosewood Rare Muscadelle	Rutherglen
99	NV Chambers Rosewood Rare Muscat	Rutherglen
98	NV Seppeltsfield Paramount Collection DP 898 Museum Reserve Aged Flor Apera	Barossa Valley
98	NV Baileys of Glenrowan Winemakers Selection Rare Old Muscat	Glenrowan
98	NV All Saints Estate Museum Muscadelle	Rutherglen
98	NV All Saints Estate Rare Muscat Museum Release	Rutherglen
98	NV Campbells Merchant Prince Rare Muscat	Rutherglen
98	NV Morris Old Premium Liqueur Muscat	Rutherglen
98	NV Pfeiffer Rare Muscat	Rutherglen
97	**Barossa Valley** NV Penfolds Grandfather Rare Tawny, **Glenrowan** NV Baileys Winemaker's Selection Rare Old Topaque, **Rutherglen** NV All Saints Estate Rare Muscadelle, NV All Saints Estate Rare Muscat, NV Campbells Isabella Rare Topaque, NV Chambers Rosewood Grand Muscat, NV Morris Old Premium Rare Muscat, NV Pfeiffer Rare Topaque, NV Stanton & Killeen Rare Muscat, NV Stanton & Killeen Rare Topaque.	

Best wineries of the regions

The nomination of the best wineries of the regions has evolved into a three-level classification (further explained on page 9). At the very top are the wineries with their names and stars printed in red; these have been generally recognised for having a long track record of excellence – truly the best of the best. Next are wineries with their stars (but not their names) printed in red, which have had a consistent record of excellence for at least the last three years. Those wineries with black stars have achieved excellence this year (and sometimes longer).

ADELAIDE HILLS

Anvers ★★★★★
Ashton Hills ★★★★★
Bird in Hand ★★★★★
BK Wines ★★★★★
Catlin Wines ★★★★★
CRFT Wines ★★★★★
Deviation Road ★★★★★
Geoff Weaver ★★★★★
Jericho Wines ★★★★★
Karrawatta ★★★★★
Lofty Valley Wines ★★★★★
Mike Press Wines ★★★★★
Mt Lofty Ranges Vineyard ★★★★★
Murdoch Hill ★★★★★
Nepenthe ★★★★★
Ochota Barrels ★★★★★
Petaluma ★★★★★
Pike & Joyce ★★★★★
Riposte ★★★★★
Romney Park Wines ★★★★★
Scott ★★★★★
Shaw + Smith ★★★★★
Sidewood Estate ★★★★★
The Lane Vineyard ★★★★★

ADELAIDE ZONE

Heirloom Vineyards ★★★★★
Hewitson ★★★★★
Patritti Wines ★★★★★
Penfolds Magill Estate ★★★★★

BALLARAT

Eastern Peake ★★★★★
Tomboy Hill ★★★★★

BAROSSA VALLEY

Balthazar of the Barossa ★★★★★
Bethany Wines ★★★★★
Caillard Wine ★★★★★
Charles Cimicky ★★★★★
Charles Melton ★★★★★
David Franz ★★★★★
Dorrien Estate ★★★★★
Dutschke Wines ★★★★★
Elderton ★★★★★
Eperosa ★★★★★
Final Cut Wines ★★★★★
First Drop Wines ★★★★★
Fox Gordon ★★★★★
Gibson ★★★★★
Glaetzer Wines ★★★★★
Glen Eldon Wines ★★★★★
Grant Burge ★★★★★
Haan Wines ★★★★★
Head Wines ★★★★★
Hemera Estate ★★★★★
Hentley Farm Wines ★★★★★
Jacob's Creek ★★★★★
John Duval Wines ★★★★★
Kaesler Wines ★★★★★
Kalleske ★★★★★
Kellermeister ★★★★★
Langmeil Winery ★★★★★
Lanz Vineyards ★★★★★
Laughing Jack ★★★★★
Massena Vineyards ★★★★★
Maverick Wines ★★★★★
Murray Street Vineyards ★★★★★
Parous ★★★★★
Penfolds ★★★★★
Peter Lehmann ★★★★★

Purple Hands Wines ★★★★★
Rockford ★★★★★
Rolf Binder ★★★★★
Saltram ★★★★★
St Hallett ★★★★★
Schubert Estate ★★★★★
Schwarz Wine Company ★★★★★
Seppeltsfield ★★★★★
Smallfry Wines ★★★★★
Sons of Eden ★★★★★
Spinifex ★★★★★
Teusner ★★★★★
Thorn-Clarke Wines ★★★★★
Tim Smith Wines ★★★★★
Tomfoolery ★★★★★
Torbreck Vintners ★★★★★
Turkey Flat ★★★★★
Two Hands Wines ★★★★★
Westlake Vineyards ★★★★★
Whistler Wines ★★★★★
Wolf Blass ★★★★★
Woods Crampton ★★★★★
Yelland & Papps ★★★★★
Z Wine ★★★★★

BEECHWORTH
A. Rodda Wines ★★★★★
Domenica Wines ★★★★★
Fighting Gully Road ★★★★★
Giaconda ★★★★★
Golden Ball ★★★★★
Indigo Wine Company ★★★★★
Sorrenberg ★★★★★

BENDIGO
Ansted & Co. ★★★★★
Bress ★★★★★
Pondalowie Vineyards ★★★★★
Turner's Crossing Vineyard ★★★★★

BLACKWOOD VALLEY
Nannup Ridge Estate ★★★★★

CANBERRA DISTRICT
Capital Wines ★★★★★
Clonakilla ★★★★★
Collector Wines ★★★★★
Eden Road Wines ★★★★★
Four Winds Vineyard ★★★★★
Helm ★★★★★

Lark Hill ★★★★★
Lerida Estate ★★★★★
Mount Majura Vineyard ★★★★★
Nick O'Leary Wines ★★★★★

CENTRAL RANGES ZONE
Swinging Bridge ★★★★★

CENTRAL VICTORIA ZONE
Mount Terrible ★★★★★

CLARE VALLEY
Annie's Lane ★★★★★
Atlas Wines ★★★★★
Clos Clare ★★★★★
Crabtree Watervale Wines ★★★★★
Gaelic Cemetery Wines ★★★★★
Greg Cooley Wines ★★★★★
Grosset ★★★★★
Jim Barry Wines ★★★★★
Kilikanoon ★★★★★
Knappstein ★★★★★
Leasingham ★★★★★
Mitchell ★★★★★
Mount Horrocks ★★★★★
O'Leary Walker Wines ★★★★★
Paulett ★★★★★
Pikes ★★★★★
Reillys Wines ★★★★★
Skillogalee ★★★★★
Steve Wiblin's Erin Eyes ★★★★★
Taylors ★★★★★
Tim Adams ★★★★★
Vickery Wines ★★★★★
Wendouree ★★★★★
Wilson Vineyard ★★★★★
Wines by KT ★★★★★

COONAWARRA
Balnaves of Coonawarra ★★★★★
Bellwether ★★★★★
Brand's Laira Coonawarra ★★★★★
Hollick ★★★★★
Katnook Coonawarra ★★★★★
Koonara ★★★★★
Leconfield ★★★★★
Lindeman's ★★★★★
Majella ★★★★★
Parker Coonawarra Estate ★★★★★
Patrick of Coonawarra ★★★★★

Penley Estate ★★★★★
Wynns Coonawarra Estate ★★★★★
Zema Estate ★★★★★

CURRENCY CREEK
Shaw Family Vintners ★★★★★

DENMARK
Apricus Hill ★★★★★
Estate 807 ★★★★★
Harewood Estate ★★★★★
Moombaki Wines ★★★★★
Rockcliffe ★★★★★
The Lake House Denmark ★★★★★

EDEN VALLEY
Brockenchack ★★★★★
Flaxman Wines ★★★★★
Gatt Wines ★★★★★
Henschke ★★★★★
Hutton Vale Farm ★★★★★
Leo Buring ★★★★★
Pewsey Vale ★★★★★
Poonawatta ★★★★★
Rileys of Eden Valley ★★★★★
Yalumba ★★★★★

FRANKLAND RIVER
Alkoomi ★★★★★
Ferngrove ★★★★★
Frankland Estate ★★★★★
Swinney Vineyards ★★★★★

GEELONG
Austins & Co ★★★★★
Banks Road ★★★★★
Bannockburn Vineyards ★★★★★
Barrgowan Vineyard ★★★★★
Bellbrae Estate ★★★★★
Brown Magpie Wines ★★★★★
Clyde Park Vineyard ★★★★★
del Rios of Mt Anakie ★★★★★
Farr | Farr Rising ★★★★★
Jack Rabbit Vineyard ★★★★★
Lethbridge Wines ★★★★★
Oakdene ★★★★★
Paradise IV ★★★★★
Provenance Wines ★★★★★
Scotchmans Hill ★★★★★
Shadowfax ★★★★★

Terindah Estate ★★★★★
Yes said the Seal ★★★★★

GEOGRAPHE
Capel Vale ★★★★★
Whicher Ridge ★★★★★
Willow Bridge Estate ★★★★★

GIPPSLAND
Bass Phillip ★★★★★
Narkoojee ★★★★★
Philippa Farr ★★★★★
Wild Dog Winery ★★★★★

GLENROWAN
Baileys of Glenrowan ★★★★★

GRAMPIANS
A.T. Richardson Wines ★★★★★
Best's Wines ★★★★★
Clarnette & Ludvigsen Wines
    ★★★★★
Grampians Estate ★★★★★
Halls Gap Estate ★★★★★
Montara ★★★★★
Mount Langi Ghiran Vineyards
    ★★★★★
Seppelt ★★★★★
The Story Wines ★★★★★

GRANITE BELT
Boireann ★★★★★
Golden Grove Estate ★★★★★
Heritage Estate ★★★★★

GREAT SOUTHERN
Byron & Harold ★★★★★
Castelli Estate ★★★★★
Forest Hill Vineyard ★★★★★
Marchand & Burch ★★★★★
Rosenthal Wines ★★★★★
Singlefile Wines ★★★★★
Staniford Wine Co ★★★★★
Trevelen Farm ★★★★★
Willoughby Park ★★★★★

HEATHCOTE
Bull Lane Wine Company ★★★★★
Chalmers ★★★★★
Downing Estate Vineyard ★★★★★

Flynns Wines ★★★★★
Graillot ★★★★★
Greenstone Vineyard ★★★★★
Heathcote Estate ★★★★★
Jasper Hill ★★★★★
La Pleiade ★★★★★
Merindoc Vintners ★★★★★
Munari Wines ★★★★★
Paul Osicka ★★★★★
Sanguine Estate ★★★★★
Tellurian ★★★★★
The Bridge Vineyard ★★★★★

HENTY
Crawford River Wines ★★★★★

HILLTOPS
Barwang ★★★★★
Chalkers Crossing ★★★★★
Freeman Vineyards ★★★★★
Moppity Vineyards ★★★★★

HUNTER VALLEY
Audrey Wilkinson ★★★★★
Bimbadgen ★★★★★
Briar Ridge Vineyard ★★★★★
Brokenwood ★★★★★
Capercaillie ★★★★★
Cockfighter's Ghost ★★★★★
Colvin Wines ★★★★★
De Iuliis ★★★★★
Eagles Rest Wines ★★★★★
First Creek Wines ★★★★★
Gartelmann Wines ★★★★★
Gundog Estate ★★★★★
Hungerford Hill ★★★★★
Keith Tulloch Wine ★★★★★
Lake's Folly ★★★★★
Leogate Estate Wines ★★★★★
Margan Family ★★★★★
Meerea Park ★★★★★
Mistletoe Wines ★★★★★
Mount Pleasant ★★★★★
Mount View Estate ★★★★★
Pepper Tree Wines ★★★★★
Peter Drayton Wines ★★★★★
Pokolbin Estate ★★★★★
Ridgeview Wines ★★★★★
Silkman Wines ★★★★★

Tallavera Grove | Carillion ★★★★★
Tamburlaine ★★★★★
Thomas Wines ★★★★★
Tinklers Vineyard ★★★★★
Tintilla Wines ★★★★★
Tulloch ★★★★★
Tyrrell's ★★★★★

KANGAROO ISLAND
Dudley Wines ★★★★★
The Islander Estate Vineyards ★★★★★

KING VALLEY
Brown Brothers ★★★★★
Wood Park ★★★★★

LANGHORNE CREEK
Angas Plains Estate ★★★★★
Bleasdale Vineyards ★★★★★
Bremerton Wines ★★★★★
John's Blend ★★★★★
Lake Breeze Wines ★★★★★

MACEDON RANGES
Bindi Wine Growers ★★★★★
Curly Flat ★★★★★
Granite Hills ★★★★★
Hanging Rock Winery ★★★★★
Lane's End Vineyard ★★★★★
Passing Clouds ★★★★★
Silent Way ★★★★★

MCLAREN VALE
Bekkers ★★★★★
Bent Creek ★★★★★
Brash Higgins ★★★★★
Cape Barren Wines ★★★★★
Chalk Hill ★★★★★
Chapel Hill ★★★★★
Clarendon Hills ★★★★★
Coates Wines ★★★★★
Coriole ★★★★★
cradle of hills ★★★★★
d'Arenberg ★★★★★
Dandelion Vineyards ★★★★★
Di Fabio Estate ★★★★★
Dowie Doole ★★★★★
Ekhidna ★★★★★
Five Geese ★★★★★
Fox Creek Wines ★★★★★

Gemtree Wines ★★★★★
Geoff Merrill Wines ★★★★★
Hardys ★★★★★
Haselgrove Wines ★★★★★
Hugh Hamilton Wines ★★★★★
Inkwell ★★★★★
Kangarilla Road Vineyard ★★★★★
Kay Brothers Amery Vineyards
   ★★★★★
Longline Wines ★★★★★
Maxwell Wines ★★★★★
McLaren Vale III Associates ★★★★★
Mitolo Wines ★★★★★
Mr Riggs Wine Company ★★★★★
Olivers Taranga Vineyards ★★★★★
Paxton ★★★★★
Penny's Hill ★★★★★
Pirramimma ★★★★★
Primo Estate ★★★★★
Reynella ★★★★★
Richard Hamilton ★★★★★
Rosemount Estate ★★★★★
Rudderless ★★★★★
Samuel's Gorge ★★★★★
SC Pannell ★★★★★
Serafino Wines ★★★★★
Shingleback ★★★★★
Shirvington ★★★★★
The Old Faithful Estate ★★★★★
Tintara ★★★★★
WayWood Wines ★★★★★
Wirra Wirra ★★★★★
Woodstock ★★★★★
Yangarra Estate Vineyard ★★★★★

MARGARET RIVER
Amelia Park Wines ★★★★★
Ashbrook Estate ★★★★★
Brookland Valley ★★★★★
Brown Hill Estate ★★★★★
Burch Family Wines ★★★★★
Cape Grace Wines ★★★★★
Cape Mentelle ★★★★★
Chapman Grove Wines ★★★★★
Churchview Estate ★★★★★
Clairault | Streicker Wines ★★★★★
Cloudburst ★★★★★
Cullen Wines ★★★★★
Deep Woods Estate ★★★★★

Devil's Lair ★★★★★
Domaine Naturaliste ★★★★★
Evans & Tate ★★★★★
Evoi Wines ★★★★★
Fermoy Estate ★★★★★
Flametree ★★★★★
Flowstone Wines ★★★★★
Flying Fish Cove ★★★★★
Forester Estate ★★★★★
Franklin Tate Estates ★★★★★
Fraser Gallop Estate ★★★★★
Grace Farm ★★★★★
Greedy Sheep ★★★★★
Happs ★★★★★
Hay Shed Hill Wines ★★★★★
Heydon Estate ★★★★★
Ibizan Wines ★★★★★
Juniper Estate ★★★★★
KarriBindi ★★★★★
Laurance of Margaret River ★★★★★
Leeuwin Estate ★★★★★
Lenton Brae Wines ★★★★★
Marq Wines ★★★★★
McHenry Hohnen Vintners ★★★★★
Mon Tout ★★★★★
Moss Wood ★★★★★
Palmer Wines ★★★★★
Pierro ★★★★★
Redgate ★★★★★
Sandalford ★★★★★
Stella Bella Wines ★★★★★
Thompson Estate ★★★★★
Umamu Estate ★★★★★
Vasse Felix ★★★★★
Victory Point Wines ★★★★★
Voyager Estate ★★★★★
Warner Glen Estate ★★★★★
Watershed Premium Wines ★★★★★
Wills Domain ★★★★★
Windows Estate ★★★★★
Wise Wine ★★★★★
Woodlands ★★★★★
Woody Nook ★★★★★
Xanadu Wines ★★★★★

MORNINGTON PENINSULA
Allies Wines ★★★★★
Avani ★★★★★
Crittenden Estate ★★★★★

Dexter Wines ★★★★★
Eldridge Estate of Red Hill ★★★★★
Elgee Park ★★★★★
Foxeys Hangout ★★★★★
Garagiste ★★★★★
Hurley Vineyard ★★★★★
Jones Road ★★★★★
Kooyong ★★★★★
Lindenderry at Red Hill ★★★★★
Main Ridge Estate ★★★★★
Merricks Estate ★★★★★
Montalto ★★★★★
Moorooduc Estate ★★★★★
Paradigm Hill ★★★★★
Paringa Estate ★★★★★
Port Phillip Estate ★★★★★
Prancing Horse Estate ★★★★★
Red Hill Estate ★★★★★
Scorpo Wines ★★★★★
Stonier Wines ★★★★★
Ten Minutes by Tractor ★★★★★
Tuck's Ridge ★★★★★
Underground Winemakers ★★★★★
Willow Creek Vineyard ★★★★★
Yabby Lake Vineyard ★★★★★

MOUNT BARKER
Gilberts ★★★★★
Plantagenet ★★★★★
Poacher's Ridge Vineyard ★★★★★
West Cape Howe Wines ★★★★★
Xabregas ★★★★★

MOUNT LOFTY RANGES ZONE
Michael Hall Wines ★★★★★

MUDGEE
Huntington Estate ★★★★★
Robert Oatley Vineyards ★★★★★
Robert Stein Vineyard ★★★★★

NAGAMBIE LAKES
Mitchelton ★★★★★
Tahbilk ★★★★★

NORTH EAST VICTORIA ZONE
Eldorado Road ★★★★★

ORANGE
Bloodwood ★★★★★

Patina ★★★★★
Philip Shaw Wines ★★★★★
Printhie Wines ★★★★★
Ross Hill Wines ★★★★★
Sons & Brothers Vineyard ★★★★★

PADTHAWAY
Morambro Creek Wines ★★★★★

PEMBERTON
Bellarmine Wines ★★★★★

PERTH HILLS
Millbrook Winery ★★★★★

PORONGURUP
Abbey Creek Vineyard ★★★★★
Castle Rock Estate ★★★★★
Duke's Vineyard ★★★★★

PYRENEES
Blue Pyrenees Estate ★★★★★
Dalwhinnie ★★★★★
DogRock Winery ★★★★★
M. Chapoutier Australia ★★★★★
Mitchell Harris Wines ★★★★★
Mount Avoca ★★★★★
Summerfield ★★★★★
Taltarni ★★★★★

QUEENSLAND COASTAL
Witches Falls Winery ★★★★★

RIVERINA
De Bortoli ★★★★★
McWilliam's ★★★★★
Nugan Estate ★★★★★

RUTHERGLEN
All Saints Estate ★★★★★
Campbells ★★★★★
Chambers Rosewood ★★★★★
Morris ★★★★★
Pfeiffer Wines ★★★★★
Stanton & Killeen Wines ★★★★★

SHOALHAVEN COAST
Coolangatta Estate ★★★★★

SOUTH AUSTRALIA
Angove Family Winemakers ★★★★★

Tapanappa ★★★★★
Wines by Geoff Hardy ★★★★★

SOUTH WEST AUSTRALIA ZONE
Kerrigan + Berry ★★★★★
Snake + Herring ★★★★★

SOUTHERN FLEURIEU
Salomon Estate ★★★★★

SOUTHERN HIGHLANDS
Centennial Vineyards ★★★★★
Tertini Wines ★★★★★

STRATHBOGIE RANGES
Fowles Wine ★★★★★
Maygars Hill Winery ★★★★★

SUNBURY
Craiglee ★★★★★
Galli Estate ★★★★★

SWAN DISTRICT
Mandoon Estate ★★★★★

SWAN VALLEY
Faber Vineyard ★★★★★
Houghton ★★★★★
John Kosovich Wines ★★★★★
Talijancich ★★★★★

UPPER GOULBURN
Delatite ★★★★★
Sedona Estate ★★★★★

TASMANIA
Bangor Estate ★★★★★
Barringwood ★★★★★
Bay of Fires ★★★★★
Bream Creek ★★★★★
Brook Eden Vineyard ★★★★★
Chatto ★★★★★
Clemens Hill ★★★★★
Craigow ★★★★★
Dalrymple ★★★★★
Dawson & James ★★★★★
Derwent Estate ★★★★★
Domaine A ★★★★★
Freycinet ★★★★★
Frogmore Creek ★★★★★
Gala Estate ★★★★★

Heemskerk ★★★★★
Holm Oak ★★★★★
Home Hill ★★★★★
House of Arras ★★★★★
Jansz Tasmania ★★★★★
Josef Chromy Wines ★★★★★
Milton Vineyard ★★★★★
Moores Hill Estate ★★★★★
Moorilla Estate ★★★★★
Morningside Vineyard ★★★★★
Pipers Brook Vineyard ★★★★★
Pooley Wines ★★★★★
Pressing Matters ★★★★★
Sinapius Vineyard ★★★★★
Stargazer Wine ★★★★★
Stefano Lubiana ★★★★★
Stoney Rise ★★★★★
Tamar Ridge | Pirie ★★★★★
Tolpuddle Vineyard ★★★★★
Velo Wines ★★★★★
Waterton Vineyards ★★★★★

VARIOUS
Ben Haines Wine ★★★★★
Echelon ★★★★★
Handpicked Wines ★★★★★
Ministry of Clouds ★★★★★
Smidge Wines ★★★★★
Stonefish ★★★★★
Twofold ★★★★★
Vinaceous Wines ★★★★★

VICTORIA
Di Sciascio Family Wines ★★★★★

WESTERN AUSTRALIA
Domaines & Vineyards ★★★★★
Larry Cherubino Wines ★★★★★

WRATTONBULLY
Terre à Terre ★★★★★

YARRA VALLEY
Bicknell fc ★★★★★
Buttermans Track ★★★★★
Carlei Estate | Carlei Green Vineyards
  ★★★★★
Chandon Australia ★★★★★
Coldstream Hills ★★★★★
Coombe Farm ★★★★★

De Bortoli ★★★★★
Dominique Portet ★★★★★
Five Oaks Vineyard ★★★★★
Gembrook Hill ★★★★★
Helen & Joey Estate ★★★★★
Helen's Hill Estate ★★★★★
Hillcrest Vineyard ★★★★★
Hoddles Creek Estate ★★★★★
In Dreams ★★★★★
Innocent Bystander ★★★★★
Jamsheed ★★★★★
Journey Wines ★★★★★
Kellybrook ★★★★★
Levantine Hill Estate ★★★★★
Mac Forbes ★★★★★
Mandala ★★★★★
Mayer ★★★★★
Medhurst ★★★★★
Mount Mary ★★★★★
Oakridge Wines ★★★★★
Out of Step ★★★★★
Pimpernel Vineyards ★★★★★
PHI ★★★★★
Punch ★★★★★
Punt Road ★★★★★
Rob Dolan Wines ★★★★★
Rochford Wines ★★★★★
St Huberts ★★★★★
Serrat ★★★★★
Seville Estate ★★★★★
Stefani Estate ★★★★★
Sticks Yarra Valley ★★★★★
Sutherland Estate ★★★★★
Tarrahill. ★★★★★
TarraWarra Estate ★★★★★
The Wanderer ★★★★★
Thick as Thieves Wines ★★★★★
Tokar Estate ★★★★★
Toolangi Vineyards ★★★★★
Trellis ★★★★★
Wantirna Estate ★★★★★
Warramunda Estate ★★★★★
Yarra Yering ★★★★★
Yarrabank ★★★★★
YarraLoch ★★★★★
Yering Station ★★★★★
Yeringberg ★★★★★

Ten of the best new wineries

Each one of these wineries making its debut in the *Wine Companion* has earned a five-star rating. They are thus the leaders of the 96 new wineries in this edition, although a number of other first-up wineries also achieved five stars. The ultimate selection criteria included the number of wines earning 95 points or above, and also value for money.

BEST NEW WINERY
Bicknell fc Yarra Valley / **PAGE 112**
See the entry for Best New Winery on page 18.

Apricus Hill Denmark / **PAGE 79**
It seems a little unfair that James and Careena Kellie, winemaker/owners of Harewood Estate, can acquire a 20-year-old vineyard, start a new estate-based vineyard, and create a new five-star winery. But they have picked the eyes out of the best blocks to make a small range of single vineyard, single varietal wines. Three of the wines scored 95 points, the fourth 94 points.

Bangor Estate Southern Tasmania / **PAGE 94**
Five generations of the Dunbabin family have farmed at Bangor; the 6200ha Forestier Peninsula property of today has 5100ha of native forest, grasslands and wetlands, dwarfing the 4ha of chardonnay, pinot noir and pinot gris. Three wines received 95 points, the other two 93 and 92 respectively.

Bent Creek McLaren Vale / **PAGE 109**
The partners of Bent Creek have established ties with growers in McLaren Vale and the Adelaide Hills, and secured the services of Tim Geddes (and his McLaren Vale winery) to make the wines. McLaren Vale Shiraz from 2010, '12 and '13 all came from vines planted in the 1930s and '40s, all rating highly, two scoring 95 points.

Catlin Wines Adelaide Hills / **PAGE 159**
Darryl Catlin grew up in the Barossa Valley, worked in Adelaide retail, and then rose from cellar hand to winemaker at Shaw + Smith. His portfolio is anchored on the Adelaide Hills, with two Clare Valley Rieslings completing the six wines tasted, two at 95 points, two at 94, and two at 93, all but one with a value symbol.

Cloudburst Margaret River / **PAGE 179**

Without question the most interesting new winery, with prices for the six wines between $200 and $250. The wines are made at Woodlands by Will Berliner, under the watchful eye of Stuart Watson. The high-class packaging of the 450 dozen of biodynamic Chardonnay, Cabernet Sauvignon and Malbec garnered three wines with 96 points, another with 95.

CRFT Wines Adelaide Hills / **PAGE 198**

Life and business partners New Zealand-born Frewin Ries and Barossa-born Candice Helbig crammed in multiple wine lives before establishing CRFT in 2012, their first vintage following in '13. Four wines at 95 and 96 points, two at 94, and two at 93 say it all: Adelaide Hills Pinot Noir, Gruner Veltliner, Gewurztraminer, Barossa Shiraz ...

Domaine Naturaliste Margaret River / **PAGE 228**

Bruce Dukes' career dates back over 25 years, its foundations built on a master's degree in viticulture and agronomy from the University of California, Davis. Having made Margaret River wines for others, in 2012 he moved to finally set up his own brand, Domaine Naturaliste, scoring 98 points with his Cabernet Sauvignon, backed up by four excellent Chardonnays and a Sauvignon Blanc Semillon.

Gala Estate East Coast Tasmania / **PAGE 276**

A 4000ha sheep station, with sixth, seventh and eighth generation custodians of the land, has an 11ha vineyard heavily skewed to pinot noir (7ha); three wines at 95 points, another two at 93 points. All the wines are estate-grown, Pinot Noir at the forefront supported by Riesling, Chardonnay and Pinot Gris.

Silkman Wines Hunter Valley / **PAGE 602**

The 1000-dozen side venture of Shaun and Liz Silkman (née Jackson), who both hold senior roles at custom crush First Creek Wines. It's a powerful team that has three wines at 96 points (one a Shiraz Pinot Noir blend), a fourth at 95, all with value symbols. The wine show record, too, is outstanding.

Ten of the best value wineries

It was an agonising task to choose between the best value wineries, which provide a brilliant snapshot of the extraordinary quality and value (or vice versa) of Australia's top wines. These would stand up to the best in the world at prices three to five times higher than those offered by these wineries, any one of which could have received top billing.

BEST VALUE WINERY
West Cape Howe Mount Barker / **PAGE 710**
See the entry for Best Value Winery on page 17.

Innocent Bystander Yarra Valley / **PAGE 347**
One of the leading wineries in the Yarra Valley, with a brilliant portfolio of wines (seven out of eight with the value symbol), a massively talented winemaker in Steve Flamsteed, the dynamism of owner Phil Sexton, and a large, brasserie-style restaurant that is always full of customers. Best take away? The bread from the wood-fired pizza oven.

Larry Cherubino Western Australia / **PAGE 388**
Larry Cherubino is never far from the top, his winery winning Winery of the Year in 2011. It's not just the spectacular array of high quality wines, but also the value for money: this year, 20 of 27 wines tasted received the value symbol; 11 were rated between 95 points and 98 points.

Mandoon Estate Swan District / **PAGE 421**
This is the venture of Allan Erceg, a highly successful real estate/shopping centre developer in Perth. Allan has bonded with winemaker Ryan Sudano; all 11 wines tasted received the value symbol, and seven rated between 95 and 97 points. This is a business that has progressed at lightning speed since its establishment in 2009, its future limitless.

Moppity Vineyards Hilltops / **PAGE 450**
Moppity has swept all before it in recent years, with a cascade of gold medals here and abroad; it also provided the grapes for the Jimmy Watson Trophy-winning Eden Road Long Road Hilltops Shiraz in 2009. Jason Brown's prior experience as a retailer has served him well in pitching the prices at a consistently enticing level.

Mount Pleasant Hunter Valley / **PAGE 462**

Mount Pleasant is going to continue to throw down the gauntlet to all other wineries in the Hunter Valley. Its offer this year is extraordinary: 14 of 17 wines tasted given value symbols, with an awesome array of wines between 97 and 98 points. When the '14 vintage reds come on-stream next year, it will surely be unstoppable.

Pepper Tree Wines Hunter Valley / **PAGE 511**

Stands close by the shoulder of Mount Pleasant, with 15 of 19 wines tasted receiving value symbols, and 12 wines between 96 and 97 points. Its advantage is a reach extending to Orange, Coonawarra and Wrattonbully, all of which contribute to its Semillon, Sauvignon Blanc, Shiraz and particularly impressive Cabernet Sauvignons.

Seppelt Grampians / **PAGE 588**

Another superstar this year, eight of its 11 wines with the value symbol, three at 97 points, and another three at 96 points, drawing on estate vineyards in Drumborg, Heathcote and the Grampians. Riesling, Chardonnay, Shiraz and Pinot Noir are all in the mix, skilled winemaking also helping.

Shingleback McLaren Vale / **PAGE 597**

The sheer consistency of the Shingleback wines, led by Shiraz from 110ha of estate vines, resulted in 14 of 17 wines tasted with value symbols. One wine at 97 and two at 96 points led the charge, albeit at higher price points. Six wines scoring 90 points or above are under $20.

Stonier Wines Mornington Peninsula / **PAGE 627**

I have to admit to being surprised by the number of wines scoring 95 points and above: 17. Yes, only ten have value symbols, but if you're in the market for high-quality, elegant Chardonnay and Pinot Noir made with extraordinary attention to detail between $45 and $55, head to Stonier.

Ten dark horses

To qualify for this category, each winery has to have received a five-star rating for the first time, and have a history of lesser ratings. Every wine growing state is represented, and eight of the ten come from different regions (the remaining two with a spread of regions). Terindah Estate is Dark Horse of the Year, and accordingly heads the list; the remaining wineries are in alphabetical order.

DARK HORSE OF THE YEAR
Terindah Estate Geelong / PAGE 651
Peter Slattery bought the 487ha property in 2001, and committed himself to the challenge of planting the vineyard, developing a restaurant, and being involved in the winemaking. He planted shiraz, pinot noir, pinot gris, picolit, chardonnay and zinfandel. Of his eight wines, three were awarded 95 points, another two 94 points, and four given the value symbol.

Di Sciascio Family Wines Victoria / PAGE 222
Matthew Di Sciascio graduated from Deakin University in 2005 as co-dux of the wine science degree, having previously graduated from Dookie Agricultural College's viticultural course. The wines come from Drumborg, Macedon Ranges and Geelong, two wines gaining the five-glass rating and all five wines the value symbol.

Dowie Doole McLaren Vale / PAGE 233
Having been on the brink, as it were, in the last three *Wine Companions*, with a four-and-a-half-star rating in those years, Norm Doole and Drew Dowie (who co-founded the winery in 1996) achieved the breakthrough this year, with three wines at 95 points, four with the value symbol. The five vineyards associated with Dowie Doole are all managed sustainably.

Greedy Sheep Margaret River / PAGE 296
When Bridget Allen purchased the vineyard in 2004 it had been planted to cabernet sauvignon, merlot, cabernet franc and malbec in '99. It pays to have a sense of humour, for in January '05 1000 sheep found their way into the vineyard, eating everything green within their reach, including unripe grapes. All three wines received 95 points and value symbols.

Heritage Estate Granite Belt / PAGE 326
Bruce and Paddy Kassulke have two estate vineyards, the cooler at Cottonvale growing white varieties, the other at Ballandean with red varieties and marsanne planted. They have navigated their way through some difficult growing seasons, including hail, but seized the opportunity provided by the excellent 2014 vintage. Five wines scored 95 or 94 points.

Reillys Wines Clare Valley / **PAGE 546**

There has never been any doubt that owners Justin Ardill (an Adelaide cardiologist) and wife Julie have unfailingly produced wines worthy of the red value symbol. 13 out of 20 wines tasted this year received the symbol, enough to have Reillys Wines as a contender for a Best Value Winery commendation. Both the 95-point wines received a value symbol, lifting its rating from the four or four-and-a-half stars of many years standing.

Sinapius Vineyard Northern Tasmania / **PAGE 604**

Vaughn Dell and Linda Morice purchased the former Golders Vineyard (planted in 1994) in 2005, and increased the plantings of pinot noir to include 13 clones and those of chardonnay to include eight clones. These new plantings are at a hyper density of 10 250 vines per hectare. All vineyard work is carried out by hand, rewarded with three wines at 95 points.

Stonefish Various / **PAGE 626**

Founder/owner Peter Papanikitas has 30 years of marketing experience, the last 15 focusing on Stonefish, a business he set up on a virtual winery basis. Stonefish rated four stars for the previous three years, but broke through this year with two splendid Barossa Shirazs from the 2012 vintage, and two keenly priced wines from Western Australia.

Underground Winemakers Mornington Peninsula / **PAGE 693**

Adrian Hennessy, Jonathon Stevens and Peter Stebbing had variously made wine in Alsace, Burgundy, Northern Italy and Swan Hill before establishing Underground Winemakers in 2004. They leased a small winery at Mount Eliza and have achieved miracles with the micro-sized winery equipment, with Pinot Noir from the Peninsula, and (inter alia) Durif and Shiraz from Northern and Central Victoria.

Whistler Wines Barossa Valley / **PAGE 713**

Brothers Martin and Chris Pfeiffer (and their families) established their winery in 1999, Martin with 25 years as a viticulturist with Southcorp, Chris with marketing skills as a publisher, and Josh Pfeiffer (Martin's son) as winemaker. Having received a four-star rating for the last three years, they broke through this year with Shiraz and Grenache at 95 points.

Australia's geographical indications

The process of formally mapping Australia's wine regions is all but complete, though it will never come to an outright halt – for one thing, climate change is lurking in the wings. The division into States, Zones, Regions and Subregions follows; those Regions or Subregions marked with an asterisk are not yet registered, and may never be, but are in common usage. The bizarre Hunter Valley GI map now has Hunter Valley as a Zone, Hunter as the Region and the sprawling Upper Hunter as a Subregion along with Pokolbin (small and disputed by some locals). Another recent official change has been the registration of Mount Gambier as a Region in the Limestone Coast Zone.

I am still in front of the game with Tasmania, dividing it into Northern, Southern and East Coast. In a similar vein, I have included Ballarat (with 15 wineries) and the Southern Eyre Peninsula (three wineries).

State/Zone	Region	Subregion
AUSTRALIA		
Australia Australian South Eastern Australia★	★ The South Eastern Australia Zone incorporates the whole of the states of NSW, Vic and Tas, and only part of Qld and SA.	
NEW SOUTH WALES		
Big Rivers	Murray Darling Perricoota Riverina Swan Hill	
Central Ranges	Cowra Mudgee Orange	
Hunter Valley	Hunter	Broke Fordwich Pokolbin Upper Hunter Valley

State/Zone	Region	Subregion
Northern Rivers	Hastings River	
Northern Slopes	New England Australia	
South Coast	Shoalhaven Coast Southern Highlands	
Southern New South Wales	Canberra District Gundagai Hilltops Tumbarumba	
Western Plains		

SOUTH AUSTRALIA

Adelaide (Super Zone, includes Mount Lofty Ranges, Fleurieu and Barossa)

State/Zone	Region	Subregion
Barossa	Barossa Valley Eden Valley	 High Eden
Far North	Southern Flinders Ranges	
Fleurieu	Currency Creek Kangaroo Island Langhorne Creek McLaren Vale Southern Fleurieu	
Limestone Coast	Coonawarra Mount Benson Mount Gambier Padthaway Robe Wrattonbully	
Lower Murray	Riverland	
Mount Lofty Ranges	Adelaide Hills	Lenswood Piccadilly Valley
	Adelaide Plains Clare Valley	 Polish Hill River★ Watervale★
The Peninsulas	Southern Eyre Peninsula★	

State/Zone	Region	Subregion
VICTORIA		
Central Victoria	Bendigo Goulburn Valley Heathcote Strathbogie Ranges Upper Goulburn	Nagambie Lakes
Gippsland		
North East Victoria	Alpine Valleys Beechworth Glenrowan King Valley Rutherglen	
North West Victoria	Murray Darling Swan Hill	
Port Phillip	Geelong Macedon Ranges Mornington Peninsula Sunbury Yarra Valley	
Western Victoria	Ballarat★ Grampians Henty Pyrenees	Great Western
WESTERN AUSTRALIA		
Central Western Australia		
Eastern Plains, Inland and North of Western Australia		
Greater Perth	Peel Perth Hills Swan District	Swan Valley

State/Zone	Region	Subregion
South West Australia	Blackwood Valley	
	Geographe	
	Great Southern	Albany
		Denmark
		Frankland River
		Mount Barker
		Porongurup
	Manjimup	
	Margaret River	
	Pemberton	
West Australian South East Coastal		

QUEENSLAND

Queensland	Granite Belt	
	South Burnett	

TASMANIA

Tasmania	Northern Tasmania★	
	Southern Tasmania★	
	East Coast Tasmania★	

AUSTRALIAN CAPITAL TERRITORY

NORTHERN TERRITORY

Varietal wine styles and regions

For better or worse, there simply has to be concerted action to highlight the link between regions, varieties and wine styles. It's not a question of creating the links: they are already there, and have been in existence for periods as short as 20 years or as long as 150 years. So here is an abbreviated summary of those regional styles (in turn reflected in the Best of the Best lists commencing on page 20).

Riesling

The link with the **Eden Valley** dates back at least to when Joseph Gilbert planted his Pewsey Vale vineyard, and quickly made its way to the nearby **Clare Valley**. These two regions stood above all others for well over 100 years, producing wines that shared many flavour and texture characteristics: lime (a little more obvious in the Eden Valley), apple, talc and mineral, lightly browned toasty notes emerging with five to 10 years bottle age. Within the last 20 or so years, the subregions of the **Great Southern** of Western Australia have established a deserved reputation for finely structured, elegant wines with wonderful length, sometimes shy when young, bursting into song after five years. The subregions are (in alphabetical order) **Albany**, **Denmark**, **Frankland River**, **Mount Barker** and **Porongurup**. **Tasmania**, too, produces high-class Rieslings, notable for their purity and intensity courtesy of their high natural acidity. Finally, there is the small and very cool region of **Henty** (once referred to as Drumborg): its exceptional Rieslings share many things with those of Tasmania.

Semillon

There is a Siamese-twin relationship between Semillon and the **Hunter Valley**, which has been producing a wine style like no other in the world for well over 100 years. The humid and very warm climate (best coupled with sandy soils not common in the region) results in wines that have a median alcohol level of 10.5% and no residual sugar, are cold-fermented in stainless steel and bottled within three months of vintage. They are devoid of colour and have only the barest hints of grass, herb and mineral wrapped around a core of acidity. Over the next five to 10 years they develop a glowing green-gold colour, a suite of grass and citrus fruit surrounded by buttered toast and honey notes. Like Rieslings, screwcaps have added decades to their cellaring life. The **Adelaide Hills** and **Margaret River** produce entirely different Semillon, more structured and weighty, its alcohol 13% to 14%, and as often as not blended with sauvignon blanc, barrel fermentation of part or all common. Finally, there is a cuckoo in the nest: Peter Lehmann in the **Barossa/Eden Valley** has adapted Hunter Valley practices, picking early, fermenting in steel, bottling early, and holding the top wine for five years before release – and succeeding brilliantly.

Chardonnay

This infinitely flexible grape is grown and vinified in all 63 regions, and accounts for half of Australia's white wine grapes and wine. Incredibly, before 1970 it was all but unknown, hiding its promise here and there (**Mudgee** was one such place) under a cloak of anonymity. It was there and in the **Hunter Valley** that the first wines labelled Chardonnay were made in 1971 (by Craigmoor and Tyrrell's). Its bold yellow colour, peaches and cream flavour and vanilla oak was unlike anything that had gone before and was accepted by domestic and export markets with equal enthusiasm. When exports took off into the stratosphere between 1985 and 1995, one half of Brand Australia was cheerful and cheap oak-chipped Chardonnay grown in the **Riverina** and **Riverland**. By coincidence, over the same period Chardonnay from the emerging cool climate regions was starting to appear in limited quantities, its flavour and structure radically different from the warm-grown, high-cropped wine. Another 10 years on, and by 2005/06 the wine surplus was starting to build rapidly, with demand for Chardonnay much less than its production. As attention swung from Chardonnay to Sauvignon Blanc, the situation became dire. Lost in the heat of battle were supremely elegant wines from most cool regions, **Margaret River** and **Yarra Valley** the leaders of the large band. Constant refinement of the style, and the adoption of the screwcap, puts these wines at the forefront of the gradually succeeding battle to re-engage consumers here and abroad with what are world-class wines.

Sauvignon Blanc

Two regions, the **Adelaide Hills** and **Margaret River**, stood in front of all others until being recently joined by **Orange**; these three produce Australia's best Sauvignon Blancs, wines with real structure and authority. It is a matter of record that Marlborough Sauvignon Blanc accounts for one-third of Australia's white wine sales; all one can say (accurately) is that the basic Marlborough style is very different, and look back at what happened with Australian Chardonnay. Margaret River also offers complex blends of sauvignon blanc and semillon in widely varying proportions, and with varying degrees of oak fermentation.

Shiraz

Shiraz, like chardonnay, is by far the most important red variety and, again like chardonnay, is tremendously flexible in its ability to adapt to virtually any combination of climate and soil/terroir. Unlike chardonnay, a recent arrival, shiraz was the most important red variety throughout the 19th and 20th centuries. Its ancestral homes were the **Barossa Valley**, the **Clare Valley**, **McLaren Vale** and the **Hunter Valley**, and it still leads in those regions. With the exception of the Hunter Valley, it was as important in making fortified wine as table wine between 1850 and 1950, aided and abetted by grenache and mourvedre (mataro). In New South Wales the **Hilltops** and **Canberra District** are producing elegant, cool-grown wines that usually conceal their power (especially when co-fermented with viognier) but not their silky length. Further north, but at a higher altitude, **Orange** is also producing fine, fragrant and spicy wines. All the other NSW regions are capable of producing Shiraz of seriously good character and quality; shiraz ripens comfortably, but quite late in the season. Polished, sophisticated wines are the result. Victoria has a cornucopia of regions at the cooler end of the spectrum; the coolest (though not too cool for comfort) are the **Yarra Valley**, **Mornington Peninsula**, **Sunbury** and **Geelong**, all producing fragrant, spicy, medium-bodied wines. **Bendigo**, **Heathcote**, **Grampians** and **Pyrenees**, more or less running east–west across the centre of Victoria, are producing some of the most exciting medium-bodied Shirazs in Australia, each with its own terroir stamp, but all combining generosity and elegance. In Western Australia, **Great Southern** and three of its five subregions, **Frankland River**, **Mount Barker** and **Porongurup**, are making magical Shirazs, fragrant and spicy, fleshy yet strongly structured. **Margaret River** has been a relatively late mover, but it, too, is producing wines with exemplary varietal definition and finesse.

Cabernet Sauvignon

The tough-skinned cabernet sauvignon can be, and is, grown in all regions, but it struggles in the coolest (notably **Tasmania**) and loses desirable varietal definition in the warmer regions, especially in warmer vintages. Shiraz can cope with alcohol levels in excess of 14.5%, but cabernet can't. In South Australia, **Coonawarra** stands supreme, its climate (though not its soil) strikingly similar to that of Bordeaux, the main difference lower rainfall. Perfectly detailed Cabernets are the result, with no need of shiraz or merlot to fill in the mid-palate, although some excellent blends are made. **Langhorne Creek** (a little warmer) and **McLaren Vale** (warmer still) have similar maritime climates, doubtless the reason why McLaren Vale manages to deal with the warmth of its summer/autumn weather. The **Eden Valley** is the most reliable of the inner regions; the other principal regions are dependent on a cool summer. From South Australia to Western Australia, where **Margaret River**, with its extreme maritime climate shaped by the warm Indian Ocean, stands tall. It is also Australia's foremost producer of Cabernet Merlot et al. in the Bordeaux mix. The texture and structure of both the straight varietal and the blend are regal, often to the point of austerity when the wines are young, but the sheer power of the underlying fruit provides the balance and guarantees the future development of the wines over a conservative 20 years, especially if screwcapped. The **Great Southern** subregions of **Frankland River** and **Mount Barker** share a continental climate that is somewhat cooler than Margaret River, and has a greater diurnal temperature range. Here Cabernet has an incisive, dark berry character and firm but usually fine tannins – not demanding merlot, though a touch of it and/or malbec can be beneficial. It is grown successfully through the centre and south of Victoria, but is often overshadowed by shiraz. In the last 20 years it has ceased to be a problem child and become a favourite son of the **Yarra Valley**; the forward move of vintage dates has been the key to the change.

Pinot Noir

The promiscuity of shiraz (particularly) and cabernet sauvignon is in sharp contrast to the puritanical rectitude of pinot noir. One sin of omission or commission, and the door slams shut, leaving the bewildered winemaker on the outside. **Tasmania** is the El Dorado for the variety, and the best is still to come, with better clones, older vines and greater exploration of the multitude of mesoclimates that Tasmania has to offer. Though it is north of Central Otago (New Zealand), its vineyards are all air conditioned by the Southern Ocean and Tasman Sea, and it stands toe-to-toe with Central Otago in its ability to make deeply coloured, profound Pinot with all the length one could ask for. Once on the mainland, Victoria's **Port Phillip Zone**, encompassing the **Geelong, Macedon Ranges, Sunbury, Mornington Peninsula** and **Yarra Valley**, is the epicentre of Australian Pinot Noir, **Henty** a small outpost. The sheer number of high-quality, elegant wines produced by dozens of makers in those regions puts the **Adelaide Hills** and **Porongurup** (also capable of producing quality Pinot) into the shade.

Other Red Varieties

There are many other red varieties in the *Wine Companion* database, and there is little rhyme or reason in the distribution of the plantings.

Sparkling Wines

The patter is eerily similar to that for pinot noir, **Tasmania** now and in the future the keeper of the Holy Grail, the **Port Phillip Zone** the centre of activity on the mainland.

Fortified Wines

Rutherglen and **Glenrowan** are the two (and only) regions that produce immensely complex, long-barrel-aged Muscat and Muscadelle, the latter called Tokay for over a century, now renamed Topaque. These wines have no equal in the world; Spain's Malaga is nearest in terms of lusciousness, but nowhere near as complex. The other producer of a wine without parallel is Seppeltsfield in the **Barossa Valley**, which each year releases an explosively rich and intense tawny liqueur style that is 100% 100 years old.

Australian vintage charts

Each number represents a mark out of 10 for the quality of vintages in each region.

red wine   white wine   fortified

NSW

2011	2012	2013	2014
Hunter Valley			
10	2	8	10
7	7	8	7
Mudgee			
6	5	7	7
8	7	8	9
Orange			
6	7	9	5
7	8	9	7
Riverina/Griffith			
6	8	7	7
7	9	8	8
Canberra District			
8	7	9	7
9	8	9	8
Southern Highlands			
6	4	7	7
7	7	8	7
Hilltops			
7	7	9	9
6	7	9	9
Tumbarumba			
6	-	8	9
7	7	9	8
Shoalhaven			
7	6	8	9
8	8	8	9

VIC

2011	2012	2013	2014
Yarra Valley			
6	10	9	7
9	9	8	8
Mornington Peninsula			
5	9	9	9
6	9	8	9
Geelong			
6	10	9	8
7	8	8	7
Macedon Ranges			
7	8	9	8
8	7	9	8
Sunbury			
6	8	9	9
7	8	9	8
Grampians			
7	9	9	9
8	8	8	9
Pyrenees			
5	9	8	8
8	7	7	8
Henty			
8	9	10	9
9	9	8	10
Bendigo			
6	9	8	9
8	8	7	7
Heathcote			
7	9	9	8
8	8	6	7

2011	2012	2013	2014
Nagambie Lakes			
6	7	9	8
8	8	7	8
Upper Goulburn			
5	8	9	9
9	7	9	9
Strathbogie Ranges			
2	7	9	6
6	7	7	7
Glenrowan			
3	7	9	9
3	6	7	7
Rutherglen			
5	9	10	7
6	10	8	6
King Valley			
5	7	8	7
7	8	8	9
Alpine Valleys			
4	7	9	7
6	9	7	8
Beechworth			
6	8	8	8
8	9	9	8
Gippsland			
6	9	8	5
8	9	8	9
Murray Darling			
1	9	8	8
4	9	7	8

SA

Region	2011	2012	2013	2014
Barossa Valley	5	10	8	7
	7	8	7	7
Eden Valley	5	10	8	8
	7	9	8	8
Clare Valley	5	9	7	8
	7	10	8	8
Adelaide Hills	3	10	9	8
	6	9	8	8
Adelaide Plains	5	8	7	7
	6	6	6	7
Coonawarra	6	8	9	8
	8	8	8	8
Padthaway	6	8	8	8
	8	8	8	9
Mount Benson & Robe	5	9	7	9
	7	9	8	9
Wrattonbully	5	9	9	9
	7	8	8	8
McLaren Vale	7	10	9	7
	8	9	8	8
Southern Fleurieu	7	9	6	8
	8	8	5	8
Langhorne Creek	7	10	9	9
	8	8	8	8
Kangaroo Island	6	10	8	8
	8	10	8	9
Riverland	5	9	8	8
	5	7	8	8

WA

Region	2011	2012	2013	2014
Margaret River	9	10	9	8
	8	8	9	9
Great Southern	9	8	7	8
	8	8	8	8
Manjimup	8	7	8	9
	8	7	9	8
Pemberton	8	8	8	9
	8	8	9	9
Geographe	9	9	6	9
	8	7	7	8
Swan District	8	9	9	8
	7	7	8	8
Peel	-	8	9	8
	-	8	9	8
Perth Hills	-	8	8	8
	-	7	10	10

QLD

Region	2011	2012	2013	2014
Granite Belt	5	10	8	9
	4	7	8	8
South Burnett	5	8	8	8
	8	7	9	7

TAS

Region	2011	2012	2013	2014
Northern Tasmania	7	8	7	8
	8	9	8	9
Southern Tasmania	8	9	8	9
	9	8	7	9

Australian vintage 2015: a snapshot

All the stars were aligned for an outstanding vintage in 2015 for most of the regions of South East Australia. The major exception was the Hunter Valley, brought down to earth by a rain-sodden summer (after two great vintages in '13 and '14).

For the rest of South East Australia, there were strikingly similar weather patterns: a dry spring after good winter rains, which meant warm soils and early budburst, followed by an at times uncomfortably cool January (especially at night, with doonas essential), then a hot, helter-skelter February as grapes ripened very quickly.

Why should this scenario result in top-quality grapes? The key was the cool January, which in fact provided the vines with ideal conditions for ripening, and – most of all – the heat that followed in February, which lead to the retention of high levels of acidity. The high temperatures in turn abruptly gave way to a cool March.

The cool regions had a more orderly vintage, harvest commencing in March and into April, well after the heat had dissipated. After the abysmal yields of '14, yields were generally on the upper side of average, which gave rise to an unexpected challenge: finding enough barrels, new or used, leading to frantic phone calls and advertisements in the *Daily Wine News*. It was to no avail: barrels were almost impossible to find.

I used the term South East Australia deliberately – for once, Western Australia's Teflon-coated climate was unpredictable – and bird pressure increased the stress.

SOUTH AUSTRALIA

The **Barossa Valley** had a vintage in two halves. Winter rainfall was good, but the driest spring since 2006 was followed by only one rainfall event in early January, as well as that month's lowest mean maximum temperature for 23 years. February was the opposite, with the highest mean maximum temperature since 2007. All varieties ripened rapidly in February, placing great pressure on tank space and on picking. A combination of circumstances saw some very high baume levels and the need for quick action in the wineries. The problems weren't universal, with vineyards and batch variation. Temperatures then fell sharply, with March around average. White wines have lovely natural acidity; the reds are strongly coloured and richly flavoured. Riesling, grenache and cabernet sauvignon are standouts. The progression of the weather in the **Eden Valley** was similar to that of the Barossa Valley, but because Eden Valley's harvest is significantly later, it avoided the hot February, enjoying a wonderful ripening period with no hot spells. Standout varieties are riesling, cabernet sauvignon and shiraz, with yields just below long-term average. **Clare Valley** shared the same weather pattern and rainfall as that of the Barossa Valley, including the frosts in both regions, which came from the dry spring weather. It was the quickest vintage seen for many years. Riesling is the standout variety, but the red wines also flourished, resulting in an overall excellent vintage with good natural acidity. **Adelaide Hills** had the best vintage in a decade. The late-season summer/autumn rain that often challenges the Hills was conspicuous for its absence, pinot gris, sauvignon blanc, chardonnay and gruner veltliner described as having exquisite quality, flavours and amazing natural acidity. Shiraz is highly aromatic, with deep purple fruit, and the potential to be among the best reds ever produced in the Hills. The overall weather sequence in **McLaren Vale** was very similar to that of the Barossa and Clare valleys. Generally dry soils made irrigation (for those with it) of prime importance. For dry-grown vines the 44mm of rain in January was a blessing. Nonetheless, the consensus was a fast and furious vintage. McLaren Vale is a red wine region first and foremost, but the retention of acidity resulted in exceptional white wines across the ever-increasing varietal range. There was a spread of opinion about the outstanding varieties: shiraz, grenache, petit verdot and cabernet sauvignon were all nominated; the unifying theme good acidity, bright fruit flavours and highly expressive varietal characters. All the wineries of **Langhorne Creek**, **Southern Fleurieu** and **Kangaroo Island** agreed that yields were low, the consequence of cold weather during flowering and the drying effect of the bursts of heat. The compressed vintage story continued; standout varieties saw all wineries choosing shiraz, two very pleased with malbec and cabernet sauvignon (excellent colour and a lovely tension between tannin and acidity). **Coonawarra** invites comparisons with 2010, '04 and '01. All agreed that the cool weather up to Christmas affected fruitset, with lower bunch numbers and very small berry size. Because Coonawarra does not start picking cabernet until mid-March (often early April), the latter stages of ripening proceeded with perfect weather. Varietal definition, elegance and freshness are all marks of a very good vintage. **Mount Benson, Robe, Wrattonbully** and **Padthaway**, all Limestone Coast neighbours, experienced similar conditions, with similar outcomes. A warmer than average spring resulted in an early and quick flowering and fruitset. Yield was down on average, but significantly better than that of 2014. Overall, the grapes ripened well with good phenological and tannin ripeness, and the continuing story of good natural acidity. Sauvignon blanc and chardonnay are the standout white varieties, cabernet sauvignon and shiraz the star reds. The **Murray Darling** had only two cycles of really hot weather; standouts have been chardonnay, viognier and shiraz, yields moderate, acidity good, with only chardonnay and merlot in excess of estimates.

VICTORIA

A close to ideal year in the **Yarra Valley**. Good winter and moderate rainfall throughout spring, along with warm spring temperatures, saw much better yields in all varieties than in 2014. Warm but not extreme temperatures continued into summer and meant a very early start to harvest. A dry March, with cool overnight temperatures, kept disease pressure low and allowed grapes to retain excellent natural acidity. Both chardonnay and pinot noir have the winemakers rubbing their hands with glee. The **Mornington Peninsula** had worries with the very cool spring and memories of 2014's poor fruitset, but temperatures warmed up just in time. A mild summer overall, with yields close to long-term average. Chardonnay and pinot noir are excellent, making this one of the best vintages of the past five years. **Geelong** received just enough rain; dry and cool conditions prevailed through to harvest, chardonnay and pinot noir the standout varieties, overall quality the best 'odd' year of the last 10. **Macedon Ranges** and **Sunbury** had a cool summer and a dry March/April, with moderate yields. Standout varieties were pinot noir ('exquisite'), chardonnay, pinot grigio and fiano. Overall quality 'fabulous'. Very few problems for **Bendigo**, although flavours didn't appear until relatively high baumes, the compensation excellent acidity. Shiraz the standout, nigh on the best for 15 years. Average winter and springs rains in **Heathcote** led into to a mild and cooler than average summer. Yields were average and picking slightly earlier than normal, despite the cooler conditions. Shiraz is the star; sangiovese, nebbiolo and montepulciano all excellent, the yields moderate. The **Grampians** had a warm and dry year, but with low yields, due to very low temperatures around budburst. A mild, dry summer and cool autumn gave shiraz great elegance and spice, albeit in smaller quantities. Winter rain was moderate in **Henty**, but the region had the driest spring since 1914. The warm, dry weather meant flowering and fruitset was perfect; vintage started March 30, with outstanding flavours in the fruit. A truly great vintage in the offing. **Pyrenees** followed the pattern, the weather through to harvest cooler than average, and with some useful rain. The yields were moderate, chardonnay, cabernet sauvignon and merlot of great quality. **Beechworth** had an excellent winter and spring rain leading up to a fine summer. Some rain in mid-January but not enough to cause any concern. Pick of varieties include pinot gris, chardonnay, shiraz and pinot noir. Chardonnay and shiraz standouts. **Nagambie Lakes** had very favourable weather throughout the growing season, although the mild conditions did lead to rapid ripening across both white and red varieties. All white wines had excellent acid retention; shiraz and cabernet sauvignon thrived in the cool conditions. Excellent winter rains in the **Strathbogie Ranges** filled the dams, and the very dry spring and summer meant no disease pressure. The mild temperatures led to excellent acidity and intense colour in the red wines. Riesling and shiraz were the standouts in a very good vintage. While the weather up to December in the **King Valley** and the **Alpine Valleys** varied across these regions, January was very cool in both, leading on to moderate temperatures through February and March, February with some rain necessitating vigilance in the vineyard, March dry and warm. Acidity and pH balance were good; prosecco, pinot grigio and chardonnay were among the standout varieties.

NEW SOUTH WALES

After two excellent to outstanding vintages in 2013 and '14, it was almost inevitable that the **Hunter Valley** would return to its vexatious worst. A warm and sunny spring was followed by a cool and wet December, January following with a mix of very hot days and more rain. February, too, saw more rain (51mm). One long-established winery abandoned the vintage, but there will be some good wine from the best vineyards and top makers. **Mudgee** had a roughly similar challenge, with above average rainfall in January, followed by eight significant rainfall events over the February to March period, chardonnay and shiraz weathering the storm better than most other varieties. **Orange** had the driest March for more than 20 years, providing a wonderful run up to and through vintage, with moderate alcohol, low pH and good acidity. Yields were generally good, chardonnay suffering most from cold conditions during flowering. Overall high quality, with riesling, cabernet franc, merlot and shiraz the best, the only caveat for chardonnay being yield, not quality, issues. The **Canberra District** had a brilliant vintage, one winery saying it was the best in the last 40 years, the weather up to harvest perfect, with day after day of glorious, sunny weather and temperatures consistently hitting the high 20s. Acid levels in the whites were excellent, the riesling destined for greatness. Shiraz was described as 'serious, soaring, utterly compelling aromas and pitch-perfect tannin structures'. The weather pattern in **Hilltops** was similar to other Central New South Wales regions; February and March were very dry, with an average of 25°C. Overall quality is good to very good, with riesling, sauvignon blanc, semillon and shiraz yielding only to cabernet sauvignon, the standout variety and ironically the only one not to provide good yields. **Tumbarumba** followed the pattern, with a warm, dry spring, January rainfall two to three times above average, with average temperatures. Rainfall tapered off in February, and March was 25% of normal. The weather was ideal from this point on, cool and dry, the only problem being the need to shoot- and bunch-thin to remove excess yield. Chardonnay was the standout, with pristine and intense flavours. Described by one winemaker as 'the best vintage since 2010, and one of the greatest vintages in Tumbarumba's short viticultural history'. The **Riverina** had a bountiful vintage of very good quality, starting January 20, finishing end March, with fewer days than normal over 35°C. Chardonnay, sauvignon blanc, verdelho and shiraz are the standouts.

WESTERN AUSTRALIA

Margaret River had abundant winter and spring rainfall, but little or no rain from November until mid-March, with significant rainfall over three days. More relevantly, it was the worst year for birds on record due to a combination of bushfires and no marri blossom. Yields were very low due to poor flowering and fruitset; chardonnay and cabernet sauvignon were standouts if picked at the right time and free of bird damage (netting the only effective control). **Great Southern** is a broad church, with five subregions spread over large distances. Yields were agreed to be low, but the percentage varied between 20% and 50%. Bird pressure made netting essential, most varieties achieved ripeness at relatively low sugar levels, riesling leading the way as the standout white variety, shiraz doing its cool-climate bit, chardonnay and pinot noir excellent in **Mount Barker**. **Manjimup** and **Pemberton** are Siamese twins; fruitset was poor due to wind and rain during flowering, down 60% on average. The Indian summer autumns of these regions did not eventuate, and in the outcome yields were down 60% on average, sauvignon blanc and shiraz the best wines in a very mixed year. **Geographe** had above average spring rain, summer dry until late rains just prior to vintage. Yields were very low, the standout varieties chardonnay and shiraz, the overall quality above average. A dry winter in **Swan Valley** preceded late spring rainfall, after which the weather turned dry and hot. An extreme heat spike on January 5 (45.5°C) was balanced by heavy, unseasonal rain in the first week of February (shades of the Hunter Valley). Yields were moderate, but with some varietal variation. Standout varieties depended on which winery was reporting: thus one said the highlight of the vintage was definitely shiraz, the other saying chardonnay, semillon, grenache and cabernet were best. **Peel** and the **Perth Hills** had broadly similar weather.

TASMANIA

The **East Coast, North** and **South** of the state sang the same song: a very good to outstanding vintage. The settled weather through November provided ideal flowering conditions (unlike 2014), resulting in good yields with well formed, even bunches. Rain fell in precisely the right time in late November, putting moisture back into soil threatening to dry out; summer temperatures were slightly warmer than the average, but noticeably cooler than 2013 and '14. There was very little disease pressure, and low overnight temperatures in the lead-up to harvest resulted in great levels of natural acid. The combination of mild and dry, cool autumn days have resulted in outstanding chardonnay and pinot noir (the state's viticultural emblems) and good riesling.

QUEENSLAND

The **Granite Belt**, by far the most important region, had a vintage it would rather forget. Spring was extremely dry, and those that did not have access to irrigation suffered poor fruitset. Hail just before Christmas devastated the western Ballandean vineyards; Golden Grove Estate, one of the stars of the region these days, lost 90% of its crop, and had to buy grapes, but even there the difficulties continued. There were periods of very hot (for the normally temperate Granite Belt) days during January and February, far from ideal conditions.

Acknowledgements

As any winemaker will tell you, no two vintages are the same. This is equally true of the *Wine Companion*. Although each edition may look superficially the same, well over 80% of the content is new – not merely updated.

A particular complication arose this year, one of my making, and in no way caused by the team responsible for the *Companion*. I have solemnly vowed that never again will writing another new book coincide with the *Companion*. *Varietal Wines* will be launched only a week after the *Companion*, its progress through to the final files delivered for printing placing enormous strain on the key players of the *Companion*.

Next year will mark a quarter of a century of service from my PA, Paula Grey. As I wrote last year, Paula is the earth mother of the *Companion*, able to charm the most difficult respondents and persuade them that they don't really need to speak to me. She is the all-important link with the programmer, John Cook, devising ways and means of blunting the ever-increasing backstage complexity of the *Wine Companion*.

Beth Anthony has been with me for 15 years, coping with the physical and mental pressure of entering into the database (and stewarding) the wines for each day's tasting, starting with the flood of wines that come in for the Top 100 tastings in September, through the dog days of the first four months of the year. It was she who was my right hand for *Varietal Wines*, collating the mass of often incomplete or inconsistent statistical information collected for the book – and typing its many drafts. It was tough going for all concerned.

Her sister Jake gave up weekend family contact to keep the juggernaut of the *Companion* going, thus creating a seven-day working week for myself. But all of this might have come to nothing were it not for Campbell Mattinson's superlative tasting notes – they are in fact poetry – for 28% of the total in the *Companion* and/or the website. What's more, he had to move house in the middle of the tastings; how he was able to do what he did is beyond my comprehension. He has my undying thanks.

So, for that matter, does Rihana Ries of Hardie Grant, who had the carriage as editor of both *Varietal Wines* and this book. She is part of a family at Hardie Grant, headed by Sandy Grant and Julie Pinkham, with Fran Berry providing another senior layer of support. Yet another is the go-to girl Annie Clemenger, forever thinking of ways to create partnerships with businesses such as Qantas, and to provide marketing support for this book and the *Wine Companion Magazine*.

Finally, there is the hidden army of Tracey, Alan and Val at Coldstream Post Office, Pam Holmes and others at Coldstream Hills.

Australian wineries and wines

A note on alphabetical order
Wineries beginning with 'The' are listed under 'T'; for example,
'The Wanderer'. Winery names that include a numeral are treated
as if the numeral is spelt out; for example, '2 Mates'
is listed under 'T'.

A. Rodda Wines ★★★★★

PO Box 589, Beechworth, Vic 3747 **Region** Beechworth
T 0400 350 135 **www.**aroddawines.com.au **Open** Not
Winemaker Adrian Rodda **Est.** 2010 **Dozens** 800 **Vyds** 2ha
Adrian Rodda has been winemaking since 1998, almost entirely working with David Bicknell at Oakridge. He was involved in the development of the superb Oakridge 864 Chardonnay, his final contribution to 864 coming in 2009. At the start of 2010 he and wife Christie, a doctor, decided to move to Beechworth, and it was no coincidence that he was a long-term friend of viticulturist Mark Walpole. Yet further coincidences came with the Smith Vineyard and winery being available for lease; he now shares it with Mark, who makes his Beechworth wines there. Even more propitious was the availability of Smith Vineyard chardonnay, planted in 1974. The quality of the portfolio has been consistently excellent.

🍷🍷🍷🍷🍷 **Willow Lake Vineyard Yarra Valley Chardonnay 2013** Classy. Dives straight in with flavour and keeps it roaring on. White peach, flint and woodsmoke flavour in excellent measure. Presence and length. Screwcap. 13% alc. **Rating** 95 **To** 2021 $38 CM

Smiths Vineyard Beechworth Chardonnay 2013 Flavours of sweet lemon barley, steel, mineral, lime sorbet and seductive, spicy, smoky oak. Excellent length through the finish. Bold but racy. Gets revs of flavour up and running and keeps the foot down throughout. Screwcap. 13% alc. **Rating** 95 **To** 2020 $38 CM

Beechworth Cuvee de Chez 2013 A 59/23/9/9% blend of cabernet, merlot, malbec and petit verdot. The bouquet and medium-bodied palate are particularly fresh, with redcurrant, cassis, bay leaf and dried herbs all in play; the tannins are still to relax, but should do so. Screwcap. 13.5% alc. **Rating** 94 **To** 2028 $36

🍷🍷🍷🍷🍷 **Aquila Audax Vineyard Tempranillo 2013 Rating** 91 **To** 2020 $36

A.T. Richardson Wines ★★★★★

94 Hard Hill Road, Armstrong, Vic 3377 **Region** Grampians
T (02) 9460 3177 **www.**atrichardsonwines.com **Open** Not
Winemaker Adam Richardson **Est.** 2005 **Dozens** 1800 **Vyds** 7ha
Perth-born Adam Richardson began his winemaking career in 1995, along the way working for Normans, d'Arenberg and Oakridge Estate. Since that time he has been appointed Director of Global Winemaking for the international premium wines division of The Wine Group, the third-largest producer in the US. He is responsible for an annual production of more than 5 million dozen from 11 countries. In 2005 he put down small roots in the Grampians region, acquiring a vineyard with shiraz from old clones from the 19th century, and riesling. The wines are exceptionally good, and given his experience and the quality of the vineyard, that should not come as a surprise.

🍷🍷🍷🍷🍷 **Hard Hill Road Great Western Shiraz 2013** When tasting Chockstone you wonder what Hard Hill Road could offer that isn't already there; the answer is the unexpected elegance, and the glimmer of red fruit of this wine; the tannins are fine and silky, the medium-bodied palate very long, new French oak lurking in the background. Screwcap. 14% alc. **Rating** 96 **To** 2033 $50 ✪

Chockstone Grampians Shiraz 2013 A classic medium to full-bodied wine; the fruit is all black, no red, purple or blue get a look in, just touches of anise and licorice; the complexity derives from the singular texture of the wine, which is grainy and cedary, but in no way bitter or angular. Screwcap. 14% alc. **Rating** 95 **To** 2038 $28 ✪

Chockstone Grampians Riesling 2014 As ever, has an extra layer – indeed layers – of lime juice fruit, balance coming easily and quickly with the crunchy, minerally acidity. Riesling abounds with bargains, but this is close to the head of the queue, ready to go. Screwcap. 11.5% alc. **Rating** 95 **To** 2030 $20 ✪

Hard Hill Road Great Western Durif 2013 A strange region for durif to bob up in, presumably estate-grown; all things are relative, and in that context, this is an elegant wine, with great light and shade through the open-weave texture to its back fruits and savoury tannins. Screwcap. 14% alc. **Rating** 94 **To** 2023 $50

Abbey Creek Vineyard ★★★★★

2388 Porongurup Road, Porongurup, WA 6324 **Region** Porongurup
T (08) 9853 1044 **Open** By appt
Winemaker Castle Rock Estate (Robert Diletti) **Est.** 1990 **Dozens** 800 **Vyds** 1.6ha
This is the family business of Mike and Mary Dilworth, the name coming from a winter creek
that runs alongside the vineyard and a view of The Abbey in the Stirling Range. The vineyard
is split between pinot noir, riesling and sauvignon blanc. The Rieslings have had significant
show success for a number of years.

🍷🍷🍷🍷🍷 **Museum Release Porongurup Riesling 2008** Scintillating. Has franked its
early promise in full. Lime, orange rind, honeysuckle and beeswax. Gets it skates
on, builds a power of flavour, then flies out through the finish. Screwcap. 12.5% alc.
Rating 97 **To** 2023 $30 CM ✪

🍷🍷🍷🍷🍷 **Museum Release Porongurup Riesling 2006** Nearing its 10th birthday and
singing a melodious song. Right in the sweet spot development-wise. Lime, toast,
spice and gentle kero complexity. Finishes long. Screwcap. 12% alc. **Rating** 95
To 2018 $30 CM ✪
Porongurup Pinot Noir 2013 Pure varietal character, long lines of spice and
tannin, and a delicious combination of sweet/savoury fruit and oak rushing up and
out through the finish. This is highly accomplished and attractive Pinot Noir, ready
to bring joy to the table now but with plenty of years up its sleeve. Screwcap.
13.5% alc. **Rating** 94 **To** 2021 $30 CM ✪

Across the Lake ★★★★

White Dam Road, Lake Grace, WA 6353 **Region** Great Southern
T 0409 685 373 **Open** By appt
Winemaker Rockcliffe (Coby Ladwig) **Est.** 1999 **Dozens** 300 **Vyds** 2ha
The Taylor family has been farming (wheat and sheep) for over 40 years at Lake Grace; a small
diversification into grapegrowing started as a hobby, but has developed into more than that
with 2ha of shiraz. They were motivated to support their friend Bill (WJ) Walker, who had
started growing shiraz three years previously, and has since produced a gold medal winning
wine. Derek and Kristie Stanton purchased the business.

🍷🍷🍷🍷🍷 **Shiraz 2012** A more than welcome return for Across the Lake, and the
continuation of the outstanding value it has always represented; faintly spicy black
fruits drive the bouquet and medium-bodied palate, the tannins ripe and balanced,
oak a bystander. Screwcap. 14.5% alc. **Rating** 93 **To** 2025 $15 ✪
Shiraz 2011 Full crimson-purple; starting to show some complexity from bottle
age, with faintly dusty/spicy overtones to the medium-bodied, supple blackberry
and blood plum fruit, the tannins and oak support totally integrated. Screwcap.
14.5% alc. **Rating** 92 **To** 2026 $15 ✪

Adelaide Winemakers ★★★★

281 Tatachilla Road, McLaren Vale, SA 5171 **Region** Adelaide Zone
T (08) 8323 6124 www.adelaidewinemakers.com.au **Open** 7 days 11–4
Winemaker Nick Haselgrove, Scott Rawlinson, Sam Watkins Warren Randall **Est.** 2010
Dozens NFP **Vyds** 418ha
After various sales, amalgamations and disposals of particular brands, Adelaide Winemakers is
owned (equally) by Nick Haselgrove, David Watkins and Warren Randall. It either owns, part-
owns or is in the process of absorbing some of the external part-ownerships of some of the
brands (The Old Faithful – see separate entry – Quorum, Blackbilly, James Haselgrove, The
Old Gentlemen, Clarence Hill, Ace High and Martins Road). Adelaide Winemakers has over
400ha of vines across Adelaide Hills (5ha), McLaren Vale (27ha), Langhorne Creek (216ha)
and Currency Creek (170ha), giving the interconnected businesses a great deal of flexibility.
Exports to the US and other major markets.

ŢŢŢŢŢ **Blackbilly McLaren Vale Shiraz 2012** Hearty serving of blackberry jam and chocolate flavours, not quite as sweet as it sounds but certainly ripe, generous and fruit-driven. Grainy, coffeed tannin plays a keen role but the fruit is always in control. Balance deserves to be noted. Value/drinking equation looks good. Screwcap. 14.5% alc. **Rating** 93 **To** 2022 $22 CM ✪

Quorum Cabernet Shiraz 2010 26 months in French and American oak, and while only 15% new, it's left an obvious trail. Coconut, peppermint and clove notes are ever-present, but so too rich plum/blackcurrant and ever-so-velvety texture. Swings and roundabouts, the finish then flushed with fruit and fine-grained tannin. Diam. 14% alc. **Rating** 93 **To** 2026 $50 CM

Blackbilly Grenache Shiraz Mourvedre 2012 65/25/10%. Warm and sweet-fruited with raspberry, dried herbs, hay and licorice flavours in good measure. Tannin is ripe and fine, but juicy drinkability, at which it's very good, is the focus of the wine's intention. Screwcap. 14.5% alc. **Rating** 91 **To** 2019 $22 CM ✪

Clarence Hill Adelaide Cabernet Sauvignon 2013 Heft, grunt, guts; whatever you want to call it, this has it. Blackberry and clove flavours pour it on, complete with meaty, brackeny tannin. Perfect accompaniment to char-grilled meats. Value too. Screwcap. 14.5% alc. **Rating** 91 **To** 2020 $18 CM ✪

Clarence Hill Reserve Langhorne Creek Cabernet 2012 Dark colour and flavour profile with dense plum, resiny vanilla and toast characters aplenty. Quite tight, almost to to point where it gets tangled in its own feet through the finish. Could go either way. Diam. 14.5% alc. **Rating** 90 **To** 2022 $40 CM

After Hours Wine ★★★★

455 North Jindong Road, Carbunup, WA 6285 **Region** Margaret River
T 0438 737 587 **www.afterhourswine.com.au Open** Fri–Mon 10–4
Winemaker Phil Potter **Est.** 2006 **Dozens** 2000 **Vyds** 8.6ha
In 2005 Warwick and Cherylyn Mathews acquired the long-established Hopelands Vineyard, planted to cabernet sauvignon (2.6ha), shiraz (1.6ha), merlot, semillon, sauvignon blanc and chardonnay (1.1ha each). The first wine was made in '06, after which they decided to completely rework the vineyard, which required many hours of physical labour. The vines were retrained, with a consequent reduction in yield and rise in wine quality and value.

ŢŢŢŢŢ **Margaret River Chardonnay 2013** An immediately attractive wine, with a full spectrum of varietal flavours from melon, pear, citrus and white peach held on a gentle cushion of creamy cashew oak; the balance and length are admirable. Screwcap. 13% alc. **Rating** 94 **To** 2020 $24 ✪

ŢŢŢŢŢ **Oliver Margaret River Shiraz 2013 Rating** 92 **To** 2021 $22 CM ✪
9 to 5 Semillon Sauvignon Blanc 2013 Rating 91 **To** 2015 $14 ✪
Margaret River Sauvignon Blanc 2014 Rating 90 **To** 2015 $18 ✪
9 to 5 Margaret River Chardonnay 2014 Rating 90 **To** 2017 $15 CM ✪

Ainsworth & Snelson ★★★★

45 Curlewis Road, Curlewis, Vic 3222 (postal) **Region** Various
T 0419 384 317 **www.ainsworthandsnelson.com Open** Not
Winemaker Brett Snelson **Est.** 2002 **Dozens** 20 000
Brett Snelson and Gregg Ainsworth say they take a handcrafted regional approach to the production of their wines. They seek to ensure that the emphasis remains on terroir, sourcing grapes from the Grampians, Geelong, Yarra Valley, Barossa and Coonawarra. Brett keeps his winemaking skills sharp with an annual vintage in Roussillon. Exports to the UK, India, Dubai, Hong Kong and China.

ŢŢŢŢŢ **Jakob's Black Magic Grampians Shiraz 2013** Full colour; has all the broody black fruits that you expect from young, well made Grampians Shiraz, likewise the firm structure and texture, the tannins (perversely, yet happily) fine-grained and balanced; tar, licorice and blackberry are the profile fruit flavours Screwcap. 14% alc. **Rating** 94 **To** 2038 $40

ŢŢŢŢŢ **Jakob's Black Magic Cabernet Sauvignon 2013 Rating** 93 **To** 2028 $40

Alkoomi ★★★★★

Wingebellup Road, Frankland River, WA 6396 **Region** Frankland River
T (08) 9855 2229 **www.**alkoomiwines.com.au **Open** 7 days 10–5
Winemaker Andrew Cherry **Est.** 1971 **Dozens** 70 000 **Vyds** 104.5ha
Established in 1971 by Merv and Judy Lange, Alkoomi has grown from a single hectare to be one of Western Australia's largest family owned and operated wineries, with a vineyard of 104.5 hectares. Now owned by Merv and Judy's daughter, Sandy Hallett and her husband Rod, Alkoomi is continuing the tradition of being a producer of high-quality varietally expressive wines which showcase the Frankland River region. Presently Alkoomi is actively reducing its environmental footprint; future plans will see the introduction of new varietals and exports to all major markets. Alkoomi operates cellar doors in Albany and the winery (which also has a function centre). Exports to all major markets.

ΨΨΨΨΨ Black Label Frankland River Riesling 2014 Estate-grown 40yo vines, and only free-run juice, gives the wine a flying start. Its intensity is exceptional, driving along the palate with high speed, the Bickford's lime juice flavours running unabated through the finish and well into the lingering aftertaste. An exceptional wine. Screwcap. 12% alc. **Rating** 97 **To** 2034 $24 ❂

ΨΨΨΨΨ Black Label Frankland River Riesling 2013 The bouquet is yet to develop intensity, but the palate is a different beast, its cascade of lime, lemon leaf and mineral immediately occupying every corner of the mouth. A classic each-way proposition: drink now, and think Chinese, or be patient for a decade or more, and think Alsace pork. Screwcap. 12.1% alc. **Rating** 95 **To** 2028 $22 ❂
Black Label Frankland River Sauvignon Blanc 2014 A blend of several small blocks on the estate vineyard, with a small portion barrel-fermented in new French oak to add complexity. A thoroughly impressive Sauvignon Blanc, brimming with passionfruit, gooseberry and grapefruit, topped and tailed with crunchy acidity. Screwcap. 12.5% alc. **Rating** 95 **To** 2018 $24 ❂
Black Label Frankland River Shiraz Viognier 2012 Estate-grown, co-fermented, and matured for 18 months in French oak (33% new). An intense, tightly focused wine, although only medium-bodied – which adds to its appeal; the fine-grained tannins help carry the blackberry and cherry fruit through to a long finish. Great value. Screwcap. 14.5% alc. **Rating** 95 **To** 2027 $24 ❂
Black Label Frankland River Cabernet Sauvignon 2012 An elegant estate-grown wine sourced from several sites on Alkoomi's extensive vineyard; an utterly classic cool-climate Cabernet, medium to full-bodied, with blackcurrant fruit, cedary oak and persistent, but integrated and balanced, cabernet tannins. Will age with grace. Screwcap. 14% alc. **Rating** 95 **To** 2027 $24 ❂

ΨΨΨΨ♀ White Label Semillon Sauvignon Blanc 2014 **Rating** 92 **To** 2016 $15 ❂
Jarrah Frankland River Shiraz 2010 **Rating** 92 **To** 2022 $45 CM
Black Label Frankland River Chardonnay 2013 **Rating** 91 **To** 2019 $24
White Label Cabernet Merlot 2012 **Rating** 91 **To** 2022 $15 ❂
White Label Frankland River Late Harvest 2014 **Rating** 90 **To** 2020 $15 ❂

All Saints Estate ★★★★★

All Saints Road, Wahgunyah, Vic 3687 **Region** Rutherglen
T 1800 021 621 **www.**allsaintswine.com.au **Open** Mon–Sat 9–5.30, Sun 10–5.30
Winemaker Dan Crane, Nick Brown **Est.** 1864 **Dozens** 25 000 **Vyds** 33.46ha
The winery rating reflects the fortified wines and table wines alike. The one-hat Terrace restaurant makes this a must-see stop for any visitor to Northeast Victoria. The towering castle façade is classified by the Historic Buildings Council. All Saints and St Leonards are owned and managed by fourth-generation Brown family members Eliza, Angela and Nicholas. Eliza is an energetic and highly intelligent leader, wise beyond her years, and highly regarded by the wine industry. Dan Crane's winemaking skills across the whole portfolio are very impressive. In May 2014 the Brown family hosted a lavish black-tie celebration of the winery's 150th anniversary. Exports to the UK, the US, Canada, Singapore and China.

ŸŸŸŸŸ Rutherglen Museum Muscadelle NV Labelled Muscadelle correctly, although the Rare is (still) labelled Tokay. Significantly more olive on the rim, but not deeper than the Rare, it has all the spiced perfume of the Rare, and also the malt and burnt toffee flavours, but builds even greater intensity and velocity on the palate, which extends the finish and aftertaste. It is based on 80yo components compared to 20+ years for the Rare, and sits outside the normal Rutherglen classification. It is only bottled on order. It shares its extraordinary length with the Museum Muscat. 18% alc. **Rating** 98 **To** 2016 $1000

Rutherglen Museum Muscat NV The ultimate in complexity and concentration; from a solera started in 1920, only 250l are released in 500 bottles of 500ml each year, the presentation doing full justice. It is a deep olive-brown, and pours reluctantly from the bottle so viscous is it. The bouquet is radically different to and more complex than that of the Rare Muscat; the palate, too, is on another level, with a fireworks display of flavours, but it is its extraordinary length that really sets it apart. Cork. 18% alc. **Rating** 98 **To** 2015 $1000

Rare Rutherglen Muscadelle NV Amber grading to near olive on the rim; a heady perfume of tea leaf, toffee and spice do justice to the intensity and drive of the palate, where malt and shortbread join the choir of the bouquet; the finish is (almost) never ending, but miraculously dries while its flavours are still with you. 375ml. Vino-Lok. 18% alc. **Rating** 97 **To** 2016 $120 ✪

Rare Rutherglen Muscat NV Darker colour than the Tokay; liqueured raisins lead the Christmas pudding and heady spice aromas of the perfumed bouquet, morphing seamlessly into treacle, raisin and Christmas pudding with hard sauce. 375ml. Vino-Lok. 18% alc. **Rating** 97 **To** 2015 $120 ✪

ŸŸŸŸŸ Grand Rutherglen Tawny NV More luscious than any Barossa Valley tawny, unless it is in the Para Tawny style. It is intensely, riotously complex, its flavours of Christmas cake, spice and burnt toffee picked up by the rancio-induced drying acidity, with an incredibly long aftertaste. It is the freshness of this finish that makes this wine so special and so great. Vino-Lok. 18% alc. **Rating** 96 **To** 2016 $38 ✪

Grand Rutherglen Muscadelle NV The faint hint of red colour at the heart of the Classic has gone, dark walnut grading to lighter olive-brown on the rim. Less luscious, but more intense and penetrating, tea leaf and burnt toffee to the fore; overall, a little more complex than the Grand Muscat. 375ml. Vino-Lok. 18% alc. **Rating** 96 **To** 2016 $72 ✪

Grand Rutherglen Muscat NV Is a neat match with the Grand Muscadelle; here it is richly fruity, with raisins, caramelised ginger and grilled nuts on the mid-palate, changing to an elegant back-palate with a pantry full of spices of Arabia; the overall balance is exceptional, especially for muscat. 375ml. Vino-Lok. 18% alc. **Rating** 96 **To** 2016 $72 ✪

Classic Rutherglen Muscadelle NV Golden brown, the clear rim showing age; exceptional complexity and depth for this (Classic) level, the bouquet showing the range of flavours to come; terrific viscosity, rolling with Christmas cake and Callard & Bowser toffee wreathed in rancio drying the finish. A massive step up from the entry point (Rutherglen) wine. 375ml. Vino-Lok. 18% alc. **Rating** 95 **To** 2016 $35 ✪

Family Cellar Marsanne 2013 Rating 94 **To** 2023 $32
Family Cellar Shiraz 2013 Rating 94 **To** 2038 $52
Alias II 2013 Rating 94 **To** 2030 $35
Rutherglen Muscadelle NV Rating 94 **To** 2016 $24 ✪
Classic Rutherglen Muscat NV Rating 94 **To** 2016 $35

ŸŸŸŸŸ Rutherglen Muscat NV Rating 93 **To** 2015 $24 ✪
Shiraz 2013 Rating 92 **To** 2033 $30
Sangiovese Cabernet 2013 Rating 92 **To** 2017 $24 ✪
Durif 2013 Rating 91 **To** 2028 $30

Allies Wines

15 Hume Road, Somers, Vic 3927 (postal) **Region** Mornington Peninsula
T 0412 111 587 **www**.allies.com.au **Open** Not
Winemaker David Chapman **Est.** 2003 **Dozens** 1000 **Vyds** 2.6ha
A former chef and sommelier, David Chapman began Allies in 2003 whilst working at
Moorooduc Estate. He aims to make Pinot Noir, emphasising the diversity of the Mornington
Peninsula by making a number of wines sourced from different townships in the region. David
spends much of his time in the vineyard, working to ensure well-exposed and positioned
bunches to achieve ripe, pure flavours and supple tannins. His winemaking focuses on simple
preservation techniques that retain the concentration and character of each vineyard. No
added yeasts, no ferment supplements, natural mlf and no fining or filtration are standard
practices. Production of Allies wines is tiny and will probably remain that way, given that any
expansion will limit the number of vines David can personally tend.

Main Ridge Mornington Peninsula Pinot Noir 2013 Picked 2 weeks
earlier than usual. The fragrant and expressive bouquet sings of red cherries and
strawberries, the elegant palate opening with more of the same before switching
gear to a distinctly savoury/foresty finish; the change does not break the line or
(of course) the length. Screwcap. 13.4% alc. **Rating** 96 **To** 2028 $39 ✪
Tuerong Mornington Peninsula Pinot Noir 2013 Bright, vivid colour; the
perfumed, spicy bouquet leads into a lively pas de deux on the palate, which is
finely structured, with plum and black cherry flavours skipping around the spicy,
savoury back-palate and finish. Screwcap. 13% alc. **Rating** 95 **To** 2028 $39
Merricks Mornington Peninsula Pinot Noir 2013 Picked a week earlier
than usual. Excellent bright crimson-purple; the bouquet and palate are fairly and
squarely in the plum spectrum, but are not the least heavy-handed; savoury/earthy
nuances are allied with fine tannins on a long, ultra-harmonious palate. Screwcap.
13.2% alc. **Rating** 95 **To** 2028 $39
Assemblage Mornington Peninsula Pinot Noir 2013 A blend of three very
different wines from purchased grapes, grapes from vineyards under rehabilitation,
and excess/declassified district ('township') vines, matured in a 3000l foudre. It
has a considerable volume of plum and black cherry fruit that fills the bouquet
and mid-palate, tweaked on the finish by a complex twist of forest/black olive.
Screwcap. 13.2% alc. **Rating** 94 **To** 2028 $30 ✪

Alta Vineyards ★★★★

102 Main Street, Hahndorf, SA 5245 **Region** Adelaide Hills
T (08) 8388 7155 **www**.altavineyards.com.au **Open** 7 days 11–5
Winemaker Sarah Fletcher **Est.** 2003 **Dozens** 6000 **Vyds** 23ha
Sarah Fletcher came to Alta with an impressive winemaking background: a degree from
Roseworthy, and thereafter seven years working for Orlando Wyndham. There she came face
to face with grapes from all over Australia, and developed a particular regard for those coming
from the Adelaide Hills. So she joined Alta, which had already established a reputation for its
Sauvignon Blanc. The portfolio has been progressively extended with varieties suited to the
cool climate of the Adelaide Hills.

Sauvignon Blanc 2014 Punchy without being overblown; lengthy without
being too lean; awash with citrus and gunmetal notes, but rightly bound by
tropical/passionfruit flavours. Screwcap. 12.5% alc. **Rating** 92 **To** 2015 $20 CM ✪
for Elsie Pinot Noir Rose 2014 Savoury release with strawberry, spice, tobacco
leaves and earth notes affording the wine a clear sense of character. Slender profile,
but complex. Screwcap. 11.5% alc. **Rating** 91 **To** 2016 $20 CM ✪

Altamont Wine Studio ★★★★

49 Peacock's Road, Lenswood, SA 5240 **Region** Adelaide Hills
T (08) 8327 4188 **www**.altamontwinestudio.com **Open** By appt
Winemaker Brendon Keys **Est.** 2012 **Dozens** 2000

Winemaker Brendon Keys was the inspiration for the establishment of Altamont Wine Studio, but has formed a partnership with Brian Gilbert, Steve Harris, Michael Sawyer and Matthew Morrissy to bring Altamont (and its associated label, Seven Deadly Vins, with Michael Sawyer the winemaker) to fruition. The business secures small but high-quality batches of Adelaide Hills fruit, thus making each wine in relatively small amounts.

ⵔⵔⵔⵔⵔ Much Loved Adelaide Hills Sangiovese 2013 Good hue; has very good varietal expression; the medium-bodied palate has that key mix of multi-spice red and sour cherry fruit and fine, but ripe, tannins in harmony with the fruit. Screwcap. 14% alc. **Rating** 93 **To** 2020 $25 ✪
Single Vineyard Adelaide Hills Sauvignon Blanc 2013 10% barrel-fermented, 10% fermented on skins, the remainder conventionally fermented in tank, the parts blended post-ferment and left on lees for 6 months. Has well above average texture and structure, any diminution in varietal character flowing directly from the way the wine was made. Screwcap. 12.5% alc. **Rating** 92 **To** 2015 $25 ✪
Single Vineyard Adelaide Hills Tempranillo 2013 Tightly wound, but promises to relax and open up its perfume and red fruits over the next couple of years; the red and black cherry flavours of the palate have a certain purity that underlines its future. Screwcap. 14% alc. **Rating** 92 **To** 2025 $25 ✪
Single Vineyard Adelaide Hills Chardonnay 2013 Obvious colour development; a complex bouquet and palate have clear winemaking thumbprints all over the place. A polarising style, but with plenty to argue about, whatever one's viewpoint. Screwcap. 12.8% alc. **Rating** 90 **To** 2016 $25

ⵔⵔⵔⵔ Single Vineyard Adelaide Hills Pinot Noir 2013 **Rating** 89 **To** 2018 $25

Amadio Wines   ★★★★

461 Payneham Road, Felixstow, SA 5070 **Region** Adelaide Hills
T (08) 8337 5144 **www**.amadiowines.com **Open** Wed–Sat 10–5.30
Winemaker Danniel Amadio **Est.** 2004 **Dozens** 75 000 **Vyds** 250ha
Danniel Amadio says he has followed in the footsteps of his Italian grandfather, selling wine from his cellar (cantina) direct to the consumer. He also draws upon the business of his parents, built not in Italy, but in Australia. Amadio Wines has substantial vineyards, primarily in the Adelaide Hills and Barossa Valley, and also contract-grown grapes from Clare Valley, McLaren Vale and Langhorne Creek, with a strong suite of Italian varieties. Exports to the UK, the US, Canada, Russia, South Korea, Singapore, Hong Kong and China.

ⵔⵔⵔⵔⵔ Heritage Selection Barossa Valley Sagrantino 2012 Matured for 12 months in used French oak. Lives up to the reputation of the variety with a fragrant bouquet, the palate with sour cherry/mint and tingling spicy flavours; good tannins add to the appeal. Cork. 14.8% alc. **Rating** 94 **To** 2022 $40

ⵔⵔⵔⵔⵔ Heritage Selection Montepulciano 2012 **Rating** 92 **To** 2020 $40
Heritage Selection Barossa Valley Aglianico 2012 **Rating** 90 **To** 2018 $40

Amato Vino   ★★★★☆

PO Box 475, Margaret River, WA 6285 **Region** Margaret River
T 0409 572 957 **www**.amatovino.com.au **Open** Not
Winemaker Brad Wehr, Contract **Est.** 2003 **Dozens** 5000
Brad Wehr has long walked on the wild side with his wines and his labels. The three brands within his portfolio are wine by brad, Mantra and Amato Vino (the last based on SA's Riverland). It's not altogether surprising that he has become the Australian importer for Bonny Doon Vineyard; some of the quirky humour of Bonny Doon is exemplified by the wine by brad label. Exports to Ireland, Canada, South Korea and Singapore.

ⵔⵔⵔⵔⵔ Mantra Margaret River Cabernet Sauvignon 2012 From a single vineyard in the Wallcliffe district; 3-day cold soak, matured for 21 months in French oak (10% new). This is Margaret River at its best, with Cabernet Sauvignons such as this: generous blackcurrant fruit, but not losing shape or detail, absorbing the oak and couched on top of the tannins. Screwcap. 13.5% alc. **Rating** 96 **To** 2037 $28 ○

Amato Teroldego 2013 Whole bunches and more than 3 weeks on skins. Unfined and unfiltered. Medium to full-bodied, with hazelnut, dark cherry, licorice and graphite flavours eventually turning towards the more floral, and herbal, end of the spectrum. Personality plus. Lines of velvety tannin just another aspect of a classy impression. Screwcap. 14.2% alc. **Rating** 94 **To** 2019 $40 CM

ŢŢŢŢŢ **Mantra Sauvignon Blanc Semillon 2014** **Rating** 93 **To** 2018 $22 ○
Mantra Margaret River Sauvignon Blanc 2014 **Rating** 92 **To** 2016 $22 ○
Margaret River Sauvignon Blanc Semillon 2014 **Rating** 92 **To** 2016 $18 ○
Amato Nebbiolo 2013 **Rating** 92 **To** 2022 $40 CM
Mantra Margaret River Chardonnay 2014 **Rating** 91 **To** 2024 $25
wine by brad Cabernet Merlot 2012 **Rating** 91 **To** 2020 $18 ○
Amato Nero d'Avola 2014 **Rating** 91 **To** 2016 $25 CM
Amato Montepulciano 2014 **Rating** 90 **To** 2019 $25 CM

Amberley   ★★★★

10460 Vasse Highway, Nannup, WA 6275 **Region** Margaret River
T 1800 088 711 **www.**amberley-estate.com.au **Open** Not
Winemaker Lance Parkin **Est.** 1986 **Dozens** NFP
Initial growth was based on its ultra-commercial, fairly sweet Chenin Blanc. Became part of Accolade, but is now simply a brand, without vineyards or winery. Exports to the UK, the US and the Pacific Islands.

ŢŢŢŢŢ **Secret Lane Margaret River Semillon Sauvignon Blanc 2014** Sits bright and clear in the glass. Announces itself aromatically from the very first. Cut grass, sweet pea, passionfruit and gunmetal. Lovely stuff. Screwcap. 12.5% alc. **Rating** 92 **To** 2016 $20 CM ○
Secret Lane Margaret River Cabernet Merlot 2013 The charm of the mid-weight wine. Mulberry and blackcurrant flavours glide through the palate, dispensing texture and flavour and, perhaps most of all, satisfaction. It's not a hefty wine, but it just feels right. Dust and bay leaf notes play to the same hand. Screwcap. 13.5% alc. **Rating** 92 **To** 2023 $20 CM ○

ŢŢŢŢ **Shiraz 2013** **Rating** 88 **To** 2017 $17 CM ○
Merlot 2013 **Rating** 88 **To** 2017 $17 CM ○

Amelia Park Wines   ★★★★★

3857 Caves Road, Wilyabrup, WA 6280 **Region** Margaret River
T (08) 9756 7007 **www.**ameliaparkwines.com.au **Open** 7 days 10–5
Winemaker Jeremy Gordon **Est.** 2009 **Dozens** 20000 **Vyds** 9.6ha
Jeremy Gordon had a winemaking career starting with Evans & Tate and thereafter Houghton, before moving to the eastern states to broaden his experience. He returned to Margaret River, and after several years he and wife Daniela founded Amelia Park wines with business partner Peter Walsh. Amelia Park initially relied on contract-grown grapes, but in 2013 purchased the Moss Brothers site in Wilyabrup, allowing the construction of a new winery and cellar door. Exports to the UK, the US, Russia and China.

ŢŢŢŢŢ **Margaret River Chardonnay 2013** Jeremy Gordon has a light touch in making Chardonnay, the wine with freshness and balance the keys to its personality, enhancing, rather than inhibiting, its varietal expression. Nine months in oak has simply been a tool allowing the focus to fix onto the seamless blend of white peach, melon and grapefruit and its blue sky finish. Screwcap. 13.5% alc. **Rating** 96 **To** 2021 $29 ○
Margaret River Sauvignon Blanc Semillon 2014 Gloriously fresh, vibrant and juicy, part wild-fermented in steel barrels; passionfruit oozes out of every pore; there are other tropical fruits and a good squeeze of lemony acidity, but all bow

down to the passionfruit. Bargain+, but drink it soon to capture the fresh flavours. Screwcap. 12.5% alc. **Rating** 95 **To** 2015 $22 ✪
Frankland River Shiraz 2013 Deep crimson-purple, it sends out a blaring call to arms: this is Frankland Shiraz, with deeply set black fruits, interwoven tannins and spikes of bramble and licorice; take me on my terms or not at all. I'm more than happy to oblige. Screwcap. 14.5% alc. **Rating** 95 **To** 2043 $29 ✪
Margaret River Cabernet Merlot 2013 Absolutely in the heart of Margaret River style for this blend, which includes small amounts of malbec and petit verdot; medium to full-bodied, with cassis/blackcurrant fruit, satin-supple tannins and integrated French oak (12 months' maturation). This is the ultimate statement of a privileged place. Screwcap. 14.5% alc. **Rating** 95 **To** 2033 $29 ✪

Amherst Winery ★★★★☆

121 High Street, Avoca, Vic 3467 **Region** Pyrenees
T 0400 380 382 **www**.amherstwinery.com **Open** W'ends & public hols 11–5
Winemaker Luke Jones, Andrew Koerner **Est.** 1989 **Dozens** 2500 **Vyds** 5ha
In 1989 Norman and Elizabeth Jones planted vines on a property with an extraordinarily rich history, commemorated by the name Dunn's Paddock. Samuel Dunn was a convict who arrived in Van Diemen's Land in 1838. He endured continuous punishment before fleeing to SA in 1846. The lease title of the property shows that Amherst Winery is sited on land once owned by Samuel Dunn. In Jan '13 son Luke and wife Rachel Jones acquired the Amherst Winery business, but not the real estate, thus the grape supply remains unchanged. Luke has a wine marketing diploma and a diploma in Wine Technology. Exports to China.

🍷🍷🍷🍷🍷 **Bonindra Vineyard Pyrenees Shiraz 2013** 15 months in French oak. Full colour; black cherry and blackberry fruit aromas and flavours reflect both the terroir and the variety, with the effortless, powerful and complex flavour profile of the northern Pyrenees; the fruit, tannins and oak are on the same page, and sing the praises of 13.5% alcohol. Screwcap. **Rating** 95 **To** 2033 $28 ✪

🍷🍷🍷🍷 **Daisy Creek Pyrenees Sauvignon Blanc 2014** **Rating** 91 **To** 2016 $16 ✪

Anderson ★★★★

1619 Chiltern Road, Rutherglen, Vic 3685 **Region** Rutherglen
T (02) 6032 8111 **www**.andersonwinery.com.au **Open** 7 days 10–5
Winemaker Howard and Christobelle Anderson **Est.** 1992 **Dozens** 2000 **Vyds** 8.8ha
Having notched up a winemaking career spanning over 50 years, including a stint at Seppelt (Great Western), Howard Anderson and family started their own winery, initially with a particular focus on sparkling wine but now extending across all table wine styles. The original estate plantings of shiraz, durif and petit verdot (6ha) have been expanded with tempranillo, saperavi, brown muscat, chenin blanc and viognier.

🍷🍷🍷🍷🍷 **Melanie 2008** Dense, inky colour; very well made vintage port style, and has a long future; lovely rich and spicy shiraz, the fortifying spirit clean and well balanced. 500ml. Vino-Lok. 17% alc. **Rating** 94 **To** 2020 $25 ✪

🍷🍷🍷🍷 **Cellar Block Shiraz 2006** **Rating** 93 **To** 2026 $35
Classic Muscat NV **Rating** 90 **To** 2015 $30

Andevine Wines ★★★★☆

247 Wilderness Road, Rothbury, NSW, 2320 **Region** Hunter Valley
T 0427 948 880 **www**.andevinewines.com.au **Open** Fri–Mon 10–5
Winemaker Andrew Leembruggen **Est.** 2012 **Dozens** NFP
Andrew Leembruggen has been a Hunter Valley boy since his cadetship at Mount Pleasant in 1998; he became a senior winemaker in 2002, remaining in that role in '10 until accepting a role within the McWilliam's group as red winemaker. He returned to lead winemaking operations for Drayton's Family Wines before his departure in '12 to create Andevine Wines. Andrew has made wine in the Rhône Valley, Bordeaux, Napa Valley and Coonawarra. There are three ranges of wines: Vineyard Reserve for 100% Hunter Valley (available exclusively

from the cellar door); Hunter Valley varietals (available exclusively through Naked Wines); and Regional Collection wines, sourced from regions across NSW.

ΨΨΨΨΨ **Reserve Hunter Valley Shiraz 2013** A Hunter Valley Shiraz in beautiful condition. Mid-weight, fresh, buoyant, slipped with plum and red/black cherry flavours, tickled with notes of earth and spice. Balance is nigh-on perfect. It's not a big wine or indeed an oak-assertive one (it saw no new oak) but it has X-factor. Screwcap. 13% alc. **Rating** 96 **To** 2028 $30 CM ✪
Reserve Hunter Valley Semillon 2014 Light touch but much promise. More mouth perfume than overt aromatics. A stream of lemony flavour, almost into sorbet territory, with a grassy, almost wheaty whisper at the fringe. Lilting length. Textural element. Grown on 30+yo vines. Impressive debut. Screwcap. 11.5% alc. **Rating** 94 **To** 2025 $30 CM ✪
Reserve Hunter Valley Chardonnay 2013 It hardly wants for anything. It has the line, the length, the flavour, the feel in the mouth. It tastes of citrus, nectarine, toasty/spicy oak and meal, but mostly it tastes of Chardonnay, fresh but complex, done very well. Screwcap. 12.8% alc. **Rating** 94 **To** 2020 $30 CM ✪

Andrew Peace Wines ★★★★

Murray Valley Highway, Piangil, Vic 3597 **Region** Swan Hill
T (03) 5030 5291 www.apwines.com **Open** Mon–Fri 8–5, Sat 12–4
Winemaker Andrew Peace, David King **Est.** 1995 **Dozens** 180 000 **Vyds** 270ha
The Peace family has been a major Swan Hill grapegrower since 1980, moving into winemaking with the opening of a $3 million winery in '96. Varieties planted include chardonnay, colombard, grenache, malbec, mataro, merlot, pinot gris, riesling, sangiovese, sauvignon blanc, semillon, tempranillo and viognier. The planting of sagrantino is the largest of only a few such plantings in Australia. Exports to all major markets.

ΨΨΨΨΨ **Australia Felix Swan Hill Sagrantino 2013** Fruit, oak and tannin, all working in harmony. This is a wine with a sense of authority. Sweet-sour cherries, spice and dried tobacco, with clips of resiny, toasty oak. Tannin is fierce but the fruit flavour has enough momentum to swing along with it. Cork. 14% alc. **Rating** 94 **To** 2025 $45 CM

ΨΨΨΨΨ **Winemakers Choice Clare Valley Riesling 2014** **Rating** 93 **To** 2024 $20 ✪
Australia Felix Swan Hill Sagrantino 2012 **Rating** 93 **To** 2022 $45 CM
Australia Felix Premium Barrel Reserve Wrattonbully Cabernet Shiraz 2013 **Rating** 91 **To** 2028 $38
Australia Felix Swan Hill Sagrantino 2011 **Rating** 91 **To** 2021 $45 CM

Angas Plains Estate ★★★★★

317 Angas Plains Road, Langhorne Creek, SA 5255 **Region** Langhorne Creek
T (08) 8537 3159 www.angasplainswines.com.au **Open** 7 days 11–5
Winemaker Peter Douglas **Est.** 1994 **Dozens** 5000 **Vyds** 15.2ha
In 1994 Phillip and Judy Cross planted a vineyard on their 40ha property, situated on the old flood plains of the Angas River, which only flows after heavy rains in its catchment of the Adelaide Hills. With the assistance of son Jason they manage the property to minimise water use and maximise the accumulation of organic matter. Skilled contract winemaking has resulted in some excellent wines from the estate-grown shiraz and cabernet sauvignon. Exports to Singapore, Hong Kong and China.

ΨΨΨΨΨ **Special Reserve Langhorne Creek Cabernet Sauvignon 2012** Estate-grown and specifically selected for maturation in 100% new French oak. The deep purple-crimson colour announces a lipsmacking wine flooded with cassis fruit on the bouquet and palate alike, the latter with fine-grained tannins, cedary oak and exceptional length. Diam. 13.5% alc. **Rating** 95 **To** 2032 $40

ΨΨΨΨΨ **Emily Cross Langhorne Creek Shiraz 2012** **Rating** 93 **To** 2028 $40 CM
Langhorne Creek Cabernet Sauvignon 2013 **Rating** 91 **To** 2030 $25 CM

Angelicus ★★★★

Lot 9 Catalano Road, Burekup, WA 6227 **Region** Geographe
T 0429 481 425 **www**.angelicus.com.au **Open** W'ends & public hols 11–4
Winemaker John Ward, Sue Ward **Est.** 1997 **Dozens** 500 **Vyds** 1.65ha
Dr John and Sue Ward moved from Sydney to WA with the aim of establishing a vineyard
and winery. They moved to the Geographe region, where they purchased a 51ha block of
granite-strewn rocky hillside facing north and west, looking towards the Indian Ocean. In
2009 they began the planting of their vines, the lion's share to grenache (bush vines, managed
biodynamically), five clones of tempranillo, and verdejo. They purchase grenache, mourvedre
and shiraz from local growers.

🍷🍷🍷🍷🍷 **Rosa 2014** Estate-grown grenache crushed and given 3 days' cold soak before
pressing. A scented, flowery bouquet, then an incisive palate, with red fruits, a
twang of citrus pith, a long, crisp finish, and a lingering aftertaste. A well made and
very interesting wine. Screwcap. 13% alc. **Rating** 94 **To** 2016 $18 ✪

🍷🍷🍷🍷🍷 **Verdejo 2014 Rating** 90 **To** 2017 $20 ✪

Angove Family Winemakers ★★★★★

Bookmark Avenue, Renmark, SA 5341 **Region** South Australia
T (08) 8580 3100 **www**.angove.com.au **Open** Mon–Fri 9–5, Sat 10–4, Sun 10–3
Winemaker Tony Ingle, Paul Kernich **Est.** 1886 **Dozens** 1 million **Vyds** 480ha
Exemplifies the economies of scale achievable in the Riverland without compromising
quality. Very good technology provides wines that are never poor and sometimes exceed their
theoretical station in life. The vast Nanya Vineyard is currently being redeveloped with changes
in the varietal mix, row orientation and a partial move to organic growing. Angove's expansion
into Padthaway (chardonnay), Watervale (riesling) and Coonawarra (cabernet sauvignon) via
long-term contracts, and the purchase of the Warboys Vineyard in McLaren Vale in 2008, have
resulted in outstanding premium wines. A large cellar door and café on the Warboys Vineyard
at the corner of Chalk Hill Rd/Olivers Rd, McLaren Vale, is open 10–5 daily. Exports to all
major markets.

🍷🍷🍷🍷🍷 **Warboys Vineyard McLaren Vale Shiraz 2013** Has all the hallmarks of old,
low-yielding vines, elaborated by the region and an unequivocally good vintage;
the heart of the wine is a supple and smooth amalgam of blackberry and satsuma
plum wrapped within a fine skein of ripe tannins and oak; the finish and aftertaste
are of very high quality. Screwcap. 14% alc. **Rating** 96 **To** 2038 $38 ✪
**Single Vineyard Limited Release Blewitt Springs McLaren Vale Shiraz
2013** From 6 rows of 65yo vines; basket-pressed, matured for 9 months in French
puncheons. Dense, deep crimson, the rim bright; an exercise in presenting power
and finesse, the calm depths of the black-fruited bouquet expanding to take
in bitter chocolate and purple fruit on the long, even, medium-bodied palate.
116 dozen made. Screwcap. 14.5% alc. **Rating** 96 **To** 2043 $38 ✪
Rare Tawny Average Age 15 Years NV A lusciously rich yet nimble mix of
fruitcake, mocha, toffee, bitter chocolate and brandy snap. Another major surprise,
winning the top-gold medal in the small volume, aged fortified tawny class in the
National Wine Show '11, causing the judges to comment 'a classic example of the
style'. 500ml. Screwcap. 19.8% alc. **Rating** 96 **To** 2016 $45 ✪
Warboys Vineyard McLaren Vale Grenache 2013 The Warboys Vineyard
is certified organic and biodynamic. The perfumed red fruits of the bouquet are
front and centre on the silky, medium-bodied palate; a beautiful rendition of
McLaren Vale Grenache, with more elegance than usual. Its balance is such that it
will live for many years, but I wouldn't criticise anyone for drinking it right now.
300 dozen made. Screwcap. 14% alc. **Rating** 96 **To** 2028 $35 ✪
Single Vineyard Limited Release Willunga McLaren Vale Shiraz 2013
From low-yielding 57yo vines; basket-pressed, matured in French puncheons for
9 months. Deep, bright colour; medium to full-bodied, the bouquet with nuances
of spice and oak underlying the fruit, the mid-palate supple before an unexpected,

but admirable, savoury/twiggy finish adding length and balance. 110 dozen made. Screwcap. 14.5% alc. **Rating** 95 **To** 2038 $38

Warboys Vineyard McLaren Vale Shiraz Grenache 2013 Good colour; a fragrant, elegant and symbiotic blend of varieties and place results in effortless complexity, with superfine but persistent tannins adding another dimension; red fruits dominate, but there is enough black fruit to provide balance and length. 400 dozen made. Screwcap. 14% alc. **Rating** 95 **To** 2028 $35 ❍

Single Vineyard Limited Release Sellicks Foothills McLaren Vale Shiraz 2013 Rating 94 To 2040 $38

Family Crest McLaren Vale Shiraz 2013 Rating 93 To 2025 $19 ❍
Family Crest McLaren Vale Cabernet Sauvignon 2013 Rating 93 To 2020 $19 ❍
Alternatus McLaren Vale Vermentino 2014 Rating 92 To 2016 $25 CM ❍
Nine Vines Grenache Shiraz Rose 2014 Rating 92 To 2015 $17 ❍
Alternatus McLaren Vale Grenache 2014 Rating 92 To 2019 $25 CM ❍
Family Crest Grenache Shiraz Mourvedre 2014 Rating 92 To 2029 $22 ❍
Alternatus McLaren Vale Carignan 2014 Rating 92 To 2019 $25 CM ❍

Angullong Wines ★★★★☆

Victoria Street, Millthorpe, NSW 2798 **Region** Orange
T (02) 6366 4300 **www.**angullong.com.au **Open** Fri–Mon & public hols 11–5
Winemaker Jon Reynolds **Est.** 1998 **Dozens** 16 000 **Vyds** 216.7ha
The Crossing family (Bill and Hatty, and third generation James and Ben) has owned a 2000ha sheep and cattle station for over half a century. Located 40km south of Orange, overlooking the Belubula Valley, more than 200ha of vines have been planted. In all, there are 15 varieties, with shiraz, cabernet sauvignon and merlot leading the way. Most of the production is sold. Exports to China.

Crossing Reserve Shiraz 2013 Power and focus with a firm-but-lengthy finish. Ripe, insistent cherry-plum, aniseed, five spice and cedar wood flavours. Immaculately presented, complex, stylish; you name it, it has it in its favour. Screwcap. 14% alc. **Rating** 96 **To** 2033 $35 CM ❍

Orange Sauvignon Blanc 2014 Rating 93 To 2015 $19 CM ❍
Fossil Hill Orange Sangiovese 2013 Rating 92 To 2019 $24 CM ❍
Fossil Hill Orange Barbera 2013 Rating 92 To 2018 $24 CM ❍
Orange Shiraz 2013 Rating 91 To 2020 $19 CM ❍
Fossil Hill Orange Shiraz Viognier 2013 Rating 91 To 2023 $25
Orange Cabernet Merlot 2013 Rating 91 To 2019 $19 CM ❍
Orange Pinot Grigio 2014 Rating 90 To 2015 $19 CM ❍

Angus the Bull ★★★☆

PO Box 611, Manly, NSW 1655 **Region** Central Victoria Zone
T (02) 8966 9020 **www.**angusthebull.com **Open** Not
Winemaker Hamish MacGowan **Est.** 2002 **Dozens** 20 000
Hamish MacGowan took the virtual winery idea to its ultimate conclusion, with a single wine (Cabernet Sauvignon) designed to be drunk with a perfectly cooked steak. Parcels of grapes are selected from regions across Victoria and SA each year, the multi-regional blend approach designed to minimise vintage variation. In 2012 a second meat-friendly wine was added. Exports to the UK, Canada, Ireland, the Philippines, Singapore, Thailand, Hong Kong and NZ.

Wee Angus Cabernet Merlot 2013 A bilingual Australian/French label extolling barbecues. Bright crimson, it is light to medium-bodied, with fresh red fruits on the mid-palate, the tannins braking loose on the back-palate, needing to be tethered to the fruit. Screwcap. 13.5% alc. **Rating** 89 **To** 2018 $19 ❍

Cabernet Sauvignon 2013 From Central Victoria. A savoury, medium-bodied wine with good varietal expression; it's a competitive world out there, and this is more akin to a sub-$20 wine. Screwcap. 14% alc. **Rating** 88 **To** 2019 $22

Annie's Lane   ★★★★★

Quelltaler Road, Watervale, SA 5452 **Region** Clare Valley
T (08) 8843 2320 www.annieslane.com.au **Open** Mon–Fri 9–5, w'ends 10–4
Winemaker Alex MacKenzie **Est.** 1851 **Dozens** NFP
The Clare Valley brand of TWE, the name coming from Annie Wayman, a turn-of-the-century local identity. The brand consistently offers wines that over-deliver against their price points. Copper Trail is the flagship release, and there are some very worthy cellar door and on-premise wines. Exports to the UK, the US and Europe.

ᵀᵀᵀᵀᵀ **Copper Trail Clare Valley Shiraz 2012** A deeply coloured wine of impressive stature; black fruits, black olive and quality oak are the drivers of the bouquet, and of the texture and structure of the palate; open fermentation and partial barrel fermentation have been all-important in shaping its mouthfeel and its impeccable length. Screwcap. 14.5% alc. **Rating** 97 **To** 2042 $70 ✪

ᵀᵀᵀᵀᵀ **Quelltaler Watervale Riesling 2014** From a block planted in '35 on the old Sarsfield Vineyard (then owned by Quelltaler). Notably fine and poised, with pure lemon/lime fruit on the long palate, lingering long on the finish and aftertaste. Screwcap. 12.5% alc. **Rating** 95 **To** 2029 $28 ✪
Quelltaler Watervale Shiraz Cabernet 2012 The bright colour and fragrant bouquet are pointers to a delicious medium-bodied blend, with its posy of red and black fruits on the bouquet and supple, harmonious palate supported by gossamer tannins. Screwcap. 14.5% alc. **Rating** 94 **To** 2027 $28 JH ✪

ᵀᵀᵀᵀᵀ **Clare Valley Shiraz 2013 Rating** 93 **To** 2025 $22 ✪
Winemaker's Blend Clare Valley Shiraz Grenache Mourvedre 2013 Rating 93 **To** 2023 $30 CM
Clare Valley Rose 2014 Rating 91 **To** 2016 $21 CM ✪
Clare Valley Cabernet Merlot 2013 Rating 91 **To** 2020 $21 CM ✪

Ansted & Co   ★★★★★

11 Flood Street, Bendigo, Vic 3550 (postal) **Region** Bendigo
T 0409 665 005 www.anstedandco.com.au **Open** Not
Winemaker Tobias Ansted **Est.** 2003 **Dozens** 550
Ansted & Co. was started as a busman's holiday by Tobias Ansted – then and now winemaker at Balgownie Estate – in 2003. Pressure of work and family commitments led to the sale of the vineyard in 2006, but with an agreement to buy back the grapes, and to manage the vineyard. Syrah was the initial planting, followed by marsanne, roussanne and viognier. Exports to China.

ᵀᵀᵀᵀᵀ **North Harcourt Vineyard Syrah 2013** A range of techniques: whole bunches, extended maceration, destemmed, open-fermented and basket-pressed, 15 months' maturation in used French puncheons. The bouquet is decidedly complex, with spice and roast meat aromas, the full-bodied palate reflecting the extended maceration component more than the whole bunches. Complex and challenging, with an unknowable future. Screwcap. 14.5% alc. **Rating** 96 **To** 2043 $35 ✪
North Harcourt Vineyard Syrah 2012 Three components: first conventionally destemmed and fermented; the second 100% whole bunches into a sealed container for 3 weeks' carbonic maceration, then opened and foot-trodden for 10 days; the third as for the first except 55 days' post-fermentation maceration; matured in French oak for 14 months. Extremely complex flavours and structure. The evolution of this wine will be fascinating to watch. 150 dozen made. Screwcap. 14% alc. **Rating** 95 **To** 2042 $35 ✪

ᵀᵀᵀᵀ **Variation No. 1 Syrah 2013 Rating** 89 **To** 2023 $20

Anvers

633 Razorback Road, Kangarilla, SA 5157 **Region** Adelaide Hills
T (08) 8374 1787 **www**.anvers.com.au **Open** Not
Winemaker Kym Milne MW **Est.** 1998 **Dozens** 10000 **Vyds** 24.5ha
Myriam and Wayne Keoghan's principal vineyard is in the Adelaide Hills at Kangarilla
(16ha of cabernet sauvignon, shiraz, chardonnay, sauvignon blanc and viognier), the second
(96-year-old) vineyard at McLarenVale (shiraz, grenache and cabernet sauvignon).Winemaker
Kym Milne has experience gained across many of the wine-producing countries in both
northern and southern hemispheres. Exports to the UK and other major markets.

The Warrior Shiraz 2012 A 67/33% blend matured for 18 months in French
oak. A very intense and powerful palate that manages to be light on its feet thanks
to the balance between fruit, oak and tannins, and the marriage of peppery, firm
black cherry of the Adelaide Hills and softer Langhorne Creek fruit on the mid-
palate. Screwcap. 14.5% alc. **Rating** 96 **To** 2035 $55 ✪
Adelaide Hills Shiraz 2013 Deep crimson-red; restrained richness is the calling
card of a high-quality, medium to full-bodied Shiraz; black fruits, spice, licorice
and oak swirl around the palate, with the finish long and very well balanced. Cork.
14.5% alc. **Rating** 95 **To** 2033 $38
Adelaide Hills Fortified Shiraz 2013 This was made with Portuguese vintage
port as a reference point, in particular the low baume keeping the accent on the
spicy black fruits and licorice of the Adelaide Hills shiraz. Easy to enjoy now,
but will only get better (more complex) over the next 5 years. 500ml. Screwcap.
18.5% alc. **Rating** 94 **To** 2028 $35

Brabo Cabernet Sauvignon 2013 **Rating** 90 **To** 2023 $14 ✪

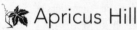 Apricus Hill

550 McLeod Road, Denmark, WA 6333 **Region** Denmark
T 0427 409 078 **www**.apricushillcom.au **Open** Fri–Mon 11–5, 7 days school hols
Winemaker James Kellie **Est.** 1995 **Dozens** 500 **Vyds** 8ha
When the then owners of Somerset Hill Vineyard, Graham and Lee Upson, placed the
vineyard on the market, James and Careena Kellie (owners of Harewood Estate) purchased the
vineyard with two purposes: first, to secure a critical fruit source for Harewood, and, second,
to make and market a small range of single-vineyard, single-varietal wines for sale exclusively
through the spectacular cellar door, with its sweeping vista.Thus Somerset Hill is now Apricus
Hill, the first four releases from 2014 offering high-quality wines.

Single Vineyard Denmark Semillon 2014 Made from free-run juice.Wines
such as this should remind the HunterValley that it is not the exclusive custodian
of riveting Semillon; indeed, at 1yo there are few Hunter Semillons I know of
with such depth and mouth-watering aftertaste. Perhaps the Hunter makers would
say they make Melbourne Cup stayers, not Golden Slipper yearlings. Screwcap.
12% alc. **Rating** 95 **To** 2024 $28 ✪
Single Vineyard Denmark Sauvignon Blanc 2014 Fermented in new French
oak, the intensity of the fruit easily handling the oak, and dominating the finish,
as it should; while the snow pea and fresh-cut grass are common varietal markers,
citrus and pink grapefruit are less so, especially as they displace tropical fruits.The
overall impact is compelling. Screwcap. 12.5% alc. **Rating** 95 **To** 2017 $28 ✪
Single Vineyard Denmark Chardonnay 2014 Fermented in new French
oak. Bright straw-green, the bouquet has some attractive flinty nuances, but it is
the supple and intense palate that steals the show, white peach and grapefruit in
a sinuous embrace, the grapefruit breaking free on the lingering aftertaste, oak an
ever-present complexing factor. Screwcap. 13% alc. **Rating** 95 **To** 2022 $28 ✪
Single Vineyard Denmark Pinot Noir 2014 Small batch-fermented and
matured in French oak.Vivid crimson-purple; the bouquet abounds with red and
black cherry aromas, the powerful palate following dutifully behind, but politely
asking for several years' grace to allow secondary flavours to emerge, as they surely
will. Screwcap. 13% alc. **Rating** 94 **To** 2024 $28 ✪

Arakoon ★★★★

7/229 Main Road, McLaren Vale, SA 5171 **Region** McLaren Vale
T (08) 8323 7339 **www**.arakoonwines.com.au **Open** By appt
Winemaker Raymond Jones **Est.** 1999 **Dozens** 3500 **Vyds** 3.5ha
Ray and Patrik Jones' first venture into wine came to nothing: a 1990 proposal for a film about the Australian wine industry with myself as anchorman. Five years too early, say the Joneses. In 1999 they took the plunge into making their own wine, and exporting it along with the wines of others. As the quality of the wines has increased, so has the originally zany labelling been replaced with simple, but elegant, labels. Exports to Sweden, Denmark, Germany, Singapore, Malaysia and China.

🍷🍷🍷🍷🍷 **Doyen Willunga Shiraz 2013** Warm and rich but well polished. Chocolate and cedar flavour flood through bitumen and blackberry. Unsubtle but well put together. Rippling tannin adds a touch of class. Screwcap. 15% alc. **Rating** 93 **To** 2024 $45 CM
Clarendon Shiraz 2013 Steps boldly into overripe territory, presenting a warm, jammy, tarry wine, bursting with both fruit flavour and seductive (dark) chocolatey oak. Integration of the various components is excellent, to the point of seamlessness, while raspberried notes at the outer edges provide much-needed brightness. In the end it's a pretty decent rendition of the inky, teeth-staining style. Screwcap. 15% alc. **Rating** 92 **To** 2024 $32 CM
Sellicks Beach Shiraz 2013 Not short on either flavour or interest. Leathery, jubey blackberry, saltbush and sweet herb flavours. It's interesting, but not always in a positive sense; it's one of those wines where you find yourself swinging for and against. It carries its alcohol well and the burst of sweet fruit is hard to resist. Screwcap. 15% alc. **Rating** 90 **To** 2020 $20 CM ✪
Lighthouse Fleurieu Shiraz Cabernet 2013 It sits at the outer edges of ripeness, and therefore carries the flavours of baked asphalt and stressed, salty herbs, but still manages a juicy, berried drinkability. It's warm with alcohol, but more than pleasant to drink. Screwcap. 15% alc. **Rating** 90 **To** 2021 $20 CM ✪

🍷🍷🍷🍷 **Vale Cru Full Bodied Red Shiraz Grenache Mourvedre 2012** Rating 89 **To** 2020 $20 CM

Aramis Vineyards ★★★★

29 Sir Donald Bradman Drive, Mile End South, SA 5031 **Region** McLaren Vale
T (08) 8352 2900 **www**.aramisvineyards.com **Open** By appt
Winemaker Scott Rawlinson **Est.** 1998 **Dozens** 10 000 **Vyds** 26ha
Aramis Vineyards was founded in 1998 by Lee Flourentzou. Located barely 2km from the Gulf of St Vincent, it is one of the coolest sites in McLaren Vale, planted to shiraz and cabernet sauvignon, the two varieties best suited to the site. This philosophy leads Aramis to source grapes from other regions that best represent each variety, including sauvignon blanc and chardonnay from Adelaide Hills and riesling from Eden Valley. After a lengthy sabbatical overseas, head winemaker Scott Rawlinson has returned. The city-based cellar door also features wines from other boutique producers. Exports to the US, Canada, greater Asia and NZ.

🍷🍷🍷🍷🍷 **Single Vineyard McLaren Vale Shiraz 2012** Dark-berried flavour infused with coffeed oak. Both are in good proportion. Satisfying and smooth with a brightish finish, courtesy of a late burst of redder-berried fruits. Fine lace work of tannin elevates it further. Screwcap. 14.5% alc. **Rating** 93 **To** 2024 $27 CM ✪
The Alliance Series Langhorne Creek McLaren Vale Sangiovese Cabernet Sauvignon 2013 This works, taking a leaf out of the Chianti book; sangiovese rules the roost, but the cabernet adds length and structure to the finish. Screwcap. 13.5% alc. **Rating** 92 **To** 2028 $35
O'Aristocratis Sparkling Syrah 2005 A celebration of the depth and complexity of McLaren Vale shiraz in layers of black plums, blackberries, licorice and black olive, lingering on a long and confident finish. The same oak treatment as Aramis' flagship The Governor Syrah is a bit too much here, though 3 years on

lees and a few in bottle have certainly helped to soften its firm, fine, tannin grip. Give it another 5–10 years yet. Disgorged July '11 Screwcap. 14.5% alc. **Rating** 92 **To** 2030 $65 TS

The Alliance Series Langhorne Creek McLaren Vale Nebbiolo Shiraz 2013 An innovative blend, but the nebbiolo still needed a little fining to provide structural balance. Screwcap. 13.5% alc. **Rating** 91 **To** 2025 $35

 Alliance Series Grenache Mataro Shiraz 2013 **Rating** 89 **To** 2020 $35
White Label McLaren Vale Shiraz 2012 **Rating** 88 **To** 2019 $20
Single Vineyard Cabernet Sauvignon 2012 **Rating** 88 **To** 2021 $27 CM

Aravina Estate   ★★★★☆

61 Thornton Road, Yallingup, WA 6282 **Region** Margaret River
T (08) 9750 1111 **www**.aravinaestate.com **Open** 7 days 10.30–4
Winemaker Jodie Opie **Est.** 2010 **Dozens** 10 000 **Vyds** 28ha
In 2010 seventh-generation Steve Tobin and family acquired the winery and vineyard of Amberley Estate from Accolade, which retained the Amberley brand. Steve has big plans for turning the property into a multifaceted resource with a host of attractions, for use as wedding ceremony areas and so forth. Exports to Indonesia, Malaysia, Hong Kong and China.

 Wildwood Ridge Reserve Margaret River Chardonnay 2014 From the oldest vines on the estate, hand-picked, whole bunch-pressed, wild-fermented. 'Underlying spicy new oak'. Has what it takes: vibrant white peach, nectarine and grapefruit, neatly balanced/integrated French oak, and squeaky/grippy (in the best sense) acidity. Screwcap. 13% alc. **Rating** 95 **To** 2026 $42

Margaret River Semillon 2014 **Rating** 93 **To** 2024 $28
Block 4 Margaret River Chenin Blanc 2014 **Rating** 93 **To** 2024 $28
Margaret River Vermentino 2014 **Rating** 92 **To** 2019 $28

Arlewood Estate   ★★★★

Cnr Bussell Highway/Calgardup Road, Forest Grove, WA 6286 **Region** Margaret River
T (08) 9755 6676 **www**.arlewood.com.au **Open** Sat 11–5
Winemaker Stuart Pym **Est.** 1988 **Dozens** 5000 **Vyds** 9.7ha
Arlewood Estate's single-vineyard wines are produced from the estate Wilyabrup vineyard and from the Forest Grove estate in the cool, southern part of Margaret River, often in small quantities. The hugely experienced and skilled Stuart Pym oversees winemaking. Exports to the UK, the US, Canada, Switzerland, Singapore, Malaysia, Hong Kong, the Philippines and China.

 Sauvignon Blanc Semillon 2014 A fragrant bouquet of snow pea and a waft of passionfruit, the palate tracking firmly in the footprints of the snow pea, grass and lemon hints of the bouquet, not the tropical. Definitely food-friendly. Screwcap. 13.5% alc. **Rating** 93 **To** 2017 $20 ✪

Cabernet Merlot 2013 Filled to the brim with juicy cassis fruit, leaving no space for either tannins or oak to gain any traction, yet is only medium-bodied. Unusual, but it's almost certain the high tide of fruit will ebb in a few years, allowing its other parts to be tasted. Screwcap. 13.5% alc. **Rating** 90 **To** 2023 $25

Armstead Estate   ★★★☆

366 Moorabbee Road, Knowsley, Vic 3523 **Region** Heathcote
T (03) 5439 1363 **www**.armsteadestate.com.au **Open** W'ends & public hols 11–5
Winemaker Peter Armstead **Est.** 2003 **Dozens** 650 **Vyds** 0.6ha
Peter Armstead had been a lifelong wine collector and consumer when he was caught up in the Ansett collapse (he had been an aircraft engineer and technical instructor). While he and partner Sharon Egan have full-time day jobs, they were able to purchase a property on the shores of Lake Eppalock. They were determined to have a small vineyard, and proceeded to

plant shiraz, marsanne and cabernet sauvignon. Peter has learned as much as possible about viticulture and winemaking, buying grapes from well-known vineyards in the region.

§§§§§ **Heathcote Cabernet Sauvignon 2012** Cuts a decent groove. Leather and blackcurrant flavour, generally well balanced, feels solid throughout and satisfying to close. Screwcap. 14.8% alc. **Rating** 90 **To** 2020 $28 CM

ArtWine   ★★★★

72 Bird in Hand Road, Woodside, SA 5244 **Region** Adelaide Hills/Clare Valley
T (08) 8389 9399 www.artwine.com.au **Open** Thurs–Mon 11–5
Winemaker Joanne Irvine **Est.** 1997 **Dozens** 3000 **Vyds** 27ha
ArtWine is the venture of Glen Kelly and wife Judy. It has two vineyards, one on Springfarm Road, Clare, the other on Sawmill Road, Sevenhill. The Springfarm Road vineyard has a 3.64ha planting of tempranillo, as well as (in descending order of size) riesling, pinot gris, cabernet sauvignon, grenache, cabernet franc, fiano, viognier and graciano. A further 2ha of fiano and 1.75ha of graciano were planted in the spring of 2011, replacing part of the cabernet block and the contoured section of the riesling block. The remainder of the cabernet sauvignon and riesling (plus cabernet franc) will be replanted over the next few years, the varieties yet to be decided. This is definitely a lateral approach by any standard. Exports to Singapore.

§§§§§ **Fiano 2014** Gets the texture right. And the flavour. Lime and apple with attractive highlights of orange blossom. Generously flavoured but also well honed through the finish. Screwcap. 12.5% alc. **Rating** 92 **To** 2015 $25 CM ✪
Tempranillo 2012 Good body of flavour. Sweet-sour cherries and chicory with seductive influence from smoky/cedary oak. Firmish but well-integrated tannin. Fruit flushes through the finish. A most attractive wine. Screwcap. 14% alc. **Rating** 92 **To** 2020 $25 CM ✪
Grumpy Old Man Reserve Grenache 2012 120 dozen produced. Strong-armed and flavoured wine. Trunks of blackberry, leather, prune and vanilla flavour, cuddled in sizeable arms of tannin. Peppery, tobacco-like notes linger through the aftertaste, though sweet/jammy fruit flavour is the main order of the day. Screwcap. 14.5% alc. **Rating** 91 **To** 2022 $60 CM

§§§§ **Graciano 2012** **Rating** 89 **To** 2018 $25 CM

Arundel Farm Estate   ★★★★☆

321 Arundel Road, Keilor, Vic 3036 **Region** Sunbury
T (03) 9338 9987 www.arundelfarmestate.com.au **Open** W'ends 10–5
Winemaker Mark Matthews, Claude Ceccomancini **Est.** 1984 **Dozens** 2000 **Vyds** 7.4ha
The first stage of the vineyard in 1984 was 0.8ha of shiraz and cabernet sauvignon. Rick Kinzbrunner of Giaconda made the first vintage, 1988, but for some years thereafter, but the enterprise lapsed until it was revived with new plantings in '96 and 2000. Today it is planted solely to shiraz and viognier. In October '11 Claude and Sandra Ceccomancini acquired the business and appointed Mark Matthews as winemaker.

§§§§§ **Sunbury Shiraz 2013** Full, bright crimson-purple; the bouquet is typical cool-climate Shiraz, with spice, pepper and licorice together with black cherry fruit, but the power and intensity of the palate is way above expectations, fine-grained tannins woven through the fruit flavours add complexity and excellent length. Will cruise past 2030. Screwcap. 14% alc. **Rating** 95 **To** 2033 $25 ✪

§§§§§ **Sunbury Viognier 2013** **Rating** 92 **To** 2017 $23 ✪

Ascella Pure Wine   ★★★☆

203 Thompsons Road, Milbrodale, NSW 2330 **Region** Hunter Valley
T (02) 6574 5275 www.ascellawine.com **Open** 7 days 10–5
Winemaker First Creek Wines (Liz Silkman) **Est.** 1999 **Dozens** 20 000 **Vyds** 32.4ha

This is a very substantial business that has only come into public focus since 2009. Ten years earlier Geoff and Barb Brown had begun to plant an organically grown vineyard; most was planted in 1999, a small amount in 2001. The grapes were sold under an ongoing contract to Tamburlaine, but in late '08 the owners turned to First Creek Wines, with Liz Silkman the lead winemaker for the new brand, Ascella Pure Wine. The name reflects the Browns' belief that organically grown grapes are inherently superior to conventionally grown grapes, and that the benefit flows through to the wines. Both have fascinating backgrounds outside the wine industry. Exports to the UK, Canada, Sweden, Japan and China.

ŸŸŸŸŸ **Reserve Hunter Valley Chardonnay 2014** Ratchets up the intensity of its sibling in terms of both fruit and French oak, but doesn't add a layer of complexity. Still, a nice wine. Screwcap. 13% alc. **Rating** 90 **To** 2019 $30

ŸŸŸŸ **Broke Fordwich Chardonnay 2014** **Rating** 88 **To** 2017 $24

Ashbrook Estate ★★★★★

379 Tom Cullity Drive, Wilyabrup, WA 6280 **Region** Margaret River
T (08) 9755 6262 www.ashbrookwines.com.au **Open** 7 days 10–5
Winemaker Catherine Edwards, Brian Devitt **Est.** 1975 **Dozens** 14500 **Vyds** 17.4ha
This fastidious producer of consistently excellent estate-grown table wines shuns publicity and is less well known than is deserved, selling much of its wine through the cellar door and to an understandably very loyal mailing list clientele. It is very much a family affair: while founder Tony Devitt retired in Nov 2013, his brother Brian is at the helm, winemaking is by his daughter Catherine, and viticulture by son Richard (also a qualified winemaker). Exports to the US, Canada, Germany, Indonesia, Japan, Singapore, Hong Kong and China.

ŸŸŸŸŸ **Margaret River Chardonnay 2013** Brilliant wine. Announces itself from the first sip. White peach and citrus notes rush into spice and nougat. The dominating aspect, though, is the wine's length, or rather the way the flavours build and then burst through the finish. Screwcap. 13.5% alc. **Rating** 95 **To** 2021 $32 CM ✪

ŸŸŸŸŸ **Margaret River Cabernet Merlot 2011** **Rating** 93 **To** 2026 $29 CM
Margaret River Semillon 2014 **Rating** 92 **To** 2018 $24 CM ✪
Margaret River Verdelho 2014 **Rating** 92 **To** 2017 $24 CM ✪
Margaret River Sauvignon Blanc 2014 **Rating** 91 **To** 2016 $24 CM
Margaret River Shiraz 2011 **Rating** 91 **To** 2022 $29 CM

Ashton Hills ★★★★★

Tregarthen Road, Ashton, SA 5137 **Region** Adelaide Hills
T (08) 8390 1243 **Open** W'ends & most public hols 11–5.30
Winemaker Stephen George **Est.** 1982 **Dozens** 1500 **Vyds** 3ha
Stephen George made Ashton Hills one of the great producers of Pinot Noir in Australia, and by some distance the best in the Adelaide Hills. With no family succession in place, he sold the business to Wirra Wirra in April 2015. It had been rumoured for some time that he (Stephen) was considering such a move, so when it was announced, there was a sigh of relief that it should pass to a business such as Wirra Wirra, with undoubted commitment to retaining the extraordinary quality of the wines made by Stephen. He will continue to live in the house on the property, and provide ongoing consulting advice.

ŸŸŸŸŸ **Estate Pinot Noir 2013** The fragrant, gently spiced bouquet and palate are akin to a miniature painting, exquisite in its detail; complete harmony is the key to this wine, its length exceptional, extended by the forest berry/forest floor overlay on the finish. Screwcap. 14% alc. **Rating** 97 **To** 2025 $60 ✪
Reserve Pinot Noir 2012 Deep crimson-purple colour, a specialty of Ashton Hills; the ultimate iron fist in a velvet glove, the fist surrounded by waves of sumptuous plum, red cherry and black cherry. The balance and harmony are utterly exceptional, the future of the wine limitless; may well prove to be one of the all-time great wines of Ashton Hills. Screwcap. 14% alc. **Rating** 97 **To** 2027 $66 ✪

ŶŶŶŶŶ **Reserve Pinot Noir 2013** Bright, full and clear colour; right in the mainstream of the Ashton Hills style, speaking with utmost clarity of its single site origin; it has prodigious length, red fruits and savoury nuances chasing each other around the stage; a pas de deux of considerable beauty. The most intense, least fleshy of the '13 quartet, its journey barely begun. Screwcap. 14% alc. **Rating** 96 **To** 2025 $90

Blend No. 2 Cemetery Block Piccadilly Valley Pinot Noir 2013 A 50/50% blend of the Griggs and estate vineyards. Powerful, intense and long, with a savoury foresty undertone to the fruit profile giving layers of flavour and textural complexity. A new wine for Ashton Hills, the Griggs Vineyard at a lower, warmer altitude. Screwcap. 14% alc. **Rating** 96 **To** 2023 $40 **☉**

Sparkling Shiraz 2008 You can feel the concentration, the deep-set texture and the inimitable flavour of ancient, dry-grown shiraz vines. Black fruits of all kinds, licorice and olives linger with remarkable line and length, enveloped by firm, drying, mouth-encapsulating tannins that are never hard or overwhelming. It will live effortlessly for decades. Disgorged Sept '14. Diam. 13% alc. **Rating** 96 **To** 2038 $40 TS **☉**

Adelaide Hills Riesling 2014 Bright straw-green; Stephen George keeps meaning to pull out the riesling and plant pinot noir in its place; I (and many others) am happy he hasn't done so; this has the clarity, precision and brilliance of a diamond, with lime, lemon and apple held together by the high-tensile stainless steel shaft of acidity. Screwcap. 13% alc. **Rating** 95 **To** 2030 $40

Blend No. 1 Cemetery Block Piccadilly Valley Pinot Noir 2013 Clones MV6 and 114 from the Griggs Vineyard next door to the Uraidla cemetery, lower and warmer than the Estate vineyard, and picked several weeks earlier. Has by some distance the deepest colour of the '13 Ashton Pinots, the palate full of plummy spicy fruit a real crowd-pleaser. Screwcap. 14% alc. **Rating** 95 **To** 2023 $40

ŶŶŶŶŸ **Piccadilly Valley Pinot Noir Brut Sauvage 2011 Rating** 92 **To** 2015 $35 TS
Piccadilly Valley Pinot Noir Salmon Brut 2011 Rating 91 **To** 2015 $35 TS

Atlas Wines   ★★★★★

PO Box 458, Clare, SA 5453 **Region** Clare Valley
T 0419 847 491 **www**.atlaswines.com.au **Open** Not
Winemaker Adam Barton **Est.** 2008 **Dozens** 3000 **Vyds** 8ha
Owner and winemaker Adam Barton had an extensive winemaking career before establishing Atlas Wines: in McLaren Vale, the Barossa Valley, Coonawarra and at the iconic Bonny Doon Vineyard in California, and most recently at Reillys Wines in the Clare Valley. He has 6ha of shiraz and 2ha of cabernet sauvignon grown on a stony ridge on the eastern slopes of the region, and also sources small batches from other distinguished sites in the Clare and Barossa valleys. The quality of the wines is extraordinarily good and extraordinarily consistent. Exports to Canada, Singapore, Hong Kong and China.

ŶŶŶŶŶ **172° Watervale Riesling 2014** From old, dry-grown vines of the Churinga Vineyard. An extremely elegant, finely chiselled Riesling, built for the long haul off the base of its crunchy acidity. Screwcap. 12% alc. **Rating** 95 **To** 2029 $28 **☉**

429° Clare Valley Shiraz 2013 Dense, inky purple-crimson, and a profound bouquet of black fruits, spice and licorice; the full-bodied palate provides more of the same, so it is telling you to leave it in peace for another 10 years or so; the balance of the fruit and tannins is good, making a 20-year future a certainty. Screwcap. 14.5% alc. **Rating** 95 **To** 2035 $38

516° Barossa Valley Shiraz 2013 Hand-picked from a single old-vine vineyard in the Ebenezer district, barrel-selected. Very deep colour; it is overflowing with blood plum, blackberry jam (without sweetness), and has a faintly savoury earthy finish that works very well. Will mature a little earlier than its Clare Valley cousin. Screwcap. 14.5% alc. **Rating** 95 **To** 2033 $38

Clare Valley Shiraz 2013 From vineyards in the White Hut district. Medium to full-bodied, it makes a powerful statement of place, albeit not with the trenchant density of its 429° sibling; while patience might reward, this is definitely the wine

to drink, leaving the more expensive (and concentrated) 429° the time it needs.
Screwcap. 14.5% alc. **Rating** 94 **To** 2028 $27 ○
The Spaniard 2012 50/30/20% tempranillo, mourvedre and grenache. A
complex wine, as befits the blend and the region, swollen with a precocious
display of red and black fruits wrapped in licorice, spice and fine-grained tannins.
Screwcap. 14.5% alc. **Rating** 94 **To** 2022 $28 ○

ŸŸŸŸŸ **Watervale Riesling 2014 Rating** 93 **To** 2024 $22 ○

Atze's Corner Wines ★★★★☆

Box 81, Nuriootpa, SA 5355 **Region** Barossa Valley
T 0407 621 989 **www**.atzescornerwines.com.au **Open** By appt
Winemaker Contract, Andrew Kalleske **Est.** 2005 **Dozens** 600 **Vyds** 30ha
The seemingly numerous members of the Kalleske family have widespread involvement in
grapegrowing and winemaking in the Barossa Valley. This venture is that of Andrew Kalleske,
son of John and Barb Kalleske. In 1975 they purchased the Atze Vineyard, which included a
small block of shiraz planted in 1912, but with additional plantings along the way, including
more shiraz in '51. Andrew purchases some grapes from the family vineyard. It has 20ha of
shiraz, with small amounts of mataro, petit verdot, grenache, cabernet, tempranillo, viognier,
petite sirah, graciano, montepulciano, vermentino and aglianico. Local boutique winemakers
provide the physical facilities for the winemaking, with Andrew involved.

ŸŸŸŸŸ **Zen Master Barossa Valley Shiraz 2012** Open-fermented, basket-pressed and
matured in new French oak for 24 months. Impenetrable black in colour, saturated
blackberry flavour, mocha/bitter chocolate and earth complexities with tips of
redcurrant. It is a giant of a wine; if you served it alongside almost any other wine
it would make the other look silly. It is the risk taken universally by all things
seeking greatness. Time alone will tell how history judges this wine, but in its
youth, it looks seriously good. Cork. 15.5% alc. **Rating** 96 **To** 2040 $140 CM

ŸŸŸŸŸ **The Bachelor 2013 Rating** 92 **To** 2021 $28 CM
The Bachelor Barossa Valley Shiraz 2012 Rating 92 **To** 2032 $26
The Giant Barossa Valley Durif 2013 Rating 92 **To** 2021 $28 CM
White Knight Vermentino 2014 Rating 91 **To** 2015 $20 CM ○
Eddies Old Vine Shiraz 2010 Rating 90 **To** 2020 $55 CM

Audrey Wilkinson ★★★★★

Oakdale, De Beyers Road, Pokolbin, NSW 2320 **Region** Hunter Valley
T (02) 4998 7411 **www**.audreywilkinson.com.au **Open** 7 days
Winemaker Jeff Byrne, Xanthe Leonard **Est.** 1866 **Dozens** 40 000 **Vyds** 35.33ha
One of the most historic properties in the Hunter Valley, set in a particularly beautiful location
and with a very attractive cellar door, has been owned by Brian Agnew and family since
2004. The wines are made from estate-grown grapes, the lion's share to shiraz, the remainder
(in descending order) to semillon, malbec, verdelho, tempranillo, merlot, cabernet sauvignon,
muscat and traminer; the vines were planted from the 1970s to the '90s. Also has a 3.45ha
McLaren Vale vineyard of merlot and shiraz. Exports to Canada, China and NZ.

ŸŸŸŸŸ **The Lake Shiraz 2013** From the best 40yo vines on the block adjacent to the
spring-fed dam. Exceptionally deep colour; it has the depth and velvety richness
expected of the '14 vintage. Its panoply of luscious black fruits will sustain its
development for a bare minimum of 30 years; oak and tannins are also in the mix,
albeit minor players. Screwcap. 14% alc. **Rating** 97 **To** 2053 $80 ○

ŸŸŸŸŸ **The Ridge Semillon 2014** Shows the power most Hunter Valley Semillons were
vested with by the vintage, and how that power can override any issue of alcohol;
the result is opulent, a word I don't think I have ever used for a 1yo Semillon;
there are layers of ripe lemongrass/Meyer lemon, almost into pink grapefruit,
minerally acidity a given. Screwcap. 12.2% alc. **Rating** 96 **To** 2034 $40 ○

Winemakers Selection Hunter Valley Shiraz 2013 A neat halfway house between The Lake planting and the entry point Shiraz; the winemaking team has been right on the money; this is in supple, mouth-filling, medium to full-bodied territory, with blackberry, dark plum and gently savoury tannins; has outstanding length and balance. Screwcap. 14% alc. **Rating** 96 **To** 2043 $36 ✪

The Oakdale Chardonnay 2014 Fermented and matured in French oak (50% new) for an unspecified period, most likely 10-12 months. Here grapefruit takes command, white peach and green apple the outriders; the line, length and balance are all exemplary. Screwcap. 12.9% alc. **Rating** 95 **To** 2027 $36

Winemakers Selection Tempranillo 2014 Adds layers to the red cherry fruit; to say tempranillo is an early-ripening variety (correct) ideally suited to the (hot) Hunter Valley climate is complete nonsense. In theory, and largely in practice, it is suited to cool climates. Screwcap. 13.9% alc. **Rating** 95 **To** 2025 $37

Winemakers Selection Hunter Valley Semillon 2014 This wine abides by the rules of the game, scintillating in its freshness, cut and poise; the flavours range from cut grass, lemongrass and spice to intense Meyer lemon and a reprise of a hint of snow pea; acidity, as ever, provides the framework. Screwcap. 11.6% alc. **Rating** 94 **To** 2029 $26 ✪

Winemakers Selection Wrattonbully Merlot Cabernet 2012 There is no question about the suitability of Wrattonbully for producing good Merlot, this wine a fine example with its floral red flower bouquet and its almost silky palate. When the new clones of merlot – 8R in particular – come on-stream, watch out. Screwcap. 14.5% alc. **Rating** 94 **To** 2030 $36

Hunter Valley Tempranillo 2014 The vintage conditions for '14 were the best for many decades, and the purity and depth of the red cherry fruit is thoroughly engaging. Screwcap. 13.8% alc. **Rating** 94 **To** 2020 $22 ✪

🍷🍷🍷🍷🍷 **Hunter Valley Shiraz 2013 Rating** 93 **To** 2033 $22 ✪
Winemakers Selection Hunter Valley Chardonnay 2014 Rating 92 **To** 2022 $26
Winemakers Selection Hunter Valley Malbec 2014 Rating 91 **To** 2024 $65

Austins & Co   ★★★★★

870 Steiglitz Road, Sutherlands Creek, Vic 3331 **Region** Geelong
T (03) 5281 1799 **www**.austinsandco.com.au **Open** By appt
Winemaker Scott Ireland **Est.** 1982 **Dozens** 20 000 **Vyds** 61.5ha
Pamela and Richard Austin have quietly built their business from a tiny base, and it has flourished. The vineyard has been progressively extended to over 60ha. Son Scott (with a varied but highly successful career outside the wine industry) took over management and ownership in 2008. Scott Ireland is full-time resident winemaker in the capacious onsite winery, and the quality of the wines is admirable Exports to the UK, Canada, Hong Kong, Japan and China.

🍷🍷🍷🍷🍷 **Kyberd Pinot Noir 2012** A little bit extra in all the right places. No lack of finesse, but powerful sour-sweet cherry-plum flavours, loaded with chalk and spice, before a finish complete with undergrowthy character, assertive tannin and inarguable length. Screwcap. 13% alc. **Rating** 96 **To** 2024 $50 CM ✪

Crue Shiraz 2014 Lays it on. Cool-climate in its flavour profile but at the plushest end of the spectrum. Blueberry, blackberry and black cherry with green fennel, pepper and violets. The full gamut. Saucy oak plays an (integrated) role too. Provokes the phrase 'riot of flavour'. Can be cellared but it's a 'why wait' wine. Screwcap. 14% alc. **Rating** 95 **To** 2028 $30 CM ✪

Riesling 2014 Boasts both elegance and intensity. The way the wine finishes is particularly impressive. Lemon, lime and spice with oodles of slatey length. Geelong is hardly a region noted for its Riesling but they're doing something very right here. Screwcap. 11.5% alc. **Rating** 94 **To** 2024 $25 CM ✪

Ellyse Chardonnay 2013 Powerful Chardonnay. Takes no prisoners through the mid-palate, but is refined and tidy to close. Overall it's impressive. Chalk, spicy oak, oatmeal and a wealth of grapefruit, apple and melon-like flavour. Straw-coloured and ready to rock. Screwcap. 13% alc. **Rating** 94 **To** 2019 $50 CM

Ireland Pinot Noir 2012 Fruit-driven but well structured. Deep cherry-plum flavour, with fresh beetroot and rhubarb. Polished and seductive. Needs time to build greater complexity but mouthfeel, balance, length and general presentation of flavour are all kicking goals. Screwcap. 13% alc. **Rating** 94 **To** 2024 $50 CM

Spencer Shiraz 2013 Begins powerfully but angles down to a slender, minerally finish. Classy, but in a youthful frump. Cakey blackberry, crushed dry leaves, fennel and woody spice. It will come into its own, but only when it's good and ready. Screwcap. 14% alc. **Rating** 94 **To** 2032 $50 CM

ᵀᵀᵀᵀᵀ **Chardonnay 2013 Rating** 93 **To** 2022 $35 CM
Geelong Pinot Noir 2013 Rating 93 **To** 2022 $35 CM
6Ft6 Shiraz 2013 Rating 93 **To** 2021 $20 CM ○
6Ft6 Pinot Noir 2013 Rating 92 **To** 2020 $20 CM ○
Greenbanks Chardonnay 2013 Rating 91 **To** 2019 $30 CM
Greenbanks Pinot Noir 2013 Rating 91 **To** 2020 $30 CM

🍇 Auswan Creek   ★★★★☆

261 Murray Street, Tanunda, SA 5352 **Region** Barossa Valley
T (02) 8203 2239 **www**.auswancreek.com.au **Open** Wed–Sun 10–5
Winemaker Ben Riggs **Est.** 2013 **Dozens** 30 000 **Vyds** 12ha
This is a relatively new wine group formed in 2013 through the merger of Inspire Vintage and Australia Swan Vintage. The jewel in the business is a 10ha vineyard in Angaston, with 1.7ha of shiraz planted in 1908, 0.86ha planted in the '60s, 5.43ha of younger shiraz, topped up with 1.76ha of cabernet sauvignon and 1.26ha of grenache. The 2ha cellar door and winery vineyard in Tanunda provide the home base. The major part of the production comes from grapes purchased from growers across SA, and Ben Riggs' experience as a winemaker needs no comment. The focus of the group is exports to Singapore, Thailand and China.

ᵀᵀᵀᵀᵀ **Governor Selection Barossa Valley Cabernet Shiraz 2012** It's supple and smooth, but cabernet doesn't let it get away that easily. Dusty, herbal notes and strings of tannin keep the wealth of plum/blackcurrant flavours well in line; truth is, it's in excellent shape from start to finish, with plenty of everything and an excess of nothing. Screwcap. 15% alc. **Rating** 95 **To** 2028 $60 CM

ᵀᵀᵀᵀᵀ **Peacock Reserve McLaren Vale Shiraz 2012 Rating** 93 **To** 2025 $60 CM
1908 Barossa Valley Shiraz 2012 Rating 90 **To** 2025 $100 CM

Avani   ★★★★★

98 Stanleys Road, Red Hill South, Vic 3937 **Region** Mornington Peninsula
T (03) 5989 2646 **www**.avanisyrah.com.au **Open** By appt
Winemaker Shashi Singh **Est.** 1987 **Dozens** 500 **Vyds** 4ha
Avani is the venture of Shashi and Devendra Singh, who have owned and operated restaurants on the Mornington Peninsula for over 25 years. This inevitably led to an interest in wine, but there was nothing inevitable about taking the plunge in 1998, and purchasing an established vineyard, Wildcroft Estate. Shashi enrolled in viticulture at Charles Sturt University, but moved across to the wine science degree course. Phillip Jones began making the Avani wines in 2000, and in '04 Shashi began working at Bass Phillip, her role in the winery steadily increasing. Changes to the vineyard increased the planting density to 4000 vines per hectare, and reduced the cropping level to a little over 1 tonne per acre. There was a move to organic in '05, and thereafter to key biodynamic practices in the vineyard. Even more radical was the decision to convert the existing plantings of five varieties to 100% shiraz. Shashi took total control of making the Avani wines at Phillip's Leongatha winery in '09, and in '12 they established their small onsite winery, of which they can be truly proud.

ᵀᵀᵀᵀᵀ **Mornington Peninsula Syrah 2013** An 8-day cold soak, 12-day wild ferment, 7 days' post-fermentation maceration, matured for 18 months in French oak

(20% new). An extremely attractive cool-climate Shiraz with a silky sheen to its supple, spicy red and black cherry fruits on the palate, the tannins a fine gauze. ProCork. 12.3% alc. **Rating** 96 **To** 2038 $75 ✪

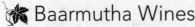

Baarmutha Wines ★★★☆

1184 Diffey Road, Beechworth, Vic 3747 **Region** Beechworth
T (03) 5728 2704 **www.**baarmuthawines.com.au **Open** By appt
Winemaker Vincent Webb **Est.** 2006 **Dozens** 170 **Vyds** 2ha
Vincent Webb is a modern-day Renaissance man. He is a graduate of oenology and viticulture at CSU, but his full-time occupation is a scheduler with Ausnet Services. He manages the vineyard and winery with 'plenty of help' from wife Sharon, and their young sons. Family and friends hand-select the fruit at harvest, and small quantities of wine are made using precisely what you would expect: a basket press, open vat fermenters, wild yeast fermentation, and maturation in new and used French oak. This is yet another start-up winery in the Beechworth region which has many attractions for both winemakers and wine consumers.

�w♀♀♀♀ **Beechworth Shiraz 2013** Silken textured, well weighted, ripe but not overdone. Air of precision. Blue and black berries, spice, sweet soy, a melt of creamy oak. Ultra fine-grained tannin. The longer you sit with it the more impressed you become. Screwcap. 13.5% alc. **Rating** 94 **To** 2022 $38 CM

♀♀♀♀ **Beechworth Shiraz 2012 Rating** 88 **To** 2019 $55 CM

BackVintage Wines ★★★★

2/177 Sailors Bay Road, Northbridge, NSW 2063 **Region** Various
T (02) 9967 9880 **www.**backvintage.com.au **Open** Mon–Fri 9–5
Winemaker Julian Todd, Nick Bulleid MW, Mike Farmilo **Est.** 2003 **Dozens** 10 000
BackVintage Wines is a virtual winery in the fullest sense; not only does it not own vineyards, nor a winery, but also it sells only through its website or by phone. The winemaking team sources parcels of bulk or bottled wines it considers represent excellent quality and value for money, and is then responsible for the final steps before the wine goes to bottle. The value for money offered by these wines is self-evident, and quite remarkable.

♀♀♀♀♀ **McLaren Vale Shiraz 2012** Wines such as this must strike fear into winemakers' hearts and gladden those of consumers, for it is ludicrously good. Archetypal McLaren Vale style, replete with blackberry, plum, a dash of chocolate and round, ripe tannins. The presence or absence of oak is irrelevant. Screwcap. 14% alc. **Rating** 94 **To** 2023 $13 ✪

♀♀♀♀♀ **Yarra Valley Pinot Noir 2013 Rating** 92 **To** 2018 $15 ✪

Baddaginnie Run ★★★★

PO Box 579, North Melbourne, Vic 3051 **Region** Strathbogie Ranges
T (03) 9348 9310 **www.**baddaginnierun.net.au **Open** Not
Winemaker Sam Plunkett **Est.** 1996 **Dozens** 2500 **Vyds** 24ha
Winsome McCaughey and Professor Snow Barlow (Professor of Horticulture and Viticulture at the University of Melbourne) spend part of their week in the Strathbogie Ranges, and part in Melbourne. The business name, Seven Sisters Vineyard, reflects the seven generations of the McCaughey family associated with the land since 1870; Baddaginnie is the nearby township. Exports to the US and China.

♀♀♀♀♀ **Reserve Strathbogie Ranges Shiraz 2009** Matured in French oak for 18 months. Has cruised along since first tasted 3 years ago, its fragrance undimmed, its fruit expression introducing red fruits alongside black, the oak a plus, the finish fresh. Screwcap. 13.5% alc. **Rating** 94 **To** 2024 $35

♀♀♀♀♀ **Single Vineyard Strathbogie Ranges Shiraz 2012 Rating** 92 **To** 2020 $24 ✪

Badger's Brook

874 Maroondah Highway, Coldstream, Vic 3770 **Region** Yarra Valley
T (03) 5962 4130 **www.**badgersbrook.com.au **Open** Wed–Sun 11–5
Winemaker Michael Warren, Gary Baldwin **Est.** 1993 **Dozens** 2500 **Vyds** 4.8ha
Situated next door to the well-known Rochford, the vineyard is planted to chardonnay, sauvignon blanc, pinot noir, shiraz (1ha each), cabernet sauvignon (0.35ha), merlot, viognier (0.2ha each), with a few rows each of roussanne, marsanne and tempranillo. The Badger's Brook wines, made onsite since 2012, are 100% estate-grown; the second Storm Ridge label uses only Yarra Valley grapes. Also houses the smart brasserie restaurant/bakery/cooking school Bella Vedere. Exports to Asia.

ΨΨΨΨΨ **Yarra Valley Tempranillo 2013** Tempranillo is an early-ripening variety in the same group as pinot noir, but is planted here, there and everywhere in Australia. Tokar Estate produced a trophy-winning wine, and it's surprising there aren't more plantings in the Yarra. This one is very welcome, and by some distance the best in the Badger's Brook portfolio. It has the full suite of cherry flavours, the mouthfeel and length likewise good. Screwcap. 13% alc. **Rating** 93 **To** 2028 $25 ✪
Yarra Valley Viognier Roussanne Marsanne 2013 Various combinations of these three varieties have a good track record in the Yarra Valley, and this continues that record. It has the length and energy of a regional Chardonnay, which is saying something. However, it does need a chance to build more flesh. Screwcap. 13% alc. **Rating** 91 **To** 2023 $22 ✪
Storm Ridge Yarra Valley Shiraz 2013 Deeply coloured; a trenchantly full-bodied Shiraz. The waves of black fruits and tannins coming from 13% cool-grown shiraz are utterly unexpected; long maceration of the must pre and post-fermentation seems the most likely explanation. If you like knife and fork styles, this is for you. Screwcap. 13.5% alc. **Rating** 90 **To** 2034 $18 ✪
Yarra Valley Cabernet Sauvignon 2012 A mix of cassis, olive, mint and oak that, somewhat improbably, comes together well, the cassis carrying the day, the tannins fine and ripe, the oak subtle. Screwcap. 13% alc. **Rating** 90 **To** 2020 $25

ΨΨΨΨ **Storm Ridge Yarra Valley Pinot Noir 2013 Rating** 89 **To** 2019 $18 ✪

Bagdad Hills

1557 Midland Highway, Bagdad, Tas 7030 **Region** Southern Tasmania
T 0408 127 004 **Open** By appt
Winemaker Winstead (Neil Snare) **Est.** 2001 **Dozens** 140 **Vyds** 2ha
Graeme and Pip Roberts, long-time residents of Tasmania, ventured into wine later in life than many. Graeme is a retired civil engineer, Pip a registered nurse; the two moved to Bagdad from Hobart. The vineyard is predominantly planted to pinot noir, with smaller amounts of sauvignon blanc, riesling and shiraz. The vineyard has been managed biodynamically since planting began in 2001, and Graeme is on the Council of Biodynamics Tasmania.

ΨΨΨΨΨ **Pinot Noir 2013** Substantially flavoured, all dark plum and black cherry, with spice ground deep into the fruit. Smoky reductive notes play a key role too, as does oak spice. After all the fanfare it feels just a little slender through the finish, but taken as a whole there's something a little fascinating about this wine. Screwcap. 13.3% alc. **Rating** 92 **To** 2022 $30 CM
Shiraz 2013 Cool-climate to the nth degree. Herbs and spices growing from its ears. Meat, cherries, kirsch, floral notes. Interesting and then some. Grows in the glass, the fruit rising, though remains challengingly cool/herbal/savoury for most drinkers. The effect of time in the cellar may surprise. Screwcap. 12.5% alc. **Rating** 90 **To** 2024 $45 CM

Baie Wines

120 McDermott Road, Curlewis, Vic 3222 **Region** Geelong
T 0400 220 436 **www.**baiewines.com.au **Open** By appt
Winemaker Robin Brockett **Est.** 2000 **Dozens** 1000 **Vyds** 6ha

Takes its name from the farming property Baie Park, owned by the Kuc family (headed by Anne and Peter) for over 30 years. In 2000 they established 2ha each of sauvignon blanc, pinot gris and shiraz, the first vintage following in '06. The vineyard is planted on north-facing slopes running down to the shore of Port Phillip Bay; the maritime influence is profound. Patriarch Peter Kuc is a GP, used to working long hours and with attention to detail, and he and agriculturist son Simon are responsible for the viticulture. Anne greets visitors at the waterfront estate, and Simon's wife Nadine is the marketing and sales force behind the business.

ΨΨΨΨΨ Bellarine Peninsula Shiraz 2013 Full, slightly diffuse, crimson-purple colour; the bouquet is full of black cherry fruit, cracked black pepper and spice, preordaining the pathway of the medium to full-bodied palate and its striking array of red, purple and blue berry flavours, all resting on a bed of spice and nigh-on perfect tannins and oak. Screwcap. 13% alc. **Rating** 95 **To** 2033 $30 ✪
Ania Bellarine Peninsula Sauvignon Blanc 2014 This is a Sauvignon Blanc with more attitude than you can poke a stick at. While there are floral aromas that can easily be described as tropical, the beautifully poised and focused palate has the rapier thrust of Riesling, thirst-quenching and pure – not the usual message of Sauvignon Blanc. Great value. Screwcap. 13% alc. **Rating** 94 **To** 2017 $20 ✪

ΨΨΨΨΨ Barrique Bellarine Peninsula Pinot Gris 2014 **Rating** 93 **To** 2017 $25 ✪
Bellarine Peninsula Rose 2014 **Rating** 92 **To** 2016 $20 ✪

Baileys of Glenrowan

★★★★★

779 Taminick Gap Road, Glenrowan, Vic 3675 **Region** Glenrowan
T (03) 5766 1600 **www.**baileysofglenrowan.com.au **Open** 7 days 10–5
Winemaker Paul Dahlenburg **Est.** 1870 **Dozens** 15 000 **Vyds** 143ha

Just when it seemed that Baileys would remain one of the forgotten outposts of the TWE group, the reverse has occurred. Since 1998 the utterly committed Paul Dahlenburg has been in charge of Baileys and has overseen an expansion in the vineyard and the construction of a 2000-tonne capacity winery. The cellar door has a heritage museum, winery viewing deck, contemporary art gallery and landscaped grounds, preserving much of the heritage value. Baileys has also picked up the pace with its Muscat and Tokay, reintroducing the Winemaker's Selection at the top of the tree, while continuing the larger-volume Founder series.

ΨΨΨΨΨ Winemakers Selection Rare Old Muscat NV Dark mahogany; essence of raisins and a whisper of orange blossom; it has flavour and texture intensity and complexity even beyond that of the Rare Topaque; all the spices in Arabia, Christmas pudding, and cognac-soaked plums; despite all this, has the essential freshness to cleanse the gloriously long finish and vibrating aftertaste. 375ml. Cork. 17.5% alc. **Rating** 98 **To** 2016 $75 ✪
1904 Block Shiraz 2013 Hand-picked and sorted bunches from the 110yo estate vineyard; open-fermented and basket-pressed. The dense colour is no surprise, nor is the powerfully fleshy palate; in the manner of old vines, the tannins are in fact fine, allowing the succulent plum and blackberry fruit free play. Given the screwcap, future generations might marvel at a 100yo varietal wine from vines planted 200 years ago. Screwcap. 14% alc. **Rating** 97 **To** 2058 $95 ✪
Winemaker's Selection Rare Old Topaque NV The extreme age is obvious from the colour, with its olive rim; the bouquet is voluminous and intensely complex, the palate incredibly luscious and complex, with multi-spice, mandarin zest, tea leaf and butterscotch flavours; the palate is like velvet, the rancio and spirit there but not obvious. A micro-sip avoided the obscenity of spitting it out when making this note. 375ml. Cork. 17.5% alc. **Rating** 97 **To** 2016 $75 ✪

ΨΨΨΨΨ Varley Shiraz 2013 Honours founder Varley Bailey, and packaged in a luxury screen-printed bottle. The wine came from separate blocks in the vineyard with a track record of excellence, and was matured in a single 2800l French cask. Deep, dense crimson-purple; has untold layers of black fruits, with flashes of licorice; it is full-bodied, yet has great balance, structure and texture; the length and persistence of the palate are exceptional. Screwcap. 14% alc. **Rating** 96 **To** 2053 $75 ⊙

1920s Block Shiraz 2013 Intense and deep crimson-purple; Paul Dahlenburg has a great touch in bringing out the best from the estate vineyards, especially this block; the colour signals the full-bodied wine to come, but not the harmony, supple balance and effortless length of the black fruits of the palate; you can certainly detect the French oak, but it is the perfect structure of the tannins that provides its balance. Screwcap. 14% alc. **Rating** 96 **To** 2053 $40 ⊙

Organic Shiraz 2013 This is the second vintage; a small percentage of co-fermented muscadelle and 18% whole bunches were used. The bouquet is fragrant; medium to full-bodied, with blackberry and plum fruit sitting on fine, balanced tannins; the element of spice in the wine reflects both the complex matrix of the fruit and the fresh fruit from the controlled alcohol; texture is also a feature. Screwcap. 14% alc. **Rating** 95 **To** 2038 $28 ⊙

Founder Series Classic Topaque NV Amber, with a slight grading to light olive on the rim proclaiming its age; abundant flavour, with Christmas cake, singed toffee and spice; the long finish is well balanced, although the sweetness continues to the mid-palate, until rancio helps dry the finish. Great care is taken to maintain the quality and style of this wine, and this is as great a bargain as any wine on the market today. Cork. 17% alc. **Rating** 95 **To** 2016 $30 ⊙

Classic Muscat NV The colour has developed past any hint of red (darker and deeper than the Topaque); a good example of the more elegant style that Paul Dahlenburg is seeking to make, with a perfumed rose petal and spice bouquet; the palate is positively elegant, without sacrificing fruit intensity or the lusciously sweet, raisined flavour; the spirit is part of the answer, also blending decisions. Great value. Cork. 17% alc. **Rating** 95 **To** 2016 $30 ⊙

Durif 2013 Rating 94 **To** 2043 $28 ⊙
Petite Sirah 2013 Rating 94 **To** 2038 $28 ⊙

ㅜㅜㅜㅜㅇ **Shiraz 2013 Rating** 93 **To** 2033 $28
ND Merlot Cabernet Sauvignon Mataro 2013 Rating 90 **To** 2035 $45

Baillieu Vineyard ★★★★

32 Tubbarubba Road, Merricks North, Vic 3926 **Region** Mornington Peninsula
T (03) 5989 7622 **www.**baillieuvineyard.com.au **Open** At Merricks General Wine Store
Winemaker Kathleen Quealy **Est.** 1999 **Dozens** 2500 **Vyds** 9.1ha
Charlie and Samantha Baillieu have re-established the former Foxwood Vineyard, growing chardonnay, viognier, pinot gris, pinot noir and shiraz. The north-facing vineyard is part of the 64ha Bulldog Run property owned by the Baillieus, and is immaculately maintained.

ㅜㅜㅜㅜㅇ **Mornington Peninsula Chardonnay 2013** Estate-grown vines 15yo, whole bunch-pressed and matured in French oak for 9 months. 75% mlf is used to impart a distinctive biscuity overtone to the fruit flavours, increasing complexity but diminishing varietal expression and drive. It's all a question of style, of swings and roundabouts, I suppose. Screwcap. 13.5% alc. **Rating** 91 **To** 2018 $30

Mornington Peninsula Pinot Noir 2012 Open-fermented and matured in French oak (20% new) for 18 months. A fresh, perfumed bouquet leads into a light-bodied Pinot, with flavours ranging between strawberry and red cherry. Given the weight of the wine, one has to wonder whether 10 months in oak might have served it better. Screwcap. 12.5% alc. **Rating** 90 **To** 2018 $35

Balgownie Estate ★★★★☆

Hermitage Road, Maiden Gully, Vic 3551 **Region** Bendigo
T (03) 5449 6222 **www.**balgownieestate.com.au **Open** 7 days 10–5
Winemaker Tony Winspear **Est.** 1969 **Dozens** 10 000 **Vyds** 35.28ha

Balgownie Estate is the senior citizen of Bendigo, having celebrated its 40th vintage in 2012. A $3 million winery upgrade coincided with a doubling of the size of the vineyard. Balgownie Estate also has a cellar door in the Yarra Valley (Yarra Glen). The Yarra Valley operation of Balgownie Estate neatly fits in with the Bendigo wines, each supporting the other. Balgownie has the largest vineyard-based resort in the Yarra Valley, with over 65 rooms and a limited number of spa suites. Exports to the UK, the US, Canada, Fiji, Hong Kong, Singapore, China and NZ.

🍷🍷🍷🍷🍷 **Limited Release Old Vine Bendigo Shiraz 2009** Hums with flavours, rattles with tannin, delights with perfume. Six years old and singing a melodious song. Blackberry, tar, mint and musky, floral tones sink into rich, luscious leather. An enthralling drink now, as it shall remain for many years to come. Screwcap. 14% alc. **Rating** 96 **To** 2029 $95 CM
Museum Release Bendigo Shiraz 2013 It's always interesting to see screwcap-sealed wines as they reach maturity. This presents as fresh, though the fruit flavours have developed steadily and as you might hope. Violets, mint, leather and blackberry, soft but beautifully shaped. Maintains an insistence through the finish. Excellent wine and resounding endorsement for the seal (not that one was needed). Screwcap. 14% alc. **Rating** 94 **To** 2024 $85 CM
Bendigo Shiraz 2012 Good colour, a splash of vanillan/coffeed oak and a wealth of grainy, tannin-shot fruit. This is a sure contender for the cellar. Sweet, ripe blackberry and violet with mint notes at modest levels. Not exactly bright, but fresh and lively enough. Indeed, all seems in excellent order. Screwcap. 14.5% alc. **Rating** 94 **To** 2032 $45 CM
Bendigo Cabernet Sauvignon 2012 Mid-weight wine in the classic mould. Fruit folded with oak and tannin. Succulent flavours of mint, blackberry, peppercorn and blackcurrant, with gently creamy oak adding a slippery smoothness. Dry tannin comes soaked in juicy fruit. Length of flavour is a feature. Screwcap. 14.5% alc. **Rating** 94 **To** 2030 $45 CM

🍷🍷🍷🍷🍷 **Bendigo Chardonnay 2013 Rating** 92 **To** 2019 $45 CM
Black Label Yarra Valley Chardonnay 2013 Rating 91 **To** 2018 $25 CM

Ballabourneen   ★★★★☆

2347 Broke Road, Pokolbin, NSW 2320 **Region** Hunter Valley
T (02) 4998 6505 **www.**ballabourneen.com.au **Open** 7 days 10–5
Winemaker Daniel Binet **Est.** 2008 **Dozens** 5000
In December 2008, young gun Daniel Binet, until that time winemaker at Capercaillie, formed a partnership with Alex Stuart OAM. The formerly low profile of Ballabourneen has lifted, the cellar door having been established in the former Evans Family Wines cellar door on what is known locally as 'The Golden Mile' of the Broke Road. Exports to the US and China.

🍷🍷🍷🍷🍷 **EDS Semillon 2014** Classic young Semillon, its whole life stretched out far in front of it; the bouquet is tight, as is the palate, but all the makings are there in big, bold letters, with lemon zest/lemongrass sinuously woven through the extreme length of the palate. Screwcap. 11% alc. **Rating** 95 **To** 2029 $30 ❂

🍷🍷🍷🍷🍷 **The Stuart Chardonnay 2014 Rating** 92 **To** 2020 $30
Shiraz 2012 Rating 92 **To** 2025 $35

Ballandean Estate Wines   ★★★★☆

Sundown Road, Ballandean, Qld 4382 **Region** Granite Belt
T (07) 4684 1226 **www.**ballandeanestate.com **Open** 7 days 9–5
Winemaker Dylan Rhymer, Angelo Puglisi **Est.** 1970 **Dozens** 12 000 **Vyds** 34.2ha
A rock of ages in the Granite Belt, owned by the ever-cheerful and charming Angelo Puglisi and wife Mary. Mary has introduced a gourmet food gallery at the cellar door, featuring foods produced by local food artisans as well as Greedy Me gourmet products made by Mary herself. 2012 was a stellar vintage for an energised Ballandean Estate, smart new labels on a portfolio of excellent wines. Exports to Taiwan.

🍷🍷🍷🍷🍷 **Messing About Granite Belt Saperavi 2013** An unqualified success, with an intriguing bouquet that drew me back again and again. Iodine? Polished leather? Cedar? Prune? None or all of the foregoing, and the palate is equally equivocal, even if the melange of flavours is fluid and enjoyable. ProCork. 14.6% alc. **Rating** 94 **To** 2033 $42
Late Harvest Sylvaner 2014 A wine that brought early fame for Ballandean Estate, although very much vintage dependent, thus not made very often. This is a very good example, with the significant residual sugar neatly balanced by acidity; sweet lime and orange juice flavours mesh really well. 375ml. Screwcap. 9.2% alc. **Rating** 94 **To** 2017 $25 ✪

🍷🍷🍷🍷🍷 **Messing About Granite Belt Fiano 2014** **Rating** 92 **To** 2020 $30
Granite Belt S.S.B. 2014 **Rating** 90 **To** 2016 $18 ✪
Opera Block Granite Belt Shiraz 2012 **Rating** 90 **To** 2020 $28
Messing About Granite Belt Shiraz Viognier 2013 **Rating** 90 **To** 2019 $24
Messing About Granite Belt Durif 2013 **Rating** 90 **To** 2028 $35

Ballycroft Vineyard & Cellars

1 Adelaide Road, Greenock, SA 5360 **Region** Barossa Valley
T 0488 638 488 **www.**ballycroft.com **Open** 7 days 11–5
Winemaker Joseph Evans **Est.** 2005 **Dozens** 250 **Vyds** 3.5ha
This micro-business is owned by Joe and Sue Evans. Joe's life on the land started in 1984 with a diploma of horticulture in nursery management, followed three years later by a viticulture degree from Roseworthy/Adelaide University. Between '92 and '99 he had various responsibilities at Rockford Wines, '92–'95 in the cellar door, '96 vintage cellar hand, and '97–'99 vineyard manager. Since that time he has been at Greenock Creek Wines.

🍷🍷🍷🍷🍷 **Small Berry New French Oak Langhorne Creek Cabernet Sauvignon 2010** Matured for 28 months in all-new French oak. 196 bottles produced, according to the back label (as strange as it seems). It's thick and porty, all blackberry pie and plum jam, with little definition or indeed structure but much in the way or thick, syrupy flavour. Cork. 14.5% alc. **Rating** 90 **To** 2022 $88 CM

🍷🍷🍷🍷 **Small Berry Old Oak Greenock Shiraz 2011** **Rating** 88 **To** 2021 $22 CM

Balnaves of Coonawarra ★★★★★

15517 Riddoch Highway, Coonawarra, SA 5263 **Region** Coonawarra
T (08) 8737 2946 **www.**balnaves.com.au **Open** Mon–Fri 9–5, w'ends 12–5
Winemaker Pete Bissell **Est.** 1975 **Dozens** 10 000 **Vyds** 68.73ha
Grapegrower, viticultural consultant and vigneron, Doug Balnaves has almost 70ha of high-quality estate vineyards. The wines are invariably excellent, often outstanding, notable for their supple mouthfeel, varietal integrity, balance and length; the tannins are always fine and ripe, the oak subtle and perfectly integrated. Coonawarra at its best. Exports to the UK, the US, Canada, Japan, Hong Kong and China.

🍷🍷🍷🍷🍷 **The Tally Reserve Cabernet Sauvignon 2013** Deeply coloured, it is the quintessence of Coonawarra Cabernet, with an immensely long palate, fruit, oak and tannins all contributing. Sometimes the oak on The Tally can seem too obvious in blind tastings with other top-flight Cabernets, but it's hard to see that happening here. The drink-to date has been shortened by the decision to use ProCork. 14.5% alc. **Rating** 97 **To** 2043 $105 ✪

🍷🍷🍷🍷🍷 **Cabernet Sauvignon 2013** From three vineyards, matured for 19 months in French oak from big-name coopers. A serious Cabernet showing just what Coonawarra can do in a top vintage; it is intense, complex and packed with cassis/blackcurrant fruit, savoury tannins and positive oak. Screwcap. 14.5% alc. **Rating** 96 **To** 2053 $42 ✪
Shiraz 2013 Matured for 19 months in big-name French coopered barrels (68% new). Consistently one of the more opulent Coonawarra Shirazs, due not

only to the amount of high-quality oak, but also (necessarily) to the depth of the black fruits and ripe tannins. Screwcap. 14.5% alc. **Rating** 95 **To** 2038 $32 **✪**

Chardonnay 2013 Balnaves is arguably the most consistent producer of Chardonnay in Coonawarra, and this elegant wine does nothing to confuse the picture. White peach and citrussy acidity glide across the tongue, the finish fresh, the oak controlled. Screwcap. 13% alc. **Rating** 94 **To** 2020 $32

Cabernet Merlot 2013 An 82/18% blend from three cabernet and two merlot vineyards; matured for 16 months in French oak (50% new). Excellent crimson-purple; the bouquet is aromatic and inviting, the palate with a balance of blackcurrant, mulberry, black olive and herbs, oak adding its own flavour as a bonus. Screwcap. 14.5% alc. **Rating** 94 **To** 2028 $28 **✪**

ҮҮҮҮ **The Blend 2013 Rating** 90 **To** 2020 $19 **✪**

Balthazar of the Barossa   ★★★★★

PO Box 675, Nuriootpa, SA 5355 **Region** Barossa Valley
T (08) 8562 2949 **www.**balthazarbarossa.com **Open** At the Small Winemakers Centre, Chateau Tanunda
Winemaker Anita Bowen **Est.** 1999 **Dozens** 1000 **Vyds** 24.93ha
Anita Bowen announced her occupation as 'a 40-something sex therapist with a 17-year involvement in the wine industry'. Anita undertook her first vintage at Mudgee, then McLaren Vale, and ultimately the Barossa; she worked at St Hallett while studying at Roseworthy. A versatile lady, indeed. As to her wine, she says, 'Anyway, prepare a feast, pour yourself a glass (no chalices, please) of Balthazar and share it with your concubines. Who knows? It may help to lubricate thoughts, firm up ideas and get the creative juices flowing!' A representative range of wines was not received for this edition, but the rating has been maintained. Exports to Canada, Singapore and China.

ҮҮҮҮ **Marananga Shiraz 2011** Matured for 24 months in French hogsheads. Holding hue remarkably well, and the fruit flavours are ripe – the problem is that the oak comes right over the top. Prayer might help, but I'm not religious. Screwcap. 14% alc. **Rating** 88 **To** 2020 $50

 # Bangor Estate   ★★★★★

20 Blackman Bay Road, Dunalley, Tas 7177 **Region** Southern Tasmania
T 0418 594 362 **www.**bangorshed.com.au **Open** 7 days 10–5
Winemaker Winemaking Tasmania **Est.** 2010 **Dozens** 900 **Vyds** 4ha
Bangor Estate's story starts in 1830, when John Dunbabin, convicted of horse stealing, was transported to Van Diemen's Land. Through sheer hard work, he earned his freedom and bought his own land, paving the way for five generations of farming at Bangor. Today it is a 6200ha property on the Forestier Peninsula in one of the most southerly parts of Tasmania, with 5100ha of native forest, grasslands and wetlands, and 35km of coastline. Both Matt and Vanessa Dunbabin have PhDs in plant ecology and plant nutrition, putting beyond question their ability to protect this wonderful property – until 2000ha were burnt in the 2013 bushfires that devastated their local town of Dunalley and surrounding areas. Bangor lost fences, stock, feed buildings and very nearly the vineyard. Time will heal this, but in the meantime they have decided to establish a cellar door in partnership with Tom and Alice Gray from Fulham Acquaculture, also badly affected by the fires. Hence the Bangor Farm 7 Oyster Shed was born. The vineyard is planted to 1.5h each of pinot noir and pinot gris, and 1ha of chardonnay.

ҮҮҮҮҮ **1830 Chardonnay 2013** Initially shy on both bouquet and palate; perhaps its balance is the explanation; the power creeps up on you, with grapefruit and mineral notes intertwined on a palate that goes on forever. Gold Tas Wine Show '15. Screwcap. 11.9% alc. **Rating** 95 **To** 2025 $38

Abel Tasman Pinot Noir 2013 A conventional Pinot Noir, bearing no relationship to the '14 Captain Spotswood. Bright crimson, it is elegant and lively; red cherry, plum and notes of forest floor all contribute to the finely honed complexity of the medium-bodied palate. Still taking shape, but its future is assured. Screwcap. 14% alc. **Rating** 95 **To** 2028 $42

Vintage 2010 A very well made Tasmanian traditional method blend of chardonnay and pinot noir. Still pale straw-green, with white flowers and juicy white peach fruit leavened by crisp acidity that draws the palate out to a classic, long finish. Diam. 12.8% alc. **Rating** 95 **To** 2020 $42

ŸŸŸŸŸ Captain Spotswood Pinot Noir 2014 Rating 93 To 2029 $29
Jimmy's Hill Pinot Gris 2014 Rating 92 To 2017 $29

Banks Road   ★★★★★

600 Banks Road, Marcus Hill, Vic 3222 **Region** Geelong
T (03) 5258 3777 **www.**banksroad.com.au **Open** Fri–Sun 11–5
Winemaker Peter Kimber, William Derham **Est.** 2001 **Dozens** 2000 **Vyds** 6ha
Banks Road is a small family-owned and operated winery on the Bellarine Peninsula. The estate vineyard is adopting biodynamic principles, eliminating the use of insecticides and moving to eliminate the use of all chemicals on the land. The new winery not only processes the Banks Road grapes, but also makes wine for other small producers in the area.

ŸŸŸŸŸ Soho Road Vineyard Barrel Select Chardonnay 2012 The vineyard is believed to be the oldest on the Bellarine Peninsula. Although the alcohol is at the lower end of the range, power and focus are obvious from the word go, with flavours of nectarine, melon and creamy cashew ex barrel fermentation. Makes its impact firmly but not ostentatiously. Screwcap. 12.5% alc. **Rating** 95 **To** 2023 $48

Soho Road Vineyard Barrel Select Pinot Noir 2012 Excellent scarlet-crimson colour; an interesting decision to choose this as the top '12 Pinot; it is more complex than Will's Selection, the fruit more savoury, and it does share the lingering finish and aftertaste. Screwcap. 12.5% alc. **Rating** 95 **To** 2020 $55

Growers Range Rice Vineyard Grampians Shiraz 2013 From a close-planted vineyard established 20 years ago by Gary Rice while working at Seppelt. Deep vivid purple; it has a fragrant purple and black fruit bouquet, and a beguilingly textured palate in a medium-bodied frame; the high-quality grapes have been handled with sensitivity in the winery, particularly given the yield of only 1 tonne per acre. Screwcap. 13.2% alc. **Rating** 95 **To** 2043 $30 ❂

Geelong Sauvignon Blanc 2013 An attractive Sauvignon Blanc, with a full spectrum of tropical fruits tempered by citrussy acidity; has excellent drive and length, the aftertaste fresh. Screwcap. 12.4% alc. **Rating** 94 **To** 2015 $24 ❂

Geelong Chardonnay 2012 A lively Chardonnay with barrel-ferment influences sufficient to provide complexity without obscuring the varietal fruit expression; the flavours are mid-range, with nectarine/white peach trimmed by crisp acidity. Will develop well. Screwcap. 12.7% alc. **Rating** 94 **To** 2022 $30 ❂

Geelong Pinot Gris 2013 Slightly less pink than the Grigio, with a hint of bronze; barrel-fermented in used oak, and fractionally less ripe fruit (or is it simply the barrel fermentation?) results in a radically different style, less exuberant, but with well above average line and length to its pear and green apple fruit. Screwcap. 13.4% alc. **Rating** 94 **To** 2017 $30 ❂

Geelong Pinot Grigio 2013 Pale blush-pink; has a startling depth to its array of pear, red cherry and peach fruit that in anyone else's language would be Pinot Gris – except, that is, for Banks Road. A touch of sweetness, from sugar or fruit immaterial, adds to the wine. Screwcap. 13.5% alc. **Rating** 94 **To** 2016 $24 ❂

ŸŸŸŸŸ Heathcote Sangiovese 2013 Rating 93 To 2020 $26 ❂
Will's Selection Pinot Noir 2012 Rating 92 To 2020 $45
Yarram Creek Geelong Chardonnay 2013 Rating 91 To 2018 $22 ❂
Geelong Pinot Grigio 2014 Rating 91 To 2016 $24
Yarram Creek Pinot Noir 2013 Rating 91 To 2019 $22 ❂
Soho Road Vineyard Pinot Noir 2013 Rating 90 To 2018 $36

Bannockburn Vineyards ★★★★★

Midland Highway, Bannockburn, Vic 3331 (postal) **Region** Geelong
T (03) 5281 1363 **www**.bannockburnvineyards.com **Open** By appt
Winemaker Matthew Holmes **Est.** 1974 **Dozens** 7000 **Vyds** 24ha

The late Stuart Hooper had a deep love for the wines of Burgundy, and was able to buy and drink the best. When he established Bannockburn, it was inevitable that pinot noir and chardonnay would form the major part of the plantings, with lesser amounts of riesling, sauvignon blanc, cabernet sauvignon, shiraz and merlot. Bannockburn is still owned by members of the Hooper family, who continue to respect Stuart's strong belief in making wines that genuinely reflect the flavours of the vineyard. Exports to Canada, China, Singapore and Hong Kong.

🍷🍷🍷🍷🍷 **De La Terre 2012** From the ultra close-planted pinot block of 10 000 vines per hectare on a north-facing slope; 100% whole bunches has been a huge success, likewise 12 months in one-third new French hogsheads, then a further 8 months in older barriques. This is reminiscent of the bouquet of young DRC Burgundies, and the palate does not disappoint. It has exceptional length and drive, with a lingering aftertaste. Destined for greatness. Screwcap. 13.5% alc. **Rating** 98 To 2037 $70 ✪

Stuart Geelong Pinot 2012 From the Olive Tree Hill Block planted in '76; 100% whole berries; 12 months in one-third new barriques, 16 months in 4yo barriques. Some forest aromas; supple, rich and round, with a spread of plum and dark cherry fruits on the long, perfectly shaped and balanced palate. The texture is silky, caressing the mouth. Will likely be drunk before the standard wine, perhaps, but not for want of quality. Screwcap. 13.5% alc. **Rating** 97 To 2032 $70 ✪

Serre 2012 Whole bunch-fermented Pinot, with 20 months in French oak (mainly used). Vivid, deep crimson; the whole-bunch fermentation (and the close planting) indelibly stamp their mark, but despite the ultra-complex nature of the wine, there is harmony wherever you look, from the bouquet through to the mid-palate, finish and aftertaste. All class. Screwcap. 12.5% alc. **Rating** 97 To 2027 $95 ✪

Geelong Shiraz 2010 100% whole-bunch fermented, matured for 2 years in used French puncheons. Has retained good colour; the freshness of the wine is a delight, as is its silky texture and – needless to say – the complexity of its smorgasbord of warmly spiced red and black fruits, oak and tannins sewn into the lining of the fruit. The cork is high-quality. 1000 dozen made. 12.5% alc. **Rating** 97 To 2035 $42 ✪

🍷🍷🍷🍷🍷 **Geelong Chardonnay 2012** Whole bunch-pressed, transferred without settling to barriques, puncheons and tank for wild yeast fermentation and 2 years' maturation on lees. Deep, but bright, yellow; a very complex wine that coasted through its long time in barrel; white peach, fig and pink grapefruit do the talking, not the oak, as one might expect; despite its complexity, has an exciting fresh finish. 1000 dozen made. Screwcap. 12.5% alc. **Rating** 96 To 2025 $57 ✪

S.R.H. 2011 From 12 rows of chardonnay planted in '76; matured for 3 years on lees in a single oak cask. Still bright straw-green, its intensity making you rear back and regroup for a second taste, the only question whether it is ripe enough, and the answer yes it is; but it's all about grapefruit and minerals on the ultra-long palate, finish and aftertaste. Screwcap. 12% alc. **Rating** 96 To 2026 $75 ✪

Geelong Pinot Noir 2013 60% Olive Tree Vineyard, 40% close-planted; 100% whole-bunch fermented, 20 months' barrel maturation (mainly used). Deeply coloured, but not star-bright; an ultra-complex and power-packed Pinot, multi-plum flavours surrounded by a palisade of whole-bunch stemmy notes. Cries out for time in bottle. Screwcap. 13% alc. **Rating** 96 To 2025 $57 ✪

Geelong Pinot Noir 2012 From 4 parcels of estate grapes, wild yeast, open-fermented. Excellent colour; skilled winemaking of high-quality fruit from a top vintage was preordained to produce a wine of exemplary quality; plummy fruit aromas and flavours are spun together on the supple and long palate. Easy to drink,

but it would be a crime to drink more than a bottle now – save as many as possible for a minimum of 5 years. Screwcap. 13.5% alc. **Rating** 96 **To** 2027 $57 ✪
De La Roche 2012 Second release ex new close-planted shiraz vineyard (10 000 vines per hectare), yielding 500 grams per vine. A super-elegant, highly fragrant spice, pepper, black cherry and blackberry compote that is deceptively light on its feet; fine, but distinctly savoury, tannins provide complexity and structure. Screwcap. 13.5% alc. **Rating** 96 **To** 2037 $65 ✪
Range 2006 The fifth release since '05. Made from the original shiraz planting of 1.66ha in '74. The sheer intensity of fruit at 9yo is as remarkable as the colour; there is an edge to the flavours that may displease some, but appeal to the majority. Cork. 14.5% alc. **Rating** 96 **To** 2026 $55 ✪
1314 a.d. Pinot Noir 2013 Rating 94 **To** 2023 $30 CM ✪
Douglas 2012 Rating 94 **To** 2030 $30 ✪

♟♟♟♟♟ **Serre 2011 Rating** 93 **To** 2020 $95
Geelong Sauvignon Blanc 2014 Rating 90 **To** 2018 $32

Bantry Grove ★★★★

25 Victoria Street, Millthorpe, NSW 2798 **Region** Orange
T (02) 6368 1036 **www.**bantrygrove.com.au **Open** Fri–Sun & Mon public hols 10–5
Winemaker Will Rikard-Bell **Est.** 1990 **Dozens** 1625 **Vyds** 12.3ha
Terrey and Barbie Johnson (and family) raise beef cattle on a property at the southern end of Orange. Seeking to diversify, the Johnsons have planted a vineyard at an elevation of 960m, making it one of the coolest in the region. The plantings began in 1990 with chardonnay and cabernet sauvignon, the latter now grafted or removed because the climate is simply too cool. Most of the 80–85-tonne production (chardonnay, merlot, sauvignon blanc, pinot noir and pinot gris) is sold to various producers making Orange-designated wines. A steadily increasing portion of the grapes is retained for the Bantry Grove label. The wines are sold through membership of Bantry Grove's Inner Circle Wine Club and local outlets.

♟♟♟♟♟ **Orange Rose 2013** Full-on salmon colour, with barely any pink on show; this and the funky bouquet strongly suggest some barrel fermentation as well as lees complexity, although no oak is mentioned on the wordy back label. Not your average style. Screwcap. 14.2% alc. **Rating** 92 **To** 2016 $22 ✪

🍇 Banyandah Estate ★★★★

PO Box 138, Trentham, Vic 3458 **Region** Macedon Ranges
T 0404 800 950 **Open** Not
Winemaker Llew Knight **Est.** 2002 **Dozens** 450 **Vyds** 2ha
Terry South is a retired solicitor with an associate degree in wine growing from CSU, and he and wife Vicki Adamson purchased Banyandah in 2001. They hired the late Bill Christophersen (who was my vineyard manager in the early days of Coldstream Hills) as a consultant for soil analysis, vineyard site, varieties, etc. They planted the vineyard with a 2.5 × 0.75m spacing and a vine density of approximately 6000 vines per ha. The vineyard is at 700m, and particularly cool, the soil deep red volcanic clay/loam. The vines have very vigorous growth, but the site does not ripen the crop until late April (mid-April in the hottest, driest years). This has meant shoot and bunch thinning to restrict the yield to 3 tonnes per ha. Prior to the 2013 vintage they sold the grapes, but in that year decided to retain the crop and secure the services of Llew Knight as contact winemaker.

♟♟♟♟♟ **Macedon Ranges Pinot Gris 2013** Skin contact has resulted in a distinctly pink hue; cold fermentation in stainless steel was followed by 5 months on lees, but no oak. Has abundant pear and stone fruit flavours, and has been well made, even if the price is ambitious. Screwcap. 13.6% alc. **Rating** 92 **To** 2015 $32

Barokes Wines

66 Lillee Crescent, Tullamarine, Vic 3043 **Region** Various
T (03) 8318 4800 **www**.wineinacan.com **Open** Not
Winemaker Steve Barics **Est.** 2003 **Dozens** 900 000
Barokes packages its wines in aluminium cans, the filling process patented. The wines show normal maturation and none of the cans used since start-up shows signs of corrosion. Wines are supplied in bulk by large wineries in South Eastern Australia, with Peter Scudamore-Smith acting as blending consultant. Year after year, my tastings give rise to tasting notes with no mention of reduction or any other fault. Exports to all major markets, success building on success, production leaping from 350 000 cases (24 cans per case) to 900 000. A significant part of this increase comes from Barokes partnership with COFO, a large Chinese state-owned entity, with many food and beverage interests and national distribution capabilities. The awards the wines win in overseas competitions can cause eyebrows to rise, but – at the very least – they confirm the quality of the wines. The most recent development, along with changes in packaging, has been the introduction of low-alcohol wines ranging between 6% and 11.5%.

Barratt

Uley Vineyard, Cornish Road, Summertown, SA 5141 **Region** Adelaide Hills
T (08) 8390 1788 **www**.barrattwines.com.au **Open** W'ends & most public hols 11.30–5
Winemaker Lindsay Barratt **Est.** 1993 **Dozens** 2000 **Vyds** 8.7ha
This is the venture of former physician Lindsay Barratt. Lindsay has always been responsible for viticulture and, following his retirement in 2001, has taken full, hands-on responsibility for winemaking (receiving a graduate diploma in oenology from the University of Adelaide in '02). The quality of the wines is excellent. Limited quantities are exported to the UK, Malaysia and Singapore.

Uley Vineyard Adelaide Hills Pinot Noir 2012 Always there, or thereabouts, and got it right in the cross-hairs in '12. The colour is good, the bouquet perfumed and spicy, the cherry fruit on the silky palate singing through to the fine tannins on the finish. Screwcap. 14% alc. **Rating** 95 **To** 2022 $41

Uley Vineyard Piccadilly Valley Chardonnay 2013 Rating 93 **To** 2022 $32

Barrgowan Vineyard

30 Pax Parade, Curlewis, Vic 3222 **Region** Geelong
T (03) 5250 3861 **www**.barrgowanvineyard.com.au **Open** By appt
Winemaker Dick Simonsen **Est.** 1998 **Dozens** 150 **Vyds** 0.5ha
Dick and Dib (Elizabeth) Simonsen began planting their shiraz (with five clones) in 1994, intending to make wine for their own consumption. With all five clones in full production, the Simonsens have a maximum production of 200 dozen, and accordingly release small quantities of Shiraz, which sell out quickly. The vines are hand-pruned, the grapes hand-picked, the must basket-pressed, and all wine movements are by gravity. The quality is exemplary.

Simonsens Bellarine Peninsula Shiraz 2013 Five estate-grown shiraz clones, the wine matured in French oak. Vivid, deep crimson-purple; a very classy cool-climate Shiraz, with a Joseph's coat array of flavours, but none going over the top; the utterly perfect bouquet leads into an intense palate with black fruits, spice, pepper, licorice and cedary oak all contributing. Has immaculate balance and length. Outstanding bargain. Diam. 13.4% alc. **Rating** 97 **To** 2043 $25 ○

Barringwood

60 Gillams Road, Lower Barrington, Tas 7306 **Region** Northern Tasmania
T (03) 6492 3140 **www**.barringwood.com.au **Open** Wed–Sun & public hols 10–5
Winemaker Josef Chromy Wines (Jeremy Dineen) **Est.** 1993 **Dozens** 1700 **Vyds** 5ha

Judy and Ian Robinson operated a sawmill at Lower Barrington, 15 minutes south of Devonport on the main tourist trail to Cradle Mountain, and when they planted 500 vines in 1993 the aim was to do a bit of home winemaking. In a thoroughly familiar story, the urge to expand the vineyard and make wine on a commercial scale soon occurred, and they embarked on a six-year plan, planting 1ha per year in the first four years and building the cellar and tasting rooms during the following two years. The recent sale of Barringwood to Neville and Vanessa Bagot should not cause any significant changes to the business.

♀♀♀♀♀ Mill Block Chardonnay 2013 Free-run juice only, fermented wild. It's a wine of excellent texture, flavour and length. Dry pears, tinned pineapple, sweet milk, peach and fruit toast. Elegant, but it makes an impression. It should develop and drink beautifully over the next handful of years. Screwcap. 12.7% alc. **Rating** 95 To 2022 $45 CM
Mill Block Pinot Noir 2013 Grown on the estate's oldest vines, the estate itself having been founded in 1998. Complexity is the name of the game here. It's all undergrowth and macerated cherry, spice and forest floor. It strikes upfront then pulls you swiftly through to a second burst of flavour on the finish. Positively impressive. Screwcap. 13.2% alc. **Rating** 95 To 2025 $45 CM

♀♀♀♀♀ Pinot Gris 2014 Rating 93 To 2015 $32 CM
Pinot Noir 2013 Rating 91 To 2023 $35 CM
Schonburger 2014 Rating 90 To 2016 $26 CM

Barton Estate ★★★☆

2307 Barton Highway, Murrumbateman, NSW 2582 **Region** Canberra District
T (02) 6230 9553 www.bartonestate.com.au **Open** W'ends & public hols 10–5
Winemaker Capital Wines, Gallagher Wines **Est.** 1997 **Dozens** 500 **Vyds** 7.7ha
Bob Furbank and wife Julie Chitty are both CSIRO plant biologists: he is a biochemist (physiologist) and she is a specialist in plant tissue culture. In 1997 they acquired the 120ha property forming part of historic Jeir Station, and have since planted 15 grape varieties. The most significant plantings are to cabernet sauvignon, shiraz, merlot, riesling and chardonnay, the Joseph's coat completed with micro quantities of other varieties.

Barton Jones Wines ★★★★

39 Upper Capel Road, Donnybrook, WA 6239 **Region** Geographe
T (08) 9731 2233 www.bartonjoneswines.com.au **Open** Fri–Mon 10.30–4.30
Winemaker Contract **Est.** 1978 **Dozens** 2000 **Vyds** 3ha
The 22ha property on which Blackboy Ridge Estate is established was partly cleared and planted to 2.5ha of semillon, chenin blanc, shiraz and cabernet sauvignon in 1978. When current owners Adrian Jones and Jackie Barton purchased the property in 2000 the vines were already some of the oldest in the region. The vineyard and cellar door are on gentle north-facing slopes, with extensive views over the Donnybrook area.

♀♀♀♀♀ The Box Seat Semillon 2013 Hand-picked from the highest part of the home vineyard; part spent 8 months in new French oak. The components have come together well, investing the wine with complexity, but not at the expense of diminishing varietal expression, and in particular the finish and aftertaste. Screwcap. 12% alc. **Rating** 94 To 2023 $23 ●

♀♀♀♀♀ The Brilliant Cut Semillon Sauvignon 2013 Rating 93 To 2016 $23 ●

Barwang ★★★★★

Barwang Road, Young, NSW 2594 (postal) **Region** Hilltops
T (02) 9722 1200 www.mcwilliamswinesgroup.com **Open** Not
Winemaker Andrew Higgins **Est.** 1969 **Dozens** NFP **Vyds** 100ha
Peter Robertson pioneered viticulture in the Young area when he planted his first vines in 1969 as part of a diversification program for his 400ha grazing property. When McWilliam's

acquired Barwang in 1989, the vineyard amounted to 13ha; today the plantings are 100ha. Wine quality has been exemplary from the word go, value for money no less so. The Barwang label also takes in 100% Tumbarumba wines, as well as Hilltops/Tumbarumba blends. Exports to Asia.

𝅘𝅥𝅘𝅥𝅘𝅥𝅘𝅥𝅘𝅥 **842 Tumbarumba Chardonnay 2013** At one with itself. Seamless. It tastes of oatmeal, citrus, white peach and river stones, a veneer of creamy/spicy/milky oak sinking speedily into the fruit as it breathes. The finish is long and assured. Irresistible drinking. Screwcap. 13% alc. **Rating** 95 **To** 2021 $65 CM

Hilltops Shiraz 2013 Looks, smells and tastes the goods. You don't expect to see such a complete cool-climate package at this price level. Dark-coloured with a purple rim; flush with black pepper, dark cherry and roasted nut overlays; herbal and complex through the finish but always within a ripe, fruit-filled context. It continues the excellent form of the 2012, and arguably betters it. Screwcap. 14% alc. **Rating** 95 **To** 2022 $23 CM **◎**

𝅘𝅥𝅘𝅥𝅘𝅥𝅘𝅥𝅘𝅥 **Tumbarumba Chardonnay 2013 Rating** 92 **To** 2019 $22 CM **◎**
Granite Track Tumbarumba Riesling 2013 Rating 91 **To** 2019 $27 CM

Barwick Estates   ★★★★☆

283 Yelverton North Road, Yelverton, WA 6281 **Region** Margaret River
T (08) 9417 5633 **www**.barwickwines.com **Open** W'ends and public hols
Winemaker Mark Thompson **Est.** 1997 **Dozens** 100000 **Vyds** 188ha
The production gives some guide to the size of the three estate vineyards. The first is the Dwalganup Vineyard in the Blackwood Valley region; the second is St John's Brook Vineyard in Margaret River; and the third is the Treenbrook Vineyard in Pemberton. Taken together, the three holdings place Barwick in the top 10 wine producers in WA. Wines are released under several labels, headed by Optimus and The Collectables. Exports to the UK, the US and other major markets.

𝅘𝅥𝅘𝅥𝅘𝅥𝅘𝅥𝅘𝅥 **White Label Margaret River Sauvignon Blanc Semillon 2014** Co-fermented with wild and cultured yeast – by definition you have no idea which prevailed; 15% barrel fermentation has added a dimension to the structure, and the flavours are a neat combination of citrus/green pea on the one hand, and tropical on the other. Screwcap. 12.5% alc. **Rating** 92 **To** 2017 $18 **◎**

Margaret River Cabernet Merlot 2012 A very firm, medium to full-bodied wine, with tannins needing to settle down, which they will do in a couple of years (Dionysus willing). Screwcap. 14.5% alc. **Rating** 92 **To** 2030 $32

White Label Cabernet Sauvignon 2013 Matured for 12 months in used French oak. Bright colour, with a fruit-filled bouquet and a fresh, well-balanced medium-bodied palate; notes of cassis are neatly couched with a hint of bay leaf and easygoing tannins. Screwcap. 14% alc. **Rating** 90 **To** 2020 $18 **◎**

𝅘𝅥𝅘𝅥𝅘𝅥𝅘𝅥 **White Label Margaret River Shiraz 2013 Rating** 89 **To** 2023 $18 **◎**

Bass Phillip   ★★★★★

Tosch's Road, Leongatha South, Vic 3953 **Region** Gippsland
T (03) 5664 3341 **www**.bassphillip.com **Open** By appt
Winemaker Phillip Jones **Est.** 1979 **Dozens** 1500
Phillip Jones handcrafts tiny quantities of superlative Pinot Noir which, at its best, has no equal in Australia. Painstaking site selection, ultra-close vine spacing and the very, very cool climate of South Gippsland are the keys to the magic of Bass Phillip and its eerily Burgundian Pinots. One of Australia's greatest small producers.

Bass River Winery   ★★★★☆

1835 Dalyston–Glen Forbes Road, Glen Forbes, Vic 3990 **Region** Gippsland
T (03) 5678 8252 **www**.bassriverwinery.com **Open** Thurs–Tues 9–5
Winemaker Pasquale and Frank Butera **Est.** 1999 **Dozens** 1500 **Vyds** 4ha

The Butera family has established 1ha each of pinot noir and chardonnay and 2ha split equally between riesling, sauvignon blanc, pinot gris and merlot, with both the winemaking and viticulture handled by the father and son team of Pasquale and Frank. The small production is principally sold through the cellar door plus to some retailers and restaurants in the South Gippsland area. Exports to Singapore.

🍷🍷🍷🍷🍷 **1835 Gippsland Chardonnay 2014** Plenty of vim and vigour. Oak and fruit are still coming together but there are good signs aplenty here. Flavours of cream, peppermint, lemon and barley meet pure, sweet white peach. Finishes lengthily. Screwcap. 13% alc. **Rating** 94 **To** 2021 $35 CM

🍷🍷🍷🍷🍷 **Gippsland Pinot Gris 2014 Rating** 93 **To** 2016 $25 CM ❂
1835 Iced Riesling 2014 Rating 90 **To** 2017 $30 CM

Battle of Bosworth

92 Gaffney Road, Willunga, SA 5172 **Region** McLaren Vale
T (08) 8556 2441 **www.**battleofbosworth.com.au **Open** 7 days 11–5
Winemaker Joch Bosworth **Est.** 1996 **Dozens** 15 000 **Vyds** 80ha
Battle of Bosworth is owned and run by Joch Bosworth (viticulture and winemaking) and partner Louise Hemsley-Smith (sales and marketing). The winery takes its name from the battle which ended the War of the Roses, fought on Bosworth Field in 1485. The vineyards were established in the early 1970s in the foothills of the Mt Lofty Ranges. The vines are fully certified A-grade organic by ACO. The label depicts the yellow soursob (*Oxalis pes-caprae*), whose growth habits make it an ideal weapon for battling weeds in organic viticulture. Shiraz, cabernet sauvignon and chardonnay account for 75% of the plantings. The Spring Seeds wines are made from estate vineyards. Exports to the UK, the US, Canada, Sweden, Norway, Belgium, Hong Kong and Japan.

🍷🍷🍷🍷🍷 **Best of Vintage NV** A certified organic 69/25/6% blend of shiraz, cabernet and petit verdot. Despite its complexity of flavour, texture and structure, it has a calm and unhurried nature, content to let it catch you before you know it, but then not relaxing its hold on you. Screwcap. 14.5% alc. **Rating** 95 **To** 2032 $50
Scarce Earth Braden's McLaren Vale Shiraz 2012 Such clever winemaking: made without any oak contact, yet complete and satisfying – and throwing all the emphasis on terroir with its pure damson plum, blackberry and dark chocolate amalgam; ripe tannins provide a softly, softly finish. Screwcap. 14.5% alc. **Rating** 94 **To** 2022 $45

🍷🍷🍷🍷🍷 **Spring Seed Morning Bride Rose 2014 Rating** 93 **To** 2016 $18 ❂
Chanticleer McLaren Vale Shiraz 2012 Rating 93 **To** 2030 $45
McLaren Vale Cabernet Sauvignon 2013 Rating 93 **To** 2028 $25 ❂
White Boar 2012 Rating 92 **To** 2027 $45
Puritan McLaren Vale Shiraz 2014 Rating 91 **To** 2016 $20 ❂

Bay of Fires

40 Baxters Road, Pipers River, Tas 7252 **Region** Northern Tasmania
T (03) 6382 7622 **www.**bayoffireswines.com.au **Open** 7 days 10–5
Winemaker Penny Jones, Richard Evans **Est.** 2001 **Dozens** NFP
Hardys purchased its first grapes from Tasmania in 1994, with the aim of further developing and refining its sparkling wines, a process that quickly gave birth to House of Arras (see separate entry). The next stage was the inclusion of various parcels of chardonnay from Tasmania in the 1998 Eileen Hardy, then the development in 2001 of the Bay of Fires brand. Bay of Fires has had outstanding success with its table wines, Pinot Noir was obvious, the other wines typically of gold medal standard. Exports to the US, Asia and NZ.

🍷🍷🍷🍷🍷 **Riesling 2014** The wine is absolutely the product of its environment, the role of the winemaker purely a QC custodian with the job of protecting the purity of the lime and apple fruit; the acidity is perfectly pitched, drawing out the palate to its exceptional length and finish. A great future lies ahead. Screwcap. 12.5% alc. Rating 96 To 2034 $35 ✪

Eddystone Point Riesling 2013 The bouquet starts quietly, with blossom and talc, and the almost succulent, lime-juicy palate builds progressively through to the finish. Gold Tas Wine Shows '14 and '15. Screwcap. **Rating** 96 **To** 2023 $26 ✪

Chardonnay 2013 Bright, gleaming straw-green; dazzlingly fresh and vibrant, but adroitly avoids the confronting acidity that can unbalance otherwise exemplary Tasmanian white wines; peach and grapefruit are balanced by subtle creamy cashew nuances ex barrel fermentation of cloudy juice; overall, an exercise in elegance. Screwcap. 13% alc. **Rating** 96 **To** 2025 $42 ✪

Pinot Noir 2013 Continues a long and distinguished line of Bay of Fires Pinots. From the Derwent Valley, Coal River and East Coast; multiple fermentation approaches and maturation in carefully controlled French oak. Red and black cherry, spice and forest floor aromas and flavours won the trophy for Best Pinot Noir at the Adelaide Wine Show '14. Screwcap. 13.5% alc. **Rating** 96 **To** 2023 $50 ✪

Bay of Fires Tasmanian Cuvee Pinot Noir Chardonnay Brut NV The wine spends 3 years on yeast lees, giving creamy brioche nuances to its bright and lively fruits, grapefruit zest and crunchy acidity adding to the complexity and length of the wine. Cork. 12.5% alc. **Rating** 95 **To** 2017 $30 ✪

Bay of Fires Tasmanian Cuvee Pinot Noir Chardonnay Rose NV A pinot noir-dominant blend that spends an average of 4 years on yeast lees. Pale, bright pink, the bouquet is charged with strawberry fruit, the palate with a distinctly savoury play on the strawberry flavours; Tasmanian acidity bounces off the brioche/almond notes engendered by the lengthy time on lees. Cork. 12.5% alc. Rating 95 To 2017 $30 ✪

Tasmanian Cuvee Rose NV Rating 94 To 2016 $30 TS ✪
Eddystone Point Pinot Noir 2013 Rating 94 To 2023 $30 ✪

ㅜㅜㅜㅜㅜ **Pinot Gris 2014** Rating 92 To 2016 $35

Bay of Shoals   ★★★☆

Cordes Road, Kingscote, Kangaroo Island, SA 5223 **Region** Kangaroo Island
T (08) 8553 0289 www.bayofshoalswines.com.au **Open** 7 days 11–5
Winemaker Jonothan Ketley **Est.** 1994 **Dozens** 1400 **Vyds** 10ha
John Willoughby's vineyard overlooks the Bay of Shoals, which is the northern boundary of Kingscote, Kangaroo Island's main town. Planting of the vineyard began in 1994 and it now comprises riesling, sauvignon blanc, savagnin, pinot gris, pinot noir, cabernet sauvignon and shiraz. In addition, 460 olive trees have been planted to produce table olives.

ㅜㅜㅜㅜㅜ **Kangaroo Island Savagnin 2014** Ribald perfume and flavour. Enters the room and lets everyone know it's there. Musk, chalk, lime/lemon, nashi pear and lactose. Interest abounds. Screwcap. 12.7% alc. **Rating** 91 **To** 2015 $20 CM ✪

ㅜㅜㅜㅜ **Kangaroo Island Riesling 2014** Rating 89 To 2019 $20 CM
Kangaroo Island Pinot Gris 2014 Rating 89 To 2015 $20 CM
Kangaroo Island Sauvignon Blanc 2014 Rating 88 To 2015 $20 CM

Beach Road   ★★★★

309 Seaview Road, McLaren Vale, SA 5171 **Region** Langhorne Creek/McLaren Vale
T (08) 8327 4547 www.beachroadwines.com.au **Open** Thurs–Mon 11–4
Winemaker Briony Hoare **Est.** 2007 **Dozens** 1500
This is the impressive venture of winemaker Briony Hoare and viticulturist Tony Hoare, who began their life partnership after meeting while studying wine science at the Roseworthy campus of Adelaide University. Their involvement in the industry dates back to the early 1990s, Briony working around Australia with many of the flagship wines of (then) Southcorp, Tony gaining extensive experience in Mildura, the Hunter Valley and McLaren Vale (where he spent five years as viticulturist for Wirra Wirra). In 2005 the pair decided to go it alone,

setting up a wine consultancy, and in '07 launching Beach Road. The focus on Italian varieties stems from Briony's vintage in Piedmont, where she worked with barbera, nebbiolo, cortese and moscato. Along the way, however, they both had a lot of exposure to grenache, shiraz and mourvedre. In 2014 Beach Road moved into its own cellar door and restaurant.

🍷🍷🍷🍷🍷 **Nero d'Avola 2013** Crushed, destemmed and open-fermented, with post-fermentation maceration; said to have spent 2 years in hogsheads (an obvious error). Good colour; rich and mouth-filling black cherry fruit, the tannins fine and supple, the finish fresh. Screwcap. 13.5% alc. **Rating** 93 **To** 2020 $45

Aglianico 2012 From the estate vineyard in Langhorne Creek; picked one month later than the last cabernet in the region. Spicy/mocha/coffee/fruitcake flavours are from the grapes, not the used French puncheons in which it spent 2 years; savoury tannins provide balance. Attractive food style. Screwcap. 13.5% alc. **Rating** 91 **To** 2016 $35

Primitivo 2012 Matured in used French hogsheads for 2 years. Distinctly savoury, with some black olive nuances; medium-bodied, with fine tannins and good length; may have lost some fruit definition in its prolonged barrel maturation. 335 dozen made. Screwcap. 14.5% alc. **Rating** 90 **To** 2016 $35

🍷🍷🍷🍷 **Greco 2013 Rating** 89 **To** 2016 $25
Fiano 2013 Rating 88 **To** 2015 $25

Beechworth Wine Estates   ★★★★

PO Box 514, Beechworth, Vic 3477 **Region** Beechworth
T (03) 5728 3340 **www**.beechworthwe.com.au **Open** Not
Winemaker Jo Marsh **Est.** 2003 **Dozens** 1260 **Vyds** 8ha
John and Joanne Iwanuch and John Allen (Joanne's brother) began the planting of the vineyard in 2003. They say Beechworth Wine Estates is a family-run and owned business, with Jo and John's four children participating in all aspects of vineyard life. Situated on the Rail Trail, 4km from Beechworth, they have planted sauvignon blanc, pinot gris, chardonnay, shiraz, cabernet sauvignon, merlot, tempranillo and sangiovese. Exports to Germany.

🍷🍷🍷🍷🍷 **Chardonnay 2012** A powerful and complex Chardonnay with nuances of White Burgundy in the way its fruit flavours are seamlessly welded into a single expression of place. Those flavours are grapefruit pith and zest, white peach and apple, which in turn are blended with oak and acidity. A snip at the price. Screwcap. 13.2% alc. **Rating** 94 **To** 2022 $25 ✪

Tempranillo 2014 A most attractive Tempranillo, especially when tasted after Nebbiolo; the colour is good, the mouthfeel very good, varietal character even better. It's as good as it ever will be right now, but won't fall over. Screwcap. 13.5% alc. **Rating** 94 **To** 2018 $28 ✪

🍷🍷🍷🍷 **Chardonnay 2014 Rating** 92 **To** 2021 $26
Reserve Merlot 2014 Rating 92 **To** 2029 $30
Shiraz 2012 Rating 90 **To** 2022 $25

Beelgara   ★★★★

Farm 576 Rossetto Road, Beelbangera, NSW 2680 **Region** Riverina
T (02) 6966 0200 **www**.beelgara.com.au **Open** Mon–Fri 10–3
Winemaker Rod Hooper, Danny Toaldo **Est.** 1930 **Dozens** 600 000
Beelgara Estate was formed in 2001 after the purchase of the 60-year-old Rossetto family winery by a group of shareholders, mostly the Toohey family. The emphasis has changed significantly, with a concerted effort to go to the right region for each variety, while still maintaining very good value for money. Exports to most major markets.

🍷🍷🍷🍷 **Black Label Clare Valley Grenache Rose 2014** One could be very unkind and say this is a good use for Clare Valley grenache. Salmon-tinged, it has a very warm-spiced bouquet, the palate fresh and full of red fruits, finishing clean, fruity and dry. Quality rose. Screwcap. 13.5% alc. **Rating** 93 **To** 2016 $18 ✪

Springview Adelaide Hills Chardonnay 2014 A well-knit Chardonnay with lashings of peachy fruit (white and yellow), toasty oak, and subliminal sweetness that it might have been better without. Best enjoyed sooner rather than later. Screwcap. 13% alc. **Rating** 90 **To** 2018 $35

ŢŢŢŢ **Black Label Adelaide Hills Sauvignon Blanc 2014** Rating 88 To 2016 $18
Springview Cabernet Sauvignon 2013 Rating 88 To 2023 $35

Bekkers ★★★★★

212 Seaview Road, McLaren Vale, SA 5171 **Region** McLaren Vale
T 0408 807 568 **www**.bekkerswine.com **Open** By appt
Winemaker Emmanuelle and Toby Bekkers **Est.** 2010 **Dozens** 400 **Vyds** 5.5ha
This brings together two high-performance, highly experienced and highly credentialled business and life partners. Husband Toby Bekkers graduated with an honours degree in applied science in agriculture from the University of Adelaide, and over the ensuing 15 years has had broad-ranging responsibilities as general manager of Paxton Wines in McLaren Vale, and as a leading exponent of organic and biodynamic viticulture. Wife Emmanuelle was born in Bandol in the south of France, and gained two university degrees, in biochemistry and oenology, before working for the Hardys in the south of France, which led her to Australia and a wide-ranging career, including Chalk Hill. Exports to the UK.

ŢŢŢŢŢ **McLaren Vale Syrah 2013** From the Hickinbotham and Gateway Vineyards; 85% destemmed, 15% whole bunches; 5-day cold soak; wild ferment; basket-pressed to French puncheons (40% new). A first-class example of McLaren Vale Shiraz, with remarkable articulation of black fruits, licorice and bitter chocolate supported and lengthened by positive fine-grained fruit and oak tannins. Screwcap. 14.5% alc. **Rating** 97 **To** 2050 $110 ◐

ŢŢŢŢŢ **McLaren Vale Syrah Grenache 2013** A 70/30% blend, the grapes from three vineyards; 20% whole bunches, the remainder destemmed and machine-sorted to remove shrivelled berries; cold soak 5 days, wild-fermented, matured in used French oak. Brightly coloured, it has strikingly savoury complexity, with red and black fruits. 97 dozen made. Screwcap. 14.5% alc. **Rating** 95 **To** 2033 $80
Grenache 2013 Hand-picked, 20% whole bunches, the remainder machine-sorted to remove shrivelled berries; matured in two used French hogsheads. No issue with the alcohol; the bouquet and palate have spicy confit red fruits ranging from strawberry to raspberry, given flavour balance by earthy/savoury tannins. 71 dozen made. Screwcap. 15% alc. **Rating** 95 **To** 2028 $80

🍂 Belford Block Eight ★★★★☆

65 Squire Close, Belford, NSW 2335 **Region** Hunter Valley
T 0410 346 300 **www**.blockeight.com.au **Open** Not
Winemaker Daniel Binet **Est.** 2012 **Dozens** 1000 **Vyds** 6ha
The existing 2ha each of semillon, shiraz and chardonnay were planted in 2000. Despite the fact that Block Eight semillon has been purchased by Brokenwood in the past, and was the single vineyard source for the 2006 Brokenwood Belford Semillon, the vineyard had been left to its own devices for two years before Jeff Ross and Todd Alexander purchased it in 2012. With the help of local consultant Jenny Bright, the vineyard was nursed back to health just in time for the celebrated 2014 vintage. With a bit more TLC, and Daniel Binet continuing to make the wines, the future should be bright.

ŢŢŢŢŢ **Reserve Hunter Valley Semillon 2014** A wine that instantaneously imposes its will on the palate, electric acidity sending a lightning fork from start to finish, with grassy nuances to the lemon zest flavours. The message is of a wine that will outlive many who cellar it. Screwcap. 11% alc. **Rating** 96 **To** 2044 $35 ◐
Estate Hunter Valley Semillon 2014 The modern expression of semillon has the best of both worlds, with far more fruit driving the bouquet and palate than the wines of (say) 30 years ago, yet not sacrificing longevity. There is an abundance

of lemon/lemongrass fruit linked to the texture and structure of crunchy, citrussy acidity. Screwcap. 11% alc. **Rating** 94 **To** 2029 $20 ○

Bellarine Estate ★★★★☆

2270 Portarlington Road, Bellarine, Vic 3222 **Region** Geelong
T (03) 5259 3310 **www.**bellarineestate.com.au **Open** 7 days 11–4
Winemaker Robin Brockett **Est.** 1995 **Dozens** 4500 **Vyds** 12ha
This business runs parallel with the Bellarine Brewing Company (which makes the only micro-brewed beer on the Bellarine Peninsula) also situated in the winery, and the extended operating hours of Julian's Restaurant, it is a popular meeting place. The vineyard is planted to chardonnay, pinot noir, shiraz, merlot, viognier and sauvignon blanc. Exports to the US.

Phil's Fetish Geelong Pinot Noir 2013 Matured for 12 months in French oak. Good hue and clarity, the highly fragrant bouquet signals the lively, fresh red, black and sour cherry fruits, plus a suggestion of plum, on the palate; a silken thread of oak and fine tannins provides complexity and structure. Screwcap. 13.6% alc. **Rating** 94 **To** 2024 $32
Two Wives Geelong Shiraz 2013 Deep purple-crimson; 'drink now or before the seven-year itch' suggests the back label, not a bad call. It is a succulent and supple wine, towards the upper end of medium-bodied, with a velvety array of blood plum/black cherry fruit, the tannins soft, the oak good. Screwcap. 13.9% alc. **Rating** 94 **To** 2033 $32

Bellarmine Wines ★★★★★

1 Balyan Retreat, Pemberton, WA 6260 **Region** Pemberton
T (08) 9842 8413 **www.**bellarmine.com.au **Open** By appt
Winemaker Dr Diane Miller **Est.** 2000 **Dozens** 5000 **Vyds** 20.2ha
This vineyard is owned by German residents Dr Willi and Gudrun Schumacher. Long-term wine lovers, the Schumachers decided to establish a vineyard and winery of their own, using Australia partly because of its stable political climate. The vineyard is planted to merlot, pinot noir, chardonnay, shiraz, riesling, sauvignon blanc and petit verdot. Exports to the UK, the US, Germany and China.

Pemberton Riesling Dry 2014 This is one of the most consistent Rieslings on the market today – and one of the very best. Lime and apple blossom aromas translate into an intense, lime juice-driven palate of prodigious length and intensity. While this version of Bellarmine's Riesling normally needs a few years to open up, this requires no such discipline. Screwcap. 12% alc. **Rating** 96 **To** 2029 $25 ○
Pemberton Riesling Half Dry 2014 A perfect rendition of off-dry Riesling in the Mosel Valley style; orange and lime blossom aromas lead into a palate that is simultaneously delicate and intense, the wine flowing in a seamless stream across and along the palate. Screwcap. 9.5% alc. **Rating** 96 **To** 2024 $25 ○
Pemberton Riesling Select 2014 As ever, Bellarmine nails the style, the 63g/l of residual sugar far from obvious on the palate, where the exotic fruit flavours (and the sweetness) are balanced to perfection by the acidity. Screwcap. 8% alc. **Rating** 96 **To** 2029 $25 ○
Pemberton Shiraz 2012 An elegant, finely structured, medium-bodied Shiraz; red cherry and plum fruits dance across the mouth, silky tannins of the highest quality adding a dimension to the delicious flavours of the fruit. One of those wines giving as much pleasure today as will in 10 years' time. Screwcap. 14% alc. **Rating** 96 **To** 2027 $28 ○
Pemberton Chardonnay 2014 An elegant, understated wine, made with a gentle hand, but don't be fooled – everything is in perfect balance, and the length of the finish is exceptional, bringing together the white flesh stone fruits, grapefruit and nutty oak. Screwcap. 13.5% alc. **Rating** 94 **To** 2021 $26 ○

Pemberton Sauvignon Blanc 2014 **Rating** 92 **To** 2015 $20 ○

Bellbrae Estate

520 Great Ocean Road, Bellbrae, Vic 3228 **Region** Geelong
T (03) 5264 8480 **www**.bellbraeestate.com.au **Open** W'ends 11–5, 7 days (Jan)
Winemaker Peter Flewellyn, David Crawford **Est.** 1999 **Dozens** 2000 **Vyds** 4.1ha
The Bellbrae Estate of 2014 is a very different business from that established in 1999.
Co-founder Richard Macdougall is now the sole owner, having purchased the small, former
sheep grazing property on which the estate vineyard was planted. In '12 the mothballed
Tarcoola Estate winery was reopened and refurbished for Bellbrae under the direction of
winemaker David Crawford and very successful vintages have been made under the Bellbrae
Estate and Longboard labels.

ΨΨΨΨΨ **Longboard Geelong Shiraz 2013** Estate-grown (2ha), cool-fermented in open
fermenters for up to 9 days; pressed straight to barrel for mlf; 12 months in 1 and
2yo French barriques. First-class cool-climate Shiraz, with a very fragrant bouquet
and supple, but intense, medium-bodied palate; red stone fruit, spice and licorice,
the tannins fine, the oak perfectly integrated. Outstanding bargain. Screwcap.
14% alc. **Rating** 96 **To** 2028 $22 ✪
Southside Geelong Sauvignon Blanc 2014 Whole bunch-pressed, cold-
settled, fermentation initiated by wild yeast, inoculated yeast added after 7 days, then
transferred for the remaining fermentation in used French barriques, 8 months'
lees stirring. All these inputs have been meticulously judged, for the flavour and
mouthfeel have exceptional intensity, length and – unusually for Sauvignon Blanc –
purity. Top-drawer stuff. Screwcap. 12.5% alc. **Rating** 95 **To** 2020 $30 ✪
Bells Geelong Syrah 2013 Open-fermented at cool temperatures for 9 days,
then pressed straight to French oak (20% new, 80% 1yo) for 14 months. The
fragrant red fruits of the bouquet flow directly onto the medium-bodied palate,
which has notable drive and focus, silky tannins drawing out the long finish.
Lovely cool-climate Shiraz. Screwcap. 14% alc. **Rating** 95 **To** 2028 $32 ✪
Longboard Geelong Pinot Noir 2013 From the 2ha estate planting,
75% MV6, 25% 777 clone; 30% whole bunches, open-fermented; 12 months'
maturation in 1 and 2yo French barriques. A delicious lipsmacking Pinot, red
cherry and spice fruits to the fore; a supple and long palate, freshness the keyword.
Excellent value. Screwcap. 14% alc. **Rating** 94 **To** 2021 $22 ✪
Bird Rock Geelong Pinot Noir 2013 Estate-grown, 75% MV6, 25% 777 clone;
70% whole bunches, mostly cool-fermented; 12 months in French oak (20% new).
Bright, full hue; the fragrant, flowery/spicy bouquet leads into a complex palate,
savoury whole-bunch notes obvious, but with plenty of red cherry/berry fruit on
the mid-palate, and on the finish and aftertaste. Well made, classy Pinot Noir, with
bell-clear varietal expression. Screwcap. 13.5% alc. **Rating** 94 **To** 2023 $36

ΨΨΨΨΨ **Boobs Geelong Chardonnay 2014** **Rating** 93 **To** 2018 $33
Longboard Geelong Sauvignon Blanc 2014 **Rating** 92 **To** 2016 $22 ✪
Longboard Geelong Chardonnay 2014 **Rating** 92 **To** 2017 $22 ✪

Bellvale Wine

95 Forresters Lane, Berrys Creek, Vic 3953 **Region** Gippsland
T 0412 541 098 **www**.bellvalewine.com.au **Open** By appt
Winemaker John Ellis **Est.** 1998 **Dozens** 5000 **Vyds** 22ha
John Ellis is the third under this name to be actively involved in the wine industry. His
background as a 747 pilot, and the knowledge he gained of Burgundy over many visits, sets
him apart from the others. He has established pinot noir (14ha), chardonnay (6ha) and pinot
gris (2ha) on the red soils of a north-facing slope. He chose a density of 7150 vines per
hectare, following as far as possible the precepts of Burgundy, but limited by tractor size, which
precludes narrower row spacing and even higher plant density. Exports to the UK, the US,
Denmark, Germany, Singapore and Japan.

ΨΨΨΨΨ **Stony Block Gippsland Pinot Noir 2013** Clear crimson; the most tightly
wound of all three Bellvale Pinots, and is the one demanding most time in

bottle – and promising the greatest reward as the firm finish softens. Screwcap. 12.7% alc. **Rating** 94 **To** 2025 $45

Quercus Vineyard Gippsland Pinot Noir 2013 Clear crimson; while all three Bellvale Pinots have precisely the same alcohol, this is distinctly firmer, presumably the consequence of more new French oak; higher acidity. Screwcap. 12.7% alc. **Rating** 94 **To** 2023 $35

ㅇㅇㅇㅇㅇ **Gippsland Pinot Noir 2013 Rating** 93 **To** 2019 $23 ✪
Athena's Vineyard Gippsland Chardonnay 2013 Rating 92 **To** 2018 $35
Gippsland Pinot Grigio 2014 Rating 90 **To** 2016 $25

Bellwether ★★★★★

PO Box 344, Coonawarra, SA 5263 **Region** Coonawarra
T 0417 080 945 **www.**bellwetherwines.com.au **Open** Not
Winemaker Sue Bell **Est.** 2009 **Dozens** 1000
When Constellation decided to sell (or mothball) its large Padthaway winery, built by Hardys little more than 10 years previously at a cost of $20 million, chief winemaker Sue Bell was summarily retrenched. In quick succession she received a $46,000 wine industry scholarship from the Grape & Wine Research Development Council to study the wine industry in relation to other rural industries in Australia and overseas, and its interaction with community and society. She also became Dux of the Len Evans Tutorial, her prize an extended trip through Bordeaux and Burgundy. She had decided to stay and live in Coonawarra, and the next stroke of good fortune was that a beautiful old shearing shed at Glenroy in Coonawarra came on the market – it will be her winery and cellar door.

ㅇㅇㅇㅇㅇ **Tamar Valley Chardonnay 2012** Hand-picked, whole bunch-pressed, wild yeast barrel-fermented and matured in French oak. This is raw power, spank me harder, I love it, stuff; its bouquet is wild and funky, and it takes control of every taste bud on the tongue; there is a moment of semi-calm before you swallow the mouthful, but it still has the last say. Screwcap. 12.5% alc. **Rating** 96 **To** 2025 $50 ✪

Tamar Valley Chardonnay 2011 Perhaps it's the vintage, perhaps it's the extra year in bottle, but either way, this is a very different proposition from the '12; it has considerable intensity and length, the flavours still in the unsweetened citrus/grapefruit mode, the acidity now and always there after providing the framework of the wine. Screwcap. 12.5% alc. **Rating** 95 **To** 2022 $50

Wrattonbully Shiraz Malbec 2013 Deep colour; an unusual bouquet, with aromas of leather (polished with soft soap), licorice and blackberry; the medium to full-bodied palate has a big bass drumbeat of black fruits, licorice and star anise; the moderate alcohol has paid big dividends in giving the wine freshness in this wild sea of flavours. Screwcap. 13.4% alc. **Rating** 95 **To** 2033 $28 ✪

Coonawarra Cabernet Sauvignon 2010 A remarkably fresh and generous Cabernet, flooded with cassis, dried herbs and an echo of regional mint; the tannins are ripe and integrated, the quality of the oak also seamlessly woven through the palate. Screwcap. 13% alc. **Rating** 95 **To** 2030 $50

ㅇㅇㅇㅇㅇ **Heathcote Vermentino 2014 Rating** 93 **To** 2020 $28
Nero d'Avola Rose 2014 Rating 91 **To** 2016 $22 ✪

Belvoir Park Estate ★★★★☆

39 Belvoir Park Road, Big Hill, Vic 3453 **Region** Bendigo
T (03) 5435 3075 **www.**belvoirparkestate.com.au **Open** W'ends 11–5
Winemaker Greg McClure **Est.** 1996 **Dozens** 1000 **Vyds** 3ha
When Greg and Mell McClure purchased Belvoir Park Estate in November 2010 from founders Ian and Julie Hall, it was in excellent condition. The house, guarded by 200-year-old red gums, overlooks the vineyard (riesling, merlot, shiraz and cabernet sauvignon). It was very much a lifestyle change for the McClures. Greg's involvement in the marketing side of many businesses is evident in the renovation and extension of the cellar door, which now includes a gallery. A new jetty has been built on the vineyard dam, and an annual wine festival is held on the first of November.

🍷🍷🍷🍷🍷 **Symphony Bendigo Shiraz Cabernet Merlot 2013** Matured in French oak for 22 months, but we are not told the blend percentages, or when the three components were blended. It is very full-bodied and very powerful, but has innate freshness courtesy of the controlled alcohol; spice, pepper and licorice components are woven through deep black fruits, the tannins perfectly balanced. Will be very long-lived. Screwcap. 13.9% alc. **Rating** 95 **To** 2043 $28 ✪
Bendigo Cabernet Sauvignon 2013 Deep, dense purple, almost no crimson; most attractive black fruits, with a texture in themselves, and a cedar/dark chocolate subset; the balance and length are exemplary. Screwcap. 13.5% alc. **Rating** 94 **To** 2028 $29 ✪

🍷🍷🍷🍷🍷 **Single Vineyard Bendigo Shiraz 2013 Rating** 93 **To** 2028 $25 ✪
Bendigo Riesling 2014 Rating 90 **To** 2018 $20 ✪

Ben Haines Wine   ★★★★★
13 Berry Street, Clifton Hill, Vic 3068 (postal) **Region** Various
T 0417 083 645 **www**.benhaineswine.com **Open** Not
Winemaker Ben Haines **Est.** 2010 **Dozens** 1800
Ben Haines graduated from the University of Adelaide in 1999 with a degree in viticulture, waiting a couple of years (immersing himself in music) before focusing on his career. An early interest in terroir led to a deliberate choice of diverse regions, including the Yarra Valley, McLaren Vale, Adelaide Hills, Langhorne Creek, Tasmania and Central Victoria, as well as time in the US and France. His services as a contract winemaker are in high demand, and his name bobs up all over the place. Exports to the US.

🍷🍷🍷🍷🍷 **Under Woods Yarra Valley Syrah 2013** Hand-picked, wild-fermented, matured for 16 months in French oak (25% new). The rich, exotically complex bouquet brings together a basket of oriental spices, dark fruits and French oak, the textured, medium to full-bodied palate with rippling tannin muscles and dark berry fruits all in balance. Diam. 13.8% alc. **Rating** 96 **To** 2033 $45 ✪
B Minor Shiraz Marsanne 2013 A 92/8% co-fermented blend, 20% whole bunches, 80% destemmed, matured for 16 months in French oak (35% new) on '12 marsanne lees. This is as juicy and as delicious as they come, with red fruit flavours soaring into the sky, and a beautifully modulated finish of silky tannins. Absurd value. Screwcap. 13.8% alc. **Rating** 96 **To** 2030 $25 ✪

🍷🍷🍷🍷🍷 **B Minor Marsanne Roussanne 2014 Rating** 90 **To** 2025 $25

Ben Potts Wines   ★★★★
Wellington Road, Langhorne Creek, SA 5255 **Region** Langhorne Creek
T (08) 8537 3029 **www**.benpottswines.com.au **Open** 7 days 10–5
Winemaker Ben Potts **Est.** 2002 **Dozens** 800
Ben Potts is the sixth generation to be involved in grapegrowing and winemaking in Langhorne Creek, the first being Frank Potts, founder of Bleasdale Vineyards. Ben completed the oenology degree at CSU, and ventured into winemaking on a commercial scale in 2002 (aged 25). Fiddle's Block Shiraz is named after great-grandfather Fiddle; Lenny's Block Cabernet Sauvignon Malbec after grandfather Len; and Bill's Block Malbec after father Bill. Exports to Hong Kong and Singapore.

🍷🍷🍷🍷🍷 **Reserve Langhorne Creek Shiraz 2012** Big end of town in both fruit and oak terms. It delivers a warm serving of licorice, malt, asphalt and coffee-cream flavour with peppermint notes shooting through the finish. Tannin has had the torque-wrench applied; it's firm and tight, but appropriate to the wealth of other goings on. Heroic style but it delivers in the end; just leave it alone for a while. Cork. 15.5% alc. **Rating** 94 **To** 2024 $80 CM

🍷🍷🍷🍷🍷 **Fiddle's Block Langhorne Creek Shiraz 2012 Rating** 91 **To** 2020 $40 CM

Bendbrook Wines

Section 19, Pound Road, Macclesfield, SA 5153 **Region** Adelaide Hills
T (08) 8388 9773 **www.**bendbrookwines.com.au **Open** By appt
Winemaker Contract **Est.** 1998 **Dozens** 2000 **Vyds** 5.5ha
John and Margaret Struik have established their vineyard on either side of a significant bend in the Angas River that runs through the property, with cabernet sauvignon on one side and shiraz on the other. The name comes from the bend in question, which is indirectly responsible for the flood that occurs every 4–5 years. The Struiks have restored what was known as the Postmaster's Residence to be their home. Exports to Hong Kong.

Adelaide Hills Chardonnay 2013 Barrel-fermented and lees-stirred, 10 months in French oak. Gleaming green-yellow, it is a complex wine sending various messages; ripe fruit is at its core, but a slightly loose line of acidity, the oak not an issue. 12.5% alc. **Rating** 90 **To** 2017 $28

Cracklin' Rosey 2014 Rating 89 **To** 2016 $18 ✪
Yarn Spinner Adelaide Hills Cabernet Shiraz 2011 Rating 88 **To** 2017 $18

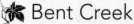 Bent Creek

13 Blewitt Springs Road, McLaren Flat, SA 5171 **Region** McLaren Vale
T (08) 8383 0414 **www.**bentcreekvineyards.com.au **Open** W'ends 12–4
Winemaker Tim Geddes, Sam Rugari, David Garrick **Est.** 1999 **Dozens** 5000
Established in 1999, today Bent Creek is a joint partnership between Sam Rugari and David Garrick, collectively with over 40 years' experience in the wine industry. They source premium fruit from vineyards in McLaren Vale (with 70-100-year-old vines) to Piccadilly Valley in the Adelaide Hills, working closely with the growers. There is an overall focus on small parcels of high-quality fruit that reflect the variety, vintage and the unique terroir each has to offer. Exports to Indonesia, Hong Kong and China.

Limited Release Reserve Shiraz 2012 Grown on vines planted in the '30s and matured in both American and French oak. Not the whopper you might expect, though it does lay down flavour aplenty. Coffee, rounds of blackberry, scorched plums and peppercorns. It's characterised as much by its shape through the mouth as it is by its density; it's taut, trim and, accordingly, impressive. Screwcap. 15% alc. **Rating** 95 **To** 2028 $65 CM

Limited Release Reserve Shiraz 2010 Produced from a 70yo dry-grown vineyard; matured for 18 months in 70% French and 30% American oak (60% new). Bent Creek regards this vintage as the best since '02, and indeed it has produced many elegant wines; this cannot be classed as elegant, but it shrugs off the alcohol warmth that destroys many wines with this alcohol level; the still-vivid colour suggests a surprisingly low pH may be the saviour, for as well as being fresh, the wine has very good varietal fruit. Screwcap. 15.4% alc. **Rating** 95 **To** 2030 $55

Bos Provincia Piccadilly Valley Pinot Gris 2013 Rating 92 **To** 2015 $28 CM
Adelaide Hills Sauvignon Blanc 2014 Rating 91 **To** 2016 $20 ✪
Black Dog McLaren Vale Shiraz 2013 Rating 91 **To** 2020 $24 CM
Nude Old Vine McLaren Vale Shiraz 2012 Rating 91 **To** 2028 $90 CM

Beresford Estates

252 Blewitt Springs Road, McLaren Flat, SA 5171 **Region** McLaren Vale
T (08) 8182 1888 **www.**beresfordwines.com **Open** Not
Winemaker Chris Dix **Est.** 1985 **Dozens** 30 000 **Vyds** 28ha
This is a sister company to Step Rd Wines in Langhorne Creek, owned and run by VOK Beverages. The estate plantings are of cabernet sauvignon and shiraz (10ha each), chardonnay (5.5ha) and grenache (2.5ha), but they account for only a part of the substantial production. Some of the wines offer excellent value. Exports to the UK, the US, Germany, Denmark, Poland, Singapore, Hong Kong and China.

ΨΨΨΨΨ **Estate Blewitt Springs McLaren Vale Cabernet Sauvignon 2013** Matured for 14–16 months in new and used French and American oak. Deeply coloured, this is a lusciously hedonistic wine with that X-factor Blewitt Springs (with its cooler climate) unfailingly delivers given responsible viticulture. This wine grows each time it is retasted. Screwcap. 14.6% alc. **Rating** 96 **To** 2038 $35 ⊙
Limited Release Shiraz 2013 Deep, inky crimson-purple; a dense, rich and powerful full-bodied shiraz, black fruits, licorice and chocolate needing to lose some puppy fat and focus on the job at hand. Lots of potential here, but needs time to grow up. Cork. 14.5% alc. **Rating** 94 **To** 2035 $60
Estate Blewitt Springs McLaren Vale Shiraz 2013 Matured for 14–16 months in new and used French and American oak. Deep, bright crimson; this has a lot going for it, the bouquet good, the medium-bodied palate better still; it is supple and very well balanced, with perfectly ripened blackberry fruit and supporting tannins. Screwcap. 14.4% alc. **Rating** 94 **To** 2033 $35
Barrel Select McLaren Vale G.S.M 2013 Hand-picked from 50yo estate bush vines. Positively coloured, it has abundant red and black fruit aromas, the medium-bodied palate precisely tracking the bouquet, adding a nice savoury/earthy twist to the finish and aftertaste. Screwcap. 14.2% alc. **Rating** 94 **To** 2025 $25 ⊙

ΨΨΨΨΨ **Single Vineyard Chardonnay 2013 Rating** 92 **To** 2020 $22 ⊙
McLaren Vale Cabernet Sauvignon 2013 Rating 92 **To** 2025 $25 ⊙

Berton Vineyard ★★★☆

55 Mirrool Avenue, Yenda, NSW 2681 **Region** Riverina
T (02) 6968 1600 **www.**bertonvineyards.com.au **Open** Mon–Fri 10–4, Sat 11–4
Winemaker James Ceccato, Bill Gumbleton **Est.** 2001 **Dozens** 1 million **Vyds** 12.14ha
The Berton Vineyard partners – Bob and Cherie Berton, Paul Bartholomaeus, James Ceccato and Jamie Bennett – have almost 100 years' combined experience in winemaking, viticulture, finance, production and marketing. 1996 saw the acquisition of a 30ha property in the Eden Valley and the planting of the first vines. Wines are released under the Berton Vineyard plus various other brands. Exports to the UK, the US, Sweden and China.

Best's Wines ★★★★★

111 Best's Road, Great Western, Vic 3377 **Region** Grampians
T (03) 5356 2250 **www.**bestswines.com **Open** Mon–Sat 10–5, Sun 11–4
Winemaker Justin Purser **Est.** 1866 **Dozens** 20 000 **Vyds** 34ha
Best's winery and vineyards are among Australia's best-kept secrets. Indeed the vineyards, with vines dating back to 1866, have secrets that may never be revealed: for example, one of the vines planted in the Nursery Block has defied identification and is thought to exist nowhere else in the world. Part of the cellars, too, go back to the same era, constructed by butcher-turned-winemaker Henry Best and his family. The Thomson family has owned the property since 1920, with Ben, the fifth generation, having taken over management from father Viv. Best's consistently produces elegant, supple wines; the Bin No. 0 is a classic, the Thomson Family Shiraz (from vines planted in 1868) magnificent. Very occasionally a Pinot Meunier (with 15% Pinot Noir) is made solely from 1866 plantings of those two varieties; there is no other Pinot Meunier of this vine age made anywhere else in the world. Justin Purser brings with him a remarkable CV, with extensive experience in Australia, NZ and (most recently) Burgundy (at Domaine de Montille). Exports to the UK, the US, Canada, Sweden, Switzerland, Singapore, Hong Kong and China.

ΨΨΨΨΨ **White Gravels Hill Great Western Shiraz 2012** From a single block on the Concogella Vineyard with a distinctly different soil and geology profile from the rest of the vineyard. A striking and fascinating wine, the intensity of its black and red cherry fruits running without any filler from the opening sip to the finish and aftertaste. Screwcap. 13.5% alc. **Rating** 96 **To** 2027 $35 ⊙
Great Western Riesling 2014 The mother vines of today's vineyard are in the Nursery Block, planted in 1866. An ultimately juicy lime essence burst of flavour

on the palate will make the wine irresistible, and its early consumption will mock the long-term cellaring potential. Screwcap. 11.5% alc. **Rating** 95 **To** 2029 $25 ✪
Bin No. 1 Great Western Shiraz 2013 Deep, dense crimson-purple; savoury/foresty nuances provide the backdrop for the black fruits and licorice aromas and flavours; maturation in large-format French oak has kept the wine fresh and firm, with a minimum 25-year future. Screwcap. 14% alc. **Rating** 94 **To** 2038 $25 ✪

Bethany Wines ★★★★★

378 Bethany Road, Tanunda, SA 5352 **Region** Barossa
T (08) 8563 2086 **www**.bethany.com.au **Open** Mon–Sat 10–5, Sun 1–5
Winemaker Geoff and Robert Schrapel **Est.** 1981 **Dozens** 25 000 **Vyds** 38ha
The Schrapel family has been growing grapes in the Barossa Valley for 140 years, and has had the winery since 1981. Nestled high on a hillside on the site of an old bluestone quarry, Geoff and Rob Schrapel produce a range of consistently well made and attractively packaged wines. Bethany has vineyards in the Barossa and Eden valleys. Exports to the UK, Europe and Asia.

🍷🍷🍷🍷🍷 **Reserve Eden Valley Riesling 2014** Quartz-white; radically different from its standard sibling – here there is concentration and intensity to its bouquet and palate alike; lemon, lime and minerally flavours drive through the palate at high speed, natural acidity the motor. Screwcap. 11.5% alc. **Rating** 95 **To** 2029 $28 ✪
LE Reserve Shiraz 2013 Deep, brilliant crimson-purple; the bouquet is brimming with predominantly black fruits allied with flecks of spice and licorice, the medium to full-bodied, savoury palate with touches of earth and bramble, but not extractive; powdery tannins shape the texture, blackberry the flavour. At every point along the way it reflects its moderate alcohol and underlying freshness. WAK screwcap. 14% alc. **Rating** 95 **To** 2043 $48
Reserve Shiraz 2012 Excellent crimson-purple hue; the expressive bouquet leads into an effortless palate, both with the same red and black fruits message; the tannins are superfine, the oak integrated. It has the balance and harmony to ensure a long and prosperous life. Cork. 14.5% alc. **Rating** 95 **To** 2037 $85

🍷🍷🍷🍷 **Old Vine Barossa Grenache 2012** **Rating** 93 **To** 2019 $20 ✪
Barossa Cabernet Sauvignon 2012 **Rating** 91 **To** 2022 $35

Between the Vines ★★★☆

452 Longwood Road, Longwood, SA 5153 **Region** Adelaide Hills
T 0417 872 538 **www**.betweenthevines.com.au **Open** W'ends & public hols 12–5
Winemaker Matt Jackman **Est.** 2013 **Dozens** 400 **Vyds** 2.3ha
The estate vineyard (2.1ha of chardonnay) was planted in 1995, and purchased by Stewart and Laura Moodie in 2006. Between then and '12 the grapes were sold to d'Arenberg for its Lucky Lizard Chardonnay. The vineyard is fully managed by Stewart and Laura, who do all the spraying/netting/wire lifting, pruning, fruit and shoot thinning, Laura having undertaken a year-long viticulture course. They employ local backpackers for labour where needed, and only bring in professional teams for the harvest. In '13, the Moodies created the Between the Vines brand, grafting 0.2ha of tempranillo (on chardonnay rootstock). Output has increased, and small quantities of Pinot Noir and Tempranillo are bottled for them under their label. The annual crush (between 4 and 10 tonnes) is taken to McLaren Vintners, where Matt Jackman makes the wine in consultation with the Moodies.

🍷🍷🍷🍷 **Single Vineyard Adelaide Hills Chardonnay 2014** Restrained winemaker inputs; subtle oak usage. A slightly funky/smoky bouquet is followed by an incisive and bright palate, white-fleshed stone fruits guarding the gate against any suggestion that the wine is a wannabe Sauvignon Blanc; has good length and persistence. Screwcap. 13% alc. **Rating** 90 **To** 2019 $18 ✪

 Bicknell fc

41 St Margarets Road, Healesville, Vic 3777 **Region** Yarra Valley
T (03) 5962 6955 **www**.bicknellfc.com **Open** Not
Winemaker David Bicknell **Est.** 2011 **Dozens** 300 **Vyds** 2.5ha
This is the busman's holiday for Oakridge chief winemaker David Bicknell and (former) viticulturist (present) wife Nicky Harris. It is focused purely on chardonnay and pinot noir, with no present intention of broadening the range, nor, indeed, the volume of production. The vintages between 2011 and '13 came, with one exception, from the Upper Yarra Valley, the exception the '13 Gippsland Pinot Noir. As from '14 all of the wines will come from Val Stewart's close-planted vineyard at the top of Prices Road, Gladysdale, planted in 1988. The partners have leased this vineyard, which will become the total focus of their business. The quality of the wines so far released has been extremely high, and there is no reason to think there will be any change in the future.

Yarra Valley Chardonnay 2013 Whole bunch-pressed to used French puncheons for wild fermentation, matured on lees for 10 months. Has a touch of reductive funk on the bouquet that is the mark of David Bicknell's best Chardonnays (and many Grand Cru White Burgundies); the river of flavours hit on the first second the wine enters the mouth, with wreathes of white peach, grapefruit and some creamy notes ex the lees contact, which don't, however, blur the message of the crunchy acidity on the finish. A masterclass in power and finesse. Screwcap. 13.3% alc. **Rating** 97 **To** 2028 $39 ○

Yarra Valley Chardonnay 2011 The wine glories in the cool vintage, tailor-made for Chardonnays. Apart from a special touch of Bicknell funk on the bouquet, it is truly impossible to say this or that aroma/flavour is more expressive than any other, which only serves to emphasise the quality of this exquisitely fine wine, the faintly chalky/grippy/citrussy acidity on the finish and aftertaste marking it as a wine of extreme class. Screwcap. 12.7% alc. **Rating** 97 **To** 2030 $32 ○

Gippsland Pinot Noir 2013 Hand-picked and sorted, wild yeast, whole berry fermentation, neither plunged nor pumped over for 28 days; pressed to used oak on gross lees for 10 months. Crystal clear crimson; a magnificently perfumed and pure bouquet, the palate living up to, if not exceeding, the promise of the bouquet; a rose garden with a profusion of red fruits, silky tannins and all the length of a great Pinot. Screwcap. 14% alc. **Rating** 97 **To** 2028 $39 ○

Yarra Valley Chardonnay 2012 Whole bunch-pressed to French puncheons for wild fermentation; matured on lees for 10 months. It's still in its infancy, but has the balance and the Yarra Valley intensity and length of flavour that will sweep it along without the slightest hesitation for not less than 10 years. That said, the balance of its grapefruit, apple and white peach fruit will encourage drinking it whenever the opportunity arises. Screwcap. 12.8% alc. **Rating** 96 **To** 2025 $39 ○

Bilgavia Wines

PO Box 246, Singleton, NSW 2330 **Region** Hunter Valley
T (02) 6574 5314 **Open** Not
Winemaker Michael McManus **Est.** 2003 **Dozens** NFP **Vyds** 17.87ha
Leona and Phil Gunter purchased Parsons Creek Farm in 2011. It covers 200ha of prime alluvial and loam land, but also terra rossa red soil for the shiraz, chardonnay, semillon and verdelho plantings. The farm has a magnificent homestead, a well-kept vineyard, and a thoroughbred horse facility. Most of the grapes are sold, with sufficient quantity retained for the Bilgavia label. They say, 'It has always been Leona's dream to one day own a vineyard and produce her own wine.'

Hunter Valley Shiraz 2013 Estate-grown, and matured in 100% new French barriques for 12 months. The wine has energy, partly from the oak, and partly fresh acidity; it will flesh out and soften over the next 5 years. Screwcap. 12.5% alc. **Rating** 90 **To** 2020 $26

Hunter Valley Pinot Noir 2014 **Rating** 88 **To** 2018 $26

Billanook Estate

280 Edward Road, Chirnside Park, Vic 3116 **Region** Yarra Valley
T (03) 9735 4484 **www.**billanookestate.com.au **Open** W'ends 10–6
Winemaker Domenic Bucci, John D'Aloisio **Est.** 1994 **Dozens** 1200 **Vyds** 15.5ha
The D'Aloisio family has been involved in the agricultural heritage of the Yarra Valley since the late 1960s, and in '94 planted the first vines on their 36ha property. The vineyard is planted to cabernet sauvignon (4.4ha), shiraz (3.3ha), chardonnay (3.2ha), sauvignon blanc (1.7ha), pinot noir (1.4ha) and merlot (1.1ha). Most of the grapes are sold to various wineries in the Valley, leaving a small percentage for the Billanook Estate label.

Yarra Valley Sauvignon Blanc 2014 Good intensity. Fresh clean flavour. Sweet red apple, passionfruit and snow peas. Attractive. Screwcap. 13.5% alc. **Rating** 89 **To** 2015 $22 CM
Yarra Valley Cabernet Sauvignon Merlot 2013 70/30% blend matured in French oak over 14 months. Dark colour and an attractive body of mid-weight flavour. Mulberry, loganberry, earth and loam, with swish smoky oak just starting to integrate. Acid feels relatively high but it aids the general impression of freshness. Harmony isn't its strongest point but it seems placed to mature well. Cork. 14.2% alc. **Rating** 89 **To** 2022 $25 CM
Yarra Valley Chardonnay 2012 Glowing straw colour; full-bodied style with malty, butterscotchy, almond-like oak on sweet peach. Slight spritz. Runs along the tongue with the softness of a kitten before finishing with a burst of cleansing citrus. Screwcap. 13% alc. **Rating** 88 **To** 2016 $25 CM
Yarra Valley Rose 2014 Bright crimson colour; fresh flavours of strawberry and red cherry with spice and fennel notes mingling throughout. Juicy. Sweet-edged. Rates high for quaffability. Screwcap. 13% alc. **Rating** 88 **To** 2015 $18 CM

Billy Button Wines

2d Anderson Street, Bright, Vic 3741 **Region** Alpine Valleys
T 0418 559 344 **www.**billybuttonwines.com.au **Open** Thurs–Sun 12–5.30
Winemaker Jo Marsh **Est.** 2014 **Dozens** 2000
Jo Marsh speaks quietly, if not diffidently, making light of the numerous awards she won during her studies for her degree in Agricultural Science (Oenology) at the University of Adelaide. She continued that habit when she won a contested position in Southcorp's (now Treasury Wine Estates) Graduate Recruitment Program; she was appointed assistant winemaker at Seppelt Great Western in 2003. By '08 she had been promoted to acting senior winemaker, responsible for all wines made onsite. In '09 she won the Graham Thorp Memorial Scholarship at the Sydney Wine Show with '05 Seppelt Salinger, the first sparkling wine she had made. The following year she won the Member's Choice and Sommelier's Choice at the Wine Society Young Winemaker of the Year Award. She also was one of the 12 wine professionals selected to participate in the Len Evans Tutorial Scholarship, from a field of over 100. After resigning from Seppelt, she became winemaker at Feathertop, and after two happy years decided to step out on her own in '14 to create Billy Button Wines. She has set up a grower network – with one exception all from the Alpine Valleys (King Valley the exception) – and made a string of excellent wines in '14, the following year making an astonishing 20 different varietal wines.

The Happy Alpine Valleys Gewurztraminer 2014 From the Happy Valley district in the Alpine Valleys; with only 50 dozen made, half going to the grapegrower, leaving 25 dozen for sale; split into two halves: one cool-fermented in stainless steel, the second with cloudy juice in a used French barrique. Has very good balance and mouthfeel, with rose petal, lychee and spice aromas and flavours. Sure-footed winemaking. Screwcap. 13% alc. **Rating** 95 **To** 2020 $25 ✪
The Feisty Alpine Valleys Friulano 2014 Rain forced picking at a lower baume than planned, and botrytis meant much care (and sorting) in the vineyard. The split processing technique was used: free-run in a used puncheon, the skin contact pressings in a used barrique. The end result is remarkably fresh and juicy,

partial mlf a brainwave. From the Dalbosco Vineyard at Porepunkah, 70 dozen made. Screwcap. 12% alc. **Rating** 94 **To** 2018 $25 ⊘

The Rustic Alpine Valleys Sangiovese 2014 Good colour; a delicious Sangiovese, flowing with red cherry, blood plum and strawberry fruit, fine-grained tannins lined up with military precision in support. Screwcap. 13.5% alc. **Rating** 94 **To** 2025 $30 ⊘

🍷🍷🍷🍷🍷 **The Versatile Alpine Valleys Vermentino 2014** **Rating** 93 **To** 2017 $25 ⊘
The Torment King Valley Riesling 2014 **Rating** 92 **To** 2034 $25 ⊘
The Affable Alpine Valleys Barbera 2014 **Rating** 92 **To** 2024 $25 ⊘

Bimbadgen   ★★★★★

790 McDonalds Road, Pokolbin, NSW 2320 **Region** Hunter Valley
T (02) 4998 4600 **www.**bimbadgen.com.au **Open** Fri–Sat 10–7, Sun–Thurs 10–5
Winemaker Rauri Donkin, Mike De Garis **Est.** 1968 **Dozens** 35000 **Vyds** 27ha
Established as McPherson Wines, then successively Tamalee, Sobels, Parker Wines and now Bimbadgen, this substantial winery has had what might be politely termed a turbulent history. It has vineyards in McDonalds Road and Palmers Lane, Pokolbin, and these produce the Bimbadgen Signature range at the top of the tree. Next comes the Regions range of a diverse selection of varietals from regions known for a given variety or varieties. Exports to the UK, Switzerland, Fiji, Taiwan, the Philippines, Hong Kong, China, Japan and NZ.

🍷🍷🍷🍷🍷 **Signature Hunter Valley Semillon 2011** Has calmly mooched along since first tasted 3 years ago, when it also received 96 points, with a 2030 drink-to date. While still incisive, and still with unsweetened lemon at its core, there is a hint of honey around the corner, but I'm pulling back its end-point a little. Screwcap. 11% alc. **Rating** 96 **To** 2026 $40 ⊘

Signature Palmers Lane Hunter Valley Semillon 2009 Last tasted 5 years ago, and has the same slashing freshness today as it had then, the same purity, the same focus. This will be prodigiously long-lived: 4 gold medals in '14 no surprise. Screwcap. 11% alc. **Rating** 96 **To** 2029 $40 ⊘

Signature Hunter Valley Semillon 2014 From the Drayton's and John Tulloch Vineyards. Has a juicy depth to its palate, as well as impressive length; Meyer lemon, lemongrass and zesty acidity give the wine an emphatic thrust. The prices of the Signature Semillons are daunting in the context of Hunter Valley Semillon, but that's not my business. Screwcap. 12% alc. **Rating** 95 **To** 2029 $40

Signature Palmers Lane Hunter Valley Semillon 2014 From the sandy loam soils on Palmers Lane. The bouquet is good, but it is the power, precision and length of the palate that is so impressive, the aftertaste likewise lingering long. Screwcap. 12% alc. **Rating** 95 **To** 2029 $40

Art Series Fume Blanc 2014 Sauvignon blanc was sourced from Orange, and the free-run (no pressing whatsoever) was drained direct to used French barriques for wild yeast fermentation and lees contact. This is a seriously good fume style, with great texture and structure to its smoky snow pea, herb and citrus flavours. Screwcap. 12.3% alc. **Rating** 95 **To** 2017 $29 ⊘

Estate Hunter Valley Shiraz Viognier 2013 A co-fermented field blend (3% viognier). This blend doesn't always work well in warm climates, but succeeds here. Bright colour; lively black and red fruit aromas and flavours have enough tannin support on the palate to suggest this might surprise with its longevity, à la Maurice O'Shea blends. Screwcap. 13.5% alc. **Rating** 95 **To** 2038 $26 ⊘

Signature Hunter Valley Chardonnay 2013 **Rating** 94 **To** 2018 $45
Signature Hunter Valley Shiraz 2013 **Rating** 94 **To** 2033 $50
Members Orange Merlot Cabernet Sauvignon 2013 **Rating** 94 **To** 2028 $32

🍷🍷🍷🍷🍷 **Estate Hunter Valley Semillon 2014** **Rating** 93 **To** 2020 $22 ⊘

Bindi Wine Growers

343 Melton Road, Gisborne, Vic 3437 (postal) **Region** Macedon Ranges
T (03) 5428 2564 **www**.bindiwines.com.au **Open** Not
Winemaker Michael Dhillon, Stuart Anderson (Consultant) **Est.** 1988 **Dozens** 2000
Vyds 6ha

One of the icons of Macedon. The Chardonnay is top-shelf, the Pinot Noir as remarkable (albeit in a very different idiom) as Bass Phillip, Giaconda or any of the other tiny-production, icon wines. The addition of Heathcote-sourced shiraz under the Pyrette label confirms Bindi as one of the greatest small producers in Australia. No new wines were received for this edition, but the rating has been maintained. Exports to the UK, the US and other major markets.

Bird in Hand

Bird in Hand Road, Woodside, SA 5244 **Region** Adelaide Hills
T (08) 8389 9488 **www**.birdinhand.com.au **Open** Mon–Fri 10–5, w'ends & public hols 11–5
Winemaker Kym Milne (MW), Peter Ruchs, Dylan Lee **Est.** 1997 **Dozens** 75000
Vyds 29ha

This very successful business took its name from a 19th-century gold mine. It is the venture of the Nugent family, headed by Dr Michael Nugent; son Andrew is a Roseworthy graduate. The family also has a vineyard in the Clare Valley, the latter providing both riesling and shiraz. The estate plantings (merlot, pinot noir, cabernet sauvignon, sauvignon blanc, riesling, shiraz) provide only part of the annual crush, the remainder coming from contract growers. In 2010, a replica Bird in Hand cellar door was opened in Dalian, in China's northeastern Liaoning province, a second following in Yingkou. Exports to all major markets.

𝑇𝑇𝑇𝑇𝑇 **Nest Egg Mt Lofty Ranges Shiraz 2012** Estate-grown, with 18 months' maturation in French oak. Intense, powerful, brooding black fruits suffused with spices, pepper, licorice and some cedar; the texture and structure are impeccable, based on fruit and oak tannins. Very classy wine. Screwcap. 14.5% alc. **Rating** 97 To 2037 $110 ✪

𝑇𝑇𝑇𝑇𝑇 **Adelaide Hills Cabernet Sauvignon 2013** Bright crimson colour is a prophetic start for an elegant and harmonious Cabernet, its cassis fruit couched in a subtle array of wild rose, bramble, black olive, savoury tannins and cedary oak; the flavours keep moving back and forth, giving the wine energy. Screwcap. 14.5% alc. **Rating** 96 To 2038 $42 ✪

Nest Egg Adelaide Hills Cabernet Sauvignon 2012 Good crimson-purple depth; an elegant, high-quality Cabernet with cassis, black olive and cedar filling the bouquet and medium-bodied palate alike; superfine tannins run throughout, but don't threaten the ascendancy of the fruit. Classy wine. 405 dozen made. Screwcap. 14.5% alc. **Rating** 96 To 2037 $110

Clare Valley Riesling 2014 The wine has maximum varietal expression; lime blossom aromas, lime zest/pith and juice flavours are all on display; the length of the wine is impeccable. Screwcap. 12% alc. **Rating** 95 To 2029 $25 ✪

Adelaide Hills Chardonnay 2014 The back label claptrap of new and old world techniques to one side, this is a high-quality Chardonnay, with intense white peach, nectarine and pink grapefruit flavours framed by just the right amount of new oak from barrel fermentation. Screwcap. 13.5% alc. **Rating** 95 To 2022 $42

Mt Lofty Ranges Shiraz 2013 Dense purple-crimson; a medium to full-bodied wine, replete with blackberry, black cherry and spice fruit couched in a fine web of tannins and well-integrated oak; balance is the key to what will be a long-lived wine of high quality. Screwcap. 14.5% alc. **Rating** 95 To 2033 $35 ✪

Adelaide Hills Merlot 2013 Matured in French oak. The bouquet is fragrant, and the medium-bodied palate has the mix of plum, cassis and spice flavours of cool-grown merlot, its wreath of fine, savoury/spicy tannins helping to extend an already long palate. When the new clones of merlot become more widespread, the reputation of the variety will no longer have to be defended. Screwcap. 14.5% alc. **Rating** 95 To 2028 $42

Adelaide Hills Pinot Gris 2014 Rating 94 To 2017 $28 ○
Nest Egg Adelaide Hills Merlot 2012 Rating 94 To 2027 $110
Adelaide Hills Montepulciano 2013 Rating 94 To 2030 $42
Adelaide Hills Nero d'Avola 2013 Rating 94 To 2030 $42

ŸŸŸŸ♀ Adelaide Hills Sauvignon Blanc 2014 Rating 93 To 2016 $25 ○
Two in the Bush Adelaide Hills Shiraz 2013 Rating 93 To 2023 $20 ○
Two in the Bush Merlot Cabernet 2013 Rating 93 To 2023 $22 ○
Adelaide Hills Arneis 2014 Rating 92 To 2017 $28
Adelaide Hills Pinot Rose 2014 Rating 91 To 2016 $25
Honeysuckle Clare Valley Riesling 2014 Rating 91 To 2024 $25
Two in the Bush Semillon Sauvignon Blanc 2014 Rating 90 To 2016 $20 ○

 # Bittern Estate

8 Bittern-Dromana Road, Bittern, Vic 3918 **Region** Mornington Peninsula
T 0417 556 529 **www.**bitternestate.com.au **Open** Not
Winemaker Alex White, Carl Tiesdell-Smith **Est.** 2013 **Dozens** 4500 **Vyds** 7ha
The Zerbe family has been involved in horticulture for many generations since arriving from Prussia in 1854, planting fruit trees in what is now suburban Melbourne. Generations later, in 1959, the family planted an apple and pear orchard called Tathravale. In '96, Gary and Karen Zerbe began planting the Bittern Vineyard on this property, the extended family, including children Matthew and Karen, their spouses and their children providing the third generation of grapegrowers. Until '13, almost all the grapes were sold to other wineries, but in that year the family produced its first full array of wine styles under the Bittern Estate label. There was an involvement with Box Stallion, but following land sales by third parties, that venture has terminated, Continuity is provided by the winemaking team of Alex White and Carl Tiesdell-Smith. Exports to China.

ŸŸŸŸŸ **Mornington Peninsula Shiraz 2013** A short cold soak, cool fermentation, 10 months' maturation in new and used French oak. A vibrantly pure and super-elegant cool-climate Shiraz, with red fruits to the fore on the long, silky medium-bodied palate. Will age slowly and with grace, a classic now or later proposition. 100 dozen made. Diam. 13.7% alc. **Rating** 94 To 2025 $30 ○

ŸŸŸŸ♀ **Mornington Peninsula Gewurztraminer 2013** Rating 93 To 2020 $20 ○
Mornington Peninsula Sauvignon Blanc 2013 Rating 92 To 2015 $20 ○
Mornington Peninsula Rose 2013 Rating 90 To 2016 $20 ○

BK Wines

Burdetts Road, Basket Range, SA 5138 **Region** Adelaide Hills
T 0410 124 674 **www.**bkwines.com.au **Open** By appt
Winemaker Brendon Keys **Est.** 2007 **Dozens** 3000
BK Wines is owned by NZ-born Brendon Keys and wife Kirsty. Brendon has packed a great deal of high and low living into the past decade, driving tractors in the UK, then managing a chalet in Val d'Isere (in the French Alps) for eight months. Bouncing between Australia and NZ before working a vintage in California with the well-known Paul Hobbs, he then helped Paul set up a winery in Argentina. Brendon's tag-line is 'wines made with love, not money', and he has not hesitated to confound the normal rules of engagement in winemaking. If he isn't remembered for this, the labels for his wines should do the trick. Exports to the UK, the US, Canada and Singapore.

ŸŸŸŸŸ **Remy Single Barrel Lenswood Pinot Noir 2013** 70% destemmed and 30% whole bunches; matured for 15 months in new French oak. The deep colour signals a Pinot of exceptional depth and power, particularly given its alcohol; the bouquet and palate bring a compote of black fruits into play, led by plum, black cherry and blueberry, lifting on the finish with a flourish that has no hint of excessive extract, but promises a long life. Screwcap. 12.5% alc. **Rating** 96 To 2023 $85

Mazi Whole Bunch Blewitt Springs Syrah 2013 Dry-grown, old vines; 100% whole-bunch fermentation without maceration for the first month; then wild yeast fermentation; pressed to new French oak for 14 months' maturation. It has a Catherine Wheel of flavours: spice, licorice, polished leather, earth, charcuterie, all embroidered on a cushion of black cherry fruit; medium-bodied, full of life. Screwcap. 13.5% alc. **Rating** 96 **To** 2025 $85

Mazi Whole Bunch Blewitt Springs Syrah 2012 The use of 100% whole bunches with shiraz polarises opinions, but for my palate it has succeeded brilliantly. The wine is no more than medium-bodied, but positively pulsates with its chorus of red fruits of every description, enhanced by silky tannins and quality oak. Screwcap. 13.5% alc. **Rating** 96 **To** 2027 $85

Sparks Whole Bunch Blewitt Springs Grenache 2013 Clear, light, crimson; will polarise opinions, for it is an outrageous attack on accepted wisdom for grenache in McLaren Vale (and the Barossa Valley); it is super-fragrant, the bouquet and palate singing soprano in unison, exulting the display of vivid red fruits/rhubarb flavours, free of the yoke of either oak or tannins. I love it. Screwcap. 12.5% alc. **Rating** 96 **To** 2020 $55 ✪

Swaby Single Vineyard Piccadilly Valley Chardonnay 2013 Bright straw-green; a fresh, elegant and expressive wine from start to finish; white peach, citrus, apple and melon are woven together by well-handled oak; the finish draws you back again and again. Screwcap. 12.5% alc. **Rating** 95 **To** 2023 $55

One Ball Single Vineyard Kenton Valley Adelaide Hills Chardonnay 2013 Rating 94 **To** 2020 $30 ✪

Saignee of Pinot Noir Lenswood Rose 2014 Rating 94 **To** 2016 $25 ✪

Gower Single Vineyard Lenswood Pinot Noir 2013 Rating 94 **To** 2023 $55

Cult Single Vineyard Lobethal Adelaide Hills Syrah 2013 Rating 94 **To** 2028 $30 ✪

Black Bishop Wines ★★★★

1 Valdemar Court, Magill, SA 5072 (postal) **Region** Adelaide Hills
T 0422 791 775 **www**.blackbishopwines.com.au **Open** Not
Winemaker Damon Koerner **Est.** 2012 **Dozens** 1200

Black Bishop was established by three mates from school, Jack Horsnell, Damon Koerner and Chris Bishop, each 27 years old. Chris has an ongoing love for Barossa Shiraz, and thought that it made sense to make his own wine rather than purchasing it from others; Damon grew up in the Watervale district of the Clare Valley, and studied oenology and viticulture at Adelaide University, working vintages across Australia and abroad since graduation; and Jack grew up living and working in Adelaide Hills hotels, often drinking (way) too much local wine. A successful small vintage from 2012 led to a significantly broader portfolio in '13, which must have brought a smile to their faces.

ΨΨΨΨΨ GSV Rose 2014 McLaren Vale and Clare. 56/24/20% grenache, shiraz and (unusually) vermentino rose. Savoury style, but there's enough fruit to hang your hat on. Strawberries and dried herbs with a melon-like edge. If you were blindfolded you'd probably pick this as a white wine. Refreshment (and texture) plus. Screwcap. 11.4% alc. **Rating** 91 **To** 2016 $20 CM ✪

Single Vineyard Barossa Valley Shiraz 2013 Fresh plum, blackberries straight from the garden, hints of meat and game, slices of fennel. Dryness to the finish is slightly exaggerated, perhaps, but the sheer drinkability of this, and freshness of fruit, is a delight. Drink young. Screwcap. 12.5% alc. **Rating** 91 **To** 2018 $25 CM

Watervale Riesling 2014 Yeasty apple and woody spice. Almost gingery. Unusual expression of the variety and region. It has a friskiness, though, an alertness, as if 'no' is a foreign concept. It just wants to go. The score is on the fence; it could go either way. Screwcap. 11.8% alc. **Rating** 90 **To** 2020 $20 CM ✪

Single Vineyard Adelaide Hills Sauvignon Blanc 2014 More about texture than flavour but there's enough here to keep you interested. Citrus, modest passionfruit, dry grass and a subtle milky note. Drinkability, once again, is high. Screwcap. 11.6% alc. **Rating** 90 **To** 2015 $20 CM ✪

GSM 2014 48/39/13% blend from McLaren Vale and Clare Valley. 'Naturally vinified'. Matured in old French puncheons. Definitely best suited to early consumption, but its freestyle flavours of raspberry, blackberry and energetic spice go down a treat. Don't expect much in the way of traditional 'structure', but do expect high drinkability. Screwcap. 13% alc. **Rating** 90 **To** 2017 $23 CM

BlackJack Vineyards

Cnr Blackjack Road/Calder Highway, Harcourt, Vic 3453 **Region** Bendigo
T (03) 5474 2355 **www**.blackjackwines.com.au **Open** W'ends & most public hols 11–5
Winemaker Ian McKenzie, Ken Pollock **Est.** 1987 **Dozens** 4000 **Vyds** 6ha
Established by the McKenzie and Pollock families on the site of an old apple and pear orchard in the Harcourt Valley, Blackjack is best known for some very good Shirazs. Despite some tough vintage conditions, BlackJack has managed to continue to produce supremely honest, full-flavoured and powerful wines, all with a redeeming edge of elegance. A representative range of wines was not received. Exports to Canada, China.

Block 6 Bendigo Shiraz 2012 Back to its best: a supple Shiraz with classic varietal fruit flavours running through the length of its medium-bodied palate; fine-grained tannins and gentle oak provide a perfectly measured framework for the fruit. Screwcap. 13.5% alc. **Rating** 94 **To** 2027 $38

 # Blaxland Vineyards

2948 Barossa Valley Way, Tanunda, SA 5352 **Region** Barossa Valley
T (08) 8304 8879 **www**.blaxwine.com.au **Open** 7 days 10–5
Winemaker Chris Polymiadis **Est.** 1995 **Dozens** 150 000 **Vyds** 675ha
Founder and owner Ron Collins has prospered mightily given the headwinds that have buffeted the Australian wine industry over the past decade. Blaxland Vineyards is the 12th-largest vineyard proprietor in Australia; it owns the 320ha Tanunda Hill Vineyard in the Barossa Valley, the 266ha Old Mundulla Vineyard in the Limestone Coast, and the 89ha St Magnus Vineyard in the Adelaide Hills. It has side-stepped the cost of establishing a winery by forming ongoing arrangements with leading wineries to make its wines meeting its cost criteria, overseen by Chris Polymiadis. The wines have enjoyed considerable success in overseas wine shows, notably in China, California and Germany. The value for money is self-evident. Exports to the UK, the US, China and Japan.

Barton Steer Shiraz 2013 Dark colour, pure blackberried/plum-shot fruit and a quick kiss of vanillan/musky oak. A steal. For drinking now. Screwcap. 14.5% alc. **Rating** 90 **To** 2018 $10 CM ✪

Barton Steer Cabernet Sauvignon 2013 Rating 88 **To** 2018 $10 CM ✪

Bleasdale Vineyards

1640 Langhorne Creek Road, Langhorne Creek, SA 5255 **Region** Langhorne Creek
T (08) 8537 3001 **www**.bleasdale.com.au **Open** Mon–Sun 10–5
Winemaker Paul Hotker, Matt Laube **Est.** 1850 **Dozens** 100 000 **Vyds** 47ha
This is one of the most historic wineries in Australia, in 2010 celebrating 160 years of continuous winemaking by the direct descendants of the Potts founding family. Not so long prior to the start of the 21st century, its vineyards were flooded every winter by diversion of the Bremer River, which provided moisture throughout the dry, cool, growing season. In the new millennium, every drop of water was counted. The vineyards have been significantly upgraded and refocused, with shiraz accounting for 45% of plantings, supported by seven other proven varieties. Bleasdale has completely revamped its labels and packaging, and has headed to the Adelaide Hills for sauvignon blanc, pinot gris and chardonnay under the direction of gifted winemaker (and viticulturist) Paul Hotker. The future of the business was greatly strengthened by the arrival of two investors in May 2013: SA family-owned pastoralist business AJ & PA McBride purchased 38%, and Monita, Bleasdale's long-term Asian distributor, 10%. Exports to all major markets.

ΨΨΨΨΨ The Iron Duke Langhorne Creek Cabernet Sauvignon 2012 Bright
crimson-purple; an immaculately crafted Cabernet, ticking each and every box;
while the blackcurrant fruit is first and foremost on the fragrant bouquet and
quite beautifully balanced and constructed medium-bodied palate, it's far from a
one-trick pony, with a swathe of hidden delights sufficient to lure even a hardened
Pinot drinker to join the party. Screwcap. 14.5% alc. **Rating** 97 To 2037 $65 ☉
Double Take Langhorne Creek Malbec 2012 This demonstrates that malbec
can make wines of the highest quality if the site and vintage are right; like a
purring Rolls Royce it effortlessly achieves domination with an extra edge to the
texture, another dimension of fruit depth. Trophy Six Nations Wine Challenge
'14 (Argentina, Australia, Chile, NZ, South Africa and the US). Screwcap. 14% alc.
Rating 97 To 2032 $65 ☉

ΨΨΨΨΨ The Powder Monkey Single Vineyard Langhorne Creek Shiraz 2013
Bright, deep colour; a velvety mouthfeel follows the symphony of gently spiced
black fruits of the bouquet; the line, length and balance are excellent, quality oak
and supple tannins handled with aplomb, giving a farewell echo of spice and
bramble on the aftertaste. Screwcap. 14.5% alc. **Rating** 96 To 2038 $65 ☉
Generations Langhorne Creek Shiraz 2013 An altogether serious Shiraz,
with sultry black fruits joined by nuances of spice and oak on the bouquet, the
full-bodied palate picking up welded-together blackberry, plum, licorice and dark
chocolate powder flavours, tannins and oak also contributing positively. Screwcap.
14.5% alc. **Rating** 95 To 2033 $35 ☉
Petrel Reserve Langhorne Creek Shiraz Cabernet Malbec 2013 A blend
that has always delivered the goods in Langhorne Creek, the only variable the
quality of the fruit. Here it is very good; there is an abundance of blackberry,
blackcurrant and plum on the impeccably balanced, medium-bodied palate;
tannins and oak both contribute in respectful fashion, not seeking to upstage the
fruit. Screwcap. 14% alc. **Rating** 95 To 2033 $30 ☉
Frank Potts 2013 Shares the bright, healthy colour of all the '13 releases; a
full-blown Bordeaux blend of 62/18/11/6/3% cabernet sauvignon, malbec,
petit verdot, cabernet franc and merlot duly delivers the goods with a beautifully
balanced array of predominantly black fruits, but not to the exclusion of some
juicy plum and red sparklets. Screwcap. 14% alc. **Rating** 95 To 2033 $35 ☉
The Riparian Vineyard Langhorne Creek Malbec 2012 From the opposite
side of the Bremer River to the Bleasdale winery. Deeply coloured, and full-
bodied, it is immaculately balanced, all the focus on the lush black fruits, not the
tannins or the alcohol. Screwcap. 14.5% alc. **Rating** 95 To 2032 $35 ☉
The Mullianna Vineyard Langhorne Creek Malbec 2012 Planted in '06
to the Potts' selection. A densely packed wine, with sombre black fruits, yet
beautifully balanced, flowing seamlessly through the long, medium-bodied palate
into the finish and aftertaste. Screwcap. 14% alc. **Rating** 95 To 2027 $35 ☉
Adelaide Hills Pinot Gris 2014 Rating 94 To 2017 $19 ☉
Mulberry Tree Cabernet Sauvignon 2013 Rating 94 To 2028 $20 ☉
The Pasquin Langhorne Creek Cabernet Sauvignon Shiraz Malbec 2013
Rating 94 To 2030 $30 ☉

ΨΨΨΨΨ **Generations Langhorne Creek Malbec 2013 Rating** 93 To 2035 $35
The Bass Hill Vineyard Clare Valley Malbec 2012 Rating 93 To 2027 $35
Second Innings Langhorne Creek Malbec 2013 Rating 92 To 2020 $20 ☉
Adelaide Hills Chardonnay 2014 Rating 91 To 2020 $25
Old Vine Verdelho 2014 Rating 91 To 2017 $29

Bloodwood   ★★★★★

231 Griffin Road, Orange, NSW 2800 **Region** Orange
T (02) 6362 5631 **www**.bloodwood.biz **Open** By appt
Winemaker Stephen Doyle **Est.** 1983 **Dozens** 4000 **Vyds** 8.43ha

Rhonda and Stephen Doyle are two of the pioneers of the Orange district, 2013 marking Bloodwood's 30th anniversary. The estate vineyards (chardonnay, riesling, merlot, cabernet sauvignon, shiraz, cabernet franc and malbec) are planted at an elevation of 810–860m, which provides a reliably cool climate. The wines are sold mainly through the cellar door and by an energetic, humorous and informatively run mailing list (see, for example, the tasting note for Big Men in Tights). Has an impressive track record across the full gamut of varietal (and other) wine styles, especially Riesling; all of the wines have a particular elegance and grace. Very much part of the high-quality reputation of Orange.

♥♥♥♥♥ **Riesling 2014** Tight control. Excellent fruit intensity. Slatey, minerally finish. If ever there was evidence that Orange is a white wine star, but arguably iffy for reds, it's the current range of Bloodwood wines. This Riesling flies an impressive flag both on the palate and through the extended finish. Screwcap. 11.5% alc. **Rating** 95 **To** 2028 $25 CM ✪

Schubert 2013 Length, interest and texture. Compelling Chardonnay. Chalk, lactose, lemon curd and stone fruit, with a velvety flex to the finish. Spicy/creamy oak keeps the silk flowing. Screwcap. 13.5% alc. **Rating** 95 **To** 2020 $30 CM ✪

♥♥♥♥♀ **Chardonnay 2014 Rating** 92 **To** 2019 $28 CM
Big Men in Tights 2014 Rating 91 **To** 2016 $18 CM ✪

Blue Pyrenees Estate   ★★★★★

Vinoca Road, Avoca, Vic 3467 **Region** Pyrenees
T (03) 5465 1111 **www**.bluepyrenees.com.au **Open** Mon–Fri 10–4.30, w'ends 10–5
Winemaker Andrew Koerner, Chris Smales **Est.** 1963 **Dozens** 60 000 **Vyds** 149ha
Forty years after Remy Cointreau established Blue Pyrenees Estate (then known as Chateau Remy), the business was sold to a small group of Sydney businessmen. It went on to celebrate its 50th anniversary in 2013. Former Rosemount senior winemaker Andrew Koerner heads the winery team. The core of the business is the very large estate plantings, most decades old, but with newer arrivals, including viognier. Blue Pyrenees has a number of programs designed to protect the environment and reduce its carbon footprint. Exports to Asia, primarily China.

♥♥♥♥♥ **Richardson Reserve Shiraz 2012** Includes 10% cabernet and 1% viognier; matured for 18 months in American oak (90% new). The sheer intensity of the blackberry and blackcurrant fruits has soaked up the oak to an astonishing degree, with no fruitcake/vanilla bean consequences; instead there is a chiselled profile very different from that of the rumbling Colin Richardson, the much-loved giant of Melbourne Food & Wine circles for decades, never a cross word coming from his lips. Diam. 14% alc. **Rating** 96 **To** 2042 $100

Estate Red 2012 A 68/22/8/2% blend of cabernet, merlot, malbec and shiraz matured for 20 months in French and American barriques (15% new). Trophy Qld Wine Show '14, gold medal Melbourne Wine Show '14. Does have some studied elegance, and is fruit (not oak) driven. Moreover, the show record of two successes is very different from one. Screwcap. 14% alc. **Rating** 95 **To** 2025 $40

Midnight Cuvee 2010 Its freshness and elegance obviously appealed to the illustrious panel of judges who awarded it the inaugural trophy for Best Australian Sparkling in Champagne at the Sparkling Wine World Championship announced Sept '14. Bright green-straw, it is fresh and well balanced, with gentle citrus notes running alongside a hint of brioche; good acidity. Cork. 12% alc. **Rating** 95 **To** 2017 $35 ✪

Reserve Shiraz 2012 Incorporates 9% of cabernet and 1% viognier, matured for 20 months in French and American barriques (10% new). The bouquet is inviting, the drive and energy of the medium to full-bodied palate even more so; while firm, there are no road blocks of dead fruit or tannins, the spice and licorice fruit given free run. Screwcap. 14% alc. **Rating** 94 **To** 2032 $40

Richardson Reserve Cabernet Sauvignon 2012 Includes 7% shiraz, matured for 20 months in French barriques (80% new). Clearly the best fruit has been used, coupled with new oak. It is a powerful, full-bodied wine that Colin Richardson would have approved of. It's far from ready now, but has the balance to repay cellaring. Diam. 14% alc. **Rating** 94 **To** 2032 $100

ŸŸŸŸŸ **Midnight Cuvee 2011 Rating** 91 **To** 2021 $35 TS
Rose 2014 Rating 90 **To** 2016 $21 ○

Blue Rock Wines ★★★★

PO Box 692, Williamstown, SA 5351 **Region** Eden Valley
T 0419 817 017 **www**.bluerockwines.com **Open** Not
Winemaker Zissis Zachopoulos **Est.** 2005 **Dozens** 4000 **Vyds** 15ha
This is the venture of the brothers Zachopoulos: Nicholas, Michael and Zissis, the last with a double degree – viticulture and wine science – from CSU. Michael and Nicholas manage the 104ha property, situated in the Eden Valley at an elevation of 475m. Most blocks are north-facing, the slopes providing frost protection with their natural air drainage, the soils likewise rich and free-draining. The vineyards have been planted so far to mainstream varieties, with an ongoing planting program extending to 8ha of tempranillo, pinot gris, pinot noir, grenache and mataro. Most of the 450–500-tonne production is the subject of a sales agreement with Grant Burge. 75 tonnes are retained each year to make the Blue Rock wines.

ŸŸŸŸŸ **Eden Valley Vineyard Series Cabernet Sauvignon 2012** A full-bodied, deeply coloured Eden Valley Cabernet, blackcurrant, spice tar and licorice bonded together by ripe, insistent tannins. These are very much in the arc of Cabernet. The sweet mystery is the price: it's one of the bargains of the year. Screwcap. 14% alc. **Rating** 94 **To** 2032 $15 ○

ŸŸŸŸŸ **Eden Valley Vineyard Series Sauvignon 2014 Rating** 92 **To** 2016 $15 ○
Eden Valley Vineyard Series Pinot Grigio 2014 Rating 90 **To** 2016 $15 ○

Boat O'Craigo ★★★★

458 Maroondah Highway, Healesville, Vic 3777 **Region** Yarra Valley
T (03) 5962 6899 **www**.boatocraigo.com.au **Open** Fri–Mon 10.30–5.30
Winemaker Rob Dolan (Contract) **Est.** 1998 **Dozens** 3000 **Vyds** 21.63ha
Steve Graham purchased the property, which is now known as Boat O'Craigo (a tiny place in a Scottish valley where his ancestors lived), in 2003. It has two quite separate vineyards: a hillside planting on one of the highest sites in the Yarra Valley, and one at Kangaroo Ground on the opposite side of the valley. Exports to Finland, China and Hong Kong.

ŸŸŸŸŸ **Black Spur Healesville Yarra Valley Sauvignon Blanc 2014** Has more to say than many Yarra Valley Sauvignon Blancs, in terms of both texture (even though solely fermented in stainless steel) and flavour; punchy citrus opens proceedings, then there's a flash of passionfruit, and a conclusion of minerally acidity, the unseen hand that provides texture. Screwcap. 13% alc. **Rating** 92 **To** 2016 $20 ○
Black Spur Healesville Yarra Valley Chardonnay 2013 The texture and mouthfeel of this wine take a millisecond to announce their presence after the wine is tasted, the flavours at an appealing midpoint between stone fruit and citrus. It doesn't need deconstruction, just a short sojourn in the fridge before cracking the cap. Screwcap. 13% alc. **Rating** 92 **To** 2020 $25 ○
Black Spur Healesville Yarra Valley Gewurztraminer 2014 Has sufficient rose petal, spice and lychee on the bouquet alone to attract followers, and the gently juicy, dry palate adds to the appeal. Screwcap. 13% alc. **Rating** 90 **To** 2017 $20 ○

ŸŸŸŸ **Black Spur Yarra Valley Pinot Noir 2013 Rating** 89 **To** 2020 $25

Boireann ★★★★★

26 Donnellys Castle Road, The Summit, Qld 4377 **Region** Granite Belt
T (07) 4683 2194 **www**.boireannwinery.com.au **Open** Fri–Sun 10–4
Winemaker Peter Stark **Est.** 1998 **Dozens** 1200 **Vyds** 1.6ha

Peter and Therese Stark have a 10ha property set among the great granite boulders and trees that are so much a part of the Granite Belt. They have planted no fewer than 11 varieties, including four that go to make the Lurnea, a Bordeaux blend; shiraz and viognier; grenache and mourvedre providing a Rhône blend; and a straight merlot. Tannat, pinot noir (French) and sangiovese, barbera and nebbiolo (Italian) make up the viticultural League of Nations. Peter is a winemaker of exceptional talent, producing cameo amounts of quite beautifully made red wines that are of a quality equal to Australia's best. Peter says he has decided to think about retiring, and has listed the property for sale.

ɤɤɤɤɤ **Granite Belt Shiraz Viognier 2013** Bright hue; a fragrant bouquet leads into a vibrant palate that has handsomely repaid the addition of viognier and maturation in French oak (50% new). It is a tribute to Peter Stark's intuitive approach, which has prevented the oak from obscuring the fruit. Screwcap. 13.5% alc. **Rating** 95 To 2023 $50

The Lurnea 2013 A 50/27/15/6/2% blend of merlot, cabernet, petit verdot, cabernet franc and tannat. Given the end of season rainfall, this is exceptional, the 50% French oak soaked up by the complex array of black and red fruits. Strongly reminiscent of Bordeaux. Screwcap. 13.5% alc. **Rating** 95 To 2028 $30 ✪

Granite Belt Cabernet Sauvignon 2013 You have to wait until the finish and aftertaste to find out what this wine has to offer; initially light cassis, mint and herb flavours manifest themselves, and the rapid expansion of those flavours comes as a surprise, as does the extreme length they engender. For the record, 25% new oak. Screwcap. 13% alc. **Rating** 95 To 2023 $28 ✪

Granite Belt Mourvedre 2013 Bright, full colour; has thoroughly enjoyed the vintage conditions; there's more flesh to the medium-bodied palate and more ripe tannins to support and add complexity to that fruit; admirable balance and length. Screwcap. 13.5% alc. **Rating** 95 To 2025 $30 ✪

Granite Belt Tannat 2013 Crimson-purple; how Peter Stark is able to produce such a diverse array of varietal wines, all with excellent rendition of varietal character, is beyond me; here is a full-bodied, full-blooded black fruit wine with sinuous tannins woven through. Screwcap. 13.5% alc. **Rating** 95 To 2033 $45

Granite Belt Shiraz 2013 An elegant wine from the first whiff through to the finish and aftertaste; the vintage had some challenges, but this hasn't precluded the spicy/peppery red and black fruits giving the wine juicy flavours bolstered by just-sufficient tannins. Screwcap. 13.5% alc. **Rating** 94 To 2023 $25 ✪

La Cima Granite Belt Sangiovese 2013 Light, but bright and clear colour; strongly varietal, with spicy/sour cherry aromas the mirror image of the palate; the tannins are evident, but firmly within the prism of Sangiovese: all present and correct. Screwcap. 12.5% alc. **Rating** 94 To 2020 $28 ✪

La Cima Superiore Granite Belt Barbera 2013 Deeper, yet more developed, colour; may have spent longer in barrel, and has the structure that its sibling lacks; the cherry fruit has a savoury/olive bite to it, all adding up to an unusually interesting Barbera. Screwcap. 13.5% alc. **Rating** 94 To 2023 $28 ✪

ɤɤɤɤɤ **La Cima Granite Belt Nebbiolo 2013** Rating 93 To 2022 $30

Botobolar ★★★

89 Botobolar Road, Mudgee, NSW 2850 **Region** Mudgee
T (02) 6373 3840 **www**.botobolar.com **Open** Thurs–Tues 11–4
Winemaker Kevin Karstrom **Est.** 1971 **Dozens** 3000 **Vyds** 19.4ha
One of the first organic vineyards in Australia, with present owner Kevin Karstrom continuing the practices established by founder (the late) Gil Wahlquist. Preservative-free reds and low-preservative dry whites extend the organic practice of the vineyard to the winery. Shiraz produces the best wines to appear under the Botobolar label, with gold medal success at the Mudgee Wine Show. A solar generator has been installed on the hill behind the winery in its first step towards lowering its carbon footprint. Exports to Denmark and Japan.

ɤɤɤɤ **Preservative Free Shiraz 2014** Organically grown on certified vineyards, and made organically. Deeply coloured, it is richly flavoured and textured, lacking a touch of polish perhaps, but revelling in the security afforded by the screwcap. Brett may always develop in a sulphur-free wine, but it's not there now. Screwcap. 12.5% alc. **Rating** 89 **To** 2016 $20

KK's Choice Mudgee Shiraz 2013 Estate-grown; matured for 20 months in American barriques. A full-bodied Shiraz in a style seldom seen these days, and which will strike a chord with some for that very reason. It can – indeed should – be given a chance to soften in bottle. Screwcap. 13.5% alc. **Rating** 89 **To** 2020 $25

Bowen Estate ★★★★

15459 Riddoch Highway, Coonawarra, SA 5263 **Region** Coonawarra
T (08) 8737 2229 **www.**bowenestate.com.au **Open** 7 days 10–5
Winemaker Emma Bowen **Est.** 1972 **Dozens** 12000 **Vyds** 33ha
Bluff-faced regional veteran Doug Bowen presides over one of Coonawarra's landmarks but he has handed over full winemaking responsibility to daughter Emma, 'retiring' to the position of viticulturist. Exports to the Maldives, Singapore, China, Japan and NZ.

♀♀♀♀♀ **Coonawarra Cabernet Sauvignon 2013** A convincing wine. High alcohol, but it comes across as well balanced. It tastes of blackcurrant, cedar wood, dusty Italian herbs and both warmed black olives and tar. It's generally eager to please, even given its ingrained ropes of firm tannin. There is, however, little doubt that if it could have been picked earlier a better result would have ensued. Screwcap. 15.5% alc. **Rating** 93 **To** 2026 $32 CM

Coonawarra Shiraz 2013 It fills the mouth with ripe, sweet, supple fruit and oak flavour but there's not a lot of magic beyond that. Blackberry and sweet plum, vanilla, chocolate. It carries the alcohol well, but even so, the finish feels simple. Screwcap. 15.5% alc. **Rating** 90 **To** 2023 $32 CM

♀♀♀♀ **Coonawarra Chardonnay 2014** **Rating** 88 **To** 2017 $23 CM

Box Grove Vineyard ★★★★

955 Avenel–Nagambie Road, Tabilk, Vic 3607 **Region** Nagambie Lakes
T 0409 210 015 **www.**boxgrovevineyard.com.au **Open** By appt
Winemaker Sarah Gough **Est.** 1995 **Dozens** 1800 **Vyds** 25ha
This is the venture of the Gough family, with industry veteran (and daughter) Sarah Gough managing the vineyard, winemaking and marketing. Having started with 10ha each of shiraz and cabernet sauvignon under contract to Brown Brothers, Sarah decided to switch the focus of the business to what could loosely be called 'Mediterranean varieties'. These days prosecco, vermentino, primitivo and roussanne (roussanne as both a table wine and a sparkling) are the main varieties, shiraz the one significant survivor of the original plantings. Exports to Asia.

♀♀♀♀♀ **Shiraz Roussanne 2012** The two varieties were estate-grown next to each other, harvested together, and co-fermented before maturation for 12 months in a mix of used and new French barriques. It works very well; there is a sprightly mouthfeel and spicy flavour to the black cherry shiraz fruit; it has very good length and balance, and doesn't require cellaring. Screwcap. 13.9% alc. **Rating** 94 **To** 2022 $28 ✪

♀♀♀♀♀ **Primitivo Saignee 2014** **Rating** 92 **To** 2016 $22 ✪
Late Harvest Viognier Roussanne 2013 **Rating** 92 **To** 2017 $22 ✪
Vermentino 2014 **Rating** 90 **To** 2017 $22
Primitivo 2013 **Rating** 90 **To** 2028 $28

Boynton's Feathertop ★★★★☆

Great Alpine Road, Porepunkah, Vic 3741 **Region** Alpine Valleys
T (03) 5756 2356 **www.**boynton.com.au **Open** 7 days 10–5
Winemaker Kel Boynton, Nick Toy **Est.** 1987 **Dozens** 8000 **Vyds** 14ha
Kel Boynton has a beautiful vineyard, framed by Mt Feathertop rising above it. The initial very strong American oak input has been softened in more recent vintages to give a better

fruit–oak balance. Kel has planted a spectacular array of varieties, headed by shiraz and pinot gris, merlot, savagnin, sauvignon blanc, nebbiolo and sangiovese, with smaller plantings of tempranillo, pinot noir, pinot meunier, vermentino, chardonnay, riesling, friulano, fiano, prosecco and semillon. Exports to Austria.

ŢŢŢŢŢ **Summit Cru Alpine Valley Riesling 2013** A surprise packet: gleaming quartz-green, it has a floral bouquet of citrus blossom followed by an elegant, lively and perfectly balanced palate, fruit and acidity entwined in a lovers' embrace. Screwcap. 11.5% alc. **Rating** 94 **To** 2023 $25 ✪
Pinot Gris 2014 Picked in two parcels, 5 days apart; the first used clear juice and cultured yeast, the second was wild-fermented on light solids, matured for 4 months on lees. All up, and impressive result, with both flavour (pear and nougat) and texture complexity. Screwcap. 13.5% alc. **Rating** 94 **To** 2016 $25 ✪

ŢŢŢŢ **Sauvignon Blanc 2014 Rating** 92 **To** 2016 $25 ✪
Limited Release Pinots 2013 Rating 91 **To** 2019 $30

Brand Group ★★★★

PO Box 18, Coonawarra, SA 5263 **Region** Coonawarra
T (08) 8736 3252 **www.**jimbrandwines.com.au **Open** Not
Winemaker Brand family, Bruce Gregory (Consultant) **Est.** 2000 **Dozens** 2000
Vyds 9.5ha
The Brand family story starts with the arrival of Eric Brand in Coonawarra in 1950. He married Nancy Redman and purchased a 24ha block from the Redman family, relinquishing his job as a baker and becoming a grapegrower. It was not until '66 that the first Brand's Laira wine was made. The family sold 50% of the Brand's Laira winery in '94 to McWilliam's, Jim Brand staying on as chief winemaker until he died in 2005, after a long battle with cancer, unable to fulfil his ambition to make quality wine under his name. Sam Brand is the fourth generation of this family, which has played a major role in Coonawarra for over 50 years, with wines made under the Jim Brand, Arm's Length Wine Co., and Ius Wines labels. To a lesser or greater degree, these businesses have a significant investment in export markets.

ŢŢŢŢŢ **Jim Brand Silent Partner Coonawarra Cabernet Sauvignon 2012** Sturdy tannin holds fresh blackcurrant and boysenberry flavours in firm place. Peppercorn, mint and tobacco-like notes add complexity. This wine isn't going anywhere in a hurry; it has mid to long-term cellarability oozing from its pores. Screwcap. 14.5% alc. **Rating** 94 **To** 2030 $33 CM

ŢŢŢŢ **Jim's Vineyard Coonawarra Shiraz 2012 Rating** 93 **To** 2025 $33 CM

Brand's Laira Coonawarra ★★★★★

Riddoch Highway, Coonawarra, SA 5263 **Region** Coonawarra
T (08) 8736 3260 **www.**brandslaira.com.au **Open** Mon–Fri 9–4.30, w'ends 10–4
Winemaker Peter Weinberg, Scott Colbert, Tim Perrin **Est.** 1966 **Dozens** NFP
Vyds 278ha
Part of a substantial investment in Coonawarra by McWilliam's, which first acquired a 50% interest from the Brand family, then increased it to 100%, and followed this with the purchase of 100ha of additional vineyard land. Significantly increased production of the smooth wines for which Brand's is known has followed. The estate plantings include the 100-year-old Stentiford block. Substantial changes for the better in the style and quality of the wines are evident with the 2012 and '13 vintages, and even more are on the way. Exports to select markets.

ŢŢŢŢŢ **One Seven One Cabernet Sauvignon 2012** A distinguished Coonawarra Cabernet with considerable cassis/blackcurrant and mulberry fruit, and also fine-grained built-in tannins that are not so commonly encountered. Perfect length, great balance. Screwcap. 14% alc. **Rating** 96 **To** 2032 $95
Old Station Riesling 2014 At one time Coonawarra had almost as much riesling planted (by Wynns) as shiraz or cabernet, but most has gone. It has a

fruit profile all of its own, with Jonathan apple and citrus sharing equal footing, supported by crisp, bright acidity. Coonawarra Riesling can perform its same magic with age as that of other regions – and this is a beautifully juicy wine to set the ball rolling. Screwcap. 12% alc. **Rating** 95 **To** 2024 $20 ✪

68 Vines Cabernet Sauvignon 2013 Cassis down to its bootstraps and up to its elbows, tannins and oak ladies in waiting. This is so full of brash fruit it's difficult to pin down now, but there is only promise in what lies ahead. Screwcap. 13% alc. **Rating** 94 **To** 2043 $60

ΨΨΨΨΨ **Foundation Chardonnay 2013** Rating 93 **To** 2020 $24 ✪
Blockers Cabernet Sauvignon 2013 Rating 91 **To** 2028 $22 ✪

Brangayne of Orange ★★★★☆

837 Pinnacle Road, Orange, NSW 2800 **Region** Orange
T (02) 6365 3229 **www**.brangayne.com **Open** Mon–Fri 11–4, Sat 11–5, Sun 11–4
Winemaker Simon Gilbert **Est.** 1994 **Dozens** 3000 **Vyds** 25.7ha
The Hoskins family (formerly orchardists) decided to move into grapegrowing in 1994 and have progressively established high-quality vineyards. Right from the outset, Brangayne has produced excellent wines across all mainstream varieties, ranging, remarkably, from Pinot Noir to Cabernet Sauvignon. It sells a substantial part of its crop to other winemakers.

ΨΨΨΨΨ **Isolde Reserve Chardonnay 2013** The best estate grapes are barrel-fermented and undergo partial mlf in French oak, the mlf working well here, leaving sufficient acidity to provide altogether superior structure to the white peach and apple flavours. Time is on its side. Screwcap. 13% alc. **Rating** 95 **To** 2022 $30 ✪

ΨΨΨΨΨ **Pinot Noir 2013** Rating 93 **To** 2021 $30
Cabernet Sauvignon 2012 Rating 93 **To** 2022 $30
Sauvignon Blanc 2014 Rating 92 **To** 2015 $22 ✪
Pinot Grigio 2014 Rating 92 **To** 2015 $20 ✪
Tristan Cabernet Sauvignon Shiraz Merlot 2012 Rating 92 **To** 2022 $32

Brash Higgins ★★★★★

California Road, McLaren Vale, SA 5171 **Region** McLaren Vale
T (08) 8556 4237 **www**.brashhiggins.com **Open** By appt
Winemaker Brad Hickey **Est.** 2010 **Dozens** 1000 **Vyds** 7ha
Move over TWE's 'vintrepreneurs', for Brad Hickey has come up with 'creator' and 'vinitor' to cover his role (together with that of partner Nicole Thorpe) in establishing Brash Higgins. His varied background, including 10 years as head sommelier at some of the best New York restaurants, then a further 10 years of baking, brewing and travelling to the best-known wine regions of the world, may provide some clue. More tangibly, he planted 4ha of shiraz, 2ha of cabernet sauvignon, and recently grafted 1ha of shiraz to nero d'Avola on his Omensetter Vineyard looking over the Willunga Escarpment. Exports to the US and Canada.

ΨΨΨΨΨ **SHZ Single Vineyard McLaren Vale Shiraz 2012** Hand-picked, basket-pressed, matured for 12 months in French hogsheads. Full purple-crimson, it has generosity built in to the tips of its toes; blackberry and a wrap of licorice and bitter chocolate are given further sustenance by ripe tannins and subtle oak; the length is a given once all the other boxes are as well ticked as here. Screwcap. 14.5% alc. **Rating** 95 **To** 2032 $37

GR/M Co-Ferment McLaren Vale Grenache Mataro 2013 A 70/30% blend of biodynamic fruit, co-fermented in an open fermenter for 14 days, matured for 8 months in French hogsheads. Good depth and hue; a complex and totally satisfying blend, with black cherry, red cherry and blood plum, in turn blessed by the beneficence of McLaren Vale chocolate. 100 dozen made. Screwcap. 14% alc. **Rating** 95 **To** 2028 $37

CBSV Single Vineyard McLaren Vale Cabernet Sauvignon 2012 Matured for 15 months in French hogsheads. Deeply coloured, this is a massive full-bodied

Cabernet that retains varietal character despite its size; blackcurrant, dried herbs, black olive and McLaren Vale dirt are all in play. Now stir in as many years of patience as possible. Screwcap. 14.5% alc. **Rating** 94 **To** 2042 $37

🍷🍷🍷🍷 R/SM Field Blend Riesling Semillon 2014 Rating 92 To 2024 $37

Brash Vineyard ★★★★

PO Box 1288, Dunsborough, WA 6281 **Region** Margaret River
T 0427 042 767 **www**.brashvineyard.com.au **Open** Not
Winemaker Bruce Dukes (Contract) **Est.** 1999 **Dozens** 250 **Vyds** 18.35ha
Brash Vineyard was established in 1998 as Woodside Valley Estate. While most of the grapes were sold to other Margaret River producers, Cabernet Sauvignon, Shiraz, Chardonnay and Merlot were made, and in '09 the Cabernet Sauvignon and the Shiraz earned the winery a 5-star rating. It is now owned by Chris and Anne Carter (managing partners, who live and work there), Brian and Anne McGuinness, and Rik and Jenny Nitert. The vineyard is now mature, and is producing high-quality fruit.

🍷🍷🍷🍷🍷 Single Vineyard Margaret River Sauvignon Blanc 2014 Watery colour with a green tinge. Settled, pure, elegant wine taken to the next tier by a final flourish of flavour. Gravel, gooseberry, spice and chalk. Fine wine from all angles. Screwcap. 12.9% alc. **Rating** 94 **To** 2016 $23 CM ✪
Single Vineyard Margaret River Cabernet Sauvignon 2013 Still counting its fingers and toes and growing into itself but there is much to be admired here already; the best well and truly yet to come. It tastes of rich blackcurrant, gravel, eucalypt and swish lacquered cedar wood, a wide paddle of tannin churning through. Screwcap. 14.3% alc. **Rating** 94 **To** 2033 $40 CM

Brave Goose Vineyard ★★★★

PO Box 852, Seymour, Vic 3660 **Region** Central Victoria Zone
T (03) 5799 1229 **www**.bravegoosevineyard.com.au **Open** By appt
Winemaker Nina Stocker **Est.** 1988 **Dozens** 250 **Vyds** 6.5ha
The Brave Goose Vineyard was planted in 1988 by former chairman of the Grape & Wine Research and Development Corporation Dr John Stocker and wife Joanne. In 1987 they found a property on the inside of the Great Dividing Range, near Tallarook, with north-facing slopes and shallow, weathered ironstone soils. They established 2.5ha each of shiraz and cabernet sauvignon, and 0.5ha each of merlot, viognier and gamay, selling the majority of the grapes, but making small amounts of Shiraz, Cabernet Merlot, Merlot, Viognier and Gamay under the Brave Goose label. The brave goose in question was the sole survivor of a flock put into the vineyard to repel cockatoos and foxes. Two decades on, Jo and John handed the reins of the operation to their winemaker daughter Nina and son-in-law John Day.

🍷🍷🍷🍷🍷 Shiraz 2012 This is a carefully managed, elegant style that befits the eminent viticultural/scientific standing of founder John Stocker. It lays the groundwork with precision, and each time you go back to the wine for a further taste, the better the balance, mouthfeel and varietal flavour spectrum work. Screwcap. 13.5% alc. **Rating** 94 **To** 2032 $25 ✪

🍷🍷🍷🍷 Cabernet Merlot 2012 Rating 93 To 2022 $25 ✪
Viognier 2013 Rating 91 To 2016 $25

Braydun Hill Vineyard ★★★☆

38–40 Hepenstal Road, Hackham. SA 5163 **Region** McLaren Vale
T (08) 8382 3023 **www**.braydunhill.com.au **Open** Thurs–Sun & public hols 11–4
Winemaker Rebecca Kennedy **Est.** 2001 **Dozens** 2000 **Vyds** 4.5ha
It is hard to imagine there would be such an interesting (and inspiring) story behind a vineyard planted between 1998 and '99 by the husband and wife team of Tony Dunn and Carol Bradley, wishing to get out of growing angora goats and into grapegrowing. The extension of the business into winemaking was totally unplanned, forced on them by the liquidation of

Normans in late 2001. With humour, courage and perseverance, they have met obstacles and setbacks which would have caused many to give up. Exports to Canada, Singapore and China.

🍷🍷🍷🍷🍷 **Single Vineyard Premium McLaren Vale Shiraz 2012** Matured in French and American oak for 2 years; gold medal Winewise Small Vignerons Awards '14. Unashamedly full-bodied, it has a bottomless pit of black fruits, yet is not over the top thanks to its moderate alcohol, which breathes life into the palate and finish. Will be very long-lived. Screwcap. 14% alc. **Rating** 94 **To** 2042 $35

🍷🍷🍷🍷 **Single Vineyard Premium McLaren Vale Shiraz 2005 Rating** 88 **To** 2017 $50

Bream Creek

Marion Bay Road, Bream Creek, Tas 7175 **Region** Southern Tasmania
T (03) 6231 4646 **www.**breamcreekvineyard.com.au **Open** At Dunalley Waterfront Café
Winemaker Winemaking Tasmania (Julian Alcorso) **Est.** 1974 **Dozens** 7000 **Vyds** 7.6ha
Until 1990 the Bream Creek fruit was sold to Moorilla Estate, but since then the winery has been independently owned and managed by Fred Peacock, legendary for the care he bestows on the vines under his direction. Fred's skills have seen an increase in production and outstanding wine quality across the range, headed by the Pinot Noir. The list of trophies and gold, silver and bronze medals won is extensive. Fred's expertise as a consultant is in constant demand.

🍷🍷🍷🍷🍷 **Riesling 2014** Sweet and generous, with lime, mandarin and spice notes rushing/flooding through the palate, seducing as they flow. It will of course develop, but it's gorgeous already. Screwcap. 12.2% alc. **Rating** 94 **To** 2022 $28 CM ○

🍷🍷🍷🍷🍷 **Chardonnay 2012 Rating** 90 **To** 2019 $29 CM
Pinot Rose 2014 Rating 90 **To** 2016 $26 CM

Bremerton Wines

Strathalbyn Road, Langhorne Creek, SA 5255 **Region** Langhorne Creek
T (08) 8537 3093 **www.**bremerton.com.au **Open** 7 days 10–5
Winemaker Rebecca Willson **Est.** 1988 **Dozens** 38 000 **Vyds** 120ha
Bremerton has been producing wines since 1988. Rebecca Willson (Chief Winemaker) and Lucy Willson (Marketing Manager) became the first sisters in Australia to manage and run a winery. With 120ha of premium vineyards (80% of which goes into their own labels), under the guiding hand of viticulturist Ron Keelan (Rebecca's husband), they grow cabernet sauvignon, shiraz, verdelho, chardonnay, sauvignon blanc, malbec, merlot and petit verdot. Exports to most major markets.

🍷🍷🍷🍷🍷 **Walter's Reserve Cabernet 2010** Grapes hand-picked from the best estate block; after extended fermentation the wine is matured for 20 months in new French barriques, individual barrels then selected and blended. It has exceptional power, concentration and drive to its savoury black fruits and ripe tannins. Will be very long-lived. Cork. 15% alc. **Rating** 96 **To** 2040 $50 ○
Old Adam Langhorne Creek Shiraz 2012 The best parcels of the best blocks, 22 months in oak. It has a spiderweb of complexity, nothing especially obvious, rather an array of spice, dark chocolate, cedar and, at the centre of the web, deep black fruit and licorice flavours; the overall balance and length are excellent. Cork. 15% alc. **Rating** 95 **To** 2027 $50
Batonnage Langhorne Creek Shiraz Malbec 2013 Matured in French oak for 14 months, lees stirred (which is more common for barrel-fermented white wines). As luscious as it is complex, with a magic carpet of predominantly black fruits, spice, and whispers of bitter chocolate and licorice; the texture may well be the result of lees stirring, and is another feature of a handsomely worked wine. Screwcap. 14.5% alc. **Rating** 95 **To** 2033 $32 ○
Special Release Langhorne Creek Tempranillo Graciano 2013 No clue about the blend percentages or vinification. Good colour; an attractive light to

medium-bodied blend of juicy red cherry and raspberry fruit. Lovely now, so don't put it in the cellar. Screwcap. 13.5% alc. **Rating** 94 **To** 2017 $24 ●
Special Release Langhorne Creek Malbec 2013 Matured in Hungarian oak, with some barrels standing out from the others from the word go, kept on lees, and ultimately selected for this wine. Excellent full crimson colour; Langhorne Creek Malbec has always had a special character, with juicy plum/raspberry flavours and soft tannins. Screwcap. 14.5% alc. **Rating** 94 **To** 2022 $24 ●

♙♙♙♙♀ Batonnage Langhorne Creek Chardonnay 2013 Rating 93 To 2020 $32
Special Release Langhorne Creek Fiano 2014 Rating 93 To 2020 $24 ●
Special Release Langhorne Creek Lagrein 2013 Rating 93 To 2020 $24 ●
Special Release Vermentino 2014 Rating 92 To 2016 $24 ●
Coulthard Cabernet Sauvignon 2013 Rating 92 To 2033 $22 ●
Special Release Graciano 2013 Rating 92 To 2018 $24 ●
Special Release Mourvedre 2013 Rating 91 To 2023 $24
Selkirk Langhorne Creek Shiraz 2013 Rating 90 To 2020 $22
Special Release Langhorne Creek Barbera 2013 Rating 90 To 2020 $24

Bress ★★★★★

3894 Harmony Way, Harcourt, Vic 3453 **Region** Bendigo
T (03) 5474 2262 **www.**bress.com.au **Open** W'ends & public hols 11–5 or by chance
Winemaker Adam Marks, Kirilly Gordon **Est.** 2001 **Dozens** 6000 **Vyds** 17ha
Adam Marks has made wine in all parts of the world since 1991, and made the brave decision (during his honeymoon in 2000) to start his own business. Having initially scoured various regions of Australia for the varieties best suited to those regions, the focus has switched to three Central Victorian vineyards: in Bendigo, Macedon Ranges and Heathcote. The Harcourt vineyard in Bendigo is planted to riesling (2ha), shiraz (1ha) and 3ha of cabernet sauvignon and cabernet franc; the Macedon vineyard to chardonnay (6ha) and pinot noir (3ha); and the Heathcote vineyard to shiraz (2ha). Exports to Hong Kong, Singapore and China.

♙♙♙♙♙ Le Grand Coq Noir Single Vineyard Macedon Chardonnay 2014 The first top-tier single-vineyard Chardonnay from Bress; whole bunch-pressed direct to two new French hogsheads for fermentation and 6 months' maturation. Intense and tightly focused fruit has soaked up the oak, grapefruit dominant, white peach in second place; has superb length and balance, and will thrive with time in bottle. Screwcap. 12% alc. **Rating** 97 **To** 2024 $80 ●

♙♙♙♙♙ Silver Chook Yarra Valley Sauvignon Blanc 2014 The Yarra Valley and sauvignon blanc aren't always the bosom buddies the climate suggests they should be, but this wine shows it can be done, and does so with a vengeance. Barrel fermentation in French oak has amplified the ripe guava, gooseberry and pink grapefruit varietal flavours, and in doing so has built flesh and structure. Screwcap. 11.5% alc. **Rating** 96 **To** 2016 $25 ●
Silver Chook Limited Release Heathcote Vermentino 2014 Half conventionally fermented in stainless steel, the other half very unconventionally as whole bunches, a feat in itself. Blending the two components has produced a complex, fresh, high-flavoured wine without a scintilla of bitterness; an outstanding success and reward for bravery. Screwcap. 12% alc. **Rating** 95 **To** 2020 $27 ●
Le Grand Coq Noir Harcourt Valley Shiraz 2013 Fascinating wine, elegant and light to medium-bodied; on the one hand intense and complex, on the other spicy/foresty nuances are woven throughout the purple fruits of the long palate; the overall balance is very good thanks to controlled tannin and oak support. Screwcap. 14.5% alc. **Rating** 95 **To** 2028 $120
Silver Chook Heathcote & Bendigo Shiraz 2013 The Bress credo is to minimise additions to wines of any kind unless essential; this is a most attractive medium-bodied Shiraz with plush black cherry and plum fruit flowing through the supple palate, making it enjoyable from day one. Screwcap. 14% alc. **Rating** 94 **To** 2023 $25 ●

♙♙♙♙♀ Gold Chook Harcourt Valley Riesling 2014 Rating 92 To 2018 $27

Brian Fletcher Signature Wines

PO Box 8385, Angel Street, South Perth, WA 6951 **Region** Margaret River
T (08) 9368 4555 **www.**brianfletcherwines.com.au **Open** Not
Winemaker Brian Fletcher **Est.** 2012 **Dozens** 9000

Brian Fletcher began his winemaking career in 1978, graduating in oenology at CSU. He had an illustrious career in eastern Australia before moving to Margaret River to become chief winemaker for Evans & Tate. He has not left the region since that time, forming a partnership with the Calneggia family, major vineyard developers and owners in the region. The wines are made under the Naked Wines umbrella, whereby Naked Wines provides the capital required to make the wines and takes them at a guaranteed price. Exports to the US.

Reserve Margaret River Chardonnay 2014 Hand-picked, whole bunch-pressed, some solids, coolish ferment, lees stirred. Is there a barrel-fermented Chardonnay that's not a reserve, I wonder? This has a slightly smoky bouquet, a finely detailed mid-palate gaining more traction on the back-palate and finish, the fruit flavours mid-range. Screwcap. 13.5% alc. **Rating** 93 **To** 2022 $27 ✪

Reserve Margaret River Shiraz 2013 Includes some whole bunches. Has very good colour, and the whole-bunch component operates to lift the bouquet's complexity, and the flavour and mouthfeel of the black fruits; the tannins are soft, the balance good. Screwcap. 14.5% alc. **Rating** 92 **To** 2030 $28

El Cid Margaret River Tempranillo 2013 It took 10 years to persuade the vines to produce a commercial crop. The colour is deep, the flavour and structure of a charging bull; Fletcher had to have patience, now it is your turn. Screwcap. 14.5% alc. **Rating** 90 **To** 2033 $45

Briar Ridge Vineyard ★★★★★

Mount View Road, Mount View, NSW 2325 **Region** Hunter Valley
T (02) 4990 3670 **www.**briarridge.com.au **Open** 7 days 10–5
Winemaker Gwyneth Olsen **Est.** 1972 **Dozens** 8000 **Vyds** 39ha

Semillon and shiraz have been the most consistent performers, underlying the suitability of these varieties to the Hunter Valley. Briar Ridge has been a model of stability, and has the comfort of substantial estate vineyards from which it is able to select the best grapes. It also has not hesitated to venture into other regions, notably Orange. In 2013 Gwyneth (Gwyn) Olsen was appointed winemaker after an impressive career in Australia and NZ. In '12 she added the distinction of graduating as Dux of the AWRI Advanced Wine Assessment course to her CV. Exports to Canada.

H.R.B. Single Vineyard Hunter Valley Shiraz Pinot Noir 2013 H.R.B. honours Hunter Valley Burgundy; no blend percentages given, but estate-grown. The light, clear colour is entirely approachable, as are the predominantly red fruits; this wine has more Burgundian notes to it than many of its predecessors in the '50s (other than those of Maurice O'Shea). Great length and elegance are the marks of a truly lovely wine. Screwcap. 13% alc. **Rating** 96 **To** 2033 $60 ✪

Dairy Hill Single Vineyard Hunter Valley Shiraz 2013 Puts a modern cut and polish onto its Stockhausen sibling, primarily through maturation in French oak puncheons, but also through more scrupulous fruit selection, which leads directly into the wine; cellaring for less than 5 years would be a mortal sin, as this is headed for a canter over the next 30 years. Screwcap. 13.5% alc. **Rating** 95 **To** 2048 $60

Dairy Hill Single Vineyard Hunter Valley Semillon 2014 Said to be made only in the best vintages from the Dairy Hill block. It has most attractive Meyer lemon aromas and flavours, with wisps of herb and mineral establishing its sense of place; the alcohol is not an issue now, but suggests a 10-year horizon. Screwcap. 12% alc. **Rating** 94 **To** 2024 $35

Briar Hill Single Vineyard Hunter Valley Chardonnay 2014 While there is no shortage of flavour, the wine has a nice overlay of savoury, grapefruity minerality to its moving parts; it is lively and fresh, with good fruit/oak balance,

and should keep its shape and length for some time yet. Screwcap. 13% alc.
Rating 94 To 2022 $35

Signature Release Karl Stockhausen Hunter Valley Shiraz 2013 Good crimson hue; it's hard to avoid the cliche 'classic Hunter Valley Shiraz', for this is precisely what the wine is: moderate alcohol; medium to full-bodied; earthy/leathery/spicy nuances to the dark berry/plum fruit; firm but not hard tannins. Will evolve wonderfully over 5–10 years and beyond. Screwcap. 13.5% alc.
Rating 94 To 2028 $35

ŶŶŶŶŶ **Fume Blanc Semillon Sauvignon Blanc 2014** Rating 93 To 2024 $22 ○
Stockhausen Hunter Valley Chardonnay 2013 Rating 93 To 2018 $28

Brick Kiln   ★★★★☆

21 Greer St, Hyde Park, SA 5061 **Region** McLaren Vale
T (08) 8357 2561 **www**.brickiln.com.au **Open** At Red Poles Restaurant
Winemaker Linda Domas, Phil Christiansen **Est.** 2001 **Dozens** 1500 **Vyds** 8ha
This is the venture of Malcolm and Alison Mackinnon, Garry and Nancy Watson, and Ian and Pene Davey. They purchased the Nine Gums Vineyard in 2001; it had been planted to shiraz in 1995–96. The majority of the grapes are sold, with a lesser portion contract-made for the partners under the Brick Kiln label, which takes its name from the Brick Kiln Bridge adjacent to the vineyard. Exports to the UK, Canada, China, Hong Kong and Singapore.

ŶŶŶŶŶ **The Ingot McLaren Vale Shiraz 2013** A selection of the best three new French hogsheads of the standard wine. Here the inky colour is more vibrant on the rim, the perfume of cedary oak matched by similar dynamics on the palate; despite all its power and intensity, the wine has great elegance, finesse and length. 99 dozen made. Screwcap. 14.7% alc. Rating 96 To 2033 $85
McLaren Vale Shiraz 2013 Fermented in 2-tonne open fermenters for 10 days, basket-pressed, 20 months in American (80%) and French hogsheads (30% new). Deep, inky colour; an unashamedly full-bodied Shiraz with black fruits, licorice, bitter chocolate and a swish of oak all contributing, easily dealing with the challenge the tannins might otherwise have posed. 1000 dozen made. Screwcap. 14.8% alc. Rating 94 To 2033 $25 ○

ŶŶŶŶŶ **McLaren Vale Sparkling 2012** Rating 90 To 2015 $26 TS

Brindabella Hills   ★★★★

156 Woodgrove Close, Wallaroo, ACT 2618 **Region** Canberra District
T (02) 6230 2583 **www**.brindabellahills.com.au **Open** W'ends, public hols 10–5
Winemaker Dr Roger Harris, Brian Sinclair **Est.** 1986 **Dozens** 1500 **Vyds** 5ha
Distinguished research scientist Dr Roger Harris presides over Brindabella Hills, which increasingly relies on estate-produced grapes, with small plantings of riesling, shiraz, chardonnay, sauvignon blanc, merlot, sangiovese, cabernet sauvignon, cabernet franc and viognier. Wine quality has been consistently impressive.

ŶŶŶŶŶ **Canberra District Riesling 2014** Slowly coming to its feet but already shows excellent poise, flavour and length. Lime, sweet green apple and floral elements do the lifting. Its best is yet to come, but soft acidity is clearly a hallmark. Screwcap. 11.5% alc. Rating 92 To 2022 $25 CM ○
Canberra District Pinot Gris 2014 Not too heady, but bursting with flavour. Nashi pear, crunchy apple and spice. Pale straw-green and sits pretty in the glass, offers enticing aromatics and then delivers on the palate. Screwcap. 13% alc. Rating 92 To 2015 $25 CM ○

Brini Estate Wines

698 Blewitt Springs Road, McLaren Vale, SA 5171 (postal) **Region** McLaren Vale
T (08) 8383 0080 **www.**briniwines.com.au **Open** Not
Winemaker Adam Hooper (Contract) **Est.** 2000 **Dozens** 3800 **Vyds** 16.4ha
The Brini family has been growing grapes in the Blewitt Springs area of McLaren Vale since
1953. In 2000 John and Marcello Brini established Brini Estate Wines to vinify a portion
of the grape production; up to that time it had been sold to companies such as Penfolds,
Rosemount Estate and d'Arenberg. The flagship Limited Release Shiraz is produced from
dry-grown vines planted in 1947, the other wines from dry-grown vines planted in '64.
Exports to Canada, Vietnam, Hong Kong and China.

Limited Release Single Vineyard Sebastian Shiraz 2010 Best old-vine
selection; matured in French and American oak for 18 months. Deep colour
despite its age; blackberry and blood plum aromas do not prepare you for the
sheer power of the full-bodied palate; here black forest fruits are the drivers,
Blewitt Springs chocolate provides the statement of place – and of the future.
Screwcap. 14.5% alc. **Rating** 95 To 2030 $50
Sebastian Single Vineyard McLaren Vale Shiraz 2009 Matured in French
and American oak for 12 months. The retention of crimson-purple hue in a
6yo wine is remarkable; here dark chocolate does make itself obvious, together
with spice, and a full hand of red and black fruits – and a touch of licorice for
good measure. '09 was in some ways a forgotten vintage, overshadowed by '10.
Screwcap. 14.5% alc. **Rating** 94 To 2029 $28 ○

Blewitt Springs Single Vineyard Shiraz 2012 Rating 93 To 2027 $21 ○
Single Vineyard McLaren Vale Grenache 2012 Rating 90 To 2022 $21 ○

Brockenchack

13/102 Burnett Street, Buderim, Qld 4556 **Region** Eden Valley
T (07) 5458 7700 **www.**brockenchack.com.au **Open** By appt
Winemaker Shawn Kalleske **Est.** 2007 **Dozens** 3000 **Vyds** 16ha
Trevor (and wife Marilyn) Harch have long been involved in liquor distribution in Qld,
owning one of Australia's leading independent liquor wholesalers. Over the years, he became
a regular visitor to the Barossa/Eden Valley, and in 1999 purchased the Tanunda Cellars Wine
Store. In 2007, Trevor and Marilyn purchased a vineyard in the Eden Valley and retained
Shawn Kalleske as winemaker. The vineyard has 8ha of shiraz, 2ha each of riesling and
cabernet sauvignon, and 1.3ha each of pinot noir, pinot gris and chardonnay. The name of the
business is appropriately Delphic. The vast majority of wines released are labelled in honour
of one or other of the Harch's family. Brockenchack comes from the first names of the four
grandchildren: Bronte, Mackenzie, Charli and Jack. Exports to Japan and NZ.

Jack Harrison Single Vineyard Eden Valley Shiraz 2012 There is no
question: good Eden Valley Shiraz has a radically different profile from most from
the Barossa Valley; there's a spicy, savoury elegance that establishes the ground rules
which highlight the varietal expression. This gains power on the silky/juicy back-
palate and finish with its array of summer berry fruits of every description. This is
a lovely wine. Screwcap. 14.5% alc. **Rating** 96 To 2037 $58 ○
William Frederick Single Vineyard Eden Valley Shiraz 2011 Exceptional
colour for an '11, bright and deep; the palate, too, proclaims its place and variety,
not the vintage; black fruits have ripe tannins interwoven throughout, the finish
long and balanced. The answer to the paradox is berry by berry selection and a
total make of 30 dozen. Screwcap. 13.5% alc. **Rating** 96 To 2036 $150
Zip Line Single Vineyard Eden Valley Shiraz 2012 A 10-day open ferment
was basket-pressed to used French hogsheads for 18 months' maturation, allowing
the high-quality fruit to convincingly express its terroir. It has exceptional length
and drive through its black fruits and complex, savoury tannins. A great vintage,
and great value. Screwcap. 14.5% alc. **Rating** 95 To 2032 $24 ○
William Frederick Single Vineyard Eden Valley Shiraz 2009 This is the
third time this wine has been tasted, and it continues its slow march towards full

maturity. Brockenchack points out that it wasn't released until May '14, and that its price has been reduced from $169.65 to $150. Eminently suited to children born in '09, even on their 30th birthday. There's no question: it's a good wine. Screwcap. 14.5% alc. **Rating** 95 **To** 2039 $150

ŶŶŶŶŶ **Mackenzie William 1896 Riesling 2014 Rating** 93 **To** 2024 $19 ✪

Broken Gate Wines ★★★☆

57 Rokeby Street, Collingwood, Vic 3066 **Region** South Eastern Australia
T (03) 9417 5757 **www**.brokengate.com.au **Open** Mon–Fri 8–5
Winemaker Josef Orbach **Est.** 2001 **Dozens** 50 000
Broken Gate is a Melbourne-based multi-regional producer, specialising in cool-climate reds and whites. Founder Josef Orbach lived and worked in the Clare Valley from 1994 to '98 at Leasingham, and completed a winemaking degree at the University of Melbourne in 2010. His is a classic negociant business, buying grapes and/or wines from various regions; the wines may be either purchased in bulk, then blended and bottled by Orbach, or purchased as cleanskins. Exports to Canada, Thailand, Singapore and China.

ŶŶŶŶŶ **Side Gate Organic Clare Valley Riesling 2014** If you want a generously flavoured Riesling with good varietal character and balance to drink now or later at a price that won't get you in strife with the bank or your partner, go no further. Screwcap. 12.5% alc. **Rating** 90 **To** 2017 $15 ✪

ŶŶŶŶ **Side Gate Adelaide Hills Sauvignon Blanc 2014 Rating** 89 **To** 2015 $15 ✪
Side Gate Geelong Pinot Noir 2012 Rating 88 **To** 2019 $17 ✪
Side Gate Mount Lofty Cabernet Shiraz 2009 Rating 88 **To** 2019 $15 ✪

Brokenwood ★★★★★

401–427 McDonalds Road, Pokolbin, NSW 2321 **Region** Hunter Valley
T (02) 4998 7559 **www**.brokenwood.com.au **Open** 7 days 9.30–5
Winemaker Iain Riggs, Stuart Hordern **Est.** 1970 **Dozens** 100 000 **Vyds** 64ha
This deservedly fashionable winery, producing consistently excellent wines, has kept Graveyard Shiraz as its ultimate flagship wine, while extending its reach through many of the best regions for its broad selection of varietal wine styles. Its big-selling Hunter Semillon provides the volume to balance the limited quantities of the flagships ILR Semillon and Graveyard Shiraz. Next there is a range of wines coming from regions including Beechworth (a major resource from the associated Indigo Vineyard), Orange, Central Ranges, McLaren Vale, Cowra and elsewhere. In 2015 Iain Riggs celebrated his 60th birthday, and his 33rd vintage at the helm of Brokenwood, offering a unique mix of winemaking skills, management of a diverse business, and an unerring ability to keep Brokenwood's high profile fresh and newsworthy. He has also contributed a great deal to various wine industry organisations. Exports to all major markets.

ŶŶŶŶŶ **ILR Reserve Hunter Valley Semillon 2009** Little or no colour change; the bouquet is quite aromatic, but still focused on primary fruit, not toast or honey; the palate is electrifying, drawing saliva from the mouth with its mix of unsweetened lemon juice/lemon zest and life-giving acidity, the DNA of great Semillon. Screwcap. 10.9% alc. **Rating** 97 **To** 2029 $70 ✪
Mistress Block Vineyard Hunter Valley Shiraz 2013 The 45yo vineyard on dark red soil is owned by Rod and Deeta McGeoch. This has a feline juiciness to its plum and black cherry fruit, with fine-grained tannins to match. This sends a big come-on message, not go away, I'm busy. By far the best of the medium-bodied Brokenwood Shirazs. Screwcap. 13.5% alc. **Rating** 97 **To** 2043 $90 ✪
Graveyard Vineyard Hunter Valley Shiraz 2013 The leader of the Brokenwood pack, matured in French oak. Deep crimson-purple; you can see the size of the castle, but the drawbridge is up, and the moat very deep. There is only one thing to do: buy as much as you/your partner can afford, and don't return for at least 5, preferably 10, years. This has the attributes of a great Graveyard, its balance and length unimpeachable. Screwcap. 13.5% alc. **Rating** 97 **To** 2053 $200

ŸŸŸŸŸ **Indigo Vineyard Beechworth Shiraz 2013** There is a warmth (in the best sense) and generosity to this supple wine, its bouquet perfumed, its medium-bodied palate filled with red and black cherry fruit, the tannins superfine, French oak singing quietly. A most attractive Shiraz from a moderate climate. Screwcap. 13.5% alc. **Rating** 96 **To** 2035 $65 ○

Maxwell Vineyard Hunter Valley Semillon 2009 Pale straw-green, little changed from its youth; the bouquet is reticent, the palate anything but, albeit very different from ILR. This wine has reached its first stage (or plenitude) of development, the fruit flavours of citrus and a hint of white peach, the acidity necessarily part of the picture. This is ready to drink, even though it has time on its side. Screwcap. 11% alc. **Rating** 96 **To** 2024 $55 ○

Oakey Creek Vineyard Hunter Valley Semillon 2013 The sandy loam soils of the vineyard are tailor-made for semillon. An immaculately balanced wine, just beginning its evolution from fresh-faced youth to adulthood. It's unusual to see a wine such as this released alongside 6-year-olds, but it does have all-important length and grip. Screwcap. 11% alc. **Rating** 95 **To** 2030 $40

Forest Edge Vineyard Orange Sauvignon Blanc 2014 There isn't another Orange Sauvignon Blanc within cooee of this wine in terms of style and (I fancy) quality. It is a bundle of nervous energy, with grapefruit the Pied Piper leading gooseberry and green pineapple as they all rush across the palate. This is definitely a Semillon lover's Sauvignon Blanc. Screwcap. 11.5% alc. **Rating** 95 **To** 2018 $28 ○

Forest Edge Vineyard Orange Chardonnay 2014 Whole bunch pressing, wild yeast fermentation and maturation in French oak have all provided strands to weave the texture and structure of this elegant Chardonnay; the fruit flavours are sotto voce, on the citrus side of the range courtesy of grapefruit juice and pith, crossing back momentarily to white peach; has all the length and balance needed for top-class Chardonnay. Screwcap. 12.5% alc. **Rating** 95 **To** 2024 $55

Indigo Vineyard Beechworth Chardonnay 2014 Dijon clones, hand-picked, whole bunches, barrel-fermented in French oak (33% new). Does nothing to challenge the view that Beechworth is a first class region for chardonnay, something often forgotten in the context of Margaret River and Yarra Valley. The perfect balance of white peach and pink grapefruit, the palate long and unhurried. Screwcap. 12.5% alc. **Rating** 95 **To** 2025 $55

Verona Vineyard Hunter Valley Shiraz 2013 Verona Vineyard is situated directly across the road from the Brokenwood winery and originally planted in '68 on red clay, it has been in Brokenwood's care for 20 years. It has a wiry strength to its structure, black fruits and earthy tannins being pulled along relentlessly. Screwcap. 13.5% alc. **Rating** 95 **To** 2038 $75

Wade Block 2 Vineyard McLaren Vale Shiraz 2013 Matured for 20 months in French oak. It's a strange day when a wine with this intensity of flavour and structure says drink me before my Hunter Valley brethren, although it's a tight call. Savoury, earthy blackberry fruit has a substrate of licorice and 70% cacao chocolate. Screwcap. 14% alc. **Rating** 95 **To** 2038 $65

Hunter Valley Semillon 2014 Rating 94 **To** 2024 $25 ○
Indigo Vineyard Beechworth Pinot Noir 2013 Rating 94 **To** 2023 $55
Hunter Valley Shiraz 2013 Rating 94 **To** 2030 $50

Bromley Wines   ★★★★

PO Box 571, Drysdale, Vic 3222 **Region** Geelong
T 0487 505 367 **www**.bromleywines.com.au **Open** Not
Winemaker Darren Burke **Est.** 2010 **Dozens** 300
In his previous life, Darren Burke worked as an intensive care nurse in Australia and the UK, but at the age of 30 he fell to the allure of wine and enrolled in the Bachelor of Applied Science (Oenology) at Adelaide University. Thereafter he successively became graduate winemaker at Orlando, then at Alkoomi Wines, fitting in a vintage in Chianti. With two successful vintages in 2005 and '06 completed, and the impending birth of wife Tammy's

first child, the couple decided to move back to the east coast. There Darren worked at several wineries on the Bellarine Peninsula before taking up his winemaking post at Leura Park Estate. Says Darren, 'The essence of Bromley is family. All our wines carry names drawn from our family history. Family is about flesh and blood, sweat and tears, love and laughter.' Exports to Singapore.

𝟗𝟗𝟗𝟗𝟗 **Aria Geelong Chardonnay 2014** Delightful style. Apple, nougat, citrus and straw flavours wash through the palate, both fresh and seamless at once. It tends towards full-bodied but its firm, almost tense finish promotes an impression of tidy control. Screwcap. 13% alc. **Rating** 93 **To** 2020 $30 CM

Geelong Pinot Noir 2013 Not quite a party, but it's a vocal gathering of flavours. Tangy tangerine and sweet-sour cherries, flings of spice. Presser mentions 'red grapefruit' and it's not a bad description. It's a vigorous Pinot Noir, sweet and savoury, almost jubey, but then positively dry through the finish. It pulls you this way and that, like watching the TV and listening to the radio at the same time. Screwcap. 12.5% alc. **Rating** 93 **To** 2022 $38 CM

Brook Eden Vineyard ★★★★★

167 Adams Road, Lebrina, Tas 7254 **Region** Northern Tasmania
T (03) 6395 6244 **www.**brookeden.com.au **Open** 7 days 11–5 Sept–May
Winemaker Winemaking Tasmania **Est.** 1988 **Dozens** 1000 **Vyds** 2.1ha
At 41° south and an altitude of 160m, Brook Eden is one of the coolest sites in Tasmania, and represents 'viticulture on the edge'. While the plantings remain small (1ha pinot noir, 0.8ha chardonnay and 0.3ha pinot gris), yield has been significantly reduced, resulting in earlier picking and better-quality grapes.

𝟗𝟗𝟗𝟗𝟗 **Pinot Noir 2012** Great saturated crimson hue; a battle royal in Tasmania between '12 and '13 Pinots; for Brook Eden, this gets a short half head victory; it has majestic depth to the dark cherry and plum fruit, yet is as supple and long in the mouth as the '13, tannins and oak doing their part, but without making a song and dance about it. Screwcap. 13.5% alc. **Rating** 96 **To** 2023 $38 ✪

Rosso 2013 Why you would want to take Pinot Noir off the front label, substitute Rosso (and its Italianate connotations) I have no idea, but the back label does admit Pinot. The wine is awash with strawberry and red cherry fruit as it glides along the tongue, spice appearing on the finish, which will increase in volume as the wine ages. Screwcap. 13.5% alc. **Rating** 95 **To** 2025 $25 ✪

Riesling 2013 The imperatives for making the wine all turn on Tasmanian acidity, thus the alcohol is moderately high, earlier picking bringing excessive acidity unless it is balanced by lots of residual sugar. Here these two parts – acidity and residual sugar – are neatly balanced, the wine showing plenty of apple and citrus fruit. Screwcap. 12.6% alc. **Rating** 94 **To** 2025 $27 ✪

Rosato 2013 Salmon-pink; a flowery strawberry bouquet suggesting pinot noir, the palate following suit. All up, there is considerable intensity to the wine. The palate is long and fruity, yet finishing dry. Very good rose. Screwcap. 13.3% alc. **Rating** 94 **To** 2016 $23 ✪

𝟗𝟗𝟗𝟗𝟗 **Jan's Tank Chardonnay 2013 Rating** 93 **To** 2023 $38

Brookland Valley ★★★★★

Caves Road, Wilyabrup, WA 6280 **Region** Margaret River
T (08) 9755 6042 **www.**brooklandvalley.com.au **Open** 7 days 10–5
Winemaker Courtney Treacher **Est.** 1984 **Dozens** NFP
Brookland Valley has an idyllic setting, plus its café and Gallery of Wine Arts, which houses an eclectic collection of wine, food-related art and wine accessories. After acquiring a 50% share of Brookland Valley in 1997, Hardys moved to full ownership in 2004; it is now part of Accolade Wines. The quality, value for money and consistency, of the wines is exemplary.

ŶŶŶŶŶ **Reserve Margaret River Cabernet Sauvignon 2012** A strictly limited production version of its estate blood brother, based on fruit and (ultimately) barrel selection. The fruit, tannin and oak balance trips towards the beautifully detailed cassis and plum fruit, and away from tannins, giving this wine the elegance its brother lacks at this stage. Screwcap. 13.5% alc. **Rating** 96 **To** 2042 $75 **◐**

Margaret River Chardonnay 2013 Estate-grown, hand-picked, whole bunch-pressed, barrel-fermented in French oak, matured on lees for 9 months. Has more elegance than many of its regional counterparts, its flavours balanced between white peach and grapefruit, with just a hint of creamy cashew. Will mature with extreme grace. Screwcap. 13.5% alc. **Rating** 95 **To** 2022 $42

Margaret River Cabernet Sauvignon Merlot 2012 Estate-grown, hand-picked, open-fermented, basket-pressed and matured in French oak for 14 months. Has a fragrant bouquet of cassis that leads directly into the flavours of the fore-palate before persistent savoury tannins provide a powerful backdrop to the cassis. Will richly repay cellaring. Screwcap. 13.5% alc. **Rating** 94 **To** 2032 $50

ŶŶŶŶŶ **Margaret River Semillon Sauvignon Blanc 2014** **Rating** 90 **To** 2016 $15 **◐**

Brown Brothers ★★★★★

Milawa–Bobinawarrah Road, Milawa, Vic 3678 **Region** King Valley
T (03) 5720 5500 **www.**brownbrothers.com.au **Open** 7 days 9–5
Winemaker Wendy Cameron, Joel Tilbrook, Cate Looney, Geoff Alexander, Chloe Earl
Est. 1885 **Dozens** Over 1 million **Vyds** 570ha
Draws upon a considerable number of vineyards spread throughout a range of site climates, ranging from very warm to very cool. An expansion into Heathcote added significantly to its armoury. In 2010 Brown Brothers took a momentous step, acquiring Tasmania's Tamar Ridge for $32.5 million. It is known for the diversity of varieties with which it works, and the wines represent good value for money. Deservedly one of the most successful family wineries – its cellar door receives the greatest number of visitors in Australia. A founding member of Australia's First Families of Wine. Exports to all major markets.

ŶŶŶŶŶ **125 Years Special Release Reserve Pinot Noir 2012** From estate-owned vineyards in the Tamar Valley and East Coast. The colour isn't deep, but the wine is fragrant and extremely intense on the long palate that provides an interplay between dark cherry flavours and spicy/savoury tannins. Screwcap. 13.5% alc. **Rating** 96 **To** 2027 $80

125 Years Special Release King Valley Shiraz Mondeuse Cabernet Sauvignon 2008 Harks back to the Everton Hills blends of '61 and '62, once having pride of place in my cellar, but I didn't know that John Charles Brown co-fermented the varieties. This rich, superbly balanced, medium-bodied wine is still very youthful, and is clearly destined for a very long life, feeding from its storehouse of smoky/spicy black fruits, these in turn sustained by ripe tannins. Screwcap. 14.5% alc. **Rating** 96 **To** 2033 $80

Limited Release Single Vineyard Heathcote Durif 2013 Ribald purple. Announces itself as alive, well, and ready to party from the first splash into the glass. It's fragrant, lively, bursting with dark fruit flavour and unafraid of both flashy oak and a hum of tannin. It's hard to know whether it's marriage material or a one-night stand; it has its paws poised over all bases. In the overall scheme, the asking price offers enormous value. Screwcap. 14% alc. **Rating** 95 **To** 2025 $21 CM **◐**

Patricia Pinot Noir Chardonnay Brut 2008 The lauded, historic Whitlands vineyard high in the alpine foothills of the King Valley infuses this outstanding vintage with an acid structure of vivacity, drive and longevity, sustaining lively lemon, pear, apple and white peach fruit. Age has drawn out its wonderfully toasty, honeyed nougat character. It's at once silky, fleshy and textured, yet resolutely tense and refreshing, making for a captivating accord, testimony to the character of site and skilled craftsmanship. Cork. 13% alc. **Rating** 94 **To** 2018 $46 TS

ŸŸŸŸŸ **18 Eighty Nine Cabernet Sauvignon 2012** Rating 91 To 2020 $19 **۞**
18 Eighty Nine Tempranillo 2013 Rating 91 To 2023 $18 **۞**
King Valley Vintage Prosecco 2014 Rating 91 To 2015 $23 TS **۞**
18 Eighty Nine Shiraz 2013 Rating 90 To 2019 $19 CM **۞**

Brown Hill Estate

Cnr Rosa Brook Road/Barrett Road, Rosa Brook, WA 6285 **Region** Margaret River
T (08) 9757 4003 **www.**brownhillestate.com.au **Open** 7 days 10–5
Winemaker Nathan Bailey, Haydn Millard **Est.** 1995 **Dozens** 3000 **Vyds** 22ha
The Bailey family is involved in all stages of wine production, with minimum outside help.
Their stated aim is to produce top-quality wines at affordable prices, via uncompromising
viticultural practices emphasising low yields. They have shiraz and cabernet sauvignon (8ha
each), semillon, sauvignon blanc and merlot (2ha each). The quality of the best wines in
the portfolio is exemplary, and the value for money of the wines selling for less than $20
is mouth-watering.

ŸŸŸŸŸ **Signature Range Bill Bailey Margaret River Shiraz Cabernet 2012**
A 50/50% blend matured for 18 months in French oak (30% new). The grapes
were picked 4 weeks later than usual (global warming?), giving the wine intensity
and length; vibrant red and black cherry are the flavour drivers, along with cassis
ex the cabernet; the ripe tannins are precisely balanced to lengthen the finish.
Screwcap. 14.5% alc. **Rating** 96 To 2032 $50 **۞**
Golden Horseshoe Margaret River Chardonnay 2014 Hand-picked and
chilled overnight, whole bunch-pressed next day, barrel-fermented in French
barriques (60% new), matured for 9 months. Fresh and vital, the wine has
relegated the oak to the backdrop, its citrus and white-fleshed stone fruit running
through the long, fine finish. Screwcap. 13.5% alc. **Rating** 95 To 2021 $35 **۞**
Croesus Reserve Margaret River Merlot 2013 Cold soak, 20% juice run off
prior to the end of ferment into barrel, then back-blended; matured 18 months
in French oak (30% new). This is a serious Merlot, with a mix of redcurrant,
blackcurrant, black olive and plum all making an appearance, finishing with
peremptory tannins. Needs patience. Screwcap. 14% alc. **Rating** 95 To 2028 $35 **۞**
Signature Range Perseverance Margaret River Cabernet Merlot 2012
A 70/30% blend with 18 months in French oak (30% new). It is very powerful
and very youthful, but has the balance to flourish over the next 5+ years before
entering its plateau; cassis, black cherry and touches of spice all point to the
grapes being picked at precisely the right time. Screwcap. 14% alc. **Rating** 95
To 2032 $50
Ivanhoe Reserve Margaret River Cabernet Sauvignon 2013 10-day
fermentation, then 20 days' maceration before pressing to tank for mlf; 18 months'
maturation in French oak. It is quite remarkable how all the details put this wine
into another category, the keywords balance and harmony, cassis fruit, cedary oak
and integrated, ripe cabernet tannins virtually taken for granted. Screwcap. 14% alc.
Rating 95 To 2033 $30 **۞**
Charlotte Margaret River Sauvignon Blanc 2014 Hand-picked, chilled
to 5°C, whole bunch-pressed; cool-fermented in stainless steel. Has sparkling
waves of gooseberry, passionfruit and snow pea, citrussy acidity on the long finish.
Exceptional value. Screwcap. 12.5% alc. **Rating** 94 To 2015 $17 **۞**
Fimiston Reserve Margaret River Shiraz 2013 Hand-picked, destemmed
and crushed to tanks, 20% drained off to barrels to finish fermentation; matured
in French oak (40% new). Strong crimson-purple; it has a complex bouquet and
medium-bodied palate, with blackberry and a juicy hint of licorice matched by
well-integrated and balanced oak. Screwcap. 14% alc. **Rating** 94 To 2028 $30 **۞**
**Signature Range Great Boulder Margaret River Cabernet Shiraz Merlot
Malbec 2012** 3 tonnes per ha, hand-picked; cabernet and merlot fermented
separately, shiraz and cabernet co-fermented; matured for 18 months in French
oak (40% new). The blend has invested the palate with both textural and flavour

complexity; black olive, spice, polished leather and cedar accompany black cherry and blackcurrant fruit. Screwcap. 14% alc. **Rating** 94 **To** 2030 $40

𝍬𝍬𝍬𝍬𝍬 **Lakeview Sauvignon Blanc Semillon 2014** Rating 93 To 2016 $17 ✪
Hannans Cabernet Sauvignon 2013 Rating 93 To 2028 $19 ✪
Morning Star Dry Light Red 2014 Rating 91 To 2015 $17 ✪

Brown Magpie Wines   ★★★★★
125 Larcombes Road, Modewarre, Vic 3240 **Region** Geelong
T (03) 5266 2147 **www**.brownmagpiewines.com **Open** 7 days Jan 11–4, w'ends 11–4 Nov–Apr
Winemaker Loretta and Shane Breheny **Est.** 2000 **Dozens** 5000 **Vyds** 9ha
Shane and Loretta Breheny's 20ha property is situated predominantly on a gentle, north-facing slope, with cypress trees on the western and southern borders providing protection against the wind. Vines were planted over 2001–02, with pinot noir (4ha) taking the lion's share, followed by pinot gris and shiraz (2.4ha each) and 0.1ha each of chardonnay and sauvignon blanc. Viticulture is Loretta's love; winemaking (and wine) is Shane's.

𝍬𝍬𝍬𝍬𝍬 **Paraparap Single Vineyard Reserve Geelong Pinot Noir 2013** Only two barrels of this deeply coloured Pinot were made, given extra months in toasty French oak. This was a correct response to layers of powerful red cherry and plum fruit; the end result is a wine of exceptional power and length. Please cellar this for at least 5 years, and you will be rewarded on earth if not in heaven. Screwcap. 14.1% alc. **Rating** 96 **To** 2025 $40 ✪
Paraparap Single Vineyard Reserve Geelong Pinot Noir 2012 Has the Brown Magpie hallmarks of style and clear-cut varietal expression. Time in bottle has brought the accompanying complexity to the fore, some forest floor alongside spicy cherry fruit. Its greatest strength is the extreme length of its palate and lingering aftertaste. Screwcap. 13.2% alc. **Rating** 96 **To** 2022 $40 ✪
Single Vineyard Geelong Shiraz 2013 Full crimson-purple; a totally delicious medium-bodied Shiraz, at once lusciously juicy, yet refined; glossy black cherry fruit is punctuated with notes of spice, licorice, and lingering juniper berry; the French oak and tannins are there, but do no more than provide a backdrop for the fruit. Screwcap. 13.9% alc. **Rating** 96 **To** 2033 $30 ✪
Modewarre Mud Single Vineyard Reserve Geelong Shiraz 2013 Makes you sit up and take notice from the first sip (or whiff); a two-barrel selection, with a fragrant dark cherry/berry bouquet, the tangy, medium-bodied palate lifted by spice, anise and vibrant fruit. Brown Magpie is on a roll. Screwcap. 13.9% alc. **Rating** 96 **To** 2033 $45 ✪
Single Vineyard Geelong Pinot Noir 2013 Good clarity and hue; Brown Magpie is a model of consistency with its elegant but satisfying style of Pinot Noir, the bouquet and palate offering a clearly varietal mix of plum and cherry fruit backed by nuances of spice and forest/truffle; the mouthfeel and balance are right on the money. Screwcap. 14% alc. **Rating** 95 **To** 2023 $27 ✪

𝍬𝍬𝍬𝍬𝍬 **Single Vineyard Geelong Rose 2014** Rating 92 To 2016 $18 ✪

Brygon Reserve   ★★★★☆
529 Osmington Road, Margaret River, WA 6280 **Region** Margaret River
T 1800 754 517 **www**.brygonreservewines.com.au **Open** W'ends 10–5
Winemaker David Longden **Est.** 2009 **Dozens** NFP
Since its establishment in 2009 by Robert and Laurie Fraser-Scott, this business has grown very rapidly, although details of its production are not available. Having originally relied on contract winemaking, it opened a winery and cellar door in February '15. The winery has its own bottling plant and bulk wine storage facilities, with at least some of the wine produced under contract elsewhere in Margaret River. The plethora of wines are under six major brands: Hummingbird, The Bruce, Brygon Reserve, Flying High, Third Wheel and Mirror Image. There are some ancillary brands used in export or special markets, thus not sold through

retail outlets in Australia. Exports to the US, Vietnam, Macau, Taiwan, Thailand, Hong Kong, Singapore and China.

ΨΨΨΨΨ **Third Wheel Reserve Margaret River Cabernet Sauvignon 2013** Bright crimson-purple colour is a sign of things to come: this is a supple, medium-bodied cabernet that has considerable purity to its cassis-dominated fruit profile; there are sufficient fine tannins, and the oak contribution is balanced. Screwcap. 13.5% alc. **Rating** 94 **To** 2027 $25 ✪

ΨΨΨΨΨ **Brygon Reserve Flying High Cabernet Merlot 2013** Rating 92 To 2028 $20 ✪
Brygon Reserve Flying High Semillon Sauvignon 2014 Rating 91 To 2017 $20 ✪
Brygon Reserve The Bruce Chardonnay 2013 Rating 90 To 2019 $20 ✪
Birds of a Feather Hummingbird Series Chardonnay 2013 Rating 90 To 2016 $20 ✪
Brygon Reserve Bin 882 Shiraz 2012 Rating 90 To 2025 $20 ✪
Brygon Reserve The Bruce Cabernet Merlot 2013 Rating 90 To 2024 $20 ✪
Birds of a Feather Hummingbird Series Cabernet Shiraz Merlot 2012 Rating 90 To 2025 $20 ✪

BTP   ★★★★

28 Jenke Road, Marananga, SA 5355 (postal) **Region** Barossa Valley/Adelaide Hills
T 0411 861 604 **Open** Not
Winemaker Tom White **Est.** 2009 **Dozens** 5000 **Vyds** 8.2ha
Owners Tom and Bridget White established Mt Jagged Wines (see separate entry) in 1989, producing cool-climate styles. In 2008 Tom decided to move outside his comfort zone, and focus on warmer climate shiraz, predominantly from the Barossa and Eden valleys. The other string to his bow is a single white wine, a blend of sauvignon blanc and pinot gris, coming from the Adelaide Hills.

ΨΨΨΨΨ **Barossa Valley Shiraz 2012** Finished fermentation in new and used French oak, matured for 14 months. Still has a deep and brightly hued colour that signals the full-bodied palate with layers of black fruits framed by spicy oak and powerful (albeit integrated) tannins. Not ready to open the door just yet. Screwcap. 14% alc. **Rating** 93 **To** 2032 $35

Buckshot Vineyard   ★★★★☆

PO Box 119, Coldstream, Vic 3770 **Region** Heathcote
T 0417 349 785 **www.**buckshotvineyard.com.au **Open** Not
Winemaker Rob Peebles **Est.** 1999 **Dozens** 700 **Vyds** 2ha
This is the venture of Meegan and Rob Peebles, and comes on the back of Rob's 20+ year involvement in the wine industry, including six vintages in Rutherglen, starting in 1993, followed by 10 years at Domaine Chandon, and squeezing in weekend work at Coldstream Hills' cellar door in '93. It is the soils of Heathcote, and a long-time friendship with John and Jenny Davies, that sees the flagship Shiraz, and a smaller amount of zinfandel (with some shiraz) coming from a small block, part of a 40ha vineyard owned by the Davies southwest of Colbinabbin. Rob makes the wines at Domaine Chandon. Exports to the US.

ΨΨΨΨΨ **Heathcote Shiraz 2012** Robust Shiraz showing strong, blackberried fruit infused with cloves and assorted dried herbs. Grunty and tannic but impeccably well balanced. Both floral notes and sweeter, jellied fruits rise in the glass as it breathes. In impeccable shape. Screwcap. 14% alc. **Rating** 94 **To** 2028 $31 CM

Bull Lane Wine Company   ★★★★★

PO Box 77, Heathcote, Vic 3523 **Region** Heathcote
T 0427 970 041 **www.**bulllane.com.au **Open** Not
Winemaker Simon Osicka **Est.** 2013 **Dozens** 400

After a successful career as a winemaker with what is now TWE, Simon Osicka, together with viticulturist partner Alison Phillips, returned to the eponymous family winery just within the eastern boundary of the Heathcote region in 2010. Spurred on by a decade of drought impacting on the 60-year-old dry-grown vineyard, and a desire to create another style of Shiraz, Simon and Alison spent considerable time visiting Heathcote vineyards with access to water in the lead-up to the '10 vintage. They ultimately decided to buy grapes from a cool slope on a vineyard owned by John Davies. It was intended that the first vintage should be in '11, but (ironically) the wet growing season precluded any idea of launching a new label with insufficient fruit flavour, so '12 (a wonderful vintage) produced the first wine. Exports to Denmark.

♥♥♥♥♥ **Heathcote Shiraz 2013** Deep, dark colour and flavour. Has its mojo rising. Peppercorns, blackberries, slinky plums and a shawl of coffeed, spicy, quality oak. Tannin adds extra revs. Excellent. Screwcap. 14.5% alc. **Rating** 95 **To** 2026 $28 CM ✪

Bulong Estate   ★★★☆

70 Summerhill Road, Yarra Junction, Vic 3797 (postal) **Region** Yarra Valley
T (03) 5967 1358 **www.**bulongestate.com.au **Open** 7 days 11–4
Winemaker Matt Carter **Est.** 1994 **Dozens** 2000 **Vyds** 31ha

Judy and Howard Carter's beautifully situated 45ha property looks down into the valley below and across to the nearby ranges, with Mt Donna Buang at their peak. Most of the grapes from the immaculately tended vineyard are sold, with limited quantities made onsite for the Bulong Estate label. The Bulong Estate restaurant, sharing the views, is open Fri–Sun. Exports to China.

♥♥♥♥♡ **Yarra Valley Pinot Gris 2014** Partial barrel fermentation and lees contact. A very good Pinot Gris; if served blind, could cause all sorts of confusion. Is it Sauvignon Blanc? Is it Chardonnay? Is it Pinot Gris, quite possibly the third choice? Whatever, a very well made Pinot Gris with real flavour, touched by complexity. Screwcap. 12.5% alc. **Rating** 93 **To** 2016 $21 ✪

♥♥♥♥ **Yarra Valley Sauvignon Blanc 2014 Rating** 89 **To** 2016 $21

Yarra Valley Pinot Noir 2013 Rating 88 **To** 2017 $26
Yarra Valley Cabernet Merlot 2012 Rating 88 **To** 2017 $24

Bundaleer Wines   ★★★★☆

PO Box 41, Hove, SA 5048 **Region** Southern Flinders Ranges
T (08) 8294 7011 **www.**bundaleerwines.com.au **Open** Little Red Grape, Sevenhill
Winemaker Angela Meaney **Est.** 1998 **Dozens** 4000 **Vyds** 7ha

Bundaleer is a joint venture between the Meaney and Spurling families, situated in an area known as Bundaleer Gardens, on the edge of the Bundaleer Forest, 200km north of Adelaide. The red wines are produced from estate plantings (equal quantities of shiraz and cabernet sauvignon are planted), the white wines from purchased grapes from the Clare Valley. The current releases from Bundaleer are a quantum leap in quality compared to those of previous years. Exports to Canada, Taiwan, Hong Kong and China.

♥♥♥♥♥ **Stony Place Clare Valley Riesling 2014** The vineyard that produces the grapes for this wine has an X-factor resulting in intense lemon and lime fruit, and even more striking citrus-linked acidity on the finish and long-lived aftertaste. A brilliant style that will age superbly, and proves the '13 was no fluke. Screwcap. 12% alc. **Rating** 95 **To** 2029 $20 ✪

ŢŢŢŢ♀ Hornsdale Mist Flinders Ranges Shiraz 2013 Rating 92 To 2021 $20
CM ○
Clare Valley Montepulciano 2014 Rating 92 To 2020 $25 CM ○

Bundaleera Vineyard

449 Glenwood Road, Relbia, Tas 7258 (postal) **Region** Northern Tasmania
T (03) 6343 1231 **Open** W'ends 10–5
Winemaker Pirie Consulting (Andrew Pirie) **Est.** 1996 **Dozens** 1000
David (a consultant metallurgist in the mining industry) and Jan Jenkinson have established
2.5ha of vines on a sunny, sheltered north to northeast slope in the North Esk Valley. The
12ha property on which their house and vineyard are established gives them some protection
from the urban sprawl of Launceston. Jan is the full-time viticulturist and gardener for the
immaculately tended property.

ŢŢŢŢ♀ Sparkling NV A sparkling Shiraz with intense black fruits of all kinds, licorice
and pepper. 18 months' maturation in older barrels and the addition of some
older Shiraz reserves heightens dark chocolate character, finely structured tannins
and persistence on an evenly balanced finish. Great value. Screwcap. 13.5% alc.
Rating 91 **To** 2016 $20 TS ○

Bunkers Margaret River Wines

1142 Kaloorup Road, Kaloorup, WA 6280 **Region** Margaret River
T (08) 9368 4555 **www**.bunkerswines.com.au **Open** Not
Winemaker Brian Fletcher **Est.** 2010 **Dozens** 5500 **Vyds** 34ha
Over the past 20+ years, Mike Calneggia has had his fingers in innumerable Margaret
River viticultural pies. He has watched some ventures succeed, and others fail, and while
Bunkers Wines (owned by Mike and Sally Calneggia) is only a small part of his viticultural
undertakings, it has been carefully targeted from the word go. It has the six mainstream
varieties (cabernet, semillon, merlot, chardonnay, sauvignon blanc and shiraz) joined by one
rising star, tempranillo, in the warm and relatively fertile northern part of the Margaret River.
He has Brian Fletcher as winemaker, and Murray Edmonds as viticulturist (both ex Evans &
Tate). Mike and daughter Amy are responsible for sales and marketing. They say, 'The world of
wine is full of serious people making serious wines for an ever-decreasing serious market ...
Bunkers wines have been created to put the "F" word back into wine: "FUN", that is.' Exports
to Canada and Hong Kong.

ŢŢŢŢ♀ Guillotines Shiraz 2013 Slightly reductive, but good value drinking. Plum,
charcoal and spice, fresh and modern, with enough power to satisfy without being
heavy or syrupy. Screwcap. 14.5% alc. **Rating** 92 **To** 2024 $20 CM ○
The Box Tempranillo 2013 Open-fermented, 25% matured in new American
oak for 1 year before blending with the stainless steel component. Purple-crimson;
the wine enters the mouth with a blast of red cherry fruit and vanillan oak,
finishing with powdery tannins. Screwcap. 14.5% alc. **Rating** 92 **To** 2018 $20 ○
Lefthanders Sauvignon Blanc Semillon 2014 Plenty of fruit around its
belly but it still manages to cut a fine figure. Lemongrass, gravel and tropical fruit
with a textural element and good push of flavour towards and through the finish.
Screwcap. 12.5% alc. **Rating** 91 **To** 2016 $20 CM ○
Honeycombs Chardonnay 2014 Night harvesting and cold-pressed clear juice
fermented in French oak result in a fresh, fruit-driven style with white peach and
melon flavours to the fore. Screwcap. 13.5% alc. **Rating** 90 **To** 2017 $20 ○

ŢŢŢŢ Bears Cabernet Merlot 2013 Rating 89 To 2019 $20 CM

Bunnamagoo Estate

603 Henry Lawson Drive, Mudgee, NSW 2850 **Region** Mudgee
T 1300 304 707 **www**.bunnamagoowines.com.au **Open** 7 days 10–4
Winemaker Robert Black **Est.** 1995 **Dozens** 60 000 **Vyds** 108ha

Bunnamagoo Estate (on one of the first land grants in the region) is situated near the historic town of Rockley. Here a 6ha vineyard planted to chardonnay, merlot and cabernet sauvignon has been established by Paspaley Pearls, a famous name in the WA pearl industry. The winery and cellar door are located at the much larger (and warmer) Eurunderee vineyard (102ha) at Mudgee. Exports to the UK, Singapore, Fiji, Papua New Guinea, Indonesia, Hong Kong and China.

ＴＴＴＴＴ **Semillon 2013** It has easily taken one step up the maturity ladder, with lime and the barest hint of honey starting to show through. The two vintages ('13 and '14) send a similar message: the wine is well worth the 5-year cellaring timeframe the Hunter Valley has established for its delayed release Semillons. Screwcap. 12.5% alc. **Rating** 93 **To** 2023 $22 ✪

1827 Handpicked Chardonnay 2013 Hand-picked, whole bunch-pressed, barrel-fermented in new and used French and Hungarian hogsheads. Has elegance and balance, but needs more intensity for higher points. Screwcap. 12.5% alc. **Rating** 93 **To** 2020 $40

Shiraz 2013 Matured in French and American oak for 14 months. The colour is very good, the fleshy, medium-bodied palate has neatly ripened plum and black cherry fruit; ripe tannins and integrated oak rounding out an attractive package. Screwcap. 13.5% alc. **Rating** 93 **To** 2033 $24 ✪

Semillon 2014 Part fermented in used French oak, part in stainless steel. Quartz-clear, it has the squeaky acidity felt on the soft tissue of the mouth – different, but not unpleasant; it adds to the mouth-watering palate and its pleasingly grippy finish. Screwcap. 12% alc. **Rating** 92 **To** 2024 $22 ✪

Kids Earth Fund Autumn Semillon 2013 No-holds-barred full-on botrytis style aged for 8 months in used French oak. There is no specific mention of its region of origin, nor of the possibility of cane cutting. It points to Riverina as its most likely birthplace, but there's no certainty. It is so rich, drinking it sooner rather than later (it has good acidity) seems a wise plan. 375ml. Screwcap. 10.5% alc. **Rating** 92 **To** 2017 $25 ✪

Riesling 2014 Has ample lime/apple/lemon varietal fruit, and acidity to give balance; just a little loosely strung. Screwcap. 11.5% alc. **Rating** 90 **To** 2020 $22

Cabernet Sauvignon Merlot 2013 Matured in new and used French hogsheads. Well made, particularly within the constraints of the Mudgee climate; there are notes of blackcurrant along with more earthy nuances, and the oak also contributes to the flavour profile. Screwcap. 14% alc. **Rating** 90 **To** 2025 $22

Pinot Noir Chardonnay 2011 Orange region pinot noir meets Mudgee chardonnay of impressive finesse for this part of the world, thanks to the cool '11 season. Firm acidity is softened by more than 3 years' lees ageing, building biscuity and ginger cake notes. It will age confidently for some years yet. A low dosage of 6.5 g/l is well balanced and nicely integrated, finishing long and characterful. Cork. 11.5% alc. **Rating** 90 **To** 2021 $30 TS

ＴＴＴＴ **Chardonnay 2013** Rating 89 To 2017 $22
Cabernet Sauvignon Shiraz Merlot 2013 Rating 89 To 2020 $22

Burch Family Wines ★★★★★

Miamup Road, Cowaramup, WA 6284 **Region** Margaret River/Denmark
T (08) 9756 5200 **www.**burchfamilywines.com.au **Open** 7 days 10–5
Winemaker Janice McDonald, Mark Bailey, Andries Mostert **Est.** 1986 **Dozens** NFP
Vyds 189.2ha
This is the renamed Howard Park, which has two vineyards: Leston in Margaret River, and Mt Barrow in Mount Barker; it also manages three vineyards. It practises mainly organic viticulture in its owned and managed vineyards, Mt Barrow with a pinot noir block established and operated using biodynamic practices. The Margaret River winery incorporates feng shui principles, and can welcome large groups for concerts, speaking events, film evenings and private parties. Burch Family Wines also operates a cellar door at Scotsdale Road, Denmark (7 days 10–4). At the top of the portfolio is Howard Park Abercrombie Cabernet Sauvignon,

then follow the Rieslings, Chardonnay and Sauvignon Blanc. Next come pairs of Shiraz and Cabernet Sauvignon under the Leston and Scotsdale labels, and the Miamup and Flint Rock regional range. MadFish is a second label, itself with three price tiers: MadFish Gold Turtle, Sideways and (the original) MadFish, covering the full varietal range. A founding member of Australia's First Families of Wine. Exports to all major markets.

ⓉⓉⓉⓉⓉ **Howard Park Scotsdale Great Southern Cabernet Sauvignon 2012** From the near-40yo estate vineyard at Mount Barker; separate lots were either pressed at dryness or given post-ferment maceration, and kept separate during 20 months' maturation in French oak (40% new). Picture perfect, not a hair out of place as the blackcurrant fruit, a touch of black olive and cedary oak flow seamlessly along the supremely elegant palate. Screwcap. 14% alc. **Rating** 97 **To** 2042 $46 ✪

ⓉⓉⓉⓉⓉ **Howard Park Porongurup Riesling 2014** From one of the oldest vineyards in Porongurup. The flowery bouquet leads into a fine, yet intense palate typical of young Porongurup Riesling; lime zest and vibrant minerally acidity run the length of the beautifully balanced palate. The end point of this lovely wine is far distant, likely later than '34. Screwcap. 12% alc. **Rating** 96 **To** 2034 $34 ✪

Howard Park Museum Release Great Southern Riesling 2010 Gleaming straw-green; an object lesson in what is to be gained by cellaring Riesling, yet with years to run yet, for this is only part-way along the road to the full maturity it will achieve (by '20) and hold without demur through another decade. The low pH and good natural acidity invest the lemon citrus flavours with a minerally mouthfeel, even as secondary hints of toast make their first tentative appearance. Screwcap. 12% alc. **Rating** 96 **To** 2030 $41 ✪

Howard Park Allingham Chardonnay 2013 Sourced from the best estate vineyard plantings in Margaret River and Mount Barker, barrel-fermented in French oak. A Chardonnay of intensity and finesse, length a given; the fruit flavours are ripe, but there is also an intriguing savoury note adding another dimension. Screwcap. 13% alc. **Rating** 96 **To** 2025 $89

Howard Park Scotsdale Great Southern Shiraz 2013 Matured in French barriques for 18 months. The wine travels a very different road from that of Leston; fresh, spicy and no more than medium-bodied, the bouquet is a symphony of red and black counterparts, the elegant palate silky smooth, and cruises through to a long and lingering finish. Screwcap. 14% alc. **Rating** 96 **To** 2035 $46 ✪

Howard Park Abercrombie Cabernet Sauvignon 2012 From Great Southern and Margaret River; wild-fermented with extended post-ferment maceration; matured in French barriques (60% new) for 20 months. This is Burch Family Wines' big dog, immensely powerful and deeply structured, blackcurrant, dried herbs and grainy tannins all competing for space and attention. Demands time, and will be very long-lived. Screwcap. 14% alc. **Rating** 96 **To** 2047 $125

Howard Park Sauvignon Blanc 2014 Free-run juice from Great Southern/ Margaret River grapes has been partially barrel-fermented, the slightly smoky bouquet leading into an intensely focused palate, with the length and clarity more frequently encountered with high-quality Riesling, a comparison heightened by attractive citrus notes that accompany stone fruit and gooseberry flavours. Screwcap. 13% alc. **Rating** 95 **To** 2017 $31 ✪

Howard Park Chardonnay 2013 Wild yeast-fermented and matured in French oak. The varietal fruit expression is fully ripe (although fresh), with white peach, melon and fig flavours, citrus sneaking in via the acidity. Has precise line, length and balance, with its future assured. Screwcap. 13% alc. **Rating** 95 **To** 2023 $54

Howard Park Leston Margaret River Shiraz 2013 Matured in new and second-use barriques for 18 months. Ticks every box: the colour very good, the bouquet an expressive mix of dark berry fruit and neatly folded oak, the medium to full-bodied palate with considerable flavour and texture complexity, the purple and black fruits graciously allowing ripe tannins and oak the curtain call. Screwcap. 14% alc. **Rating** 95 **To** 2033 $46

Howard Park Mount Barker Riesling 2014 Rating 94 **To** 2029 $33
MadFish Gold Turtle Margaret River Semillon Sauvignon Blanc 2014 **Rating** 94 **To** 2017 $25 ✪

MadFish Gold Turtle Margaret River Chardonnay 2014 Rating 94
To 2021 $25 ✪
Howard Park Flint Rock Mount Barker Chardonnay 2012 Rating 94
To 2019 $27 CM ✪
MadFish Shiraz 2012 Rating 94 To 2022 $18 ✪
Howard Park Miamup Margaret River Cabernet Sauvignon 2013
Rating 94 To 2028 $28 ✪
Howard Park Leston Margaret River Cabernet Sauvignon 2012
Rating 94 To 2037 $46

♟♟♟♟♟ Howard Park Miamup Chardonnay 2014 Rating 93 To 2025 $28
Howard Park Flint Rock Chardonnay 2014 Rating 93 To 2024 $28
MadFish Shiraz Pinot Noir Rose 2014 Rating 93 To 2016 $18 ✪
MadFish Gold Turtle Cabernet Merlot 2013 Rating 93 To 2028 $25 ✪

Burge Family Winemakers   ★★★★☆

1312 Barossa Way, Lyndoch, SA 5351 **Region** Barossa Valley
T (08) 8524 4644 **www.**burgefamily.com.au **Open** Fri, Sat, Mon 10–5
Winemaker Rick Burge **Est.** 1928 **Dozens** 3500 **Vyds** 10ha
Burge Family Winemakers, with Rick Burge at the helm (not to be confused with
Grant Burge, although the families are related), has established itself as an icon producer
of exceptionally rich, lush and concentrated Barossa red wines. 2013 marked 85 years of
continuous winemaking by three generations of the family. Exports to Canada, Germany,
Belgium, The Netherlands, Hong Kong, Singapore and Japan.

♟♟♟♟♟ Olive Hill Barossa Valley Shiraz 2012 Estate-grown, spending 12 months in
new and used French (Allier) barriques. The bouquet sets the antennae waving
with its promise (duly delivered) of plush blackberry fruit, quality oak entirely
integrated on the medium-bodied palate, the tannins ripe and soft. The best for
many years. The cork is perfect. 13.8% alc. Rating 95 To 2032 $30 ✪
Draycott Barossa Valley Shiraz 2012 There's a freshness to the '12 Burge
Family reds that has been missing at times in the past. It's pure Barossan fruit doing
the talking, sans overt oak and with all its faculties intact. Joy of life in a red wine
bottle. Mix of black and red berries, licorice, gritty tannin and a firm confidence
to the finish. It's an excellent Draycott. Cork. 14.5% alc. Rating 94 To 2025
$35 CM

♟♟♟♟♟ Olive Hill Premium Semillon 2014 Rating 93 To 2020 $26 CM ✪
Clochemerle Grenache Shiraz Mourvedre 2012 Rating 93 To 2021 $18
CM ✪
Draycott Barossa Valley Merlot 2012 Rating 93 To 2022 $25 ✪
Wilsford Founders Reserve Three Generations Blend Old Tawny
Port NV Rating 93 To 2015 $38
Garnacha Barossa Valley Grenache 2010 Rating 92 To 2020 $25 ✪
The Homestead Cabernet Sauvignon 2012 Rating 91 To 2022 $30 CM
Olive Hill Barossa Valley Mourvedre 2012 Rating 90 To 2025 $25

Burke & Wills Winery

3155 Burke & Wills Track, Mia Mia, Vic 3444 **Region** Heathcote
T (03) 5425 5400 **www.**wineandmusic.net **Open** By appt
Winemaker Andrew Pattison, Robert Ellis **Est.** 2003 **Dozens** 1500 **Vyds** 3.4ha
After 18 years at Lancefield Winery in the Macedon Ranges, Andrew Pattison moved his
operation a few miles north in 2004 to set up Burke & Wills Winery at the southern edge of
Heathcote, continuing to produce wines from both regions. With vineyards at Mia Mia and
Redesdale, he now has 2ha of shiraz, 1ha of cabernet sauvignon and Bordeaux varieties and
0.4ha of gewurztraminer. He still sources a small amount of Macedon Ranges fruit from his
former Malmsbury vineyard; additional grapes are contract-grown in Heathcote.

🍷🍷🍷🍷🍷 **Vat 1 French Oak Heathcote Shiraz 2013** Hand-picked, open-fermented and plunged, basket-pressed, matured in 1yo French oak for 12 months. Deep, vivid crimson; Heathcote at its best, the bouquet with glints of spice sewn through the dark fruit aromas, spice and black pepper allied with licorice on the medium to full-bodied palate; it has length and balance, its power coming strictly from the fruit and oak, not tannins per se. Screwcap. 14% alc. **Rating** 95 **To** 2038 $32 ❂

🍷🍷🍷🍷🍷 **Mia Mia Heathcote Gewurztraminer 2014 Rating** 93 **To** 2020 $25 ❂
Dig Tree Heathcote Viognier 2014 Rating 90 **To** 2016 $18 ❂

Burnbrae   ★★★☆

548 Hill End Road, Mudgee, NSW 2850 **Region** Mudgee
T (02) 6373 3504 **www**.burnbraewines.com.au **Open** 7 days 10–4
Winemaker Lisa Bray **Est.** 1968 **Dozens** 5400 **Vyds** 6ha
Tony and Jill Bryant were broadacre farmers who had a long-held dream of having a vineyard and winery. Following the sale of the family farm in the 1990s Tony studied viticulture and marketing, and went on to manage wineries in the Mudgee area before starting his own viticultural consultancy business. In 2004 he and Jill were able to take the final step by purchasing Burnbrae. Exports to Singapore and China.

🍷🍷🍷🍷🍷 **Mudgee Shiraz Viognier 2013** Life and power. This will keep most red drinkers happy. Blackberry, five spice and violet-like flavours provide plenty to chew on. Licoricey/leathery tannin curls through the finish. Very good. Screwcap. 13.9% alc. **Rating** 92 **To** 2022 $25 CM ❂

🍷🍷🍷🍷 **Jilly's Pick Chardonnay 2014 Rating** 89 **To** 2017 $30 CM

 # Buttermans Track   ★★★★★

PO Box 82, St Andrews, Vic 3761 **Region** Yarra Valley
T 0425 737 839 **www**.buttermanstrack.com.au **Open** Not
Winemaker James Lance, Gary Trist **Est.** 1991 **Dozens** 600 **Vyds** 2.13ha
I became intimately acquainted with Buttermans Track in the latter part of the 1980s when Coldstream Hills, at that stage owned by my wife Suzanne and myself, purchased grapes from the Roberts family's Rising Vineyard. I had to coax a 3-tonne truck with almost no brakes and almost no engine to tackle the hills and valleys of the unsealed Buttermans Track. Louise and Gary Trist began planting a small vineyard in 1991 on a small side road just off the Buttermans Track. Between then and '03 they established 0.86ha of pinot noir, 0.74ha of shiraz and 0.53ha of sangiovese. The first tiny yield of 400kg of pinot noir was sold to a boutique winery in the Yarra Valley, and the Trist family continued to sell the grapes to Yarra Valley wineries until '08. From that year onwards a small parcel of sangiovese was retained for the Buttermans Track label, which has now extended to include the other two varieties. The quality of the 2012 and '13 vintage wines is of the highest order.

🍷🍷🍷🍷🍷 **Yarra Valley Shiraz 2012** 75% crushed, 25% whole bunches, open-fermented 11 days on skins, matured in French hogsheads (30% new) for 18 months. Deep crimson-purple; this is a picture-perfect example of cool-climate Shiraz, with blackberry, plum, licorice and spice all clamouring for recognition, oak patrolling the boundaries of the challenges of the fruit. 135 dozen made. Screwcap. 12.5% alc. **Rating** 95 **To** 2033 $32 ❂
Yarra Valley Sangiovese 2013 Open fermenters, wild yeast, matured for 18 months in used French oak. Very good colour for Sangiovese, both in depth and hue; the palate, likewise, has an extra degree of power to the dark cherry fruits promised by the bouquet; the length and overall balance are thoroughly impressive. Major surprise packet. Screwcap. 13.7% alc. **Rating** 95 **To** 2028 $32 ❂

🍷🍷🍷🍷🍷 **Yarra Valley Pinot Noir 2013 Rating** 92 **To** 2020 $40

Buxton Ridge ★★★★

88 Seal Rock Road, Buxton, Vic 3711 **Region** Upper Goulburn Valley
T (03) 5774 7117 **www.**buxtonridge.com **Open** W'ends & public hols 10–5
Winemaker Michael Gelbert **Est.** 1996 **Dozens** 1300 **Vyds** 3ha
The story of Buxton Ridge is long and complicated, with sorrow and hardship, but also extraordinary tenacity. In 1996 Lorna and IT consultant husband Wolf-Ruediger Gelbert purchased a 2ha property. The first shiraz was planted in Nov '96; Wolf retired in Oct '97, and in November that year planted small quantities of sauvignon blanc, pinot noir, merlot and more shiraz. Every weekend was spent with the endless tasks of a young vineyard. Wolf died unexpectedly from a heart attack in July '98, leaving an embryonic vineyard and a building site where their dream house had only advanced to the stage of a leaky cellar. Their youngest son Michael wanted to continue, and with input from friends and experts, the business progressed, with small blocks either side of the original vineyard purchased and more vines planted. Oscar Rosa and Nick Arena from Mount Cathedral Wines took Michael under their wing, and he has made all the red wines since 2005, with Marysville an important local market. Then came the '09 bushfires, the destruction of that year's vintage by smoke, and the loss of the '11 vintage thanks to the cold and wet spring and summer.

🍷🍷🍷🍷🍷 **Lorna Grace Pinot Noir 2010** Open-fermented, hand-plunged, 18 months' maturation in new and used French oak. Impressive wine, developing slowly, but with surefootedness. Ample plum and black cherry fruit team with touches of spice and forest floor; good oak integration aids length and balance. Screwcap. 14% alc. **Rating** 94 **To** 2020 $25 ✪

🍷🍷🍷🍷🍷 **Katie Maree Sauvignon Blanc 2012 Rating** 93 **To** 2016 $20 ✪
Central Victorian Shiraz 2012 Rating 93 **To** 2032 $25 ✪
Molly Jean Methode Traditionelle Blanc de Noir 2008 Rating 93 **To** 2016 $29
Michael Wolf Merlot 2012 Rating 92 **To** 2020 $25 ✪

Byrne Vineyards ★★★☆

PO Box 15, Kent Town BC, SA 5071 **Region** South Australia
T (08) 8132 0022 **www.**byrnevineyards.com.au **Open** Not
Winemaker Peter Gajewski, Phil Reedman MW **Est.** 1963 **Dozens** 35 000 **Vyds** 384ha
Byrne Vineyards is a family-owned wine business. The Byrne family has been involved in the SA wine industry for three generations, with vineyards spanning SA's prime wine-producing regions, including Clare Valley, Eden Valley, Adelaide Plains and Riverland. The vines vary from 20 to over 50 years of age. Exports to the UK, Canada, France, Germany, Denmark, Sweden, Norway, Thailand, the Philippines, Singapore, Japan and China.

🍷🍷🍷🍷🍷 **Reserve Clare Valley Shiraz 2013** Deep, inky purple; the palate is as chock full of black fruits, tar, licorice, oak and tannins as the colour suggests. A full-bodied Magimix style, needing some years to allow light and shade to develop. Screwcap. 14.8% alc. **Rating** 91 **To** 2033 $25

🍷🍷🍷🍷 **Reserve Clare Valley Cabernet Sauvignon 2012 Rating** 89 **To** 2020 $25

Byron & Harold ★★★★★

PO Box 408, Denmark, WA 6333 **Region** Great Southern
T 0402 010 352 **www.**byronandharold.com.au **Open** Not
Winemaker Luke Eckersley **Est.** 2011 **Dozens** 6500 **Vyds** 26ha
The owners of Byron & Harold make a formidable partnership, covering every aspect of winemaking, sales and marketing, and business management and administration. Paul Byron and Ralph (Harold) Dunning together have more than 65 years of experience in the Australian wine trade, working at top levels for some of the most admired wineries and wine distribution companies. Andrew Lane worked for 20 years in the tourism industry, including in a senior role with Tourism Australia, leading to the formation of the Wine Tourism Export Council. More recently he developed the family vineyard (Wandering Lane). Luke Eckersley

has a Bachelor of Science in oenology and viticulture, has worked in Europe and the US, then at Forest Hill and Rockcliffe. Rose Eveson began her working life in the airline industry before moving to Denmark, managing the cellar doors at Goundrey and Plantagenet. Then followed a degree in wine marketing from the University of Adelaide, and a move to West Cape Howe and Forest Hill Vineyard. Exports to China.

ΨΨΨΨΨ **The Partners Mount Barker Pinot Noir 2014** Some wines are sent to stagger you. This is one such wine. It's in complete control of its world. Sweet-sour, perfumed, fruit-filled and savoury, with long elegant strings of tannin marshalling the wine's forces before stretching out into tomorrow. Screwcap. 13.5% alc. Rating 96 To 2024 $35 CM ✪

The Partners Great Southern Shiraz 2012 Spearmint and choc notes play leading roles to an immensely fragrant play of well-ripened fruit flavour. Berries, cherries, leather and licorice notes, fresh and succulent, give the palate a sense of controlled abundance. We have a producer and a half on our hands here. Screwcap. 14.5% alc. Rating 96 To 2030 $35 CM ✪

Rose & Thorns Great Southern Shiraz 2013 Thoroughly delicious Shiraz. It sights the sweet spot of red wine drinkability and zeroes in on it. Blackberry jubes and spices, redcurrant and fennel. Fine tannin, flecked with spice. A prettiness, but a substance too. There is simply a great deal to both admire and enjoy here. Screwcap. 14% alc. Rating 95 To 2027 $28 CM ✪

Rose & Thorns Mount Barker Riesling 2014 Elegant from head to foot. Impressive along the way. Apple, slate and talc with sunny, floral nuances. Shows quite a bit of colour but you'd not know it from the taste of it. Gorgeous style. Screwcap. 12.5% alc. Rating 94 To 2024 $28 CM ✪

ΨΨΨΨΩ **The Partners Mount Barker Riesling 2014** Rating 93 To 2021 $28 CM
Duncan's Patch Cabernet Sauvignon 2013 Rating 92 To 2023 $28 CM

Caillard Wine   ★★★★★

5 Annesley Street, Leichhardt, NSW 2040 (postal) **Region** Barossa Valley
T 0433 272 912 **www.**caillardwine.com **Open** Not
Winemaker Dr Chris Taylor, Andrew Caillard MW **Est.** 2008 **Dozens** 700
Andrew Caillard MW has had a long and varied career in wine, including vintages at Brokenwood and elsewhere, but has also taken the final step of making his own wine, with the support of wife Bobby. Andrew says the inspiration to make Mataro (and now Shiraz) came while writing the background for the Penfolds' The Rewards of Patience tastings. He learnt that both Max Schubert and John Davoren had experimented with mataro, and that the original releases of Penfolds St Henri comprised a fair percentage of the variety. For good measure, Andrew's great (times four) grandfather, John Reynell, planted one of Australia's first vineyards at Reynella, around 1838. Exports to Hong Kong and China.

ΨΨΨΨΨ **Barossa Valley Shiraz 2013** Sourced from two vineyards near Stockwell; open-fermented and basket-pressed to a combination of new and used French barriques for 15 months prior to bottling. An altogether serious Shiraz, sending a consistent message from start to finish, with luscious, layered dark fruits, licorice and cedar in a velvety, perfectly balanced palate. There is not even a glimmer of dead fruit. Screwcap. 14.8% alc. Rating 96 To 2038 $50 ✪

Mataro 2013 Very good crimson colour; more supple and well proportioned than most single-variety Mataros; the savoury tannins are there, but there is a rich vein of spicy, dark fruits running through the length of the medium-bodied, elegant palate. Screwcap. 14.5% alc. Rating 95 To 2025 $50

Calabria Family Wines   ★★★★☆

1283 Brayne Road, Griffith, NSW 2680 **Region** Riverina
T (02) 6969 0800 **www.**calabriawines.com.au **Open** Mon–Fri 8.30–5, w'ends 10–4
Winemaker Bill Calabria, Emma Norbiato, Tony Steffania, Jeremy Nascimben, Sam Trimboli **Est.** 1945 **Dozens** NFP **Vyds** 55ha

Along with a number of Riverina producers, Calabria Family Wines (until 2014 known as Westend Estate) has successfully lifted both the quality and the packaging of its wines. Its 3 Bridges range, which has an impressive array of gold medals to its credit, is anchored on estate vineyards. Calabria Family Wines is moving with the times, increasing its plantings of durif, and introducing aglianico, nero d'Avola, and St Macaire (on the verge of extinction, and once grown in Bordeaux, this 2ha is the largest planting in the world). Equally importantly, it is casting its net over the Canberra District, Hilltops and King Valley, premium regions, taking this one step further by acquiring a 12ha vineyard in the Barossa Valley. A producer that consistently delivers exceptional value for money across the entire range. Exports to the UK, the US and other major markets, including China.

ŸŸŸŸŸ **The Iconic Grand Reserve Barossa Valley Shiraz 2012** Deeply coloured, this comes from 100yo vines, matured in new French oak, and presented in a deluxe dedicated bottle. The new French oak has clasped its hands around the blackberry/black cherry flavours in no uncertain fashion; it is this, not tannins or ripe fruit, that calls for time. Cork. 14% alc. **Rating** 96 **To** 2037
3 Bridges Barossa Valley Shiraz 2013 Pressed to finish its fermentation in new French and American oak, plus 18 months' maturation. Deep crimson-purple; a full-bodied Shiraz that starts off life with that precious attribute of balance – balance in its structure and texture, fruit flavour and oak; tannins, too, are exactly weighted. All this awaits a wine that is certain to improve impressively over the next 5–10 years. Screwcap. 14.5% alc. **Rating** 94 **To** 2033 $25 ✪
3 Bridges Botrytis Semillon 2012 Orange-gold; the grapes for this wine must have had an extraordinary level of botrytis, and hence baume; it has creme brulee with a thick burnt sugar crust, cumquat and mandarin flavours, the resulting baume/acid/alcohol balance very good indeed. 375ml. Screwcap. 12% alc. **Rating** 94 **To** 2017 $25 ✪
Fortified Durif 2013 A surprise: less robust and deep than its Durif base might suggest, the answer lying partly with the brandy spirit used to fortify the wine, and partly with the relatively dry style (more Portuguese than Australian). Screwcap. 18% alc. **Rating** 94 **To** 2043 $40

ŸŸŸŸŸ **3 Bridges Golden Mist Botrytis 2008** Rating 93 **To** 2016 $25 ✪
Calabria Bros. Barossa Shiraz 2013 Rating 91 **To** 2020 $25
3 Bridges Durif 2013 Rating 91 **To** 2023 $25
Cool Climate Series Hilltops Shiraz 2013 Rating 90 **To** 2018 $15 ✪

Caledonia Australis | Mount Macleod ★★★★

PO Box 626, North Melbourne, Vic 3051 **Region** Gippsland
T (03) 9329 5372 **www.**southgippslandwinecompany.com **Open** Not
Winemaker Mark Matthews **Est.** 1995 **Dozens** 4500 **Vyds** 16.18ha
Mark and Marianna Matthews acquired Caledonia Australis in 2009. Mark is a winemaker with vintages in numerous wine regions around the world. He works as a winemaking teacher, and also runs a contract winemaking business. Marianna has experience with major fast-moving consumer goods brands globally. The Matthews have converted the main chardonnay block to certified organic, and are rehabilitating around 8ha of wetlands with the local catchment authority. Exports to Canada and Japan.

ŸŸŸŸŸ **Caledonia Australis Gippsland Pinot Noir 2013** Savoury spice, rhubarb, quite mellow but with an appreciable shoot of flavour to close. Foresty notes as highlights and lots of tangy, juicy acidity. Not one for the long term, but will drink well over the next few years. Screwcap. 13.6% alc. **Rating** 91 **To** 2019 $28 CM
Mount Macleod Chardonnay 2013 Full-bodied through the mid-palate with fennel, melon and fig notes aplenty. Not quite as convincing through the finish, but not far off. Generally well balanced. Noticeably complex, but not forced or exaggerated. Return to form. Screwcap. 14% alc. **Rating** 90 **To** 2018 $19 CM ✪

Campbells

★★★★★

Murray Valley Highway, Rutherglen, Vic 3685 **Region** Rutherglen
T (02) 6033 6000 **www**.campbellswines.com.au **Open** Mon–Sat 9–5, Sun 10–5
Winemaker Colin Campbell, Tim Gniel, Julie Campbell **Est.** 1870 **Dozens** 36 000
Vyds 72ha

Campbells has a long and rich history, with five generations of the family making wine for over 140 years. There were difficult times: phylloxera's arrival in the Bobbie Burns Vineyard in 1898; the Depression of the 1930s; and premature deaths. But the Scottish blood of founder John Campbell has ensured that the business has not only survived, but quietly flourished. Indeed, there have been spectacular successes in unexpected quarters (white table wines, especially Riesling) and expected success with Muscat and Topaque. 99-point scores from Robert Parker and a 100-point score from Harvey Steiman (Wine Spectator) put Campbells in a special position. It is fair to say that the nigh-on half-century fourth-generation stewardship of Malcolm and Colin Campbell has been the most important in the history of the winery, but the five members of the fifth generation all working in the business are well equipped to move up the ladder when Colin and/or Malcolm decide to retire. A founding member of Australia's First Families of Wine. Exports to the UK, the US, China and other major markets.

🍷🍷🍷🍷🍷 **Merchant Prince Rare Muscat NV** Wines of this intensity can be a life-changing experience. If it was any thicker or denser it would be impossible to pour. It has might but it also has glory: it packs bags of tarry, toffeed, burnt fruits and honeyed flavours, but still manages to skip through the palate at a speed more youthful wines often cannot manage. Few wines, the world over, come as guaranteed to impress as this. Screwcap. 18% alc. **Rating** 98 **To** 2016 $130 CM ❂
Isabella Rare Topaque NV A deep well of flavour, preserved and kept fresh to make the weight on our shoulders seem lighter. If you look deep into this wine's olive-mahogany hues you're likely to glimpse an insight into human existence. Such is the profound depth of flavour. Toffee apples, sweet tea, raisins and stone fruits dried and shrivelled. There's a tar-like thickness here; a burst of lime/toffee treacle. Screwcap. 18% alc. **Rating** 97 **To** 2016 $135 CM ❂

🍷🍷🍷🍷🍷 **Grand Rutherglen Muscat NV** Intense leather, malt, black tea and burnt honey flavours with brighter notes of dried orange peel and apricot. Dense, dark Christmas cake character, in-shot with roasted nuts. They release these treasures each year; they're raved over routinely; they must never be taken for granted. Screwcap. 17.5% alc. **Rating** 96 **To** 2016 $68 CM ❂
The Sixties Block 2013 Fantastic release. A step up in class for this label. Fresh, polished, dark-berried fruits, licks of woody spice, peppercorns and slippery, smoky oak. Floral influences, succulent feel throughout, plenty of grunt but with a modern face. Screwcap. 14.5% alc. **Rating** 95 **To** 2030 $30 CM ❂
Bobbie Burns Rutherglen Shiraz 2013 Richness and personality. Excellent release. Blackberry, iodine, leather and toast, with musky notes adding an extra layer of appeal. Grainy, earthen tannin gives it an authoritative stamp. Excellent value. Screwcap. 14.5% alc. **Rating** 94 **To** 2028 $22 CM ❂
Limited Release Rutherglen Durif 2012 Builds up a power of flavour and then oozes it down through to a licoricey, leathery conclusion. This will not disappoint any of its fans, and may win a few more. Violet, bitumen and thick blackberry flavour, complemented by grainy, almost sandy tannin. Decant now, or cellar for as long as you desire. Screwcap. 14% alc. **Rating** 94 **To** 2035 $28 CM ❂
Rutherglen Topaque NV It's quite extraordinary that the 'entry level' topaque is this good. It takes deliciousness to new levels. Fresh with apricot, spicy fruit cake, toffee and tea flavours, it's sweet and honeyed but lively, and it feels tremendously good to drink. Price is madness, in a rational world. Screwcap. 17.5% alc. **Rating** 94 **To** 2016 $19 CM ❂
Liquid Gold Classic Rutherglen Topaque NV Old sweet material brimful with life. If we were introduced to these wines anew we would find them miraculous. Tea, dried apricot, honey and dark, intense butterscotch. Sweet but champing at the bit to please, and to entertain. Screwcap. 17.5% alc. **Rating** 94 **To** 2016 $38 CM

🍷🍷🍷🍷🍷 The Brothers Rutherglen Shiraz 2013 Rating 93 To 2028 $60 CM
The Barkly Rutherglen Durif 2013 Rating 93 To 2033 $60 CM
Classic Rutherglen Muscat NV Rating 93 To 2016 $38 CM
Select Parcels Rutherglen Tempranillo 2012 Rating 92 To 2021 $28 CM
Rutherglen Muscat NV Rating 92 To 2016 $19 CM ✪
Limited Release Rutherglen Roussanne 2014 Rating 91 To 2016 $30 CM

Cannibal Creek Vineyard

260 Tynong North Road, Tynong North, Vic 3813 **Region** Gippsland
T (03) 5942 8380 **www.**cannibalcreek.com.au **Open** 7 days 11–5
Winemaker Patrick Hardiker **Est.** 1997 **Dozens** 3000 **Vyds** 5ha
Patrick and Kirsten Hardiker moved to Tynong North in 1988, initially grazing beef cattle, but aware of the viticultural potential of the sandy clay loam and bleached subsurface soils weathered from the granite foothills of the Black Snake Ranges. Plantings began in 1997, using organically based cultivation methods; varieties include pinot noir, chardonnay, sauvignon blanc, merlot and cabernet sauvignon. The family established the winery in an old farm barn built in the early 1900s by the Weatherhead family, with timber from Weatherhead Hill (visible from the vineyard); it also houses the cellar door. Exports to Hong Kong.

🍷🍷🍷🍷🍷 Sauvignon Blanc 2014 It works as a straight fruit-driven white but it has more to offer if you're inclined to look. Of most note is its elegant, structural length. It curls with lemon pith, grapefruit and lemongrass notes extending appreciably out through the finish. Screwcap. 12% alc. **Rating** 93 To 2016 $28 CM
Chardonnay 2012 A very neatly made and balanced Chardonnay, with white peach, nectarine and fig flavours the drivers, French oak influences held in restraint. Good now, good later. Screwcap. 13% alc. **Rating** 92 To 2020 $28
Pinot Noir 2013 Clear crimson-purple; red and black cherry fruit on the bouquet is joined by some bramble/stemmy notes on the palate; needs a little more focus. Screwcap. 13.7% alc. **Rating** 90 To 2020 $32

Capanno

PO Box 1310, Double Bay, NSW 1360 **Region** Southern Highlands
T 0417 569 544 **www.**capanno.com.au **Open** Not
Winemaker Eden Road Wines (Nick Spencer) **Est.** 2004 **Dozens** 230 **Vyds** 1.2ha
This is the weekend and holiday retreat of Cameron Jones and Jody Williams. Capanno is the Italian word for 'shed', and is an allusion to the series of architect-designed (almost industrial) pavilions that together make up the house. The vineyard was planted close to and around the house, a foreground to the mountains beyond, which, in their words, 'provide a fantastic backdrop for afternoon drinks around the bocce court with great friends'. The vineyard gives equal space to pinot gris and pinot noir clones 115 and 777. Notwithstanding the small production, the wines are sold to restaurants and wine bars in Sydney, Melbourne and Canberra.

🍷🍷🍷🍷🍷 Single Vineyard Pinot Noir 2013 Full, clear and bright hue; perfectly ripened and evolved varietal character courtesy of red and black cherry fruit; good length, still needing a few years to develop spice and other secondary flavours, and will undoubtedly do so. Screwcap. 13% alc. **Rating** 93 To 2023 $35

Cape Barren Wines ★★★★★

PO Box 738, North Adelaide, SA 5006 **Region** McLaren Vale
T (08) 8267 3292 **www.**capebarrenwines.com **Open** By appt
Winemaker Rob Dundon **Est.** 1999 **Dozens** 8500 **Vyds** 14.5ha
Cape Barren was founded in 1999 by Peter Matthews, who worked tirelessly to create wines of distinction from some of the oldest vineyards in McLaren Vale. Peter sold the business in late 2009 to Rob Dundon and Tom Adams, who together have amassed in excess of 50 years' experience in winemaking, viticulture and international sales. Wines are sourced from 3ha of

80–85-year-old grenache at Blewitt Springs, 4.5ha of 120-year-old unirrigated shiraz at McLaren Flat, and 4ha of chardonnay plus 3ha of sauvignon blanc in the Adelaide Hills. Exports to the US, Canada, Switzerland, Vietnam, the Philippines, Singapore, Taiwan, Hong Kong, Thailand, Japan and China.

ŸŸŸŸŸ **Old Vine Reserve Release McLaren Vale Shiraz 2012** From two vineyards; matured for 18 months in French hogsheads. Archetypal full-bodied McLaren Vale Shiraz, saturated with black fruits and dark chocolate, the tannins, oak and alcohol mere facts of life; an effortless celebration of place and variety. Cork. 15% alc. Rating 96 To 2042 $38 **☺**

Native Goose McLaren Vale Shiraz 2013 Emphasises McLaren Vale's ability to produce Shiraz that has many of the characteristics of cool-climate grapes, aided in this instance by excellent control of oak and tannins, leaving the blackberry and nuanced bitter chocolate fruit flavours centre stage. Screwcap. 14.5% alc. **Rating** 94 To 2033 $23 **☺**

Old Vine Reserve Release McLaren Vale Shiraz 2013 Substantial in every way. Dense with blackberry and fresh, roasted coffee flavours. Brings alcohol warmth along with the flavours, but the overall balance is so good that the motion of quality is carried. Melt of chocolatey tannin completes a powerful picture. Cork. 15% alc. **Rating** 94 To 2028 $40 CM

ŸŸŸŸŸ **Native Goose Chardonnay 2013** Rating 92 To 2018 $23 CM **☺**
Native Goose McLaren Vale GSM 2012 Rating 92 To 2021 $23 CM **☺**

Cape Bernier Vineyard ★★★★

230 Bream Creek Road, Bream Creek, Tas 7175 **Region** Southern Tasmania
T (03) 6253 5443 **www.**capebernier.com.au **Open** By appt
Winemaker Winemaking Tasmania (Julian Alcorso) **Est.** 1999 **Dozens** 1800 **Vyds** 4ha
Andrew and Jenny Sinclair took over from founder Alastair Christie in 2014. The vineyard plantings consist of 2ha of pinot noir (including three Dijon clones), 1.4ha of chardonnay and 0.6ha of pinot gris on a north-facing slope with spectacular views of Marion Bay. The property is one of several in the region that are changing from dairy and beef cattle to wine production and tourism. The coastal vineyard benefits from the moderating effects of the sea in Tasmania's generally cool climate. Exports to Singapore.

ŸŸŸŸŸ **Pinot Noir 2012** Open vat-fermented with wild yeast; spent 9 months in 'multi-age' French puncheons. Very good colour; the rich, full-bodied (in Pinot terms) palate has strong plum and black cherry fruit coming through in layers on the back-palate and savoury finish. Screwcap. 13.5% alc. **Rating** 94 To 2021 $42

ŸŸŸŸŸ **Chardonnay 2012** Rating 93 To 2020 $42
La Frontiere Cuvee Brut Rose 2011 Rating 91 To 2016 $42 TS
Pinot Rose 2014 Rating 91 To 2016 $30

Cape Grace Wines ★★★★★

281 Fifty One Road, Cowaramup, WA 6284 **Region** Margaret River
T (08) 9755 5669 **www.**capegracewines.com.au **Open** 7 days 10–5
Winemaker Mark Messenger (Consultant) **Est.** 1996 **Dozens** 2000 **Vyds** 6.25ha
Cape Grace can trace its history back to 1875, when timber baron MC Davies settled at Karridale, building the Leeuwin lighthouse and founding the township of Margaret River; 120 years later, Robert and Karen Karri-Davies planted the vineyard to chardonnay, shiraz and cabernet sauvignon, with smaller amounts of merlot, semillon and chenin blanc. Robert is a self-taught viticulturist; Karen has over 15 years of international sales and marketing experience in the hospitality industry. Winemaking is carried out on the property; consultant Mark Messenger is a veteran of the Margaret River region. Exports to Singapore and China.

ŸŸŸŸŸ **Margaret River Cabernet Sauvignon 2012** Estate-grown, hand-picked, basket-pressed, matured in French barriques. A stylish Cabernet with fruit, oak and tannins neatly aligned; the flavours are juicy, with cassis to the fore, and oak on the long, medium-bodied palate. Screwcap. 13.5% alc. **Rating** 96 **To** 2028 $50 ✪

Margaret River Cabernet Franc 2013 You can see why the winemaking team decided to save this Cabernet Franc for separate maturation and bottling; only Margaret River makes this single varietal so well, with its wonderfully juicy red fruits on the bouquet and palate alike, given just enough structure by silken tannins on the finish. 70 dozen made. Screwcap. 12.9% alc. **Rating** 95 **To** 2023 $40

Margaret River Cabernet Shiraz 2013 Estate-grown, with all the winemaking bells and whistles, including French oak. The blend works very well, with an almost chocolatey richness and suppleness to the flavours; the textural mouthfeel and structure are both exemplary. Screwcap. 13.8% alc. **Rating** 94 **To** 2033 $25 ✪

Cape Jaffa Wines

459 Limestone Coast Road, Mount Benson via Robe, SA 5276 **Region** Mount Benson
T (08) 8768 5053 **www**.capejaffawines.com.au **Open** 7 days 10–5
Winemaker Anna and Derek Hooper **Est.** 1993 **Dozens** 15 000 **Vyds** 22.86ha
Cape Jaffa was the first of the Mount Benson wineries, its winery made from local rock (between 800 and 1000 tonnes are crushed each year). Cape Jaffa's fully certified biodynamic vineyard provides 50% of production, with additional fruit sourced from a certified biodynamic grower in Wrattonbully. Having received the Advantage SA Regional Award in '09, '10 and '11 for its sustainable initiatives in the Limestone Coast, Cape Jaffa is now a Hall of Fame inductee. Winemaker Anna Hooper was named South Australian Rural Woman of the Year '13 for her commitment to sustainability. Exports to the UK, Canada, Thailand, the Philippines, Hong Kong, Singapore and China.

🍷🍷🍷🍷🍷 **Epic Drop Limestone Coast Shiraz 2012** A seriously good Shiraz from the temperate climate of Mount Benson/Limestone Coast; it's positively vibrant, with spice, pepper and licorice threaded through its abundant black and red fruits in manner strongly reminiscent of the Northern Rhône Valley; great length, line and balance. Screwcap. 14.5% alc. **Rating** 96 **To** 2037 $35 ✪

La Lune Mount Benson Shiraz 2013 Estate-grown, open-fermented in concrete tanks with 14 days' post-fermentation maceration, 22 months in French and American oak. A densely packed wine with the flavours of seemingly lower than 14.5% alcohol providing freshness and a racy mouthfeel. Very unusual, but also very food-friendly. Diam. 14.5% alc. **Rating** 94 **To** 2033 $60

🍷🍷🍷🍷🍷 **Wrattonbully Pinot Gris 2014 Rating** 93 **To** 2015 $26 ✪

Cape Mentelle

Wallcliffe Road, Margaret River, WA 6285 **Region** Margaret River
T (08) 9757 0888 **www**.capementelle.com.au **Open** 7 days 10–4.30
Winemaker Robert Mann, Paul Callaghan, Evan Thompson **Est.** 1970 **Dozens** 105 000
Vyds 166ha
Part of the LVMH (Louis Vuitton Möet Hennessy) group. Cape Mentelle is firing on all cylinders, with the winemaking team fully capitalising on the extensive and largely mature vineyards, which obviate the need for contract-grown fruit. It is hard to say which of the wines is best; the ranking, such as it is, varies from year to year. That said, Sauvignon Blanc Semillon, Chardonnay, Shiraz and Cabernet Sauvignon lead the portfolio, and Cape Mentelle is one of those knocking on the door the the Winery of the Year Award. Exports to all major markets.

🍷🍷🍷🍷🍷 **Margaret River Cabernet Sauvignon 2012** Berry-sorted before fermentation of 30 days on skins; 18 months in French oak (50% new). This is a glorious Cabernet, its blackcurrant, cedar and spice bouquet leading into a seamless, perfectly balanced palate with cassis and redcurrant fruit framed by cedary oak. The amazing tannins, softly woven into the fabric of the fruit, give this wine its ultimate class. Screwcap. 14% alc. **Rating** 98 **To** 2052 $92 ✪

Wallcliffe 2012 55/45% estate-grown sauvignon blanc and semillon barrel-fermented in French oak (35% new). Three vineyard sections are picked and separately fermented, with a selection of the best barrels at the end of the process. The precocious display of fruit throughout has easily absorbed the oak, leaving lemongrass, citrus and a wisp of lime marmalade offset by cleansing natural acidity. Bred to stay. Screwcap. 13% alc. **Rating** 97 **To** 2022 $46 ○

Margaret River Chardonnay 2013 Predominantly from the estate vineyard, hand-picked, whole bunch-pressed, barrel-fermented in French barriques (one-third new), part wild, part cultured, yeast-fermented, matured for 9 months with weekly battonage. Gleaming straw-green; a super-elegant, yet extremely complex, wine, with pink grapefruit to the fore, balanced in both texture and flavour by buttery brioche. Screwcap. 13% alc. **Rating** 97 **To** 2023 $46 ○

ᵧᵧᵧᵧᵧ **Wilyabrup 2012** 45/33/24% cabernet sauvignon, merlot and cabernet franc, destemmed and berry-sorted, then fermented for up to 30 days; matured in French barriques (40% new) for 16 months. A high-toned, savoury wine with plum, tobacco and cedar all in play, the tannins fine, the balance impeccable. Screwcap. 13.5% alc. **Rating** 95 **To** 2035 $52

Margaret River Sauvignon Blanc Semillon 2014 A 58/42% blend machine-harvested at night; most cold-fermented in stainless steel, with 7% of the blend fermented in new and used French barriques; both components given 4 months of lees contact. There is an array of citrus and tropical fruit aromas and flavours, but it is the electricity of the intense palate that is the defining feature of the wine. Screwcap. 12.5% alc. **Rating** 94 **To** 2017 $31

ᵧᵧᵧᵧᵧ **Trinders Cabernet Merlot 2013 Rating** 93 **To** 2025 $35 CM

Cape Naturaliste Vineyard ★★★★☆

1 Coley Road (off Caves Road), Yallingup, WA 6282 **Region** Margaret River
T (08) 9755 2538 www.capenaturalistevineyard.com.au **Open** 7 days 10.30–5
Winemaker Ian Bell, Bruce Dukes, Craig Brent-White **Est.** 1997 **Dozens** 4500
Vyds 9.7ha
Cape Naturaliste Vineyard has a long and varied history going back 150 years, when it was a coach inn for travellers journeying between Perth and Margaret River. Later it became a dairy farm, and in 1970 a mining company purchased it, intending to extract nearby mineral sands. The government stepped in and declared the area a national park, whereafter (in 1980) Craig Brent-White purchased the property. The vineyard is planted to cabernet sauvignon, shiraz, merlot, semillon and sauvignon blanc, and is run on an organic/biodynamic basis. Exports to Singapore and Indonesia.

ᵧᵧᵧᵧᵧ **Single Vineyard Margaret River Shiraz 2013** Matured in French barriques for 14 months. A ravishingly vibrant and lively Shiraz that is also elegant and detailed, offering a range of flavours more commonly found in seriously cool climates, with black cherry and a charcuterie/savoury edge on the back-palate and finish. Tension and vinosity. Screwcap. 14.6% alc. **Rating** 96 **To** 2043 $25 ○

Torpedo Rocks Reserve Single Vineyard Margaret River Cabernet Sauvignon 2011 Hand-picked, mlf in barrel, matured for 2 years in barrel. It is a rich and complex wine, threaded by tannins and cocooned in French oak; there is plenty of cassis fruit, but there is a question about the amount of oak. Screwcap. 14.7% alc. **Rating** 94 **To** 2031 $60

ᵧᵧᵧᵧᵧ **Single Vineyard Sauvignon Blanc 2014 Rating** 91 **To** 2016 $18 ○

Capel Vale ★★★★★

118 Mallokup Road, Capel, WA 6271 **Region** Geographe
T (08) 9727 1986 www.capelvale.com **Open** 7 days 10–4
Winemaker Daniel Hetherington **Est.** 1974 **Dozens** 50 000 **Vyds** 90ha

Established by Perth-based medical practitioner Dr Peter Pratten and wife Elizabeth in 1974. The first vineyard adjacent to the winery was planted on the banks of the quiet waters of Capel River. The very fertile soil gave rise to extravagant vine growth, providing 95% of the winery's intake until the mid-1980s. The viticultural empire has since been expanded, spreading across Geographe (15ha), Mount Barker (15ha), Pemberton (32ha) and Margaret River (28ha); the most recent arrivals are petit verdot, sangiovese, tempranillo and nebbiolo. Exports to all major markets.

ŸŸŸŸŸ **Black Label Cabernet Sauvignon 2013** From the Scholar Vineyard in Margaret River. It's firm and powerful. It tastes of tar, blackberry, bay leaves and dry licorice, and indeed dryness is something of a theme. It's certainly not sweet in its profile in any way. Heavy chains of tannin tow the wine out through the heads and into the drinking future. It's not lively, or fresh, or seductive, but it is suited to cellaring. Screwcap. 14% alc. **Rating** 94 **To** 2030 $50 CM

ŸŸŸŸŸ **Black Label Margaret River Chardonnay 2014** Rating 93 To 2019 $50 CM
Regional Series Margaret River Cabernet Sauvignon 2013 Rating 93 To 2028 $27 CM ✪
Regional Series Pemberton Semillon Sauvignon Blanc 2014 Rating 92 To 2021 $25 ✪
Regional Series Margaret River Chardonnay 2013 Rating 92 To 2018 $25 CM ✪

Capercaillie   ★★★★★

4 Londons Road, Lovedale, NSW 2325 **Region** Hunter Valley
T (02) 4990 2904 **www**.capercailliewine.com.au **Open** 7 days 10–4.30
Winemaker Peter Lane **Est.** 1995 **Dozens** 7000 **Vyds** 8ha
A highly successful winery in terms of the quality of its wines, as well as their reach outwards from the Hunter Valley. The Capercaillie wines have always been well made, with generous flavour. Following the example of Brokenwood, its fruit sources are spread across South Eastern Australia, although the portfolio includes high-quality wines that are 100% Hunter Valley. The business is owned by Winston Wine Pty Ltd, a rapidly growing Chinese-owned wine business. Exports to the UK, Dubai and China.

ŸŸŸŸŸ **The Ghillie 2013** From the 70yo estate vineyard on red volcanic soils; open-fermented, matured for 14 months in French hogsheads (30% new). The harmony of the wine is exceptional: you would never guess (unless, you were a devotee of the Hunter Valley) that this comes from a very warm region. The purity of the fruit and the finesse of the tannins are impeccable. Screwcap. 13% alc. **Rating** 96 To 2038 $60 ✪
Brycefield Hunter Valley Chardonnay 2013 From the estate Brycefield Vineyard in the Lovedale district; free-run juice was cool barrel-fermented in French oak (50% new). An elegant and fresh wine, very much in the modern style, with white-flesh stone fruit and grapefruit flavours in a perfectly balanced, supple palate. Screwcap. 13% alc. **Rating** 95 To 2023 $32 ✪
Hunter Valley Shiraz 2013 A very good Hunter Valley vintage that has everything a Shiraz from the Hunter should have; it effortlessly caresses the mouth with dark berry fruits, fine, ripe tannins and perfectly judged French oak (30% new) from 13 months' maturation. Screwcap. 13% alc. **Rating** 95 To 2033 $35 ✪
Ceilidh Shiraz 2013 McLaren Vale (85%) and Hunter Valley shiraz given 14 months' maturation in all-American oak. Toasty, roasted characters play on blackberry and peppercorn flavour, with bitter choc and clove notes never too far away. Maintains a firmness throughout. The motor's running at high revs but it comes across as a purring rumble. Has a certain irresistibility as a result. Screwcap. 14.5% alc. **Rating** 95 To 2032 $50 CM
The Creel 2014 Light straw-green; proclaims its regional and (semillon) varietal make-up from the first whiff through to its finish and aftertaste; only the free-run juice from the protected environment of the Bucher tank press was used. Precision

and focus are the hallmarks, lemon/lemongrass/chalky acidity the flavours. Screwcap. 11.4% alc. **Rating** 94 **To** 2024 $45

Brycefield Hunter Valley Chardonnay 2014 A yeast with high aromas was used; barrel-fermented in 50% new French oak. The colour is a little forward, the palate decidedly not, with an elegance that is part juicy, part airy. Good stuff for a dinner conversation. Screwcap. 12.6% alc. **Rating** 94 **To** 2020 $32

The Clan 2012 Cabernet sauvignon, cabernet franc and merlot from the southern foothills of the Barossa Valley. It maintains an elegant profile as it offers flavours of blackberry, bitumen, fragrant herbs and crushed, smoked, dry eucalyptus leaves. It's fragrant, powerful but not heavy, and is unashamed in its promotion of complexity/savouriness ahead of sheer fruit force. More power to it. Screwcap. 14.5% alc. **Rating** 94 **To** 2026 $50 CM

Capital Wines ★★★★★

42 Cork Street, Gundaroo, NSW 2620 **Region** Canberra District
T (02) 6236 8555 **www**.capitalwines.com.au **Open** Mon–Fri 10–5, w'ends 9–5
Winemaker Andrew McEwin **Est.** 1986 **Dozens** 5000 **Vyds** 5ha
This is the venture of Mark and Jennie Mooney (of the Royal Hotel at Gundaroo) and Andrew and Marion McEwin (of Kyeema Wines). They joined forces to found Capital Wines, which purchased Kyeema Wines and related contract winemaking in 2008. The venture has seen the creation of The Ministry Series wines, with clever graphic design and generally invigorated marketing efforts. The estate vineyard is still an important source, supplemented by grape purchases. The cellar door operates in conjunction with the Grazing Restaurant in Gundaroo, in the 1830s stone stables.

ϘϘϘϘϘ **Gundaroo Vineyard Canberra District Riesling 2014** Wine of Show at the Canberra Regional Wine Show. Slashing style with scintillating length. Lemon, apple, mineral and bath salt notes, rind and floral aspects present too. Thrilling wine. Screwcap. 11.1% alc. **Rating** 96 **To** 2026 $28 CM ✪
Kyeema Vineyard Reserve Canberra District Shiraz Viognier 2013 In some ways it's exotically delicious drinking right now; in others it needs a good sleep in a cool, dark place. It's perfumed, meaty, crackles with dry, crunchy leaves, has a tangy, cranberried character that bursts through the finish with a razzle of licorice, black cherry, violets and five spice. In short, it's personality-laden, and a fascinating experience to sit with, and take in. But it has other delights in store, in time. Screwcap. 14.5% alc. **Rating** 96 **To** 2032 $52 CM ✪

ϘϘϘϘϘ **The Whip Canberra District Riesling 2014** Rating 93 To 2021 $19 CM ✪
Kyeema Vineyard Tempranillo Shiraz 2013 Rating 92 To 2022 $36 CM
The Foreign Minister Sangiovese 2013 Rating 91 To 2020 $25 CM
The Black Rod 2011 Rating 91 To 2021 $36 CM

Carlei Estate | Carlei Green Vineyards ★★★★★

1 Alber Road, Upper Beaconsfield, Vic 3808 **Region** Yarra Valley/Heathcote
T (03) 5944 4599 **www**.carlei.com.au **Open** W'ends 11–6
Winemaker Sergio Carlei **Est.** 1994 **Dozens** 10000 **Vyds** 2.25ha
Sergio Carlei has come a long way, graduating from home winemaking in a suburban garage to his own (commercial) winery in Upper Beaconsfield. Carlei Estate falls just within the boundaries of the Yarra Valley. Along the way Carlei acquired a Bachelor of Wine Science from CSU, and established a vineyard with organic and biodynamic accreditation adjacent to the Upper Beaconsfield winery, plus 7ha in Heathcote. Contract winemaking services are now a major part of the business. Exports to the US, Singapore and China.

ϘϘϘϘϘ **Estate Directors' Cut Central Victoria Shiraz 2007** A barrel selection that spent 24 months in oak. Deep crimson-purple; looks as if it might have the secret to eternal youth, so plush and rich is its panoply of velvety black fruits, licorice, spice and pepper; the tannins and oak both contribute to the total package. Diam. 14.9% alc. **Rating** 96 **To** 2032 $90

Estate Nord Heathcote Shiraz 2012 Red Cambrian soil; a 5-day cold soak, destemmed berries then wild-fermented plus post-fermentation maceration for 25 days, matured for 10 months in French oak (40% new). Deep crimson-purple, a full-bodied, layered palate brings pepper, licorice and bitter chocolate into play, backed by ripe tannins. Diam. 14.9% alc. **Rating** 95 **To** 2037 $149

Estate Sud Heathcote Shiraz 2012 Decomposed granite soils; identical making to the Estate Nord other than slightly longer on skins. A fragrant berry bouquet, and a lighter and softer medium to full-bodied palate will be ready well before Nord, although it still has an attractive web of red and black fruits, licorice and spice. Diam. 14.7% alc. **Rating** 95 **To** 2032 $69

ŶŶŶŶŶ **Estate Pinot Noir 2012 Rating** 92 **To** 2020 $49
Green Vineyards Heathcote Shiraz 2012 Rating 92 **To** 2025 $30
Green Vineyards Cardinia Ranges Pinot Gris 2013 Rating 90 **To** 2016 $27
Green Vineyards Cardinia Ranges Pinot Noir 2012 Rating 90 **To** 2019 $27

Caroline Hills

489 Norman Road, Yahl, SA 5291 **Region** Mount Gambier
T (08) 8725 8857 **www.**carolinehills.com.au **Open** By appt
Winemaker Terry Strickland **Est.** 1988 **Dozens** 300 **Vyds** 5.2ha
This is the venture of Helen and Terry Strickland, who started the ball rolling when they planted 100 cabernet sauvignon rootlings in 1988. The intention was to learn how to grow vines and make some wine for their own consumption. The original plan of a Bordeaux blend was soon abandoned with the realisation that the climate was far too cool; the present plantings are much more suited to the region. They walk around the red wine (other than pinot noir) problem by purchasing shiraz and merlot from Padthaway. Most of their own production is sold to larger wineries in Coonawarra, but they have established a winemaking facility in a disused shearing shed, and have expanded the facility with a barrel store and an underground cellar. The property has a large rambling country garden which is open from time to time.

ŶŶŶŶŶ **Mount Gambier Pinot Noir 2013** Machine-harvested, crushed, destemmed, 4-day cold soak, open-fermented, plunged 7 days, matured for 12 months in French oak. Light colour, but the hue is good; the bouquet is fragrant, the flavours with a pleasantly edgy/savoury undertow reflecting the very cool climate; delicious red fruits float over that undertow. Screwcap. 12.5% alc. **Rating** 93 **To** 2020 $35

Mount Gambier Chardonnay 2013 From vines planted in '82, the first in Mount Gambier; crushed and destemmed, 10-day ferment with yeast and mlf culture added, 12 months in a mix of French and American oak. A lively, fresh and zesty wine with more grapefruit than stone fruit, but none the worse for that. Screwcap. 12.7% alc. **Rating** 90 **To** 2020 $18 **○**

Casa Freschi

PO Box 1412, Ashton, SA 5137 **Region** Langhorne Creek
T 0409 364 569 **www.**casafreschi.com.au **Open** Not
Winemaker David Freschi **Est.** 1998 **Dozens** 2000 **Vyds** 7.55ha
David Freschi graduated with a degree in oenology from Roseworthy College in 1991 and spent most of the decade working in California, Italy and NZ. In 1998 he and his wife decided to trade in the corporate world for a small family-owned winemaking business, with a core of 2.4ha of vines established by his parents in '72; an additional 1.85ha of nebbiolo is now planted adjacent to the original vineyard. Says David, 'The names of the wines were chosen to best express the personality of the wines grown in our vineyard, as well as to express our heritage.' A second 3.2ha vineyard has been established in the Adelaide Hills, planted to chardonnay, pinot gris, riesling and gewurztraminer. Exports to Singapore and the Philippines.

ŶŶŶŶŶ **Adelaide Hills Chardonnay 2013** Wild yeast-fermented in barrel, 14 months sur lie, bottled unfined. Thoroughly interesting wine. The flavours: of hazelnuts,

cracked wheat, nectarine and citrus. The texture: satiny. The length: it sings with juicy, slinky flavour. Screwcap. 13% alc. **Rating** 94 **To** 2019 $45 CM
Langhorne Creek Nebbiolo 2012 Wild yeast-fermented, macerated for 28 days in open fermenters; unfined and unfiltered. Light body on a sturdy frame. Delicate flavours of mint, dark cherry, soy, twigs and tar. Floral overtones. Beautifully integrated in all respects. Cork. 13.5% alc. **Rating** 94 **To** 2024 $55 CM

ՊՊՊՊՋ **Ragazzi Adelaide Hills Chardonnay 2014** Rating 92 To 2020 $27
La Signorina 2013 Rating 92 To 2016 $30 CM
La Signora 2013 Rating 92 To 2028 $45

Cascabel ★★★★

Rogers Road, Willunga, SA 5172 (postal) **Region** McLaren Vale
T (08) 8557 4434 **www**.cascabelwinery.com.au **Open** Not
Winemaker Susana Fernandez, Duncan Ferguson **Est.** 1997 **Dozens** 2500 **Vyds** 4.9ha
Cascabel's proprietors, Duncan Ferguson and Susana Fernandez, have planted a mosaic of southern Rhône and Spanish varieties. The choice of grapes reflects the winemaking experience of the proprietors in Australia, the Rhône Valley, Bordeaux, Italy, Germany and NZ – and also Susana's birthplace, Spain. Production has moved steadily towards the style of the Rhône Valley, Rioja and other parts of Spain. Since December '14 the business has been quietly on the market. Exports to the UK, the US, Hong Kong, Japan and China.

ՊՊՊՊՊ **El Sendero 2012** Tempranillo fermented in stainless steel with some whole bunches before being left to macerate on skins for 2 weeks; then into French oak, 40% new, for 15 months' maturation. Silky smooth but light on its feet, with cherry and coffee cream flavours tripping through the mouth. Shows its oak but overcomes it at the same time. Intricately woven with tannin. Succulent finish. Essence of the variety. Screwcap. 14% alc. **Rating** 93 **To** 2021 $32 CM
Tipico 2013 Light, perfumed and elegant with aromatic herbs leading into curranty fruit flavour. Ripe but not heavy. Food stye as a genuine rather than backhanded compliment. Highlights of blueberry and violet. Moreish. Shiraz/Grenache/Mourvedre. Screwcap. 14% alc. **Rating** 92 **To** 2021 $27 CM
McLaren Vale Carignan 2013 It's a wine you just want to drink. It's juicy with acidity and sweet-sour red-berried fruits, and while there are flashes of tonic-like dried herbs, promoting a kind of savoury complexity, its fruity drinkability is its ace. Screwcap. 14.5% alc. **Rating** 92 **To** 2019 $32 CM
McLaren Vale Roussanne 2014 Barrel-fermented and matured in old French oak. You'd be hard pressed to pick the influence, even texturally, though it's more savoury than fruity and it runs with slatey length. Elegant. Screwcap. 13% alc.
Rating 91 **To** 2016 $25 CM

Casella Wines ★★★★

Wakely Road, Yenda, NSW 2681 **Region** Riverina
T (02) 6961 3000 **www**.casellawines.com.au **Open** Not
Winemaker Alan Kennett, Peter Mallamace **Est.** 1969 **Dozens** 12 million **Vyds** 1397ha
A modern-day fairytale success story, transformed overnight from a substantial, successful but non-charismatic business making 650 000 dozen in 2000. Its opportunity came when leading US distributor WJ Deutsch & Sons formed a partnership with Casella and, for the first time, imported wines as well as distributing them. The partners built their US presence at a faster rate than any other brand in history. It has been aided in all markets by making small batches (500 dozen or so) of Reserve and Limited Release wines, prices ranging from $10 to $100 across its product range. It is not generally realised just how large its estate vineyards are; the principal plantings are of pinot noir, merlot, semillon, sauvignon blanc, riesling, pinot gris, cabernet sauvignon and shiraz. Exports to all major markets.

ՊՊՊՊՊ **1919 Shiraz 2007** The '10 Limited Release and the '08 sibling of this wine have cork wine stains, each different from the others, but a great concern for wines of this price. Many of the SA wines of '07 were very tough, but not this wine, which has good mouthfeel to its abundant plum and blackberry fruit, finishing with fine tannins and quality oak. Far better than the other 1919 wines on release. Wrattonbully. 14% alc. **Rating** 95 **To** 2027 $100

Y Y Y Y Y **Limited Release Cabernet Sauvignon 2010** Rating 90 To 2018 $45

Castagna ★★★★☆

88 Ressom Lane, Beechworth, Vic 3747 **Region** Beechworth
T (03) 5728 2888 **www.**castagna.com.au **Open** By appt
Winemaker Julian Castagna, Adam Castagna **Est.** 1997 **Dozens** 1800 **Vyds** 4ha
Julian Castagna is an erudite and totally committed disciple of biodynamic grapegrowing and winemaking. While he acknowledges that at least part of the belief in biodynamics has to be intuitive, he also seeks to understand how the principles and practices enunciated by Rudolf Steiner in 1924 actually work. He purchased two egg-shaped, food-grade concrete tanks, each holding 900 litres. They are, he says, 'the most perfect shape in physics', and in the winery reduce pressure on the lees and deposit the lees over a larger surface area, which, he believes, will eliminate the need for batonnage. He has been joined by son Adam, who is responsible for the 400 dozen or so of Adam's Rib made each year, complementing the production of Castagna. Exports to the UK, France, Spain, Denmark, South Korea, Hong Kong, China and Japan.

Y Y Y Y Y **Genesis Syrah 2012** Shiraz with 2% viognier. Not quite as sweet/intense as the best prior releases but arguably more complex. It's both an entirely satisfying and an intriguing wine. Red cherries, blackberries, a flash of aniseed, cedary oak and both dried leaf and smoke-like notes. Highly aromatic; it draws you in; it deserves to be enjoyed from a large-bowled glass. Diam. 13.5% alc. **Rating** 95 **To** 2025 $75 CM

Ingenue 2013 A hot year has produced a restrained Viognier. It's a good outcome. The power is still there, the textural flavours of fennel, roses, super-fresh apricot and spice. But it's keeping some of its thoughts to itself, rather than insisting we hear everything at once. It's a most becoming look, and wine. Diam. 14% alc. **Rating** 94 **To** 2018 $55 CM

Y Y Y Y Y **Grower Selection Roussanne 2013** Rating 93 To 2019 $35 CM

Castelli Estate ★★★★★

380 Mount Shadforth Road, Denmark, WA 6333 **Region** Great Southern
T (08) 9364 0400 **www.**castelliestate.com.au **Open** 7 days 10–5
Winemaker Mike Garland **Est.** 2007 **Dozens** 5000
Castelli Estate will cause many small winery owners to go green with envy. When Sam Castelli purchased the property in late 2004, he was intending simply to use it as a family holiday destination. But because there was a partly constructed winery he decided to complete the building work and simply lock the doors. However, wine was in his blood, courtesy of his father, who owned a small vineyard in Italy's south. The temptation was too much, and in 2007 the winery was commissioned, with 20 tonnes of Great Southern fruit crushed under the Castelli label, and annual increases thereafter. Fruit is sourced from some of the best vineyards in WA, situated in Frankland River, Mount Barker, Pemberton and Porongurup. Exports to Singapore and China.

Y Y Y Y Y **Il Liris Rouge 2012** A 56/37/7% blend of cabernet, shiraz and malbec. This is winemaking of a high standard, even if (oak to one side) it is merely ensuring that the quality of the grapes has been property protected. The flavours cover much of the red fruit spectrum, with cassis, black cherry and blackberry woven seamlessly together on a vivid tapestry, high-quality oak and ripe tannins doing the rest. Screwcap. 14.9% alc. **Rating** 97 **To** 2042 $70 ❂

Y Y Y Y Y **Empirica Pemberton Fume Blanc 2014** Extended skin contact/ cold soak, partial wild barrel fermentation with high solids, explains how this exceptional Sauvignon Blanc was made. This really is barrel-fermented

Loire Valley/Dageneau-inspired, and duly delivered; notwithstanding all of its complexity, it has a piercing and pure finish. Screwcap. 13.3% alc. **Rating** 96 To 2025 $32 ✪

Il Liris Chardonnay 2013 Super cool-grown Chardonnay. Let it speak after the first taste, and let the flavour impact rumble around your mouth, stripping saliva as it gyrates again and again. Conventional measurements or descriptions of the Aladdin's cave of flavours really don't add much: you either get this wine or you don't. Screwcap. 12.4% alc. **Rating** 96 To 2025 $55 ✪

Great Southern Shiraz 2013 Vibrant purple-crimson; a perfectly built cool-grown Shiraz, making you wonder why you would look elsewhere; the bouquet is highly expressive, the counterbalance of the red and black fruits, spice, pepper, fine-grained tannins and French oak perfectly judged. Screwcap. 14.3% alc. **Rating** 96 To 2033 $32 ✪

Frankland River Cabernet Sauvignon 2013 Regal Cabernet with blackcurrant fruit at the heart of a multilayered and complex array of typical firm tannins, dried herbs and cedary tannins; the balance is immaculate, but the wine sings out for patience. Screwcap. 14.6% alc. **Rating** 96 To 2033 $32 ✪

Pemberton Chardonnay 2014 Vibrant, but a little deeper than most when 11 months old; barrel-ferment inputs are immediately obvious, providing aroma/flavour complexity, structure and texture likewise. Struck match, grapefruit zest and toasty oak have come together with unexpected poise, bordering on outright finesse. Quite a journey. Screwcap. 13.3% alc. **Rating** 95 To 2024 $32 ✪

Checkmate Pemberton Margaret River Sauvignon Blanc Semillon 2014 **Rating** 94 To 2017 $20 ✪

Empirica Pemberton Pinot Gris 2014 **Rating** 94 To 2017 $32

Empirica Uvaggio 2012 **Rating** 94 To 2027 $32

♟♟♟♟♟ **Checkmate Cabernet Merlot 2013** **Rating** 93 To 2025 $20 ✪

Castle Rock Estate   ★★★★★

2660 Porongurup Road, Porongurup, WA 6324 **Region** Porongurup
T (08) 9853 1035 **www**.castlerockestate.com.au **Open** 7 days 10–5
Winemaker Robert Diletti **Est.** 1983 **Dozens** 4500 **Vyds** 11.2ha

An exceptionally beautifully sited vineyard (riesling, pinot noir, chardonnay, sauvignon blanc, cabernet sauvignon and merlot), winery and cellar door on a 55ha property with sweeping vistas from the Porongurups, operated by the Diletti family. The standard of viticulture is very high, and the vineyard itself is ideally situated. The two-level winery, set on a natural slope, maximises gravity flow. The Rieslings have always been elegant and have handsomely repaid time in bottle; the Pinot Noir is the most consistent performer in the region; the Shiraz is a great cool-climate example; and Chardonnay has joined a thoroughly impressive quartet, elegance the common link. Rob Diletti's excellent palate and sensitive winemaking mark Castle Rock as one of the superstars of WA. Exports to China.

♟♟♟♟♟ **Porongurup Riesling 2014** Quartz-white; opens demurely, but by the time you begin to think the only thing the wine needs is a few years in the cellar, it starts tapping insistently on your taste buds, the finish building focus and intensity courtesy of lemon and mineral acidity, the aftertaste providing a reprise. Screwcap. 12% alc. **Rating** 96 To 2029 $25 ✪

A&W Reserve Porongurup Riesling 2013 From 30yo estate vines yielding 5t/ha; whole bunch-pressed and fermented with light solids. Archetypal Castle Rock Estate style, still very fine and delicate until you register the electricity of the finish and aftertaste, a foundation for its 20-year future. Screwcap. 12% alc. **Rating** 95 To 2035 $30 ✪

Diletti Chardonnay 2012 Estate-grown, hand-picked, wild-fermented and matured in French oak for 10 months. A distinguished, perfectly made Chardonnay that is just starting to hit its straps; white peach, nectarine and gentle citrus fill the palate and long finish. Screwcap. 13% alc. **Rating** 95 To 2022 $30 ✪

Great Southern Pinot Noir 2013 From 27yo estate vines yielding 3.7t/ha; 8% was separately whole-bunch fermented, then back-blended with the remainder after it had completed fermentation in French oak (35% new). Striking crimson-purple; the wine cries out for a minimum of 3 years in bottle as the savoury plum fruit yields up the spice and violets locked in its tight embrace. Will have a long and distinguished future. Screwcap. 13.5% alc. **Rating** 94 **To** 2025 $35

�♀ Skywalk Great Southern Riesling 2014 Rating 92 To 2020 $20 ✪
Porongurup Sauvignon Blanc 2014 Rating 91 To 2016 $20 ✪
Great Southern Chardonnay 2014 Rating 91 To 2018 $20 ✪

Catherine Vale Vineyard   ★★★☆

656 Milbrodale Road, Fordwich, NSW 2330 **Region** Hunter Valley
T (02) 6579 1334 **www**.catherinevale.com.au **Open** W'ends & public hols 10–5
Winemaker Hunter Wine Services **Est.** 1994 **Dozens** 1500 **Vyds** 4.45ha
Former schoolteachers Bill and Wendy Lawson have established Catherine Vale as a not-so-idle retirement venture. The lion's share of the vineyard planting is to chardonnay and semillon, with smaller amounts of verdelho, arneis, dolcetto and barbera. The Lawsons chose to plant the latter three varieties after visiting the Piedmont region of Italy, pioneering the move to these varieties in the Hunter Valley. In 2012 Wendy received an OAM for her work in tourism, the environment and viticulture.

♥♥♥♥♀ **Verdelho 2013** The still pale colour doesn't hint at the extra level of fruit flavours the wine has, tropical fruits with a distinct ring of citrus holding them together. Well above the normal ruck of Verdelho. Screwcap. 12.3% alc. **Rating** 91 **To** 2017 $16 ✪

♥♥♥♥ Grantham Reserve Semillon 2013 Rating 89 To 2020 $18 ✪

 # Catlin Wines   ★★★★★

39B Sydney Road, Nairne, SA 5252 **Region** Adelaide Hills
T 0411 326 384 **www**.catlinwines.com.au **Open** Not
Winemaker Darryl Catlin **Est.** 2013 **Dozens** 1000
Darryl Catlin grew up in the Barossa Valley with vineyards as his playground, picking bush-vine grenache for pocket money as a child. Various stints with Saltram, the Australian Bottling Company and Vintner Imports followed in his 20s, before he moved on to gain retail experience at Adelaide's Royal Oak Cellar, London's Oddbins and McKay's Macquarie Cellars. The next stage was studying for a winemaking degree while working at Adelaide's East End Cellars. Then followed a number of years at Shaw + Smith, rising from cellar hand to winemaker, finishing in 2012 and allowing him to establish his own business the following year. Exports to the UK.

♥♥♥♥♥ **Single Vineyard Adelaide Hills Shiraz 2013** Whole berries, with some whole bunches, fermented and left on skins for prolonged post-fermentation maceration. Deep crimson-purple; black cherry fruit is swathed in superfine, but persistent, tannins ex the long maceration – which has not been overdone. This has the style to flourish in bottle for decades. Screwcap. 14% alc. **Rating** 95 **To** 2033 $45
Single Vineyard Dry Grown Clare Valley Riesling 2013 Whole bunch-pressed, wild-fermented, on lees for 4 months. A very powerful Riesling that Rheingau winemakers would like and respect; it has a storehouse to feed on as it develops slowly over the next 15+ years, its citrussy acidity on the finish dangerously appealing, potentially cutting its life short. Screwcap. 12.7% alc. **Rating** 95 **To** 2030 $30 ✪
Single Vineyard Adelaide Hills Sauvignon Blanc 2013 Hand-picked, whole bunch-pressed, wild-fermented in French barriques for 84 days then 3 further months on lees. This is a wine almost entirely concerned with structure, looking to Bordeaux not Marlborough for inspiration. Length is its strength. Screwcap. 13% alc. **Rating** 94 **To** 2016 $30 ✪
Single Vineyard Adelaide Hills Montepulciano 2013 Extended maceration before maturation in French oak. Good depth to the colour; the maceration

has certainly given the wine a tannin-based structure to go with the strongly spicy plum fruit. While there is much interest in Montepulciano, what we need is mature vines and older vintages to see just how well it fits into the Australian landscape. Screwcap. 13.5% alc. **Rating** 94 **To** 2020 $30 **☼**

♀♀♀♀♀ The Molly Mae Clare Valley Riesling 2014 **Rating** 93 **To** 2024 $16 **☼**
The Molly Mae Gruner Veltliner 2014 **Rating** 93 **To** 2017 $16 **☼**

Centennial Vineyards   ★★★★★

'Woodside', 252 Centennial Road, Bowral, NSW 2576 **Region** Southern Highlands
T (02) 4861 8722 **www**.centennial.net.au **Open** 7 days 10–5
Winemaker Tony Cosgriff **Est.** 2002 **Dozens** 10 000 **Vyds** 28.65ha
Centennial Vineyards, a substantial development jointly owned by wine professional John Large and investor Mark Dowling, covers 133ha of beautiful grazing land, with the vineyard planted to pinot noir (6.21ha), chardonnay (7.14ha), sauvignon blanc (4.05ha), tempranillo (3.38ha), pinot gris (2.61ha) and smaller amounts of savagnin, riesling, arneis, gewurztraminer and pinot meunier. Production from the estate vineyards is supplemented by purchases of grapes from other regions. Tony Cosgriff has not hesitated to source grapes from Orange to meet the challenge of Southern Highlands' capricious weather. Exports to the US, Denmark, Singapore, China and South Korea.

♀♀♀♀♀ Reserve Single Vineyard Chardonnay 2012 Grown on the Rowley Vineyard
    at Orange. Straw-yellow colour, flinty aromatics, powerful fruit and oak through
    the palate. Textbook example of a complex style. Builds it up and then brings
    it home. Racy but rich, with a lively parade of textures and flavours. Screwcap.
    13.8% alc. **Rating** 95 **To** 2018 $28 CM **☼**
    Reserve Single Vineyard Shiraz 2013 Bright-but-dark colour; licoricey heart
    of flavour, though, with cherry-plum and violets in support; flings of spice without
    anything too overt; integrated smoky/saucy oak; fine-grained tannin and a lengthy
    finish. In all, a beautiful Shiraz. Diam. 14.7% alc. **Rating** 95 **To** 2025 $30 CM **☼**
    Reserve Single Vineyard Shiraz Viognier 2013 Excellent colour, bright
    and dark, with the flavour to match. It tastes of plum, black olive, dark chocolate
    and spice, the viognier both obvious and well applied at once. It has good length
    and fine, assertive tannin, but where it really builds its appeal is via silken, supple
    mouthfeel. Diam. 14.6% alc. **Rating** 94 **To** 2023 $30 CM **☼**

♀♀♀♀♀ Reserve Single Vineyard Pinot Noir 2013 **Rating** 93 **To** 2020 $28 CM
    Reserve Single Vineyard Sangiovese 2013 **Rating** 93 **To** 2019 $30 CM
    House Block Pinot Noir 2013 **Rating** 91 **To** 2020 $25 CM
    House Block Gewurztraminer 2014 **Rating** 90 **To** 2016 $24 CM
    Reserve Single Vineyard Arneis 2013 **Rating** 90 **To** 2015 $25 CM
    Old Block Savagnin 2013 **Rating** 90 **To** 2016 $20 CM **☼**
    Reserve Single Vineyard Barbera 2013 **Rating** 90 **To** 2018 $30 CM
    Limited Blanc de Blancs NV **Rating** 90 **To** 2016 $39 TS

Ceravolo Estate   ★★★★

Suite 5, 143 Glynburn Road, Firle, SA 5070 **Region** Adelaide Plains/Adelaide Hills
T (08) 8336 4522 **www**.ceravolo.com.au **Open** Not
Winemaker Joe Ceravolo, Michael Sykes **Est.** 1985 **Dozens** 15 000 **Vyds** 23.5ha
Dentist turned vigneron and winemaker Joe Ceravolo, and wife Heather, have been producing single-vineyard wines from their 16ha estate on the Adelaide Plains since 1999, enjoying wine show success with Shiraz, Petit Verdot, Merlot and Sangiovese. Their son Antony, and wife Fiona, have joined to take their family business into the next generation. The Ceravolos have also established vineyards (7.5ha) around their home in the Adelaide Hills, focusing on Italian varieties such as primitivo, picolit, pinot grigio, dolcetto, barbera and cortese. Wines are released under Ceravolo and St Andrews Estate labels. Exports to all major markets.

ŸŸŸŸŸ **Adelaide Plains Petit Verdot 2011** Matured in French oak. Petit verdot is an extraordinary variety, able to deliver depth of colour and richness of flavour even in (or due to?) a vintage such as this. Blackberry, black cherry and blackcurrant flavours all sing together. Cork. 15% alc. **Rating** 92 **To** 2021 $25 ○

Adelaide Hills Cortese 2014 Well made; it has an appealing floral bouquet and a nicely weighted palate, with nuances of stone fruit and apple. It could surprise with a year or two in bottle. Screwcap. 12.5% alc. **Rating** 90 **To** 2020 $22

Ceres Bridge Estate ★★★★

84 Merrawarp Road, Stonehaven, Vic 3221 **Region** Geelong
T (03) 5271 1212 **Open** By appt
Winemaker Challon Murdock **Est.** 1996 **Dozens** 500 **Vyds** 7.4ha
Challon and Patricia Murdock began the long, slow and at times very frustrating process of establishing their vineyard in 1996. They planted 1.8ha of chardonnay in that year, but 50% of the vines died over the next two years in the face of drought and inadequate water supply. Instead of deciding it was all too difficult, they persevered by planting 1.1ha of pinot noir in 2000, with replanting in '01, and then in '05 signified their intention to become serious by planting shiraz, nebbiolo, sauvignon blanc, viognier, tempranillo and pinot grigio. Those vines are now mature, the nebbiolo, in particular, proving its worth.

ŸŸŸŸŸ **Geelong Nebbiolo 2013** A very creditable effort with a notoriously difficult variety. The colour is good (for Nebbiolo) and the medley of cherry flavours has an appropriately savoury backdrop. Screwcap. 12.5% alc. **Rating** 93 **To** 2018 $25 ○

Geelong Pinot Noir 2012 Matured in French barriques. The colour is still deep and youthful, the complex bouquet and palate ruled by foresty plum/wild berry aromas and flavours. A wine of left field character, perhaps, but not diminished by that, and remains very good value. Screwcap. 13.7% alc. **Rating** 92 **To** 2019 $20 ○

Chaffey Bros Wine Co ★★★★☆

26 Campbell Road, Parkside, SA 5063 (postal) **Region** Barossa Valley
T 0417 565 511 **www.chaffeybros.com Open** Not
Winemaker Daniel Chaffey Hartwig **Est.** 2008 **Dozens** 20 000
Chaffey Bros was co-founded by Daniel Chaffey Hartwig, whose great-uncle Bill Chaffey founded Seaview Wines in McLaren Vale, and who was himself a descendant of the Chaffey brothers who came to Australia to create the Riverina and Riverland regions by designing and implementing the original irrigation schemes. Daniel, born and raised in the Barossa Valley, picked grapes during school holidays, and later on worked at Penfolds' cellar door. After eight years of selling and helping other people create wine labels, he became a bulk wine merchant dealing in both Australian and overseas wines and wineries and also developing a range of branded wines. Exports to the UK, Canada and China.

ŸŸŸŸŸ **This Is Not Your Grandma's Eden Valley Riesling 2014** Chalky, crunchy aspect to the finish is the icing on the cake. Intense lime, lemon and bath salt flavours make for a powerful impression. Spray of herbs in the background. Funky label, classic flavours. Screwcap. 12.5% alc. **Rating** 95 **To** 2022 $22 CM ○

Tessellation Eden Valley Riesling 2014 It whispers sweetness in your ear but there are more significant qualities to focus on. Apple, pear and lime flavours of good dimension sing harmoniously through a well-organised, well-powered palate. There's a bite of extra flavour on the finish. From three vineyards, includes 7g residual, and is clearly the result of a fine palate on top of fine vineyard sources. Screwcap. 11.5% alc. **Rating** 94 **To** 2020 $24 CM ○

The Super Barossa is Shiraz + Cabernet Sauvignon 2013 Stern but flavoursome. Strings of smoky, minerally tannin are visible throughout, yet the drama of the fruit still plays to good effect. Blueberry, coffee, blackberry and violet-like notes. It lifts and expands as it breathes in the glass/bottle; a stint in the decanter does it no harm. Screwcap. 14.5% alc. **Rating** 94 **To** 2026 $35 CM

♟♟♟♟♀ Synonymous Barossa = Shiraz 2013 Rating 93 To 2022 $25 CM ✪
Battle for Barossa La Resistance Grenache Syrah Mourvedre 2014
Rating 93 To 2021 $25 CM ✪
Battle for Barossa La Conquista! Tempranillo + Garnacha 2014
Rating 92 To 2019 $25 CM ✪

Chain of Ponds   ★★★★☆

Adelaide Road, Gumeracha, SA 5233 **Region** Adelaide Hills
T (08) 8389 1415 **www**.chainofponds.com.au **Open** Mon–Fri 10–4
Winemaker Greg Clack **Est.** 1993 **Dozens** 25 000
The Chain of Ponds brand has been separated from its 200ha of vineyards, which were among the largest in the Adelaide Hills. It has contract growers throughout the region for its various labels. Exports to the UK, the US, Canada, Singapore, Hong Kong, the Philippines and China.

♟♟♟♟♟ The Ledge Adelaide Hills Shiraz 2012 From two vineyards, with row and vine selection pre-harvesting; 2-day cold soak of crushed grapes in open fermenters, 7 days on skins, 20 months' oak maturation. A top-flight example of the synergy between Adelaide Hills and shiraz; the bouquet is alive with pepper, spice, licorice and black fruits, the medium-bodied, but intense and long, palate preserving all the complexity and fruit of the bouquet. Screwcap. 13.5% alc. Rating 96 To 2032 $38 ✪
Black Thursday Adelaide Hills Sauvignon Blanc 2014 There is an incisive mouthfeel, part due to 8% semillon, the flavours running from lemongrass and snow pea through to stone fruit/tropical, all this achieved in a fluid, seamless line. Great value. Screwcap. 12% alc. **Rating** 94 To 2016 $20 ✪
First Lady Barrel Fermented Adelaide Hills Sauvignon Blanc 2013 25% wild-fermented with full solids, 75% clarified juice with special fruit-enhancing yeast strain, fermentation completed in barrel, plus 9 months' maturation. Full straw-green; a Sauvignon Blanc wanting to be a Chardonnay, a role reversal if ever there was one. It has already hit the point of maximum flavour development while retaining acidity. Screwcap. 12.5% alc. **Rating** 94 To 2017 $38

♟♟♟♟♀ Corkscrew Rd Adelaide Hills Chardonnay 2013 Rating 92 To 2020 $38
Novello Adelaide Hills Rose 2014 Rating 92 To 2016 $16 ✪

Chalk Hill   ★★★★★

58 Field Street, McLaren Vale, SA 5171 **Region** McLaren Vale
T (08) 8323 6400 **www**.chalkhill.com.au **Open** Not
Winemaker Emmanuelle Bekkers **Est.** 1973 **Dozens** 20 000 **Vyds** 89ha
The growth of Chalk Hill has accelerated after passing from parents John and Diana Harvey to grapegrowing sons Jock and Tom. Both are heavily involved in wine industry affairs in varying capacities. Further acquisitions mean the vineyards now span each district of McLaren Vale, planted to both the exotic (savagnin, barbera and sangiovese) and mainstream (shiraz, cabernet sauvignon, grenache, chardonnay and cabernet franc) varieties. The Alpha Crucis series is especially praiseworthy. Exports to most markets: to the US under the Alpha Crucis label, to Canada under the Wits End label.

♟♟♟♟♟ Alpha Crucis Winemakers' Series Tom Harvey McLaren Vale Shiraz 2012 Definitely at the luscious end of the spectrum. It doesn't pour, it oozes. Thick blackberry jam, milk chocolate and raspberry, with splashes of anise, coffee grounds, condensed milk and cloves. When you're in this kind of form you can hardly have too much of a good thing. Besides, it all melts in your mouth. A combination of words you rarely see but which are entirely appropriate here: a robust delicacy. Screwcap. 15% alc. Rating 96 To 2030 $60 CM ✪
Alpha Crucis McLaren Vale Syrah 2012 Bright but intense. It aptly presents as a star in a dark sky. Bitumen, graphite, saturated plum and clove; it's on the finish where floral, musky, whiter stone fruit characters beam through, lightening the

mood. This is a substantial wine, with fruit and oak proving a powerhouse team. Screwcap. 15% alc. **Rating** 96 **To** 2035 **$85** CM

Alpha Crucis Winemakers' Series Peter Schell McLaren Vale Shiraz 2013 Heady but mesmerising. The word 'exotic' springs immediately to mind. Saturated plum and blackberry, orange rind, smoked meats, fresh fennel and crushed dry spices. It works up a glorious head of steam and then pours down and through the finish, complete with integrated tannin of superfine form. Screwcap. 14.5% alc. **Rating** 96 **To** 2033 **$60** CM ✪

Alpha Crucis Winemakers' Series Mike Brown McLaren Vale Shiraz 2013 Dark, inky colour. Lascivious fruit profile. Saturated plum, graphite, cloves and sweet, milky, smoky cedar. It roars and it croons and does everything in its power to win you over. Voluptuous but framed by fine-grained tannin. Screwcap. 15% alc. **Rating** 95 **To** 2030 **$60** CM

Alpha Crucis Winemakers' Series Bec Willson McLaren Vale Shiraz 2013 Tremendous concentration of fruit. Blackberry, asphalt, chocolate and a ribald assortment of dried spices. Soft in the mouth but not loose. Floral notes add another facet. Warm-hearted but ultra generous in the flavour it delivers. Screwcap. 15% alc. **Rating** 95 **To** 2030 **$60** CM

Alpha Crucis McLaren Vale Shiraz 2012 Grown on the Hickinbotham Vineyard at Clarendon. Intensely licoricey and blackberried with saltbush and a flood of smoky oak in support. Strong, muscular style. It doesn't flow, it flexes. Arms of tannin complete the picture. At the start of a long life. Screwcap. 15% alc. **Rating** 95 **To** 2035 **$85** CM

Alpha Crucis Winemakers' Series Corrina Wright McLaren Vale Shiraz 2013 Rich, swanky red with both red and black-berried fruit lighting up the palate. Texture is ultra smooth, spice and chocolate/coconut notes help fill it out, and clovey tannin then wraps it all up, pretty as a picture. A wealth of flavour and texture. Screwcap. 15% alc. **Rating** 95 **To** 2035 **$60** CM

Alpha Crucis Winemakers' Series Steve Grimley McLaren Vale Shiraz 2013 **Rating** 94 **To** 2030 **$60** CM

🍷🍷🍷🍷🍷 **Luna McLaren Vale Shiraz 2013** **Rating** 93 **To** 2023 **$18** CM ✪
McLaren Vale Cabernet Sauvignon 2013 **Rating** 92 **To** 2023 **$25** CM ✪
The Procrastinator 2013 **Rating** 92 **To** 2020 **$18** CM ✪

Chalkers Crossing ★★★★★

285 Grenfell Road, Young, NSW 2594 **Region** Hilltops
T (02) 6382 6900 **www**.chalkerscrossing.com.au **Open** Mon–Fri 9–5
Winemaker Celine Rousseau **Est.** 2000 **Dozens** 14 000 **Vyds** 27ha

Chalkers Crossing's Rockleigh Vineyard was planted in 1996–97, and is supplemented by purchased grapes from Tumbarumba. Winemaker Celine Rousseau was born in France's Loire Valley, trained in Bordeaux and has worked in Bordeaux, Champagne, Languedoc, Margaret River and the Perth Hills. This Flying Winemaker (now an Australian citizen) has exceptional skills and dedication. In 2012 a subsidiary of a substantial Hong Kong-based company (Nice Link Pty Ltd) acquired Chalkers Crossing, and has appointed Celine Rousseau as manager of the business in addition to her prior and continuing role as winemaker. Exports to the UK, Canada, Germany, Denmark, Sweden, Singapore, China and Hong Kong.

🍷🍷🍷🍷🍷 **Tumbarumba Chardonnay 2014** Grapefruit, white peach and nectarine ring bell-clear throughout, oak a largely irrelevant adjunct. While thoroughly enjoyable now, will flourish in bottle for a minimum of 10 years. Screwcap. 13% alc. **Rating** 95 **To** 2024 **$25** ✪

Hilltops Cabernet Sauvignon 2013 Excellent crimson-purple; the bouquet is pure, with perfectly presented cabernet fruit, the palate following suit; cassis and a hint of black olive/bramble flavours are supported by controlled tannins. This is the vineyard speaking with utmost clarity. Screwcap. 13.5% alc. **Rating** 95 **To** 2028 **$30** ✪

Hilltops Semillon 2014 Fermented in French barriques, then on lees for 10 months. A very good Semillon, in a different style from any other in Australia. The impact of the oak is on texture, with more mouthfeel, yet not impairing the varietal expression; lemon juice and lemongrass flavours are sustained by brisk acidity on the long palate. Exceptional value. Screwcap. 13% alc. **Rating** 94 To 2024 $18 ✪

ⵡⵡⵡⵡⵡ **Hilltops Riesling 2014 Rating** 93 To 2024 $18 ✪
Hilltops Shiraz 2013 Rating 93 To 2025 $30
CC2 Hilltops Shiraz 2014 Rating 92 To 2029 $18 ✪

Chalmers ★★★★★

PO Box 2263, Mildura, Vic 3502 **Region** Heathcote
T 0400 261 932 **www.chalmerswine.com.au Open** Not
Winemaker Sandro Mosele (Contract) **Est.** 1989 **Dozens** 7500 **Vyds** 26.5ha
Following the 2008 sale of their very large vineyard and vine nursery propagation business, the Chalmers family has refocused its wine businesses. All fruit comes from the 80ha property on Mt Camel Range in Heathcote, which provides the grapes for the individual variety, single-vineyard Chalmers range (Vermentino, Fiano, Greco, Lambrusco, Rosato, Nero d'Avola, Sagrantino and Aglianico). The entry level Montevecchio label is based around blends and more approachable styles. The Chalmers and Montevecchio wines continue to be made at Kooyong. A second vineyard at Mildura is a contract grapegrower, other than a small nursery block housing the Chalmers' clonal selections. In '13 a program of micro-vinification of the rarer, and hitherto unutilised, varieties from the Nursery Block was introduced.

ⵡⵡⵡⵡⵡ **Heathcote Fiano 2013** Has real attitude and assured character. Almond/peach kernel/pear and minerally acidity run through the length of the intense palate. This should leave no one in doubt about the long-term future of the variety in moderate Australian conditions. Screwcap. 13.5% alc. **Rating** 95 To 2019 $35 ✪
Sagrantino Appassimento 2013 Fascinating wine; the sagrantino sun-dried for weeks so that there was no obvious juice in the conventional sense, then crushed, macerated and pressed (all with great difficulty) to produce the juice to be fermented (at over 20° baume, I would guess) to ultimately produce this deeply coloured, intensely rich and sweet red dessert wine. 375ml. Screwcap. 13% alc. Rating 95 To 2035 $49
Heathcote Rosato 2014 Wild yeast-fermented aglianico in old oak. Pale salmon coloured, soft, fragrant, succulent and well flavoured, but crisp and clear through the finish. Places high emphasis on pure drinkability, using texture, raspberried fruit and a dry, savoury finish. Screwcap. 12.5% alc. **Rating** 94 To 2016 $25 CM ✪
Le Sorelle Heathcote Shiraz 2013 Good colour; the decision to pick a little earlier than most Heathcote producers in most vintages gives this wine a fragrant bouquet and a light to medium-bodied palate; there is a mix of red fruits and savoury tannins. There is a minor question whether the grapes needed a few more days on the vine. Screwcap. 13% alc. **Rating** 94 To 2028 $33
Arturo Heathcote Malbec 2013 Deep crimson-purple; a powerful, strongly structured wine that has the blood plum flavour of the variety, backed by ripe tannins and quality oak. This will age with aplomb for years to come. Screwcap. 14% alc. **Rating** 94 To 2028 $33

ⵡⵡⵡⵡⵡ **Heathcote Vermentino 2014 Rating** 93 To 2020 $25 ✪
Heathcote Greco 2014 Rating 93 To 2016 $29 CM
Montevecchio Rosso 2013 Rating 91 To 2020 $23 ✪
Heathcote Nero d'Avola 2013 Rating 90 To 2020 $29

Chambers Rosewood ★★★★★

Barkly Street, Rutherglen, Vic 3685 **Region** Rutherglen
T (02) 6032 8641 **www.chambersrosewood.com.au Open** Mon–Sat 9–5, Sun 10–5
Winemaker Stephen Chambers **Est.** 1858 **Dozens** 8000 **Vyds** 50ha

Chambers' Rare Muscat and Rare Muscadelle (or Topaque or Tokay, what's in a name?) are the greatest of all in the Rutherglen firmament, the other wines in the hierarchy also magnificent. Stephen Chambers comes into the role as winemaker, the sixth generation of the Chambers family. Exports to the UK, the US, Belgium, Sweden, South Korea, Singapore, China and NZ.

ΨΨΨΨΨ **Rare Rutherglen Muscadelle NV** Dark mahogany; the impact of the wine in the mouth is as extraordinary as that of the Rare Muscat; a micro-sip floods the senses as they go into overdrive trying to capture the myriad of interlocking flavours. The everlasting finish and aftertaste are the keys to this wine: it is not just the 5% of so of the oldest component (say 90 years), but the 5% of the most youthful (say 5–6 years) that, with a skill worthy of Michelangelo, have given the wine the vibrant freshness drawing you back again and again, but without diminishing its complexity. 375ml. Screwcap. 18% alc. **Rating** 99 **To** 2016 $250 ✪
Rare Rutherglen Muscat NV Dense mahogany; incredibly concentrated and complex, yet has a quicksilver lightness on the back-palate; the layers of flavour are almost countless. This wine is truly something that all wine lovers must experience at least once in their lives; one sip was taken for this entire note and the flavour is still building. 375ml. Screwcap. 18% alc. **Rating** 99 **To** 2016 $250 ✪
Grand Rutherglen Muscat NV The olive rim to a walnut-brown heart of the colour sets the scene; the heady essence of raisin bouquet pushes any discussions of the fortifying spirit to the back row; in its place there is an Arabian bazaar of spices, with a nod to Turkish baklava, then a rolling wave of Christmas pudding with a garnish of dark chocolate and caramelised rose nuts. The ultimate magic lies in the freshness of the finish. Screwcap. 19% alc. **Rating** 97 **To** 2016 $55 ✪

ΨΨΨΨΨ **Old Vine Rutherglen Muscadelle NV** This is a very good Muscadelle, with the Chambers stamp all over it. Interestingly, Chambers has elected to take it out of the standard Rutherglen classification system, and rely on 'old vine' as much as 'old wine' – although the wine has obvious age to its array of cold tea, toffee, spice and Christmas cake flavours. From a price point of view, it's equivalent to Grand. 375ml. Screwcap. 17.5% alc. **Rating** 96 **To** 2016 $55 ✪

ΨΨΨΨΨ **Rutherglen Muscadelle NV Rating** 92 **To** 2015 $17 ✪
Rutherglen Muscat NV Rating 90 **To** 2016 $18 ✪

Chandon Australia   ★★★★★

727 Maroondah Highway, Coldstream, Vic 3770 **Region** Yarra Valley
T (03) 9738 9200 **www**.chandon.com.au **Open** 7 days 10.30–4.30
Winemaker Dan Buckle, Glenn Thompson **Est.** 1986 **Dozens** 120 000 **Vyds** 139ha
Established by Möet & Chandon, this is one of the two most important wine facilities in the Yarra Valley; the tasting room has a national and international reputation, having won a number of major tourism awards in recent years. The sparkling wine product range has evolved, and there has been increasing emphasis placed on the table wines, now released under the Chandon label. An energetic winemaking team under the leadership of Dan Buckle has maintained the high-quality standards. Exports to all major markets.

ΨΨΨΨΨ **Barrel Selection Yarra Valley Chardonnay 2011** A high-quality example of Yarra Valley Chardonnay from a great white wine vintage; the cool conditions gave Chardonnay a fragrance and a wholly positive intensity that will see these wines stand proud over the years ahead; here fruit, oak and acidity are fused together, and will never break apart. Screwcap. 12.5% alc. **Rating** 96 **To** 2026 $40 ✪
Blanc de Blancs 2010 Doesn't disclose the cool-climate regions from which it comes, nor the (obviously long) time it spent on tirage; it has exceptional length and drive to its grapefruit, white peach and apple flavours, the fresh, zesty aftertaste particularly appealing. Cork. 12.5% alc. **Rating** 96 **To** 2020 $41 ✪
Barrel Selection Yarra Valley Chardonnay 2014 The power of elegance. White peach, grapefruit, flint and almond milk flavours shoot through the palate, light on their feet at all times and yet exuding presence and exhibiting length. Screwcap. 13% alc. **Rating** 95 **To** 2021 $40 CM

Barrel Selection Yarra Valley Pinot Noir 2013 A barrel selection of the best lots of estate-grown fruit that spent 12 months in French oak. Bright crimson, it has a svelte offering of black cherry, red cherry and plum fruit, tannins and oak invisibly mended through the palate. Begs to be cellared, allowing the largely latent spices free play. Screwcap. 13.5% alc. **Rating** 95 **To** 2025 $46

Vintage Collection Les Trois Rose 2010 Rose of such grace and refinement is rare. The elegance and energy of Coal River Valley (Tasmania) and Whitlands plateau (King Valley) chardonnay have been masterfully fused with 12% pinot noir red wine from Upper Yarra Valley, in a pristine, understated and focused style of rose petal, red cherry, strawberry hull and pink pepper. 3.5 years on lees has heightened mineral texture and subtle complexity on a finish of impeccable balance. One of the most exciting new Australian sparkling wines this year. Disgorged Dec '13. Screwcap. 12.5% alc. **Rating** 95 **To** 2015 $45 TS

Barrel Selection Pinot Meunier 2014 Made from the oldest vines on the estate's 'home' Yarra Valley vineyard. First release. More than mere quirk value. Fragrant and tangy with a dry, structural finish. There's perfume from both fruit and oak, woody herb notes, and generally enough flavour, though it feels minimalist, in a stylish way. Straight, well-pitched lines. Screwcap. 13% alc. **Rating** 94 **To** 2022 $46 CM

ȲȲȲȲȲ **Yarra Valley Chardonnay 2014 Rating** 93 **To** 2020 $23 CM ✪
Pinot Gris 2014 Rating 93 **To** 2015 $25 ✪
Pinot Noir Rose 2014 Rating 93 **To** 2016 $20 ✪
Yarra Valley Pinot Noir 2014 Rating 93 **To** 2021 $31 CM
Yarra Valley Pinot Noir 2013 Rating 93 **To** 2020 $31
Yarra Valley Shiraz 2013 Rating 93 **To** 2024 $31 CM
Sparkling Pinot Noir Shiraz NV Rating 92 **To** 2016 $32 TS
Vintage Brut Rose 2011 Rating 91 **To** 2015 $41 TS
Brut NV Rating 91 **To** 2016 $32 TS

Chapel Hill   ★★★★★

1 Chapel Hill Road, McLaren Vale, SA 5171 **Region** McLaren Vale
T (08) 8323 8429 **www**.chapelhillwine.com.au **Open** 7 days 11–5
Winemaker Michael Fragos, Bryn Richards **Est.** 1973 **Dozens** 5000 **Vyds** 44ha
A leading medium-sized winery in the region. Owned since 2000 by the Swiss Thomas Schmidheiny group, which owns the respected Cuvaison winery in California and vineyards in Switzerland and Argentina. Wine quality is unfailingly excellent. The production comes from estate plantings of shiraz, cabernet sauvignon, chardonnay, verdelho, savagnin, sangiovese and merlot plus contract grown grapes. Exports to all major markets.

ȲȲȲȲȲ **The Vicar McLaren Vale Shiraz 2013** From four blocks, open-fermented, basket-pressed to French hogsheads (22% new) for 20 months. Two blocks are on the Inkwell Vineyard, and the colour is indeed inky; by some distance the fullest-bodied and richest of the four '13 Chapel Hill Shirazs, but keeps its shape and balance, with a layered and plush palate, soused plum and black fruits, the tannins ripe, the oak keeping its end up. Screwcap. 14.7% alc. **Rating** 96 **To** 2048 $75 ✪

The Chosen House Block McLaren Vale Shiraz 2013 From a 0.8ha block planted in '77; open-fermented, basket-pressed to French hogsheads (15% new) for 19 months. Deep crimson-purple; medium to full-bodied, it has cascades of luscious black fruits and a hint of chocolate; the texture of the palate is quite exceptional. Screwcap. 14.7% alc. **Rating** 96 **To** 2048 $65 ✪

McLaren Vale Shiraz 2013 Open-fermented, basket-pressed. Good colour; takes a millisecond to establish its sense of place and variety; at the full end of medium-bodied, it has very good balance and texture, its luxuriant black fruits trimmed by bitter chocolate and ripe tannins; has impeccable length. Screwcap. 14.5% alc. **Rating** 95 **To** 2038 $30 ✪

The Chosen Road Block McLaren Vale Shiraz 2013 Scarce Earth. Open-fermented, basket-pressed to French hogsheads (12% new) for 19 months.

A very expressive fruit-laden bouquet and palate, plum to the fore, blackberry in attendance; here, too, there is excellent texture and structure to a medium-bodied Shiraz with perfectly ripened flavours and integrated oak. Screwcap. 14.7% alc. Rating 95 To 2043 $65

The Chosen Gorge Block McLaren Vale Cabernet Sauvignon 2013 Open-fermented, basket-pressed, matured in French hogsheads (20% new) for 19 months. A more elegant medium-bodied wine, still with intensity and focus to its cassis/blackcurrant fruit, and lengthened on the palate by fine, savoury tannins. Screwcap. 14.6% alc. Rating 95 To 2040 $65

McLaren Vale Mourvedre 2013 Open-fermented, hand-plunged, basket-pressed, matured in French puncheons and hogsheads (17% new) for 17 months. Very deep colour for the variety, and the depth of flavour is also excellent, avoiding excess tannins. I love Chapel Hill's description 'brooding ambition and an introverted decadence'. This walks the finest line between finesse and brawny power with nonchalance. Screwcap. 14.5% alc. Rating 95 To 2033 $30 ○

Parson's Nose McLaren Vale Shiraz 2013 Rating 94 To 2023 $16 ○

Bush Vine McLaren Vale Grenache 2013 Rating 94 To 2028 $30 ○

Parson's Nose McLaren Vale Cabernet Sauvignon 2013 Rating 94 To 2027 $18 ○

McLaren Vale Cabernet Sauvignon 2013 Rating 94 To 2035 $30 ○

♟♟♟♟♟ **Sangiovese Rose 2014** Rating 92 To 2016 $18 ○
Chardonnay 2014 Rating 90 To 2018 $16 ○
Grenache Shiraz Mourvedre 2013 Rating 90 To 2020 $20 ○

Chapman Grove Wines ★★★★★

29 Troy Street, Applecross, WA 6153 **Region** Margaret River
T (08) 9364 3885 **www**.chapmangrove.com.au **Open** Not
Winemaker Bruce Dukes (Contract) **Est.** 2005 **Dozens** 10 000 **Vyds** 32ha
A very successful venture under the control of CEO Ron Fraser. The wines come from the estate vineyards planted to chardonnay, semillon, sauvignon blanc, shiraz, cabernet sauvignon and merlot. The wines have three price levels: at the bottom end, the Dreaming Dog red varietals and blends; in the middle, the standard Chapman Grove range; and, at the top, ultra-premium wines under the Atticus label. Exports to Canada, Hong Kong, Singapore, the Philippines, Taiwan and China.

♟♟♟♟♟ **Atticus Single Vineyard Margaret River Chardonnay 2013** As much about elegance as power, though there's certainly no shortage of the latter. Such clean lines here. Lactose, dry pear, apple, oatmeal and white peach. There's oak here but it's seamlessly woven. Fluid finish. Beautiful expression of Margaret River. Screwcap. 13.3% alc. Rating 96 To 2022 $60 CM ○
Reserve Margaret River Semillon Sauvignon Blanc 2014 All flint and gunmetal. Sees time in oak and is accordingly textural and soft, but not so that it curbs the juicy flow of flavour. A reserve wine with its drinkability intact; notable for that reason alone. Screwcap. 12.5% alc. Rating 95 To 2018 $30 CM ○
Margaret River Semillon Sauvignon Blanc 2014 Pretty as a picture; complete with a sturdy frame. Texture, flavour, interest, length. Gravel, passionfruit pulp, spice and lemongrass. Makes an impression from the outset but maintains a sense of proportion and balance. Finish just keeps the momentum going. Screwcap. 12.9% alc. Rating 94 To 2018 $22 CM ○
Reserve Margaret River Chardonnay 2013 It's turned out well. It has presence and sweetness of fruit but it's elegant and lengthy. Peach, grapefruit, toast and chalk. Modern style, but rich pickings. Screwcap. 13.3% alc. Rating 94 To 2020 $30 CM ○

♟♟♟♟♟ **Margaret River Sauvignon Blanc 2014** Rating 92 To 2016 $22 CM ○
Reserve Cabernet Sauvignon 2013 Rating 91 To 2025 $30 CM

Charles Cimicky

Hermann Thumm Drive, Lyndoch, SA 5351 **Region** Barossa Valley
T (08) 8524 4025 **www.**charlescimickywines.com.au **Open** Tues–Fri 10.30–3.30
Winemaker Charles Cimicky **Est.** 1972 **Dozens** 20 000 **Vyds** 25ha

These wines are of very good quality, thanks to the sophisticated use of good oak in tandem with high-quality grapes. Historically, Cimicky was happy to keep an ultra-low profile, but he has relented sufficiently to send some (very impressive) wines. Exports to the US, Canada, Switzerland, Germany, Malaysia and Hong Kong.

ㅇㅇㅇㅇㅇ The Autograph Barossa Valley Shiraz 2012 Barossa at its effortless best, with deep black fruit aromas on the bouquet, the earth/mocha/leather spotlights to the abundant black fruits of the medium-bodied palate telling you to enjoy some bottles over the next 10 years, but keep some for the magic that will unfold another 10 years on. Screwcap. 14.5% alc. **Rating** 95 **To** 2037 $30 ✪

The Autograph Barossa Valley Shiraz 2013 Inky purple-crimson, this is a very good full-bodied Shiraz, the fruit so concentrated that it doesn't allow any heat ex the alcohol to escape, the front door of the palate bolted shut. If you are prepared to give the wine a bare minimum of 10, better still, 20, years, go for it. Screwcap. 15% alc. **Rating** 94 **To** 2053 $35

Barossa Valley Durif 2013 Deep, inky crimson, almost back in its centre; the full-bodied structure and depth throw down the challenge: when will the wine welcome visitors? Perhaps the cork is a clue, not so much that it may slightly hasten the development of the wine, rather that it may be headed north (China or thereabouts). 15% alc. **Rating** 94 **To** 2053 $38

ㅇㅇㅇㅇㅇ Trumps Barossa Valley Shiraz 2013 **Rating** 92 **To** 2025 $18 ✪

Charles Melton

Krondorf Road, Tanunda, SA 5352 **Region** Barossa Valley
T (08) 8563 3606 **www.**charlesmeltonwines.com.au **Open** 7 days 11–5
Winemaker Charlie Melton **Est.** 1984 **Dozens** 15 000 **Vyds** 32.6ha

Charlie Melton, one of the Barossa Valley's great characters, with wife Virginia by his side, makes some of the most eagerly sought à la mode wines in Australia. There are 7ha of estate vineyards at Lyndoch, 9ha at Krondorf and 1.6ha at Light Pass, the lion's share shiraz and grenache, and a small planting of cabernet sauvignon. An additional 30ha property was purchased in High Eden, with 10ha of shiraz planted in 2009, and a 5ha field planting of grenache, shiraz, mataro, carignan, cinsaut, picpoul and bourboulenc was planted in '10. The expanded volume has had no adverse effect on the quality of the rich, supple and harmonious wines. Exports to all major markets.

ㅇㅇㅇㅇㅇ Grains of Paradise Shiraz 2012 Matured for 2 years in new American barriques. Superb colour, and a pure bouquet heralding the plum and black cherry fruit of the precisely balanced and detailed palate, the American oak totally appropriate for the fruit flavours. While very different in terms of flavour, it is one of a pair with Voices of Angels. Screwcap. 14.5% alc. **Rating** 97 **To** 2047 $65 ✪

Voices of Angels Shiraz 2012 From a vineyard at Mt Pleasant on the border of the Adelaide Hills, matured for 2 years on lees in new French barriques. A supremely elegant, medium-bodied Shiraz, which quietly fills every crevice of the mouth with its insistent red berry fruits and beautifully integrated oak; it is, of course, easy to enjoy the hell out of this wine on its own, and when compared to Grains of Paradise, you see the mastery of Charles Melton. Screwcap. 14.5% alc. **Rating** 97 **To** 2042 $65 ✪

ㅇㅇㅇㅇㅇ Barossa Valley Rose of Virginia 2014 Vivid puce; a tailor-made 60/16/13/7/4 % blend of grenache, cabernet sauvignon, petit meunier, shiraz and pinot. There are few better roses than this in Aus or, for that matter, in France or Spain. The red berry flavours literally shimmer in the mouth, lightly but insistently exploring every corner, then finishing as brightly as a sunlit spring day. Screwcap. 12% alc. **Rating** 96 **To** 2015 $24 ✪

Nine Popes 2012 GSM matured for 26 months on lees in French barriques
(25% new). Always a trailblazer, and remains so today with the vibrancy of its
multifaceted, predominantly red-fruited palate; it is willowy, yet firm, and has
prodigious length, tannin and oak precisely placed and balanced. Screwcap.
14.5% alc. **Rating** 96 **To** 2037 $70 ✪

ΨΨΨΨΨ The Kirche 2012 **Rating** 92 **To** 2017 $35

Charles Sturt University Winery ★★★★

McKeown Drive, Wagga Wagga, NSW 2650 **Region** Orange/Riverina
T (02) 6933 2435 **www.**winery.csu.edu.au **Open** Mon–Fri 11–5, w'ends 11–4
Winemaker Stanton & Killeen **Est.** 1977 **Dozens** 10 000 **Vyds** 25.1ha
In May 2015 Charles Sturt University announced it had discontinued making commercial
wine, and – unable to secure the sale or lease of its vineyards in Wagga Wagga and Orange – was
removing the vines and returning the land to pasture. The experimental winery and associated
0.4ha vineyard at Wagga Wagga are being retained for education and research purposes.
A similar decision was taken by Roseworthy Agricultural College several decades ago.

ΨΨΨΨΨ **Reserve Orange Chardonnay 2012** Developed yellow colour but fresh in the
mouth. Stone fruit, oatmeal and grapefruit with an appropriate clip of toasty/spicy
oak. Fruit flavour rings cleanly, and clearly, through the finish. Screwcap. 11.5% alc.
Rating 93 **To** 2017 $28 CM
Shiraz 2013 Gundagai/Wagga. Heroic style but most attractive. Meaty and
spicy with substantial blackberry, iodine, clove and toast flavour. Rustic finish but
outstanding concentration given the price. Screwcap. 14% alc. **Rating** 91 **To** 2020
$15 CM ✪
Cabernet Sauvignon Merlot 2013 Gundagai. Mid-weight blackberry,
chocolate and clove flavours with a light sprinkle of dried sweet herbs. Feels beefy
and substantial with more concentration than is usual at the price. Good buying/
drinking to be had. Screwcap. 14.2% alc. **Rating** 90 **To** 2020 $15 CM ✪
Reserve Sparkling 2010 Pinot noir (almost two-thirds, the balance chardonnay)
takes the lead in a rich and intense style of notable toasty/biscuity character and
full straw hue, having built more secondary complexity during 42 months on
lees than might be expected, rendering 10g/l dosage a little more than it needs.
It retains vitality, cool Tumbarumba acid line and good persistence. Disgorged
June '14. Screwcap. 11.8% alc. **Rating** 90 **To** 2015 $28 TS

Charnwood Estate ★★★★

253 Burrundulla Road, Mudgee, NSW 2850 (postal) **Region** Mudgee
T (02) 6372 4577 **www.**charnwoodestate.com.au **Open** Not
Winemaker Jacob Stein **Est.** 2004 **Dozens** 960 **Vyds** 2ha
In 2004 Greg Dowker planted the vineyard on a historic property just 5 minutes from the
centre of Mudgee, nestled at the foot of the surrounding hills of the Cudgegong Valley. He
has established shiraz (1.5ha) and merlot (0.5ha), the wines contract-made by former Flying
Winemaker Jacob Stein.

ΨΨΨΨΨ **Mudgee Semillon Sauvignon Blanc 2014** A blend of Mudgee semillon
(presumably 85%) and Orange sauvignon blanc that works very well indeed; the
lemon and lemongrass notes of the semillon flow into a nice burst of tropical fruit
on the mid-palate, semillon coming again on the finish. Very keen price. Screwcap.
11.5% alc. **Rating** 90 **To** 2016 $18 ✪
Mudgee Shiraz 2013 Matured in French and American hogsheads for
12 months. This is a nice Shiraz, red fruits to the fore, black to the rear, all
abounding with life, and supported by positive contributions from both oak and
tannins. Screwcap. 13.5% alc. **Rating** 90 **To** 2020 $25

Chartley Estate   ★★★

38 Blackwood Hills Road, Rowella, Tas 7270 **Region** Northern Tasmania
T (03) 6394 7198 **www.**chartleyestatevineyard.com.au **Open** Not
Winemaker Winemaking Tasmania (Julian Alcorso) **Est.** 2000 **Dozens** 1250
The Kossman family began the establishment of 2ha each of pinot gris, sauvignon blanc and
pinot noir, and 1ha of riesling, in 2000. Some attractive wines from each variety have been
made. Exports to Taiwan.

🍷🍷🍷🍷   **Black Crow Pinot Noir 2013** There is charry oak on the bouquet, which is
also obvious on the palate, but this doesn't destroy the forest fruit flavours. Patience
may be rewarded. Screwcap. 13% alc. **Rating** 88 **To** 2017 $28

Chatto   ★★★★★

PO Box 54, Cessnock, NSW 2325 **Region** Southern Tasmania
T (02) 4990 8660 **www.**chattowines.com **Open** Not
Winemaker Jim Chatto **Est.** 2000 **Dozens** 300 **Vyds** 1.5ha
Jim Chatto is recognised as having one of the very best palates in Australia, and has proved to
be an outstanding winemaker. He and wife Daisy have long wanted to get a small Tasmanian
Pinot wine business up and running, but having moved to the Hunter Valley in 2000, it took
six years to find a site that satisfied all of the criteria Jim considers ideal. It is a warm, well-
drained site in one of the coolest parts of Tasmania, looking out over Glaziers Bay. So far they
have planted nine clones of pinot noir, with a 5000 vines per hectare spacing. This will be a
busman's holiday for some years to come, following his appointment as chief winemaker for
McWilliam's Wine Group.

🍷🍷🍷🍷🍷   **Isle Pinot Noir 2014** The first release of 50 dozen bottles, 60 magnums from
the best part of the estate. Clones 777, 115 and 8048, matured for 11 months in
1yo French oak. Bright, full purple-crimson, this is a world apart from the varietal
Pinot Noir, more powerful, complex and deep, black cherry and plum driving the
palate. Will develop superbly. Screwcap. 13.5% alc. **Rating** 96 **To** 2029 $75 ✪
Pinot Noir 2014 The third release. Takes in the remainder of the vineyard,
clones 777, 8048, 115, 114, 2051 and MV6 (in that order), plus 20% from a
neighbouring vineyard; matured for 11 months in French oak (33% new).
150 dozen made. Bright crimson-purple; fragrant cherry and plum blossom
aromas foretell a beautifully sculpted, long and fine palate, the fruit having eaten
the oak, the tannins a fine filigree. Screwcap. 13.5% alc. **Rating** 95 **To** 2024 $50

Cherry Tree Hill   ★★★★

Hume Highway, Sutton Forest, NSW 2577 **Region** Southern Highlands
T (02) 8217 1409 **www.**cherrytreehill.com.au **Open** 7 days 9–5
Winemaker Anton Balog (Contract) **Est.** 2000 **Dozens** 4000 **Vyds** 14ha
The Lorentz family, then headed by Gabi Lorentz, began the establishment of the Cherry Tree
Hill vineyard in 2000 with the planting of 3ha each of cabernet sauvignon and riesling; 3ha
each of merlot and sauvignon blanc followed in '01, and, finally, 2ha of chardonnay in '02.
The inspiration was childhood trips on a horse and cart through his grandfather's vineyard
in Hungary, and Gabi's son (and current owner) David completes the three-generation
involvement as manager of the business.

🍷🍷🍷🍷🍷   **Riesling 2013** Southern Highlands has a continental climate that is suited to
riesling, so the varietal flavours of this wine should not surprise. It is a tad soft,
and might have profited from earlier picking, but it does make the wine enjoyable
right now. Screwcap. 12% alc. **Rating** 90 **To** 2017 $30
Sauvignon Blanc 2013 While the impact of the wine is light-bodied, the
gooseberry, lychee and tropical fruits are distinctly varietal, as is the lemony acidity
on the finish. Screwcap. 12.9% alc. **Rating** 90 **To** 2015 $20 ✪

🍷🍷🍷🍷   **Diana Reserve Chardonnay 2011 Rating** 88 **To** 2016 $35

Chestnut Grove

Chestnut Grove Road, Manjimup, WA 6258 **Region** Manjimup
T (08) 9722 4255 **www.**chestnutgrove.com.au **Open** 7 days 10–4
Winemaker David Dowden **Est.** 1988 **Dozens** 15 000 **Vyds** 40ha
A substantial vineyard that commenced in 1987, with a winery constructed in '98, Chestnut
Grove has come full circle from founder Vic Kordic and sons Paul and Mark, to Australian
Wine Holdings in 2002, and back to the Kordics in '09 under the umbrella of Manjimup
Wine Enterprises Pty Ltd. Mark is general manager of the wine business. All of the 2011
red wines released in 2014 have extensive wine staining along the sides of the corks. Exports
to China.

Sauvignon Blanc 2014 Has considerable drive and intensity to its fresh aromas
and flavours, citrus to the fore, but with a spread ranging from savoury/herbal to
tropical; refreshing acidity lengthens the finish and aftertaste. Screwcap. 13.5% alc.
Rating 94 To 2016 $20 ✪

Estate Manjimup Chardonnay 2013 Rating 93 To 2018 $20 ✪
Reserve Manjimup Chardonnay 2011 Rating 92 To 2017 $40
Reserve Manjimup Cabernet Merlot 2011 Rating 92 To 2020 $40
Sauvignon Blanc 2013 Rating 91 To 2016 $20 ✪
Estate Manjimup Chardonnay 2014 Rating 91 To 2018 $20 ✪
Estate Manjimup Verdelho 2014 Rating 90 To 2016 $20 ✪
Estate Manjimup Pinot Noir 2013 Rating 90 To 2023 $20 ✪
Estate Manjimup Merlot 2013 Rating 90 To 2018 $20 ✪

Chris Ringland

9 Stone Chimney Creek Road, Flaxmans Valley, SA 5353 **Region** Eden Valley
T (08) 8564 3233 **www.**chrisringland.com **Open** By appt
Winemaker Chris Ringland **Est.** 1989 **Dozens** 500 **Vyds** 2.05ha
The wines made by Chris Ringland for his eponymous brand were at the very forefront of
the surge of rich, old-vine Barossa Shirazs discovered by Robert Parker. As a consequence
of very limited production, and high-quality (albeit polarising) wine, the wine assumed
immediate icon status. The production of 500 dozen does not include a small number of
magnums, double-magnums and imperials that are sold each year. The addition of 0.5ha of
shiraz planted in 1999, joining the 1.5ha planted in 1910 has had little practical impact on
availability. Exports to the US, Canada, Belgium, Spain, Singapore and NZ.

Reservation Barossa Valley Shiraz 2012 This is the ultimate quandary: if
you can handle 16% alcohol (presumably at a steak house), it's a good example
of its breed; if you can't, don't put your head in the lion's jaws. The points are for
lovers of full-bodied Shiraz, not far distant from vintage port. Screwcap. 16% alc.
Rating 94 To 2037 $65

CR Barossa Shiraz 2013 Rating 90 To 2033 $30

Chrismont ★★★★☆

251 Upper King River Road, Cheshunt, Vic 3678 **Region** King Valley
T (03) 5729 8220 **www.**chrismont.com.au **Open** 7 days 10–5
Winemaker Warren Proft **Est.** 1980 **Dozens** 23 500 **Vyds** 100ha
Arnie and Jo Pizzini's substantial vineyards in the Cheshunt and Whitfield areas of the upper
King Valley have been planted to riesling, sauvignon blanc, chardonnay, pinot gris, cabernet
sauvignon, merlot, shiraz, barbera, sagrantino, marzemino and arneis. The La Zona range ties
in the Italian heritage of the Pizzinis and is part of the intense interest in all things Italian. It
also produces a Prosecco, contract-grown in the King Valley. A new cellar door and restaurant
is planned to open in spring 2015. Exports to the Philippines.

La Zona King Valley Sagrantino 2013 Sagrantino often demands something
of the drinker and this release is in that category. It's a forceful, strenuous wine,

tiring if you're of a certain mind but rewarding if you're of another. Hulking tannin takes centre stage, or seems to, while flavours of plum, dried herbs, leather, roasted nuts and aniseed fight it out for second place. There's plenty to brood on here. Screwcap. 13% alc. **Rating** 94 **To** 2026 $30 CM ○

King Valley Riesling 2014 Rating 92 To 2022 $16 CM ○
La Zona King Valley Pinot Grigio 2014 Rating 92 To 2015 $22 CM ○
King Valley Pinot Gris 2013 Rating 92 To 2016 $26 CM
La Zona King Valley Rosato 2014 Rating 92 To 2016 $18 CM ○
King Valley Merlot 2013 Rating 92 To 2022 $24 CM ○
La Zona King Valley Sangiovese 2013 Rating 92 To 2022 $26 CM
King Valley Petit Manseng 2012 Rating 90 To 2016 $26 CM

Churchview Estate   ★★★★★

8 Gale Road, Metricup, WA 6280 **Region** Margaret River
T (08) 9755 7200 **www**.churchview.com.au **Open** Mon–Sat 10–5
Winemaker Greg Garnish **Est.** 1998 **Dozens** 25 000 **Vyds** 65ha
The Fokkema family, headed by Spike Fokkema, immigrated from The Netherlands in the 1950s. Business success in the following decades led to the acquisition of the 100ha Churchview Estate property in '97, and to the progressive establishment of substantial vineyards (65ha planted to 15 varieties). Exports to all major markets.

St Johns Limited Release Margaret River Cabernet Sauvignon Malbec Merlot 2013 60/25/15%. Authoritative wine with purple fruit aplenty. Tannin cracks a wide smile from the mid-palate onwards. Blackcurrant, boysenberry and bay leaves. Dry, hulking, muscular; its best days are far ahead of it. Screwcap. 14.5% alc. **Rating** 96 **To** 2035 $35 CM ○
The Bartondale Margaret River Chardonnay 2013 Specific rows hand-picked; whole bunch-pressed, 100% wild-fermented in a mix of French oak (barriques and puncheons). Lives up to expectations with white peach, nectarine and melon fruit, integrated oak and gentle natural acidity. Will develop at a leisurely pace. Screwcap. 12.5% alc. **Rating** 95 **To** 2022 $45
The Bartondale Margaret River Cabernet Sauvignon 2012 Specific rows were hand picked, with 10% malbec included. The colour is very good, fermentation and maceration extended for 45 days before transfer to 100% French barriques; not fined or filtered. Shows what the estate can produce, with feisty spicy cassis flavours balanced by pleasantly savoury tannins and cedary oak. Screwcap. 14.5% alc. **Rating** 95 **To** 2032 $55
The Bartondale Margaret River Chardonnay 2014 Hand-picked from selected rows. Wild-fermented in barrel. Unfined. Combines power and grace with aplomb. Grapefruit, lime, white peach and blossomy notes. Sweet/spicy oak plays a subservient role. Everything in the right order, in the right place. Screwcap. 13% alc. **Rating** 94 **To** 2022 $55 CM
St Johns Limited Release Margaret River Cabernet Sauvignon Malbec Petit Verdot 2012 A 65/20/15% blend matured in used French barriques. Is complex and medium-bodied, with a convincing tapestry of blackcurrant, redcurrant and blueberry fruit flavours given texture and structure by ripe tannins and well-integrated oak. Screwcap. 14.5% alc. **Rating** 94 **To** 2032 $35
St Johns Limited Release Margaret River Malbec 2013 They made 20 barrels of Malbec; this is the best four. It saw French oak for 16 months, though none of that oak was new. It's a wine of understated charm. Flavours of leather, blackberry and bay leaf sidle through the palate, in no particular hurry but with a clear sense of direction. It's a confident wine, well structured and mannered, with just enough upfront fruit to satisfy and more than enough length. Screwcap. 14.5% alc. **Rating** 94 **To** 2022 $35 CM

The Bartondale Margaret River Shiraz 2012 Rating 93 To 2027 $55
The Bartondale Cabernet Sauvignon 2013 Rating 93 To 2035 $55 CM
St Johns Limited Release Viognier 2014 Rating 91 To 2016 $35 CM

Margaret River Cabernet Sauvignon 2012 Rating 90 To 2017 $20
St Johns Limited Release Riesling 2014 Rating 90 To 2019 $35 CM

Ciavarella Oxley Estate ★★★★

Evans Lane, Oxley, Vic 3678 **Region** King Valley
T (03) 5727 3384 **www.**oxleyestate.com.au **Open** Mon–Sat 9–5, Sun 10–5
Winemaker Tony Ciavarella **Est.** 1978 **Dozens** 2500 **Vyds** 1.6ha
Cyril and Jan Ciavarella's vineyard was begun in 1978, with plantings being extended over the years. One variety, aucerot, was first produced by Maurice O'Shea of McWilliam's Mount Pleasant 60 or so years ago; the Ciavarella vines have been grown from cuttings collected from an old Glenrowan vineyard before the parent plants were removed in the mid-1980s. Tony Ciavarella left a career in agricultural research in mid-2003 to join his parents at Ciavarella. Cyril and Jan retired in 2014, Tony and wife Merryn taking over management of the winery.

🍷🍷🍷🍷🍷 **Reserve Shiraz 2012** Good depth and hue to the colour; has more depth than most King Valley Shirazs; spice, pepper, tobacco leaf (the power of suggestion?) and black cherry run strong and clear through the bouquet and palate, with anise lurking in the background; the tannins are all that one can ask for, ripe and balanced. Screwcap. 14.3% alc. **Rating** 94 **To** 2027 $40

🍷🍷🍷🍷🍷 **Shiraz Viognier 2012** Rating 92 To 2019 $22
Zinfandel 2013 Rating 91 To 2018 $28

Circe Wines ★★★★☆

PO Box 22, Red Hill, Vic 3937 **Region** Mornington Peninsula
T 0417 328 142 **www.**circewines.com.au **Open** Not
Winemaker Dan Buckle **Est.** 2010 **Dozens** 800 **Vyds** 2.9ha
Circe Wines (Circe was a seductress and minor goddess of intoxicants in Homer's *Odyssey*) is the partnership of winemaker Dan Buckle and marketer Aaron Drummond, very much a weekend and holiday venture, inspired by their mutual love of Pinot Noir. They have a long-term lease of a vineyard in Hillcrest Road, not far from Paringa Estate, Tucks Ridge and Montalto. 'Indeed,' says Dan, 'it is not far from the Lieu-dit "Buckle" Vineyard my dad planted in the 1980s.' Circe has 1.2ha of vines, half chardonnay and half MV6 pinot noir. They have also planted 1.7ha of pinot noir (MV6, Abel, 777, D2V5 and Bests' Old Clone) at a vineyard in William Road, Red Hill. Dan Buckle's real job is chief winemaker at Chandon Australia. Exports to the UK.

🍷🍷🍷🍷🍷 **Pinot Noir 2013** The satsuma plum of the bouquet, with a hint of fruit spice in the background, impacts immediately the wine enters the mouth; the balance is faultless, but the wine begs to be left to its own devices for a year or two, and will richly repay those who listen. Screwcap. 13% alc. **Rating** 95 **To** 2023 $40
Hillcrest Road Vineyard Mornington Peninsula Pinot Noir 2013 Bright, clear colour; the bouquet is very fragrant, with gently spiced red cherry aromas; the accent on the palate is purity of expression, and a gentle hand on the tiller. Very different from the '12. Screwcap. 13% alc. **Rating** 94 **To** 2023 $65

🍷🍷🍷🍷🍷 **Whinstone Vineyard Pinot Noir 2013** Rating 91 To 2023 $65

Citadine Wines ★★★★

5 Beverley Street, Cheltenham, Vic 3192 (postal) **Region** Yarra Valley/Mornington Peninsula
T 0407 100 313 **www.**citadine.com.au **Open** Not
Winemaker Kirby Siemering **Est.** 2008 **Dozens** 400
Citadine is the venture of Kirby Siemering, who is fully entitled to append 'Dr' to his name, but chooses not to do so. He obtained his PhD in microbiology and genetics, and for four years worked and lived in the UK heading a team that sequenced the genome of a wine yeast. During that period he visited many of the wine regions of Europe, and on his return to Australia in 1999, began the CSU wine science course. He subsequently worked vintages at Warramate and Jamsheed.

♀♀♀♀♀ **Red Hill Chardonnay 2013** Rich and heady. Lime, white peach and
butterscotch with an ooze of spice. Hits you between the eyes for flavour.
Screwcap. 13.5% alc. **Rating** 91 **To** 2019 $28 CM
Yarra Valley Syrah 2012 Single vineyard, wild yeast-fermented in small batches
with varying amounts of whole bunches; matured for 12 months in used French
barriques. An elegant and precisely weighted and structured wine, barely crossing
the threshold into medium-bodied territory. Needs a little more flesh on the mid-
palate for top points. Screwcap. 13% alc. **Rating** 91 **To** 2022 $34

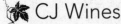 CJ Wines

60 Spiller Road, Lethbridge, Vic 3332 **Region** Geelong
T 0408 474 833 **Open** Not
Winemaker David Crawford **Est.** 2014 **Dozens** 4000
CJ Wines may be a virtual winery, owning neither vineyards or winery, but it makes up for
that with its people power. There may be only two partners, but their experience and skills
cover all the bases needed, while keeping costs to a bare minimum. It is in this way that they
are able to sell wines to the consumer for $15 a bottle which would cost $20+ when made
by conventional operators. The 'C' stands for (David) Crawford, the winemaker half of the
duo, 'J' for (Phil) Joiner, the marketer. David has 28 vintages under his belt, starting with 12
in Rutherglen, then a seachange with three at Taltarni/Clover Hill, the next eight as senior
winemaker at Willow Bridge Estate in Geographe, before moving back to Vic to Bellbrae
Estate in Geelong, where he is currently employed. Phil began his career in the glory days
of Mildara Blass/Beringer Blass, followed by work guiding smaller wine businesses for over
20 years. The Geelong St Erth Pinot Noir and Heathcote Redcastle Shiraz are both single-
vineyard wines, but the emphasis is on the value for money the wines offer.

♀♀♀♀♀ **Redcastle Single Vineyard Heathcote Shiraz 2013** Available from Dan
Murphy nationwide, explaining the quality/price equation – excellent. Black
fruits, spice and fruitcake sit well with the American oak in which the wine was
matured; the balance, supple mouthfeel and length are all spot on. Screwcap.
14% alc. **Rating** 91 **To** 2028 $17 ❂

♀♀♀♀ **St Erth Geelong Pinot Noir 2012** Rating 89 **To** 2015 $15 ❂
St Erth Geelong Pinot Noir 2013 Rating 88 **To** 2015 $15 ❂

Clairault | Streicker Wines ★★★★★

3277 Caves Road, Wilyabrup, WA 6280 **Region** Margaret River
T (08) 9755 6225 **www.**streickerwines.com.au **Open** 7 days 10–5
Winemaker Bruce Dukes **Est.** 2002 **Dozens** 15 000 **Vyds** 146.09ha
This multifaceted business is owned by New York resident John Streicker. It began in 2002
when he purchased the Yallingup Protea Farm and Vineyards. This was followed by the
purchase of the Ironstone Vineyard in '03, and finally the Bridgeland Vineyard, which has one
of the largest dams in the region: 1km long and covering 18ha. The Ironstone Vineyard is
one of the oldest vineyards in Wilyabrup. In April 2012 Streicker acquired Clairault, bringing
a further 40ha of estate vines, including 12ha now over 35 years old. The two brands are
effectively run as one venture. A large part of the grape production is sold to winemakers in
the region. Exports to the US, Canada, Dubai, Malaysia, Singapore, Hong Kong and China.

♀♀♀♀♀ **Streicker Bridgeland Block Margaret River Syrah 2011** Open-fermented,
matured for 18 months in French oak. This is gold-plated class from start to finish.
Superb colour is the first signal, the come-hither bouquet continuing the message,
but it is the palate that sweeps all before it: black fruits of every description,
cedar, spice and licorice are fused together, the balance and length utterly perfect.
Screwcap. 14% alc. **Rating** 97 **To** 2041 $43 ❂

♀♀♀♀♀ **Streicker Bridgeland Block Margaret River Syrah 2012** Back label text
is quite amusing; it's worth a look. The wine is serious, though, with cloves, nuts
and spice notes churning through intense black cherry and pepper, smoky oak

then clinching the deal. Assertive tannin, complex flavour, convincing power; it's excellent from every angle. Screwcap. 14.1% alc. **Rating** 96 **To** 2032 $43 CM ✪
Streicker Ironstone Block Old Vine Margaret River Chardonnay 2012 Shows its oak, no two ways about it, but the length of flavour here is exceptional. The fruit tastes of white peach, pineapple and nashi pear; the oak of cream and smoky cedar wood. It all combines to power on through the finish in blazing style. Screwcap. 14% alc. **Rating** 96 **To** 2020 $41 CM ✪
Streicker Ironstone Block Old Vine Margaret River Cabernet Sauvignon 2011 Dark colour with a crimson rim; penetrating fruit flavour, blackcurrant and gravel with studs of peppercorn; a swagger of tannin to close. This is in a good place, and has age-worthiness running through its veins. Screwcap. 14.1% alc. **Rating** 95 **To** 2032 $45 CM
Clairault Estate Margaret River Chardonnay 2013 A beautiful wine. Not in any way overdone. Pear, grapefruit and white peach flavours melt into blanched almonds and wood spice. It's charming in a pristine way; it finishes long. Screwcap. 13% alc. **Rating** 95 **To** 2020 $38 CM

🍷🍷🍷🍷♀ **Clairault Sauvignon Blanc Semillon 2014 Rating** 93 **To** 2017 $22 CM ✪
Streicker Bridgeland Block Margaret River Sauvignon Semillon 2013 Rating 93 **To** 2016 $35 CM
Clairault Margaret River Chardonnay 2013 Rating 93 **To** 2019 $27 CM ✪
Clairault Cabernet Sauvignon Merlot 2013 Rating 93 **To** 2025 $22 CM ✪
Clairault Cabernet Sauvignon 2013 Rating 93 **To** 2024 $27 CM ✪
Clairault Cellar Release Petit Verdot 2012 Rating 93 **To** 2021 $35 CM

Clare Wine Co   ★★★★

PO Box 852, Nuriootpa, SA 5355 **Region** Clare Valley
T (08) 8562 4488 **www.**clarewineco.com.au **Open** Not
Winemaker Reid Bosward, Stephen Dew **Est.** 2008 **Dozens** 5000 **Vyds** 30.5ha
An affiliate of Kaesler Wines, its primary focus is on exports. Its vines are predominantly given over to shiraz (15ha) and cabernet sauvignon (9.5ha). It also has 3.8ha of riesling and 2.2ha of semillon, but no chardonnay, which is presumably purchased from other Clare Valley growers. The business is growing rapidly. Exports to Malaysia, Singapore, Hong Kong and China.

🍷🍷🍷🍷♀ **Cabernet Sauvignon 2012** Estate-grown from Polish Hill and Watervale districts; matured for 12 months in barriques (20% new French). A robust and powerful Cabernet with bell-clear varietal definition, and the gold-plated guarantee of improvement in bottle for a minimum of 5–8 years. Screwcap. 14% alc. **Rating** 91 **To** 2027 $25
Watervale Riesling 2014 In the mainstream of Watervale style: abundant lime and lemon blossom aromas precisely reflected on the generous palate with enough acidity to provide balance and length. Screwcap. 11% alc. **Rating** 90 **To** 2020 $25
Shiraz 2012 Fermented in stainless steel for 7 days, then transferred to French oak (25% new) for 12 months' maturation. A potent, full-bodied wine; black fruits, earth, tar and a strong tannin presence are somewhat rustic, but this is as honest as they come. A Cliff Young wine. Screwcap. 15% alc. **Rating** 90 **To** 2027 $25

Clarendon Hills

Brookmans Road, Blewitt Springs, SA 5171 **Region** McLaren Vale
T (08) 8363 6111 **www.**clarendonhills.com.au **Open** By appt
Winemaker Roman Bratasiuk **Est.** 1990 **Dozens** 15 000 **Vyds** 63ha
Age and experience, it would seem, have mellowed Roman Bratasiuk – and the style of his wines. Once formidable and often rustic, they are now far more sculpted and smooth, at times bordering on downright elegance. Roman took another major step by purchasing a 160ha property high in the hill country of Clarendon at an altitude close to that of the Adelaide Hills. Here he has established a vineyard with single-stake trellising similar to that used on the steep slopes of Germany and Austria; it produces the Domaine Clarendon Syrah. He makes up to

20 different wines each year, all consistently very good, a tribute to the old vines. Exports to the US and other major markets.

ŶŶŶŶŶ **Astralis 2012** The price is stratospheric but so too is the quality. This mounts a watertight case. Voluminous fruit, dense in colour and concentration, large bones of supporting tannin and a resounding finish. Such super-sweet concentration isn't for everyone, but when it's done like this it creates a universe for you to immerse yourself in; it's as all-encompassing as it is compelling. Syrah. Cork. 14.5% alc. **Rating** 98 **To** 2040 $400 CM

ŶŶŶŶŶ **Brookman Syrah 2012** Its inky profile sets the tone from the outset. This thickset red oozes saltbush, concentrated blackberry and spice box flavours, though for all its depth and intensity it still manages room for brighter redcurrant and raspberry notes. Tannin is fine but insistent, alcohol warmth is never far away but never over the top, and oak handling is light, sure and positive. Ripping quality. Cork. 14.5% alc. **Rating** 96 **To** 2028 $95 CM

Sandown Cabernet Sauvignon 2012 Slippery smooth, slated with tannin, substantially fruited and seductive. This year you're on a winner with Sandown. Cassis, earth, mint and flecks of tobacco. How long do you have? Chances are it will live longer than that. Cork. 14.5% alc. **Rating** 96 **To** 2040 $75 CM ✪

Piggott Range Clarendon Syrah 2012 First bottle corked. Second bottle offered a warm parade of firm, hay-infused, blackberried flavour, one-dimensional in many ways but a stunning dimension it is. A wall of flavour with a wall of tannin melted into the back-palate. Dark chocolate notes are neatly shrouded by the darkness of the fruit. Cork. 14.5% alc. **Rating** 95 **To** 2030 $200 CM

Onkaparinga Clarendon Syrah 2012 Tremendous fruit intensity is met by a wave of tannin. It's a muscle-bound style and a champion of it. Bitter chocolate characters are everywhere through the wine, in a positive sense, but kirsch, bitumen and dark leather notes are the drivers. Long future awaits. Cork. 14.5% alc. **Rating** 95 **To** 2035 $95 CM

Kangarilla Grenache 2012 Grenache with guts. Prune, licorice and spearmint notes, overlaid with chocolatey/creamy oak. It's sweet, but dense and firm. The word 'monumental' springs to mind. If the cork holds out, it will live a long life. 14.5% alc. **Rating** 95 **To** 2035 $65 CM

Hickinbotham Syrah 2012 Almost fully stained cork. Dense plum, earth, asphalt and blackberry with clovey oak giving a masterclass on fruit–oak integration. Dense but remains bright and lively. Filigreed tannin does the wine's credentials no harm. 14.5% alc. **Rating** 95 **To** 2030 $90 CM

Onkaparinga Grenache 2012 Sturdy, structured grenache. Carries the expected raspberry and sweet licorice flavours but gravelly, grainy, almost sandy tannin adds an entirely different complexion. Will age. Has a bit of gravitas. Cork. 14.5% alc. **Rating** 95 **To** 2024 $85 CM

Hickinbotham Grenache 2012 Rating 94 **To** 2022 $50 CM
Clarendon Grenache 2012 Rating 94 **To** 2028 $50 CM

ŶŶŶŶŶ **Domaine Clarendon Syrah 2012 Rating** 93 **To** 2022 $41 CM
Moritz Clarendon Syrah 2012 Rating 93 **To** 2021 $80 CM
Liandra Syrah 2012 Rating 93 **To** 2025 $70 CM
Romas Grenache 2012 Rating 93 **To** 2021 $100 CM
Hickinbotham Cabernet Sauvignon 2012 Rating 93 **To** 2040 $90 CM
Bakers Gully Syrah 2012 Rating 92 **To** 2022 $50 CM
Brookman Cabernet Sauvignon 2012 Rating 92 **To** 2026 $70 CM

Clarnette & Ludvigsen Wines ★★★★★

Westgate Road, Armstrong, Vic 3377 **Region** Grampians
T 0409 083 833 **www**.clarnette-ludvigsen.com.au **Open** By appt
Winemaker Leigh Clarnette **Est.** 2003 **Dozens** 650 **Vyds** 15.5ha
Winemaker Leigh Clarnette and viticulturist Kym Ludvigsen's career paths crossed in late 1993 when both were working for Seppelt, Kym with a 14ha vineyard in the heart of the

Grampians, all but 1ha of chardonnay, 0.5ha of viognier and 0.25ha of riesling planted to rare clones of shiraz, sourced from old plantings in the Great Western area. They met again in 2005 when both were employed by Taltarni. The premature death of Kym in '13 was widely reported, in no small measure due to his (unpaid) service on wine industry bodies. With next generations on both sides, the plans are to continue the business. Exports to China.

ŦŦŦŦŦ **Grampians Riesling 2014** A tour de force in balancing residual sugar and titratable acidity; the bouquet gives little idea about the palate to follow; it is here that lime juice, lemon zest and apple skin join forces and drive through the long, lingering palate, its acidity adding to the mouth-watering quality of the wine. A 20-year future is assured. Screwcap. 11.5% alc. **Rating** 96 **To** 2034 $23 ✪
Grampians Shiraz 2013 Made with old clone St Ethels, unique to the Grampians. Glorious deep purple-crimson; the bouquet is complex and tantalising, dark forest fruits and spice to the fore, the medium-bodied palate with tightly controlled power and immaculate balance, the flavours tracking the bouquet in a steady stream from start to finish. Screwcap. 14% alc. **Rating** 95 **To** 2033 $35 ✪

ŦŦŦŦŦ **Grampians Viognier 2013 Rating** 90 **To** 2016 $23

Claymore Wines ★★★★

7145 Horrocks Way, Leasingham, SA 5452 **Region** Clare Valley
T (08) 8843 0200 **www**.claymorewines.com.au **Open** 7 days 10–5
Winemaker Donna Stephens, Marnie Roberts **Est.** 1998 **Dozens** 12 000 **Vyds** 27ha
Claymore Wines is the venture of a medical professional who imagined that it would lead the way to early retirement (which, of course, it did not). The starting date depends on which event you take: the first 4ha vineyard at Leasingham purchased in 1991 (with 70-year-old grenache, riesling and shiraz); '96, when a 16ha block at Penwortham was purchased and planted to shiraz, merlot and grenache; '97, when the first wines were made; or '98, when the first releases came onto the market. The labels are inspired by U2, Pink Floyd and Lou Reed. Exports to the UK, Canada, Denmark, Malaysia, Singapore, Taiwan, Hong Kong and China.

ŦŦŦŦŦ **Joshua Tree Watervale Riesling 2014** Classic Watervale, with a fragrant and floral bouquet leading into a palate that has considerable grip and attitude; the flavours are in the citrus family, from the familiar lime to the less familiar grapefruit; it has remarkable texture given a no-tricks fermentation, and will develop well. Screwcap. 12% alc. **Rating** 94 **To** 2024 $22 ✪
You'll Never Walk Alone Grenache Mataro Shiraz 2013 A 68/23/9% blend from the dry-grown estate Penwortham vineyard, the grenache and mataro co-fermented, the shiraz component determined by blending trials after 12 months in American oak (10% new). Has more weight, texture and structure than most Clare Valley blends of these varieties, with blackberry, plum and red cherry fruit all contributing. Screwcap. 14.5% alc. **Rating** 94 **To** 2025 $22 ✪

ŦŦŦŦŦ **Dark Side of the Moon Clare Valley Shiraz 2012 Rating** 93 **To** 2027 $25 ✪
Black Magic Woman Reserve Cabernet 2012 Rating 92 **To** 2022 $35 CM
Walk on the Wild Side Shiraz 2013 Rating 91 **To** 2019 $22 CM ✪

Clemens Hill ★★★★★

686 Richmond Road, Cambridge, Tas 7170 **Region** Southern Tasmania
T (03) 6248 5587 **www**.clemenshill.com.au **Open** By appt
Winemaker Winemaking Tasmania **Est.** 1994 **Dozens** 3500 **Vyds** 8ha
Clemens Hill is now jointly owned by Aurelia D'Ettorre and Dr Rob Ware. Rob has over 20 years' experience in the Tasmanian wine industry, having been a partner with Fred Peacock at Bream Creek since 1989. Clemens Hill now has two vineyards: the estate property with pinot noir, sauvignon blanc and semillon, and the Tashinga Vineyard, also in the Coal River area, but with a different climate, bringing chardonnay and additional pinot noir. A representative range of wines was not received for this edition, but the rating has been maintained.

ΨΨΨΨΨ **Aurelia Chardonnay 2013** Flinty Chablis style; crisp fruit, green apple/
citrus flavours, the oak not obvious; line and balance are its strong points; hangs
together very well. From the estate-owned Tashinga Vineyard. Screwcap. 12.7% alc.
Rating 94 **To** 2022 $55

Clonakilla ★★★★★

Crisps Lane, Murrumbateman, NSW 2582 **Region** Canberra District
T (02) 6227 5877 **www.**clonakilla.com.au **Open** 7 days 10–5
Winemaker Tim Kirk, Bryan Martin **Est.** 1971 **Dozens** 17 000 **Vyds** 13.5ha
The indefatigable Tim Kirk, with an inexhaustible thirst for knowledge, is the winemaker and
manager of this family winery founded by his father, scientist Dr John Kirk. It is not at all
surprising that the quality of the wines is excellent, especially the Shiraz Viognier, which has
paved the way for numerous others to follow, but remains the icon. Demand for the wines
outstrips supply, even with the 1998 acquisition of an adjoining 20ha property by Tim and
wife Lara Kirk, and planted to shiraz and viognier; the first Hilltops Shiraz being made in 2000,
from the best Hilltops vineyards; the 2007 purchase by the Kirk family of another adjoining
property, and the planting of another 1.8ha of shiraz, plus 0.4ha of grenache, mourvedre and
cinsaut; and in the same year, the first vintage of O'Riada Shiraz. Exports to all major markets.

ΨΨΨΨΨ **O'Riada Canberra District Shiraz 2014** This has class stamped all over it
from the moment you first taste it, sweeping away any necessity to describe the
colour or bouquet; it creates a sparkling river of dark fruits that run from the tip
of the tongue through to the elegant, but oh so complex, finish and aftertaste.
Exhilarating. Screwcap. 13.5% alc. **Rating** 97 **To** 2045 $45 ✪

ΨΨΨΨΨ **Murrumbateman Syrah 2013** From the warmest spot on the estate, the top
half of T & L Block, planted in '99. Destemmed, not crushed; wild ferment, no
viognier; 1 months on skins; 15 months in very tight grain French oak (33% new).
The bright colour and fragrant bouquet introduce an exceptionally complex wine,
fruit and tannins embracing each other, framed by quality oak. Will develop and
live for decades. Screwcap. 14% alc. **Rating** 96 **To** 2038 $110
Shiraz Viognier 2014 The bright hue and perfumed bouquet run true to type
for this modern classic, setting the bar for the co-fermented blend several years
ago. It has a set of flavours that are unique, and can fool even expert tasters in blind
tastings; its cross-thatched flavours (not textures) need careful navigation. Screwcap.
13.5% alc. **Rating** 96 **To** 2034 $110
Canberra District Riesling 2014 This is succulent, smoky, complex and pure.
Difficult to ask for more. Moreish flavours of lime, sweet pear, apple skin and slate.
Floral aromatics. Super. Screwcap. 12.5% alc. **Rating** 95 **To** 2025 $28 CM ✪
Canberra District Viognier 2014 A very small crop, largely due to spring frost
and rain welcoming the '14 vintage birth, gave rise to an intensely flavoured and
tautly featured and structured wine; it takes the palate onto a seldom traversed
path, with apricot, lime and orange skin flavours, acidity beating a tattoo on the
finish. Screwcap. 13.5% alc. **Rating** 95 **To** 2018 $55
Hilltops Shiraz 2014 Deep crimson-purple; unlike the colour, the moderate
alcohol gives no clue about the wine, which is full to the brim with saturnine
black fruits, the tannins part of the wine's DNA; says Tim Kirk on the back label
'Ten years in a cool cellar would do it no harm at all'; my only question is what
about 20 years? Screwcap. 14% alc. **Rating** 95 **To** 2034 $35 ✪
Ballinderry 2013 A 42/35/23% blend of cabernet franc, merlot and cabernet
sauvignon. Brilliant crimson-purple; back to where it all began, and with intense
style. That sure touch of Tim Kirk in giving balance, texture and structure is very
obvious here, the tannins silky, the oak in positive support. Screwcap. 14% alc.
Rating 95 **To** 2030 $55
Tumbarumba Chardonnay 2014 Rating 94 **To** 2025 $45

ΨΨΨΨΩ **Murrumbateman Pinot Noir 2014 Rating** 92 **To** 2023 $55

Clos Clare

45 Old Road, Watervale, SA 5452 **Region** Clare Valley.
T (08) 8843 0161 **www**.closclare.com.au **Open** W'ends & public hols 11–5
Winemaker Sam and Tom Barry **Est.** 1993 **Dozens** 700 **Vyds** 2ha
Clos Clare was acquired by the Barry family in 2008. Riesling continues to be made from the
2ha unirrigated section of the original Florita Vineyard (the major part of that vineyard was
already in Barry ownership) and newly introduced red wines are coming from a 49-year-old
vineyard beside the Armagh site. Exports to the UK.

Watervale Riesling 2014 From a 44yo dry-grown vineyard, hand-picked,
chilled overnight, then whole bunch-pressed. Apple and lemon blossom fragrance
sets the scene for a particularly elegant and focused palate; while still in a primary
phase, and very delicate, it has utterly perfect line, length and balance. Screwcap.
11.5% alc. **Rating** 95 **To** 2029 $26 ✪

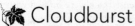 Cloudburst

PO Box 1294, Margaret River, WA 6285 **Region** Margaret River
T (08) 6323 2333 **www**.cloudburstwine.com **Open** Not
Winemaker Will Berliner **Est.** 2005 **Dozens** 450 **Vyds** 5ha
An extremely interesting new winery. Will Berliner and wife Alison Jobson spent several
years in Australia searching for a place that resonated with them, and on their first visit
to Margaret River were immediately smitten, drawn by its biodiversity, beaches, farms,
vineyards, community and lifestyle. When they purchased their land in 2004 they hadn't the
slightest connection with wine and no intention of ever getting involved. Will explains he
had organic gardens since his teen years, has kept bees for decades, and been the steward of
forests he owns in the US, studying related subjects at university level. Within 12 months his
perspective had entirely changed, and in '05 he began green manuring the vineyard site and
applying biodynamic preparations, seeking to build microbial life in the soil. They planted the
vineyard as if it were a garden, with short rows, and initially planted 0.2ha of each of cabernet
sauvignon and chardonnay, and 0.1ha of malbec. By 2018 the vineyard will have doubled in
size, but without changing the varieties or their proportions. The packaging is truly striking
and imaginative, and one is tempted to say the same thing of the prices of the wines. The
unseen hand is that of the Watson family, the wines being made at Woodlands by Will under
the watchful eye of Stuart Watson. Exports to the US.

Margaret River Chardonnay 2014 Bright straw-green; Cloudburst has
either managed to secure some top-flight grapes and/or had the wines made
very skilfully; either way, both this and its Cabernet Sauvignon have great purity
and tightly controlled winemaking at every point along the way. White flowers,
grapefruit and high tensile acidity are the keys to this wine. Screwcap. 13.5% alc.
Rating 96 **To** 2026 $200
Margaret River Cabernet Sauvignon 2013 Pale crimson-purple; a striking
black bottle with a single word on the screen-printed gold label: 'Cloudburst'.
This is a very well made Margaret River Cabernet, with purity and focus its
watchwords; cassis and bay leaf fruit sits in a frame of firm, but not dry, tannins; has
impressive length. Screwcap. 13.2% alc. **Rating** 96 **To** 2043 $250
Margaret River Cabernet Sauvignon 2012 Ritzy packaging to one side, an
outstanding feature of this wine is its exceptionally supple mouthfeel. Having said
that, the purity of the varietal expression lays convincing claim to being more
striking than the mouthfeel. Then there is the perfection of the balance. It goes on
and on. Screwcap. 13.5% alc. **Rating** 96 **To** 2037 $250
Margaret River Malbec 2013 Bright crimson; an impeccably made wine
without a single blemish in its complexion, the bouquet and palate deliver the
same message: clearly varietal plum with fine tannins and quality oak. Screwcap.
13.1% alc. **Rating** 95 **To** 2027 $225
Margaret River Malbec 2012 This has slightly brighter colour than its '13
counterpart, and a more lively bouquet and palate; whether this faint emission of
mint and herbal adds positive interest to an otherwise serene wine (à la '13) is a

moot point. The breathtaking prices of all the Cloudburst wines is another matter. Screwcap. 13% alc. **Rating** 94 **To** 2022 $225

♟♟♟♟♟ **Margaret River Chardonnay 2013 Rating** 91 **To** 2020 $200

Clovely Estate   ★★★★

Steinhardts Road, Moffatdale via Murgon, Qld 4605 **Region** South Burnett
T (07) 3876 3100 **www**.clovely.com.au **Open** 7 days 10–4
Winemaker Luke Fitzpatrick, Sarah Boyce **Est.** 1997 **Dozens** 25 000 **Vyds** 173.76ha
Clovely Estate has the largest vineyards in Qld, with immaculately maintained vines at two locations in the Burnett Valley. There are 140ha of red grapes (including 60ha of shiraz) and 34ha of white grapes. The attractively packaged wines are sold in various styles at various price points. The estate also has a second cellar door at 210 Musgrave Road, Red Hill (open Tues–Sat 11–7). Exports to Denmark, Papua New Guinea, Taiwan and China.

♟♟♟♟♟ **Double Pruned South Burnett Shiraz 2013** Intense blackberry infused with clove, peppercorn and woodsmoke. It doesn't look particularly dark in the glass but there's a wealth of flavour to tuck into on the palate. Neither complexity nor persistence can be faulted. Screwcap. 14.5% alc. **Rating** 94 **To** 2026 $65 CM

♟♟♟♟♟ **Left Field South Burnett Semillon 2013 Rating** 92 **To** 2020 $25 CM

Clover Hill   ★★★★☆

60 Clover Hill Road, Lebrina, Tas 7254 **Region** Northern Tasmania
T (03) 5459 7900 **www**.cloverhillwines.com.au **Open** By appt
Winemaker Robert Heywood, Loic Le Calvez **Est.** 1986 **Dozens** 12 000 **Vyds** 23.9ha
Clover Hill was established by Taltarni in 1986 with the sole purpose of making a premium sparkling wine. It has 23.9ha of vineyards (chardonnay, pinot noir and pinot meunier) and its sparkling wine quality is excellent, combining finesse with power and length. The American owner and founder of Clos du Val (Napa Valley), Taltarni and Clover Hill has brought these businesses and Domaine de Nizas (Languedoc) under the one management roof, the group known as Goelet Wine Estates. Exports to the UK, the US and other major markets.

♟♟♟♟♟ **Blanc de Blancs Late Disgorged 2001** Signature Blanc de Blancs at the prime of its life, testimony to the stamina of chardonnay from Clover Hill's Piper's River vineyard. A bright, full straw hue and well-poised preserved lemon and white peach fruit are upheld confidently by a beautifully poised acid line, energised by partial retention of malic acidity. Batonnage in tank, partial use of oak and, most importantly, 8 years of lees age followed by 4 years in bottle post-disgorgement have created a seamless, creamy and silky palate, slowly building a faintly smoky allure of ginger, brioche and lemon butter. A low dosage of 6.4g/l is well integrated. Disgorged Mar '10. Screwcap. 13% alc. **Rating** 95 **To** 2019 $150 TS

Clyde Park Vineyard   ★★★★★

2490 Midland Highway, Bannockburn, Vic 3331 **Region** Geelong
T (03) 5281 7274 **www**.clydepark.com.au **Open** 7 days 11–5
Winemaker Terry Jongebloed **Est.** 1979 **Dozens** 6000 **Vyds** 10.1ha
Clyde Park Vineyard, established by Gary Farr but sold by him many years ago, has passed through several changes of ownership. Now owned by Terry Jongebloed and Sue Jongebloed-Dixon, it has significant mature plantings of pinot noir (3.4ha), chardonnay (3.1ha), sauvignon blanc (1.5ha), shiraz (1.2ha) and pinot gris (0.9ha), and the quality of its wines is consistently exemplary. Exports to the UK and Hong Kong.

♟♟♟♟♟ **Geelong Pinot Noir 2014** There have been only occasional entry point Pinots as good as this, and don't feel cheated if you find the Block wines were all purchased the moment they were offered to mailing list customers, for this is a mighty Pinot in its own right: brilliant colour, a super-fragrant bouquet, a palate full of pinot fruit (plum and cherry), great texture and structure, great length and great balance. Screwcap. 13% alc. **Rating** 96 **To** 2024 $35 **⊙**

Block D Geelong Pinot Noir 2014 From a very steep slope of dark volcanic clay over limestone, planted in '98; hand-picked, wild-fermented with 40% whole bunches, matured for 10 months in French oak (40% new). Deep crimson-purple, this immediately proclaims the low yield of the vintage from the cool spring. Each bottle drunk now or inside 5 years is vinous sacrilege; seldom do you come across a Pinot with such power that retains shape and mouthfeel. Wholly within the Pinot church. Screwcap. 13% alc. **Rating** 96 **To** 2029 $65 **⊙**

Block F Geelong College Pinot Noir 2014 A 0.7ha block planted in '89 by Gary Farr to MV6, yielding half a tonne from the whole block; wild yeast open-fermented, matured in a 2yo French hogshead. 30 dozen made. Brilliant colour; this is in more familiar Pinot territory, intense and focused red and black cherry fruit precision-driving the long, medium-bodied palate. It has excellent balance, and is an escape route from the sheer power of Block D. Screwcap. 13.5% alc. **Rating** 96 **To** 2024 $65 **⊙**

Geelong Sauvignon Blanc 2014 A very classy, rich and complex Sauvignon Blanc, abounding with ripe tropical fruits, reigned in by citrussy acidity. Two clones are hand-picked; the two portions are fermented separately, with a portion fermented in barrel, and the wine is then blended and bottled early to maintain freshness. Screwcap. 12% alc. **Rating** 95 **To** 2016 $25 **⊙**

Block B3 Geelong Chardonnay 2014 Hand-picked from vines planted '95, whole bunch-pressed, wild-fermented in French hogsheads (33% new), on lees for 11 months, a small percentage of mlf. 50 dozen made. The numbers simply don't add up: 50 dozen = 1.5 hogsheads, yet 33% new would imply three hogsheads. This shouldn't distract from an elegantly powerful Chardonnay that ticks the boxes in terms of length, varietal expression and length. Screwcap. 13% alc. **Rating** 95 **To** 2024 $60

Geelong Shiraz 2014 Says to its '14 Pinot siblings, 'anything you can do, I can do better'. This is full-bodied and very intense, despite its modest alcohol; that said, it is distinctly cool-climate, its suite of black fruit flavours laced up with licorice, pepper and persistent tannins. A long and prosperous life ahead. Screwcap. 13% alc. **Rating** 95 **To** 2044 $35 **⊙**

♥♥♥♥♀ **Geelong Chardonnay 2014 Rating** 91 **To** 2020 $35
Geelong Pinot Gris 2014 Rating 91 **To** 2017 $30

Coal Valley Vineyard ★★★★

257 Richmond Road, Cambridge, Tas 7170 **Region** Southern Tasmania
T 0407 224 543 **www.**coalvalley.com.au **Open** Wed–Mon 11–5
Winemaker Alain Rousseau, Todd Goebel **Est.** 1991 **Dozens** 1495 **Vyds** 4.5ha
Since acquiring Coal Valley Vineyard in 1999, Gill Christian and Todd Goebel have increased the original 1ha hobby vineyard to pinot noir (2.3ha), riesling, cabernet sauvignon, merlot, chardonnay and tempranillo. More remarkable were Gill and Todd's concurrent lives: one in India, the other in Tasmania (flying over six times a year), and digging 4000 holes for the new vine plantings. Todd makes the Cabernet Sauvignon onsite, and dreams of making all the wines. Exports to Canada.

♥♥♥♥♀ **Museum Release Riesling 2007** Has fulfilled its early promise. Still features a daring line of acidity but the flavours positively sing, and the length is outstanding. Screwcap. 11.6% alc. **Rating** 93 **To** 2019 $30 CM
Barilla Bay Pinot Noir 2014 Vastly different from the '13 release. This is pretty and upfront with bright aroma and flavour on full, open show. Plum, forest-mint and dark cherry flavours swoosh attractively through the palate. High value and drinkability. Screwcap. 13.5% alc. **Rating** 93 **To** 2020 $25 CM **⊙**
Old Block 375 Pinot Noir 2013 From the estate's original pinot noir block, planted in '91. It displays a complex array of flavours but is essentially a wine built

on structure and length. Its best years are ahead of it. Depth, intensity and a clear acid/tannin framework. Screwcap. 14% alc. **Rating** 93 **To** 2024 $37 CM

Pinot Noir 2013 Impressive Pinot Noir. Stands up to be counted. Cherry-plum, coffee, spice and blueberry notes offer a flavoursome ride. Chalky tannin provides the ramp to a higher quality level. Some very good wines coming out of this estate. Screwcap. 14% alc. **Rating** 93 **To** 2022 $36 CM

TGR Riesling 2014 Balanced on a pinhead. Attractive and easygoing, but the thrilling finish helps to set it apart. Sweetish lime, barley and lemon. A very good example of the off-dry style. Screwcap. 9% alc. **Rating** 93 **To** 2023 $28 CM

Riesling 2014 Elegant and floral. Almost feels supple as it rolls along your tongue. Slate, apple and lime, perhaps some chalkiness. Beautiful drinking. Soft. Screwcap. 12.1% alc. **Rating** 92 **To** 2021 $29 CM

Barilla Bay Pinot Noir 2013 Brooding, stewy Pinot Noir, all game, spice and matching plum, light in colour but with plenty of presence. Still sorting itself out but looks promising. Screwcap. 13.5% alc. **Rating** 92 **To** 2022 $25 CM ○

Museum Release Riesling 2008 In a good place. Well developed and at its peak, but still with plenty of drive from orange peel and lime-like flavour. Generous body of flavour. Screwcap. 11.5% alc. **Rating** 91 **To** 2017 $30 CM

TGR Riesling 2013 TGR = 20g/l residual sugar. Acidity and sweetness, both in appropriate measure. Lime and lemon with a ripe, grapey deliciousness. A kind of earthy spiciness. Easy drinkability almost goes without saying. Screwcap. 9% alc. **Rating** 91 **To** 2023 $28 CM

Chardonnay 2013 Delicious lactose, fennel and lemon curd flavours, combined with spicy oak, though whether there is enough fruit flesh here is debatable. The next few years will answer the question. Screwcap. 12.8% alc. **Rating** 90 **To** 2021 $35 CM

Coates Wines   ★★★★★

PO Box 859, McLaren Vale, SA 5171 **Region** McLaren Vale
T 0417 882 557 **www**.coates-wines.com **Open** Not
Winemaker Duane Coates **Est.** 2003 **Dozens** 1500

Duane Coates has a Bachelor of Science, a Master of Business Administration and a Master of Oenology from Adelaide University; for good measure he completed the theory component of the Masters of Wine degree in 2005. Having made wine in various parts of the world, and in SA, he is more than qualified to make and market Coates wines. Nonetheless, his original intention was to simply make a single barrel of wine employing various philosophies and practices outside the mainstream; there was no plan to move to commercial production. The key is organically grown grapes; a low level of new oak (20–30%) is also part of the picture. Exports to the US, Canada, Germany and Sweden.

ŸŸŸŸŸ   **Robe Vineyard The Malbec 2013** Single vineyard; wild yeast-fermented for 20 days, matured for 18 months in French oak (25% new). Deep crimson-purple; this is a surprise packet, the velvety folds of perfectly balanced plum fruit filling the mouth, with hauntingly juicy/spicy notes on the finish and aftertaste. Screwcap. 14% alc. **Rating** 96 **To** 2028 $25 ○

Adelaide Hills Chardonnay 2013 Single vineyard; wild yeast-fermented with fine solids in new (66%) and 1yo French barriques, aged on lees for 16 months with natural mlf, no stirring. A focused and elegant wine, balance the key, but also having exemplary length to its white stone fruit flavours; the lingering finish and aftertaste also score. Screwcap. 13.5% alc. **Rating** 95 **To** 2020 $35 ○

McLaren Vale Syrah 2012 This comes from two vineyards at Blewitt Springs and Willunga, 30–80yo; matured in 30% new French and 70% used French and Russian oak for 2 years, plus 6 months' bottle age. Powerful and focused, immaculate balance and length engendering elegance, with a mix of black cherry, licorice and spice flavours. Screwcap. 14.5% alc. **Rating** 95 **To** 2028 $30 ○

The Consonance Red 2012 A 62/38% blend of shiraz and cabernet sourced from McLaren Vale and Langhorne Creek; on skins 14–20 days, 33 months in French barriques (20% new). Bright colour; a very elegant wine of coherence and finesse, its multitude of inputs all synergistic and symbiotic freshness the key, controlled alcohol the origin of all this. 400 dozen made. Screwcap. 14% alc. **Rating** 95 **To** 2027 $25 ✪

Langhorne Creek The Cabernet Sauvignon 2012 The yield of only 5t/ha from 30+yo vines provides concentration and structure, 22 months in 75% new French oak adding complexity without compromising the varietal fruit expression. A high-quality Cabernet, its savoury black fruits and ripe tannins right on the money. Screwcap. 14% alc. **Rating** 95 **To** 2032 $30 ✪

Clare Valley Sangiovese 2010 Pre-fermentation cold soak, then 10-day wild fermentation; 20 months' maturation in French oak (10% new); bottled unfined/ unfiltered. Has retained excellent hue, the red and sour cherry fruit supported by the tannins giving expected structure and length. High-quality Sangiovese. 240 dozen made. Screwcap. 13.5% alc. **Rating** 95 **To** 2020 $25 ✪

Adelaide Hills The Sauvignon Blanc 2014 Rating 94 **To** 2019 $25 ✪
McLaren Vale Langhorne Creek The Syrah 2012 Rating 94 **To** 2027 $25 ✪
McLaren Vale The Reserve Syrah 2012 Rating 94 **To** 2037 $75
The Iberian 2012 Rating 94 **To** 2022 $30 ✪

Cobaw Ridge   ★★★★☆

31 Perc Boyers Lane, Pastoria, Vic 3444 **Region** Macedon Ranges
T (03) 5423 5227 **www**.cobawridge.com.au **Open** Thurs–Mon 12–5
Winemaker Alan Cooper **Est.** 1985 **Dozens** 800 **Vyds** 5ha

When the Coopers started planting in the early 1980s there was scant knowledge of the best varieties for the region, let alone the Cobaw Ridge site. They have now settled on four varieties, chardonnay and syrah always being part of the mix. Lagrein and close-planted, multi-clonal pinot noir are more recent arrivals to thrive. Son Joshua has breezed through the Wine Science degree at Adelaide University with multiple distinctions; in 2012 he crammed in vintages with Tyrrell's, Heathcote Estate/Yabby Lake and Domaine de la Vougeraie (Burgundy). Cobaw Ridge is now fully certified biodynamic, and all winery operations are carried out according to the biodynamic calendar. Exports to Canada and China.

♆♆♆♆♆ **Pinot Noir 2013** All MV6 clone. 55 dozen made. Certified biodynamic, nil additives (save sulphur at bottling), unfined and unfiltered. Cobaw Ridge Pinot always has plenty of attitude; this release is no exception. It's ripped with meaty spice and sweet-sour cherry, carries an overt tanginess, and while pretty with foresty florals is also grunty with smoky tannin. It's as much Cobaw as Pinot Noir; meant as a compliment. Diam. 13.7% alc. **Rating** 94 **To** 2024 $60 CM

♆♆♆♆♀ **Chardonnay 2013 Rating** 91 **To** 2019 $50 CM

Cockfighter's Ghost   ★★★★★

DeBeyers Road, Pokolbin, NSW 2321 **Region** Hunter Valley
T (02) 4993 3688 **www**.cockfightersghost.com.au **Open** 7 days 10–5
Winemaker Jeff Byrne, Xanthe Leonard **Est.** 1988 **Dozens** 40 000 **Vyds** 16ha

Ever the professional, David Clarke had taken steps towards the sale of Poole's Rock prior to his death in April 2012. Discussions with neighbour Brian Agnew, owner of Audrey Wilkinson, led to agreement between the Clarke and Agnew families for Poole's Rock to be acquired by the Agnew interests. Audrey Wilkinson keeps its separate identity, but the changes have been rung for Poole's Rock. The winery is now known as Cockfighter's Ghost, Poole's Rock and Firestick brands forming part of the Cockfighter's Ghost business. Exports to the US, Canada, Sweden and China.

♆♆♆♆♆ **Poole's Rock Hunter Valley Semillon 2014** The kingpin of a trio of '14 Semillons from Cockfighter's Ghost, and worth every dollar (as are the two much cheaper versions). This is a flavour elaboration of the cheapest in the range, not the mid-priced Reserve, rippling with power and structure, layer upon layer of lemon, lemon curd, lemongrass and a royal crown of zesty acidity. Screwcap. 12% alc. **Rating** 97 **To** 2034 $45 ✪

ΨΨΨΨΨ **Cockfighter's Ghost Reserve Hunter Valley Semillon 2014** This wine has a sylph-like elegance and finesse, with Meyer lemon, herb and lemon zest gliding along the railroad of acidity that runs all the way to a far horizon. Screwcap. 11.9% alc. **Rating** 95 **To** 2029 $26 **◐**
Cockfighter's Ghost Hunter Valley Semillon 2014 This is the real deal: a Semillon already showing its muscle and backbone; it is full to the brim with lemongrass and lemon citrus fruit, and while it has a 20-year timeframe, there is no reason to feel guilty about cracking a bottle tonight. Indeed, buy a dozen and drink half, cellar half. Screwcap. 11.5% alc. **Rating** 94 **To** 2025 $22 **◐**
Cockfighter's Ghost Reserve Wrattonbully Langhorne Creek Merlot Cabernet 2012 An attractive wine, the colour still vivid and clear; there is a juicy flow of cassis and forest berry fruits, and well-balanced tannins to provide structure; the oak is unobtrusive. Screwcap. 14.5% alc. **Rating** 94 **To** 2027 $36

ΨΨΨΨΩ **Cockfighter's Ghost Reserve Shiraz 2014 Rating** 92 **To** 2034 $36
Cockfighter's Ghost Shiraz 2013 Rating 91 **To** 2025 $22 **◐**
Cockfighter's Ghost Sauvignon Blanc 2014 Rating 90 **To** 2016 $22

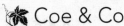 Coe & Co   ★★★☆

Cooba East Station, Dollar Vale Road, Eurongilly, NSW 2663 (postal) **Region** Gundagai
T 0427 245 272 **www**.coeandcowines.com.au **Open** Not
Winemaker Nick Spencer, Andrew McEwin, Antonio D'Onise **Est.** 2014 **Dozens** 5000
Vyds 52ha
Jim and Karen Coe are the current generation of several to own and run the Cooba East Station cattle grazing property. In 2003 they established 52ha of vines, and from the outset have operated on a strict sustainability philosophy (and practice). They have placed a perpetual covenant on 485ha of a grassy woodland and mountain that rises behind and directly above the vineyard. This has created a major wildlife habitat, and all the vineyard operations are similarly focused. Solar power is used, chemical sprays are kept to a minimum, and the wines are made offsite on the facilities run by various of their contract winemakers. Exports to the UK.

ΨΨΨΨΩ **Covenant Gundagai Shiraz 2013** Bright colour. A very attractive Shiraz; the bouquet is expressive, promising the perfectly ripened fruit of the palate; there is finesse in the way the fruit, new oak and ripe tannins interact, and push past the finish onto the aftertaste. Screwcap. 13.5% alc. **Rating** 93 **To** 2028 $38

ΨΨΨΨ **Leaning Cow Gundagai Shiraz 2014 Rating** 89 **To** 2025 $18 **◐**

Cofield Wines   ★★★★

Distillery Road, Wahgunyah, Vic 3687 **Region** Rutherglen
T (02) 6033 3798 **www**.cofieldwines.com.au **Open** Mon–Sat 9–5, Sun 10–5
Winemaker Damien Cofield, Brendan Heath **Est.** 1990 **Dozens** 13 000 **Vyds** 15.4ha
Sons Damien (winery) and Andrew (vineyard) have taken over responsibility for the business from parents Max and Karen. Collectively, they have developed an impressively broad-based product range with a strong cellar door sales base. The Pickled Sisters Café is open for lunch Wed–Mon (tel (02) 6033 2377). A 20ha property at Rutherglen, purchased in 2007, is planted to shiraz, durif and sangiovese. Exports to China.

ΨΨΨΨΨ **Provincial Parcel Beechworth Chardonnay 2013** Fruit and oak are taking their time to mesh, yet already there's an elegant lilt to this. Citrus, white peach, lactose and sweet oak create an impression of power before pulsing out through the finish. Persistence is a prime marker of its quality. Needs a year or two but there's something good building here. Screwcap. 13% alc. **Rating** 94 **To** 2019 $36 CM
Provincial Parcel Rutherglen Durif 2013 Glowing purple. Presents a modern, polished, slinky-smooth face within a sturdy tannin framework. Bright ripe

berries on hay and sawdust and violet. Now or later; is a ripper drink either way. Screwcap. 13.7% alc. **Rating** 94 **To** 2025 $39 CM

ΨΨΨΨ **Minimal Footprint Quartz Vein Shiraz 2013** Rating 92 To 2022 $30 CM
Rutherglen Shiraz 2013 Rating 91 To 2021 $26 CM
Rutherglen Durif 2012 Rating 91 To 2022 $24 CM

Coldstream Hills   ★★★★★

31 Maddens Lane, Coldstream, Vic 3770 **Region** Yarra Valley
T (03) 5960 7000 **www**.coldstreamhills.com.au **Open** 7 days 10–5
Winemaker Andrew Fleming, Greg Jarratt, James Halliday (Consultant) **Est.** 1985
Dozens 25 000 **Vyds** 100ha
Founded by the author, James Halliday, Coldstream Hills is now a small part of Treasury Wine Estates, with 100ha of owned estate vineyards as its base, three in the Lower Yarra Valley, and two in the Upper Yarra Valley. Chardonnay and Pinot Noir continue to be the principal focus; Merlot came on-stream in 1997, Sauvignon Blanc around the same time, Reserve Shiraz later still. Vintage conditions permitting, Chardonnay and Pinot Noir are made in Reserve, Single Vineyard and varietal forms (at three price levels). In addition, Amphitheatre Pinot Noir was made in tiny quantities in '06 and '13. In 2010 a multimillion-dollar winery was erected around the original winery buildings and facilities; it has a capacity of 1500 tonnes. There is a plaque in the fermentation area commemorating the official opening on 12 October 2010 and naming the facility the 'James Halliday Cellar'. Exports to the UK, the US and Singapore.

ΨΨΨΨΨ **Reserve Yarra Valley Chardonnay 2013** It's not just neat and tidy; it has views that stretch on and on. It's beautifully ordered and structured and yet its flavours have reach and flare. Bran, white peach, struck match and citrus line up and march precisely along the palate before kicking off their heels and bursting through the finish. Screwcap. 13% alc. **Rating** 96 **To** 2022 $60 CM ✪
Reserve Pinot Noir 2013 Estate-grown from the famed Amphitheatre and G Blocks, the fruit vinified in small open fermenters. This is a controlled, cellar-worthy release with terrific persistence of flavour. Cherry-plum, inshot spice, cloves, satsuma plum, bacon. Softness to the fruit, firmness to the tannin, chalkiness to the finish. It plays its hand on a few fronts (whole bunches, oak, spice, fruit) but keeps them in strict formation, a military flyover of flavour and texture. Nothing short of a stellar release. Screwcap. 13.5% alc. **Rating** 96 **To** 2030 $85 CM
Deer Farm Vineyard Pinot Noir 2013 Cedar-spice oak. Sweet-sour fruit. Macerated cherry, mint, ground spice, plum. Velvety Pinot Noir in fruit terms and also in tannin terms. Feels seductive as plush flavours roll through the mouth. Cream, coffee, spice, cherry plum, chicory. This wine will not have any trouble attracting attention/fans; quite rightly so. Screwcap. 13.5% alc. **Rating** 96 **To** 2025 $50 CM ✪
Rising Vineyard Chardonnay 2013 There's a peaches and cream aspect to this but there are also more sophisticated layers. Dry pear, oatmeal, fennel, toasty oak and grapefruit, with a sprightly, smoky minerality adding dare to the finish. Length is excellent. So too mouthfeel. Beautiful drinking now or anytime over at least the next 5 years. Screwcap. 13% alc. **Rating** 95 **To** 2022 $45 CM
Deer Farm Vineyard Chardonnay 2013 A wine of elegant power. It's lazy with fennel, fresh sweet peach and oatmeal notes, all completely unhurried and enticing to be around. You can relax in its company, even as the finish treats you to a bit of dazzle. Screwcap. 13.5% alc. **Rating** 95 **To** 2021 $45 CM
The Esplanade Yarra Valley Pinot Noir 2013 The overall class of this wine is something to behold. It has so many things to offer: flavours of rhubarb, cherry-plum, chalk, green herbs, tobacco and woodsmoke for starters. But the gentle creaminess of oak, and an accompanying plushness, allows funk and game notes to sit snug in the polished display. Tannin is fine and well balanced but firm; the wine presents as fresh and fragrant but destined to cellar well; and persistence is exemplary. Everything suggests time in the cellar will bring rich rewards. Screwcap. 13.5% alc. **Rating** 95 **To** 2026 $50 CM

Yarra Valley Pinot Noir 2013 Rating 94 To 2024 $35 CM
Yarra Valley Pinot Noir 2012 Rating 94 To 2024 $35 CM
Reserve Yarra Valley Shiraz 2012 Rating 94 To 2027 $45 CM

ꭹꭹꭹꭹꭹ Yarra Valley Chardonnay 2013 Rating 93 To 2018 $35 CM

Coliban Valley Wines ★★★

313 Metcalfe–Redesdale Road, Metcalfe, Vic 3448 **Region** Heathcote
T 0417 312 098 **www**.colibanvalleywines.com.au **Open** W'ends 10–5
Winemaker Helen Miles **Est.** 1997 **Dozens** 300 **Vyds** 4.4ha
Helen Miles, who has a degree in science, and partner Greg Miles have planted 2.8ha of shiraz, 1.2ha of cabernet and 0.4ha of merlot near Metcalfe, in the cooler southwest corner of Heathcote. The granitic soils and warm climate allow organic principles to be used successfully. The shiraz is dry-grown, while the cabernet sauvignon and merlot receive minimal irrigation.

ꭹꭹꭹꭹ **Heathcote Shiraz 2012** Clear colour; this is lighter-bodied than most Heathcote Shirazs, with a savoury backdrop to its red fruits; just a little too far towards light-bodied. Screwcap. 13.5% alc. **Rating** 88 **To** 2020 $25

 # Collalto ★★★

Lot 99, Adelaide–Lobethal Road, Lobethal, SA 5241 **Region** Adelaide Hills
T +44 207 910 8300 **www**.collalto.com.au **Open** Not
Winemaker Revenir (Peter Leske) **Est.** 2006 **Dozens** 1200 **Vyds** 8ha
To say this is a business with a difference is a masterly understatement. It has a real vineyard of 5.5ha of pinot noir and 2.5ha of chardonnay planted in 2001; a real viticulturist (Damon Koerner), and a real winemaker (Peter Leske). Its two owners (who grew up in the Adelaide Hills) are London-based QC James Drake, and Scott Drake, Professor of Architecture in the international program in design and architecture at Chulalongkorn University in Bangkok. Most of the grapes are sold to Petaluma, but enough to make 1200 dozen or so a year is held back. The name Collalto describes the high vineyard, and is also a tribute to their mother Palimira (née Tosolini) whose father came from the village of that name just north of Udine, in north-eastern Italy. Exports to the UK.

ꭹꭹꭹꭹ **Adelaide Hills Chardonnay 2013** Still pale straw-quartz, and still locked up in itself; it is difficult to assess how much varietal fruit will appear with development in bottle, so quiescent is it now. Screwcap. 13% alc. **Rating** 89 **To** 2020 $35
Adelaide Hills Chardonnay 2012 Has profited from extra time in bottle, but the fruit is largely in a citrus/grapefruit spectrum, and still lacks complexity. Finesse is all very well, but there has to be substance. Screwcap. 13% alc. **Rating** 88 **To** 2017 $35
Adelaide Hills Pinot Noir 2013 The Collalto style has an element of minty/green acidity that marks the finish and aftertaste, made obvious due to the light-bodied structure of the palate; that said, there are some attractive savoury red fruit notes to the bouquet and palate. Riper fruit might well deal with the acidity issue. Screwcap. 13% alc. **Rating** 88 **To** 2018 $35

Collector Wines

12 Bourke Street, Collector, NSW 2581 (postal) **Region** Canberra District
T (02) 6116 8722 **www**.collectorwines.com.au **Open** Not
Winemaker Alex McKay **Est.** 2007 **Dozens** 3000
Owner and winemaker Alex McKay makes exquisitely detailed wines, bending to the dictates of inclement weather on his doorstep, heading elsewhere if need be. He was part of a talented team at BRL Hardy's Kamberra Winery, and when it was closed down by Hardys' new owner CHAMP, decided to stay in the district, He is not known to speak much, and when he does, his voice is very quiet. So you have to remain alert to appreciate his unparalleled sense of humour. No such attention is needed for his wines, which are consistently excellent, their elegance appropriate for their maker. Exports to The Netherlands and Japan.

ΨΨΨΨΨ Tiger Tiger Chardonnay 2013 Shows Tumbarumba to full advantage; French oak fermentation and maturation has simply added a necklace to show off the beauty of the fresh grapefruit and white peach medley of the long, lingering palate. Screwcap. 12.9% alc. **Rating** 95 **To** 2027 $39

Lamp Lit Marsanne 2013 An 86/8/6% blend of marsanne, roussanne and viognier, whole bunch-pressed and fermented in used French oak; full mlf, and lees contact for 8 months. The oak has impacted more on mouthfeel than flavour; the wine has real presence in the mouth, with delicious lemony acidity on the finish and aftertaste. Screwcap. 12.9% alc. **Rating** 95 **To** 2034 $33 ✪

Reserve Shiraz 2013 Light, clear hue; fills in almost all the gaps of Marked Tree Red; while its boundaries are drawn by savoury elegance, there are attractive, high-toned red fruits in the centre of the field, and a distinct kick of intensity on the finish. Screwcap. 13.2% alc. **Rating** 94 **To** 2028 $59

ΨΨΨΨΨ Rose Red City Sangiovese 2013 **Rating** 92 **To** 2020 $33
Marked Tree Red Shiraz 2013 **Rating** 90 **To** 2023 $27

🍇 Colmar Estate   ★★★★

790 Pinnacle Road, Orange, NSW 2800 **Region** Orange
T 0419 977 270 **www**.colmarestate.com.au **Open** Wed–Sun & public hols 10.30–5
Winemaker Chris Derrez, Lucy Maddox **Est.** 2013 **Dozens** 1000 **Vyds** 5.9ha
You don't have to look far for the inspiration behind the name when you find that owners Bill Shrapnel and his wife Jane have long loved the wines of Alsace: Colmar is the main town in that region. The Shrapnels realised a long-held ambition when they purchased an established, high-altitude (980m) vineyard in May 2013. Everything they have done has turned to gold, notably grafting cabernet sauvignon to pinot noir, merlot to chardonnay, and shiraz to pinot gris. The plantings are now 1.51ha of pinot noir (clones 777, 115 and MV6), 1.25ha of chardonnay (clones 95, 96 and P58), 1.22ha of sauvignon blanc and lesser quantities of riesling, pinot gris and traminer. Chris Derrez and Lucy Maddox continue to make the wines, the 2014 Sauvignon Blanc winning the trophy for Best Young Sauvignon Blanc at the NSW Wine Awards '14, following on its gold medal at the Orange Wine Show '14.

ΨΨΨΨΨ Orange Sauvignon Blanc 2014 Excellent intensity. Gets the overall balance right too. Fresh herbs, lemongrass, gunmetal and gooseberry. Packs the flavours in but is not inelegant. Screwcap. 12% alc. **Rating** 94 **To** 2015 $24 CM ✪

Orange Pinot Rose 2014 Estate-grown. Pale puce hue; the perfumed rose fragrance is striking, the delicate, crisp and dry palate with excellent length. Come into my garden, said the spider to the fly. Screwcap. 12.5% alc. **Rating** 94 **To** 2016 $26 ✪

ΨΨΨΨ Orange Pinot Gris 2014 **Rating** 89 **To** 2016 $26

Colvin Wines   ★★★★★

19 Boyle Street, Mosman, NSW 2088 (postal) **Region** Hunter Valley
T (02) 9908 7886 **www**.colvinwines.com.au **Open** Not
Winemaker Andrew Spinaze, Mark Richardson **Est.** 1999 **Dozens** 500 **Vyds** 5.2ha
In 1990 Sydney lawyer John Colvin and wife Robyn purchased the De Beyers Vineyard, which has a history going back to the second half of the 19th century. By 1967, when a syndicate bought 35ha of the original vineyard site, no vines remained. The syndicate planted semillon on the alluvial soil of the creek flats and shiraz on the red clay hillsides. Up to 1998 all the grapes were sold to Tyrrell's, but since '99 quantities have been made for the Colvin Wines label. These include Sangiovese, from a little over 1ha of vines planted by John in '96 because of his love of the wines of Tuscany.

ΨΨΨΨΨ De Beyers Vineyard Hunter Valley Semillon 2008 Has fulfilled the promise it showed when last tasted 4 years ago. It has now entered the plateau of perfection it will hold for another 10 years, building honey to join the intense lime zest flavours it has always had. Screwcap. 10.4% alc. **Rating** 95 **To** 2023 $30 ✪

De Beyers Vineyard Hunter Valley Shiraz 2005 First tasted 6 years ago, and has grown and prospered much as anticipated, the black fruits, plum, earth and spice filling the mouth. What hasn't changed is the price (a paltry $2 a bottle increase) and the drink-to date. Screwcap. 13.5% alc. **Rating** 95 **To** 2020 $40

Condie Estate ★★★★☆

480 Heathcote–Redesdale Road, Heathcote, Vic 3523 **Region** Heathcote
T 0404 480 422 **www**.condie.com.au **Open** W'ends & public hols 11–5
Winemaker Richie Condie **Est.** 2001 **Dozens** 1500 **Vyds** 6.8ha

Richie Condie worked as a corporate risk manager for a multinational company off the back of a Bachelor of Commerce degree, but after establishing Condie Estate, completed several viticulture and winemaking courses, including a diploma of winemaking at TAFE Dookie. Wife Rosanne is an audiologist, with a Bachelor of Science degree, her love of good food and wine greatly influenced by her Italian heritage. Having first established 2.4ha of shiraz, they followed with 2ha of sangiovese and 0.8ha of viognier. In 2010 they purchased a 1.6ha vineyard that had been planted in 1990, 5km southwest of Heathcote on Wild Duck Creek, where they have established a winery and cellar door. Flynns Wines, where Richie worked with Greg Flynn as a cellar hand for three vintages, marked the transition to making their own wines. Richie gives the best possible advice to anyone thinking of going into wine production: 'Go and work in a small vineyard and winery for at least one year before you start out for yourself. You need to understand how much hard physical work is involved in planting a vineyard, looking after it, making the wine, and then selling it. While it is hard work, it is most satisfying.' The proof of the pudding is in the eating, with excellent wine quality.

🍷🍷🍷🍷🍷 **The Max Heathcote Shiraz 2012** And we're off to the races. Strong malty/vanillan/cedary oak running through a wealth of rich fruit. The back label suggests that it's elegant; it's almost anything but, but it's certainly impressive. Plum, spearmint, cakey blackberry, fresh cherries, red and black. It's a heady, sweet-fruited, almost exaggerated style, but there remains a liveliness here; an irrepressibility; a jubilance. Screwcap. 14.5% alc. **Rating** 95 **To** 2028 $47 CM

🍷🍷🍷🍷 **The Gwen Heathcote Shiraz 2013** **Rating** 93 **To** 2024 $27 CM ✪
Giarracca Heathcote Sangiovese 2013 **Rating** 93 **To** 2020 $30 CM

Cooks Lot ★★★★☆

Ferment, 87 Hill Street, Orange, NSW 2800 **Region** Orange
T (02) 9550 3228 **www**.cookslot.com.au **Open** Tues–Sat 11–5
Winemaker Duncan Cook **Est.** 2002 **Dozens** 4000

Duncan Cook began making wines for his eponymous brand in 2002, while undertaking his oenology degree at CSU. He completed his degree in '10, and now works with a number of small growers from Orange wishing to be part of the production of wines with distinctive regional character. In '12 Duncan transferred his business from Mudgee to Orange, current releases focusing on grapes grown in Orange. The price for value ratio is exceptionally good. Exports to China.

🍷🍷🍷🍷🍷 **Allotment No. 333 Orange Riesling 2014** Trophy Orange Wine Show '14. Reminiscent of a Rheingau Riesling, with a strong, slatey/minerally texture and structure matching the Granny Smith apple and lime zest fruit; interesting wine. Great value. Screwcap. 11% alc. **Rating** 95 **To** 2024 $20 ✪

Lot 9999 Orange Cabernet Sauvignon 2013 There is no mistaking the variety; after opening with a mix of redcurrant and blackcurrant, positive cabernet tannins sweep through on the finish. I'm not concerned about the balance, which is good, and the components will fuse neatly over the next few years. Screwcap. 13.5% alc. **Rating** 95 **To** 2023 $20 ✪

Lot 365 Orange Rose 2014 Produced from shiraz; destemmed, crushed, the juice was given limited skin contact to extract colour. The scented raspberry/strawberry bouquet and the Turkish delight nuances on the palate point to grenache contributing at least part of the cepage; the fresh, slightly peppery, finish adds a final dimension. Screwcap. 13% alc. **Rating** 94 **To** 2016 $20 ❂

🍷🍷🍷🍷🍷 **Allotment No. 589 Semillon Sauvignon 2014** Rating 90 To 2016 $20 ❂

Coola Road
★★★☆

Private Mail Bag 14, Mount Gambier, SA 5291 **Region** Mount Gambier
T 0487 700 422 **www**.coolaroad.com **Open** Not
Winemaker John Innes, Peter Douglas, Sue Bell **Est.** 2013 **Dozens** 1000 **Vyds** 103.5ha
Thomas and Sally Ellis are the current generation of the Ellis family that has owned the Coola grazing property on which the vineyard is now established for over 160 years. They began planting the vineyard in the late 1990s with pinot noir, and have since extended the range to include sauvignon blanc, chardonnay, riesling and pinot gris. As the largest vineyard owner in the region, they decided they should have some of the grapes vinified to bring further recognition to the area. If global warming should recommence and increase significantly, this very cool region will stand to gain.

🍷🍷🍷🍷🍷 **Single Vineyard Sauvignon Blanc 2014** Has a bit of spark about it. A freshness, a zip. It essentially tastes of passionfruit, green apple and sweet pea but it's the overall perk of it that has you wanting more. Screwcap. 11.5% alc. **Rating** 91 **To** 2016 $20 CM ❂

🍷🍷🍷🍷 **Single Vineyard Riesling 2014** Rating 89 To 2019 $20 CM

Coolangatta Estate
★★★★★

1335 Bolong Road, Shoalhaven Heads, NSW 2535 **Region** Shoalhaven Coast
T (02) 4448 7131 **www**.coolangattaestate.com.au **Open** 7 days 10–5
Winemaker Tyrrell's **Est.** 1988 **Dozens** 5000 **Vyds** 10.5ha
Coolangatta Estate is part of a 150ha resort with accommodation, restaurants, golf course, etc; some of the oldest buildings were convict-built in 1822. The standard of viticulture is exceptionally high (immaculate Scott Henry trellising), and the contract winemaking is wholly professional. Coolangatta has a habit of bobbing up with medals at Sydney and Canberra wine shows, with gold medals for its mature Semillons. In its own backyard, Coolangatta has won the trophy for Best Wine of Show at the South Coast Wine Show for 13 consecutive years.

🍷🍷🍷🍷🍷 **Individual Vineyard Wollstonecraft Semillon 2014** The vineyard has amassed 92 trophies and 150 gold medals to date. Winemaking by Tyrrell's, and sandy soils, plus a maritime climate, explain the enduring qualities of the Coolangatta Semillons. This is a typically pure example, with lemongrass/wax/citrus aromas and flavours underwritten on the palate by crunchy acidity. Screwcap. 11.8% alc. **Rating** 96 **To** 2025 $25 ❂
Aged Release Estate Grown Semillon 2005 The front and back labels are those used on its first release in '05, its second release in '10 and now its third release. The touch of CO_2 noted in '10 is still just apparent, intensifying its unsweetened grapefruit zest and low alcohol. Screwcap. 10.2% alc. **Rating** 96 **To** 2018 $50 ❂
Semillon 2014 Counterintuitively picked a week earlier than its Individual Vineyard sibling, with slightly more flesh, softer acidity and more citrus flavours; this all adds up to an earlier drinking style, although cellaring will only benefit it over the next 5 years. Screwcap. 12% alc. **Rating** 94 **To** 2020 $25 ❂

🍷🍷🍷🍷🍷 **Alexander Berry Chardonnay 2014** Rating 90 To 2017 $25

Coombe Farm
★★★★★

673–675 Maroondah Highway, Coldstream, Vic 3770 **Region** Yarra Valley
T (03) 9739 0173 **www**.coombeyarravalley.com.au **Open** 7 days 10–5
Winemaker Nicole Esdaile **Est.** 1999 **Dozens** 8000 **Vyds** 60ha

Coombe Farm was once the home of legendary soprano Dame Nellie Melba and is still owned and operated by her direct descendants, the Vestey family. The Coombe Farm vineyard was established in the 1990s. Cellar doors are situated in two unique locations. The original cellar door is at 11 St Huberts Road and is situated on the vineyard. In addition, Coombe - The Melba Estate, is situated behind the hedge of Melba's Coombe Cottage property in Coldstream. The newly restored historic motor house and stable block is home to a second cellar door as well as a 150-seat restaurant, a provedore store stocking products made onsite, and a photographic and written history of the international career of Dame Nellie Melba. Exports to the UK and China.

Tribute Series Armstrong Yarra Valley Merlot 2013 Estate-grown; matured in French barriques for 12 months. Very good colour, and picks up where its varietal sibling leaves off; the bouquet is commanding, the palate intense, the varietal character of the kind found in Bordeaux. A convincing selection of the best blocks and best barrels. Screwcap. 13% alc. **Rating** 96 **To** 2028 $60

Yarra Valley Chardonnay 2013 Mendoza and P58 clones were separately fermented and matured in French oak (20% new), and 10% went through mlf, a barrel selection blended shortly prior to bottling to produce a thoroughly elegant Chardonnay with perfect varietal fruit expression and a crisp, lively finish. Screwcap. 13% alc. **Rating** 95 **To** 2023 $35 ✪

Tribute Series Fullerton Yarra Valley Pinot Noir 2013 MV6 clone; matured in French oak (55% new) for 11 months. A complex and mouth-filling Pinot reflecting the great vintage, but still in its infancy; there are red and purple fruits on the one hand, finesse and length on the other. Will be a distinguished wine in a year or two thanks to its length. Screwcap. 13% alc. **Rating** 95 **To** 2025 $55

Yarra Valley Pinot Gris 2014 Hand-picked over several days; free-run juice was tank-fermented, the pressings fermented in used oak. Has well above average intensity and complexity to its flavour profile (pear, apple, citrus) and texture. Screwcap. 12.5% alc. **Rating** 94 **To** 2017 $25 ✪

Yarra Valley Merlot 2013 **Rating** 92 **To** 2023 $30

 # Cooter & Cooter   ★★★☆

82 Almond Grove Road, Whites Valley, SA 5172 **Region** McLaren Vale
T 0438 766 178 **www**.cooter.com.au **Open** Not
Winemaker James Cooter **Est.** 2012 **Dozens** 800 **Vyds** 23ha

James and Kimberley Cooter have taken the slow road to establishing their business; the cursive script on the wine labels has been that of various Cooter businesses in South Australia since 1847. James came from a family with a modern history of more than 20 years in the wine industry – he is the son of Colin Cooter from Lengs & Cooter. Kimberley is also a hands-on winemaker, having spent the early years of her craft with father Walter Clappis, a veteran McLaren Vale winemaker. In 2005 they headed for the US, working in California's Sonoma Valley, and returned, much invigorated, to continue winemaking with Walter at The Hedonist. Now, with 20 vintages between them, they have established their own vineyard on the southern slopes of Whites Valley, McLaren Vale, with views to the coast. It has 18ha of shiraz and 3ha of cabernet sauvignon planted in 1996, and 2ha of old-vine grenache planted in the 1950s. They also buy Clare Valley grapes to make (what else) riesling.

Watervale Riesling 2014 Bright straw-green; a thoroughly friendly Riesling, already showing plenty of ripe lime/lemon fruit on the bouquet and palate alike; its low pH will provide a foundation for future development if that's your bag. Screwcap. 12% alc. **Rating** 93 **To** 2024 $22 ✪

McLaren Vale Shiraz 2013 **Rating** 89 **To** 2023 $22

Coppabella of Tumbarumba   ★★★★☆

424 Tumbarumba Road, Tumbarumba, NSW 2653 (postal) **Region** Tumbarumba
T (02) 6382 7997 **www**.coppabella.com.au **Open** Not
Winemaker Jason Brown **Est.** 2011 **Dozens** 4000 **Vyds** 71.9ha

Coppabella is owned by Jason and Alecia Brown, best known in the wine industry as owners of the highly successful Moppity Vineyards in Hilltops. They became aware of the quality of Tumbarumba chardonnay and pinot noir, in particular the quality of the grapes from the 71ha Coppabella vineyard, when purchasing grapes for the Moppity Vineyards business. This was the second vineyard (established in 1993) by the region's founder, Ian Cowell, but frost and other problems led him to lease the vineyard to Southcorp, an arrangement that continued until 2007. The reversion of the management of the vineyard coincided with several failed vintages, and this precipitated a decision by the owner to close the vineyard and remove the vines. In October '11, at the last moment, the Browns purchased the vineyard, and have since invested heavily in it, rehabilitating the vines and grafting a number of blocks to the earlier ripening Dijon clones of pinot noir and chardonnay. Coppabella is run as an entirely separate venture from Moppity, and it is already on the road to emulating the success of Moppity.

ΨΨΨΨΨ **Sirius Chardonnay 2013** All about the fruit. The quality of it. The reach. There's nothing particularly rich here but it glistens and gleams its way through to a very long finish, convincing at every step along the way, and that's all it needs to do now. The rest is ahead of it. Screwcap. 12.5% alc. **Rating** 95 **To** 2021 $60 CM
The Crest Single Vineyard Chardonnay 2013 Brilliant acidity and length, lactose notes aplenty, wheatgerm and toasty oak complexity. Some may find the overt mlf influence exaggerated; others will swoon. It feels exceptionally dry but it doesn't feel lean; it feels powerful. It's certainly not a wine to be dismissed lightly. Screwcap. 13% alc. **Rating** 94 **To** 2020 $30 CM ✪

ΨΨΨΨΨ **Single Vineyard Pinot Noir 2014 Rating** 92 **To** 2019 $20 CM ✪
The Crest Single Vineyard Pinot Noir 2014 Rating 91 **To** 2020 $30 CM

Coriole   ★★★★★

Chaffeys Road, McLaren Vale, SA 5171 **Region** McLaren Vale
T (08) 8323 8305 **www**.coriole.com **Open** Mon–Fri 10–5, w'ends & public hols 11–5
Winemaker Alex Sherrah **Est.** 1967 **Dozens** 32 000 **Vyds** 48.5ha
While Coriole was not established until 1967, the cellar door and gardens date back to 1860, when the original farm houses that now constitute the cellar door were built. The oldest shiraz forming part of the estate plantings dates back to 1917, and since '85, Coriole has been an Australian pioneer of sangiovese and – more recently – the Italian white variety fiano. Shiraz has 65% of the plantings, and it is for this variety that Coriole is best known. Exports to all major markets.

ΨΨΨΨΨ **Old House Single Vineyard McLaren Vale Shiraz 2013** From a 30yo vineyard. It shows intensity, spice and elegance even in a context of warming alcohol. Licorice, plum, graphite and clove flavours, with grated woody spices expanding the show. Toasty/spicy oak gets it all into smooth line. No question over its quality. Screwcap. 14.5% alc. **Rating** 95 **To** 2028 $55 CM
Willunga Single Vineyard McLaren Vale Shiraz 2013 A Scarce Earth release. From a 95yo vineyard at Willunga. Fragrant but not at the expense of power. Gravel, florals and spice introduce heartier notes of raspberry and blackberry. Has a sandy, grainy aspect to its texture. Not the density of the Old House release but prettier and no lesser in quality. Screwcap. 14.5% alc. **Rating** 95 **To** 2028 $55 CM
Estate Grown McLaren Vale Shiraz 2012 Open-fermented, hand-plunged and matured in French hogsheads. The Coriole style comes through consistently in all its red wines, right in the slot of medium body, black fruits taking centre stage, sending a measured, unhurried message about its place. Screwcap. 14% alc. **Rating** 95 **To** 2032 $30 ✪
McLaren Vale Sangiovese 2013 The '85 pioneer of sangiovese in Australia. Vine maturity is obvious, starting with the healthy colour, then continuing through with tastes of just about every cherry in the book, rounded off with a balanced helping of savoury, but fine tannins beckoning fine pasta or a risotto. Screwcap. 14% alc. **Rating** 95 **To** 2023 $25 ✪

McLaren Vale Fiano 2014 Has the energy, drive and flavour intensity to reinforce the idea that fiano has a real future in Australia's temperate regions; it has remarkable length, and grip (in the best sense) from its lemon zest fruit. Screwcap. 12.5% alc. **Rating** 94 **To** 2019 $25 ○

Estate Grown McLaren Vale Shiraz 2013 Light and shade. The grunt of blackberry, the sweet relief of raspberry. Both combine here with earth, spice and creamy oak to present a pitch-perfect expression of modern McLaren Vale shiraz. Screwcap. 14.5% alc. **Rating** 94 **To** 2028 $30 CM ○

Lloyd Reserve McLaren Vale Shiraz 2012 The slick of vanillan, resiny, coffeed oak is substantial and ultimately wins the day on palate. That said, if you'd like some fruit with your oak you get plenty here, with saturated plum, asphalt and jammy blackberry flavours roaring throughout. Assertive tannin sniffs the prevailing winds and enters with force. It's not much fun now, but given (lots of) time it should perform. Screwcap. 14.5% alc. **Rating** 94 **To** 2037 $80 CM

Mary Kathleen Reserve McLaren Vale Cabernet Merlot 2012 Excellence has become this wine's middle name. Softer and more user-friendly than some versions but its intent is equally serious. It tastes of dark, bitter chocolate and blackberry, saltbush and assorted dry herbs. Tannin is neatly tucked into the fruit but that's not to suggest there isn't a firm hand on the tiller; everything about this wine feels controlled and sure. Screwcap. 14% alc. **Rating** 94 **To** 2030 $60 CM

Vita Reserve McLaren Vale Sangiovese 2012 Stern-faced Sangiovese with tannin rutted through and a pruney warmth to the finish. Drinkability doesn't seem high on its agenda and accordingly, it gives the impression that it's trying too hard. But the combination of dark cherry and leather with polished oak is a good one, and as it rests/breathes in the glass a glimpse into an exciting future is afforded. Its day will come; it needs a few years. Screwcap. 14.5% alc. **Rating** 94 **To** 2024 $60 CM

ΨΨΨΨΨ **McLaren Vale Nero d'Avola 2014** Rating 93 To 2017 $25 ○
Redstone McLaren Vale Shiraz 2013 Rating 91 To 2020 $22 CM ○
McLaren Vale Barbera 2014 Rating 91 To 2018 $25 CM

Cornelia Creek Wines   NR

1557 O'Dea Road, Koyuga, Vic 3622 **Region** Goulburn Valley
T (03) 5859 2211 www.corneliacreekwines.com.au **Open** W'ends 11–5
Winemaker Peter Beckingham **Est.** 2007 **Dozens** 550
Lou Dumar spent his formative years on a family farm and vineyard in northern Italy. When he migrated to Australia he continued to work as a mechanical engineer, but in 1984 purchased a sadly neglected 160ha property, formerly used as part of a productive sheep station. Lou planted a 1.6 ha vineyard to shiraz, cabernet sauvignon, pinot noir, merlot and brunello, retiring to live on the farm in 2011 with wife Merilyn. They now manage all the vineyard activities. In the early years the grapes were supplied to long-term friend and winemaker Peter Beckingham, who continues to make the wines.

Cosmo Wines   ★★★☆

32 Warrs Avenue, Preston, Vic 3072 **Region** Yarra Valley
T 0408 519 461 www.cosmowines.com.au **Open** By appt
Winemaker Lindsay Corby **Est.** 2008 **Dozens** 2000
Lindsay Corby started with fruit winemaking while still at high school, and in 1985 enrolled at CSU, gaining qualifications in viticulture and wine science. Thereafter he gained practical experience in various roles, including cellar door sales, laboratory work and vineyard management, leading in turn to teaching 'the art and science of the vine and wine' at La Trobe University and managing the small campus vineyard. In 2008 he found his first (and hopefully permanent) home at Bianchet Winery, where he makes the Bianchet wines, and the Cosmo wines (all of which are made from purchased grapes). Exports to China.

ΨΨΨΨ **Reserve Yarra Valley Shiraz 2013** From the Coranderk Vineyard, fermented with all pressings and 10% cabernet franc with 'a high level of oak blocks added', then retained in stainless steel. Deep crimson-purple; the technique achieves a lot at minimal cost, but at the end of the day, there's not much texture or mouthfeel. Screwcap. 13.7% alc. **Rating** 89 **To** 2020 $40

Reserve Yarra Valley Cabernet Sauvignon 2012 Similar making regime to the Shiraz, with some shiraz included. Significantly oak-sweetened, which diminishes the sense of place, but adds to the volume of flavour; it's hard to deny that the wine has its charms. Screwcap. 13% alc. **Rating** 89 **To** 2027 $35

Courabyra Wines

805 Courabyra Road, Tumbarumba, NSW 2653 **Region** Tumbarumba
T (02) 6948 2462 **www**.courabyrawines.com **Open** W'ends 10–4
Winemaker Alex McKay, Nick Spencer **Est.** 2010 **Dozens** NFP **Vyds** 36.3ha
This significant development in the Tumbarumba region brings together brother and sister Cathy Gairn and Stephen Morrison, although it has taken 25 years for the two families to form Courabyra Wines. Cathy and husband Brian purchased their land in 1985, and moved there permanently in '87. After planting their 8.3ha vineyard to pinot noir, chardonnay and pinot meunier in '93, Cathy moved on to formal viticultural studies. Investment banker Stephen always came to help at harvest time. After looking for an appropriate cool-climate vineyard for many years, he found one under his nose, at 157 Courabyra Road, in 2010. This is the oldest vineyard in Tumbarumba, established in 1981 by the region's founder, Ian Cowell, and thereafter for two decades owned by what is now TWE. Now known as Revee Estate, pinot noir (16ha) and chardonnay (8ha) take the lion's share of the plantings, with lesser amounts of sauvignon blanc, pinot gris and pinot meunier. The decision to label the wines 805 and 157 is obvious enough.

🍷🍷🍷🍷🍷 **805 Late Disgorged Tumbarumba Pinot Noir Chardonnay Pinot Meunier 2002** An impressively pale and bright medium straw hue after a full decade on lees, this blend (of almost two-thirds pinot noir, chardonnay and a touch of meunier) has attained that marvellous place where the buttery silkiness and roast nut character of bottle age melds gracefully with the cool focus of high-altitude Tumbarumba white citrus and stone fruits. The accord is enticing, magnificently silky and impeccably polished, right at its peak. Disgorged Aug '12. Cork. 13% alc. **Rating** 95 **To** 2017 $65 TS

805 Late Disgorged Pinot Noir Chardonnay Pinot Meunier 2001 A magnificently toasty and secondary style, after 11 years of lees maturity, yet upholding the cool, high-altitude citrus definition of Tumbarumba. It's spicy and characterful, proclaiming its 60% pinot noir dominance (with 30% chardonnay and 10% meunier), yet retaining focus and streamlined definition, only now beginning to dry out on the finish, in the twilight of a glorious life. Disgorged Aug '12. Cork. 13% alc. **Rating** 94 **To** 2016 $75 TS

🍷🍷🍷🍷🍷 **805 Pinot Noir Chardonnay Pinot Meunier 2008** Rating 93 To 2018 $45 TS

Cowaramup Wines

19 Tassel Road, Cowaramup, WA 6284 **Region** Margaret River
T (08) 9755 5195 **www**.cowaramupwines.com.au **Open** By appt
Winemaker Naturaliste Vintners (Bruce Dukes) **Est.** 1995 **Dozens** 5000 **Vyds** 17ha
Russell and Marilyn Reynolds run a biodynamic vineyard with the aid of sons Cameron (viticulturist) and Anthony (assistant winemaker). Plantings began in 1996 and include merlot, cabernet sauvignon, shiraz, semillon, chardonnay and sauvignon blanc. Notwithstanding low yields and the discipline that biodynamic grapegrowing entails, wine prices are modest. Wines are released under the Reserve, Clown Fish and New School labels.

🍷🍷🍷🍷🍷 **Reserve Limited Edition Margaret River Chardonnay 2012** Estate-grown and matured for 12 months in new French oak. A supremely elegant, fine and well-balanced wine, developing slowly and surely, with even more time before the wine plateaus; citrus, stone fruit, oak and acidity all contribute to the result. Screwcap. 12.5% alc. **Rating** 96 **To** 2022 $30 ❂

ΨΨΨΨ️ **Clown Fish Sauvignon Semillon 2014** Rating 92 To 2020 $20 ✪
Clown Fish Shiraz 2012 Rating 91 To 2020 $20 ✪
Clown Fish Cabernet Merlot 2012 Rating 90 To 2023 $20 ✪

Coward & Black Vineyards ★★★★☆

448 Tom Cullity Drive, Wilyabrup, WA 6280 **Region** Margaret River
T (08) 9755 6355 **www**.cowardandblack.com.au **Open** 7 days 9–5
Winemaker Clive Otto (Contract) **Est.** 1998 **Dozens** 3000 **Vyds** 9.5ha
Patrick Coward and Martin Black have been friends since they were five years old. They
acquired a property directly opposite Ashbrook and on the same road as Vasse Felix, and began
the slow establishment of a dry-grown vineyard; a second block followed five years later. In
all there are 2.5ha each of cabernet sauvignon and shiraz, and 1.5ha each of chardonnay,
semillon and sauvignon blanc. The cellar door is integrated with another of their businesses,
the Margaret River Providore. The result is an organic vegetable garden, 1000 olive trees and
an 80-seat restaurant serving food that has attracted praise from all and sundry since the word
go, incorporating vegetables and fruit straight from the organic garden.

ΨΨΨΨΨ **Margaret River Semillon Sauvignon Blanc 2014** A precisely detailed, fresh
wine, each component allowed to express itself; semillon gets in first with its
lemon citrus/snow pea flavours, passionfruit and green pineapple following. Don't
deconstruct it, just drink it. Screwcap. 12.3% alc. **Rating** 94 To 2017 $20 ✪
Margaret River Chardonnay 2014 Bright straw-green; the fruit has made
light work of 9 months' maturation in new French oak; it is strongly grapefruit-
accented, and I find no problem with that – it's a recurrent flavour with cool-
grown chardonnay. Others may disagree, looking for more stone fruit, but so be it.
Screwcap. 13.4% alc. **Rating** 94 To 2035 $29 ✪

ΨΨΨΨ️ **Margaret River Show Shiraz 2013** Rating 92 To 2020 $28

Crabtree Watervale Wines ★★★★★

North Terrace, Watervale SA 5452 **Region** Clare Valley
T (08) 8843 0069 **www**.crabtreewines.com.au **Open** 7 days 10.30–4.30
Winemaker Kerri Thompson **Est.** 1979 **Dozens** 6000 **Vyds** 13.2ha
Crabtree is situated in the heart of the historic and iconic Watervale district, the tasting
room and courtyard (set in the produce cellar of the original 1850s homestead) looking out
over the estate vineyard. The winery was founded in 1984 by Robert Crabtree, who built a
considerable reputation for medal-winning Riesling, Shiraz and Cabernet Sauvignon. In 2007
the winery was purchased by an independent group of wine enthusiasts, the winery firmly
continuing in the established tradition of estate-grown premium wines (Robert remains
a shareholder).

ΨΨΨΨΨ **Riesling 2014** Precision, purity and persistence are the three Ps that define this
classy Riesling; hand-picked, but we don't know whether it was whole bunch-
pressed or not, arguably an irrelevant detail anyway. It is flooded with zesty
lemon and lime flavours on the long palate, acidity just as it should be. Screwcap.
12.5% alc. **Rating** 96 To 2029 $26 ✪
Shiraz 2013 Direct from the notebook: distinctive. Quality from start to finish.
Long life ahead. Raw meat, black cherry and blackberry, various dried peppers
and smoke-like nuances. Absolute quality. Firm, raking tannin. No shortage of
personality. Screwcap. 14% alc. **Rating** 96 To 2032 $28 CM ✪
Cabernet Sauvignon 2013 Deep dark colour, plenty of flavour, feels gutsy
throughout but not in any way loose or undisciplined. Impressive wine. Cassis,
eucalypt, smoky/cedary oak and various floral characters. Assured through the
finish. Tannin builds up a head of steam; cellar time is required but the quality is
there. Screwcap. 13.5% alc. **Rating** 95 To 2035 $28 CM ✪

ΨΨΨΨ️ **Hilltop Vineyard Cabernet 2013** Rating 93 To 2024 $22 CM ✪
Hilltop Vineyard Riesling 2014 Rating 90 To 2020 $21 ✪

cradle of hills

76 Rogers Road, Sellicks Hill, SA, 5174 **Region** McLaren Vale
T (08) 8557 4023 **www.**cradle-of-hills.com.au **Open** By appt
Winemaker Paul Smith **Est.** 2009 **Dozens** 900 **Vyds** 6.88ha
Paul Smith's introduction to wine was an unlikely one: the Royal Australian Navy, and in particular the wardroom cellar at the tender age of 19. A career change took Paul to the world of high-performance sports, and he met his horticulturist wife Tracy. From 2005 they travelled the world with their two children, spending a couple of years in Europe, working in and learning about the great wine regions, and how fine wine is made. For his part, Paul secured a winemaking diploma, and they now have almost 7ha of cabernet sauvignon and shiraz (roughly 50% each). They supplement the shiraz with grenache and mourvedre to make their Route de Bonheur (Road to Happiness) grenache mourvedre shiraz blend.

Row 23 McLaren Vale Shiraz 2013 Micro-parcels of estate fruit picked over 3 days early to mid-March for red and black fruit flavours, 15° baume; open-fermented, matured for 18 months in new and used French puncheons. This is a joyously full-bodied Shiraz, with the promised fruit complexity and more; the tannins and oak contributions play second fiddle to the fruit. 65 dozen made. Screwcap. 14.5% alc. **Rating** 95 **To** 2038 $45

Maritime McLaren Vale Cabernet Shiraz 2012 A 67/33% blend, open-fermented, hand-plunged, post-fermentation maceration, matured in used French hogsheads on lees for 24 months, then racked/returned for a further 6 months. Has retained excellent hue; the maceration has worked to perfection, giving a firm, ripe tannin framework for a brimful glass of luscious blackcurrant and blackberry fruit. Screwcap. 14.5% alc. **Rating** 95 **To** 2042 $29 ❂

GiGi McLaren Vale Grenache Rose 2014 A 90/10% blend of grenache and mourvedre; hand-picked and sorted, lightly crushed, 24 hours' skin contact, basket-pressed to tank for 6 months on fine lees for mlf. The blend works very well, with energy and drive, the finish prolonged by crisp acidity. 100 dozen made. Screwcap. 13.5% alc. **Rating** 94 **To** 2016 $19 ❂

Darkside McLaren Vale Shiraz Mourvedre 2012 70% shiraz, 25% mourvedre, 5% grenache, hand-sorted, hand-plunged, 2 weeks' post-fermentation maceration, basket-pressed to used puncheons, on lees for 12 months, racked, then a further 18 months in oak. The result has a creamy texture, with such deep fruit that it has overall balance. Whether 6 months less in oak would have been better is a question without answer. Screwcap. 14.5% alc. **Rating** 94 **To** 2032 $29 ❂

Wild Child Adelaide Hills Chardonnay 2014 **Rating** 93 **To** 2021 $25 ❂

Craiglee ★★★★★

Sunbury Road, Sunbury, Vic 3429 **Region** Sunbury
T (03) 9744 4489 **www.**craiglee.com.au **Open** Sun & public hols 10–5
Winemaker Patrick Carmody **Est.** 1976 **Dozens** 2500 **Vyds** 9.5ha
A winery with a proud 19th-century record, Craiglee recommenced winemaking in 1976 after a prolonged hiatus. Produces one of the finest cool-climate Shirazs in Australia, redolent of cherry, licorice and spice in the better (warmer) vintages, lighter-bodied in the cooler ones. Mature vines and improved viticulture have made the wines more consistent (except 2011) over the past 10 years or so. Exports to the UK, the US, Italy, Hong Kong and China.

Sunbury Chardonnay 2014 Richness and generosity, but ultimately it's all about the finish. This is a beautifully persistent wine. It tastes of roasted nuts, white peach, grapefruit and chalk, its seams of cedary oak hovering. The finish, almost entirely fruit, rings on and on. Screwcap. 13.5% alc. **Rating** 95 **To** 2021 $35 CM ❂

Sunbury Chardonnay 2012 'Made by natural processes that reflect the flavours specific to the site' says the back label. Make of that what you will, but the outcome in the glass is excellent, led by the juicy, crisp grapefruit, white peach and melon flavours; bright acidity and subtle oak provide the finishing touches. Screwcap. 13.5% alc. **Rating** 95 **To** 2020 $35 ❂

Sunbury Viognier 2013 Sets you back on your heels. This is a high-quality offering. Complex and funky yet essentially and appropriately fruit-driven. Struck match, apricot, slate and hay-like notes. Pure apricot and spice as a finishing push. Outstanding. Screwcap. 13.5% alc. **Rating** 95 **To** 2016 $35 CM ✪

Sunbury Shiraz 2013 Composed. Keeping it all close to its chest for now. Dark cherries, roasted meats, black pepper and smoky oak; beautifully integrated and teamed. Lift of redder berries, inching into florals. Tannin has the whip held aloft, ready to crack. Screwcap. 13.5% alc. **Rating** 95 **To** 2035 $55 CM

Sunbury Shiraz 2012 Relatively light but bright crimson-purple hue; there is an almost Pinot-like fragrance and delicacy to the bouquet of shimmering red fruits; the balance and mouthfeel of the light to medium-bodied palate is perfect, making the wine one of those with an almost indefinite drinking span, starting now. Screwcap. 13.5% alc. **Rating** 95 **To** 2032 $55

Sunbury Chardonnay 2013 Warm year, but an elegant release. Oak is tucked seamlessly into the fruit. Spice, white peach, a drive of citrussy acidity. Textbook Craiglee Chardonnay but with perhaps a measure of elegance beyond the norm. Toast and oatmeal-like notes linger on the aftertaste. In fine form. Screwcap. 13.5% alc. **Rating** 94 **To** 2021 $35 CM

Sunbury Viognier 2014 Bursting with flavour and style. Slatey and spicy. Not overdone, but plenty of power. Screwcap. 13.5% alc. **Rating** 94 **To** 2016 $35 CM

LTV Shiraz Viognier 2012 Lightish in Shiraz terms but it shows power beyond its depth/concentration of fruit. It's savoury, silken and firm with cranberried/black cherried flavour. Indeed the more you taste it the more it draws you in. Smoky oak and spiced meat notes add to the interest. Quite exquisite. Screwcap. 13.5% alc. **Rating** 94 **To** 2026 $40 CM

♥♥♥♥♡ **Sunbury Viognier 2012 Rating** 93 **To** 2015 $35 CM
LTV Shiraz 2013 Rating 93 **To** 2023 $40 CM

Craigow ★★★★★

528 Richmond Road, Cambridge, Tas 7170 **Region** Southern Tasmania
T (03) 6248 5379 www.craigow.com.au **Open** 7 days Christmas to Easter (except public hols)
Winemaker Winemaking Tasmania (Julian Alcorso) **Est.** 1989 **Dozens** 800 **Vyds** 8.75ha
Hobart surgeon Barry Edwards and wife Cathy have moved from being grapegrowers with only one wine to a portfolio of several wines, while continuing to sell most of their grapes. Craigow has an impressive museum release program; the best are outstanding, while others show the impact of sporadic bottle oxidation (a diminishing problem with each vintage now under screwcap).

♥♥♥♥♡ **Chardonnay 2013** Needs time to build flesh but its line and length seem sound. Lemon, apple and white peach notes of moderate intensity shoot crisply through the palate, the linger of flavour the most impressive feature; for now. Screwcap. 12.7% alc. **Rating** 92 **To** 2020 $29 CM

Pinot Noir 2010 Excellent intensity and length. Displays violets, stewed cherries, stems, beetroot and an assortment of dried herbs/spices. It feels both warm and cool, fresh and slightly baked. Complex is one way to describe it. Tannin is in healthy supply, as is intrigue. Screwcap. 13.8% alc. **Rating** 92 **To** 2020 $34 CM

Craneford ★★★★

Moorundie Street, Truro, SA 5356 **Region** Barossa Valley
T (08) 8564 0003 www.cranefordwines.com **Open** Mon–Fri 10–5, w'ends by appt
Winemaker Carol Riebke, John Glaetzer (Consultant) **Est.** 1978 **Dozens** 50 000
Since Craneford was founded it has undergone a number of changes of both location and ownership. The biggest change came in 2004 when the winery, by then housed in the old country fire station building in Truro, was expanded and upgraded. In '06 John Glaetzer joined the team as consultant winemaker, with Carol Riebke the day-to-day winemaker. Quality

grapes are sourced from contract growers, and production has doubled – amazing in these tough times. Exports to all major markets.

Barossa Valley Cabernet Sauvignon 2013 Very good colour; skilled winemaking, carefully sourced grapes, a benison of aromatic oak and a good vintage have all conspired to produce a very good wine at a very fair price. Screwcap. 14.5% alc. **Rating** 94 **To** 2033 $28 ✪

Barossa Valley Shiraz 2013 Rating 93 **To** 2028 $28
Barossa Valley GSM 2013 Rating 92 **To** 2028 $24 ✪
Allyson Parsons Shiraz 2013 Rating 91 **To** 2023 $20 ✪
Allyson Parsons Cabernet Sauvignon 2013 Rating 90 **To** 2023 $20 ✪

Cranswick Wines

1 Waiwera Street, McMahon's Point, NSW 2060 (postal) **Region** South Eastern Australia
T (02) 9929 3954 **www.**cranswickwinesaustralia.com **Open** Not
Winemaker Various **Est.** 2008 **Dozens** 100 000 **Vyds** 1000ha
While the establishment date is shown as 2008, the Cranswick brand was created in 1991 when owner Graham Cranswick-Smith initiated a management buy-out of Diageo's bulk winemaking facility in the Riverina. Since then it has diversified by also marketing its own broad range of wines (Cranswick Lakefield, Cranswick Estate and Cranswick Sarus) from cabernet sauvignon, merlot, shiraz, chardonnay, sauvignon blanc, pinot grigio, colombard and semillon. Exports to all major markets.

Estate Riverina Botrytis Semillon 2010 Bright gold; the impact of clean botrytis is immediate; the wine is complex, well balanced (not too sweet) and still fresh. These wines often develop at a rate of knots – this hasn't done so. 375ml. Screwcap. 10.5% alc. **Rating** 91 **To** 2017 $10 ✪

Crawford River Wines

741 Hotspur Upper Road, Condah, Vic 3303 **Region** Henty
T (03) 5578 2267 **www.**crawfordriverwines.com **Open** By appt
Winemaker John and Belinda Thomson **Est.** 1975 **Dozens** 4000 **Vyds** 11.5ha
Time flies, and it seems incredible that Crawford River celebrated its 40th birthday in 2015. Once a tiny outpost in a little-known wine region, Crawford River is a foremost producer of Riesling (and other excellent wines) thanks to the unremitting attention to detail and skill of its founder and winemaker, John Thomson (and moral support from wife Catherine). His talented elder daughter Belinda has returned part-time after completing her winemaking degree and working along the way in Marlborough (NZ), Bordeaux, Ribera del Duero (Spain), Bolgheri and Tuscany, and the Nahe (Germany), with Crawford River filling in the gaps. She continues working in Spain, effectively doing two vintages each year. Younger daughter Fiona is in charge of sales and marketing. Exports to the UK and South-East Asia.

Reserve Riesling 2004 When I tasted this wine as part of a vertical tasting of all the Crawford River Rieslings in Aug '09 I gave it 97 points (although it and one or two others had not been released – this is in fact the first commercial release). It has the power of a great Rheingau and the finesse of a great Mosel Riesling, the multiplication of intensity × length giving rise to an astronomical number. Screwcap. 12.5% alc. **Rating** 98 **To** 2026 $92 ✪
Riesling 2014 If you have the opportunity to taste this and the Young Vines it is essential you taste the Young Vines first, and rhapsodise about it before moving onto this wine, because its sheer intensity and extreme length are in the realm of the gods and their ambrosia and nectar. This is a dry Riesling equivalent of Tokaji Essencia. Screwcap. 13% alc. **Rating** 97 **To** 2039 $43 ✪

Young Vines Riesling 2014 Bright, pale quartz-green; citrus blossom fills the bouquet with just a flash of apple blossom for good measure; the palate is simply a joy to taste, as these 15-years-young vines are doing what most 50yo vines in other riesling regions cannot. The length and balance are perfect. Screwcap. 13% alc. **Rating** 96 **To** 2034 $28

Museum Release Riesling 2006 Could easily be mistaken for a 1 or 2yo Riesling if served blind. A faint touch of CO_2 is in play with the purity of the lime and mineral-like acidity pure Crawford River. Will make a fine 21st birthday gift for anyone born in '06. Screwcap. 13% alc. **Rating** 96 **To** 2027 $70

Cielo 2013 100% fermented in French barriques, other than some cigar-shaped barrels that are longer and narrower than a standard 225l barrique with a capacity of 285l, which led to greater lees contact without stirring. Only Crawford River could produce a Sauvignon Blanc with this intensity and length, although tasted blind you might be chasing down a lot of blind alleys before you guessed its varietal origin. Screwcap. 13% alc. **Rating** 95 **To** 2020 $30

Cabernet Franc 2013 The first vintage, simply too good to go into the cabernet blend. Destemmed, 6-day cold soak, wild-fermented, pressed when dry, matured for 1 year in used French oak. You can see why Crawford River wanted to keep the wine separate: it is outrageously juicy, yet has great shape and structure to its redcurrant fruits and a spider web of fine-spun tannins. Screwcap. 13.5% alc. **Rating** 95 **To** 2028 $35

Semillon Sauvignon Blanc 2012 Rating 94 **To** 2022 $24

ŢŢŢŢŢ **Cabernet Sauvignon 2008 Rating** 92 **To** 2028 $46

Credaro Family Estate   ★★★★☆

2175 Caves Road, Yallingup, WA 6282 **Region** Margaret River
T (08) 9756 6520 **www**.credarowines.com.au **Open** 7 days 10–5
Winemaker Dave Johnson **Est.** 1993 **Dozens** 10 000 **Vyds** 120ha
The Credaro family first settled in Margaret River in 1922, migrating from Northern Italy. Initially a few small plots of vines were planted to provide the family with wine in the European tradition. However, things began to change significantly in the '80s and '90s, and changes have continued through to 2015. The most recent has been the acquisition of a 40ha property, with 18ha of vineyard, in Wilyabrup (now called the Summus Vineyard) and the expansion of winery capacity with 300 000 litres of additional tank space. Credaro now has seven separate vineyards (120ha in production), spread throughout the Margaret River: Credaro either owns or leases each property and grows/manages the vines with its own viticulture team. It has its own mechanical harvester, and makes all the wine in its 1200-tonne winery. There are no purchases of fruit from other vineyards. The wines are produced in two ranges: Beach Head and Credaro Family Estate. Exports to China.

ŢŢŢŢŢ **Margaret River Shiraz 2012** Determined Shiraz with an element of brute force to the fruit profile but enough softness to give early drinkers a chance. What it really needs is time to soften. Dense dark chocolate, blackcurrant and blackberry flavours with pangs of smoked sawdust and coffee-cream. Strikes a pose for the camera, in that it wants you to admire it, but it does have the looks. Screwcap. 13.8% alc. **Rating** 95 **To** 2030 $35 CM

ŢŢŢŢŢ **Margaret River Cabernet Merlot 2012 Rating** 93 **To** 2024 $28 CM
Margaret River Sauvignon Blanc 2014 Rating 91 **To** 2016 $20 CM
Beach Head Sauvignon Semillon 2014 Rating 91 **To** 2016 $18 CM
Beach Head Margaret River Shiraz 2013 Rating 90 **To** 2019 $19 CM

🍃 CRFT Wines   ★★★★★

PO Box 197, Aldgate, SA 5154 **Region** Adelaide Hills
T 0413 475 485 **www**.crftwines.com.au **Open** Not
Winemaker Candice Helbig, Frewin Ries **Est.** 2012 **Dozens** 1200
Life and business partners NZ-born Frewin Ries and Barossa-born Candice Helbig crammed multiple wine lives into a relatively short period before giving up secure jobs and establishing CRFT in time for their inaugural 2013 vintage. Frewin started with four years at Cloudy Bay before heading to St Emilion, then to the iconic Pinot Noir maker in Sonoma, Williams

Selyem, then four years with Kingston Estate, and subsequent years as a contract winemaker. Candice is a sixth-generation Barossan, trained as a laboratory technician, spent eight years with Hardys, gaining her degree in oenology and viticulture from CSU, then to Boar's Rock and Mollydooker in 2011, and now CRFT. The 2013 vintage produced a Gewurztraminer, a Gruner Veltliner, three Pinot Noirs and three Shirazs. They say growth will come from additional single vineyards rather than by increasing the size of the make of any particular wine. They share the Lenswood Winery (the original Nepenthe Winery) with other kindred spirits. A shed-cum-cellar door is in the planning stage, as is the possibility of planting some gruner veltliner, a variety they find as fascinating as I find this duo.

ΨΨΨΨΨ **Fechner Vineyard Moculta Shiraz 2013** Matured in 55% French, 45% American oak (75% new); grown on 900 million-year-old gravel soils. As far removed from the Cemetery Vineyard Ebenezer Shiraz as the sun from the moon, this is all about elegance and intensity, with fruit and oak spices to the fore, but leaving ample opportunity for the tangy cherry, plum and blackberry fruits to state their case. Screwcap. 13.5% alc. **Rating** 96 **To** 2033 $65 ❂

K1 Vineyard Kuitpo Gruner Veltliner 2013 Whole bunch-pressed and cool-fermented in stainless steel with lees contact. Has the classic waft of white pepper and fresh pear on the bouquet; the palate has excellent mouthfeel, line, length and drive, all making this on a par with Riesling if given time in the cellar; its aftertaste is already long. Screwcap. 12% alc. **Rating** 95 **To** 2023 $29 ❂

Chapel Valley Vineyard Piccadilly Valley Pinot Noir 2013 From a south-facing slope of clones 114 and 115; 4-day cold soak, slightly less new French oak (35%), otherwise identical making to its siblings. The bouquet has notes of bramble and earth, plus an unexpected, but undoubted, waft of orange peel; the palate has great depth, but also impressive length. Needs less time to open up, but will live and flourish for as long. Screwcap. 13.5% alc. **Rating** 95 **To** 2025 $45

Little Hill Vineyard Seppeltsfield Shiraz 2013 Here the oak is 60% French, 40% American (75% new), the fruit grown on a west-facing slope, made identically to its Shiraz siblings. Brilliant crimson-purple; it has an utterly seductive bouquet, medium-bodied mouthfeel, and delicious black and red fruit flavours; the oak is evident, but perfectly integrated. The wine makes a good case for consumption sooner rather than later, but its balance guarantees a long life. Screwcap. 14.5% alc. **Rating** 95 **To** 2028 $45

Arranmore Vineyard Piccadilly Valley Pinot Noir 2013 All the CRFT Pinot Noirs are made the same way: hand-picked, open-fermented, 20% whole bunches, 6-day cold soak, then warm fermentation, pressed directly to French oak (40% new), 10 months' maturation. Black cherry, spice, and a nice touch of forest ex whole bunches; well balanced and long in the mouth. Has all of the breed and balance to repay a minimum of 5 years' cellaring. 154 dozen made, clones 114 and 115. Screwcap. 13.5% alc. **Rating** 94 **To** 2025 $45

Cemetery Vineyard Ebenezer Shiraz 2013 All CRFT Shirazs are open-fermented, hand-plunged 2–3 times daily, and pressed directly to barrel for 11 months, with some minor differences in the oak, here 60% French, 40% American (60% new). In classic full-blooded and full-bodied black-fruited style, the fruit having made short work of the new oak; tarry tannins round off a very good full-bodied wine. 149 dozen made. Screwcap. 15% alc. **Rating** 94 **To** 2033 $49

ΨΨΨΨΨ **K1 Vineyard Kuitpo Gewurztraminer 2013** **Rating** 93 **To** 2017 $27 ❂
Budenberg Vineyard Pinot Noir 2013 **Rating** 93 **To** 2025 $39

Crisford Winery ★★★

556 Hermitage Road, Pokolbin, NSW 2022 **Region** Hunter Valley
T 0412 564 943 **www.**crisfordwines.com.au **Open** Not
Winemaker Neal Crisford **Est.** 1990 **Dozens** 300 **Vyds** 2.5ha
Carol and Neal Crisford have established a vineyard of merlot and cabernet franc. Neal produces educational videos on wine used in TAFE colleges and by other wine educators. The wine is sold through the Hunter Valley Wine Society.

🍷🍷🍷 **Reserve Hunter Valley Cabernet Franc Merlot Cabernet Sauvignon 2011** Open-fermented, matured in French oak. A most unusual blend anywhere in Australia, and especially the Hunter Valley; in the end minty/savoury notes outfox the underlying cassis fruit, but it's far from disgraced. Screwcap. 13.1% alc. **Rating** 88 **To** 2020 $22

Crittenden Estate   ★★★★★

25 Harrisons Road, Dromana, Vic 3936 **Region** Mornington Peninsula
T (03) 5981 8322 **www.crittendenwines.com.au Open** 7 days 10.30–4.30
Winemaker Rollo Crittenden **Est.** 1984 **Dozens** 7000 **Vyds** 4.8ha
Garry Crittenden was one of the pioneers on the Mornington Peninsula, establishing the family vineyard over 30 years ago, and introducing a number of avant garde pruning and canopy management techniques. In the manner of things, much has changed – and continues to change – in cool-climate vineyard management. Grafting unsuitable varieties (notably cabernet sauvignon) to clonally selected pinot noir, moving from spur to cane pruning, lowering the height of the cordon, eliminating herbicides and synthetic fertilisers, onsite production of compost, and green mulching with inter-row crops, have all been undertaken. While pinot noir and chardonnay remain the principal focus, Garry's constant desire to push envelopes saw the establishment of a range of Italian varietals (Pinocchio) and Iberian Peninsula varieties (Los Hermanos). Winemaking has now returned to the family vineyard on the Mornington Peninsula in a newly built facility, with son Rollo Crittenden very much in charge. Exports to the UK and the US.

🍷🍷🍷🍷🍷 **The Zumma Chardonnay 2013** The bright straw-green colour augurs well for a wine that is indeed the best of the Crittenden Estate trio of '13 Chardonnays, with a classic white peach/grapefruit assemblage underwritten by crisp, minerally acidity; has the requisite length. Screwcap. 13.2% alc. **Rating** 95 **To** 2025 $50
The Zumma Pinot Noir 2013 From the best grapes from the best vines in the family vineyards, all Crittenden Estate Pinots vinified the same way. Curious pricing, this much cheaper than Cris de Coeur; it has profound plummy fruit on the bouquet and a full-bodied (in Pinot terms) palate, where complex savoury tannins come thundering through; there is enough fruit to provide balance for those tannins. Pinot is a broader church than many realise. Screwcap. 13.5% alc. **Rating** 95 **To** 2025 $50
Kangerong Pinot Noir 2013 The Crittenden family planted the Kangerong Vineyard in '82, run biologically (sic); wild yeast-fermented, bottled unfined and unfiltered, standard practice for Crittenden Estate. While strongly flavoured and structured, dark fruits, tannins and oak run in supple stream across the palate. Will repay patience for 2–3 years. Screwcap. 13.5% alc. **Rating** 95 **To** 2025 $40
Peninsula Pinot Noir 2013 Wild yeast-fermented; no filtration or fining. Very good deep colour; a powerful, full-bodied wine (by pinot standards) with a long future as the dark pools of plummy fruit open up; in every sense a cellaring special from a very good Pinot vintage. Screwcap. 13.7% alc. **Rating** 94 **To** 2023 $34

🍷🍷🍷🍷🍷 **Peninsula Chardonnay 2013** Rating 93 To 2023 $34
Cri de Coeur Pinot Noir 2013 Rating 92 To 2023 $70
Kangerong Chardonnay 2013 Rating 91 To 2019 $40

Cullen Wines   ★★★★★

4323 Caves Road, Wilyabrup, WA 6280 **Region** Margaret River
T (08) 9755 5277 **www.cullenwines.com.au Open** 7 days 10–4.30
Winemaker Vanya Cullen, Trevor Kent **Est.** 1971 **Dozens** 20 000 **Vyds** 49ha
One of the pioneers of Margaret River, and has always produced long-lived wines of highly individual style from the mature estate vineyards. The vineyard has progressed beyond organic to biodynamic certification and, subsequently, has become the first vineyard and winery in Australia to be certified carbon neutral. This requires the calculation of all of the carbon used and carbon dioxide emitted in the winery; the carbon is then offset by the planting of new trees. Winemaking is in the hands of Vanya Cullen, daughter of the founders; she is possessed

of an extraordinarily good palate. It is impossible to single out any particular wine from the top echelon; all are superb. Exports to all major markets.

ΨΨΨΨΨ **Diana Madeline 2013** A bright crimson 73/20/7% blend of cabernet, merlot and franc, aged for an average of 17 months in French barriques (60% new). There is no doubt this is Cullen's greatest wine, and one of Australia's greatest cabernet blends, the only real competition coming from other Margaret River blends. The bouquet is perfumed, the palate fluid and graceful, notwithstanding the intensity of its cassis et al. fruits, which give the wine its awesome length, fine tannins its balance. Screwcap. 13% alc. **Rating** 98 **To** 2043 $115 ✪

ΨΨΨΨΨ **Kevin John 2013** Hand-picked chardonnay on a biodynamic flower day; whole bunch-pressed and wild-fermented in French oak and an egg, with a completely spontaneous fermentation before maturation for 7 months in French oak (30% new). It has brightness and life from the natural acidity remaining after the mlf, the fruit flavours drawn from both citrus and stone fruit inputs. Screwcap. 14% alc. **Rating** 96 **To** 2030 $105

Cullen Vineyard Margaret River Sauvignon Blanc Semillon 2014
An estate-grown 64/36% blend; wild-fermented and matured in French oak (70% new) for 6 months, no acid additions made. It is quite extraordinary how the wine has absorbed the oak, perhaps one of the factors emboldening Vanya Cullen to suggest a 15-year cellaring proposition – not so scary if you look at 15yo White Bordeaux. Screwcap. 13.5% alc. **Rating** 95 **To** 2024 $35 ✪

Mangan Vineyard Margaret River Merlot Malbec Petit Verdot 2014
A densely coloured 38/55/27% blend matured in French oak (35% new) for an average of 6 months. It is a profound wine, still newborn, but with all the boxes ticked: a cascade of cassis/blackcurrant, plum, firm tannins (in balance) and a long finish. Screwcap. 13.5% alc. **Rating** 95 **To** 2034 $29 ✪

Mangan East Block 2013 A deep and bright 58/52% blend of petit verdot and malbec. As with all Cullen wines, wild-fermented; matured for 17 months in used French oak. Very different from the other Cullen wines, reflecting its varietal composition, the tannins and black fruits of the petit verdot balanced by the richer, plummier malbec. The blend works very well, and it will be fascinating to watch its development. Screwcap. 13% alc. **Rating** 95 **To** 2038 $55

ΨΨΨΨΩ **Mangan Vineyard Semillon Sauvignon 2014 Rating** 93 **To** 2024 $29

🍇 Cultivar Wines   ★★★★☆

60 Spiller Road, Lethbridge, Vic 3222 **Region** Heathcote
T 0409 337 151 **www**.cultivar.com.au **Open** Not
Winemaker David Crawford **Est.** 2012 **Dozens** 750
Cultivar is the venture of industry veteran David Crawford and wife Meaghan, David with 25 years' experience across the entire Australian wine industry. The term 'cultivar' is technically a more appropriate word than 'variety' (according to Jancis Robinson), but is seldom used outside South Africa. For David, clones are in fact all-important, and, after a protracted search, he found a vineyard first planted in 1991 to clone PT23, with subsequent plantings of the well-known SA1654 clone and a mutated version of PT23 (Mt Ida). David has leased the former Tarcoola Estate winery in conjunction with Bellbrae Estate, and this is where the Cultivar wines are made. The two wines from 2012 show very different characteristics. The wine simply labelled Heathcote Shiraz is in fact a blend of 40% each of SA1654 and the clonally mutated Mt Ida PT23 clone, together with 20% of the unaltered PT23. The Cutout is a 70% blend of PT23 and 30% SA1654.

ΨΨΨΨΨ **Heathcote Shiraz 2012** A 40/40/20% clonal blend that is radically different from its Cutout sibling; the dark berry fruit is deeper and marries perfectly with over a year in French barriques (20% new, 80% 1yo); an excellent medium-bodied Heathcote Shiraz, reflecting the excellent vintage, and with a long life ahead, however enjoyable it is now. Screwcap. 14.5% alc. **Rating** 95 **To** 2032 $32 ✪

ΨΨΨΨΩ **The Cutout Heathcote Shiraz 2012 Rating** 90 **To** 2022 $17 ✪

Cumulus Wines

PO Box 41, Cudal, NSW 2864 **Region** Orange
T (02) 6390 7900 **www**.cumuluswines.com.au **Open** During Orange Food Week (Apr)
and Wine Week (Oct)
Winemaker Debbie Lauritz, Matt Atallah **Est.** 2004 **Dozens** NFP **Vyds** 508ha
Cumulus Wines is majority owned by the Berardo Group of Portugal (which has numerous
wine investments in Portugal, Canada and Madeira). Over 500ha of mature vineyards focus on
shiraz, cabernet sauvignon, chardonnay and merlot. The wines are released under three brands:
Rolling, from the Central Ranges Zone; Climbing, solely from Orange fruit; and Cumulus,
super-premium from the best of the estate vineyard blocks. One of an increasing number of
wineries to use lightweight bottles. The annual crush varies between 3000 and 6000 tonnes,
and if all of the harvest was vinified it would result in between 210 000 and 420 000 dozens.
Exports to the UK, the US and other major markets.

ȚȚȚȚȚ **Six Hundred Above Orange Merlot 2013** The hue is bright and clear, the
varietal expression on both bouquet and palate equally clear; dark cherry, plum,
black olive and bramble are synergistically interwoven, framed by ripe tannins. Is
Cumulus' best Merlot to date. Screwcap. 13.5% alc. **Rating** 95 **To** 2028 $30 ✪
Cumulus Orange Chardonnay 2013 Barrel-fermented and lees-stirred in
French oak. Full-on grapefruit and lesser white peach, together with crisp acidity
are the drivers of this tightly focused Chardonnay, oak relegated to the back seat.
Screwcap. 13.5% alc. **Rating** 94 **To** 2021 $33

ȚȚȚȚȚ **Six Hundred Above Orange Chardonnay 2013** **Rating** 92 **To** 2019 $30
Rolling Grenache Shiraz Mourvedre 2013 **Rating** 92 **To** 2019 $17 CM ✪
Climbing Orange Merlot 2013 **Rating** 91 **To** 2030 $19 ✪
Climbing Orange Shiraz 2013 **Rating** 90 **To** 2017 $19 ✪
Rolling Central Ranges Shiraz 2013 **Rating** 90 **To** 2019 $17 CM ✪

Cupitt's Winery

58 Washburton Road, Ulladulla, NSW 2539 **Region** Shoalhaven Coast
T (02) 4455 7888 **www**.cupittwines.com.au **Open** Wed–Sun 10–5
Winemaker Rosie, Wally & Tom Cupitt **Est.** 2007 **Dozens** 2000 **Vyds** 4ha
Griff and Rosie Cupitt run a combined winery and restaurant complex, taking full advantage
of the location on the south coast of NSW. Rosie studied oenology at CSU and has more
than a decade of vintage experience, taking in France and Italy; she also happens to be
the Shoalhaven representative for Slow Food International. The Cupitts have 4ha of vines
centred on sauvignon blanc, cabernet franc and semillon, and also buy viognier and shiraz
from Tumbarumba, shiraz, chardonnay and sauvignon blanc from the Southern Highlands,
and verdelho from Canowindra (Cowra). Rosie has been joined in the winery by sons Wally
and Tom.

ȚȚȚȚȚ **Dusty Dog Shiraz 2013** 2% viognier was arguably excess to requirements
though there's little question this is a slashing wine. Perfumed, spicy, rich with
cherry-plum flavour, and both clovey and minerally to close. Perfumed tannin
draws back through the wine. Stone fruit notes become more apparent as it
breathes, but there's a whole lot of goodness embedded in this wine. Screwcap.
13.6% alc. **Rating** 95 **To** 2025 $48 CM

ȚȚȚȚȚ **Sangiovese 2013** **Rating** 93 **To** 2021 $32 CM
Slaughterhouse Red 2013 **Rating** 92 **To** 2023 $30 CM
Carolyn's Cabernet 2013 **Rating** 92 **To** 2025 $30 CM
Estate Grown Semillon 2014 **Rating** 90 **To** 2020 $25 CM
Alphonse Sauvignon 2014 **Rating** 90 **To** 2016 $28 CM
Rosie's Rose 2014 **Rating** 90 **To** 2016 $25 CM

Curly Flat ★★★★★

263 Collivers Road, Lancefield, Vic 3435 **Region** Macedon Ranges
T (03) 5429 1956 **www**.curlyflat.com **Open** W'ends 12–5
Winemaker Phillip Moraghan, Matt Regan **Est.** 1991 **Dozens** 6000 **Vyds** 13ha
Phillip Moraghan and Jenifer Kolkka began developing Curly Flat in 1991, drawing in part on Phillip's working experience in Switzerland in the late '80s, and with a passing nod to Michael Leunig. With ceaseless help and guidance from the late Laurie Williams (and others), they have painstakingly established an immaculately trained 8.5ha of pinot noir, 3.5ha of chardonnay and 1ha of pinot gris, and a multi-level, gravity-flow winery. Exports to the UK, Japan and Hong Kong.

🍷🍷🍷🍷🍷 **The Curly Chardonnay 2012** The initial fruit selection has some bearing, but the main differences from the varietal wine are 100% new oak, and 85% mlf (taking acidity down from 9.1g/l at harvest to 6.8g/l in the bottle). Pale green-straw; as fresh as a daisy, with delicious white peach and grapefruit flavours that have made light work of the 100% new oak; its length (in particular) and balance are perfect. Screwcap. 13.8% alc. **Rating** 97 **To** 2030 $55 ✪

🍷🍷🍷🍷🍷 **Chardonnay 2013** Whole bunch-pressed, fermented in French oak (52% new), 18 months' maturation, 20% mlf. Bright, light straw-green; in the typically tightly wound Curly Flat style: very, very long and well-balanced, fruit – not oak – in the driver's seat. The attention to detail is awesome, more than almost any other Australian Chardonnay. Screwcap. 13% alc. **Rating** 96 **To** 2028 $42 ✪

Pinot Noir 2012 Estate-grown; open-fermented, 4% whole bunches, 3-day cold soak, wild yeast, 20 days on skins, French oak (25% new) for 20 months. The bright crimson colour and fragrant bouquet lead into a supple, full-flavoured (cherry/plum/spice) palate with immaculate length and balance. Will stand tall against its forebears. Screwcap. 14.2% alc. **Rating** 96 **To** 2025 $50 ✪

Chardonnay 2012 Estate-grown, hand-picked, whole bunch-pressed with 25% passed through rollers for texture/flavour impact; wild yeast-fermented, 65% mlf in 33% new French oak. Bright green-gold; the bouquet is complex and nutty, the palate crisp and lively, with grapefruit, white peach and minerally acidity each given equal space on the palate. WAK screwcap. 14% alc. **Rating** 95 **To** 2022 $42

The Curly Pinot Noir 2012 Clones 114 and 115; hand-picked, 100% whole bunches, 5-day cold soak, 29 days of pre, during and post-fermentation, matured for 20 months in French oak (65% new). The light crimson colour is perfectly clear, an appropriate introduction for a delicately embroidered palate that, against the odds, has kept the oak impact under total control; red fruits dominate early on, but savoury/briary nuances on the finish provide a satisfying conclusion. Screwcap. 14% alc. **Rating** 95 **To** 2027 $64

Williams Crossing Chardonnay 2013 The only obvious difference from its big brother is the near absence of new oak (2% compared to 52%) as a result of barrel declassification, so the similarities are greater than the differences. Citrus (grapefruit), apple (Granny Smith) and stone fruit (white peach) offer roughly equal amounts. Screwcap. 12.9% alc. **Rating** 94 **To** 2025 $27 ✪

Williams Crossing Pinot Noir 2013 Picked 19 Mar to 8 Apr, destemmed, 3-day cold soak, wild-fermented for 14–18 days, 12 months' maturation in used French oak. A serious junior brother to The Curly, its colour bright and clear, the bouquet and palate both poised and detailed, the red fruits already shimmering. Screwcap. 13.6% alc. **Rating** 94 **To** 2025 $30 ✪

Curtis Family Vineyards ★★★☆

514 Victor Harbor Road, McLaren Vale, SA 5171 **Region** McLaren Vale
T 0439 800 484 **www**.curtisfamilyvineyards.com **Open** Not
Winemaker Mark and Claudio Curtis **Est.** 1973 **Dozens** 10 000
The Curtis family traces its history back to 1499 when Paolo Curtis was appointed by Cardinal de Medici to administer Papal lands in the area around Cervaro. (The name Curtis is

believed to derive from Curtius, a noble and wealthy Roman empire family.) The family has been growing grapes and making wine in McLaren Vale since 1973, having come to Australia some years previously. Exports to the US, Canada, Thailand and China.

ŶŶŶŶŶ **Gold Label McLaren Vale Shiraz 2010** Unashamedly full-bodied, with lavish helpings of fruit and oak, a touch of discipline from savoury tannins on the finish. If the Diam stays true, will develop over many years; against the odds, it has balance and length. 14% alc. **Rating** 91 **To** 2025 $70

d'Arenberg ★★★★★

Osborn Road, McLaren Vale, SA 5171 **Region** McLaren Vale
T (08) 8329 4888 **www.**darenberg.com.au **Open** 7 days 10–5
Winemaker Chester Osborn, Jack Walton **Est.** 1912 **Dozens** 270 000 **Vyds** 197.2ha
Nothing, they say, succeeds like success. Few operations in Australia fit this dictum better than d'Arenberg, which has kept its almost 100-year-old heritage while moving into the 21st century with flair and élan. At last count the d'Arenberg vineyards, at various locations, have 24 varieties planted, as well as 120 growers in McLaren Vale. There is no question that its past, present and future revolve around its considerable portfolio of richly robed red wines, Shiraz, Cabernet Sauvignon and Grenache being the cornerstones, but with over 20 varietal and/or blend labels. The quality of the wines is unimpeachable, the prices logical and fair. It has a profile in both the UK and the US that far larger companies would love to have. d'Arenberg celebrated 100 years of family grapegrowing in '12 on the property that houses the winery, cellar door and restaurant. A founding member of Australia's First Families of Wine. Ridiculous wine names the only downside. Exports to all major markets.

ŶŶŶŶŶ **The Beautiful View Grenache 2012** Superb retention of colour; a powerhouse of exceptional concentration and focus more common with Shiraz than Grenache; there are as many black fruit notes as red, sealed together by the glue of fine, persistent tannins. Screwcap. 14.3% alc. **Rating** 97 **To** 2027 $103 ✪
The Blewitt Sands McLaren Vale Grenache 2012 The cooler climate of the Blewitt Springs district gives this wine exceptional intensity, with a strong savoury/spicy carpet for the primary grenache fruit flavours; the tannins also play an important role, oak merely a vehicle to bring the wine to the point where it is ready to bottle. Screwcap. 14.4% alc. **Rating** 97 **To** 2032 $103 ✪

ŶŶŶŶŶ **Scarce Earth The Amaranthine Single Vineyard Shiraz 2012** As with all the Scarce Earth Shirazs, has deep colour; an awesomely powerful and rich wine, black fruits, licorice and fresh-turned earth aromas and flavours; the palate is long and distinguished (it's no surprise this vineyard should also constitute an important part of Dead Arm), the tannins firm, but not aggressive. Screwcap. 14.6% alc. **Rating** 96 **To** 2042 $99
Scarce Earth The Eight Iron Single Vineyard Shiraz 2012 Open-fermented, foot-trodden and basket-pressed. The bouquet is distinctive, with some iodine and bitter chocolate aromas; the palate is full-bodied, but not without polish, fruit, oak and tannins moulded together, the finish long and balanced. The style of d'Arenberg's Scarce Earth is different (to a large degree from terroir, not quality). Screwcap. 14.6% alc. **Rating** 96 **To** 2037 $99
Scarce Earth Tyche's Mustard Single Vineyard Shiraz 2012 There is no question about it: the bouquet has mustard seed and earth aromas, the palate picking up the same mustard nuance; the result is a savoury wine (hitherto blended in small proportions with other d'Arenberg top reds), yet has remarkable finesse. Screwcap. 14.6% alc. **Rating** 96 **To** 2032 $99
The Fruit Bat Single Vineyard Shiraz 2012 A spicy, earthy bouquet; the medium to full-bodied palate has tension and movement, with notes of herb, spice and earth on the finish of a wine with X-factor. Screwcap. 14.4% alc. **Rating** 96 **To** 2042 $103
The Little Venice Single Vineyard Shiraz 2012 Dark chocolate, coffee, licorice and black fruits; good texture, mouthfeel and balance; harmonious; one of the best. Screwcap. 14.5% alc. **Rating** 96 **To** 2042 $103

The Vociferate Dipsomaniac Single Vineyard Shiraz 2012 Rich and full, but retains shape and balance; blackberry and licorice fruit, persistent, dusty tannins, good length. Screwcap. 14.6% alc. **Rating** 96 **To** 2047 $103

The Sardanapalian Single Vineyard Shiraz 2012 Instantly attractive bouquet, then an extra dimension of intensity and drive without sacrificing harmony; all the flavour boxes ticked. Screwcap. 14.4% alc. **Rating** 96 **To** 2037 $103

J.R.O. Afflatus Single Vineyard Shiraz 2012 Medium to full-bodied; oak and spice components are obvious on the bouquet; accelerates markedly on the juicy back-palate and finish. Screwcap. 14.5% alc. **Rating** 95 **To** 2042 $103

The Swinging Malaysian Single Vineyard Shiraz 2012 Has good intensity, focus and length; McLaren Vale dark chocolate comes through strongly, and the texture is good. Screwcap. 14.8% alc. **Rating** 95 **To** 2042 $103

The Other Side Single Vineyard Shiraz 2012 Attractive, open structure/movement/mouthfeel; spice, licorice, earth and black fruits interwoven. Screwcap. 14.7% alc. **Rating** 95 **To** 2037 $103

The Coppermine Road Cabernet Sauvignon 2011 How this was achieved in '11 is anyone's guess, other than vigilant viticulture and nerves of steel in delaying the picking. It has an extra edge to its varietal expression thanks to the cool temperatures (rain to one side), blackcurrant/cassis the driver, savoury olive and bay leaf in the rear seat. A very good wine. Screwcap. 14.3% alc. **Rating** 95 **To** 2031 $65

The Piceous Lodestar Single Vineyard Shiraz 2012 **Rating** 95 **To** 2042 $103

The Sisypheanic Euphoria Single Vineyard Shiraz 2012 **Rating** 94 **To** 2032 $103

Shipsters' Rapture Single Vineyard Shiraz 2012 **Rating** 94 **To** 2042 $103

Scarce Earth The Blind Tiger Single Vineyard McLaren Vale Shiraz 2012 **Rating** 94 **To** 2047 $103

Museum Cellar Release d'Arry's Original Shiraz Grenache 2006 **Rating** 94 **To** 2020 $30 ⊘

The Custodian Grenache 2012 **Rating** 94 **To** 2022 $18 ⊘

The Derelict Vineyard Grenache 2010 **Rating** 94 **To** 2021 $30 CM ⊘

Dal Zotto Wines ★★★★

Main Road, Whitfield, Vic 3733 **Region** King Valley
T (03) 5729 8321 **www.dalzotto.com.au** **Open** 7 days 10–5
Winemaker Michael Dal Zotto **Est.** 1987 **Dozens** 15 000 **Vyds** 48ha
The Dal Zotto family is a King Valley institution; ex-tobacco growers, then contract grapegrowers, they are now primarily focused on their Dal Zotto range. Led by Otto and Elena, and with sons Michael and Christian handling winemaking and sales/marketing respectively, the family is producing increasing amounts of wine of consistent quality from its substantial estate vineyard. The cellar door is in the centre of Whitfield, and is also home to their Trattoria (open weekends).

♟♟♟♟♟ Strathbogie Ranges Riesling 2013 An interesting floral/talc bouquet is followed by a brightly flavoured lime, lemon and herb palate with admirable length and balance, the fruit surging on the finish. Will this sell for $60 in 11 years' time? It is likely to be even better than the '04 Museum Release King Valley Riesling. Screwcap. 12.5% alc. **Rating** 94 **To** 2023 $18 ⊘

Museum Release King Valley Riesling 2004 The colour is still remarkably light and bright; the bouquet raises the question of some pyrazine influence, but the palate blows this away with its barrage of ripe citrus flavours, and a cunningly hidden touch of residual sugar. Screwcap. 12% alc. **Rating** 94 **To** 2020 $60

♟♟♟♟♟ King Valley Arneis 2014 **Rating** 93 **To** 2017 $27 ⊘
King Valley Pinot Grigio 2014 **Rating** 92 **To** 2016 $19 ⊘
King Valley Nebbiolo 2012 **Rating** 91 **To** 2017 $50
Pucino King Valley Prosecco 2014 **Rating** 91 **To** 2015 $23 TS ⊘
King Valley Garganega 2014 **Rating** 90 **To** 2016 $24

Dalfarras ★★★★

PO Box 123, Nagambie, Vic 3608 **Region** Nagambie Lakes
T (03) 5794 2637 **www**.tahbilk.com.au **Open** At Tahbilk
Winemaker Alister Purbrick, Alan George **Est.** 1991 **Dozens** 6400 **Vyds** 20.97ha
The personal project of Alister Purbrick and artist wife Rosa (née Dalfarra), whose paintings adorn the labels of the wines. Alister, of course, is best known as winemaker at Tahbilk (see separate entry), the family winery and home, but this range of wines is intended to (in Alister's words) 'allow me to expand my winemaking horizons and mould wines in styles different from Tahbilk'.

♥♥♥♥♥ **Tempranillo 2013** Mid-weight with cherry-plum and chocolate flavours of decent dimension. It doesn't overcomplicate the issue; quite simply it both feels and tastes good. Value and then some. Screwcap. 12.4% alc. **Rating** 91 **To** 2020 $18 CM ✪
Arneis 2014 Dry and slatey with stone fruit and red apple notes adding a prettiness. No shortage of dry-but-perfumed appeal. Screwcap. 11.5% alc. **Rating** 90 **To** 2015 $17 CM ✪
Savinno 2013 Straw-coloured; oxidative notes give oomph to green melon and nectarine flavours. Texture, mouthfeel, a sense of power; it's a good offering, especially given the price. Screwcap. 13% alc. **Rating** 90 **To** 2015 $17 CM ✪
Garnacha 2013 Attractive expression of the variety. Raspberry, licorice and earth flavours with the perk of dried, woody spice. A curl of chewy tannin. Versatile style, at home both at the dinner table or on the couch in front of the screen of your choice. Screwcap. 14% alc. **Rating** 90 **To** 2019 $18 CM ✪

♥♥♥♥ **Vermentino 2014 Rating** 89 **To** 2015 $17 CM ✪

Dalrymple ★★★★★

1337 Pipers Brook Road, Pipers Brook, Tas 7254 **Region** Northern Tasmania
T (03) 6382 7229 **www**.dalrymplevineyards.com.au **Open** Not
Winemaker Peter Caldwell **Est.** 1987 **Dozens** 4000 **Vyds** 17ha
Dalrymple was established many years ago by the Mitchell and Sundstrup families; the vineyard and brand were acquired by Hill-Smith Family Vineyards in late 2007. Plantings are split between pinot noir and sauvignon blanc, and the wines are made at Jansz Tasmania. In September 2010 Peter Caldwell was appointed as 'Vigneron', responsible for the vineyard, viticulture and winemaking. He brought with him 10 years' experience at Te Kairanga Wines (Martinborough, NZ), and 2 years with Josef Chromy Wines. His knowledge of pinot noir and chardonnay is obviously comprehensive. In Dec '12 Hill-Smith Family Vineyards acquired the 120ha property on which the original Frogmore Creek Vineyard was established; 10ha of that property is pinot noir specifically for Dalrymple.

♥♥♥♥♥ **Single Site Bicheno Pinot Noir 2013** Good depth to the hue; has a very complex bouquet with spiced plum leading the charge, and a totally delicious mouth-filling array of the same spiced plum, black cherry, sweet tannins (oxymoron, I know) and a touch of plum cake. Plenty to feed on as the wine ages. Screwcap. 14% alc. **Rating** 96 **To** 2025 $61 ✪
Single Site Coal River Pinot Noir 2013 Light, bright, clear colour; both the bouquet and palate have an extra dimension of racy aroma and flavour, with spicy plum and black cherry to the fore. Needs, but will richly repay, time in bottle. Screwcap. 13.5% alc. **Rating** 95 **To** 2025 $61
Cave Block Pipers River Chardonnay 2013 Cut with the brilliance of a diamond by natural acidity; fruit aromas and flavours in the citrus sphere, not stone fruit – perhaps a touch of apple and pear to leaven the grapefruit loaf. Will develop at its own pace. Screwcap. 12.5% alc. **Rating** 94 **To** 2025 $37
Pipers River Pinot Noir 2013 A spicy/savoury bouquet points the way for the textured savoury palate, with more foresty/stemmy notes than Cottage Block, but not to the exclusion of fruit. Screwcap. 13.5% alc. **Rating** 94 **To** 2025 $34

Cottage Block Pinot Noir 2013 A fragrant, red berry-filled bouquet leads onto a fresh and juicy palate revelling in a smorgasbord of red, purple and blue fruits, the tannins silky and fine. Screwcap. 13.5% alc. **Rating** 94 **To** 2020 $57

ȲȲȲȲȲ Pipers River Sauvignon Blanc 2014 Rating 92 To 2026 $26

Dalwhinnie ★★★★★
448 Taltarni Road, Moonambel, Vic 3478 **Region** Pyrenees
T (03) 5467 2388 **www**.dalwhinnie.com.au **Open** 7 days 10–5
Winemaker David Jones, Rachel Gore **Est.** 1976 **Dozens** 4500 **Vyds** 26ha
David and Jenny Jones are making wines with tremendous depth of fruit flavour, reflecting the relatively low-yielding but very well maintained vineyards. A 50-tonne high-tech winery now allows the wines to be made onsite. In 2011 David and Jenny celebrated 30 years of winemaking at Dalwhinnie with a superb series of vertical tastings. Exports to the UK and other major markets.

ȲȲȲȲȲ **Moonambel Cabernet 2013** Exceptionally dense crimson-purple showing through on the rim; blackcurrant/cassis fruit is perfectly matched with and by ripe, persistent tannins and quality oak. Will surely be one of the great Dalwhinnie Cabernets as it slowly matures over the next 20+ years. Screwcap. 14% alc. **Rating** 97 **To** 2043 $55 ✪

ȲȲȲȲȲ **Moonambel Shiraz 2013** Saturated crimson; the classic breeding lines on full display; black fruits of every description fill the medium-bodied palate, with spicy/cedary tannins rippling the surface from start to finish. Already very distinguished, and headed to greatness. Screwcap. 13.8% alc. **Rating** 96 **To** 2043 $60 ✪
Moonambel Chardonnay 2013 Glowing, bright green-straw; this is a rich and powerful Chardonnay, the French oak in which it was barrel-fermented obvious, but not to a fault, and will be addressed by time; melon, fig and citrus flavours are dominant in the fruit spectrum. Screwcap. 14% alc. **Rating** 94 **To** 2023 $42
Forest Hut Viognier 2014 A quasi-Rhône 85/15% blend of viognier and roussanne from an interplanted block. The roussanne adds acidity and freshness without depriving the viognier of a voice – stone fruit and a hint of fresh ginger. May surprise with age. Screwcap. 13.5% alc. **Rating** 94 **To** 2017 $40

Dandelion Vineyards ★★★★★
PO Box 138, McLaren Vale, SA 5171 **Region** McLaren Vale
T (08) 8556 6099 **www**.dandelionvineyards.com.au **Open** Not
Winemaker Elena Brooks **Est.** 2007 **Dozens** NFP **Vyds** 124.2ha
This is a highly impressive partnership between Peggy and Carl Lindner (40%), Elena and Zar Brooks (40%), and Fiona and Brad Rey (20%). It brings together vineyards spread across the Adelaide Hills, Eden Valley, Langhorne Creek, McLaren Vale, Barossa Valley and Fleurieu Peninsula. Elena is not only the wife of industry dilettante Zar, but also a gifted winemaker. Exports to all major markets.

ȲȲȲȲȲ **Wonderland of the Eden Valley Riesling 2014** From vines planted in 1912, tended by Colin Kroehn since he was 20, so for 66 of his 86 years. There is a silky (a strange word for Riesling) power and intense focus to the lime, lemon and apple fruit of the palate, still building power long after you have swallowed it/spat it out, the latter the sacrilege of tasting. Screwcap. 11% alc. **Rating** 96 **To** 2034 $60 ✪
Fairytale of the Barossa Rose 2013 Hand-picked from 85yo grenache vines, the free-run juice from a basket press, wild yeast-fermented in used French oak, plus 12 weeks' lees contact without mlf. Trophy Sydney Wine Show '14. Plays the refrain of grenache to perfection, the fragrant bouquet and light-footed palate with red cherry, touches of spice and raspberry all coalescing into a seamless whole. Screwcap. 13% alc. **Rating** 96 **To** 2015 $30 ✪
Wishing Clock of the Adelaide Hills Sauvignon Blanc 2014 Hand-selected (how not?), but apart from this, vinification all directed to the successful capture of

every skerrick of the considerable volume of varietal tropical fruit; has line, length and balance, ticking all the boxes along the way. Screwcap. 12% alc. **Rating** 95 To 2016 $27 ⊙

Lionheart of the Barossa Shiraz 2012 Hand-picked, crushed, wild yeast open-pot fermentation for 8 days, hand-plunging; 18 months in predominantly used French oak. While medium to full-bodied, the wine has elegance and freshness, with no hint of alcohol-induced warmth on the finish, and a particularly attractive bouquet – blackberry, plum and licorice fruits – and supple, but persistent tannins. Screwcap. 14% alc. **Rating** 95 To 2032 $30 ⊙

Red Queen of the Eden Valley Shiraz 2012 From a single vineyard, exactly 100 years old; hand-picked; one-third whole bunches in the bottom of small open pots, two-thirds crushed on top; hand-plunged 11 days; 30 months in 50/50% new and 1yo French barriques. Needs time for the oak to settle down, but the intensity of the black fruits guarantees this will happen, the tannins already in balance. Screwcap. 14.5% alc. **Rating** 95 To 2037 $100

Lioness of McLaren Vale Shiraz 2012 Hand-picked and whole-bunch fermented in open pots, hand-plunged for 12 days; spent 2 years in French oak (80% used, 20% new). Dense, yet vivid, crimson-purple; the powerful full-bodied palate is stacked full of layers of black fruits, licorice and dark chocolate, the tannins ripe and balanced, sustaining the long finish. A cellar special. Screwcap. 14.5% alc. **Rating** 95 To 2032 $30 ⊙

Menagerie of the Barossa Grenache Shiraz Mataro 2012 Rating 94 To 2020 $30 ⊙

Pride of the Fleurieu Peninsula Cabernet Sauvignon 2013 Rating 94 To 2030 $27 ⊙

March Hare of the Barossa Mataro 2012 Rating 94 To 2022 $30 ⊙

ɔɔɔɔɔ **Enchanted Garden Riesling 2014** Rating 93 To 2028 $27 ⊙
Lionheart of the Barossa Shiraz 2013 Rating 93 To 2028 $27 ⊙

Darlington Vineyard ★★★★

Holkham Court, Orford, Tas 7190 **Region** Southern Tasmania
T (03) 6257 1630 **www**.darlingtonvineyard.com.au **Open** 7 days 10–5
Winemaker Frogmore Creek **Est.** 1993 **Dozens** 800 **Vyds** 1.6ha
Peter and Margaret Hyland planted a little under 2ha of vineyard in 1993, on the Freycinet coast. The first wines were made from the '99 vintage, forcing retired builder Peter to complete their home so that the small building in which they had been living could be converted into a cellar door. The vineyard looks out towards the settlement of Darlington on Maria Island, the site of Diego Bernacchi's attempt to establish a vineyard in the 1880s – he tried to lure investors by attaching artificial bunches of grapes to his vines. Darlington Vineyard is now owned by Paul and Louise Stranan.

ɔɔɔɔɔ **Pinot Noir 2013** Full, clear colour; good focus and drive; the palate has spice and forest nuances to its dark cherry fruit, providing a good finish. Screwcap. 13% alc. **Rating** 90 To 2020 $29

David Franz ★★★★★

PO Box 677, Tanunda, SA 5352 **Region** Barossa Valley
T 0419 807 468 **www**.david-franz.com **Open** By appt
Winemaker David Franz Lehmann **Est.** 1998 **Dozens** 5000 **Vyds** 39.17ha
David Franz (Lehmann) is one of Margaret and Peter Lehmann's sons, and took a very circuitous path around the world before establishing his eponymous winery. Wife Nicki accompanied him on his odyssey and they, together with three children, two dogs, a mess of chickens and a surly shed cat, all happily live together in their house and winery. The utterly unique labels stem from (incomplete) university studies in graphic design; his degree in hospitality business management is less relevant, for visits to the winery, aka the shed, are strictly by appointment only. An extended family of five share the work in the vineyard and the shed. Exports to the UK, the US, Canada and China.

ŸŸŸŸŸ Cellar Release Eden Valley Riesling 2010 Whole-bunch basket-pressed, wild fermentation of juice with full solids, 6 months on lees. The wine has fully repaid the investment in holding it for re-release. It is classic Eden Valley, with lemon and lime leaf aromas; the palate is full of citrus and slate notes, all immaculately balanced. Screwcap. 12.5% alc. **Rating** 95 **To** 2025 $32 ✪

Long Gully Road Ancient Vine Semillon 2013 From 127yo vines. David Franz has (seemingly) managed to control his desire to push every known (and unknown) boundary, and let the awesome power of the fruit express itself. Potent lemon/lemongrass acidity is balanced by just a whisper of honey and the crackle of hay. Screwcap. 12.8% alc. **Rating** 95 **To** 2033 $22 ✪

Marg's Blood Semillon 2012 Hand-picked, whole bunch-pressed, 15% barrel-fermented in used French oak, the balance in stainless steel, on completion kept at 4°C for 12 months. Honours mother Margaret Lehmann and her love of Semillon, and does so handsomely. It fills the mouth with fully ripe varietal fruit enhanced by a hint of the barrel-ferment component; the result is a complete wine that doesn't demand patience, but will run whatever course you set it. Screwcap. 11.8% alc. **Rating** 95 **To** 2022 $25 ✪

Survivor Vines Red Rose 2013 Hold your breath; a deep-coloured rose from a mixed block of 90yo shiraz, white frontignan, grenache, semillon, mataro, plus a few more, co-harvested and co-fermented after a carbonic maceration in tubs, then pressed and fermented in stainless steel, held in the same tank for 12 months at 14.4°C. Complex flavours and texture are no surprise; the potent red fruits have a strong, lemony/spicy/savoury twist to the dry palate. Screwcap. 12.7% alc. **Rating** 95 **To** 2017 $22 ✪

Alexander's Reward Cabernet Sauvignon Shiraz 2010 A 75/25% blend from both estate vineyards; 18–30 days in open fermenters; matured for 30 months in new and used French and American oak. Some colour shift, but well within expectations; a complex wine (no surprise), with an array of blackcurrant fruit girdled by oak that is, of course, obvious, yet fits with the fruit. 100 dozen made, 1000 bottles this release. Screwcap. 14.3% alc. **Rating** 95 **To** 2020 $45

Brother's Ilk Moskos' Birdwood Vineyard Adelaide Hills Chardonnay 2013 Hand-picked, basket-pressed, wild-fermented in used oak, then to new and used French hogsheads for 12 months. Vibrantly fresh and crisp, with pointed natural acidity. Should thrive with a few more years in bottle, and hold thereafter. Screwcap. 12.8% alc. **Rating** 94 **To** 2020 $45

Benjamin's Promise Shiraz 2010 From two vineyards; 18-day maceration/ fermentation, hand-plunged, matured for 30 months in new and used French oak. Exceptional generosity and richness, but at this point the oak is very obvious, and the question is whether the fruit or oak will emerge the victor. Screwcap. 14.6% alc. **Rating** 94 **To** 2030 $45

Alternative View Shiraz 2010 A two (new French) barrel selection made 12 months after vintage of the richest, most dense wine in the cellar, and matured for a total of 48 months. Has retained very good colour, hue and depth; takes no prisoners, with very ripe fruit and French oak trying to stare each other down, tannins like ladies in waiting. For the long haul. Total make 55 dozen, 40 dozen this release. Screwcap. 15% alc. **Rating** 94 **To** 2030 $100

Benjamin's Promise Cellar Release Shiraz 2007 Extraordinary colour for an '07, with no loss of primary hues. Most '07 Barossa Shirazs had tough tannins, but here mocha and plum cake, and 36 months in French oak, smother the tannins sufficiently to provide balance, the only issue a tweak of warmth from the alcohol. Screwcap. 14.8% alc. **Rating** 94 **To** 2027 $85

Georgie's Walk Cellar Release Cabernet Sauvignon 2007 From two blocks in the Stelzer Vineyard; 18 days' fermentation/maceration; matured 32 months in new and used American oak; held in the cellar for 5 years. Where the cassis fruit comes from, or how it is still so prominent is part of the David Franz mystery and mastery of his style, but don't give it the chance to fade away. 576 bottles this release. Screwcap. 14.4% alc. **Rating** 94 **To** 2017 $75

ŸŸŸŸŸ Eden Edge 2014 **Rating** 93 **To** 2020 $17 ✪

David Hook Wines

Cnr Broke Road/Ekerts Road, Pokolbin, NSW 2320 **Region** Hunter Valley
T (02) 4998 7121 **www.davidhookwines.com.au Open** 7 days 10–5
Winemaker David Hook **Est.** 1984 **Dozens** 10 000 **Vyds** 8ha
David Hook has over 25 years' experience as a winemaker for Tyrrell's and Lake's Folly, also
doing the full Flying Winemaker bit with jobs in Bordeaux, the Rhône Valley, Spain, the US
and Georgia. The estate-owned Pothana Vineyard has been in production for over 25 years,
and the wines made from it are given the 'Old Vines' banner. This vineyard is planted on the
Belford Dome, an ancient geological formation that provides red clay soils over limestone on
the slopes, and sandy loams along the creek flats; the former for red wines, the latter for white.

🍷🍷🍷🍷🍷 **Old Vines Pothana Vineyard Belford Semillon 2014** Hand-picked, whole
bunch-pressed, cold-settled juice, then tank-fermented at 15°C, short lees contact.
It is extraordinary how Hunter Valley Semillon at this (normal) alcohol can have
such effortless and persistent power so young, yet in no way compromise its future.
A national treasure, but will still have the living daylights taxed out of it. 250 dozen
made. Screwcap. 10.5% alc. **Rating** 95 **To** 2039 $25 ⚫
Old Vines Pothana Vineyard Belford Shiraz 2013 Hand-picked, open-
fermented, hand-plunged, basket-pressed, 12 months in French oak. This is a
great example of what Hunter Valley Shiraz is all about: medium-bodied, with
a distinctive earthy/leathery edge to both the bouquet and the savoury finish.
Not necessarily a great wine, but absolutely true to the faith. 500 dozen made.
Screwcap. 13.5% alc. **Rating** 94 **To** 2038 $40

🍷🍷🍷🍷🍷 **Hunter Valley Shiraz 2014 Rating** 93 **To** 2029 $18 ⚫
Reserve De Novo Rosso 2013 Rating 93 **To** 2023 $30
Reserve Central Ranges Barbera 2013 Rating 92 **To** 2023 $30
Pothana Vineyard Belford Pinot Noir 2014 Rating 90 **To** 2022 $30

Dawson & James

★★★★★

1240B Brookman Road, Dingabledinga, SA 5172 **Region** Southern Tasmania
T (08) 8556 7326 **www.dawsonjames.com.au Open** Not
Winemaker Peter Dawson, Tim James **Est.** 2010 **Dozens** 900
Peter Dawson and Tim James had long and highly successful careers as senior winemakers for
Hardys/Accolade wines. Tim jumped ship first, becoming managing director of Wirra Wirra
for seven years until 2007, while Peter stayed longer. Now both have multiple consulting roles.
They have both long had a desire to grow and make wine in Tasmania, a desire which came
to fruition in '10. The wines so far released have all been of the highest quality. Exports to
the UK and Singapore.

🍷🍷🍷🍷 **Pinot Noir 2013** Sourced from the Meadowbank Vineyard in the Derwent Valley.
Good colour and clarity is a promising start, the wine rapidly building on that
with its utterly seductive and delicious red cherry and strawberry fruit that caresses
the mouth; the end result is exceptional purity, oak and tannins present, but largely
unseen. Screwcap. 12.8% alc. **Rating** 97 **To** 2025 $58 ⚫

🍷🍷🍷🍷 **Chardonnay 2013** Still pale, bright straw-green; sourced from the Meadowbank
Vineyard and impeccably made; the Tasmanian acidity of 7.1g/l has been secreted
in the fruit flavours by some sleight of hand, not by the high-quality French oak
in which it was fermented and matured. This is still a baby, with years to grow,
although will not necessarily become more beautiful. Gold Tas Wine Show '15.
Screwcap. 12.9% alc. **Rating** 96 **To** 2025 $48 ⚫

Dawson's Patch

71 Kallista–Emerald Road, The Patch, Vic 3792 (postal) **Region** Yarra Valley
T 0419 521 080 **www.dawsonspatch.com.au Open** Not
Winemaker Jody Dawson, Martin Siebert **Est.** 1996 **Dozens** 300 **Vyds** 1.2ha

James and Jody Dawson own and manage this vineyard at the southern end of the Yarra Valley, planted to pinot noir (0.7ha) and chardonnay (0.5ha). The climate here is particularly cool, and the grapes do not normally ripen until late April. Jody has completed a degree in viticulture through CSU. The tiny handcrafted production (Chardonnay and Pinot Noir) is sold through local restaurants and cellars in the Olinda/Belgrave/Emerald area.

Yarra Valley Pinot Noir 2012 90% destemmed, 10% whole bunches, cold-soaked for 5 days, wild yeast-fermented, matured for 22 months in French oak (20% new). Bright and clear colour; a strong savoury/stemmy character runs through the length of the palate, posing the question whether the grapes were picked a little too soon. Screwcap. 13% alc. **Rating** 90 **To** 2020 $28

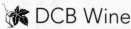 # DCB Wine

505 Gembrook Road, Hoddles Creek, Vic 3139 **Region** Yarra Valley
T 0419 545 544 **www.dcbwine.com.au Open** Not
Winemaker Chris Bendle **Est.** 2013 **Dozens** NFP
DCB is a busman's holiday for Chris Bendle, currently a winemaker at Hoddles Creek Estate, where he has been since 2010. He has previously made wine in Tasmania, NZ and Oregon, thus he is the right person to provide wines that are elegant, affordable, and reward the pleasure of drinking (Chris's aim). It should be said that the two wines so far made have had sophisticated winemaking behind the wine in the glass.

Yarra Valley Chardonnay 2013 Complex but full of fruit. Strong grapefruit and citrus rind flavours lead into struck match, spicy oak and peach. There's a lot going on here. Despite its length, there's certainly nothing lean about it. Impressive. Screwcap. 13% alc. **Rating** 93 **To** 2020 $20 CM ✪
Yarra Valley Pinot Noir 2013 Grown in the Upper Yarra. Bottled unfined and unfiltered. Light on its feet, complex, you could almost call it sordid, but you could also call it juicy and cranberried and delicious. Bands of tannin keep it all feeling neat and tidy. It doesn't try too hard and yet there's a tension to the way it flows along the palate. Screwcap. 13% alc. **Rating** 90 **To** 2020 $20 CM ✪

De Bortoli

De Bortoli Road, Bilbul, NSW 2680 **Region** Riverina
T (02) 6966 0100 **www.debortoli.com.au Open** Mon–Sat 9–5, Sun 9–4
Winemaker Darren De Bortoli, Julie Mortlock, John Coughlan **Est.** 1928
Dozens 4.5 million **Vyds** 311.5ha
Famous among the cognoscenti for its superb Noble One, which in fact accounts for only a minute part of its total production, this winery turns out low-priced varietal and generic wines that are invariably competently made. They come in part from estate vineyards, but also from contract-grown grapes. The rating is in part a reflection of the exceptional value for money offered across the range. In June 2012 De Bortoli received a $4.8 million grant from the Federal Government's Clean Technology Food and Foundries Investment Program. This grant supports an additional investment of $11 million by the De Bortoli family in their project called 'Re-engineering Our Future for a Carbon Economy'. De Bortoli is a founding member of Australia's First Families of Wine. Exports to all major markets.

Noble One Botrytis Semillon 2013 Golden-orange; has that tsunami of luscious honey crumble and preserved cumquat flavours as it enters the mouth, but then changes tack with a burst of fresh citrus on the finish that provides freshness. My only concern is the colour. Best drink sooner rather than later. 375ml. Screwcap. 10.5% alc. **Rating** 95 **To** 2016 $33 ✪
Noble One Botrytis Semillon 2011 Burnt orange-gold colour; the colour suggests a particularly rich Noble One, but in fact it is less full-bodied and luscious than expected; tangy acidity underlies the burnt crème brûlée and poached fig/crystallised citrus fruit flavours. A very interesting wine, ready now. Screwcap. 11% alc. **Rating** 95 **To** 2016 $33 ✪

Black Noble NV Absolutely unique wine, tasting the same with this bottling, with its own outlandish charm – and drinkability. Dark aged mahogany; an absolutely unique barrel-aged Botrytis Semillon (ex Noble One) with hyper-intense fruit cleansed by volatile acidity – counterintuitive, of course. Overall, a sauvage note to its unique mouthfeel. 500ml. WAK screwcap. 17.5% alc. **Rating** 94 To 2016 $38

ŸŸŸŸŸ **Old Boys 21 Years Old Barrel Aged Tawny NV** Rating 93 To 2016 $45
Deen De Bortoli Vat Series No 1 Durif 2012 Rating 91 To 2018 $13 ✪
Deen Vat Series No 9 Cabernet 2013 Rating 90 To 2020 $13 ✪

De Bortoli (Hunter Valley)   ★★★☆

532 Wine Country Drive, Pokolbin, NSW 2320 **Region** Hunter Valley
T (02) 4993 8800 **www**.debortoli.com.au **Open** 7 days 10–5
Winemaker Matt Burton **Est.** 2002 **Dozens** 10 000 **Vyds** 36ha
De Bortoli extended its wine empire in 2002 with the purchase of the former Wilderness Estate, giving it an immediate and significant presence in the Hunter Valley courtesy of the 26ha of established vineyards, including semillon vines over 40 years old. The subsequent purchase of the adjoining 40ha property increased the size of the business. The intention is to convert the vineyards to biological farming practices, with composting and mulching already used to reduce the need for irrigation. Exports to all major markets.

ŸŸŸŸ **Hunter Valley Merlot 2013** It's an awesome display of De Bortoli's winemaking reach when it's able to produce a Hunter Valley Merlot that has clear varietal character – cassis and plum – and a twist of cedar and tobacco to add allure. Bus loads of visitors to the cellar door will take away bus loads of the wine. Screwcap. 12.5% alc. **Rating** 89 To 2018 $20
Murphy's Vineyard Semillon 2014 Fresh and crisp, slippery tactile acidity framing the lemongrass fruit; needs a bit more urgency and energy. Very strange pricing (identical to the '07), twice confirmed with De Bortoli. Screwcap. 11.5% alc. **Rating** 88 To 2018 $35
Murphy's Vineyard Semillon 2007 Bright green-straw; light and fresh, nowhere near the end of its journey, but now (and in the future) lacks intensity. A peculiar bitterness. Screwcap. 11% alc. **Rating** 88 To 2020 $35

De Bortoli (Victoria)   ★★★★★

Pinnacle Lane, Dixons Creek, Vic 3775 **Region** Yarra Valley
T (03) 5965 2271 **www**.debortoliyarra.com.au **Open** 7 days 10–5
Winemaker Stephen Webber, Sarah Fagan, Andrew Bretherton **Est.** 1987
Dozens 350 000 **Vyds** 397ha
The quality arm of the bustling De Bortoli group, run by Leanne De Bortoli and husband Steve Webber, ex-Lindemans winemaker. The top label (De Bortoli), the second (Gulf Station) and the third (Windy Peak) offer wines of consistently good quality and excellent value – the complex Chardonnay and the Pinot Noirs are usually of outstanding quality. The volume of production, by many times the largest in the Yarra Valley, simply underlines the quality/value for money ratio of the wines. The business also owns 170ha in the King Valley, the best grapes going to the Windy Peak label, the surplus going to the parent winery in the Riverina. Exports to all major markets.

ŸŸŸŸŸ **Estate Grown Yarra Valley Pinot Noir 2014** In perfect shape and form. Sets the pitch between savouriness, dryness and fruitiness to an exquisite level. A riot of spices, cherries, smoke and herb notes rush through the palate and explode through the finish. Reductive notes work admirably in the context of the style/wine. Fantastic release. Screwcap. 13% alc. **Rating** 96 To 2024 $30 CM ✪
Estate Grown Yarra Valley Pinot Noir 2013 Clear, bright crimson; Steve Webber was, I believe, the author of 'attention to detail' to describe one of the keys to fine wine, and this is a shining example of that virtue. Every aspect of the purity

of the Pinot Noir flavour, its silky texture and its balance, line and length is in full view. A truly lovely wine. Screwcap. 13% alc. **Rating** 96 **To** 2025 $30 ✪

Section A8 Syrah 2013 Superb expression of cool-climate shiraz. Composed, complex and complete. Roasted nuts, aged meats, sweet-sour cherry and rhubarb flavours lead to a peppery, grainy, beautifully persistent finish. Class right down to its fingers and toes. Screwcap. 14% alc. **Rating** 96 **To** 2032 $50 CM ✪

Estate Grown Yarra Valley Shiraz 2012 The grapes were sourced from 6 estate vineyards, attesting to the unequalled extent of De Bortoli's holdings in the Yarra Valley; each parcel was fermented and matured separately until final blending. An immaculate medium-bodied Shiraz, reflecting the top vintage and De Bortoli's sensitive winemaking, its chorus of red fruits and spiced backed by silky tannins and subtle French oak. Screwcap. 13% alc. **Rating** 95 **To** 2027 $30 ✪

Este Vintage Cuvee 2008 Is an elegantly restrained and subtle sparkling. 6 years of lees age creating a beautifully textured and creamy style, with rising ginger cake, nougat, honey and mixed spice orbiting a focused core of lemon and beurre bosc pear. Sustained by seamlessly integrated acidity, balanced dosage and great persistence, it has the potential for further improvement. Disgorged Nov '14. Diam. 12.7% alc. **Rating** 94 **To** 2015 $40 TS

Villages Fume Blanc 2014 Texture and flavour. Harmonious white with nothing too overt and yet plenty to hold onto. Nettle, stone fruits, gunmetal and honeysuckle. Pristine. Screwcap. **Rating** 94 **To** 2018 $22 CM ✪

Riorret The Abbey Yarra Valley Pinot Noir 2013 Savoury and stemmy at heart but bursting with a combination of boysenberry and cherry-like fruit. There's a keen freshness to this, a friskiness. It puts lightness of touch to powerful effect. Velvety tannin finesses its way through the finish. In short, it's immaculate. Diam. **Rating** 94 **To** 2023 $40 CM

Estate Grown Yarra Valley Shiraz 2013 Fronts up and performs its tricks with a minimum of fuss. Cherry-plum fruit splashed with black pepper and cloves, all given a light lacquering of spicy French oak. Feels, tastes and performs exactly as you would hope. Screwcap. 13.5% alc. **Rating** 94 **To** 2026 $30 CM ✪

La Boheme Act Four Yarra Valley Syrah Gamay 2013 Surely the only such blend in the world. It has good colour, but even better fragrance, full of flowery red fruits. The palate ratchets the impact up further again, with savoury/foresty tannins underlying the copious red fruit flavours, and adding to the length of the wine. Screwcap. 13.5% alc. **Rating** 94 **To** 2018 $20 ✪

🍷🍷🍷🍷🍷 **Vinoque Oval Vineyard Pinot Blanc 2014** Rating 93 To 2018 $24 ✪
Vinoque Yarra Valley Nebbiolo Rose 2014 Rating 93 To 2016 $22 ✪
Gulf Station Yarra Valley Pinot Noir 2013 Rating 93 To 2020 $18 ✪
Villages Pinot Noir 2013 Rating 93 To 2021 $22 CM ✪
Riorret Ponderosa Vineyard Pinot Noir 2012 Rating 93 To 2023 $42 CM
La Boheme Act Four Yarra Valley Syrah Gamay 2014 Rating 93 To 2020 $20 CM ✪
Melba Lucia 2012 Rating 93 To 2020 $22 ✪
Vinoque Art Martin Vineyard Sangiovese 2013 Rating 93 To 2023 $24 ✪
Estate Grown Yarra Valley Chardonnay 2013 Rating 92 To 2021 $30 CM
Villages Chardonnay 2013 Rating 92 To 2018 $22 CM ✪
BellaRiva Sangiovese 2013 Rating 92 To 2019 $15 CM ✪
Rococo Yarra Valley Blanc de Blancs NV Rating 92 To 2015 $22 TS ✪

De Iuliis ★★★★★

1616 Broke Road, Pokolbin, NSW 2320 **Region** Hunter Valley
T (02) 4993 8000 **www.**dewine.com.au **Open** 7 days 10–5
Winemaker Michael De Iuliis **Est.** 1990 **Dozens** 10 000 **Vyds** 30ha
Three generations of the De Iuliis family have been involved in the establishment of their vineyard. The family acquired a property at Lovedale in 1986 and planted 18ha of vines in '90, selling the grapes from the first few vintages to Tyrrell's but retaining increasing amounts

for release under the De Iuliis label. In '99 the land on Broke Road was purchased, where a winery and cellar door were built prior to the 2000 vintage. In '11 the business purchased 12ha of the long-established Steven Vineyard in Pokolbin. Winemaker Michael De Iuliis completed postgraduate studies in oenology at the Roseworthy campus of Adelaide University and was a Len Evans Tutorial scholar. He has lifted the quality of the wines into the highest echelon.

🍷🍷🍷🍷🍷 **Steven Vineyard Hunter Valley Shiraz 2013** This celebrated vineyard was planted on red volcanic soils in '68. The perfumed bouquet of red fruits and spices, not unlike Pinot Noir, leads into a vibrant medium-bodied palate that positively vibrates with its intense red berry fruits and spices; as it ages with grace, other flavours will join the band. Screwcap. 12.5% alc. **Rating** 97 **To** 2043 $40 ✪

🍷🍷🍷🍷🍷 **Hunter Valley Semillon 2014** The wine has enough zesty citrus and lemongrass fruit to encourage immediate consumption, or to be left for 5 years to move into its second life of lemon curd and lightly browned toast. Put simply, great each-way odds. Screwcap. 11.2% alc. **Rating** 95 **To** 2024 $18 ✪
Sunshine Vineyard Hunter Valley Semillon 2014 This is the replanted vineyard that provided the great Lindeman Semillons of the '40s, '50s and '60s, the likes of which we have not seen for 50 years. This wine holds out great promise for the future as the vines mature, its purity and depth of varietal expression flawless. Screwcap. 11.5% alc. **Rating** 95 **To** 2034 $25 ✪
Hunter Valley Shiraz 2013 Excellent colour; a wine that is comfortable in its skin, effortlessly demonstrating what Hunter Valley Shiraz is all about: plum, blackberry, fresh earth, polished leather and soft tannins all encompassed in a medium-bodied, perfectly balanced framework. Great now or in 20 years' time. Screwcap. 13.3% alc. **Rating** 94 **To** 2033 $25 ✪

🍷🍷🍷🍷🍸 **LDR Vineyard Hunter Valley Shiraz Touriga 2013** Rating 92 **To** 2023 $40

De Salis Wines   ★★★★

Lofty Vineyard, 125 Mount Lofty Road, Nashdale, NSW 2800 **Region** Orange
T 0403 956 295 **www**.desaliswines.com.au **Open** 7 days 11–5
Winemaker Charles Svenson **Est.** 1999 **Dozens** 3500 **Vyds** 8.76ha
This is the venture of research scientist Charles (Charlie) Svenson and wife Loretta. Charlie became interested in winemaking when, aged 32, he returned to study microbiology and biochemistry at UNSW. His particular area of interest (for his PhD) was the yeast and bacterial fermentation of cellulosic waste to produce ethanol. In 2009, after a prolonged search, Charlie and Loretta purchased a vineyard first planted in 1993 and known as Wattleview. At 1050m, it is the highest vineyard in the Orange GI, with pinot noir (6 clones), chardonnay, merlot, pinot meunier and sauvignon blanc.

🍷🍷🍷🍷🍸 **Wild Fume Blanc 2013** Whole bunch-pressed, wild yeast fermentation initiated in tank, then to used French barriques for 6 months' maturation. Primarily concerned with structure and texture, which are both good; there are nuances of gooseberry and passionfruit to keep the variety in the tasting frame. Screwcap. 12.5% alc. **Rating** 92 **To** 2016 $32
Wild Chardonnay 2013 Harvested the same day as its sibling; encouraged to start wild yeast fermentation in tank, transferred to new and used French oak for 12 months with weekly lees stirring. Wild yeast fermentation does give more conviction on the finish. Screwcap. 12.8% alc. **Rating** 91 **To** 2017 $38
Chardonnay 2013 Hand-picked from a single block, whole bunch-pressed, the juice settled for 24 hours before fermentation in French oak (35% new). Curiously, has the concentration and complexity the red wines lack. Some custard apple flavours raise the question of a hint of sweetness, partially answered by acidity. Either way, is ready now. Screwcap. 12.8% alc. **Rating** 90 **To** 2016 $42
St Em M 2012 An 80/15/5% blend of merlot, cabernet sauvignon and cabernet franc. The colour is light, but bright, the light to medium-bodied palate with cassis to the fore, herbs and fine-grained tannins bringing up the rear. Is just ripe enough to get it over the line. Drink up. Screwcap. 13.6% alc. **Rating** 90 **To** 2018 $38

St Em F 2012 A 70/28/2% blend of cabernet sauvignon, cabernet franc and merlot. The colour is light but bright, and fruits of the light to medium-bodied palate are enjoyable, with notes of blackcurrant, cedar and spice. Drink now while it retains that freshness. Screwcap. 13.4% alc. **Rating** 90 **To** 2018 $46

Deakin Estate ★★★★

Kulkyne Way, via Red Cliffs, Vic 3496 **Region** Murray Darling
T (03) 5018 5555 www.deakinestate.com.au **Open** Not
Winemaker Frank Newman **Est.** 1980 **Dozens** 205 000 **Vyds** 350ha
This is owned by Freixenet of Spain, along with Katnook Estate. For over 10 years, Dr Phil Spillman steered the development of Deakin Estate, his rather large shoes to be filled by Frank Newman. He has had a long and varied career, starting at Penfolds working alongside Max Schubert, then Angove (for more than a decade) and BRL Hardy at Renmano. The very large production of Deakin Estate, with an enlarged range of brands, is only part of the story: with other labels produced at the estate, the annual crush of 2500 tonnes for Deakin is doubled, as is the production of bottled wines under those other labels.

ΨΨΨΨΩ **Viognier 2014** This really is a surprise: it has crystal clear varietal character in a stone fruit spectrum (apricot to peach), and has length that is not dependent on phenolics. Terrific value. Screwcap. 13.5% alc. **Rating** 91 **To** 2016 $10 ✪
Cabernet Sauvignon 2013 If there's a better Cabernet at $10 on the market I would go jump. It not only has clear varietal expression, but also has texture and structure to go hand in hand with cassis fruit, oak from staves or chips no doubt, but good. Screwcap. 13.5% alc. **Rating** 91 **To** 2020 $10 ✪
Azahara Pinot Grigio 2014 Crisp and lively, with bright acidity; nashi pear, apple and a faint tickle of fresh ginger; good acidity aids the length and finish. Screwcap. 12% alc. **Rating** 90 **To** 2016 $15 ✪

ΨΨΨΨ **La La Land Tempranillo 2013** **Rating** 89 **To** 2018 $16 ✪
La La Land Malbec 2013 **Rating** 89 **To** 2017 $16 ✪

Deep Woods Estate ★★★★★

889 Commonage Road, Yallingup, WA 6282 **Region** Margaret River
T (08) 9756 6066 www.deepwoods.com.au **Open** Wed–Sun 11–5, 7 days during hols
Winemaker Julian Langworthy, Dan Stocker **Est.** 1987 **Dozens** 30 000 **Vyds** 16ha
Owned by Perth businessman Peter Fogarty and family, who also own Lake's Folly in the Hunter Valley, and Millbrook in the Perth Hills. The 32ha property has 16ha plantings of cabernet sauvignon, shiraz, merlot, cabernet franc, chardonnay, sauvignon blanc, semillon and verdelho. Exports to Germany, Malaysia, Singapore, Japan and China.

ΨΨΨΨΨ **Reserve Margaret River Chardonnay 2013** Hand-picked, whole bunch-pressed and fermented in new and used French oak with lees stirring, and ultimately a selection of the best barrels. The complex bouquet and palate both avoid over-the-top flourishes, resulting in an elegant, impeccably balanced wine, with white stone fruit and nuances of cashew running through the palate and finish. Winner of the James Halliday Chardonnay Challenge '14. Screwcap. 13.5% alc. **Rating** 98 **To** 2023 $35 ✪
Reserve Margaret River Cabernet Sauvignon 2013 Exceptional crimson-purple; Julian Langworthy has a rare touch, particularly with cabernet and chardonnay, an unlikely couple outside Margaret River, and even within it when Julian's wines are on show. This has the elegance and symmetry of Bordeaux in good vintages before they were all pumped up on Parkeresque steroids. Screwcap. 14% alc. **Rating** 97 **To** 2043 $60 ✪
Wilyabrup 2012 100% cabernet sauvignon. Has more purple in its crimson colour than Yallingup; there is a silky succulence to the mouthfeel of the pure cassis flavours, the fragrance of the bouquet heightened retrospectively by the medium-bodied palate; the tannins are superfine, the oak handling perfect, the length prodigious. Screwcap. 14.5% alc. **Rating** 97 **To** 2037 $125 ✪

ΨΨΨΨΨ **Block 7 Reserve Margaret River Shiraz 2013** Matured for 18 months in new
and used French oak, which is still flexing its muscles, but before too long will
have to gracefully give way to the supple, but intense, black cherry and black berry
fruit; the handling of the tannins has been critical in giving the wine its stamp of
ultimate quality. Screwcap. 14.5% alc. **Rating** 95 **To** 2033 $45
Margaret River Cabernet Sauvignon Merlot 2013 From estate blocks
planted in '87, separately picked, vinified and matured in new and used French
oak before being blended. A luscious fruit-driven wine, awash with juicy cassis and
redcurrant fruit, yet retains focus and elegance thanks to measured alcohol and
skilled winemaking. Screwcap. 14% alc. **Rating** 95 **To** 2033 $35 ✪
Yallingup 2012 100% cabernet sauvignon. Has good colour, albeit slightly
less bright than Wilyabrup; the palate is more immediately complex in its fruit
dimensions, and ripe tannins more obvious in a balanced, full-bodied wine; there is
also a greater range of flavours, and this may yet throw down a greater challenge in
time than it does today. Screwcap. 14.5% alc. **Rating** 95 **To** 2037 $125
Margaret River Chardonnay 2014 Rating 94 **To** 2019 $20 ✪
Harmony Margaret River Rose 2014 Rating 94 **To** 2016 $15 ✪

ΨΨΨΨΨ **Margaret River Shiraz et al 2013 Rating** 93 **To** 2028 $20 ✪
Margaret River Sauvignon Blanc 2014 Rating 91 **To** 2016 $20 ✪
Ivory Semillon Sauvignon Blanc 2014 Rating 90 **To** 2016 $15 ✪

 DEGEN ★★★★

365 Deasys Road, Pokolbin, NSW 2320 **Region** Hunter Valley
T 0427 078 737 **www.**degenwines.com.au **Open** W'ends 10–5
Winemaker Various contract **Est.** 2001 **Dozens** 1880 **Vyds** 4.5ha
In June 1997 marine engineer Tom Degen, together with IT project manager wife Jean, took
a weekend drive to the Hunter Valley with no particular plan in mind, but as a consequence
of that drive, became the owners of an 11ha wild, heavily wooded bush block, dotted with
boulders, with no fencing or water. The weekend drive became an every weekend drive to
mount their John Deere tractor and slowly but surely clear tonnes of timber, remove the
boulders, build a dam and work the soil. I know all about that, having done the same thing
in 1970/71 (creating what became Brokenwood). In Sept 2001 they planted 1.8ha of shiraz,
1.7ha chardonnay and 1ha semillon, and by '13 opened the DEGEN vineyard, cellar door and
Vine Stay (accommodating 4 guests).

ΨΨΨΨΨ **Hunter Valley Semillon 2007** Full gleaming green-gold; you don't have to wait
for this: lime, honey and toast are now all on display, acidity seemingly melted
away (it can't, of course). Screwcap. 11.8% alc. **Rating** 91 **To** 2017 $25
Nicolas Estate Reserve Hunter Valley Shiraz 2011 Matured for 14 months
in French and American oak. Has retained a youthful colour, but the oak is
swamping the fruit at this stage; it will settle down to a degree, but it's unlikely the
wine will ever achieve balance; the tannins ex the ripe (too ripe?) fruit add to the
message. Screwcap. 14% alc. **Rating** 90 **To** 2026 $35
Single Vineyard Hunter Valley Shiraz 2006 Matured in French oak for
18 months. Very bright colour for a 9yo wine; the oak is evident, but so are
the chirpy red fruits of the brisk palate. A blend of the '06 and '11 would be
interesting – so much so I made an ex tempore blend, which was by some
distance the best of the three. Screwcap. 12.7% alc. **Rating** 90 **To** 2021 $39

del Rios of Mt Anakie ★★★★★

2320 Ballan Road, Anakie, Vic 3221 **Region** Geelong
T (03) 9497 4644 **www.**delrios.com.au **Open** W'ends 10–5
Winemaker John Durham, Gus del Rio **Est.** 1996 **Dozens** 3500 **Vyds** 17ha
Gus del Rio, of Spanish heritage, established a vineyard in 1996 on the slopes of Mt Anakie,
northwest of Geelong (chardonnay, pinot noir, cabernet sauvignon, sauvignon blanc, shiraz,
merlot and marsanne). The wines are made onsite in the fully equipped winery, which
includes a bottling and labelling line able to process over 150 tonnes. Exports to China.

ŸŸŸŸŸ Geelong Shiraz 2013 88% crushed, 12% whole bunches, open-fermented, racked to French oak (38% new), 50% on lees for a further 12 months. Deep, dense, yet bright colour; the bouquet is all Côte Rôtie, with black fruits, spice, licorice and roasted meat nuances, the promise fulfilled by the medium to full-bodied palate. Screwcap. 14% alc. **Rating** 96 **To** 2038 $32 ✪

Geelong Cabernet Sauvignon 2013 Crushed to open fermenters with pump-over until day 5, then 20 further days on skins, maturation in new (35%) and used French oak. An altogether serious Cabernet, with blackcurrant, bay leaf and firm (not dry) tannins on the long, stylish palate, oak the bouquet garni. Screwcap. 14% alc. **Rating** 95 **To** 2028 $32 ✪

Geelong Sauvignon Blanc 2013 Whole bunch-pressed, 50% tank-fermented with cultured yeast, 50% wild yeast-fermented in used oak, both parcels matured for 9 months before blending. The approach has worked to perfection, ripe tropical fruits put on a leash to restrain their desire to go over the top. Excellent value for a drink-now style that has lots to offer lunchtime discussion. Screwcap. 13.2% alc. **Rating** 94 **To** 2015 $22 ✪

Mayhem @ Anakie Chardonnay 2013 Hand-picked, whole bunch-pressed straight to barrel (25% new) for wild yeast fermentation, 8 months in oak. It has gleaming varietal character, grapefruit and white peach to the fore, sustained by crisp acidity and very well handled oak. Excellent value, and can be left in the cellar at leisure. Screwcap. 13% alc. **Rating** 94 **To** 2020 $22 ✪

ŸŸŸŸŸ Mayhem @ Anakie Pinot Noir 2013 **Rating** 90 **To** 2017 $22

Delatite ★★★★★

26 High Street, Mansfield, Vic 3722 **Region** Upper Goulburn
T (03) 5775 2922 **www.**delatitewinery.com.au **Open** 7 days 11–5
Winemaker Andy Browning **Est.** 1982 **Dozens** 5000 **Vyds** 26ha
With its sweeping views across to the snow-clad Alps, this is uncompromising cool-climate viticulture. Increasing vine age (many of the plantings are well over 25 years old), and the adoption of organic (and partial biodynamic) viticulture, seem also to have played a role in providing the red wines with more depth and texture; the white wines are as good as ever; all are wild yeast-fermented. In 2011 Vestey Holdings Limited, the international pastoral giant, acquired a majority holding in Delatite, and has said it represents one of 'what we hope will be a number of agricultural businesses here'. Exports to Denmark, China, Japan and Malaysia.

ŸŸŸŸŸ Polly's Block Reserve Chardonnay 2013 Wild yeast-fermented in 100% new French oak, extended lees contact and maturation. By some distance the most complex of the Delatite '13 Chardonnays, the intensity of the fruit handsomely absorbing the new oak, and twisting it (the oak) to its own advantage on the long and vibrant palate. Screwcap. 13.5% alc. **Rating** 95 **To** 2023 $39

Pinot Gris 2014 Has a positive and appealing varietal expression, nashi pear to the fore, wisps of green apple behind the pear. All works well in a very good example of Pinot Gris. Screwcap. 13% alc. **Rating** 95 **To** 2016 $25 ✪

Pinot Gris 2013 Fermented with wild yeast in large oak barrels. Full-on gris, for sure, Alsace not so distant; as well as an abundance of fruit and a creamy mid-palate, there is vital acidity on the finish; whether this is natural or added is irrelevant. The 8-year cellaring guide is interesting. Screwcap. 13% alc. **Rating** 95 **To** 2027 $25 ✪

ŸŸŸŸŸ High Ground Sauvignon Blanc 2014 **Rating** 93 **To** 2016 $17 ✪
Riesling 2013 **Rating** 92 **To** 2022 $25 CM ✪
Chardonnay 2013 **Rating** 91 **To** 2020 $25
High Ground Pinot Grigio 2013 **Rating** 91 **To** 2016 $17 ✪
Shiraz Rose 2014 **Rating** 91 **To** 2016 $20 ✪
High Ground Pinot Noir 2013 **Rating** 91 **To** 2020 $19 ✪
High Ground Chardonnay 2013 **Rating** 90 **To** 2018 $17 ✪

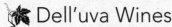 Delinquente Wine Co

36 Brooker Terrace, Richmond, SA 5033 **Region** Riverland
T 0437 876 407 **www.**delinquentewineco.com **Open** Not
Winemaker Various **Est.** 2013 **Dozens** 600
A Hollywood actress was famous for saying 'I don't care what they say about me as long as
they spell my name right.' Con-Greg Grigoriou might say 'I don't care how bad people think
my wine labels are as long as they remember them.' They certainly set a new high-water mark
in Australia. Con-Greg grew up on a vineyard in the Riverland, and spent a lot of time in
wineries, with his father and grandfather, and has decided to concentrate on southern Italian
grape varieties. 2014 production was 8 tonnes (600 dozen bottles), and it's pretty clear it's a
virtual winery operation, buying fruit from growers who share his vision and having the wine
made wherever he is able to find a facility prepared to assist in the making of micro-quantities.
Fortune favours the bold, and if you wish to read more, visit www.delinquentewineco.com.

ΨΨΨΨ   Pretty Boy Riverland Nero d'Avola Rosato 2014 Bright crimson;
strawberries drive the bouquet and palate; some residual sugar on the finish is
balanced by acidity. Easy to drink. Screwcap. 13% alc. **Rating** 89 **To** 2015 $20
The Bullet Dodger Riverland Montepulciano 2014 I can't believe a label
such as this will work; it is the worst of a bad lot. Behind the façade is the
power of montepulciano to deliver colour and flavour even when grown in the
Riverland, joining durif et al. Screwcap. 14% alc. **Rating** 89 **To** 2017 $20

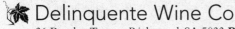 Dell'uva Wines ★★★★☆

194 Richards Road, Freeling, SA 5372 **Region** Barossa Valley
T (08) 8525 2245 **www.**delluvawines.com.au **Open** By appt
Winemaker Wayne Farquhar **Est.** 2014 **Dozens** 1500 **Vyds** 20ha
Owner and winemaker Wayne Farquhar moved from horticulture to viticulture, acquiring his
first vineyard in 1979. His viticultural career was low-key for a number of years, but having
tasted wines from all over the world over a decade of business travel, he decided to establish
Dell'uva wines off the back of his existing (conventional) vineyard on the western ridge of
the Barossa Valley. In short order he established small plots of an A–Z of varieties: aglianico,
albarino, ansonica, arinto, barbera, cabernet sauvignon, caniolo nero, carmenere, carnelian,
chardonnay, dolcetto, durif, fiano, freisca, garnacha, graciano, grillo, lagrein, merlot, marsanne,
mencia, montepulciano, moscato bianco, mourvedre, negroamaro, nero d'Avola, pinot blanc,
pinot grigio, pinot noir, primitivo, roussanne, sagrantino, sangiovese, saperavi, shiraz, tannat,
tempranillo, touriga nacional, verdejo, vermentino, verdicchio, viognier. With only 20ha
available, the production of each wine is necessarily limited, the vinification as unconventional
as the vineyard mix, utilising barrels, ceramic eggs, demijohns and tanks. The winemaking
techniques have been chosen to throw maximum attention onto the inherent quality of the
varieties, and this story has a long way to run.

ΨΨΨΨΨ   Barossa Graciano 2012 Bright purple-crimson; a spicy, almost flowery, bouquet
leads into a light to medium-bodied, particularly attractive, juicy palate of plum
and blackcurrant fruit supported by fine-grained tannins. A very elegant surprise.
Cork. 14.5% alc. **Rating** 95 **To** 2022 $35 ✪
Barossa Barbera 2012 Good colour; cherry and mulberry fruits on the fragrant
bouquet and palate have none of the edgy acidity that the variety can produce;
in the full Dell'uva line-up, one of the most elegant wines. Screwcap. 14% alc.
Rating 94 **To** 2022 $24 ✪
Barossa Petite Sirah 2012 Dense purple-crimson; the typical powerful
clenched fist of durif (as we know it in this country) is presented in an ultra-heavy
bottle; the tannins of durif are built-in cupboards, part of the room, and indivisible.
Cork. 14.5% alc. **Rating** 94 **To** 2032 $85
Barossa Montepulciano 2012 An interesting wine, its medium body at odds
with its intensity and the spread of red and black fruits; the tannins are good,
French oak in play. Cork. 13.5% alc. **Rating** 94 **To** 2025 $35

🍷🍷🍷🍷🍷 Barossa Tempranillo Garnacha 2012 Rating 93 To 2025 $24 ◎
Barossa Dolcetto 2012 Rating 93 To 2022 $24 ◎
Barossa Primitivo 2012 Rating 93 To 2022 $30
Barossa Saperavi 2012 Rating 93 To 2032 $55
Barossa Lagrein 2012 Rating 93 To 2022 $55
Barossa Merlot 2012 Rating 92 To 2027 $24 ◎
Barossa Syrah 2012 Rating 91 To 2027 $30

Della Fay Wines ★★★★

3276 Caves Road, Yallingup, WA 6284 **Region** Margaret River
T (08) 9755 2747 **www**.kellysvineyard.com.au **Open** By appt
Winemaker Michael Kelly **Est.** 1999 **Dozens** 3000 **Vyds** 8ha
This is the venture of the Kelly family, headed by district veteran Michael Kelly, who gained his degree in wine science from CSU before working at Seville Estate and Mount Mary and Domaine Louis Chapuis in Burgundy, then coming back to WA working for Leeuwin Estate and Sandalford. From there he became the long-term winemaker at Fermoy Estate, but he and his family laid the ground for their own brand, buying prime viticultural land in Caves Road, Yallingup, in 1999. They planted 2ha each of cabernet sauvignon, nebbiolo and sauvignon blanc, and 1ha each of chardonnay and vermentino. Shiraz from the Geographe region is also included. 'Della Fay' honours the eponymous Kelly family matriarch. Exports to The Netherlands, South Korea, Singapore and China.

🍷🍷🍷🍷🍷 Geographe Shiraz 2012 Rockets out of the blocks with satsuma plum, hazelnut and dense blackberried flavour. This is good stuff. It pours on the fruit but has a roasted, twiggy savouriness as well. It's good now and will definitely be good later. Alcohol isn't a major factor in the wine. What terrific value. Screwcap. 15% alc. **Rating** 94 To 2027 $20 CM ◎

🍷🍷🍷🍷🍷 Margaret River Chardonnay 2013 Rating 92 To 2018 $25 CM ◎

Deonte Wines ★★★★

15 Mary Street, Hawthorn, Vic 3122 **Region** Various
T (03) 9819 4890 **www**.deontewines.com.au **Open** By appt
Winemaker Benjamin Edwards, Jolian Segell **Est.** 2012 **Dozens** 10 000
This is the venture of Zhijun (George) Hu, who has started a virtual winery with the primary purpose of exporting to China and elsewhere in South-East Asia. The initial focus has been on the Yarra Valley, Coonawarra and the Barossa Valley, shiraz figuring prominently, either as a single variety, or as part of a blend with cabernet sauvignon. Having neither a vineyard nor a winery affords George maximum flexibility in purchasing grapes and/or bulk wine. Exports to China.

🍷🍷🍷🍷🍷 Reserve 710 Barossa Valley Shiraz 2013 Matured in new and used French oak. Is the best of the '13 Deonte Shirazs; it is full-bodied, but all the components are in balance; it has supple black fruits and well-integrated French oak; the tannins are just where they should be, the future assured. Screwcap. 14.2% alc. **Rating** 93 To 2033 $50

Exceptional Barrels McLaren Vale Shiraz 2013 Matured in French hogsheads. Generously flavoured and well balanced; a textbook McLaren Vale Shiraz, medium-bodied, with blackberry, plum and some dark chocolate; good tannins and oak integration. Screwcap. 14.5% alc. **Rating** 90 To 2023 $50

Exceptional Parcel Langhorne Creek Shiraz 2012 40yo vines. Maturation in new French (80%) and American hogsheads for 14 months; just about obscures the alcohol, with savoury black fruits, earth and licorice the first line of defence, attractive grainy tannins the second line. Screwcap. 15% alc. **Rating** 90 To 2027 $40

🍷🍷🍷🍷 Estate 512 Shiraz Cabernet 2013 Rating 89 To 2028 $32
Delish 320 Limestone Coast Shiraz 2013 Rating 88 To 2019 $19

Derwent Estate

329 Lyell Highway, Granton, Tas 7070 **Region** Southern Tasmania
T (03) 6263 5802 **www**.derwentestate.com.au **Open** Mon–Fri 10–4
Winemaker Winemaking Tasmania **Est.** 1992 **Dozens** 2500 **Vyds** 10.08ha
Three generations of the Hanigan family are involved in the management of their historic
Mt Nassau property, owned by the family since 1913. Given that over the last 100 years the
property has at various times been involved with sheep, cattle, vegetable production, quarrying
and the production of lime, the addition of viticulture in '92 was not surprising. The vineyard
has grown in stages, some of the grapes bound for Bay of Fires and Penfolds Yattarna. The
grapes retained by Derwent Estate have produced consistently good wines. A representative
range of wines was not received for this edition, but the rating has been maintained.

♟♟♟♟♟ **Pinot Gris 2014** Full pink ex skin contact; strawberry-like bouquet is not simply
the power of suggestion, carrying through to the striking palate. Gold Tas Wine
Show '15. Screwcap. 13.8% alc. **Rating** 95 **To** 2017 $25 ✪

Deviation Road ★★★★★

207 Scott Creek Road, Longwood, SA 5153 **Region** Adelaide Hills
T (08) 8339 2633 **www**.deviationroad.com **Open** 7 days 10–5
Winemaker Kate and Hamish Laurie **Est.** 1999 **Dozens** 6000 **Vyds** 11.05ha
Deviation Road was created in 1998 by Hamish Laurie, great-great-grandson of Mary Laurie,
SA's first female winemaker. He initially joined with father Dr Chris Laurie in '92 to help
build the Hillstowe Wines business; the brand was sold in 2001, but the Laurie family retained
the vineyard, which now supplies Deviation Road with its grapes. Wife Kate joined the
business in '01, having studied winemaking and viticulture in Champagne, then spent four
years at her family's Stone Bridge winery in Manjimup. All the wines come from the family
vineyards. It also has 3ha of pinot noir and shiraz at Longwood, where its cellar door is situated.
Exports to the UK, the US and Hong Kong.

♟♟♟♟♟ **Reserve Adelaide Hills Chardonnay 2013** From Dijon clones. Has truly
excellent focus, balance and elegance, adding intensity and drive to lengthen the
palate and underwrite the future of a wine with a delicious balance of stone fruit
and citrus. Screwcap. 12% alc. **Rating** 95 **To** 2023 $45
Beltana Adelaide Hills Blanc de Blancs 2009 Estate-grown and aged,
traditional method, hand-riddled and disgorged on the estate, it spends 5 years
on tirage. The varietal fruit expression of chardonnay is captured notwithstanding
the long time on cork, amplified by time in bottle post-disgorgement. 11.5% alc.
Rating 95 **To** 2020 $75
Loftia Adelaide Hills Vintage Brut 2012 70/30% pinot noir and chardonnay
made by the traditional method, spending at least 2 years on tirage. It has multiple
layers of strawberry, nectarine and apple aromas and flavours, the balance and
length very good. Yet further time on lees (and on cork) will be rewarded.
12.5% alc. **Rating** 94 **To** 2020 $42

♟♟♟♟♟ **Adelaide Hills Sauvignon Blanc 2014 Rating** 93 **To** 2015 $21 ✪
Adelaide Hills Pinot Gris 2014 Rating 91 **To** 2015 $28
Altair Adelaide Hills Brut Rose NV Rating 91 **To** 2015 $32 TS

Devil's Corner

The Hazards Vineyard, Sherbourne Road, Apslawn, Tas 7190 **Region** East Coast Tasmania
T (03) 6257 8881 **www**.brownbrothers.com.au **Open** 7 days 10–5 Nov–Apr
Winemaker Tom Wallace **Est.** 1999 **Dozens** 70 000 **Vyds** 175ha
This is one of the separately managed operations of Brown Brothers' Tasmanian interests,
taking The Hazards Vineyard as its chief source of supply. That vineyard is planted to pinot
noir, chardonnay, sauvignon blanc, pinot gris, riesling, gewurztraminer and savagnin. The avant
garde, striking and (for me) attractive labels mark a decided change from the past, and also
distinguish Devil's Corner from the other Tasmanian activities of Brown Brothers. Exports to
all major markets.

ŢŢŢŢŢ Riesling 2014 This has a fragrant citrus blossom bouquet, the palate powerful, full of classic Bickford's lime juice – acid no more than a balancing act; delicious now, better still later. Screwcap. 12.5% alc. **Rating** 94 **To** 2024 $20 ⊙

ŢŢŢŢŢ Riesling 2011 **Rating** 93 **To** 2031 $18 ⊙
Resolution Pinot Noir 2013 **Rating** 92 **To** 2023 $30
Sauvignon Blanc 2014 **Rating** 90 **To** 2016 $18 ⊙
Chardonnay 2014 **Rating** 90 **To** 2019 $20 ⊙

Devil's Lair ★★★★★

Rocky Road, Forest Grove via Margaret River, WA 6285 **Region** Margaret River
T 1300 651 650 **www**.devils-lair.com **Open** Not
Winemaker Oliver Crawford **Est.** 1981 **Dozens** NFP
Having rapidly carved out a high reputation for itself through a combination of clever packaging and impressive wine quality, Devil's Lair was acquired by Southcorp in 1996. The estate vineyards have been substantially increased since, now with sauvignon blanc, semillon, chardonnay, cabernet sauvignon, merlot, shiraz, cabernet franc and petit verdot, supplemented by grapes purchased from contract growers. An exceptionally successful business; production has increased from 40 000 dozen to many times greater, in no small measure due to its Fifth Leg and Dance With the Devil wines. Exports to the UK, the US and other major markets.

ŢŢŢŢŢ 9th Chamber Margaret River Cabernet Sauvignon 2011 Cabernet reaching for the stratosphere and placing its fingertips fairly in the vicinity. This takes the flesh and bone of Devil's Lair Cabernet Sauvignon and adds rippling muscle. Blackcurrant, black olive, truffle, sweetly spiced oak, peppercorn and brighter, almost pretty, redcurrant notes. There's a dusting of chocolate too; the flavours here flex and contract, relax and unveil, in waves. Gravelly tannin maintains a firm rule. Persistence: it looks tomorrow in the eye. Screwcap. **Rating** 98 **To** 2040 $120 CM ⊙

ŢŢŢŢŢ Margaret River Cabernet Sauvignon 2013 Pure dark fruit, smart oak and a spread of ripe, fine-grained tannin; quality franked in full. Margaret River cabernet tinkered and tailored into immaculate shape. Blackcurrant, bay leaves, woodsmoke and sugarless chocolate; the sweetness of ripe fruit rushes through the veins of both the tannin and acid; this is classical from all angles. Screwcap. 14% alc. **Rating** 96 **To** 2035 $50 CM ⊙
Margaret River Chardonnay 2013 Scintillating Chardonnay. Length is its signature detail, but the flood of mid-palate flavour is a close second. Grapefruit, pure peach, citrus and brilliant fennel. Spicy/cedary oak swirls throughout. Immediately impressive but the finish then sails on. Screwcap. 13% alc. **Rating** 95 **To** 2021 $50 CM

ŢŢŢŢŢ The Hidden Cave Cabernet Shiraz 2013 **Rating** 93 **To** 2028 $23 ⊙
Fifth Leg Sauvignon Blanc Semillon 2014 **Rating** 92 **To** 2015 $18 ⊙
The Hidden Cave Sauvignon Semillon 2014 **Rating** 92 **To** 2016 $23 CM ⊙
The Hidden Cave Chardonnay 2014 **Rating** 92 **To** 2018 $23 ⊙
Dance with the Devil Cabernet 2013 **Rating** 92 **To** 2020 $25 CM ⊙
Dance with the Devil Chardonnay 2014 **Rating** 91 **To** 2018 $25 CM
Fifth Leg Rose 2014 **Rating** 91 **To** 2016 $18 CM ⊙
Fifth Leg Shiraz 2013 **Rating** 91 **To** 2019 $18 CM ⊙
Fifth Leg Cabernet Shiraz Merlot 2013 **Rating** 90 **To** 2019 $18 CM ⊙

Dexter Wines ★★★★★

210 Foxeys Road, Tuerong, Vic 3915 (postal) **Region** Mornington Peninsula
T (03) 5989 7007 **www**.dexterwines.com.au **Open** Not
Winemaker Tod Dexter **Est.** 2006 **Dozens** 1600 **Vyds** 7.1ha
Through a series of events, Tod Dexter arrived in the US with the intention of enjoying some skiing; having done that, he became an apprentice winemaker at Cakebread Cellars, a well-known Napa Valley winery. After seven years he returned to Australia and the Mornington

Peninsula, and began the establishment of the vineyard in 1987, planted to pinot noir (4ha) and chardonnay (3.1ha). To keep the wolves from the door he became winemaker at Stonier, and leased his vineyard to Stonier. Having left Stonier to become Yabby Lake winemaker, and spurred on by turning 50 in 2006 (and at the urging of friends), he and wife Debbie established the Dexter label. Exports to the UK, the US and Norway.

🍷🍷🍷🍷🍷 **Mornington Peninsula Pinot Noir 2013** Over half clone MV6; destemmed whole berries, open fermenters; part wild, part cultured yeasts; hand-plunged until 2–3 days post-fermentation; 10 months in French barriques (21% new). It has a highly expressive bouquet and palate, red and black cherry, plum, forest and bramble all contributing to a Pinot with many years to go. Screwcap. 13.5% alc. **Rating** 96 **To** 2025 $50 ✪
Mornington Peninsula Chardonnay 2013 A distinguished quartet of clones hand-picked, whole bunch-pressed to tank for settling, then to French barriques (25% new, 35% 1yo, the remainder older) May–Aug, stirred every 2 weeks until mlf (70%) completed. Tod knows the Mornington Peninsula better than most, and his decision on mlf was faultless. A wine with excellent varietal definition despite its complexity. Screwcap. 13% alc. **Rating** 95 **To** 2023 $40

Di Fabio Estate ★★★★★

5 Valleyview Drive, McLaren Vale, SA 5171 (postal) **Region** McLaren Vale
T (08) 8383 0188 **www**.difabioestatewines.com.au **Open** Not
Winemaker Goe Di Fabio **Est.** 1994 **Dozens** 6000 **Vyds** 38.91ha
Di Fabio Estate is the venture of brothers Goe and Tony Di Fabio. Their parents Giovanni and Maria Di Fabio purchased their first vineyard in McLaren Vale in 1966 (with a tradition stretching back further to Italy) and became long-term contract grapegrowers for other winemakers. The business carried on by their sons has a 56ha property at McLaren Vale and 8.5ha at Waikerie. The plantings are dominated by 12.5ha of grenache, 10.5ha of shiraz, and 3.6ha of mourvedre; petit verdot, merlot, chardonnay, cabernet franc, sauvignon blanc and semillon are also grown. Exports to Macau, Singapore and China.

🍷🍷🍷🍷🍷 **Bush Vine McLaren Vale Shiraz 2013** A full-bodied but well-crafted (an overused word, but deserved here) shiraz that proclaims its region, vintage and variety in equal measure. Its supple, mouth-filling array of blackberry, satsuma plum, dark chocolate and mocha flavours are sustained by ripe tannins and oak. A classy wine from Blewitt Springs. Screwcap. 15% alc. **Rating** 95 **To** 2033 $37
Bush Vine McLaren Vale Shiraz 2012 From Blewitt Springs. Has retained excellent colour; the fragrant bouquet introduces a medium-bodied palate that is at once juicy and creamy in its mouthfeel, the flavours running from red to black, with a spicy/savoury/dark chocolate back-palate and finish; more elegant than the '13. Screwcap. 14.5% alc. **Rating** 95 **To** 2027 $37

Di Sciascio Family Wines ★★★★★

2 Pincott Street, Newtown, Vic 3220 **Region** Various Vic
T 0417 384 272 **www**.disciasciofamilywines.com.au **Open** Not
Winemaker Matthew Di Sciascio, Andrew Santarossa **Est.** 2012 **Dozens** 1000
Matthew Di Sciascio's journey through wine has been an odyssey of Homeric proportions. His working life began as an apprentice boilermaker in his father's business. In 1991 he accompanied his father on a trip to Italy, where a shared bottle of wine in the kitchen of his uncle sowed the seed that flowered back in Australia, helping with garage winemaking by his father and friends. In '97, the vinous pace increased, with vineyard work in the Yarra Valley and enrolment in Dookie Agricultural College's viticultural course. It accelerated further with the establishment of Bellbrae Estate in Geelong, and enrolling (in 2002) in the new Deakin University Wine and Science degree, graduating in '05 as co-dux, with a vintage at the celebrated Masciarelli Winery in Abruzzo as the prize. In Dec '10 the responsibility for seriously ill parents and a young daughter led to the decision to sell his share of Bellbrae to his financial partners, and (in '12) to start this venture.

ΨΨΨΨΨ **D'Sas Drumborg Riesling 2014** Drumborg (in the Henty region) produces wonderful Riesling: its climate is the coolest in Australia, Tasmania included. It has intense lime juice flavours that float on a foundation of crisp acidity and low pH. This is an irresistible wine. Screwcap. 11.8% alc. **Rating** 95 **To** 2024 $24 **◐**
D'Sas Drumborg Pinot Gris 2014 The climate grabs pinot gris by the scruff of its neck, forcing it to ripen with layers of rarely encountered depth of flavour, even though the nashi pear, citrus zest and apple are varietal. This is a wine drinker's Pinot Gris, exuding attitude. Screwcap. 12.7% alc. **Rating** 95 **To** 2016 $24 **◐**
D'Sas Macedon Ranges Gewurztraminer 2014 Very well made; the rose petal, spicy bouquet leads into a perfectly balanced palate with more rose petal, spice and Turkish delight flavours set in a wreath of soft acidity. Screwcap. 12.5% alc. **Rating** 94 **To** 2025 $24 **◐**

ΨΨΨΨΨ **D'Sas RS50 Drumborg Riesling 2014** **Rating** 93 **To** 2020 $24 **◐**
D'Sas Geelong Semillon 2014 **Rating** 92 **To** 2024 $22 **◐**

DiGiorgio Family Wines ★★★★☆

Riddoch Highway, Coonawarra, SA 5263 **Region** Coonawarra
T (08) 8736 3222 **www.**digiorgio.com.au **Open** 7 days 10–5
Winemaker Peter Douglas **Est.** 1998 **Dozens** 25000 **Vyds** 353.53ha
Stefano DiGiorgio emigrated from Abruzzo, Italy, in 1952. Over the years, he and his family gradually expanded their holdings at Lucindale. In '89 he began planting cabernet sauvignon (99ha), chardonnay (10ha), merlot (9ha), shiraz (6ha) and pinot noir (2ha). In 2002 the family purchased the historic Rouge Homme winery and its surrounding 13.5ha of vines, from Southcorp. Since that time the Coonawarra plantings have been increased to almost 230ha, the lion's share to cabernet sauvignon. The enterprise offers full winemaking services to vignerons in the Limestone Coast Zone. Exports to all major markets.

ΨΨΨΨΨ **Emporio Coonawarra Merlot Cabernet Sauvignon Cabernet Franc 2013** The combination of ripe, almost luscious fruit/oak flavour and assertive tannin here works quite significantly well. It tastes of blackcurrant, black olive, green herbs and swish, chocolatey oak, before succumbing to a firm, dry finish. Both whistles and bells. Screwcap. 14.5% alc. **Rating** 94 **To** 2030 $23 CM **◐**

ΨΨΨΨΨ **Coonawarra Cabernet Sauvignon 2013** **Rating** 93 **To** 2029 $23 CM **◐**
Coonawarra Cabernet Sauvignon 2012 **Rating** 92 **To** 2026 $23 CM **◐**
Coonawarra Tempranillo 2013 **Rating** 92 **To** 2021 $23 CM **◐**
Emporio Coonawarra Merlot Cabernet Sauvignon Cabernet Franc 2012 **Rating** 91 **To** 2026 $23 CM **◐**
Kongorong Riesling 2014 **Rating** 90 **To** 2022 $19 CM **◐**
Lucindale Sparkling Merlot 2012 **Rating** 90 **To** 2020 $19 TS **◐**

Dinny Goonan ★★★★☆

880 Winchelsea–Deans Marsh Road, Bambra, Vic 3241 **Region** Geelong
T 0438 408 420 **www.**dinnygoonan.com.au **Open** 7 days Jan, w'ends Nov–Jun
Winemaker Dinny and Angus Goonan **Est.** 1990 **Dozens** 1200 **Vyds** 5.5ha
The establishment of Dinny Goonan dates back to 1988, when Dinny bought a 20ha property near Bambra, in the hinterland of the Otway Coast. Dinny had recently completed a viticulture diploma at CSU, and initially a wide range of varieties was planted in what is now known as the Nursery Block, to establish those best suited to the area. As these came into production Dinny headed back to CSU, where he completed a wine science degree. Production is focused on shiraz and riesling, with more extensive planting of these varieties.

ΨΨΨΨΨ **Museum Release Riesling 2009** When first tasted in '10, the wine was precise, and folded in on itself with lemon and apple flavours enhanced by minerally acidity; demanding time. 4 years later it is still as fresh and crisp as a daisy. Screwcap. 12.5% alc. **Rating** 94 **To** 2020 $26 **◐**

Single Vineyard Shiraz 2013 Includes a small percentage of viognier. A vibrant and highly perfumed cool-grown Shiraz, with a kaleidoscope of spicy pepper, fresh cherry and fine, savoury tannins. Screwcap. 14.5% alc. **Rating** 94 **To** 2028 $27 ◎

♀♀♀♀♀ **Semillon Sauvignon 2014 Rating** 93 **To** 2017 $25 ◎
Single Vineyard Riesling 2014 Rating 91 **To** 2024 $25
Cabernets 2013 Rating 90 **To** 2028 $25

Dionysus Winery   ★★★★

1 Patemans Lane, Murrumbateman, NSW 2582 **Region** Canberra District
T (02) 6227 0208 www.dionysus-winery.com.au **Open** W'ends & public hols 10–5
Winemaker Michael O'Dea **Est.** 1998 **Dozens** 1000 **Vyds** 4ha
Michael and Wendy O'Dea founded the winery while they had parallel lives as public servants in Canberra; they have now retired, and devote themselves full-time to the winery. They purchased their property in 1996, and planted chardonnay, sauvignon blanc, riesling, viognier, merlot, pinot noir, cabernet sauvignon and shiraz between '98 and 2001. Michael has completed an associate degree in winemaking at CSU, and is responsible for viticulture and winemaking; Wendy has completed various courses at the Canberra TAFE and is responsible for wine marketing and (in their words) 'nagging Michael and being a general slushie'.

♀♀♀♀♀ **Canberra District Riesling 2014** Every time I taste a high-quality Canberra District Riesling such as this I berate myself for not including the region in a standard roll call of honour for the variety. The wine has a delicate intensity (an ultimate oxymoron, I realise), with its fine lime/lemon fruit starting with a light touch, then accelerating through to the end of the palate and aftertaste without missing a beat. Screwcap. 11.2% alc. **Rating** 95 **To** 2029 $20 ◎

♀♀♀♀ **Canberra District Shiraz 2013 Rating** 89 **To** 2017 $25
Canberra District Tempranillo 2013 Rating 89 **To** 2016 $25

Disaster Bay Wines   ★★★☆

133 Oaklands Road, Pambula, NSW 2549 **Region** South Coast Zone
T (02) 6495 6869 **Open** Not
Winemaker Dean O'Reilly, Nick O'Leary **Est.** 2000 **Dozens** 200 **Vyds** 1.2ha
Dean O'Reilly has a 15-year background in the distribution of fine table wines, culminating in employment by Möet Hennessy Australia. In 2009 he was one of 12 wine professionals selected to participate in the week-long Len Evans Tutorial. The wines are made with Nick O'Leary; the grapes come from the block owned by Dean adjacent to the Pambula River.

♀♀♀♀♀ **Deano's Vino Tumbarumba Pinot Noir 2013** Full colour, deep and bright in Pinot terms; buckets of varietal fruit – plum and morello cherry – lay down the foundations for the wine to build complexity over the next few years; real potential here. Screwcap. 13% alc. **Rating** 92 **To** 2023 $40

♀♀♀♀ **Sauvignon Blanc Semillon 2014 Rating** 89 **To** 2016 $22

Doc Adams   ★★★★☆

2/41 High Street, Willunga, SA 5172 **Region** McLaren Vale
T (08) 8556 2111 www.docadamswines.com.au **Open** By appt
Winemaker Adam Jacobs **Est.** 2005 **Dozens** 5000 **Vyds** 27ha
Doc Adams is a partnership between viticulturist Adam Jacobs and orthopaedic surgeon Dr Darren Waters (and their wives). Adam graduated from CSU with a degree in viticulture and has had over 20 years' experience as a consultant viticulturist. Darren has grown low-yielding shiraz vines in McLaren Vale since 1998, using all of his time off from his surgical practice. Exports to China.

🍷🍷🍷🍷🍷 McLaren Vale GSM 2013 The three varieties are usually synergistic in McLaren Vale, but here brilliantly so; the colour is vibrant, the flavours a chorus of red fruits and Cherry Ripe on the finish; the tannins are soft, but important. Gold medal McLaren Vale Wine Show '14. Screwcap. 14.3% alc. **Rating** 95 **To** 2023 $20 ⊗

🍷🍷🍷🍷🍷 McLaren Vale Cabernet Sauvignon 2013 **Rating** 90 **To** 2025 $20 ⊗

Dodgy Brothers ★★★★☆

PO Box 655, McLaren Vale, SA 5171 **Region** McLaren Vale
T 0450 000 373 **www**.dodgybrotherswines.com **Open** Not
Winemaker Wes Pearson **Est.** 2010 **Dozens** 2000
This is a partnership between Canadian-born Flying Winemaker Wes Pearson, viticulturist Peter Bolte and grapegrower Peter Sommerville. Wes graduated from the University of British Columbia's biochemistry program in 2008, along the way working at wineries including Chateau Leoville Las Cases in Bordeaux. In '08 he and his family moved to McLaren Vale, and after working at several wineries, he took up a position at the Australian Wine Research Institute as a sensory analyst. Peter Bolte has over 35 vintages in McLaren Vale under his belt, and was the original Dodgy Brother. Peter's vineyard provides cabernet sauvignon, cabernet franc and petit verdot for the Dodgy Brothers Bordeaux blend. Exports to Canada.

🍷🍷🍷🍷🍷 McLaren Vale Grenache Shiraz Mataro 2013 A 70/18/12% blend. No more than medium-bodied, but is a lively and energetic assemblage of a full suite of red and black fruits, supported by firm but balanced tannins. 630 dozen made. Screwcap. 14.5% alc. **Rating** 94 **To** 2020 $28 ⊗
DODG McLaren Vale Sangiovese 2014 A Super Tuscan style 87/13% sangiovese and merlot blend with 30% whole bunches and sophisticated use of different species of yeasts; matured in used French and Hungarian hogsheads. Persistent sangiovese tannins are woven through red fruit flavours, demurely asking for a bowl of pasta or risotto. Screwcap. 13.5% alc. **Rating** 94 **To** 2018 $22 ⊗
McLaren Vale Mataro 2013 Co-fermented with 13% grenache; 10 days on skins, basket-pressed to 2 used French hogsheads; neither fined or filtered. Pretty neat example, avoiding the grippy tannins that mataro can inflict, spicy red fruits to the fore. 65 dozen made. Screwcap. 13.8% alc. **Rating** 94 **To** 2020 $29 ⊗

🍷🍷🍷🍷🍷 McLaren Vale Shiraz 2013 **Rating** 90 **To** 2033 $29

Dog Trap Vineyard ★★★★

262 Dog Trap Road, Yass, NSW 2582 **Region** Canberra District
T (02) 6226 5898 **www**.dogtrapvineyard.com.au **Open** By appt
Winemaker Dr Dennis Hart, Dr Roger Harris **Est.** 1996 **Dozens** 1000 **Vyds** 6.1ha
The somewhat ghoulish name and label illustration is a reminder of bygone days when wild dogs were caught in traps in much the same way as rabbits. It certainly means the name of the venture will be remembered. Planting of the vineyard began in 1996. The property was purchased by Dr Dennis Hart and Ms Julian White in 2003, and until '06 the grapes were sold. The first wines were made in '08. Shiraz and cabernet sauvignon were the initial plantings; more recently, riesling and pinot gris were added.

🍷🍷🍷🍷🍷 Entente 2013 A 75/25% blend of cabernet and shiraz matured in American and French oak. The colour is bright, and the medium-bodied blend works well, providing synergy between blackberry and blackcurrant fruits; has enough tannin structure for future development. Screwcap. 14% alc. **Rating** 91 **To** 2023 $20 ⊗
Canberra District Shiraz 2012 The back label discloses the presence of cabernet (necessarily less than 15%); light to medium-bodied fresh wine with red cherry, plum and black cherry fruit, French oak in the background, fine-grained tannins in measured support on the finish. Animal liberationists won't warm to the label, but it's a point of difference. Screwcap. 12.5% alc. **Rating** 90 **To** 2020 $18 ⊗

🍷🍷🍷🍷 Canberra District Cabernet Sauvignon 2012 **Rating** 89 **To** 2017 $18 ⊗

DogRidge Wine Company

129 Bagshaws Road, McLaren Flat, SA 5171 **Region** McLaren Vale
T (08) 8383 0140 **www**.dogridge.com.au **Open** 7 days 11–5
Winemaker Fred Howard **Est.** 1991 **Dozens** 10 000 **Vyds** 56ha

Dave and Jen Wright had a combined background of dentistry, art and a CSU viticultural degree when they moved from Adelaide to McLaren Flat to become vignerons. They inherited vines planted in the early 1940s as a source for Chateau Reynella fortified wines, and their vineyards now range from 2001 plantings to some of the oldest vines in the immediate district. At the McLaren Flat vineyards, DogRidge has 60+-year-old shiraz and grenache. Part of the grape production is retained, part is sold. Quality at one end, value- packed at the other end. Exports to the UK, the US and other major markets.

PPPPP The Pup McLaren Vale Sauvignon Blanc 2014 Achieves the absolutely impossible in providing a juicy, vibrant Sauvignon Blanc from McLaren Vale. It has a full hand of tropical fruits, with squeaky, tactile acidity bringing notes of citrus into play with a joker on the finish. Screwcap. 13% alc. **Rating** 94 **To** 2016 $18 ✪
Square Cut McLaren Vale Cabernet 2013 From vines over 60yo, uncommon (for cabernet) in McLaren Vale. The vivid crimson-purple colour flies a flag of confidence, and doesn't deceive; the initial flavours are flush with cassis, then persistent, fine tannins add a savoury dimension that is pure cabernet to its bootstraps. Screwcap. 14.5% alc. **Rating** 94 **To** 2033 $25 ✪

PPPPP Old Mates McLaren Vale Grenache Shiraz 2013 **Rating** 93 **To** 2023 $25 ✪
Shirtfront McLaren Vale Shiraz 2013 **Rating** 92 **To** 2030 $25 ✪
The Pup McLaren Vale Cabernet Merlot 2013 **Rating** 92 **To** 2028 $18 ✪
The Pup Shiraz 2013 **Rating** 91 **To** 2023 $18 ✪
Running Free McLaren Vale Grenache Rose 2014 **Rating** 90 **To** 2015 $25

DogRock Winery ★★★★★

114 De Graves Road, Crowlands, Vic 3377 **Region** Pyrenees
T 0409 280 317 **www**.dogrock.com.au **Open** By appt
Winemaker Allen Hart **Est.** 1999 **Dozens** 500 **Vyds** 6.2ha

This is the micro-venture (but with inbuilt future growth to something slightly larger) of Allen (now full-time winemaker) and Andrea (viticulturist) Hart. Having purchased the property in 1998, the planting of shiraz, riesling, tempranillo, grenache, chardonnay and marsanne began in 2000. Given Allen's former post as research scientist/winemaker with Foster's, the attitude taken to winemaking is unexpected. The estate-grown wines are made in a low-tech fashion, without gas cover or filtration, the Harts saying 'all wine will be sealed with a screwcap and no DogRock wine will ever be released under natural cork bark'. DogRock installed the first solar-powered irrigation system in Australia, capable of supplying water 365 days a year, even at night or in cloudy conditions.

PPPPP Degraves Road Vineyard Shiraz 2013 Hand-picked, open-fermented 8 days; 16 months' French oak (60% new); only 40 dozen made. Has even greater intensity than its cheaper sibling to its array of sombre black fruits, licorice and foresty tannins. Great bargain. Screwcap. 14% alc. **Rating** 96 **To** 2038 $35 ✪
Shiraz 2013 Hand-picked; wild yeast open-fermented; 6–7 days on skins, basket-pressed, 14 months in 60% new oak (85% French, 15% American). Exceptional deep crimson-purple colour; layer upon layer of blackberry, plum and licorice fruit on the medium to full-bodied palate; savoury tannins provide exactly the right response to the well of fruit. Screwcap. 14% alc. **Rating** 95 **To** 2033 $25 ✪
Riesling 2014 From a high-altitude (800m) vineyard in the King Valley; cold-fermented with a specific yeast; held on lees for 4 months. A striking wine, its texture, structure and mouth-wateringly bone-dry finish sending a coherent message – bring on the food. Screwcap. 12.5% alc. **Rating** 94 **To** 2024 $22 ✪

PPPPP Degraves Road Vineyard Del Doce Al Uno 2013 **Rating** 93 **To** 2023 $38
Pyrenees Grenache 2013 **Rating** 92 **To** 2020 $25 ✪

Domaine A

105 Tea Tree Road, Campania, Tas 7026 **Region** Southern Tasmania
T (03) 6260 4174 **www.**domaine-a.com.au **Open** Mon–Fri 10–4
Winemaker Peter Althaus **Est.** 1973 **Dozens** 5000 **Vyds** 11ha
The striking black label of the premium Domaine A wine, dominated by the single multicoloured 'A', signified the change of ownership from George Park to Peter Althaus many years ago. The wines are made without compromise, and reflect the low yields from the immaculately tended vineyards. They represent aspects of both Old World and New World philosophies, techniques and styles. Exports to the UK, Canada, Denmark, Switzerland, Taiwan, Hong Kong, Singapore, Japan and China.

Domaine Asmara ★★★★☆

Gibb Road, Toolleen, Vic 3551 **Region** Heathcote
T (03) 5433 6133 **www.**domaineasmara.com **Open** 7 days 9–6.30
Winemaker Sanguine Estate **Est.** 2008 **Dozens** 2000 **Vyds** 12ha
Chemical engineer Andreas Greiving had a lifelong dream to own and operate a vineyard, and the opportunity came along with the global financial crisis. He was able to purchase a vineyard planted to shiraz (7ha), cabernet sauvignon (2ha), cabernet franc, durif and viognier (1ha each), and have the wines contract-made. The venture is co-managed by dentist wife Hennijati. Exports to the UK and China.

♥♥♥♥♥ **Reserve Heathcote Cabernet Sauvignon 2013** An impressive Cabernet with an unusual stamp of elegance that will serve it well in the years ahead; there is a totally delicious fusion of cassis with fine-grained cabernet tannins on the long, medium-bodied palate; the oak handling has been especially dextrous. Cork. 14.5% alc. **Rating** 95 **To** 2033 $45
Reserve Heathcote Shiraz 2012 Good colour; aromas of spice, licorice and dark fruits are directly translated on the medium to full-bodied palate, which has focus, intensity and length; overall savoury flavours, texture and structure come mainly from both fruit and tannins, but oak also plays a role. Screwcap. 14.8% alc. **Rating** 94 **To** 2027 $49

♥♥♥♥♀ **Private Collection Heathcote Shiraz 2013 Rating** 92 **To** 2033 $35
Private Reserve Heathcote Durif 2013 Rating 92 **To** 2033 $59

Domaine de Binet

477 Lovedale Road, Lovedale, NSW 2320 **Region** Hunter Valley
T 0418 211 378 **Open** Fri–Mon 10–4
Winemaker Daniel Binet **Est.** 2013 **Dozens** 2000
Domaine de Binet is effectively owned by Ballabourneen, which is in turn owned by Alex Stuart OAM and Daniel Binet. Binet and Stuart decided they should extend the portfolio of wines into some of the newer varieties and styles becoming popular with the younger, but aspiring, wine demographic. The problem they foresaw was the risk of confusing the long-term Ballabourneen customers used to mainstream Hunter Valley wines. So they moved to set up a separate business, with a separate address and cellar door. A further point of difference was the decision to look to other regions on a come and go basis.

♥♥♥♥♥ **Hunter Valley Tempranillo 2013** Rated in the same early ripening group as pinot noir, tempranillo has no business being in the Hunter Valley, let alone producing a wine with this depth of crimson colour; it has exceptional drive, line and length, and is bursting with cherry fruit. No one could fail to enjoy this wine. Screwcap. 14% alc. **Rating** 95 **To** 2020 $25 ✪
Hunter Valley Pinot Grigio 2014 Has a startling pink hue, every bit as deep as most roses; 20% drained to oak for fermentation, the balance in stainless steel. The juicy flavours live up to the promise of the colour, with strawberries and citrus to the fore. Screwcap. 14.5% alc. **Rating** 94 **To** 2016 $25 ✪

Petit Verdot 2013 There's no question about the sledge-hammer petit verdot in this wine, Hunter Valley the dominant influence, but that doesn't matter – petit verdot has proved time and time again it enjoys warm to hot growing conditions. Hunter Valley/McLaren Vale. Screwcap. 14.5% alc. **Rating** 94 **To** 2020 $25 ❂

▼▼▼▼▽ **Barbera Nebbiolo Grenache 2012 Rating** 92 **To** 2020 $25 ❂

Domaine Epis   ★★★★☆

812 Black Forest Drive, Woodend, Vic 3442 **Region** Macedon Ranges
T (03) 5427 1204 **Open** By appt
Winemaker Stuart Anderson **Est.** 1990 **Dozens** NA
Three legends are involved in the Domaine Epis and Epis & Williams wines, two of them in their own lifetime. They are long-term Essendon guru and former player Alec Epis, who owns the two quite separate vineyards and brands; Stuart Anderson, who directs winemaking, with Alec doing all the hard work; and the late Laurie Williams, the father of viticulture in the Macedon region and the man who established the Flynn & Williams vineyard in 1976. Alec Epis purchased that vineyard from Laurie Williams in '99, and as a mark of respect (and with Laurie's approval) continued to use his name, in conjunction with his own. The Cabernet Sauvignon comes from this vineyard, the Chardonnay and Pinot Noir from the vineyard at Woodend, where a small winery was built in 2002.

▼▼▼▼▼ **Macedon Ranges Chardonnay 2013** Totally unforced. Flavour flows sweetly; freely. Ripe pear, barley, grapefruit and green melon. Toasty, chalky, minerally complexity. Opens the throttle on the finish and lets it ride on out. Diam. 13.3% alc. **Rating** 95 **To** 2021 $45 CM
Macedon Ranges Pinot Noir 2013 Reliability is the middle name of Epis Pinot Noir, and from a good vintage it was never going to miss the party. This release is supple and soft with clean acid tang and clear peppery tones. It's light without being in any way lacking, presenting a suave combination of cherry, pine, undergrowth and cranberry flavours. Highly drinkable now, but its best years are ahead of it. Diam. 13.2% alc. **Rating** 94 **To** 2025 $70 CM

▼▼▼▼▽ **The Williams Vineyard 2002 Rating** 93 **To** 2019 $65 CM

 # Domaine Naturaliste   ★★★★★

Cnr Hairpin Road/Bussell Highway, Carbunup, WA 6280 **Region** Margaret River
T (08) 9755 1188 **www.domainenaturaliste.com.au** **Open** Not
Winemaker Bruce Dukes **Est.** 2012 **Dozens** 2800
Bruce Dukes' career dates back over 25 years, its foundations built around a degree in agronomy from the University of WA, followed by a master's degree in viticulture and agronomy from the University of California, Davis. Stemming directly from this was a four-year stint at Francis Ford Coppola's iconic Niebaum-Coppola winery in the Napa Valley. Back in WA he worked with a consultancy and contract winemaking business in Margaret River in 2000. The winery was set up to handle small and large amounts of fruit, but it was not until 2012 that he moved to set up his own winemaking business, Domaine Naturaliste.

▼▼▼▼▼ **Rebus Cabernet Sauvignon 2012** 94/6% cabernet sauvignon and merlot, fermented and matured separately in French barriques (33% new) for 12 months. Strikingly pure, it speaks with utmost clarity of its place, the gloriously fine texture underpinned by perfectly handled tannins. A wine of the highest quality, the aftertaste lingering for minutes. Screwcap. 13.8% alc. **Rating** 98 **To** 2042 $28 ❂

▼▼▼▼▼ **Sauvage Sauvignon Blanc Semillon 2013** A two-thirds/one-third blend, fermented (part wild yeast) and matured in used French puncheons for 12 months. Bright green-straw; shows the hallmark juxtaposition of finesse and complexity achieved so consistently by Bruce Jukes; no component of fruit, oak and/or acidity breaks out, allowing the line and length free play. Screwcap. 13% alc. **Rating** 95 **To** 2018 $28 ❂

Floris Chardonnay 2013 From the Floris Vineyard at the southern end of Margaret River; fermented and matured in French barriques (33% new) for 10 months, lees-stirred and partial mlf. Intense grapefruit flavours attest to the cool vineyard conditions and the retention of natural acidity. Makes a curtsey to Burgundy, and will relish more time in bottle. Screwcap. 13.5% alc. **Rating** 95 To 2023 $28 ○

Artus Chardonnay 2013 Promotes itself (on the back label) as rich with butterscotch and French oak but it's more refined than it makes out. Better to over- than under-deliver in this regard. It's slightly backward and enclosed but there's power here, coiled, green melon and white peach, oatmeal and toasty oak keeping a close eye. It will venture out in its own sweet time. Screwcap. 13.5% alc. **Rating** 94 To 2022 $43 CM

♀♀♀♀♀ **Purus Margaret River Chardonnay 2013** Rating 93 To 2022 $43 CM

Domaine Rogha Crois Wines ★★★★

73 Joe Rocks Road, Bungendore, NSW 2621 **Region** Canberra District
T 0411 228 839 **www.drcwine.com.au Open** By appt
Winemaker Malcolm Burdett, Andrew McEwin **Est.** 1998 **Dozens** 400 **Vyds** 2ha
David and Lyn Crossley purchased their property on the Lake George escarpment in 1998, planting clonally selected pinot noir, pinot gris, cabernet franc and merlot over the following 2 years, their inspiration the pioneering work done by Dr Edgar Riek. The vineyard is on a steep hillside at 800–840m, often snow-covered in winter, but protected from frosts by its slope. The small size of the vineyard facilitates micro-management of the vines throughout the year. The name is Gaelic for 'quality cross'.

♀♀♀♀♀ **Silver Label Pinot Noir 2013** Fragrant fruit, blueberry and dark/stewy cherry, leads into a succulent, well-contained palate. It's far short of a century, but puts some good runs on the board. Herbal/stem notes add complexity. Supple texture adds to the appeal. Screwcap. 13.9% alc. **Rating** 90 To 2021 $28 CM

Barrel Select Pinot Noir 2011 Second release of a Barrel Select. Tight, controlled wine, riddled with sap and cool-year personality. Little sunlight, much twigs and spice, but with a fan of velvety flavour through the finish. It's not much fun now but you wouldn't write it off; even as a 3yo it hasn't properly cleared its throat yet. Screwcap. 12.6% alc. **Rating** 90 To 2022 $53 CM

Conti's Tower 2013 70% cabernet franc/30% merlot. Fresh and flavoursome with excellent vitality of fruit. Boysenberry and blueberry notes, some spice, a dusting of milk chocolate. Chewy, fragrant, flavoursome and fun. Screwcap. 13.7% alc. **Rating** 90 To 2020 $25 CM

♀♀♀♀ **Pinot Gris 2013** Rating 89 To 2015 $25 CM
Pinot Noir Chardonnay Cuvee 2011 Rating 88 To 2016 $37 TS

Domaines & Vineyards ★★★★★

PO Box 6096, Swanbourne, WA 6010 **Region** Various WA
T (08) 6555 3280 **www.dandv.com.au Open** Not
Winemaker Robert Bowen **Est.** 2009 **Dozens** 10 000
One of the best-known winemakers in WA is Rob Bowen, with over 35 years' experience with several of WA's leading wineries, most recently Houghton. In 2009 he joined forces with a team of viticulturists led by David Radomilijac and other agricultural experts, who collectively furnish the project with an extensive range of knowledge and expertise. The theme is to produce premium wines with a strong sense of place through a virtual winery exercise, all grapes to be hand-picked from the best available vineyards in the Margaret River and Pemberton regions of southern WA. Two ranges of wines are produced: Robert Bowen (from Margaret River and Pemberton) and Pemberley (from the Pemberley Farms Vineyard owned by David). Exports to the UK, the US, China, Singapore and Hong Kong.

99999 **Robert Bowen Margaret River Cabernet Sauvignon 2012** Hand-picked from a 2ha vineyard on the Wilyabrup/Yallingup border, open-fermented and matured for 20 months in new and second-use French barriques, 300 dozen made. A sumptuous Cabernet flooded with cassis, but enough tannins and oak to provide texture, structure and balance for the long haul for those able to keep their hands off it in the shorter term. Screwcap. 14.5% alc. **Rating** 96 **To** 2042 $60 **○**
Pemberley Pemberton Chardonnay 2014 Hand-picked, whole bunch-pressed, wild yeast barrel-fermented and matured for 9 months in new and 1yo French barriques. It has wonderful energy and precision within a medium-bodied frame, white peach and grapefruit jockeying for pole position. Will richly repay cellaring over the next few years. Screwcap. 13.5% alc. **Rating** 95 **To** 2024 $30 **○**
Robert Bowen Margaret River Chardonnay 2011 Developing slowly. Whole bunch-pressed, the juice taken straight to new and used French oak oak for wild yeast fermentation; matured for 9 months in oak with partial mlf. Elegance and length are its watchwords. Screwcap. 14% alc. **Rating** 95 **To** 2026 $60
Pemberley Pemberton Sauvignon Blanc 2014 A strikingly juicy style, with Meyer lemon and finely wrought acidity taking the front of stage, partial barrel fermentation inputs hiding in the wings, but detectable nonetheless. A Sauvignon Blanc to gladden the hearts of Semillon devotees, and won't keep them waiting too long. Screwcap. 13% alc. **Rating** 94 **To** 2016 $25 **○**
Pemberley Pemberton Pinot Noir 2012 Alcohol is high-ish for a Pinot Noir but it more than makes up for it in both complexity and straightforward deliciousness. Plums, sweet-sour cherries, nuts and a polished veneer of cedary oak. A taut acid line and gusts of tannin keep the wine feeling dry and firm. Reductive notes work here as a positive. Most attractive drinking package. Screwcap. 14.5% alc. **Rating** 94 **To** 2021 $30 CM **○**

99997 **Pemberley Pinot Noir Rose 2014** **Rating** 93 **To** 2016 $25 **○**
Pemberley Sauvignon Blanc 2013 **Rating** 92 **To** 2016 $25 CM **○**
Pemberley Chardonnay 2013 **Rating** 91 **To** 2018 $30 CM
Robert Bowen Pemberton Sauvignon Blanc 2012 **Rating** 90 **To** 2016 $35

Domaines Tatiarra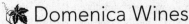

2 Corrong Court, Eltham, Vic 3095 (postal) **Region** Heathcote
T 0428 628 420 **www.**tatiarra.com **Open** Not
Winemaker Ben Riggs **Est.** 1991 **Dozens** 4000 **Vyds** 13.4ha
Domaines Tatiarra Ltd. is an unlisted public company, its core asset being a 60ha property of Cambrian earth identified and developed by Bill Hepburn, who sold it to the company in 1991. It produces only one varietal wine: Shiraz. The majority of the wine comes from the Tatiarra (an Aboriginal word meaning 'beautiful country') property, but the Trademark Shiraz is an equal blend of McLaren Vale and Heathcote wine. The wines are made at the Scotchmans Hill winery in Geelong, with Ben Riggs commuting between there and McLaren Vale as required. Exports to the UK, the US, Canada, Denmark, Switzerland, Singapore and China.

99999 **Trademark Heathcote McLaren Vale Shiraz 2012** The bouquet is both expressive and complex, reflecting the 50/50% regional contributions; spice, mocha, sweet leather and black fruits are all present on both bouquet and palate; counterintuitively, the tannins are more obvious here than in the Caravan of Dreams, and make a positive contribution, combining with savoury bitter chocolate notes ex McLaren Vale. Screwcap. 15% alc. **Rating** 94 **To** 2032 $62

99997 **Caravan of Dreams Shiraz Pressings 2012** **Rating** 93 **To** 2020 $62
Cambrian Heathcote Shiraz 2012 **Rating** 91 **To** 2025 $33

🍇 Domenica Wines

651 Wangaratta–Beechworth Road, Beechworth, Vic 3747 **Region** Beechworth
T (03) 5728 1612 **www.**domenicawines.com.au **Open** By appt
Winemaker Peter Graham **Est.** 2012 **Dozens** 1500 **Vyds** 5ha

Domenica Wines is the reincarnation of the previous Ergo Sum joint venture between Rick Kinzbrunner, Michel Chapoutier and Peter Graham. Domenica was established in 2012 when Peter Graham purchased the shares of Kinzbrunner and Chapoutier, and he is now the sole owner and winemaker of the business. He has already had 15 years of winemaking in Beechworth, and in particular worked both growing and making the wines from the (now) Domenica vineyard since it first produced fruit. Shiraz, roussanne and marsanne are considered by Peter Graham to have a natural affinity with the warm, dry summers, granitic soils, slopes and altitude provided by Beechworth. Beechworth's two major varieties are shiraz and chardonnay, and these are cornerstones for Domenica Wines.

ΤΤΤΤΤ   ...Ergo Sum Shiraz 2012 Meat, bones, flesh and silken skin. This has the gamut covered. It's a powerful wine, as much savoury as sweet, with kirsch, black pepper, ground cloves and powerful anise. More than the descriptors, though, is the impact this wine has: it's a wine of presence. It's heavy enough to have a gravity, but elegant enough to preach restraint. It's entirely worthy of your best glassware or, indeed, prized space in your cellar. Cork. 14% alc. **Rating** 96 **To** 2032 $75 CM ❂
Beechworth Roussanne Marsanne 2013 Rich and luscious with various stone fruits, spices and a rocky minerality ricocheting around the palate. Powerful flavour continues on through the finish. One to seek out. Screwcap. 13.5% alc. **Rating** 95 **To** 2018 $40 CM
Beechworth Chardonnay 2013 Grown on the Warner vineyard. Production of 6 barrels. Pure and powerful with tangy grapefruit, nectarine, toast, mineral and dirt/funk notes. Finishes spicy, almost redolent of ginger. No need to wait; it drinks gorgeously now. Screwcap. **Rating** 94 **To** 2019 $40 CM
Beechworth Shiraz 2012 Excellent red in the spicy/peppery style. No lack of bold, blueberried/black-cherried flavour but then meaty, smoky, peppery and generally complex as the wave of flavour rumbles through the finish. Screwcap. 13.7% alc. **Rating** 94 **To** 2027 $44 CM

ΤΤΤΤΥ   Two Cells Beechworth Shiraz 2012 **Rating** 93 **To** 2022 $25 CM ❂
Beechworth Roussanne Marsanne 2012 **Rating** 92 **To** 2016 $40 CM

Dominique Portet ★★★★★

870–872 Maroondah Highway, Coldstream, Vic 3770 **Region** Yarra Valley
T (03) 5962 5760 **www**.dominiqueportet.com **Open** 7 days 10–5
Winemaker Ben Portet **Est.** 2000 **Dozens** 15 000 **Vyds** 4.3ha
Dominique Portet was bred in the purple. He spent his early years at Chateau Lafite (where his father was régisseur) and was one of the first Flying Winemakers, commuting to Clos du Val in the Napa Valley, where his brother was winemaker. He then spent over 20 years as managing director of Taltarni and Clover Hill. After retiring from Taltarni, he moved to the Yarra Valley, a region he had been closely observing since the mid-1980s. In 2001 he found the site he had long looked for and built his winery and cellar door, planting a quixotic mix of viognier, sauvignon blanc and merlot next to the winery. Son Ben is now executive winemaker, leaving Dominique with a roving role as de facto consultant and brand marketer. Ben (35) has a winemaking CV of awesome scope, covering all parts of France, South Africa, California and four vintages at Petaluma. Exports to the UK, Canada, Denmark, India, Dubai, Hong Kong, Singapore, Malaysia, China and Japan.

ΤΤΤΤΤ   Origine Yarra Valley Chardonnay 2013 Sourced from mature vines in the Upper Yarra Valley. The complex bouquet and vibrant palate set the scene for a high-quality Chardonnay that progressively builds flavour through the entire length of the palate and lingering aftertaste; the oak for the barrel ferment has been astutely chosen and used, leaving the varietal fruit expression undimmed. Screwcap. 13.5% alc. **Rating** 95 **To** 2023 $40
Origine Pyrenees Cabernet Sauvignon 2013 A far softer, and more fluid, release than the inaugural 2012, though there's been no real sacrifice in cellarability. This is a beautifully balanced and fruited wine. It's all blackcurrant, mint, tobacco leaves and dust, the integration of smoky-sweet oak quite impeccable. A modern

expression of Pyrenees cabernet, moulded along classic lines. Screwcap. 13.6% alc. **Rating** 95 **To** 2033 $40 CM

Yarra Valley Brut Rose LD NV A traditional method blend of pinot noir, chardonnay and pinot meunier. 'LD' here doesn't stand for 'late disgorged', but 'light dosage'. Abundant mousse persists long after the wine is poured; it has plentiful red fruits offset by citrus and brioche. Diam. 13% alc. **Rating** 94 **To** 2017 $28 ✪

🍷🍷🍷🍷🍷 **Yarra Valley Sauvignon Blanc 2014** Rating 93 To 2016 $28 CM
Fontaine Yarra Valley Pyrenees Rose 2014 Rating 92 To 2015 $22 ✪
Brut Rose NV Rating 92 To 2015 $28 TS

Dorrien Estate   ★★★★★

Cnr Barossa Valley Way/Siegersdorf Road, Tanunda, SA 5352 **Region** Barossa Valley
T (08) 8561 2200 **www**.cellarmasters.com.au **Open** Not
Winemaker Corey Ryan (Chief) **Est.** 1982 **Dozens** 1 million
Dorrien Estate is the physical base of the vast Cellarmasters network that is the largest direct-sale outlet in Australia. It also makes wine for many producers across Australia at its modern winery, which has a capacity of 14.5 million litres in tank and barrel; however, a typical make of each wine will be little more than 1000 dozen. Most of the wines made for others are exclusively distributed by Cellarmasters. Acquired by Woolworths in May 2011.

🍷🍷🍷🍷🍷 **Black Wattle Vineyards Icon Mount Benson Cabernet Sauvignon 2012**
A wine to settle in with. It flows and struts, is easy to take and is demanding all at once. It tastes of blackcurrant, boysenberry, fresh mint and smoky oak, and comes complete with a sheer shift of assertive tannin. But nothing feels out of place; it all teams and talks as one. Balanced wines always drink well young; so too this. But it has a long life ahead. Screwcap. 14.5% alc. **Rating** 96 **To** 2035 $46 CM ✪
Dorrien Estate Bin 1A Shiraz 2012 Made from grapes grown in Mount Benson, Langhorne Creek and Wrattonbully. It's a bobby-dazzler of a wine, lush with both fruit and oak, impeccably well balanced, rippling with tannin and lengthy. Bold and beautiful. Screwcap. 14.5% alc. **Rating** 95 **To** 2028 $38 CM
Black Wattle Vineyards Mount Benson Cabernet Sauvignon 2012
Excellent colour, flavour and length. Blackcurrant, twiggy herbs and integrated smoky oak, all well teamed and working in the one direction. Firm, assertive tannin completes a strong, muscular impression. Quality nailed to the wall. Screwcap. 14.5% alc. **Rating** 95 **To** 2030 $33 CM ✪
Mockingbird Hill Clare Valley Cabernet Sauvignon Malbec 2012 A Clare Valley blend made famous by Leasingham Bin 56 and Wendouree. This is a very good example, its plush texture and black fruit flavour profile a delight, oak and tannins buried in the fruit. Screwcap. 14.5% alc. **Rating** 95 **To** 2025 $24 ✪
Dorrien Estate Bin 1A Chardonnay 2013 Made with grapes sourced from Tasmania, Adelaide Hills, Margaret River, Tumbarumba and Mount Gambier. All that blending and effort has created a slim arrow of a wine, as much acid and oak as fruit at this early stage, though it's not underdone; it's simply built for the patient. Grapefruit, citrus and steel are the drivers of a very long finish. If drinking now, decant. Screwcap. 13% alc. **Rating** 94 **To** 2020 $31 CM
Redemption Canberra District Shiraz 2013 Lively and lifted with spice and sweet ripe cherry/fennel flavours aplenty. Beautiful to drink. No mention of viognier but it would be surprising if there wasn't at least a dab of it here. Whisper of nutty oak. Works a treat. Screwcap. 14.5% alc. **Rating** 94 **To** 2023 $28 CM ✪
Mockingbird Hill Reserve Clare Valley Shiraz 2013 Pure silk. Rich blackberry, saturated plum, robes of sweet vanilla. It's not a new formula, but when it's done well, as it is here, it's very hard to resist. Screwcap. 15% alc. **Rating** 94 **To** 2025 $28 CM ✪

🍷🍷🍷🍷🍷 **Yarra View Reserve Pinot Noir 2013** Rating 93 To 2021 $33 CM
Tolley Elite Shiraz 2012 Rating 93 To 2022 $38 CM

Dorrien Estate Bin 1 Shiraz 2012 Rating 93 To 2025 $44 CM
Black Wattle Mount Benson Shiraz 2012 Rating 93 To 2024 $33 CM
Mockingbird Hill Clare Valley Riesling 2014 Rating 92 To 2022 $21 CM ✪
Dorrien Estate Bin 1A Pinot Noir 2013 Rating 92 To 2019 $38 CM
Krondorf Growers Barossa Shiraz 2013 Rating 92 To 2022 $27 CM
Krondorf Symmetry Old Vine Shiraz 2012 Rating 92 To 2028 $45 CM
Black Wattle Mount Benson Cabernet 2011 Rating 92 To 2024 $46 CM
Mockingbird Hill Clare Valley Cabernet Sauvignon Malbec 2013
Rating 92 To 2025 $24 CM ✪
John Glaetzer Stonyfell Black Shiraz 2013 Rating 91 To 2020 $28 CM
Shark's Block McLaren Vale Shiraz 2012 Rating 91 To 2021 $40 CM

Dowie Doole ★★★★★

276 California Road, McLaren Vale, SA 5171 **Region** McLaren Vale
T (08) 8323 8875 **www**.dowiedoole.com **Open** 7 days 10–5
Winemaker Chris Thomas **Est.** 1996 **Dozens** 25 000 **Vyds** 44.35ha
Dowie Doole was born of the frustration following the 1995 vintage, which led friends Norm
Doole and Drew Dowie to form a partnership to take control over the destiny of their grapes.
In '98, Leigh Gilligan, a McLaren Vale veteran, was appointed to take overall control of the
business, and joined the partnership. Founding winemaker Brian Light has stepped back to a
consultancy role following the appointment of Chris Thomas as winemaker. Sami Gilligan,
Lulu Lunn and Dave Gartelmann share responsibility for the five vineyards in which Dowie
Doole has an interest, all managed using sustainable viticulture practices. Exports to the UK,
the US, Canada, Denmark, Germany, Hong Kong, Thailand and China.

🍷🍷🍷🍷🍷 **Reserve McLaren Vale Shiraz 2012** Made in the same way as Cali Road,
except 3 days of post-fermentation maceration and French, not American oak.
A really attractive example of a '12 McLaren Vale Shiraz, the quality of the fruit
enhanced by the French oak, not threatened by it. The fact that these vines
are over 40yo (compared to 15yo for Cali Road) also contributes much to the
equation. Diam. 14.5% alc. **Rating** 96 To 2037 $60 ✪
**Scarce Earth The Architect The Fruit of the Vine McLaren Vale Shiraz
2012** Matured in 2yo French barriques for 24 months. The extent to which this
portrays a particular part of McLaren Vale is moot, but it certainly tells you loud
and clear that it is from McLaren Vale. It is medium-bodied, the tannins soft and
pliant, the fruit flavours seductively sweet, but it is the chocolate wrapping that
starts and finishes the palate. It is very, very seductive, drinking well now, but with
decades (or more) in front of it. Diam. 14.5% alc. **Rating** 95 To 2029 $45
G&T McLaren Vale Garnacha & Tempranillo 2014 Good colour; the
fragrant bouquet is but an 'on your mark' command, the vibrantly fresh, yet
complex, light to medium-bodied palate racing through the 'set, go' sequence;
there are spices of all kinds woven like sequins into the Thai silk of licorice and
dark fruits on the palate. Screwcap. 14% alc. **Rating** 95 To 2020 $25 ✪
McLaren Vale Cabernet Sauvignon 2013 The synergy between cabernet
and McLaren Vale has been demonstrated on countless occasions over the decades,
and this wine isn't going to challenge that line; just when you think it's a little too
chocolatey, black fruits assert themselves with the assistance of insidious tannins
that are there before you realise it. Screwcap. 14% alc. **Rating** 94 To 2020 $25 ✪

🍷🍷🍷🍷🍷 **McLaren Vale Shiraz 2013** Rating 93 To 2033 $25 ✪
Cali Road McLaren Vale Shiraz 2012 Rating 92 To 2027 $35

Downing Estate Vineyard ★★★★★

19 Drummonds Lane, Heathcote, Vic 3523 **Region** Heathcote
T (03) 5433 3387 **www**.downingestate.com.au **Open** W'ends & public hols 11–5
Winemaker Rob Ellis **Est.** 1994 **Dozens** 1700 **Vyds** 10ha

Bob Downing purchased 24ha of undulating land in 1994, and has established a dry-grown vineyard planted to shiraz (7.2ha), cabernet sauvignon (2.4ha) and merlot (0.4ha). Exports to Canada, Singapore and China.

ŶŶŶŶŶ **Reserve Heathcote Shiraz 2012** Finely balanced and structured red and black cherry fruit spent 12 months in new French oak, but has not missed a step; the oak has drawn out the fruit on the long finish, rather than dominating proceedings. 140 dozen made. Screwcap. 13% alc. **Rating** 96 **To** 2027 $85

Reserve Heathcote Cabernet Sauvignon 2012 While sharing many, if not all, of the characters of its standard sibling, this wine lifts the intensity of expression by several notches, 22 months' maturation in new French barriques being met on equal terms by cassis fruit. Screwcap. 14% alc. **Rating** 95 **To** 2027 $85

Geoffrey's Blend 2012 An estate-grown 50/50% blend of cabernet sauvignon and shiraz. The colour is excellent, as are the balance and mouthfeel of this delicious medium-bodied wine; black and red fruits of every persuasion figure somewhere along the journey, the tannins ample, but soft, the oak balanced and integrated. Screwcap. 13.5% alc. **Rating** 95 **To** 2032 $30 ✪

Heathcote Cabernet Sauvignon 2012 A gold medal and trophy from the Heathcote Wine Show '14 isn't a bad introduction to a perfectly balanced wine, with varietal fruit, oak and tannins playing synergistic roles; has the harmony young Cabernets often lack. Screwcap. 14.3% alc. **Rating** 94 **To** 2027 $30 ✪

ŶŶŶŶŸ **Heathcote Shiraz 2012 Rating** 92 **To** 2022 $30
Heathcote Merlot 2012 Rating 90 **To** 2020 $25

Drayton's Family Wines   ★★★★☆

555 Oakey Creek Road, Cessnock, NSW 2321 **Region** Hunter Valley
T (02) 4998 7513 **www.draytonswines.com.au Open** Mon–Fri 8–5, w'ends 10–5
Winemaker Edgar Vales, Max and John Drayton **Est.** 1853 **Dozens** 50 000 **Vyds** 72ha
This substantial Hunter Valley producer has suffered more than its share of misfortune over the years, but has risen to the challenges. Edgar Vales is the chief winemaker after previous experience as assistant winemaker with David Hook and First Creek Wines. His arrival has coincided with the release of a range of high-quality wines. Exports to Ireland, Vietnam, Singapore, Taiwan and China.

ŶŶŶŶŶ **Vineyard Reserve Pokolbin Semillon 2010** Gleaming green-quartz; just cruising along on its journey to full maturity and complexity; the citrus/lemon flavours are particularly attractive, and you can sense the next stage of honey and toast around the corner. Screwcap. 11% alc. **Rating** 95 **To** 2025 $30 ✪

ŶŶŶŶŸ **Joseph Hunter Valley Shiraz 2007 Rating** 93 **To** 2027 $70
Vineyard Reserve Pokolbin Chardonnay 2012 Rating 91 **To** 2018 $30

Driftwood Estate   ★★★★☆

3314 Caves Road, Wilyabrup, WA 6282 **Region** Margaret River
T (08) 9755 6323 **www.driftwoodwine.com.au Open** 7 days 10–5
Winemaker Hugh Warren **Est.** 1989 **Dozens** 15 000
Driftwood Estate is a well-established landmark on the Margaret River scene. Quite apart from offering a brasserie restaurant capable of seating 200 people (open 7 days for lunch and dinner) and a mock Greek open-air theatre, its wines feature striking and stylish packaging and opulent flavours. The winery architecture is, it must be said, opulent rather than stylish. Exports to the UK, Singapore and China.

ŶŶŶŶŸ **Artifacts Margaret River Cabernet Sauvignon 2012** Flavoursome wine with curls of tannin lending an air of importance. Blackcurrant and bitumen, bold and stern, with gravelly, pepperminty tannin motoring throughout. Will not fall over in a hurry. Screwcap. 15.1% alc. **Rating** 93 **To** 2026 $30 CM

Oceania Meritage 2012 Medium-bodied, but at the lighter end of the term. Perfumed blueberry and violet scents lead to a refreshing palate showing game, blueberry and dried herb flavours. Quite tannic given its lighter profile, but it's a pretty wine nonetheless. Screwcap. 15% alc. **Rating** 91 **To** 2020 $30 CM

ŦŦŦŦ   The Collection Cabernet Merlot 2012 Rating 89 To 2020 $20 CM
Margaret River Classic White 2014 Rating 88 To 2015 $20 CM
Artifacts Margaret River Shiraz 2012 Rating 88 To 2022 $25 CM

Dromana Estate ★★★★☆

555 Old Moorooduc Road, Tuerong, Vic 3933 **Region** Mornington Peninsula
T (03) 5974 4400 **www**.dromanaestate.com.au **Open** Not
Winemaker Duncan Buchanan **Est.** 1982 **Dozens** 30 000 **Vyds** 53.9ha
Since it was established over 30 years ago, Dromana Estate has always been near or at the cutting edge, both in marketing terms and in terms of development of new varietals, most obviously the Italian range under the 'i' label. Dromana Estate is owned by the investors of a publicly listed company, operating under the name of Mornington Winery Group Limited. It includes the Dromana Estate, Mornington Estate and David Traeger (see separate entry) labels. Expanded production has seen export markets increase. Exports to the US, Canada and China.

ŦŦŦŦŦ   Pinot Noir 2012 From Tuerong Park Vineyards, 83% MV6 clone; wild yeast-fermented in open vats, macerated for 16–19 days; 10 months' maturation in used (91%) and new oak. Good colour and clarity; a supple and smooth rendition of black cherry and plum varietal fruit, the tannins and oak management precisely handled. Screwcap. 13.6% alc. **Rating** 95 **To** 2020 $35 ✪
Chardonnay 2012 Clones P58 (41%) and I10V1 (59%); wild yeast-fermented in new (27%) and used French oak, plus 10 months' maturation. Full straw colour; has very good drive, intensity and focus, with grapefruit/citrus zest overtones to the stone fruit and apple flavours, the new oak totally integrated. Good now, but has the structure for cellaring. Screwcap. 12.9% alc. **Rating** 94 **To** 2020 $35
Viognier 2014 Hand-picked; fermented in stainless steel with cultured yeast, matured in used oak for 7 months. Bright green-quartz, it breaks all the rules, especially with its zesty, vibrant finish. There's not much apricot on the palate, but enough stone fruit to satisfy. Screwcap. 12.4% alc. **Rating** 94 **To** 2017 $32
Syrah 2013 Wild yeast open-fermented, 35 days on skins, matured in used oak for 17 months, 'spared filtration'. Vivid crimson-purple, the fragrant bouquet and light to medium-bodied palate are all about finesse, elegance and harmony; red and black cherries provide the core, with a delicate web of spices and fine tannins on the finish. Screwcap. 14% alc. **Rating** 94 **To** 2028 $80
Mornington Estate Shiraz 2012 88% shiraz from three Mornington Peninsula vineyards and 12% sangiovese; destemmed to open pots; part wild, part cultured yeast ferments; 22 months in new (10%) and used oak. The scented, spicy red and black fruit aromas lead into an elegant, medium-bodied palate, red fruits asserting themselves on the silky finish. Screwcap. 13.5% alc. **Rating** 94 **To** 2022 $24 ✪

ŦŦŦŦ̦   Pinot Noir 2013 Rating 93 To 2022 $39
Chardonnay 2013 Rating 92 To 2030 $39
Mornington Estate Pinot Noir 2013 Rating 91 To 2023 $25
Mornington Estate Chardonnay 2012 Rating 90 To 2017 $24

Drummonds Corrina Vineyard ★★★★

85 Wintles Road, Leongatha South, Vic 3953 **Region** Gippsland
T (03) 5664 3317 **www**.drummondwines.com.au **Open** W'ends 10–5
Winemaker Bass Phillip **Est.** 1983 **Dozens** NA **Vyds** 3ha
The Drummond family organically grow 1ha each of pinot noir and sauvignon blanc, and 0.5ha each of cabernet sauvignon and merlot, all established slowly without the aid of irrigation. The viticultural methods are those practised by Phillip Jones, who makes the wines for Drummonds: north–south row orientation, leaf plucking on the east side of the rows, low

yields, and all fruit picked by hand. Similarly restrained winemaking methods (no pumping, no filters and low SO_2) follow in the winery.

ŢŢŢŢŢ **Premium South Gippsland Pinot Noir 2012** Made at Bass Phillip – and the ProCork is branded 2012 Bass Phillip! It has spicy/savoury/rose petal aromas; the palate is only light to medium-bodied, but it has good length. Given the dry-grown 30yo vineyard and the '12 vintage, one might have expected more depth. 12.5% alc. **Rating** 91 **To** 2019 $45

Dudley Wines   ★★★★★

1153 Willoughby Road, Penneshaw, Kangaroo Island 5222 **Region** Kangaroo Island
T (08) 8553 1333 **www.**dudleywines.com.au **Open** 7 days 10–5
Winemaker Brodie Howard **Est.** 1994 **Dozens** 3500 **Vyds** 14ha
Jeff and Val Howard own Dudley Wines and its three vineyards on Kangaroo Island's Dudley Peninsula: the Porky Flat Vineyard, Hog Bay River and Sawyers. It is the quirky vineyard names that give the wines their distinctive identities. The Howards not only look after viticulture, but also join in the winemaking process. Most of the wines are sold through licensed outlets on Kangaroo Island.

ŢŢŢŢŢ **Porky Flat Kangaroo Island Shiraz 2012** Has excellent colour, with spiced black plum fruit aromas, a lively medium-bodied palate bringing spice and licorice onto the agenda in addition to the bouquet; there is a juicy finesse to the wine that is most appealing. Screwcap. 14.5% alc. **Rating** 95 **To** 2032 $28 ✪
Hog Bay River Kangaroo Island Cabernet Sauvignon 2013 Whereas riesling doesn't enjoy a maritime climate, it's a case of a duck to water for cabernet; it gives the varietal expression an autocratic twist, with briary/dried herb nuances that fit well in the overall flavour, especially when the alcohol is controlled, as it is here. This is a manicured Cabernet that doesn't need any town crier to announce its arrival. Screwcap. 14% alc. **Rating** 95 **To** 2033 $28 ✪

ŢŢŢŢŢ **Pink Bay Kangaroo Island Rose 2014 Rating** 90 **To** 2016 $18 ✪

Duke's Vineyard   ★★★★★

Porongurup Road, Porongurup, WA 6324 **Region** Porongurup
T (08) 9853 1107 **www.**dukesvineyard.com **Open** 7 days 10–4.30
Winemaker Robert Diletti **Est.** 1998 **Dozens** 3500 **Vyds** 10ha
When Hilde and Ian (Duke) Ranson sold their clothing manufacturing business in 1998, they were able to fulfil a long-held dream of establishing a vineyard in the Porongurup subregion of Great Southern with the acquisition of a 65ha farm at the foot of the Porongurup Range. They planted shiraz and cabernet sauvignon (3ha each) and riesling (4ha). Hilde, a successful artist, designed the beautiful, scalloped, glass-walled cellar door sales area, with its mountain blue cladding. Great wines at great prices.

ŢŢŢŢŢ **Magpie Hill Reserve Riesling 2014** You almost need GPS assistance to chart the distance between the start of the flavours and the finish. This is astonishingly persistent and therefore impressive. Apple, sweet lime, dry spice and slate. Whoosh. This is good. Screwcap. 11.5% alc. **Rating** 97 **To** 2035 $30 CM ✪

ŢŢŢŢŢ **Magpie Hill Reserve Cabernet Sauvignon 2013** A bit of the old Cabernet swagger here. It loads up the fruit but has a firm, grainy, muscular hand of tannin visible in its holster at all times. Blackcurrant, asphalt, peppercorns and a swoosh of well-integrated smoky oak. Will make old bones. Screwcap. 13.7% alc. **Rating** 95 **To** 2033 $35 CM ✪
Magpie Hill Reserve Shiraz 2013 Maintains a measured approach but there's plenty of fruit, spice, body and length to be enjoyed here. It's simply playing these aspects close to its chest in its youth. Dark cherry, aniseed and blackberry flavours, velvety tannin, and a crush of dry spice to the aftertaste. Exemplary. Screwcap. 13.8% alc. **Rating** 94 **To** 2028 $35 CM

Invitation Winemaker Michael Staniford Cabernet Sauvignon 2013 Same fruit as the Magpie Hill Reserve; different winemaker. Both wines are excellent. Coconut oak sits just above pure cabernet fruit flavour: blackcurrant, bay leaves and tar. Seems sweeter and slightly less defined than the Magpie Hill, though splitting hairs of course. Screwcap. 14% alc. **Rating** 94 **To** 2033 $35 CM

ŸŸŸŸŸ Single Vineyard Riesling 2014 Rating 93 To 2026 $25 CM ●
Single Vineyard Shiraz 2013 Rating 93 To 2025 $26 CM ●
Single Vineyard Rose 2014 Rating 90 To 2015 $20 CM ●
Single Vineyard Autumn Riesling 2014 Rating 90 To 2020 $25 CM

Dutschke Wines ★★★★★

Lot 1 Gods Hill Road, Lyndoch, SA 5351 **Region** Barossa Valley
T (08) 8524 5485 **www**.dutschkewines.com **Open** By appt
Winemaker Wayne Dutschke **Est.** 1998 **Dozens** 6000 **Vyds** 67ha
Wayne Dutschke spent over 20 years working in Australia and overseas for companies large and small before joining his uncle (and grapegrower) Ken Semmler to form Dutschke Wines. In addition to outstanding table wines, he has a yearly release of fortified wines; these sell out overnight, and have received stratospheric points from Robert Parker Jr. The property has been owned by the Semmler family for five generations, each married in the adjacent church. Exports to the US, Canada, Denmark, Germany and The Netherlands.

ŸŸŸŸŸ **St Jakobi Single Vineyard Lyndoch Barossa Valley Shiraz 2013**
An altogether stylish medium to full-bodied Barossa Valley Shiraz, with blackberry, plum, bitter chocolate (70% cacao) and balanced tannins. Built for the long haul, but can be approached earlier. Screwcap. 14.6% alc. **Rating** 94 **To** 2033 $38
GHR Neighbours Barossa Valley Shiraz 2013 The energy and drive of this Shiraz sets it apart from the run of the Barossa mill; it may be that the hillside vineyards on Gods Hill Road are the starting point, but sensitive winemaking also plays a role in preserving the freshness of the medium-bodied palate. Screwcap. 14.5% alc. **Rating** 94 **To** 2030 $30 ●

ŸŸŸŸŸ **SAMI St Jakobi Vineyard Lyndoch Barossa Valley Cabernet Sauvignon 2013** Rating 92 To 2033 $30

 # Eagles Rest Wines ★★★★★

Lot 1, 534 Oakey Creek Road, Pokolbin, NSW 2320 **Region** Hunter Valley
T 0413 942 743 **www**.eaglesrestwines.com.au **Open** 7 days 10–5
Winemaker PJ Charteris **Est.** 2007 **Dozens** 5000 **Vyds** 17.9ha
Eagles Rest has flown under the radar since its establishment eight years ago, and still does. The 'current owner' wishes to remain anonymous, although winemaker PJ Charteris is anything but. He was second in charge to Iain Riggs at Brokenwood for many years, and both his palate and his knowledge of the finest wines in the world were the bedrock for his formidable skills as a winemaker. He arrived after the wines tasted for this edition of the *Wine Companion* were made, so the future can only bring further fame for the business. For the record, the estate is planted to semillon, chardonnay and shiraz.

ŸŸŸŸŸ **Gully Block Hunter Valley Semillon 2009** Extraordinarily pale quartz-green; the bouquet has flowered magically over the past 6 years, full of lemongrass, talc and (yes) a faint waft of lavender; the palate is commensurately intense and complex, with grapefruit pith, dried herbs and crunchy acidity. Screwcap. 11% alc. **Rating** 95 **To** 2025 $35 ●
Shed Block Hunter Valley Shiraz 2010 The bright, deep colour sends a signal that this is worth paying close attention to; it is at the upper end of medium-bodied, replete with a mosaic of red and black fruits, fine-grained, gently savoury tannins and integrated oak. It has length and perfect balance, guaranteeing a long and prosperous life. Screwcap. 13.1% alc. **Rating** 95 **To** 2040 $40

Hunter Valley Shiraz 2010 Has that almost airy elegance of modest alcohol typical of many Hunter Valley Shirazs, and at 5yo is still fresh and lively; black cherry, fine tannins, hints of Hunter Valley earth give this a real sense of place – and purpose. It's a good wine. Screwcap. 12.8% alc. **Rating** 94 **To** 2030 $35

ǧǧǧǧǧ Gully Block Hunter Valley Semillon 2013 **Rating** 92 **To** 2026 $25 ○
Maluna Block Hunter Valley Shiraz 2009 **Rating** 92 **To** 2029 $50
Dam Block Hunter Valley Chardonnay 2012 **Rating** 90 **To** 2018 $30
Hunter Valley Chardonnay 2012 **Rating** 90 **To** 2018 $23

Eastern Peake   ★★★★★

67 Pickfords Road, Coghills Creek, Vic 3364 **Region** Ballarat
T (03) 5343 4245 **www.**easternpeake.com.au **Open** 7 days 11–5
Winemaker Owen Latta **Est.** 1983 **Dozens** 1500 **Vyds** 5.6ha
Norm Latta and Di Pym established Eastern Peake, 25km northeast of Ballarat on a high plateau overlooking the Creswick Valley, over 20 years ago. In the early years the grapes were sold, but the 5.6ha of vines are now dedicated to the production of Eastern Peake wines. Son Owen Latta has been responsible for the seismic increase in the quality of the wines, marking the 30th anniversary of the winery in fine style in 2013.

ǧǧǧǧǧ **Walsh Block Tres Ancienne Pinot Noir 2012** 20yo vines. One barrel only.
50% whole bunch, wild yeast, 8 weeks' post-ferment maceration. It's a stern, tannic style in some ways but the structure does not come at the expense of flavour and/ or personality. There's much to tuck into here; to contemplate, even. Cranberry, mocha, boysenberry and satsuma plum notes, its laces tied with complex dry spice. It presents a pretty face to the world but its IQ is high, its future worth tracking. Screwcap. 13% alc. **Rating** 96 **To** 2027 $70 CM ○
Block P58 Chardonnay 2013 The block of P58 clone chardonnay at Eastern Peake, now 22yo, has always been fermented separately but blended into the estate wine. This year, to celebrate the estate's 30th year, one barrel was kept separate. It picked a good season to turn 30. This is a scintillating wine, rich but with excellent thrust of juicy flavour and acidity through the finish. Lime, chalk, lemon and apple with a gentle, integrated milky-creaminess. Outstanding length too. Screwcap. 12.5% alc. **Rating** 96 **To** 2022 $45 CM ○
Morillion Block 89 OBC Pinot Noir 2013 26yo vines, one barrel produced, no whole bunches. Tangy style, not light but not heavy, with spice, boysenberry and juicy sour-sweet cherries sluicing through the palate. Tannin creeps up on you, as indeed does flavour; it saves its best for last. The freshness here, and for that matter the polish, is quite exquisite. Screwcap. **Rating** 95 **To** 2025 CM
Walsh Block Syrah 2013 10yo vines, 10% whole bunch, wild yeast. Cool-climate flavours are tattooed on its sleeve but there's no lack of oomph. Black cherry edging into plum with green garden herbs and roasted, nutty characters aplenty. Wine as a kind of exotic foodstuff. Savoury, herbal, fresh and altogether fascinating. Screwcap. 13% alc. **Rating** 95 **To** 2027 $40 CM
Block I10V5 Chardonnay 2013 It has a certain irresistibility. It's full of lime, sweet barley, custard and milk-like notes and it feels slippery and smooth throughout. It went through full mlf and the effect is noticeable, but it sings with citrussy acidity too. You could call it flavoursome, but mostly it's a mouth-watering style. Screwcap. 12.5% alc. **Rating** 94 **To** 2019 $45 CM
Intrinsic Pinot Noir 2013 Perfumed and pretty, satiny to the touch, amply fruited but all the while as fresh as a cool autumn morning. Beautiful style of wine, admirably executed. The word 'heavy' is a foreign concept. Wines like this are why people love drinking, and drinking, Pinot Noir. Screwcap. 13% alc. **Rating** 94 **To** 2023 $40 CM
Mount Block Pinot Noir 2012 Two barrels selected from the youngest block, which is 20yo. Wild yeast, 10% whole bunch, 8 weeks' post-ferment maceration, 14 months in oak. Tangy, fragrant style but with an underlying power. Sweet boysenberry, sour cherry, meaty, bacony characters and dried spice. Lively. Almost

nervy. Tense tannin too. Interest aplenty. Screwcap. 13% alc. **Rating** 94 **To** 2022 $45 CM

ΥΥΥΥΥ The Don Pinot Noir 2013 Rating 93 To 2022 $40 CM
Intrinsic Chardonnay 2012 Rating 92 To 2018 $40 CM
Red Basalt Block Pinot Noir 2013 Rating 91 To 2020 $40 CM

Echelon ★★★★★

68 Anzac Street, Chullora, NSW 2190 **Region** Various
T (02) 9722 1200 **www**.echelonwine.com.au **Open** Not
Winemaker Various **Est.** 2009 **Dozens** NFP
Echelon is the brainchild of Nicholas Crampton, a wine marketer who understands wine (by no means a usual occurrence). He persuaded McWilliam's (Echelon's owner) to give free rein to his insights, and enlisted the aid of winemaker Corey Ryan. Brands under the Echelon umbrella are Last Horizon (single-vineyard wines from Tasmania, made by Adrian Sparks), Partisan (from McLaren Vale), Armchair Critic and Under & Over (from established vineyards in the best regions) and Zeppelin (made by Corey Ryan and Kym Teusner, sourced from Barossa vineyards owned by Teusner or Sons of Eden, and often up to 80 years old). Few wineries in Australia so over-deliver on quality at their price point.

ΥΥΥΥΥ Last Horizon Tamar Valley Pinot Noir 2013 Destemmed and cold-soaked for 6 days pre-fermentation before 10 months' maturation in mainly used French oak. The bouquet is expressive, but it is the palate that sets this wine apart, the fruit coating the mouth with red and blue fruit flavours that run from the tip of the tongue to the lingering aftertaste that won't go away, Tasmanian acidity cunningly woven through. Screwcap. 13% alc. **Rating** 95 **To** 2023 $24 ❂
Last Horizon Huon Valley Pinot Noir 2013 Five clones, hand-picked, 80% destemmed, 20% whole bunches, matured for 9 months in French barriques (35% new), 208 dozen made. Clear crimson; the complex bouquet and the drive of the palate repay the decisions made in the winery; red and black cherry, wild strawberry and superfine tannins; the new oak is well integrated, and adds to the package. Screwcap. 13.5% alc. **Rating** 95 **To** 2023 $42
Last Horizon Coal River Riesling 2013 Hand-picked and whole bunch-pressed, liberating only free-run juice (500l per tonne, not 700l) and cool-fermented. Has the almost painful diamond-cut Tasmanian acidity, with no obvious residual sugar. Glorious summer seafood style, a wine of unashamed place. Screwcap. 12.5% alc. **Rating** 94 **To** 2029 $32
Last Horizon Tamar Valley Chardonnay 2012 Wild-fermented on full solids in French barriques (35% new), minimal mlf. The acid backbone of the wine is all-important, white peach/grapefruit draped over part of it, barrel-ferment inputs the other; simply because it is the backbone, it pulls all the components together into a single, fluid stream. Screwcap. 13.5% alc. **Rating** 94 **To** 2022 $37
Zeppelin Big Bertha Barossa Valley Shiraz 2013 Produced from old vines; open-fermented, basket-pressed. An unusual wine, intense and very powerful, yet not hot nor with any dead fruit; savoury/spicy flavours dance along the palate and into the finish and aftertaste. Screwcap. 14.5% alc. **Rating** 94 **To** 2027 $19 ❂

ΥΥΥΥΥ Partisan Communication Road Shiraz 2012 Rating 93 To 2028 $41 CM
Zeppelin Eden Valley Riesling 2014 Rating 92 To 2022 $21 CM ❂
Partisan McLaren Vale Shiraz 2013 Rating 92 To 2030 $18 ❂
Last Horizon East Coast Pinot Gris 2013 Rating 91 To 2015 $24
Under & Over Heathcote Shiraz 2012 Rating 90 To 2020 $14 ❂

Eclectic Wines ★★★★☆

687 Hermitage Road, Pokolbin, NSW 2320 (postal) **Region** Hunter Valley
T 0410 587 207 **www**.eclecticwines.com.au **Open** At Hunter Valley Gardens Cellars
Winemaker First Creek Wines, David Hook, Neil Pike **Est.** 2001 **Dozens** 3000

This is the venture of Paul and Kate Stuart, nominally based in the Hunter Valley, where they live and have a vineyard planted to shiraz and mourvedre; 'nominally', because Paul's 30 years in the wine industry have given him the marketing knowledge to sustain the purchase of grapes from various regions, including Canberra and interstate. He balances the production and sale of his own wines under the Eclectic label while also acting as an independent marketing and sales consultant to other producers, selling his clients' wine in different markets from those in which he sells his own. Exports to The Netherlands and China.

ΨΨΨΨΨ **Pewter Label Hunter Valley Semillon 2014** Waxy texture, citrussy flavour and a lengthy, lilting finish. Hunter Semillon can make quality look so easy. Elegance personified. Screwcap. 12% alc. **Rating** 93 **To** 2021 $25 CM ✪
Pewter Hunter Valley Shiraz Mourvedre 2014 More length than breadth. Tangy cherry, mineral and earth flavours of light to medium weight are the main offering, the finish awash with tasty acidity. Creamy vanillan oak helps smooth the ride. Screwcap. 13.5% alc. **Rating** 90 **To** 2019 $35 CM

ΨΨΨΨ **Adelaide Hills Sauvignon Blanc 2014** Rating 89 To 2015 $25 CM
Pewter Label Hunter Valley Verdelho 2014 Rating 88 To 2015 $25 CM
Hunter Valley Merlot 2013 Rating 88 To 2017 $28 CM

Eden Hall

6 Washington Street, Angaston, SA 5353 **Region** Eden Valley
T 0457 686 010 **www.edenhall.com.au Open** 7 days 11–5
Winemaker Kym Teusner, Christa Deans **Est.** 2002 **Dozens** 2000 **Vyds** 32.3ha
David and Mardi Hall purchased the historic Avon Brae estate in 1996. The 120ha property has been planted to cabernet sauvignon (the lion's share, with 13ha), riesling (9.25ha), shiraz (6ha) and smaller plantings of merlot, cabernet franc and viognier. The majority of the production is contracted to Yalumba, St Hallett and McGuigan Simeon, with 10% of the best grapes held back for the Eden Hall label. Exports to the US, Malaysia and China.

ΨΨΨΨΨ **Block 4 Shiraz 2013** Superb example of the variety and of the region. Full-bodied but silken, ripped with inky blueberry and blackberry fruit flavour but alive with violet, fresh mint and assorted garden herbs. Deep and wise but sharp as a tack. Cut with rocky, minerally, smoky tannin. At the riper end of the spectrum, sure, but a powerhouse wine, a perfumed steamroller, and with a long future ahead. Screwcap. 14.5% alc. **Rating** 97 **To** 2035 $40 CM ✪

ΨΨΨΨΨ **Riesling 2014** 'From low yielding vines high in the rocky outcrops of the Eden Valley.' So says the back label. When you taste the wine it suddenly seems like an evocative, nigh on powerful, statement. This is an electric wine, quartz-like, intense but more than that. It has presence and it makes a statement, but you'd swear, on tasting it, that you can tell it's come from rocky terrain. Screwcap. 11.5% alc. **Rating** 94 **To** 2025 $22 CM ✪

ΨΨΨΨΨ **Block 3 Cabernet Sauvignon 2013** Rating 93 To 2028 $40 CM
Springton Shiraz 2013 Rating 92 To 2022 $25 CM ✪

Eden Road Wines

3182 Barton Highway, Murrumbateman, NSW 2582 **Region** Canberra District
T (02) 6226 8800 **www.edenroadwines.com.au Open** Wed–Sun 11–4
Winemaker Nick Spencer, Hamish Young **Est.** 2006 **Dozens** 9500 **Vyds** 3ha
The name of this business, now entirely based in the Canberra District, reflects an earlier stage of its development, when it also had a property in the Eden Valley. That has now been separated, and Eden Road's operations since 2008 centre on Hilltops, Canberra District and Tumbarumba. Eden Road has relocated to Murrumbateman, where it purchased the former Doonkuna winery and mature vineyard, marketing greatly assisted by winning the Jimmy Watson Trophy '09. Exports to the UK, the US, the Maldives and Hong Kong.

ΨΨΨΨΨ **Maragle Chardonnay 2014** Pure as the driven snow. It takes line and length and adds x-factor. Pear and apple with the flesh of peaches and the cream of oak.

Feel and flavour work majestically and harmoniously, resulting in outstanding persistence. Screwcap. 12.6% alc. **Rating** 96 **To** 2022 $40 CM ✪

Maragle Chardonnay 2013 Hand-picked from the Maragle Vineyard in Tumbarumba at an elevation of 430m on Feb 22; fermented and matured in French barriques (35% new) for 12 months. Bright straw-green; there is more mouthfeel here than that of Courabyra, and the fruit flavours lean towards grapefruit, the oak eaten by the power of that fruit, the finish so balanced that it is everlasting. 100 dozen made. Screwcap. 13% alc. **Rating** 96 **To** 2023 $50 ✪

Gundagai Syrah 2013 Smashing wine. Medium-bodied and nutty, with iodine and black cherry fruit gushing through the palate at speed. There's beauty to be found at all points along the line here but the finish is where the star shines brightest. It drips juicily and lingers appreciably. A landmark wine for the Gundagai region. Screwcap. 13% alc. **Rating** 96 **To** 2030 $50 CM ✪

Courabyra Tumbarumba Chardonnay 2014 Over and over, to the point of routine, Eden Road proves itself an outstanding producer. This offers lactose, chalk, white peach, orange rind and both oatmeal and spice complexities. Such descriptions of course do the deliciousness of it all an injustice. Though it's more than that too: its elegant length is superb. Screwcap. 12.8% alc. **Rating** 95 **To** 2021 $40 CM

Courabyra Tumbarumba Chardonnay 2013 Spent 18 months on lees in a stainless steel tank. Bright straw-green; vividly demonstrates that unoaked Chardonnay can fire the imagination and the palate (just as Chablis can); green apple, lime, white peach flesh and skin, and wondrous acidity. 100 dozen made. Screwcap. 12.5% alc. **Rating** 95 **To** 2023 $50

Tumbarumba Chardonnay 2013 Made from grapes grown on the Maragle and Courabyra vineyards. It's a gorgeous Chardonnay. Complete. Texture, zip, flavour and length. Lemon curd, stone fruits, spice, fennel and cedar, with lengthy flavours of grapefruit and toasted meal setting sail on the finish. Screwcap. 13% alc. **Rating** 95 **To** 2021 $50 CM

Hilltops Syrah 2013 Bright crimson-purple, it has a highly fragrant and expressive bouquet of red and black cherries, blood plums and spice; the medium-bodied palate is supple, long and perfectly balanced, fresh acidity and fine tannins the staples for a long life. Screwcap. 13.5% alc. **Rating** 95 **To** 2033 $50

The Tumblong Syrah 2013 You could measure this wine's spiciness in volts. It's charged with black pepper, cured meats, crushed leaves and baked earth notes. Savoury plus. Perfumed too. There's a cranberried, raspberried, plummy fruitiness gliding beneath the riot of treble. The finish is long, sinewy and dry. Quite stunning. Screwcap. 13.5% alc. **Rating** 95 **To** 2024 $30 CM ✪

The Barton Syrah 2013 Sourced from a single vineyard on the Barton Highway. All French oak, none of it new. Characterised by five spice and a mix of black/white pepper notes on a pure, plush bed of black cherried fruit. Classic Canberra Shiraz/Syrah. Mid-weight and colour but full of conviction on both the nose and the palate. Screwcap. 13.5% alc. **Rating** 95 **To** 2026 $30 CM ✪

94 Block Syrah 2013 Lightish crimson colour; riddled with white pepper; savoury first and fruity second, though the silk of the cherry/plum flavours here is captivating in itself. There's almost a cranberried tanginess to this wine; it's certainly lively. Fennel, cured meat and assorted dry spice notes slowly build an impression of significant complexity. It's not a heavy wine in any way but its premium quality is certain. Screwcap. 13.3% alc. **Rating** 95 **To** 2028 $100 CM

Museum Release Canberra Riesling 2010 Rating 94 **To** 2021 $30 CM ✪
The Long Road Chardonnay 2013 Rating 94 **To** 2021 $27 CM ✪
Courabyra Pinot Noir 2014 Rating 94 **To** 2022 $35 CM
Canberra Syrah 2013 Rating 94 **To** 2028 $60 CM

Edenmae Estate Wines ★★★☆

7 Miller Street, Springton, SA 5235 **Region** Eden Valley
T (08) 8568 2098 **www.**edenmae.com.au **Open** Fri–Sun 10–5
Winemaker David Redhead **Est.** 2007 **Dozens** 1800 **Vyds** 12ha

In 2006 David and Michelle Redhead moved from Melbourne to the Barossa, thence moving to work in various parts of the world but always returning to the Barossa. They purchased a 36ha property on the southernmost crest of the Eden Valley, long known as Holmes Estate Wines, abandoned for three years. Hard work has restored it to its former glory, with tree lots, dams and open areas for alpaca, lambs, ponies, geese and hens, and it is managed on organic principles. The varied nature of the property lends itself to farm stay, which is one of its attractions. There are 4ha each of riesling and shiraz, and 2ha each of pinot noir and cabernet sauvignon, most around 40 years old, with some 10-year-old shiraz and 30-year-old pinot.

ΨΨΨΨ **Single Vineyard Eden Valley Pinot Noir 2013** Incredible colour for a Pinot Noir. Dark purple black with corresponding licorice and black-berried fruit flavours, almost tending towards jam. It's quite delicious, if hardly at all varietal. Screwcap. 14.5% alc. **Rating** 89 **To** 2020 $28 CM

1847 | Yaldara Wines   ★★★★☆

PO Box 919, Rowland Flat, SA 5352 **Region** Barossa Valley
T (08) 8524 5328 **www**.eighteenfortyseven.com **Open** By appt
Winemaker Derek Fitzgerald **Est.** 1996 **Dozens** 50 000 **Vyds** 53.9ha
1847 is wholly owned by Treasure Valley Wines Pty Ltd, which is Chinese-owned. The year is that when Barossa pioneer Johann Gramp planted his first vines in the region. There is in fact no other connection between Gramp and the business he established with that of 1847 Wines. It (1847 Wines) has 80ha of estate vineyards in the general vicinity of the original plantings by Johann Gramp. Derek Fitzgerald became winemaker in 2012, after eight vintages at Thorn-Clarke Wines and one at Robert Oatley Vineyards in Mudgee. A 1000-tonne winery was built for the '14 vintage, handling the core production destined to sell at $35 a bottle or more, together with new varieties and blends. This will be underpinned by the acquisition of Chateau Yaldara in '14 providing a major face and massively enhanced production facilities. Exports to China.

ΨΨΨΨΨ **Pappy's Barossa Valley Cabernet Sauvignon 2012** '12 was a particularly good vintage for cabernet in the Barossa Valley (joining a throng of regions and varieties through SA). It has a purity and a balance that can only be achieved in stellar vintages, cassis a fluid line running the length of the tongue and into the aftertaste. Cork. 14.8% alc. **Rating** 95 **To** 2037 $35 ✪

ΨΨΨΨῈ **Home Block Barossa Valley Petit Verdot 2012** **Rating** 90 **To** 2032 $35

Ekhidna   ★★★★★

Cnr Kangarilla Road/Foggo Road, McLaren Vale, SA 5171 **Region** McLaren Vale
T (08) 8323 8496 **www**.ekhidnawines.com.au **Open** 7 days 11–5
Winemaker Matthew Rechner **Est.** 2001 **Dozens** 3500
Matt Rechner entered the wine industry in 1988, spending most of the years since at Tatachilla in McLaren Vale, starting as laboratory technician and finishing as operations manager. Frustrated by the constraints of large winery practice, he decided to strike out on his own in 2001 via the virtual winery option. His long experience has meant he is able to buy grapes from high-quality producers. Exports to China.

ΨΨΨΨΨ **Rarefied McLaren Vale Shiraz 2012** Matured in French barriques (10% new) for over 24 months, a completely justified time, for the colour is still deep, the bouquet and palate positively luxuriant, with seductive black fruits revelling in the combined impact of McLaren Vale dark chocolate, oak and ripe tannins. Screwcap. 14.5% alc. **Rating** 97 **To** 2042 $90 ✪

ΨΨΨΨΨ **Linchpin McLaren Vale Shiraz 2013** Matured in new (20%) and used oak. Bright, deep crimson-purple; the region and variety walk hand in hand on the velvety medium to full-bodied palate, the finish emphatic, but in a remarkably silky and fresh way. Screwcap. 14.5% alc. **Rating** 95 **To** 2038 $40

McLaren Vale GSM 2014 Equal amounts of the varieties were matured in used French and American barriques. This is a blasphemously good $20 wine, blowing 90% of GSMs over $20 out of the value for money water; it has intensity, grace, glistening red fruits and fine tannins. It's no sin to drink it here and now, but it won't fall over any time soon. Screwcap. 14.5% alc. **Rating** 95 **To** 2024 $20 **○**

♥♥♥♥♡ **McLaren Vale Shiraz 2013 Rating** 90 **To** 2028 $23

Elderton ★★★★★

3–5 Tanunda Road, Nuriootpa, SA 5355 **Region** Barossa Valley
T (08) 8568 7878 **www**.eldertonwines.com.au **Open** Mon–Fri 10–5, w'ends, hols 11–4
Winemaker Richard Langford **Est.** 1982 **Dozens** 45 000 **Vyds** 75ha
The founding Ashmead family, with mother Lorraine supported by sons Allister and Cameron, continues to impress with their wines. The original source was 30ha of fully mature shiraz, cabernet sauvignon and merlot on the Barossa floor; subsequently 16ha of Eden Valley vineyards (shiraz, cabernet sauvignon, chardonnay, zinfandel, merlot and roussanne) were incorporated into the business. The Rohrlach Vineyard, with 75-year-old shiraz, is under long-term lease and managed by the Ashmead family. Energetic promotion and marketing in Australia and overseas are paying dividends. Elegance and balance are the keys to these wines. Exports to all major markets.

♥♥♥♥♥ **Command Single Vineyard Barossa Shiraz 2012** From a vineyard planted in 1894, picked in five small parcels over 4 weeks; part fermented in open fermenters, part concluding its fermentation in new American and French puncheons. Command indeed; elegant, but brooking no argument, the X-factor of the fruit at once obvious, yet undefinable; certain it is that its balance and depth are beyond approach, the oak and tannins seamlessly joining the fruit. Screwcap. 14.5% alc. **Rating** 97 **To** 2050 $110 **○**
Ashmead Single Vineyard Barossa Cabernet Sauvignon 2013 From 70yo vines, hand-picked, open-fermented, matured for 18 months in French oak. The quality of the fruit shines through with absolute varietal conviction, bringing cassis onto centre stage, quality oak and well-managed tannins the last touches. Screwcap. 14% alc. **Rating** 97 **To** 2045 $100 **○**

♥♥♥♥♥ **Neil Ashmead Grand Tourer Barossa Valley Shiraz 2013** From a 50yo single estate block; open-fermented in wax-lined vats; finished fermentation in new French hogsheads, held on gross lees for 15 months. Made in a very different idiom from the other '13 Elderton Shirazs: lighter in colour, body and red fruit profile. Screwcap. 14% alc. **Rating** 95 **To** 2028 $75
High Altitude Barossa Shiraz 2012 Matured in used French and American oak for 12 months. The lovely fruit expression on the medium-bodied palate explains why Elderton purchased this vineyard. The wine caresses the mouth, the flavours of plum, red and black cherry running through to the finish and aftertaste, tannins and oak barely visible. Screwcap. 14% alc. **Rating** 95 **To** 2027 $24 **○**
Western Ridge Barossa Valley Grenache Carignan 2013 The Helbeg Vineyard was acquired in '10, and included the grenache (planted '69) and carignan (planted 1915). The light, clear colour reflects the varietal make-up, the moderate alcohol (in the grenache field normally 15–16.5%) reflects an elegant wine that leaves no doubt about its varietal foundations, and is a pleasure to drink right now. Screwcap. 14.5% alc. **Rating** 95 **To** 2020 $55
Barossa Cabernet Sauvignon 2013 Estate-grown vines 35–50yo; matured for 22 months in French hogsheads. Quite apart from the rarity of cabernet vines of this age, the viticultural skill in managing growth through to picking at this baume/alcohol level is the cornerstone for a strongly varietal Cabernet treated with utmost respect in the winery. Screwcap. 14% alc. **Rating** 95 **To** 2035 $34 **○**
Ode to Lorraine Barossa Cabernet Sauvignon Shiraz Merlot 2012
A 58/31/11% blend from vines planted between 1914 and '98, matured for 24 months in French and American oak. Focused winemaking has corralled all the disparate parcels onto an elegant, medium-bodied palate, with a gently

savoury lining to the predominantly purple and black fruits. Screwcap. 14.5% alc.
Rating 95 **To** 2032 $55

Barossa Shiraz 2013 Open-fermented in waxed concrete vats with header boards, matured in American puncheons for 22 months. Full-bodied, but doesn't lose balance; black fruits have soaked up such of the new oak (if any) as was used, the end result generous complexity. Screwcap. 14.5% alc. **Rating** 94 **To** 2035 $34

Eden Valley Riesling 2014 Rating 94 **To** 2029 $24 **❍**

Greenock One Barossa Valley Shiraz 2013 Rating 94 **To** 2033 $34

Greenock Two Barossa Valley Shiraz Mourvedre Grenache 2013
Rating 94 **To** 2028 $34

High Altitude Barossa Cabernet Sauvignon 2014 Rating 94 **To** 2029 $24 **❍**

Eldorado Road

1317 Eldorado Road, Eldorado, Vic 3678 (postal) **Region** North East Victoria Zone
T (03) 5725 1698 **www**.eldoradoroad.com.au **Open** Not
Winemaker Paul Dahlenburg, Lauretta Schulz **Est.** 2010 **Dozens** 600 **Vyds** 4ha
Paul Dahlenburg (nicknamed Bear), Lauretta Schulz (Laurie) and their children have leased a 2ha block of shiraz planted in the 1890s with rootlings supplied from France (doubtless grafted) in the wake of phylloxera's devastation of the Glenrowan and Rutherglen plantings. Bear and Laurie knew about the origins of the vineyard, which was in a state of serious decline after years of neglect. The owners of the vineyard were aware of its historic importance and were more than happy to lease it. Four years of tireless work in the vineyard, reconstructing the old vines, has finally resulted in tiny amounts of exceptionally good shiraz; they have also planted a small area of nero d'Avola and durif.

ΨΨΨΨΨ Onyx Durif 2013 Open-fermented, matured in French oak. Deep crimson-purple; it's the magic of durif that it can be grown in Rutherglen, have alcohol near 15%, and still have a savoury elegance to the black fruits of its medium to full-bodied palate, its tannins perfectly balanced and integrated. Screwcap. 14.9% alc. **Rating** 95 **To** 2035 $35 **❍**

Eldredge   ★★★★☆

Spring Gully Road, Clare, SA 5453 **Region** Clare Valley
T (08) 8842 3086 **www**.eldredge.com.au **Open** 7 days 11–5
Winemaker Leigh Eldredge **Est.** 1993 **Dozens** 5000 **Vyds** 20.9ha
Leigh and Karen Eldredge have established their winery and cellar door in the Sevenhill Ranges at an altitude of 500m above Watervale. The mature estate vineyard is planted to shiraz, cabernet sauvignon, merlot, riesling, sangiovese and malbec. Both the Rieslings and red wines have had considerable wine show success in recent years. Exports to the UK, the US, Canada, Singapore and China.

ΨΨΨΨΨ The Reserve Clare Valley Malbec 2013 Incredible wine. Monumentally tannic, and if that's not your thing, then look away now. Fresh, bright, succulent and in no way (otherwise) overdone, the cherry/plum/leather/mint-like fruit crowing its quality in the liveliest of voices. A Malbec for Nebbiolo lovers, perhaps, complete with floral nuances. For those of a certain persuasion, the $30 asking price is almost daylight robbery. Screwcap. 14% alc. **Rating** 96 **To** 2035 $30 CM **❍**

Blue Chip Clare Valley Shiraz 2013 Follows the script established for this wine decades ago: ripe, but not overripe fruit and 18 months' maturation in new American oak, it abounds with black fruits, plum cake and mocha neatly balanced by firm, gently savoury tannins. Screwcap. 14.8% alc. **Rating** 94 **To** 2028 $30 **❍**

Gilt Edge Clare Valley Shiraz 2010 Cellar door only. Matured in French oak for 40 months. Grown on the estate's oldest vines. It's a warm, slightly soupy red with asphalt, chocolate, spearmint, lavender and porty blackberry flavours pouring through the palate. Alcohol is obvious, but the flood of sweet fruit is so significant it more or less carries it. Tannin flexes through the finish. Rich, and then some. Screwcap. 14.6% alc. **Rating** 94 **To** 2030 $75 CM

RL Clare Valley Cabernet Sauvignon 2012 Deep crimson-purple; includes some malbec and shiraz; matured in a mix of French and American oak. The quality of the vintage shines through this medium to full-bodied Cabernet, filling the palate with black fruits and berries, relegating tannins to a back seat role, the oak likewise. WAK screwcap. 14.5% alc. **Rating** 94 **To** 2037 $30 ✪

 JD Clare Valley Sangiovese 2012 Rating 93 **To** 2027 $25 ✪
 Clare Valley Riesling 2014 Rating 91 **To** 2024 $18 ✪

Eldridge Estate of Red Hill ★★★★★

120 Arthurs Seat Road, Red Hill, Vic 3937 **Region** Mornington Peninsula
T 0414 758 960 **www**.eldridge-estate.com.au **Open** Mon–Fri 12–4, w'ends & hols 11–5
Winemaker David Lloyd **Est.** 1985 **Dozens** 800 **Vyds** 2.8ha
The Eldridge Estate vineyard was purchased by David and (the late) Wendy Lloyd in 1995. Major retrellising work has been undertaken, changing to Scott Henry, and all the wines are estate-grown and made. David has also planted several Dijon-selected pinot noir clones (114, 115 and 777), which have been contributing since 2004; likewise the Dijon chardonnay clone 96. Attention to detail permeates all he does in vineyard and winery. Exports to the US.

 Clonal Blend Pinot Noir 2013 A 6-clone blend that wastes no time in establishing its authority. Finely structured and intensely fruited, the bouquet and palate are joined at the hip; gently savoury red fruits have a fine web of tannins, boding well for its long-term future. Screwcap. 14% alc. **Rating** 96 **To** 2030 $75 ✪
 Single Clone 96 Chardonnay 2013 There is no question that clone 96 adds a dimension to the structure and flavour of the fruit, grapefruit edging in front of the stone fruit and melon contributions; as with its sibling, the oak management has been faultless. Screwcap. 13.5% alc. **Rating** 95 **To** 2025 $45
 Pinot Noir 2013 Has the brilliant, deep colour of all Eldridge's '13 Pinots; powerful, with black cherry, plum and some briar interwoven with the supple mouthfeel; has a pleasing touch of forest on the finish. Screwcap. 14% alc. **Rating** 95 **To** 2025 $55
 Gamay 2013 Deep but bright purple-crimson; waste not, want not: every aroma and flavour compound has been retained, making this dark berry-fruited wine as good as any Australian Gamay I have tasted. It is reminiscent of some 1947 Beaujolais I tasted in the late '60s. Screwcap. 13.5% alc. **Rating** 95 **To** 2025 $38
 Single Clone Pinot Noir 2013 MV6. Red and black cherries to the fore on the very fragrant bouquet; a supple, bordering on velvety, palate with a sinuous mouthfeel, and great length and balance. The most welcoming of three Pinots and a Gamay made by Eldridge in '13. Screwcap. 14% alc. **Rating** 95 **To** 2023 $55
 Chardonnay 2013 A very well made wine, tightly focused and detailed, fruit, oak and acid harmoniously singing the same tune; the fruit flavours cover both stone fruit and citrus, reflecting astute handling of the barrel fermentation (and choice of oak). Screwcap. 13.5% alc. **Rating** 94 **To** 2023 $40

Elgee Park ★★★★★

24 Junction Road, Merricks North, Vic 3926 **Region** Mornington Peninsula
T (03) 5989 7338 **www**.elgeeparkwines.com.au **Open** At Merricks General Wine Store
Winemaker Geraldine McFaul (Contract) **Est.** 1972 **Dozens** 1600 **Vyds** 4.4ha
The pioneer of the Mornington Peninsula in its 20th-century rebirth, owned by Baillieu Myer and family. The vineyard is planted to riesling, chardonnay, viognier (some of the oldest vines in Australia), pinot gris, pinot noir, merlot and cabernet sauvignon. The vineyard is set in a picturesque natural amphitheatre with a northerly aspect looking out across Port Phillip Bay towards the Melbourne skyline. A representative range of wines was not received for this edition, but the rating has been maintained.

 Family Reserve Mornington Peninsula Pinot Noir 2012 Light, but bright and fresh colour; an elegant Pinot with dark cherry and savoury/brambly/forest floor flavours making equal contributions; it has good length, line and balance. Screwcap. 13% alc. **Rating** 94 **To** 2019 $45

Ellender Estate ★★★☆

Leura Glen, 260 Green Gully Road, Glenlyon, Vic 3461 **Region** Macedon Ranges
T (03) 5348 7785 www.ellenderwines.com.au **Open** W'ends & public hols 11–5
Winemaker Graham Ellender **Est.** 1996 **Dozens** 420 **Vyds** 3.75ha
Graham and Jenny Ellender have established pinot noir (2.7ha), chardonnay (1ha), sauvignon blanc (0.2ha) and pinot gris (0.1ha). Wine style is restricted to those varieties true to the ultra-cool climate of the Macedon Ranges. Exports to the United Arab Emirates.

ᵀᵀᵀᵀᵀ **Macedon Ranges Chardonnay 2013** Nicely wrought wine; white peach, nectarine and grapefruit have equal billing, the finish lively and juicy, the oak subtle. There may be a grain or two of residual sugar, but that's of small moment. Screwcap. 12% alc. **Rating** 92 **To** 2020 $27

ᵀᵀᵀᵀ **Macedon Ranges Pinot Noir 2012 Rating** 89 **To** 2022 $45

Ellis Wines ★★★☆

3025 Heathcote–Rochester Road, Colbinabbin, Vic 3559 (postal) **Region** Heathcote
T 0401 290 315 www.elliswines.com.au **Open** Not
Winemaker Guy Rathjen **Est.** 1998 **Dozens** 700 **Vyds** 54.6ha
Bryan and Joy Ellis own this family business, daughter Raylene Flanagan is the sales manager, and seven of the vineyard blocks are named after family members. For the first 10 years the Ellises were content to sell the grapes to a range of distinguished producers. However, since then a growing portion of the crop has been vinified.

ᵀᵀᵀᵀᵀ **Premium Heathcote Shiraz 2012** Estate-grown, matured for 14 months in new and 1yo French barriques, two selected for this wine. An alternative face for Heathcote, giving no hint of its alcohol; clear, fresh colour, the bouquet and light to medium-bodied palate have spicy/savoury red and black fruits at play, the finish well balanced. Screwcap. 14.9% alc. **Rating** 94 **To** 2025 $30

ᵀᵀᵀᵀᵀ **Signature Label Heathcote Shiraz 2012 Rating** 92 **To** 2027 $24 ❂

Elmswood Estate ★★★★☆

75 Monbulk–Seville Road, Seville, Vic 3139 **Region** Yarra Valley
T (03) 5964 3015 www.elmswoodestate.com.au **Open** W'ends 12–5
Winemaker Han Tao Lau **Est.** 1981 **Dozens** 3000 **Vyds** 8.5ha
Planted to cabernet sauvignon, chardonnay, merlot, sauvignon blanc, pinot noir, shiraz and riesling on the red volcanic soils of the far southern side of the Yarra Valley. The cellar door operates from 'The Pavilion', a fully enclosed glass room situated on a ridge above the vineyard, with 180° views of the Upper Yarra Valley. It seats up to 110 guests, and is a popular wedding venue. Exports to Hong Kong and China.

ᵀᵀᵀᵀᵀ **Yarra Valley Sauvignon Blanc 2014** Fermented in French oak, but its quality rests squarely on the quality of the fruit. It's exemplary, bordering on exciting. Musky sweet oak leads into citrus, grapefruit, passionfruit and lime zest notes. Sweet perfume and flavour from oak is noticeable, indeed, but the cut and drive of this wine are excellent. Screwcap. 13.3% alc. **Rating** 94 **To** 2016 $25 CM ❂
Yarra Valley Chardonnay 2014 Good intensity. Nectarine, apple and pear flavour with a zingy, limey burst to close. There's a fruit sweetness here but there's also plenty of drive and length. Oak has been sympathetically handled. Makes you sit up and take notice. Screwcap. 13.2% alc. **Rating** 94 **To** 2020 $30 CM ❂

ᵀᵀᵀᵀᵀ **Yarra Valley Pinot Noir 2013 Rating** 93 **To** 2020 $30 CM
Yarra Valley Cabernet Sauvignon 2013 Rating 93 **To** 2025 $35 CM
Yarra Valley Chardonnay 2013 Rating 92 **To** 2019 $30 CM
Yarra Valley Riesling 2014 Rating 90 **To** 2017 $25 CM

Eloquesta

10 Stroud Avenue, Dubbo, NSW 2830 (postal) **Region** Mudgee
T 0458 525 899 **www**.eloquesta.com.au **Open** Not
Winemaker Stuart Olsen **Est.** 2008 **Dozens** 1200 **Vyds** 6ha

The full name of the business is Eloquesta by Stuart Olsen, Stuart being the sole owner and winemaker. He is a trained scientist and teacher, gaining winemaking experience since 2000, variously working at Cirillo Estate, Lowe Family Wines and Torbreck, as well as at a German winery in the Rheinhessen. His aim in Mudgee is to make the two varieties that he believes grow consistently well year after year in the cooler foothills of Mudgee and Rylstone: Shiraz and Petit Verdot, with an occasional bucket of Viognier.

Mudgee Shiraz Petit Verdot 2011 Whole bunch-fermented. Aged in multi-region oak. Bottled with minimal sulphur. It's a perfumed, lively wine with a bit of the 'come hither' about it. It's seductive. Oak has been reined right back with this release, allowing dark berry and floral notes free flight. Spice notes are the icing on the cake. Screwcap. 14.5% alc. **Rating** 91 **To** 2020 $32 CM

A Boy with Fruit No.1 NV **Rating** 89 **To** 2018 $28 CM

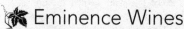 Eminence Wines **NR**

234 Burders Lane, Whitlands, Vic 3733 **Region** King Valley
T 0433 277 211 **www**.eminencewines.com.au **Open** Not
Winemaker Contract **Est.** 2008 **Dozens** 1000 **Vyds** 16ha

In 1998 David and Sharon Burder planted 8ha of chardonnay (clones I10V1 and 76), 5ha of pinot noir (clones 114, 115 and MV6), 2ha of pinot gris and 1ha of pinot meunier, backed by 5-year grape supply agreements with Yalumba and Brown Brothers. Daughter Clare began her wine life working in vineyards and cellar doors in the King Valley, thereafter in Melbourne at The Prince Wine Store. In 2008 she started Eminence by working with local winemakers to produce Pinot Gris, Pinot Meunier, Rose and Pinot Noir under the Le Peche Mignon brand, and vintage sparkling under The Assembly brand. The wines are all made at the King Valley Wines Cooperative, where Clare can call upon the winemakers for technical help. In the meantime, Tony Jordan has come on board to help Clare assemble the sparkling wines. At 870m, the vineyard is one of the highest, if not the highest, in Australia, and wind and rain can wreak havoc. She has '12 and '13 in bottle, maturing on cork, and plans to release an NV Pinot Meunier Brut in the next 18 months. Further out, a cellar door and basic winery feature in a 5-year plan. As well as making the wines, she has been front and central in distribution (now with Firebrand in Melbourne) and also teaches wine appreciation courses through her business, The Humble Tumbler (www.thehumbletumbler.com.au).

Eperosa

24 Maria Street, Tanunda, SA 5352 **Region** Barossa Valley
T 0428 111 121 **www**.eperosa.com.au **Open** By appt
Winemaker Brett Grocke **Est.** 2005 **Dozens** 800 **Vyds** 9.1ha

Eperosa owner Brett Grocke qualified as a viticulturist in 2001, and, through Grocke Viticulture, consults and provides technical services to over 200ha of vineyards spread across the Barossa Valley, Eden Valley, Adelaide Hills, Riverland, Langhorne Creek and Hindmarsh Valley. He is ideally placed to secure small parcels of organically managed grapes, hand-picked, whole bunch-fermented and foot-stomped, and neither filtered nor fined. The wines are of impeccable quality – the use of high-quality, perfectly inserted, corks will allow the wines to reach their full maturity decades hence.

Elevation Eden Valley Shiraz 2013 From three Eden Valley vineyards, open-fermented, foot-stomped, plunged, wild yeast-fermented, on skins 14 days, new and used French oak 12+ months. 105 dozen made. Glory be, a wine of rare purity and intensity, a Brideshead Revisited style that slowly, but inexorably unrolls its tapestry of black fruits, gleaming beads of juice, and fine-grained tannins. Screwcap. 13% alc. **Rating** 97 **To** 2053 $40 ✪

YYYYY **L.R.C. Greenock Barossa Valley Shiraz 2013** From a single boundary row, open-fermented, wild yeast-fermented, in one French oak barrel, includes 1% of riesling and 0.5% of mataro, 33 dozen made. A miniature painting, every tiny detail faithfully recorded, provides a picture of this single row of vines with a solitary riesling and a random scatter of mataro vines. A living treasure from the Barossa, picked at the perfect moment. Cork. 13.3% alc. **Rating** 96 **To** 2053 $45 **☉**
Stonegarden Eden Valley Grenache 2013 From one of Australia's oldest vineyards, planted in 1858, this from bush-vine grenache planted in 1860 – from 1858 to 1962 Oscar Seppelt and his descendants owned and ran the now decayed winery, and the (now) rehabilitated vineyard. Grenache doesn't come bigger than this, the alcohol woven into the fabric of the palate, with its glossy black and red fruits. Cork. 15.4% alc. **Rating** 96 **To** 2043 $80
Synthesis Barossa Valley Mataro Grenache Shiraz 2013 47% Barossa Valley mataro, 45% Barossa Valley grenache and 8% Eden Valley shiraz; open-fermented for 14 days, matured in new and used French oak on full lees. Excellent colour; a vividly fragrant bouquet and equally expressive palate, supple, silky and endlessly satisfying, drawing saliva each time it is retasted. 200 dozen made. Cork. 13.2% alc. **Rating** 96 **To** 2033 $30 **☉**
Totality Barossa Valley Mataro Shiraz 2013 The Barossa Valley mataro (78%) fits so seamlessly with the Eden Valley shiraz (22%) it is nigh on impossible to engage in any useful deconstruction of either flavour or structure. Despite its (typical) modest alcohol, this has more raw power than the other wines in the portfolio, the tannins seamlessly folded into the starless night of black fruits. 203 dozen made. Cork. 13.5% alc. **Rating** 94 **To** 2038 $35

Eppalock Ridge   ★★★★☆

6 Niemann Street, Bendigo, Vic 3550 (postal) **Region** Heathcote
T 0409 957 086 **www**.eppalockridge.com.au **Open** Not
Winemaker Don Lewis, Narelle King, Rod Hourigan **Est.** 1979 **Dozens** 3000
Sue and Rod Hourigan gave up their careers in fabric design and television production at the ABC in 1976 to chase their passion for fine wine. This took them first to McLaren Vale, with Sue working in the celebrated Barn Restaurant, and Rod starting at d'Arenberg; over the next three hectic years both worked vintages at Pirramimma and Coriole while undertaking the first short course for winemakers at what is now CSU. They then moved to Redesdale in '79 and established Eppalock Ridge on a basalt hilltop overlooking Lake Eppalock. The 10ha of shiraz, cabernet sauvignon, cabernet franc and merlot are capable of producing wines of high quality, 2013 compelling evidence of that ability.

YYYYY **Heathcote Shiraz 2013** Sturdy, dense and inky. No prisoners taken. Concentrated plum, blackberry jam, toast, roasted nuts and gum leaf flavours. Needs a few years but has a long life ahead of it. For all its might, it's beautifully put together. Screwcap. 15% alc. **Rating** 95 **To** 2028 $30 CM **☉**
Susan's Selection Shiraz Cabernet Merlot 2013 Warm with alcohol but terrific depth of fruit. Dense plum and blackcurrant with side serves of mint, olive and choc-cream. Framework of tannin both keeps it tidy and adds to the impression of heft. Serve with protein. Screwcap. 15.5% alc. **Rating** 94 **To** 2028 $25 CM **☉**

Ernest Hill Wines   ★★★★☆

307 Wine Country Drive, Nulkaba, NSW 2325 **Region** Hunter Valley
T (02) 4991 4418 **www**.ernesthillwines.com.au **Open** 7 days 10–5
Winemaker Mark Woods **Est.** 1999 **Dozens** 6000 **Vyds** 12ha
This is part of a vineyard originally planted in the early 1970s by Harry Tulloch for Seppelt Wines; it was later renamed Pokolbin Creek Vineyard, and later still (in '99) the Wilson family purchased the upper (hill) part of the vineyard, and renamed it Ernest Hill. It is now planted to semillon, shiraz, chardonnay, verdelho, traminer, merlot, tempranillo and chambourcin. Exports to the US and China.

ΨΨΨΨΨ William Henry Reserve Premium Hunter Shiraz 2013 Bright crimson-purple; absolutely deserves the Reserve name; the bouquet and palate reflect maturation in French oak for 12 months, but it is still the fruit of the medium-bodied palate that gives the wine its special mouthfeel, and an array of supple cherry, plum and blackberry flavours; fresh earth and sweet leather give regional authenticity. Lovely wine. Diam. 13.2% alc. **Rating** 95 **To** 2033 $50

Alexander Reserve Premium Hunter Chardonnay 2014 Similar to Chicken Shed Chardonnay in many ways, except new French oak was used for partial barrel fermentation and maturation. Fresh fruit flavours are the key, in turn derived from old vines. Screwcap. 13.5% alc. **Rating** 94 **To** 2020 $35

ΨΨΨΨΨ Chicken Shed Chardonnay 2014 **Rating** 92 **To** 2018 $25 ✪

Ernest Schuetz Estate Wines ★★★★

Edgel Lane, Mudgee, NSW 2850 **Region** Mudgee
T 0402 326 612 **www**.ernestschuetzestate.com.au **Open** W'ends 10.30–4.30
Winemaker Jacob Stein **Est.** 2003 **Dozens** 4300 **Vyds** 4.1ha

Ernest Schuetz's involvement in the wine industry started in 1988 at the age of 21. Working in various liquor outlets and as a sales representative for Miranda Wines, McGuigan Simeon and, later, Watershed Wines, gave him an in-depth understanding of all aspects of the wine market. In 2003 he and wife Joanna purchased the Arronvale Vineyard (first planted in '91), at an altitude of 530m. When the Schuetzs acquired the vineyard it was planted to merlot, shiraz and cabernet sauvignon, and they have since grafted 1ha to riesling, pinot blanc, pinot gris, zinfandel and nebbiolo. The estate plantings are complemented by other varieties purchased from other growers.

ΨΨΨΨΨ Family Reserve Mudgee Black Syrah 2012 Hand-picked from two vineyards, matured for 16 months in American and Hungarian oak (30% new), 160 dozen made. Has delicious red fruits on the bouquet, changing gear on the palate, with black fruits joining the party, supported by finely detailed tannins; the oak sits well, more so than expected. Screwcap. 13.5% alc. **Rating** 94 **To** 2030 $30 ✪

ΨΨΨΨΨ Terra X Semillon Sauvignon Blanc 2014 **Rating** 91 **To** 2017 $18 ✪
Saint Rose Mudgee Dry Rose 2013 **Rating** 91 **To** 2016 $28
Family Reserve Black Merlot 2012 **Rating** 91 **To** 2020 $30
Saint Isabel Chardonnay Pinot Blanc Gris 2013 **Rating** 90 **To** 2023 $38

Espier Estate ★★★☆

Room 1208, 401 Docklands Drive, Docklands, Vic 3008 **Region** South Eastern Australia
T (03) 9670 4317 **www**.jnrwine.com **Open** Mon–Fri 9–5
Winemaker Sam Brewer **Est.** 2007 **Dozens** 25 000

This is the venture of Robert Luo and Jacky Lin, owners of JNR Wine Group, which in turn owns Espier. Sam Brewer has worked for Southcorp and De Bortoli, and in the US and China, and has been closely linked with the business since its establishment. The principal focus of the business is export to Asian countries, with China and Hong Kong the main areas. Much of the volume is linked to contract-made wines under the Espier Estate label, with prices ranging from entry level to those befitting premium regional styles. Heathcote is the focus for the latter, the entry to mid-level sourced from across South Eastern Australia. Exports to Asia.

ΨΨΨΨΨ Feel Reserve Padthaway Shiraz 2012 Alive with dark fruit flavour. Choc-mint, smooth and generous, melts into ripe blackberry, asphalt and plum. Full-bodied but doesn't feel over the top. Very little tannin to speak of. The flavours just ooze on through. Cork. 14.5% alc. **Rating** 92 **To** 2020 $28 CM

ΨΨΨΨ Feel Reserve Heathcote Shiraz 2013 **Rating** 89 **To** 2020 $28
Old Vine Reserve Shiraz 2008 **Rating** 88 **To** 2019 $25 CM

Estate 807 ★★★★★

807 Scotsdale Road, Denmark, WA 6333 **Region** Denmark
T (08) 9840 9027 **www**.estate807.com.au **Open** Thurs–Sun 10–4
Winemaker James Kellie, Mike Garland **Est.** 1998 **Dozens** 1500 **Vyds** 4.2ha
Dr Stephen Junk and Ola Tylestam purchased Estate 807 in 2009. Stephen was a respected embryologist in IVF, while Ola came from a financial background. They chose the property due to its good range of pinot noir and chardonnay clones (there are also plantings of cabernet sauvignon and sauvignon blanc). Farm animals are used in the vineyard: chickens and ducks eat the pests and sheep and alpacas provide manure and keep the vineyard neat and tidy.

ΨΨΨΨΨ **Frankland River Riesling 2014** A very good example of Great Southern Riesling's ability to marry crisp, crunchy acidity with fruit flavours that seem sweet despite being totally dry; the more traditional areas of SA don't have this structure. I love the poise of this wine. Screwcap. 11.5% alc. **Rating** 95 **To** 2029 $23 **◐**
Reserve Chardonnay 2014 The bouquet reflects barrel fermentation, while the very elegant and expressive palate runs through the full range of white peach, nectarine, melon and grapefruit, the oak well balanced and integrated. A bird's song, not a big bass drum. Screwcap. 13.3% alc. **Rating** 95 **To** 2020 $29 **◐**
Mount Barker Riesling 2014 A fragrant bouquet leads into a palate that puts lime, lemon, green apple and a touch of citrus peel into play. The extra degree of alcohol (compared to the Frankland River version) gives the wine more depth, but the length remains the same. Screwcap. 12.5% alc. **Rating** 94 **To** 2027 $24 **◐**
Sauvignon Blanc 2014 The back label caused me to sneer, with its seven fruit flavours, until I tasted the wine, which is indeed endowed with a seductive array of flavours ranging through citrus, stone fruit and tropical; best of all, it finishes fresh and lively. Screwcap. 12.5% alc. **Rating** 94 **To** 2017 $20 **◐**
Pixie's Sweet Riesling 2014 Lively and vibrantly fresh, with lime juice and passionfruit, lightly sweetened, acidity running the show. Sure to age well, changing character as it does. Screwcap. 10.5% alc. **Rating** 94 **To** 2024 $20 **◐**

ΨΨΨΨΨ **Reserve Pinot Noir 2013 Rating** 92 **To** 2021 $30
Peb's Red Pinot Noir 2013 Rating 90 **To** 2018 $25
Reserve Cabernet Sauvignon 2012 Rating 90 **To** 2023 $30

Evans & Tate ★★★★★

Cnr Metricup Road/Caves Road, Wilyabrup, WA 6280 **Region** Margaret River
T (08) 9755 6244 **www**.evansandtate.com.au **Open** 7 days 10.30–5
Winemaker Matthew Byrne, Lachlan McDonald **Est.** 1970 **Dozens** NFP **Vyds** 12.3ha
The 40-year history of Evans & Tate has been one of constant change and, for decades, expansion, acquiring large wineries in SA and NSW. For a series of reasons, nothing to do with the excellent quality of its Margaret River wines, the empire fell apart in 2005; it took an interminable time before McWilliam's finalised its acquisition of the Evans & Tate brand, cellar door and vineyards (and since a part share in the winery) in December '07. Remarkably, wine quality was maintained through the turmoil. Exports to all major markets.

ΨΨΨΨΨ **Redbrook Margaret River Chardonnay 2012** Hand-picked at dawn, the bunches chilled to 5°C, then whole bunch-pressed direct to French puncheons for wild yeast fermentation on full solids. This is one of the most aristocratic Margaret River Chardonnays, more savoury than fruity, but still a panegyric to the variety, finesse and length are its foundations. Screwcap. 13% alc. **Rating** 96 **To** 2025 $45 **◐**
Redbrook Margaret River Chardonnay 2013 Seamless and refined. This is a far more elegant display than is the norm for this label. It's bright and complex with plenty of grapefruit, citrus, pear and apple flavour, a splash of tinned tropical fruits blooming on the finish. Oak and fruit sit hand-in-glove and the lengthy, refreshing trail of fruit flavour extending out through the finish is impressive. Screwcap. 13% alc. **Rating** 95 **To** 2021 $45 CM

Redbrook Margaret River Cabernet Sauvignon 2012 In tiptop form. Classic Cabernet flavours and structure. Blackcurrant, gravel, lead pencil/chocolate, smoky tobacco and bay leaf. Flows more or less effortlessly through the mouth but the undertow of tannin is not insignificant, no matter how deeply sunk into the fruit it is. Persistence more than passes the test. Ticks all the way along the line. Screwcap. 13.9% alc. **Rating** 95 **To** 2032 $45 CM

Breathing Space Margaret River Sauvignon Blanc 2014 A bright, crisp, fresh and lively bouquet and palate precisely reflect the terroir of Margaret River, and its symbiotic union with sauvignon blanc; a delicious wine, even for those whose palates are becoming jaded by the tsunami of Sauvignon Blanc from NZ. Screwcap. 12.5% alc. **Rating** 94 **To** 2016 $19 ✪

Pemberton Chardonnay 2013 A wine of elegant power. It tastes of green melon, grapefruit and apple, with only modest input from spicy oak; it hardly needs the adornment. It's fruity and succulent but exudes a calm authority in the length of its finish. Screwcap. 13.3% alc. **Rating** 94 **To** 2020 $32 CM

Redbrook Margaret River Shiraz 2012 Oak has been reined in over the years though its presence is still no doubt felt; as a positive. Fruit intensity is not an issue here, but it's surprising how elegantly this presents, with blackberries, violets and black cherries pouring through the palate, sweeping trails of firm, grainy tannin along for the ride. It needs time to mellow, but the ingredients are no doubt here. Screwcap. 14% alc. **Rating** 94 **To** 2028 $45 CM

Breathing Space Margaret River Cabernet Sauvignon 2013 Sets the cat among the pigeons: high-quality Margaret River Cabernet is not meant to be sold for $19. This elegant, medium-bodied wine has a great bouquet, and an equally impressive palate with a relaxed mix of black and redcurrant fruit, cedary oak and precisely managed tannins. Screwcap. 14.5% alc. **Rating** 94 **To** 2025 $19 ✪

Margaret River Cabernet Sauvignon 2012 Highly cellarworthy. Strong fruit and strong tannin. Cassis, gum leaf, smoky oak and gravel. Establishes its credentials then settles in for the long, slow haul. It's in dock for now, its tannin coiled, its fruit stacked and stored. It will be many years before we see its best. Screwcap. 14.2% alc. **Rating** 94 **To** 2042 $100 CM

🍷🍷🍷🍷🍷 **Metricup Road Shiraz 2012** Rating 93 To 2022 $24 CM ✪
Metricup Road Semillon Sauvignon Blanc 2013 Rating 92 To 2016 $24 ✪
Metricup Road Cabernet Merlot 2013 Rating 92 To 2025 $24 CM ✪
Margaret River Malbec 2013 Rating 92 To 2021 $36 CM
Karridale Margaret River Chardonnay 2014 Rating 91 To 2019 $28 CM
Breathing Space Cabernet Sauvignon 2012 Rating 91 To 2017 $19 ✪

Evoi Wines   ★★★★★

92 Dunsborough Lakes Drive, Dunsborough, WA 6281 **Region** Margaret River
T 0407 131 080 **www**.evoiwines.com **Open** By appt
Winemaker Nigel Ludlow **Est.** 2006 **Dozens** 8000
NZ-born Nigel Ludlow has a Bachelor of Science in human nutrition, but after a short career as a professional triathlete, he turned his attention to grapegrowing and winemaking, with a graduate diploma in oenology and viticulture from Lincoln University, NZ. Time at Selaks Drylands winery was a stepping stone to Flying Winemaking stints in Hungary, Spain and South Africa, before returning as senior winemaker at Nobilo. He thereafter moved to Vic, finally to Margaret River. It took time for Evoi to take shape, the first vintage of chardonnay made in the lounge room of his house. By 2010 the barrels had been evicted to more conventional storage, and since '14 the wines have been made in leased space at a commercial winery. Quality throughout has been exceptional. Exports to the UK and Hong Kong.

🍷🍷🍷🍷🍷 **Reserve Chardonnay 2013** Hand-picked, whole bunch-pressed, partial wild-yeast and malolactic fermentations in French barriques. The Evoi style is near-unique, its intensity and bright acidity illuminating the layered complexity of the palate; here grapefruit (juice and skin) start the ball rolling, next white peach and nectarine appear, then creamy cashew and fig on the prodigiously long finish Screwcap. 13.5% alc. **Rating** 97 **To** 2023 $52 ✪

ŶŶŶŶŶ Cabernet Sauvignon 2013 Open-fermented, pressed to finish fermentation in French oak. A fine, harmonious and perfectly balanced wine making Cabernet a pleasure, not a duty, to drink. Moreover, you can do this today or in 10 years' time. Screwcap. 14.5% alc. **Rating** 95 **To** 2028 $32 ○

The Satyr Reserve 2012 A blend of cabernet sauvignon, petit verdot, merlot and malbec, with a full-on impact, notwithstanding that the components finished primary fermentation and mlf in French oak, normally softening the tannins; however, the cascade of black fruits will not yield to those tannins, and the long-term future of the wine is assured. Screwcap. 14.5% alc. **Rating** 94 **To** 2037 $49

ŶŶŶŶŶ art by Evoi Sauvignon Semillon 2014 **Rating** 92 **To** 2015 $18 ○

Faber Vineyard   ★★★★★

233 Haddrill Road, Baskerville, WA 6056 **Region** Swan Valley
T (08) 9296 0209 **www**.fabervineyard.com.au **Open** Fri–Sun 11–4
Winemaker John Griffiths **Est.** 1997 **Dozens** 2500 **Vyds** 4.5ha
John Griffiths, former Houghton winemaker, now university lecturer and consultant, teamed with wife Jane Micallef to found Faber Vineyard. They have established shiraz, verdelho (1.5ha each), brown muscat, chardonnay and petit verdot (0.5ha each). Says John, 'It may be somewhat quixotic, but I'm a great fan of traditional warm-area Australian wine styles, wines made in a relatively simple manner that reflect the concentrated ripe flavours one expects in these regions. And when one searches, some of these gems can be found from the Swan Valley.' Exports to Hong Kong and China.

ŶŶŶŶŶ Reserve Swan Valley Shiraz 2012 Rigid lines of tannin keep rolls of licorice, coffee grounds and asphalt-like flavour in trim, taut shape. It's no mean feat. It's a wine with a dark, heady heart of flavour and lots of it, but it's also a wine with no real alcohol warmth: a cool-head-in-a-crisis kind of wine. Creamy oak hovers without ever getting in the way. The longer you sit with this wine the grander it seems. Cork. 14.5% alc. **Rating** 95 **To** 2030 $71 CM

Swan Valley Grenache 2014 This puts a completely new face on the general impression of Swan Valley red wine. It's delicate, pretty and perfumed with a cruise of tannin and inbuilt complexity. It has berried fruit, not heavy but sweet and appealing, matched to twiggy herb and crushed fennel seed notes. The longer you look, the more you see, the more you like. Screwcap. 14% alc. **Rating** 95 **To** 2023 $33 CM ○

ŶŶŶŶŶ Dwellingup Semillon 2014 **Rating** 93 **To** 2024 $29
Dwellingup Chardonnay 2013 **Rating** 93 **To** 2019 $31 CM
Frankland River Cabernet Sauvignon 2013 **Rating** 93 **To** 2025 $55 CM
Petit Verdot 2013 **Rating** 93 **To** 2021 $29 CM
Riche Swan Valley Shiraz 2014 **Rating** 92 **To** 2024 $27 CM
Dwellingup Mourvedre 2014 **Rating** 92 **To** 2021 $33 CM
Dwellingup Mourvedre 2013 **Rating** 92 **To** 2020 $33 CM
Donnybrook Durif 2013 **Rating** 92 **To** 2023 $36
Dwellingup Malbec 2013 **Rating** 91 **To** 2020 $33 CM
Swan Verdelho 2014 **Rating** 90 **To** 2022 $19 ○

Fairbrossen Estate   ★★★★

51 Carmel Road, Carmel, WA 6076 **Region** Perth Hills
T 0410 105 915 **www**.fairbrossenestate.com.au **Open** Fri–Sun 10–4
Winemaker Matthew Bowness **Est.** 2011 **Dozens** 2500 **Vyds** 5.2ha
Matt Bowness was the winemaker at Sittella Wines for 8 years, guiding it to numerous show awards, and together with father Ken, the pair was able to secure a small property in Margaret River, planting vines in 1994. This was followed by a Perth Hills vineyard planted 10 years later. The grapes from both vineyards were sold until 2008, but in that year a very small amount was made while working at Sittella. Matt relinquished his position with Sittella in '11 to establish Fairbrossen Estate, and the winery was built for the first harvest in '12. Matt

says, 'Our family origins are from the Lake District in the north-west of England where big appetites are common. A phrase often expressed at the completion of very hearty meals is "I'm fair brossen", meaning, quite literally, "I am full to bursting!".'

馨馨馨馨馨 **Margaret River Cabernet Sauvignon 2012** From the family vineyard in Wilyabrup planted in '96; matured for 18 months in French barriques. That's pretty good breeding, and the wine doesn't disappoint: strong cassis and cedar flavours drive the long palate, the tannins exactly measured. Screwcap. 13.6% alc. **Rating** 94 **To** 2027 $22 ❂

馨馨馨馨馨 **Perth Hills Tempranillo 2012** Rating 90 To 2019 $22

Farmer's Daughter Wines ★★★☆

791 Ulan Road, Mudgee, NSW 2850 **Region** Mudgee
T (02) 6373 3177 **Open** Mon–Fri 9–5, Sat 10–5, Sun 10–4
Winemaker Liz and Greg Silkman **Est.** 1995 **Dozens** 8000 **Vyds** 17.6ha
The intriguingly named Farmer's Daughter Wines is a family-owned vineyard, named for the daughters of Lance and Gwen Smith, who originally planted grapes for sale, looking to retirement. Retirement, they say, has now become a 10-day week. Part of the production from the vineyard, planted to shiraz (8ha), cabernet sauvignon, merlot and chardonnay (3.2ha each), is sold to other makers, but the majority is made for the Farmer's Daughter label. Exports to the US, Canada, Vietnam and China.

馨馨馨馨馨 **Reserve Mudgee Shiraz 2011** Has some savoury elegance to its medium-bodied palate; juicy red fruits, fine-grained tannins and well-integrated oak all add up to the right answer. There's no need for patience: take the Farmer's Daughter into your vinous arms tonight. Screwcap. 12.7% alc. **Rating** 90 **To** 2021 $40

馨馨馨馨 **Mudgee Semillon Sauvignon Blanc 2014** Rating 89 To 2016 $25
Mudgee Shiraz 2013 Rating 89 To 2018 $22

Farmer's Leap Wines ★★★☆

41 Hodgson Road, Padthaway, SA 5271 **Region** Padthaway
T (08) 8765 5155 **www.**farmersleap.com **Open** Not
Winemaker Renae Hirsch **Est.** 2004 **Dozens** 10 000 **Vyds** 295.4ha
Scott Longbottom and Cheryl Merrett are third-generation farmers in the Padthaway region. They commenced planting the vineyard in 1995 on the family property, now planted to shiraz, cabernet sauvignon, chardonnay and merlot. Initially the majority of the grapes were sold, but increasing quantities held for the Farmer's Leap label have seen production rise from 2500 dozen to its present level. Exports to Canada, Singapore, South Korea, Japan, Taiwan, Hong Kong and China.

馨馨馨馨馨 **Padthaway Shiraz 2013** Hearty, well-polished red of widespread appeal. Sweet aniseed and blackberry flavours set up the spinnaker and sail for home, with woody cloves and toasty oak hanging over the sides in encouragement. Lots of power to tuck into here. Screwcap. 14.5% alc. **Rating** 92 **To** 2020 $23 CM ❂

馨馨馨馨 **Padthaway Chardonnay 2014** Rating 88 To 2016 $23 CM
Random Shot Cabernet 2013 Rating 88 To 2018 $17 CM ❂

Farr | Farr Rising ★★★★★

27 Maddens Road, Bannockburn, Vic 3331 **Region** Geelong
T (03) 5281 1733 **www.**byfarr.com.au **Open** Not
Winemaker Nick Farr **Est.** 1994 **Dozens** 5500 **Vyds** 13.8ha
By Farr and Farr Rising continue to be separate brands from separate vineyards, the one major change from previous years being that Nick Farr has assumed total responsibility for both labels, leaving father Gary free to pursue the finer things in life without interruption. This has in no way resulted in any diminution in the quality of the Pinot Noir, Chardonnay, Shiraz

and Viognier made. The vineyards are based on ancient river deposits within the Moorabool Valley. There are six different soils spread across the Farr property, with the two main types being rich, friable red and black volcanic loam, and limestone, which dominates the loam in some areas. The other soils are quartz gravel through a red volcanic soil, ironstone (called buckshot) in grey sandy loam with a heavy clay base, sandstone base and volcanic lava. The soil's good drainage and low fertility are crucial in ensuring small yields of intensely flavoured fruit. Exports to the UK, Canada, Denmark, Sweden, Hong Kong, Singapore, Taiwan, the Maldives, China and Japan.

ŢŢŢŢŢ **Sangreal by Farr Geelong Pinot Noir 2013** The vineyard was planted in '94 to clones 114 and 115, mutated into a 'Sangreal' clone. Made with 50–70% whole bunches, and 60–70% new oak maturation for 18 months. Another very different iteration of Pinot, the multifaceted bouquet with both red and black fruits in play, the same perfumed vehicle as Farr Rising, the palate of remarkable elegance and finesse, with exactly the right balance between pure pinot fruit flavours and structure ex the whole bunches. Cork. 13% alc. **Rating** 97 **To** 2028 $80 ✪

By Farr Shiraz 2012 4% viognier is co-fermented, with 20% whole bunches and 19 days on skins prior to pressing. Bright colour; here the bouquet and palate both have an intense black fruit headstone; the texture is, quite simply, brilliant, with fruit and tannins so finely interwoven they defy deconstruction; the depth of the palate is profound, the balance flawless in terms of both flavour and structure. Cork. 13.5% alc. **Rating** 97 **To** 2042 $60 ✪

ŢŢŢŢŢ **By Farr Chardonnay 2013** Same site as Sangreal Pinot Noir; Dijon clones and P58, hand-picked, whole bunch-pressed juice and solids to French oak (30% new) for wild yeast fermentation, stirred to start mlf, 11 months from picking to bottling. Why in god's name throw the wine to the cork wolves? It's a beautiful, power-packed, tangy, yet fine, Chardonnay that will be dead in the water in 10 years' time. I'll put my house on the outcome. 13% alc. **Rating** 96 **To** 2018 $75 ✪

Farr Rising Geelong Pinot Noir 2013 The vineyard was planted in '01, with MV6, 114 and 115 clones all on a large mixture of rootstocks; hand-picked and sorted in the vineyard, open-fermented with 60–70% destemmed, fermented and matured in Allier oak (25% new) for 18 months. Highly fragrant, the palate brimming with red fruits of every kind, before sliding gracefully into a silken web of tannins on the finish. Diam. 13.5% alc. **Rating** 96 **To** 2025 $47 ✪

Tout Pres by Farr Pinot Noir 2012 From a 1ha vineyard in an amphitheatre with three different soil types, 6 clones mutated into a single Tout Pres clone planted at 7300 vines per ha. Normally 100% whole bunches in a single 5-tonne open fermenter. An imperious Pinot with deep colour, purple and black fruits sewn seamlessly together, perfect tannins in the same tapestry; impeccable length and balance. Cork. 13% alc. **Rating** 96 **To** 2032 $110

Farr Rising Geelong Shiraz 2013 Planted in '94, on the warmest site on the vineyard; 10–15% whole bunches, 18 days' fermentation/maceration, French oak (10% new) for 18 months. Nick knows how to play the whole bunch card better than any of the other players in Australia, using only 10–15%, but there are levels of flavour complexity running through the savoury/spicy black fruit flavours directly stemming (no pun intended) from the whole bunches, the faintly grippy finish likewise. Diam. 13.5% alc. **Rating** 96 **To** 2033 $43 ✪

Farrside by Farr Geelong Pinot Noir 2013 From clones 114, 115, 667 and MV6; hand-picked and sorted, 60–70% destemmed before a 4-day cold soak, wild-yeast ferment for 12 days, pigeaged 2–3 times daily, matured for 18 months in French oak (50–60% new). Significantly more powerful and intense than its Farr Rising sibling. This is the big dog of the trio, with everything needed for a 20-year future. Cork. 13.5% alc. **Rating** 96 **To** 2033 $80

By Farr Viognier 2012 Crushed and foot-stomped on skins for 2 hours, pressed, cooled and straight to barrel with solids for 10 months' maturation. It has bountiful apricot, peach and vanilla varietal fruit achieved without phenolics, but with fresh acidity cleaning the finish, oak a means, not an end. But, oh that bloody cork. 12% alc. **Rating** 95 **To** 2019 $60

Fergusson ★★★★☆

82 Wills Road, Yarra Glen, Vic 3775 **Region** Yarra Valley
T (03) 5965 2237 **www.**fergussonwinery.com.au **Open** 7 days 11–5
Winemaker Rob Dolan **Est.** 1968 **Dozens** 2000 **Vyds** 6ha
One of the very first Yarra wineries to announce the rebirth of the Valley, now best known
as a favoured destination for tourist coaches, offering hearty fare in comfortable surroundings
and wines of both Yarra and non-Yarra Valley origin. For this reason the limited quantities of
its estate wines are often ignored, but they should not be.

🍷🍷🍷🍷🍷 Jeremy Reserve Yarra Valley Shiraz 2012 Estate-grown 45yo vines; open-
fermented and matured in French and American oak for 18 months. A wine
bubbling with joy, red cherry, plum and blueberry fruits built on a foundation of
superfine tannins and good acidity. A return after a long absence from the *Wine
Companion*. Screwcap. 13% alc. **Rating** 95 **To** 2027 $35 ✪

🍷🍷🍷🍷🍷 Benjamyn Reserve Yarra Valley Cabernet 2012 **Rating** 92 **To** 2027 $40

Fermoy Estate ★★★★★

838 Metricup Road, Wilyabrup, WA 6280 **Region** Margaret River
T (08) 9755 6285 **www.**fermoy.com.au **Open** 7 days 10–5
Winemaker Jeremy Hodgson, Coralie Lewis **Est.** 1985 **Dozens** 16 000 **Vyds** 17ha
A long-established winery with 17ha of semillon, sauvignon blanc, chardonnay, cabernet
sauvignon and merlot. The Young family acquired Fermoy Estate in 2010, and built a new,
larger cellar door which opened in '13, signalling the drive to increase domestic sales.
Notwithstanding its significant production, it is happy to keep a relatively low profile, however
difficult that may be given the quality of the wines. In October '14 senior winemaker Liz
Dawson resigned with the impending birth of her second child: after 10 years in the role, and
lifting Fermoy Estate's reputation ever higher, she decided family had to come first. Jeremy
Hodgson brings with him a first class honours degree in oenology and viticulture, and a
CV encompassing winemaking roles with Wise Wines, Cherubino Consultancy and, earlier,
Plantagenet, Houghton and Goundrey Wines. Exports to the US, Europe and Asia.

🍷🍷🍷🍷🍷 Reserve Cabernet Sauvignon 2013 Rolls back the curtains on a wealth
of well-placed fruit and tannin. A director's cut of a wine: nothing seems
compromised for short-term gain, it's all about longevity. Cool boysenberry and
blackcurrant with garden herbs and chocolate, but it's not a wine for flavour-
spotting; it's at one with itself. Screwcap. 14% alc. **Rating** 96 **To** 2040 $65 CM ✪
Chardonnay 2014 Such elegance, such length. It unfolds at its own pace, leaving
flavours of wheat, grapefruit, toast and white peach in its delicious wake. Lengthy,
citrussy acidity smiles out from behind that veil of fruit; there's a promise here
of fun both now and for years to come. Screwcap. 13% alc. **Rating** 95 **To** 2020
$30 CM ✪
Merlot 2013 It takes time to break the ice but allow this to breathe and it
tells you some things. It's a fine merlot. Filigreed tannin and grassy notes make
statements in themselves, but ripe plum and blackcurrant fruit are the scene
stealers. It's a charming style, not overdone; mid-weight but balanced and
thoughtfully well designed. Screwcap. 14% alc. **Rating** 94 **To** 2026 $25 CM ✪
Cabernet Sauvignon 2013 It has something serious to say but it elects to
croon it; no shouting. Accordingly, it makes for an excellent dinner table guest.
Blackcurrant, melted dark chocolate, modest gravelly notes and oak spice. Presents
as a seamless whole. Screwcap. 14% alc. **Rating** 94 **To** 2028 $35 CM

🍷🍷🍷🍷🍷 Semillon 2014 **Rating** 91 **To** 2016 $25 CM
Cabernet Sauvignon Merlot 2013 **Rating** 91 **To** 2020 $22 CM ✪
Sauvignon Blanc 2014 **Rating** 90 **To** 2016 $25 CM

Fernfield Wines ★★★★

112 Rushlea Road, Eden Valley, SA 5235 **Region** Eden Valley
T 0402 788 526 **www.**fernfieldwines.com.au **Open** Fri–Mon 11–4
Winemaker Rebecca and Scott Barr **Est.** 2002 **Dozens** 1500 **Vyds** 0.7ha
The establishment date of 2002 might, with a little poetic licence, be shown as 1864. Bryce Lillecrapp is the fifth generation of the Lillecrapp family; his great-great-great-grandfather bought land in the Eden Valley in 1864, subdividing it in 1866, establishing the township of Eden Valley and building the first house, Rushlea Homestead. Bryce restored this building and opened it in 1998 as a bicentennial project; it now serves as Fernfield Wines' cellar door. Ownership has now passed on to daughter Rebecca Barr and husband Scott, who have increased production.

🍷🍷🍷🍷🍷 **Eden Valley Riesling 2014** Bright straw-green; abounds with lime juice fruit aromas and flavours, but retains elegance; a thoroughly impressive wine showing why the Eden Valley gained such a reputation for its Rieslings decades ago. Screwcap. 12.1% alc. **Rating** 94 **To** 2025 $21 ✪

🍷🍷🍷🍷🍷 **Adelaide Hills Sauvignon Blanc 2014 Rating** 93 **To** 2015 $21 ✪
Old River Red Eden Valley Shiraz 2013 Rating 93 **To** 2033 $34

Ferngrove ★★★★★

276 Ferngrove Road, Frankland River, WA 6396 **Region** Frankland River
T (08) 9855 2378 **www.**ferngrove.com.au **Open** Mon–Sat 10–4
Winemaker Kim Horton **Est.** 1998 **Dozens** NFP **Vyds** 340ha
Known for producing consistent examples of cool-climate wines across multiple price brackets, the Ferngrove stable includes the Stirlings, Orchid, Frankland River and Symbols ranges. Ferngrove Wine Group enjoys the benefits of majority international ownership, but remains Australian-run. The success of the business is reflected in the increase in the estate vineyard area from 210ha to 340ha. Exports to all major markets.

🍷🍷🍷🍷🍷 **Cossack Riesling 2014** High-quality grapes reflect a high-quality vineyard site, and the high-quality wine reflects sensitive and respectful handling in the winery; the balance and length both underwrite the future of the wine, and the rewards to be gained from cellaring. Screwcap. 12.5% alc. **Rating** 94 **To** 2025 $23 ✪
Dragon Shiraz 2013 Pours the fruit on but maintains an elegance. A silken, almost creamy serving of red/black cherries, peanuts and chocolate with a firm hand of olivey, spicy tannin. Certainly needs time, but looks pretty swish in its youth. Screwcap. 14% alc. **Rating** 94 **To** 2030 $32 CM
Dragon Shiraz 2012 Luscious style, knows what it's about, black pepper laced through hearty blackberry and black cherry but with suppleness as a keen consideration throughout. Smoky, minerally tannin of the ultra fine-grained variety. Screwcap. 13.5% alc. **Rating** 94 **To** 2026 $32 CM
Majestic Cabernet Sauvignon 2012 Succulent Cabernet, true to its variety and region, with tannin, herbs, refreshing acidity and a pure burst of boysenberry/cassis-like fruit. Doesn't put a foot wrong. In the overall scheme the value here isn't half bad. Screwcap. 13.5% alc. **Rating** 94 **To** 2032 $32 CM

🍷🍷🍷🍷🍷 **Limited Release Cabernet Sauvignon 2013 Rating** 93 **To** 2022 $20 CM ✪
Limited Release Malbec 2013 Rating 93 **To** 2022 $20 CM ✪
King Frankland River Malbec 2012 Rating 93 **To** 2023 $32 CM
Frankland River Shiraz 2012 Rating 92 **To** 2022 $20 ✪
Majestic Cabernet Sauvignon 2013 Rating 92 **To** 2026 $32 CM
King Frankland River Malbec 2013 Rating 91 **To** 2022 $32 CM
Frankland River Malbec Rose 2014 Rating 90 **To** 2016 $20 CM ✪

Fighting Gully Road ★★★★★

319 Whorouly South Road, Whorouly South, Vic 3735 **Region** Beechworth
T (03) 5727 1434 **www**.fightinggully.com **Open** By appt
Winemaker Mark Walpole, Adrian Rodda **Est.** 1997 **Dozens** 1500 **Vyds** 8.3ha
Mark Walpole and partner Carolyn De Poi began the development of their Aquila Audax
Vineyard in 1997. It is situated between 530m and 580m above sea level: the upper-eastern
slopes are planted to pinot noir and the warmer western slopes to cabernet sauvignon; there
are also small quantities of shiraz, tempranillo, sangiovese and merlot.

ⓉⓉⓉⓉⓉ **Chardonnay 2013** From the illustrious Smiths Vineyard, wild yeast-fermented in
mainly used French barriques, and aged on lees for 10 months. It has the refined
concentration of French white Burgundies, its flavour spectrum perfectly balanced
between white peach and grapefruit. A very long life ahead. Screwcap. 13% alc.
Rating 97 To 2025 $32 ✪

ⓉⓉⓉⓉⓉ **Rose 2014** A blend of sangiovese and shiraz from Beechworth, Alpine Valleys
and Heathcote; wild yeast-fermented in used French barriques, then matured for
8 months in those barriques. Pale pink; a highly spiced and perfumed bouquet,
then a graceful palate, fruit-sweet, finishing clean and dry. Terrific winemaking
skills on display. Screwcap. 13.5% alc. Rating 95 To 2016 $22 ✪
Shiraz 2012 First and foremost, a Shiraz that is all about finesse and length,
entering the mouth almost surreptitiously, ending with a flourish of spiced red
fruits. Needed a touch more upfront. Screwcap. 13.2% alc. Rating 94 To 2025 $32
Sangiovese 2013 The very good colour suggests a Sangiovese with impressive
attitude; sour cherry duels with morello cherry, herbs and black olive tannins
(not dry or raspy) stop the attention wandering elsewhere. Screwcap. 14% alc.
Rating 94 To 2023 $28 ✪

ⓉⓉⓉⓉⓉ **Aquila 2013** Rating 93 To 2017 $22 CM ✪
Tempranillo 2011 Rating 93 To 2021 $28 CM
Aglianico 2012 Rating 93 To 2021 $38 CM
Beechworth Pinot Noir 2013 Rating 90 To 2021 $25 CM

Final Cut Wines ★★★★★

1a Little Queen Street, Chippendale, NSW 2008 (postal) **Region** Barossa Valley
T (02) 9690 0286 **www**.finalcutwines.com **Open** Not
Winemaker David Roe, Alex Head (Consultant) **Est.** 2004 **Dozens** 4000
The names of the wines point to the involvement of owners David Roe and Les Lithgow
in the film industry. Theirs is a virtual winery (likewise appropriate to the cinema), the wines
made from high-quality, contract-grown grapes. David becomes involved in vintage, but it is
otherwise long-distance winemaking from the directors' studio in Sydney. It should come as
no surprise to find the wines are of high quality. Exports to the US, Canada and the Far East.

ⓉⓉⓉⓉⓉ **Take Two Shiraz 2013** Two puncheons of Seppeltsfield (the place, not the
winery) Shiraz. A fascinating wine with many of the indicia of cool-region Shiraz;
no more than medium-bodied, with jaunty, spicy fruit profile to its fragrant
bouquet, and purple fruits on the palate; a gentle hand in the winery has ensured
fine tannins and perfectly integrated oak. Screwcap. 13.9% alc. Rating 97 To 2033
$45 ✪

Fire Gully ★★★★

Metricup Road, Wilyabrup, WA 6280 **Region** Margaret River
T (08) 9755 6220 **www**.firegully.com.au **Open** By appt
Winemaker Dr Michael Peterkin **Est.** 1988 **Dozens** 5000 **Vyds** 13.4ha
A 6ha lake created in a gully ravaged by bushfires gave the name. In 1998 Mike Peterkin of
Pierro purchased it, and manages the vineyard in conjunction with former owners Ellis and
Margaret Butcher. He regards the Fire Gully wines as entirely separate from those of Pierro:

the plantings are cabernet sauvignon, merlot, shiraz, semillon, sauvignon blanc, chardonnay, viognier and chenin blanc. Exports to all major markets.

🍷🍷🍷🍷🍷 **Sauvignon Blanc Semillon 2014** Gets the mix pretty right. Mid-weight flavour, soft texture, spicy florals on a bed of thistles and tropical fruit. Finishes with a flourish. Screwcap. 12.5% alc. **Rating** 92 **To** 2016 $25 CM ✪
Chardonnay 2013 Both refreshing and hefty. Buttery notes meet yellow stone fruits. Crisp, acidic, firmish finish. Tries to be all things to all folks, and manages the task fairly well. Screwcap. 13% alc. **Rating** 91 **To** 2018 $32 CM
Shiraz 2012 There's a lot to like about this. It's well fruited and flush with savoury character. Flavours of plum, dark cherry, meat, cracked black pepper and crushed dry leaves put on a display. It's one of those medium-weight wines that seems to fight attractively beyond its weight; until perhaps the finish, where alcohol seems fractionally too keen. Screwcap. 15% alc. **Rating** 91 **To** 2021 $32 CM

Firetail   ★★★★

21 Bessell Road, Rosa Glen, WA 6285 **Region** Margaret River
T (08) 9757 5156 **www**.firetail.com.au **Open** 7 days 11–5
Winemaker Contract **Est.** 2002 **Dozens** 1600 **Vyds** 5.3ha
Electrical engineer Jessica Worrall and chemical engineer Rob Glass worked in the oil and gas industry in Australia and The Netherlands for 20 years before making a staged move into grapegrowing and the establishment of Firetail. Their first move was the planting of a small vineyard of merlot in Geographe, which produced its first wine in 2003; a more important move was the acquisition of a somewhat neglected vineyard (and rammed-earth house) in Margaret River. Here the Geographe merlot is supplemented by semillon, sauvignon blanc and cabernet sauvignon, the Margaret River plantings dating back to 2004. Jessica is in the final stages of completing her Masters of Viticulture at the University of Melbourne while managing the vineyard and the wine production, and Rob balances the demands of the wine sales and marketing with consulting for the liquid natural gas business. Exports to Hong Kong, Japan and China.

🍷🍷🍷🍷🍷 **Just Desserts 2012** 77/23% late harvest botrytis semillon and sauvignon blanc. Luscious mandarin, cumquat, apricot and vanilla flavours are balanced by citrussy acidity. Well made: the botrytis infection was devoid of black rot. Drink up while it is still fresh. 375ml. Screwcap. 11.4% alc. **Rating** 94 **To** 2015 $18 ✪

🍷🍷🍷🍷🍷 **Margaret River Semillon 2013** Rating 92 **To** 2020 $19 ✪
Margaret River Cabernet Sauvignon 2013 Rating 90 **To** 2023 $28
Margaret River Cabernet Sauvignon 2012 Rating 90 **To** 2018 $27

First Creek Wines   ★★★★★

600 McDonalds Road, Pokolbin, NSW 2320 **Region** Hunter Valley
T (02) 4998 7293 **www**.firstcreekwines.com.au **Open** 7 days 10–5
Winemaker Liz and Greg Silkman **Est.** 1984 **Dozens** 35 000
First Creek Wines is the brand of First Creek Winemaking Services, a major contract winemaker (over 25 clients). Winemaker Liz Silkman (née Jackson) had an exceptional year in 2011: she was a finalist in the Gourmet Traveller Winemaker of the Year awards, winner of the Hunter Valley Winemaker of the Year, and won Best Red Wine of Show at the NSW Wine Awards for the Winemakers Reserve Shiraz 2010. At the James Halliday Chardonnay Challenge '12, the First Creek Winemakers Reserve Chardonnay 2011 was named top Hunter Valley Chardonnay, adding to its prior triple-trophy record. Exports to the UK, Sweden and China.

🍷🍷🍷🍷🍷 **Winemaker's Reserve Chardonnay 2014** Scintillating. Struck match notes are infused through white peach, citrus and grapefruit. Medium in weight but with real presence. Texturally it pours on the silk, though it's threaded with frisky acidity. Quite a treat. Screwcap. 12.6% alc. **Rating** 96 **To** 2019 $60 CM ✪

Winemaker's Reserve Semillon 2014 It pushes impressively through the finish. It's a slow train at first but the steam builds, as does the momentum, until it's irrepressible. Lemon, wax and a smidge of cut grass. Cellarability written all over it. Screwcap. 11.5% alc. **Rating** 95 **To** 2025 $45 CM

ŸŸŸŸŸ **Semillon 2014 Rating** 91 **To** 2022 $22 CM ○
Chardonnay 2013 Rating 90 **To** 2018 $25 CM

First Drop Wines ★★★★★

Beckwith Park, Tanunda Road, Nuriootpa, SA 5355 **Region** Barossa Valley
T (08) 8562 3324 **www**.firstdropwines.com **Open** Wed–Sat 10–4
Winemaker Matt Gant **Est.** 2005 **Dozens** 10 000
The First Drop Wines of today has been transformed since its establishment in 2005. It now has a real winery, part of the old Penfolds winery at Nuriootpa, shared with Tim Smith Wines. The group of buildings is now called Beckwith Park, in honour of the man who did so much groundbreaking work for Penfolds (Ray Beckwith OAM, who died in 2012, but not before his 100th birthday; his other recognition came in the form of the Maurice O'Shea Award). Exports to the UK, the US, Canada, Denmark, Japan, Hong Kong, Singapore and NZ.

ŸŸŸŸŸ **The Cream Barossa Valley Shiraz 2012** Generosity and complexity; black fruits have outstanding texture, structure, balance and – above all – length. One of those wines that manages to fill the mouth with flavour, and not palling with repeated sips, simply revealing more. Cork. 14.5% alc. **Rating** 96 **To** 2042 $100
Mere et Fils Adelaide Hills Chardonnay 2013 Whole bunch-pressed, wild yeast-fermented in François Frères oak, lees stirred/contacted for 6 months. Bright straw-green, it is an elegant and restrained style, with excellent balance between grapefruit/white peach fruit, oak and crisp acidity on the finish. Screwcap. 12.5% alc. **Rating** 95 **To** 2023 $25 ○
Mother's Milk Barossa Shiraz 2013 Deep crimson-purple; this is a Shiraz that is elegant, yet full-bodied, with a panoply of black and purple fruits, spices of all kinds, a nice touch of integrated oak, a whisper of licorice, and fine tannins. All good, as they say. Screwcap. 14.5% alc. **Rating** 95 **To** 2035 $25 ○
Fat of the Land Single Vineyard Greenock Barossa Valley Shiraz 2012 Savoury, twiggy, earthy aromas are replayed on the opening stanzas of the palate before pleasantly grippy tannins exert their influence, the aftertaste changing gear again to juicy fruit. Cork. 14.5% alc. **Rating** 95 **To** 2037 $75
Fat of the Land Ebenezer Single Vineyard Barossa Valley Shiraz 2012 All four of the '12 First Drop subregion Shirazs are of similar deep colour, and all have perfect corks, perfectly inserted. Choc-mint characters come through strongly on the bouquet, and the palate stays closely aligned to those characters; foresty tannins keep its line intact. Cork. 14.5% alc. **Rating** 95 **To** 2037 $75
Minchia Adelaide Hills Montepulciano 2012 Is very similar to the Catlin '13 Montepulciano, not the least in its powerful structure; here black fruits, licorice, spice and tannins all whirl around and along the palate. It is the spice that is most alluring, and each time the wine is retasted, it reveals more about its inner self – which is all good, very good. Screwcap. 14.5% alc. **Rating** 95 **To** 2022 $38
Two Percent Barossa Shiraz 2013 Rating 94 **To** 2028 $38
Fat of the Land Seppeltsfield Single Vineyard Barossa Valley Shiraz 2012 Rating 94 **To** 2032 $75
Mother's Ruin McLaren Vale Cabernet Sauvignon 2013 Rating 94 **To** 2028 $25 ○

ŸŸŸŸŸ **Vivo d'Adelaide Hills Arneis 2014 Rating** 93 **To** 2019 $25 ○
McLaren Vale Touriga Nacional 2013 Rating 93 **To** 2020 $25 ○
Half & Half Barossa Shiraz Monastrell 2013 Rating 91 **To** 2020 $25

Five Geese

389 Chapel Hill Road, Blewitt Springs, SA 5171 (postal) **Region** McLaren Vale
T (08) 8383 0576 **www.fivegeese.com.au Open** Not
Winemaker Mike Farmilo **Est.** 1999 **Dozens** 5000 **Vyds** 28ha

Sue Trott is devoted to her Five Geese wines, which come from vines planted in 1927 and
'65 (shiraz, cabernet sauvignon, grenache and mataro), nero d'Avola a more recent arrival. She
sold the grapes for many years, but in '99 decided to create her own label and make a strictly
limited amount of wine from the pick of the vineyards, which are run on organic principles.
The quality of the wines, and their value for money, is exemplary. Exports to the UK, South
Korea and Singapore.

♥♥♥♥♥ **The Gander's Blend Old Vine Grenache Shiraz 2013** 80% grenache/20%
shiraz. Full-bodied, throaty expression of this blend. Flooded with ripe, sweet
raspberry and saturated plum with mint and five-spice notes finally getting a word
in edgeways through the finish. Grainy, earthen, licoricey tannin, and an ample
serve of it. Quite a star. Screwcap. 14.5% alc. **Rating** 95 **To** 2026 $25 CM ◎
The Pippali Old Vine Shiraz 2012 Blewitt Springs shiraz. Firm, solid,
substantial Shiraz. Quality written all over it. Value almost goes without saying.
Blackberry, earth, saltbush and smoky oak. Excellent integration of the various
components. Tannin comes in a block but the fruit is up to the task. Screwcap.
14.5% alc. **Rating** 94 **To** 2026 $25 CM ◎
Jon's Block Reserve Blewitt Springs Shiraz 2012 Juice and impact. A firm
sense of structural integrity. This gutsy, blackberried wine comes coated in toasty
vanillan oak and blessed with velvety-smooth texture. Round after round of
flavour. Cork. 14.5% alc. **Rating** 94 **To** 2030 $35 CM
Sue's Paddock Reserve Blewitt Springs Grenache 2013 Remarkably pretty,
well-structured, seductive Grenache. Fruit is the hero here. Warm ripe raspberry,
rose petals, earth and sweet spice with the lightest kiss of musky vanillan. Would
drink well from a Burgundy glass. Screwcap. 15% alc. **Rating** 94 **To** 2022 $35 CM

♥♥♥♥♡ **Jen's Block Reserve Cabernet 2012 Rating** 91 **To** 2022 $35 CM
McLaren Vale Cabernet 2012 Rating 91 **To** 2020 $20 CM ◎

Five Oaks Vineyard ★★★★★

60 Aitken Road, Seville, Vic 3139 **Region** Yarra Valley
T (03) 5964 3704 **www.fiveoaks.com.au Open** W'ends & public hols 10–5
Winemaker Wally Zuk **Est.** 1995 **Dozens** 1000 **Vyds** 3ha

Wally Zuk and wife Judy run all aspects of Five Oaks – far removed from Wally's background
in nuclear physics. He has, however, completed the wine science degree at CSU, and is thus
more than qualified to make the Five Oaks wines. The lion's share of the vineyard is planted
to cabernet sauvignon (2.6ha), with 0.2ha each of riesling and merlot. Exports to Canada,
Macau, Hong Kong and China.

♥♥♥♥♥ **Yarra Valley Cabernet Sauvignon 2013** Spent 16 days in open fermenters,
18 months in French oak (90% new). Excellent, vibrant colour; a splendidly
juicy attack of cassis on the palate makes you sit up and either wave or salute, the
choice is yours; the impact continues through to the back-palate, joined there by
fine-grained tannins and well-integrated, cedary oak. Worth every dollar, and then
some. Screwcap. 13.7% alc. **Rating** 96 **To** 2033 $30 ◎
Yarra Valley Merlot 2013 Open-fermented, matured in 100% new oak for
18 months. Good colour; a wine that encapsulates the suitability of the Yarra Valley
climate for the variety; has the pure (in classic terms) cassis and black olive flavour
duopoly top-quality Merlot should have, tannins very much in the back row; they
have gobbled up the oak. Screwcap. 13.2% alc. **Rating** 95 **To** 2033 $35 ◎

♥♥♥♥ **Yarra Valley Merlot 2012 Rating** 89 **To** 2019 $30 CM

Flametree

Cnr Caves Road/Chain Avenue, Dunsborough, WA 6281 **Region** Margaret River
T (08) 9756 8577 **www.**flametreewines.com **Open** 7 days 10–5
Winemaker Cliff Royle, Julian Scott **Est.** 2007 **Dozens** 20 000
Flametree, owned by the Towner family (John, Liz, Rob and Annie), has had extraordinary
success since its first vintage in 2007. The usual practice of planting a vineyard and then finding
someone to make the wine was turned on its head: a state-of-the-art winery was built, and
grape purchase agreements signed with growers in the region. Gold medal after gold medal
and trophy after trophy followed, topped by the winning of the Jimmy Watson Trophy with
its first red wine, the 2007 Cabernet Merlot. If all this were not enough, Flametree has since
secured the services of former long-serving winemaker at Voyager Estate, Cliff Royle. Exports
to the UK, Indonesia, Malaysia, the Philippines and Singapore.

ŸŸŸŸŸ Jeremy John Margaret River Cabernet Sauvignon Malbec 2011
Deep crimson-purple; a selection of the best parcels from the '11 vintage, itself a
memorable year; intense blackcurrant fruit is layered with plum ex the malbec, and
supported by plentiful, but ripe, tannins, French oak adding yet another dimension.
This wine will still be kicking goals 40 years on from its vintage; give it a chance
for at least 10 years. Screwcap. 14% alc. **Rating** 97 **To** 2051 $80 ✪

ŸŸŸŸŸ S.R.S. Karridale Sauvignon Blanc 2014 Free-run juice, wild yeast-fermented
in stainless steel and French oak. This approach works well in building mouthfeel
without taking the edge off the passionfruit, guava and grapefruit flavours of the
totally seductive palate. Screwcap. 13% alc. **Rating** 95 **To** 2016 $33 ✪
S.R.S. Wallcliffe Margaret River Chardonnay 2014 Clearly barrel-fermented
and matured, although we are told nothing of its elevage. Here the fruit density
is very good, even though the alcohol is restrained, and layered complexity is
achieved with ease, tangy grapefruit leading green apple, white peach and pear.
Screwcap. 13% alc. **Rating** 95 **To** 2029 $55
S.R.S. Frankland River Shiraz 2012 Superb colour, then a perfumed bouquet
with black fruits, licorice and pepper/spice, the full-bodied palate with excellent
balance and length. Just embarking on what will be a very long and prosperous
life. Screwcap. 14.5% alc. **Rating** 95 **To** 2042 $55
Embers Margaret River Sauvignon Blanc 2014 The fragrant bouquet and
richly endowed palate provide a vivid portrait of Margaret River sauvignon blanc,
with a complex array of citrus, stone fruit and tropical fruits balanced by crisp,
gently herbal acidity. Screwcap. 13% alc. **Rating** 94 **To** 2016 $20 ✪
Margaret River Sauvignon Blanc Semillon 2014 An exercise in precision
and discipline, almost glittering in its mouthfeel and structure; snow pea, capsicum,
lemon, guava and green pineapple are held in an embrace of crunchy acidity.
Screwcap. 13% alc. **Rating** 94 **To** 2020 $24 ✪

ŸŸŸŸŸ Margaret River Chardonnay 2014 **Rating** 93 **To** 2022 $25 ✪
Family Tree Wine Club Natalie Margaret River Malbec 2013 **Rating** 93
To 2020 $22 ✪

Flaxman Wines

Lot 535 Flaxmans Valley Road, Angaston, SA 5353 **Region** Eden Valley
T 0411 668 949 **www.**flaxmanwines.com.au **Open** By appt
Winemaker Colin Sheppard **Est.** 2005 **Dozens** 1500 **Vyds** 2ha
After visiting the Barossa Valley for over a decade, Melbourne residents Colin Sheppard
and wife Fi decided on a seachange, and in 2004, found a small, old vineyard overlooking
Flaxmans Valley. It consists of 1ha of 60+ and 90-year-old riesling, 1ha of 65+ and 90-year-
old shiraz and a 0.8ha of 60+-year-old semillon. The vines are dry-grown, hand-pruned and
hand-picked, and treated – say the Sheppards – as their garden. Yields are restricted to under
4 tonnes per hectare, and exceptional parcels of locally grown grapes are also purchased.
Colin has worked at various Barossa wineries for many years, and his attention to detail (and

understanding of the process) is reflected in the consistently high quality of the wines. An onsite winery and cellar door are planned for the near future.

🍷🍷🍷🍷🍷 **Reserve Eden Valley Cabernet 2013** Flaxman rarely uses 'Reserve'; matured for 20 months in French oak. You can see the reason for the Reserve name and the price – there is simply no way you would pick this as anything but a classic cool-climate region wine, its juicy cassis fruit with a wreath of superfine tannins, both line and length faultless. Screwcap. 13.5% alc. **Rating** 96 **To** 2043 $100

Eden Valley Riesling 2014 Picked slightly riper than recent vintages, and spent longer on lees; tiny crop with above-average concentration; green apple, lime zest and crunchy acidity give the wine more presence than usual early in what will be a long life. Screwcap. 11.5% alc. **Rating** 95 **To** 2029 $27 🲔

Estate Eden Valley Shiraz 2012 From estate vines up to 85yo, 3/4 tonne per acre, open-fermented, matured in French oak (33% new) for 24 months. All the bells and whistles; the very intense fruit is swathed in French oak at the moment, but the fruit will triumph 5–10 years down the track, the wine with an indefinite future. 90 dozen made. Screwcap. 14% alc. **Rating** 95 **To** 2052 $55

The Stranger Barossa Shiraz Cabernet 2013 An 80/20% blend, shiraz from Gomersal matured in American oak, cabernet from Moculta matured in French oak, both for 20 months. The secret to this wine is, without question, its low alcohol (by Barossa Valley standards), giving the palate a magic carpet ride of freshness and fruit intensity, making the oak (and the tannins) nigh-on irrelevant. Screwcap. 13.5% alc. **Rating** 94 **To** 2028 $38

🍷🍷🍷🍷🍷 **Paladin Barossa Valley Shiraz 2013 Rating** 90 **To** 2028 $22

Flint's of Coonawarra   ★★★★

Flint Road, Coonawarra, SA 5263 **Region** Coonawarra
T (08) 8736 5046 **www**.flintsofcoonawarra.com.au **Open** By appt
Winemaker Contract **Est.** 2001 **Dozens** 2000 **Vyds** 84ha
Six generations of the Flint family have lived and worked in Coonawarra since 1840. Damian Flint and his family began the development of 84ha of cabernet sauvignon, shiraz and merlot in 1989, but it was not until 2000 that they decided to have a small portion of cabernet sauvignon contract-made. Damian and Sue oversee the day-to-day running of both the vineyard and the farm, with Matthew, who studied viticulture in the Barossa, managing the vineyard.

🍷🍷🍷🍷🍷 **Gammon's Crossing Cabernet Sauvignon 2012** Clear varietal character and profile. Stern, dusty tannin, mulberry and blackcurrant, tips of mint and cedar wood. Builds a sense of authority as it travels through the mouth. Screwcap. 14% alc. **Rating** 93 **To** 2025 $20 CM 🲔

Rostrevor Shiraz 2012 Slippery-smooth, creamy texture, carrying with it an ample serving of mint, choc and plum flavour. Fine tannin completes a job well done. Can easily be consumed now. Screwcap. 13% alc. **Rating** 91 **To** 2021 $20 CM 🲔

Flowstone Wines   ★★★★★

Lot 16 Bussell Highway, Forrest Grove, WA 6286 **Region** Margaret River
T 0487 010 275 **www**.flowstonewines.com **Open** By appt
Winemaker Stuart Pym **Est.** 2013 **Dozens** 700 **Vyds** 2.25ha
Flowstone is the venture of Stuart Pym and Phil Giglia. Stuart's involvement with wine commenced in 1983, when he moved to Margaret River to help his parents establish their vineyard and winery in Wilyabrup (since sold and now Hay Shed Hill). Lengthy winemaking careers at Voyager Estate (1991–2000), Devil's Lair (2000–08) and Stella Bella (2008–13), were rounded out with concurrent vintage work overseas. Phil is a self-confessed wine tragic, his fascination starting at the University of WA's Wine Club. The two met at a Margaret River Great Estates lunch in the late '90s, and hatched the idea of starting a small business. It finally took shape in '03 when the property was purchased. 0.5ha of chardonnay was planted the

following year, the remainder in '09. Estate grapes are augmented by contract-grown grapes. The attention to detail of the venture is typified by the appeal of the label design, the labels themselves made from 81% limestone, the remainder bonding resin (there is no wood fibre or pulp). Best New Winery Award '15 *Wine Companion*.

🍷🍷🍷🍷🍷 Sauvignon Blanc 2012 Follows closely in the thoroughly unorthodox, but brilliantly successful, '11 inaugural release: barrel fermentation and 11 months' oak maturation, then 18 months in bottle prior to release. The synergy between the grape and the vinification, orchestrated by winemaker Stuart Pym, is spectacularly successful; the flavours are a Joseph's Coat of complexity, yet indivisible. Zesty acidity means the wine will outlast almost all other Sauvignon Blancs. Screwcap. 12.5% alc. **Rating** 97 **To** 2022 $30 ✪

Queen of the Earth Chardonnay 2011 From the 0.5ha planting in '04; fermentation and mlf in French oak (50% new); 17 months in barrel; once bottled, held for 36 months before release. Counterintuitively, elegance and finesse, rather than complexity, define the character of this wine, and underwrite its extreme length. A quite beautiful display of perfectly ripened chardonnay vinified by a master. Screwcap. 13% alc. **Rating** 97 **To** 2025 $55 ✪

Queen of the Earth Cabernet Sauvignon 2011 Hand-picked from a single dry-grown vineyard in Wilyabrup; open-fermented in 1-tonne pots, 17 days' post-fermentation maceration, matured for 3 years in new French barriques, plus 15 months' bottle age, 9 dozen made. Briefly tries to hide its beauty, but has to let the rivulets of cassis caress the tongue and cheeks of the mouth, supported by persistent, but extraordinarily fine, silky tannins. Screwcap. 14% alc. **Rating** 97 **To** 2041 $74 ✪

🍷🍷🍷🍷🍷 Sauvignon Blanc 2013 Hand-picked from a single 20yo vineyard at Karridale in southern Margaret River, whole bunch-pressed, fermented in used oak barrels and one new 600l demi muid, 11 months' maturation before bottling followed by 18 months' bottle maturation. Gleaming straw-green, it has all the layered complexity and depth that is the touchstone of its '12 predecessor, unlike any other Sauvignon Blanc in Australia. Screwcap. 12.5% alc. **Rating** 96 **To** 2020 $32 ✪

Queen of the Earth Chardonnay 2012 The second (1.3 tonnes) vintage from the home block, hand-picked, whole bunch-pressed, fermented in French barriques (50% new, 50% 1yo), matured for 18 months, plus a further 24 months in bottle, 90 dozen made. A beautifully detailed wine, all its components perfectly lined up, flowing seamlessly across the palate, stone fruit tempered by just so citrussy acidity, the oak absorbed. Screwcap. 13% alc. **Rating** 96 **To** 2025 $55 ✪

Chardonnay 2011 Hand-picked, whole bunch-pressed, fermented in French oak (15% new), with natural mlf; 11 months in oak. Gleaming green-gold; the cashew/walnut complexity of the bouquet carries through to the palate, but here takes second place to its intense pink grapefruit core. Awesome second-tier wine. Screwcap. 12.5% alc. **Rating** 96 **To** 2024 $35 ✪

Cabernet Sauvignon Touriga 2010 The cabernet comes from a 25yo vineyard in Wilyabrup, the touriga from a 35yo patch of vines in Yallingup. The parcels were separately open-fermented, and thereafter spent 2 years in French oak (20% new); once blended and bottled, the wine was held for 2 years prior to release. While the Queen of the Earth Cabernet Sauvignon makes no secret of its autocratic provenance, this is an immediately and unequivocally joyous blend of cassis and small red fruits, its tannins fine and soft. Screwcap. 13.5% alc. **Rating** 96 **To** 2025 $35 ✪

Gewurztraminer 2012 Gleaming straw-green; made from 35+yo vines, and takes Margaret River by the hand to head off to Alsace; the way the flavour builds progressively through to the finish is wholly impressive, as is the spicy lychee varietal expression. Screwcap. 13.5% alc. **Rating** 95 **To** 2020 $30 ✪

Queen of the Earth Cabernet Sauvignon 2010 From a single dry-grown vineyard in Wilyabrup planted in the late '70s; hand-picked, open-fermented and macerated for 3 weeks thereafter; pressed to new French barriques and left there for 3 years; 85 dozen made. The result is a wine that nods to the Right Bank of

Bordeaux, with foresty/savoury notes at ease with the autocratic black fruits of cabernet. Screwcap. 14% alc. **Rating** 95 **To** 2030 $75

Cabernet Sauvignon Touriga 2011 A 70/30% blend separately made, but using similar steps: open-fermented in 1-tonne pots, cabernet 14 days' post-fermentation maceration, touriga 11 days, pressed to French barriques (20% new) for 24 months, blended with a further 2 years in bottle, 350 dozen made. This is left field, but irresistible with its array of cedar, spice and cassis in utter harmony, each flattering the other. Screwcap. 13.5% alc. **Rating** 95 **To** 2031 $35 ✪

Margaret River Chardonnay 2012 Rating 94 **To** 2022 $35

Flying Fish Cove ★★★★★

Caves Road, Wilyabrup, WA 6284 **Region** Margaret River
T (08) 9755 6600 **www**.flyingfishcove.com **Open** 7 days 11–5
Winemaker Simon Ding **Est.** 2000 **Dozens** 21 000 **Vyds** 25ha

Flying Fish Cove has two strings to its bow: contract winemaking for others, and the development of its own brand, partly based on 25ha of estate plantings. The long-serving winemakers both had a circuitous journey before falling prey to the lure of wine. Simon Ding finished an apprenticeship in metalwork in 1993, and took off to see the world; some of his employment was in restaurants and bars, which sparked his interest in wine. On returning to Australia in '96 he obtained a Bachelor of Science Degree and joined the Flying Fish Cove team in 2000. Damon Easthaugh has always lived in WA, spending seven years studying law (among other things) at the University of WA. Law did not have the same appeal as winemaking, and Damon became a founding member of the winery. Exports to the US and Malaysia.

🍷🍷🍷🍷🍷 **Prize Catch Cabernet Sauvignon 2013** It's not flashy, but it's seriously good. The way the tannin here integrates or co-ordinates with the fruit is worth the price of admission in itself. Pencils, cassis, mint, tobacco and slippery, creamy cedar. The effect of the whole is much greater than the sum of its parts. Brooding and tannic but not with succulence; it remains lively. Vital. Screwcap. 14.5% alc. **Rating** 98 **To** 2040 $95 CM ✪

🍷🍷🍷🍷🍷 **Prize Catch Chardonnay 2013** Tangy acidity pushes this into challenging waters but taken as a whole there is no choice but to herald a terrific release of Margaret River Chardonnay. This is a wine to make you stop and take stock. It's all pear, grapefruit, lemon barley and sweet/spicy cedar wood, but the way it builds as it moves through the mouth and then sizzles out through the finish is quite something. Screwcap. 13% alc. **Rating** 96 **To** 2022 $95 CM

The Wildberry Reserve Shiraz 2013 Dense crimson-purple; from the estate vineyard in Wilyabrup, and Wildberry connotes the best Shiraz of the vintage; open-fermented and French oak-matured, this brings sensuous black fruits framed by fine-grained but persistent tannins, part oak, part fruit-derived. Will be prodigiously long-lived. Screwcap. 14.5% alc. **Rating** 96 **To** 2050 $40 ✪

The Wildberry Reserve Cabernet Sauvignon 2013 More than a little fancy. Flesh, power, tannin and reach. This is a cracking release. Currants, chocolates, lead pencil and tobacco. It's classically flavoured, brimful really, but it also locks into a determined groove through the finish. Exciting future ahead. Screwcap. 14.5% alc. **Rating** 96 **To** 2035 $40 CM ✪

Cabernet Sauvignon 2012 Strikes the chord and the flavours launch in harmony. This has a delicious pitch to it. It's an amalgam of blackcurrant, earth, black olives and bay leaves, though what sets it apart is the way chocolatey oak plays in with the fruit and how curls of dry, leafy tannin impart an authoritative feel. Screwcap. 14% alc. **Rating** 95 **To** 2028 $45 CM

The Wildberry Reserve Chardonnay 2013 In a very good place. Rich but elegant. Heads out in search of quality and length but stops to make sure that drinkability is all sorted. Grapefruit, white peach, citrus and toasty/spicy oak. A sure provider of pleasure. Screwcap. 13% alc. **Rating** 94 **To** 2019 $40 CM

ΨΨΨΨΨ Wildberry Reserve Semillon 2014 Rating 93 To 2017 $40 CM
4 Boards Semillon Sauvignon Blanc 2013 Rating 92 To 2015 $18 ✪
Chardonnay 2013 Rating 92 To 2018 $22 ✪
Cabernet Sauvignon Merlot 2013 Rating 92 To 2023 $22 CM ✪

Flynns Wines ★★★★★

Lot 5 Lewis Road, Heathcote, Vic 3523 **Region** Heathcote
T (03) 5433 6297 **www**.flynnswines.com **Open** Fri 10–3, w'ends 11–5
Winemaker Greg and Natala Flynn **Est.** 1999 **Dozens** 2000 **Vyds** 4.12ha
Greg and Natala Flynn spent 18 months searching for their property, which is 13km north of
Heathcote on red Cambrian soil. They have established shiraz, sangiovese, verdelho, cabernet
sauvignon and merlot. Greg is a Roseworthy marketing graduate, and has had 24 years
working at the coal face of retail and wholesale businesses, interweaving 10 years of vineyard
and winemaking experience, supplemented by the two-year Bendigo TAFE winemaking
course. Just for good measure, wife Natala has joined in the vineyard and winery, and likewise
completed the TAFE course. The rating is based on the quality, and (exceptional) value
for money.

ΨΨΨΨΨ Lewis Road Heathcote Shiraz 2013 Open-fermented, 12 months' maturation
in French and American oak. Deeply coloured, it encapsulates everything
Heathcote can offer in a year not hit by drought; a sumptuous layered palate
of predominantly black fruits and a flutter of spice before fine, savoury tannins
provide a logical conclusion. Screwcap. 14.5% alc. Rating 95 To 2033 $24 ✪
Irena's Heathcote Verdelho 2013 Hand-picked, 20% barrel-fermented in new
French barriques and matured for a short time thereafter. Bright straw-green; it
has excellent citrussy acidity on the finish, and made thus will prosper with bottle
age, although there is enough stone fruit and green banana to please here and now.
Screwcap. 14% alc. Rating 94 To 2020 $26 ✪

ΨΨΨΨΨ Jimmy Junior Heathcote Shiraz 2013 Rating 92 To 2020 $17 ✪
Heathcote Viognier 2014 Rating 91 To 2016 $28
Heathcote Vermentino 2013 Rating 91 To 2016 $22 ✪

Forbes & Forbes ★★★★☆

30 Williamstown Road, Springton, SA 5235 **Region** Eden Valley
T (08) 8568 2709 **www**.forbeswine.com.au **Open** At Taste Eden Valley, Angaston
Winemaker Colin Forbes **Est.** 2008 **Dozens** 400 **Vyds** 5ha
This venture is owned by Colin and Robert Forbes, and their respective partners. Colin says,
'I have been in the industry for a "frightening" length of time', beginning with Thomas Hardy
& Sons in 1974. The winemaking is carried out in the shed owned by McLean's Farm. While
Colin is particularly attached to riesling, the property owned by the partners in Eden Valley
has 2ha each of riesling and merlot, and 1ha of cabernet sauvignon.

ΨΨΨΨΨ Cellar Matured Eden Valley Riesling 2009 Wonderful, light quartz-green
colour; a lemon blossom and frangipani bouquet leads into a totally delicious and
fresh Riesling, still in its development trajectory, but it's no crime to drink the
wine now. Screwcap. 11% alc. Rating 96 To 2020 $27 ✪

ΨΨΨΨΨ Single Vineyard Eden Valley Riesling 2014 Rating 91 To 2020 $21 ✪

Forest Hill Vineyard ★★★★★

Cnr South Coast Highway/Myers Road, Denmark, WA 6333 **Region** Great Southern
T (08) 9848 0000 **www**.foresthillwines.com.au **Open** 7 days 10–4
Winemaker Michael Ng **Est.** 1965 **Dozens** 19 000 **Vyds** 65ha
This family-owned business is one of the oldest 'new' winemaking operations in WA, and
was the site for the first grape plantings in Great Southern in 1965. The Forest Hill brand
became well known, aided by the fact that a '75 Riesling made by Sandalford from Forest
Hill grapes won nine trophies. The quality of the wines made from the oldest vines on the

property is awesome (released under the numbered vineyard block labels). Exports to Taiwan, Hong Kong, Singapore and China.

ΨΨΨΨΨ **Block 1 Mount Barker Riesling 2014** Such penetration. Such a flourish of citrus/grapefruit/orange rind/mineral flavour and acidity through the finish. Such undeniable quality. Brilliant. Screwcap. 13% alc. **Rating** 97 **To** 2030 $40 CM ✪

ΨΨΨΨΨ **Block 8 Mount Barker Chardonnay 2012** It flares with flavour before swanning through the finish; power at the hand of elegance. Grapefruit, white peach, lemon curd and oak spice, a thrilling wire of lemony acidity pulling it long/tight. Screwcap. 13.5% alc. **Rating** 95 **To** 2021 $50 CM
Estate Great Southern Shiraz 2013 Supple but sturdy. Plums, cherries, sweet milk chocolate, aniseed and peppercorn. Boasts both volume and spread of flavour. Fine-grained tannin, leaning towards the assertive side, is more than just a tidying influence; it's a future. Screwcap. 13.5% alc. **Rating** 95 **To** 2028 $30 CM ✪
Block 9 Mount Barker Shiraz 2011 Non-aggressive complexity. You can take from this as much as you wish. Cherry-plum fruit, briary aspects, chicory and cloves and small goods. Silty tannin is a key and seductive feature, as is well-integrated smoky/coffeed/creamy oak. Supple, elegant and with just enough power. Screwcap. 14.5% alc. **Rating** 95 **To** 2030 $60 CM
Estate Mount Barker Cabernet Sauvignon 2013 Essence of cabernet. It flows with blackcurrant, lead pencil, dried tobacco and peppercorn flavours. There's an earthiness here too, in a juicy context. And yet tannin, lacy and integrated, has not been eschewed. Screwcap. 13.5% alc. **Rating** 95 **To** 2033 $35 CM ✪
Estate Mount Barker Riesling 2014 Rating 94 **To** 2024 $28 CM ✪

ΨΨΨΨΨ **Block 5 Cabernet Sauvignon 2012 Rating** 93 **To** 2030 $65 CM
Estate Mount Barker Gewurztraminer 2014 Rating 92 **To** 2017 $28 CM
Highbury Fields Sauvignon Blanc 2014 Rating 92 **To** 2016 $25 CM ✪
Estate Great Southern Chardonnay 2014 Rating 92 **To** 2018 $32 CM

Forester Estate ★★★★★

1064 Wildwood Road, Yallingup, WA 6282 **Region** Margaret River
T (08) 9755 2788 **www**.foresterestate.com.au **Open** By appt
Winemaker Kevin McKay, Todd Payne **Est.** 2001 **Dozens** 25 000 **Vyds** 33.5ha
Forester Estate is owned by Kevin and Jenny McKay, with a 500-tonne winery, half devoted to contract winemaking, the other half for the Forester label. Winemaker Todd Payne has had a distinguished career, starting in the Great Southern, thereafter the Napa Valley, back to Plantagenet, then Esk Valley in Hawke's Bay, plus two vintages in the Northern Rhône Valley, one with esteemed producer Yves Cuilleron in 2008. His move back to WA completes the circle. The estate vineyards are planted to sauvignon blanc, semillon, chardonnay, cabernet sauvignon, shiraz, merlot, petit verdot, malbec and alicante bouschet. Exports to Japan.

ΨΨΨΨΨ **Home Block Shiraz 2012** Hand-picked; 3% whole bunches into the bottom of the fermenter, 7 days on skins; pressed to new and used French barrels, 50% with full solids; 21 months' maturation, held in bottle for 18 months. A very elegant wine that seeks to hide its light under a bushel, but once you have tasted it twice, it can hide no more, its delicious red fruits, silky texture and length exposed. Screwcap. 13.5% alc. **Rating** 96 **To** 2027 $40 ✪
Cabernet Sauvignon 2012 91/4/3/2% cabernet sauvignon, cabernet franc, merlot and petit verdot, hand-picked and open-fermented (with header boards), with maceration/fermentation of batches for between 7 and 30 days; matured for 22 months in new and used French oak. Very much in the pure, precisely detailed Forester Cabernet style, marrying finesse with vibrant cassis fruit, cedar and powdery tannins. Screwcap. 14% alc. **Rating** 96 **To** 2032 $38 ✪
Sauvignon Blanc 2014 Hand-picked in the early morning and processed immediately, 40% with cultured yeast in stainless steel, the balance fermented in used French barriques, 33% of the blend with wild yeast. It has great tactile

qualities, with the grass, green pea and nettle flavours of prior vintages, and the same fresh, crisp finish. Screwcap. 13.5% alc. **Rating** 95 **To** 2016 $27 ⚪

Semillon Sauvignon Blanc 2014 A 61/39% blend, largely fermented in stainless steel in separate batches with different cultured yeasts, 4% barrel-fermented in used French barriques. The highly expressive bouquet is in a typical Margaret River range of snow pea, nettle and tropical fruit, and is followed by an exceptionally intense vinous replay of the bouquet in the flavours of the long palate and dry finish. Screwcap. 13.5% alc. **Rating** 95 **To** 2016 $24 ⚪

Yelverton Reserve Cabernet 2012 91/4.5/2.5/2% cabernet, franc, petit verdot and merlot; headed down, 30 days on skins, 21 months in French oak. Has an exceptionally complex myriad of flavours; the questions are how much is oak, and how much dark fruits and tannins, how much 13.5% alcohol, and how much new French oak? In the end, the whole package can't be usefully deconstructed, and doesn't need to be. Screwcap. 13.5% alc. **Rating** 95 **To** 2037 $62

Shiraz 2011 Open-fermented with heading-down boards; 10 days on skins, then 50% to new and used French barriques, the remainder kept in stainless steel; blended and bottled after 24 months. Stacked with blood plum and blackberry fruit on the fragrant bouquet and medium-bodied palate; with positive tannin support. Screwcap. 14% alc. **Rating** 94 **To** 2026 $24 ⚪

Cabernet Merlot 2012 54/36/6/2/2% cabernet, merlot, petit verdot, malbec and franc, fermentation and mlf completed in new and used French barriques. An elegant, neatly groomed wine, the Bordeaux blend coming together in a synergistic whole; the tannins are sufficiently fine to make this a now or later style. Screwcap. 14% alc. **Rating** 94 **To** 2027 $24 ⚪

🍷🍷🍷🍷🍷 **Margaret River Shiraz 2012** Rating 91 **To** 2020 $24

Foster e Rocco ★★★★

PO Box 438, Heathcote, Vic 3523 **Region** Heathcote
T 0407 057 471 **www**.fostererocco.com.au **Open** Not
Winemaker Adam Foster, Lincoln Riley **Est.** 2008 **Dozens** 2500
Long-term sommeliers and friends Adam Foster and Lincoln Riley have established a business that has a very clear vision: food-friendly wine based on the versatility of sangiovese. They make their wine at Syrahmi, building it from the ground up, with fermentation in both stainless steel and a mixture of used French oak barrels. Exports to the US, Japan and China.

🍷🍷🍷🍷🍷 **Heathcote Rose 2014** Pale salmon-pink; an arresting bouquet with some smoky/savoury/funky notes woven through the red and sour cherry mix on the long, dry palate. Screwcap. 13.8% alc. **Rating** 94 **To** 2016 $25 ⚪

🍷🍷🍷🍷🍷 **Nuovo Heathcote Sangiovese 2014** Rating 93 **To** 2016 $25 ⚪

Four Winds Vineyard ★★★★★

9 Patemans Lane, Murrumbateman, NSW 2582 **Region** Canberra District
T 0432 060 903 **www**.fourwindsvineyard.com.au **Open** W'ends 10–5
Winemaker Jaime and Bill Crowe **Est.** 1998 **Dozens** 1500 **Vyds** 11.9ha
Graeme and Suzanne Lunney conceived the idea for Four Winds in 1997, planting the first vines in '98, moving to the property full-time in '99, and making the first vintage in 2000. Daughter Sarah looks after events and promotions, and youngest daughter Jaime, complete with a degree in forensic biology, has joined husband Bill in the winery. She brings with her several years' experience with the former Kambera winery, and three vintages in the Napa Valley.

🍷🍷🍷🍷🍷 **Tom's Block Canberra District Shiraz 2013** This wine announces Four Winds Vineyard as a Shiraz producer of class, and of note. It's a breakthrough wine. It has the flesh and the fantasy, the fruit and the peppery spice, and comes raked with the kind of dry, uncompromised, integral tannin that will see it mature well over many years. Screwcap. 14.2% alc. **Rating** 96 **To** 2033 $45 CM ⚪

Canberra District Riesling 2014 Rapier acidity, floral notes, steel and a cutting burst of lime. It's uncompromising, but it's intense, long and pure. Screwcap. 11.2% alc. **Rating** 95 **To** 2030 $22 CM ○

ŢŢŢŢŢ **Canberra District Shiraz 2013 Rating** 93 **To** 2021 $25 CM ○
Canberra District Sangiovese 2013 Rating 91 **To** 2020 $25 CM

Fowles Wine

Cnr Hume Freeway/Lambing Gully Road, Avenel, Vic 3664 **Region** Strathbogie Ranges
T (03) 5796 2150 **www.**fowleswine.com **Open** 7 days 9–5
Winemaker Victor Nash, Lindsay Brown **Est.** 1968 **Dozens** 60 000 **Vyds** 145ha
This family-owned winery is led by Matt Fowles, with chief winemaker Victor Nash heading the winemaking team. The large vineyard is primarily focused on riesling, chardonnay, shiraz and cabernet sauvignon, and also includes sauvignon blanc, pinot noir, merlot, semillon, viognier, gewurztraminer, savagnin, tempranillo, lagrein, arneis, vermentino, pinot gris and sangiovese. Marketing is energetic, with the well-known Ladies Who Shoot Their Lunch label available as large posters, the wines also available presented in a 6-bottle gun case. Exports to the UK, the US, Canada and China.

ŢŢŢŢŢ **Ladies who Shoot their Lunch Riesling 2014** Fermentation in a used 5400l French oak vat, the addition of 2% muscat of Alexandria, and the retention of 5g/l of residual sugar have all come together seamlessly in a wine with length and real personality; the flavours ripple through citrus, apple and minerally acidity. Screwcap. 12.2% alc. **Rating** 95 **To** 2024 $35 ○
Ladies Who Shoot Their Lunch Strathbogie Ranges Shiraz 2012 A more than worthy successor to the '10, here with even greater intensity and length to the vibrant mix of red fruits, spice and fine, savoury tannins of the medium-bodied palate. It will relish a few more years in the bottle, but hold its form for years thereafter. Screwcap. 13.5% alc. **Rating** 95 **To** 2032 $35 ○
Upton Run Reserve Single Vineyard Strathbogie Ranges Shiraz 2008 From a single block on the estate vineyard at an elevation of 503m. It has relished the time in bottle, allowing the development of gently earthy, spicy secondary flavours within the moderate alcohol mainframe of the medium-bodied palate; excellent length and balance. Cork. 14% alc. **Rating** 95 **To** 2023 $75
Stone Dwellers Strathbogie Ranges Cabernet Sauvignon 2010 A thoroughly impressive Cabernet reflecting the very good vintage that clearly suited the extensive Fowles cabernet planting down to the ground. This is a vibrantly fresh and elegant wine that will retain this freshness for years to come, tannins at no stage threatening the balance. Screwcap. 14% alc. **Rating** 95 **To** 2030 $25 ○
Ladies Who Shoot Their Lunch Chardonnay 2013 From two vineyards, picked 6–20 Mar; half wild yeast-fermented, half cultured yeast, French oak of various sizes (30% new), with stirring, small portion mlf. A suitably complex wine has emerged, with good drive and tension through to the bright, zesty finish. Screwcap. 13.7% alc. **Rating** 94 **To** 2021 $35
Stone Dwellers Limited Release Vermentino 2013 A delicious tangy, zesty wine with all manner of citrus elements at play, couched within a framework of minerally acidity; the length of the finish is likewise impressive. Screwcap. 12% alc. **Rating** 94 **To** 2016 $22 ○
Stone Dwellers Shiraz 2013 Proclaims its (relatively) cool region, the savoury/ spicy bouquet perfectly reflected in the medium-bodied palate; here notes of sour plum, anise and blackberry come together, oak and tannins providing carefully managed support. Screwcap. 14% alc. **Rating** 94 **To** 2028 $25 ○
The Exception Late Harvest Viognier 2013 The grapes were approaching 18° baume by the time of harvest, and the fermentation was stopped with a high level of residual sugar. Bright, deep straw-green, verging on gold; the striking feature of the wine is the way it has preserved its apricot varietal character, with just a hint of cumquat; a touch more acidity would have made a great wine. Screwcap. 10.5% alc. **Rating** 94 **To** 2019 $30 ○

ΨΨΨΨΨ Upton Run Reserve Riesling 2008 Rating 91 To 2018 $35
Stone Dwellers Riesling 2014 Rating 90 To 2024 $22
Stone Dwellers Sauvignon Blanc 2014 Rating 90 To 2015 $22

Fox Creek Wines ★★★★★

Malpas Road, McLaren Vale, SA 5171 **Region** McLaren Vale
T (08) 8557 0000 **www.foxcreekwines.com Open** 7 days 10–5
Winemaker Scott Zrna, Ben Tanzer **Est.** 1995 **Dozens** 45 000 **Vyds** 21ha
Fox Creek has made a major impact since coming on-stream late in 1995. It is the venture
of the extended Watts family, headed by Jim (a retired surgeon). Moves are afoot to introduce
organic practices in the vineyards, with trials of an organically registered herbicide derived
from pine oil for weed control. Although Fox Creek is not organic, they use sustainable
vineyard practices, avoiding all systemic chemicals. The wines have enjoyed considerable show
success. Exports to all major markets.

ΨΨΨΨΨ Old Vine Shiraz 2013 From a single vineyard planted 103 years before this
vintage. The deep colour is as it should be, and the complex array of aromas and
flavours are a direct legacy of the very old vines. Black cherry, satsuma plum,
licorice, dark chocolate and spice are all in tune with each other, leaving the way
clear for the supple tannins and oak to make their impact on this beautiful example
of medium-bodied Shiraz. Screwcap. 14.5% alc. **Rating** 97 To 2043 $50 ✪

ΨΨΨΨΨ Reserve Shiraz 2013 A barrel-by-barrel selection from the best of the vintage.
The deep purple-crimson hue introduces a full-bodied Shiraz of extreme
complexity and power; the fruit flavours are uncompromisingly black, the tannins
integral to the overall style and quality of the wine, oak also well in play. Demands
respect and time. Screwcap. 14.5% alc. **Rating** 96 To 2043 $75 ✪
Short Row Shiraz 2013 The bouquet does not prepare you for the naked power
of the full-bodied palate with its onrush of black fruits, bitter chocolate and potent,
dusty tannins. Approach with caution, armed with a large char-grilled T-bone
steak. Screwcap. 14.5% alc. **Rating** 95 To 2038 $32 ✪
Shiraz 2013 Deep, inky crimson-purple colour doesn't lie: this is all about full-
bodied regional Shiraz from a very good vintage, with black fruits, a slash of
bitter chocolate and ripe tannins embedded in the fruit; the oak contribution is
incidental. Screwcap. 14.5% alc. **Rating** 94 To 2028 $23 ✪
Reserve Shiraz 2012 Trophies and gold medals in wine shows in France, Spain
and Germany (two) make a major splash on the bottle. A barrel selection, oak
oozing from every pore, milk chocolate tannins adding to the flavour and texture.
A dry red wine for those with a sweet tooth; time in bottle will reward. Screwcap.
14.5% alc. **Rating** 94 To 2032 $75
Duet Cabernet Merlot 2012 Has a string of gold, silver and bronze medals
from international wine competitions and shows. A 64/36% blend, with all
components finishing their fermentation in used French and American oak,
matured for 19 months thereafter. The cabernet is as dominant as the percentage
split suggests (if not more so), with pure blackcurrant fruit, black olive and
balanced tannins. Well priced. Screwcap. 14.5% alc. **Rating** 94 To 2027 $23 ✪

ΨΨΨΨΨ Chardonnay 2014 Rating 93 To 2020 $23 ✪
JSM Shiraz Cabernet Sauvignon Cabernet Franc 2012 Rating 92 To 2022
$23 ✪
Vermentino 2014 Rating 90 To 2016 $23

Fox Gordon ★★★★★

44 King William Road, Goodwood, SA 5034 **Region** Barossa Valley/Adelaide Hills
T (08) 8377 7707 **www.foxgordon.com.au Open** Not
Winemaker Natasha Mooney **Est.** 2000 **Dozens** 10 000
This is the venture of Sam and Rachel Atkins (née Fox) and winemaker Natasha (Tash)
Mooney. Tash has had first-class experience in the Barossa Valley, particularly during her

time as chief winemaker at Barossa Valley Estate. The partners initially produced only small quantities of high-quality wine, allowing them time to look after their children; the venture was planned in the shade of the wisteria tree in Tash's back garden. The grapes come from dry-grown vineyards farmed under biodiversity principles. Classy packaging adds the final touch. Exports to the UK, Canada, Germany, India, Singapore, Hong Kong and China.

🍷🍷🍷🍷🍷 **Abby Adelaide Hills Viognier 2014** Not at all in your face and yet with plenty of personality. It's a fine line between pleasure and pain, and this walks it. Ginger spice, stone fruits, grapefruit and orange blossom; it provides a most enjoyable experience. Screwcap. 13% alc. **Rating** 93 **To** 2016 $23 CM ✪

Sassy Adelaide Hills Sauvignon Blanc 2014 Back label describes it as 'contagiously cheerful' and that pretty much sums it up. It offers a mouthful of flavour and fragrance: apple, tropical fruit, rockmelon and Turkish delight characters. Crowd-pleasing. Screwcap. 12% alc. **Rating** 91 **To** 2015 $19 CM ✪

King Louis Barossa Valley Cabernet Sauvignon 2012 Dark colour and good depth of flavour. Concern is that it all seems a bit lifeless. Flavours display tar, blackberry and bay leaf characters and while it's both varietal and hearty enough, it's more resistible than you'd hope at the price. Perhaps it's in a dull spot. Screwcap. 13.9% alc. **Rating** 91 **To** 2025 $60 CM

Charlotte's Web Adelaide Hills Pinot Grigio 2014 It sits somewhere between Grigio and Gris style-wise. It certainly offers abundant apple, pear and nectarine-like fruit flavour, the finish then a burst a citrus. Perfumed and generous. Screwcap. 13.2% alc. **Rating** 90 **To** 2015 $23 CM

Foxeys Hangout   ★★★★★

795 White Hill Road, Red Hill, Vic 3937 **Region** Mornington Peninsula
T (03) 5989 2022 www.foxeys-hangout.com.au **Open** W'ends & public hols 11–5
Winemaker Tony and Michael Lee **Est.** 1998 **Dozens** 5000 **Vyds** 3.4ha
This is the venture of Tony Lee and journalist wife Cathy Gowdie. Cathy explains where it all began: 'We were not obvious candidates for a seachange. When we talked of moving to the country, friends pointed out that Tony and I were hardly back-to-nature types. "Do you own a single pair of shoes without heels?" asked a friend. At the end of a bleak winter, we bought an old farmhouse on 10 daffodil-dotted acres at Red Hill and planted a vineyard.' They planted pinot noir, chardonnay, pinot gris and shiraz on the north-facing slopes of the old farm.

🍷🍷🍷🍷🍷 **Shiraz 2013** Deep, vivid crimson-purple; the perfumed bouquet attests to the wild yeast co-fermentation of a small percentage of viognier uplifting the chorus of red and black fruits wreathed with cool-grown spice and pepper; the super-elegant palate is as intense as it is long. A worthy successor to the '12. Screwcap. 13.5% alc. **Rating** 97 **To** 2038 $45 ✪

🍷🍷🍷🍷🍷 **Kentucky Road 777 Pinot Noir 2013** The leash is long but it's definitely there. It's a ribald Pinot Noir in its flavour profile but structurally it's taut and trim. Winemaker Tony Lee says it tastes of 'chocolate, chilli and anise', and whether or not you agree, it gives an insight into its exotic profile. It's sappy, spicy, quite deep yet frisky, tangy, alive. If you're a Pinot fancier you will fancy this. Screwcap. 13.5% alc. **Rating** 96 **To** 2023 $60 CM ✪

White Gates Vineyard Pinot Noir 2013 It's a pretty, floral wine, immediately attractive and interesting, the conversation lively from the first hello. At no point thereafter do you feel let down. Deep cherry, boysenberry, sap and spice, with liquid toast/spice oak adding a beautiful extra. One sip and you never want to leave. Screwcap. 13.5% alc. **Rating** 96 **To** 2025 $60 CM ✪

Scotsworth Farm Pinot Noir 2013 Made from 15yo MV6-clone vines. It has both a lightness of touch and a strength to its personality. Treat it as a pushover and you'll be on your back in a blink. Sappy cherries, floral overtones, autumnal herbs and spices, bowls of strawberries and plums and strings of sinewy tannin. Quite outstanding. Screwcap. 13.5% alc. **Rating** 96 **To** 2025 $60 CM ✪

Chardonnay 2013 Has more complexity, mouthfeel and weight than many Mornington Chardonnays, with cloudy juice, wild yeast barrel ferment; this provides an impressive crosscut between white peach/grapefruit on the one hand, and savoury/acid nuances on the other. Screwcap. 13% alc. **Rating 95 To 2023** $35 ✪

White Gates Vineyard Chardonnay 2013 Wild yeast-fermented, full solids, no mlf. Sweet, sunny, generous style with length to burn. Peach, white peach and clips of high-class oak. Makes it all look easy. Screwcap. 13.5% alc. **Rating 94 To 2020** $45 CM

Pinot Gris 2014 Immaculate in all respects. Flavoured but not too heavily so, textured but not oily, refreshing but more than that. Chalk, spice and pear with a barley sugar-like aspect. A most pleasurable wine. Screwcap. 13.5% alc. **Rating 94 To 2016** $28 CM ✪

Pinot Noir 2013 Spice, cherry and plum contend for equal billing on the bouquet and palate alike; the wine has plenty of flesh, and has the balance to prosper over the next 2–3 years as the spices become even more evident. Screwcap. 13.5% alc. **Rating 94 To 2020** $35

�♟♟♟♙ **Late Harvest Pinot Gris 2013 Rating** 93 **To** 2017 $28 CM

Frankland Estate   ★★★★★

Frankland Road, Frankland, WA 6396 **Region** Frankland River
T (08) 9855 1544 **www.franklandestate.com.au Open** Mon–Fri 10–4, public hols & w'ends by appt
Winemaker Hunter Smith, Brian Kent **Est.** 1988 **Dozens** 15 000 **Vyds** 34.5ha
A significant operation, situated on a large sheep property owned by Barrie Smith and Judi Cullam. The vineyard has been established progressively since 1988; the introduction of an array of single-vineyard Rieslings has been a highlight, driven by Judi's conviction that terroir is of utmost importance, and the soils are indeed different. The Isolation Ridge Vineyard is now organically grown. Frankland Estate has held important International Riesling tastings and seminars over the past decade. Exports to all major markets.

♟♟♟♟♟ **Isolation Ridge Vineyard Riesling 2014** Light straw-green; an exceptionally scented, blossom-filled bouquet, including wild flowers as well as citrus and apple; a very intense and sculptured palate, with squeaky acidity running throughout. Likely to have a very low pH, and has a commensurately long palate. Screwcap. 11.7% alc. **Rating 97 To 2034** $35 ✪

♟♟♟♟♟ **Poison Hill Vineyard Riesling 2014** Apple, citrus blossom, talc and wild flowers don't necessarily warn you of the intensity of the palate, but the pH of 2.83 certainly does; the finish surges on and on, with a mix of mineral, citrus and green apple. Screwcap. 12.5% alc. **Rating 96 To 2034** $30 ✪

Netley Road Vineyard Riesling 2014 Light straw-green; citrus blossom, plus notes of herb; a finely structured and immaculately balanced palate, lime, lemon juice and mineral notes all interwoven; the acidity and balance guarantee a distinguished future. Screwcap. 13% alc. **Rating 95 To 2029** $30 ✪

Isolation Ridge Vineyard Cabernet Sauvignon 2012 Good hue; an autocratic Cabernet demanding to be taken on its own terms; black fruits, bramble and persistent tannins, all true varietal markers. Screwcap. 14% alc. **Rating 95 To 2027** $27 ✪

Olmo's Reward 2012 A long-established estate 70/18/12% blend of cabernet franc, cabernet sauvignon and petit verdot. The hue is bright, and the bouquet and palate live up to it in no uncertain fashion, with a bevy of red fruits and cassis woven through with fine, almost spicy, tannins and a waft of French oak. Screwcap. 14.5% alc. **Rating 95 To 2027** $45

♟♟♟♟♙ **Marsanne 2014 Rating** 93 **To** 2034 $27 ✪
Rocky Gully Riesling 2014 Rating 92 **To** 2024 $18 ✪
Rocky Gully Sauvignon Blanc 2014 Rating 91 **To** 2015 $18 ✪
Rocky Gully Shiraz 2013 Rating 91 **To** 2018 $18 ✪

Franklin Tate Estates ★★★★★

Gale Road, Kaloorup, WA 6280 **Region** Margaret River
T (08) 9267 8555 **www**.franklintateestates.com.au **Open** Not
Winemaker Rory Clifton-Parks **Est.** 2010 **Dozens** 30 000 **Vyds** 101.11ha
This is the second business established by Franklin and Heather Tate since the demise of
Evans & Tate. In 2007 they came up with Miles From Nowhere (see separate entry), but this
is a quite separate venture, with 101ha of vines (Miles From Nowhere has 47ha). The lion's
share of the plantings go to sauvignon blanc and semillon (24ha each), chardonnay (22ha),
shiraz (17ha) and cabernet sauvignon (8ha), with minor plantings of verdelho, petit verdot and
viognier. Rory Clifton-Parks has been the winemaker for both incarnations. It's not surprising
to see five Asian markets, and Canada, as the export focus. Exports to Canada, Malaysia,
Singapore, Thailand, Hong Kong and China.

ＴＴＴＴＴ **Tate Alexanders Vineyards Reserve Shiraz 2013** Value plus. Impressive
colour and depth of flavour, but it's not just grunty (though it is that); it's also
polished, stylish and presentable in any company. Blackberry, peanuts, garden
herbs and swish cedar wood. Just enough fine-grained tannin. A find. Screwcap.
14.5% alc. **Rating** 95 **To** 2027 $24 CM ✪
Tate Alexanders Vineyard Reserve Cabernet Sauvignon 2013 You
wouldn't expect this quality at this price to last. Make hay while you can. It's a
beautiful Margaret River Cabernet, highly aromatic, smooth-skinned, tannic in an
integrated way, awash with blackcurrant, gravel and bay leaf flavours, slipped with
chocolatey/pencilly oak. Screwcap. 14.5% alc. **Rating** 95 **To** 2030 $24 CM ✪

ＴＴＴＴＹ **Tate Cabernet Merlot 2013 Rating** 91 **To** 2019 $16 CM ✪

Fraser Gallop Estate ★★★★★

493 Metricup Road, Wilyabrup, WA 6280 **Region** Margaret River
T (08) 9755 7553 **www**.frasergallopestate.com.au **Open** By appt
Winemaker Clive Otto, Kate Morgan **Est.** 1999 **Dozens** 11 000 **Vyds** 20ha
Nigel Gallop began the development of the vineyard in 1999, planting cabernet sauvignon,
semillon, petit verdot, cabernet franc, malbec, merlot, sauvignon blanc and multi-clone
chardonnay. The vines are dry-grown with modest yields, followed by kid-glove treatment in
the winery. The first vintage was 2002. With Clive Otto (formerly of Vasse Felix) on board, a
300-tonne winery was built in '08, with highly qualified assistant Kate Morgan joining the
team from that vintage. Right from the word go, the wines have had richly deserved success
in wine shows and journalists' reviews. Exports to the UK, Canada, Switzerland, Germany,
Indonesia, Singapore, Hong Kong and China.

ＴＴＴＴＴ **Parterre Semillon Sauvignon Blanc 2013** A 65/35% blend, wild yeast-
fermented in new and used French oak, and matured for 9 months in that oak. This
takes all the best characters of Margaret River SSB, and adds a layer of opulence
that only Cullen gets close to emulating. It is the result of immaculate viticulture
and sensitive winemaking. Screwcap. 13% alc. **Rating** 97 **To** 2028 $30 ✪

ＴＴＴＴＴ **Parterre Wilyabrup Cabernet Sauvignon 2012** An estate-grown and bottled
Cabernet, including 7% petit verdot and 4% each of merlot and malbec. It has
considerable attitude, with crisply detailed and framed flavours that progressively
gain velocity as they move across the palate towards the emphatic, balanced, finish.
Screwcap. 14% alc. **Rating** 96 **To** 2042 $42 ✪
Semillon Sauvignon 2014 The ultimate synergy that Margaret River gives this
blend has no parallel elsewhere in Australia, and France has to work hard. There is
a diamond-cut brilliance to the profusion of lemon/lemon zesty/crunchy acidity
of the semillon and the guava/tropical fruits following demurely behind. Partial
barrel fermentation has played a role, but where that starts and finishes isn't easy
to pick. Screwcap. 12% alc. **Rating** 95 **To** 2025 $23 ✪

ＴＴＴＴＹ **Margaret River Chardonnay 2014 Rating** 93 **To** 2020 $24 ✪

Freeman Vineyards ★★★★★

101 Prunevale Road, Prunevale, NSW 2587 **Region** Hilltops
T (02) 6384 4299 **www**.freemanvineyards.com.au **Open** By appt
Winemaker Dr Brian Freeman, Xanthe Freeman **Est.** 2000 **Dozens** 5000 **Vyds** 103ha
Dr Brian Freeman has spent much of his life in research and education, in the latter role as head of CSU's viticulture and oenology campus. In 2004 he purchased the 30-year-old vineyard previously known as Demondrille. He has also established a vineyard next door, and in all has 14 varieties that range from staples such as shiraz, cabernet sauvignon, semillon and riesling through to more exotic, trendy varieties such as tempranillo, and on to corvina and rondinella. He has long had an interest in the effect of partial drying of grapes on the tannins and was easily able to obtain a prune dehydrator to partially raisin the two varieties.

ŶŶŶŶŶ **Altura Vineyard Nebbiolo 2013** A Nebbiolo you accept or reject on its terms, no negotiations on the table; it has the rectitude of a mother superior, the tannins testing one's faith, but doing so fully understanding the need for some pleasure as a reward – and the complexity of the full family of cherry flavours, from sour to morello, does just that. Screwcap. 13.5% alc. **Rating** 95 **To** 2028 $35 ✪
Prosecco 2014 Made from young vines, but it soars in the glass. This is a beauty. Flavours of lemon delicious, custard apples, wax and yellow stone fruit give the wine both richness and more than a little strut. It's tangy and pert too, and beautifully dry. Great drinking. Cork. 12% alc. **Rating** 95 **To** 2016 $23 CM ✪
Altura Vineyard Cabernet Sauvignon 2012 This elegant, medium-bodied Cabernet comes from Hilltops; there has been no attempt to over-extract or over-elaborate; this is just what the terroir should give: varietal fruit expression in a demure red berry fashion, fine, earthy tannins just so. Screwcap. 13.5% alc. **Rating** 94 **To** 2022 $25 ✪

ŶŶŶŶŶ **Secco Rondinella Corvina 2011 Rating** 93 **To** 2021 $35
Fortuna Pinot Grigio Plus 2013 Rating 91 **To** 2016 $25

Freycinet ★★★★★

15919 Tasman Highway via Bicheno, Tas 7215 **Region** East Coast Tasmania
T (03) 6257 8574 **www**.freycinetvineyard.com.au **Open** 7 days 10–5 Nov–Apr,
10–4 May–Oct
Winemaker Claudio Radenti, Lindy Bull **Est.** 1980 **Dozens** 7000 **Vyds** 14.83ha
The Freycinet vineyards are situated on the sloping hillsides of a small valley. The soils are brown dermosol on top of Jurassic dolerite, and the combination of aspect, slope, soil and heat summation produces red grapes with unusual depth of colour and ripe flavours. One of the foremost producers of Pinot Noir, with an enviable track record of consistency – rare in such a temperamental variety. The Radenti (sparkling), Riesling and Chardonnay are also wines of the highest quality. In 2012 Freycinet acquired part of the neighbouring Coombend property from Brown Brothers. The 42ha property extends to the Tasman Highway, and includes a 5.75ha mature vineyard and a 4.2ha olive grove. Exports to the UK and Singapore.

ŶŶŶŶŶ **Pinot Noir 2013** Sulky, brooding Pinot Noir with quality oozing from its pores. Smoky, sappy perfume, rose petals, berries and a power of cherry-plum fruit, but for all its muscle it remains vigorous and athletic, supple, everything massaged and alert at once. Outstanding wine by any criteria. Screwcap. 14% alc. **Rating** 97 **To** 2030 $75 CM ✪

ŶŶŶŶŶ **Pinot Noir 2012** This was my favourite in the first flight of Stonier's '15 SIPNOT event. Deeply coloured crimson-purple, it has a highly expressive bouquet, spice woven through the luscious dark fruits of the powerful and distinguished palate. Fermented for 8–10 days with 5% whole bunches, it spent 16 months in French barriques (27% new). Screwcap. 13.5% alc. **Rating** 96 **To** 2022 $75 ✪

Riesling 2014 Complex even in its youth. Apple and grapefruit with spice notes and green herbs. Excellent intensity and length. Drive through the finish is most impressive. Screwcap. 13% alc. **Rating** 95 **To** 2026 $30 CM ✪
Chardonnay 2013 Estate-grown, fully mature vines, hand-picked and barrel-fermented and matured for 10 months in French oak (20% new) have produced an elegant wine with harmony its centrepiece; stone fruit and melon are supported by oak and some citrus, the sometimes awkward Tasmanian acidity posing no problems. Screwcap. 13.5% alc. **Rating** 95 **To** 2023 $40
Louis Chardonnay 2013 No lack of length but no lack of flavour either. That famed Tasmanian acidity rides again. Pear, honeysuckle, sweet lime and toast with oatmeal and powdered milk notes rising as the wine breathes. In excellent shape. Screwcap. 13.5% alc. **Rating** 94 **To** 2019 $28 CM ✪

🍷🍷🍷🍷 **Sauvignon Blanc 2014 Rating** 93 **To** 2016 $29 CM
Louis Pinot Noir 2013 Rating 92 **To** 2023 $37 CM

Frog Choir Wines ★★★★☆

PO Box 635, Margaret River, WA 6285 **Region** Margaret River
T 0427 777 787 **www**.frogchoir.com **Open** Not
Winemaker Naturaliste Vintners (Bruce Duke) **Est.** 1997 **Dozens** 250 **Vyds** 1.2ha
Kate and Nigel Hunt have a micro vineyard equally split between shiraz and cabernet sauvignon. It has immaculate address credentials: adjacent to Leeuwin Estate and Voyager Estate, 6km from the Margaret River township. The hand-tended vines are grown without the use of insecticides. Exports to France and Thailand.

🍷🍷🍷🍷🍷 **Margaret River Cabernet Shiraz 2008** A 54/46% blend; the wine is incredibly youthful in its colour, fragrance and its wanton display of bright red and black fruits; oak and tannins are accessories after the fact. This is as delicious as it is freakish. Screwcap. 14.5% alc. **Rating** 95 **To** 2023 $25 ✪

🍷🍷🍷🍷 **Margaret River Cabernet Shiraz 2007 Rating** 92 **To** 2022 $25 ✪

Frogmore Creek ★★★★★

699 Richmond Road, Cambridge, Tas 7170 **Region** Southern Tasmania
T (03) 6248 4484 **www**.frogmorecreek.com.au **Open** 7 days 10–5
Winemaker Alain Rousseau, John Bown **Est.** 1997 **Dozens** 18000 **Vyds** 55ha
Frogmore Creek is a Pacific Rim joint venture, the owners being Tony Scherer of Tasmania and Jack Kidwiler of California. The business has grown very substantially, first establishing its own organically managed vineyard, and thereafter by a series of acquisitions. First was the purchase of the Hood/Wellington Wines business previously owned by Andrew Hood; next was the purchase of the large Roslyn Vineyard near Campania; and finally (in Oct 2010) the acquisition of Meadowbank Estate, where the cellar door is now located. In Dec '12 the original Frogmore Creek vineyard was sold to Hill-Smith Family Vineyards. Exports to the US, Japan, Indonesia and South Korea.

🍷🍷🍷🍷🍷 **Iced Riesling 2013** The grapes were crushed for an overnight cold soak to increase aroma and flavour extraction, then lightly pressed to tank for freeze concentration until the baume reached 19°, transferred to oak for wild yeast fermentation while the residual sugar of 197g/l remained, then cross-flow filtered and bottled. A glorious interplay between lemon and honey. 375ml. Screwcap. 7% alc. **Rating** 96 **To** 2025 $26 ✪
FGR Riesling 2014 Beautiful essence of Bickford's lime juice, with a hint of passionfruit; utterly perfect balance of residual sugar and acidity. Frogmore Creek pioneered this style in Tasmania well over 10 years ago, the winemaking skilled (and complex). Screwcap. 10.2% alc. **Rating** 95 **To** 2025 $24 ✪
FGR Riesling 2013 The wine that launched a 1000 ships over 15 years ago. Cold-fermented, then cross-flow filtered while it still retained 48g/l of residual sugar, a less important figure than the pH of 2.87 (and titratable acidity of 8.4g/l).

A reflex action caused me to swallow the wine, so delicious are its juicy lime fruit flavours. Screwcap. 10.2% alc. **Rating** 95 **To** 2023 $24 ✪

Cuvee Evermore 2008 A celebration of Tasmanian pinot noir, fruity, rich and powerful, layered with succulent white peach and yellow mirabelle plums. Barrel and bottle maturation has furnished layers of mixed spice, roasted almond and brioche complexity. Lemon zest freshness holds out impressively at 6yo, neatly tempered by well-integrated dosage. Diam. 12% alc. **Rating** 95 **To** 2018 $38 TS

Chardonnay 2013 Grown in the Coal River Valley; barrel-fermented and kept on lees for 10 months. Has excellent length, texture and balance, poised between grapefruit and white peach, acidity a positive contributor. Screwcap. 13% alc. **Rating** 94 **To** 2023 $30 ✪

🍷🍷🍷🍷♀ **Fume Blanc Sauvignon Blanc 2014 Rating** 93 **To** 2015 $28
42°S Pinot Noir 2014 Rating 91 **To** 2019 $28
42°S Pinot Noir 2013 Rating 91 **To** 2020 $28
Pinot Noir 2010 Rating 91 **To** 2020 $36
42°S Unoaked Chardonnay 2011 Rating 90 **To** 2018 $25

Gabriel Horvat Wines ★★★★

No. 9, 37–39 East Street, Daylesford, Vic 3460 **Region** Macedon Ranges
T 0429 585 129 **www**.horvatwines.com **Open** Mon–Tues 11–5, Fri–Sat 11–late, Sun 12–4
Winemaker Gabriel Horvat **Est.** 2005 **Dozens** 1000
Gabriel Horvat grew up in the Pyrenees town of Landsborough, and after finishing school, worked for several years in local vineyards before beginning a winemaking degree in 2000 at CSU. He subsequently decided to discontinue studying for that degree, instead gaining practical and philosophical education in traditional methods in his father's winery (Horvat). He began developing his own labels, and eventually moved to set up his own small winery in Daylesford. Situated in the middle of town, his venture extends to a boutique wine store focusing on the wines of Western Victoria, a wine bar and music venue. The premises are named 'W.I.N.E. is a 4 letter word', his operating company called Liberated Winemakers.

🍷🍷🍷🍷♀ **Native Youth Shiraz 2012** A powerful, yet well-balanced Shiraz; black fruits on the bouquet and palate are leavened by notes of spice, licorice and earth; good length and balance. Screwcap. 13.3% alc. **Rating** 91 **To** 2027 $25
Native Youth Cabernet Sauvignon 2013 From the Pyrenees and Grampians. Sombre black flavours of licorice, blackberry, earth and leather drive the full-bodied palate. It is quite simply not ready yet, but should relax over the next 5+ years. Screwcap. 13.6% alc. **Rating** 91 **To** 2028 $26

Gaelic Cemetery Wines ★★★★★

PO Box 54, Sevenhill, SA 5453 **Region** Clare Valley
T (08) 8843 4370 **www**.gaelic-cemeterywines.com **Open** Not
Winemaker Neil Pike, Steve Baraglia **Est.** 2005 **Dozens** 1500 **Vyds** 6.5ha
This is a joint venture between winemaker Neil Pike, viticulturist Andrew Pike and Adelaide retailers Mario and Ben Barletta. It hinges on a single vineyard owned by Grant Arnold, planted in 1996, adjacent to the historic cemetery of the region's Scottish pioneers. Situated in a secluded valley of the Clare hills, the low-cropping vineyard, say the partners, 'is always one of the earliest ripening shiraz vineyards in the region and mystifyingly produces fruit with both natural pH and acid analyses that can only be described as beautiful numbers'. The result is hands-off winemaking and maturation for 24 months in new and used Burgundian barriques. Exports to the UK, the US, Canada, Germany, Singapore, Taiwan, Hong Kong and China.

🍷🍷🍷🍷🍷 **Celtic Farm Clare Valley Riesling 2014** Length and balance are immediately obvious, less so the way it builds flavour and length, until the aftertaste brings home the quality of citrus/green varietal fruit. Great value. This wine could easily outlast its Premium sibling. Screwcap. 11% alc. **Rating** 95 **To** 2029 $22 ✪

Premium Clare Valley Riesling 2014 The front label is black (its Celtic Farm sibling is white), but otherwise gives no clue until you read the back label, which has 'Premium' in bold print. When you taste it the impact of the fruit is immediate and generous, sweet lime juice coating the mouth, balanced by acidity on a dry finish. Screwcap. 11.5% alc. **Rating** 95 **To** 2029 $35 ❖

ㅜㅜㅜㅜ **Clare Valley Shiraz 2010 Rating** 89 **To** 2030 $80

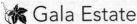

Gala Estate   ★★★★★

14891 Tasman Highway, Cranbrook, Tas 4814 **Region** East Coast Tasmania
T 0408 681 014 **www.**galaestate.com.au **Open** 7 days 10–4 (closed winter)
Winemaker Winemaking Tasmania **Est.** 2008 **Dozens** 2500 **Vyds** 11ha
This vineyard is situated on a 4000ha sheep station, with the sixth, seventh and eight generations headed by Robert and Patricia (Amos) Greenhill, custodians of the land granted to Adam Amos in 1821; it is recognised as the second-oldest family business in Tasmania. The 11ha vineyard is heavily skewed to pinot noir (7ha), the remainder planted (in descending order of area) to chardonnay, pinot gris, riesling, shiraz and sauvignon blanc. The main risk is spring frost, and overhead spray irrigation serves two purposes: to provide adequate moisture for early season growth, and frost protection at the end of the growing season. All of the viticultural work is carried out by the family. Given that the vines were not planted until 2008, Gala Estate has a bright future. I am strongly of the view that its modest success in wine shows so far does not fully reflect the quality of the wines.

ㅜㅜㅜㅜㅜ **Pinot Gris 2013** Still pale quartz; Pinot Gris was fast out of the blocks in Tasmania, but little understood at first; this is a very good example of Gris, with a richness to the texture, nashi pear and a hint of fresh ginger; the acidity is balanced, even soft. Screwcap. 13.6% alc. **Rating** 95 **To** 2021 $28 ❖
Pinot Noir 2011 More purple to its colour than Young Vine. Remarkable. The vintage was much better than that of southern Vic, but it was no bed of roses; this is a delicious Pinot, with elegance, length and a bouquet garni accompanying its silky red fruits. Screwcap. 13.5% alc. **Rating** 95 **To** 2028 $37
Late Harvest Riesling 2012 Tasmania does so well with this style, its acidity crying out for the residual sugar, and vice versa. Marries intensity with elegance and length, thanks to its balance, Bickford's lime juice and lemon sherbet providing the flavours. Will coast through and grow over the next decade. Screwcap. 10.5% alc. **Rating** 95 **To** 2022 $28 ❖

ㅜㅜㅜㅜㅜ **Young Vine Pinot Noir 2013 Rating** 93 **To** 2025 $28
Pinot Noir Chardonnay NV Rating 93 **To** 2020 $35
Riesling 2013 Rating 91 **To** 2023 $28

Galafrey   ★★★★

Quangellup Road, Mount Barker, WA 6324 **Region** Mount Barker
T (08) 9851 2022 **www.**galafreywines.com.au **Open** 7 days 10–5
Winemaker Kim Tyrer **Est.** 1977 **Dozens** 4000 **Vyds** 13.1ha
Galafrey makes wines with plenty of robust, if not rustic, character, drawing grapes in the main from estate plantings. Following the death of husband/father/founder Ian Tyrer, Kim and Linda Tyrer have taken up the reins, announcing, 'There is girl power happening at Galafrey Wines!' There is a cornucopia of back vintages available at the cellar door. Exports to China.

ㅜㅜㅜㅜㅜ **Dry Land Reserve Mount Barker Riesling 2014** Fruit selection, and only free-run juice, produces a wine that deserves the Reserve tag. Finely structured, and bone dry, the mix of lime and grapefruit flavours is underlined by crisp acidity. Certain to flourish with time. Screwcap. 11.5% alc. **Rating** 93 **To** 2024 $28
Dry Grown Mount Barker Merlot 2012 Microscopic black printing on a dark grey label needs a searchlight in a restaurant. Old dry-grown vines and the cool climate join to produce a wine with abundant cassis and black olive fruit, the tannins neatly balanced. Screwcap. 13% alc. **Rating** 93 **To** 2027 $30

Dry Grown Mount Barker Cabernet Sauvignon 2012 35yo dry-grown vines have produced a wine that doesn't take a backwards step – but then that's the autocratic nature of most high-quality young Cabernets. Thus the blackcurrant fruit, bramble and earthy notes are all framed by firm tannins. Patience will be rewarded. Screwcap. 14% alc. **Rating** 92 **To** 2027 $30

ΨΨΨΨ   **Mount Barker Riesling 2014 Rating** 88 **To** 2020 $20

Gallagher Wines   ★★★★☆

2770 Dog Trap Road, Murrumbateman, NSW 2582 **Region** Canberra District
T (02) 6227 0555 **www**.gallagherwines.com.au **Open** W'ends & public hols 10–5
Winemaker Greg Gallagher **Est.** 1995 **Dozens** 2000 **Vyds** 2ha
Greg Gallagher was senior winemaker at Taltarni for 20 years, working with Dominique Portet. He began planning a change and, together with wife Libby, established a small vineyard at Murrumbateman in 1995, now with 1ha each of chardonnay and shiraz. Between '99 and 2004 Greg was winemaker at CSU, and now acts as both winemaker and consultant for a dozen or so wineries in or near the Canberra District.

ΨΨΨΨΨ   **Canberra District Shiraz 2013** Strong colour; immediately stamps its class with a perfect display of cool-grown shiraz that effortlessly reached optimum varietal flavour; medium-bodied and supple, it has spicy black cherry and plum fruit, ripe but silky tannins and subtle oak. Deserves its gold medal at the Canberra District Wine Show '14. Screwcap. 13.6% alc. **Rating** 95 **To** 2028 $30 **○**

ΨΨΨΨ♀   **Canberra District Riesling 2014 Rating** 92 **To** 2024 $22 **○**
    Canberra District Sauvignon Blanc 2014 Rating 90 **To** 2015 $20 **○**

Galli Estate   ★★★★★

1507 Melton Highway, Plumpton, Vic 3335 **Region** Sunbury
T (03) 9747 1444 **www**.galliestate.com.au **Open** 7 days 11–5
Winemaker Ben Ranken **Est.** 1997 **Dozens** 10 000 **Vyds** 160ha
Galli Estate has two vineyards: Heathcote, which produces the red wines (Shiraz, Sangiovese, Nebbiolo, Tempranillo, Grenache and Montepulciano), and the cooler climate vineyard at Plumpton, producing the whites (Chardonnay, Pinot Grigio, Sauvignon Blanc and Fiano). All wines are estate-grown and made. Exports to Canada, Singapore, China and Hong Kong.

ΨΨΨΨΨ   **Pamela 2012** Produced from the four Dijon chardonnay clones; whole bunch-pressed, fermented and matured in French oak. Bright straw-green; it has purity and length, the balance exact. Screwcap. 12.5% alc. **Rating** 95 **To** 2022 $60
    Adele Fiano 2013 Wild yeast-fermented. The grapes are estate-grown at Sunbury, and this is one of the best Fianos I've so far seen from Australia. It is vibrantly fresh, with a supple mid-palate, and zesty citrussy acidity on the long palate. The climate is right. Screwcap. 12% alc. **Rating** 95 **To** 2016 $38
    Adele Syrah 2013 Small batch wild yeast-fermented with 40% whole bunches. The very complex bouquet ranges through red and black fruits, cinnamon and charcuterie; the palate is equally complex, retracing the characters of the bouquet, all attesting to the cool Sunbury region and the high percentage of whole bunches in the ferment. Screwcap. 14.5% alc. **Rating** 95 **To** 2033 $38
    Adele Tempranillo 2013 Small batch, 30% whole bunches, wild yeast-fermented. This has unusual depth and texture for the more usual linear style of the variety, the cherries dark, not red, and plum also in the picture. It's looking for a meal, and could be transformed by the right dish. Screwcap. 14.5% alc. **Rating** 94 **To** 2028 $38

ΨΨΨΨ♀   **Camelback Heathcote Shiraz 2013 Rating** 93 **To** 2023 $20 **○**
    Tempranillo Grenache Mourvedre 2013 Rating 93 **To** 2023 $20 **○**
    Artigiano Sunbury Pinot Grigio 2014 Rating 91 **To** 2016 $20 **○**
    Camelback Rose 2014 Rating 91 **To** 2016 $20 CM **○**
    Sunbury Cabernet Sauvignon Merlot 2013 Rating 91 **To** 2025 $20 **○**

Gallows Wine Co   ★★★★

Lennox Road, Carbunup River, WA 6280 **Region** Margaret River
T (08) 9755 1060 **www**.gallows.com.au **Open** 7 days 10–5
Winemaker Charlie Maiolo, Neil Doddridge **Est.** 2008 **Dozens** 11 000 **Vyds** 27ha
This is the venture of the Maiolo family, headed by winemaker Charlie. The macabre name
is that of one of the most famous surf breaks on the Margaret River coast. The vineyard is
planted to semillon, sauvignon blanc, chardonnay, pinot noir, shiraz, merlot and cabernet
sauvignon. The site climate is strongly influenced by Geographe Bay, 5km to the north, and
facilitates the production of wines with a large spectrum of flavours and characteristics.

ＹＹＹＹＹ **The Bommy Margaret River Semillon Sauvignon Blanc 2014** Excellent
intensity. Hits and runs with flavour. Gravel, snow pea, passionfruit and a flash of
woodsmoke. Some class. Screwcap. 13% alc. **Rating** 93 **To** 2016 $26 CM ✪
The Bommy Margaret River Chardonnay 2013 Flint, spice, smoke and then
grapefruit and peach. It comes with all guns blazing. It works, though you find
yourself flinching at first. More brimstone than fire. Hard to look away in the end;
it has an allure beyond logic. Screwcap. 14% alc. **Rating** 92 **To** 2018 $28 CM
The Bommy Margaret River Shiraz 2012 Saucy-sweet oak on ripe, fleshy
fruit. It's easy to be seduced. Vanilla cream, plum, peppermint and dry licorice
notes. Not particularly dark in colour but good power through the palate. Smooth
operator. Screwcap. 14% alc. **Rating** 92 **To** 2021 $31 CM
Carpark Merlot Shiraz 2013 Slips into a groove and taps out a fine tune of
flavour. This is good drinking and value. It's mellifluous, shot with juicy currants,
and slipped with dust and chocolate notes. It's entirely successful at delivering
supple, mid-weight fruit flavour. Screwcap. 13.5% alc. **Rating** 91 **To** 2018 $19
CM ✪
The Bommy Margaret River Cabernet Sauvignon 2012 Mid-weight and
curranty with delicious peppermint-cream flavours riding over the top. Ripe and
soft as it rolls along the tongue. Certainly no need to cellar this; it's drinking well
already. Screwcap. 14% alc. **Rating** 91 **To** 2020 $31 CM

ＹＹＹＹ **Carpark Cabernet Sauvignon Merlot 2010 Rating** 88 **To** 2019 $19 CM

Gapsted   ★★★★

3897 Great Alpine Road, Gapsted, Vic 3737 **Region** Alpine Valleys
T (03) 5751 1383 **www**.gapstedwines.com.au **Open** 7 days 10–5
Winemaker Shayne Cunningham, Michael Cope-Williams, Tony Pla Bou, Daniela
Neumann **Est.** 1997 **Dozens** 130 000 **Vyds** 256.1ha
Gapsted is the major brand of the Victorian Alps Winery, which started life (and continues)
as large-scale contract winemaking facilities. However, the quality of the wines made for its
own brand (Gapsted) has led to the expansion of production not only under that label, but
also under a raft of cheaper, subsidiary labels. Its substantial vineyards extend across the Alpine
Valleys and (mostly) the King Valley. Exports to the UK, Denmark, Sweden, Norway, the
United Arab Emirates, Hong Kong, Singapore, China and Japan.

ＹＹＹＹＹ **Limited Release King Valley Alpine Valleys Petit Manseng 2014** There's
a lot going on here: honeysuckle, lime and spice aromas, apricot kernel and
peach on the palate; it is highly textural, and jam-packed with interest. Screwcap.
12.9% alc. **Rating** 94 **To** 2020 $25 ✪

ＹＹＹＹＹ **Ballerina Canopy Sauvignon Blanc 2014 Rating** 90 **To** 2016 $19 ✪
Limited Release Barbera 2013 Rating 90 **To** 2023 $31

Garagiste   ★★★★★

4 Lawrey Street, Frankston, Vic 3199 (postal) **Region** Mornington Peninsula
T 0439 370 530 **www**.garagiste.com.au **Open** Not
Winemaker Barnaby Flanders **Est.** 2006 **Dozens** 2000 **Vyds** 3ha

Barnaby Flanders was a co-founder of Allies Wines (see separate entry) in 2003, with some of the wines made under the Garagiste label. Allies has now gone its own way, and Barnaby has a controlling interest in the Garagiste brand. The focus is on the Mornington Peninsula, and in particular grapes from the sand-based soils of Tuerong and Moorooduc in the north, the brown loam/red volcanic soils of Merricks and Merricks North in the middle, and the red volcanic soils of Red Hill and Main Ridge in the most elevated southern sector. The wines are made with wild yeasts, minimal handling, and are bottled without fining or filtration. Exports to Singapore, Hong Kong and China.

ＹＹＹＹＹ **Merricks Mornington Peninsula Chardonnay 2013** Complete wine. Intense, complex and lengthy. Flavoursome but frisky, barley, lime, white peach and apple, the input from spicy, nutty oak both seductive and well judged. The combination of savouriness and sweetness brings immense pleasure, but it's the length of flavour that gets the heart racing. Screwcap. 13% alc. **Rating** 97 **To** 2021 $40 CM ❂
Terre de Feu Mornington Peninsula Pinot Noir 2013 First release. Grown on 19yo vines at Merricks. 100% whole bunches. Wild yeast, 25 days on skins, unfined and unfiltered, production of 700 bottles. The wine itself lays down the law. This is a commanding wine, full of both authority and nuance, with smoky, sinewy, savoury elements combined to perfection with powerful cherry-plum fruit and roasted, nutty oak. Some wines make you sit back and marvel; this is one such. Screwcap. 13.5% alc. **Rating** 97 **To** 2026 $75 CM ❂

ＹＹＹＹＹ **Merricks Mornington Peninsula Pinot Noir 2013** Impresses from the outset. It has that extra something. It flourishes and fans out through the finish, never a bad sign, but in getting there it offers generous flavours of dark cherry, coffee grounds, spice and undergrowth. Tannin is fine but authoritative. Clearly an upper-echelon release. Screwcap. 13.5% alc. **Rating** 96 **To** 2026 $45 CM ❂
Le Stagiaire Mornington Peninsula Pinot Gris 2014 Rich and honeyed with sweet pear, apple and spice flavours piled on. It's hedonistic, but it's very good. There's a textural element too, but the flare of flavour is what it's all about. Importantly, it stays honeyed and well directed throughout. Screwcap. 13.5% alc. **Rating** 94 **To** 2015 $28 CM ❂

ＹＹＹＹＹ **Balnarring Pinot Noir 2013 Rating** 93 **To** 2022 $45 CM
Le Stagiaire Pinot Noir 2013 Rating 92 **To** 2022 $30 CM

Garbin Estate ★★★★

209 Toodyay Road, Middle Swan, WA 6056 **Region** Swan Valley
T (08) 9274 1747 **www.**garbinestatewines.com.au **Open** 7 days 11–5.30
Winemaker Peter Garbin **Est.** 1956 **Dozens** 4500 **Vyds** 10ha
Duje Garbin, winemaker and fisherman from a small island near the Dalmatian coast in the Adriatic Sea, migrated to WA in 1937; in '56 he purchased the Middle Swan property on which Garbin Estate stands. When he retired in the early '90s, son Peter took over what was a thoroughly traditional small business, and embarked on a massive transition: a new cellar door and processing area, upgraded major plant and equipment, and the establishment of a vineyard in Gingin. A former design draughtsman, Peter is now full-time winemaker, backed up by wife Katrina, assistant winemaker, and sons Joel and Adam. Exports to China.

ＹＹＹＹＹ **Vigneron Series Verdelho 2014** Bright straw-green; while retaining varietal identity, has more freshness and zest than most, the reason why it won a gold medal at the Swan Valley Wine Show '14. Will age well. Screwcap. 12.9% alc. **Rating** 94 **To** 2020 $17 ❂

Garners Heritage Wines ★★★★

54 Longwood–Mansfield Road, Longwood East, Vic 3666 **Region** Strathbogie Ranges
T (03) 5798 5513 **Open** W'ends 11–4
Winemaker Lindsay Brown **Est.** 2005 **Dozens** 500 **Vyds** 1.8ha
Leon and Rosie Garner established Garners Heritage Wine in 2005, celebrating their tenth anniversary in 2015. The 1.8ha boutique vineyard may be small, and the newest in the

Strathbogie Ranges, but it has produced high class Shirazs. Although the region is classified as cool-climate, the property is at the base of the mountain range, where the warm summers are ideal for growing shiraz. A very small amount is exported to Hong Kong.

ΨΨΨΨΨ **Strathbogie Ranges Shiraz 2013** Big but bright. A flood of cherry-plum flavour comes roaring through the palate, accompanied by dry, surging tannin. Spearmint and musk notes add lift. Alcohol is taken in its stride. Excellent. Screwcap. 15% alc. **Rating** 93 **To** 2021 $28 CM
Reserve Strathbogie Ranges Shiraz 2012 Dense colour. Looks and smells promising. Ripe plum and blackberry flavours with a coating of slippery-smooth, creamy vanillan oak. Crowd-pleasing, but it has the structure and depth to be that and more. Good now but it has a future. Diam. 14.1% alc. **Rating** 92 **To** 2022 $34 CM

Gartelmann Wines ★★★★★

701 Lovedale Road, Lovedale, NSW 2321 **Region** Hunter Valley
T (02) 4930 7113 **www**.gartelmann.com.au **Open** Mon–Sat 10–5, Sun 10–4
Winemaker Jorg Gartelmann, Liz Silkman **Est.** 1970 **Dozens** 7000
In 1996 Jan and Jorg Gartelmann purchased what was previously the George Hunter Estate – 16ha of mature vineyards, most established by Oliver Shaul in '70. In a change of emphasis, the vineyard was sold, and Gartelmann now sources its grapes from the Hunter Valley and other NSW regions, including the cool Rylstone area in Mudgee. Exports to the US, Germany, Singapore and China.

ΨΨΨΨΨ **Benjamin Hunter Valley Semillon 2011** Half comes from vines on alluvial creek flats in Pokolbin, the other half from the Upper Hunter. Has already fulfilled part of the potential it showed 3 years ago. Then it had a delicious, albeit unusual, amalgam of sweetened lemon juice, orange peel and near-tropical flavours, the acid balance excellent. The length has increased significantly, taking it into top-flight quality. Screwcap. 11% alc. **Rating** 95 **To** 2023 $30 ✪
Mudgee Petit Verdot 2013 A blend of 85% petit verdot and 15% Clare Valley cabernet; no details on oak maturation (if any used). The blend has worked well, with satsuma plum and a dash of blackcurrant fruit; the mouthfeel is supple, and the balance good. 372 dozen made. Screwcap. 15% alc. **Rating** 94 **To** 2019 $35

ΨΨΨΨΨ **Mudgee Phillip Alexander 2013 Rating** 93 **To** 2025 $25 ✪
Benjamin Hunter Valley Semillon 2014 Rating 92 **To** 2024 $25 ✪
Jesse Mudgee Shiraz 2013 Rating 92 **To** 2028 $30
Jessica Hunter Valley Verdelho 2014 Rating 90 **To** 2016 $20 ✪
Jonathan Mudgee Cabernet Sauvignon 2013 Rating 90 **To** 2020 $30

Gatt Wines ★★★★★

417 Boehms Springs Road, Flaxman Valley, SA 5235 **Region** Eden Valley
T (08) 8564 1166 **www**.gattwines.com **Open** Not
Winemaker David Norman **Est.** 1972 **Dozens** 8000 **Vyds** 50.65ha
When you read the hyperbole that sometimes accompanies the acquisition of an existing wine business, about transforming it into a world-class operation, it is easy to sigh and move on. When Ray Gatt acquired Eden Springs, he proceeded to translate words into deeds. As well as the 19.82ha Eden Springs Vineyard, he also acquired the historic Siegersdorf Vineyard (19.43ha) on the Barossa floor, and the neighbouring Graue Vineyard (11.4ha). The change of name from Eden Springs to Gatt Wines in 2011 was sensible. Exports to Denmark, Germany, South Korea, Hong Kong, Japan and China.

ΨΨΨΨΨ **High Eden Single Vineyard Riesling 2013** The bouquet is filled with citrus and apple blossom to the point of outright perfume, and the Thai silk suite of shimmering flavours is the mirror image of the bouquet. Delicious Riesling. Screwcap. 12% alc. **Rating** 95 **To** 2028 $30 ✪
Accent Barossa Valley Viognier 2014 Gatt goes pot hunting in offshore wine competitions with astounding success, far less in Australia. Here the picture

is reversed, with top gold at the Adelaide Wine Show '14 and blue-gold at the Sydney International Wine Competition '14. Simply cool-fermented with 2 months on lees, it is very crisp and fresh, the length of the palate and aftertaste its strength. Lovely wine. Screwcap. 13% alc. **Rating** 95 **To** 2017 $20 ✪

High Eden Single Vineyard Riesling 2014 Good Eden Valley expression of place, with lemon foremost, but leaving room for apple and lime to also wave their hands; the balance and length of the wine can't be faulted. Screwcap. 11.5% alc. **Rating** 94 **To** 2024 $30 ✪

Accent Barossa Valley Tempranillo 2012 Spent 7 days on skins; matured for 12 months in used French and American hogsheads. I wouldn't argue much about its gold at the Melbourne International Wine Competition '14. It is fresh, with a mix of red and black cherry, and a pleasing airbrush of tannins on the finish. Screwcap. 13.5% alc. **Rating** 94 **To** 2022 $25 ✪

ŶŶŶŶŶ **High Eden Cabernet Sauvignon 2012** Rating 93 To 2042 $60
High Eden Single Vineyard Shiraz 2012 Rating 92 To 2032 $60
Barossa Valley Cabernet Sauvignon 2012 Rating 91 To 2032 $60
Old Vine Barossa Valley Shiraz 2012 Rating 90 To 2032 $100
Accent Barossa Valley Sangiovese 2012 Rating 90 To 2019 $25

Gembrook Hill ★★★★★

Launching Place Road, Gembrook, Vic 3783 **Region** Yarra Valley
T (03) 5968 1622 **www**.gembrookhill.com.au **Open** By appt
Winemaker Timo Mayer, Andrew Marks **Est.** 1983 **Dozens** 2500 **Vyds** 6ha
Ian and June Marks established Gembrook Hill, one of the oldest vineyards in the coolest part of the Upper Yarra Valley, and harvested some weeks later than the lower parts of the region. Son Andrew assists Timo Mayer on the winemaking front, each also having his own labels (see separate entries for The Wanderer and Mayer). The northeast-facing vineyard is in a natural amphitheatre; the low-yielding sauvignon blanc, chardonnay and pinot noir are not irrigated. The minimal approach to winemaking produces wines of a consistent style with finesse and elegance. Exports to the UK, Denmark, Japan and Malaysia.

ŶŶŶŶŶ **Yarra Valley Sauvignon Blanc 2013** The cooler Upper Yarra, and its red soil, are more suited to sauvignon blanc than the Lower Yarra. The bouquet has a beautiful expression of the variety, tropical fruits, citrus and even a touch of white peach, the palate providing more of the same without apparent effort. No one could dislike this style. Screwcap. 13% alc. **Rating** 95 **To** 2016 $33 ✪

Yarra Valley Pinot Noir 2013 Bright and deeply coloured; the bouquet is pure, the palate of blood plum varietal fruit with a wreath of fine-grained, gently savoury tannins; the balance and length are impeccable, and it would be a pity not to give the wine time (2–3 years) to come into full flower. Diam. 13.5% alc. **Rating** 95 **To** 2023 $50

Blanc de Blancs 2010 The enduring stamina of high Upper Yarra chardonnay on parade. The hue is a youthfully pale straw and the palate captures an energy that promises decades of potential. 5 years (4 on lees) has done little to subdue primary white citrus zest and tense acidity, though it has built impressive texture and creamy mouthfeel and subtle nuances of almond meal. Length is impressive. Patience. Diam. 12.5% alc. **Rating** 94 **To** 2030 $55 TS

ŶŶŶŶŶ **Village Yarra Valley Pinot Noir 2012** Rating 92 To 2020 $28

Gemtree Wines ★★★★★

167 Elliot Road, McLaren Flat, SA 5171 **Region** McLaren Vale
T (08) 8323 8199 **www**.gemtreewines.com **Open** 7 days 10–5
Winemaker Mike Brown, Joshua Waechter **Est.** 1998 **Dozens** 50 000 **Vyds** 138.47ha
Gemtree is a family-owned winery dedicated to growing better wine – naturally. Paul and Jill Buttery established the Gemtree vineyards in McLaren Vale in 1980. Now their son Andrew runs the business, their daughter Melissa Brown (née Buttery) is the biodynamic viticulturist

and her husband, Mike Brown, is the chief winemaker. Mike's philosophy is minimal intervention across all stages of the winemaking process to produce wines which are powerful and express the characteristics of each variety and the region. The vineyards are certified organic and farmed biodynamically and the wine portfolio is of high quality. Gemtree wines are exported to the UK, the US, Canada, Brazil, Sweden, Indonesia, South Korea, Vietnam, Hong Kong, China and NZ.

ΨΨΨΨΨ **Ernest Allan McLaren Vale Shiraz 2013** 20 months in French oak. Drinking this is like wrapping your mouth in velvet. It's plush, smooth, offers folds and layers of flavour, and is both comforting and warming. It's rich with syrupy plum, blackberry, milk chocolate and woodsmoke, and comes draped with fine, integrated tannin. Swallow, and the pulse of flavour keeps beating on. Screwcap. 14.5% alc. **Rating** 96 **To** 2033 $40 CM ❂
Obsidian McLaren Vale Shiraz 2012 Made from the top 1% of Gemtree's shiraz production. 3 years in French oak. All the best treatment, and then thrown to the cork wolves. It's a monumental wine, thick with fruit and oak, the power of blueberry and blackberry flavour affording tremendous intensity. Peppermint notes add lift, sawdusty oak adds spunk, and rivers of tannin set the wine on a firm course. Length is as confident as everything else about the wine. Indeed the momentum of quality here is quite something. 14% alc. **Rating** 96 **To** 2036 $70 CM ❂
Uncut McLaren Vale Shiraz 2013 Attacks with flavour and doesn't let up. Inky, blackberried, clovey characters power throughout, tempered only by fruit-drenched tannin, saltbush complexity and meaty/smoky oak. It's almost exactly the wine you'd hope it to be. Screwcap. 14.5% alc. **Rating** 94 **To** 2026 $25 CM ❂
Scarce Earth Stage 7 McLaren Vale Shiraz 2012 Wow: the wine steps up to the plate the second it enters the mouth; intense spicy savoury characters grudgingly make way for black fruits. Biodynamic principles (not formally adopted/certified) are used in the vineyard, another variable in the Scarce Earth series. Screwcap. 14.5% alc. **Rating** 94 **To** 2022 $35

ΨΨΨΨΨ **Gemstone Shiraz 2013 Rating** 91 **To** 2018 $16 CM ❂
Cinnabar McLaren Vale GSM 2014 Rating 91 **To** 2019 $20 CM ❂
Luna Temprana McLaren Vale Tempranillo 2014 Rating 91 **To** 2017 $18 ❂
Dragon's Blood McLaren Vale Shiraz 2013 Rating 90 **To** 2020 $16 CM ❂

Geoff Merrill Wines   ★★★★★

291 Pimpala Road, Woodcroft, SA 5162 **Region** McLaren Vale
T (08) 8381 6877 **www**.geoffmerrillwines.com.au **Open** Mon–Fri 10–5, Sat 12–4
Winemaker Geoff Merrill, Scott Heidrich **Est.** 1980 **Dozens** 65 000 **Vyds** 45ha
If Geoff Merrill ever loses his impish sense of humour or his zest for life, high and not-so-high, we shall all be the poorer. The product range consists of three tiers: premium (varietal); Reserve, being the older wines, reflecting the desire for elegance and subtlety of this otherwise exuberant winemaker; and, at the top, Henley Shiraz. Exports to all major markets.

ΨΨΨΨΨ **Henley McLaren Vale Shiraz 2006** You can easily drink this now, but the rip of integrated tannin provides a long future. It's awash with complex spice and leather characters, yet forceful through the finish. Licorice, tobacco and dark chocolate notes continue the developed-but-youthful theme. Sweeter citrus candy flavours complete an exotic picture. Cork. 14.5% alc. **Rating** 95 **To** 2024 $150 CM
Bush Vine McLaren Vale Shiraz Grenache Mourvedre 2010 A 57/35/8% blend, the components utterly synergistic; the result is a spicy, savoury elegance that bodes well for the long life ahead of a wine that has made light of its 4 years to date; the oak, tannin and alcohol management could not have been improved on, the fruit expression a delight. Screwcap. 14.5% alc. **Rating** 95 **To** 2030 $25 ❂
Reserve Chardonnay 2013 An 80/20% blend from McLaren Vale and Coonawarra; sensitive use of French oak (8 months' maturation) has protected the elegance of the white peach, apple and melon fruit; good acidity also builds length. Screwcap. 13.5% alc. **Rating** 94 **To** 2019 $31

🍷🍷🍷🍷🍷 Bush Vine McLaren Vale Grenache Rose 2014 Rating 93 To 2016 $21 ○
Parham Cabernet Merlot 2006 Rating 92 To 2021 $40
Jacko's Blend McLaren Vale Shiraz 2010 Rating 91 To 2020 $28 CM
Fleurieu Cabernet Merlot 2010 Rating 91 To 2022 $21 CM ○
Fleurieu Cabernet Shiraz 2010 Rating 91 To 2018 $21 ○

Geoff Weaver ★★★★★

2 Gilpin Lane, Mitcham, SA 5062 (postal) **Region** Adelaide Hills
T (08) 8272 2105 **www**.geoffweaver.com.au **Open** Not
Winemaker Geoff Weaver **Est.** 1982 **Dozens** 3000 **Vyds** 12.3ha
This is the business of one-time Hardys chief winemaker Geoff Weaver. This vineyard was
established between 1982 and '88, and invariably produces immaculate Riesling and Sauvignon
Blanc, and one of the longest-lived Chardonnays to be found in Australia. The beauty of the
labels ranks supreme with Pipers Brook. Exports to the UK, Hong Kong and Singapore.

🍷🍷🍷🍷🍷 Lenswood Sauvignon Blanc 2014 Dry-grown 37yo vines give moderate yields
at low pH levels; an aromatic, flowery bouquet leads into a crisp, juicy palate that
continues to accelerate all the way through to the finish and aftertaste. Fastidious
winemaking has thrown all the emphasis on varietal fruit. A master of his art.
Screwcap. 12% alc. Rating 96 To 2016 $25 ○
Ferus Lenswood Sauvignon Blanc 2013 Estate-grown, wild yeast-fermented
in French barriques and aged on lees for 12 months. It seems clear the oak is
either totally or largely used, for its impact is on texture and structure, leaving
the varietal fruit to express itself with a savoury framework in support. Screwcap.
13% alc. Rating 95 To 2017 $41

Ghost Rock Vineyard ★★★★☆

1055 Port Sorrell Road, Northdown, Tas 7307 **Region** Northern Tasmania
T (03) 6428 4005 **www**.ghostrock.com.au **Open** Wed–Sun & public hols 11–5,
7 days Dec–Feb
Winemaker Jeremy Dineen (Contract) **Est.** 2001 **Dozens** 2800 **Vyds** 16ha
Cate and Colin Arnold purchased the former Patrick Creek Vineyard (planted in 1989) in
2001. This was the springboard for the family-owned business to progressively acquire three
vineyards, open a cellar door, a tourist centre, and, most recently, erect a 100-tonne winery
and regional interpretation centre. The home vineyard is situated among the patchwork
fields of sassafras to the south, and the white sands of the Port Sorell Peninsula to the north.
The vineyards now total 16ha, planted to pinot gris, pinot noir, sauvignon blanc, chardonnay
and riesling.

🍷🍷🍷🍷🍷 Pinot Gris 2014 This has a complex, funky bouquet, unusual for Pinot Gris,
then a powerful and potent nashi pear palate. Gold Tas Wine Show '15. Screwcap.
13% alc. Rating 94 To 2018 $33

🍷🍷🍷🍷🍷 Sauvignon Blanc 2014 Rating 92 To 2016 $28 CM
Riesling 2014 Rating 91 To 2020 $35 CM
Two Blocks Pinot Noir 2013 Rating 90 To 2017 $36

Giaconda ★★★★★

30 McClay Road, Beechworth, Vic 3747 **Region** Beechworth
T (03) 5727 0246 **www**.giaconda.com.au **Open** By appt
Winemaker Rick Kinzbrunner **Est.** 1985 **Dozens** 3000 **Vyds** 5.5ha
These wines have a super-cult status and, given the small production, are extremely difficult
to find; they are sold chiefly through restaurants and via their website. All have a cosmopolitan
edge befitting Rick Kinzbrunner's international winemaking experience. The Chardonnay
is one of Australia's greatest, and is made and matured in the underground wine cellar hewn
out of granite. This permits gravity flow, and a year-round temperature range of 14–15°C,
promising even more for the future. Exports to the UK and the US.

ŸŸŸŸŸ Estate Chardonnay 2013 Bright straw-green; has the hallmark faintly funky bouquet, and the effortlessly silky, immaculately balanced, and long palate for which Giaconda is rightly revered. No one fruit flavour dominates, all drawn into the spell of the palate, as is the oak. It's perfectly possible to deconstruct a wine such as this, and equally easy to label that process sacrilege. Just revel in its harmony. Screwcap. 13.5% alc. **Rating** 97 **To** 2033 $139 **✪**

ŸŸŸŸŸ Nantua Les Deux Chardonnay 2013 100 dozen made. Not entirely estate-grown though on tasting it, you're unlikely to care. Has a chalky/minerally flavour/texture but the flood of barley, lime, peach and pear drop flavours provide the main seduction. Smoky, leesy characters add both layers and complexity. Power and finish. Screwcap. 13.5% alc. **Rating** 94 **To** 2019 $44 CM

McClay Road Beechworth King Valley Nebbiolo 2012 Part from the late Guy Darling's vineyard in the King Valley, and part from a small Beechworth producer. This is high-quality Nebbiolo, created to honour Guy Darling by his son and Rick Kinzbrunner. Very good colour; a perfumed rose garden bouquet, a detailed red fruit palate that leaves it until the last few seconds for the tannins to appear. Exclusive to Dan Murphy, but not made for Dan Murphy, simply purchased after they tasted it. Screwcap. 13.9% alc. **Rating** 94 **To** 2032 $50

ŸŸŸŸ Pinot Noir 2013 Rating 89 **To** 2019 $89

Gibson   ★★★★★

190 Willows Road, Light Pass, SA 5355 **Region** Barossa Valley
T (08) 8562 3193 **www**.gibsonwines.com.au **Open** 7 days 11–5
Winemaker Rob Gibson **Est.** 1996 **Dozens** 10 000 **Vyds** 14.2ha
Rob Gibson spent much of his working life as a senior viticulturist for Penfolds, involved in research tracing the characters that particular parcels of grapes give to a wine, which left him with a passion for identifying and protecting what is left of the original vineyard plantings in Australia. He has a vineyard in the Barossa Valley at Light Pass (merlot), and one in the Eden Valley (shiraz and riesling), and also purchases grapes from McLaren Vale and the Adelaide Hills. Exports to Germany, Denmark, Hong Kong and China.

ŸŸŸŸŸ Eden Valley Riesling 2014 Right on the money for its diamond-clear expression of variety and place; it is full of Rose's lime juice flavours, yet has freshness and intensity to its structure and finish courtesy of its low pH, good acidity, and low alcohol. Screwcap. 10.9% alc. **Rating** 95 **To** 2034 $21 **✪**

Reserve Shiraz 2013 Matured in French oak for 18 months, and a barrel selection of the best barrels. Excellent, bright colour; a very stylish medium to full-bodied wine with polished black fruits running through the long, perfectly balanced palate and aftertaste. Needs time. Screwcap. 14.5% alc. **Rating** 95 **To** 2038 $48

Adelaide Hills Pinot Gris 2013 This is a Gris with near-boundless energy, of itself both good (fruit intensity and length) and bad (lack of varietal fruit). Having written these words, it occurs to me it could be all good, and retasting underlines this, for it's a Riesling in drag, the lemony acidity of its back-palate and finish very impressive. Screwcap. 13.9% alc. **Rating** 94 **To** 2023 $21 **✪**

The Dirtman Barossa Shiraz 2013 A blend of northern Barossa Valley and Eden Valley grapes. Bright crimson-purple; elegant and medium-bodied, with a touch of fresh fragrance to its bouquet and palate, red fruits holding hands with black, tannins and oak contributions in support roles. More or less ready now. Screwcap. 14.5% alc. **Rating** 94 **To** 2028 $30 **✪**

ŸŸŸŸŸ The Smithy Barossa Shiraz Cabernet 2012 Rating 93 **To** 2027 $27 **✪**
Reserve Merlot 2012 Rating 93 **To** 2027 $47

gilbert by Simon Gilbert

PO Box 773, Mudgee, NSW 2850 **Region** Orange/Mudgee
T (02) 6373 1371 **www.**thegilbertsarecoming.com.au **Open** Not
Winemaker Simon and Will Gilbert **Est.** 2010 **Dozens** 3500 **Vyds** 25.81ha
For some time now Simon Gilbert has devoted himself to his consultancy and wine brokering
business Wineworks of Australia. As that business has grown, Simon has returned to the
winery wearing his Wineworks of Australia hat, overseeing the winemaking of the estate-
grown grapes, all exported. Separate from his consultancy business, he has established gilbert
by Simon Gilbert, and also makes the wines for this label at the same winery. Distribution is
limited to specialist wine retailers and restaurants. Exports to Hong Kong and China.

ŸŸŸŸŸ **Mudgee Orange Saignee Sangiovese Shiraz Barbera Rose 2014**
Distinctly savoury-accented and distinctly good at it. Pale salmon colour, awash
with cherry and herb/spice flavours, and dashed with fennel. Would be at home at
the lunch table. Screwcap. 12% alc. **Rating** 91 **To** 2016 $24 CM

Gilberts

30138 Albany Highway, Kendenup via Mount Barker, WA 6323 **Region** Mount Barker
T (08) 9851 4028 **www.**gilbertwines.com.au **Open** Wed–Mon 10–5
Winemaker Plantagenet (Cath Oates) **Est.** 1980 **Dozens** 3000 **Vyds** 13.5ha
Once a part-time occupation for sheep and beef farmers Jim and Beverly Gilbert, but now
a full-time and very successful one. The mature vineyard (shiraz, chardonnay, riesling and
cabernet sauvignon), coupled with contract winemaking at Plantagenet, has long produced
very high-class Riesling, and now also makes excellent Shiraz. The 3 Devils Shiraz is named
in honour of their sons. Exports to Singapore.

ŸŸŸŸŸ **Hand Picked Mount Barker Chardonnay 2013** From 28yo estate vines.
Barrel fermentation in mainly used French oak has worked well, providing texture,
but leaving the fruit free to express itself on what is a very long palate, that classic
mix of grapefruit and stone fruit sustained by a shaft of steely acidity running
through from start to finish. Screwcap. 13.5% alc. **Rating** 95 **To** 2020 $25 ✪
Reserve Mount Barker Shiraz 2012 The wine takes the quality of the 3 Devils
Shiraz onto another level through fruit selection and maturation (7 months in
French oak, 30% new). There is a savoury complexity to the dominance of black
fruits, oak and fruit tannins combining to create a complex texture. A great future
in store. Screwcap. 14.5% alc. **Rating** 95 **To** 2032 $30 ✪
Mount Barker Riesling 2014 A wine with an enviable record going back
20 years, and quietly exceeding the confidence such a history merits. Has lime and
apple blossom aromas and flavours, the latter etched by minerally acidity on the
long, harmonious finish. It will repay patience many times over, no matter how
enjoyable it is now. Screwcap. 12% alc. **Rating** 94 **To** 2029 $22 ✪
3 Devils Mount Barker Shiraz 2012 Very good colour; estate-grown grapes
from 35yo vines have delivered the goods, maturation in used oak no issue; the
medium-bodied palate has red and black cherry, blackberry and a splash of spice,
the mouthfeel and supple length reflecting skilled winemaking. Fantastic value.
Screwcap. 14.5% alc. **Rating** 94 **To** 2025 $18 ✪

ŸŸŸŸŸ **Mount Barker Rose 2014** Rating 92 To 2015 $20 ✪
3 Lads Cabernet Sauvignon 2012 Rating 92 To 2022 $25 ✪

Gilligan

PO Box 235, Willunga, SA 5172 **Region** McLaren Vale
T 0412 423 131 **www.**gilligan.com.au **Open** Not
Winemaker Mark Day, Leigh Gilligan **Est.** 2001 **Dozens** 1000 **Vyds** 5.74ha
Leigh Gilligan is a marketing veteran, mostly with McLaren Vale wineries (including Wirra
Wirra). The Gilligan family has just over 4ha of shiraz and 0.4ha each of grenache, mourvedre,
marsanne and roussanne, selling part of the production. In 2001 they persuaded next-door

neighbour Drew Noon to make a barrel of Shiraz, which they drank and gave away. Realising they needed more than one barrel, they have migrated to Mark Day's Koltz Winery at Blewitt Springs. Exports to the UK, the US, Canada, Germany, Denmark, Thailand and Hong Kong.

ȘȘȘȘȘ McLaren Vale Shiraz Grenache Mourvedre 2013 Good colour; the bouquet and (in particular) the palate have a spread of flavours that are well into left field, with crushed walnut at one end, iodine mineral at the other; these flavours stay in the mouth for several breaths before diminishing. What to make of this? I don't know is the unhelpful answer. Screwcap. 15% alc. **Rating** 91 **To** 2023 $25
McLaren Vale Roussanne Marsanne 2013 Full straw-green; this is a blend that has potential; the trick is to decide when to pick if you are looking for longevity (and hence the maximum return). This may prove to be about right, with its nice chalky acidity. Screwcap. 13.5% alc. **Rating** 90 **To** 2023 $25

Gioiello Estate ★★★★

PO Box 250, Tullamarine, Vic 3043 **Region** Upper Goulburn
T 0437 240 502 **www**.gioiello.com.au **Open** Not
Winemaker Scott McCarthy (Contract) **Est.** 1987 **Dozens** 3500 **Vyds** 8.97ha
The Gioiello Estate vineyard was established by a Japanese company and originally known as Daiwa Nar Darak. Planted between 1987 and '96, it accounts for just under 9ha on a 400ha property of rolling hills, pastures, bushland, river flats, natural water springs and billabongs. Now owned by the Schiavello family, the vineyard continues to produce high-quality wines, the introduction of Syrah a major success.

ȘȘȘȘȘ Old Hill Upper Goulburn Chardonnay 2013 Mid-weight, more about juicy momentum than power, flavours of bran and nectarine, input from oak but lines of fruit and acid are the drivers. One of those wines that just grows and grows on you. Screwcap. 13.8% alc. **Rating** 93 **To** 2020 $45 CM
Reserve Upper Goulburn Cabernet Merlot 2012 Can we still use the words 'claret style'? This gives the words 'medium weight' a good name. It's curranty and pencil-like with input from tobacco and green (but not unripe) herbs. It saunters along, or seems to, but has enough cleansing acidity and tension through the finish to promote a sense of good order. Now or mid-term, it should drink very well. Screwcap. 13.2% alc. **Rating** 92 **To** 2022 $28 CM

Gipsie Jack Wine Co ★★★★

1509 Langhorne Creek Road, Langhorne Creek, SA 5255 **Region** Langhorne Creek
T (08) 8537 3029 **www**.gipsiejack.com.au **Open** 7 days 10–5
Winemaker John Glaetzer, Ben Potts **Est.** 2004 **Dozens** 7000
The partners of Gipsie Jack are John Glaetzer and Ben Potts, who made a little over 500 dozen from two growers in their inaugural vintage in 2004. Glaetzer and Potts say, 'We want to make this label fun, like in the "old days". No pretentiousness, no arrogance, not even a back label. A great wine at a great price, with no discounting.' Exports to Switzerland, Hong Kong, Singapore and China.

ȘȘȘȘȘ Langhorne Creek Shiraz 2013 A jungle of ripe, sweet berries comes dressed in a well-cut suit. This lays on full-bodied flavour, all saturated plum and mint, before turning tidy and respectable on the finish, mostly courtesy of fine-grained, well-positioned tannin. The value bells are ringing. Screwcap. 14.6% alc. **Rating** 94 **To** 2022 $18 CM ◎

ȘȘȘȘȘ Langhorne Creek Malbec 2013 Rating 93 **To** 2021 $18 CM ◎
The Terrier Shiraz Cabernet 2013 Rating 91 **To** 2020 $18 CM ◎
Cabernet Sauvignon 2013 Rating 90 **To** 2019 $18 CM ◎

Girraween Estate

41 Hickling Lane, Wyberba, Qld 4383 **Region** Granite Belt
T (07) 4684 3186 **www**.girraweenestate.com.au **Open** W'ends & public hols 10–5
Winemaker Mike Hayes, Steve Messiter **Est.** 1985 **Dozens** 600 **Vyds** 3.5ha
In 2009 Steve Messiter and wife Lisa Barter purchased Bald Mountain from its founders, Denis and Jackie Parsons. Steve is a chemical engineer with a Masters degree and has studied winemaking, and has overseen the complete rejuvenation of the vineyard, including the removal of the lyre trellis and 40% of the vines and the construction of a new winery in 2013. Mike Hayes (Symphony Hill) advises on vineyard management and makes the wine.

Cabernet Sauvignon 2013 Open-fermented with extended post-fermentation maceration; matured for 14 months in new and used French hogsheads. Good wine, with clear blackcurrant/cassis fruit, balanced and ripe tannins and a nice infusion of cedary oak. Screwcap. 13.5% alc. **Rating** 93 **To** 2028 $28
Reserve Chardonnay 2013 Fermented in stainless steel, matured in new French oak. Theoretically this approach shouldn't work, and should leave the oak unintegrated. Well, it has worked here, the white peach, nectarine and fig fruit given structure and context by the oak. Screwcap. 13% alc. **Rating** 91 **To** 2018 $35
Shiraz Cabernet 2013 A 60/40% blend. Very good purple-crimson; the spicy/peppery edge to the blackberry/blackcurrant fruits of the bouquet and medium-bodied palate bespeaks the cool climate. Needs a little more tannin support, but is a very creditable wine. Screwcap. 13.5% alc. **Rating** 90 **To** 2020 $22

GISA

578 The Parade, Auldama, SA 5072 **Region** South Australia
T (08) 8338 2123 **www**.gisa.com.au **Open** Not
Winemaker Mat Henbest **Est.** 2006 **Dozens** 10 000
Mat and Lisa Henbest have chosen a clever name for their virtual winery – GISA stands for Geographic Indication South Australia – neatly covering the fact that their grapes come variously from the Adelaide Hills (Semillon, Sauvignon Blanc and Chardonnay), Clare Valley (Riesling), McLaren Vale (Shiraz Viognier) and Barossa Valley (Reserve Shiraz). It in turn reflects Mat's long apprenticeship in the wine industry, working in retail while he pursued tertiary qualifications, thereafter wholesaling wine to the retail and restaurant trade. He then moved to Haselgrove, where he spent five years working closely with the small winemaking team, refining his concept of style, and gaining experience on the other side of the fence of the marketing equation. Exports to China.

Piccadilly Chardonnay 2014 Texture, flavour and length. The impression of quality is clear. There's almost a chalkiness to the finish, but there's plenty of stone fruit, apple and toast flavours, with a gentle almond milk character adding that something extra. Walk up starter in the quality chardonnay stakes. Screwcap. 13% alc. **Rating** 94 **To** 2019 $30 CM ✪

Round Barossa Valley Shiraz 2013 **Rating** 91 **To** 2022 $22 CM ✪

Gisborne Peak ★★★★

69 Short Road, Gisborne South, Vic 3437 **Region** Macedon Ranges
T (03) 5428 2228 **www**.gisbornepeakwines.com.au **Open** 7 days 11–5
Winemaker John Ellis **Est.** 1978 **Dozens** 2000 **Vyds** 5.5ha
Bob Nixon began the development of Gisborne Peak way back in 1978, planting his dream vineyard row by row. (Bob is married to Barbara Nixon, founder of Victoria Winery Tours.) The tasting room has wide shaded verandahs, plenty of windows and sweeping views. The vineyard is planted to pinot noir, chardonnay, semillon, riesling and lagrein.

Macedon Ranges Riesling 2014 Well made, and given Granite Hills' proud record, this tightly structured and finely detailed Riesling will develop year by

year for a decade as its lime, lemon, apple and mineral notes all flourish. Screwcap.
12.8% alc. **Rating** 94 **To** 2024 $27 ✪

🍷🍷🍷🍷♀ **Two Block Blend LE Pinot Noir 2012 Rating** 92 **To** 2022 $35
Macedon Ranges Chardonnay 2013 Rating 91 **To** 2023 $28

Glaetzer Wines   ★★★★★

PO Box 824 Tanunda, SA 5352 **Region** Barossa Valley
T (08) 8563 0947 **www**.glaetzer.com **Open** Not
Winemaker Ben Glaetzer **Est.** 1996 **Dozens** 15000 **Vyds** 20ha
With a family history in the Barossa Valley dating back to 1888, Glaetzer Wines was established
by father Colin after 30 years of winemaking experience, reflected in his appointment as
a Baron of the Barossa. Son Ben worked in the Hunter Valley and as a Flying Winemaker
in many of the world's wine regions before returning to Glaetzer Wines and assuming the
winemaking role. The wines are made with great skill and abundant personality. Exports to
all major markets.

🍷🍷🍷🍷🍷 **Bishop Barossa Valley Shiraz 2013** From the Ebenezer district of the Barossa
Valley, and made in the inimitable plush and velvety style of Ben Glaetzer, dripping
with black fruits, oak and soft, ripe tannins; retains remarkable equilibrium in
the face of the cornucopia of flavours, and no heat from the alcohol. Screwcap.
15% alc. **Rating** 95 **To** 2033 $33 ✪
Amon-Ra Unfiltered Barossa Valley Shiraz 2013 From vines 50–130yo,
yield 2t/ha; open-fermented, matured for 16 months in 100% new hogsheads,
95% French. Dense, deep inky crimson-purple; this is archetypal Amon-Ra, with
black fruits, licorice, oak and almost anything more you care to name; takes no
prisoners – you are either in or out. Cork. 15.5% alc. **Rating** 95 **To** 2043 $100

🍷🍷🍷🍷♀ **Wallace Barossa Valley Shiraz Grenache 2013 Rating** 93 **To** 2020 $23
CM ✪
Anaperenna 2013 Rating 92 **To** 2028 $52

Glandore Estate   ★★★★☆

1595 Broke Road, Pokolbin, NSW 2320 **Region** Hunter Valley
T (02) 4998 7140 **www**.glandorewines.com **Open** 7 days 10–5
Winemaker Duane Roy **Est.** 2004 **Dozens** 4000 **Vyds** 8ha
Glandore Estate is the reincarnation of the Brokenback Vineyard established as part of The
Rothbury Estate in the early 1970s, but it had an even longer history. It was purchased by
legendary grapegrowers Mick and Jack Phillips in the '30s, and given the Glandore name.
Owners David Madson, John Cambridge and Peter McBeath, who acquired the property in
2004 (with existing chardonnay vines), have extended the plantings with savagnin, semillon
and viognier.

🍷🍷🍷🍷🍷 **Elliott Semillon 2006** More development in the hue than the '08, although still
healthy and bright; the first toasty edge to the citrus and honey fruit makes for a
wine that has now entered a plateau it should hold for another 10 years if you are
so minded. Screwcap. 10.7% alc. **Rating** 95 **To** 2026 $35 ✪

🍷🍷🍷🍷♀ **Regional Series Hunter Valley Semillon 2014 Rating** 93 **To** 2029 $23 ✪
Elliott Semillon 2008 Rating 93 **To** 2023 $35
Regional Series Hunter Valley Savagnin 2014 Rating 92 **To** 2019 $23 ✪

Glen Eldon Wines   ★★★★★

143 Nitschke Road, Krondorf, SA 5352 **Region** Barossa Valley
T (08) 8568 2644 **www**.gleneldonwines.com.au **Open** By appt
Winemaker Richard Sheedy **Est.** 1997 **Dozens** 6000 **Vyds** 50ha
Owners Richard and Mary Sheedy (and their four children) have established the Glen Eldon
property in the Eden Valley. The shiraz and cabernet sauvignon come from their vineyards in

the Barossa Valley; viognier and merlot are contract-grown; the riesling is from the Eden Valley. Exports to the US, Canada and China.

ŶŶŶŶŶ   **Black Lady Shiraz 2012** A blend of Glen Eldon's Twisted Trunk Reserve Barossa Shiraz and Munari's Lady Pass Heathcote Shiraz. This has complexity written all over it in big black letters, yet with a juicy, open-weave mouthfeel, the fruits purple and black, the medium-bodied palate with exceptional balance and length. The best so far made. Cork. 14.5% alc. **Rating** 97 **To** 2037 $110 ✪

ŶŶŶŶŶ   **Twisted Trunk Reserve Shiraz 2010** Open-fermented, basket-pressed, matured for 24 months in new and used French and American oak, then a further 24 months in older oak. Dense crimson-purple; an uncompromisingly full-bodied Shiraz, but its foundations have been laid with care; inky, but supple, fruit and fine tannins are in great balance. The one caveat is the cork, the bottle laid on its side too soon after insertion, the quality of the cork mediocre. 14.5% alc. **Rating** 96 **To** 2035 $95
Dry Bore Barossa Shiraz 2012 Matured for 18–24 months in French and American oak. Holding its colour very well; the deliberate use of 'Barossa' suggests a blend of Barossa Valley and Eden Valley fruit, and its full-bodied and rich palate supports that hypothesis; a certain cool darkness to the fruit and the absence of that on the finish is also consistent. However, what really matters is the quality of the wine, which is very good, with a long life ahead. Screwcap. 14.5% alc. **Rating** 95 **To** 2042 $30 ✪
Eight Barrels Single Vineyard Eden Valley Shiraz 2012 Composed of the finest barrels from a single block on the estate vineyard. The colour is deep but bright, the bouquet a complex amalgam of spicy black fruits and oak, the palate dense and power-packed, with multiple layers of black fruits, licorice, tar, ripe tannins and oak tumbling over each other. Simply has to be cellared for 5+ years. ProCork. 14.5% alc. **Rating** 94 **To** 2032 $30 ✪

ŶŶŶŶ   **Barossa Shiraz Mataro 2012 Rating** 89 **To** 2032 $30

GlenAyr ★★★

Back Tea Tree Road, Richmond, Tas 7025 **Region** Southern Tasmania
T (03) 6260 2388 **www**.glenayrwines.com.au **Open** Mon–Fri 8–5
Winemaker Contract **Est.** 1975 **Dozens** 500 **Vyds** 3.1ha
GlenAyr intends to carry on in the wake of the sale of the Tolpuddle Vineyard to Shaw + Smith. It has retained its original vineyard (planted in 1975), with chardonnay, pinot noir, shiraz, cabernet merlot and riesling. GlenAyr had the enviable distinction of selling half of the shiraz that won the Jimmy Watson Trophy '11 to Glaetzer-Dixon Wines for their Mon Pere label.

ŶŶŶŶ   **Riesling 2013** The wine has abundant flavour, but, unusually for Tasmania, not enough line for higher points, its acidity soft, not vibrant. Screwcap. 11.7% alc. **Rating** 88 **To** 2018 $22

Glenguin Estate ★★★★☆

Milbrodale Road, Broke, NSW 2330 **Region** Hunter Valley

T (02) 6579 1009 **www**.glenguinestate.com.au **Open** 7 days 10–5
Winemaker Robin Tedder MW, Rhys Eather **Est.** 1993 **Dozens** 2000 **Vyds** 6ha
Glenguin Estate was established by the Tedder family, headed by Robin Tedder MW, close to Broke and adjacent to Wollombi Brook. The backbone of the production comes from 20-year-old plantings of semillon and shiraz. Tannat (1ha) and a new planting of grafted semillon, with cuttings from Braemore/HVD, complete the picture. Vineyard manager Andrew Tedder, who has considerable experience with organics and biodynamics, is overseeing the ongoing development of Glenguin's organic program. Exports to NZ.

♀♀♀♀♀ **Semillon 2014** Grown on 1.21 hectares of 26yo vines, planted in sandy loam soils. It's remarkably accessible in its youth. It tastes of pear and lemon drops with a gently waxy edge, the mid-palate succulent and eager to please. Despite its cellaring qualities there's no real need to wait on this; it's delicious now. Screwcap. 11.5% alc. **Rating** 92 **To** 2021 $25 CM ✪

♀♀♀♀ **School House Block Shiraz 2013 Rating** 88 **To** 2022 $40 CM

Glenwillow Wines   ★★★★☆

Bendigo Pottery, 146 Midland Highway, Epsom, Vic 3551 **Region** Bendigo
T 0428 461 076 **www**.glenwillow.com.au **Open** Fri–Mon 11–5
Winemaker Greg Dedman, Adam Marks **Est.** 1999 **Dozens** 750 **Vyds** 2.8ha
Peter and Cherryl Fyffe began their vineyard at Yandoit Creek, 10km south of Newstead, in 1999, planting 1.8ha of shiraz and 0.3ha of cabernet sauvignon, later branching out with 0.6ha of nebbiolo and 0.1ha of barbera. The vineyard, planted on a mixture of rich volcanic and clay loam interspersed with quartz and buckshot gravel, has an elevated north-facing aspect, which minimises the risk of frost. Wines are released under the elegantly designed Glenwillow label.

♀♀♀♀♀ **Bendigo Shiraz 2012** Estate-grown, hand-picked and matured for 15 months in new and used French oak. A full-bodied and rich wine with blackberry/plum engaged in a battle with the oak, tannins applauding from the sideline; the very good colour and depth to the fruit bode well for the future. Made by Greg Dedman. Screwcap. 14% alc. **Rating** 95 **To** 2037 $25 ✪
Reserve Bendigo Shiraz 2012 The best 6 rows of vines were hand-picked and foot-trodden, with some whole bunches remaining. Elegant and medium-bodied, this is as far away in style as one can imagine from a single vineyard to its sibling made by Greg Dedman, this made by Adam Marks. Silky and supple, it will drink well whether young or old. Screwcap. 14.5% alc. **Rating** 94 **To** 2027 $48
Bendigo Cabernet Sauvignon 2012 Interesting wine; maturation in new and used French oak has already invested the wine with the cedary characters that normally don't appear for at least 5 years, yet there is no sign of premature development in what is an impressive cabernet with a full range of blackcurrant, olive, bramble and earthy flavours. Screwcap. 14% alc. **Rating** 94 **To** 2027 $25 ✪

♀♀♀♀ **Bendigo Nebbiolo d'Yandoit 2013 Rating** 89 **To** 2023 $28

Goaty Hill Wines   ★★★★☆

530 Auburn Road, Kayena, Tas 7270 **Region** Northern Tasmania
T 1300 819 997 **www**.goatyhill.com **Open** 7 days 11–5
Winemaker Jeremy Dineen (Contract) **Est.** 1998 **Dozens** 5000 **Vyds** 19.5ha
Kristine Grant, Markus Maislinger and Natasha and Tony Nieuwhof are close friends from two families who moved from Victoria to make wine in the pristine climate of the Tamar Valley. Most of the estate-grown grapes are now made into the Goaty Hill brand, although they still sell some of their premium sparkling fruit to Jansz Tasmania. There aren't any goats on the property, but there is, according to the owners, a friendly collection of children and dogs.

♀♀♀♀♀ **Chardonnay 2013** Classy chardonnay; fruit is the driver, oak subtle; white peach and melon flavours, with a long, lingering finish underwritten by Tasmanian acidity. Gold Tas Wine Show '15. Screwcap. **Rating** 95 **To** 2021 $36

Golden Ball   ★★★★★

1175 Beechworth–Wangaratta Road, Beechworth, Vic 3747 **Region** Beechworth
T (03) 5727 0284 **www**.goldenball.com.au **Open** By appt
Winemaker James McLaurin **Est.** 1996 **Dozens** 850 **Vyds** 4ha
The vineyard is on one of the original land grants in the Beechworth region, planted by James and Janine McLaurin in 1996, mainly to shiraz, cabernet sauvignon, merlot and malbec, with lesser plantings of petit verdot, sagrantino and savagnin. The wines are aged in one-third new

French oak, the remainder 2–3 years old. The low yields result in intensely flavoured wines, which are to be found in a Who's Who of Melbourne's best restaurants and a handful of local and Melbourne retailers. Exports to Singapore.

🍷🍷🍷🍷🍷 **là-bas Beechworth Chardonnay 2013** From Smiths Vineyard, planted '78; fermented for 17 months in French oak (35% new). It has incredible drive, intensity and length to its grapefruit, green apple and white peach palate, yet it's not the least heavy, and with the screwcap to safeguard it, will have a minimum 15-year life span. Screwcap. 13% alc. **Rating** 97 **To** 2030 $55 ✪

🍷🍷🍷🍷🍷 **Gallice Beechworth Cabernet Merlot Malbec 2012** A wine with attitude, although it's quite restrained in the way it expresses itself; the interplay between cassis, herb, spice and earth constantly shifts its centre point, but never its length or balance. Diam. 13.5% alc. **Rating** 95 **To** 2032 $55

🍷🍷🍷🍷🍷 **Cherish a la provencale 2014 Rating** 93 **To** 2016 $28
Beechworth Shiraz 2012 Rating 93 **To** 2027 $55

Golden Grove Estate ★★★★★

Sundown Road, Ballandean, Qld 4382 **Region** Granite Belt
T (07) 4684 1291 **www**.goldengroveestate.com.au **Open** 7 days 9–4
Winemaker Raymond Costanzo **Est.** 1993 **Dozens** 4000 **Vyds** 12.4ha
Golden Grove Estate was established by Mario and Sebastian Costanzo in 1946, producing stone fruits and table grapes. The first wine grapes (shiraz) were planted in '72, but it was not until '85, when ownership passed to son Sam and his wife Grace, that the use of the property began to change. In '93 chardonnay and merlot joined the shiraz, followed by cabernet sauvignon, sauvignon blanc and semillon. The baton has been passed down another generation to Ray Costanzo, who has lifted the quality of the wines remarkably, and has also planted tempranillo, durif, barbera, malbec, mourvedre, vermentino and nero d'Avola. Its consistent wine show success over recent years with alternative varieties is impressive.

🍷🍷🍷🍷🍷 **Vintage Grand Reserve Granite Belt Mourvedre 2012** Hits the mark from the first whiff and the first sip, but you only realise just how outstanding it is once you experience the finish, and – even more – the aftertaste. There is a rainbow of red and dark forest fruits, a garland of spices and a farewell of cedary tannins, all encouraging you to repeat the process until the bottle is finished. The best Granite Belt red I have ever tasted, and from a variety that isn't easy to manipulate. Screwcap. 14.5% alc. **Rating** 97 **To** 2032 $55 ✪

🍷🍷🍷🍷🍷 **Vintage Grand Reserve Granite Belt Shiraz 2012** Still has vivid crimson colour, and is an object lesson in combining elegance, finesse and extreme length; the aromas and flavours hover between red and black fruits, the tannins silky smooth, but persistent, oak in its due place. A great vintage has produced a great wine. Screwcap. 14.5% alc. **Rating** 96 **To** 2032 $45 ✪
Granite Belt Semillon 2009 Semillon and shiraz have been part of the development of the Granite Belt from its earliest days. Some colour development; picked at the optimum moment, the wine has classic lemon/lemongrass/ honeysuckle flavours embraced by minerally acidity; 4 years young, with years to go. Screwcap. 11.6% alc. **Rating** 95 **To** 2020 $20 ✪
Granite Belt Semillon Sauvignon 2014 A 62/38% blend, wild yeast-fermented in new French oak. Wonderfully vibrant and juicy, improbably with some of the lime/citrus flavours of top-quality Riesling (the semillon at work), finishing with a burst of tropical fruits. Screwcap. 12.8% alc. **Rating** 95 **To** 2019 $18 ✪
Granite Belt Chardonnay 2013 The retro technique of 24-hour skin contact reflects Ray Costanzo's ability to make decisions outside the square, for the skin contact has not made the wine coarse or flabby. Half was wild yeast barrel-fermented in new and 1yo French oak, and here too the result is felicitous, for the overall driver of an energetic wine is fresh fruit. Screwcap. 12.8% alc. **Rating** 94 **To** 2020 $26 ✪

ŸŸŸŸ♀ Granite Belt Vermentino 2014 Rating 93 To 2019 $26 ✪
Granite Belt Durif 2013 Rating 92 To 2023 $30
Granite Belt Rose 2014 Rating 91 To 2015 $16 ✪
Accommodation Creek Mediterranean Red 2013 Rating 91 To 2020
$18 ✪
Granite Belt Barbera 2013 Rating 91 To 2020 $24

Golding Wines   ★★★★☆

52 Western Branch Road, Lobethal, SA 5241 **Region** Adelaide Hills
T (08) 8389 5120 **www**.goldingwines.com.au **Open** 7 days 11–4
Winemaker Michael Sykes, Darren Golding **Est.** 2002 **Dozens** 8000 **Vyds** 18.52ha
The Golding family has lived in the Lobethal area for several generations, and has trimmed
its once larger viticultural holdings to concentrate on the Western Branch Road vineyard,
planted to sauvignon blanc, savagnin, chardonnay, pinot gris and pinot noir. Exports to the UK,
the US, Canada, Hong Kong, the Philippines, Malaysia, Singapore and China.

ŸŸŸŸŸ Cascara Adelaide Hills Savagnin 2013 Fascinating wine. Spicy yet fruity,
textural but full of zip. Barley, lime, apricot, wax and spice. It's complex but
effortless at the same time. Immensely easy to drink, even as you muse on it.
Screwcap. 12.5% alc. **Rating** 95 To 2017 $35 CM ✪

ŸŸŸŸ♀ Francesca Adelaide Hills Savagnin 2013 Rating 92 To 2016 $35 CM
The Merchant Adelaide Hills Merlot 2013 Rating 91 To 2019 $22 CM ✪
Block 2 Adelaide Hills Chardonnay 2013 Rating 90 To 2018 $35 CM
The East End Adelaide Hills Rose 2013 Rating 90 To 2016 $22 CM
The Purveyor Adelaide Hills Pinot Noir 2013 Rating 90 To 2019 $22 CM

Gomersal Wines   ★★★★

Lyndoch Road, Gomersal, SA 5352 **Region** Barossa Valley
T (08) 8563 3611 **www**.gomersalwines.com.au **Open** 7 days 10–5
Winemaker Barry White, Peter Pollard **Est.** 1887 **Dozens** 8500 **Vyds** 20ha
The 1887 establishment date has a degree of poetic licence. In 1887 Friedrich W Fromm
planted the Wonganella Vineyards, following that with a winery on the edge of the Gomersal
Creek in 1891; it remained in operation for 90 years, finally closing in 1983. In 2000 a group
of friends 'with strong credentials in both the making and consumption end of the wine
industry' bought the winery and re-established the vineyard, planting 17ha of shiraz, 2ha of
mourvedre and 1ha of grenache via terraced bush vines. The Riesling comes from purchased
grapes. Exports to the US, Ireland, The Netherlands, Hong Kong and China.

ŸŸŸŸŸ Estate Grown Barossa Valley Shiraz 2012 Fermented and macerated on skins
for 12 days, matured in new French hogsheads for 26 months, only 394 dozen
made. The wine is of high quality, but is simply not ready to drink; the parts are
in balance, but there are gaping holes in the mortar intended to join the fruit, oak
and tannins together. Screwcap. 15% alc. **Rating** 94 To 2052 $50

ŸŸŸŸ♀ Barossa Valley Shiraz 2012 Rating 91 To 2025 $17 ✪
Reserve Barossa Valley Shiraz 2012 Rating 91 To 2032 $25

Goona Warra Vineyard   ★★★★

790 Sunbury Road, Sunbury, Vic 3429 **Region** Sunbury
T (03) 9740 7766 **www**.goonawarra.com.au **Open** By appt
Winemaker John Barnier, Emmett Andersen **Est.** 1863 **Dozens** 3000 **Vyds** 6.92ha
A historic stone winery, originally established under this name by a 19th-century Victorian
premier. Excellent tasting facilities, an outstanding venue for weddings and receptions. Exports
to China.

ŸŸŸŸŸ Sunbury Sauvignon Blanc Semillon 2014 A 70/30% blend, hand-picked,
whole bunch-pressed, cool-fermented in stainless steel plus 5% barrel-fermented.

A very well made wine with great drive and energy, sauvignon blanc relishing the structural support from the semillon and the barrel fermentation, leaving it free to showpiece its passionfruit and kiwifruit flavours on the lingering palate. Screwcap. 12.5% alc. **Rating** 94 **To** 2018 $22 ✪

Sunbury Chardonnay 2014 Hand-picked, whole bunch-pressed, wild yeast-fermented in French barriques, 6 months' lees contact, no mlf. This is a deliciously mouth-filling style, with sweet nectarine and white peach fruit to the fore obligingly filling any of the empty crevices that may have been there. Balance is the key. Screwcap. 13% alc. **Rating** 94 **To** 2024 $27 ✪

Gooree Park Wines   ★★★

Gulgong Road, Mudgee, NSW 2850 **Region** Mudgee
T (02) 6378 1800 **www.**gooreepark.com.au **Open** Mon–Fri 10–5, w'ends 11–4
Winemaker Andrew Ewart **Est.** 2008 **Dozens** 2500 **Vyds** 546ha
Gooree Park Wines is part of a group of companies owned by Eduardo Cojuangco, other companies including a thoroughbred horse stud and a pastoral enterprise and vineyards based in Mudgee and Canowindra. Eduardo's interest in all forms of agriculture has resulted in the planting of over 500ha of vines, starting with the Tullamour Vineyard in Mudgee in 1996, Fords Creek in Mudgee in '97, and Mt Lewis Estate at Canowindra in '98. A cellar door was opened in 2008.

🍷🍷🍷🍷 **Sauvignon Blanc 2014** Eager to please. Ready to go. Ripe tropical fruit and cooked flavours load the palate up with fruity appeal. Screwcap. 12.5% alc. **Rating** 89 **To** 2015 $18 CM ✪
Cabernet Rose 2014 Bright copper, almost into bricking territory. Dry, herbal nuances float through cidery berry flavours. Good food style. Screwcap. 12% alc. **Rating** 89 **To** 2016 $18 CM ✪
Cabernet Sauvignon 2013 Solid hit of curranty flavour. Bay leaf notes emphasise the variety. Slight dip through the mid-palate and a drying finish, but there's plenty of substance here. Screwcap. 13.9% alc. **Rating** 88 **To** 2020 $18 CM

Grace Farm   ★★★★★

741 Cowaramup Bay Road, Gracetown, WA 6285 **Region** Margaret River
T (08) 9384 4995 **www.**gracefarm.com.au **Open** By appt
Winemaker Jonathan Mettam **Est.** 2006 **Dozens** 3000 **Vyds** 8.17ha
Situated in the Wilyabrup district, in the Cowaramup Brook valley, Grace Farm is the small, family-owned vineyard of Elizabeth and John Mair, taking its name from the nearby coastal hamlet of Gracetown. Situated beside picturesque natural forest, the vineyard is planted to cabernet sauvignon, chardonnay, sauvignon blanc and semillon. Viticulturist Tim Quinlan conducts tastings (by appointment), offering an insight into Grace Farms's sustainable viticultural practices.

🍷🍷🍷🍷🍷 **Margaret River Cabernet Sauvignon 2013** Gold medals Margaret River and Perth Wine Shows '14. It is immediately obvious why the wine has consistently risen to the top in what are always highly competitive classes in wine shows; it has deeply layered cassis fruit and complementary oak, yet retains elegance, the finish unusually supple for Cabernet. Screwcap. 14.5% alc. **Rating** 96 **To** 2033 $30 ✪
Reserve Margaret River Cabernet Sauvignon 2013 The best parcels from four estate blocks. It has vivid, deep purple-crimson colour, and is more intense and structured than its estate sibling; it is akin to a 2yo First Growth Bordeaux: its quality is laid out in stark letters, but it's a long way from being even half-ready to drink. Screwcap. 14.5% alc. **Rating** 96 **To** 2048 $50 ✪
Margaret River Sauvignon Blanc Semillon 2014 Trophies WA and Perth Wine Shows '14. Partially barrel-fermented, it has tropical fruits at its heart, given structure and authority by lemongrass and snow pea flavours surrounding the heart; outstanding value. Screwcap. 12.8% alc. **Rating** 95 **To** 2020 $21 ✪
Margaret River Chardonnay 2014 Hand-picked, whole bunch-pressed to French barriques. Bright quartz-green; a very elegant and expressive wine,

winemaker, variety and place all contributing to the outcome; it has great length, and will grow another leg in bottle over the next few years. Screwcap. 13.5% alc. Rating 95 To 2024 $30 ✪

Graillot ★★★★★

19–21 Russell Street, Abbotsford, Vic 3067 (postal) **Region** Heathcote
T 1300 610 919 **www.**graillotaustralia.com.au **Open** Not
Winemaker Alain Graillot, Sandro Mosele **Est.** 2010 **Dozens** 900 **Vyds** 3.3ha
Graillot is owned by Robert Walters, well known for his role with Bibendum Wine Co., which (inter alia) imports fine wines from various parts of Europe, with France to the fore. He has imported the wines of Alain Graillot, one of the superstars of the northern Rhône Valley (in Crozes-Hermitage) for many years. The two become good friends during that time, and in 2010 that friendship took a new turn with the establishment of Graillot. There are two wines made each year, the first simply labelled Syrah, the second Project Syrah No. 2.

🍷🍷🍷🍷🍷 Heathcote Syrah 2013 The interplay of warm and cool-climate characters is quite beautiful. Pepper and spice notes abound but in a context of fresh, ripe, blackberry and black cherry flavour. Licks of fennel, smoke and violet are part of the show and there's a hum of fine tannin from at least the mid-palate onwards. It gives up the flavours but then draws them all back in; controlled; classical. Screwcap. 13% alc. **Rating** 96 **To** 2033 $46 CM ✪
Project Syrah No. 2 2013 The hits keep coming, This is another fine, sophisticated release. Black pepper and clove notes thread through a myriad of both savoury and fruit-filled characters: licorice, black cherry, meat, green herbs, peppercorn and violets among them. It flows in decisive manner towards a structured, spice-riddled finish. It will live for many years but, being so well balanced, drinks well young. Screwcap. 13% alc. **Rating** 95 **To** 2028 $32 CM ✪

Grampians Estate ★★★★★

1477 Western Highway, Great Western, Vic 3377 **Region** Grampians
T (03) 5354 6245 **www.**grampiansestate.com.au **Open** 7 days 10–5
Winemaker Hamish Seabrook, Don Rowe, Tom Guthrie **Est.** 1989 **Dozens** 1400
Vyds 8ha
Graziers Sarah and Tom Guthrie began their diversification into wine in 1989, but their core business continues to be fat lamb and wool production. Both activities were ravaged by the 2006 bushfires, but each has recovered, that of their grapegrowing and winemaking rising like a phoenix from the ashes. They have acquired the Garden Gully winery at Great Western, giving them a cellar door and a vineyard with 2.4ha of 130-year-old shiraz and 3ha of 80-year-old riesling. Exports to Singapore, China and Japan.

🍷🍷🍷🍷🍷 The Longest Drive Shiraz 2013 From a single vineyard in the Pyrenees. Highly focused and intense, the black fruits, plus spice, pepper and licorice, run true throughout the bouquet and long drive of the palate, tannins perfectly pitched. Screwcap. 14% alc. **Rating** 95 **To** 2033 $30 ✪
Streeton Reserve Shiraz 2010 Hand-picked from the St Ethel and Mafeking Vineyards. Has held its bright hue very well; no more than medium-bodied, it nonetheless has remarkable intensity in the savoury half of the field, spicy fruits on the other half. It's one of those wines that will go on and on. Screwcap. 14% alc. Rating 95 To 2035 $60
Grenache 2013 From Great Western. Light, but bright hue; it has a highly fragrant red berry bouquet and an intense palate, obviously Grenache, but with a freshness, zest and fruit grip different from the normal profile of Grenache. Jam-packed with interest. Screwcap. 13.5% alc. **Rating** 94 **To** 2028 $25 ✪

🍷🍷🍷🍷🍷 GST 2013 **Rating** 93 **To** 2030 $28
Mafeking Gold Chardonnay 2013 Rating 90 To 2018 $22

Granite Hills ★★★★★

1481 Burke and Wills Track, Baynton, Vic 3444 **Region** Macedon Ranges
T (03) 5423 7273 **www**.granitehills.com.au **Open** 7 days 11–6
Winemaker Llew Knight, Ian Gunter **Est.** 1970 **Dozens** 5000 **Vyds** 12.5ha
Granite Hills is one of the enduring classics, pioneering the successful growing of riesling and shiraz in an uncompromisingly cool climate. It is based on riesling, chardonnay, shiraz, cabernet sauvignon, cabernet franc, merlot and pinot noir (the last also used in its sparkling wine). The Rieslings age superbly, the Shiraz the forerunner of the cool-climate school in Australia.

🍷🍷🍷🍷🍷 **Tor Riesling 2013** From the oldest, lowest-yielding vines on the property. Tor
means rocky outcrop; central to the Knight Granite Hills experience. The wine
is a strong straw-green; has more than a little spritz; takes risks with green, herbal
elements but pours on lime, slate, lemon pith and assorted blossomy elements.
Interest, intensity and length. You can ask for little more. Screwcap. 13% alc.
Rating 96 **To** 2026 $45 CM ✪
Knight Riesling 2013 The intense bouquet of citrus blossom leads into a
piercing palate with a seamless fusion of lime, apple and slatey acidity. The acidity
underwrites a 20-year future for the wine, its statement of the very cool place of
its birth plain for all to see. Screwcap. **Rating** 96 **To** 2034 $25 ✪
Knight Riesling 2014 Pristine expression of the variety. Lime and florals, spice
and talc. Rind-like burst on the finish gives it that extra something. Clean, zesty
length. Screwcap. 12.5% alc. **Rating** 94 **To** 2026 $25 CM ✪

🍷🍷🍷🍷🍸 **Knight Shiraz 2008 Rating** 93 **To** 2025 $35 CM

Grant Burge ★★★★★

279 Krondorf Road, Barossa Valley, SA 5352 **Region** Barossa Valley
T (08) 8563 3700 **www**.grantburgewines.com.au **Open** 7 days 10–5
Winemaker Grant Burge, Craig Stansborough **Est.** 1988 **Dozens** 400 000 **Vyds** 356ha
Grant and Helen Burge established the eponymous Grant Burge business in 1988. By a series of astute vineyard purchases and unrelenting sales and marketing by the duo, it grew to being one of the largest family-owned wine businesses in the valley. In February 2015, Accolade Wines announced it had acquired the Grant Burge brand, Burge and Rathbone Fine Wine Merchants, and the historic Krondorf Winery. The 356ha of vineyards remain in family ownership, and will continue to supply premium grapes to the Accolade-owned business. Grant Burge will also play an ongoing role as a brand ambassador.

🍷🍷🍷🍷🍷 **Thorn Eden Valley Riesling 2014** Lipsmacking, layered and powerful; the
bouquet is very flowery, filled with spring blossom aromas, the palate bursting with
Bickford's lime juice flavours that continue in an unbroken stream through to the
finish and (notably) the aftertaste. Screwcap. 12.5% alc. **Rating** 95 **To** 2029 $24 ✪
Cameron Vale Barossa Cabernet Sauvignon 2012 Grant Burge and chief
winemaker Craig Stansborough proposed that this may be the best vintage ever
(upstaging the late Murray Tyrrell, who only ever got to vintage of the century
level). This is a blue-blood Cabernet, with elegance, length and intensity all
wrapped up in blackcurrant and cedar flavours, supported by fine tannins through
the finish and aftertaste. Screwcap. 14% alc. **Rating** 95 **To** 2027 $28 ✪
Filsell Old Vine Barossa Shiraz 2012 Opaque, dense crimson-purple; the
Filsell Vineyard is nearing its 100th birthday, and '12 was a vintage to dream of.
This full-bodied Shiraz is densely packed with sooty, brooding black fruits, copious
tannins and some oak. It is 10 years away from nearing its best; the points are for
the wine today, and will be considerably higher down the track. Screwcap. 14% alc.
Rating 94 **To** 2042 $45
Daly Road Barossa Shiraz Mourvedre 2013 While the colour doesn't set the
pulse racing, this wine reveals more and more each time it is retasted, both in terms
of its complexity and length. The overall flavour profile is savoury and spicy; there
are lively red cherry and fresh plum fruits, the package given life and lift by the
moderate alcohol and fine tannins. Screwcap. 14% alc. **Rating** 94 **To** 2033 $25 ✪

ŸŸŸŸŸ East Argyle Pinot Gris 2014 Rating 92 To 2016 $24 ✪
Mt 0° Grampians Alpine Valley Shiraz 2012 Rating 91 To 2022 $25
Blanc de Noirs Méthode Traditionelle Brut NV Rating 91 To 2015 $41 TS
5th Generation Shiraz 2013 Rating 90 To 2020 $21 ✪

Greedy Sheep   ★★★★★

PO Box 530, Cowaramup, WA 6284 **Region** Margaret River
T (08) 9755 7428 **www**.greedysheep.com.au **Open** Not
Winemaker Dave Johnson **Est.** 2005 **Dozens** 4000 **Vyds** 6ha
When Bridget Allen purchased the Greedy Sheep property in 2004 it had been planted to
cabernet sauvignon, merlot, cabernet franc and malbec in 1999. It pays to have a sense of
humour, for in January '05 1000 sheep found their way into the vineyard, eating everything
green within their reach, including unripe grapes, which must have challenged their digestion.
Bridget also purchases fruit from her twin sister's vineyard, a mere 3km away.

ŸŸŸŸŸ Single Vineyard Alchemy Chardonnay 2014 Dry-grown, hand-picked,
whole bunch-pressed, wild yeast-fermented in French oak. All of its winemaking
inputs are evident, but have worked like a charm; it is complex, savoury and long,
with an overriding elegance to its mouthfeel. Gold medal Hobart Wine Show '14.
Screwcap. 13.5% alc. **Rating** 95 To 2024 $30 ✪
Single Vineyard Shiraz 2013 Gold medals Perth Wine Show '14 and Decanter
World Wine Awards '14 emphasise the coming of age of shiraz in Margaret River.
There is an array of vibrant cherry and plum fruits allied with licorice and spice
on the medium-bodied, yet richly endowed palate; French oak and fine tannins
provide precise support. Screwcap. 13.5% alc. **Rating** 95 To 2028 $30 ✪
Cabernet Merlot 2011 Strong crimson-purple; a supple, smooth, medium-
bodied wine with nigh-on perfect integration of cassis, plum fruit, French oak and
superfine tannins. A gold medal from the Sydney Wine Show '14 fully deserved.
Screwcap. 14% alc. **Rating** 95 To 2026 $24 ✪

 # Greenock Estate   ★★★

Lightpass Road, Angaston, SA 5355 **Region** Barossa Valley
T (08) 6365 5822 **www**.gewines.com **Open** Not
Winemaker Steve Kurtz **Est.** 1948 **Dozens** NFP
The establishment date is that of the Kurtz Family vineyards, which supply Greenock Estate
with its grapes. The first Greenock Estate wine was made in 2002, and the first wines reached
Asia in 2009. Exports to Hong Kong and Macau.

ŸŸŸŸ   Premium Selection Barossa Valley Shiraz 2013 Full of contradictions and
questions: first up is the price in the context of its presumed district origin and
slick packaging; next is the light (although bright) colour; then the light-bodied
palate. Altogether strange. Cork. 14% alc. **Rating** 88 To 2017 $15 ✪

Greenstone Vineyard   ★★★★★

319 Whorouly South Road, Whorouly South, Vic 3735 **Region** Heathcote
T (03) 5727 1434 **www**.greenstoneofheathcote.com **Open** By appt
Winemaker Sandro Mosele (Contract), Alberto Antonini, Mark Walpole **Est.** 2002
Dozens 2500 **Vyds** 20ha
This is one of the most interesting ventures to emerge over the past decade, bringing together
David Gleave MW, born and educated in Canada, now a long-term UK resident, co-founder
of Liberty Wines and who writes widely about the wines of Italy; Alberto Antonini, a graduate
of the University of Florence, and Italian Flying Winemaker; and Mark Walpole, for 20 years
manager of Brown Brothers' 700ha of vineyards before retiring in 2010. The partners chose
what they considered an outstanding vineyard site on the red soil of the Heathcote region, and
duly planted 17ha of shiraz, 2ha of sangiovese and 1ha of monastrell (mourvedre). Exports to
the UK, the US and other major markets.

♀♀♀♀♀ Rosso di Colbo Heathcote Sangiovese 2013 Wild yeast open-fermented, matured in large-format used French oak; a small injection of colorino also in the mix. This is a more complete Sangiovese than most others, with texture running alongside structure, the fruit spectrum as much black cherry as red. Drink now or much later. Screwcap. 13.5% alc. **Rating** 95 **To** 2023 $28 **☉**

Greg Cooley Wines ★★★★★

Lot 1 Main North Road, Clare, SA 5453 **Region** Clare Valley
T (08) 8843 4284 **www**.gregcooleywines.com.au **Open** 7 days 11–4
Winemaker Greg Cooley **Est.** 2002 **Dozens** 3000
Greg Cooley explains, 'All my wines are named after people who have been of influence to me in my 45 years and their influence is as varied as the wine styles – from pizza shop owners, to my greyhound's vet and South Australian author Monica McInerney.' I have to confess that I am taken by Greg's path to glory, because my move through law to wine was punctuated by the part-ownership of two greyhounds that always wanted to run in the opposite direction from the rest of the field.

♀♀♀♀♀ Valerie Beh Single Vineyard Riesling 2014 Not only single vineyard, but 11 specific rows of one of the highest blocks above Watervale. It combines finesse and power, which may seem oxymoronic, but reflects the finesse of the citrus blossom and citrus flavour, and the power of the stony/minerally acidity. A wine that cries out for a minimum of 5+ years in bottle, but has such appeal it will largely fall to vinocide. Screwcap. 12% alc. **Rating** 95 **To** 2029 $23 **☉**
Dad & Meads Clare Valley Grenache Shiraz 2013 A 60/40% blend matured for 12 months in French oak (30% new). There are exceptions to any rule, but this is a particularly obvious example, its galaxy of red fruit flavours rich and supple, without the least hint of confection. Indeed, when I tasted the wine I thought I had picked up the wrong glass. As an extra, it has uncommon balance and synergy between the two varieties. Screwcap. 14% alc. **Rating** 95 **To** 2028 $25 **☉**
Museum Release Valerie Beh Clare Valley Riesling 2008 Pale, bright straw-green; still amazingly delicate and fresh, with a mix of citrus juice, pith and zest, plus green apple; its fruit–acid balance is impeccable. If you belatedly decide you should have some birth-year wine for your child or godchild, you could do a lot worse than this (and no one need know how little it cost). Screwcap. 12.5% alc. **Rating** 94 **To** 2026 $25 **☉**
Monica, Macca & Moo Clare Valley Shiraz 2013 Matured for 15 months in French and American oak (60% new), 230 dozen made. A succulent, rich and layered palate is framed by (and built on) integrated but obvious oak; some may cavil at this, but I think it's a positive contribution to a wine with very good overall balance and mouthfeel. Screwcap. 14% alc. **Rating** 94 **To** 2033 $30 **☉**

♀♀♀♀♀ The Gloria Southern Fleurieu Pinot Grigio 2014 **Rating** 93 **To** 2016 $23 **☉**

Groom ★★★★☆

28 Langmeil Road, Tanunda, SA 5352 (postal) **Region** Barossa Valley
T (08) 8563 1101 **www**.groomwines.com **Open** Not
Winemaker Daryl Groom **Est.** 1997 **Dozens** 2100 **Vyds** 27.8ha
The full name of the business is Marschall Groom Cellars, a venture owned by David and Jeanette Marschall and their six children, and Daryl and Lisa Groom and their four children. Daryl was a highly regarded winemaker at Penfolds before he moved to Geyser Peak in California. Years of discussion between the families resulted in the purchase of a 35ha block of bare land adjacent to Penfolds' 130-year-old Kalimna Vineyard. Shiraz was planted in 1997, giving its first vintage in '99. The next acquisition was an 8ha vineyard at Lenswood in the Adelaide Hills, planted to sauvignon blanc. In 2000, 3.2ha of zinfandel was planted on the Kalimna Bush Block. Exports to the US, Canada, Hong Kong, Taiwan and China.

♀♀♀♀♀ Barossa Valley Shiraz 2012 Matured for 20 months in American (55%) and French (45%) oak, 30% new. Deep colour; the complex black fruits of the bouquet multiply on the full-bodied palate, framed by generous, although integrated, oak; a whisk of savoury licorice provides light and shade on the finish. Cork. 14.9% alc. **Rating** 94 **To** 2032 $49

YYYY Adelaide Hills Sauvignon Blanc 2014 **Rating** 93 **To** 2016 $24 ○
Bush Block Barossa Valley Zinfandel 2013 **Rating** 93 **To** 2020 $30

Grosset ★★★★★

King Street, Auburn, SA 5451 **Region** Clare Valley
T (08) 8849 2175 **www**.grosset.com.au **Open** Wed–Sun 10–5 from Sept for approx 6 weeks
Winemaker Jeffrey Grosset, Brent Treloar **Est.** 1981 **Dozens** 11 000 **Vyds** 22.2ha
Jeffrey Grosset has assumed the unchallenged mantle of Australia's foremost Riesling maker in the wake of John Vickery stepping back to a consultancy role for Richmond Grove. Grosset's pre-eminence in Riesling making is recognised both domestically and internationally; however, he merits equal recognition for the other wines in his portfolio: Semillon Sauvignon Blanc from Clare Valley/Adelaide Hills, Chardonnay and Pinot Noir from the Adelaide Hills; and Gaia, a Bordeaux blend from the Clare Valley. These are all benchmarks. His quietly spoken manner conceals a steely will. Trial plantings (2ha) of fiano, aglianico, nero d'Avola and petit verdot (plus one or two more varieties planned) suggest some new wines may be gestating. Exports to all major markets.

YYYYY Polish Hill Clare Valley Riesling 2014 A super-elegant, beautifully balanced and poised Riesling that becomes steadily more impressive with each sip, the flavours of lime and lemon wreathed by slatey acidity. It has years of improvement in front of it, but one can hardly be blamed for enjoying it now. Screwcap. 12.5% alc. **Rating** 97 **To** 2034 $54 ○

YYYYY Alea Clare Valley Riesling 2014 Only just off-dry, the fruit intensity wrapping both residual sugar and acidity in its folds; as the wine develops in bottle over the next 15+ years that sweetness will cease to be obvious as all of the multitude of flavour inputs become one. Screwcap. 12.5% alc. **Rating** 96 **To** 2034 $36 ○
Clare Valley Adelaide Hills Semillon Sauvignon Blanc 2014 A 75/25% blend; 600 dozen made. Jeff Grosset believes this is one of the most appealing releases of this wine in recent year; early-picked Clare semillon gives the wine its texture and structure, but doesn't blur the tropical fruits of the Adelaide Hills sauvignon blanc; the two parts are joined symbiotically and synergistically. Screwcap. 12.5% alc. **Rating** 96 **To** 2019 $35 ○
Piccadilly Adelaide Hills Chardonnay 2013 500 dozen produced. Grown on the same vines as the initial 1993 release. Partial mlf. Cutting style but its best is clearly all before it. Slate, citrus, spice, seashells and creamy oak. A wine of terrific momentum and class. Screwcap. 13.5% alc. **Rating** 95 **To** 2024 $62 CM
Apiana 2014 Fiano and semillon from the Watervale Vineyard. You might think fiano and semillon was a long-established blend, but this is quite certainly the first, stacked with ultra-delicious citrus and honey fruit (apiana is Latin for bees). 180 dozen made. Screwcap. 12.7% alc. **Rating** 95 **To** 2020 $40
Adelaide Hills Pinot Noir 2013 Foot-stomped, some stalks, warm-fermented, unfined. Silken texture, quite bold upfront but tangy and bright in general, almost cranberried. Fresh plum and stewed cherry notes, spice, extra polish from cedary/smoky oak. Tense on the finish, as if it's not quite ready to reveal itself properly. An interesting future awaits. Screwcap. 13.5% alc. **Rating** 95 **To** 2024 $74 CM
Gaia 2012 75% cabernet sauvignon, 25% cabernet franc. Highly expressive wine, medium weight but full of character. Juicy blackcurrant and black cherry, dust and herb/floral notes, smoky oak and ripples of fine, spicy, almost peppery tannin. Tangy Cabernet but quite beautiful. Monty for the cellar. Screwcap. 13.7% alc. **Rating** 95 **To** 2035 $79 CM

Grove Estate Wines

4100 Murringo Road, Young, NSW 2594 **Region** Hilltops
T (02) 6382 6999 **www**.groveestate.com.au **Open** 7 days 10–5
Winemaker Brian Mullany **Est.** 1989 **Dozens** 4000 **Vyds** 46ha

The Grove Estate partners of the Mullany, Kirkwood and Flanders families purchased the then unplanted property situated on volcanic red soils at an elevation of 530m with the intention of producing premium cool-climate wine grapes for sale to other winemakers. Over the ensuing years plantings included cabernet sauvignon, shiraz, merlot, zinfandel, barbera, sangiovese, petit verdot, chardonnay, semillon and nebbiolo. In 1997 a decision was taken to retain a small amount of cabernet sauvignon and have it vinified under the Grove Estate label, and the winemaking gathered pace thereafter. Exports to China.

 **Sommita Hilltops Nebbiolo 2013** It has become clear that the climate of the Hilltops region is particularly well suited to the high-spirited and demanding nature of nebbiolo; here Brian Mullany's experience with Italian varieties completes the circle. While retaining its autocratic personality, the sour cherry/red cherry fruit is utterly enticing, and the tannins are freakishly well behaved. Screwcap. 13.5% alc. **Rating** 95 **To** 2033 $50

The Cellar Block Hilltops Shiraz Viognier 2013 Bright, clear crimson; the fragrant bouquet is full of lifted red fruits and spice, typical of shiraz and viognier grown in a temperate climate; it is a wine about elegance, not power, and will give pleasure from day one. Screwcap. 13.5% alc. **Rating** 94 **To** 2023 $35

The Partners Reserve Cabernet Sauvignon 2012 Fermented and then matured in new and used French oak for 24 months, a time-consuming approach if (as it seems) the whole primary fermentation was indeed in the oak in which maturation took place. The result is a complex wine with blackcurrant and black olive fruit and a lingering, savoury finish. Screwcap. 14% alc. **Rating** 94 **To** 2027 $35

Late Harvest Viognier 2013 This is a pretty smart late harvest Viognier at any price, let alone this. It has abundant concentration and complexity underpinning the apricot and peach fruit, the sweetness tempered by cleansing acidity. These wines are expensive to grow and make, underlining the price/quality equation. 375ml. Screwcap. 10.5% alc. **Rating** 94 **To** 2019 $19

Growers Gate

PO Box 238, Berri, SA 5343 **Region** Riverland
T (08) 8583 2286 **www**.growersgate.com.au **Open** Not
Winemaker Peter Dawson **Est.** 2010 **Dozens** 35 000

Growers Gate is owned by CCW Co-operative Ltd., the largest grape supply co-operative in Australia, growing approximately 15% of Australia's total annual wine grape production. In 2009 the CCW Growers decided they would use their combined vineyard resources to produce their own brand and they appointed Peter Dawson, former BRL Hardy chief winemaker, to assist with the creation of Growers Gate. The range consists of Sauvignon Blanc, Chardonnay, Cabernet Sauvignon and Shiraz, all from SA. Exports to Japan, China, Canada and Germany.

Gumpara Wines ★★★★

410 Stockwell Road, Light Pass, SA 5355 **Region** Barossa Valley
T 0419 624 559 **www**.gumparawines.net.au **Open** By appt
Winemaker Mark Mader **Est.** 1999 **Dozens** 500 **Vyds** 21.53ha

In 1856 the Mader family left Silesia to settle in SA, acquiring a 25ha property at Light Pass. Over the generations, farming and fruit growing gave way to 100% grapegrowing; six generations later, in 2000, Mark Mader produced the first wine under the Gumpara label. After success with Shiraz, Mark branched out into Semillon made from a small parcel of almost 90-year-old estate vines. The portfolio may be small, but it's certainly diverse, with Vermentino and a range of fortified wines (Tawny Grenache, Liqueur Semillon and Liqueur Frontignac).

🍷🍷🍷🍷🍷 **Mader Reserve Barossa Valley Shiraz 2012** Crushed to open fermenters, fermentation completed in French hogsheads (65% new), then matured for 18 months in those hogsheads. The intensity of the fruit and the successful use of oak manages to provide sufficient balance to carry the alcohol. Cork. 15.5% alc. **Rating** 94 **To** 2030 $50

Gundog Estate ★★★★★

101 McDonalds Road, Pokolbin, NSW 2320 **Region** Hunter Valley
T (02) 4998 6873 **www**.gundogestate.com.au **Open** 7 days 10–5
Winemaker Matthew Burton **Est.** 2006 **Dozens** 6000 **Vyds** 5ha
Matt Burton makes four different Hunter Semillons and Shirazs from the Hunter Valley and Murrumbateman. He and wife Renee run the cellar door from the historic Pokolbin school house, next to the old Rosemount/Hungerford Hill building on McDonalds Road. They are also constructing a cellar door at the Gundaroo family property (in the Canberra District) owned by parents Sharon and Geoff, which has 2.5ha each of chardonnay and cabernet sauvignon. The Burton McMahon wines are a joint collaboration between Matt Burton and Dylan McMahon of Seville Estate.

🍷🍷🍷🍷🍷 **Indomitus Rutilus Canberra District Shiraz 2013** Whole bunch-fermented with 4% viognier; 12 months in used French oak. The colour is vivid and bright, the bouquet perfumed and spicy, the palate elegant and supple, but with a stamp of authority that will underwrite a long future, however attractive the wine is now. 50 dozen made. Screwcap. 13% alc. **Rating** 96 **To** 2028 $45 ✪

Poacher's Hunter Valley Semillon 2014 From two vineyards in the heart of Pokolbin, made in such a way as to maximise the quality of the fruit, with free-run juice, cold-settling and racking, and a cool ferment. It has exemplary length and intensity, citrus, lemongrass and acidity tightly wound together from start to finish. Screwcap. 11% alc. **Rating** 95 **To** 2029 $30 ✪

Burton McMahon Yarra Valley Chardonnay 2014 From the red soils of the Seville/Upper Yarra districts; hand-picked, sorted, whole bunch-pressed, settled, and racked to French puncheons (30% new) for wild yeast fermentation and 10 months' maturation. It has exceptional drive and intensity, grapefruit and minerally acidity the drivers, but plenty of action from the passengers, including apple, white peach and a fine gauze of oak. Screwcap. 13% alc. **Rating** 95 **To** 2024 $36

Burton McMahon Yarra Valley Pinot Noir 2014 Hand-picked, open-fermented, 30% whole bunches, 4-day cold soak, wild yeast-fermented, in 30% new French hogsheads and puncheons. A high-toned, expressive bouquet with spice and red fruits lays out a roadmap for the palate which, while on the light side, provides red fruits (cherry, wild strawberry), spices, and a perfectly judged touch of forest ex the whole bunches. Screwcap. 13% alc. **Rating** 95 **To** 2024 $36

Hunter's Shiraz 2014 From three vineyards planted '48 to '74; 304 days' cold soak, fermentation peaking at 32°C for 5–7 days, matured in French puncheons (30% new) for 9 months. Bright crimson. This is a piercing Shiraz that has bright, shiny red fruits and crisp acidity. For the geeks, the alcohol is in fact 13.7%, and the acidity is 6.8g/l. The '14 Shirazs are going to show endless iterations of Hunter Valley style on a magic carpet ride. Screwcap. 14% alc. **Rating** 95 **To** 2034 $35 ✪

Smoking Barrel Red 2014 A deep crimson blend of 50/50% Hunter Valley and Canberra District shiraz. This has more profound fruit, with cool-climate black cherry, plum and spice taking the lead, but with the Hunter Valley contribution still obvious. Here the actual alcohol is 14.2%, and suits the wine, adding gravitas (not dead fruit/warmth). Time alone will show which is the better wine – at the moment they are locked. Screwcap. 14% alc. **Rating** 95 **To** 2034 $30 ✪

Canberra District Shiraz 2013 Open-fermented for 10 days, matured in French puncheons (30% new) for 12 months. Deep colour; a fragrant bouquet semaphores the vibrant cool-climate black cherry, blackberry and spiced fruit that has effortlessly absorbed the oak, and rides handsomely on the bed of ripe, fine tannins. Screwcap. 13.5% alc. **Rating** 95 **To** 2028 $40

Marksman's Canberra District Shiraz 2013 Fruit-sorted in the vineyard and winery; extended cold soak, then matured in French puncheons for 16 months. Bright, light crimson; an aromatic bouquet of red and black cherry fruit, plus obvious quality oak, then a precisely calibrated palate where the fruit exercises control over the oak, Made for the long haul, balance and length its strengths. Screwcap. 13.5% alc. Rating 95 To 2033 $60

Wild Hunter Valley Semillon 2014 Rating 94 To 2024 $30 ✪

ΥΥΥΥΥ Indomitus Albus Hunter Valley Semillon 2014 Rating 93 To 2020 $45
Canberra District Rose 2014 Rating 93 To 2015 $25 ✪
Squire's Gundagai Canberra District Shiraz 2013 Rating 91 To 2028 $30
Hunter Valley Off-Dry Semillon 2014 Rating 91 To 2020 $25

🍇 Guthrie Wines   ★★★★

661 Torrens Valley Road, Gumeracha, SA 5253 Region Adelaide Hills
T 0413 332 083 www.guthriewines.com.au Open Not
Winemaker Hugh Guthrie Est. 2012 Dozens 700
This is the venture of Hugh and Sarah Guthrie, established over 2012–13. Growing up on his family's farm in the Adelaide Hills, Hugh developed an early interest in the wines and vineyards of the region, completing a Masters of Oenology at the University of Adelaide before working in wineries around Australia and abroad. Most recently he was a winemaker at The Lane Vineyard, winner of many awards for its wines. Sarah's interest has always been more about drinking than making wine, and her work as an anaesthetist and mother is already a full-time job. Looking after the business side of Guthrie Wines mops up any of her spare time. In 2014 Hugh held his breath, jumped, quit his day job, and became full-time winemaker at Guthrie Wines.

ΥΥΥΥΥ Obtenu Bois Adelaide Hills Sauvignon Blanc 2013 Hand-picked from a single vineyard at Aldgate; whole bunch-pressed direct to used French hogsheads for a wild-yeast ferment followed by 12 months' undisturbed lees contact. It has excellent texture and mouthfeel, the flavours herbal/savoury, not tropical, dry White Bordeaux the inspiration. Screwcap. 12.5% alc. Rating 94 To 2016 $27 ✪

ΥΥΥΥΥ Walk the Line Single Barrel Nebbiolo 2013 Rating 92 To 2019 $30
The Little Things Sauvignon Blanc 2014 Rating 91 To 2015 $22 ✪

Haan Wines   ★★★★★

148 Siegersdorf Road, Tanunda, SA 5352 Region Barossa Valley
T (08) 8562 4590 www.haanwines.com.au Open Not
Winemaker James Irvine (Contract) Est. 1993 Dozens 3500 Vyds 16.3ha
Hans and Fransien Haan established their business in 1993 when they acquired a vineyard near Tanunda. The plantings are shiraz (5.3ha), merlot (3.4ha), cabernet sauvignon (3ha), viognier (2.4ha), cabernet franc (1ha) and malbec, petit verdot and semillon (0.4ha each). Oak undoubtedly plays a role in the shaping of the style of the Haan wines, but it is perfectly integrated, and the wines have the fruit weight to carry the oak. Exports to the UK, China and other major markets.

ΥΥΥΥΥ Barossa Valley Merlot Prestige 2012 Matured for 2 years in French barriques. There is no other Merlot on the Australian market that has the opulence of this wine, which in itself mightn't be a cause for celebration, but it also has freshness to its bevy of fruit flavours, and a particularly compelling varietal finish and aftertaste. Diam. 14.5% alc. Rating 95 To 2030 $65
Wilhelmus 2012 An 86/95/5% blend of cabernet, merlot, franc, malbec and petit verdot matured in new and 1yo French barriques. Keeps the flame of the Haan style burning brightly, and does so with elegance, respecting the bright array of cassis flavours. Diam. 14% alc. Rating 95 To 2032 $65

ΥΥΥΥΥ Semillon Sauvignon Blanc 2014 Rating 93 To 2016 $20 ✪
Barossa Valley Shiraz Prestige 2012 Rating 93 To 2028 $65

Barossa Valley Viognier Ratafia NV Rating 92 To 2016 $20 ✪
Barossa Valley Shiraz Cabernet Sauvignon 2013 Rating 91 To 2025 $25
Barossa Valley Shiraz 2013 Rating 90 To 2038 $25

Hahndorf Hill Winery ★★★★☆

38 Pain Road, Hahndorf, SA 5245 **Region** Adelaide Hills
T (08) 8388 7512 **www.**hahndorfhillwinery.com.au **Open** 7 days 10–5
Winemaker Larry Jacobs **Est.** 2002 **Dozens** 5000 **Vyds** 6.5ha
Larry Jacobs and Marc Dobson, both originally from South Africa, purchased Hahndorf
Hill Winery in 2002. Larry gave up a career in intensive care medicine in 1988 when he
bought an abandoned property in Stellenbosch, and established the near-iconic Mulderbosch
Wines. When Mulderbosch was purchased at the end of '96, the pair migrated to Australia
and eventually found their way to Hahndorf Hill. In '06, their investment in the winery and
cellar door was rewarded by induction into the South Australian Great Tourism Hall of Fame.
In '07 they began converting the vineyard to biodynamic status, and they were one of the
first movers in implementing a carbon offset program. Having successfully grown and made
multi medal-winning blaufrankisch wines, they have successfully imported three clones of
gruner veltliner from Austria, and their first vintage was made in '10. While all of Hahndorf
Hill's wines won gold or silver medals in '14, the greatest success went to their Austrian and
Germanic varieties, mainly in alternative variety and similar shows, the trollinger blend Rose
rising above the rest with a trophy and gold medal for the Best Rose at the Adelaide Hills
Wine Show '14. Exports to the UK, Singapore and China.

ҮҮҮҮҮ **Single Vineyard Shiraz 2012** Ripe Shiraz influenced clearly by both toasty
oak and eucalypt characters. Cherry-plum and blackberry, woody spice, saucy
barbecue-like oak. It's not a blockbuster, and at this early stage it seems heavy-
handed; but not so much that time shouldn't be able to iron it out. Fruit quality is
excellent. Screwcap. 14% alc. **Rating** 93 To 2026 $35 CM
GRU Gruner Veltliner 2014 Continues its excellent run of recent form. This
is a white wine of feel, flavour and interest. It tastes of stone fruit, crushed spice/
white pepper, Turkish delight and crunchy apple. It's fleshy and fun but there's a bit
more to it besides. Screwcap. 12% alc. **Rating** 92 To 2017 $28 CM
Blueblood Blaufrankisch 2013 Light but insistent. Juicy fruit meets throaty,
spicy tannin, though the juiciness of the fruit clearly cuts through to victory.
Sweet-sour cherries, Christmas cake, cinnamon. Interesting wine from various
angles. Screwcap. 14% alc. **Rating** 92 To 2018 $40 CM
Pinot Grigio 2014 Modest-but-attractive scents, medium-weight palate,
everything right and proper and in good working order. Spice, nashi pear and
apple. Crisp and contained. Screwcap. 12.5% alc. **Rating** 91 To 2015 $25 CM
Sauvignon Blanc 2014 Lively both aromatically and to taste. Melon and tropical
fruit flavours with modest input from lemongrass and spice. This will keep most
white drinkers happy. Screwcap. 13% alc. **Rating** 90 To 2015 $23 CM
White Mischief 2014 Gruner with a modest amount of residual sugar. Body of
grapey flavour turns slatey and spicy on the finish. Screwcap. 12% alc. **Rating** 90
To 2016 $23 CM
Rose 2014 Made principally with German grape trollinger. Pale crimson-copper,
complex aromatics, juicy and acidic on the palate. Undergrowth, sweet strawberry,
spice and hay-like notes. It works, if clearly outside the norm; a wine for wild hair
days. Screwcap. 13% alc. **Rating** 90 To 2015 $23 CM

ҮҮҮҮ **Zsa Zsa Zweigelt Rose 2014** Rating 89 To 2016 $25 CM

 Halls Gap Estate ★★★★★

4113 Ararat–Halls Gap Road, Halls Gap, Vic 3381 **Region** Grampians
T 0413 595 513 **www.**hallsgapestate.com.au **Open** Wed–Mon 10–5
Winemaker Duncan Buchanan **Est.** 1969 **Dozens** 2000 **Vyds** 10.5ha
I first visited this vineyard when it was known as Boroka Vineyard (having been established
in 1969), and marvelled at the location in the wild country of Halls Gap. It wasn't wildly

successful, but when Mount Langi Ghiran acquired it in 1998 it had already changed its name to The Gap Vineyard. It was a useful adjunct to Mount Langi Ghiran for a while, but by 2013 it had long outlived its original purpose. It was then that the opportunity arose for the Drummond family, led by Aaron, to purchase the somewhat rundown vineyard. They moved quickly; while the '13 vintage was made by Kate Petering at Mount Langi Ghiran, the blending, vineyard management and future vintages are all being controlled under contract by Circe Wines (Aaron Drummond's partnership business with Dan Buckle). At the start of '14 Dan and Aaron hired Duncan Buchanan (ex Dromana Estate viticulturist and winemaker), giving him the dual task of managing their Mornington Peninsula vineyards, and spending all-important time at Halls Gap. Considering the rapidly moving pieces on the chess board, the quality of the two wines from '13 is quite special.

⦿⦿⦿⦿⦿ **Fallen Giants Vineyard Shiraz 2013** Open-fermented, 10 days on skins, matured for 18 months in French oak (15% new). Vivid crimson-purple hue; the wine is Grampians to the tips of its toes, black fruits subtly permeated with notes of pepper, licorice and spice carried in a web of ultrafine, but persistent, tannins. Screwcap. 14% alc. **Rating** 95 **To** 2033 $30 ✪

Fallen Giants Vineyard Cabernet Sauvignon 2013 Open-fermented with 18 days on skins, matured for 18 months in French oak (20% new). It has crystal clear cassis varietal fruit on its bouquet and palate, with touches of briar and black olive wound through in conjunction with tannins and cedary oak. 400 dozen made. Screwcap. 14% alc. **Rating** 95 **To** 2033 $30 ✪

Hamelin Bay   ★★★★☆

McDonald Road, Karridale, WA 6288 **Region** Margaret River
T (08) 9758 6779 www.hbwines.com.au **Open** 7 days 10–5
Winemaker Julian Scott **Est.** 1992 **Dozens** 10000 **Vyds** 23.5ha
The Hamelin Bay vineyard was established by the Drake-Brockman family, pioneers of the region. Richard Drake-Brockman's great-grandmother, Grace Bussell, is famous for her courage when, in 1876 aged 16, she rescued survivors of a shipwreck not far from the mouth of the Margaret River. If this were not enough, Richard's great-grandfather Frederick, known for his exploration of the Kimberley, read about the feat in Perth's press and rode 300km on horseback to meet her – they married in 1882. Hamelin Bay's vineyard and winery is located within a few kilometres of Karridale, at the intersection of the Brockman and Bussell Highways, which were named in honour of both these pioneering families. Exports to the UK, Canada, Malaysia, Singapore and China.

⦿⦿⦿⦿⦿ **Five Ashes Reserve Chardonnay 2012** A chardonnay that reflects the cool climate of Karridale in southern Margaret River. Its perfect balance of white stone fruit, melon and pink grapefruit framed by high-quality French oak is impressive enough, but it is the way the flavours accelerate on the finish and lingering aftertaste that gives this wine its special quality. Screwcap. 13% alc. **Rating** 97 **To** 2025 $49 ✪

⦿⦿⦿⦿⦿ **Five Ashes Vineyard Shiraz 2011** Significant serve of dark fruit and assertive tannin, almost too much of each though in tandem it works. Toasty oak is folded in, its minor reductive influence fostering an impression of complexity, and the finish lingers appreciably. Needs time, but is quite impeccable. Screwcap. 14% alc. **Rating** 94 **To** 2030 $32 CM

⦿⦿⦿⦿⦾ **Five Ashes Vineyard Sauvignon Blanc 2014 Rating** 93 **To** 2017 $24 ✪
Five Ashes Vineyard Chardonnay 2013 Rating 93 **To** 2019 $30 CM
Rampant Red Shiraz Merlot Cabernet 2011 Rating 93 **To** 2021 $19 ✪
Five Ashes Vineyard Cabernet 2011 Rating 93 **To** 2026 $32 CM
Five Ashes Vineyard Semillon Sauvignon Blanc 2014 Rating 92 **To** 2017 $24 CM ✪
Five Ashes Vineyard Merlot 2013 Rating 91 **To** 2028 $24 CM
Main Break Cabernet Merlot 2011 Rating 90 **To** 2018 $19 ✪

Handpicked Wines

18/2 Park Street, Sydney, NSW 2000 (postal) **Region** Various
T (02) 9475 7888 **www**.handpickedwines.com **Open** By appt
Winemaker Gary Baldwin, Peter Dillon **Est.** 2001 **Dozens** 50 000 **Vyds** 63ha
Handpicked is part of DMG Fine Wines, a global wine business with its head office based in
Australia. Its roots go back over 50 years to the Taiwanese fish markets, and the vision of Ming
Guang Dong, who built a successful broad-based business. His four children were educated
in either the UK, Australia or Singapore, and today they are all involved in the business,
with William Dong at the helm. Having worked with what became Handpicked Wines,
he bought the business with the aim of creating great wines from great regions under one
label. Today it makes wines in Italy, Chile, France and Spain, but the main arm is Australia,
where Handpicked has 33ha in the Yarra Valley, 18ha in the Mornington Peninsula and 12ha
in the Barossa Valley. It secured the services of Gary Baldwin as executive chief winemaker,
and constructed a winery at the company's flagship Capella Vineyard at Bittern, on the
Mornington Peninsula, destined to become the hospitality base for the business. In November
2014, Peter Dillon was successfully headhunted to assist Gary Baldwin; Dillon has established
his credentials as a winemaker of the highest quality over the past 12 years. Exports to Italy,
the Philippines, South Korea, Japan, Hong Kong and China.

⟡⟡⟡⟡⟡ **Capella Vineyard Mornington Peninsula Pinot Noir 2013** From two small
blocks on the estate Capella Vineyard, fruit-thinned to 2.5 tonnes per hectare. Has
wonderful drive and length, riding on the back of purity, intensity and layered
elegance, oak merely an echo. Trophy Best Wine of Show, Mornington Peninsula
Wine Show '14. Screwcap. 13.9% alc. **Rating** 97 **To** 2025 $80 ✪

⟡⟡⟡⟡⟡ **Regional Selections Eden Valley Riesling 2013** 70% from 100+yo vines
on the northeast-facing slope of the Woodman Vineyard, 30% from 30yo vines;
hand-picked, whole bunch-pressed, cultured yeast to give enhanced aromas. The
floral bouquet and exquisitely delicate, but fully formed, palate shows Eden Valley
and very old vines at their best; its balance ensures this will be a great wine in its
youth, full maturity and old age. Screwcap. 11.3% alc. **Rating** 96 **To** 2033 $34 ✪
Collection Heathcote Shiraz 2013 Three clones, separately fermented, a small
portion with whole bunches, matured for 15 months in new and used barriques.
Deep crimson-purple, its power and complexity stand side by side; black fruits, star
anise and licorice with a sunbeam of red fruit on the palate, the tannins persistent
but fine. Screwcap. 13.6% alc. **Rating** 96 **To** 2038 $70 ✪
Collection Margaret River Cabernet Merlot 2012 Hand-picked from
vineyards mainly in Wilyabrup; matured in French and American oak (25% new).
Deeply coloured, it coats every corner of the mouth with its elegant, but intense,
blend of cassis, cedar and dried herbs; despite its power, it is immaculately balanced.
Screwcap. 13.9% alc. **Rating** 96 **To** 2042 $70 ✪
Highbrow Hill Vineyard Yarra Valley Cabernet Sauvignon 2013 Bright
hue; a fragrant, rich cassis-filled bouquet opens the way for a supple medium-
bodied palate, with a delicious reprise of the cassis of the bouquet and superfine,
albeit persistent, tannins; its length and balance can only be described as gracious.
Screwcap. 14.3% alc. **Rating** 96 **To** 2033 $80
Collection Tasmania Pinot Noir 2013 From four vineyards, two on the east
side of the Tamar, two on the opposite side, predominantly French clones 114,
115 and 777; made by Fran Austin at Delamere. Exceptionally rich and layered
dark fruits/plum on the mid-palate, then a foresty/savoury finish and great length.
Screwcap. 13.8% alc. **Rating** 96 **To** 2025 $50 ✪
Collection Mornington Peninsula Chardonnay 2013 Made at Willow
Creek by Geraldine McFaul, 50% ex the Capella Vineyard, 50% from the Red
Hill district; 70% wild-fermented in 30% new French barriques. Has texture and
bite to its intense display of grapefruit and minerally acidity, the finish long and
satisfying, the oak totally integrated. Screwcap. 13.6% alc. **Rating** 95 **To** 2023 $45
Collection Barossa Valley Shiraz 2012 Fermented for 10 days in open and
static fermenters, matured in hogsheads for 24 months; made in collaboration with

Rolf Binder. A smooth silk and velvet medium-bodied palate, with black fruits, supple tannins and totally integrated oak. A gracious Barossa Valley Shiraz from a great vintage. Screwcap. 14% alc. **Rating** 95 **To** 2032 $70

Collection Margaret River Cabernet Sauvignon 2013 From Wilyabrup. Like all the Handpicked wines, uses quality fruit and experienced winemaking to deliver the goods; the fragrant bouquet is followed by a complex medium to full-bodied palate with black foresty fruits married to cedary oak and persistent, fine-grained tannins. An assured future. Cork. 13.9% alc. **Rating** 95 **To** 2038 $70

Regional Selections Clare Valley Riesling 2013 Rating 94 **To** 2028 $34
Collection Yarra Valley Cabernet Sauvignon 2013 Rating 94 **To** 2028 $70
Regional Selections Margaret River Cabernet Sauvignon 2013 Rating 94 **To** 2028 $34

♈♈♈♈♈ **Yarra Valley Pinot Noir 2013 Rating** 93 **To** 2021 $55 CM

Hanging Rock Winery ★★★★★

88 Jim Road, Newham, Vic 3442 **Region** Macedon Ranges
T (03) 5427 0542 **www**.hangingrock.com.au **Open** 7 days 10–5
Winemaker Robert Ellis **Est.** 1983 **Dozens** 20 000 **Vyds** 14.5ha

The Macedon area has proved marginal in spots, and the Hanging Rock vineyards, with their lovely vista towards the Rock, are no exception. John Ellis thus elected to source additional grapes from various parts of Victoria to produce an interesting and diverse range of varietals at different price points. In 2011 John's children Ruth and Robert returned to the fold: Robert has an oenology degree from Adelaide University, since then working as a Flying Winemaker in Champagne, Burgundy, Oregon and Stellenbosch. More recently he worked as winemaker at Hewitson, before coming back to Hanging Rock to take over winemaking responsibilities from father John. Ruth has a degree in wine marketing from Adelaide University. Exports to the UK, the US and other major markets.

♈♈♈♈♈ **The Jim Jim Macedon Ranges Sauvignon Blanc 2014** The vines, planted adjacent to the winery in '81, were hand-picked over 3 days; this, together with 10% barrel fermentation, has built impressive complexity and intensity into the mix of fruits from citrus and stone fruit through to tropical; citrussy acidity ties the knot on the finish. Screwcap. 13.5% alc. **Rating** 94 **To** 2016 $28 ●

Macedon Ranges Pinot Noir 2013 Primarily sourced from the low-yielding Jim Jim Vineyard, it has good colour; savoury/spicy overtones to the red fruits of the bouquet and palate alike put their stamp on this wine, reflecting the inclusion of 33% whole bunches in the open fermenters, wild yeast another factor. Screwcap. 14% alc. **Rating** 94 **To** 2020 $35

Macedon Rose Brut NV A pinot noir–chardonnay blend made using the traditional method; the components are barrel-fermented and aged before blending and tiraged; the vibrant pink colour comes from pinot noir table wine used with the dosage. The wine has very good persistence, length and grip. Diam. 12% alc. **Rating** 94 **To** 2018 $30 ●

 # Hanrahan Estate ★★★★☆

3 Hexham Road, Gruyere, Vic 3770 **Region** Yarra Valley
T 0421 340 810 **www**.hanrahan.net.au **Open** Fri–Mon 11–5
Winemaker Yering Station (Willy Lunn) **Est.** 1997 **Dozens** 1800 **Vyds** 9.11ha

Bev Cowley (Ansett Cabin Manager) and long-term partner Bill Hanrahan (Ansett Captain) began the establishment of their vineyard in 1997 on what was previously a cattle grazing property. The idea was to have a more relaxing lifestyle away from the Ansett international service that flew for several years throughout Asia. They retained former Coldstream Hills vineyard manager Bill Christophersen to design and lay out the vineyard, planting 5ha of pinot noir, 3.3ha of shiraz and 0.8ha of chardonnay. The quality of the grapes led to a contract with Yering Station, and their label was launched in 2002 with the support of Yering Station winemaker Tom Carson. Following the tragic death of husband Bill in 2007, Bev has thrown herself tirelessly into the development of the project, helped by family and friends, and in particular by Dave Willis, her vineyard manager. Bev has also worked with Yarra Ranges Tourism, and introduced a concept called Reverse BYO® – you bring your own food and Bev provides the wine and other beverages, resulting in many picnic spots around the estate.

♥♥♥♥♥ **Yarra Valley Chardonnay 2013** Oak-fermented and matured. Pale, bright straw-green; this is all Yarra Valley with its focus, intensity and great length; the fruit was picked at precisely the right moment, its legacy a seamless array of white peach, almond and grapefruit, with a surprise pristine delicacy to the finish. Screwcap. 13% alc. **Rating** 95 **To** 2023 $38
Yarra Valley Chardonnay 2012 Bright straw-green; a dyed-in-the-wool Yarra Valley Chardonnay with juicy white peach fruit surrounded by citrussy acidity giving it length of flavour. Lovely wine, barrel-ferment oak merely a vehicle. Screwcap. 13% alc. **Rating** 94 **To** 2025 $38
Yarra Valley Shiraz 2013 Bright crimson hue; a bouquet of red and black cherries and spice leads into a vibrantly juicy medium-bodied palate, fine-grained tannins balanced to perfection, the oak integrated and balanced. Screwcap. 14% alc. **Rating** 94 **To** 2028 $38

♥♥♥♥♡ **Yarra Valley Pinot Noir 2013** **Rating** 93 **To** 2025 $42

Happs ★★★★★

575 Commonage Road, Dunsborough, WA 6281 **Region** Margaret River
T (08) 9755 3300 **www**.happs.com.au **Open** 7 days 10–5
Winemaker Erl Happ, Mark Warren **Est.** 1978 **Dozens** 15 000 **Vyds** 35.2ha
One-time schoolteacher, potter and winemaker Erl Happ is the patriarch of a three-generation family. More than anything, Erl has been a creator and experimenter, building the self-designed winery from mudbrick, concrete form and timber, and making the first crusher. In 1994 he began an entirely new 30ha vineyard at Karridale, planted to no less than 28 varieties, including some of the earliest plantings in Australia of tempranillo. The Three Hills label is made from varieties grown at this vineyard. Erl passed on to son Myles a love of pottery, and Happs Pottery now has four potters, including Myles. Exports to the US, Denmark, The Netherlands, Malaysia, Hong Kong, China and Japan.

♥♥♥♥♥ **Margaret River Sauvignon Blanc Semillon 2014** Wild yeast barrel fermentation and lees ageing has produced a blend that first and last is gloriously wild, throwing chunks of flavour at you from all directions; citrussy acidity eventually providing a modicum of discipline. Great stuff. Screwcap. 13.5% alc. **Rating** 95 **To** 2020 $24 ✪
Three Hills Eva Marie 2013 This is an altogether more serious and studied SSB than its Margaret River sibling; while the extra year in bottle has played a role, it has not diminished the intensity, nor broken the line of the palate. This has the autocratic mien of a cool-grown Cabernet: 'I'm simply not interested in getting into an argument with you.' Screwcap. 12% alc. **Rating** 95 **To** 2023 $27 ✪
Margaret River Chardonnay 2013 Fermented and matured in French oak. This could easily fly under the radar; it has a delicious, pure and focused fruit line of grapefruit, white peach and melon, and a light-footed finish. Screwcap. 13% alc. **Rating** 94 **To** 2023 $24 ✪

♥♥♥♥♡ **Margaret River Merlot 2014** **Rating** 93 **To** 2020 $15 ✪
Cabernet Sauvignon 2013 **Rating** 92 **To** 2023 $24 ✪
VP Very Particular Semillon 2013 **Rating** 91 **To** 2020 $15 ✪

Harcourt Valley Vineyards ★★★★☆

3339 Calder Highway, Harcourt, Vic 3453 **Region** Bendigo
T (03) 5474 2223 **www**.harcourtvalley.com.au **Open** 7 days 11–5
Winemaker Quinn Livingstone **Est.** 1975 **Dozens** 2500 **Vyds** 4ha

Harcourt Valley Vineyards (planted 1975) has the oldest planting of vines in the Harcourt Valley. Using 100% estate-grown fruit Quinn Livingstone (second-generation winemaker) is making a number of small-batch wines from the property. Minimal fruit handling is used in the winemaking process. A new tasting area overlooks the vines, with a large window that allows visitors to see the activity in the winery. Founder Barbara Broughton died in '12, aged 91, and Quinn's mother, Barbara Livingstone, has now retired. Exports to China.

ŸŸŸŸŸ **Barbara's Bendigo Shiraz 2013** Richness and character. Sturdy flavours of plum, earth and peppercorn meet the prettiness of violet and sweet oak. Tannin curls authoritatively throughout. In total command. Screwcap. 14% alc. **Rating** 95 To 2025 $25 CM ✪
Limited Release Bendigo GSM 2013 An unusual blend from this region, but an unqualified success, uncommon elegance its watch words. There are red fruits ranging from cherry through to raspberry, supported by the finest imaginable tannins, subtle oak and gently cleansing acidity. Screwcap. 14.9% alc. **Rating** 94 To 2023 $25 ✪

ŸŸŸŸŸ **Heathcote Shiraz 2013** Rating 93 To 2022 $25 CM ✪
Limited Release Tempranillo 2014 Rating 93 To 2019 $25 CM ✪
Single Vineyard Bendigo Cabernet 2012 Rating 92 To 2026 $60 CM

Hardys   ★★★★★
202 Main Road, McLaren Vale, SA 5171 **Region** McLaren Vale
T (08) 8329 4124 **www.**hardys.com.au **Open** Mon–Fri 10–4.30, Sat 10–5, Sun 11–5
Winemaker Paul Lapsley (Chief) **Est.** 1853 **Dozens** NFP
The 1992 merger of Thomas Hardy and the Berri Renmano group may have had some elements of a forced marriage, but the merged group prospered over the next 10 years. So successful was it that a further marriage followed in early 2003, with Constellation Wines of the US the groom, BRL Hardy the bride, creating the largest wine group in the world (the Australian arm was known as Constellation Wines Australia, or CWA); but it is now part of the Accolade Wines group. The Hardys wine brands are headed by Thomas Hardy Cabernet Sauvignon, Eileen Hardy Chardonnay, Pinot Noir and Shiraz; then the Sir James range of sparkling wines; next the HRB wines, the William Hardy quartet; then the expanded Oomoo range and the Nottage Hill wines. The quality (and the prices) of the fine wines couldn't be better. Exports to all major markets.

ŸŸŸŸŸ **HRB Riesling 2014** D659 Clare Valley and Tasmania. The mouth-watering intensity of the palate, its finish and aftertaste are a superb illustration of the synergy that can come from regional blends; here the spearing acidity of Tasmania lifts and enhances the lime and lemon fruit of the Clare Valley to make a Riesling of the highest class. Screwcap. 12.5% alc. **Rating** 97 To 2034 $30 ✪
Eileen Hardy McLaren Vale Shiraz 2010 100% McLaren Vale from 106yo vines in Upper Tintara and from McLaren Flat. Open-fermented with pneumatic pigeage/punch down, 3 days' cold soak, 14 days on skins. The vivid, deep crimson-purple hue tells of an intense mix of blackberry and blackcurrant flavours, with breathtaking texture, the ultimate fist in an iron glove. A 25-year life span is extremely conservative. Screwcap. 14% alc. **Rating** 97 To 2035 $125 ✪
Thomas Hardy Cabernet Sauvignon 2012 70% Coonawarra, 27% Margaret River and 3% McLaren Vale, a blend Roger Warren would have been proud of. Margaret River contributes cassis, herbs and spices; Coonawarra an elusive touch of mint, olives and acidity; McLaren Vale a hint of dark chocolate. The cumulative effect is a wine with a fragrant, cedary bouquet, the tannins superfine and mouth-watering. All up, shoulders up convincingly to Bordeaux. Screwcap. 14.1% alc. **Rating** 97 To 2042 $130 ✪

ŸŸŸŸŸ **Eileen Hardy Yarra Valley Tasmania Pinot Noir 2013** Here the Yarra Valley provides 70%, Tasmania 30%, both wild yeast-fermented, the Yarra component with 35% whole bunches, Tasmania with 25%. It has glorious colour, and a profusion of strawberry and blueberry fruit sustained by tannins so supple they provide a silky conclusion. Screwcap. 13.5% alc. **Rating** 96 **To** 2025 $95

Eileen Hardy Tasmania Yarra Valley Chardonnay 2013 65% Tasmanian and 35% Yarra Valley grapes, hand-picked and wild yeast barrel-fermented, the Yarra component with no mlf, the Tasmanian portion with mlf. The blend was made after 10 months in barrel, the wine settled with 4 months in tank. It has a super-intense, pure, flinty bouquet, the palate a waltz for two, white peach from the Yarra Valley, grapefruit from Tasmania, piercing in its intensity and purity. Screwcap. 13% alc. **Rating** 96 **To** 2023 $95

HRB Chardonnay 2013 D657 Yarra Valley and Pemberton. There is definite synergy in the blend, even if it's the Yarra Valley that provides most of the flavour and the glue; grapefruit is in the driving seats, but there's a special texture to the mouthfeel, part fruit, part oak-derived. Screwcap. 13.5% alc. **Rating** 95 **To** 2025 $30 ✪

HRB Chardonnay 2012 D655 Pemberton, Yarra Valley and Margaret River. A convincing demonstration of the synergies of regional blending, but not losing the seamless progression of the wine from the bouquet through to the aftertaste; all the best qualities of present-day Chardonnay, with its panoply of white peach, citrus and cashew flavours. Screwcap. 13.5% alc. **Rating** 95 **To** 2022 $30 ✪

HRB Pinot Gris 2013 D656 Yarra Valley and Tasmania. Goes where angels fear to tread, asking that it be taken seriously, very seriously. A fragrant and flowery bouquet feeding off apple and pear blossom leads into a true Gris palate that has texture built by significant lees contact, citrus framing the nashi pear and apple at the heart of the wine. Screwcap. 12.5% alc. **Rating** 95 **To** 2017 $30 ✪

HRB Shiraz 2013 D654 McLaren Vale, Clare Valley and Frankland River. Open-fermented, basket-pressed. McLaren Vale dark chocolate and black fruit richness, the Clare Valley providing some mint and fine, firm tannins, Frankland the pepper, violets and soft black fruit finish. The sum of the parts is greater than the whole, brought together and bonded on the full-bodied palate by persistent, ripe tannins that also add texture. Screwcap. 13.5% alc. **Rating** 95 **To** 2043 $39

HRB Cabernet Sauvignon 2013 Bin D645 Margaret River contributes cassis and herbal notes, Coonawarra choc-mint ripeness and Frankland River power and definition, says the back label, and that is exactly right. A seriously good Cabernet for prolonged cellaring, but will be approachable soonish. Screwcap. 13.5% alc. **Rating** 95 **To** 2038 $39

Starve Dog Lane Clare Valley Riesling 2014 Rating 94 **To** 2029 $20 ✪

♟♟♟♟♟ **William Hardy Barossa Valley Shiraz 2013 Rating** 93 **To** 2028 $21 ✪
Insignia Coonawarra Cabernet Sauvignon 2013 Rating 92 **To** 2028 $18 ✪
Starve Dog Lane Clare Valley Cabernet Sauvignon 2012 Rating 92 **To** 2025 $20 ✪
Insignia Adelaide Hills Chardonnay 2014 Rating 91 **To** 2019 $18 ✪

Harewood Estate   ★★★★★

Scotsdale Road, Denmark, WA 6333 **Region** Denmark
T (08) 9840 9078 **www.**harewood.com.au **Open** Fri–Mon 10–4, 7 days school hols
Winemaker James Kellie, Paul Nelson **Est.** 1988 **Dozens** 15 000 **Vyds** 19.2ha
In 2003 James Kellie, responsible for the contract making of Harewood's wines since 1998, purchased the estate with his father and sister as partners. A 300-tonne winery was constructed, offering both contract winemaking services for the Great Southern region and the ability to expand the Harewood range to include subregional wines. In January 2010 James, together with wife Careena, purchased his father's and sister's shares in the business; they are now 100% owners. Exports to the UK, the US, Denmark, Switzerland, Indonesia, Hong Kong, Malaysia, Macau, Singapore, China and Japan.

♟♟♟♟♟ **Reserve Great Southern Semillon Sauvignon Blanc 2014** Loads up the gun and lets you have it. Perfume, texture and flavour but not at the expense of elegance or, indeed, length. Nettle, tropical fruit, flint, woodsmoke and herbs. It's exotic and classical at once. Screwcap. 13% alc. **Rating** 96 **To** 2020 $28 CM ✪

Great Southern Chardonnay 2013 Barrel-fermented in French oak, and lees-stirred during maturation in barrel. Gleaming straw-green; the bouquet has touches of burnt match acting as a positive, but it is the intensity and length of the palate that is so striking; pink grapefruit and white peach are supported by crisp acidity, echoes of the oak somewhere in the background. Screwcap. 13.5% alc. Rating 96 To 2025 $27 ◆

Frankland River Riesling 2014 Single vineyard, made from free-run juice. A deliciously full-flavoured Riesling, with intense lime fruit and a subliminal touch of sweetness sewn into the flavour. Great all-purpose wine, all occasions and any time. Screwcap. 12% alc. Rating 95 To 2027 $22 ◆

Denmark Riesling 2014 Intense apple and lime flavours put their foot to the floor from the outset and keep it there all the way through a lengthy, chalky finish. Textbook. Screwcap. 12% alc. Rating 95 To 2028 $21 CM ◆

Reserve Great Southern Chardonnay 2013 It rolls with flavour and unfurls on the finish. Satisfaction goes without saying; excitement is the thing. Lime, grapefruit and white peach flavours, aided by smoky/spicy oak, build and seduce through the palate before kicking again. No need to wait; tuck in. Screwcap. 13.5% alc. Rating 95 To 2020 $34 CM ◆

ΥΥΥΥΥ **Porongurup Riesling 2014** Rating 93 To 2025 $21 CM ◆
Mount Barker Riesling 2014 Rating 93 To 2024 $21 CM ◆
Great Southern Shiraz 2013 Rating 93 To 2021 $21 CM ◆
Reserve Cabernet Sauvignon 2012 Rating 93 To 2024 $34 CM
Great Southern Shiraz Cabernet 2013 Rating 92 To 2020 $21 CM ◆
Sauvignon Blanc Semillon 2014 Rating 91 To 2015 $21 CM ◆
F-Block Great Southern Pinot Noir 2013 Rating 91 To 2018 $21 CM ◆
Reserve Great Southern Shiraz 2012 Rating 91 To 2021 $34 CM
Denmark Pinot Noir 2014 Rating 90 To 2019 $21 CM ◆
Reserve Denmark Pinot Noir 2012 Rating 90 To 2019 $45 CM

 Harrison's   NR

565 Racecourse Road, Winnaleah, Tas 7265 **Region** Northern Tasmania
T 0438 585 148 **www**.hpinot.com **Open** By appt
Winemaker Duncan Farquhar, David Calvert **Est.** 2002 **Dozens** 150 **Vyds** 0.3ha
This is very definitely a labour of love, with no intention of getting a financial return on the vast amount of knowhow being accumulated on the new clones of pinot noir coming from Burgundy via the Dijon University/Bernard clonal selection trials. The work that Duncan Farquhar has done was a central plank in the establishment of the Tasmanian Pinot Noir Forum in 1998, and ongoing research thereafter. Another unique feature of the operation is that it is in a new Tasmanian district, 60km further east than the Pipers Brook vineyards, but more inland than Pipers Brook. It has one particular advantage – abundant water from the Winnaleah irrigation scheme – even though in the normal course (after the establishment period) the vineyards do not require irrigation. The wines are made in the Dysart winery of David Calvert, who has a similarly small pinot noir-focused vineyard called Bonnie Vue. For the time being hands-on management of the vineyard has passed to Marc McLaughlin, while Duncan has moved to Wagga Wagga and lectures at CSU in vineyard establishment.

Hart & Hunter   ★★★★☆

Gabriel's Paddock, 463 Deasys Road, Pokolbin, NSW 2325 **Region** Hunter Valley
T 0401 605 219 **www**.hartandhunter.com.au **Open** Thurs–Sun 10–4
Winemaker Damien Stevens **Est.** 2009 **Dozens** 2000
This is the venture of winemaking couple Damien Stevens and Jodie Belleville, with partners Daniel and Elle Hart. The grapes are purchased from growers within the Hunter, with the emphasis on single-vineyard wines and small-batch processing. Damien and Jodie look after the winemaking and Australian sales side of the business, Daniel and Elle fly the flag for Hart & Hunter in the UK and Ireland, looking after UK distribution, and tasting events. The venture has had significant wine show success. Exports to the UK.

🍷🍷🍷🍷🍷 **Single Vineyard Series Oakey Creek Semillon 2014** Lean and elegant. A wine that seems in no hurry, and yet still manages to push lemony, waxy flavour out through the finish, a quick twirl as a glimpse into the future. Lemongrass notes make a gentle play, as do more exotic notes of fennel and mandarin blossom. Screwcap. 10.5% alc. **Rating** 93 **To** 2023 $30 CM

Single Vineyard Series The Remparts Semillon 2014 Light straw-green. Intriguing nose of lemongrass and brine, replicated in the mouth though added to by flavours of citrus and stone. Pristine young Semillon, complex already but with plenty more to come. Screwcap. 11.2% alc. **Rating** 93 **To** 2022 $30 CM

Single Vineyard Series Twenty Six Rows Chardonnay 2014 Peach, citrus and stone fruit flavours roll through the mouth, supported appropriately by spicy-sweet oak. Ironed, combed and ready for dinner. Screwcap. 12.5% alc. **Rating** 92 **To** 2019 $40 CM

Hart of the Barossa ★★★★☆

Cnr Vine Vale Road/Light Pass Road, Tanunda, SA 5352 **Region** Barossa Valley
T 0412 586 006 **www.**hartofthebarossa.com.au **Open** By appt
Winemaker Michael and Alisa Hart, Troy Kalleske **Est.** 2007 **Dozens** 2200 **Vyds** 6.5ha
The ancestors of Michael and Alisa Hart arrived in SA in 1845, their first address (with seven children) a hollow tree on the banks of the North Para River. Michael and Alisa personally tend the vineyard, which is the oldest certified organic vineyard in the Barossa Valley, and includes a patch of 110-year-old shiraz. The quality of the wines coming from these vines is exceptional; unfortunately, there is only enough to fill two hogsheads a year (66 dozen bottles). The other wines made are also impressive, particularly given their prices. Exports to Germany, Hong Kong, Taiwan and China.

🍷🍷🍷🍷🍷 **The Faithful Limited Release Old Vine Shiraz 2012** From four half-rows planted in 1902, enough for two new French hogsheads, 24 months' maturation. The colour is excellent, and the seamless fusion between the bouquet and palate likewise; the French oak is obvious, but it will sink back into intense red and black cherry fruit given time. Screwcap. 14.3% alc. **Rating** 96 **To** 2037 $79

🍷🍷🍷🍷🍷 **Limited Release Semillon 2007 Rating** 92 **To** 2017 $22 ❂

Harvey River Estate ★★★★

Third Street, Harvey, WA 6220 **Region** Geographe
T (08) 9729 2085 **www.**harveyriverestate.com.au **Open** 7 days 10–4
Winemaker Stuart Pierce **Est.** 1999 **Dozens** 20 000 **Vyds** 18.5ha
This highly focused business is owned by Kevin Giovanni. It has 15ha of chardonnay, shiraz and cabernet sauvignon in Geographe and 3.5ha of cabernet sauvignon, chardonnay and tempranillo in Margaret River, plus contract growers with spread throughout Geographe, Blackwood Valley and Margaret River. Exports to the UK, the US, Canada, Singapore and China.

🍷🍷🍷🍷 **Bridge Estate Geographe Sauvignon Blanc Semillon 2014** Pale straw-green; mid-intensity flavours of cut grass, passionfruit, wax and honeysuckle. Makes a positive impression. Screwcap. 13.2% alc. **Rating** 89 **To** 2017 $15 CM ❂

Billy Goat Hill Estate Geographe Sauvignon Blanc 2014 A steely grassiness meets the flesh of tropical fruits. 20% was fermented and matured in oak but it's left little trace, save a gentle softness. Reasonable push through the finish. Screwcap. 13% alc. **Rating** 88 **To** 2015 $17 CM ❂

Bridge Estate Geographe Merlot 2013 Soft-textured and awash with blackberry and eucalypt oil flavours/scents. Decent value. Screwcap. 14.5% alc. **Rating** 88 **To** 2018 $15 CM ❂

Haselgrove Wines

187 Sand Road, McLaren Vale, SA 5171 **Region** McLaren Vale
T (08) 8323 8706 **www.**haselgrove.com.au **Open** By appt
Winemaker Greg Clack, Matthew Copping **Est.** 1981 **Dozens** 40 000 **Vyds** 9.7ha
This is a winery on the move. The catalyst for change was the purchase of the business in
February 2008 by four Italian-Australian industry veterans: Don Totino, Don Luca, Tony
Carrocci and Steve Maglieri. They have completely changed the product range, its price and
its presentation: the Legend Series $75 to $150, the Origin Series at $35, and First Cut at
$18. Then there is the very large custom crush facility which provides all important cash flow.
Exports to Canada, Malaysia, South Korea, Hong Kong, China and NZ.

🍷🍷🍷🍷🍷 The Cruth McLaren Vale Shiraz 2012 Two parcels from Seaview and two
from McLaren Flat were crushed to open fermenters; 3-day cold soak; on skins
for 8 days; pressed direct to new and used French oak for 18 months' maturation;
a barrel selection made for this wine. It has enormous concentration of blackberry,
black cherry, spice, bitter chocolate and cedar, but no harsh tannins whatsoever.
May well outlive its cork. 14.5% alc. **Rating** 97 **To** 2037 $150 ⊙

🍷🍷🍷🍷🍷 Scarce Earth The Ambassador McLaren Vale Shiraz 2012 All the proceeds
of sale of the 118 dozen made of this selection of the best parcels from the estate
vineyard go to Variety. A seriously good, medium to full-bodied Shiraz flooded
with black fruits, a twist of dark chocolate, good oak and excellent ripe tannins.
Bottle no. 1353 of 1416. Cork. 14.5% alc. **Rating** 96 **To** 2032 $85
Switch GSM McLaren Vale Grenache Shiraz Mourvedre 2013 An utterly
compelling example of the synergy that can be achieved in McLaren Vale with this
blend, in general unequalled by other regions (there are always exceptions). The
colour is great, the ultra-evocative bouquet with a tantalising mix of red and black
fruits, smoky charcuterie and dark chocolate, the palate welding all this into a cool,
savoury whole. Screwcap. 14.5% alc. **Rating** 95 **To** 2030 $35 ⊙
Twist McLaren Vale Primitivo 2013 Open-fermented for 7 days, then
11 months in French oak (25% new) completing primary and secondary
fermentation. This is a very good Primitivo, rich and fleshy, but neither hot nor
with dead fruit; the tannins are exceptional, as are the length and balance, the slurp
of red fruits on the finish a delight. Screwcap. 15% alc. **Rating** 95 **To** 2027 $30 ⊙
First Cut McLaren Vale Shiraz 2013 Deep crimson-purple; full to the brim
with strongly regional, strongly varietal fruit on both the bouquet and the medium
to full-bodied palate; black fruits, bitter chocolate and licorice dance hand in hand
on the palate. Screwcap. 14.5% alc. **Rating** 94 **To** 2028 $19 ⊙
Verdict McLaren Vale Petit Verdot 2012 Says Haselgrove, 'The '11 vintage
was the first made, and the '12 vintage will be the last time this wine is ever made',
but with no explanation whatsoever. It has all the gravitas of Petit Verdot, with its
deep folds of black fruits, fleshy tannins and regional dark chocolate all in balance.
Screwcap. 13% alc. **Rating** 94 **To** 2029 $30 ⊙

🍷🍷🍷🍷🍷 Staff Adelaide Hills Chardonnay 2013 **Rating** 93 **To** 2018 $30
The Old Nut Fortified NV **Rating** 93 **To** 2016 $40
Bradan Adelaide Hills Pinot Noir 2013 **Rating** 90 **To** 2017 $30

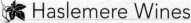 Haslemere Wines

PO Box 308, Angaston, SA 5353 **Region** Eden Valley
T (08) 8564 1314 **www.**haslemerewines.com **Open** Not
Winemaker Mark Maxwell (Contract) **Est.** 2014 **Dozens** 1240 **Vyds** 58.7ha
Haslemere Wines had its origins in 1993, when John Wade's father, Bob Wade, and friend
Brian Miles planted their Eden Valley vineyard. Bob Wade died later that year, and since
that time John has worked with Brian to manage the site. Brian in turn passed away in
2014, and his son Peter is now in charge of viticulture. The vineyard (chardonnay, shiraz,
cabernet sauvignon, riesling and sauvignon blanc) had been under long-term contract with
Treasury Wine Estates. John is now taking a small part of the production of the vineyard

to grow and make a little over 1200 dozen bottles of wine a year. Mark Maxwell has been appointed contract winemaker, John describing him as 'my guiding star – a great palate and a top operator'.

ΨΨΨΨ♀ **Samuel's Row Eden Valley Riesling 2014** Glowing straw-green; generous, ripe Bickford's lime juice flavours make this an early-drinking style without reducing its capacity to age well over the next 5+ years. Screwcap. 12% alc. **Rating** 90 **To** 2020 $22

Hastwell & Lightfoot   ★★★★☆

204 Foggos Road, McLaren Vale, SA 5171 **Region** McLaren Vale
T (08) 8323 8692 **www**.hastwellandlightfoot.com.au **Open** By appt
Winemaker James Hastwell **Est.** 1988 **Dozens** 4500 **Vyds** 16ha
Established in 1988 by Mark and Wendy Hastwell and Martin and Jill Lightfoot. Having initially sold much of the production, they have made a significant commitment to the Hastwell & Lightfoot brand, producing wines from estate-grown varieties. The vines are grafted onto devigorating rootstocks that restrain the development of dead fruit characters in warmer seasons. James Hastwell, son of Mark and Wendy, has his winery just 2km from the vineyard. Exports to the UK, Canada, Denmark, Norway, Germany, Malaysia, Taiwan, Singapore and China.

ΨΨΨΨΨ **38 Days 2012** A blend of cabernet and shiraz. The focus is on a cool-ferment and post-ferment maceration for 38 days, lengthy, but not unprecedented. It has not extracted an overburden of tannins; on the contrary, they are fine, leaving the juicy blackcurrant and blackberry fruits ample opportunity to play tag with each other on the long palate. Screwcap. 13.5% alc. **Rating** 95 **To** 2032 $40

ΨΨΨΨ♀ **McLaren Vale Shiraz 2012 Rating** 93 **To** 2027 $23 ✪
McLaren Vale Cabernet Sauvignon 2012 Rating 92 **To** 2032 $23 ✪

Hay Shed Hill Wines   ★★★★★

511 Harmans Mill Road, Wilyabrup, WA 6280 **Region** Margaret River
T (08) 9755 6046 **www**.hayshedhill.com.au **Open** 7 days 9–5
Winemaker Michael Kerrigan **Est.** 1987 **Dozens** 24 000 **Vyds** 18.55ha
Mike Kerrigan, former winemaker at Howard Park, acquired the business in late 2006 (with co-ownership by the West Cape Howe syndicate) and is now the full-time winemaker. He had every confidence he could dramatically lift the quality of the wines, which is precisely what he has done. Exports to the UK, the US, Singapore, Malaysia, Hong Kong and China.

ΨΨΨΨΨ **Block 6 Margaret River Chardonnay 2013** This is in the heart of the grand complexity of Margaret River Chardonnay style, with exceptional depth of flavour and structure amplified by the old vines and the Gingin clone; white peach, nectarine and fig fruit and creamy cashew notes are balanced by crisp, firm acidity. Screwcap. 13% alc. **Rating** 96 **To** 2023 $40 ✪
G40 Mount Barker Riesling 2014 The G40 name heralds 40g/l of residual sugar in the wine; the remarkable feature of this Riesling is the way that crunchy/ rocky acidity is as obvious as the sweetness, the fruit in a lime, grapefruit and green apple spectrum standing proudly above the residual sugar and acidity. Is earmarked for greatness in 10 years' time. Screwcap. 9% alc. **Rating** 96 **To** 2034 $25 ✪
Block 1 Margaret River Semillon Sauvignon Blanc 2014 Barrel-fermented in used French oak, matured for 9 months. Margaret River makes a challenging task for eastern Australia seem ridiculously easy, although it's true that the quality of the grapes is the all-important starting point. The wine has presence and gravitas, the lemon/citrus/mineral flavours given texture by the oak, without diminishing the fruit flavours. Screwcap. 12% alc. **Rating** 95 **To** 2018 $30 ✪
Block 6 Margaret River Chardonnay 2014 Estate-grown, only free-run juice used, fermented in new (30%) and used French barriques, matured for a further 10 months, no stirring or mlf. Elegance and balance are the keys to a Chardonnay

that side-steps many of the big hitters from Margaret River. Screwcap. 13% alc.
Rating 95 **To** 2024 $40

Margaret River Chardonnay 2013 Straw-green; has all the gravitas expected
of the Gingin clone grown in Margaret River, making light work of barrel
fermentation and maturation, but no lees stirring or mlf; white peach, melon and
fig flavours have exceptional mouthfeel thanks to the acidity, with Chablis-like
punch. Screwcap. 13% alc. **Rating** 95 **To** 2020 $28 ●

Margaret River Cabernet Sauvignon 2013 An 86/10/4% blend of cabernet
sauvignon, malbec and cabernet franc, standard Hay Shed Hill vinification, then
French oak for 13 months. All about complexity, built on the fruit blend, the
tannin structure, the oak and the terroir. A quintessential Margaret River style;
there are even better examples, but you have to pay three or four times as much to
get one. Screwcap. 14% alc. **Rating** 95 **To** 2028 $28 ●

Block 2 Margaret River Cabernet Sauvignon 2012 Destemmed, open-
fermented with pump-overs, 10 days' post-fermentation maceration, matured in
French oak for 18 months. Vivid crimson-purple colour introduces a Cabernet's
Cabernet, full of blackcurrant fruits ringed by the autocratic tannins that are
unique to the variety. Because the balance is there, patience (which is essential)
will be richly rewarded. Screwcap. 14% alc. **Rating** 95 **To** 2047 $55

Margaret River Chardonnay 2014 Rating 94 **To** 2029 $28 ●

Margaret River Cabernet Merlot 2013 Rating 93 **To** 2028 $22 ●
Margaret River Sauvignon Blanc Semillon 2014 Rating 92 **To** 2016 $22 ●
Margaret River Shiraz Tempranillo 2013 Rating 92 **To** 2020 $22 ●
Pitchfork Margaret River Cabernet Merlot 2013 Rating 92 **To** 2020 $17 ●

Head in the Clouds ★★★★

36 Neate Avenue, Belair, SA 5052 **Region** Adelaide Hills
T 0404 440 298 **www.**headintheclouds.com **Open** Not
Winemaker Tom Robinson **Est.** 2008 **Dozens** 250
This is the part-time business of winemaker Tom Robinson and sales manager Ashley
Coats. In a potential demarcation dispute, Tom Robinson won the Gourmet Traveller Wine
Magazine New Wine Writer Award '12, and holds a Masters degree in French literature. Each
of them has a part-time teaching job at Mercedes College, Tom lecturing in French, Ashley
head of the Arts Faculty. Tom's journey through wine is a prodigious one, covering the US for
many years, and more recently, Australia. With a production of 250 dozen, they had travelled
below the Halliday radar, but have been making wines under the Head in the Clouds banner
since 2008.

McLaren Vale Old Vine Grenache 2012 Clear crimson-red; a deliciously
fragrant and fresh wine, its red fruit core exactly what Grenache is all about; the
mouthfeel is supple, the finish long. The one pity is that only 65 dozen were made.
Screwcap. 14.5% alc. **Rating** 94 **To** 2020 $30 ●

Adelaide Hills Fiano 2012 Rating 90 **To** 2016 $22
Inkwell Vineyard McLaren Vale Zinfandel 2012 Rating 90 **To** 2017 $30

Head Wines ★★★★★

Lot 1 Stonewell Road, Stonewell, SA 5352 **Region** Barossa Valley
T 0413 114 233 **www.**headwines.com.au **Open** By appt Feb–Apr
Winemaker Alex Head **Est.** 2006 **Dozens** 5000 **Vyds** 7.5ha
Head Wines is the intriguing and highly focused venture of Alex Head, who came into the
wine industry in 1997 with a degree in biochemistry from Sydney University. Experience
in fine wine retail stores, wholesale importers and an auction house was followed by vintage
work at wineries he particularly admired: Tyrrell's, Torbreck, Laughing Jack and Cirillo Estate.
The naming of the wines reflects his fascination with Côte-Rôtie in the Northern Rhône
Valley. The two facing slopes in Côte-Rôtie are known as Côte Blonde and Côte Brune,
sometimes combining grapes from the two slopes as Côte Brune et Blonde. Head's Blonde

comes from an east-facing slope in the Stonewell area, while The Brunette comes from a very low-yielding vineyard in the Moppa area. In each case, open fermentation (with whole bunches included) and basket-pressing precedes 15 months in seasoned French hogsheads. Exports to Denmark, The Netherlands and Japan.

ΨΨΨΨΨ **The Brunette Barossa Valley Shiraz 2013** From a single east-facing vineyard, full morning sun, no afternoon sun, 100% destemmed, 3-week wild yeast fermentation and maceration, 1 year in French hogsheads and barriques (40% new). A wine of immediate authority, but with a heart of pure gold; forest berries and spices spin a web of sheer pleasure. Screwcap. 14% alc. **Rating** 97 To 2038 $60 ✪

ΨΨΨΨΨ **The Blonde Stonewell Barossa Valley Shiraz 2013** Destemmed and open-fermented with 3% viognier skins, 21-day wild yeast fermentation, matured for 1 year in French puncheons (50% new). Deep and bright colour; seduces every nook and cranny of the mouth, silky red red fruits coming in waves; the new French oak has been totally absorbed into the fabric of the wine; terrific overall texture. Screwcap. 14% alc. **Rating** 96 To 2038 $50 ✪

Ancestor Vine Springton Eden Valley Grenache 2013 From a 155yo vineyard at 400m. Bright, clear crimson-purple; Grenache seldom has tannin structure, but this has it, adding to the beautiful bouquet and spiced red fruits of the palate. Can be enjoyed now, but has an exciting future when you think about Rhône Valley Grenache. Screwcap. 14.5% alc. **Rating** 96 To 2033 $100

Head Red Barossa Valley Shiraz 2013 The ultimate Barossa blend, a barrel cull from the Blonde, Brunette and Contrarian, with 10 separate district parcels plus small amounts of grenache, mataro and old-vine cabernet sauvignon. This has an almost airy lightness to its silky red fruit palate; there is no reason to hold back from enjoying the hell out of it right now. Great value. Screwcap. 14% alc. **Rating** 95 To 2033 $25 ✪

Springton Eden Valley Riesling 2014 Very good quality fruit has been expertly handled to lock in every bit of flavour; lime is ascendant on the flowery bouquet, and even more on the full, juicy palate. Maturity will add another leg for those who prefer 5yo Riesling. Screwcap. 11% alc. **Rating** 94 To 2024 $23 ✪

The Contrarian Moculta Eden Valley Shiraz 2013 Alex Head says this allows foot crushing of whole bunches and, of course, wild yeast fermentation. It is radically different from the other wines in the Head portfolio, with an abundance of stalky tannins giving rise to a savoury, mouth-watering finish – Head says he has a special affinity for this wine. Screwcap. 13.8% alc. **Rating** 94 To 2028 $35

Old Vine Krondorf Barossa Valley Grenache 2013 From vines planted in '42, matured in a 20yo 2500l foudre with 10% whole bunches, 90% destemmed, plunged daily for 2 weeks. The Head magic gives the wine intensity and texture, not blowsy confection; its raspberry and red berry fruit has a translucent web of superfine tannins. Screwcap. 14.5% alc. **Rating** 94 To 2023 $40

Nouveau Marananga Barossa Valley Touriga Montepulciano 2014 An unoaked 65/35% blend that exactly meets Alex Head's agenda: a perfumed bouquet (cherry blossom, rose petals and spice) and a black cherry palate that is light and fresh, but also has saliva-generating tannins. A mini tour de force designed for drinking right now, but has a sneaky 'real wine' power within. Screwcap. 13% alc. **Rating** 94 To 2018 $20 ✪

Heafod Glen Winery   ★★★★☆

8691 West Swan Road, Henley Brook, WA 6055 **Region** Swan Valley
T (08) 9296 3444 **www.**heafodglenwine.com.au **Open** Wed–Sun 10–5
Winemaker Liam Clarke **Est.** 1999 **Dozens** 2500 **Vyds** 3ha
A combined vineyard and restaurant business, each set on outdoing the other, each with major accolades. Founder Neil Head taught himself winemaking, but in 2007 employed Liam Clarke (with a degree in viticulture and oenology), and a string of significant show successes for Verdelho, Viognier and Reserve Chardonnay has followed. Chesters Restaurant has received many awards over the years. Exports to Japan.

🍷🍷🍷🍷🍷 HB2 Vineyard Semillon 2014 Hand-picked, whole bunch-pressed and fermented in French oak. Pale straw-green; the winemaking has worked perfectly, lifting the wine out of the ruck in no uncertain fashion; tangy citrus fruit is strongly varietal, and given structure and mouthfeel by the oak. Screwcap. 12.1% alc. Rating 95 To 2029 $27 ○

HB2 Vineyard Verdelho 2014 Cold-fermented in stainless steel with selected cultured yeast; as well as a mix of fruit salad, the wine has a grainy note from the acidity. Screwcap. 12.5% alc. Rating 94 To 2017 $27 ○

HB2 Vineyard Cabernet Shiraz 2010 A 72/28% blend assembled shortly prior to bottling. A tour de force for the very hot Swan Valley climate, early picking the key to its success; the palate is at once elegant and complex, with multi-fruits, spice, herbs and mocha all part of the mix. Gold medal Australian Small Winemakers Show '14. Screwcap. 13.6% alc. Rating 94 To 2025 $35

🍷🍷🍷🍷🍷 HB2 Vineyard Viognier 2014 Rating 93 To 2016 $29

Heartland Wines   ★★★★

The Winehouse, Wellington Road, Langhorne Creek, SA 5255 **Region** Langhorne Creek
T (08) 8333 1363 **www.**heartlandwines.com.au **Open** 7 days 10–5
Winemaker Ben Glaetzer **Est.** 2001 **Dozens** 50000 **Vyds** 200ha
A joint venture of industry veterans: winemakers Ben Glaetzer and Scott Collett, and wine industry management specialist Grant Tilbrook. Heartland focuses on Cabernet Sauvignon and Shiraz from Langhorne Creek, John Glaetzer (head winemaker at Wolf Blass for over 30 years, and Ben's uncle) liaising with growers and vineyards he has known for over three decades, the wines made by Ben at Barossa Vintners. Director's Cut is the flagship release. Exports to all major markets.

🍷🍷🍷🍷🍷 Shiraz 2013 Not a hair out of place. Hearty blackberry and tar flavours come laced with chocolate and peppercorn. Attacks with flavour from the start and doesn't let go. Screwcap. 14.5% alc. Rating 91 To 2019 $18 CM ○

Dolcetto & Lagrein 2013 Enough oomph to appeal to Shiraz drinkers and the character to make it a generally irresistible choice. This label has been putting out mid-table hits for years but this season's release ramps up the weight and in the process, the 'selling proposition'. Cloves, tar, musk and black cherries, with herbal nuances nestled into the sweet fruit. Tidy tannin and tasty at every turn. Screwcap. 14.5% alc. Rating 91 To 2020 $20 CM ○

Spice Trader Shiraz Cabernet Sauvignon 2013 Lines them up and knocks them down. Good value drinking to be tucked into here. It offers sweet plummy, clovey fruit with an edge of bitumen, floral highlights then giving a gutsy wine a bit of prettiness. Screwcap. 14.5% alc. Rating 90 To 2020 $16 CM ○

Heathcote Estate   ★★★★★

98 High Street, Heathcote, Vic 3523 **Region** Heathcote
T (03) 5433 2488 **www.**yabbylake.com **Open** 7 days 10–5
Winemaker Tom Carson, Chris Forge **Est.** 1998 **Dozens** 5000 **Vyds** 34ha
Heathcote Estate and Yabby Lake Vineyards are owned by the Kirby family, of Village Roadshow Ltd. They purchased a prime piece of Heathcote red Cambrian soil in 1999, planting shiraz (30ha) and grenache (4ha), the latter an interesting variant on viognier. The wines are matured exclusively in French oak (50% new). The arrival of the hugely talented Tom Carson as Group Winemaker has added lustre to the winery and its wines. The cellar door, situated in an old bakery in the Heathcote township, provides a relaxed dining area. Exports to the US, the UK, Canada, Sweden, Singapore, Hong Kong and China.

🍷🍷🍷🍷🍷 Single Vineyard Shiraz 2013 This wine peers down at the landscape of ready drinkability, age-worthiness, individuality and regional good faith, and then proceeds to walk the fine line between them all. It is its own self and it will appeal to many because of that; it's as ironic as it is true. Bright raspberries, dark blackberries, peppercorns and cedar spice; all these flavours and more. It works, quite beautifully. Screwcap. 14% alc. Rating 95 To 2032 $45 CM

Heathcote Winery

183–185 High Street, Heathcote, Vic 3523 **Region** Heathcote
T (03) 5433 2595 **www**.heathcotewinery.com.au **Open** 7 days 10–5
Winemaker David Main **Est.** 1978 **Dozens** 8000 **Vyds** 15.25ha

The cellar door of Heathcote Winery is situated in the main street of Heathcote, housed in a restored miner's cottage built by Thomas Craven in 1854 to cater for the huge influx of goldminers. The winery is immediately behind the cellar door, and processed the first vintage in 1983, following the planting of the vineyards in '78. Stephen Wilkins is the principal shareholder, supported by Colin Gaetjens and Carol Russo, Wilkins commenting, 'The reality is we are family owned.' Shiraz and Shiraz Viognier now account for 90% of the production.

Slaughter House Paddock Shiraz 2013 It's a wine of impact and class. It has depth, ripe but not overripe fruit, a veneer of slippery-smooth American oak and firm-but-juicy length. Peppermint and choc notes are a key feature, and in the overall context they work beautifully. Simultaneously cellarworthy and moreish. Screwcap. 14.3% alc. **Rating** 94 **To** 2028 $50 CM

Single Vineyard Heathcote Shiraz 2013 Harvested from the original Heathcote Winery vineyard. Matured in all French oak. One smell/taste and it makes you wonder why French oak (exclusively) isn't employed more often with the estate's fruit; it makes for such a harmonious match. Blue and black-berried fruit, cloves, ink and cedar wood. Seamless and delicious. Able to be enjoyed now or well into the future. Screwcap. 14.3% alc. **Rating** 94 **To** 2026 $50 CM

Mail Coach Shiraz 2013 Rating 92 **To** 2022 $35 CM
The Wilkins Shiraz 2010 Rating 92 **To** 2024 $95 CM
Mail Coach Viognier 2014 Rating 91 **To** 2016 $28 CM
Mail Coach Viognier 2013 Rating 91 **To** 2016 $28

Heathvale

★★★★☆

300 Saw Pit Gully Road, via Keyneton, SA 5353 **Region** Eden Valley
T (08) 8564 8248 **www**.heathvale.com **Open** At Taste Eden Valley, Angaston
Winemaker Trevor March, Chris Taylor (Consultant) **Est.** 1987 **Dozens** 600 **Vyds** 10ha

The origins of Heathvale go back to 1865, when William Heath purchased the property, building the homestead and establishing the vineyard. The wine was initially made in the cellar of the house, which still stands on the property (now occupied by owners Trevor and Faye March). The vineyards were re-established in 1987, and consist of shiraz, cabernet sauvignon, riesling, sagrantino and tempranillo. Between 2011 and '12 fundamental changes for the better took place. Stylish new labels are but an outward sign of the far more important changes to wine style, with winemaking now under the control of consultant Chris Taylor (Quattro Mano) and the introduction of French oak, 30% new in most instances. Exports to China.

The Reward Eden Valley Barossa Shiraz 2013 Deep, vivid crimson-purple; the palate confirms the promises of the bouquet, with imperious black fruits surging with spice, pepper and licorice, the tannin structure providing a classy backdrop, oak lending yet further support. This is a seriously good Shiraz that has ticked each and every box. Screwcap. 14.8% alc. **Rating** 96 **To** 2043 $50

The Encounter Eden Valley Barossa Cabernet Sauvignon 2013 Full crimson-purple; the bouquet is flush with blackcurrant fruit plus spice and oak nuances; the full-bodied palate shadows the bouquet, reinforcing, but not going beyond, the path laid down by the bouquet – and didn't need to do so. Patience may be hard, but it's needed for maximum results. Screwcap. 14.5% alc. **Rating** 94 **To** 2038 $40

The Belief Eden Valley Sagrantino 2013 Rating 92 **To** 2033 $35

Hedberg Hill

701 The Escort Way, Orange, NSW 2800 **Region** Orange
T 0429 694 051 **www**.hedberghill.com.au **Open** W'ends 10–5
Winemaker Philip Kerney **Est.** 1998 **Dozens** 700 **Vyds** 5.6ha
Peter and Lee Hedberg have established their hilltop vineyard (880m altitude) 4km west of Orange, with 0.8ha each of cabernet sauvignon, merlot, tempranillo, chardonnay, viognier, sauvignon blanc and riesling. The cellar door has great views of Mt Canobolas and the surrounding valleys. The appointment of Phil Kerney as winemaker has seen a significant improvement in quality.

Claudia's Orange Viognier 2013 Aged in used French barriques. This is a considerable achievement: it really does have clear-cut apricot/orange/peach blossom aromas and flavours; it also is a little cluttered on the finish (no surprise), and you wonder whether a small acid adjustment might have made it even better. Screwcap. 13% alc. **Rating** 92 **To** 2020 $22 ✪
Lara's Orange Chardonnay 2013 Wild yeast barrel-fermented. There is a controlled complexity to the flavour and structure, with white stone fruits, grapefruit zest and green apple all contributing; the oak has been a means to an end, not an end in itself. Screwcap. 13% alc. **Rating** 91 **To** 2020 $22 ✪
Peter's Orange Riesling 2014 Its early picking has resulted in minerally acidity that frames the unsweetened citrus fruit; it has good length, and will fill out over the next 3+ years. Screwcap. 11.2% alc. **Rating** 90 **To** 2020 $18 ✪

Orange Late Harvest Riesling 2012 **Rating** 89 **To** 2015 $22

Heemskerk

131 Cascade Road, South Hobart, Tas 7004 (postal) **Region** Tasmania
T 1300 651 650 **www**.heemskerk.com.au **Open** Not
Winemaker Charles Hargraves **Est.** 1975 **Dozens** NFP
The Heemskerk brand established by Graham Wiltshire when he planted the first vines in 1965 (in the Pipers River region) is a very different business these days. It is part of TWE, and sources its grapes from vineyards including the Riversdale Vineyard in the Coal River Valley for riesling; the Lowestoft Vineyard in the Derwent Valley for pinot noir; and the Tolpuddle Vineyard in the Coal River Valley for chardonnay.

Abel's Tempest Chardonnay 2012 An impressive Tasmanian Chardonnay at this price. The backbone is the steely acidity of most Tasmanian white wines, but there is ample flesh to the intense fusion of citrus zest and pith, white stone fruits and a hint of melon. Its best years are still down the track. Screwcap. 13% alc. **Rating** 95 **To** 2020 $25 ✪
Coal River Valley Riesling 2014 Rock-solid quality. It bursts with lime, red apple and orange blossom aroma/flavour and just keeps charging through, barely slowing to finish. Screwcap. 11.5% alc. **Rating** 95 **To** 2025 $50 CM
Coal River Valley Chardonnay 2013 Reserved and tight with oatmeal, citrus, fennel, white peach and chalky/smoky spice through the finish. Just enough weight and personality but more than enough focus and length. Will develop slowly, in Chardonnay terms. Screwcap. 13% alc. **Rating** 94 **To** 2023 $50 CM

Abel's Tempest Chardonnay 2013 **Rating** 93 **To** 2020 $25 CM ✪
Coal River Valley Pinot Noir 2012 **Rating** 93 **To** 2022 $60 CM
Abel's Tempest Pinot Noir 2013 **Rating** 92 **To** 2021 $32 CM
Coal River Valley Chardonnay Pinot Noir 2010 **Rating** 92 **To** 2020 $60 TS
Coal River Valley Chardonnay Pinot Noir 2009 **Rating** 92 **To** 2019 $60 TS

Heggies Vineyard

Heggies Range Road, Eden Valley, SA 5235 **Region** Eden Valley
T (08) 8561 3200 **www**.heggiesvineyard.com **Open** By appt
Winemaker Peter Gambetta **Est.** 1971 **Dozens** 15 000 **Vyds** 62ha

Heggies was the second of the high-altitude (570m) vineyards established by the Hill-Smith family. Plantings on the 120ha former grazing property began in 1973; the principal varieties are riesling, chardonnay, viognier and merlot. There are then two special plantings: a 1.1ha reserve chardonnay block, and 27ha of various clonal trials. Exports to all major markets.

ŦŦŦŦŦ **Eden Valley Riesling 2014** Picked 1–20 Mar, attesting to both the size of the vineyard and winemaking decisions. The balance and conjunction between the apple/citrus blossom aromas, the dancing citrus flavours and the crisp acidity are exactly as they should be. Drink now by all means, but do hide a few bottles from yourself. Screwcap. 12% alc. **Rating** 95 **To** 2029 $25 ✪

ŦŦŦŦŦ **Eden Valley Chardonnay 2013 Rating** 92 **To** 2020 $30

Heidenreich Estate   ★★★★☆

PO Box 99, Tanunda, SA 5352 **Region** Barossa Valley
T (08) 8563 2644 **www.**heidenreichvineyards.com.au **Open** By appt
Winemaker Noel Heidenreich, Sarah Siddons **Est.** 1998 **Dozens** 2000 **Vyds** 47.3ha
The Heidenreich family arrived in the Barossa in 1857, with successive generations growing grapes ever since. It is now owned and run by Noel and Cheryl Heidenreich who, having changed the vineyard plantings and done much work on the soil, were content to sell the grapes from their 45ha (at three different sites) of shiraz, cabernet sauvignon, cabernet franc, viognier and chardonnay until 1998, when they and friends crushed a tonne in total of shiraz, cabernet sauvignon and cabernet franc. Since that time, production has soared; much is exported to San Diego (US), and a little sold locally, the remainder exported to Hong Kong and China.

ŦŦŦŦŦ **The Old School Principals Barossa Valley Shiraz 2013** A full-flavoured, full-bodied palate brings copious quantities of blackberry, plum and anise to the party; the wine has excellent length. A long future available, free of charge. Screwcap. 14.5% alc. **Rating** 95 **To** 2033 $30 ✪

ŦŦŦŦŦ **The Old School Masters Barossa Valley Cabernet Merlot 2013 Rating** 90 **To** 2028 $25

Heifer Station   ★★★★

PO Box 5082, Orange, NSW 2800 **Region** Orange
T 0407 621 150 **www.**heiferstation.com **Open** Not
Winemaker Daniel Shaw, Charles Svenson **Est.** 1999 **Dozens** 1500 **Vyds** 24.3ha
Founders Phillip and Michelle Stivens both grew up on the land, but spent over 25 years in the corporate world, Phillip as owner-operator of real estate offices in Parkes and Orange, Michelle working in the Attorney-General's Department. When their five adult children left the nest, they decided to retire to the land and grow fat cattle, and when Heifer Station, a property Phillip had admired for years, came onto the market they did not hesitate to purchase it. There was an existing 25ha vineyard, planted in 1998, barely visible through the blackberries, and their intention was to remove the vines. But locals argued they should not do so, pointing to the ideal soils: red loam over limestone. After much contemplation, they agreed to give the vineyard a chance to prove its worth. It has indeed proved its worth, and a cellar door will be built and opened once a pending development application has been approved.

ŦŦŦŦŦ **Orange Shiraz 2013** Shape, form, generous splashes of black pepper and a core of black cherried fruit. And a very good version thereof. Bunchy and savoury, but it brings a whoosh of fruit along with it. Screwcap. 13.5% alc. **Rating** 92 **To** 2024 $25 CM ✪
Orange Pinot Noir 2013 Grown at nearly 900m above sea level on vines planted in 1998. Light colour but an expressive release, and quite wonderfully fragrant, with strawberry and red cherry notes bouncing this way and that, helped along on both the nose and the palate by creamy, smoky oak. Spice notes play

a role too, though the expressive, juicy fruit is centre stage on the palate too. Screwcap. 13.2% alc. **Rating** 91 **To** 2019 $25 CM

Orange Chardonnay 2014 Sits in a sweet zone between lean and racy and flavoursome. Cedary, slippery oak lends a helping hand to fruit flavours of nectarine, honeysuckle and apple. Drinks well; oak upfront but elegance wins out in the end. Screwcap. 13% alc. **Rating** 90 **To** 2019 $28 CM

Orange Pinot Gris 2014 Plenty of flavour and appeal. Exhibits clear notes of pear cider, honeysuckle and candied ginger. Textured finish, helped along by a whisper of spicy oak. Screwcap. 13.2% alc. **Rating** 90 **To** 2015 $28 CM

Orange Merlot 2013 Nutty oak influences work in well with the main medium-weight, black cherried flavours. Bay leaf and assorted spice notes are on camera but by no means lead players. Overall, it delivers pretty handily. Screwcap. 13.5% alc. **Rating** 90 **To** 2020 $24 CM

Heirloom Vineyards

Salopian Inn, Cnr Main Rd/McMurtrie Road, McLaren Vale, SA 5171 **Region** Adelaide **T** (08) 8556 6099 **www.**heirloomvineyards.com.au **Open** 7 days 10–5
Winemaker Elena Brooks **Est.** 2004 **Dozens** NFP

This is (yet another) venture for Zar Brooks and his wife Elena. They met during the 2000 vintage, and one thing led to another, as they say. Dandelion Vineyards and Zonte's Footstep came along first, and continue, but other partners are involved in those ventures (they are also co-owners of the Salopian Inn, with the cellar door in the restaurant). The lofty aims here are to preserve the best of tradition, the unique old vineyards of SA, and to champion the best clones of each variety, embracing organic and biodynamic farming. I don't doubt for one moment the sincerity of the underlying sentiments, but there's a fair degree of Brooksian marketing spin involved. Exports to all major markets.

ŶŶŶŶŶ **Barossa Shiraz 2013** Deep colour; this is a luscious and velvety full-bodied Shiraz, black fruits shading out any possibility of red fruits getting a look in; it is far from one-dimensional, ripe tannins and oak adding to (not competing with) the fruit. This will serenely cruise on over several decades without losing its compass. Screwcap. 14.5% alc. **Rating** 96 **To** 2043 $40 ✪

Eden Valley Shiraz 2012 Excellent hue and depth; speaks loudly of its place (and the great vintage), its blackberry, spice and licorice fruit aromas and flavours driving through to the finish and aftertaste with ultimate precision, leaving the mouth fresh and asking for more. Gold medal International Wine Competition, London '13, a serious show. Screwcap. 14% alc. **Rating** 96 **To** 2042 $80

Eden Valley Riesling 2014 Pale straw-green; sometimes I see the primary difference between Eden Valley and Clare Valley as a function of taste, other times mouthfeel; obviously there are some shared attributes, but here the first-up message is the supple, focused mouthfeel, the second the lemongrass flavours magically reminiscent of Hunter Valley Semillon. All up, a wine of great delicacy and potential beauty. Screwcap. 12% alc. **Rating** 95 **To** 2032 $30 ✪

Eden Valley Riesling 2013 Bright, light straw-green; the pure lime-infused bouquet leads into an immaculately balanced and structured palate, citrus and apple flavours set within a wreath of stony, minerally acidity. Give it 5 years to really strut its stuff. Screwcap. 12% alc. **Rating** 95 **To** 2023 $30 ✪

Adelaide Hills Sauvignon Blanc 2013 Bright, light colour; the bouquet is expressive, with a mix of kiwifruit, apple and passionfruit, but pales into insignificance once the wine enters the mouth, driving intensely along the palate and accelerating on the finish and aftertaste. Adelaide Hills sings as clearly as ever. Screwcap. 12.5% alc. **Rating** 95 **To** 2016 $30 ✪

Adelaide Hills Chardonnay 2014 Doesn't miss the bullseye, establishing its credentials from the word go. It has a tight mineral core of citrussy acidity that provides the foundation for white peach/nectarine fruit, and lengthens the palate in fine style; oak has been pushed to one side by this display, which is all good. Screwcap. 13% alc. **Rating** 95 **To** 2025 $30 ✪

Barossa Shiraz 2012 The bouquet and supple, smooth, medium-bodied palate are both utterly harmonious, dark fruits, cedary oak and rounded tannins so seamlessly woven together that the wine is already totally enjoyable, yet is on a long plateau of perfection. Screwcap. 14.5% alc. **Rating** 95 **To** 2032 $40

Adelaide Hills Tempranillo 2013 The Adelaide Hills region is very well suited to the variety. Fragrant, supple and silky red cherry, and some black cherry flavours sweep along the palate in a full-blown charm offensive. Total seduction, and there's no need for foreplay. Screwcap. 13.5% alc. **Rating** 95 **To** 2028 $40

Adelaide Hills Sauvignon Blanc 2014 Rating 94 **To** 2018 $30 ○

Adelaide Hills Pinot Grigio 2013 Rating 94 **To** 2016 $30 ○

Adelaide Hills Pinot Noir 2014 Rating 94 **To** 2025 $40

Adelaide Hills Pinot Noir 2013 Rating 94 **To** 2020 $40

Helen & Joey Estate ★★★★★

12–14 Spring Lane, Gruyere, Vic 3770 **Region** Yarra Valley
T 0410 234 688 **www**.hjestate.com.au **Open** Mon & Fri 11–5, w'ends 11–5
Winemaker Rob Dolan **Est.** 2011 **Dozens** 7000 **Vyds** 33.7ha

This is the venture of Helen Xu, who purchased the large Fernando Vineyard on Spring Lane (next to Yeringberg) in 2010. It is planted to pinot noir, cabernet sauvignon, merlot, chardonnay, pinot gris, shiraz and sauvignon blanc. Helen's background is quite varied. She has a Masters degree in analytical chemistry, and was a QA manager for Nestlé for several years. She now owns a business in Shanghai, working with textile ink development together with husband Joey, and they currently split their time between China and Australia. They work closely with Wine Australia, and are active members of the Yarra Valley Winegrowers Association. Exports to China.

ΨΨΨΨΨ **Alena Single Vineyard Yarra Valley Cabernet Sauvignon Merlot 2013** A 66/34% blend matured in French barriques and hogsheads (30% new). A barrel selection, and the richest and most powerful of the three Helen & Joey '13 Cabernet Merlot blends; the bouquet is of the highest quality, and despite its power, the medium-bodied palate is immaculately balanced; cassis, oak and bay leaf are in play through its length, the tannins fine. Screwcap. 13.5% alc. **Rating** 96 **To** 2033 $41 ○

Alena Single Vineyard Yarra Valley Cabernet Sauvignon 2013 A short maceration post-fermentation, then to French barriques and hogsheads (20% new) for 12 months, this wine a barrel selection. Bright crimson-purple, it is a very, very good Cabernet that speaks equally of its place and variety with calm authority, signing off with a smile of cassis. Screwcap. 13% alc. **Rating** 96 **To** 2038 $40 ○

Layla Yarra Valley Chardonnay 2013 Hand-picked, whole bunch-pressed, fermented in small and large-format French oak, 50% mlf, 10 months' maturation on lees, 500 dozen made. Pale straw-green, it has the Yarra Valley birthmark (and birthright) length to its palate; its finesse is also of a high order, fresh, crisp fruit seamlessly stitched to the oak. Perhaps it needs a bit more emotion. Screwcap. 12.5% alc. **Rating** 94 **To** 2020 $27 ○

Alena Single Vineyard Yarra Valley Pinot Noir 2013 A barrel selection of the best barrels of the vintage. Deep, bright crimson; the cherry and plum fruit has good mouthfeel and balance, but is biding its time before revealing the secondary spicy notes that are around the corner. Screwcap. 13% alc. **Rating** 94 **To** 2023 $45

Layla Single Vineyard Yarra Valley Pinot Noir 2013 Hand-picked, 48-hour cold soak, pressed to 1yo French and American oak for 12 months' maturation. Good hue, although less dense than Alena; this has more spice and texture to its red and black cherry fruit than its more expensive sibling, but is less intense, and will hit its peak much sooner. Screwcap. 13% alc. **Rating** 94 **To** 2020 $34

Layla Single Vineyard Yarra Valley Cabernet Sauvignon Merlot 2013 A 62/38% blend matured for 12 months in a mix of oak (5% new) and stainless steel. Bright hue; an impressive blend, fruit, oak and tannins all carefully balanced; cassis is by far the dominant flavour, given context and structure by fine-grained tannins and oak. Screwcap. 13% alc. **Rating** 94 **To** 2027 $29 ○

ŶŶŶŶŶ Layla Cabernet Sauvignon 2013 Rating 93 To 2028 $29
Inara Merlot Cabernet Sauvignon 2013 Rating 92 To 2020 $19 ✪
Layla Shiraz 2013 Rating 90 To 2020 $31
Inara Cabernet Sauvignon 2013 Rating 90 To 2020 $19 ✪

Helen's Hill Estate ★★★★★

16 Ingram Road, Lilydale, Vic 3140 **Region** Yarra Valley
T (03) 9739 1573 **www**.helenshill.com.au **Open** 7 days 10–5
Winemaker Scott McCarthy **Est.** 1984 **Dozens** 15 000 **Vyds** 53ha
Helen's Hill Estate is named after the previous owner of the property, Helen Fraser. Venture partners Andrew and Robyn McIntosh and Roma and Allan Nalder combined childhood farming experience with more recent careers in medicine and finance to establish and manage the day-to-day operations of the estate. It produces two labels: Helen's Hill Estate and Ingram Rd, both labels made onsite. Scott McCarthy started his career early by working vintages during school holidays before gaining diverse and extensive experience in the Barossa and Yarra valleys, Napa Valley, Languedoc, the Loire Valley and Marlborough. The winery, cellar door complex and elegant 140-seat restaurant command some of the best views in the valley. Exports to Hong Kong, the Maldives and China.

ŶŶŶŶŶ Breachley Block Single Vineyard Yarra Valley Chardonnay 2014 Estate-grown, hand-picked, wild yeast-fermented in new and used French barriques with lees stirring. Excellent wine, with the length and intensity that is the hallmark of the Yarra Valley; it is fruit-driven, with pink grapefruit and white peach sharing the wine's billboard, complexed by good acidity and savoury notes on the finish. Screwcap. 13.1%alc. Rating 95 To 2024 $35
Long Walk Single Vineyard Yarra Valley Pinot Noir 2013 From clones MV6, 114 and 115, open-fermented with cultured (Burgundy) yeast. The colour is relatively light, but bright crimson, the latter the clue to the wine's vibrant cherry fruit and its intensity; the bouquet evolves after 10 or 15 minutes to put the seal on the deal in no uncertain fashion, falling into step with the very long finish. Diam. 12% alc. Rating 95 To 2023 $35
Ingram Rd Yarra Valley Pinot Grigio 2014 Lilts along nicely and then kicks with flavour (and class) through the finish. Winning style. Dry pear and citrus, spice and chalk. Shows many wannabes how it's done. Screwcap. 12.9% alc. Rating 94 To 2016 $20 CM ✪
Ingram Rd Yarra Valley Pinot Noir 2013 Once again it applies the blowtorch to the value equation. It's varietal, complex enough and quite exquisitely well composed. It's like a set of well-chosen words. Sweet-sour cherry, cranberry, dried herbs, sap. Oak aids texture and polish more than flavour, though oak spice through the finish is hard to resist. The words 'fleshy' and 'fresh' are apt here. Screwcap. 12.8% alc. Rating 94 To 2020 $20 CM ✪

ŶŶŶŶŶ Ingram Rd Cabernet Merlot 2012 Rating 92 To 2024 $20 CM ✪
Ingram Rd Chardonnay 2014 Rating 91 To 2019 $20 CM ✪

Helm ★★★★★

19 Butt's Road, Murrumbateman, NSW 2582 **Region** Canberra District
T (02) 6227 5953 **www**.helmwines.com.au **Open** Thurs–Mon 10–5
Winemaker Ken and Stephanie Helm **Est.** 1973 **Dozens** 5000 **Vyds** 17ha
Ken Helm is an energetic promoter of his wines and of the Canberra District generally. For some years now his wines have been of the highest standard, the Rieslings receiving conspicuous show success and critical acclaim. Plantings have steadily increased, with riesling (8ha), cabernet sauvignon (6ha), shiraz, gewurztraminer and chardonnay (1ha each), plus smaller plantings of other varieties. Exports to Macau and Hong Kong.

ŶŶŶŶŶ Tumbarumba Riesling 2014 Bright green-straw; the wine has some instantly appealing Germanic fruit overtones, coating the mouth in the best possible way with interwoven lime/tropical/acid flavours. Drinking well right now, and will hold if you wish. Screwcap. 11% alc. **Rating** 95 **To** 2020 $26 ✪

Classic Dry Canberra District Riesling 2014 Classic Helm style, with lime/lemon/apple blossom aromas, then a tightly focused and structured palate, the flavours evenly distributed from the first sip to the aftertaste. Good now, but better still in 5 years. Screwcap. 11.5% alc. **Rating** 95 **To** 2024 $35 ✪

Premium Canberra District Cabernet Sauvignon 2013 Matured for 2 years in French oak (50% new). This is by some distance the best Cabernet Ken Helm (and daughter Stephanie) have produced. It has a cedary autocracy wrapped around a heart of cassis and bay leaf; the tannins are firm, but completely ripe, and the finish is long and detailed. Screwcap. 13.5% alc. **Rating** 95 **To** 2033 $52

Central Ranges Riesling 2014 The flowery bouquet is attractive, but the wine defines itself on the elegant, perfectly balanced palate; here lime juice and lime leaf are held within a fine web of crisp acidity, the finish clean and bracing. Screwcap. 12% alc. **Rating** 94 **To** 2020 $26 ✪

▼▼▼▼▽ **Half Dry Canberra District Riesling 2014** Rating 91 To 2020 $26

Hemera Estate   ★★★★★

1516 Barossa Valley Way, Lyndoch, SA 5351 **Region** Barossa Valley
T (08) 8524 4033 **www.**hemeraestate.com.au **Open** 7 days 10–5
Winemaker Alex Peel **Est.** 1999 **Dozens** 15 000 **Vyds** 44ha
Ross Estate was purchased in 2013 by Winston Wine Pty Ltd, the local branch of a major Chinese wine distributor. It operates 100 wine stores throughout China, and has also purchased the Golden Grape Wine Estate in Oakey Creek Road, Pokolbin (with a long and not particularly distinguished track record during the time it was owned by the giant German Pieroth wine company), and the Lovedale-based Capercaillie vineyard, winery and brand. In the wake of the purchase of Ross Estate, its name was changed to Hemera. Exports to the US, Canada, Denmark, Germany, Hong Kong and China.

▼▼▼▼▼ **Limited Release Block 3A Barossa Valley Shiraz 2013** Matured in new French oak for 15 months. Bright crimson-purple; it has revelled in its marriage with oak, its medium to full-bodied palate long and confident, with red and black fruits both thrusting themselves forward. Screwcap. 14.5% alc. **Rating** 95 **To** 2038 $65

Tier 1 Barossa Shiraz Cabernet Sauvignon 2010 Premium parcels from selected press cycles were diverted to conclude fermentation in 100% new French oak. Amazingly, bright and youthful colour; this is heaven on a stick for oak lovers, the intense blackberry and blackcurrant fruit digging in for the long haul. The points reflect my uncertainty about judgement day 30 years hence. Screwcap. 14.5% alc. **Rating** 95 **To** 2045 $125

Old Vine Barossa Grenache 2013 Part from the estate's 101yo plantings, part from a 70yo vineyard, both in the southern foothills of the Barossa Valley. Bright, light crimson-red; there is no argument about the intensity of the fruit, simply the confection of the Turkish delight notes on the finish. Yes, it's a function of place, variety and alcohol, but this ought to be a gold medal wine, and doesn't make it. Screwcap. 15.5% alc. **Rating** 94 **To** 2028 $35

▼▼▼▼▽ **Limited Release Lyndoch 2013** Rating 90 To 2023 $50
Limited Release Barossa Cabernet Franc 2013 Rating 90 To 2025 $50

Henry's Drive Vignerons   ★★★★☆

41 Hodgson Road, Padthaway, SA 5271 **Region** Padthaway
T (08) 8765 5251 **www.**henrysdrive.com **Open** 7 days 10–4
Winemaker Kim Jackson **Est.** 1998 **Dozens** 65 000 **Vyds** 94.9ha
Named after the proprietor of the 19th-century mail coach service that once ran through their property, Henry's Drive Vignerons is the wine operation established by Kim Longbottom and her late husband Mark. Kim is continuing to build the family tradition of winemaking,

with brands such as Henry's Drive, Parson's Flat, The Trial of John Montford, Dead Letter Office, Pillar Box, Morse Code and The Postmistress. Exports to the UK, the US, Canada, Denmark, Singapore, China and NZ.

🍷🍷🍷🍷🍷 **Padthaway Shiraz Cabernet 2012** Given the same terroir, the same climate, and shiraz the dominant part of the blend, it is not surprising the wine should have the same tide marks – especially the dark chocolate – as its Shiraz sibling. But, and it's a big but, the cabernet does make its mark with some savoury cassis notes that add to the picture. Screwcap. 14.5% alc. **Rating** 94 **To** 2030 $35

🍷🍷🍷🍷🍷 **Pillar Box Padthaway Shiraz 2012 Rating** 93 **To** 2025 $20 ○
Padthaway Shiraz 2012 Rating 93 **To** 2037 $35
Pillar Box Cabernet Sauvignon 2012 Rating 93 **To** 2022 $20 ○

Henschke   ★★★★★

1428 Keyneton Road, Keyneton, SA 5353 **Region** Eden Valley
T (08) 8564 8223 **www**.henschke.com.au **Open** Mon–Fri 9–4.30, Sat 9–12
Winemaker Stephen Henschke **Est.** 1868 **Dozens** 30 000 **Vyds** 121.72ha
Regarded as the best medium-sized red wine producer in Australia, Henschke has gone from strength to strength over the past three decades under the guidance of winemaker Stephen and viticulturist Prue Henschke. The red wines fully capitalise on the very old, low-yielding, high-quality vines and are superbly made with sensitive but positive use of new small oak: Hill of Grace is second only to Penfolds Grange as Australia's red wine icon (since 2005 sold with a screwcap). A founding member of Australia's First Families of Wine. Exports to all major markets.

🍷🍷🍷🍷🍷 **Mount Edelstone 2012** Deep purple-crimson; this is a blue-blood aristocratic Shiraz, certain in its supreme power, length and balance, and not going out to prove anything. If anyone doubts its quality now, the scales will fall from their eyes over the decades ahead, as it will be recognised by all and sundry as one of the greatest Mount Edelstones. Screwcap. 14.5% alc. **Rating** 98 **To** 2062 $140 ○
Hill Of Grace 2010 Mesmerising wine. Exotic. Blackcurrant, truffles, licorice, leather and a stemmy rendition of five spice, the tumble of flavours clipping through the palate at a steady pace before gathering to meet on the finish; and there a flourish of complex flavour and tannin is unleashed. Medium to full-bodied but with a powerful persona; it's not a safe wine, it has some dare. Luxury is rarely so interesting. Screwcap. 14.5% alc. **Rating** 97 **To** 2040 $650 CM
Keyneton Euphonium 2012 A magic combination of a cascade of black and red fruit flavours with supreme elegance and balance, the complex blend of shiraz, cabernet sauvignon, merlot and cabernet franc at once fused yet synergistic. The best Euphonium yet. Screwcap. 14% alc. **Rating** 97 **To** 2035 $50 ○
Cyril Henschke 2010 Full purple-crimson; an 84/13/3% blend of cabernet sauvignon, merlot and cabernet franc, first bottled as a single wine in '78. The blend, and the cooler climate of the Eden Valley, lend themselves to this elegant, medium-bodied wine, with a full hand of blackcurrant and forest fruits, integrated French oak, and fine, but persistent and balanced, tannins. This is a particularly good vintage. Screwcap. 14% alc. **Rating** 97 **To** 2040 $140 ○

🍷🍷🍷🍷🍷 **Green's Hill Adelaide Hills Riesling 2014** Has an utterly beguiling combination of flavour and delicacy, which in turn translates into balance and intensity as you are drawn back again and again to the lime and lemon fruit; crisp, minerally acidity lengthens the finish. Screwcap. 12.5% alc. **Rating** 96 **To** 2029 $26 ○
Tappa Pass Vineyard Selection Eden Valley Shiraz 2012 Full crimson-purple; a beautifully textured and weighted wine, a faultless definition of what a medium-bodied Shiraz should be; dusty red and black cherry fruit, glints of spice and pepper; silky tannins and perfectly integrated oak. Vino-Lok. 14.5% alc. **Rating** 96 **To** 2042 $85

Julius Eden Valley Riesling 2014 A powerful wine proclaiming its integrity; citrus fruit and leaf aromas open the door to the palate of crisp green apple, lime/lemon and sustained acidity. Screwcap. 11.5% alc. **Rating** 95 To 2029 $32 ✪

Abbots Prayer Vineyard 2010 A 68/32% blend of merlot and cabernet sauvignon with excellent colour, open-fermented in the square vats Henschke uses for all their red wines, and matured in French oak. It is an elegant and precise wine, with cassis fruit on a foundation of firm, but not dry or abrasive, tannins. Will age with guaranteed charm. Vino-Lok. 14.5% alc. **Rating** 95 To 2040 $80

Peggy's Hill Eden Valley Riesling 2014 Rating 94 To 2020 $19 ✪

Johanne Ida Selma Lenswood Blanc de Noir MD NV Rating 94 To 2015 $50 TS

ҶҶҶҶҶ **Croft Adelaide Hills Chardonnay 2013 Rating** 93 To 2018 $40 CM
Henry's Seven 2013 Rating 93 To 2022 $33 CM
Johann's Garden 2013 Rating 93 To 2020 $45 CM
Littlehampton Pinot Gris 2014 Rating 92 To 2015 $30 CM
Giles Adelaide Hills Pinot Noir 2013 Rating 92 To 2022 $50 CM
Joseph Hill Gewurztraminer 2014 Rating 91 To 2019 $30 CM
Eleanor's Cottage Eden Valley Adelaide Hills Sauvignon Blanc Semillon 2014 Rating 90 To 2017 $20 CM ✪

Hentley Farm Wines   ★★★★★

Cnr Jenke Road/Gerald Roberts Road, Seppeltsfield, SA 5355 **Region** Barossa Valley
T (08) 8562 8427 **www**.hentleyfarm.com.au **Open** 7 days 11–5
Winemaker Andrew Quin **Est.** 1999 **Dozens** 15 000 **Vyds** 38.21ha
Keith and Alison Hentschke purchased Hentley Farm in 1997, as an old vineyard and mixed farming property. Keith has thoroughly impressive credentials, having studied agricultural science at Roseworthy, graduating with the Gramp Hardy Smith Memorial Prize for Most Outstanding Student, later adding an MBA. During the 1990s he had a senior production role with Orlando, before moving on to manage Fabal, one of Australia's largest vineyard management companies. A total of 38.2ha were planted between 1999 and 2005. In '04 an adjoining 6.5ha vineyard, christened Clos Otto, was acquired. Shiraz dominates the plantings, with 32.5ha. Situated on the banks of Greenock Creek, the vineyard has red clay loam soils overlaying shattered limestone, lightly rocked slopes and little topsoil. Joining Keith in the vineyard and winery are Greg Mader as viticulturist, and Andrew Quin as winemaker, both with very impressive CVs. 2015 *Wine Companion* Winery of the Year. Exports to the US and other major markets.

ҶҶҶҶҶ **H Block Shiraz 2013** Hentley Farm takes no prisoners. The logic of the construction of the wines in the winery is irrefutable. This is full-bodied in every way, but its black fruits, earth and licorice move on ball bearings as they roll along the palate until meeting ripe tannins. At no time are there any dead fruit flavours – they are juicy and fresh. Cork. 14.8% alc. **Rating** 97 To 2048 $145 ✪

The Beauty Shiraz 2013 Co-fermented with 2.5% viognier. Deep, full crimson; this is V8 power, but the engine is idling; fragrant cherry and plum aromas fold quietly into the medium-bodied palate; here black fruits join those of the bouquet, the mouth-watering, superfine, but persistent, tannins drawing out the finish for an aeon. Screwcap. 14% alc. **Rating** 97 To 2043 $60 ✪

Clos Otto Shiraz 2013 Exceptionally deep, powerful and full-bodied; blackberry, blackcurrant, licorice, tar and dark chocolate gambol across the luxurious palate, tannin and oak with secondary roles; in Hentley Farm style, manages to massage the mouth so thoroughly that it throws off any idea of dead fruit or excessive extract. Cork. 14.6% alc. **Rating** 97 To 2053 $165

The Creation Shiraz 2013 The usual deep crimson colour, but from that point on follows its own drumbeat; there is a brightness and freshness to the black fruits allied with notes of cedar, spice and dark chocolate. I hesitate to say the word 'elegance' with Hentley Farm, but this comes close. Cork. 14.6% alc. **Rating** 97 To 2048 $115 ✪

Museum Release The Beauty Shiraz 2010 A dreadnought-weight bottle. The hue is that of a 2yo wine, not 5yo; a particularly distinguished example of full-bodied Barossa single-vineyard Shiraz; the balance, length, texture and structure are all flawless, but the freshness of the finish and aftertaste is its most remarkable quality. Cork. 14.5% alc. **Rating** 97 **To** 2039 $73 ✪

Museum Release The Creation Shiraz Cabernet 2010 A 73/27% blend from a single block (H Block), then barrel-selected by winemaker Andrew Quin. Deeply coloured, it has multiple layers of black fruits, yet no dead fruit or alcohol heat; it has such good balance that it could be described as elegant, however improbable that may seem. Cork. 15.5% alc. **Rating** 97 **To** 2040 $220

♟♟♟♟♟ **Museum Release The Beast Shiraz 2010** Deep, dense colour; this defeats the laws of alcohol, with black fruits, licorice and spice coursing through the full-bodied palate, sweeping all before them, promising an immensely long life. I wish there wasn't wine staining down one side of the cork. 15.5% alc. **Rating** 96 **To** 2040 $105

The Quintessential Shiraz Cabernet 2013 Vivid crimson. A synergistic 70/30% blend; shiraz, almost regardless of its percentage, was always going to open proceedings with its rich, velvety fruit, cabernet preordained to provide the tannins and freshness to drive the finish and aftertaste; oak is hiding somewhere in the bushes. Screwcap. 14.7% alc. **Rating** 96 **To** 2043 $60 ✪

Eden Valley Riesling 2014 From a single block at an elevation of 420m; two methods of pre-fermentation clarification were used for all but a small amount; part-fermented on crushed skins before pressing for fermentation to proceed on full solids. This has contributed to the power of the finish and aftertaste of a very complex wine. Screwcap. 12% alc. **Rating** 95 **To** 2020 $23 ✪

Shiraz 2014 Blended from different blocks within the estate vineyard. Deep purple-crimson, it underscores the supreme quality of the vineyard, for this could pass muster as a Reserve release thanks to the layered array of red and black fruits, rounded tannins and quality oak; the balance is such that it can be enjoyed now or much later. Screwcap. 14.8% alc. **Rating** 95 **To** 2034 $27 ✪

The Beast Shiraz 2013 Awesomely powerful, with a tsunami of sombre black fruits, licorice and tannins to match, overwhelming you the moment the wine enters the mouth. It is, of course, full-bodied, and doesn't have the fluid grace of the other Hentley Farm '13 Shirazs. It is indeed a beast, but will repay those who put their faith in the high-quality corks used by Henley Farm. 14.8% alc. **Rating** 95 **To** 2038 $84

Cabernet Sauvignon 2014 By focusing on cool sites with an easterly aspect, Hentley Farm maximises its ability to produce Cabernet with clear-cut varietal character at moderate alcohol levels in most vintages, and that is what it has done here. Blackcurrant, dried herbs and perfectly pitched tannins all come up with the right answer. Screwcap. 14.5% alc. **Rating** 95 **To** 2039 $27 ✪

Black Beauty Sparkling Shiraz NV Achieving colour, depth and intensity while retaining finesse and softness in sparkling shiraz is no easy juggling act, and Hentley Farm has nailed it here, all the more admirable with the temperamental '11 as the base vintage. Shiraz is co-fermented with 3% viognier, aged in barrel for 30 months and on lees in bottle for 12 months. Luscious and deep in black fruit and licorice profile, and at the same time creamy in fine bead and silky in fine-grained tannin structure, backed by well-gauged dark chocolate oak. Crown seal. 14% alc. **Rating** 95 **To** 2017 $60 TS

The Skinbone Barossa Valley Grenache Rose 2014 **Rating** 94 **To** 2016 $20 ✪

Museum Release Clos Otto Barossa Valley Shiraz 2009 **Rating** 94 **To** 2020 $200

The Marl Barossa Valley Grenache 2014 **Rating** 94 **To** 2020 $21 ✪

The Stray Mongrel 2014 **Rating** 94 **To** 2029 $28 ✪

Premiere Barossa Valley Cabernet Sauvignon 2014 **Rating** 94 **To** 2024 $27 ✪

von Kasper Barossa Valley Cabernet Sauvignon 2013 **Rating** 94 **To** 2038 $85

Henty Estate
★★★★☆

657 Hensley Park Road, Hamilton, Vic 3300 (postal) **Region** Henty
T (03) 5572 4446 **www**.henty-estate.com.au **Open** Not
Winemaker Peter Dixon **Est.** 1991 **Dozens** 1400 **Vyds** 7ha

Peter and Glenys Dixon have hastened slowly with Henty Estate. In 1991 they began the planting of 4.5ha of shiraz, 1ha each of cabernet sauvignon and chardonnay, and 0.5ha of riesling. In their words, 'we avoided the temptation to make wine until the vineyard was mature', establishing the winery in 2003. Encouraged by neighbour John Thomson, they have limited the yield to 3–4 tonnes per hectare on the VSP-trained, dry-grown vineyard.

♟♟♟♟♟ Edward Shiraz 2012 20% whole bunches, basket-pressed and then into 100% new oak. It shows this oak, but also tannin and grunt not seen in the other wines. This is the vision realised. Fresh fruit, cool in style but dark enough, with garden mint and spicy cedar wood. What the effects of time do should be a fascinating journey to watch. Screwcap. 13.2% alc. **Rating** 95 **To** 2028 $35 CM ❂

♟♟♟♟♀ Shiraz 2013 Rating 93 **To** 2023 $25 CM ❂
Cabernet Sauvignon 2013 Rating 92 **To** 2025 $25 CM ❂

Herbert Vineyard
★★★★

Bishop Road, Mount Gambier, SA 5290 **Region** Mount Gambier
T 0408 849 080 **www**.herbertvineyard.com.au **Open** By appt
Winemaker David Herbert **Est.** 1996 **Dozens** 550 **Vyds** 2.4ha

David and Trudy Herbert have planted 1.9ha of pinot noir, and a total of 0.5ha of cabernet sauvignon, merlot and pinot gris (the majority of the pinot noir is sold for sparkling wine). They have built a two-level (mini) winery overlooking a 1300-square metre maze, which is reflected in the label logo.

♟♟♟♟♟ Mount Gambier Pinot Noir 2013 Wild yeast-fermented and matured in French oak. Bright, clear purple-crimson; an altogether elegant wine with fragrant red fruits and a fine, silky palate with considerable fruit purity; its elegance puts it on a different pedestal from Barrel #7, but it is of similar quality. Screwcap. 13.6% alc. **Rating** 94 **To** 2021 $26 ❂
Barrel #7 Mount Gambier Pinot Noir 2013 Wild yeast-fermented and matured in a single 1yo French barrel. Good hue; the bouquet is fragrant, bordering on perfumed, the palate with very good drive and focus; dark cherry/plum and spicy oak are knitted together. The most powerful and complex of the '13 Herbert Vineyard Pinots. Screwcap. 14% alc. **Rating** 94 **To** 2025 $30 ❂

♟♟♟♟♀ Square Mile Mount Gambier Pinot Noir 2013 Rating 92 **To** 2022 $25 ❂
Barrel Number 1 Mount Gambier Pinot Noir 2012 Rating 92 **To** 2019 $39

Heritage Estate
★★★★★

Granite Belt Drive, Cottonvale, Qld 4375 **Region** Granite Belt
T (07) 4685 2197 **www**.heritagewines.com.au **Open** 7 days 9–5
Winemaker John Handy **Est.** 1992 **Dozens** 3000 **Vyds** 10ha

Heritage Estate (owned by Bryce and Paddy Kassulke) has two estate vineyards in the Granite Belt, one at Cottonvale (north) at an altitude of 960m, where it grows white varieties, and the other at Ballandean, a slightly warmer site where red varieties and marsanne are planted. Heritage Estate has been a prolific award-winner in various Qld wine shows and (I am pleased to report) it has invested in a new bottling line enabling it to use screwcaps. After a series of difficult vintages, with the Cottonvale vineyard, predominantly planted to white varieties, hit by hail in 2013, Heritage Estate has bounced back impressively, taking full advantage of the excellent vintage. A winery to watch.

♟♟♟♟♟ Granite Belt Fiano 2014 A first crop from vines grafted in '12; wild yeast-fermented in used French barriques, and on stirred lees for 3 months. A gold medal winner at the Australian Small Winemakers Show, no award at the Alternative Varieties Show because, so said the judges, it lacked varietal character. Bright straw-green, it leaves no doubt that the learned judges at the latter show were on another planet, for the intensity and length of the finish, mineral and crabapple intertwined, is memorable Screwcap. 12.5% alc. **Rating** 95 **To** 2024 $45

Single Vineyard Granite Belt Shiraz 2014 From 50yo vines. The deep colour stems from 2 weeks of pre and 4 weeks of post-fermentation maceration, then maturing in French hogsheads (75% new). A power-packed Shiraz, from a vineyard that produces deep colour, amplified by the maceration. While desperately young, it has the balance to ensure that the parade of black fruits will remain in line and in step for many years. Screwcap. 14% alc. **Rating** 95 **To** 2034 $30 ○

Granite Belt Chardonnay 2014 The first vintage for 3 years (due to hail). Whole bunch-pressed, wild yeast-fermented in French oak (40% new), matured on lees for 10 months, the new oak portion transferred to used oak after 4 months. Bright straw-green; this is a powerful, well made, mouth-filling style punching well above its 13% alcohol. Screwcap. **Rating** 94 **To** 2024 $45

Wild Ferment Marsanne 2013 From 25yo vines at Ballandean; fermented in used French oak and matured on lees for 12 months. Young Marsanne seldom has the depth of flavour or the supple mouthfeel this wine has (Tahbilk and Yeringberg honourably excepted). A high level of care and skill from vine to glass have kept the varietal apple, citrus and honeysuckle fruit, guarded by chalky acidity, that makes this wine special. Screwcap. 13.6% alc. **Rating** 94 **To** 2020 $30 ○

Reserve Granite Belt Tempranillo 2014 Made in a Joven style, only 5 months in used French oak. Brilliant crimson colour, and lives up to the promise of that colour in the mouth (and bouquet) with silky smooth red cherry fruits and fine tannins: the Spanish girl with a red hibiscus behind her ear. Screwcap. 13.2% alc. **Rating** 94 **To** 2018 $25 ○

♟♟♟♟ **Cabernet Sauvignon 2013 Rating** 89 **To** 2020 $30
Petite White Muscat a Petits Grains 2013 Rating 89 **To** 2016 $20

Heritage Wines   ★★★☆

399 Seppeltsfield Road, Marananga, SA 5355 **Region** Barossa Valley
T (08) 8562 2880 **www**.heritagewinery.com.au **Open** Mon–Fri 10–5, w'ends 11–5
Winemaker Stephen Hoff **Est.** 1984 **Dozens** 4000 **Vyds** 8.3ha
A little-known winery that deserves a wider audience, for veteran owner/winemaker Stephen Hoff is apt to produce some startlingly good wines. At various times the Riesling (from old Clare Valley vines), Cabernet Sauvignon and Shiraz (now the flag-bearer) have all excelled. The vineyard is planted to shiraz (5.5ha), cabernet sauvignon (2.5ha) and malbec (0.3ha). Exports to the UK, the US, Thailand, Hong Kong, Malaysia and Singapore.

♟♟♟♟♟ **Rossco's Shiraz 2010** Charry, chocolatey, raisiny red. Shiraz from a hot oven. Thick tar and blackberry flavours attack the palate and don't let go until long after you've swallowed. Alcohol warmth is apparent, there's no getting around it, but it sits comfortably in line with the overall style of the wine. Big, porty end of town, but it does pack the flavour in. Cork. 15.3% alc. **Rating** 93 **To** 2023 $48 CM

♟♟♟♟ **Barossa Semillon 2014 Rating** 88 **To** 2017 $15 CM ○

Hesketh Wine Company   ★★★★

28 The Parade, Norwood, SA 5067 **Region** Various
T (08) 8232 8622 **www**.heskethwinecompany.com.au **Open** Not
Winemaker Phil Lehmann **Est.** 2006 **Dozens** 20 000
Headed by Jonathon Hesketh, this is part of WD Wines Pty Ltd, which also owns Parker Coonawarra Estate and St John's Road in the Barossa Valley. Jonathon spent 7 years as the Global Sales & Marketing Manager of Wirra Wirra, two and a half years as General Manager of Distinguished Vineyards in NZ, working with the Möet Hennessy wine and champagne portfolio, plus the Petaluma group. He also happens to be the son of Robert Hesketh, one

of the key players in the development of many facets of the SA wine industry. The focus of Hesketh has changed significantly, with a series of wines exploring new varietal regional matches. Exports to the US, the EU and Hong Kong.

ŸŸŸŸŸ Barossa Valley Touriga 2014 They're onto something here. It has a different flavour profile, which is part of the attraction, but it has more to offer than mere 'difference'. It's well weighted, is both floral and sour-sweet, shows cola notes and fresh, crunchy cherries. It drinks quite beautifully young but it could go anywhere, and any way, with a few years under its belt. Screwcap. 14% alc. **Rating** 92 To 2020 $25 CM ☻

ŸŸŸŸ Mezzo Tatiara District Shiraz Mataro 2014 Rating 89 To 2020 $19 ☻
Barossa Valley Tempranillo 2013 Rating 89 To 2019 $25 CM
Lenswood Pinot Grigio 2014 Rating 88 To 2015 $25 CM
Barossa Valley Montepulciano 2013 Rating 88 To 2018 $25 CM

Hewitson   ★★★★★
1 Seppeltsfield Road, Dorrien, SA 5355 **Region** Adelaide Zone
T (08) 8212 6233 **www**.hewitson.com.au **Open** 7 days 9–5
Winemaker Dean Hewitson **Est.** 1996 **Dozens** 35 000 **Vyds** 4.5ha
Dean Hewitson was a winemaker at Petaluma for 10 years, during which time he managed to do three vintages in France and one in Oregon as well as undertaking his Masters at the University of California, Davis. It is hardly surprising that the wines are immaculately made from a technical viewpoint. Dean sources 30-year-old riesling from the Eden Valley and 70-year-old shiraz from McLaren Vale; he also makes Barossa Valley Mourvedre from vines planted in 1853 at Rowland Flat, and Barossa Valley Shiraz and Grenache from 60-year-old vines at Tanunda. Exports to the UK, the US and other major markets.

ŸŸŸŸŸ The Mother Vine Single Vineyard Barossa Valley Shiraz 2013 Luscious release but in no way unrefined. More than a bit of class. Dense plum, woodsmoke, bitter chocolate and chicory favours flood into the mouth, build a deal of momentum and then push concertedly out through the finish. Fine, grainy, earthen tannin makes its presence felt, as indeed does smoky, cedary oak. This is a quite superb release. Screwcap. 14.5% alc. **Rating** 96 To 2035 $49 CM ☻
The Mad Hatter Single Vineyard McLaren Vale Shiraz 2012 From vines with an average age of 50 years; fermented for 4 weeks in an upright vat, followed by 20 months in new French barriques. Makes up big time for the decision not to make an '11, its flavours positively explosive, sparks ricocheting in all directions, but always within a coherent, elegant framework; has great length into the bargain. Screwcap. 14% alc. **Rating** 96 To 2032 $49 ☻
The Mother Vine Single Vineyard Barossa Valley Shiraz 2012 From vines grafted with buds taken from a single vine planted in 1853; matured for 20 months in new and used French barriques. The claim of unique DNA is debatable, but the quality and character of this beautifully sculpted and weighted medium-bodied wine are not; the flavours run in a juicy blackberry and licorice spectrum, supported by fine tannins. Screwcap. 14% alc. **Rating** 96 To 2035 $49 ☻
Old Garden Mourvedre 2012 Luscious release. Brimful of dark, leathery, berried fruit, loaded with fennel and spice, both characterful and persistent. Tannin has a minerally edge, a sophistication. Orange-peel notes dance about. The bold and the beautiful in one. Super. Screwcap. 14% alc. **Rating** 96 To 2030 $120 CM
Basham's Beach Single Vineyard Fleurieu Tempranillo 2012 This is only the second release in 10 years; matured in new and used French barriques for 10 months, it is Tempranillo on a scale normally encountered in the warmer parts of Rioja, with rich dried cherry and spice flavours, and very good tannin structure. Screwcap. 14.5% alc. **Rating** 95 To 2027 $49
Gun Metal Eden Valley Riesling 2014 Showing beautiful form. Upfront lime juice, gunmetal, lime leaf and spice flow effortlessly but persuasively all the way through to a compelling finish. Purity and detail but no lack of deliciousness. Screwcap. 11.5% alc. **Rating** 94 To 2024 $28 CM ☻

The Mad Hatter Single Vineyard McLaren Vale Shiraz 2013 Warm with alcohol but an ever-so-seductive offering. Explosive blackberried fruit with bass notes of tar; treble of saltbush and dried woody spice. Oak has mostly soaked straight into the fruit, though a semblance of creamy, musky vanillan remains, and has a most positive influence. Screwcap. 14.5% alc. **Rating** 94 **To** 2028 $49 CM

ＹＹＹＹＹ **Ned & Henry's Barossa Valley Shiraz 2013 Rating** 93 **To** 2024 $28 CM
LuLu Adelaide Hills Sauvignon Blanc 2014 Rating 90 **To** 2016 $23 CM

Heydon Estate   ★★★★★

325 Tom Cullity Drive, Wilyabrup, WA 6280 **Region** Margaret River
T (08) 9755 6995 **www**.heydonestate.com.au **Open** 7 days 10–5
Winemaker Mark Messenger **Est.** 1988 **Dozens** 1800 **Vyds** 10ha
Margaret River dentist and cricket tragic George Heydon and wife Mary have been involved in the region's wine industry since 1995. They became 50% partners in Arlewood, and when that partnership was dissolved in 2004 they retained the property and the precious 2ha of cabernet sauvignon and 2.5ha of Gingin clone chardonnay planted in '88. Additional plantings from '95 include Dijon chardonnay clones, sauvignon blanc, semillon, shiraz and petit verdot. The estate is now biodynamic, near neighbour Vanya Cullen having inspired the decision. Exports to the UK, Singapore and Hong Kong.

ＹＹＹＹＹ **W.G. Grace Single Vineyard Margaret River Cabernet Sauvignon 2009**
Good retention of colour; a rich and pliant Cabernet, with almost velvety layers of fruit upholstering the mid-palate, ripe tannins providing the innersprings. A truly lovely Cabernet, great today or in 30 years – the choice is yours. Screwcap. 14.2% alc. **Rating** 97 **To** 2042 $60 ○

ＹＹＹＹＹ **The Willow Single Vineyard Margaret River Chardonnay 2011** A nigh-on perfect depiction of Margaret River chardonnay's ability to provide depth and complexity while retaining discipline; a case of still water running deep and unruffled, the crystalline acidity almost hidden. Screwcap. 13.8% alc. **Rating** 95 **To** 2020 $50
The Willow Single Vineyard Margaret River Chardonnay 2010
A particularly rich and complex wine; ripe stone fruit has a buttery/toasty/creamy backdrop, oak joining with the fruit to provide this. Screwcap. 13.5% alc. **Rating** 94 **To** 2019 $50
The Sledge Single Vineyard Margaret River Shiraz 2012 Estate shiraz planted in '88; this also has 4% viognier, which lifts the bouquet, introducing exotic garrigue scents; the palate is long, shapely and elegant, the finish with fine-grained tannins and evident French oak. Screwcap. 14% alc. **Rating** 94 **To** 2027 $40

ＹＹＹＹＹ **The Urn Botrytis Semillon 2012 Rating** 93 **To** 2020 $35

 # Hidden Valley Forest Retreat   ★★★★

162 Haag Road, Carbunup River, WA 6280 **Region** Margaret River
T (08) 9755 1066 **www**.yourhiddenvalley.com **Open** Not
Winemaker Bernie Stanlake **Est.** 2010 **Dozens** 400 **Vyds** 1.9ha
John and Sally Glover settled on this secluded property over 15 years ago, growing table grapes, and also establishing five eco lodges scattered through the 60ha property. None is within sight of any others thanks to the mini-valleys, and typical Margaret River trees and shrubs. The decision to diversify led to the planting of 1.2ha of cabernet sauvignon and 0.7ha of sauvignon blanc, the first vintage of cabernet following in 2010, sauvignon blanc in '11.

ＹＹＹＹＹ **Daisy Sauvignon Blanc 2014** Pale straw-green; tropical fruits are the business of the day, passionfruit and guava rounded up by a touch of Meyer lemon; a wine that grows each time it is retasted, the acidity on the finish precisely balanced. Drink asap. Screwcap. 13.5% alc. **Rating** 92 **To** 2016 $23 ○
Daisy Sauvignon Blanc 2011 Interesting wine. While not reaching out to the development of fleshy richness, is not showing the least sign of vegetal break-up,

nor of its alcohol; the flavours are in no man's land, and where they will ultimately go is anyone's guess. Screwcap. 13.5% alc. **Rating** 90 **To** 2015 $23
Lucy Cabernet Sauvignon 2011 As with the '12, oak has been used to advantage, but with more fruit to start with; there are notes of cassis on the medium-bodied palate, and it hardly need be said that the tannins are fine. Good early drinking style. Screwcap. 14% alc. **Rating** 90 **To** 2020 $23

♥♥♥♥ Daisy Sauvignon Blanc 2012 Rating 89 To 2015 $23

Higher Plane   ★★★★☆

165 Warner Glen Road, Forest Grove, WA 6286 **Region** Margaret River
T (08) 9755 9000 www.higherplanewines.com.au **Open** At Juniper Estate
Winemaker Mark Messenger **Est.** 1996 **Dozens** 2000 **Vyds** 14.55ha
In late 2006 Higher Plane was purchased by the late Roger Hill and Gillian Anderson (of Juniper Estate), but kept as a stand-alone brand, with different distributors, etc. The Higher Plane vineyards are planted to all of the key varieties: chardonnay and sauvignon blanc are foremost, with cabernet sauvignon, merlot, tempranillo, fiano, semillon, cabernet franc, malbec and petit verdot making up the rest of the plantings. Exports to Hong Kong.

♥♥♥♥♥ **Margaret River Cabernet Sauvignon 2011** An 86/8/5/1% blend of cabernet, malbec, franc and petit verdot; cold-soaked 5 days, fermented/macerated 10–32 days, matured for 18 months in French barriques (45% new). The winemaking approach in maximising structure – especially tannins – has certainly worked. The wine is still not ready to drink, but there is adequate fruit density to keep it in form until the tannins begin to soften. Screwcap. 14.5% alc. **Rating** 95 **To** 2041 $50

♥♥♥♥♡ **South by Southwest Semillon Sauvignon Blanc 2014** Rating 93 To 2016 $21 ✪
South by Southwest Cabernet Merlot 2012 Rating 91 To 2020 $22 ✪

Hill-Smith Estate   ★★★★

Flaxmans Valley Road, Eden Valley, SA 5235 **Region** Eden Valley
T (08) 8561 3200 www.hillsmithestate.com **Open** By appt
Winemaker Teresa Heuzenroeder **Est.** 1979 **Dozens** 5000 **Vyds** 12ha
The vineyard sits at an altitude of 510m, providing a cool climate that extends the growing season; rocky, acidic soil, coupled with winter rainfall and dry summers, results in modest crops. As an added bonus, the vineyard is surrounded by conservation park. Other Hill-Smith wines have been given a home here.

♥♥♥♥♥ **Adelaide Hills Chardonnay 2013** Light straw-green; an elegant, perfectly balanced Chardonnay that has soaked up the oak in which it was fermented, leaving the stone fruit, melon and grapefruit flavours as free as a bird, the finish bright and fresh. A barrel selection. Screwcap. 13% alc. **Rating** 94 **To** 2023 $30 ✪

♥♥♥♥♡ **Eden Valley Sauvignon Blanc 2014** Rating 93 To 2017 $22 ✪
Eden Valley Chardonnay 2013 Rating 91 To 2018 $23 ✪

Hillbillé   ★★★★☆

Blackwood Valley Estate, Balingup Road, Nannup, WA 6275 **Region** Blackwood Valley
T (08) 9481 0888 www.hillbille.com **Open** By appt
Winemaker Naturaliste Vintners (Bruce Dukes) **Est.** 1998 **Dozens** 5000 **Vyds** 18ha
Gary and Rai Bettridge have planted chardonnay, shiraz, cabernet sauvignon, merlot, semillon, sauvignon blanc and viognier on their 75ha family property. The vineyard is situated in the Blackwood Valley between Balingup and Nannup, which the RAC describes as 'the most scenic drive in the southwest of WA'. Part of the grape production is sold to other makers, the remainder vinified for the Hillbillé label. Exports to Japan, Singapore, Hong Kong and China.

♥♥♥♥♥ **Signature James Brittain Shiraz Viognier 2012** Fluid fruit flavour but an overall impression of substance. Silken texture, cherry-plum flavours, bright presentation throughout and a slide of licoricey tannin. Impressed more and more as it breathed in the glass. Screwcap. 14% alc. **Rating** 95 **To** 2030 $48 CM

🍷🍷🍷🍷♀ **Signature James Brittain Cabernet 2012** Rating 93 To 2028 $48 CM
Signature James Brittain Merlot 2012 Rating 92 To 2026 $48 CM
Estate Merlot 2012 Rating 90 To 2019 $18 CM ○

Hillcrest Vineyard ★★★★★

31 Phillip Road, Woori Yallock, Vic 3139 **Region** Yarra Valley
T (03) 5964 6689 **www**.hillcrestvineyard.com.au **Open** By appt
Winemaker David and Tanya Bryant **Est.** 1970 **Dozens** 800 **Vyds** 8.1ha
The small, effectively dry-grown vineyard was established by Graeme and Joy Sweet, who ultimately sold it to David and Tanya Bryant. The pinot noir, chardonnay, merlot and cabernet sauvignon grown on the property have always been of the highest quality and, when Coldstream Hills was in its infancy, were particularly important resources for it. For some years the wines were made by Phillip Jones (Bass Phillip), but the winemaking is now carried out onsite by David and Tanya Bryant. Exports to Singapore.

🍷🍷🍷🍷🍷 **Premium Yarra Valley Pinot Noir 2013** 50% new French oak. Extremely deep colour; one of those rare Pinots that are full-bodied, but not clumsy; resounding with drumbeats of black cherry and satsuma plum, quality oak also playing a role. It makes only one request: like '99 Burgundies, give me as much time as your heart, wallet and other basic instincts will allow. The high-quality cork should go the distance. 12.8% alc. **Rating** 97 **To** 2030 $70 ○

🍷🍷🍷🍷🍷 **Village Yarra Valley Pinot Noir 2013** 25% new French oak. Full colour; a richly robed and utterly seductive style with a velvet brocade of plum fruit on the palate following with utmost clarity the message delivered by the bouquet, but with a nice twang to the finish and aftertaste. Great value. 175 dozen made. Diam. 13% alc. **Rating** 96 **To** 2025 $25 ○
Premium Yarra Valley Chardonnay 2013 50% new François Frères oak, 50 dozen made. Has more intensity and acidity than Village, although the oak is no more obvious; here there are some citrus notes to accompany the white peach and nectarine fruit. Cork. 12.5% alc. **Rating** 95 **To** 2023 $70
Premium Yarra Valley Cabernet Sauvignon Merlot 2013 A 65/35% estate blend only bottled in magnums; matured in François Frères oak (50% new) for 12 months. The medium-bodied wine caresses the mouth with its juicy cassis fruit, the tannins persistent, but superfine, the high-quality oak both balanced and integrated. Cork. 13.2% alc. **Rating** 95 **To** 2038 $160

🍷🍷🍷🍷♀ **Village Yarra Valley Chardonnay 2013** Rating 92 To 2020 $25 ○

Hither & Yon ★★★★☆

17 High Street, Willunga, SA 5172 **Region** McLaren Vale
T (08) 8556 2082 **www**.hitherandyon.com.au **Open** 7 days 11–4
Winemaker Richard Leask **Est.** 2012 **Dozens** 4000 **Vyds** 90ha
Brothers Richard and Malcolm Leask arrived as youngsters in McLaren Vale in the 1970s, following a family move from the Hunter Valley. Since father Ian Leask established the first family vineyard in '80, a further six sites spread across McLaren Vale have been added. Currently 13 varieties are planted over 90ha, with more plantings planned. In 2011 Richard and Malcolm started the Hither & Yon label, focusing on small single-vineyard parcels, which change each year depending on the vintage and site. Richard manages all the vineyards and makes the wines, Malcolm handles production, sales and the historic cellar door. The labels feature the brand's ampersand, created by a different artist for each wine.

🍷🍷🍷🍷🍷 **McLaren Vale Shiraz Cabernet 2013** The 75% shiraz and 25% cabernet components were separately fermented and matured until final blending, the shiraz in new French hogsheads, the cabernet in used French barriques. It is unequivocally full-bodied, with a tsunami of blackberry and blackcurrant fruit,

oak and plush tannins, but isn't hot. Matched with a large steak and shared by four would be a winner. Screwcap. 14.9% alc. **Rating** 95 **To** 2033 $35 **۞**
McLaren Vale Grenache Mataro 2013 A 73/27% blend from 2 vineyards. This is a wine that could only come from McLaren Vale; it has both red and black fruits that are at once juicy, but given a framework of fruit-derived texture and structure guaranteeing the future, however enjoyable it may be right now. And the price is right. Screwcap. 14.6% alc. **Rating** 94 **To** 2023 $25 **۞**
McLaren Vale Cabernet Sauvignon Petit Verdot 2012 A 92/8% blend that spent 21 months in a mix of used French oak of various sizes. An impressive wine with a multilayered, full-bodied palate. Will handsomely repay patience. Screwcap. 13.7% alc. **Rating** 94 **To** 2032 $35

ΨΨΨΨΨ **McLaren Vale Shiraz 2012** Rating 93 **To** 2027 $50
McLaren Vale Young Shiraz 2014 Rating 90 **To** 2033 $22
McLaren Vale Aglianico 2013 Rating 90 **To** 2018 $27

Hobbs of Barossa Ranges ★★★★☆

Cnr Flaxman's Valley Road/Randalls Road, Angaston, SA 5353 **Region** Barossa Valley
T 0427 177 740 **www**.hobbsvintners.com.au **Open** At Artisans of Barossa
Winemaker Pete Schell, Chris Ringland (Consultant) **Est.** 1998 **Dozens** 1100
Vyds 6.22ha
Hobbs of Barossa Ranges is the high-profile, if somewhat challenging, venture of Greg and Allison Hobbs. The estate vineyards revolve around 1ha of shiraz planted in 1908, 1ha planted in '88, 1ha planted in '97 and 1.82ha planted in 2004. In '09 0.4ha of old white frontignac was removed, giving space for another small planting of shiraz. The viticultural portfolio is completed with 0.6ha of semillon planted in the 1960s, and an inspired 0.6ha of viognier ('88). All of the wines made by Peter Schell (at Spinifex) push the envelope. The only conventionally made wine is the Shiraz Viognier, with a production of 130 dozen. Gregor, an Amarone-style Shiraz in full-blooded table wine mode, and a quartet of dessert wines are produced by cane cutting followed by further desiccation on racks. The Grenache comes from a Barossa floor vineyard, the Semillon, Viognier and White Frontignac from estate-grown grapes. Exports to the US, France, The Netherlands, Russia, Taiwan, Hong Kong and China.

ΨΨΨΨΨ **1905 Shiraz 2012** Hand-picked from vines planted in 1905, and spent 24 months in new French oak. Overflows with flavour from the first sip to the aftertaste, yet the alcohol is not a distraction; likewise, it is full-bodied, but not extractive. A tribute to very old vines in a great vintage. 180 dozen made. Diam. 15.1% alc. Rating 96 **To** 2042 $130
Tin Lids Shiraz Cabernet Sauvignon 2012 A 70/30% blend sourced from the Barossa Ranges, hand-picked and open-fermented before 18 months in used oak. This medium-bodied wine has fresh and bright blackberry and blackcurrant flavours allied with hints of spice. Screwcap. 14.6% alc. **Rating** 94 **To** 2027 $50

ΨΨΨΨΨ **Tango Shiraz Viognier 2012** Rating 93 **To** 2027 $110
With Freckles Viognier 2013 Rating 92 **To** 2017 $31
Gregor Shiraz 2012 Rating 92 **To** 2032 $130

Hochkirch Wines ★★★★

Hamilton Highway, Tarrington, Vic 3301 **Region** Henty
T (03) 5573 5200 **Open** 11–5 by appt
Winemaker John Nagorcka **Est.** 1997 **Dozens** 4000 **Vyds** 8ha
Jennifer and John Nagorcka have developed Hochkirch in response to the very cool climate: growing season temperatures are similar to those in Burgundy. A high-density planting pattern was implemented, with a low fruiting wire taking advantage of soil warmth in the growing season, and the focus was placed on pinot noir (5ha), with lesser quantities of riesling, chardonnay, semillon and shiraz. The Nagorckas have moved to certified biodynamic viticulture and the vines are not irrigated. Exports to Japan.

♥♥♥♥♀ Tarrington Vineyards Pinot Noir 2012 It has a bright, natural feel. It flows, unfettered, its notes of dried herbs and sap running through its veins rather than coming emblazoned on its skin. It doesn't have a lot of force but it's not insipid; it goes about its business with an air of ambivalence. Sour cherry notes mutter throughout. You have to listen closely, but there's some intrigue here. Cork. 12.9% alc. **Rating** 93 **To** 2022 $38 CM

Riesling 2013 Glowing straw colour. and tastes developed for its age. Difficult to know whether it's the wine or the cork. Lime juice and blossom, honeysuckle and lemongrass. Piercing finish. 11.5% alc. **Rating** 91 **To** 2020 $27 CM

Maximus Pinot Noir 2012 The hazy shades of autumn. This fairly puts savouriness and complexity far ahead of brightness and overt fruit. It's smoky, murky, spicy and run with rhubarb-like flavour, with black woody/twiggy cherries flowing beneath. Aromas are caught in a fog but the palate has plenty going on. Cork. 12.9% alc. **Rating** 91 **To** 2022 $40 CM

Hoddles Creek Estate ★★★★★

505 Gembrook Road, Hoddles Creek, Vic 3139 **Region** Yarra Valley
T (03) 5967 4692 **www**.hoddlescreekestate.com.au **Open** By appt
Winemaker Franco D'Anna, Chris Bendle **Est.** 1997 **Dozens** 20 000 **Vyds** 33.3ha
The D'Anna family has established a vineyard on the property that has been in the family since 1960. The vineyards (chardonnay, pinot noir, sauvignon blanc, cabernet sauvignon, pinot gris, merlot and pinot blanc) are hand-pruned and hand-harvested, and a 300-tonne, split-level winery was built in 2003. Son Franco is the viticulturist and inspired winemaker; he started to work in the family liquor store at 13, graduating to chief wine buyer by the time he was 21, then completed a Bachelor of Commerce degree at Melbourne University before studying viticulture at CSU. A vintage at Coldstream Hills, then two years' vintage experience with Peter Dredge at Witchmount, and Mario Marson (ex Mount Mary) as mentor in the '03 vintage, has put an old head on young shoulders. The Wickhams Rd label uses grapes from an estate vineyard in Gippsland, and purchased grapes from the Yarra Valley and Mornington Peninsula. 2015 *Wine Companion* Best Value Winery. Exports to The Netherlands, Singapore, Japan and China.

♥♥♥♥♥ 1er Yarra Valley Chardonnay 2013 The very complex bouquet immediately grabs attention, barrel fermentation the playmaker bringing overt (but balanced) oak into the equation; the intensity and extreme length of the palate are of the highest order, grapefruit providing a mouth-watering finale; acidity is a given, and guarantees a long life ahead. Screwcap. 13.2% alc. **Rating** 97 **To** 2028 $40 ◐

1er Yarra Valley Pinot Noir 2013 The top Pinot from Hoddles Creek Estate, with a strict selection process and a little more new oak, made in small quantities. Exceptional colour; the perfumed, silky nature of the wine is encapsulated in one word: harmony, which you might also call supreme balance. Small red fruits at its core, superfine tannins and restrained oak underwriting its structure and longevity. Screwcap. 13.2% alc. **Rating** 97 **To** 2028 $45 ◐

♥♥♥♥♥ Wickhams Road Yarra Valley Chardonnay 2014 Light straw-green; has the same balance and mouthfeel as Wickhams Road Gippsland Chardonnay, here with white peach and melon joined by some grapefruit, all three flavours seamlessly stitched together to give the wine that extra touch of length. Ludicrously good value. Screwcap. 12.7% alc. **Rating** 95 **To** 2024 $18 ◐

Yarra Valley Chardonnay 2013 Yet another example of the serious over-delivery of quality that made Hoddles Creek Estate the Best Value Winery in the 2015 *Wine Companion*. There is not a hair out of place in this beautifully composed and balanced wine; the fruit is at optimum ripeness and freshness, the oak almost invisible in terms of flavour, but present in structure. Screwcap. 13.2% alc. **Rating** 95 **To** 2023 $20 ◐

Yarra Valley Pinot Noir 2013 The bright, clear crimson-purple colour is what other Pinot makers aspire to. Absolutely on the bull's eye; barely any need to go past the plum and cherry varietal fruit of the bouquet to assess its quality; the perfectly balanced and very long palate is every bit as impressive. There's no greater value on the market, and the wine will become even better with 3+ years in bottle. Screwcap. 13.2% alc. **Rating** 95 **To** 2023 $20 ✪

Wickhams Road Gippsland Chardonnay 2014 The usual immaculate balance and proportion, the picking date a key decision; white peach and nectarine are the drivers of the flavour, fresh acidity second up; the barrel fermentation has, of course, played a role. Screwcap. 12.7% alc. **Rating** 94 **To** 2022 $18 ✪

Hoggies Estate Wines ★★★★

Stentiford Vineyard, Lot 95 Skinner Road, Coonawarra, SA 5263 **Region** Coonawarra
T (08) 8736 3268 **www**.hoggieswine.com **Open** By appt
Winemaker Gavin Hogg **Est.** 1996 **Dozens** 10 000 **Vyds** 27.5ha

A complicated story. Founded by Gavin Hogg and Mike Press in 1996 and based on an 80ha vineyard in the Wrattonbully region, the Kopparossa label was born in 2000. The vineyard (not the brand) was sold in '02, and Mike retired to build his eponymous winery and vineyard in the Adelaide Hills. Various twists and turns followed between then and '09, when Gavin purchased a 24ha vineyard on the Murray River, adjacent to his parents' vineyard; the majority of the fruit from the Hoggies Vineyard is used for Hoggies Estate brand, and for various private labels. The Kopparossa wines come from the 3.5ha estate vineyard in Coonawarra. Exports to the UK, the US, Canada, The Netherlands, Poland, Vietnam, Hong Kong and China.

🍷🍷🍷🍷🍷 **Kopparossa Estate Shiraz 2012** Substantial hit of fruit flavour. Drinking this is like sinking into a big comfy chair. Plum, mint, raspberry and slippery, smoky oak. Matured in both French and American oak but fruit flavour remains in control. Much here to enjoy. Screwcap. 14% alc. **Rating** 93 **To** 2022 $29 CM

Kopparossa Vintage Reserve Coonawarra Shiraz 2012 Matured in all new oak, French and American, for 2 years. Heightened mintiness with toast and ripe, intense plum in behind. Lots of promises upfront and delivers on most of them. Firm finish. You wouldn't call it modern, but you would say that it works. Cork. 14% alc. **Rating** 93 **To** 2024 $50 CM

🍷🍷🍷🍷 **Coonawarra Sauvignon Blanc 2014** **Rating** 89 **To** 2016 $15 CM ✪

Kopparossa Vintage Reserve Coonawarra Cabernet Sauvignon 2012 **Rating** 89 **To** 2024 $50 CM

Olivia Coonawarra Cabernet Sauvignon 2012 **Rating** 88 **To** 2019 $19 CM

Kopparossa Estate Cabernet Sauvignon 2012 **Rating** 88 **To** 2020 $29 CM

Hollick ★★★★★

Riddoch Highway, Coonawarra, SA 5263 **Region** Coonawarra
T (08) 8737 2318 **www**.hollick.com **Open** Mon–Fri 9–5, w'ends & public hols 10–5
Winemaker Ian Hollick, Joe Cory **Est.** 1983 **Dozens** 30 000 **Vyds** 87ha

In April 2014 the Hollick family announced that a major investment had been made in their business by the large Chinese group Hong Kong Yingda Investment Co. Ltd. Involved in hospitality and tourism in China, part of its business involves vineyard and winery operations. The Hollick family will continue to own a part of the business, and will continue to manage it in the same way as usual. Major benefits to Hollick are working capital and access to the Chinese market; and Hong Kong Yingda Investment Co. Ltd will gain expertise from the Hollick family. Exports to most major markets.

🍷🍷🍷🍷🍷 **Shiraz 2013** Made from the estate Wrattonbully vineyard, matured for 12 months in French and American oak. Deep crimson-purple, this is full to the rafters with juicy black fruits, licorice and bitter chocolate, the tannins obvious, but fleshy. Altogether impressive. Screwcap. 14.5% alc. **Rating** 95 **To** 2035 $25 ✪

Ravenswood Cabernet Sauvignon 2012 Estate-grown; matured in new oak, mainly French, for 18 months. The colour is slightly turbid, although the hue is good; the bouquet transmits the oak, the palate fighting back thanks to its considerable length and balance, cassis insisting that it's the most important feature of the wine. Screwcap. 14.5% alc. **Rating** 95 **To** 2032 $77

The Nectar 2014 Off to the left, of course, but this botrytised riesling is always good; the Hollick team have got the vineyard and winery in sync, for there are many things that could go wrong with it – but haven't; the combination of lime, cumquat and honeyed sweetness balanced by acidity is very good indeed. 375ml. Screwcap. 10.5% alc. **Rating** 94 **To** 2020 $25 ✪

Bond Road Chardonnay 2013 **Rating** 93 **To** 2021 $25 ✪

Hollydene Estate ★★★★

3483 Golden Highway, Jerrys Plains, NSW 2330 **Region** Hunter Valley
T (02) 6576 4021 **www.**hollydeneestate.com **Open** 7 days 9–5
Winemaker Matt Burton **Est.** 1965 **Dozens** 2000 **Vyds** 40ha
Karen Williams has three vineyards and associated properties, all established in the 1960s. They are Hollydene Estate, Wybong Estate and Arrowfield, the latter one of the original vinous landmarks in the Upper Hunter. The three vineyards produce grapes for the Juul and Hollydene Estate labels. Exports to Indonesia and China.

Juul Blanc de Blancs 2008 It's exciting to find a sparkling at this price with more than 6 years on lees. It needs it, too, with a tightly honed spine of lemon juice acidity only beginning to soften. It holds an impressively pale straw hue for its age, carrying admirable primary citrus fruit, only beginning to reveal almond complexity, and promising a very long life. Elegantly honed texture and subtle, seamlessly integrated dosage confirm skilful craftsmanship. Disgorged Nov '14. Diam. 12.5% alc. **Rating** 93 **To** 2023 $30 TS
Blanc de Noirs 2008 A full straw hue and all the toasty, biscuity complexity of 6 years on lees overlays a bright acid line and tangy morello cherry fruit of this pinot noir and meunier blend. It lingers with elegant persistence and integrity, with a low dosage of 6g/l neatly integrated. Skilfully assembled and great value. Disgorged Nov '14. Diam. 12.5% alc. **Rating** 92 **To** 2020 $30 TS

Holm Oak ★★★★★

11 West Bay Road, Rowella, Tas 7270 **Region** Northern Tasmania
T (03) 6394 7577 **www.**holmoakvineyards.com.au **Open** 7 days 11–5
Winemaker Rebecca Duffy **Est.** 1983 **Dozens** 10 000 **Vyds** 11.62ha
Holm Oak takes its name from its grove of oak trees, planted around the beginning of the 20th century and originally intended for the making of tennis racquets. Winemaker Rebecca Duffy, daughter of owners Ian and Robyn Wilson, has extensive winemaking experience in Australia and California, and husband Tim, a viticultural agronomist, manages the vineyard (pinot noir, cabernet sauvignon, chardonnay, riesling, sauvignon blanc and pinot gris, with small amounts of merlot, cabernet franc and arneis). Exports to Canada, Norway and Japan.

The Wizard Chardonnay 2013 Hand-picked, whole bunch-pressed to tank to settle for 24 hours, then to French oak (50% new, 50% 1yo) for wild-yeast ferment, 50% mlf, 12 months in oak, only 2 barrels made. The mlf has taken the edge off the acerbic acid Tasmanian Chardonnay can have, allowing white peach and nectarine free play among the creamy, nutty nuances of the wine. Very well made. Screwcap. 13% alc. **Rating** 96 **To** 2028 $60 ✪
Riesling 2014 Only Tasmania produces Riesling with this electric acidity that ignites the palate and aftertaste; lemon zest and pith are tracked by grapefruit, the finish almost painful, and certainly mouth-watering in its intensity. 30% fermented in a Numblot egg. Screwcap. 12% alc. **Rating** 95 **To** 2029 $25 ✪
Chardonnay 2013 Whole bunch-pressed, wild yeast-fermented, 20% in a 600l Numblot egg for 8 months, the balance in oak (30% new), 30% mlf. It's a very lively wine, and will fit well with the most obvious food matches, but you wonder whether, given its natural acidity, 13% alcohol might have been a better approach. That said, time is on its side. Screwcap. 12.5% alc. **Rating** 94 **To** 2023 $30 ✪

Pinot Gris 2014 Pale pink; pinot gris grown in the right climate; nashi pear, apple and even a hint of strawberry; good length, balance and aftertaste. Screwcap. 12% alc. **Rating** 94 **To** 2017 $25 ✪

The Wizard Pinot Noir 2013 From 6 rows of 1 estate block; 70% destemmed, 30% whole bunches, wild yeast-fermented, pressed direct to barrel (50% new, 40% 1yo), a selection of 10 barrels Dec '13, the blended wine given a further 6 months in oak. Bright, full, but clear crimson-purple; the fragrant bouquet and supple red-fruited fore-palate are followed by an emphatic finish. Let it make its point, but don't be bullied into drinking the next bottle in less than 3 years. Screwcap. 13% alc. **Rating** 94 **To** 2025 $60

♟♟♟♟♀ **Arneis 2014 Rating** 92 **To** 2024 $25 ✪
Sauvignon Blanc 2014 Rating 90 **To** 2016 $25
Ilex Pinot Noir 2014 Rating 90 **To** 2016 $22

Home Hill   ★★★★★

38 Nairn Street, Ranelagh, Tas 7109 **Region** Southern Tasmania
T (03) 6264 1200 **www**.homehillwines.com.au **Open** 7 days 10–5
Winemaker Gilli and Paul Lipscombe **Est.** 1994 **Dozens** 2000 **Vyds** 5ha
Terry and Rosemary Bennett planted their first 0.5ha of vines in 1994 on gentle slopes in the beautiful Huon Valley. Between '94 and '99 the plantings were increased to 3ha of pinot noir, 1.5ha of chardonnay and 0.5ha of sylvaner. Home Hill has had great success with its exemplary Pinot Noir, a consistent multi-trophy and gold medal winner in the ultra-competitive Tasmanian Wine Show.

♟♟♟♟♟ **Kelly's Reserve Pinot Noir 2013** Excellent colour; the bouquet has vibrant red and dark cherry fruit with plum also in the mix; the palate opens with gloriously supple, smooth and seductive red fruits, lulling you into Pinot dreamland before the earthy/spicy power of the tannins accompany the finish and aftertaste. Gold medal Tas Wine Show '15. Screwcap. 14.1% alc. **Rating** 97 **To** 2028 $60 ✪

♟♟♟♟♟ **Estate Pinot Noir 2013** Very good colour; the red label seems fitting (its other siblings have white labels) once the power of the wine on the bouquet and palate have made their considerable impact; black cherries, savoury spices, persistent tannins and an impressively long palate are in the heartland of the long-lived Home Hill style. Screwcap. 13.9% alc. **Rating** 96 **To** 2025 $36 ✪

Kelly's Reserve Chardonnay 2013 Estate-grown, hand-picked, whole bunch-pressed, matured for 10 months in French oak (30% new). A high-class Chardonnay by any standards; while the alcohol is low, the fruit is fully ripe and has absorbed the oak without effort; citrus and stone fruit respect the role each plays in the wine. Screwcap. 13.1% alc. **Rating** 95 **To** 2023 $30 ✪

Landslide Pinot Noir 2013 Even the third tier of Home Hill has more than many first-tier wines; the colour is bright and clear, the bouquet intensely fragrant, and the palate explores red and black cherries, spices and raspberries, which are set against a backdrop of silky, yet persistent, tannins. By far the most approachable now, and over the next 5 years, before its senior siblings are prepared to welcome you. Screwcap. 13.9% alc. **Rating** 95 **To** 2020 $25 ✪

Kelly's Reserve Late Harvest Sticky 2010 Well, this is one answer to the Sylvaner conundrum, for it is a smart wine; still bright green-straw, still fresh and balanced, still with delicious lime juice fruit behind the sweetness. 375ml. Screwcap. 9.9% alc. **Rating** 95 **To** 2020 $22 ✪

Unwooded Chardonnay 2013 After almost 2 years, almost devoid of colour, and of course, devoid of oak – but far from devoid of flavour or texture; pink grapefruit, white peach and lime/lemon aromas and flavours drive the long palate. Time still on its side. Screwcap. 12.9% alc. **Rating** 94 **To** 2019 $24 ✪

♟♟♟♟♀ **Rose 2013 Rating** 92 **To** 2015 $23 ✪

Honey Moon Vineyard

135 Church Hill Road, Echunga, SA 5153 **Region** Adelaide Hills
T 0438 727 079 **www**.honeymoonvineyard.com.au **Open** By appt
Winemaker Jane Bromley, Hylton McLean **Est.** 2004 **Dozens** 600 **Vyds** 1.2ha
Jane Bromley and Hylton McLean planted 0.4ha each of pinot noir (clones 777, 114 and 115)
and shiraz (selected from two old vineyards known for their spicy fruit flavours) in 2003. The
moon is a striking feature in the landscape, particularly at harvest time when, as a full moon,
it appears as a dollop of rich honey in the sky – hence the name. The first vintage was '05,
but Jane has been making wine since '01, with a particular interest in Champagne; Hylton
is a winemaker, wine science researcher and wine educator with over 20 years' experience.

♀♀♀♀♀ **Extra Adelaide Hills Pinot Noir 2013** Well composed and deeply fruited.
Sweet cranberry, plum and red cherry with shots of clove and spicy oak. Tannin
works to batten it all mostly down, though the ripeness of the fruit has an
irrepressibility to it. It will drink better again in a few years but there's much here
to admire/enjoy. Screwcap. 14.2% alc. **Rating** 92 **To** 2021 $50 CM

Horner Wines

12 Shedden Street, Cessnock, NSW 2325 **Region** Hunter Valley
T 0427 201 391 **www**.nakedwines.com.au **Open** Not
Winemaker Ashley Horner **Est.** 2013 **Dozens** 5900 **Vyds** 12ha
Horner Wines is the family venture of Ashley and Lauren Horner, with viticultural input
from Glen and Josephine Horner. It began when verdelho, chardonnay, viognier and shiraz
were planted; the vineyard is now fully certified organic. Grapes are also sourced from organic
vineyards in Orange and Cowra. Ashley had a 14-year career working at Rosemount Estate,
Penfolds, Kamberra Estate, Saint Clair (NZ) and Mount Pleasant, ultimately becoming
winemaker at Tamburlaine and completing a Diploma in Wine Technology at Dookie
College. Wife Lauren has a degree in hospitality/tourism, and is now involved in the running
of Horner Wines. The move from grapegrowing to winemaking was precipitated by the fall
in demand for grapes, and they sell the wines through www.nakedwines.com.au.

♀♀♀♀♀ **Little Jack Organic Sauvignon Blanc 2014** Absolutely stacked to the brim
with every tropical fruit in the business, the biggest surprise the lively, juicy acidity
on the finish. A list of fruits is to deconstruct a wine that deserves better. Screwcap.
11.4% alc. **Rating** 92 **To** 2016 $17 ○
Family Reserve Late Harvest Viognier 2014 Late-harvested, but its sweetness
comes from stopping the ferment (in barrel) when the sugar/acid balance is
correct. The decision was well taken, but the remarkable thing is how clearly the
apricot varietal character comes through. A fresh, moderately sweet, and lively
wine. 375ml. Screwcap. 8% alc. **Rating** 91 **To** 2017 $26
Family Reserve Viognier 2014 A mix of wild and cultured yeast, oak and
stainless steel, and lees contact options used – no doubt about the effort in the
winery. Against all the odds, viognier has been cajoled into behaving itself, with
a gentle display of stone fruit/apricot flavours, the finish clean and well balanced.
Bottle no. 3143 of 3300. Screwcap. 13.5% alc. **Rating** 90 **To** 2017 $23

♀♀♀♀ **Family Reserve Chardonnay 2014 Rating** 89 **To** 2018 $24
Little Jack Organic Riesling 2014 Rating 88 **To** 2017 $17 ○

Horseshoe Vineyard

Horseshoe Road, Horseshoe Valley via Denman, NSW 2328 **Region** Hunter Valley
T (02) 6547 3528 **Open** By appt
Winemaker John Hordern **Est.** 1969 **Dozens** 1500 **Vyds** 3.5ha
Horseshoe Vineyard, owned and operated by John and Wendy Hordern and family, was
established by Bob Hordern with cuttings of semillon and shiraz from Penfolds Wybong Park
vineyard; further plantings of chardonnay, semillon and shiraz were made in following years.
Roseworthy graduate John Hordern gained experience at Wybong Estate and Arrowfield

before founding Hunter Wine Services with Rex D'Aquino in 2001. Riesling and Sauvignon Blanc are made from purchased grapes from Orange. Exports to the UK and China.

ΥΥΥΥ **Premium Reserve Chardonnay 2013** Straw-coloured, with strong notes of lactose and creamy oak, matched more or less harmoniously to white peach and nectarine. Pushes well through the finish. Screwcap. 12.5% alc. **Rating** 89 **To** 2019 $25 CM

Premium Reserve Hunter Valley Semillon 2013 Forward in its development and already offering flavours of wax, honeycomb and ripe citrus. Enjoyable now but not one for the cellar. Screwcap. 11% alc. **Rating** 88 **To** 2018 $25 CM

Houghton ★★★★★

148 Dale Road, Middle Swan, WA 6065 **Region** Swan Valley
T (08) 9274 9540 **www**.houghton-wines.com.au **Open** 7 days 10–5
Winemaker Ross Pamment **Est.** 1836 **Dozens** NFP

Houghton's reputation was once largely dependent on its (then) White Burgundy, equally good when young or 5 years old. In the last 20 years its portfolio has changed out of all recognition, with a kaleidoscopic range of high-quality wines from the Margaret River, Frankland River, Great Southern and Pemberton regions to the fore. The Jack Mann and Gladstones red wines stand at the forefront, the Wisdom range covering all varietal bases in great style. Nor should the value-for-money Stripe brand be ignored. To borrow a saying of the late Jack Mann, 'There are no bad wines here.' With a history of more than 175 years, its future now lies in the hands of Accolade Wines. Exports to the UK and Asia.

ΥΥΥΥΥ **Thomas Yule Frankland River Shiraz 2012** Hand-picked, open-fermented, matured in French oak. As elegant and classy as they come, it has intensity, focus, length and drive, yet the motor is just idling; the juicy fruit flavours are as much in the red as the black spectrum, the tannins and French oak perfectly balanced. Screwcap. 14% alc. **Rating** 97 **To** 2040 $75 ✪

Gladstones Margaret River Cabernet Sauvignon 2012 One of the best of a long line of distinguished Cabernets under the Gladstones label. Vivid crimson-purple, its bouquet offers cassis, violets and cedar, its palate so harmonious it is almost luminous, fruit, tannins and oak locked in an embrace that neither man nor time will put asunder. Screwcap. 14% alc. **Rating** 97 **To** 2047 $77 ✪

ΥΥΥΥΥ **Thomas Yule Frankland River Shiraz 2011** Open-fermented and matured in high-quality French oak (much new), this unashamedly full-bodied wine is laden with black fruits, licorice, earth and rounded tannins. Leave alone for at least 5 years. Screwcap. 14% alc. **Rating** 96 **To** 2041 $75 ✪

CW Ferguson Great Southern Cabernet Malbec 2012 CW Ferguson was the owner/winemaker of Houghton from 1863 to 1911, and employed George Mann (father of Jack Mann) as winemaker, providing a direct link of well over 100 years. This is a fragrant and elegant wine, bordering on juicy, reflecting open fermentation, gentle extraction, and maturation in high-quality French oak. Screwcap. 14% alc. **Rating** 96 **To** 2037 $77

Wisdom Pemberton Sauvignon Blanc 2014 Short-term maturation on lees in tank following a cool ferment. A gallant price for an unoaked Sauvignon Blanc, doubtless based on its fragrant and lively display of tropical fruits, passionfruit and gooseberry to the fore, lemony acidity providing balance and length. Screwcap. 13% alc. **Rating** 95 **To** 2017 $34 ✪

Jack Mann Cabernet Sauvignon 2012 A classic, pure exposition of cabernet, with blackcurrant, bay leaf and dried herbs on the bouquet and palate, fine, but decidedly persistent cabernet tannins making sure you don't get off the hook too easily. So relax, and try to enjoy it, but realise this is a 30-year wine. Screwcap. 14% alc. **Rating** 95 **To** 2042 $115

Wisdom Margaret River Cabernet Sauvignon 2012 Is tighter and purer than many of its Margaret River siblings, blackcurrant fruit and garden herbs riding high, wide and handsome; the French oak has been carefully (and correctly)

judged, joining hands with firm tannins for the long journey ahead. Screwcap.
13.2% alc. **Rating** 95 To 2032 $37
Crofters Frankland River Shiraz 2013 Rating 94 To 2030 $19 ✪
Crofters Frankland River Cabernet Sauvignon 2012 Rating 94 To 2020
$19 ✪

🍷🍷🍷🍷🍷 **Crofters Pemberton Margaret River Sauvignon Blanc Semillon 2013**
Rating 93 To 2020 $19 ✪
Crofters Chardonnay 2013 Rating 92 To 2017 $19 ✪
Margaret River Cabernet Sauvignon 2013 Rating 92 To 2025 $19 ✪
Margaret River Cabernet Merlot 2012 Rating 90 To 2022 $19 ✪

House of Arras ★★★★★

Bay of Fires, 40 Baxters Road, Pipers River, Tas 7252 **Region** Northern Tasmania
T 1800 088 711 **www**.houseofarras.com.au **Open** 7 days 10–5
Winemaker Ed Carr **Est.** 1995 **Dozens** NFP
The rise and rise of the fortunes of the House of Arras has been due to two things: first, the
exceptional skills of winemaker Ed Carr, and second, its access to high-quality Tasmanian
chardonnay and pinot noir. While there have been distinguished sparkling wines made in
Tasmania for many years, none has so consistently scaled the heights of Arras. The complexity,
texture and structure of the wines are akin to that of Bollinger RD and Krug; the connection
stems from the 7–10 years the wines spend on lees prior to disgorgement.

🍷🍷🍷🍷🍷 **Blanc de Blancs 2004** Pale straw-green, notwithstanding 8 years on tirage in
traditional method; it has extraordinary balance, finesse and varietal citrus blossom
and white peach purity. It is even better than it was when first disgorged, and will
continue to develop in bottle, sustained by its acidity. Cork. 12.5% alc. **Rating** 97
To 2020 $80 ✪

🍷🍷🍷🍷🍷 **Rose 2005** A pinot noir–chardonnay blend made using the traditional method,
and spending at least 6 years on tirage. Salmon pink; forest strawberries, nectarine
and brioche are swathed in finely balanced Tasmanian acidity, the dosage calibrated
to the last microgram, and helping provide a deliciously spicy farewell. Cork.
12.5% alc. **Rating** 96 To 2020 $80
Blanc de Blancs 2005 Arras Blanc de Blancs upholds the elegance and
endurance of Tasmanian chardonnay in subtle yellow stone fruit and white citrus
definition, overlaying it with considerable layers of secondary and tertiary character
and silky, buttery mouthfeel. Beautifully poised and carefully crafted, '05 is a
magnificent vintage for this cuvee. Cork. 12.5% alc. **Rating** 95 To 2020 $80 TS
Rose 2006 A copper salmon hue reflects considerable maturity, yet it upholds
poise and balance in contrasting the lively strawberry, pink pepper and red apple
fruit of pinot noir (two-thirds of the blend, the balance chardonnay) with the roast
nut and burnt butter allure of age. Firm, fine tannins provide definition without
dryness to a long and sculpted finish. It's engaging now, with the structure to age
longer still. Cork. 12.5% alc. **Rating** 94 To 2021 $80 TS

🍷🍷🍷🍷🍷 **A by Arras Premium Cuvee NV** Rating 92 To 2016 $25 TS ✪
Brut Elite NV Rating 91 To 2015 $50 TS

House of Cards ★★★★☆

3220 Caves Road, Yallingup, WA 6282 **Region** Margaret River
T (08) 9755 2583 **www**.houseofcardswine.com.au **Open** 7 days 10–5
Winemaker Travis Wray **Est.** 2011 **Dozens** 4000 **Vyds** 12ha
House of Cards is owned and operated by Elizabeth and Travis Wray, the youngest
winemaking team in Margaret River. The name of the winery is a reflection of the gamble
that all viticulturists and winemakers face every vintage: 'You have to play the hand you are
dealt by Mother Nature.' They are involved in every aspect of the business, from growing the
grapes to marketing and sales. They only use estate-grown grapes, open-top fermentation,

hand-plunging and manual basket-pressing. It's certainly doing it the hard way, but it must seem all worthwhile when they produce wines of such quality.

ŸŸŸŸŸ **Limited Release Ace of Spades 2013** A 50/50% blend of cabernet and malbec; hand-picked, open-fermented, 10% drained off, 35 days' extended maceration, matured for 18 months in French oak (40% new). The plummy malbec, sexy oak and the cassis of the cabernet all come together like beads of mercury running together with no effort, and contrary to your wishes. Don't try to resist the irresistible. Cork. 14.6% alc. **Rating** 96 **To** 2033 $65 ✪

The Joker Single Vineyard Margaret River Sauvignon Blanc 2014 A prime example of the depth that Margaret River achieves with its sauvignon blanc, even without any oak fermentation or maturation. Grapefruit and ginger provide an unexpected first-up trick, followed by snow pea and strongly minerally acidity on the long finish. Screwcap. 12.3% alc. **Rating** 94 **To** 2016 $21 ✪

The Royals Single Vineyard Margaret River Chardonnay 2014 Wild yeast-fermented in French oak (30% new). The House of Cards style carries through between the otherwise disconnected polarities of cabernet and chardonnay – a direct precision that is full of confidence and self-belief. This has a long way to go until it reaches its potential. Screwcap. 13.5% alc. **Rating** 94 **To** 2024 $36

The Joker Single Vineyard Margaret River Cabernet Merlot 2013 A 64/36% blend, open-fermented, hand-plunged and matured in French barriques for 12 months. Vivid crimson-purple; a complex, full-bodied wine with a storehouse of savoury fruits and tannins to sustain it for many years to come. Needs time to settle down, which it will do, because the balance is good. Screwcap. 14.3% alc. **Rating** 94 **To** 2028 $21 ✪

The Royals Single Vineyard Margaret River Cabernet Sauvignon 2013 Hand-picked and sorted, open-fermented, 35 days' post-fermentation maceration, matured for 18 months in French oak (30% new). The impact of the extreme maceration is very interesting, for the tannins are resolved, and there are dried herb/bay leaf nuances running through its blackcurrant fruit. The result is a tightly framed, but ultra-classic style that brooks no argument. Screwcap. 14.4% alc. **Rating** 94 **To** 2033 $39

ŸŸŸŸŸ **The Joker Single Vineyard Shiraz 2013** **Rating** 90 **To** 2025 $21 ✪

Howard Vineyard   ★★★★☆

53 Bald Hills Road, Nairne, SA 5252 **Region** Adelaide Hills
T (08) 8188 0203 **www**.howardvineyard.com **Open** Fri–Sun 10–5
Winemaker Tom Northcott **Est.** 2005 **Dozens** 6000 **Vyds** 60ha

This dates back to the late 1990s, with the establishment of two vineyards at different locations in the Adelaide Hills. The Schoenthal Vineyard near Lobethal, at an elevation of 440–500m, is planted primarily to sauvignon blanc and chardonnay, with smaller amounts of pinot noir and pinot gris. The Howard Vineyard is at a lower elevation, and the slightly warmer site has been planted to sauvignon blanc, chardonnay, semillon, cabernet sauvignon, shiraz, viognier and cabernet franc. The grapes not required for the Howard Vineyard label are sold to other winemakers. Tom Northcott graduated with a Bachelor of Viticulture and Oenology from Adelaide University, having completed vintages in Languedoc (France) and with Grant Burge, Peter Lehmann, Houghton and Bay of Fires. Exports to Hong Kong and China.

ŸŸŸŸŸ **Amos Adelaide Hills Cabernet Sauvignon 2013** It's drinking beautifully already and yet it has longevity stitched into its seams. It's an outstanding release. Pure, concentrated blackcurrant, drives of chocolate, assorted dust, dark olive and spice and a casual smattering of herbs. It's mostly, though, characterised by a casual, almost offhand sense of precision. Screwcap. 13.9% alc. **Rating** 96 **To** 2030 $60 CM ✪

Picnic Adelaide Hills Rose 2014 Made with 100% cabernet franc. Seductive, cranberried, tangy fruit, bursting with life and flavour, jellied and sweet-fruited

through the mid-palate but with a keen savoury twist from there onwards. Value plus. Screwcap. 12.5% alc. **Rating** 94 **To** 2015 $18 CM ✪
Amos Adelaide Hills Shiraz 2013 Substantial Shiraz. Fully ripe. Liqueured plums, dried herbs, layers of liquid chocolate and cedar spice. It's simple but immensely supple; it drinks well now but for greater complexities time will be your friend. Screwcap. 13.8% alc. **Rating** 94 **To** 2026 $60 CM

ŢŢŢŢŢ **Picnic Adelaide Hills Shiraz Cabernet 2013 Rating** 92 **To** 2023 $18 CM ✪
Picnic Adelaide Hills Sauvignon Blanc 2014 Rating 91 **To** 2015 $18 CM ✪
Amos Adelaide Hills Chardonnay 2014 Rating 91 **To** 2017 $35 CM

Hugh Hamilton Wines ★★★★★

94 McMurtrie Road, McLaren Vale, SA 5171 **Region** McLaren Vale
T (08) 8323 8689 **www**.hughhamiltonwines.com.au **Open** 7 days 11–5
Winemaker Peter Leske **Est.** 1991 **Dozens** 18 000 **Vyds** 22.41ha
In 2014, fifth-generation family member Hugh Hamilton handed over the reins to daughter Mary, the sixth generation of the family. It was she who developed the irreverent black sheep packaging. But it's more than simply marketing: the business will continue to embrace both mainstream and alternative varieties, its 85-year-old shiraz and 65-year-old cabernet sauvignon at its Blewitt Springs vineyard providing the ability to develop the Pure Black label. This reflects changes in the way the vines are trellised, picking and fermenting in small open fermenters, using gravity for wine movements, and maturation in high-quality French oak. The cellar door is lined with the original jarrah from Vat 15 of the historic Hamilton's Ewell winery, the largest wooden vat ever built in the southern hemisphere.

ŢŢŢŢŢ **Black Blood III Black Sheep Vineyard Old Vine McLaren Vale Shiraz 2013** Adds a layer of prettiness to the enormity of fruit. Saturated plum, licorice and asphalt flavour with choc cream and violet notes. Long chains of tannin come injected with inky fruit. Warm but not warming. Heroic style done (very) well. Screwcap. 14.5% alc. **Rating** 96 **To** 2032 $70 CM ✪
Pure Black Shiraz 2010 Open-fermented, hand-plunged, matured in French oak, a 5-barrel selection from a total of 250 (2% of the total make). Deep and vibrant crimson-purple; the wine itself is also superb, with a freshness suggesting alcohol in the 13.5% range; the mouthfeel is fine and supple thanks to ultra fine-grained tannins, the flavours of black fruits, cedar, spice and licorice. Presentation to match. Cork. 14.5% alc. **Rating** 96 **To** 2045 $180
The Mongrel McLaren Vale Sangiovese 2013 Exceptional hue and clarity; 12 months in used French barriques a very good decision; perfect sour cherry/red cherry fruit; long, silky tannins sign and deliver a terrific sangiovese. Screwcap. 14.5% alc. **Rating** 96 **To** 2023 $24 ✪
Tonnellerie Damy Single Barrel Shiraz 2013 Bold but elegant. Feels generally seamless. Has an all-round spiciness despite the ooze of plummy, black-berried fruit. Not quite as saucy/sexy as the François Frères version but far less obvious. Fine wine. Screwcap. 14.5% alc. **Rating** 95 **To** 2030 $50 CM
Tonnellerie Remond Single Barrel Shiraz 2013 Well-integrated but plush. Halfway in style between the François Frères and Damy versions. Sex appeal and integration. Dark plums and woodsmoke, velvety blackberry and resin. It coats the mouth with luscious flavour but remains well mannered at all times. Length is assured. 24 dozen made. Screwcap. 14.5% alc. **Rating** 95 **To** 2030 $50 CM
Jekyll & Hyde McLaren Vale Shiraz Viognier 2013 Impressive wine. Perfumed and spice-riven though there's plenty of leathery, plummy, licoricey flavour on display. It feels soft and sturdy at once, its natural exuberance well tethered to firm, flavour-filled tannin. Coffeed oak adds a darkness to the performance. It's excellent from many angles. Screwcap. 15% alc. **Rating** 95 **To** 2025 $50 CM
Tonnellerie François Frères Single Barrel Shiraz 2013 Rating 94 **To** 2030 $50 CM

Black Blood I Cellar Vineyard McLaren Vale Shiraz 2013 Rating 94
To 2032 $70 CM
Oddball McLaren Vale Saperavi 2013 Rating 94 To 2025 $50 CM

ŶŶŶŶŸ The Scoundrel Tempranillo 2013 Rating 93 To 2019 $25 CM ✪
Black Blood II Church Vineyard Shiraz 2013 Rating 91 To 2025 $70 CM
Black Ops Shiraz Mataro Saperavi 2013 Rating 91 To 2020 $30 CM
The Villain Cabernet Sauvignon 2013 Rating 91 To 2022 $30 CM
Members Only Shearer's Cut Black Sheep Block McLaren Vale Shiraz
2013 Rating 90 To 2019 $25 CM

Hugo ★★★★☆

246 Elliott Road, McLaren Flat, SA 5171 **Region** McLaren Vale
T (08) 8383 0098 **www.**hugowines.com.au **Open** Mon–Fri 10–5, Sat 12–5, Sun 10.30–5
Winemaker John Hugo **Est.** 1982 **Dozens** 7000 **Vyds** 25ha
Came from relative obscurity to prominence in the late 1980s with some lovely ripe, sweet
reds, which, while strongly American oak-influenced, were quite outstanding. It picked up
the pace again after a dull period in the mid-'90s, and has made the most of the recent run of
good vintages. The estate plantings include shiraz, cabernet sauvignon, chardonnay, grenache
and sauvignon blanc, with part of the grape production sold to others. Exports to the UK
and Canada.

ŶŶŶŶŶ Reserve McLaren Vale Shiraz 2012 From the first estate plantings in '51;
finished its fermentation in American and French oak. This is no-holds-barred,
boots and all, full-bodied; blackberry fruit is caught on a wave of oak that rolls
towards the shore and crashes onto a beach of tannins. All that said, the wine
has the balance needed to reach its destiny 30+ years away. Screwcap. 14.5% alc.
Rating 96 To 2045 $50 ✪

ŶŶŶŶŸ McLaren Vale Cabernet Sauvignon 2012 Rating 91 To 2029 $25
McLaren Vale Cabernet Sauvignon 2013 Rating 90 To 2030 $25

Hungerford Hill ★★★★★

1 Broke Road, Pokolbin, NSW 2320 **Region** Hunter Valley
T (02) 4998 7666 **www.**hungerfordhill.com.au **Open** Sun–Thurs 10–5, Fri–Sat 10–6
Winemaker Adrian Lockhart **Est.** 1967 **Dozens** 2000 **Vyds** 5ha
Since acquiring Hungerford Hill a decade ago, the Kirby family has sought to build on the
Hungerford Hill story that began over 40 years ago. James Kirby was involved in his family's
engineering business during its growth to become one of Australia's leading automotive
refrigeration and air-conditioning manufacturers. The winemaking team continues to make
wines from the Hunter Valley and from the cool-climate regions of Hilltops and Tumbarumba.
The cellar door complex sits at the gateway to the Hunter Valley at One Broke Road, and has
been the recipient of significant awards. Exports to all major markets.

ŶŶŶŶŶ Heavy Metal 2013 A blend of shiraz and cabernet from McLaren Vale,
Coonawarra, Hunter and Barossa valleys. Deep crimson-purple hue; seek and ye
shall find all you want from this particularly distinguished blend of varieties and
regions: every one of those regions had a top-class vintage, and it shows in the
profound depth of the wine, built with blackberry, blackcurrant, iodine, plum and
anise. Screwcap. 14.5% alc. Rating 97 To 2048 $55 ✪

ŶŶŶŶŶ Epic Barossa Valley Shiraz 2013 Matured in new French and American oak
for 18 months. Single-vineyard release. Modest alcohol but fully and elegantly ripe.
Flavours of coffee-cream, blackberry and sweet raspberry sluice juicily through the
palate, backed by olive and ground dry spice notes. Complex but not aggressively
so. Feathered tannin rather than the full brakes. As much about poise as impact.
Screwcap. 13% alc. Rating 95 To 2030 $120 CM
Hunter Valley Semillon 2014 Pure, intense, racy, and very long; a terrific young
Semillon, busily stripping saliva from the mouth long after it is swallowed or

ejected (in tasting mode); the crunchy acidity is particularly good, and is one of the guarantors of the future of the wine. Screwcap. 11% alc. **Rating** 95 To 2029 $27 ⊙

Heavy Metal Shiraz 2013 Blend of 68% shiraz and 32% cabernet from McLaren Vale, Coonawarra, and Hunter and Barossa valleys. Sweet-edged in general but dry and savoury through the finish. Classic style, classically executed. Blackcurrant, blackberry, leather, earth and beef stock with an overlay of creamy oak. Mounts the argument and wins the case. Screwcap. 14.5% alc. **Rating** 95 To 2030 $55 CM

Tumbarumba Chardonnay 2011 The wine is developing at a leisurely pace thanks to its near-perfect balance and line, rather than power and complexity, although the latter will build as the palate continues to develop. Comparisons to Chablis have some validity. Screwcap. 12.4% alc. **Rating** 94 To 2021 $33

Gundagai Shiraz 2013 An elegant and brightly flavoured medium-bodied Shiraz that utterly belies its alcohol; matured in new and used French oak for 11 months; red and black cherry aromas and flavours have a distinct garnish of black pepper and a hint of oak; the tannins are graceful and balanced. Screwcap. 14.6% alc. **Rating** 94 To 2028 $28 ⊙

Hunter Valley Shiraz 2013 The bespoke suit displays the elegant, medium-bodied array of bright fruits, spice and earth to perfection. It steps out with the knowledge of the Hunter Valley's ability to develop without the slightest risk for 20+ years, but won't object to being tried on for size at any point along the way. Screwcap. 13.7% alc. **Rating** 94 To 2038 $36

Cote D'Or Hunter Valley Shiraz 2011 Surely the use of Côte D'Or has been made illegal under the terms of the EU Wine Agreement, and is on a par for confusion with the Blackberry Semillon name. Marketing stupidity to one side, this is a very elegant Hunter Shiraz, as long as it is elegant, red and black fruits with freshness and regional typicity. Screwcap. 14% alc. **Rating** 94 To 2036 $65

ҬҬҬҬҬ **Tumbarumba Pinot Gris 2014** Rating 93 To 2018 $27 ⊙
Blackberry Hunter Valley Semillon 2011 Rating 92 To 2026 $55
Orange Merlot 2013 Rating 92 To 2025 $35
Hilltops Cabernet Sauvignon 2013 Rating 91 To 2028 $35

Huntington Estate   ★★★★★

Ulan Road, Mudgee, NSW 2850 **Region** Mudgee
T 1800 995 931 **www.**huntingtonestate.com.au **Open** Mon–Sat 10–5, Sun 10–4
Winemaker Tim Stevens **Est.** 1969 **Dozens** 15 000 **Vyds** 43.8ha
Since taking ownership of Huntington Estate from the founding Roberts family, Tim Stevens has sensibly refrained from making major changes. The policy of having older vintage wines available is continuing, making the cellar door a first port of call for visitors to Mudgee. On the other side, the Music Festival suffers only one problem: there are not enough tickets to satisfy the demand. It really has a well-deserved life of its own, and will do so for years to come. Most Successful Exhibitor Mudgee Wine Show '12 and '13. Exports to China.

ҬҬҬҬҬ **Tim Stevens Signature Bin 14 Shiraz 2009** The deep colour sends a message that is received loud and clear with the first sip of the vividly fresh black cherry/blackberry fruit flavours; the tannins are precisely balanced, oak a conveyance for the fruit. Lovely wine. Screwcap. 13.9% alc. **Rating** 96 To 2034 $40 ⊙

Basket Dried Shiraz 2013 Picked at 11°C baume and dried in baskets for 6 weeks. A very interesting and wholly successful Amarone style. Because of the path it has taken, there are none of the confit/dead fruit characters that often stalk wines with this level of alcohol; instead there are savoury/licorice/bitter chocolate elements that all add to the appeal, and without any tannin penalty. Screwcap. 15% alc. **Rating** 95 To 2038 $60

ҬҬҬҬҬ **Shiraz 2011** Rating 93 To 2025 $26 ⊙
Block 3 Cabernet Sauvignon 2012 Rating 93 To 2032 $70

Special Reserve Shiraz 2012 Rating 92 To 2027 $38
Special Reserve Cabernet Sauvignon 2012 Rating 92 To 2027 $38
Semillon 2014 Rating 91 To 2025 $24
Cabernet Sauvignon 2011 Rating 91 To 2022 $27

Hurley Vineyard ★★★★★

101 Balnarring Road, Balnarring, Vic 3926 **Region** Mornington Peninsula
T (03) 5931 3000 **www**.hurleyvineyard.com.au **Open** 1st w'end each month 11–5
Winemaker Kevin Bell **Est.** 1998 **Dozens** 1000 **Vyds** 3.5ha

It's never as easy as it seems. Despite leading busy city lives, Kevin Bell and wife Tricia Byrnes have done most of the hard work in establishing Hurley Vineyard themselves, with family and friends. Most conspicuously, Kevin has completed the Applied Science (Wine Science) degree at CSU, drawing on Nat White for consultancy advice, and occasionally from Phillip Jones of Bass Phillip and Domaine Fourrier in Gevrey Chambertin. He has not allowed a significant heart issue to prevent him continuing with his first love.

🍷🍷🍷🍷🍷 Garamond Mornington Peninsula Pinot Noir 2013 The prettiest of the three releases, but there's been no sacrifice in power. Rose petal, strawberry and assorted spice notes lead into a powerful palate juiced with black cherry and plum. Tannin manages to be both assertive and velvety at once; it exerts discipline via its presence, without having to do/say much. Length, complete with foresty undergrowth notes, is assured. Diam. 14.5% alc. **Rating** 95 To 2021 $80 CM
Estate Mornington Peninsula Pinot Noir 2013 Pinot Noir with more than a little presence to it. Brooding black cherried fruit is the main driver of this effect, though a rich vein of earthen, velvety, almost leathery tannin amplifies the impression. Not a pretty wine, but a substantial and lengthy one. Diam. 13.9% alc. **Rating** 94 To 2021 $45 CM
Hommage Mornington Peninsula Pinot Noir 2013 Substantial flavour, but not heavy in any way. Cherry-plum and chalk flavours meet pepper spice, aged meat and more foresty notes. Chains of tannin work through the wine, adding a sense of both gravity and control. Yet to really blossom but it no doubt will. Diam. 14.4% alc. **Rating** 94 To 2021 $70 CM

Hutton Vale Farm ★★★★★

Stone Jar Road, Angaston, SA 5353 **Region** Eden Valley
T (08) 8564 8270 **www**.huttonvale.com **Open** By appt
Winemaker Kym Teusner **Est.** 1960 **Dozens** 600 **Vyds** 27ha

John Howard Angas arrived in SA in 1843, and inter alia gave his name to Angaston, purchasing and developing significant farming property close to the still embryonic town. He named part of this Hutton Vale, and it is this property that is now owned and occupied by his great-great-grandson John and wife Jan Angas. In 2012, the Angas family and Teusner Wines shook hands on a new partnership arrangement, under which the Angases grow the grapes, and Kym Teusner is responsible for the winemaking, sales and marketing of Hutton Vale wines. The vineyards in question first caught Kym's attention when he was at Torbreck, and he fulfilled a long-term ambition with the new agreement. Just when the future seemed assured, the vineyards were badly affected by a grass fire in August '14. While much of the vineyard will ultimately be regenerated, some of the oldest grenache vines were completely destroyed, as were 55 of the magnificent 500yo gum trees that are part of the striking landscape of Hutton Vale. Small quantities of its wines are exported to China.

🍷🍷🍷🍷🍷 Eden Valley Riesling 2014 Water-white, the spotless bouquet and immaculately balanced palate all pointing in precisely the same direction – just leave it in peace at the moment, and allow the latent lime and apple fruit to come out of hiding. It's rare that you find a wine with so much promise despite the delicacy of today. Screwcap. 12% alc. **Rating** 95 To 2034 $27 ✪

Eden Valley Cabernet Sauvignon 2010 Hutton Vale wines have been made at Teusner since '12; this cabernet was made at Torbreck. It's as slippery as it is seductive, coated in classy, cedary oak but driven by a rush of pure, curranty, mint-infused fruit. Dark and luscious with a dry linger of flavour. It will be adored by many, and not unreasonably so. Screwcap. 15% alc. **Rating** 95 **To** 2028 $75 CM

Eden Valley Riesling 2012 Intensity and length. Lime juice and kaffir lime leaf flavours lead into a slatey, talc-like finish. It will cellar, but it's both delicious and impressive young. Screwcap. 12% alc. **Rating** 94 **To** 2024 $27 CM ○

Eden Valley Shiraz 2010 Bold, fruit-driven, plum and tar-flavoured wine with smoky, earthen flashes about the edges. Warm and rich, with some raisiny notes, but generally well balanced. At all points, enjoyable. Ultra-fine seams of tannin complete a seamless picture. Screwcap. 15% alc. **Rating** 94 **To** 2026 $75 CM

Eden Valley Grenache Mataro 2010 Warm, rich and supple. Full-bodied in the take-no-prisoners vein, but it builds such momentum of flavour and flows so effortlessly that it's hard not to be caught up in the rush. Tar, raspberry, clove and earth, with a heart of leathery, licoricey blackberry. Not at all hard to take. Screwcap. 15% alc. **Rating** 94 **To** 2022 $75 CM

Ibizan Wines ★★★★★

PO Box 1525, Margaret River, WA 6285 **Region** Margaret River
T (08) 9757 5021 **www.**ibizanwines.com.au **Open** Not
Winemaker Naturaliste Vintners (Bruce Dukes) **Est.** 2000 **Dozens** 1000 **Vyds** 7.7ha
Brian and Michelle Lowrie found a vineyard in the beautiful but seldom visited Upper Chapman Valley district of Margaret River in 2000. It had 2.7ha of cabernet sauvignon believed to have been planted in 1976, and 5ha of semillon and sauvignon blanc planted in the early '80s. Until '10 the grapes were sold, but in that year the semillon and sauvignon blanc were vinified for Ibizan Wines, and had immediate and significant show success. The name, incidentally, comes from the two red cloud kelpies who have faithfully kept company with Brian and Michelle in the vineyard over the years. They resemble the Egyptian Ibizan hounds who looked after the pharoahs, hence the Egyptian eye on the striking labels.

ΨΨΨΨΨ **Old Vine Margaret River Cabernet Sauvignon 2013** This is a very good Cabernet even by the exalted length of the Margaret River yardstick; both texture (satin brocade) and flavour (cassis concentrate) make an immediate impact when the wine enters the mouth, and keep their mojo through to the finish and aftertaste. Screwcap. 13.5% alc. **Rating** 95 **To** 2043 $27 ○

Margaret River Semillon Sauvignon Blanc 2014 Two trophies Perth Wine Show '14 for Best Semillon Sauvignon Blanc and Best White Wine. It will have appealed to the judges because it is impeccably balanced, its quite delicate flavours effortlessly achieved, lemongrass and snow pea to the fore. Screwcap. 12.4% alc. **Rating** 95 **To** 2017 $22 ○

Idavue Estate ★★★★

470 Northern Highway, Heathcote, Vic 3523 **Region** Heathcote
T 0429 617 287 **www.**idavueestate.com **Open** W'ends 10.30–5
Winemaker Andrew and Sandra Whytcross **Est.** 2000 **Dozens** 600 **Vyds** 5.7ha
Owners and winemakers Andrew and Sandra Whytcross both undertook a two-year winemaking course through the Bendigo TAFE; with assistance from son Marty, they also look after the vineyard, which is planted to shiraz (3ha), cabernet sauvignon (1.9ha), and semillon and chardonnay (0.4ha each). The red wines are made in typical small-batch fashion with hand-picked fruit, hand-plunged fermenters and a basket press.

ΨΨΨΨΨ **Heathcote Shiraz 2012** Sited at the base of Mt Ida, hence the winery name. Beefy blackberry and cloves with top notes of violet. Super intense, concentrated wine leaving nothing to the imagination. Vanillan oak is present, but as a melt rather than as a flamboyant display. Eucalypt through the aftertaste. You have to admire its sheer power and weight. Screwcap. 14% alc. **Rating** 94 **To** 2027 $30 CM ○

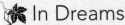 In Dreams

179 Glenview Road, Yarra Glen, Vic 3775 **Region** Yarra Valley
T (03) 8413 8379 **www**.indreams.com.au **Open** Not
Winemaker Nina Stocker **Est.** 2013 **Dozens** 3000
In Dreams is well named, because it is a project that has been 'fizzing away' for nearly eight
years. It is the venture of Nina Stocker (daughter of eminent scientist Dr John Stocker) and
Callie Jemmeson. Their combined winemaking experience has been gained in the Yarra Valley,
Rhône Valley, Barolo, Emilia Romana, California, Alentejo, Central Otago and Marlborough.
The wines are made predominantly from Upper Yarra Valley fruit, hand-picked and small
batch-fermented. Winemaking takes place in a micro winery within the framework of a larger
winery in Yarra Glen.

ŸŸŸŸŸ Yarra Valley Chardonnay 2014 Its Pinot Noir sibling may not have had
enough intensity, but no such issues raise their head here. This is a marvellous
expression of Yarra Valley chardonnay, packed with grapefruit and white peach
on its bouquet and very long palate, the barrel-ferment oak inputs just so. It will
probably be at its best over the next 5 years, for has been fast out of the blocks.
Screwcap. 13.5% alc. **Rating** 95 **To** 2020 $23 ✪
Yarra Valley Pinot Noir 2013 As striking a label as I've seen for years, and a
very interesting story behind the label. This is a seriously good young Pinot, with a
seriously good future. It is flooded with all manner of red fruits, but retains supple,
elegant mouthfeel; its length and balance are the foundation stones of its future.
Screwcap. 13.5% alc. **Rating** 95 **To** 2025 $28 ✪

ŸŸŸŸŸ Yarra Valley Chardonnay 2013 **Rating** 91 **To** 2016 $25

Indigo Wine Company ★★★★★

1221 Beechworth–Wangaratta Road, Everton Upper, Vic 3678 **Region** Beechworth
T (03) 5727 0233 **www**.indigovineyard.com.au **Open** Wed–Sun 11–4
Winemaker Stuart Horden, Marc Scalzo **Est.** 1999 **Dozens** 2600 **Vyds** 46.15ha
Indigo Wine Company has a little over 46ha of vineyards planted to 11 varieties, including the
top French and Italian grapes. The business was and is primarily directed to growing grapes
for sale to Brokenwood, but since 2004 increasing amounts have been vinified for the Indigo
label. The somewhat incestuous nature of the whole business sees the Indigo wines being
made at Brokenwood (Marc Scalzo makes the Pinot Grigio).

ŸŸŸŸŸ Secret Village Beechworth Chardonnay 2014 This provides an altogether
different picture from the Alpine Valleys/Beechworth blend; it is complex from
start to finish, with white peach opening the bowling, grapefruit waiting its turn;
the barrel-ferment oak is more obvious, the texture and structure harmonious.
Screwcap. 13.5% alc. **Rating** 95 **To** 2026 $50
Beechworth Pinot Noir 2014 Very good colour; spice and plum are interwoven
from the bouquet through to the finish and aftertaste; Beechworth can be
unkind to pinot, but not this year – its texture and structure are admirable, pinot
expression sure-footed and long. Will flourish with a few more years' bottle age no
matter how good it is now. Screwcap. 13.4% alc. **Rating** 95 **To** 2027 $35 ✪
Secret Village Beechworth Shiraz 2013 Arguably shiraz and Beechworth
make the ideal couple, over and above all except chardonnay from Giaconda and
Smiths Vineyard (planted '78). Bright crimson-purple; this trips along the tongue,
liberating juicy red fruits, spices and finely worked tannins. A truly lovely wine.
Screwcap. 13.5% alc. **Rating** 95 **To** 2033 $50
Viognier 2014 Clever winemaking, capturing apricot, peach and even a hint of
fresh ginger, yet altogether avoiding phenolics. Screwcap. 12.5% alc. **Rating** 94
To 2020 $32

ŸŸŸŸŸ Chardonnay 2014 **Rating** 93 **To** 2021 $30
Beechworth Sangiovese 2014 **Rating** 92 **To** 2018 $32

Ingoldby ★★★☆

GPO Box 753, Melbourne, Vic 3001 **Region** McLaren Vale
T 1300 651 650 **www**.ingoldby.com.au **Open** Not
Winemaker Kate Hongell **Est.** 1983 **Dozens** 48 000 **Vyds** 37ha
Part of TWE, with the wines now having a sole McLaren Vale source. Over the years Ingoldby has produced some excellent wines, which can provide great value for money.

♥♥♥♥♀ **McLaren Vale Shiraz 2013** A loyal soldier in the service of McLaren Vale. The colour is good, the multi-berry aromas and fruit flavours ranged between purple and black, oak and tannins keeping the show on the road. Screwcap. 14.5% alc. **Rating** 90 **To** 2028 $20 ✪

♥♥♥♥ **McLaren Vale Grenache Shiraz 2013** Rating 89 **To** 2021 $20
McLaren Vale Cabernet Sauvignon 2012 Rating 89 **To** 2027 $20

Inkwell ★★★★★

PO Box 33, Sellicks Beach, SA 5174 **Region** McLaren Vale
T 0430 050 115 **www**.inkwellwines.com **Open** By appt
Winemaker Dudley Brown **Est.** 2003 **Dozens** 800 **Vyds** 12ha
Inkwell was born in 2003 when Dudley Brown returned to Australia from California and bought a rundown vineyard on the serendipitously named California Road. He inherited 5ha of neglected shiraz, and planted an additional 7ha to viognier (2.5ha), zinfandel (2.5ha) and heritage shiraz clones (2ha). The five-year restoration of the old vines and establishment of the new reads like the ultimate handbook for aspiring vignerons, particularly those who are prepared to work non-stop. The reward has been rich. Dudley is adamant the production will be capped at 1000 dozen; almost all the grapes are sold. Exports to the US and Canada.

♥♥♥♥♥ **I&I McLaren Vale Shiraz 2012** Creamy, ripe, voluptuous Shiraz. Fresh through the finish but awash with dark-berried flavour for the most part. Cloves and other woody spice notes. Fruit-shot tannin. Comes at you in waves. Made from estate-grown fruit and matured in French oak, though 85% of this oak is used/old. Fruit shines in all its dark glory. Screwcap. 14.5% alc. **Rating** 95 **To** 2025 $40 CM
Perfect Day McLaren Vale Shiraz 2012 4% primitivo. Name is 'in memory of Lou Reed'. Straightforward blackberry, blueberry and chocolate flavours but excellent density, texture and fruit purity. Inky. Succulent. Tannin buried in the fruit. Superb drinkability. Screwcap. 14.6% alc. **Rating** 95 **To** 2024 $40 CM
Black and Blue Late Harvest Fortified Zinfandel 2012 375ml. 260 bottles made. Matured in very old barrels. If you expected it to be concentrated with sweetness, you'd be bang on. It's a wild ride of prune and licorice, blackberry jam and brandy, though the spirit feels ultra clean and it all flushes out well through the finish. It's balanced. Which, given the extreme hedonism on display, is no mean feat. Diam. 21.5% alc. **Rating** 94 **To** 2020 $35 CM

♥♥♥♥♀ **Road to Joy Shiraz Primitivo 2012** Rating 92 **To** 2023 $25 CM ✪
Blonde on Blonde Viognier 2013 Rating 90 **To** 2017 $21 CM ✪
The Infidel McLaren Vale Primitivo 2012 Rating 90 **To** 2024 $30 CM

Innocent Bystander ★★★★★

336 Maroondah Highway, Healesville, Vic 3777 **Region** Yarra Valley
T (03) 5962 6111 **www**.innocentbystander.com.au **Open** 7 days 9 until late
Winemaker Phil Sexton, Steve Flamsteed **Est.** 1997 **Dozens** 49 000 **Vyds** 45ha
Innocent Bystander is owned by accomplished brewer and winemaker Phil Sexton. A pioneer in both industries, Phil co-founded Matilda Bay and Little Creatures breweries and Devil's Lair winery in Margaret River. Innocent Bystander produces distinctive wines from its Yarra Valley vineyards, each a symbiotic expression of variety and region. Giant Steps focuses on single-vineyard wines, showcasing some of the Yarra Valley's finest sites. The wines are fastidiously produced at its winery in the heart of Healesville, providing a busy backdrop

behind the soaring glass walls for visitors to its must-visit award-winning restaurant and cellar door. Exports to the UK, the US and other major markets.

♟♟♟♟♟ Giant Steps Tarraford Vineyard Chardonnay 2013 The impact of this wine is achieved by stealth, the balance between fruit and acidity sheer perfection, leaving the flavours of white peach and nectarine to insinuate themselves on the long, lingering palate and aftertaste in the fashion that is the hallmark of Yarra Valley Chardonnay at its best. Screwcap. 13% alc. **Rating** 97 **To** 2023 $45 ⊘

♟♟♟♟♟ Giant Steps Sexton Vineyard Chardonnay 2013 Made with a gimlet-like precision and focus; intense grapefruit zest, white peach and peach skin, and underlying acidity, combine to sop up the oak, barrel fermentation simply a means to the end of a complete wine. Screwcap. 13.2% alc. **Rating** 96 **To** 2023 $45 ⊘

Giant Steps Applejack Vineyard Yarra Valley Pinot Noir 2013 Bright, deep and clear crimson; the bouquet is very fragrant, the palate brimming with plum and red and black cherry fruit, yet retaining a fluid grace. A worthy successor to the acclaimed trophy-winning '12. Screwcap. 13.5% alc. **Rating** 96 **To** 2023 $50 ⊘

Mea Culpa Yarra Valley Syrah 2013 From the old Tarraford Vineyard, with an apparently unique clone; hand-picked and 100% whole bunch wild yeast-fermented, peaking at 32°C, matured for 14 months in new and used French puncheons. Vibrant crimson-purple; a fragrant, almost perfumed bouquet with exotic spice and pepper notes is taken to another level by the silk and velvet of the dark fruits of the palate. A micro-millimetre more tannin thrust on the finish might have yielded another point. Screwcap. 13.5% alc. **Rating** 96 **To** 2033 $60 ⊘

Giant Steps Sexton Vineyard Yarra Valley Merlot 2013 Hand-picked, destemmed, fermentation peaking at 32°C, hand-plunged, fermenters sealed for 3-week skin maceration after fermentation complete, matured for 12 months in French oak (40% new), Bright crimson-purple; this is the real Merlot deal, its cassis fruit with veins of dark spice, bramble and black olive running through it. Screwcap. 14% alc. **Rating** 96 **To** 2035 $40 ⊘

Giant Steps Harry's Monster 2013 Bright, deep crimson; a powerful, intense, yet perfectly balanced array of black, blue and red berry fruits; the tannins are woven through the dominant fruit display, new oak used with discretion. A wholly satisfying medium to full-bodied wine with an assured future. Screwcap. 14% alc. **Rating** 96 **To** 2038 $55 ⊘

Giant Steps Sexton Vineyard Yarra Valley Pinot Noir 2013 Very good colour; a vibrantly savoury Pinot, with cherry-accented fruit woven through a spicy/foresty palate of excellent length and persistence. Will richly reward 5 years in the cellar. Screwcap. 13.5% alc. **Rating** 95 **To** 2025 $50

♟♟♟♟♀ Pinot Gris 2014 **Rating** 93 **To** 2016 $20 ⊘

Irvine   ★★★★☆

PO Box 308, Angaston, SA 5353 **Region** Eden Valley
T (08) 8564 1046 www.irvinewines.com.au **Open** At Taste Eden Valley, Angaston
Winemaker Joanne Irvine **Est.** 1980 **Dozens** 9000 **Vyds** 9.5ha
Industry veteran Jim Irvine, who has successfully guided the destiny of so many SA wineries, quietly introduced his own label in 1991. The land (purchased in '80) from which the wines are sourced was planted in '83 to an eclectic mix of merlot (4.2ha), chardonnay (3.1ha), pinot gris (1ha), petit meslier, zinfandel (0.5ha each) and tannat (0.2ha). The flagship is the rich Grand Merlot. Jim has stepped back to allow daughter Joanne to receive the recognition and praise for the wines she makes for the brand (and, for that matter, others). Exports to the UK, Germany, Switzerland, Taiwan, Malaysia, Singapore, Hong Kong and China.

♟♟♟♟♀ Reserve Eden Valley Zinfandel 2012 Sweet and ripe but not to be discounted. This release has a bit of extra something. It tastes of aniseed, jubey blackberry, dust and dry spice, but the fine-grained tannin is integrated to say the least. Much pleasure to be had here. Screwcap. 15% alc. **Rating** 93 **To** 2022 $45 CM

Estate Eden Valley Merlot 2012 Unsurprisingly, Joanne Irvine produces Merlot with the same profile as that previously made by father Jim, rich and velvety, with some barrel-ferment input serving to integrate the oak. A wine made to be enjoyed for what it is, without introspection or undue delay. Screwcap. 14.5% alc. **Rating** 92 **To** 2022 $30

Eden Valley Pinot Gris 2014 More than enough flavour and more than enough texture. Red apples, nashi pears and chalky spice. Fragrant nose; dry food-friendly palate. Screwcap. 13.5% alc. **Rating** 91 **To** 2015 $25 CM

ŸŸŸŸ   **Springhill Barossa Merlot 2012 Rating** 89 **To** 2017 $20

J&J Wines
★★★★☆

Lot 115 Rivers Lane, McLaren Vale, SA 5172 **Region** McLaren Vale
T (08) 8339 9330 **www**.jjvineyards.com.au **Open** Third Thurs each month 10.30–5.30
Winemaker Winescope (Scott Rawlinson) **Est.** 1998 **Dozens** 5000 **Vyds** 5.5ha
J&J is owned and operated by three generations of the Mason family. The estate vineyards are organically managed, but are significantly supplemented by contract-grown grapes. It has come a long way since 2004, when some of the estate grapes were not purchased and were vinified to make wine for the private use of the family. Exports to Hong Kong.

ŸŸŸŸŸ   **Rivers Lane Reserve McLaren Vale Shiraz 2012** Single-vineyard wine, organically grown. Robust style. Strong flavours of blackberry, coffee-cream, mint and ripe, sweet plum. Fine tannin. Big end of town but not without finesse. Screwcap. 14% alc. **Rating** 95 **To** 2026 $50 CM

Rivers Lane McLaren Vale Shiraz 2012 Hearty but exuberant. Flooded with clovey, blackberried flavour. Edged with both sweetness and smoky, earthen flavour. Impressive in all respects. Full-frontal attack on the value equation. Screwcap. 14% alc. **Rating** 94 **To** 2024 $25 CM ❂

ŸŸŸŸŸ   **Adelaide Hills Sauvignon Blanc 2014 Rating** 92 **To** 2015 $19 CM ❂
Boots Hill McLaren Vale Shiraz 2013 Rating 90 **To** 2020 $20 CM ❂

Jack Estate
★★★★☆

15025 Riddoch Highway, Coonawarra, SA 5263 **Region** Coonawarra
T (08) 8736 3130 **www**.jackestate.com **Open** 7 days 10–5
Winemaker Shannon Sutherland, Jarred Stringer **Est.** 2011 **Dozens** 9000 **Vyds** 221ha
The Lees family has been involved in agriculture for over a century, but it was left to Adrian and Dennise Lees (and their son Matthew) to make the transition from general agriculture to viticulture. The business was formally established in 2011, when the family was able to acquire the large Mildara Blass winery and barrel storage to accommodate the Limestone Coast-sourced wines, and the far larger amount from the Murray Darling region, where the family owns 220ha of vineyard (plus 1ha of cabernet sauvignon in Coonawarra). Rachel Lees is responsible for marketing, Matthew (with a degree in civil engineering) is the winery manager. Exports to the UK, the US and China.

ŸŸŸŸŸ   **Mythology Coonawarra Shiraz 2012** Open-fermented, 26 months' maturation in new and used French and American oak. A complex wine that certainly shows its sojourn in oak, but has enough savoury blackberry and mulberry fruits to sustain that oak; the tannins are fine, and underpin the length of the palate. Luxury packaging with a first-class cork. 14% alc. **Rating** 95 **To** 2032 $55

Mythology Coonawarra Cabernet Sauvignon 2012 Matured for 26 months in predominantly French oak. A full-bodied Cabernet with savoury/earthy black fruits, earth, a dab of Coonawarra mint and black olive flavours, well harnessed by oak (cedar and vanilla) and balanced tannins. The cork is as poor as that of the Shiraz is good. 14% alc. **Rating** 94 **To** 2027 $55

ŸŸŸŸŸ   **Coonawarra Cabernet Sauvignon 2013 Rating** 91 **To** 2025 $25

Jack Rabbit Vineyard   ★★★★★

85 McAdams Lane, Bellarine, Vic 3221 **Region** Geelong
T (03) 5251 2223 **www.**jackrabbitvineyard.com.au **Open** 7 days 10–5
Winemaker Nyall Condon **Est.** 1989 **Dozens** 8000 **Vyds** 2ha
Jack Rabbit vineyard is owned by David and Lyndsay Sharp of Leura Park Estate. Its 2ha
of vineyards (planted equally to pinot noir and cabernet sauvignon), take second place to
its Restaurant at Jack Rabbit, plus the House of Jack Rabbit tasting room, cellar door and
café (open 7 days for lunch, Fri–Sat for dinner). The estate vineyards are supplemented by
contract-grown fruit.

ＹＹＹＹＹ   Bellarine Peninsula Pinot Noir 2013 A Cabernet bottle shape is uncommon,
but it didn't stop the wine winning a gold medal and trophy at the Geelong Wine
Show '14. Bright crimson-purple, it has good varietal expression throughout the
bouquet and palate; seamless plum and cherry fruit are the vectors, the finish with
a silky texture and a touch of savoury bramble to add length and complexity.
Screwcap. 13.8% alc. **Rating** 95 To 2023 $35 ✪
Bellarine Peninsula Shiraz 2013 Full crimson-purple; a generously built
wine, but retains shape and balance; has an abundance of plum and black cherry
interlocked with ripe tannins and positive French oak on the medium to full-
bodied palate. Gold medal Geelong Wine Show '14. Screwcap. 13.5% alc.
Rating 95 To 2033 $35 ✪

ＹＹＹＹ   Bellarine Peninsula Riesling 2014 **Rating** 89 To 2017 $30
Bellarine Peninsula Merlot 2013 **Rating** 89 To 2018 $35
Bellarine Peninsula Chardonnay 2013 **Rating** 88 To 2016 $35
Bellarine Peninsula Pinot Grigio 2014 **Rating** 88 To 2015 $35

Jacob's Creek   ★★★★★

Barossa Valley Way, Rowland Flat, SA 5352 **Region** Barossa Valley
T (08) 8521 3000 **www.**jacobscreek.com **Open** 7 days 10–5
Winemaker Bernard Hickin **Est.** 1973 **Dozens** NFP **Vyds** 1600ha
Jacob's Creek is one of the largest-selling brands in the world, and the global success of the
base range has had the perverse effect of prejudicing many critics and wine writers who fail
(so it seems) to objectively look behind the label and taste what is in fact in the glass. Jacob's
Creek has multiple ranges, and all the wines have a connection, direct or indirect, with Johann
Gramp, who built his tiny stone winery on the banks of the creek in 1847. The ranges include
Heritage (Johann Shiraz Cabernet, Steingarten Riesling, Reeves Point Chardonnay and
Centenary Hill Barossa Shiraz); then St Hugo; Reserve (all major varietals); and Classic (ditto).
Exports include the UK, the US, Canada and China, and other major markets.

ＹＹＹＹＹ   St Hugo Vetus Purum Barossa Shiraz 2010 Made in tiny quantities and
only sold in airport shops in Australia, Asia and the US; the packaging is at a level
only previously seen with top-end Special Bin Penfolds reds. It is an outstanding
wine, still amazingly youthful, with a cascade of plum, blackberry, licorice and
multi-spice flavours on the very long, superbly balanced and focused palate. Cork.
14.9% alc. **Rating** 97 To 2040 $188

ＹＹＹＹＹ   St Hugo Vetus Purum Coonawarra Cabernet Sauvignon 2010 As
expected, a wine of considerable quality, breed and finesse; harmony and balance
are its keywords, its varietal character expressed through its cassis and spice fruit.
Not a hair out of place, but doesn't have the same intensity as its Barossa Valley
Shiraz sibling. Cork. 14.9% alc. **Rating** 96 To 2026 $188
Reeves Point Shiraz 2010 Dense red purple. Plush of fruit but sturdy of tannin.
It means business from the outset, delivering powerful plum, peppercorn and
creamy/minty oak flavour in sizeable measure all the way through. Red berry
and spice notes add a keenness to the finish. No-holds-barred but top quality.
Screwcap. 14.1% alc. **Rating** 95 To 2025 $32 CM ✪

Centenary Hill Barossa Valley Shiraz 2010 Anchored on old-vine fruit from multiple vineyard sources; has entered into its first phase of development, with spicy/earthy nuances beneath intense black fruits; the tannins are impeccable, as is the oak handling. Screwcap. 14.2% alc. **Rating** 94 **To** 2025 $82

Double Barrel Coonawarra Cabernet Sauvignon 2012 The palate makes up for a quiet bouquet in no uncertain fashion, with cassis to the fore, and given complexity by touches of Coonawarra earth and herb; classy, integrated and balanced tannins add depth and length. Screwcap. 14.6% alc. **Rating** 94 **To** 2025 $25 ✪

Reeves Point Cabernet Sauvignon 2012 Kangaroo Island cabernet, matured in French oak, old and new. Straight lines of tannin run through minty, curranty, boysenberried fruit flavour. It's fresh, dusty, varietal and built to age. Tannin perhaps leans towards the overly assertive, but there's no question this is impressive. Screwcap. 13.2% alc. **Rating** 94 **To** 2030 $32 CM

▼▼▼▼▽ **Reeves Point Chardonnay 2013** Rating 93 To 2018 $32 CM
Reserve Barossa Shiraz 2013 Rating 93 To 2021 $19 CM ✪
Double Barrel Barossa Shiraz 2012 Rating 93 To 2022 $25 ✪
Reserve Cabernet Sauvignon 2013 Rating 92 To 2021 $19 CM ✪
Double Barrel Cabernet Sauvignon 2013 Rating 92 To 2018 $25 CM ✪
Reserve Limited Edition Margaret River Cabernet Sauvignon 2012 Rating 91 To 2021 $19 CM ✪

JaJa   ★★★★

PO Box 3015, Strathmore, Vic 3041 **Region** Barossa Valley
T 0411 106 652 **www**.jaja.com.au **Open** Not
Winemaker Troy Kalleske (Contract) **Est.** 2003 **Dozens** 500
Brothers Bert and Pierre Werden are the faces behind www.winestar.com.au, which they describe as Australia's leading online fine wine retailer. While it seemed a natural progression for them to develop JaJa as a family label, they say, 'Being in retail was a huge advantage in learning what not to do.' On the positive side was the decision to concentrate on Barossa shiraz, the Stonewell subdistrict, 50-year-old vines, and the services of Troy Kalleske as winemaker. Exports to Singapore and Hong Kong.

▼▼▼▼▼ **JaJa Barossa Shiraz 2010** Still full, bright and deep purple-crimson; carries its alcohol with ease, full of blackberry, plum cake and licorice fruit on the medium to full-bodied palate; the oak and tannins are present, providing balanced support and promising a long life. Screwcap. 14.8% alc. **Rating** 94 **To** 2030 $30 ✪

 # James & Co. Wines   ★★★★

359 Cornishtown Road, Rutherglen, Vic 3685 **Region** Beechworth
T (02) 6032 7556 **www**.jamesandcowines.com.au **Open** Not
Winemaker Ricky James **Est.** 2011 **Dozens** 450
Ricky and Georgie James intended to buy land in Beechworth, and establish a vineyard planted primarily to sangiovese. They say, 'Serendipity led us to Mark Walpole, and we were given the chance to purchase fruit from his Fighting Gully Road Vineyard.' In the meantime, they had set up their home in Rutherglen, and intend to float between the two regions – in their words, 'James & Co. is a winery with a vineyard of no fixed address.' The underlying aim is to produce a lighter-bodied red wine than is usually found in Rutherglen.

▼▼▼▼▽ **Beechworth Sangiovese 2012** Light, but bright, colour; a lively and no-apologies-asked-for style, only medium-bodied in overall weight, but with red cherry/berry fruit disputing primacy with savoury, yet fine, tannins. Fun to be front row, ringside. Screwcap. 14% alc. **Rating** 93 **To** 2022 $35

Beechworth Sangiovese Rose 2014 Dry, textural, savoury-accented style. Pale salmon-crimson colour. Cherries, crushed leaves, aniseed and spice. No lack of power. Screwcap. 14% alc. **Rating** 92 **To** 2016 $18 CM ✪

Beechworth Sangiovese Cabernet 2013 Fleshy blend with just enough savoury spiciness to offset the rush of jubey, berried flavour. Fine run of tannin suggests it will age mid-term but there's no real reason to wait; it's lipsmackingly enjoyable now. Screwcap. 14% alc. **Rating** 92 **To** 2020 $22 CM ✪
Beechworth Sangiovese Cabernet 2012 A 65/35% blend. Essentially jubey and licoricey with an edge of savoury spice. Screwcap. 14% alc. **Rating** 90 **To** 2019 $22 CM

James Estate ★★★★

951 Bylong Valley Way, Baerami, NSW 2333 **Region** Hunter Valley
T (02) 6547 5168 **www.**jamesestatewines.com.au **Open** 7 days 10–4.30
Winemaker Graeme Scott **Est.** 1997 **Dozens** 15 000 **Vyds** 86ha
James Estate has had an unsettled corporate existence at various times since 1997, but has now straightened the ship under the new ownership of Sydney-based businessman, Sam Fayad. Graeme Scott continues in the role of senior winemaker (with his key staff), which bodes well for the future as the winemaking team under his guidance has appreciably lifted wine quality in recent years. Graeme arrived with an impressive Hunter Valley CV, having worked with Jim Chatto and Ross Pearson at First Creek, and at Rothbury Estate before that. The vineyard is planted to shiraz, cabernet sauvignon, merlot, petit verdot, cabernet franc, semillon, chardonnay and verdelho. Cellar doors operate at Baerami, in the Upper Hunter, and at 1210 Hermitage Road, Pokolbin, in the Lower Hunter Valley.

🍷🍷🍷🍷🍷 **Reserve Semillon 2014** Classic Hunter Semillon in every respect: a touch of herb on the bouquet, then intense lemon/lemongrass/grapefruit flavours couched in electric acidity that draws out the palate for a lingering finish. The best is yet to come. Screwcap. 11.5% alc. **Rating** 94 **To** 2029 $23 ✪

Jamieson Estate ★★★★

PO Box 6598, Silverwater, NSW 2128 **Region** Mudgee
T (02) 9737 8377 **www.**jamiesonestate.com.au **Open** Not
Winemaker James Manners **Est.** 1998 **Dozens** 1000 **Vyds** 10ha
Generations of the Jamieson family have been graziers in the region for 150 years, and were able to select 100ha of the most suitable soil from their property on which to establish their vineyard. Beginning in 1998, they planted 89ha of vines, selling the grapes to leading wineries in the region. When the buyers did not renew their contracts, they removed 79ha of vines (leaving 10ha of shiraz), and are now producing small quantities of Semillon Sauvignon Blanc, Chardonnay, Shiraz and Cabernet Sauvignon. Exports to Taiwan and China.

🍷🍷🍷🍷🍷 **Guntawang Shiraz 2013** Mid-weight wine, fruit-driven and blackberried/black cherried for the most part before a savoury, peppery finish. Slight dip at the start of the back-palate but the combination of fruit and spice here has been done well. Screwcap. 14.5% alc. **Rating** 91 **To** 2021 $22 CM ✪

Jamiesons Run ★★★★

Coonawarra Wine Gallery, Riddoch Highway, Coonawarra, SA 5263 **Region** Coonawarra
T (08) 8737 1300 **www.**jamiesonsrun.com.au **Open** 7 days 10–5
Winemaker Andrew Hales **Est.** 1987 **Dozens** NFP
The wheel has turned full circle for Jamiesons Run. It started out as a single-label, mid-market, high-volume brand developed by Ray King during his time as CEO of Mildara. It grew and grew until Mildara, having many years since been merged with Wolf Blass, decided to rename the Mildara Coonawarra winery Jamiesons Run, with the Mildara label just one of a number falling under the Jamiesons Run umbrella. Now the Jamiesons Run winery is no more – Foster's sold it, but retained the brand; the cellar door has moved to shared accommodation at the Coonawarra Wine Gallery. Exports to Asia.

🍷🍷🍷🍷🍷 **Mildara Coonawarra Cabernet Shiraz 2012** A once-famous label (Mildara, not Jamiesons Run) courtesy of Peppermint Pattie, the '63 Cabernet. This is an elegant light to medium-bodied wine with fine tannins in support of its predominantly red-berry fruits, a testament to the vintage. Screwcap. 14% alc. **Rating** 93 **To** 2027 $30

Limestone Coast Cabernet Shiraz Merlot 2012 Rating 89 To 2017 $15 ○

Jamsheed   ★★★★★

157 Faraday Street, Carlton, Vic 3053 (postal) **Region** Yarra Valley
T 0409 540 414 **www.**jamsheed.com.au **Open** Not
Winemaker Gary Mills **Est.** 2003 **Dozens** 1000
Jamsheed is the venture of Gary Mills, proprietor of Simpatico Wine Services, a boutique contract winemaking company established at the Hill Paddock Winery in Healesville. The primary focus is on shiraz (aka syrah) from high-quality Victorian regions, made using indigenous/wild yeasts and minimal handling techniques. The name, incidentally, is that of a Persian king, recorded in the Annals of Gilgamesh.

Pyren Pyrenees Syrah 2013 It has all bases covered. Feel, flavour, complexity and length. You can sink into this one and quite happily lose yourself. Dark plum, menthol, violets and aromatic herbs. It coats the mouth with flavour and then just carries on. Layers, folds, spices and fruit. Undergrowth. Heart of darkness. Refined brilliance. Diam. 13% alc. **Rating** 97 **To** 2035 $54 CM ○

Beechworth Syrah 2013 Pepper, assorted spice, stems and licoricey/ blackberried fruit. Pure Beechworth and pure Jamsheed. Dry, smokin' tobacco notes. Assertive minerally tannin. Floral lift. Nails quality to the wall. Diam. 14.5% alc. **Rating** 96 **To** 2030 $54 CM ○
Seville Syrah 2013 Still sorting itself out but it's bound to mature like a charm. Woodsmoke, intense blackberry and black cherry, fennel and a spray of green garden herbs. Velvety texture carries it all along. Modest input from white pepper and clove. Balance is spot on. Diam. 13.5% alc. **Rating** 95 **To** 2030 $54 CM
Garden Gully Great Western Syrah 2013 Savoury but substantial. Eucalypt, intense black cherry, super-ripe plum and then a slide of cloves, peppers and salts. Assertive meaty tannin. The concentration of fruit, and associated length, here is most impressive. Diam. 14.5% alc. **Rating** 94 **To** 2028 $54 CM

Pepe le Pinot Noir 2014 Rating 89 To 2019 $26 CM
Harem La Syrah 2013 Rating 89 To 2021 $22 CM

Jane Brook Estate Wines   ★★★★☆

229 Toodyay Road, Middle Swan, WA 6056 **Region** Swan Valley
T (08) 9274 1432 **www.**janebrook.com.au **Open** 7 days 10–5
Winemaker Mark Baird **Est.** 1972 **Dozens** 20 000 **Vyds** 18.2ha
Beverley and David Atkinson have worked tirelessly to build up the Jane Brook Estate wine business over the past 40 years. All wines are produced from the estate vineyards in Swan Valley (6.5ha) and Margaret River (11.7ha). Exports to China.

Shovelgate Vineyard Margaret River Cabernet Sauvignon 2011 At the upper end of ripeness but a substantially flavoured release, all blackcurrant, blackberry and asphalt with peppercorn characters popping through the finish. Tannin is fine but mostly sunk into the fruit, and earthen, almost loganberried nuances help build complexity. Completely primary but just starting to mellow. Screwcap. 14.2% alc. **Rating** 93 **To** 2023 $35 CM
Shovelgate Vineyard Margaret River Chardonnay 2011 Straw colour; fluid mix of pear, yellow stone fruit and citrus flavour with a healthy complement of toasty, sweet oak. Drinking at its peak now but still has a couple of years up its sleeve. Linger of citrussy flavour on the finish is most enjoyable. Screwcap. 13.5% alc. **Rating** 91 **To** 2017 $35 CM

Back Block Shiraz 2013 Rating 89 To 2021 $28 CM

Jansz Tasmania ★★★★★

1216b Pipers Brook Road, Pipers Brook, Tas 7254 **Region** Northern Tasmania
T (03) 6382 7066 www.jansztas.com **Open** 7 days 10–4.30
Winemaker Louisa Rose **Est.** 1985 **Dozens** 38000 **Vyds** 30ha

Jansz is part of Hill-Smith Family Vineyards, and was one of the early sparkling wine labels in Tasmania, stemming from a short-lived relationship between Heemskerk and Louis Roederer. Its 15ha of chardonnay, 12ha of pinot noir and 3ha of pinot meunier correspond almost exactly to the blend composition of the Jansz wines. It is the only Tasmanian winery entirely devoted to the production of sparkling wine (although the small amount of Dalrymple Estate wines is also made here), and is of high quality. Part of the former Frogmore Creek Vineyard purchased by Hill-Smith Family Vineyards in Dec 2012 is dedicated to the needs of Jansz Tasmania. Exports to all major markets.

ꙮꙮꙮꙮꙮ **Single Vineyard Vintage Chardonnay 2008** Achieving an exacting and captivating balance between elegant restraint, fruit presence, lees maturity and zesty freshness is the high-wire act of sparkling winemaking, and this is one of Australia's most sublime performances this year. Poise and complexity meet graceful subtlety, seamlessly juxtaposing the rich complexity of barrel fermentation with all the elegance of Tasmanian chardonnay, drawing into a honed vector of lively acidity, deep mineral texture and magnificent persistence. Take (another) bow, Natalie Fryar. Just 2244 bottles. Screwcap. 12.5% alc. **Rating** 96 **To** 2018 $65 TS ❂
Single Vineyard Vintage Chardonnay 2009 Attaining elegance in the midst of characterful expression and grand complexity is one of the ultimate challenges of sparkling winemaking. Natalie Fryar has achieved all three here with consummate flair, upholding the crunch of primary lemon, apple and pear, becoming black cherry in time, gracefully polishing all this with the ginger cake, mixed spice and burnt butter nuances of 5 years of lees maturity. Outstanding length, line and an inherent core of structural confidence are upheld, with a focused, incisive acid line uniting with well-gauged phenolic grip to promise a grand future in the cellar. Just 1212 bottles. Cork. 12% alc. **Rating** 95 **To** 2021 $65 TS
Premium Vintage Rose 2010 The finest two blocks of pinot noir in the Jansz vineyard, entirely fermented in old barrels, aged on lees in bottle and, unusually, only then stained elegantly with red wine at disgorgement, the recipe for the most compelling rose in the country. It unites the elegant watermelon, strawberry hull and guava fruit of fresh Tasmanian pinot noir with the savoury depth and texture of barrel fermentation, creating a rose that is complex and multifaceted yet at every moment upholding a graceful elegance, finely mineral-accented mouthfeel and focused assurance. Screwcap. 12% alc. **Rating** 95 **To** 2016 $48 TS
Premium Vintage Late Disgorged 2005 An almost equal blend of chardonnay and pinot noir from the Jansz vineyard, 40% barrel-fermented. There's real power and generosity on display in this low-cropping, cool, dry vintage – think fig and grilled pineapple. 4 years on lees brings honey on toast, and even notes of truffles to the party. This is not a simple aperitif tipple, but a full-bodied sparkling white wine of sumptuous generosity, enduring persistence and creamy, silky mouthfeel. It retains impeccable control and determination at every moment of this captivating fanfare. Screwcap. 12% alc. **Rating** 94 **To** 2015 $50 TS

ꙮꙮꙮꙮ꙯ **Premium Vintage Late Disgorged 2006** Rating 93 To 2021 $56 TS
Premium Vintage Cuvee 2009 Rating 92 To 2024 $47 TS
Premium Vintage Rose 2011 Rating 92 To 2016 $53 TS
Premium Rose NV Rating 91 To 2016 $32 TS

Jarretts of Orange | See Saw Wine ★★★

Annangrove Park, 4 Nanami Lane, Cargo, NSW 2800 **Region** Orange
T (02) 6364 3118 www.seesawwine.com **Open** By appt **Vyds** 170ha
Winemaker Contract **Est.** 1995 **Dozens** 4000

Justin and Pip Jarrett have established one of the largest vineyards in the Orange region. Varieties include chardonnay (51ha), sauvignon blanc (28ha), shiraz and merlot (22ha ea), pinot gris (15ha), cabernet sauvignon (14ha), pinot noir (11ha), gewurztraminer and prosecco (3ha ea), and marsanne (2ha). They also provide management and development services to growers of another 120ha in the region. A substantial part of the annual production is sold to others. One of the purchasers of Jarretts' grapes was See Saw, a venture owned by Hamish MacGowan (of Angus the Bull) and Andrew Margan. In 2014 Hamish and Andrew decided to concentrate on other wine activities, and Jarretts of Orange was the logical purchaser.

ŸŸŸŸ **See Saw Pinot Gris 2014** From two distinctly different blocks; some lees contact and stirring prior to bottling. A pretty wine with just enough varietal expression to satisfy the Gris classification. Screwcap. 12.1% alc. **Rating** 89 **To** 2015 $25
See Saw Pinot Noir 2014 Made from MV6 and 777 clones. Bright, clear crimson-purple; a mix of red and black cherry plus a touch of plum; the finish exposes some brittle, green acidity, suggesting it was picked a little too soon. Screwcap. 12.8% alc. **Rating** 89 **To** 2019 $25

Jasper Hill ★★★★★

Drummonds Lane, Heathcote, Vic 3523 **Region** Heathcote
T (03) 5433 2528 **www.**jasperhill.com **Open** By appt
Winemaker Ron Laughton, Emily McNally **Est.** 1979 **Dozens** 2500 **Vyds** 26.5ha
The red wines of Jasper Hill are highly regarded and much sought after. Over the past decade drought has caused some variation in style and weight, but as long as vintage conditions allow, these are wonderfully rich and full-flavoured wines. The vineyards are dry-grown and are managed organically. Exports to the UK, the US, Canada, France, Denmark, Hong Kong and Singapore.

ŸŸŸŸŸ **Emily's Paddock Shiraz Cabernet Franc 2013** Good colour, deep and bright; a wine of immediate class, the bouquet with an expressive, complex array of dark fruits, spice and warm earth, the palate adding lively twists of licorice and bitter chocolate; the mouthfeel is outstanding, fine tannins and quality oak adding their imprint. Cork. 14.5% alc. **Rating** 97 **To** 2038 $105 ✪

ŸŸŸŸŸ **Georgia's Paddock Shiraz 2013** Deep, bright, crimson-purple; the bouquet offers a complex array of black fruits, spice, licorice and a hint of smoked meat, the full-bodied palate fulfilling the promises of the bouquet; dusty tannins join with the extravagant fruit, and the wine cries out for time. A gold-plated certainty to repay discipline many times over. Cork. 14.5% alc. **Rating** 96 **To** 2050 $80
Georgia's Paddock Heathcote Nebbiolo 2013 Good hue and depth; a convincing sequel to the '12, even if not scaling the absolute heights of that wine; the bouquet is very fragrant, violets, rose petals and cedar to the fore; and the palate creates great tension between the savoury/spicy notes and the dark cherry-accented fruit. Cork. 13% alc. **Rating** 96 **To** 2030 $68 ✪

jb Wines ★★★☆

PO Box 530, Tanunda, SA 5352 **Region** Barossa Valley
T 0408 794 389 **www.**jbwines.com **Open** By appt
Winemaker Joe Barritt **Est.** 2005 **Dozens** 700 **Vyds** 18ha
The Barritt family has been growing grapes in the Barossa since the 1850s, but this particular venture was established in 2005 by Lenore, Joe and Greg Barritt. It is based on shiraz, cabernet sauvignon and chardonnay (with tiny amounts of zinfandel, pinot blanc and clairette) planted between 1972 and '03. Greg runs the vineyard operations; Joe, with a Bachelor of Agricultural Science degree from Adelaide University, followed by 10 years of winemaking in Australia, France and the US, is now the winemaker. Exports to Hong Kong.

ŸŸŸŸŸ **Cabernet Sauvignon 2011** A dusty bouquet of old books in a library is way amiss as a lead into the cassis-charged fruit of the palate. How this was achieved from '11 is a sweet mystery. Screwcap. 14.4% alc. **Rating** 92 **To** 2021 $25 ✪

♥♥♥♥   Future Perfect Syrah Primitivo NV Rating 89 To 2016 $20
Lola Barossa Valley Zinfandel 2012 Rating 89 To 2020 $25

Jeir Creek   ★★★★

122 Bluebell Lane, Murrumbateman, NSW 2582 **Region** Canberra District
T (02) 6227 5999 www.jeircreekwines.com.au **Open** Thurs–Mon & hols 10–5
Winemaker Rob Howell **Est.** 1984 **Dozens** 3000 **Vyds** 8ha
Rob and Kay Howell, owner–founders of Jeir Creek, celebrated 25 years of involvement
in 2009. Rob runs the technically advanced winery, while Kay looks after the cellar door.
Predominantly an estate-based business, the plantings comprise chardonnay, cabernet
sauvignon (2ha each), riesling, sauvignon blanc, shiraz (1ha each) and smaller plantings of pinot
noir, viognier and muscat.

♥♥♥♥♥   Canberra District Riesling 2014 Medium-intensity lime and slate flavours
build progressively through the palate before reaching a zesty peak. Will age but
no real reason to wait; it's drinking well already. Screwcap. 12.4% alc. **Rating** 91
To 2020 $25 CM

Jericho Wines   ★★★★★

13 Seacombe Cresecent, Seacombe Heights, SA 5047 (postal) **Region** Adelaide Hills
T 0499 013 554 www.jerichowines.com.au **Open** Not
Winemaker Neil and Andrew Jericho **Est.** 2012 **Dozens** 1500
Neil Jericho made wine for over 35 years in Victoria, mainly in the Rutherglen and King
Valley regions, interspersed with stints in Portugal. In this venture the whole family is in
play, with wife Kaye, a 'vintage widow'; eldest daughter Sally, who worked for Wine Australia
for 10 years after working in the Clare Valley, then obtaining marketing and accounting
degrees from the University of Adelaide; and son Andrew, who obtained his Bachelor of
Oenology from the University of Adelaide (in 2003), having worked for 10 years in McLaren
Vale, but then moved outside the square for experience at the highly regarded Grace Vineyard
in the Shanxi Province of China. Son Kim was torn between oenology and hospitality courses
and graphic design, and opted for the latter, providing help with label and point-of-sale design.
Jericho's Single Vineyard McLaren Vale Shiraz '13 won two important trophies at the McLaren
Vale Wine Show '14: Best McLaren Vale Shiraz, and Best Small Producer.

♥♥♥♥♥   Single Vineyard McLaren Vale Shiraz 2013 From a vineyard in the Seaview
district with a steep southern slope, yielding 2 tonnes per acre; fermented for
8 days, then 12 months in new and used French oak. An altogether classy wine
with a sinuous dance between blackberry, plum, bitter chocolate and savoury
tannins. 415 dozen made. Diam. 14% alc. **Rating** 96 To 2034 $35 **O**
Single Vineyard Adelaide Hills Syrah 2013 From a north-facing vineyard
(340m) yielding only 0.5 tonnes per acre; fermented with 10% stalks and 34 days
on skins; 10 months in used French oak. Exceptionally intense, even better than
the '12, with a piercing array of black fruits, and superb tannins providing both
texture and structure. 325 dozen made. Diam. 13% alc. **Rating** 96 To 2033 $35 **O**
Single Vineyard Adelaide Hills Fume Blanc 2014 Barrel-fermented in used
French oak. Its bouquet is fragrant, and essentially driven by the passionfruit/
tropical fruit that appears on entry to the palate, before the flavours morph into
insistent citrus on the finish and lingering aftertaste. 420 dozen made. Screwcap.
12.5% alc. **Rating** 94 To 2018 $25 **O**

♥♥♥♥♥   Single Vineyard Tempranillo 2014 Rating 93 To 2018 $25 **O**
Selected Vineyards Adelaide Hills Fiano 2014 Rating 92 To 2018 $25 **O**

Jester Hill Wines   ★★★★☆

292 Mount Stirling Road, Glen Aplin, Qld 4381 **Region** Granite Belt
T (07) 4683 4380 www.jesterhillwines.com.au **Open** 7 days 10–5
Winemaker Stephen Oliver, Michael Bourke **Est.** 1993 **Dozens** 2000 **Vyds** 7.3ha

A family-run vineyard situated in the pretty valley of Glen Aplin in the Granite Belt. Owners Michael and Ann Bourke aim to concentrate on small quantities of premium-quality wines reflecting the full-bodied style of the region. Most recently they have planted sangiovese and roussanne.

ΥΥΥΥΥ **Touchstone Petit Verdot 2011** Matured in French and American oak. Petit verdot goes everywhere, paying no attention to rain (here a deluge), hail or shine (little thereof). It has layers of blackberry, plum and copious tannins – which will throw in the towel first? Screwcap. 15% alc. **Rating** 91 **To** 2031 $30

Touchstone Sangiovese 2013 Bright hue; doesn't have the same magic as the '12, but nor was the overall vintage as good; nonetheless, there are red cherry/sour cherry fruits and savoury tannins to provide clear-cut varietal character. Screwcap. 12% alc. **Rating** 90 **To** 2016 $25

Jim Barry Wines ★★★★★

33 Craigs Hill Road, Clare, SA 5453 **Region** Clare Valley
T (08) 8842 2261 **www.**jimbarry.com **Open** Mon–Fri 9–5, w'ends, hols 9–4
Winemaker Peter Barry, Tom Barry **Est.** 1959 **Dozens** 80 000 **Vyds** 249ha
The patriarch of this highly successful wine business, Jim Barry, died in 2004, but the business continues under the active management of several of his many children, led by the irrepressible Peter Barry. The ultra-premium release is The Armagh Shiraz, with the McCrae Wood red wines not far behind. Jim Barry Wines is able to draw upon mature Clare Valley vineyards, plus a small holding in Coonawarra. After studying and travelling, third-generation winemaker Tom and commercial manager Sam Barry have joined the business, launching The Barry Bros label, Tom celebrating by winning the Gourmet Traveller Wine Young Winemaker of the Year '13. A founding member of Australia's First Families of Wine. Exports to all major markets.

ΥΥΥΥΥ **The Armagh Shiraz 2009** The vineyard was planted in '68, a drought year requiring each vine to be hand-watered by the family from drums on the back of a tractor, an investment in blood, sweat and tears that has been handsomely repaid. 'Elegance' is a word not usually associated with wines having the dimension of Armagh, but it applies here, yet without betraying the birthright of a wine with exceptional depth to its fusion of dark berries, spices and toasty oak, the latter in the manner of Grange, obvious yet integrated and balanced. Cork. 14.5% alc. **Rating** 96 **To** 2049 $240

The Florita Clare Valley Riesling 2014 From the best rows in the Florita Vineyard. There is a flowery fragrance to the bouquet, and it comes as no surprise to find that the lime juice flavours impact immediately with the first sip. The drive continues through the intense, very long palate and aftertaste, thanks to crisp acidity, not residual sugar. Screwcap. 12.5% alc. **Rating** 95 **To** 2029 $45

Pb Coonawarra Clare Valley Cabernet Shiraz 2010 Coonawarra cabernet sauvignon (60%) and Clare Valley shiraz (40%) with a Schubertian ancestry. The first impression is of elegant complexity, but the afterburners turn on as you reach the finish of the palate, with the tannins of Coonawarra cabernet and the decadent confit ripeness of Clare shiraz. It really needs time, and I hope the corks are better than the one in this bottle. 14.9% alc. **Rating** 95 **To** 2035 $60

The Lodge Hill Riesling 2014 One of the highest vineyards in the Clare Valley, at 480m. Classic dry Clare style, with lemon, lime and apple blossom aromas, the strongly structured palate following suit with a base of chalky/minerally acidity. Screwcap. 11.7% alc. **Rating** 94 **To** 2024 $22 ☉

The McRae Wood Clare Valley Shiraz 2012 I suspect this wine is in transition, and has closed down for its annual holidays; there is nothing amiss, but the black fruits, integrated tannins and oak should be speaking more clearly. Given the vintage and the provenance of the wine, sure to emerge in a year or two. Screwcap. 14% alc. **Rating** 94 **To** 2032 $55

ΥΥΥΥΥ **The Lodge Hill Shiraz 2013 Rating** 93 **To** 2033 $22 ☉
Watervale Riesling 2014 Rating 92 **To** 2020 $19 ☉

Jinglers Creek Vineyard

288 Relbia Road, Relbia, Tas 7258 (postal) **Region** Northern Tasmania
T (03) 6344 5121 **www**.jinglerscreekvineyard.com.au **Open** Thurs–Sun 11–5
Winemaker Bass Fine Wines (Guy Wagner) **Est.** 1998 **Dozens** 250 **Vyds** 2ha
The name dates back to the early 1800s and to the activities of an escaped convict who terrorised the Relbia settlement, stealing from settlers, including their horses. The practice was known as horse jingling and the adjacent creek soon adopted the name it has had ever since. The vineyard is now owned by Mat and Jane Usher, who sensibly have seen no reason to change its name. They have 1.8ha of pinot noir, and small plantings of pinot gris, sauvignon blanc and chardonnay.

Chardonnay 2010 Interesting: gleaming straw-green; bottled in June '10, strongly suggests no oak was used, and the wine in the glass doesn't raise a contrary argument, just proving that if you are going to cellar an unoaked Chardonnay, make sure it is from Tasmania. Screwcap. 13.5% alc. **Rating** 89 **To** 2016 $24

Pinot Gris 2014 A distinct pink tinge to the colour; has followed the kiwi game of leaving some residual sugar partially balanced by acidity. Good for the cellar door. Screwcap. 12.5% alc. **Rating** 88 **To** 2015 $24

Jirra Wines at Jeir Station

Jeir Station, 2443 Barton Highway, Yass, NSW 2582 **Region** Canberra District
T (02) 6227 5671 **www**.jirrawines.com.au **Open** Not
Winemaker Canberra Winemakers **Est.** 2007 **Dozens** 1500 **Vyds** 4ha
The present-day Jeir Station, while a substantial 120ha, was once part of a 6500ha grazing property owned by the Johnston family between 1825 and 1918. The old homestead was built around 1835 by convict labour, and still stands today. In 2000 present owners Colin and Kay Andrews planted shiraz, cabernet sauvignon, chardonnay, viognier and sangiovese, and have the wines contract-made by Rob Howell and Greg Gallagher of Canberra Winemakers.

Shiraz 2013 Snappy value for a $16 wine, the best of the current releases. It has good colour, and an impressive generosity to its mid-palate fruits of black cherry and blackberry; fine tannins and a farewell of French oak complete the picture – except for the great value. Screwcap. 14.3% alc. **Rating** 92 **To** 2025 $16 **☉**

Shiraz Viognier 2008 Co-fermented. This – coupled with its alcohol – provides a wine of extreme power, delicacy and finesse a universe away. That said, it has good balance and complexity, and makes a strong case to be cellared for decades. Screwcap. 14.9% alc. **Rating** 90 **To** 2038 $18 **☉**

Cabernet Merlot 2013 Rating 89 **To** 2028 $16 **☉**

John Duval Wines

PO Box 622, Tanunda, SA 5352 **Region** Barossa Valley
T (08) 8562 2266 **www**.johnduvalwines.com **Open** At Artisans of Barossa
Winemaker John Duval **Est.** 2003 **Dozens** 7000
John Duval is an internationally recognised winemaker, having been the custodian of Penfolds Grange for almost 30 years as part of his role as chief red winemaker at Penfolds. In 2003 he established his eponymous brand; he continues to provide consultancy services to clients all over the world. While his main focus is on old-vine shiraz, he has extended his portfolio with other Rhône varieties. Exports to all major markets.

Eligo Barossa Valley Shiraz 2012 It's deceptive how firm and well scaffolded this wine is. It's a flood of rich, ripe, dark-hearted fruit, all blackberry and anise, peppercorn and coffee, and it feels so fluid that at first you barely notice the tannin at all. It's only on closer investigation (all in the line of duty) that you start to notice the strings. It can be consumed now or much later; it will take either option in its stride. Cork. 14.5% alc. **Rating** 96 **To** 2032 $120 CM

Entity Barossa Shiraz 2013 Tastes of dark, sweet-centred blackberry, chocolate, mocha and ground spices, but the way it combines freshness and depth is the thing; and then there's the way guy ropes of flavour-packed tannin stake a deep hold, aiming to keep everything in place both now and long into the future. Screwcap. 14.5% alc. **Rating** 95 **To** 2030 $50 CM

Annexus Barossa Valley Grenache 2013 Intense red and black-berried flavours, sweet but not confected and with layer after layer of savoury spice, tannin and assorted other delights. Terrific Grenache. Smoky, almost gravelly aftertaste. Length. Screwcap. 14.5% alc. **Rating** 95 **To** 2025 $70 CM

Plexus Marsanne Roussanne Viognier 2013 50% finished fermentation in French oak (10% new), matured in oak for 6 months, the remainder aged in tank on yeast lees. The abundant texture and structure are remarkable until one remembers John Duval's long career at Penfolds, with responsibility for Grange. Screwcap. 13.5% alc. **Rating** 94 **To** 2020 $30 ❂

Plexus Barossa Valley Shiraz Grenache Mourvedre 2013 In beautiful condition and shape. It tastes beautiful. Raspberry, blueberry and blackberry, no alarms or surprises, complemented by woody spice and fine, smoky oak. Everything is where it should be – and where you'd hope it to be. Screwcap. 14.5% alc. **Rating** 94 **To** 2025 $40 CM

♟♟♟♟♟ **Plexus Marsanne Roussanne Viognier 2014 Rating** 92 **To** 2017 $30 CM

John Gehrig Wines ★★★★

Oxley–Milawa Road, Oxley, Vic 3678 **Region** King Valley
T (03) 5727 3395 **www.**johngehrigwines.com.au **Open** 7 days 10–5
Winemaker Ross Gehrig **Est.** 1976 **Dozens** 5600 **Vyds** 85ha
The Gehrig family has been making wine for five generations in Rutherglen, but in August 2011 the shape and size of the business increased exponentially. The purchase of an 80ha vineyard from Rutherglen Winemakers saw estate plantings rise from 6ha to 85ha; the vineyard purchased by Gehrig has a rich history, with an 1870 building known as Snarts Winery operating until the 1940s. Heritage listed, it has been restored and now operates as the cellar door. Work continues to rehabilitate the vineyard; part is used for the significantly increased John Gehrig production, the remainder of the grapes are sold.

♟♟♟♟♟ **RG King Valley Riesling 2011** A generous Riesling, already drawing near to its best, infused with ripe lime flavours and good acidity. Released a year after the '13. Screwcap. 11% alc. **Rating** 94 **To** 2021 $32

♟♟♟♟♟ **Grand Tawny NV Rating** 90 **To** 2016 $32

John Kosovich Wines ★★★★★

Cnr Memorial Ave/Great Northern Hwy, Baskerville, WA 6056 **Region** Swan Valley
T (08) 9296 4356 **www.**johnkosovichwines.com.au **Open** 7 days 10–5.30
Winemaker Anthony Kosovich **Est.** 1922 **Dozens** 4000 **Vyds** 10.9ha
John Kosovich Wines operated as Westfield Wines until 2003, when it changed its name to honour John's 50th vintage. The name change did not signify any change in either philosophy or direction for this much-admired producer of gloriously complex Rare Muscats. The 7.4ha of old vines in the Swan Valley accompany 3.5ha established in Pemberton in 1989. Son Anthony joined his father in 1994.

♟♟♟♟♟ **Reserve Pemberton Cabernet Malbec 2013** An 85/15% blend, hand-plunged and matured in new and used French oak for 12 months, only 4 barrels made each year. It is bright coloured, the fruit flavours and mouthfeel utterly delicious; cassis and plum marry with subtle French oak and feathery tannins. Screwcap. 13.5% alc. **Rating** 95 **To** 2028 $38

Old Vineyard Swan Valley Malbec 2010 From vines planted in '80. Deep colour. It is full of cooked plum, spice and vanilla, but is not tannic or alcoholic. In a very different style from Wendouree, but of near equal quality. Screwcap. 14% alc. **Rating** 95 **To** 2025 $70

Pemberton Chardonnay 2014 Supple, elegant and fresh, it has the white peach and nectarine fruit of its cool region; the oak is purely a means to an end, not an end in itself. A strong argument to capture all the fruit freshness before it is blunted. Screwcap. 13% alc. **Rating** 94 **To** 2020 $36

Bottle Aged Reserve Swan Valley Chenin Blanc 2010 Chenin Blanc made in stainless steel has the capacity to improve out of sight with 5 years' bottle age in the same way as Semillon and Marsanne. Still as fresh as a daisy, it is light on its feet, but with real length and texture – and it's not done yet. Screwcap. 13.5% alc. **Rating** 94 **To** 2020 $35

 Chenin Blanc 2014 **Rating** 90 **To** 2016 $22

John's Blend ★★★★★

18 Neil Avenue, Nuriootpa, SA 5355 (postal) **Region** Langhorne Creek
T (08) 8562 1820 **www**.johnsblend.com.au **Open** At The Winehouse, Langhorne Creek
Winemaker John Glaetzer **Est.** 1974 **Dozens** 1170 **Vyds** 23ha

John Glaetzer was Wolf Blass's right-hand man almost from the word go, the power behind the throne of the three Jimmy Watson trophies awarded to Wolf Blass Wines ('74, '75, '76) and the small matter of 11 Montgomery trophies for the Best Red Wine at the Adelaide Wine Show. This has always been a personal venture on the side, as it were, by John and wife Margarete, officially sanctioned, of course, and needing little marketing effort. Exports to Canada, Switzerland, Indonesia, Singapore and Japan.

♀♀♀♀♀ **Margarete's Langhorne Creek Shiraz 2012** The concentration of black-berried fruit here is phenomenal. It's graded with grainy, coffeed, earthen tannin too. There's oak but it's integrated; the wine is saturated with flavour but it remains keen and fresh. A long future awaits, cork permitting. 14.5% alc. **Rating** 96 **To** 2032 $35 CM ✪

Jones Road ★★★★★

2 Godings Road, Moorooduc, Vic 3933 **Region** Mornington Peninsula
T (03) 5978 8080 **www**.jonesroad.com.au **Open** W'ends 11–5
Winemaker Sticks (Travis Bush) **Est.** 1998 **Dozens** 7500 **Vyds** 26.5ha

It's a long story, but after establishing a very large and very successful herb-producing business in the UK, Rob Frewer and family migrated to Australia in 1997. By a circuitous route they ended up with a property on the Mornington Peninsula, planting pinot noir and chardonnay, then pinot gris, sauvignon blanc and merlot; they have since leased another vineyard at Mt Eliza, and purchased Ermes Estate in 2007.

♀♀♀♀♀ **Nepean Chardonnay 2013** A selection of the best estate-grown chardonnay, winemaking much the same as its junior sibling. While retaining freshness and precision, the fruit here is more juicy and polished, not quite as angular. Screwcap. 12.5% alc. **Rating** 97 **To** 2028 $55 ✪

♀♀♀♀♀ **Chardonnay 2013** Hand-picked, whole bunch-pressed and wild yeast-fermented in new and used French barriques. Has more singular potency and precision than many Mornington Peninsula Chardonnays; it has great length and drive, grapefruit and white peach to the fore. This is a serious Chardonnay with a great future. Screwcap. 12.5% alc. **Rating** 96 **To** 2028 $32 ✪

Nepean Pinot Noir 2013 Full, clear crimson-purple; the bouquet is at once fragrant and focused, setting the scene for the drive and precision of the long palate, its red fruits straying from pure cherry to a touch of the arcane world of cassis, the aftertaste lingering. Screwcap. 13% alc. **Rating** 94 **To** 2028 $55

♀♀♀♀♀ Pinot Gris 2013 **Rating** 93 **To** 2018 $26 ✪

Josef Chromy Wines

370 Relbia Road, Relbia, Tas 7258 **Region** Northern Tasmania
T (03) 6335 8700 **www.**josefchromy.com.au **Open** 7 days 10–5
Winemaker Jeremy Dineen **Est.** 2004 **Dozens** 30 000 **Vyds** 60ha

Joe Chromy just refuses to lie down and admit that the wine industry in Tasmania is akin to a financial black hole in space. After escaping from Czechoslovakia in 1950, establishing Blue Ribbon Meats, using the proceeds of that sale to buy Rochecombe and Heemskerk vineyards, then selling those and establishing Tamar Ridge before it, too, was sold, Joe is at it again; this time he's invested $40 million in a wine-based business. If this were not remarkable enough, Joe is in his 80s, and has recovered from a major stroke. The foundation of the new wine business is the Old Stornoway Vineyard, with 60ha of mature vines, the lion's share to pinot noir and chardonnay. Chromy's grandson, Dean Cocker, is business manager of the restaurant, function and wine centre, which has spectacular views over White Hills to Ben Lomond, the vineyard and the lakes. The homestead is now a dedicated wine centre and cellar door, offering WSET (Wine & Spirit Education Trust) courses. Exports to the UK, Canada, Sweden, Poland, the Czech Republic, Indonesia, Japan and China.

ZDAR Riesling 2011 Pale straw-green; proclaims its Tasmanian citizenship from the first sip, acidity ricocheting around the mouth, playing hide-and-seek with citrus and apple fruit before the chase sorts itself out on the long finish and aftertaste. Screwcap. 12.5% alc. **Rating** 95 **To** 2021 $55

Chardonnay 2013 Has the vibrancy that comes from Tasmanian acidity; it provides a light for the grapefruit and nectarine fruit flavours to shine by, walnut a further adornment ex the oak. Screwcap. 13.5% alc. **Rating** 95 **To** 2020 $34 ✪

ZDAR Chardonnay 2012 Hand-picked, whole bunch-pressed direct to French oak (33% new) for fermentation with a mix of wild and cultured yeasts, matured for 11 months, the first 7 months with lees stirring. It has layered richness to the white peach fruit before the thrust of grapefruit acidity comes through on the finish and aftertaste. Due for release March '16 – an unusual gambit to delay release until 4yo. Screwcap. 13.1% alc. **Rating** 95 **To** 2020 $55

Chardonnay 2014 Barrel-fermented in French oak; the wine launches into a kamikaze attack on the palate, fuelled by Tasmanian acidity. As it ages, other flavours will develop: white peach and some toasty cashew notes, presently lying low, will come to the surface. Screwcap. 13.5% alc. **Rating** 94 **To** 2024 $36

ZDAR Pinot Noir 2012 Good depth of colour typical of Tasmania; a complex, powerful wine that is still seeking to repel all boarders; it starts well on the bouquet and entry to the mouth before stem tannins take control of the back-palate and finish. Has prospects, especially given its release date of March '16. Screwcap. 14% alc. **Rating** 94 **To** 2022 $55

Riesling 2014 Rating 93 **To** 2024 $28
Pinot Gris 2014 Rating 93 **To** 2016 $26 ✪
PEPIK Chardonnay 2014 Rating 92 **To** 2020 $25 ✪
Pinot Noir 2013 Rating 92 **To** 2020 $36
Vintage 2009 Rating 92 **To** 2015 $42 TS
Tasmania Cuvee Methode Traditionale NV Rating 92 **To** 2018 $30
Botrytis 2014 Rating 92 **To** 2024 $28

Joshua's Fault Wines

Amorelle, 1725 Murrumbateman Road, Gundaroo, NSW 2620 **Region** Canberra District
T 0407 077 663 **www.**joshuasfault.com.au **Open** By appt
Winemaker Chris Joshua **Est.** 1995 **Dozens** 500 **Vyds** 4.5ha

Joshua's Fault was established by Chris and Sophie Joshua 10 years ago, but flew under the radar for a decade, largely – but not entirely – because its main focus was growing high-quality grapes for local and Hunter Valley wineries. The name is not like Lake's Folly, a whimsical, self-deprecating word play. It derives from two major geological faultlines that run north–south either side of the vineyard. They were created 40 million years ago, and provide ideal viticultural soil. Chris completed a Diploma of Viticulture at CSU, and purchased the property in 1994, initially planting cabernet and chardonnay with numerous clones. Later plantings of shiraz and merlot took the total to 4.5ha, and each year they retain sufficient grapes to make 500 dozen bottles. They plan to open the cellar door on a regular basis as their children get older.

TTTTT **Amorelle Dry Red 2009** This is the first blend of cabernet, shiraz and merlot, and will only be made in the best years. The colour is remarkably vibrant, the medium-bodied palate with precisely the fresh cassis and redcurrant fruit the colour suggests; the tannins are fine, but do provide sufficient structure for the wine to continue to prosper. Screwcap. 13.5% alc. **Rating** 93 **To** 2024 $42
Rose 2014 100% cabernet sauvignon. Pale puce colour, with a fresh red berry bouquet; the palate is refreshingly crisp and dry, with a faint echo of the savoury nature of cabernet adding to the complexity of a well made wine. Screwcap. 13% alc. **Rating** 90 **To** 2016 $18 ✪
Cabernet Sauvignon 2008 Exceptional retention of colour, and, for that matter, varietal definition; it is attractively savoury, with a freshness suggesting a low pH, and redcurrant more than blackcurrant on its light to medium-bodied palate. Screwcap. 13.6% alc. **Rating** 90 **To** 2023 $28

TTTT **Chardonnay 2013** **Rating** 89 **To** 2017 $28
Shiraz 2013 **Rating** 88 **To** 2017 $26

Journey Wines ★★★★★

1a/29 Hunter Road, Healesville, Vic 3777 (postal) **Region** Yarra Valley
T 0427 298 098 **www**.journeywines.com.au **Open** Not
Winemaker Damian North **Est.** 2011 **Dozens** 2500
The name chosen by Damian North for his brand is particularly appropriate given the winding path he has taken before starting (with his wife and three youngish children) his own label. Originally a sommelier at Tetsuya's when it was still at Rozelle (and at Pier), he was inspired to enrol in the oenology course at CSU, gaining his first practical winemaking experience as assistant winemaker at Tarrawarra Estate for a number of years. Then, with family in tow, he moved to Oregon's Benton-Lane Winery to make pinot noir for several years, before returning to become winemaker at Leeuwin Estate for five years, indulging in his other vinous passion, chardonnay. The wheel has turned full circle as the family has returned to the Yarra Valley, securing 2ha of chardonnay, 2.5ha of pinot noir and 2ha of shiraz under contract arrangements with three distinguished vineyards, and making the wines at Medhurst. Exports to Hong Kong.

TTTTT **Heathcote Shiraz 2013** 75% destemmed, 25% whole bunches, wild yeast open-fermented with 15 days on skins, matured for 16 months in French barriques (33% new). Manages to combine complexity and power with elegance and balance; a compote of black fruit flavours is laced with licorice, a touch of tar, and authoritative tannins. Will be very long-lived, kicking more goals along the way. Screwcap. 13.5% alc. **Rating** 96 **To** 2043 $40 ✪
Yarra Valley Pinot Noir 2013 Wild yeasts, open-fermented with 20% whole bunches, 9 months in French barriques (20% new). Light, clear red-purple; a very well made Pinot, the bouquet fragrant, the palate seductively supple and long, red fruits dominant until a pleasing savoury echo of the whole bunches appears on the finish. Screwcap. 13% alc. **Rating** 95 **To** 2022 $34 ✪

TTTTT **Yarra Valley Chardonnay 2013** **Rating** 93 **To** 2025 $34

Journeys End Vineyards ★★★★

Level 7, 420 King William Street, Adelaide, SA 5000 (postal) **Region** South Eastern Australia
T 0431 709 305 **www**.journeysendvineyards.com.au **Open** Not
Winemaker Ben Riggs (Contract) **Est.** 2001 **Dozens** 10 000
An interesting virtual winery, which, while focused on McLaren Vale shiraz, also has contracts for other varieties in the Adelaide Hills and Langhorne Creek. The Shiraz comes in four levels and, for good measure, uses five different clones to amplify the complexity that comes from

having grapegrowers in many different parts of McLaren Vale. Exports to the UK, the US, Malaysia, Singapore, Hong Kong, China and NZ.

ΥΥΥΥ **The Return Watervale Riesling 2009** Glowing straw-green. Developed but drinking well. Lime jelly, lemongrass, mandarin and kaffir lime. Bright presentation of flavour. Ready to go. Screwcap. 12% alc. **Rating** 92 **To** 2019 $25 CM ✪
Three Brothers Reunited Shiraz 2012 While the wine always offers good value, it exceeds itself here, thanks in part to the superb vintage, and in part to the skill (and grower contacts) of winemaker Ben Riggs. It is only just medium-bodied, a plus for early drinking, the plum, licorice and small black fruits supple and smooth. Screwcap. 14.5% alc. **Rating** 91 **To** 2018 $11 ✪
Coonawarra Station Cabernet Sauvignon 2010 Much drinking pleasure to be tucked into here. Peppermint, blackcurrant and sweet boysenberry fruit flavour is given a seductive boost by coffeed oak. Game and tobacco notes play about the edges; it's just starting to mellow out. Drink soonish. Screwcap. 14.5% alc. **Rating** 90 **To** 2019 $20 CM ✪

Juniper Estate ★★★★★

98 Tom Cullity Drive, Cowaramup, WA 6284 **Region** Margaret River
T (08) 9755 9000 **www.**juniperestate.com.au **Open** 7 days 10–5
Winemaker Mark Messenger **Est.** 1973 **Dozens** 12 000 **Vyds** 19.5ha
When Roger Hill and Gillian Anderson purchased the Wrights' vineyard in 1998, the 10ha vineyard was already 25 years old, but in need of retrellising and a certain amount of nursing to bring it back to health. All of that has happened, along with the planting of additional shiraz and cabernet sauvignon. The Juniper Crossing wines use a mix of estate-grown grapes and grapes from other Margaret River vineyards, while the Juniper Estate releases are made only from the estate plantings. The death of Roger Hill in a traffic accident in May '13 was (obviously) not foreseen, but wife Gillian continues running Juniper Estate and Higher Plane. Exports to the UK, the US, Ireland, Canada, Hong Kong, the Philippines, Singapore and NZ.

ΥΥΥΥΥ **Margaret River Aquitaine 2013** A 60/40% blend of sauvignon blanc and semillon, wild yeast barrel-fermented, matured for 10 months in French barriques (25% new). Yes, this is a blend that Margaret River produces well and consistently, but this wine adds a further dimension to the blend; it is at once intense and complex, yet with finesse and elegance; the oak, wild yeast, lees, sauvignon blanc and semillon all contribute to a seamless stream of bright flavour. Screwcap. 13% alc. **Rating** 96 **To** 2020 $30 ✪
Margaret River Shiraz 2012 Estate-grown, hand-picked in batches over 9 days and cold-soaked, matured in French hogsheads (40% new) for 18 months, a barrel selection for the final blend. A lovely wine, effortlessly ticking all the boxes, leaving red and black cherry fruit free rein to fill the bouquet and fore-palate, the fruit in turn allowing superfine tannins and high-quality oak to line up in support. Screwcap. 14.5% alc. **Rating** 96 **To** 2032 $38 ✪
Margaret River Cabernet Sauvignon 2011 From 52yo cabernet vines (87%), malbec (6%), franc (6%) and petit verdot (3%); 5 days' cold soak, fermentation/maceration 10–31 days, matured for 18 months in French barriques (50% new). The colour is still primary crimson-purple, the bouquet and flavours of cassis/blackcurrant interwoven with notes of bramble, cedar, bay leaf and perfectly weighted tannins. Screwcap. 14% alc. **Rating** 96 **To** 2036 $60 ✪
Margaret River Semillon 2013 Barrel-fermented, 50% with wild yeast, 50% inoculated, matured for 10 months in French barriques (33% new). Here the refrain is of elegance, purity and balance, a testimonial to the cleverness of controlling and balancing all of the inputs, ending up with a Semillon that waits until the finish and aftertaste to explode into life (and lingering flavour). Screwcap. 13% alc. **Rating** 95 **To** 2023 $30 ✪
Margaret River Chardonnay 2013 In the hallmark Juniper style, where all the complexity of the winemaking approach melts like ice in the noon-day sun, leaving a perfectly formed, perfectly balanced and elegant Chardonnay that simply needs time to burst into full song. Screwcap. 13% alc. **Rating** 95 **To** 2025 $38

Juniper Crossing Margaret River Cabernet Sauvignon 2012 From estate declassified barrels and some younger vine material; includes 8% malbec and 2% petit verdot; matured for 15 months in French oak (25% new). There's no escaping the hedonism of this wine; it fills the mouth with a cornucopia of red and black fruits, spices, ripe tannins and quality oak all in perfect balance, the next glass coming soon. Screwcap. 14% alc. **Rating** 95 **To** 2025 $25 ○

Juniper Crossing SSB 2014 Rating 94 **To** 2016 $20 ○
Juniper Crossing Chardonnay 2014 Rating 94 **To** 2025 $22 ○
Margaret River Aquitaine Rouge 2012 Rating 94 **To** 2037 $38
Juniper Crossing Tempranillo 2013 Rating 94 **To** 2023 $22 ○

ΨΨΨΨΨ **Juniper Crossing Shiraz 2013 Rating** 93 **To** 2028 $22 ○
Juniper Crossing Merlot 2012 Rating 93 **To** 2022 $22 ○
Juniper Crossing Cabernet Merlot 2012 Rating 93 **To** 2022 $20 ○

Just Red Wines   ★★★★

2370 Eukey Road, Ballandean, Qld 4382 **Region** Granite Belt
T (07) 4684 1322 **www.**justred.com.au **Open** W'ends & public hols 10–5
Winemaker Michael Hassall **Est.** 1998 **Dozens** 1500 **Vyds** 2.6ha
Tony, Julia and Michael Hassall have planted shiraz and merlot (plus cabernet sauvignon, tannat and viognier not yet in production) at an altitude of just under 900m. They minimise the use of chemicals wherever possible, but do not hesitate to protect the grapes if weather conditions threaten an outbreak of mildew or botrytis. The Hassalls' daughter, Nikki, was very much involved in the creation of the vineyard, and was driving back from university to be there for the first day of picking. In the ultimate cruel finger of fate, the car crashed and she was killed. After a pause, wine production has been resumed.

ΨΨΨΨΨ **Granite Belt Tannat 2014** Vivid, full crimson-purple; easily the best of the Just Red releases, with bright fruits encased in velvety tannins; will repay cellaring, although the balance is such that it can be enjoyed now. Screwcap. 13.2% alc. **Rating** 94 **To** 2029 $35

ΨΨΨΨΨ **Granite Belt Shiraz Viognier 2014 Rating** 90 **To** 2020 $25

Kaesler Wines   ★★★★★

Barossa Valley Way, Nuriootpa, SA 5355 **Region** Barossa Valley
T (08) 8562 4488 **www.**kaesler.com.au **Open** 7 days 11–5
Winemaker Reid Bosward **Est.** 1990 **Dozens** 20000 **Vyds** 50ha
The first members of the Kaesler family settled in the Barossa Valley in 1845. The vineyards date back to 1893, but the Kaesler family ownership ended in 1968. After several changes, the present (much-expanded) Kaesler Wines was acquired by a small group of investment bankers (who have since acquired Yarra Yering), in conjunction with former Flying Winemaker Reid Bosward and wife Bindy. Reid's experience shows through in the wines, which now come from estate vineyards, 40ha adjacent to the winery, and 10ha in the Marananga area. The latter includes shiraz planted in 1899, with both blocks seeing plantings in the 1930s, '60s, then each decade through to the present. Exports to all major markets.

ΨΨΨΨΨ **Old Bastard Barossa Valley Shiraz 2012** Sourced from a block on the estate vineyard at Nuriootpa planted in 1893; hand-picked and matured in French oak (35% new, 65% 1yo); vinification 'a closely guarded secret'. A fragrant bouquet of red, purple and black fruits tightly spun together in a fine coat of black chocolate; shares the medium-bodied elegance of Alte Reben, with even more freshness on the lingering finish. A special wine. Cork. 14.5% alc. **Rating** 98 **To** 2047 $220

The Bogan 2012 From 1899 and 1965 estate plantings, matured in French (75%) and American oak for 15 months. An exceptional pedigree reflected in a Shiraz of rare elegance, balance and finesse; its supple, medium-bodied palate is almost lipsmacking, so juicy is it, but there is no shortage of texture or structure. Cork. 14% alc. **Rating** 97 **To** 2045 $50 ○

Alte Reben Barossa Valley Shiraz 2012 From the estate 3.7ha vineyard at Marananga planted in 1899, a national treasure; hand-picked, 8 days on skins, matured in new (35%) and used French oak for 20 months. The most surprising feature of the wine is its sheer elegance and light to medium body; its length and superfine tannins and oak will sustain it for as long as the cork lasts. 14% alc. **Rating** 97 **To** 2042 $150 ✪

WOMS Shiraz Cabernet 2010 From shiraz planted in '61 and cabernet planted in '85, each separately vinified and matured in new French oak for 18 months, with a barrel by barrel selection – hence weapon of mass selection. Dense purple-crimson; velvety, supple fruit simultaneously reaches every corner of the mouth, the trifecta of rich black fruits, oak and tannins a guaranteed stayer and winner. Cork. 14.5% alc. **Rating** 97 **To** 2045 $70 ✪

ⓎⓎⓎⓎⓎ **Old Vine Barossa Valley Semillon 2014** Vines planted in '60, the wine with inspiration from the Hunter Valley, Graves (Bordeaux) and the Barossa Valley. Early picking resulted in an extremely low pH (2.79), yet curiously left a tapestry of flavours of citrus of all kinds, and a supple mouthfeel feeding into a long, crisp finish. Screwcap. 10.5% alc. **Rating** 95 **To** 2024 $22 ✪

Old Vine Barossa Valley Shiraz 2012 Spends 10 days on skins, then 23 months in French oak (30% new). A very different mouthfeel from Alte Reben and Old Bastard, unequivocally full-bodied, built on a scaffold of tannins, with layers of black fruits and tannins. This needs more time in bottle, but has the balance to repay patience. Cork. 14.5% alc. **Rating** 95 **To** 2032 $80

Avignon Barossa Valley Grenache Shiraz 2012 A medium-bodied 86/14% blend of 83yo grenache and 52yo shiraz. The flavours of red and black cherry fruit have no hint of confection; the tannins are fine and ripe, the oak integrated. Comes with a back label request to decant, I'm not quite sure why. Screwcap. 15% alc. **Rating** 95 **To** 2027 $35 ✪

Barossa Valley Viognier 2013 Rating 94 **To** 2017 $25 ✪
Stonehorse Shiraz 2012 Rating 94 **To** 2022 $25 ✪
Stonehorse Grenache Mourvedre Shiraz 2012 Rating 94 **To** 2022 $22 ✪

🍇 Kakaba Wines ★★★★☆

PO Box 348, Hahndorf, SA 5245 **Region** Adelaide Hills
T 0438 987 010 www.kakaba.com.au **Open** Not
Winemaker Greg Clack **Est.** 2006 **Dozens** 7000

When I send an email to a new winery for the *Companion*, I ask what inspired the vigneron to entertain the folly of starting a new winery. Chris Milner, with wife Jill in tow, responded by saying, '… it has been an enjoyable journey and, incredible as it may seem, moderately profitable, which I attribute to having zero overheads (no vineyards and no winery), zero employees (Jill and I don't get paid) and zero bank debt (too much debt will kill you every time!)'. He had the great advantage of having worked in the wine business since the late 1990s, mainly in the finance and commercial operations of various businesses. In 2006 there was an opportunity to source premium wine from the Adelaide Hills, and sell it to other wineries as bulk either during vintage or shortly thereafter. This worked very well in '06 and '07, but then came the super-abundant vintage of '08, with supply exceeding demand. Because of his wisdom the business survived, and continued, finally moving to bottle some wine under its own labels, Cat's Eyes and Milner of Hahndorf. In '13 they appointed Greg Clack as winemaker and gave him some good French oak. This resulted in the Reserve range, and the Cabernet Sauvignon winning the trophy for Best Cabernet at the Adelaide Hills Wine Show '14.

ⓎⓎⓎⓎⓎ **Reserve Shiraz 2013** Finished fermentation in and matured in French oak (60% new) for 18 months. The excellent crimson colour heralds a medium-bodied wine that ticks all the boxes of a cool-grown Shiraz that has made light of the new oak; the fragrant bouquet of spicy, peppery black cherry is at one with the beautifully fine and detailed palate, the finish exceptionally long. Screwcap. 14% alc. **Rating** 95 **To** 2035 $33 ✪

Reserve Cabernet Sauvignon 2013 An altogether welcoming style of Cabernet, with cassis, bay leaf and unusually soft (for Cabernet) and persistent tannins; the wine is dry, but the cassis has a seductive sweetness to it, and it will all be consumed long before its drink-to date. Screwcap. 14% alc. **Rating** 94 **To** 2028 $33

❢❢❢❢❢ **Milner of Hahndorf The Sculptor Sangiovese 2013** Rating 90 To 2017 $18 ✪

Kalleske   ★★★★★

6 Murray Street, Greenock, SA 5360 **Region** Barossa Valley
T (08) 8563 4000 **www.**kalleske.com **Open** 7 days 10–5
Winemaker Troy Kalleske **Est.** 1999 **Dozens** 15 000 **Vyds** 48ha
The Kalleske family has been growing and selling grapes on a mixed farming property at Greenock for 140 years. Sixth-generation Troy Kalleske, with brother Tony, established the winery and created the Kalleske label in 1999. The vineyard is planted to shiraz (27ha), grenache (6ha), mataro (2ha), chenin blanc, durif, viognier, zinfandel, petit verdot, semillon and tempranillo (1ha each). The vines vary in age, with the oldest dating back to 1875, and the overall average age is around 50 years; all grown organically. Exports to all major markets.

❢❢❢❢❢ **Greenock Single Vineyard Barossa Valley Shiraz 2013** A more tannic release than we've come to expect under this label, though the fruit in support here is exciting. This is a Barossa Shiraz for the ages. Mighty but meticulously well crafted, awash with blueberry, blackberry, saltbush and coffee-cream flavour, and boasting a finish that sets sail for tomorrow. Classic. Screwcap. 14.5% alc. **Rating** 98 **To** 2043 $40 CM ✪

❢❢❢❢❢ **Root Biodynamic Barrel Project Shiraz 2013** Deep, dark and brooding. Ropes of tannin. Quite distinct and different from the 'fruit' version of the same wine. Blackberry and dark chocolate flavours abound. Profound wine. Screwcap. 14.5% alc. **Rating** 96 **To** 2035 $50 CM ✪
Johann Georg Old Vine Single Vineyard Shiraz 2012 Monumental in some ways, seamless in others. Thick leather, blackberry and mocha notes lead through to a long, supple, well-mannered and even-tempered finish. Brute in a tuxedo. Quite exemplary. Screwcap. 14% alc. **Rating** 96 **To** 2035 $120 CM
Moppa Barossa Valley Shiraz 2013 Includes 10% petit verdot and 5% viognier. blended rather than co-fermented. There's certainly nothing shy or dull about the fruit here. Purple-black, dark berried, toasty, slightly spicy. Incredibly fresh and juicy and yet the tannin profile has not been compromised. Biodynamically grown. Screwcap. 14.5% alc. **Rating** 95 **To** 2026 $28 CM ✪
Fruit Biodynamic Barrel Project Shiraz 2013 The oak was coopered on a 'fruit' day, according to the biodynamic calendar. Perhaps it's the power of suggestion, but this wine certainly tastes of fruit; dried peel and apricot, essentially into Christmas cake territory. These characters are backed by a wealth of blackberried, chocolatey, smooth-skinned flavours. BD experiments aside, the wine is excellent. Screwcap. 14.5% alc. **Rating** 95 **To** 2030 $50 CM
Merchant Single Vineyard Barossa Valley Cabernet Sauvignon 2013 Burly Cabernet with essence-like fruit flavour. Big revs of berry-soaked tannin, blackcurrant and truffle, mint and clovey herbs. Fruit builds tremendous momentum before tannin applies the brakes. Monty for the cellar. Screwcap. 13.5% alc. **Rating** 95 **To** 2030 $28 CM ✪
Buckboard Single Vineyard Barossa Valley Durif 2013 You'd think butter wouldn't melt in its mouth, judging by the velvety softness of the fruit, but the wine's iron chains of tannin are a force to be reckoned with. Durif is fast proving to be a star of the Kalleske estate. Saturated plum, tar, vanilla and chicory notes with dark, brooding extension of fruit out through the finish. Screwcap. 15% alc. **Rating** 95 **To** 2025 $24 CM ✪
JMK Shiraz VP 2014 Impressive balance and style; relatively dry and spicy, with complex fruit and oak. Seriously good. Bred to stay. Screwcap. 18% alc. **Rating** 95 **To** 2034 $23 ✪

Barossa Valley Rosina 2014 Rating 94 To 2015 $19 CM ✪
Pirathon by Kalleske Shiraz 2013 Rating 94 To 2021 $23 CM ✪
Flower Biodynamic Barrel Project Shiraz 2013 Rating 94 To 2030 $50 CM
Old Vine Single Vineyard Barossa Valley Grenache 2013 Rating 94
To 2024 $45 CM
Clarry's Barossa Valley GSM 2014 Rating 94 To 2025 $20 CM ✪

Kangarilla Road Vineyard ★★★★★

Kangarilla Road, McLaren Vale, SA 5171 **Region** McLaren Vale
T (08) 8383 0533 **www.**kangarillaroad.com.au **Open** Mon–Fri 9–5, w'ends 11–5
Winemaker Kevin O'Brien **Est.** 1997 **Dozens** 65 000 **Vyds** 14ha
In Jan 2013 Kangarilla Road founders Kevin O'Brien and wife Helen succeeded in breaking the mould for a winery sale, and crafted a remarkable win–win outcome. They sold their winery and surrounding vineyard to Gemtree Vineyards, which has had its wine made at Kangarilla Road since '01 under the watchful eye of Kevin. The O'Briens have retained their adjacent JOBS Vineyard and the Kangarilla Road wines continue to be made by Kevin at the winery. Luck of the Irish, perhaps. Exports to the UK, the US and other major markets.

ŶŶŶŶŶ Q McLaren Vale Shiraz 2012 This is full-bodied, but has convincing shape, texture and balance; there are quality sultry black fruits, oak and tannins, none going over the top, but all contributing, dark chocolate conspicuous by its absence. All in all, a tour de force. Screwcap. 14.5% alc. **Rating** 96 To 2042 $70 ✪
Black St Peters McLaren Vale Zinfandel 2013 Tasted alongside its basic McLaren Vale sibling, one has to concede alcohol at this level has to be accepted at face value, and the wine tasted without prejudice. For this has a wonderfully exotic array of spices woven through its predominantly red fruits. Top-quality Zinfandel with impressive balance. Screwcap. 16% alc. **Rating** 96 To 2025 $70 ✪
Alluvial Fans McLaren Vale Shiraz 2013 The vignerons of McLaren Vale continue to gnaw on the bones of their belief that the myriad soils and subsoil/ parent rocks can be seen in their wines. Tasting the grapes, the wine while it's fermenting, and as it matures in barrel and then in bottle gives them a reference library that the taster/consumer does not have. All I can see is a wine that shrieks of McLaren Vale, with vivid black and red fruits and dark chocolate flavours, and that is of obvious quality. Screwcap. 14.5% alc. **Rating** 95 To 2043 $45
Blanche Point Formation McLaren Vale Shiraz 2013 Deeply, vividly coloured and stacked full of flavour from go to whoa; ultra-typical high-quality McLaren Vale Shiraz, black fruits and dark chocolate doing the heavy lifting; it is marginally rounder in the mouth than Alluvial Fans, but the intensity of the two wines means that repeated tastings of each tend to anaesthetise the palate. Screwcap. 14.5% alc. **Rating** 95 To 2043 $45

ŶŶŶŶŶ McLaren Vale Shiraz 2013 Rating 93 To 2033 $25 ✪
McLaren Vale Sangiovese 2013 Rating 93 To 2030 $30
Adelaide Hills Pinot Grigio 2014 Rating 92 To 2015 $20 CM ✪
Duetto 2014 Rating 92 To 2016 $25 CM ✪
McLaren Vale Cabernet Sauvignon 2013 Rating 92 To 2025 $25 ✪
McLaren Vale Primitivo 2013 Rating 92 To 2020 $30

Karatta Wines ★★★★

292 Clay Wells Road, Robe, SA 5276 **Region** Robe
T (08) 8735 7255 **www.**karattawines.com.au **Open** W'ends & hols 11–4
Winemaker Duane Coates **Est.** 1994 **Dozens** 4000 **Vyds** 39.6ha
Owned by David and Peg Woods, Karatta Wines is named after Karatta House, one of Robe's well-known heritage-listed icons. Built in 1858, Karatta House was occupied by the South Australian Governor, Sir James Fergusson, during the summers of 1868 to '71. Vineyards include the 12 Mile Vineyard and Tenison Vineyard, both in the Robe region.

ŸŸŸŸŸ **Robe Shiraz 2013** Matured in French barriques (40% new). Brilliant crimson-purple; flush with black cherry and blackberry on the supple, medium to full-bodied palate, it eats, breathes and sleeps value for money. If you are looking for a $20 wine to lay down for someone's year of birth, this does the trick, for it also has length and balance. How anyone can spend so much money on oak is beyond my ken. Screwcap. 13.8% alc. **Rating** 94 **To** 2034 $20 ✪

ŸŸŸŸŸ **Robe Cabernet Sauvignon 2013 Rating** 93 **To** 2028 $20 ✪

Karrawatta   ★★★★★

818 Greenhills Road, Meadows, SA 5201 **Region** Adelaide Hills/Langhorne Creek
T (08) 8537 0511 **www**.karrawatta.com.au **Open** By appt
Winemaker Mark Gilbert **Est.** 1996 **Dozens** 925 **Vyds** 46ha
Mark Gilbert is the great-great-great-grandson of Joseph Gilbert, who established the Pewsey Vale vineyard (and winery) in 1847. What is not generally known is that Joseph Gilbert had named the property Karrawatta, a name already in use for another property. The right to use the name was decided on the toss of a coin in a local SA pub, forcing Gilbert (who lost) to relinquish the Karrawatta name and adopt Pewsey Vale instead. The Karrawatta of today is not in the Barossa Ranges, but the Adelaide Hills; there is a neat coincidence here, because in 1847 Pewsey Vale was the highest vineyard planting in SA, and Mark Gilbert's Karrawatta is one of the highest plantings in the Adelaide Hills. It is true he only has 14ha of vines here, and 32ha in Langhorne Creek, but never let facts get in the way of a good story.

ŸŸŸŸŸ **Limited Edition Dairy Block Adelaide Hills Shiraz 2013** Exciting release from a newish label, though it's grown on mature vines. It's a complex, spicy red with bold, exuberant fruit stuffing. Red and black berries, swish cedary oak, crushed leaves and a modest smattering of black pepper. Both substantial and thoroughly stylish. Screwcap. 14.5% alc. **Rating** 95 **To** 2024 $38 CM
Limited Edition Christo's Paddock Langhorne Creek Cabernet Sauvignon 2013 Substantial fruit weight and length to match. This certainly covers the bases. Blackcurrant, syrupy plum, melted milk chocolate and mint. It oozes and slides but has tension and tannin to close; it's a beauty. Screwcap. 14.7% alc. **Rating** 95 **To** 2035 $54 CM
Anna's Adelaide Hills Sauvignon Blanc 2014 Aged on lees in old French oak with some mlf. Fruit intensity comes across as diamond-cut. Passionfruit, cut grass, hay and apple. Terrific fruit purity but textural, smoky, spicy too. Excellent quality. Screwcap. 12% alc. **Rating** 94 **To** 2016 $26 CM ✪
Limited Edition Joseph Langhorne Creek Shiraz 2013 It offers a power of fruit and oak but it does so with a firm sense of control. Black berries, coffee grounds, dark chocolate and a warm rumble of flavour-filled tannin. Raspberried brightness on top. Excellent. Screwcap. 14.6% alc. **Rating** 94 **To** 2030 $54 CM

ŸŸŸŸŸ **Sophie's Hill Pinot Grigio 2014 Rating** 93 **To** 2016 $26 CM ✪

KarriBindi   ★★★★★

111 Scott Road, Karridale, WA 6288 (postal) **Region** Margaret River
T (08) 9758 5570 **www**.karribindi.com.au **Open** Not
Winemaker Kris Wealand **Est.** 1997 **Dozens** 2000 **Vyds** 32.05ha
KarriBindi is owned by Kevin, Yvonne and Kris Wealand. The name is derived from Karridale and the surrounding karri forests, and from Bindi, the home town of one of the members of the Wealand family. In Nyoongar, 'karri' means strong, special, spiritual, tall tree and 'bindi' means butterfly, hence the label's picture of a butterfly soaring through karri trees. The Wealands have established sauvignon blanc (15ha), chardonnay (6.25ha), cabernet sauvignon (4ha), plus smaller plantings of semillon, shiraz and merlot. KarriBindi supplies a number of high-profile Margaret River wineries, reserving approximately 20% for their own label.

ŸŸŸŸŸ **Margaret River Chardonnay 2013** Hand-picked, whole bunch-pressed, fermented and matured in French barriques (40% new), a deserved gold medal

Adelaide Wine Show '14. In the deceptively light style of KarriBindi, despite its new oak; deceptive because this is a Chardonnay that is all about length, marrying intensity with finesse. Screwcap. 12.6% alc. **Rating** 95 **To** 2023 $30 ○

Margaret River Shiraz 2011 From a north-facing slope of karri loam and gravel soils, matured for 10 months in French barriques, 30% new; gold medal Melbourne Wine Awards '13. Elegance personified, and must have stood out like a beacon amid South Eastern Australian Shirazs from the same vintage; it is (only) medium-bodied, but the cherry and blackberry fruits positively sing. Screwcap. 13.7% alc. **Rating** 95 **To** 2026 $25 ○

Margaret River Sauvignon Blanc 2014 10% barrel-fermented in new French barriques. Still gin-clear, and is deliciously bright, breezy and fresh on the bouquet and palate alike; passionfruit and grapefruit are the fruit markers, the acidity crisp and crunchy, the barrel-ferment component largely lost in the wash. Great value. Screwcap. 12.4% alc. **Rating** 94 **To** 2019 $20 ○

ΨΨΨΨ **Margaret River Semillon Sauvignon Blanc 2014** **Rating** 93 **To** 2020 $20 ○

Kate Hill Wines ★★★★

101 Glen Road, Huonville, Tas 7109 (postal) **Region** Southern Tasmania
T (03) 6223 5641 **www**.katehillwines.com.au **Open** Not
Winemaker Kate Hill **Est.** 2008 **Dozens** 1000
When Kate Hill (and husband Charles) came to Tasmania in 2006, Kate had worked as a winemaker in Australia and overseas for 10 years. Kate's wines are made from a number of vineyards across southern Tasmania, the aim being to produce approachable, delicate wines. Exports to the UK and Singapore.

ΨΨΨΨ **Pinot Noir 2012** While 3yo, the colour is still deep, and only slightly developed; the bouquet is full of plum, cherry and spice, the palate moving trenchantly to the forest floor for its message. Reading the tea leaves of its future isn't at all easy, so there needs to be some head-scratching. Screwcap. 14% alc. **Rating** 92 **To** 2022 $35

Katnook Coonawarra ★★★★★

Riddoch Highway, Coonawarra, SA 5263 **Region** Coonawarra
T (08) 8737 0300 **www**.katnookestate.com.au **Open** Mon–Sat 10–5, Sun 11–5
Winemaker Wayne Stehbens **Est.** 1979 **Dozens** 90000 **Vyds** 198ha
Second in size (in the region) to Wynns Coonawarra Estate, Katnook has made significant strides since its acquisition by Freixenet, the Spanish Cava producer; at one time selling most of its grapes, it now sells a maximum of 10%. The historic stone woolshed in which the second vintage in Coonawarra (1896) was made, and which has served Katnook since 1980, has been restored. Likewise, the former office of John Riddoch has been fully restored and is now the cellar door, and the former stables now serve as a function area. Well over half the total estate plantings are cabernet sauvignon and shiraz, other varieties of importance being chardonnay, merlot, sauvignon blanc and pinot noir. The Odyssey Cabernet Sauvignon and Prodigy Shiraz are the icon duo at the top of a multitiered production. Exports to all major markets.

ΨΨΨΨ **Prodigy Shiraz 2010** As ever, a careful selection of the best parcels of estate grapes. It's in unmistakable Prodigy style, oak prominent, but there is also supple plum, cherry and licorice fruit of quite exceptional length, making this the best Prodigy since '02. Screwcap. 14.5% alc. **Rating** 96 **To** 2040 $100

Estate Cabernet Sauvignon 2012 In immaculate form. Fresh fruit, firm tannin, oak folded snugly within. Both longevity and pleasure are assured. It tastes of blackcurrant, boysenberry, spearmint and an assortment of red berries and dry, leafy herbs. Tannin flicks firmly through the finish, as it should with a wine of this gravity. Screwcap. 13.5% alc. **Rating** 95 **To** 2032 $40 CM

Estate Merlot 2012 Lavishly flavoured and smooth to the touch. It's a powerhouse rendition but the style here will be right up the alley of many a Merlot devotee. Plum, coffee, tobacco and dried herbs, with a creamy, chocolatey

coating of flavour slipped over the top. Tannin runs at fairly high revs; this isn't
going anywhere in a hurry, and will develop over many years. Screwcap. 13.5% alc.
Rating 94 **To** 2030 $40 CM

🍷🍷🍷🍷♀ Estate Shiraz 2012 **Rating** 92 **To** 2026 $40 CM
Founder's Block Cabernet Sauvignon 2013 **Rating** 92 **To** 2023 $22 CM ◐
Founder's Block Cabernet Sauvignon 2012 **Rating** 92 **To** 2021 $22 CM ◐
Squire's Blend Cabernet Merlot 2012 **Rating** 91 **To** 2024 $22 CM ◐
Select Series Limited Edition Shiraz 2013 **Rating** 90 **To** 2021 $22 CM

Kay Brothers Amery Vineyards ★★★★★

57 Kays Road, McLaren Vale, SA 5171 **Region** McLaren Vale
T (08) 8323 8211 www.kaybrothersamerywines.com **Open** Mon–Fri 9–5, w'ends 11–5
Winemaker Colin Kay, Andy Coppard **Est.** 1890 **Dozens** 10 000 **Vyds** 22ha
A traditional winery with a rich history and just over 20ha of priceless old vines; while the
white wines have been variable, the red wines and fortified wines can be very good. Of
particular interest is Block 6 Shiraz, made from vines over 120 years old; both vines and wines
are going from strength to strength. Celebrated its 125th anniversary in 2015. Exports to the
US, Canada, Switzerland, Germany, Malaysia, Hong Kong, Singapore, South Korea and China.

🍷🍷🍷🍷🍷 Block 6 McLaren Vale Shiraz 2012 Fred and Herbert Kay planted 4.8ha of
cuttings from Hardys' Tintara Vineyard in 1892; this comes from the surviving
1.6ha, made in open fermenters built in 1896, matured for 20 months in new
American and Baltic oak. A full-bodied, black-fruited wine as gnarly as the ancient
vines, but none the worse for that. Screwcap. 14.5% alc. **Rating** 95 **To** 2052 $80
Hillside McLaren Vale Shiraz 2012 The vines come from cuttings of the
120yo vines on Block 6, re-establishing the 4.85ha Hillside Vineyard. Open-
fermented, basket-pressed, matured for 20 months in American and Baltic oak.
Deep crimson-purple; full-bodied, but more approachable than Block 6, its
brooding black fruits and bitter chocolate balanced by good tannin and oak,
providing a very long palate. Screwcap. 14.5% alc. **Rating** 95 **To** 2037 $40
Cuthbert McLaren Vale Cabernet Sauvignon 2012 Open-fermented, with
extended maceration post-fermentation before being basket-pressed; matured for
18 months in new French and Bulgarian oak. Deep, healthy colour; the varietal
expression overwhelms any regional impact, making this an impressive wine;
the use of 100% new oak has been fully justified. A long life ahead from a great
vintage. Screwcap. 14.5% alc. **Rating** 95 **To** 2037 $45
Basket Pressed McLaren Vale Shiraz 2013 An archetypal full-bodied wine
proclaiming its varietal and regional breeding with foghorn loudness. Multiple
layers of black fruits and slabs of dark chocolate wreathed in ripe, balanced tannins.
Will be exceptionally long-lived thanks as much to its balance as to its power.
Screwcap. 14% alc. **Rating** 94 **To** 2050 $25 ◐

🍷🍷🍷🍷♀ Ironmonger 2011 **Rating** 93 **To** 2021 $30
Basket Pressed McLaren Vale Nero d'Avola 2013 **Rating** 91 **To** 2018 $25

Keith Tulloch Wine ★★★★★

Hermitage Road, Pokolbin, NSW 2320 **Region** Hunter Valley
T (02) 4998 7500 www.keithtullochwine.com.au **Open** 7 days 10–5
Winemaker Keith Tulloch, Joel Carey **Est.** 1997 **Dozens** 10 000 **Vyds** 7.4ha
Keith Tulloch is, of course, a member of the Tulloch family, which has played a leading role
in the Hunter Valley for over a century. Formerly a winemaker at Lindemans and Rothbury
Estate, he developed his own label in 1997. There is the same almost obsessive attention to
detail, the same almost ascetic intellectual approach, the same refusal to accept anything but the
best as that of Jeffrey Grosset. Exports to the UK, the US, Canada, Sweden and Hong Kong.

🍷🍷🍷🍷🍷 Field of Mars Block 2A Hunter Valley Semillon 2014 Leaner, racier
expression than the Block 3B. Both the style and the flavours themselves serve to

emphasis the finish, which is classically long and lemony, with herbal notes tucked deep within. Taut, tense personality builds further on this impression. In short, it's outstanding. Screwcap. 11% alc. **Rating** 96 **To** 2026 $45 CM **○**

The Kester Hunter Valley Shiraz 2013 Grown on a single vineyard. Extra level of fruit power and push through the finish. It's a 'make you sit up straighter' wine. It tastes of kirsch and black cherry with fresh leather and dark, grainy earth notes cruising through. Tannin is fine, floral and reasonably pushy, but integrated. There are gamey notes here but they work as positives. It's a beauty. Screwcap. 13.8% alc. **Rating** 96 **To** 2032 $68 CM **○**

Field of Mars Block 3B Hunter Valley Semillon 2014 Pure, effortless flavour. Fennel, lemongrass, wax and lime. Already showing well. It's enough to make you sit back and marvel. Screwcap. 11.5% alc. **Rating** 95 **To** 2022 $45 CM

Hunter Valley Semillon 2014 Opening the curtains of a morning to find a pure blue sky; opening a bottle of this is a similar experience. Fresh, crisp, pure and full of promise; you take a sip and suddenly feel optimistic about the future. Lemon and lemonade, mineral and lemongrass. That's a lot of citrussy zing, partly why it darts so convincingly through the finish. There are textural beginnings here too; everything in its due place. Screwcap. 11.5% alc. **Rating** 95 **To** 2025 $28 CM **○**

Field of Mars Hunter Valley Chardonnay 2014 The flavours are full but they run within tightly controlled lines. This is a prime example of Hunter Valley Chardonnay. It tastes of peach, flint, chalk and nectarine, with spicy oak adding a light kiss and little more. Classy. Delicious drinking. Length plus. Screwcap. 13.5% alc. **Rating** 95 **To** 2020 $60 CM

Hunter Valley Chardonnay 2014 Rating 94 **To** 2019 $32 CM

♟♟♟♟♟ **Museum Release Semillon 2008 Rating** 92 **To** 2019 $45 CM
Tawarri Vineyard Hunter Valley Shiraz 2013 Rating 92 **To** 2028 $45 CM
The Wife Hunter Valley Shiraz 2013 Rating 92 **To** 2022 $55 CM
Museum Release Kester Shiraz 2007 Rating 92 **To** 2025 $85 CM
Forres Blend 2013 Rating 92 **To** 2025 $38 CM

Kellermeister   ★★★★★

Barossa Valley Highway, Lyndoch, SA 5351 **Region** Barossa Valley
T (08) 8524 4303 **www.**kellermeister.com.au **Open** 7 days 9.30–5.30
Winemaker Mark Pearce **Est.** 1976 **Dozens** 30 000 **Vyds** 20ha
Since joining Kellermeister from Wirra Wirra in 2009, Mark Pearce has successfully worked through challenging times to ensure the survival of the winery and its brands; and upon the retirement of founders Ralph and Val Jones in late '12, the Pearce family acquired the business. Surrounded by a young, close-knit team, Mark is committed to continuing to build on the legacy that the founders began almost 40 years ago. His winemaking focus is on continuing to preserve Kellermeister's best wines, while introducing new wines, made with the intention of expressing the purity of the provenance of the Barossa. Exports to the US, Canada, Switzerland, Denmark, Israel, Taiwan, China and Japan.

♟♟♟♟♟ **Black Sash Barossa Valley Shiraz 2012** From 100yo vines at Ebenezer. Exudes calm authority from the outset, and keeps the focus and intensity of its bouquet on track; the remarkable feature of the full-bodied palate is the half suggestion of cool–climate fruit backed by fine tannins and quality oak. The key to this wine is its extreme length. Screwcap. 14% alc. **Rating** 97 **To** 2042 $65 **○**

♟♟♟♟♟ **Dry Grown Barossa Shiraz 2013** An imposing wine, its colour warning of the intensity to come; black fruits, dark chocolate, bramble, briar and tar are welded together on the full-bodied palate; tannin and oak are locked within the wine, useful hostages for the decades ahead. Cork. 14.5% alc. **Rating** 96 **To** 2038 $35 **○**

Wild Witch Barossa Shiraz 2012 Giant bottles are all very well, but I would walk a crooked mile to avoid this wine if I were a sommelier trying to pour it at a restaurant. If Black Sash is calm, this is wildly extroverted, in its element in a Harry Potter world, its luscious black fruits flooding the palate; I have to acknowledge that the finish is perfectly weighted, verging on outright elegance. Screwcap. 14.5% alc. **Rating** 96 **To** 2052 $85

Wild Witch Barossa Shiraz 2011 Breaks each and every rule for the vintage, with good colour, abundant red and black fruits, and a long, fresh, supple palate. A brave move to sit it alongside the towering power of the '12, but (particularly if served blind) this might appeal more to many of its consumers, and you don't have to lock it away for decades. Screwcap. 14.5% alc. **Rating** 94 **To** 2027 $85

ŸŸŸŸŸ **Threefold Farm Missy Moo Mataro 2012** Rating 93 To 2032 $45
The Curtain Raiser Barossa Tempranillo 2014 Rating 92 To 2028 $27
The Wombat General Riesling 2014 Rating 91 To 2020 $22 ✪

Kellybrook   ★★★★★

Fulford Road, Wonga Park, Vic 3115 **Region** Yarra Valley
T (03) 9722 1304 www.kellybrookwinery.com.au **Open** 7 days 11–5
Winemaker Philip and Darren Kelly, Rob Hall **Est.** 1962 **Dozens** 3000 **Vyds** 8.5ha
The vineyard is at Wonga Park, one of the gateways to the Yarra Valley, and has a picnic area and a full-scale restaurant. A very competent producer of both cider and apple brandy (in Calvados style) as well as table wine. When it received its winery licence in 1970, it became the first winery in the Yarra Valley to open its doors in the 20th century, a distinction often ignored or forgotten (by this author as well as others). The arrival of Rob Hall, former Mount Mary winemaker, has seen the quality of the wines increase dramatically.

ŸŸŸŸŸ **Estate Yarra Valley Shiraz 2013** Estate-grown, the vines 40yo. A classic Shiraz, no more than medium-bodied, but with a supple and very long display of red berries, blood plums, spice and a whisk of licorice couched in a gently savoury tannin framework. The benefit of moderate alcohol cannot be over-emphasised. Diam. 13% alc. **Rating** 96 **To** 2038 $40 ✪

Estate Yarra Valley Pinot Noir 2013 Strong, clear crimson-purple; this has the light and shade its '14 sibling presently lacks; it's not a heavyweight, but there's a lot to explore in the complex web of dark cherry fruits, spices, bramble and forest floor; very good overall length and line. Diam. 13% alc. **Rating** 95 **To** 2023 $40

Yarra Valley Rose 2014 Made from cabernet sauvignon, picked at low baume. Salmon-pink; a particularly complex, savoury rose, with bramble, spice and red fruits driving the bouquet and palate alike; a long, textured palate, and a pleasingly dry finish. Very good value. Screwcap. 12.7% alc. **Rating** 94 **To** 2016 $18 ✪

Yarra Valley Cabernet Sauvignon 2013 A perfumed and elegantly detailed light to medium-bodied Cabernet that sends an immediate 'drink me quick' message on its deceptively long palate, flooded with cassis fruit, unburdened by cranky tannins. Screwcap. 12.5% alc. **Rating** 94 **To** 2023 $27 ✪

ŸŸŸŸŸ **Estate Yarra Valley Chardonnay 2013** Rating 92 To 2023 $35
Yarra Valley Pinot Noir 2014 Rating 91 To 2020 $27
Yarra Valley Shiraz 2013 Rating 91 To 2023 $27
Yarra Valley Cabernet Merlot 2010 Rating 90 To 2020 $27

Kelman Vineyard   ★★★★

2 Oakey Creek Road, Pokolbin, NSW 2320 **Region** Hunter Valley
T (02) 4991 5456 www.kelmanvineyard.com.au **Open** 7 days 9–4
Winemaker Jeff Byrne **Est.** 1999 **Dozens** 1600 **Vyds** 9.3ha
Kelman Vineyard is a California-type development: a 40ha property has been subdivided into 80 residential development lots, with vines wending between the lots, which are under common ownership. Part of the chardonnay was grafted to shiraz before coming into full production, and the vineyard has the potential to produce 8000 dozen bottles per year. In the meantime, each owner receives 12 dozen a year.

ŸŸŸŸŸ **Hunter Valley Semillon Sauvignon Blanc 2014** Delicious white wine. Dry and lengthy but with just enough fruit to satisfy. Citrus, lemongrass and melon. Prawns beckon. Screwcap. 11.7% alc. **Rating** 92 **To** 2017 $18 CM ✪

Hunter Valley Semillon 2014 Light but elegant, with lemon and subtle grass notes swishing through the palate. Nothing out of place. Screwcap. 11.6% alc. **Rating** 90 **To** 2020 $18 CM ✪

Hunter Valley Chardonnay 2014 Stone fruit and more tropical flavours matched to sweet, custardy oak. Mid-weight, clean and accessible, with pangs of fruit to the finish. Cuts a pretty decent figure. Screwcap. 13.5% alc. **Rating** 90 **To** 2017 $22 CM

Kelvedon ★★★★

PO Box 126, Swansea, Tas 7190 **Region** East Coast Tasmania
T (03) 6257 8283 www.kelvedonestate.com.au **Open** Not
Winemaker Winemaking Tasmania (Julian Alcorso) **Est.** 1998 **Dozens** 2000 **Vyds** 9ha
Jack and Gill Cotton began planting the Kelvedon Vineyard with 1ha of pinot noir in 1998. The Cotton family has owned and managed the historic East Coast property since 1829, grapegrowing coming very late in the piece. The plantings were extended in 2000–01 by an additional 5ha, half to pinot noir and half to chardonnay, followed by a further 2ha of chardonnay in '10; 1ha of sauvignon blanc has also been established to provide a second wine under the Kelvedon label. The chardonnay and 1ha of pinot noir plantings are under contract to Accolade Wines.

🍷🍷🍷🍷🍷 **Pinot Noir 2013** Full, deep colour, following in the footsteps of the '12. The bouquet is complex, as are the spicy/savoury dark fruit flavours of the palate, and the long finish. Screwcap. **Rating** 94 **To** 2023

🍷🍷🍷🍷🍷 **Sauvignon Blanc 2014 Rating** 90 **To** 2016 $27
Chardonnay 2012 Rating 90 **To** 2020 $37

Kerrigan + Berry ★★★★★

PO Box 221, Cowaramup, WA 6284 **Region** South West Australia Zone
T (08) 9755 6046 www.kerriganandberry.com.au **Open** At Hay Shed Hill
Winemaker Michael Kerrigan, Gavin Berry **Est.** 2007 **Dozens** 1200
Owners Michael Kerrigan and Gavin Berry have been making wine in WA for a combined period of over 40 years, and say they have been most closely associated with the two varieties that in their opinion define WA: riesling and cabernet sauvignon. This is strictly a weekend and after-hours venture, separate from their respective roles as chief winemakers at Hay Shed Hill and West Cape Howe. They have focused on what is important, and explain, 'We have spent a total of zero hours on marketing research, and no consultants have been injured in the making of these wines.' Exports to the UK, the US, Singapore and China.

🍷🍷🍷🍷🍷 **Mt Barker Great Southern Riesling 2014** From the historic Langton Vineyard planted in the '70s; free-run juice. Quartz-white; the bouquet is fresh and clean, but gives little clue about the quite beautiful palate to follow, which is perfectly balanced, and has pure lime and apple – even a wisp of passionfruit – already on enticing display. Screwcap. 11.5% alc. **Rating** 96 **To** 2034 $30 ✪
Mt Barker Margaret River Cabernet Sauvignon 2011 A 50/50% blend of the two regions, eloquently demonstrating just how compatible the union can be; Margaret River provides the fleshy mid-palate, Mount Barker the finely boned structure and notes of cassis, the finish a duet between two tenors, oak and tannins providing the beat. Screwcap. 14% alc. **Rating** 95 **To** 2031 $70

Kidman Wines ★★★☆

13713 Riddoch Highway, Coonawarra, SA 5263 **Region** Coonawarra
T (08) 8736 5071 www.kidmanwines.com.au **Open** 7 days 10–5
Winemaker Sid Kidman **Est.** 1984 **Dozens** 6000 **Vyds** 17.2ha
Sid Kidman planted the first vines on the property in 1971, and has been managing the vineyard ever since. Over the years it has grown to include cabernet sauvignon, shiraz, riesling and sauvignon blanc. The cellar door is housed in the old stables on the Kidman property; they

were built in 1859 and are a great link with the district's history. Susie and Sid have recently been joined by their son George, who becomes the fourth generation of the Kidman family to be involved with the property. Exports to Malaysia and China.

ΨΨΨΨ **Coonawarra Shiraz 2012** Fully reflects the excellent vintage; its 18 months in American oak and substantial alcohol should (in theory) not give the result achieved; it is mouth-filling, but not hot, nor is the vanilla/coconut American oak particularly obvious. Screwcap. 15% alc. **Rating** 92 **To** 2022 $20 ⊙

ΨΨΨΨ **Coonawarra Cabernet Sauvignon 2012 Rating** 89 **To** 2018 $22
Coonawarra Riesling 2013 Rating 88 **To** 2017 $16 ⊙

Kilikanoon   ★★★★★

Penna Lane, Penwortham, SA 5453 **Region** Clare Valley
T (08) 8843 4206 **www**.kilikanoon.com.au **Open** 7 days 11–5
Winemaker Kevin Mitchell, Barry Kooij **Est.** 1997 **Dozens** 80 000 **Vyds** 330ha
Kilikanoon has travelled in the fast lane since winemaker Kevin Mitchell established it in 1997 on the foundation of 6ha of vines he owns with father Mort. With the aid of investors, its 80 000-dozen production comes from over 300ha of estate-owned vineyards, and access to the best grapes from a total of 2266ha across SA. Between 2013 and early '14 all links between Kilikanoon and Seppeltsfield were ended; the sale of Kilikanoon's share in Seppeltsfield, together with the sale of Kilikanoon's Crowhurst Vineyard in the Barossa Valley, led to the purchase by Kilikanoon of the winery which it had previously leased, and purchase of the Mount Surmon Vineyard. Exports to most major markets.

ΨΨΨΨΨ **Crowhurst Reserve Barossa Valley Shiraz 2012** It could be called delicious but that might give the wrong impression. It is intensely fruited, weighty, inky, all black coal and blackberry with seams of dark earth and mocha flavour. There's no getting off lightly here. It's an earth wine with a sweet, fruit-filled heart, and while it swings joyously through the palate, bones of tannin are tucked neatly but firmly into the wine's deep flesh. Rarely is wine such a complete package. Screwcap. 14.5% alc. **Rating** 97 **To** 2035 $120 CM ⊙

ΨΨΨΨΨ **Exodus Barossa Valley Shiraz 2013** Entirely French oak-matured, and the result is entirely seamless. They've nailed this one. Black berries, coal, cloves and woodsmoke, dense but supple, with massaged tannin rippling through the majority of the wine. The quality was born in the vineyard, but the winemaking is particularly skilful. Screwcap. 14.5% alc. **Rating** 96 **To** 2033 $40 CM ⊙
The Duke Reserve Clare Valley Grenache 2012 Grown on 80+yo vines (and some over 100). The word 'beast' springs to mind … until its charms start to work on you. Sweet, grainy, earthen and authoritative flavours motor through the palate, seducing as much as impressing as they go. There's a sizeable churn of tannin here too, but the fruit squelches deep into it, making for juicily profound drinking. Screwcap. 14.5% alc. **Rating** 95 **To** 2028 $80 CM
Killerman's Run Clare Valley Grenache Shiraz Mataro 2013 Worth championing. Effortless, balanced, bright-fruited and spice-laden. Cherries, aniseed, twigs, raspberries and cloves. Just enough firmness. Beautiful wine at a beautiful price. Screwcap. 14.5% alc. **Rating** 95 **To** 2023 $20 CM ⊙
Mort's Block Clare Valley Riesling 2014 Combines flavour with length. Lime and lavender with an assortment of dried spices. Such juicy drinkability. Crystal clear quality. Screwcap. 12.5% alc. **Rating** 94 **To** 2025 $23 CM ⊙
Prophecy Clare Valley Shiraz 2013 Style and substance. Matured in all French oak. Supple flavours of blackberry, plum, eucalypt and boysenberry. Clovey oak plays a role too, as do notes of peppercorn and general dried spice. Watch the waves of flavour; there's a rip of tannin lurking beneath. This is very good. Screwcap. 14.5% alc. **Rating** 94 **To** 2033 $44 CM
Green's Vineyard Barossa Valley Shiraz 2012 It's a more modest, even elegant, style than you might expect. Supple red and black-berried fruit, fresh

tar, smoky oak and a general slipperiness of texture. Sound, satisfying length. Everything in its right place. Screwcap. 14.5% alc. **Rating** 94 **To** 2032 $80 CM
Oracle Clare Valley Shiraz 2012 Interesting release. The flavour profile is slightly different from what you might imagine and/or expect. There's a thick stream of licorice, blackberry, cloves and sappy, cedary oak, but the unexpected appears in the form of truffle, plus heightened blackcurrant and leather notes. It doesn't lessen the wine; it makes it distinctive. Importantly, at all points this wine feels fresh and fine. Screwcap. 14.5% alc. **Rating** 94 **To** 2028 $80 CM

ᵀᵀᵀᵀᵎ **Killerman's Run Clare Valley Shiraz 2013** Rating 93 To 2021 $20 CM ✪
Kavel's Flock Barossa Valley Shiraz 2013 Rating 92 To 2020 $18 CM ✪
Killerman's Run Cabernet Sauvignon 2013 Rating 92 To 2022 $20 CM ✪

Killerby ★★★★

4259 Caves Road, Wilyabrup, WA 6280 **Region** Margaret River
T (08) 9755 5983 **www**.killerby.com.au **Open** 7 days 10–5
Winemaker Marco Pinares **Est.** 1973 **Dozens** NFP **Vyds** 4ha
Owned by Ferngrove Wine Group since 2008, Killerby has relaunched, opening its architect-designed 'Cellar Store' (with one of the longest tasting benches in Australia) in 2013. With a variety of local produce available, it pays homage to the history of the Killerby family (in the late 1930s, Benjamin George Lee Killerby established a general store to supply the pioneers of the region, with grandson Dr Benjamin Barry Killerby planting one of the first vineyards in Geographe in '73).

ᵀᵀᵀᵀᵀ **Margaret River Sauvignon Blanc 2014** Fermented and matured for 3 months in new and used French oak. Barrel-ferment characters are certainly evident, but the fruit is not overwhelmed; its aromas and flavours have an admirably balanced mix of grass/citrus on the one hand, tropical/passionfruit on the other. A year or two in bottle will do no harm. Screwcap. 13% alc. **Rating** 94 **To** 2017 $26 ✪

ᵀᵀᵀᵀᵎ **The Foundations Cabernet Sauvignon 2012** Rating 93 To 2032 $60
Margaret River Chardonnay 2013 Rating 92 To 2023 $30

Killiecrankie Wines ★★★★

103 Soldier Road, Ravenswood, Vic 3453 **Region** Bendigo
T (03) 5435 3155 **www**.killiecrankiewines.com **Open** W'ends 11–5
Winemaker John Monteath **Est.** 2000 **Dozens** 300 **Vyds** 1ha
John Monteath moved to the Bendigo region in 1999 to pursue his interest in viticulture and winemaking, and while helping to establish the vineyard from which the grapes are sourced, gained experience at Water Wheel, Heathcote Estate, Balgownie and Blackjack. The vineyard is planted to four shiraz clones, and is the backbone of the Bendigo wine. The small crop is hand-picked, with the resultant wines made in true garagiste style. Small parcels of premium fruit are also sourced from meticulously tended vineyards in Bendigo and Heathcote.

ᵀᵀᵀᵀᵀ **Montspear Heathcote Shiraz 2013** Deep crimson-purple; the dark, sombre fruits of the bouquet, with hints of tar and licorice come through with power, yet grace, on the medium to full-bodied palate. Here spice and pepper join the flavours signalled by the bouquet, and the balance and texture are very good. A bargain with a long future. Screwcap. 14% alc. **Rating** 94 **To** 2038 $20 ✪

ᵀᵀᵀᵀᵎ **Montspear Heathcote Shiraz 2012** Rating 92 To 2027 $20 ✪
Lola Montez Tempranillo 2014 Rating 90 To 2016 $25

King River Estate ★★★☆

3556 Wangaratta–Whitfield Road, Wangaratta, Vic 3678 **Region** King Valley
T (03) 5729 3689 **www**.kingriverestate.com.au **Open** 7 days 11–5
Winemaker Trevor Knaggs **Est.** 1996 **Dozens** 3000 **Vyds** 17.6ha

Trevor Knaggs, with assistance from father Colin, began the establishment of King River Estate in 1990, making the first wines in '96. The initial plantings of 3.3ha each of chardonnay and cabernet sauvignon were followed by 8ha of merlot and 3ha of shiraz. More recent plantings have extended the varietal range to include verdelho, viognier, barbera and sangiovese. Biodynamic practices are used in the vineyard. Exports to China and Singapore.

🍷🍷🍷🍷🍷 **King Valley Sagrantino 2012** A good example of a variety (and wine) that has successfully made the trip from central Italy to Northeast Victoria; there are tangy cherry, spice, blueberry and plum flavours with a fine web of tannins in support. Diam. 14% alc. **Rating** 91 **To** 2022 $35

Kingston Estate Wines   ★★★☆

Sturt Highway, Kingston-on-Murray, SA 5331 **Region** South Australia
T (08) 8243 3700 **www.**kingstonestatewines.com **Open** By appt
Winemaker Bill Moularadellis, Brett Duffin, Helen Foggo, Donna Hartwig **Est.** 1979
Dozens 70 000 **Vyds** 500ha

Kingston Estate, under the direction of Bill Moularadellis, has its production roots in the Riverland region, but also has long-term purchase contracts with growers in the Clare Valley, the Adelaide Hills, Coonawarra, Langhorne Creek and Mount Benson. It has also spread its net to take in a wide range of varietals, mainstream and exotic, under a number of brands at various price points. Exports to all major markets.

🍷🍷🍷🍷🍷 **Adelaide Hills Sauvignon Blanc 2014** Hand-picked at night, cold-fermented in stainless steel. Has very attractive tropical fruits anchored on passionfruit, with a surrounding support of crisp acidity and a tweak of lemon zest. Great value. Screwcap. 11% alc. **Rating** 91 **To** 2016 $15 ✪

Kirrihill Wines   ★★★★☆

12 Main North Road, Clare, SA 5453 **Region** Clare Valley
T (08) 8842 4087 **www.**kirrihillwines.com.au **Open** 7 days 10–4
Winemaker Hamish Seabrook, Marnie Roberts **Est.** 1998 **Dozens** 30 000

Kirrihill is a large development, with an 8000-tonne, $12 million winery, as well as a role as a contract maker for several producers. Focused on the Clare Valley and Adelaide Hills, grapes are sourced from specially selected parcels of Kirrihill's 1300ha of managed vineyards, as well as the Edwards and Stanway families' properties in these regions. The Regional Range comprises blends of both regions, while the Single Vineyard Selection Series aims to elicit a sense of place from the chosen vineyards. The Alternative range features varieties such as fiano, vermentino, montepulciano, nebbiolo, tempranillo and sangiovese. Exports to all major markets.

🍷🍷🍷🍷🍷 **Tullymore Vineyard Clare Valley Shiraz 2012** An exceptional vineyard at an altitude of 450m; partial cold soak in open fermenters, cool-fermented, and matured in French oak (35% new). While dense and full-bodied, its black fruits and black olive flavours remain supple and well balanced. Can be enjoyed now or in the distant future. Screwcap. 14.8% alc. **Rating** 96 **To** 2052 $25 ✪

🍷🍷🍷🍷🍷 **Regional Range Clare Valley Riesling 2014 Rating** 93 **To** 2022 $16 CM ✪
Vineyard Selection Series Riesling 2014 Rating 91 **To** 2022 $20 CM ✪
Regional Range Clare Valley Shiraz 2013 Rating 91 **To** 2024 $18 CM ✪

Knappstein   ★★★★★

2 Pioneer Avenue, Clare, SA 5453 **Region** Clare Valley
T (08) 8841 2100 **www.**knappstein.com.au **Open** Mon–Fri 9–5, w'ends 11–4
Winemaker Glenn Barry **Est.** 1969 **Dozens** 40 000 **Vyds** 114ha

Knappstein's full name is Knappstein Enterprise Winery & Brewery, reflecting its history before being acquired by Petaluma, and since then part of Lion Nathan's stable. The substantial mature estate vineyards in prime locations supply grapes both for the Knappstein brand and for wider Petaluma use. Exports to all major markets.

ŶŶŶŶŶ **Block 5 Enterprise Vineyard Clare Valley Cabernet Sauvignon 2012** An effortless Cabernet, building layers of complexity each time you return to it; redcurrant, blackcurrant, olive, bay leaf, fine tannins and cedary French oak are all in harmony – so much so that it can be enjoyed tonight as much as in 30 years' time. Screwcap. 13.5% alc. **Rating** 97 **To** 2042 $85 ✪

ŶŶŶŶŶ **Slate Creek Vineyard Watervale Riesling 2014** Proclaims its quality right from the outset; it fills the senses with its intense lime and grapefruit flavours that race through the palate, never losing sight of the finish line. Screwcap. 12.5% alc. **Rating** 96 **To** 2034 $30 ✪

Ackland Vineyard Watervale Riesling 2014 It is very different from Bryksy's Hill Vineyard, with more power and depth without losing any of its focus or definition; here lime juice flavours edge up close to grapefruit on the back-palate. Amazing how two vineyards planted on the same soil in the same district can be so different. Screwcap. 12.5% alc. **Rating** 95 **To** 2034 $32 ✪

The Mayor's Vineyard Shiraz 2013 Whatever shortcomings there may be with this wine, they originate in the vineyard, not the winery; what is there is elegant and most attractive, with some red fruits (not common in the Clare Valley) joining the purple and black flavour spectrum, the tannins and oak well balanced, the finish and aftertaste seductive. Screwcap. 13% alc. **Rating** 95 **To** 2028 $46

The Insider Limited Release Clare Valley Shiraz Malbec 2013 70/30% blend of shiraz and malbec, fermented with a portion of whole bunches. Highly successful result. Firm, chewy, splashed with spice, twigs, and various savoury elements, but underpinned by strong red and black-berried fruit flavours. Succulent, grippy complexity. Screwcap. 13% alc. **Rating** 95 **To** 2024 $27 CM ✪

Enterprise Vineyard Clare Valley Cabernet Sauvignon 2012 Good colour; a medium to full-bodied dissertation on Clare Valley cabernet from a classic vintage, given total care and access to good-quality French oak; it is unequivocally varietal and immaculately balanced, with fruit, French oak and tannins all contributing to the whole. Screwcap. 13.5% alc. **Rating** 95 **To** 2032 $46

Bryksy's Hill Vineyard Watervale Riesling 2014 Rating 94 **To** 2029 $32

Clare Valley Shiraz 2013 Rating 94 **To** 2023 $22 ✪

Clare Valley Cabernet Sauvignon 2012 Rating 94 **To** 2027 $22 ✪

ŶŶŶŶŶ **Hand Picked Clare Valley Riesling 2014 Rating** 93 **To** 2020 $20 ✪

Knee Deep Wines   ★★★★☆

160 Johnson Road, Wilyabrup, WA 6280 **Region** Margaret River
T (08) 9755 6776 **www**.kneedeepwines.com.au **Open** 7 days 10–5
Winemaker Bruce Dukes **Est.** 2000 **Dozens** 7500 **Vyds** 20ha
Perth surgeon and veteran yachtsman Phil Childs and wife Sue acquired a 34ha property in Wilyabrup in 2000. This was planted to chardonnay (3.2ha), sauvignon blanc (4ha), semillon (1.48ha), chenin blanc (4ha), cabernet sauvignon (6.34ha) and shiraz (1.24ha). The name, Knee Deep Wines, was inspired by the passion and commitment needed to produce premium wine and as a tongue-in-cheek acknowledgement of jumping in 'boots and all' during a testing time in the wine industry, the grape glut building more or less in tune with the venture.

ŶŶŶŶŶ **Kim's Limited Release Margaret River Chardonnay 2012** Made by Bob Cartwright. Searingly good. Flesh, fantasy, flavour. Peach, grapefruit, a thrill of citrus and intriguing notes of cornflake, oatmeal, toast and wood spice. Builds immediately on the front palate then whooshes in mouth-watering style all the way through to an extended finish. Screwcap. 14% alc. **Rating** 95 **To** 2021 $45 CM

Margaret River Shiraz 2012 Classy Shiraz. Complex. Reductive, smoky, almost rubbery notes run smoothly into seductive flavours of kirsch, black cherry, stringy herbs and swish, peanutty oak. Fine-but-assertive tannin ripples throughout. Excellent release. Screwcap. 14.5% alc. **Rating** 94 **To** 2026 $28 CM ✪

ŶŶŶŶŶ **Margaret River Sauvignon Blanc 2014 Rating** 91 **To** 2016 $22 CM ✪
Margaret River Cabernet Merlot 2013 Rating 90 **To** 2020 $24 CM

Knotting Hill Estate Vineyard ★★★★☆

247 Carter Road, Wilyabrup WA 6280 **Region** Margaret River
T (08) 9755 7733 **www.**knottinghill.com.au **Open** 7 days 11–5
Winemaker Flying Fish Cove (Simon Ding) **Est.** 1997 **Dozens** 3500 **Vyds** 37.5ha
The Gould family has been farming in WA since 1907, and still owns the land grant taken up on their arrival from Scotland. In '97 two generations of the family decided to diversify, and acquired Knotting Hill, their Wilyabrup property. In '98, using their extensive farming background, they propagated 56 000 cuttings in an onsite nursery, supervised plantings, created a 5.5ha dam, and built the 45m bridge entry to the local limestone cellar door. In 2002 they leased the wheat farm, and have since devoted all their time to Knotting Hill. The spectacular vineyard setting is established on a natural amphitheatre, with the lake at the bottom.

🍷🍷🍷🍷🍷 **Margaret River Cabernet Sauvignon 2012** Deep colour; has that depth and richness that Margaret River seems to bestow on all those who ask politely; it is so supple it is impossible to deny its charms, cassis by the yard, and ripe tannins to preserve its future. Screwcap. 14% alc. **Rating** 95 **To** 2032 $38

🍷🍷🍷🍷🍷 **Margaret River Semillon Sauvignon Blanc 2014 Rating** 93 **To** 2020 $20 ✪
Margaret River Cabernet Malbec 2014 Rating 91 **To** 2020 $28

Koonara ★★★★★

44 Main Street, Penola, SA 5277 **Region** Coonawarra
T (08) 8737 3222 **www.**koonara.com **Open** 7 days 10–6
Winemaker Peter Douglas **Est.** 1988 **Dozens** 8000 **Vyds** 9ha
Koonara is a sister, or, more appropriately, a brother company to Reschke Wines. The latter is run by Burke Reschke, Koonara by his brother Dru. Both are sons of Trevor Reschke, who planted the first vines on the Koonara property in 1988. Peter Douglas, formerly Wynns' chief winemaker before moving overseas for some years, has returned to the district and is consultant winemaker. Since 2013 Koonara have leased and managed the Kongorong Partnership Vineyard in Mount Gambier, which had previously sold its grapes to Koonara. Exports to Canada, Singapore and China.

🍷🍷🍷🍷🍷 **The Big Guns Coonawarra Shiraz 2012** Matured for 24 months in French hogsheads. A seriously good Shiraz, wielding its power through persuasion, not brute force; high-quality French oak is certainly obvious, but the waves of black fruits and ripe tannins carry the oak – or vice versa. Extended cellaring will be handsomely repaid. Diam. 14.2% alc. **Rating** 96 **To** 2047 $100
The Head Honcho Coonawarra Cabernet Sauvignon 2012 24 months in French oak, a selection of the best barrels. Even more concentrated and focused than the Family Reserve Ambriel's Gift, with more blackcurrant fruit and more tannins. A long way away from being ready to drink, but has the all-important balance to justify cellaring. Diam. 13.9% alc. **Rating** 95 **To** 2042 $100
Angel's Peak Coonawarra Shiraz 2012 Bright, deep crimson-purple; lives up to the promise of the colour with both the bouquet and palate full of ripe black cherry and blackberry fruit, which at this stage has better balance (qua oak) than the Family Reserve Ezra's Gift, and has a particularly appealing juicy intensity to the finish. Screwcap. 14% alc. **Rating** 94 **To** 2027 $20 ✪
Ambriel's Gift Family Reserve Coonawarra Cabernet Sauvignon 2012 2.5 tonnes per ha, 24 months in French oak. Inky purple-crimson; an uninhibited, full-bodied Cabernet with layered and powerful blackcurrant fruit, oak and tannins all speaking from the same page. Screwcap. 13.9% alc. **Rating** 94 **To** 2027 $40

🍷🍷🍷🍷🍷 **Family Reserve Ezra's Gift Shiraz 2012 Rating** 93 **To** 2032 $35
Angel's Peak Cabernet Sauvignon 2013 Rating 92 **To** 2033 $20 ✪

Koonowla Wines

18 Koonowla Road, Auburn, SA 5451 **Region** Clare Valley
T (08) 8849 2270 **www**.koonowla.com **Open** W'ends & public hols 10–5, Mon–Fri by appt
Winemaker O'Leary Walker Wines **Est.** 1997 **Dozens** 5000 **Vyds** 48.77ha
Koonowla is a historic Clare Valley property; situated just east of Auburn, it was first planted
with vines in the 1890s, and by the early 1900s was producing 60 000 litres of wine annually.
A disastrous fire in '26 destroyed the winery and wine stocks, and the property was converted
to grain and wool production. Replanting of vines began in '85, and accelerated after Andrew
and Booie Michael purchased the property in '91; there are now almost 50ha of cabernet
sauvignon, riesling, shiraz, merlot and semillon. In an all-too-familiar story, the grapes were
sold until falling prices forced a change in strategy; now a major part of the grapes is vinified
by the infinitely experienced David O'Leary and Nick Walker. Exports to the UK, the US,
Scandinavia, Malaysia, China and NZ.

ŸŸŸŸŸ **Clare Valley Cabernet Sauvignon 2012** Has the fruit and has the structure.
Varietal character is in the bag too. Blackcurrant, dust, tobacco and eucalypt.
Grainy tannin takes the reins and pulls the fruit through. Not a huge wine, but a
good option for the cellar. Screwcap. 14.5% alc. **Rating** 93 **To** 2026 $22 CM ✪
The Ringmaster Clare Valley Riesling 2014 Zesty and lime-driven with
a chalky dryness to the finish. Length is very good. As is the value. Screwcap.
12% alc. **Rating** 92 **To** 2021 $15 CM ✪
Clare Valley Riesling 2014 Bright green-straw; interesting wine; already shows
some advanced characters, but there is no hint of oxidation; the flavours are in a
grapefruit spectrum (no bad thing) as much as lime, allied with some spicy notes.
Screwcap. 12% alc. **Rating** 90 **To** 2017 $19 ✪

ŸŸŸŸ **The Ringmaster Clare Valley Shiraz 2012 Rating** 88 **To** 2019 $15 CM ✪
The Ringmaster Cabernet 2012 Rating 88 **To** 2019 $15 CM ✪

Kooyong

★★★★★

PO Box 153, Red Hill South, Vic 3937 **Region** Mornington Peninsula
T (03) 5989 4444 **www**.kooyongwines.com.au **Open** At Port Phillip Estate
Winemaker Sandro Mosele **Est.** 1996 **Dozens** 9300 **Vyds** 33.4ha
Kooyong, owned by Giorgio and Dianne Gjergja, released its first wines in 2001. The vineyard
is planted to pinot noir (20ha), chardonnay (10.4ha) and, more recently, pinot gris (3ha).
Winemaker Sandro Mosele is a graduate of CSU, and has a deservedly high reputation. He
also provides contract winemaking services for others. The Kooyong wines are made at the
state-of-the-art winery of Port Phillip Estate, also owned by the Gjergjas. Exports to the UK,
the US, Canada, Sweden, Norway, Singapore, Hong Kong, Japan and China.

ŸŸŸŸŸ **Single Vineyard Selection Farrago Chardonnay 2013** Flinty edges, but the
soar of fruit is the thing. Grapefruit, apple and white peach with a shining wire
of citrussy acidity strung from start to finish. Creamy oak. Gorgeous persistence.
Good enough to spellbind. Screwcap. 13.5% alc. **Rating** 96 **To** 2021 $60 CM ✪
Single Vineyard Selection Ferrous Pinot Noir 2013 Promises a big story
from the outset, all showy oak and velvety fruit, but once the opening number
has died down a web of finer details is revealed, and there the mesmerising
begins. This needs a little time, but it has tight sleeves and all the right cards
tucked therein. Plums, cherries, steel, spice, polished cedarwood and subtle foresty
elements. It's long, fine and more simply, fantastic to spend time with. Screwcap.
14% alc. **Rating** 96 **To** 2023 $75 CM ✪
Single Vineyard Selection Meres Pinot Noir 2013 Polish, power and poise.
Depth of fruit and flavour but it never becomes bogged down; it keeps flowing
with cherry-plum and chicory flavour, notes of coffee grounds and undergrowth
more than enough to raise your pulse. Excellent length. Terrific wine. Screwcap.
13.5% alc. **Rating** 96 **To** 2025 $75 CM ✪
Single Vineyard Selection Faultline Chardonnay 2013 Fluid but complex.
Smoky and flinty as it flushes pear, apple, chalk and white peach flavour through

the palate. Style, substance and length. Elegant face of Mornington chardonnay. Screwcap. 13% alc. **Rating** 95 **To** 2020 $60 CM

Estate Mornington Peninsula Pinot Noir 2013 Wild with aroma and flavour. Spice, stalk, garden herbs and then dark, juicy plum and black cherry. Call me anything but don't call me simple. Smoky oak slips suggestively under the covers of the fruit. Tremendous drinking from a range of angles. Screwcap. 13.5% alc. **Rating** 95 **To** 2020 $53 CM

Estate Mornington Peninsula Chardonnay 2013 Fleshy pear, apple, grapefruit and cashew flavours make for both stylish and delicious drinking. At all points it feels bright, balanced and eager to please, though flinty notes through the finish underline its inherent sophistication. Builds as it rests in the glass; a standout for this label. Screwcap. 13.5% alc. **Rating** 95 **To** 2020 $42 CM

Massale Mornington Peninsula Pinot Noir 2013 Rating 94 To 2020 $32
Single Vineyard Selection Haven Pinot Noir 2013 Rating 94 To 2024 $75 CM

Krinklewood Biodynamic Vineyard

712 Wollombi Road, Broke, NSW 2330 **Region** Hunter Valley
T (02) 6579 1322 **www**.krinklewood.com **Open** W'ends 10–5
Winemaker Damien Stevens, Rod Windrim **Est.** 1981 **Dozens** 4000 **Vyds** 19.9ha
Krinklewood is a family-owned certified biodynamic organic winery. Every aspect of the property is managed in a holistic and sustainable way, Rod Windrim's extensive herb crops, native grasses and farm animals all contributing to biodynamic preparations to maintain healthy soil biology. The small winery is home to a Vaslin Bucher basket press and two Nomblot French fermentation eggs, a natural approach to winemaking.

Basket Press Chardonnay 2013 Glowing straw colour but fresh and zippy. Alive with struck match, challengingly so, with citrus and assorted melon-like fruit flavours rushing through the palate. Sweet, spicy oak plays a role too. Complex, insistent, thrilling wine. Screwcap. 12.5% alc. **Rating** 95 **To** 2020 $38 CM

Semillon 2014 Rating 92 To 2022 $24 CM ✪
Chardonnay 2013 Rating 91 To 2020 $28
Francesca Rose 2014 Rating 90 To 2016 $24 CM

Kurrajong Downs

Casino Road, Tenterfield, NSW 2372 **Region** New England
T (02) 6736 4590 **www**.kurrajongdownswines.com **Open** Thurs–Mon 9–4
Winemaker Symphony Hill (Mike Hayes) **Est.** 2000 **Dozens** 2000 **Vyds** 4.4ha
Jonus Rhodes arrived at Tenterfield in 1858, lured by the gold he mined for the next 40 years, until his death in '98. He was evidently successful, for the family now runs a 2800ha cattle-grazing property, on which Lynton and Sue Rhodes began the development of their vineyard, at an altitude of 850m, in 1996. Plantings include pinot noir, shiraz, cabernet sauvignon, chardonnay, semillon, gewurztraminer and tempranillo.

Louisa Mary Semillon 2014 A well made Semillon with abundant varietal expression, intensity and drive, in no small measure due to the altitude of 860m and the cold nights preserving life-giving acidity, backing the lemon/lemongrass flavours of the long palate. Screwcap. 11.5% alc. **Rating** 93 **To** 2025 $18 ✪

Kurtz Family Vineyards

731 Light Pass Road, Angaston, SA, 5353 **Region** Barossa Valley
T 0418 810 982 **www**.kurtzfamilyvineyards.com.au **Open** By appt
Winemaker Steve Kurtz **Est.** 1996 **Dozens** 1800 **Vyds** 15.04ha
The Kurtz family vineyard is at Light Pass, with 9ha of shiraz, the remainder planted to chardonnay, cabernet sauvignon, semillon, sauvignon blanc, petit verdot, grenache, mataro and malbec. Steve Kurtz has followed in the footsteps of his great-grandfather Ben Kurtz, who first

grew grapes at Light Pass in the 1930s. During a career working first at Saltram, and then at Foster's until 2006, Steve gained invaluable experience from Nigel Dolan, Caroline Dunn and John Glaetzer, among others. Exports to the US, Canada, Macau and China.

🍷🍷🍷🍷🍷 **Boundary Row Barossa Valley Cabernet Sauvignon 2012** So much to like. It's bright but deep, supple but firm, complex and yet moreish. Smoky/creamy oak, blackcurrant, bay leaves, sweet boysenberry and dust. It all slips deliciously along the tongue. Will cellar, but no compelling reason to wait. Screwcap. 14.5% alc. Rating 95 To 2025 $25 CM ✪

🍷🍷🍷🍷🍷 **Boundary Row Barossa Valley Shiraz 2012** Rating 93 To 2025 $25 CM ✪
Schmick Barossa Shiraz 2010 Rating 93 To 2035 $80 CM
Boundary Row Barossa Valley 2012 Rating 92 To 2022 $25 CM ✪
Seven Sleepers Barossa Valley Shiraz 2013 Rating 91 To 2020 $18 CM ✪

Kyneton Ridge Estate ★★★★☆

90 Blackhill School Road, Kyneton, Vic 3444 **Region** Macedon Ranges
T (03) 5422 7377 www.kynetonridge.com.au **Open** W'ends & public hols 10–5
Winemaker John and Luke Boucher **Est.** 1997 **Dozens** 1200 **Vyds** 4ha
Established by John Boucher and partner Pauline Russell in the shadow of Black Mountain, an ideal environment for pinot noir and chardonnay vines. With five generations of winemaking behind them, John and Luke Boucher continue the quest for quality and refinement. They maintain the traditional hand-making processes that complement the character of the wines; new facilities have recently been introduced to enhance the production process for the sparkling wines. The additional production capacity gives the opportunity to source additional suitable quality parcels of shiraz and cabernet sauvignon from Macedon and Heathcote.

🍷🍷🍷🍷🍷 **Premium Macedon Ranges Pinot Noir 2013** Open-fermented after a long cold soak, hand-plunged and basket-pressed, matured in French oak. Has ample colour, the bouquet full of rich plum fruit, the palate both deep and complex, with sparklets of spice and forest stitched through the plum. Will cellar very well. Screwcap. 13.5% alc. Rating 94 To 2023 $38
Heathcote Shiraz 2010 Has continued to prosper since first tasted over 2 years ago, its regional – and varietal – expression most impressive, with black fruits liberally studded with licorice and pepper, the tannins ensuring a long life. A gold medal at the Daylesford Wine Show '13 added to its trophy in '11. Screwcap. 15% alc. Rating 94 To 2030 $45

🍷🍷🍷🍷🍷 **Macedon Ranges Cabernet Sauvignon 2010** Rating 92 To 2020 $35
Macedon Ranges Cabernet Sauvignon 2013 Rating 91 To 2023 $30

La Bise ★★★★

PO Box 918, Williamstown, SA 5351 **Region** Adelaide Hills/Southern Flinders
T 0439 823 251 www.labise.com.au **Open** Not
Winemaker Natasha Mooney **Est.** 2006 **Dozens** 1500
This is a reasonably significant busman's holiday for Natasha Mooney, a well-known and highly regarded winemaker whose 'day job' (her term) is to provide winemaking consultancy services for some of SA's larger wineries. This allows her to find small, unique parcels of grapes that might otherwise be blended into large-volume brands. She manages the arrangements so that there is no conflict of interest, which allows her to make wines that are about fruit and vineyard expression. She aims for mouthfeel and drinkability without high alcohol, and for that she should be loudly applauded.

🍷🍷🍷🍷🍷 **Le Petite Frais Rose 2014** A blend of sangiovese, tempranillo and shiraz. The bouquet is positively perfumed with rose petals to the fore, the palate tangy and fresh as a daisy. Exciting rose. Screwcap. 13.5% alc. Rating 94 To 2016 $19 ✪

🍷🍷🍷🍷🍷 **Organic Southern Flinders Shiraz 2010** Rating 92 To 2025 $19 ✪
Adelaide Hills Chardonnay 2014 Rating 90 To 2018 $19 ✪

La Curio ★★★★☆

Cnr Foggo Road/Kangarilla Road, McLaren Vale, SA 5171 **Region** McLaren Vale
T (08) 8323 7999 **www.**lacuriowines.com **Open** By appt
Winemaker Adam Hooper **Est.** 2003 **Dozens** 1500
Adam Hooper purchases small parcels of grapes from vineyards in McLaren Vale with an average age of 40 years, the oldest 120 years, the wines made at Redheads Studio in McLaren Vale. The manacles depicted on the striking label are those of Harry Houdini, and the brand proposition is very cleverly worked through. Winemaking techniques, too, are avant garde, and highly successful. Exports to the UK, Canada, Sweden and Hong Kong.

99999 **Reserve Shiraz 2012** Average vine age 80 years, oldest 120; open fermenters, hand-plunged, matured in new and used French and American hogsheads for 18 months. Has the intensity and focus expected from such old vines; blackberry and black cherry fruit is complexed by threads of bitter chocolate and licorice, the whole package convincing. Screwcap. 14.5% alc. **Rating** 95 **To** 2032 $31

99999 **Reserve Bush Vine Grenache 2012** **Rating** 93 **To** 2022 $27 ❂
The Selfie Aglianico Rose 2014 **Rating** 92 **To** 2016 $17 ❂

La Linea ★★★★☆

36 Shipsters Road, Kensington Park, SA 5068 (postal) **Region** Adelaide Hills
T (08) 8431 3556 **www.**lalinea.com.au **Open** Not
Winemaker Peter Leske **Est.** 2007 **Dozens** 3500 **Vyds** 9ha
La Linea is a partnership of several experienced wine industry professionals, including Peter Leske and David LeMire MW. Peter was among the first to recognise the potential of tempranillo in Australia, and his knowledge of it is reflected in the three wine styles made from the variety: Tempranillo Rose, Tempranillo blended from several Adelaide Hills vineyards, and Norteno, from a single vineyard at the northern end of the Hills. Two Rieslings are produced under the Vertigo label: TRKN (short for trocken), and the off-dry 25GR (25g/l residual sugar).

99999 **Vertigo TRKN Adelaide Hills Riesling 2013** Pale straw-ish colour. Grown at altitude in the Adelaide Hills. Floral style, as much stone fruit and slate as citrus, but making a clear impression of power/concentration. Sizzles through the finish. Just when you think it's about to stop, the palate keeps motoring on. Screwcap. 12% alc. **Rating** 94 **To** 2025 $26 CM

99999 **Vertigo 25GR Adelaide Hills Riesling 2013** **Rating** 92 **To** 2021 $24 CM ❂
Adelaide Hills Tempranillo 2013 **Rating** 92 **To** 2023 $27

La Pleiade ★★★★★

c/- Jasper Hill, Drummonds Lane, Heathcote, Vic 3523 **Region** Heathcote
T (03) 5433 2528 **Open** By appt
Winemaker Ron Laughton, Michel Chapoutier **Est.** 1998 **Dozens** 500 **Vyds** 9ha
This is the joint venture of Michel and Corinne Chapoutier and Ron and Elva Laughton. In spring 1998 a vineyard of Australian and imported French shiraz clones was planted. The vineyard is run biodynamically, and the winemaking is deliberately designed to place maximum emphasis on the fruit quality. Exports to the UK, the US, France, Singapore and Hong Kong.

99999 **Heathcote Shiraz 2012** The clear, full crimson-purple colour has that intangible quality that promises much, the expectations more than fulfilled on the bouquet and palate. This is a beautifully wrought (I would used 'crafted' but that is nauseously overused in marketing blah) medium-bodied wine, effortlessly uncoiling its array of red fruits through the length of the palate, an exercise in restrained elegance. Cork. 13.5% alc. **Rating** 97 **To** 2035 $75

Lake Breeze Wines   ★★★★★

Step Road, Langhorne Creek, SA 5255 **Region** Langhorne Creek
T (08) 8537 3017 **www**.lakebreeze.com.au **Open** 7 days 10–5
Winemaker Greg Follett **Est.** 1987 **Dozens** 20 000 **Vyds** 90ha

The Folletts have been farmers at Langhorne Creek since 1880, and grapegrowers since the 1930s. Part of the grape production is sold, but the quality of the Lake Breeze wines is exemplary, with the red wines particularly appealing. Lake Breeze also owns and makes the False Cape wines from Kangaroo Island. Exports to the UK, Canada, Switzerland, Denmark, Germany, Vietnam, Singapore, Hong Kong, Japan and China.

ŸŸŸŸŸ **The Drake Langhorne Creek Shiraz Cabernet Sauvignon 2010** A 70/30% blend that has retained exceptional colour, and similar freshness on the bouquet and palate; surely it can't be 5yo, but it is. The balance and integration of the full array of perfectly ripened black fruits effortlessly uncoils as the wine travels along the supple, medium-bodied palate. This is Langhorne Creek royalty: the Drake should be made the Duke. Screwcap. 14.5% alc. **Rating** 97 **To** 2030 $70 ✪

ŸŸŸŸŸ **Arthur's Reserve Langhorne Creek Cabernet Sauvignon Petit Verdot Malbec 2012** An 86/9/5% blend matured for 22 months in new French oak, 250 dozen made. It has excellent colour, still youthful, as is the bouquet and, even more, the beautifully tempered palate; it is only medium-bodied, but has perfect balance and great length. Screwcap. 14% alc. **Rating** 96 **To** 2042 $38 ✪
Section 54 Langhorne Creek Shiraz 2013 Open-fermented and matured for 18 months in French oak. Brightly coloured; the bouquet is complex, with dark berry fruits and a fragrant, warm infusion of quality oak; the palate adds licorice and bitter chocolate to the equation, underlining the complexity (and future) of the wine. Screwcap. 14.5% alc. **Rating** 95 **To** 2033 $24 ✪
Winemaker's Selection Langhorne Creek Shiraz 2013 An immaculately balanced and shaped medium-bodied palate, oak and tannin support for the fruit precisely measured. It may be churlish to say so, but it doesn't have the X-factor of Section 54. Screwcap. 14.5% alc. **Rating** 94 **To** 2030 $38
Langhorne Creek Cabernet Sauvignon 2013 From 45yo vines. The good depth to the colour signals a wine with all the deliciously soft and fleshy mid-palate fruit Langhorne Creek can provide, yet leaving it with fine, savoury tannins to highlight its varietal character. Screwcap. 14% alc. **Rating** 94 **To** 2028 $25 ✪
False Cape The Captain Cabernet Sauvignon 2012 A cool-grown Cabernet of considerable distinction; blackcurrant fruit is given stature and texture by nigh-on perfect tannins giving the flavour profile an edge of bay leaf/black olive. Has time on its side. Screwcap. 14% alc. **Rating** 94 **To** 2032 $30 ✪

ŸŸŸŸŸ **Winemaker's Selection Cabernet 2012** **Rating** 93 **To** 2022 $25 ✪
Reserve Langhorne Creek Chardonnay 2014 **Rating** 92 **To** 2019 $24 ✪
Bernoota Shiraz Cabernet 2013 **Rating** 92 **To** 2023 $22 ✪
Bullant Cabernet Merlot 2013 **Rating** 92 **To** 2023 $17 ✪
False Cape Unknown Sailor Cabernet Merlot 2012 **Rating** 90 **To** 2020 $20 ✪

Lake Moodemere Vineyards   ★★★

12 Moodemere Road, Rutherglen, Vic 3685 **Region** Rutherglen
T (02) 6032 9449 **www**.moodemerewines.com.au **Open** Mon, Thurs, Fri, Sat 10–5
Winemaker Michael Chambers **Est.** 1995 **Dozens** 3000 **Vyds** 20.74ha

Michael and Belinda Chambers are sixth-generation members of the famous Chambers family of Rutherglen, and Michael considers himself fortunate to have been mentored by grandfather Bill Chambers. The vineyards include the Italian grape variety biancone, a vineyard specialty made in a light-bodied late-harvest style. The cellar door has moved to the original homestead built in the 1850s (home to four generations of the Chambers family, including Bill and Michael), with panoramic views of Lake Moodemere.

♥♥♥♥ Rutherglen Moodemere Muscat NV The colour isn't deep, nor are the flavours especially concentrated; it is distinctly varietal, with raisins to the fore; its finish is quite sweet, and seems low in rancio for Grand Muscat (as the back label shows). 500ml. Cork. 17.5% alc. **Rating** 89 **To** 2016 $32

Lake's Folly   ★★★★★

2416 Broke Road, Pokolbin, NSW 2320 **Region** Hunter Valley
T (02) 4998 7507 **www**.lakesfolly.com.au **Open** 7 days 10–4 while wine available
Winemaker Rodney Kempe **Est.** 1963 **Dozens** 4500 **Vyds** 12.2ha
The first of the weekend wineries to produce wines for commercial sale, long revered for its Cabernet Sauvignon and nowadays its Chardonnay. Very properly, terroir and climate produce a distinct regional influence and thus a distinctive wine style. Lake's Folly no longer has any connection with the Lake family, having been acquired some years ago by Perth businessman Peter Fogarty. Peter's family company previously established the Millbrook Winery in the Perth Hills and has since acquired Deep Woods Estate in Margaret River, so is no stranger to the joys and agonies of running a small winery.

♥♥♥♥♥ Hill Block Chardonnay 2014 Barrel-fermented in French oak. The Hill Block vines are now mature, giving a wine with slightly greater intensity, grip and length than the original plantings. 150 dozen made. Screwcap. 14% alc. **Rating** 96 **To** 2024 $80
Hunter Valley Chardonnay 2014 Barrel-fermented in French oak (33% new) with extended lees contact during maturation. Bright straw-green; a distinguished and complex wine with layers of flavour, but no soft stone fruit notes. Simply has to be vine age (and site) that distinguishes it from all Hunter Valley Chardonnays (other than Tyrrell's). Screwcap. 14.5% alc. **Rating** 95 **To** 2020 $65
Hunter Valley Cabernets 2013 A 60/22/12/6% blend of cabernet, shiraz, petit verdot and merlot. A typically elegant Folly, and has taken full advantage of the vintage; cassis, redcurrant, cedar and wisp of earth typical of the Hunter Valley are all to be had. Cork. 12.6% alc. **Rating** 95 **To** 2033 $65

Lambert Vineyards   ★★★★

810 Norton Road, Wamboin, NSW 2620 **Region** Canberra District
T (02) 6238 3866 **www**.lambertvineyards.com.au **Open** Thurs–Sun 10–5
Winemaker Steve and Ruth Lambert **Est.** 1998 **Dozens** 4000 **Vyds** 10ha
Ruth and Steve Lambert have established riesling (2.5ha), pinot noir, pinot gris (2ha each), merlot (1.5ha), chardonnay (1ha), cabernet sauvignon and shiraz (0.5ha each). Steve makes the many wines onsite, and does so with skill and sensitivity.

♥♥♥♥♥ Riesling 2013 No tricks to the winemaking: clean juice fermented with cultured yeast in temperature-controlled stainless steel tanks. Shows – yet again – how the continental climate of Canberra is an ideal home for the variety; it has intense citrus and citrus zest flavours, squeaky acidity responsible for this particular (attractive) mouthfeel. Screwcap. 12.5% alc. **Rating** 94 **To** 2023 $22 ○

♥♥♥♥ Pinot Gris 2013 Rating 89 **To** 2016 $24
Pinot Noir 2013 Rating 89 **To** 2019 $25

Lambrook Wines   ★★★★

6 Coorara Avenue, Payneham South, SA 5070 **Region** Adelaide Hills
T 0437 672 651 **www**.lambrook.com.au **Open** By appt
Winemaker Adam Lampit, Michael Sykes **Est.** 2008 **Dozens** 5000
This is a virtual winery created by husband and wife team Adam and Brooke Lampit. With almost two decades of industry experience between them, they began purchasing sauvignon blanc, shiraz and pinot noir (for sparkling) in 2008. Adam's experience has come through working with Stonehaven, Norfolk Rise and Bird in Hand.

♟♟♟♟♟ **Adelaide Hills Chardonnay 2013** Hand-picked, whole bunch-pressed and fermented in French oak. Gleaming green-quartz, it has good intensity, line and length, the flavours running through nectarine, white peach and a touch of grapefruit. Screwcap. 13% alc. **Rating** 92 **To** 2019 $30

Amelia Rose Adelaide Hills Shiraz 2012 Dense, dark colour with black cherry, licorice and asphalt flavours oozing through the palate. Not a lot of room for nuance, but refreshing acidity and assorted dried herb notes keep the attraction ticking over. Screwcap. 14.5% alc. **Rating** 92 **To** 2022 $40 CM

Lamont's Winery ★★★★☆

85 Bisdee Road, Millendon, WA 6056 **Region** Swan Valley
T (08) 9296 4485 **www**.lamonts.com.au **Open** Thurs–Sun 10–5
Winemaker Digby Leddin **Est.** 1978 **Dozens** 7000 **Vyds** 2ha
Corin Lamont is the daughter of the late Jack Mann, and oversees the making of wines in a style that would have pleased her father. Lamont's also boasts a superb restaurant run by granddaughter Kate Lamont. The wines are going from strength to strength, utilising both estate-grown and contract-grown (from southern regions) grapes. Lamont's restaurant in Perth, open for lunch and dinner Mon–Fri, offers food of the highest quality, and is superbly situated. The Margaret River cellar door is open 7 days 11–5 for wine tasting, sales and lunch.

♟♟♟♟♟ **Frankland Dessert Riesling 2013** This is a wine of presence and power, utterly unlike the banal late-picked/off dry styles. The juice was freeze-concentrated, a technique that increases both sugar and acidity, leaving them in balance; a wonderful aperitif on a summer's day, a piece of fresh fruit the perfect match. Screwcap. 8.5% alc. **Rating** 95 **To** 2018 $30 ✪

Mount Barker Riesling 2014 Zesty, lively and fresh; unsweetened lemon and lime flavours repeat the bouquet, braced by minerally acidity; has excellent length and balance, and will richly repay extended cellaring. Screwcap. 12% alc. **Rating** 94 **To** 2029 $25 ✪

Margaret River Cabernet Sauvignon 2013 A potent, powerful, medium to full-bodied Cabernet with a mix of blackcurrant, black olive, dried herb and varietal tannins. Has all the makings, but needs time to soften and open up – which it will most assuredly do. Screwcap. 13.8% alc. **Rating** 94 **To** 2035 $35

Family Reserve 2013 A blend of malbec and shiraz from Geographe and cabernet sauvignon from Margaret River. Good depth to the colour and to the dense black fruits; despite that density, the wine flows evenly through the mouth, and has the balance to reward prolonged cellaring if that is your wish. Screwcap. 14% alc. **Rating** 94 **To** 2028 $30 ✪

♟♟♟♟♟ **Quartet 2013 Rating** 90 **To** 2020 $18 ✪

Landaire ★★★★☆

PO Box 14, Padthaway, SA 5271 **Region** Padthaway
T 0417 408 147 **www**.landaire.com.au **Open** Not
Winemaker Pete Bissell **Est.** 2012 **Dozens** 1000 **Vyds** 200ha
David and Carolyn Brown have been major grapegrowers in Padthaway over the past 18 years, David having been brought up with a vineyard and farming background, Carolyn with a background in science. Landaire has evolved from a desire after many years of growing grapes at their Glendon Vineyard to select small quantities of the best grapes and have them vinified by Pete Bissell, chief winemaker at Balnaves. It has proved a sure-fire recipe for success.

♟♟♟♟♟ **Single Vineyard Vermentino 2014** Estate-grown, hand-picked, whole bunch-pressed, 85% fermented on solids for 2 weeks in tank, 15% in used French barriques. A very powerful wine with lemon blossom and pith notes on the long, lingering finish. Screwcap. 13.5% alc. **Rating** 94 **To** 2016 $26 ✪

Single Vineyard Tempranillo 2014 Estate-grown and hand-picked; 25% whole bunch inclusion, with 4-day cold soak and a total of 14 days on skins; a small portion went to new and used French oak, the remainder kept in tank. The approach has succeeded brilliantly, the spicy bouquet with red berry aromas, the palate with cherry and some almost sweet/creamy tannins, an oxymoron of a description if ever there was one. Screwcap. 14% alc. **Rating** 94 **To** 2025 $26 **○**

Lane's End Vineyard

885 Mount William Road, Lancefield, Vic 3435 **Region** Macedon Ranges
T (03) 5429 1760 **www**.lanesend.com.au **Open** By appt
Winemaker Howard Matthews, Kilchurn Wines **Est.** 1985 **Dozens** 400 **Vyds** 2ha
Pharmacist Howard Matthews and family purchased the former Woodend Winery in 2000, with 1.8ha of chardonnay and pinot noir (and a small amount of cabernet franc) dating back to the mid-1980s. The cabernet franc has been grafted over to pinot noir (with a mix of four clones), and the chardonnay now totals 1ha. Howard has been making the wines for over a decade.

⚑⚑⚑⚑⚑ Macedon Ranges Chardonnay 2013 Whole bunch-pressed, 100% barrel-fermented (25% new French), 50% mlf, 11 months' maturation. This is seriously good winemaking at work, for all the inputs are seamlessly joined, none more obvious than any other, except to say the often-difficult mlf has been particularly well judged. The result is a classy cool-climate Chardonnay with a long future. Screwcap. 13% alc. **Rating** 96 **To** 2028 $33 **○**
Macedon Ranges Pinot Noir 2013 90% destemmed, 10% whole bunch, open pot, wild yeast, hot fermentation, pressed to French oak (40% new) for completion of fermentation and 11 months' maturation. Bright and clear colour; this is a delicious Pinot from its bouquet through to the aftertaste; the fine and supple palate has an uncommon purity to its display of pinot red fruits, the finish bright and beckoning. Screwcap. 13% alc. **Rating** 96 **To** 2023 $38 **○**
Isanda Macedon Ranges Chardonnay 2013 The intensity and length of the palate is explained by the pH of 3.02 and titratable acidity of 7.5g/l; this make-up explains the apparently minerally flavours, although there is no mineral take-up into the fruit; the wine is bracingly complex, and will have a fascinating future. Screwcap. 12.5% alc. **Rating** 94 **To** 2025 $28 **○**

⚑⚑⚑⚑⚐ Macedon Ranges Cabernet Franc Merlot 2012 Rating 92 **To** 2018 $23 **○**
Cottage Macedon Ranges Chardonnay 2014 Rating 91 **To** 2018 $21 **○**

Langmeil Winery ★★★★★

Cnr Para Road/Langmeil Road, Tanunda, SA 5352 **Region** Barossa Valley
T (08) 8563 2595 **www**.langmeilwinery.com.au **Open** 7 days 10.30–4.30
Winemaker Paul Lindner, Tyson Bitter **Est.** 1996 **Dozens** 35 000 **Vyds** 31.4ha
Vines were first planted at Langmeil (which possesses the oldest block in Australia) in the 1840s, and the first winery on the site, known as Paradale Wines, opened in 1932. In '96, cousins Carl and Richard Lindner with brother-in-law Chris Bitter formed a partnership to acquire and refurbish the winery and its 5ha vineyard (planted to shiraz, and including 2ha planted in 1843). Another vineyard was acquired in '98, which included cabernet sauvignon and grenache. In late 2012 the Lindner family put a succession plan into action: Richard and Shirley Lindner, and their sons Paul and James, have acquired 100% ownership of the business. In terms of management, little changes: Paul has been chief winemaker and James the sales and marketing manager since the winery began in 1996. Exports to all major markets.

⚑⚑⚑⚑⚑ The Freedom 1843 Barossa Shiraz 2012 169yo vines, open-fermented, basket-pressed, 2 years in French oak. A brilliant exposition of elegance and balance: the idea that very old vines produce full-bodied thick fruit is 100% wrong – this has a gloriously juicy palate with both red and black fruits running through an extremely long palate. Mouth-watering purity. You should kneel in the presence of a wine such as this. Screwcap. 14.5% alc. **Rating** 98 **To** 2042 $125 **○**

⚑⚑⚑⚑⚑ Orphan Bank Barossa Shiraz 2012 Original vines planted 1860, 10 rows relocated after 150 years; basket-pressed, open-fermented, matured for 2 years in

French oak. Unsurprisingly rich and layered blackberry/blackcurrant fruit with notes of earth and licorice, yet all this comes in a measured way. Excellent oak and tannin balance. Screwcap. 14.5% alc. **Rating** 96 **To** 2042 $50 ✪

The Fifth Wave Barossa Grenache 2012 The vines are more than 70yo, classed as survivor vines by the Barossa Valley Charter. This is a very good Grenache, reflecting the great vintage, and also what may be a change in the winemaking philosophy, seeking finesse as well as flavour; there are no cooked or confection flavours whatsoever. Screwcap. 14.5% alc. **Rating** 95 **To** 2022 $40

Eden Valley Dry Riesling 2014 From 35yo vines. Has an abundance of juicy lime fruit, making it a now or later proposition; the acidity is balanced, but won't guarantee a multi-decade life. Screwcap. 11.5% alc. **Rating** 94 **To** 2024 $25 ✪

The Long Mile Barossa Shiraz 2013 A potent, medium to full-bodied Shiraz with multiple layers of blackberry, plum and licorice sandwiched between ripe tannins and integrated oak. Screwcap. 14.5% alc. **Rating** 94 **To** 2033 $25 ✪

🍷🍷🍷🍷🍷 **Jackaman's Barossa Cabernet Sauvignon 2012** Rating 93 To 2032 $50
Live Wire Medium Sweet Barossa Riesling 2014 Rating 93 To 2024 $20 ✪
Valley Floor Shiraz 2012 Rating 92 To 2022 $30 CM

Lanz Vineyards ★★★★★

220 Scenic Road, Lyndoch, SA 5351 **Region** Barossa Valley
T 0417 858 967 **www**.lanzvineyards.com **Open** By appt
Winemaker Michael Paxton **Est.** 1998 **Dozens** 500 **Vyds** 16ha

The major part of the grape production is sold to premium producers in the Barossa Valley. However, Marianne and Thomas Lanz take enough of the grapes to make their Shiraz and Grenache Shiraz Mourvedre. Their choice of Michael Paxton as winemaker is no accident; he is a committed biodynamic grower (as is his father, David) and the Lanzs are aiming at the 'three L' wine style: Lower alcohol, Lower intervention, and Lower carbon footprint. Exports to Switzerland, Germany and Singapore.

🍷🍷🍷🍷🍷 **Limited Edition The Grand Reserve Barossa Valley Shiraz 2012** Hand-picked, destemmed, open-fermented, hand-plunged, 10 days on skins, part finished in barrel, 20 months in 33% new French, 33% new American, 33% in used French oak. This is an outstanding Shiraz in every respect: colour, balance, length, and above all, its perfect evocation of supple black-fruited shiraz, the tannins smooth and velvety, all framed by quality oak. Screwcap. 13.8% alc. **Rating** 97 **To** 2037 $39 ✪

Lark Hill ★★★★★

521 Bungendore Road, Bungendore, NSW 2621 **Region** Canberra District
T (02) 6238 1393 **www**.larkhillwine.com.au **Open** Wed–Mon 10–5
Winemaker Dr David, Sue and Chris Carpenter **Est.** 1978 **Dozens** 4000 **Vyds** 10.5ha

The Lark Hill vineyard is situated at an altitude of 860m, offering splendid views of the Lake George escarpment. The Carpenters have made wines of real quality, style and elegance from the start, but have defied all the odds (and conventional thinking) with the quality of their Pinot Noirs in favourable vintages. Significant changes have come in the wake of son Christopher gaining three degrees, including a double in wine science and viticulture through CSU, and the biodynamic certification of the vineyard. They have also planted 1ha of gruner veltliner; it is hard to understand why there have been so few plantings of this high-quality Austrian variety. In 2011 Lark Hill purchased one of the two Ravensworth vineyards from Bryan Martin, with plantings of sangiovese, shiraz, viognier, roussanne and marsanne; they will also be converting it (renamed Dark Horse) to biodynamic farming. Exports to the UK.

🍷🍷🍷🍷🍷 **Canberra District Riesling 2014** Biodynamic wine grown in a continental climate that is right up riesling's alley. The flowery bouquet leads into a long, particularly well balanced palate, lime and lemon fruits aplenty, and framed by crisp, crunchy acidity. Screwcap. 11.5% alc. **Rating** 95 **To** 2029 $35 ✪

Canberra District Chardonnay 2014 Biodynamic. Wild yeast fermentation in French oak (a small amount new) and 9 months' maturation on lees has worked very well, the varietal fruit expression mouth-wateringly intense and persistent, the softening effect of prolonged lees contact barely perceptible; the length of the palate is excellent. Screwcap. 12.5% alc. **Rating** 95 **To** 2024 $40

Canberra District Gruner Veltliner 2014 May not have the same instant varietal signal of white pepper as it does in its home base, but it does have overall varietal character, gently mouth-filling, and with length and balance. Screwcap. 12.5% alc. **Rating** 94 **To** 2024 $45

🍷🍷🍷🍷 **Canberra District Shiraz Viognier 2014** **Rating** 91 **To** 2020 $35

Larry Cherubino Wines ★★★★★

15 York Street, Subiaco, WA 6008 **Region** Western Australia
T (08) 9382 2379 **www**.larrycherubino.com **Open** Not
Winemaker Larry Cherubino **Est.** 2005 **Dozens** 8000 **Vyds** 120ha

Larry Cherubino has had a particularly distinguished winemaking career, first at Hardys Tintara, then Houghton, and thereafter as consultant/Flying Winemaker in Australia, NZ, South Africa, the US and Italy. He has developed three ranges: at the top is Cherubino (Riesling, Sauvignon Blanc, Shiraz and Cabernet Sauvignon); next The Yard, five single-vineyard wines from WA; and at the bottom the Ad Hoc label, all single-region wines. The range and quality of his wines is extraordinary, the prices irresistible. The runaway success of the business has seen the accumulation of 120ha of vineyards, the appointment of an additional winemaker, and Larry's own appointment as Director of Winemaking at Robert Oatley Vineyards. The delphic one-liners on the back labels are a further challenge. Exports to the UK, the US, Canada, Ireland, Switzerland, Hong Kong, South Korea, Singapore, China and NZ.

🍷🍷🍷🍷🍷 **Cherubino Frankland River Cabernet Sauvignon 2013** Hand-picked and sorted, cooled overnight, fermentation and maceration for 6 weeks with minimal pump-overs, the ferment peaking at 27°C; pressed, 7 days' settling before taken to French oak for 17 months. Full purple-crimson; the bouquet sends out an immediate alert of what lies in store with the palate; its power and length are effortless, the flavours of cassis and dried herbs. Quite beautiful, but it is the utterly exceptional texture and structure that take this wine into the stratosphere. Screwcap. 14.5% alc. **Rating** 98 **To** 2053 $110 ✪

🍷🍷🍷🍷🍷 **Cherubino Margaret River Chardonnay 2014** Hand-picked, whole bunch-pressed direct to new and used oak for wild yeast fermentation. The green tint to the colour is a come-on for a wine that doesn't really need foreplay, so intense and deep is its orchestra of fruits, quality oak the conductor's baton. Cost has not been a consideration in building this wine. Screwcap. 12.5% alc. **Rating** 96 **To** 2024 $49 ✪

Cherubino Laissez Faire Syrah 2013 Hand-picked and sorted, wild yeast-fermented, 6 months in used French oak, no additions except SO_2. Deeply coloured, the bouquet is powerful, the full-bodied palate even more so, opening with a panoply of sombre black fruits, then picking up spicy, savoury briary nuances, all careering through to the punctuated finish. If it's syrah, it's Côte Rôtie sans viognier. Screwcap. 13.8% alc. **Rating** 96 **To** 2043 $39 ✪

The Yard Riversdale Frankland River Cabernet Sauvignon 2013 Hand-picked, sorted, fermentation in small fermenters, fermented and macerated for 4 weeks, matured in new and 1yo French oak for 8 months. It is a distinguished wine, speaking loud and clear about its terroir, with juicy blackcurrant/cassis/black olive equally penetrating. A modern evocation of Frankland River cabernet with its cleaning finish and aftertaste. Screwcap. 14.5% alc. **Rating** 96 **To** 2038 $35 ✪

Ad Hoc Avant Gardening Frankland Cabernet Sauvignon Malbec 2013 Outside of Wendouree, Australia's finest Cabernet Malbecs have come from the Riversdale Vineyard; this must be close-on the best-value cabernet blend on the market today, its palate ablaze with juicy red berry, plum and cassis fruit, the tannins relegated to the outfield, oak likewise. Screwcap. 14% alc. **Rating** 96 To 2028 $21 ○

Cherubino Porongurup Riesling 2014 Hand-picked and made with the usual Cherubino deceptive hands-off protocols, not far removed from natural winemaking, except that the result is as far removed from yellow wine as the sun from the moon. Classic Porongurup, all about finesse and length, the finish crisp and bone dry, citrus and mineral appearing on the aftertaste. Watch this space 5 years hence. Screwcap. 11.5% alc. **Rating** 95 **To** 2034 $35 ○

Cherubino Pemberton Sauvignon Blanc 2014 While the wine has the usual Cherubino freshness and lightness of touch, there is both textural and flavour complexity from wild yeast barrel fermentation in new French oak. The flavours are best described as semi-tropical, but with a gently savoury backdrop. Screwcap. 13% alc. **Rating** 95 **To** 2015 $35 ○

The Yard Channybearup Vineyard Pemberton Sauvignon Blanc 2014 Has more intensity and power than is usual for Larry Cherubino, and this appears to be a direct reflection of the mature Channybearup Vineyard, the flavours in a cut grass/snow pea/fresh asparagus spectrum, with an overarching skein of lemony acidity. Screwcap. 13.5% alc. **Rating** 95 **To** 2016 $25 ○

The Yard Acacia Vineyard Frankland River Shiraz 2013 In the heartland of Cherubino style, supremely elegant, and with sotto voce complexity; here cedary/woodsy/earthy/spicy notes all accompany the black fruits; Cherubino disdains elevated fruit ripeness, forceful tannins and obvious new oak. Screwcap. 14% alc. **Rating** 95 **To** 2028 $35 ○

The Yard Riversdale Vineyard Frankland River Shiraz 2013 Bright crimson-purple, the colours nailed to the Cherubino mast for all his Frankland Shirazs; here there are accents of almost cassis-like fruit on the bouquet, the palate engaged in a hide-and-seek game for the fruit, the tannins and the oak, all of which come and go in an ultimately savoury framework. Screwcap. 14% alc. **Rating** 95 **To** 2033 $35 ○

Ad Hoc Middle of Everywhere Frankland River Shiraz 2013 Full crimson-purple; this is a full-bodied Shiraz with Frankland River stamped all over it; a deep stream of inky black fruits, licorice, cracked pepper and spice flows through the palate, ultimately arriving at the finish with as much power as it had at the start of its journey. One of the bargains of the year. Screwcap. 14% alc. **Rating** 95 **To** 2038 $21 ○

Cherubino Cowaramup Cabernet Sauvignon 2013 Hand-picked and sorted, matured in French oak for 10 months. Bright crimson; it would seem there's a fair amount of new oak within the blackcurrant and redcurrant fruit, ripe tannins also having their say. Totally satisfactory as a whole. Screwcap. 13.8% alc. **Rating** 95 **To** 2033 $49

Ad Hoc Straw Man Sauvignon Semillon 2014 **Rating** 94 **To** 2017 $21 ○
Pedestal Semillon Sauvignon 2014 **Rating** 94 **To** 2016 $25 ○
Cherubino Laissez Faire Chardonnay 2014 **Rating** 94 **To** 2022 $29 ○

Latta ★★★★

47 Pickfords Road, Coghills Creek, Vic 3364 **Region** Macedon Ranges
T 0408 594 454 **www.**lattavino.com.au **Open** By appt
Winemaker Owen Latta **Est.** 2012 **Dozens** 600

This is the culmination of a long-standing desire of Owen Latta to make wines from small plantings in the Pyrenees, Grampians and Macedon regions. Eastern Peake, owned by the Latta family, makes wine from the Ballarat region, and the rationale was to avoid confusing the nature of the two operations. He says he has empathy with the growers he works with from when he and his father were themselves contract grapegrowers for others. The degree of that empathy is fortified by the fact that the growers have been known to the Latta family for over 15 years. The wines are, to put it mildly, unconventional.

ⵟⵟⵟⵟⵟ **Olandezos Gisborne Pinot Noir 2013** Pinot Noir in a Riesling bottle. Full of sweet, lifted fruit, almost jellied in its sweetness but tempered by notes of spice, foresty herbs and woodsmoke. Extends appreciably through the finish. Comes complete with an undergrowthy complexity. It's not short on interest. Screwcap. 13% alc. **Rating** 92 **To** 2021 $50 CM

Olandezos Sur Lie Gisborne Sauvignon Blanc 2013 Wild yeast, mlf, low sulphur, 17 months on full lees, unfined and unfiltered. Straw-coloured and complex with yeasty lemongrass, thistle and green melon flavours. Has an earthiness, almost a gaminess. Sits well outside the mainstream. Worth a look. Screwcap. 13% alc. **Rating** 90 **To** 2015 $35 CM

ŸŸŸŸ　Reflection Dextrous Batch Cluster Contact Project – OzA 2013 **Rating** 89 **To** 2015 $50 CM

Laughing Jack　★★★★★

194 Stonewell Road, Marananga, SA 5355 **Region** Barossa Valley
T (08) 8562 3878 www.laughingjackwines.com.au **Open** By appt
Winemaker Shawn Kalleske **Est.** 1999 **Dozens** 3000 **Vyds** 38.88ha
The Kalleske family has many branches in the Barossa Valley. Laughing Jack is owned by Shawn, Nathan, Ian and Carol Kalleske, and Linda Schroeter. The lion's share of the vineyard is planted to shiraz, with lesser amounts of semillon and grenache. Vine age varies considerably, with old dry-grown shiraz the jewel in the crown. A small part of the grape production is taken for the Laughing Jack Shiraz. As any Australian knows, the kookaburra is also called the laughing jackass, and there is a resident flock of kookaburras in the stands of blue and red gums surrounding the vineyards. Exports to Malaysia, Hong Kong and China.

ŸŸŸŸŸ　Greenock Barossa Valley Shiraz 2012 The '11 was declassified, making this
the follow-up to the excellent '10. It's in the same quality league. Matured in
both French and American oak, it offers an impressive march of coffee-cream,
blackberry, plum and clove flavour, a raspberried brightness picking out the finish.
It's a wine that doesn't take a backward step yet manages to keep its cool/remain
stylish throughout. Screwcap. 14.5% alc. **Rating** 95 **To** 2032 $40 CM

Moppa Hill Barossa Valley Shiraz 2013 There's a volume of flavour here but
it's not overdone; there's even a suggestion of elegance. Dark, roasted plums, toast,
peppercorns and bitter chocolate. It's dense but not dull; there's a freshness to
the way its oozes through the mouth. Modern and traditional at once. Screwcap.
14.5% alc. **Rating** 94 **To** 2030 $35 CM

ŸŸŸŸŸ　Jack's Barossa Valley Shiraz 2013 **Rating** 92 **To** 2023 $23 CM ✪

Laurance of Margaret River　★★★★★

3518 Caves Road, Wilyabrup, WA 6280 **Region** Margaret River
T (08) 9755 6199 www.laurancewines.com **Open** 7 days 11–5
Winemaker Naturaliste Vintners (Bruce Dukes) **Est.** 2001 **Dozens** 8000 **Vyds** 23ha
Founder and chairwoman Dianne Laurance is the driving force behind this family-owned business. The 100ha property has vines (planted in 1996 to three clones of chardonnay, plus sauvignon blanc, shiraz, cabernet sauvignon, semillon and merlot), beautiful gardens, artwork and sculptures. The quality of the wines can be lost behind the unusual bottles, reminiscent of Perrier-Jouët's Belle Epoque deluxe Champagne. Exports to Singapore, Hong Kong, Malaysia, Thailand and China.

ŸŸŸŸŸ　Chardonnay 2012 Estate-grown, and very much in the Laurance style; barrel-
fermented then matured in French oak for 9 months. Attractive regional fruit,
with grapefruit, white peach and creamy/nutty nuances running through to the
well-balanced finish. Screwcap. 13.5% alc. **Rating** 95 **To** 2020 $34 ✪

Rose 2014 Grenache rose is common in McLaren Vale/Barossa Valley, but rare
in WA. Vivid puce; the highly aromatic bouquet and juicy palate are driven by
raspberry and sour cherry fruit, the long finish crisp and dry. Assured winemaking,
Laurance has the recipe right. Screwcap. 13% alc. **Rating** 94 **To** 2016 $27 ✪

Shiraz 2012 Estate-grown; 7t/ha; 15 months in French oak. Relatively light colour; fragrant red cherry aromas, allied with some oak spice, lead into an elegant, light to medium-bodied palate that surprises with its length and intensity. Drink now or much later. Screwcap. 14% alc. **Rating** 94 **To** 2027 $32
Merlot 2012 Has the studied elegance of Laurance Merlot, its supple, medium-bodied mouthfeel presenting a mix of spice, redcurrant and cassis fruit with an unusual cut of blood orange acidity to freshen the finish and aftertaste. Screwcap. 13.3% alc. **Rating** 94 **To** 2022 $27 ✪

ϷϷϷϷϙ **Semillon Sauvignon Blanc 2014 Rating** 92 **To** 2016 $20 ✪

Laurel Bank ★★★★

130 Black Snake Lane, Granton, Tas 7030 **Region** Southern Tasmania
T (03) 6263 5977 **www.**laurelbankwines.com.au **Open** By appt
Winemaker Winemaking Tasmania (Julian Alcorso) **Est.** 1987 **Dozens** 1100 **Vyds** 3.5ha
Laurel (hence Laurel Bank) and Kerry Carland's north-facing vineyard, overlooking the Derwent River, is planted to sauvignon blanc, riesling, pinot noir, cabernet sauvignon and merlot. They delayed the first release of their wines for some years and (by virtue of the number of entries they were able to make) won the trophy for Most Successful Exhibitor at the Hobart Wine Show. Things have settled down since; wine quality is very reliable.

ϷϷϷϷϙ **Sauvignon Blanc 2014** It's strange how the Tasmanian Wine Show throws up so many featureless wines in the Sauvignon Blanc class, yet wines from the class can look the real deal when tasted alone. This is a general observation; I don't know whether Laurel Bank was entered in the show. Regardless, this has good fruit depth, and while it's not overly tropical, the kiwi and gooseberry flavours are distinctly varietal. Screwcap. 13.2% alc. **Rating** 92 **To** 2016 $22 ✪
Pinot Noir 2012 Very deep colour, so deep you think you have grabbed the wrong bottle. Moving on to the bouquet and palate you become even more confused; the only Tasmanian Pinots with this level of extract I can remember are Steve Hyde's Rotherhythe Pinots of the late '80s, his and this wine Dr Samuel Johnson's apocryphal dog. Screwcap. 13.6% alc. **Rating** 92 **To** 2020 $33
Riesling 2014 Fresh and lively; lime leaves and lemon sherbet, the acidity far less obvious than in many young Tasmanian Rieslings, meaning there's no need to wait. Screwcap. 11.7% alc. **Rating** 90 **To** 2016 $22

ϷϷϷϷ **Pinot Noir 2013 Rating** 89 **To** 2021

Leasingham ★★★★★

PO Box 57, Clare, SA 5453 **Region** Clare Valley
T 1800 088 711 **www.**leasingham-wines.com.au **Open** Not
Winemaker Paul Lapsley **Est.** 1893 **Dozens** NFP
Leasingham has experienced death by a thousand cuts. First, its then owner, CWA, sold its Rogers Vineyard to Tim Adams in 2009, and unsuccessfully endeavoured to separately sell the winemaking equipment and cellar door, while retaining the winery. In January '11 Tim Adams was able to buy the winery, cellar door and winemaking equipment, making the once-proud Leasingham a virtual winery (or brand). Exports to the UK and Canada.

ϷϷϷϷϷ **Classic Clare Provis Vineyard Shiraz 2010** French barrique-matured for 18 months, then bottle-matured for a further 2 years prior to release. This is a mighty, mouth-filling full-bodied Shiraz, with a medley of succulent black fruit flavours and a touch of McLaren Vale-like dark chocolate lurking in the shadows. Its greatest attribute is its savoury complexity on the finish, balancing the opulence of the mid-palate fruit. Screwcap. 14% alc. **Rating** 97 **To** 2040 $61 ✪

ϷϷϷϷϙ **Bin 61 Clare Valley Shiraz 2012 Rating** 93 **To** 2027 $27 ✪
Bin 56 Clare Valley Cabernet Malbec 2012 Rating 93 **To** 2026 $27 ✪

Leconfield

Riddoch Highway, Coonawarra, SA 5263 **Region** Coonawarra
T (08) 8737 2326 **www**.leconfieldwines.com **Open** Mon–Fri 11–4.30, w'ends 11–4
Winemaker Paul Gordon, Tim Bailey **Est.** 1974 **Dozens** 25 000 **Vyds** 43.7ha

Sydney Hamilton purchased the unplanted property that was to become Leconfield in 1974, having worked in the family wine business for over 30 years until his retirement in the mid-'50s. When he acquired the property and set about planting it, he was 76, and reluctantly bowed to family pressure to sell Leconfield to nephew Richard in '81. Richard has progressively increased the vineyards to their present level, over 75% to cabernet sauvignon, for long the winery's specialty. Exports to the UK, Canada, Denmark, Switzerland, Belgium, Japan, Malaysia, Hong Kong, Singapore, the Philippines, Vietnam, China and NZ.

🍷🍷🍷🍷🍷 **Coonawarra Cabernet Sauvignon 2013** 4% cabernet franc and maturation for 18 months in new and used French oak have brought out maximum varietal expression in its regional context, where mint and mulberry are often part of the mix; it is medium-bodied, with firm cabernet tannins, the oak largely a bystander. Screwcap. 14.5% alc. **Rating** 94 To 2028 $33

🍷🍷🍷🍷🍷 **McLaren Vale Shiraz 2013 Rating** 93 To 2024 $25 CM ✪
Old Vines Coonawarra Riesling 2014 Rating 92 To 2023 $25 CM ✪
Coonawarra Merlot 2013 Rating 92 To 2023 $25 CM ✪
Syn Rouge Sparkling Shiraz NV Rating 90 To 2018 $18 TS ✪

Leeuwin Estate ★★★★★

Stevens Road, Margaret River, WA 6285 **Region** Margaret River
T (08) 9759 0000 **www**.leeuwinestate.com.au **Open** 7 days 10–5
Winemaker Paul Atwood, Tim Lovett, Phil Hutchinson **Est.** 1974 **Dozens** 50 000
Vyds 121ha

This outstanding winery and vineyard is owned by the Horgan family, founded by Denis and Tricia, who continue their involvement, but with son Justin Horgan general manager. The Art Series Chardonnay is, in my opinion, Australia's finest example, based on the wines of the last 30 vintages. The move to screwcap brought a large smile to the faces of those who understand just how superbly the wine ages. The large estate plantings, coupled with strategic purchases of grapes from other growers, provide the base for high-quality Art Series Cabernet Sauvignon and Shiraz; the hugely successful, quick-selling Art Series Riesling and Sauvignon Blanc; and lesser-priced Prelude and Siblings wines. Exports to all major markets.

🍷🍷🍷🍷🍷 **Art Series Margaret River Chardonnay 2012** If price wasn't a concern we'd all just want to drink bucket loads of this. It's all class and quality but the drinkability factor is extremely high. It's like sitting with someone expert in the art of conversation; it makes you laugh and cry and lean in closer. Fruit, oak, texture, acidity, length: a hand full of aces, neatly arranged, trim and terrific. Screwcap. 14% alc. **Rating** 97 To 2025 $94 CM ✪

🍷🍷🍷🍷🍷 **Art Series Margaret River Shiraz 2012** Has a bit of swagger about it. It's meaty and shot with pure, ripe plum flavour, but while the tannin is velvety and well integrated, it flexes its muscle from the mid-palate onwards, inspiring confidence in the process. You're in sure hands here. Clove, leaf and spice notes play a role, but overall the wine presents as seamless. Screwcap. 14% alc. **Rating** 95 To 2030 $38 CM

Prelude Vineyards Chardonnay 2013 Freshness and flavour. The two need not be mutually exclusive. This shows spicy oak laced through pear and grapefruit, dripping with juice. It's immediately appealing and seductive yet it has reach and drive. Incredibly moreish. Screwcap. 13.5% alc. **Rating** 94 To 2020 $32 CM
Art Series Margaret River Cabernet Sauvignon 2011 Makes a fist at effortlessness. Supple blackcurrant and choc flavours glide into bay leaf and clove. Mid-weight but juicy. Builds a good amount of momentum as it rolls through the

mouth. Shape, mouthfeel and length. Elegance is its middle name. Should mature
well. Screwcap. 13.5% alc. **Rating** 94 To 2028 $65 CM

ΥΥΥΥΥ **Art Series Sauvignon Blanc 2014** Rating 93 To 2017 $30 CM
Siblings Margaret River Shiraz 2012 Rating 93 To 2022 $23 CM ✪
Pinot Noir Chardonnay Brut 2011 Rating 91 To 2021 $33 TS
Art Series Margaret River Riesling 2014 Rating 90 To 2020 $22 CM

Left of Centre ★★★★☆

98 Bolwanna Park Drive, Bolwannah, NSW 2320 (postal) **Region** Hunter Valley
T 0414 595 239 **www.**leftofcentrewines.com.au **Open** Not
Winemaker Nick and Sarah Connaughton **Est.** 2013 **Dozens** 250
Left of Centre has nothing to do with Nick and Sarah Connaughton's political beliefs; rather
it is intended to reflect the simple philosophy of buying fruit from the best vineyards and
making the best possible wine because they believe in the old adage that great wine starts in
the vineyard. Collectively, they have 20 vintages of experience, starting in the Hunter Valley
in 1996 (Sarah, straight out of school to Parker Wines) and Nick in 2004 (spending six years
working for Peter Lehmann before moving to the Hunter Valley for the '09 vintage). In the
interim Sarah gained years of experience in the lower and upper Hunter before moving to
the lure of the wine world with Wine Planet and Vintage Cellars, thereafter working vintages
at a roll call of honour in SA. They truly have all the bases covered.

ΥΥΥΥΥ **Hunter Valley Shiraz 2014** Hand-picked from 70yo vines on the Howard
family vineyard, matured for 10 months in French oak. Red fruit dominance isn't
common for the Hunter Valley, but the earthy undertone certainly is; the wine
has a finely detailed structure, and the red fruits do emerge comfortably in front
of the tannins. One of the early tastings of '14 Shiraz, and this doubly interesting.
Screwcap. 12.5% alc. **Rating** 95 To 2034 $35 ✪
Hunter Valley Chardonnay 2014 From the Rothbury Creek Vineyard;
hand-picked, whole bunch-pressed, fermented in French oak, matured on lees
for 9 months, no mlf. This is a smart Hunter Valley Chardonnay, full of life and
drive, grapefruit/melon/white peach to the fore, oak left well behind. Screwcap.
12.5% alc. **Rating** 94 To 2024 $30 ✪

ΥΥΥΥΥ **Hunter Valley Shiraz 2013** Rating 91 To 2023 $35
Hunter Valley Chardonnay 2013 Rating 90 To 2017 $30

Lenton Brae Wines ★★★★★

3887 Caves Road, Margaret River, WA 6285 **Region** Margaret River
T (08) 9755 6255 **www.**lentonbrae.com **Open** 7 days 10–6
Winemaker Edward Tomlinson **Est.** 1982 **Dozens** NFP **Vyds** 9ha
The late architect Bruce Tomlinson built a strikingly beautiful winery (heritage-listed by the
Shire of Busselton), now in the hands of winemaker son Edward (Ed), who consistently makes
elegant wines in classic Margaret River style. A midwinter (French time) trip to Pomerol
in Bordeaux to research merlot is an indication of his commitment. Exports to Indonesia,
Singapore and China.

ΥΥΥΥΥ **Margaret River Semillon Sauvignon Blanc 2014** Mostly unoaked, but
8% of the wine is oak-matured. Whatever they're doing, they're doing it right. It's
intense but flowing, is awash with passionfruit pulp and gunmetal notes, has a bit
of the come hither about it and yet does not lack sophistication. Composed and
complete. Screwcap. 13.5% alc. **Rating** 95 To 2017 $25 CM ✪
Wilyabrup Semillon Sauvignon Blanc 2012 Intense, tightly wound wine.
Smoky, lemony and thistle-like with sweet nectarine itching to show itself
fully. Restraint is the name of the game. Coiled power. Oak plants a wet kiss so
accurately that it's at one with the fruit. Fresh but with a grand future in front of
it. Screwcap. 12.5% alc. **Rating** 95 To 2021 $50 CM

Wilyabrup Chardonnay 2012 Elegant power. White peach and grapefruit with oatmeal and sweet/spicy oak. Unfurls slowly in the glass but once it's at full stretch it's impressive. Length, texture and fruit power to burn, but mannered at all points along the way. Screwcap. 13% alc. **Rating** 95 **To** 2020 $55 CM

Southside Margaret River Chardonnay 2014 It's almost impossible to criticise this wine. It announces itself upfront, maintains the gaze, then shoots out impressively through the finish. You don't just drink it, you catch up with it. Flavours are in the lemon barley, pear drop, fennel and nectarine spectrum, with clips of lactose, light cedar wood and chalk, though the truth is that it presents more or less seamlessly. A refreshing burst of acidity to the finish completes the pretty picture. Screwcap. 13.5% alc. **Rating** 94 **To** 2020 $24 CM ✪

Margaret River Shiraz 2013 Generously fruited Shiraz with enough of a savoury edge to keep the interest levels high. Plum, dark cherry and liberal oak with peppercorn and dried spice. Feels velvety throughout. Screwcap. 14% alc. **Rating** 94 **To** 2026 $30 CM ✪

Wilyabrup Cabernet Sauvignon 2012 Fluid Cabernet boasting cassis and mulberry flavour flanked by bay leaf and ground spice. Creamy oak has an exuberant influence but as the wine breathes the fruit shines further and further through it. Tannin and overall balance suggest this wine has many years up its sleeve. Screwcap. 14.5% alc. **Rating** 94 **To** 2032 $60 CM

♼♼♼♼♼ **Margaret River Cabernet Merlot 2013** Rating 92 **To** 2022 $24 CM ✪

Leo Buring   ★★★★★

Sturt Highway, Nuriootpa, SA 5355 **Region** Eden Valley/Clare Valley
T 1300 651 650 **Open** Not
Winemaker Peter Munro **Est.** 1934 **Dozens** NFP
Between 1965 and 2000, Leo Buring was Australia's foremost producer of Rieslings, with a rich legacy left by former winemaker John Vickery. After veering away from its core business with other varietal wines, it has now been refocused as a specialist Riesling producer. Top of the range are the Leopold Derwent Valley and the Leonay Eden Valley Rieslings, under a changing DW bin no. (DWQ for '13, DWR for '14 etc), supported by Clare Valley and Eden Valley Rieslings at significantly lower prices, and expanding its wings to Tasmania and WA.

♼♼♼♼♼ **Leonay Riesling 2014** DWR 18. From three vineyards in Watervale. This is a seriously good Riesling. The bouquet is filled with lemon and lime blossom aromas, the perfectly balanced palate picking up the promised citrus flavours, its mouthfeel shaped by glorious, slightly talcy, acidity that provides texture to go with the flavour profile Screwcap. 12.5% alc. **Rating** 96 **To** 2034 $40 ✪

Leopold Tamar Valley Riesling 2014 DWR 20. Now and in the future from the estate White Hills Vineyard southeast of Launceston. The flowery, citrus blossom bouquet leads into lazy intensity as totally delicious lime juice flavours roll along the mouth through to the finish and aftertaste. Screwcap. 12% alc. **Rating** 96 **To** 2029 $40 ✪

Eden Valley Riesling Dry 2014 Estate-grown; picked after 14 Feb rain between 26 Feb and 13 Mar. Quartz-green; in the best tradition of the Leo Buring style, lime juice cut and lengthened by perfectly balanced acidity. Terrific value. Screwcap. 12% alc. **Rating** 94 **To** 2025 $20 ✪

♼♼♼♼♼ **Medium Sweet Eden Valley Riesling 2014** Rating 93 **To** 2029 $20 ✪
Clare Valley Dry Riesling 2014 Rating 90 **To** 2020 $20 ✪

Leogate Estate Wines   ★★★★★

1693 Broke Road, Pokolbin, NSW 2320 **Region** Hunter Valley
T (02) 4998 7499 **www.leogate.com.au** **Open** 7 days 10–5
Winemaker Mark Woods **Est.** 2009 **Dozens** 12 000 **Vyds** 64ha
Since purchasing the substantial Brokenback Vineyard in 2009 (a key part of the original Rothbury Estate, with vines over 40 years old), Bill and Vicki Widin have wasted no time.

Initially the Widins leased the Tempus Two winery, but prior to the '13 vintage they completed the construction of their own winery and cellar door. They have also expanded the range of varieties, supplementing the long-established 30ha of shiraz, 25ha of chardonnay and 3ha of semillon with between 0.5 and 2ha of each of verdelho, viognier, gewurztraminer, pinot gris and tempranillo. Have had a string of wine show successes for their very impressive portfolio.

🍷🍷🍷🍷🍷 **The Basin Reserve Hunter Valley Shiraz 2013** In Hunter Valley terms, the colour is an exceptionally deep purple-crimson; the 45yo vines are east-facing, catching the morning sun, and this is the most concentrated and focused of the '13 Leogate Shirazs. All are French oak-matured, but that oak is particularly finely balanced and integrated here; the flavours span black cherry, spice and sparklets of tar and earth. Will live forever. Screwcap. 14% alc. **Rating** 97 **To** 2058 $115 ○

🍷🍷🍷🍷🍷 **Western Slopes Reserve Hunter Valley Shiraz 2013** Very good crimson-purple colour; the tantalising multifaceted bouquet is matched in complexity by the medium-bodied, but intense, palate; earthy/savoury tannins wend their way through the red and black fruits that progressively appear on the way through to the finish and aftertaste. Screwcap. 14% alc. **Rating** 96 **To** 2053 $115
Creek Bed Reserve Hunter Valley Semillon 2011 The price has risen from $19 to its present level since I first tasted the wine in Sept '11; the only thing yet to happen is the development of honey and toast; the points have risen from 94 to 95. Screwcap. 11% alc. **Rating** 95 **To** 2021 $30 ○
Creek Bed Reserve Hunter Valley Chardonnay 2013 A civilised Chardonnay, varietal fruit, oak and acidity all coming harmoniously together on the well-balanced and long palate, the sign-off a neat burst of citrussy acidity. Screwcap. 13% alc. **Rating** 95 **To** 2023 $38
Creek Bed Reserve Semillon 2014 Like many young high-quality Semillons, it sneaks up on you, the bouquet with faint wisps of lemon blossom, the wine entering the mouth without a fanfare of trumpets, but accelerating ever faster as it travels along the palate. A perfect building block for development in bottle over a decade or more. Screwcap. 11% alc. **Rating** 94 **To** 2029 $30 ○
Vicki's Choice Reserve Hunter Valley Chardonnay 2012 From a single block in the original Brokenback Vineyard. An elegant wine that only suffers in comparison with Australia's very best cool-climate Chardonnays. Screwcap. 13% alc. **Rating** 94 **To** 2020 $38
Brokenback Vineyard Hunter Valley Shiraz 2013 Bright crimson; spicy, earthy, leathery red fruit nuances can be detected through the supple, dense palate and bouquet; a medium to full-bodied Hunter Valley Shiraz with an indefinite future; the texture is a feature, the structure also very good. Screwcap. 13.5% alc. **Rating** 94 **To** 2038 $40
Brokenback Vineyard Dirt Boys' Choice Hunter Valley Shiraz Viognier 2013 The back label is ambiguous on the question of co-fermentation, but regardless, the bouquet is full of red fruits, cedar and spice, the lively palate offering red fruits to anyone stopping to enquire along the way, the French oak delicate, the tannins superfine. Screwcap. 13% alc. **Rating** 94 **To** 2030 $40

🍷🍷🍷🍷 **Brokenback Vineyard Hunter Valley Rose 2014 Rating** 89 **To** 2016 $22

Lerida Estate

The Vineyards, Old Federal Highway, Lake George, NSW 2581 **Region** Canberra District
T (02) 6295 6640 **www.**leridaestate.com.au **Open** 7 days 10–5
Winemaker Malcolm Burdett **Est.** 1997 **Dozens** 6000 **Vyds** 7.93ha
Lerida Estate, owned by Jim Lumbers and Anne Caine, owes a great deal to the inspiration of Dr Edgar Riek, planted as it is immediately to the south of his former Lake George vineyard, and also planted mainly to pinot noir (there are also smaller plantings of pinot gris, chardonnay, shiraz, merlot, cabernet franc and viognier). The Glenn Murcutt–designed winery, barrel room, cellar door and café complex has spectacular views over Lake George. Exports to China.

ŢŢŢŢŢ Lake George Canberra District Botrytis Pinot Gris 2013 A rare wine, but
a great example of botrytis at work, concentrating the flavours of the normally
bland Pinot Gris to expose rivers of preserved lemon, cumquat, pear and apricot,
the lusciousness balanced by the essential acidity. Not easy to make so well. 375ml.
Screwcap. 11.5% alc. **Rating** 95 **To** 2018 $35 **○**
Lake George Canberra District Shiraz Viognier 2013 It doesn't lack
substance, but its lean, smoky minerality is all elegance and class. It's clearly a wine
of a classic vintage. Dark cherries, beetroot, flings of wood spice, assorted herbs,
roasted nuts and a long, lingering, sinewy finish. Screwcap. 14.2% alc. **Rating** 95
To 2030 $50 CM
Canberra District Shiraz 2013 Peak release. Complex but inviting. Smoky,
meaty and savoury at heart and yet ripped with fleshy plum and dark cherry
flavour. Generally seamless before an expansive finish. Screwcap. 14.1% alc.
Rating 94 **To** 2025 $27 CM **○**

ŢŢŢŢ♀ Cullerin Lake George Pinot Noir 2012 **Rating** 93 **To** 2018 $35
Lake George Pinot Noir 2013 **Rating** 92 **To** 2020 $27 CM
Josephine Lake George Pinot Noir 2012 **Rating** 92 **To** 2021 $75 CM
Lake George Chardonnay 2013 **Rating** 91 **To** 2019 $25 CM
Lake George Pinot Noir Rose 2014 **Rating** 91 **To** 2016 $17 CM **○**
Canberra District Shiraz 2012 **Rating** 91 **To** 2017 $26

Lethbridge Wines   ★★★★★

74 Burrows Road, Lethbridge, Vic 3222 **Region** Geelong
T (03) 5281 7279 **www.**lethbridgewines.com **Open** Mon–Fri 11–3, w'ends 11–5
Winemaker Ray Nadeson, Maree Collis, Alexander Byrne **Est.** 1996 **Dozens** 5000
Vyds 7ha
Lethbridge was founded by scientists Ray Nadeson, Maree Collis and Adrian Thomas. In
Ray's words, 'Our belief is that the best wines express the unique character of special places.'
As well as understanding the importance of terroir, the partners have built a unique straw-bale
winery, designed for its ability to recreate the controlled environment of cellars and caves in
Europe. Winemaking is no less ecological: hand-picking, indigenous yeast fermentation, small
open fermenters, pigeage (foot-stamping) and minimal handling of the wines throughout
the maturation process are all part and parcel of the highly successful Lethbridge approach.
Ray also has a distinctive approach to full-blown chardonnay and pinot noir. There is also a
contract winemaking limb to the business. Exports to the UK.

ŢŢŢŢŢ Indra 2012 A deeply coloured and highly aromatic Shiraz with strong spicy,
peppery notes, but not at the expense of the array of foresty black fruits; the
palate is, if anything, even more filled with flavour, part dark fruits, part distinctive
Lethbridge tannins; length and balance are a given. Screwcap. 14% alc. **Rating** 97
To 2030 $95 **○**

ŢŢŢŢŢ Mietta 2012 Full colour; a Pinot that proclaims its class from the first whiff of
cherry blossom morphing smoothly into dark cherry and plum fruit on the long,
perfectly balanced palate; you can sense the spicy complexity that will come with
further bottle age. One out of the box. Screwcap. 13% alc. **Rating** 96 **To** 2025 $95
Hugo George 2012 70/25/5% sangiovese, merlot and cabernet franc, the blend
well known in Tuscany. There is a complex array of cherry and smoky charcuterie
aromas and flavours; assured winemaking has precisely gauged the contribution
of ripe tannins (even at this alcohol level) and French oak. Screwcap. 13% alc.
Rating 96 **To** 2032 $85
Chardonnay 2013 Hand-picked, whole bunch-pressed to new French
puncheons for wild yeast fermentation and mlf, then taken to French oak
(30% new) for a further 11 months on lees. An opulent and complex Chardonnay
with stone fruit, melon and fig in a creamy/toasty matrix, oak evident but
integrated and balanced. Screwcap. 13.5% alc. **Rating** 95 **To** 2023 $40

Allegra 2012 Bright straw-gold; a finely structured and textured Chardonnay; white peach, a hint of toasty oak and ripe citrus are held together by admirable acidity; it is this, and the likely low pH, that give the wine its streak of tactile minerally acidity. Screwcap. 13.5% alc. **Rating** 95 **To** 2022 $85

Pinot Noir 2013 Ray Nadeson is a master builder of full-bodied, long-lived Pinot, deep in colour, resounding with poached plum and black cherry fruit, the tannins ripe and the oak lost in the oceans of flavour. Screwcap. 14% alc. **Rating** 95 **To** 2023 $42

Shiraz 2013 A potent, unequivocally full-bodied Shiraz, reflecting its place (in Geelong) and its maker to equal degrees; there is an abundance of black fruits, licorice and bramble, welded together by powerful tannins. Made for the child born today who will live for 150 years. Screwcap. 13.5% alc. **Rating** 95 **To** 2043 $42

 Pinot Gris 2014 Rating 93 **To** 2015 $30 CM
Dr Nadeson Riesling 2013 Rating 93 **To** 2023 $30
Chardonnay 2012 Rating 90 **To** 2016 $42

Leura Park Estate   ★★★★☆

1400 Portarlington Road, Curlewis, Vic 3222 **Region** Geelong
T (03) 5253 3180 **www.**leuraparkestate.com.au **Open** W'ends 10.30–5, 7 days Jan
Winemaker Darren Burke **Est.** 1995 **Dozens** 5000 **Vyds** 15.94ha
Leura Park Estate's vineyard is planted to chardonnay (50%), pinot noir, pinot gris, sauvignon blanc and shiraz. Owners David and Lyndsay Sharp are committed to minimal interference in the vineyard, and have expanded the estate-grown wine range (Sauvignon Blanc, Pinot Gris, Chardonnay, Pinot Noir and Shiraz) to include Vintage Grande Cuvee. The next step was the erection of a winery prior to the 2010 vintage, leading to increased production and ongoing wine show success. Exports to South Korea and Singapore.

 Limited Release Block 1 Reserve Chardonnay 2012 The bouquet is lively, with a controlled touch of funk adding to its appeal; the palate takes proceedings one step further, with perfectly defined varietal fruit (white peach, pink grapefruit) and a compelling finish. Screwcap. 13.7% alc. **Rating** 95 **To** 2022 $45

25 d'Gris Bellarine Peninsula Pinot Gris 2014 Pale pink-bronze; seductive style, with pear and peach fruit allied with exotic spices; has texture, tied neatly together by a skein of citrussy acidity on the finish. Good wine. Screwcap. 13.8% alc. **Rating** 94 **To** 2016 $30 ✪

Bellarine Peninsula Shiraz 2013 Rating 91 **To** 2028 $45
Vintage Grande Blanc de Blanc 2013 Rating 91 **To** 2016 $30 TS
Bellarine Peninsula Sauvignon Blanc 2014 Rating 90 **To** 2015 $30
Bellarine Peninsula Viognier 2013 Rating 90 **To** 2016 $30

Levantine Hill Estate   ★★★★★

Level 1, 461 Bourke Street, Melbourne, Vic 3000 **Region** Yarra Valley
T (03) 8602 0831 **www.**levantinehill.com.au **Open** Not
Winemaker Paul Bridgeman **Est.** 2009 **Dozens** 4400 **Vyds** 23.6ha
This is the most ambitious project in the Yarra Valley since the establishment of Domaine Chandon a quarter of a century ago. It is the venture of Lebanese-born Elias (Eli) Jreissati and wife Colleen, Eli having amassed a fortune as a property developer, that business continuing apace. Levantine Hill has two vineyards, the larger and older established by Soo & Son in 1995, and purchased by Levantine Hill in 2010. It not only has 18ha of productive vines, but also has a frontage to the Maroondah Highway, and – at the bottom of a very steep hill – to the Yarra River. The second vineyard fronts Hill Road with a little over 5ha of young vines. All the major varieties of the Yarra Valley are planted on one or other of the two vineyards, but the Soo & Son vineyard is the more important from a business viewpoint. It is destined to provide space for a cellar door, restaurant and winery designed by Fender Katsalidis, who created Hobart's avant garde, and technically awesomely challenging MONA (Museum of

Old and New Art), and the Eureka Tower in Melbourne. The ground-hugging, futuristic buildings, their roof line reminiscent of a stealth bomber, will be visible from the Maroondah Highway, and easily accessed via Hill Road.

ΨΨΨΨΨ Samantha's Paddock Melange Traditionelle 2012 85/10/3/1/1% cabernet sauvignon, merlot, cabernet franc, malbec and petit verdot. An immaculately balanced, medium-bodied wine with a wreath of small-berry fruits around superfine, but persistent tannins and cedary oak. The keynote is elegance. The use of a cheap twin-top cork is inexplicable, contrary to the very expensive heavyweight bottle. 12.5% alc. **Rating** 96 **To** 2032 $125

Yarra Valley Cabernet Sauvignon 2013 Mid-weight but the intensity feels good and there's no question that it's complex. Indeed the word 'authority' springs to mind. An assortment of dried and green herbs, smoky oak, blackcurrant and redcurrant, with superfine tannin adding texture and surety. Class act from start to finish. Screwcap. 13.5% alc. **Rating** 95 **To** 2028 $80 CM

Yarra Valley Rose 2014 92% cabernet, 7% pinot and 1% cabernet franc and petit verdot; harvest ran from 14 Feb to 17 Apr (astonishing). A dry, savoury, very complex rose with a brambly/twiggy bouquet and a long, well-balanced palate. Screwcap. 13.5% alc. **Rating** 94 **To** 2016 $35

Yarra Valley Pinot Noir 2013 Clones MV6 and D2V5; 9 months in French oak (30% new). A fresh and lively Pinot with bright red and black cherry on the bouquet; the long, linear palate needs time for complexity to develop. It will be long-lived, so be patient. Screwcap. 13% alc. **Rating** 94 **To** 2023 $80

Yarra Valley Syrah 2013 Fine-grained wine. Intricate quality. Succulent cherry-plum laced with white pepper and sweet, smoky oak. As contradictory as this might sound, it's impossible not to notice this wine's elegance. Clovey bitterness on the finish is not a negative. Screwcap. 13.5% alc. **Rating** 94 **To** 2025 $80 CM

ΨΨΨΨΨ Yarra Valley Sauvignon Blanc Semillon 2014 Rating 92 To 2017 $35 CM

Lightfoot & Sons   ★★★★☆

Myrtle Point Vineyard, 717 Calulu Road, Bairnsdale, Vic 3875 **Region** Gippsland
T (03) 5156 9205 www.lightfootwines.com **Open** Thurs–Sun 11–4
Winemaker Alastair Butt, Tom Lightfoot **Est.** 1995 **Dozens** 4000 **Vyds** 29.3ha
Brian and Helen Lightfoot have established pinot noir, shiraz, chardonnay, cabernet sauvignon and merlot, the lion's share to pinot noir and shiraz. The soil is very similar to that of Coonawarra, with terra rossa over limestone. Most of the grapes are sold (as originally planned) to other Vic winemakers. With the arrival of Alastair Butt (formerly of Brokenwood and Seville Estate), but supported by son Tom, production has increased, and may well rise further. Second son Rob has also come on board, bringing 10 years' experience in sales and marketing.

ΨΨΨΨΨ Single Block Gippsland Chardonnay 2013 This wine comes from a block within a single vineyard planted to the Dijon clone 96; wild yeast-fermented and matured in French oak. It is a beautiful wine, full of the delicious white peach fruit, tempered by citrussy acidity, that this clone gives; the oak handling has been perfectly judged. Screwcap. 13.2% alc. **Rating** 96 **To** 2025 $48 ✪

Single Block Gippsland Pinot Noir 2013 The colour is deep, the bouquet redolent of cherry and soused plum fruit, French oak somewhere in the mix; the intense, layered palate provides more of the same, with a supplementary message: allow time for the wine to relax. Full of potential. Screwcap. 13.5% alc. **Rating** 94 **To** 2023 $48

Myrtle Point Single Vineyard Gippsland Lakes Merlot 2013 Bright colour; as Merlots go, this has some appeal with its mix of cassis, plum and black olive; indeed, it's one of those wines that sneaks up on you, insisting its length should be praised, its French oak and fine tannins likewise. The pity is only 75 dozen made. Screwcap. 13.9% alc. **Rating** 94 **To** 2028 $25 ✪

ŸŸŸŸ♀ **Myrtle Point Single Vineyard Rose 2014** Rating 93 To 2016 $20 ✪
Myrtle Point Single Vineyard Pinot Noir 2013 Rating 93 To 2020 $28 CM
Myrtle Point Chardonnay 2013 Rating 91 To 2020 $25
Myrtle Point Shiraz 2013 Rating 90 To 2023 $25
Myrtle Point Cabernet Sauvignon 2013 Rating 90 To 2028 $25

Lillian   ★★★★

Box 174, Pemberton, WA 6260 **Region** Pemberton
T (08) 9776 0193 **Open** Not
Winemaker John Brocksopp **Est.** 1993 **Dozens** 320 **Vyds** 3.2ha
Long-serving (and continuing consultant) viticulturist to Leeuwin Estate John Brocksopp has
established 2.8ha of the Rhône trio of marsanne, roussanne and viognier, and 0.4ha of shiraz.
He is also purchasing grapes form other growers in Pemberton. Exports to Japan.

ŸŸŸŸŸ **Pemberton Marsanne Roussanne 2011** 65% marsanne, 35% roussanne.
Straw-yellow; rich and creamy, with peach and spice notes rushing to the scene.
Full-bodied but lengthy; the creek of minerally flavour running through the finish
is beguiling. Screwcap. 13.5% alc. **Rating** 94 To 2018 $20 CM ✪

ŸŸŸŸ♀ **Lefroy Brook Pinot Noir 2013** Rating 93 To 2021 $27 CM ✪
Lefroy Brook Chardonnay 2012 Rating 90 To 2019 $27 CM

Lillypilly Estate   ★★★★☆

47 Lillypilly Road, Leeton, NSW 2705 **Region** Riverina
T (02) 6953 4069 **www.**lillypilly.com **Open** Mon–Sat 10–5.30, Sun by appt
Winemaker Robert Fiumara **Est.** 1982 **Dozens** 10 000 **Vyds** 27.9ha
Botrytised white wines are by far the best offering from Lillypilly, with the Noble Muscat
of Alexandria unique to the winery; these wines have both style and intensity of flavour and
can age well. Table wine quality is always steady – a prime example of not fixing what is not
broken. Exports to the UK, the US, Canada and China.

ŸŸŸŸŸ **Family Reserve Noble Blend 2011** Remarkable concentration of flavour. Adds
shape and structure to the pomp of the palate. Pure dry and nectar-like apricot is
threaded by a sizzle of sweet lime. Almost unbearably sweet, but ever so good at it.
375ml. Screwcap. 11% alc. **Rating** 94 To 2019 $39 CM
Museum Series Limited Release Noble Blend 2002 Like stepping into
another world. Fully mature, golden-brown in colour, toffee and tangerine,
cumquat and apricot, with lime darting into the depths. Buying an experience as
much as a drink. 375ml. Screwcap. 12.5% alc. **Rating** 94 To 2017 $75 CM

ŸŸŸŸ♀ **Noble Blend 2012** Rating 91 To 2020 $33 CM
Vermentino 2014 Rating 90 To 2015 $17 CM ✪
Sweet Harvest 2013 Rating 90 To 2020 $19 CM ✪

Lindeman's (Coonawarra)   ★★★★★

Coonawarra Wine Gallery, Riddoch Highway, Coonawarra, SA 5263 **Region** Coonawarra
T (08) 8737 1300 **www.**lindemans.com **Open** 7 days 10–5
Winemaker Brett Sharpe **Est.** 1908 **Dozens** NFP
Lindeman's Coonawarra vineyards have assumed a greater importance than ever thanks to the
move towards single-region wines. The Coonawarra Trio of Limestone Ridge Vineyard Shiraz
Cabernet, St George Vineyard Cabernet Sauvignon and Pyrus Cabernet Sauvignon Merlot
Cabernet Franc are all of high quality.

ŸŸŸŸŸ **Coonawarra Trio Limestone Ridge Vineyard Shiraz Cabernet 2013**
Decidedly curious: the back label is voluminous, but gives no explanation of the
Trio (nor does the front label), nor any basic facts (eg the percentage of the blend).
The colour is excellent, the bouquet and palate likewise; blackberry, blackcurrant

and mulberry are the flavour vectors of the medium to full-bodied palate, although oak also has its say. Lovely wine. Screwcap. 14% alc. **Rating** 96 **To** 2043 $70 ⊕

Coonawarra Trio St George Vineyard Cabernet Sauvignon 2013 Full crimson-purple; the vibrant cassis of the bouquet and palate has that distinctive touch of mint that appears in many Coonawarra red wines despite the relative dearth of gum trees; the palate has excellent drive and purity, oak and tannins lined up in perfectly calculated support. Screwcap. 14% alc. **Rating** 96 **To** 2048 $70 ⊕

Coonawarra Trio Pyrus Cabernet Sauvignon Cabernet Franc Malbec 2013 Dense purple-crimson; this completes a very impressive vintage Trio, with luscious folds of black, purple and red fruits, ranging from cassis to plum, a chorus of almost sweet tannins and quality oak rounding out the finish. Screwcap. 14% alc. **Rating** 96 **To** 2033 $70 ⊕

ΨΨΨΨ   **Rouge Homme Shiraz Cabernet 2012 Rating** 88 **To** 2017 $16 CM ⊕

Lindeman's (Hunter Valley)   ★★★★☆

McDonalds Road, Pokolbin, NSW 2320 **Region** Hunter Valley
T (02) 4993 3700 **www**.lindemans.com.au **Open** 7 days 10–5
Winemaker Wayne Falkenberg, Brett Sharpe **Est.** 1843 **Dozens** NFP

Just when I expected it least, Lindeman's has produced some seriously good wines from the Hunter Valley, and one half of the Lindeman's winemaking or marketing side (without talking to the other half) has exhumed some of the Bin number systems that were used in the glory days of the 1960s, admittedly without total consistency. Thus for white wines, 50 or 55 were the last two digits used for what was named Riesling, 70 for what was named White Burgundy, and 75 for what was called Chablis; with the shiraz-based wines, the last two digits were 00, 03 or 10. The most famous were the 1965 Claret and Burgundy releases Bin 3100 and Bin 3110, the most famous Chablis 1967 Bin 3475. Exports to all major markets.

ΨΨΨΨΨ   **Limited Release Reserve Hunter Valley Shiraz 2013** Bin 1300. An elegant and focused Shiraz, with a fragrant bouquet ranging through black cherry, spice and a touch of sweet leather; the tannins are high-quality, fine, but persistent. It's great to see the remnants of the Ben Ean Vineyard performing so well. This will run and run, the drink-to date conservative. Screwcap. 12.5% alc. **Rating** 95 **To** 2038 $50

Hunter Valley Semillon 2014 Bin 1455. This may not scale the heights of the great Lindeman wines of the '60s from the Sunshine Vineyard, but it's a very good Semillon with a guaranteed development path over the next 20 years as it moves from its tightly structured present profile to honeyed richness, but always with a shaft of lemony acidity. Screwcap. 11.5% alc. **Rating** 94 **To** 2034 $30 ⊕

ΨΨΨΨ̣   **Hunter Valley Shiraz 2013 Rating** 92 **To** 2033 $30

Lindeman's (Karadoc)   ★★★

44 Johns Way, Karadoc, Vic 3496 **Region** Murray Darling
T (03) 5051 3285 **www**.lindemans.com.au **Open** 7 days 10–4.30
Winemaker Wayne Falkenberg **Est.** 1974 **Dozens** NFP

The production centre for many of the TWE premium (an elastic term) wines, variously making and/or bottling them. The very large winery also allows all-important economies of scale, and is the major processing centre for TWE's beverage wine sector (casks, flagons and low-priced bottles). Exports to all major markets.

ΨΨΨΨ   **Bin 65 Chardonnay 2014** Straightforward flavour with a whisper of sophistication. A deserved leader at its price point. It tastes of peach, nectarine, citrus and cut grass with a gentle (and attractive) smokiness about the edges. It's not exactly packed with flavour, but it's fresh and satisfying. Screwcap. 13.5% alc. **Rating** 88 **To** 2016 $10 CM ⊕

Lindenderry at Red Hill ★★★★★

142 Arthurs Seat Road, Red Hill, Vic 3937 **Region** Mornington Peninsula
T (03) 5989 2933 **www**.lindenderry.com.au **Open** W'ends 11–5
Winemaker Barnaby Flanders **Est.** 1999 **Dozens** 1000 **Vyds** 3.35ha
Lindenderry at Red Hill is a sister operation to Lancemore Hill in the Macedon Ranges and
Lindenwarrah at Milawa. It has a five-star country house hotel, conference facilities, a function
area, day spa and restaurant on 16ha of gardens, but also has a little over 3ha of vineyards,
planted equally to pinot noir and chardonnay more than 15 years ago. Notwithstanding the
reputation of the previous contract winemakers for Lindenderry, the range and quality of
the wines now being made by Barney Flanders is the best yet. He has made the most of the
estate-grown grapes in Mornington Peninsula and Macedon, adding cream to the cake by
sourcing some excellent Grampians shiraz.

♥♥♥♥♥ **Grampians Shiraz 2013** This is a majestic Grampians Shiraz, with that edge to
the black fruits reminiscent of Côte Rôtie, an edge partly ex pepper, licorice and
spice, but going even further. Screwcap. 13.5% alc. **Rating** 96 **To** 2048 $35 ✪
Mornington Peninsula Chardonnay 2013 Has all the fluid grace of well-
made Mornington Peninsula Chardonnay on display; barrel fermentation has
provided the groundwork of complexity, the intense white peach/grapefruit
brooking no argument. Screwcap. 13% alc. **Rating** 95 **To** 2023 $35 ✪
Macedon Ranges Pinot Gris 2014 Skilled winemaking invests this wine
with texture, structure and flavour, even intensity – not a word often used with
Pinot Gris; the actual flavours are in the usual nashi pear/apple range, it's just
their vigour. This could well upset the café lunch conversation. Screwcap. 13% alc.
Rating 95 **To** 2018 $30 ✪
Mornington Peninsula Pinot Noir 2013 Good colour, not quite as bright as
its Macedon Ranges sibling; plum and cherry fruit inhabit a complex and textured
palate with a complex foresty twang on the finish. Bred to say, 'Vive la différence'.
Screwcap. 13.5% alc. **Rating** 95 **To** 2023 $40
Macedon Ranges Pinot Noir 2013 Bright, clear crimson-purple; red cherry
and multi-spice fragrance is translated directly and exactly on the lively palate; a
delicious wine, flavours sinuously weaving their way across the mouth. Screwcap.
13% alc. **Rating** 95 **To** 2023 $40

♥♥♥♥♡ **Macedon Ranges Pinot Noir Rose 2014 Rating** 93 **To** 2017 $25 ✪

Linfield Road Wines ★★★★☆

65 Victoria Terrace, Williamstown, SA 5351 **Region** Barossa Valley
T (08) 8524 7355 **www**.linfieldroadwines.com **Open** 7 days 10–5
Winemaker Daniel Wilson, Natasha Mooney **Est.** 2002 **Dozens** 2500 **Vyds** 19ha
Linfield Road produces small batches of single-vineyard wines from the Wilson family
vineyard at Williamstown. The story began in 1860 when Edmund Major Wilson planted
the first vines on the outskirts of Williamstown. Since Edmund's first plantings, the Wilson
family has fostered a viticulture tradition that now spans five generations; three generations
of the family currently live and work on the property, located at the very southern edge of
the Barossa. It is situated high above the valley floor, with cooler nights and longer ripening
periods. This results in elegant red and white wines with good structure. Exports to Canada,
Malaysia, Singapore, Japan and China.

♥♥♥♥♥ **The Stubborn Patriarch Shiraz 2013** Smooth-talking Shiraz with quite a
lot to say. Beefy blackberry, raspberry, toasty oak and a smattering of fragrant dry
herbs. Inky heart of flavour but remains bright and focused. Texture is a given.
Entirely satisfying. Screwcap. 14.9% alc. **Rating** 94 **To** 2026 $28 CM ✪
Edmund Major Reserve 100 Year Old Vines Barossa Shiraz 2013 Rich
and chocolatey. It doesn't exactly hide its alcohol, but it does keep your attention
diverted. Thick, saturated plum, mocha and dark chocolate with a sweet core of
tar and fresh blackberry. Makes all its statements with a booming voice. Screwcap.
15.6% alc. **Rating** 94 **To** 2030 $55 CM

ŶŶŶŶ♀ The Pruner Single Vineyard Grenache 2014 Rating 93 To 2020 $30 CM
The Black Hammer Cabernet 2013 Rating 93 To 2028 $26 CM ✪
Edmund Major Reserve 100 Year Old Vines Barossa Shiraz 2012
Rating 92 To 2024 $55 CM

Lino Ramble ★★★★

2 Hall St, McLaren Vale, SA 5171 (postal) **Region** McLaren Vale
T 0409 553 448 **www**.linoramble.com.au **Open** Not
Winemaker Andy Coppard **Est.** 2012 **Dozens** 700
After 20 years of working for other wine companies, big and small, interstate and
internationally, the last 7 years with Kay Brothers, Andy Coppard yearned for the opportunity
to start his own business. However, he needed a partner, and found her at Kay Brothers, where
she (Angela Townsend) was business manager; she is now Lino Ramble's first employee. They
say, 'We've climbed on top of the dog kennel, tied a cape around our necks, held our breaths,
and jumped.' Their first vintage was 2012, with 350 dozen bottles, and a similar volume made
in '13. They doubled that for the '14 vintage, and hope to double it again in '15. And if you
are curious about the name (as I was), the story has overtones of James Joyce's stream of
consciousness mental rambles.

ŶŶŶŶŶ Treadlie McLaren Vale Grenache Shiraz Mataro 2013 Wild yeast-fermented,
basket-pressed, not fined. Light, but bright, colour; it has a striking palate, which
weaves juicy fruit with spicy/savoury tannins to create drive and length. A very
smart wine. 181 dozen made. Screwcap. 14% alc. **Rating** 94 **To** 2023 $28 ✪

ŶŶŶŶ♀ Ludo Roussanne Marsanne Viognier 2013 Rating 93 To 2025 $28

Lisa McGuigan Wines ★★★★

18 College St, Sydney, NSW 2000 (postal) **Region** Various
T 0418 424 382 **www**.lisamcguiganwines.com **Open** Not
Winemaker Liz Silkman, Lisa McGuigan **Est.** 2010 **Dozens** 6000
Lisa McGuigan is a fourth-generation member of a famous Hunter Valley winemaking
dynasty, started many decades ago by Perc McGuigan, and more recently (and perhaps more
famously) led by Brian McGuigan. In 1999 Lisa started Tempus Two from her garage, and
under the McGuigan-Simeon (now Australian Vintage) umbrella, the volume rose to 250 000
dozen before she left in 2007 to start a retail wine business. In 2010 she turned full circle,
starting her own business in the Hunter Valley, and using the winemaking skills of Liz Silkman,
whom she had headhunted for Tempus Two, and who is now also chief winemaker at First
Creek Wines.

ŶŶŶŶ♀ Adelaide Hills Pinot Noir 2013 Made in the Hunter Valley; destemmed grapes
fermented and macerated for 20 days, then matured for 10 months in used French
oak. The colour is excellent, the bouquet fragrant, the palate focused and long,
full to the brim with red and black cherry fruit, with a hint of forest that will add
complexity with age. Screwcap. 13.5% alc. **Rating** 93 **To** 2023 $30
Orange Pinot Gris 2013 No frills: whole bunch-pressed, clear juice cool-
fermented in stainless steel before early bottling. Has considerable flavour, with
pear and a subliminal touch of fresh ginger on the long finish (with a whisper of
residual sugar?). Screwcap. 13% alc. **Rating** 90 **To** 2015 $30

Little Bridge ★★★

106 Brooks Road, Bywong, NSW 2621 **Region** Canberra District
T (02) 6236 9620 **www**.littlebridgewines.com.au **Open** W'ends 11–4
Winemaker Various contract **Est.** 1996 **Dozens** 1000 **Vyds** 5.5ha
Little Bridge is a partnership between long-term friends John Leyshon, Rowland Clark,
John Jefferey and Steve Dowton. There are 2ha of chardonnay, pinot noir, riesling and merlot
planted at Folly Run; 2ha of shiraz, cabernet sauvignon, sangiovese, cabernet franc and malbec
at Mallaluka; and 1.5ha of riesling, chardonnay and mourvedre at Brooks Creek. Canberra

Winemakers makes the white wines, Lark Hill the Pinot Noir, and Mallaluka the other reds. Steve purchased Brooks Creek Vineyard in 2009 (largely derelict, and now rehabilitated), and it is here that the Little Bridge cellar door is situated.

�◦4 **Canberra District Cabernet Shiraz Sangiovese 2013** One-third of each variety, estate-grown and matured in French barriques for 12 months. The light to medium-bodied palate has a contrasting mix of red fruits offset by savoury/spicy elements. Needs a little patience. Screwcap. 13.7% alc. **Rating** 89 **To** 2020 $20

Little Cathedral ★★★★

PO Box 1188, Thornbury, Vic 3071 **Region** Upper Goulburn
T 0412 581 912 **www**.littlecathedral.com.au **Open** Not
Winemaker Caroline Mooney **Est.** 1996 **Dozens** 200 **Vyds** 3.25ha
The Little Cathedral vineyard was planted in 1996 under the lee of the striking Cathedral Ranges at Taggerty. It has been established on a gentle north-facing slope at an altitude of 280m, and should irrigation be required, it comes from the gin-clear Little River, a mountain stream that originates deep within the forest that the vineyard backs onto. Since Madge Alexandra and Anna Pickworth acquired the property in 2006, it has been a sharp learning curve about the challenges of nature. Happily, they have surmounted the hurdles of inclement weather and bushfires, and with the winemaking skills of Caroline Mooney to boot, the ability of the vineyard to produce excellent Pinot Noir is beyond doubt.

♀♀♀♀♀ **Pinot Noir Rose 2013** Salmon-pink; winemaker Caroline Mooney has thrown the rule book out the window and made this with 100% whole bunch fermentation; the end result is a complex, savoury, dusty wine, the impact of the stems adding texture and structure. A rose to be sipped with food. Screwcap. 12.7% alc. **Rating** 93 **To** 2016 $22 ✪
Pinot Noir 2013 Composed of 15% whole bunch, 35% whole berry, 50% crushed fruit; matured in French oak (15% new). It has excellent colour, and a fresh, zesty palate. To be hypercritical, it needs an extra 0.5% alc. to give more weight and flesh to an undeniably elegant palate. Screwcap. 13% alc. **Rating** 93 **To** 2019 $30

Little River Estate ★★★★

c/- 147 Rankins Road, Kensington, Vic 3031 (postal) **Region** Upper Goulburn
T 0418 381 722 **Open** Not
Winemaker Philip Challen, Oscar Rosa, Nick Arena **Est.** 1986 **Dozens** 250 **Vyds** 2.5ha
Philip (a chef and hotelier) and Christine Challen began the establishment of their vineyard in 1986 with the planting of 0.5ha of cabernet sauvignon. Several years later, 2ha of chardonnay (and a few vines of pinot noir) followed. Vineyard practice and soil management are based on organic principles; there are low yields, notwithstanding the age of the vines.

♀♀♀♀♀ **Forgotten Hero 2011** Petit verdot grown at Colbinabbin (the centre of the Heathcote region), matured in new French oak for 12 months. Its elevage in new French oak may have been a gamble, but it produced an elegant and immediately enjoyable wine with bright fruit flavours and fine, persistent tannins. Screwcap. 14.5% alc. **Rating** 93 **To** 2025 $25 ✪
Reserve Shiraz 2008 Light colour, but has retained good hue; the light to medium-bodied palate shows no impact from the March heatwave, doubtless helped by the moderate cool climate of Taggerty. There are lively red fruit flavours cushioned by fine tannins, and the wine is à point right now. Screwcap. 14% alc. **Rating** 90 **To** 2018 $30

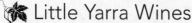 Little Yarra Wines

PO Box 2311, Richmond South, Vic 3121 **Region** Yarra Valley
T 0401 228 196 **www**.littleyarra.com.au **Open** Not
Winemaker Dylan McMahon (Contract) **Est.** 2013 **Dozens** 450 **Vyds** 1.2ha

This is a family partnership between Ian, Pip and Matt Pattison and Pip's sister Mary Padbury. The Pattisons previously operated a vineyard and winery in the Macedon Ranges (Metcalfe Valley Wines), but could not resist buying the Little Yarra Wines property and its plantings of 0.6ha each of pinot noir and chardonnay. The quality of the grapes also allowed them to secure Dylan McMahon as winemaker, with input from Matt.

ΨΨΨΨΨ **Chardonnay 2014** Whole bunch-pressed and fermented in French hogsheads on light solids (30% new), kept in barrel for 10 months. Has all the immediacy and impact of top-quality Yarra Valley Chardonnays; the tangy, zesty fruit is positively mouth-watering, its grapefruit and white peach flavours striking pure and equally long. Screwcap. 13.1% alc. **Rating** 95 **To** 2024 $35 ✪
Pinot Noir 2014 Clones 777 (25%) and MV6 (75%), hand-picked and fermented separately, 777 with whole bunches, MV6 destemmed, a 3-day cold soak, then fermented; matured in French hogsheads (30% new) for 10 months. Highlights the concentration of '14, stacked with plum and black cherry, and will respond very well to 3+ years in bottle. Screwcap. 13.5% alc. **Rating** 94 **To** 2025 $35

Littles   ★★★

363 Palmers Lane, Pokolbin, NSW 2321 **Region** Hunter Valley
T (02) 4998 7626 **www**.littleswines.com.au **Open** Not
Winemaker Rhys Eather (Contract) **Est.** 1984 **Dozens** 1500 **Vyds** 17.7ha
Littles is managed by the Kindred family, the ownership involving a number of investors. The winery has mature vineyards planted to semillon (7.2ha), shiraz (5.55ha), chardonnay (1.21ha), cabernet sauvignon (1.82ha), pinot noir (1.42ha) and marsanne (0.5ha).

ΨΨΨΨ **Reserve Hunter Valley Semillon 2013** Grassy and tight. Sweet pea, asparagus, gravel and spice notes lead into a run of citrus, before grassier notes once again take control. Pent up at present; needs time to relax. Screwcap. 11% alc. **Rating** 88 **To** 2023 $25 CM
Block 5 Reserve Hunter Valley Cabernet Sauvignon 2011 Fresh fruit flavour, mulberry and boysenberry with a gently currant edge. Full of dusty, gamey and herbal nuances, but it still swings freely through the finish. Screwcap. 13% alc. **Rating** 88 **To** 2022 $35 CM

Littore Family Wines   ★★★☆

265 Ballan Road, Moorabool, Vic 3221 **Region** Geelong
T (03) 5228 4888 **www**.littorewines.com.au **Open** 7 days 10–5
Winemaker David Thompson, Toby Wanklyn **Est.** 1997 **Dozens** 1.5m **Vyds** 1416ha
Littore Family Wines was founded by Mario and Aurora Littore on the Murray River near Mildura, the first vineyard named Jindalee, meaning 'bare hill'. A decade later the winery capacity was increased from 3 million to 13 million litres (15 000 tonnes). Sons Vince and David had purchased the Idyll Vineyard (now Jindalee Estate) near Geelong, which is now the headquarters of the group, and oversaw the expansion in the Riverland (here the group owns 1400ha planted to 23 varieties; the Geelong vineyards are a paltry 16ha). The wines now come under a number of labels for domestic and numerous export markets.

ΨΨΨΨΨ **Idyll Geelong Shiraz 2013** Deeply coloured and powerfully built on the foundations of some of the oldest vines in Geelong, oozing jet-black fruits, anise, tar and – of course – tannins. All are in balance, the future a gold-plated certainty. Screwcap. 14% alc. **Rating** 94 **To** 2043 $25 ✪

Livewire Wines   ★★★★☆

PO Box 369, Portarlington, Vic 3223 **Region** Geelong
T 0439 024 007 **Open** Not
Winemaker Anthony Brain **Est.** 2011 **Dozens** 600
Anthony Brain started working life as a chef, but in the late 1990s 'took a slight bend into the wine industry'. He started gathering experience in the Yarra Valley, and simultaneously

started oenology studies at CSU. Margaret River followed, as did time in SA before returning to the Yarra, working at De Bortoli from 2003 to '07 (undertaking vintages in the Hunter, King and Yarra valleys). Five vintages as winemaker at Bellarine Estate followed, giving him 'a platform and understanding of the Geelong region and the opportunity to learn more about sites, viticulture and winemaking decisions'. In '13 he resigned from Bellarine Estate, having made some of his own Livewire wines on the way through.

ŸŸŸŸŸ **The Blood of Hipsters 2 2014** A blend of sangiovese and shiraz from Heathcote, here (surely) with oak – indeed quality oak – involved. Has terrific crimson-purple colour, and although the wine is medium-bodied at best, the black cherry fruit has nuanced tannins and oak that wander unhurried along the palate. Screwcap. 13.2% alc. **Rating** 95 **To** 2029 $25 ✪

Geelong Pinot Noir 2013 From the 36yo Innisfail Vineyard (90%) and the Barwon Vineyard (10%); matured for 10 months in French oak. Fresh red fruits (strawberry and red cherry) drive the bouquet and elegant, well-balanced palate with a fresh, supple mouthfeel. Screwcap. 12.8% alc. **Rating** 94 **To** 2021 $32

Grampians Shiraz 2014 Intense deep purple-crimson; a newborn baby, chock-full of black fruits and plums, balanced by swaddling clothes of almost creamy, soft tannins and quality oak. Obviously, will grow with more time in bottle. Screwcap. 13.5% alc. **Rating** 94 **To** 2034 $32

The Blood of Hipsters 2014 A 65/35% blend of tempranillo and shiraz from Heathcote made in the Spanish Joven style, fermented in stainless steel and bottled early. It succeeds admirably, focusing all the attention on the fruit. Drink over the next 2–3 years, and everyone's a winner, with the bright cherry/plum fruit in full ascendancy. Screwcap. 13.4% alc. **Rating** 94 **To** 2018 $25 ✪

ŸŸŸŸŸ **Rose 2014 Rating** 92 **To** 2016 $22 ✪
Jolt Geelong Pinot Noir 2013 Rating 91 **To** 2023 $22 ✪

Lloyd Brothers   ★★★★☆

34 Warners Road, McLaren Vale, SA 5171 **Region** McLaren Vale
T (08) 8323 8792 **www**.lloydbrothers.com.au **Open** 7 days 11–5
Winemaker Ross Durbidge **Est.** 2002 **Dozens** 5000 **Vyds** 38ha
Lloyd Brothers Wine and Olive Company is owned and operated by David and Matthew Lloyd, third-generation McLaren Vale vignerons. Their 25ha estate overlooks the township, and is planted to 12ha shiraz, 0.8ha bush-vine grenache and 0.4ha bush-vine mataro (plus sauvignon blanc, chardonnay, pinot gris and shiraz in the Adelaide Hills). The shiraz planting allows the creation of a full range of styles, including Rose, Sparkling Shiraz, Fortified Shiraz and Estate Shiraz, along with the White Chalk Shiraz, so named because of the white chalk used to mark each barrel during the classification process. Exports to the UK.

ŸŸŸŸŸ **Grenache 2013** Whole berry-fermented, and given extended maceration post-fermentation; basket-pressed, and matured in French oak, some new. A fragrant, supple and silky celebration of the variety, with joyous red fruits on the bouquet and palate alike. Screwcap. 14.5% alc. **Rating** 95 **To** 2023 $30 ✪

Cabernet Sauvignon 2013 An attractive example of McLaren Vale Cabernet, with a complex array of black fruits, dark chocolate and black olive aromas and flavours woven together on the medium-bodied palate. The best is yet to come. Screwcap. 14.5% alc. **Rating** 94 **To** 2029 $30 ✪

Mataro 2013 It is a splendidly sturdy wine, and the 10 to 15-year cellaring window suggested by Lloyd Brothers is on the mark, reinforced by its excellent hue. Screwcap. 14.5% alc. **Rating** 94 **To** 2028 $30 ✪

ŸŸŸŸŸ **Estate McLaren Vale Shiraz 2013 Rating** 93 **To** 2028 $30
The Winery Door Shiraz Cabernet 2013 Rating 91 **To** 2028 $15 ✪
Adelaide Hills Sauvignon Blanc 2014 Rating 90 **To** 2015 $20 ✪

Lobethal Road Wines

2254 Onkaparinga Valley Road, Mount Torrens, SA 5244 **Region** Adelaide Hills
T (08) 8389 4595 **www**.lobethalroad.com **Open** W'ends & public hols 11–5
Winemaker Michael Sykes (Contract) **Est.** 1998 **Dozens** 5500 **Vyds** 5.1ha
Dave Neyle and Inga Lidums bring diverse but very relevant experience to the Lobethal
Road vineyard, the lion's share planted to shiraz (3.1ha), with smaller amounts of chardonnay,
tempranillo, sauvignon blanc and graciano. Dave has been in vineyard development and
management in SA and Tasmania since 1990. Inga brings 25 years' experience in marketing
and graphic design in Australia and overseas, with a focus on the wine and food industries.
The property is managed with minimal chemical input.

ŸŸŸŸŸ Bacchant Adelaide Hills Chardonnay 2013 Relatively pale colour but a rich,
        rewarding style. Pear, peach and citrus notes with bass notes of grapefruit. Creamy/
        spicy oak feathers seductively throughout. Holds a fine tune from start to finish.
        Screwcap. 13.2% alc. **Rating** 94 **To** 2019 $45 CM
        Bacchant Adelaide Hills Shiraz 2012 Sweet, almost jellied, blackberried fruits
        lead into a complex web of spice and smoked meat-like notes. It's like going for
        a walk and exploring a new trail. Fine spicy tannin talks a good game and the
        aftertaste is all roasted nuts and peppercorns. An excellent offering. Screwcap.
        14% alc. **Rating** 94 **To** 2024 $45 CM

ŸŸŸŸŸ Adelaide Hills Sauvignon Blanc 2014 **Rating** 92 **To** 2015 $22 CM ◐
        Adelaide Hills Pinot Gris 2014 **Rating** 91 **To** 2015 $22 CM ◐
        Adelaide Hills Shiraz 2013 **Rating** 90 **To** 2020 $25 CM

Lofty Valley Wines ★★★★★

100 Collins Road, Summertown, SA 5141 **Region** Adelaide Hills
T 0400 930 818 **www**.loftyvalleywines.com.au **Open** By appt
Winemaker Various **Est.** 2004 **Dozens** 600 **Vyds** 3ha
Medical practitioner Brian Gilbert began collecting wine when he was 19, flirting with the
idea of becoming a winemaker before being headed firmly in the direction of medicine by his
parents. Thirty or so years later he purchased a blackberry and gorse-infested 12ha property in
the Adelaide Hills, eventually obtaining permission to establish a vineyard. Chardonnay (2ha)
was planted in 2004, and 1ha of pinot noir in '07, both on steep slopes. Exports to Singapore.

ŸŸŸŸŸ Lani's View Adelaide Hills Chardonnay 2012 Hand-picked, barrel-fermented
        and matured for 9 months in new and used French oak. This is a seriously
        delicious Chardonnay, its texture positively silky so supple is it; white peach
        flavours rule the roost, having absorbed all the oak, and power the long finish.
        Screwcap. 13% alc. **Rating** 96 **To** 2025 $40 ◐
        Collins Class II Adelaide Hills Pinot Noir 2013 Wild yeast-fermented with
        30% whole bunches, matured in French oak (30% new). There is impressive
        complexity to the fruit flavours that seem to oscillate between cherry and plum
        in a tantalising play in the mouth, yet don't lose coherence; the oak has been well
        handled/balanced. Screwcap. 13% alc. **Rating** 95 **To** 2023 $59
        Collins Class Adelaide Hills Pinot Noir 2012 A very attractive Pinot sharing
        many of the characteristics of its '13 Class II sibling, perhaps slanted slightly more
        in the plum spectrum, but with the same dynamic interface with red cherry.
        Excellent balance and mouthfeel to a wine with the certainty of even more
        complexity over coming years. Screwcap. 13% alc. **Rating** 95 **To** 2022 $59

ŸŸŸŸŸ Lani's View Adelaide Hills Chardonnay 2013 **Rating** 93 **To** 2017 $40
        Ascent Adelaide Hills Chardonnay 2013 **Rating** 91 **To** 2016 $32

Logan Wines ★★★★

Castlereagh Highway, Apple Tree Flat, Mudgee, NSW 2850 **Region** Mudgee
T (02) 6373 1333 **www**.loganwines.com.au **Open** 7 days 10–5
Winemaker Peter Logan **Est.** 1997 **Dozens** 45 000

Logan is a family-owned and operated business with emphasis on cool-climate wines from Orange and Mudgee. The business is run by husband and wife team Peter (winemaker) and Hannah (sales and marketing). Wines are released from three ranges: Logan (from Orange), Weemala and Apple Tree Flat. Exports to the UK, the US, Japan and other major markets.

ΨΨΨΨΨ **Orange Sauvignon Blanc 2014** The bouquet is striking in its intensity, with asparagus, herb and peach skin aromas; the palate provides a totally logical continuation of those characters, the finish dry and fresh. Screwcap. 12.5% alc. **Rating** 94 **To** 2017 $23 ○

ΨΨΨΨΨ **Weemala Central Ranges Merlot 2012 Rating** 93 **To** 2018 $19 ○
Weemala Orange Riesling 2014 Rating 91 **To** 2017 $20 CM ○
Orange Cabernet Merlot 2012 Rating 91 **To** 2022 $28
Hannah Orange Rose 2014 Rating 90 **To** 2016 $23
Ridge of Tears Orange Shiraz 2012 Rating 90 **To** 2021 $45 CM

Lonely Vineyard   ★★★★

61 Emmett Road, Crafers West, SA 5152 (postal) **Region** Eden Valley
T 0413 481 163 **www**.lonelyvineyard.com.au **Open** Not
Winemaker Michael Schreurs **Est.** 2008 **Dozens** 400 **Vyds** 1.5ha
This is the venture of winemaker Michael Schreurs and Karina Ouwens, a commercial lawyer from Adelaide. Daughter Amalia Schreurs can 'hoover a box of sultanas in record time' while Meesh, the family cat, 'treats Karina and Amalia well, and Michael with the contempt he deserves. As cats do.' One or other of the partners (perhaps both) has a great sense of humour. Michael's winemaking career in Australia began with Seppelt Great Western winery for three years, followed by six years at Henschke, and, more recently, The Lane Vineyard in the Adelaide Hills, backed up by stints in Burgundy, the Rhône Valley, the US and Spain.

ΨΨΨΨΨ **Eden Valley Riesling 2014** Clean and crisp with pure lime and talc flavours shooting through the palate. Leafy spice notes add complexity to the aftertaste. Textbook. Screwcap. 12.5% alc. **Rating** 93 **To** 2022 $26 CM ○
Montepulciano 2013 Substantial flavour, mix of boysenberry and plum jam with a leatheriness to both its flavour and texture. Grainy tannin helps build another layer. Flings of spice likewise. Each step placed deliberately but firmly. Light colour, but more than meets the eye. Screwcap. 13.5% alc. **Rating** 92 **To** 2019 $36 CM
Eden Valley Shiraz 2012 Fragrant, savoury-accented red with five spice, cloves and floral notes making a persuasive pitch on the nose. Palate offers more of the same, with the introduction of dry licorice and saltbush. Manages to be both pretty and steady at once. Screwcap. 13.5% alc. **Rating** 91 **To** 2022 $36 CM

Long Yarn Wines   ★★★★

90 Chalk Hill Road, McLaren Vale, SA 5171 **Region** McLaren Vale
T (08) 8323 8623 **www**.longyarnwines.com **Open** 7 days 10–5
Winemaker Jess Hardy **Est.** 2005 **Dozens** 10000 **Vyds** 12ha
Long Yarn Wines is a family-operated wine business. It makes wines under two labels: the widely distributed Long Yarn range and the cellar door-only wines of Stamford & Clark. In addition to managing the Loom Wine business, owner Steve Grimley consults to UK-based Direct Wines (the largest direct marketer of wine in the world) and is in charge of making and sourcing their Australian range. Jess Hardy was appointed winemaker and manager of the business in 2013. Exports to the UK, the US and Japan.

ΨΨΨΨΨ **Long Yarn Eden Valley Riesling 2014** Straw-green. Accessible flavours of lime and apple with bath salt notes contributing both texture and complexity. Steal of a price. There'll be no complaints if you serve this. Screwcap. 12% alc. **Rating** 90 **To** 2019 $14 CM ○

Long Yarn Adelaide Hills Pinot Grigio 2014 Tangy pear and apple flavour with the merest slip of fruit sweetness. Drinks well. Slight creaminess does the wine no harm. Excellent value. Screwcap. 12% alc. **Rating** 90 **To** 2015 $14 CM ☼

� Long Yarn McLaren Vale Shiraz 2013 **Rating** 89 **To** 2017 $14 CM ☼

Longline Wines ★★★★★

PO Box 28, Old Noarlunga, SA 5168 **Region** McLaren Vale/Adelaide Hills
T 0415 244 124 **www.**longlinewines.com.au **Open** Not
Winemaker Paul Carpenter **Est.** 2013 **Dozens** 880
The name reflects the changing nature of the Carpenter family's activities. 40 years ago Bob Carpenter gave up his job as a bank manager, becoming a longline fisherman at Goolwa; this was in turn replaced by a move to McLaren Vale for farming activities. Son Paul graduated from Adelaide University and began his professional life as a cereal researcher for the university, but a vintage job at Geoff Merrill Wines at the end of his university studies led to the decision to switch to winemaking. Over the next 20 years he worked both locally and internationally, in the Rhône Valley and Beaujolais, and at Archery Summit in Oregon. Back in Australia he worked for Hardys, and is currently a winemaker at Wirra Wirra. Together with partner Martine, he secured small parcels of outstanding grapes from four grower vineyards of grenache and shiraz (three vineyards in McLaren Vale, the fourth in the Adelaide Hills).

♥♥♥♥♥ Blood Knot Shiraz 2013 A synergistic 60/40% blend from McLaren Vale and Adelaide Hills, the outcome very impressive, iron fist in velvet glove stuff. The beautifully presented black cherry, blackberry and spice fruits seem more closely linked to Adelaide Hills than McLaren Vale, but that's not worth debating given the sheer class, balance and length of the palate. A ridiculous bargain. Screwcap. 14% alc. **Rating** 96 **To** 2043 $26 ☼
Wicker Basket Adelaide Hills Shiraz 2013 Vivid crimson; this is an exercise in studied elegance, far removed from Blood Knot; spice, pepper and black licorice underpin the red and black cherry fruit flavours, superfine tannins rippling through the medium-bodied palate. I feel guilty in not giving this wine the same (or better) points than Blood Knot, so blame my perfidious palate. Screwcap. 13.7% alc. **Rating** 95 **To** 2038 $45
Bimini Twist Grenache Rose 2014 Half was fermented and stored in barrel; the other was fermented to dryness on skins and then run to old oak. The result has a clear textural element and more than a little complexity. It tastes of earth, spice, sweet raspberry and woodsmoke, in that order, with a lipsmacking dryness to the finish. Immaculate and delicious. Screwcap. 13% alc. **Rating** 94 **To** 2016 $20 CM ☼
Albright McLaren Vale Grenache 2013 It doesn't put a foot wrong. This is the kind of release that makes you wonder why old-vine Australian Grenache isn't more hotly contested in the marketplace. It offers a mix of red and black cherries, raspberry and earth, with an attractive fling of dried herbs. Oak plays next to no role. Moreish. Screwcap. 14.5% alc. **Rating** 94 **To** 2022 $26 CM ☼

❧ Lost Buoy Wines ★★★★

PO Box 156, Aldinga Beach, SA 5173 **Region** McLaren Vale
T 0400 505 043 **www.**lostbuoywines.com.au **Open** Not
Winemaker Phil Christiansen **Est.** 2010 **Dozens** 1500 **Vyds** 6ha
Originally called Lion Point Wines, the name change forced by Lion Nathan. Seeking a new name for the 3.2ha of grenache and 2.8ha of shiraz planted at the turn of the century, and saved from property developers when the local Kelley family stepped in, the Lost Buoy name stems from the coastal location of the estate vineyard, perched high on the cliff top at Port Willunga's Lion Point. The wines are released at two price levels: the entry point Lost at Sea range (The Edge Shiraz and Gulf View Sauvignon Blanc) are made from grapes purchased from other growers, the Preserver range of Cliff Block Grenache and Lion Point Shiraz from the estate vineyard. Winemaker Phil Christiansen has long-time experience in the region.

ΨΨΨΨΨ **Lion Point McLaren Vale Shiraz 2012** A very impressive debut, even allowing for the head start given by the vintage. There is an immediately appealing conjunction of black fruits, with more savoury, spicy elements on the long, well-balanced, medium-bodied palate; 14 months in used oak was the right call. Screwcap. 14.5% alc. **Rating** 94 **To** 2027 $35

ΨΨΨΨΨ **Gulf View Adelaide Hills Sauvignon Blanc 2014 Rating** 93 **To** 2015 $15 ✪
Cliff Block McLaren Vale Grenache 2012 Rating 90 **To** 2018 $35

Lou Miranda Estate ★★★★☆

1876 Barossa Valley Way, Rowland Flat, SA 5352 **Region** Barossa Valley
T (08) 8524 4537 **www.loumirandaestate.com.au Open** Mon–Fri 10–4.30, w'ends 11–4
Winemaker Lou Miranda, Janelle Zerk **Est.** 2005 **Dozens** 20 000 **Vyds** 23.29ha
Lou Miranda's daughters Lisa and Victoria are the driving force behind the estate, albeit with continuing hands-on involvement from Lou. The jewels in the crown of the estate plantings are 0.5ha of mourvedre planted in 1897 and 1.5ha of shiraz planted in 1907. The remaining vines have been planted gradually since '95, the varietal choice widened by cabernet sauvignon, merlot, chardonnay and pinot grigio. Exports to the UK, the US, and other major markets.

ΨΨΨΨΨ **Limited Edition Old Vine Barossa Valley Shiraz 2010** It's also called Selected Vineyard, but how many names can a koala bear? The wine itself is a flashy display of showy oak and luscious fruit, the oak all spearmint and coffee-cream, the fruit inky and blackberried and dripping with dark plum. Tannin is a supporting bone, buried deep in the wine's flesh. Every sip brings further confirmation of its quality. Cork. 15% alc. **Rating** 96 **To** 2032 $55 CM ✪
Angel's Vineyard Old Vine Barossa Valley Shiraz Mourvedre 2012
110yo vines. Thick blackberry and tar flavours with a clear band of alcohol stretching out across the wine's horizon. Sweet but not too sweet; licoricey without tending into cola; oak influenced but happily married to the fruit. Picking date may not have been optimum but it's still produced an intensely seductive wine. Screwcap. 14.5% alc. **Rating** 94 **To** 2026 $55 CM

ΨΨΨΨΨ **The Fine Selection Shiraz 2012 Rating** 91 **To** 2019 $22 CM ✪
Individual Vineyard Sagrantino 2012 Rating 91 **To** 2021 $35 CM
Leone Barossa Valley Pinot Grigio 2014 Rating 90 **To** 2015 $22 CM

Lowe Wines ★★★★☆

Tinja Lane, Mudgee, NSW 2850 **Region** Mudgee
T (02) 6372 0800 **www.lowewine.com.au Open** 7 days 10–5
Winemaker David Lowe, Liam Heslop **Est.** 1987 **Dozens** 17 000 **Vyds** 41.3ha
Lowe Wines has undergone a number of changes in recent years, the most recent the acquisition of Louee and its two vineyards. The first is at Rylstone, led by shiraz, cabernet sauvignon, petit verdot and merlot, with chardonnay, cabernet franc, verdelho and viognier making up the balance. The second is on Nullo Mountain, bordered by the Wollemi National Park, at an altitude of 1100m, high by any standards, and often the coolest location in Australia. Lowe Wines continues with its organic profile. The Tinja property has been in the Lowe family ownership for five generations. Exports to the UK and Japan.

ΨΨΨΨΨ **Icon Nullo Mountain Riesling 2012** The elevation of the vineyard delivers an intense and striking Riesling of exceptional length, lime and unsweetened lemon juice flavours girdled by minerally acidity that intensifies on the finish. Will be very long-lived. Screwcap. 10.5% alc. **Rating** 96 **To** 2027 $45 ✪
Louee Museum Release Nullo Mountain Rylstone Riesling 2008
Gleaming green–gold, surprisingly developed for a wine under screwcap; it has a toasty bouquet, and an elegant, crisp palate that ends any suggestion of oxidation. Its future development will be built around its acidity, not its fruit. Screwcap. 12.5% alc. **Rating** 94 **To** 2020 $45

Museum Release Block 5 Mudgee Shiraz 2009 The colour is very good for its age; aromas and flavours of bramble, earth and leather are woven through the black fruits of the medium-bodied palate, adding a touch of licorice; has lots of character and sense of place. Cork. 14% alc. **Rating** 94 **To** 2020 $75

♀♀♀♀♀ **Nullo Mountain Pinot Gris 2014** Rating 91 To 2016 $30
Organic Block 8 Mudgee Shiraz 2012 Rating 91 To 2025 $35
Museum Release Mudgee Zinfandel 2005 Rating 91 To 2017 $125
Tinja Mudgee Riesling 2014 Rating 90 To 2020 $22

Luke Lambert Wines ★★★★☆

PO Box 1297, Healesville, Vic 3777 **Region** Yarra Valley
T 0448 349 323 **www**.lukelambertwines.com.au **Open** By appt
Winemaker Luke Lambert **Est.** 2003 **Dozens** 1500 **Vyds** 6ha
Luke Lambert graduated from CSU's wine science course in 2002, aged 23, cramming in winemaking experience at Mount Pleasant, Coldstream Hills, Mount Prior, Poet's Corner, Palliser Estate in Martinborough, and Badia di Morrona in Chianti. He purchases grapes from quality-conscious growers in the Yarra Valley and Heathcote. He has now settled in the Yarra Valley, leasing slightly less than 1ha of Heathcote nebbiolo, and larger amounts of Yarra Valley shiraz and nebbiolo. The wines are wild yeast-fermented and bottled without fining or filtration. Exports to the UK, the US, Canada, Norway, Singapore and Japan.

♀♀♀♀♀ **Yarra Valley Chardonnay 2013** A flinty bouquet, very tangy and zesty, with grapefruit to the fore pulling the length of the palate out to the far horizon. Stylish Yarra Valley Chardonnay by any standards. Diam. 12.5% alc. **Rating** 95 **To** 2023 $32 ✪
Yarra Valley Syrah 2013 A very complex, multifaceted bouquet and palate in typical Luke Lambert style, 40% whole bunches one of the playmakers. The result is an eagle's nest of interlocking savoury black fruits and fruit and stem tannins coming from all quarters. Diam. 13.5% alc. **Rating** 94 **To** 2030 $40

M. Chapoutier Australia ★★★★★

141–143 High Street, Heathcote, Vic 3523 **Region** Pyrenees/Heathcote
T (03) 5433 2411 **www**.mchapoutieraustralia.com **Open** 7 days 10–5
Winemaker Michel Chapoutier **Est.** 1998 **Dozens** 10 000 **Vyds** 50ha
M. Chapoutier Australia is the eponymous offshoot of the famous Rhône Valley producer. The business focuses on vineyards in the Pyrenees, Heathcote and Beechworth, with collaboration from Ron Laughton of Jasper Hill and Rick Kinzbrunner of Giaconda. After first establishing a vineyard in Heathcote adjacent to Jasper Hill (see La Pleiade), Chapoutier purchased the Malakoff Vineyard in the Pyrenees to create Domaine Terlato & Chapoutier (the Terlato & Chapoutier joint venture was established in 2000; Terlato still owns 50% of the Malakoff Vineyard). In '09 Michel Chapoutier purchased two neighbouring vineyards, Landsborough Valley and Shays Flat; all these are now fully owned by Domaine Tournon. (Domaine Tournon consists of Landsborough and Shays Flat Vineyards in the Pyrenees and Lady's Lane Vineyard in Heathcote.) Exports to all major markets.

♀♀♀♀♀ **Tournon Lady's Lane Vineyard Heathcote Shiraz 2013** Crunchingly dry and tannic. Powder keg of a wine. It's an understatement to say that it's more savoury than sweet, but even so, there's still a considerable amount of tarry, blackberried, licoricey flavour here. Gum leaves, smoke, black pepper, hazelnut and graphite characters fly hither and thither; even the tannin comes thoroughly infused. It really needs time. Cork. 14.5% alc. **Rating** 95 **To** 2028 $50 CM
Tournon Lady's Lane Vineyard Heathcote Shiraz 2012 Cuts a fine figure. Burly, grumpy tannin but the fruit has more than enough watts to cater for it. Blackberry and gun smoke, graphite and crushed dry leaves. Cracked black pepper, set deep into the fruit. Tannin is assertive, there's no two ways about it. but it never feels anything other than appropriate. Plenty of length, too. Cork. 13.5% alc. **Rating** 95 **To** 2030 $50 CM

Tournon Shays Flat Vineyard Pyrenees Shiraz 2013 Turns on the power by establishing and maintaining a heart of dark fruit flavour. It's grunty but it's also polished and immaculately well presented. Plum, mint, savoury herbs and a wave of robust tannin; it tastes and feels good now but it has a long journey ahead. Screwcap. 14.5% alc. **Rating** 94 **To** 2028 $34 CM

Domaine Terlato & Chapoutier lieu dit Malakoff Pyrenees Shiraz 2012 Deep colour and flavour but sinewy, dry and herbal through the finish. Handy combination, or it is when done well, as it is here. Dark cherry, plum and blackberry add the stuffing; meat and iodine notes another dimension, while bitter chocolate and roasted nut characters do nothing but emphasise the quality of the offering. Cork. 13.5% alc. **Rating** 94 **To** 2026 $40 CM

Domaine Terlato & Chapoutier L-Block Pyrenees Shiraz 2011 It's flashed with white pepper, roasted nuts and clove notes and comes complete with kirsch and truffle fruit/weight/complexity. It's all quite fascinating. It's a relatively small wine with a big personality; it's a wine to provoke comment. The 2011 vintage is a kind of lesson for us all; many of the best, or memorable, or most affecting, things are sprung from difficulty. This wine makes you ponder such things, anyway. Cork. 13.5% alc. **Rating** 94 **To** 2020 $65 CM

ŸŸŸŸ♀ **Tournon Mathilda Blanc 2013** Rating 91 To 2016 $16 CM ❂
Tournon Mathilda Shiraz 2013 Rating 91 To 2019 $16 CM ❂
Tournon Mathilda Blanc 2014 Rating 90 To 2016 $16 CM ❂
Domaine Terlato & Chapoutier Shiraz Viognier 2012 Rating 90 To 2019 $18 CM ❂

Mac Forbes ★★★★★

Graceburn Wine Room, 11a Green Street, Healesville, Vic 3777 **Region** Yarra Valley
T (03) 9818 8099 **www**.macforbes.com **Open** Thurs–Sun 11–7, Sun 11–5
Winemaker Mac Forbes, Austin Black **Est.** 2004 **Dozens** 4500
Mac Forbes cut his vinous teeth at Mount Mary, where he was winemaker for several years before heading overseas in 2002. He spent two years in London working for Southcorp in a marketing liaison role, then travelled to Portugal and Austria to gain further winemaking experience. He returned to the Yarra Valley prior to the '05 vintage, purchasing grapes for the two-tier portfolio: first, the Victorian range (employing unusual varieties or unusual winemaking techniques); and second, the Yarra Valley range of multiple terroir-based offerings of Chardonnay and Pinot Noir. Exports to the UK, the US, Spain, Sweden and Norway.

ŸŸŸŸŸ **Hoddles Creek Chardonnay 2013** Hand-picked grapes are destemmed and crushed before pressing, wild yeast fermentation and maturation in new and used oak. The bouquet and palate have some struck match/flint nuances, but are built around intense grapefruit and white fruit flavours, oak seamlessly absorbed by the fruit. ArdeaSeal. 12.5% alc. **Rating** 97 **To** 2028 $50 ❂
Woori Yallock Chardonnay 2013 Crushed and destemmed hand-picked grapes are wild yeast-fermented and matured for 10 months in new and used French oak. The bouquet is very complex, the palate with tightly focused power driving the minerally/grapefruit flavours of the palate, reflecting the very low pH; has exceptional length. ArdeaSeal. 13% alc. **Rating** 97 **To** 2028 $50 ❂

ŸŸŸŸŸ **Woori Yallock Pinot Noir 2013** Hand-picked 24 Feb, 10% whole bunch, hand-sorted, foot-stomped; 11 months in new and used French oak. Light, bright colour; has more fruit intensity and weight than its siblings, red and black cherry to the fore, the tannins superfine, the oak totally integrated; very good overall balance and length. ArdeaSeal. 13.1% alc. **Rating** 96 **To** 2020 $70 ❂
Hugh 2012 A blend of cabernet, merlot, cabernet franc, petit verdot and malbec; matured in French barriques and casks. As elegant as they come, but not at the expense of flavour or ripeness; everything about this wine is precisely judged and proportioned. I wish I could be confident about the closure. ArdeaSeal. 12.5% alc. **Rating** 96 **To** 2032 $70 ❂

RS7 Strathbogie Ranges Riesling 2014 Substantial colour; an extremely powerful and tightly focused Riesling with an array of grated lime skin, spice and herb, fermented in both cask and tank; 7g/l of residual sugar is perfectly balanced by the titratable acidity of 7.65g/l. Screwcap. 12.6% alc. **Rating** 95 **To** 2029 $30 ✪
Wesburn Pinot Noir 2013 10% whole bunch, 90% destemmed, open, wild yeast-fermented; 11 months in new and used French oak; no fining/filtration. A fragrant bouquet with spicy undertones to the fruit leads into a savoury palate that belies the unusually low alcohol; dark plum/black cherry carry the day over persistent tannins. ArdeaSeal. 12.2% alc. **Rating** 95 **To** 2020 $70
RS33 Strathbogie Ranges Riesling 2014 Elegance and intensity hand in glove; lime, mineral and zest carry the 33g/l of residual sugar with ease, and the length is wonderful, picked up by minerally acidity on the finish. Screwcap. 10.8% alc. **Rating** 95 **To** 2029 $35 ✪
Yarra Valley Chardonnay 2013 Rating 94 **To** 2020 $30 CM ✪
Yarra Valley Pinot Noir 2013 Rating 94 **To** 2021 $30 CM ✪
Coldstream Pinot Noir 2013 Rating 94 **To** 2017 $50

Macaw Creek Wines ★★★☆

Macaw Creek Road, Riverton, SA 5412 **Region** Mount Lofty Ranges Zone
T (08) 8847 2657 **www**.macawcreekwines.com.au **Open** By appt
Winemaker Rodney Hooper **Est.** 1992 **Dozens** 10 000 **Vyds** 10ha
Geoff (aka Mad Dog) Munzberg, a third-generation grapegrower, joined with Jeremy and Heidi Holmes, Aaron and Kirsty Brasher and son Matthew to create Mad Dog Wines. Management has now passed to Matthew (also carrying the 'mad dog' mantle) after a 25-year apprenticeship. The purchase of a neighbouring vineyard in 2006 has led to the inclusion of some 100-year-old vine fruit, and the range has been extended with small amounts of Sangiovese Exports to Canada and China.

🍷🍷🍷🍷🍷 **Em's Table Premium Organic Preservative Free Shiraz 2013** Awash with fresh, primary fruit flavour. Cherries, apples and plums. Not particularly weighty but there's more than enough volume to the fruit flavours. Washes cleanly and satisfyingly through the finish. Excellent option for those looking to avoid SO_2. Screwcap. 14% alc. **Rating** 90 **To** 2015 $19 CM ✪

🍷🍷🍷🍷 **Reserve Shiraz Cabernet 2008 Rating** 89 **To** 2018 $29 CM
Mount Lofty Ranges Cabernet Shiraz 2012 Rating 88 **To** 2019 $17 CM ✪

McGuigan Wines ★★★★☆

Cnr Broke Road/McDonalds Road, Pokolbin, NSW 2321 **Region** Hunter Valley
T (02) 4998 7400 **www**.mcguiganwines.com.au **Open** 7 days 9.30–5
Winemaker Peter Hall, James Evers **Est.** 1992 **Dozens** 1.5 million
McGuigan Wines is an Australian wine brand operating under parent company Australian Vintage Ltd. McGuigan represents four generations of Australian winemaking, and while its roots are firmly planted in the Hunter Valley, its vine holdings extend across SA, from the Barossa Valley to the Adelaide Hills and the Eden and Clare valleys, into Victoria and NSW. McGuigan Wines' processing facilities operate out of three core regions: the Hunter Valley, Sunraysia and the Barossa Valley, with its super-premium grapes from the Barossa, Adelaide Hills and adjacent regions processed at Chateau Yaldara for the medium term. Exports to all major markets.

🍷🍷🍷🍷🍷 **The Philosophy 2010** Cabernet sauvignon and shiraz (the blend proportions not specified) from the Eden and Clare valleys; spent 2 years in French and American oak. Still has brilliant primary colour; the complex bouquet, with black fruits, armchair leather and pipe tobacco, and the freshness and precision of the intense palate, link back to the colour, each explaining the other; the length is prodigious, the balance perfect. Diam. 13.5% alc. **Rating** 97 **To** 2040 $150 ✪

🍷🍷🍷🍷🍷 **The Shortlist Hunter Valley Semillon 2014** The reputation McGuigan has for making Semillons that mature magnificently adds needless emphasis in the case of this wine, its intensity and quality plain for all to see; lemongrass, lemon zest and slashing minerally acidity will underwrite the far distant point of its best drink-by date. Screwcap. 10.5% alc. **Rating** 96 To 2044 $29 ❂

The Shortlist Eden Valley Riesling 2014 A wine with a very good track record, and it's not hard to see why; a minerally frame holds the fine, yet intense, lime/lemon fruit in perfect balance; the finish is full of life, but makes it perfectly clear that this will be a great wine in the future. Low-yielding vines are the lynchpin. Screwcap. 12% alc. **Rating** 95 To 2034 $29 ❂

Farms Barossa Valley Shiraz 2012 A very, very well made Shiraz from old vines still flourishing; black fruits are festooned with spices, a passing touch of licorice and sympathetic vanillan oak; the tannins are so fine they give rise to a silky mouthfeel. Lovely medium-bodied wine. Cork. 14.5% alc. **Rating** 95 To 2035 $75

The Shortlist Barossa Valley GSM 2012 Open-fermented 7–10 days, matured for 16 months in new and 1yo French and American oak. Bright and clearly coloured, this has rarely encountered energy and life to its rhapsodic display of red and black cherry, satsuma plum, spice and fine-grained tannins. Terrific value. Screwcap. 14.5% alc. **Rating** 95 To 2032 $29 ❂

Personal Reserve Hunter Ridge Vineyard Chardonnay 2014 Very well made, in the upper echelon of Hunter Valley Chardonnay; the nectarine and white peach fruit has mouth-watering citrussy acidity, and has effortlessly sopped up the oak. Doesn't need to be cellared, but will gain complexity. Diam. 13% alc. **Rating** 94 To 2024 $35

The Shortlist Adelaide Hills Chardonnay 2013 Gleaming straw-green, it has the length and grip Adelaide Hills confers on many of its best Chardonnays, the grip giving emphasis to its array of cool-grown chardonnay characteristics. Screwcap. 13.5% alc. **Rating** 94 To 2023 $29 ❂

The Shortlist Barossa Valley Shiraz 2012 Open-fermented for 7–10 days, matured in new French and American oak. It has a welcoming bouquet and a supple, medium-bodied palate with perfectly ripened black cherry and blackberry fruits that have sopped up the oak and easily carry the tannins. Lovely wine, appealing price. Screwcap. 14.5% alc. **Rating** 94 To 2032 $29 ❂

The Shortlist Coonawarra Cabernet Sauvignon 2012 Speaks with utmost clarity of its place of origin, with that bay leaf/earth/mint undertone to strong cassis fruit, which is by no means a fault; the oak, too, has been well handled, not challenging the fruit. Screwcap. 13.5% alc. **Rating** 94 To 2027 $29 ❂

🍷🍷🍷🍷🍷 **Hand Made Langhorne Creek Shiraz 2012** Rating 92 To 2027 $45
The Shortlist Montepulciano 2013 Rating 92 To 2020 $30 CM

McHenry Hohnen Vintners ★★★★★

5962 Caves Road, Margaret River, WA 6285 **Region** Margaret River
T (08) 9757 7600 **www**.mchv.com.au **Open** 7 days 10.30–4.30
Winemaker Trent Carroll **Est.** 2004 **Dozens** 10 000 **Vyds** 56ha
McHenry Hohnen is owned by the McHenry and Hohnen families, sourcing grapes from four vineyards owned by various members of the families. Vines have been established on the McHenry, Calgardup Brook, Rocky Road and McLeod Creek properties. A significant part of the grape production is sold to others (including Cape Mentelle). The family members with direct executive responsibilities are leading Perth retailer Murray McHenry and Cape Mentelle founder and former long-term winemaker David Hohnen. Exports to the UK, Ireland, Sweden, Indonesia, Japan, Singapore, Hong Kong and NZ.

🍷🍷🍷🍷🍷 **Rocky Road Vineyard Margaret River Cabernet Sauvignon 2012** Estate-grown in the coolest, southern part of Margaret River, the stone fermenter has 15% whole bunch inclusion, with partial wild yeast, and 5 weeks on skins. A fascinating wine, giving the autocratic nature of cabernet free play to express itself. Thus it is matured in old, inert oak, but lacks nothing in its interlocking cassis/blackcurrant fruit, black olive and earthy tannins drawing out the finish. Screwcap. 14.5% alc. **Rating** 96 To 2042 $49 ❂

Rolling Stone 2012 28.5% each of cabernet, malbec, merlot and 14.5% petit verdot. This is a wine of awesome proportions, yet is so well balanced there are moments of elegance, and the blackcurrant, blueberry and blackberry fruit flavours will feed off the reservoir of tannins as the wine slowly wends its way to full maturity decades hence. Screwcap. 14.7% alc. **Rating** 96 **To** 2042 $90

Rocky Road Vineyard Margaret River Chardonnay 2013 Whole bunch-pressed, natural yeast, matured in French barriques (20% new) for 10 months. While well and truly elegant, is a little more open, white peach first up, grapefruit in hot pursuit; shakes itself off on the aftertaste in best canine fashion. Screwcap. 13.5% alc. **Rating** 95 **To** 2024 $40

Rocky Road Margaret River Semillon Sauvignon Blanc 2014 A 69/31% blend, 90% fermented in stainless steel, 10% in a new French oak foudre, all left on lees for 6 months. Has considerable complexity and richness, and is given length and authority by the semillon. This is real wine at a token price. Screwcap. 12.8% alc. **Rating** 94 **To** 2020 $20 ✪

Rocky Road Margaret River Semillon Sauvignon Blanc 2013 Bright straw-green; has a greater depth and volume of flavour, and more texture, than many; while semillon is the major partner, stone fruit and tropical flavours ex the sauvignon blanc are welded onto the semillon to provide a seamless stream. Screwcap. 12.5% alc. **Rating** 94 **To** 2016 $20 ✪

Rocky Road Margaret River Shiraz 2013 Open-fermented in stainless steel and concrete vats, the final stages of fermentation and 9 months' maturation in French oak (10% new), barrels selected for blending/bottling. Deeply coloured, its bouquet and palate are peppered with black fruits, with a spicy/savoury twist calling 'bring on one of David Hohnen's cows'. Great value. Screwcap. 14.5% alc. **Rating** 94 **To** 2030 $25 ✪

Rocky Road Margaret River Cabernet Merlot 2013 65% cabernet, 25% merlot, and 5% each of malbec and shiraz; partial wild ferment, stone fermenter, hand-plunged and basket-pressed. Deeply coloured and richly robed, the flavours straddle blackcurrant, dark cherry and blackberry, neatly offset by fine-grained tannins on the finish. Screwcap. 14.5% alc. **Rating** 94 **To** 2028 $25 ✪

Margaret River Cabernet Merlot 2012 Deep crimson-purple; 50/42/4/4% cabernet sauvignon, merlot, petit verdot and malbec; a prime example of the synergy that Margaret River creates with this blend; cabernet providing the blackcurrant fruit and sustained, ripe tannins, merlot filling the mid-palate with softer red fruits; oak plays a minor role in bringing cohesion to the finish. Screwcap. 14.5% alc. **Rating** 94 **To** 2027 $25 ✪

Rocky Road Vineyard Margaret River Zinfandel 2012 A whole berry ferment in stainless steel, hand-plunged/pumped over, basked-pressed to used French oak to complete fermentation. Shows the barrel ferment to advantage, giving the wine a spicy tobacco edge to the red and purple fruits, and softening the tannins. Screwcap. 14.5% alc. **Rating** 94 **To** 2022 $40

🍷🍷🍷🍷🍷 **Burnside Vineyard Chardonnay 2013** **Rating** 93 **To** 2023 $40
Calgardup Brook Vineyard Chardonnay 2013 **Rating** 93 **To** 2023 $40
Amigos Shiraz Grenache Mataro 2011 **Rating** 93 **To** 2021 $27 ✪

McIvor Estate ★★★★☆

80 Tooborac–Baynton Road, Tooborac, Vic 3522 **Region** Heathcote
T (03) 5433 5266 **www**.mcivorestate.com.au **Open** W'ends & public hols 10–5
Winemaker Various contract **Est.** 1997 **Dozens** 2000 **Vyds** 5.3ha

McIvor Estate is situated at the base of the Tooborac Hills, at the southern end of the Heathcote wine region, 5km southwest of Tooborac. Gary and Cynthia Harbour have planted 5.3ha of marsanne, roussanne, shiraz, cabernet sauvignon, merlot, nebbiolo and sangiovese.

🍷🍷🍷🍷🍷 **Giannisceddu 2013** This 85/15% blend of sangiovese and cabernet comes from the Super Tuscan wine template. But – obviously enough – this is Central Victoria, and there was no guarantee the wine would succeed as seamlessly and fluidly as this, the different fruit vices of sangiovese (red cherry) and cabernet (cassis) occupying centre stage so gracefully that tannins are left with nothing to say. Screwcap. 13.8% alc. **Rating** 95 **To** 2028 $60

Heathcote Sangiovese 2013 This and Giannisceddu weren't tasted next to each other, and should have been; this seems more powerful, but that's inherently improbable. Black and red cherry flavours are deep, but underneath there's a carpet of savoury tannins, more obvious than in the Giannisceddu. Whatever, a Sangiovese of distinction. Screwcap. 13.6% alc. **Rating** 94 **To** 2028 $30 ✪

Nebbiolo 2013 The hue is bright and clear, although light; it's when you taste Nebbiolo like this that the affinity with Pinot Noir (often lost in a sea of drying tannins) is obvious; bright forest fruits (mainly red) are finely etched, their inherent power easy to miss. Screwcap. 13.4% alc. **Rating** 94 **To** 2030 $35

McKellar Ridge Wines

Point of View Vineyard, 2 Euroka Avenue, Murrumbateman, NSW 2582
Region Canberra District
T 0409 789 861 **www.**mckellarridgewines.com.au **Open** Sun 12–5 Sept–Jun
Winemaker Dr Brian Johnston **Est.** 2000 **Dozens** 600 **Vyds** 5.5ha
Dr Brian Johnston and his wife Janet are the partners in McKellar Ridge Wines. Brian has completed a postgraduate diploma in science at CSU, focusing on wine science and wine production techniques. The wines come from low-yielding mature vines (shiraz, cabernet sauvignon, chardonnay, merlot and viognier) and have had significant show success. They are made using a combination of traditional and new winemaking techniques, the emphasis on fruit-driven styles.

🍷🍷🍷🍷🍷 **Canberra District Riesling 2014** Piercing Riesling, apple, citrus and slate, softened at least in its early-drinking appeal by floral nuances. Powerful through the finish. Suggestions of inbuilt complexity, even at this early stage. Screwcap. 12% alc. **Rating** 94 **To** 2026 $22 CM ✪

🍷🍷🍷🍷🍷 **Canberra District Merlot Shiraz Rose 2014** Rating 93 To 2015 $20 CM ✪
Canberra District Shiraz Viognier 2013 Rating 92 To 2026 $30 CM
Trio Cabernet Franc Merlot 2013 Rating 92 To 2033 $30 CM
Canberra District Pinot Noir 2013 Rating 91 To 2022 $30 CM

McLaren Vale III Associates

309 Foggo Road, McLaren Vale, SA 5171 **Region** McLaren Vale
T 1800 501 513 **www.**mclarenvaleiiiassociates.com.au **Open** Mon–Fri 9–5, w'ends 11–5
Winemaker Brian Light, Campbell Greer **Est.** 1999 **Dozens** 12 000 **Vyds** 34ha
McLaren Vale III Associates is a very successful boutique winery. Its signature wine is Squid Ink Shiraz. Mary Greer, Managing Director, Reg Wymond, Director, and Brian Light, Winemaker, have over 80 years' combined experience in the wine industry. An impressive portfolio of estate-grown wines allows them control over quality and consistency, and thus success in Australian and international wine shows. Exports to the US, Canada, Indonesia, Hong Kong, Singapore, South Korea, Japan and China.

🍷🍷🍷🍷🍷 **Giant Squid Ink Reserve Shiraz 2010** Last/first tasted 3 years ago, the colour is still bright and deep, the palate fresh and vibrant, having shaken off its puppy fat. Unquestionably a very good wine, still with its sense of place undimmed, its seamless black fruits, dark chocolate, oak and fine-grained tannins on the same page. Screwcap. 14.5% alc. **Rating** 96 **To** 2040 $150

Backbone GSM 2012 A 70/25/5% blend of grenache, shiraz and mourvedre; the components were fermented and matured separately, the final blend made after 16 months and further matured in 1–4yo oak. Good hue; a tangy wine, full of personality, with a brew of red and black berries, spice and earth. Screwcap. 14.5% alc. **Rating** 95 **To** 2027 $35 ✪

The Descendant of Squid Ink Shiraz 2013 Matured for 9 months in used American oak, the emphasis on the fruit; deeply coloured, it is on the upper side of medium-bodied, with a tapestry of black fruits, dark chocolate and plum cake;

the balance is good, the future of the wine assured, so give it at least some of the time it deserves. Screwcap. 14.5% alc. **Rating** 94 **To** 2033 $35

🍷🍷🍷🍷🍷 **Renaissance Merlot Cabernet Petit Verdot 2011** Rating 93 To 2021 $25 **۞**
Four Score Grenache 2013 Rating 91 To 2023 $35

McLean's Farm   ★★★★☆

barr–Eden Vineyard, Menglers Hill Road, Tanunda, SA 5352 **Region** Eden Valley
T (08) 8564 3340 **Open** W'ends 10–5
Winemaker Bob and Wilma McLean **Est.** 2001 **Dozens** 6000 **Vyds** 5.3ha
The ever-convivial, larger-than-life Bob McLean covered a lot of wine turf until his death on 9 April 2015. Many people, myself included, were good friends of Bob, and all of us are immensely saddened by his death. There will doubtless be some changes in the structure of the business, but at the time of going to print, decisions were still being taken. Exports to the UK.

🍷🍷🍷🍷🍷 **Barossa Master Shiraz 2012** Slinky soft, rich and chocolatey with saturated blackberry, leather, ground coffee and dark earth flavours galore. Pours on the flavours and then keeps pouring some more. Screwcap. 14.5% alc. **Rating** 94 To 2026 $52 CM

🍷🍷🍷🍷🍷 **Eden Valley Riesling 2014** Rating 93 To 2020 $21 CM **۞**
Reserve Barossa Shiraz 2012 Rating 92 To 2021 $26 CM

McLeish Estate   ★★★★☆

462 De Beyers Road, Pokolbin, NSW 2320 **Region** Hunter Valley
T (02) 4998 7754 **www.mcleishhunterwines.com.au Open** 7 days 10–5
Winemaker Andrew Thomas (Contract) **Est.** 1985 **Dozens** 8000 **Vyds** 17.3ha
Bob and Maryanne McLeish have established a particularly successful business, based on estate plantings of semillon, chardonnay, verdelho, shiraz, merlot and cabernet sauvignon. The wines are of consistently high quality, and more than a few have accumulated show records leading to gold medal-encrusted labels. The quality of the grapes is part of the equation, the other the skills of contact winemaker Andrew Thomas. 2015 marked McLeish Estate's 30th vintage. Over the years, there have been 30 trophies, 76 gold, 66 silver, and 80 bronze medals, the majority won in the Hunter Valley Wine Show and Sydney Wine Show. Exports to the UK, the US and Asia.

🍷🍷🍷🍷🍷 **Hunter Valley Semillon 2014** Let no one say young Semillon is devoid of flavour – this has it in capital letters; sure, lemon juice and zest link hands with the acidity, but there are other fruits haunting the bouquet and flitting across the palate. These are the dots for you to join as you taste the wine – more easily in 5 years' time, but fun right now. Screwcap. 11% alc. **Rating** 95 To 2029 $20 **۞**

🍷🍷🍷🍷🍷 **Reserve Hunter Valley Chardonnay 2014** Rating 93 To 2020 $30
Semillon Sauvignon Blanc 2014 Rating 92 To 2016 $18 **۞**
Hunter Valley Chardonnay 2013 Rating 91 To 2020 $25

McPherson Wines   ★★★★☆

6 Expo Court, Mount Waverley, Vic 3149 **Region** Nagambie Lakes
T (03) 9263 0200 **www.mcphersonwines.com.au Open** Not
Winemaker Jo Nash **Est.** 1993 **Dozens** 375 000 **Vyds** 262ha
McPherson Wines is, by any standards, a substantial business. Its wines are largely produced for the export market, with enough sales in Australia to gain some measure of recognition here. Made at various locations from the estate vineyards and supplemented with contract-grown grapes, they represent very good value. For the record, McPherson Wines is a joint venture between Andrew McPherson and Alister Purbrick (Tahbilk), both of whom have had a lifetime of experience in the industry. Quality is unfailing good. Exports to all major markets.

ŶŶŶŶŶ **Princess Butterfly Marsanne 2013** An exceptional young Marsanne, its quality created primarily in the vineyard, although experienced winemaking has also helped the cause; a lovely mix of honeysuckle and tangy lemony acidity, and the length of a Hunter Semillon. Screwcap. 12.5% alc. **Rating** 95 **To** 2023 $22 ✪

MWC Shiraz Mourvedre 2013 A 95/5% blend matured in French oak. Has everything one might wish for at this price; the supple, medium to full-bodied palate provides a reprise of the gently spicy black cherry/berry aromas of the bouquet, adding savoury tannins (probably from the mourvedre) to provide both texture and length. Screwcap. 14.5% alc. **Rating** 94 **To** 2028 $19 ✪

ŶŶŶŶŶ **Basilisk Central Victoria Shiraz Mourvedre 2013** Rating 93 To 2020 $18 ✪
MWC Pinot Gris 2014 Rating 90 To 2016 $19 ✪
Lucie's Promise Rose 2014 Rating 90 To 2016 $11 ✪

McWilliam's ★★★★★

Jack McWilliam Road, Hanwood, NSW 2680 **Region** Riverina
T (02) 6963 3400 **www**.mcwilliams.com.au **Open** Mon–Fri 10–4, Sat 10–5
Winemaker Jim Chatto (chief) plus team **Est.** 1916 **Dozens** NFP **Vyds** 455.7ha
The best wines to emanate from the Hanwood winery are in whole or part from other regions, notably the Hilltops, Coonawarra, Yarra Valley, Tumbarumba, Margaret River and Eden Valley. As McWilliam's viticultural resources have expanded, it has been able to produce regional blends from across Australia of startlingly good value. The winery rating is strongly reliant on the exceptional value for money of the Hanwood Estate and Inheritance brands. The value of McWilliam's Mount Pleasant (Hunter Valley), Barwang (Hilltops), Brand's Laira (Coonawarra) and Evans & Tate (Margaret River) will become ever more apparent as the ability of these brands to deliver world-class wines at appropriate prices (from both McWilliam's point of view and that of domestic or international customers) is leveraged by group chief winemaker Jim Chatto. A founding member of Australia's First Families of Wine, 100 per cent owned by the McWilliam family. Exports to all major markets.

ŶŶŶŶŶ **Appellation Series Tumbarumba Chardonnay 2014** Nailed to the quality mast. Lean but fleshy, with apple, spice and white peach flavours sizzling through the palate. Long. Pure. A beautiful expression of its region. Screwcap. 13% alc. **Rating** 95 **To** 2020 $24 CM ✪

Appellation Series Hilltops Cabernet Sauvignon 2013 Body of flavour is excellent; so too the wine's balance and length. Value alert. Blackcurrant, mint, creamy oak and dark olive. Gets it right. Excellent drinking. Screwcap. 14% alc. **Rating** 94 **To** 2024 $24 CM ✪

ŶŶŶŶŶ **Tightrope Walker Chardonnay 2013** Rating 93 To 2019 $22 CM ✪
Hanwood Estate 1913 Durif 2013 Rating 93 To 2023 $25 CM ✪
Hanwood Estate 1913 Touriga 2013 Rating 92 To 2020 $25 CM ✪
Tightrope Walker Pinot Noir 2013 Rating 91 To 2023 $24

Maddens Rise ★★★★

Cnr Maroondah Highway/Maddens Lane, Coldstream, Vic 3770 **Region** Yarra Valley
T (03) 9739 1977 **www**.maddensrise.com **Open** Fri–Mon 11–5
Winemaker Anthony Fikkers **Est.** 1996 **Dozens** 2000 **Vyds** 22.5ha
Justin Fahey has established a vineyard planted to pinot noir (three clones), chardonnay (two clones), cabernet sauvignon, merlot, shiraz and viognier. Planting began in 1996, but the first wines were not released until 2004. The vines are grown using organic/biological farming practices that focus on soil and vine health, low yields and hand-picking to optimise the quality. Part of the grape production is sold to other Yarra Valley wineries.

ŶŶŶŶŶ **Yarra Valley Chardonnay 2012** Rich with fruit and oak, more of the latter than of the former though it's well integrated, with peach, oatmeal and pineapple filed into sweet cashew, lactose and cedar-spice. It certainly doesn't take any backward steps and, in the end, proves that it doesn't need to. It simply works. Screwcap. 12.2% alc. **Rating** 91 **To** 2017 $27 CM

Reserve Yarra Valley Pinot Noir 2012 Hits the spot in terms of texture and flavour without ever quite hitting the heights. Cherry-plum, forest and dry herbs with perfumed cranberry-like notes rising through the finish. No shortage of drinking appeal. Screwcap. 12.7% alc. **Rating** 91 **To** 2021 $45 CM

♀♀♀♀ **Yarra Valley Pinot Noir 2012 Rating** 89 **To** 2019 $27 CM
Yarra Valley Shiraz 2011 Rating 89 **To** 2019 $27 CM
Yarra Valley Cabernet Sauvignon 2011 Rating 88 **To** 2019 $27 CM
Yarra Valley Nebbiolo 2011 Rating 88 **To** 2019 $40 CM

Magpie Estate   ★★★★☆

PO Box 126, Tanunda, SA 5352 **Region** Barossa Valley
T (08) 8562 3300 **www**.magpieestate.com **Open** Not
Winemaker Rolf Binder, Noel Young **Est.** 1993 **Dozens** 7000
This is a partnership between Rolf Binder and Cambridge (UK) wine merchant Noel Young. Conceived in the early 1990s when grenache and mourvedre were largely forgotten varieties, the two Rhône-philes have adopted that great larrikin of the Australian sky – the magpie – as their mascot for the brand. Fruit is sourced from around 15 different growers, each batch kept separate, enabling many blend options; the winemaking approach is of minimal intervention, with little new oak. Rolf and Noel say they have a lot of fun making the wines, but are also serious about quality and delivering value for money. Exports to the UK, the US, Canada, Austria, Finland, Belgium and the Bahamas.

♀♀♀♀♀ **Rag & Bones Eden Valley Riesling 2014** A floral, blossom-filled bouquet, then a fruit-packed and intense palate, lime and minerally acidity brooking no argument. Great now, but if you can keep your hands off it, there's even more in store. Screwcap. 12.5% alc. **Rating** 95 **To** 2024 $25 ✪
The Malcolm Barossa Valley Shiraz 2010 A massively rich, full-bodied Shiraz, the colour showing little change 5 years from harvest; the bouquet speaks of inky black fruits, the palate adding licorice, and persistent tannins giving texture and balance to the fruit. The cork has been perfectly inserted, with no hint of wine travel down the sides, so the wine will live for decades for those lovers of big, bosomy Barossa Valley reds. 15% alc. **Rating** 94 **To** 2040 $150
The Fakir Barossa Valley Grenache 2012 Aged in a small amount of new French oak, the remainder used. Light but bright crimson; this is as pure an evocation of grenache as you could hope for at twice the price, red fruits of every description on display, acidity and subtle oak giving the wine texture and structure. Great bargain. Screwcap. 14% alc. **Rating** 94 **To** 2022 $20 ✪
The Wit & Shanker Barossa Valley Cabernet Sauvignon 2012 Still retains primary crimson-purple colour; I am convinced that if you want the Barossa Valley to produce elegant Cabernet with clear varietal expression, the alcohol cannot (or should not) exceed 14%, and this would be a good witness in prosecuting my case. Blackcurrant fruit has a nice touch of dried herb merging with the fine tannins of the gently savoury finish. Screwcap. 14% alc. **Rating** 94 **To** 2027 $25 ✪

♀♀♀♀♀ **The Sack Barossa Valley Shiraz 2012 Rating** 93 **To** 2027 $30
The Call Bag Mourvedre Grenache 2012 Rating 93 **To** 2018 $25 ✪
The Black Sock Barossa Valley Mourvedre 2012 Rating 92 **To** 2020 $25 ✪
The Black Craft Barossa Valley Shiraz 2013 Rating 90 **To** 2023 $18 ✪
The Mixed Thing 2013 Rating 90 **To** 2016 $25

Main Ridge Estate   ★★★★★

80 William Road, Red Hill, Vic 3937 **Region** Mornington Peninsula
T (03) 5989 2686 **www**.mre.com.au **Open** Mon–Fri 12–4, w'ends 12–5
Winemaker Nat White **Est.** 1975 **Dozens** 1200 **Vyds** 2.8ha
Quietly spoken and charming founder/owners Nat and Rosalie White preside over their immaculately maintained vineyard and equally meticulously run winery. Their site is a particularly cool one, and if global warming proves to be a permanent part of the landscape,

they say they will not be complaining. The estate is (quietly) on the market, and could be sold at any time, but Nat and Rosalie are still building their shore-side retirement house, so aren't in a hurry to sell what is one of the jewels of the Peninsula.

ΨΨΨΨΨ **Mornington Peninsula Chardonnay 2013** Gleaming straw-green; in classic Main Ridge Estate style with layers of fruit (mlf playing an important role) achieved at a modest alcohol, and with no sense that the wine is over the top, blowsy or whatever. This is the Makybe Diva of the Chardonnay world. Screwcap. 13% alc. **Rating** 96 **To** 2022 $55 **○**

Half Acre Mornington Peninsula Pinot Noir 2013 Deeper colour than The Acre; signals its intentions with the first whiff of the black cherry and plum bouquet, building on that with the powerful, yet fluid, palate where the fruit flavours run amok, satsuma plum to the fore, black cherries also featuring. Screwcap. 13.5% alc. **Rating** 96 **To** 2028 $80

The Acre Mornington Peninsula Pinot Noir 2013 Totally destemmed, wild yeast, 18 days on skins, 17 months' maturation in new and used French oak. Light, bright crimson; a flowery, spicy bouquet, then a long and intense palate, with red fruits intersected by savoury/spicy tannins and quality oak. Screwcap. 13.5% alc. **Rating** 94 **To** 2023 $70

Maipenrai Vineyard & Winery ★★★★

1516 Sutton Road, Sutton, NSW 2620 (postal) **Region** Canberra District
T (02) 8588 1217 **www**.maipenrai.com.au **Open** Not
Winemaker Brian Schmidt **Est.** 2000 **Dozens** 250 **Vyds** 1.1ha
What a story this is, far too rich for just a few lines. It begins at Harvard, in 1992–93, where American-born Brian Schmidt and (now) wife (Australian) Jennifer Gordon were both working on their PhDs. Brian is presently a Laureate Fellow at the Australian National University's Mount Stromlo Observatory and in 2011 won the Nobel Prize for Astronomy. Prior to emigrating to Canberra in '95, he had formed a research team of 20 astronomers on five continents who used distant exploding stars to trace the expansion of the universe back in time; between then and now he has been awarded a constellation of awards and fellowships, undeterred by the tragic destruction of Mount Stromlo in the Canberra bushfires of '03. In 1999 he and Jennifer purchased a property with a beautiful sloped hillside, and planted six clones of pinot noir; he was 33 at the time, and figured that by the time he was ready to retire, the vineyard would be well and truly into the prime of its life. An astronomer's view indeed. A 0.1ha trial of ultra-close spaced shiraz and viognier is underway.

ΨΨΨΨ **Canberra District Pinot Noir 2012** Murky colour. Complex aromatics. Spice, florals, meat and ripe strawberries. Palate is all sweet-sour spiciness, savoury to its back teeth but lively, fruity and tannic. Lots going on. Should be an interesting ride over the coming few years. From the wettest and coolest growing season on record. Vino-Lok. 13.2% alc. **Rating** 89 **To** 2021 $33 CM

Majella ★★★★★

Lynn Road, Coonawarra, SA 5263 **Region** Coonawarra
T (08) 8736 3055 **www**.majellawines.com.au **Open** 7 days 10–4.30
Winemaker Bruce Gregory **Est.** 1969 **Dozens** 25 000 **Vyds** 55ha
Majella is one of the foremost grapegrowers in Coonawarra, with important vineyards, principally shiraz and cabernet sauvignon, plus a little riesling and merlot. The Malleea is one of Coonawarra's greatest wines, The Musician one of Australia's most outstanding red wines selling for less than $20. Exports to the UK, the US and other major markets.

ΨΨΨΨΨ **Coonawarra Shiraz 2012** Traces its roots back to the Woodley Treasure Chest series of the '40s and '50s, its balance and mouthfeel immaculate; red and black fruits vie for prominence, the combination putting oak and tannins into a pure, balanced support role. This is old money speaking, and great value. Screwcap. 14.5% alc. **Rating** 96 **To** 2032 $30 **○**

Coonawarra Cabernet Sauvignon 2012 A near-perfect rendition of Coonawarra Cabernet, blackcurrant the central pillar, herb, mint and earth nuances spread around that pillar simply adding complexity to a distinguished wine with a very long future ahead. Screwcap. 14.5% alc. **Rating** 95 **To** 2032 $33 ✪

♟♟♟♟ The Musician Cabernet Shiraz 2013 **Rating** 92 **To** 2019 $18 CM ✪
Coonawarra Sparkling Shiraz 2008 **Rating** 91 **To** 2023 $30 TS
Minuet NV **Rating** 91 **To** 2020 $30 TS
Coonawarra Riesling 2014 **Rating** 90 **To** 2023 $17 CM ✪

Malcolm Creek Vineyard ★★★★

33 Bonython Road, Kersbrook, SA 5231 **Region** Adelaide Hills
T (08) 8389 3619 **www**.malcolmcreekwines.com.au **Open** By appt
Winemaker Peter Leske, Michael Sykes **Est.** 1982 **Dozens** 1000 **Vyds** 2ha
Malcolm Creek was set up as the retirement venture of Reg Tolley, who decided to upgrade his retirement by selling the venture to Bitten and Karsten Pedersen in 2007. The wines are invariably well made and develop gracefully; they are worth seeking out, and are usually available with some extra bottle age at a very modest price. Exports to the UK, the US, Denmark, Malaysia and China.

♟♟♟♟ Adelaide Hills Chardonnay 2013 Clipped by sweet, toasty oak but the fruit flavours here work a treat. Pear, citrus and white peach, sunny and ripe, with juicy acidity keeping it all fresh. Screwcap. 13.5% alc. **Rating** 92 **To** 2017 $25 CM ✪
Adelaide Hills Sauvignon Blanc 2014 In fine fettle. More textural than you might expect but sweet, musky, tropical fruit flavour is its main thing. Importantly, these flavours are tempered by notes of cut grass and lime zest; overall it's both well balanced and tasty. Screwcap. 13% alc. **Rating** 91 **To** 2015 $20 CM ✪
Ashwood Estate Adelaide Hills Cabernet Sauvignon 2010 Some wines just give you what you want without any mucking around. This is of that ilk, though there's nothing rough and ready about it; there's polish aplenty here. It tastes of blackcurrant, violets, spearmint and sweet, clovey oak, with dusty tannin ribbing through the finish. Cork. 14% alc. **Rating** 91 **To** 2022 $25 CM

♟♟♟♟ The Reginald Blanc de Blanc 2011 **Rating** 88 **To** 2015 $35 TS

Mandala ★★★★★

1568 Melba Highway, Dixons Creek, Vic 3775 **Region** Yarra Valley
T (03) 5965 2016 **www**.mandalawines.com.au **Open** 7 days 10–5
Winemaker Scott McCarthy, Andrew Santarossa, Charles Smedley **Est.** 2007
Dozens 8000 **Vyds** 29ha
Mandala is owned by Charles Smedley, who acquired the established vineyard in 2007. The estate vineyard has vines up to 20 years old, but the spectacular restaurant and cellar door complex is a more recent addition. The vineyards are primarily at the home base, Dixons Creek, with chardonnay (8ha), cabernet sauvignon (6ha), sauvignon blanc and pinot noir (4ha each), shiraz (2ha) and merlot (1ha). There is a separate 4ha vineyard planted entirely to pinot noir with an impressive clonal mix at Yarra Junction.

♟♟♟♟ The Compass Yarra Valley Chardonnay 2012 Hand-picked and sorted before whole bunch pressing to French oak for a cool ferment and 16 months' maturation. A classy wine, still in the first flush of youth when 3yo; white peach is all-important in establishing the parameters of what is a very pure and lovely Chardonnay. Screwcap. 12.5% alc. **Rating** 96 **To** 2022 $50 ✪
Butterfly Yarra Valley Cabernet Sauvignon 2012 A brilliant purple-crimson rim to the colour. Everything comes together in this excellent Cabernet; blackcurrant/cassis fruit is in the driver's seat, cushioned by finely strung tannins and just the right amount of savoury nuances to the overall flavour, oak buried somewhere in the mix. Screwcap. 13% alc. **Rating** 96 **To** 2032 $50 ✪

Yarra Valley Pinot Noir 2013 From the estate Yarra Junction vineyard (70%) and 30% from Dixons Creek; a 4-clone mix with multiple picking dates Feb–Mar; destemmed to open fermenters, then 12 months in French oak (30% new). Barrel selection has resulted in an intense bouquet and palate, with juicy cherry fruit and a lingering finish. Screwcap. 13% alc. **Rating** 95 **To** 2023 $28 ✪

Yarra Valley Chardonnay 2013 Hand-picked, separately vinified clones 76, 95, 96 and 11OV1; wild yeast-fermented in French barriques, with 25% mlf. Vivid green hue; stone fruit and citrus provide fruit flavour complexity, the oak and mlf adding a touch of brioche. Screwcap. 13% alc. **Rating** 94 **To** 2020 $28 ✪

The Matriarch Yarra Valley Pinot Noir 2013 This wine has deeper colour than The Prophet, indeed, deeper than most '13 Yarra Valley Pinots; the bouquet is of black cherry and plum, the substantial palate carrying on the dark fruits message. Screwcap. 14% alc. **Rating** 94 **To** 2025 $50

Yarra Valley Merlot 2013 A prime example of Yarra Valley Merlot, and of the synergy that exists between variety and place, the flavours of cassis (foremost) and plum with a very attractive skein of spice and olive, oak and tannins in their due place. Screwcap. 13.5% alc. **Rating** 94 **To** 2028 $39

ＹＹＹＹＹ **The Prophet Yarra Valley Pinot Noir 2013 Rating** 93 **To** 2020 $50
Yarra Valley Rose 2014 Rating 92 **To** 2015 $20 ✪
Yarra Valley Shiraz 2013 Rating 92 **To** 2028 $28

Mandalay Estate   ★★★★

Mandalay Road, Glen Mervyn via Donnybrook, WA 6239 **Region** Geographe
T (08) 9732 2006 **www**.mandalayroad.com.au **Open** 7 days 11–5
Winemaker John Griffiths, Peter Stanlake (Contract) **Est.** 1997 **Dozens** 500 **Vyds** 4.2ha
Tony and Bernice O'Connell left careers in science and education to establish plantings of shiraz, chardonnay, zinfandel, cabernet sauvignon on their property in 1997 (followed by durif). A hands-on approach with low yields has brought out the best characteristics of the grape varieties and the region.

ＹＹＹＹＹ **Mandalay Road Stump Block Shiraz 2014** Fleshy and perfumed, with blackberry, toast, peppercorn and choc-mint flavours combining into a most attractive package. Balanced and sure-footed with obvious, immediate appeal but no lack of either structure or complexity. Screwcap. 14.5% alc. **Rating** 92 **To** 2022 $25 CM ✪

Mandalay Road Lindsay's Folly Cabernet Shiraz 2014 Offers attractive fruit flavours of blackcurrant, boysenberry and bay leaf and does so without tricks or pretence; it's clean and pure, with sound, dry length. Screwcap. 14.3% alc. **Rating** 92 **To** 2026 $25 CM ✪

Mandalay Road Persimmon Paddock Cabernet Sauvignon 2014 Sinewy wine with tannin dragging blackcurrant, green tobacco and earthen flavours along with it. When the fruit catches up and pulls ahead, which it should do before long, it will be all the better for it. Indeed it's a wine that could easily surprise given some cellar time. Screwcap. 13.9% alc. **Rating** 90 **To** 2024 $25 CM

Mandalay Road Durif 2013 A flood of loose-knit berried flavours roll lusciously along the tongue. Bright disposition despite its inky, dark colour. Slinky-smooth. Screwcap. 13.6% alc. **Rating** 90 **To** 2019 $30 CM

Mandoon Estate   ★★★★★

10 Harris Road, Caversham, WA 6055 **Region** Swan District
T (08) 9274 4346 **www**.mandoonestate.com.au **Open** 7 days 11–4
Winemaker Ryan Sudano **Est.** 2009 **Dozens** 3500 **Vyds** 6.07ha
Mandoon Estate, headed by Allan Erceg, has made a considerable impression with its wines in a very short space of time. In 2008 the family purchased a 13.2ha site in Caversham in the Swan Valley, on a property that had remained in the hands of the Roe family since its initial settlement in the 1840s. Construction of the winery was completed in time for the

first vintage in '10. Winemaker Ryan Sudano has metaphorically laid waste in Australian wine shows with the quality of the wines he has made. By the end of 2014 Mandoon had won 34 trophies, 72 gold, 60 silver and 111 bronze medals, including five trophies in the Qantas Wine Show of WA 2014, its '12 Reserve Cabernet Best Wine of Show.

TTTTT **Reserve Research Station Margaret River Cabernet Sauvignon 2012**
The grapes come from a small 38yo planting of cabernet sauvignon by the State Government as part of the Research Station's experiments to ascertain the varieties best suited to the region. The Bramley Vineyard (as it was known) has been restored by Mandoon, and the old vines have given this beautifully structured and utterly pure evocation of cabernet sauvignon, blackcurrant fruit to the fore, tannins and oak lined up in magisterial support. Screwcap. 14.5% alc. **Rating** 97 To 2042 $45 ✪

TTTTT **Reserve Frankland River Shiraz 2013** Open-fermented for 14 days, then matured for 18 months in French oak. Vibrant, full crimson-purple colour signals a juicy and intense array of blackberry, black cherry, licorice and spice held within a finely spun web of ripe tannins. Will outlive your patience. Screwcap. 14.5% alc. **Rating** 96 To 2038 $33 ✪
Reserve Frankland River Shiraz 2012 There is a wholly admirable consistency to the style and the quality of Mandoon's Reserve Frankland River Shiraz; this is a particularly elegant and supple evocation of the black cherry, blackberry and multi-spice flavour profile, silky tannins and a touch of French oak completing a wine of true quality. Screwcap. 14.5% alc. **Rating** 96 To 2032 $33 ✪
Margaret River Cabernet Merlot 2013 From what was the Research Station in Margaret River, which has some of the oldest vines in the region; matured in French oak. The supple, medium-bodied palate follows in the tracks of the bouquet with its spotless array of cassis, redcurrant and gently savoury tannins. Exceptional bargain. Screwcap. 14% alc. **Rating** 96 To 2029 $24 ✪
Reserve Research Station Margaret River Cabernet Sauvignon 2013 Bright crimson-purple; impeccable winemaking provides a brilliant display of cassis fruit, French oak and tannins in disciplined support. This wine really highlights the synergy between the region and variety. Brilliant stuff. Screwcap. 14% alc. **Rating** 96 To 2038 $63 ✪
Old Vine Swan Valley Shiraz 2013 Old dry-grown vines produce this ultra-deep crimson-purple colour; the bouquet and palate are driven by sombre black fruits, the French oak in which the wine was matured folded within the bosom; winemaker Ryan Sudano shows exceptional skill in the way he has kept this wine balanced, supple and fresh. Screwcap. 14.5% alc. **Rating** 95 To 2033 $25 ✪
Old Vine Swan Valley Grenache 2013 **Rating** 94 To 2020 $22 ✪
Old Vine Swan Valley Grenache 2012 **Rating** 94 To 2025 $22 ✪

TTTTP **Swan Valley Verdelho 2014** **Rating** 93 To 2025 $19 ✪
Margaret River Sauvignon Blanc 2014 **Rating** 91 To 2015 $19 ✪

Mandurang Valley Wines   ★★★☆

77 Fadersons Lane, Mandurang, Vic 3551 **Region** Bendigo
T (03) 5439 5367 **www**.mandurangvalleywines.com.au **Open** W'ends 11–5
Winemaker Wes Vine, Steve Vine **Est.** 1995 **Dozens** 4000 **Vyds** 2.5ha
Wes and Pamela Vine planted their first vineyard at Mandurang in 1976 and started making wine as a hobby. Commercial production began in '93, and an additional vineyard was established in '97. Wes (a former school principal) became full-time winemaker in '99. Son Steve has progressively taken greater responsibility for the winemaking, while Wes is spending more time developing export markets. Pamela manages the cellar door café, established in 2001 and extended in '05. Exports to China.

TTTTP **Bendigo Shiraz 2012** Deeply coloured; the expressive black fruits of the bouquet fill the full-bodied palate; here blackberry compote, tar, licorice and robust tannins all complete for space in a tightly packed parcel that will repay the patience needed. Diam. 14.4% alc. **Rating** 93 **To** 2027 $28

Mansfield Wines ★★★★

201 Eurunderee Lane, Mudgee, NSW 2850 **Region** Mudgee
T (02) 6373 3871 **www**.mansfieldwines.com.au **Open** Thurs–Tues & public hols 10–5
Winemaker Bob Heslop **Est.** 1975 **Dozens** 1000 **Vyds** 5.5ha
Ian McLellan and family purchased Mansfield Wines from his cousin Peter Mansfield in late 1997. The original plantings, which included chardonnay, frontignac, sauvignon blanc, cabernet sauvignon, merlot and shiraz, were removed, to be replaced by a Joseph's coat patchwork of savagnin, vermentino, petit manseng, parellada, tempranillo, touriga, zinfandel and tinta cao, supported by grenache, mourvedre and pedro ximinez. Souzao and carignan are more recent arrivals.

🍷🍷🍷🍷🍷 **Firetail 2013** A 45/40/5% blend of garnacha, shiraz and monastrel. Don't think about it twice: this offers exceptional value. The colour is full and bright; there is a symphony of red and black fruits on the supple medium-bodied palate, with embedded fine-grained tannins on the long, balanced finish. Diam. 13% alc. **Rating** 94 **To** 2020 $19 ✪

🍷🍷🍷🍷🍷 **Touriga Nacional 2012 Rating** 93 **To** 2022 $23 ✪

Marchand & Burch ★★★★★

241 Scotsdale Road, Denmark, WA 6333 **Region** Great Southern
T (08) 9848 2345 **www**.burchfamilywines.com.au **Open** 7 days 10–4
Winemaker Janice McDonald, Pascal Marchand **Est.** 2006 **Dozens** 1100 **Vyds** 8.46ha
A joint venture between Canadian-born and Burgundian-trained Pascal Marchand and Burch Family Wines. Grapes are sourced from single vineyards, and in most cases, from single blocks within those vineyards (4.51ha of chardonnay and 3.95ha of pinot noir, in each case variously situated in Mount Barker and Porongurup). Biodynamic practices underpin the viticulture in the Australian and French vineyards, and Burgundian viticultural techniques have been adopted in the Australian vineyards (eg narrow rows and high-density plantings, Guyot pruning, vertical shoot positioning, and leaf and lateral shoot removal). Exports to the UK, the US and other major markets.

🍷🍷🍷🍷🍷 **Villages Chardonnay 2014** Hand-picked from Porongurup vineyards and shows the magic of this subregion, with the extra integrity and precision it seems to give all varieties grown there; here there is a chorus of trumpets announcing the mouth-watering, vivid pink grapefruit and peach fruit flavours that have devoured the oak. Screwcap. 13% alc. **Rating** 96 **To** 2025 $38 ✪
Porongurup Chardonnay 2013 Hand-picked, whole bunch-pressed, wild yeast-fermented in French oak; the result is a resplendently complex Chardonnay with white stone fruit, creamy cashew and bright acidity forming a circle of continuous flavours. Screwcap. 13% alc. **Rating** 96 **To** 2022 $73 ✪
Mount Barrow Mount Barker Pinot Noir 2013 Ticks all the boxes, and a nice endorsement of John Gladstones' belief in the benefits of increased temperatures in lockstep with increased CO_2; red cherry fruit on the bouquet. The palate has a complex carpet of spice and earth, drawing out the finish, providing complexity and a vigorous finish. Screwcap. 13.5% alc. **Rating** 95 **To** 2028 $50

Margan Family ★★★★★

1238 Milbrodale Road, Broke, NSW 2330 **Region** Hunter Valley
T (02) 6579 1317 **www**.margan.com.au **Open** 7 days 10–5
Winemaker Andrew Margan **Est.** 1997 **Dozens** 30 000 **Vyds** 98ha
Andrew Margan, following in his father's footsteps, entered the wine industry over 20 years ago, working as a Flying Winemaker in Europe, then for Tyrrell's. Andrew and wife Lisa now

have almost 100ha of fully mature vines at their Ceres Hill property at Broke, and lease the nearby Vere Vineyard. Wine quality is consistently good. Exports to the UK, Germany, Norway, Indonesia, Malaysia, Vietnam, Hong Kong and China.

🍷🍷🍷🍷🍷 **Limited Release Semillon 2014** While the Hunter Valley winemakers were (and remain) justifiably over the moon about the quality of the '14 Shiraz, the quality of the '14 Semillons is also very good, with the opportunity to leave the grapes unpicked until the baume and acid levels said it was time. Slightly higher alcohol levels have been the outcome, but as is the case here, the wines have great power, precision and length. Screwcap. 12.5% alc. **Rating** 95 **To** 2027 $30 ✪
Aged Release Semillon 2010 This is on a slow-moving conveyor belt that will smoothly and uninterruptedly move it to the point of peak complexity down the time track years hence. The lemony/minerally flavours are yet to show signs of honey or toast, and it may be they will never assume an important role, but it's quite certain there is plenty of petrol in the tank to take it even further forward. Screwcap. 11% alc. **Rating** 95 **To** 2025 $40

🍷🍷🍷🍷 **Hunter Valley Semillon 2014 Rating** 93 **To** 2029 $15 ✪
Hunter Valley Chardonnay 2014 Rating 92 **To** 2019 $15 ✪
Hunter Valley Shiraz Saignee Rose 2014 Rating 91 **To** 2016 $15 ✪
Hunter Valley Shiraz 2013 Rating 90 **To** 2020 $20 ✪

Margaret Hill Vineyard   ★★★★☆

18 Northcote Avenue, Balwyn, Vic 3103 (postal) **Region** Heathcote
T (03) 9836 2168 **www**.guangtiangroup.com.au **Open** Not
Winemaker Ben Portet (Contract) **Est.** 1996 **Dozens** 1100 **Vyds** 12.5ha
Formerly known as Toolleen Vineyard, the name Margaret Hill Vineyard was chosen by owner Linchun Bao (and wife Chunye Qiu) after they acquired the business from the Huang family in 2010. They have upgraded the vineyard equipment and irrigation system, and are restoring full health and vigour to the vineyard, which is equally split between cabernet sauvignon and shiraz. Wines are released under the Margaret Hill and Kudo labels. The quality of the vineyard, and the skill of contract winemaker Ben Portet, have together been responsible for the high quality of the wines. Exports to China.

🍷🍷🍷🍷🍷 **Kudo Heathcote Shiraz 2013** Hand-picked, matured in French oak for 10 months. Complexity is my name, the wine intones: spice, pepper, anise, black cherry, blackberry and fine, savoury tannins, oak also in the frame of a compelling, medium-bodied Shiraz. Cork. 14.2% alc. **Rating** 95 **To** 2038 $80

Marq Wines   ★★★★★

PO Box 1415, Dunsborough, WA 6281 **Region** Margaret River
T 0411 122 662 **www**.marqwines.com.au **Open** Not
Winemaker Mark Warren **Est.** 2011 **Dozens** 2000
Mark Warren has a degree in wine science from CSU and a science degree from the University of WA; to complete the circle, he is currently lecturing in wine science and wine sensory processes at Curtin University, Margaret River. He also has 26 years' experience in both the Swan Valley and Margaret River, and his current major commercial role is producing the extensive Happs range as well as wines under contract for several other Margaret River brands. When all of this is added up, he is responsible for 60 to 70 individual wines each year, now including wines under his own Marq Wines label. A quick look at the list of Vermentino, Fiano, Wild & Worked Sauvignon Blanc Semillon, Wild Ferment Chardonnay, Rose, Gamay, Tempranillo, Malbec, and Cut & Dry Shiraz (Amarone style) points to the underlying philosophy: an exploration of the potential of alternative varieties and unusual winemaking methods by someone with an undoubted technical understanding of the processes involved.

🍷🍷🍷🍷🍷 **Wild and Worked Margaret River Sauvignon Blanc Semillon 2014** Wild yeast barrel-fermented and who knows what else. It's right on the money from the opening whiff and sip through to the almost frightening power and intensity of the multifaceted display of lemon citrus juice, pith and zest on the finish and aftertaste. Screwcap. 12.8% alc. **Rating** 95 **To** 2022 $25 **✪**

Serious Margaret River Rose 2014 Grenache is given skin contact, then wild yeast barrel-fermented. A mouth-watering rose with both length and depth of red berry fruits building on the foundation of the bouquet; it is at once fruity, yet dry, faintly citrussy acidity drawing out the fresh, inviting finish. Screwcap. 13% alc. **Rating** 95 **To** 2017 $25 **✪**

Cut and Dry Margaret River Shiraz 2013 Margaret River shiraz is taken to Italy for inspiration; picked at normal baume, the grapes are then dried on straw mats. Savoury black chocolate and licorice flavours are laid over blackberry varietal fruit. Why the wine shouldn't be a hotbed of dead fruit is a mystery; given points for its mastery of the style. Screwcap. 15.5% alc. **Rating** 95 **To** 2033 $35 **✪**

Margaret River Malbec 2013 This Malbec doesn't take things lying down. It's a wine with a robust personality. It tastes of leather, blackcurrant, cloves and chocolate/chicory with firm fingers of tannin pinning it safely to the ground. Assured palate and finish. A few years in the bottle will bring greater complexity and expression to the nose. A standout in Malbec circles. Screwcap. 14.2% alc. **Rating** 95 **To** 2024 $28 CM **✪**

Wild Ferment Margaret River Chardonnay 2013 Wild fermentation has resulted in a (deliberately) funky bouquet with strong flinty aromas that are lost in the notably fresh and vibrant palate, picked with pinpoint precision between the citrus and the stone fruit arc. A go-anywhere, any-time style. Screwcap. 12.9% alc. **Rating** 95 **To** 2023 $28 **✪**

♟♟♟♟♟ **Margaret River Fiano 2014 Rating** 93 **To** 2016 $25 **✪**
Margaret River Vermentino 2014 Rating 92 **To** 2020 $25 **✪**
Margaret River Gamay 2013 Rating 91 **To** 2018 $25
Petit Manseng 2013 Rating 90 **To** 2016 $28 CM
Margaret River Tempranillo 2013 Rating 90 **To** 2023 $28

Massena Vineyards ★★★★★

PO Box 643, Angaston, SA 5353 **Region** Barossa Valley
T (08) 8564 3037 **www**.massena.com.au **Open** At Artisans of Barossa
Winemaker Jaysen Collins **Est.** 2000 **Dozens** 3000 **Vyds** 4ha
Massena Vineyards draws upon 1ha each of mataro (mourvedre), saperavi, petite syrah and tannat at Nuriootpa, also purchasing grapes from other growers. It is an export-oriented business, although the wines can also be purchased by mail order, which, given both the quality and innovative nature of the wines, seems more than ordinarily worthwhile. Exports to the US, Switzerland, Denmark, South Korea, Hong Kong and China.

♟♟♟♟♟ **Barossa Valley Primitivo 2013** In California, the best Primitivos are made by those who learn how to correctly gauge the ripeness of the fruit, for berries on the same bunch can range from green to black. The Massena team has judged this to perfection, the perfumed bouquet leading into a palate with red fruits to the fore, black fruits on the back-palate, and silky tannins on the finish. Screwcap. 14.5% alc. **Rating** 96 **To** 2025 $30 **✪**

Barossa Valley Mataro 2013 Mataro is not an easy variety to handle on its own, tending to be bolshie. Here a top site and experienced winemaking has harnessed its power, providing a full-bodied palate that is still well balanced; sultry black fruits side-step the tannins with a little bit of help from the oak maturation. Screwcap. 14.5% alc. **Rating** 95 **To** 2028 $30 **✪**

Massoni ★★★★

30 Brasser Avenue, Dromana, Vic 3936 **Region** Pyrenees/Mornington Peninsula
T (03) 5981 0711 **www**.massoniwines.com **Open** By appt 10–4.30
Winemaker Fred Ursini, Robert Paul, Phil Kittle **Est.** 1984 **Dozens** 25 000 **Vyds** 269ha

Massoni is a substantial business owned by the Pellegrino and Ursini families, and is a venture with two completely distinct arms. In terms of vineyard and land size, by far the larger is the GlenKara vineyard in the Pyrenees (269ha). It also has 8.5ha on the Mornington Peninsula where Massoni started, and where it gained its reputation. In 2012 Massoni purchased the former Tucks Ridge/Red Hill winemaking facility at Dromana. Exports to China.

Mornington Peninsula Chardonnay 2012 It smells and tastes seductive from the first sip. Oak, citrus and nectarine flavours, but it's more characterised by its poise, its balance, its effortless flow of varietal flavour. Chalky grip to the finish completes an entirely positive impression. Screwcap. 13.5% alc. **Rating** 94 **To** 2019 $25 CM ❂

Mornington Peninsula Pinot Noir 2012 Rating 92 To 2022 $30 CM
Pyrenees Ranges Cabernet Merlot 2012 Rating 90 To 2024 $25 CM

Maverick Wines ★★★★★

981 Light Pass Road, Vine Vale, Moorooroo, SA 5352 **Region** Barossa Valley
T (08) 8563 3551 www.maverickwines.com.au **Open** By appt
Winemaker Ronald Brown, Will Thompson **Est.** 2004 **Dozens** 14 000 **Vyds** 61.7ha
This is the very successful venture of Ronald Brown, Jeremy Vogler and Adrian Bell. Taking advantage of excess grape production in Australia, the partners have acquired four vineyards in key areas of the Eden Valley and Barossa Valley, with vines ranging in age from 40 to over 140 years. Maverick has achieved listings in top restaurants and fine wine retailers in Australia and internationally. Exports to the UK, the US and other major markets.

Trial Hill Eden Valley Shiraz 2012 Biodynamically grown, and a good advertisement for that discipline. A vibrantly alive wine, with a cornucopia of red fruits, warm spices and black pepper; the tannins are superfine, the oak integrated and the finish is very long. Cork. 13.5% alc. **Rating** 96 **To** 2032 $80
Twins Barossa Shiraz 2012 Twins from 4 estate vineyards? Never mind, this is a vibrant, multifaceted wine, its bouquet and medium-bodied palate opening with a collage of red and black fruits, then with rising intensity through to the finish and aftertaste. Andrew Caillard MW's lovely painting on the label captures the spirit of the wine. Great value. Screwcap. 14.5% alc. **Rating** 95 **To** 2027 $25 ❂
Greenock Rise Barossa Valley Shiraz 2012 This is one of those wines that defy the laws of gravity, imparting its array of blackberry and soused plum fruit without breaking into fire on the finish. You are still left to wonder how many (or few) glasses you could drink during a single meal, but Maverick Wines would say 'so what'. Cork. 15.5% alc. **Rating** 95 **To** 2032 $70
Paraview Shiraz 2011 Barossa Valley pearls from the '11 vintage are less common than those from McLaren Vale. Here you find the hallmarks of the cool vintage, but not the rainfall; scrupulous fruit selection from vines protected from moulds and/or botrytis is the key. Cork. 13.5% alc. **Rating** 94 **To** 2026 $50
Twins Barossa Valley Cabernet Sauvignon Merlot Petit Verdot Cabernet Franc 2012 From the estate Barossa Ridge Vineyard, matured in French barriques for 18 months. It's not an easy varietal ride for the Barossa, but in '12 many things were possible: a very well balanced wine, leaving no doubt about the thrust of its blend. Screwcap. 14.2% alc. **Rating** 94 **To** 2032 $27 ❂

Ahrens' Creek Barossa Valley Grenache 2012 Rating 92 To 2032 $150
The Maverick Barossa Shiraz 2012 Rating 90 To 2052 $250

Maximus Wines ★★★★☆

Cnr Foggo Road/Penny's Road, McLaren Vale, SA 5171 **Region** McLaren Vale
T (08) 8323 8777 www.maximuswinesaustralia.com.au **Open** Fri–Mon 11–4
Winemaker Rowland Short **Est.** 2007 **Dozens** 2000 **Vyds** 1.82ha
Sailing master Rowland Short, having run one of Australia's most successful sailing schools, decided (in his words) 'to brave the choppy waters of the Australian wine industry' by

establishing Maximus Wines in partnership with wife Shelley. They purchased an already-planted shiraz vineyard, and built a cellar door into the side of a hill, with a maturation cellar underneath. Grapes are purchased from other vineyards in McLaren Vale, including from vines up to 150 years old.

ΨΨΨΨΨ **McLaren Vale Tempranillo & Grenacha 2013** Hearty but slippery smooth. A wine with much to recommend it. It's tannic and structural but not at the expense of domination of the fruit. It offers fresh, ripe raspberry and plum notes, but gives savouriness and spiciness free rein. The finish has a bit of flex to it; a suggestion that it could do more if it wanted or needed to. Quality drinking. Screwcap. 14.6% alc. **Rating** 95 **To** 2021 $30 CM ❂
Premium McLaren Vale Shiraz 2013 Spends 16 months in a combination of French and American oak. Hefty wine, but it has its hands firmly on the controls. Deepset flavours of coal, blackberry and milk chocolate, with violet-like notes lightening the mood. A crash of tannin lands through the finish but it keeps pouring the flavour on. Screwcap. 14.6% alc. **Rating** 94 **To** 2026 $25 CM ❂

ΨΨΨΨΨ **McLaren Vale Cabernet Sauvignon 2013** **Rating** 93 **To** 2025 $25 CM ❂
Old Vine McLaren Vale Mourvedre 2013 **Rating** 93 **To** 2021 $30 CM
Premium McLaren Vale GSM 2013 **Rating** 92 **To** 2021 $25 CM ❂

Maxwell Wines   ★★★★★

Olivers Road, McLaren Vale, SA 5171 **Region** McLaren Vale
T (08) 8323 8200 **www.**maxwellwines.com.au **Open** 7 days 10–5
Winemaker Andrew Jericho, Mark Maxwell **Est.** 1979 **Dozens** 24000 **Vyds** 40ha
Maxwell Wines has carved out a reputation as a premium producer in McLaren Vale. The brand has produced some excellent red wines in recent years. The majority of the vines on the estate were planted in 1972, and include 19 rows of the highly regarded Reynella Selection cabernet sauvignon. The Ellen Street shiraz block in front of the winery was planted in '53. During vintage, visitors to the elevated cellar door can watch the gravity-flow operations in the winery. Owned and operated by Mark Maxwell. Exports to all major markets.

ΨΨΨΨΨ **Eocene Ancient Earth McLaren Vale Shiraz 2012** Grown on a single block of vines planted on the corner of Olivers and Chalk Hill roads in 1953. This was matured in all French oak, none of it spanking new but all of it only 1yo. It's balanced, grippy, chock full of dark-berried fruit and yet smooth as a caress as it rolls along the tongue. It needs time for the oak to melt further into the fruit but its quality is obvious. Screwcap. 14.6% alc. **Rating** 95 **To** 2035 $45 CM
Eight Bells Reserve McLaren Vale Shiraz 2012 Good colour; a generous wine from its bouquet through to its finish and aftertaste, giving its place and variety equal billing; supple black fruits are wrapped in a thin coat of dark chocolate, and supported by integrated tannins and quality oak. Can't ask for more. Screwcap. 13.3% alc. **Rating** 95 **To** 2032 $45
Minotaur Reserve McLaren Vale Shiraz 2012 Threatens to overdo it without ever quite overstepping the mark. End result is a substantial, inky, brooding wine with tar and saturated blackberry flavours pulled tight by iron chains of tannin. Saltbush and thick, toasty oak also make a clear impression. Cork permitting, this will live and develop well for a very long time. 14.8% alc. **Rating** 94 **To** 2035 $75 CM

ΨΨΨΨΨ **Lime Cave McLaren Vale Cabernet 2012** **Rating** 93 **To** 2028 $40 CM
Little Demon Shiraz Grenache 2013 **Rating** 92 **To** 2020 $17 CM ❂
Little Demon Cabernet Malbec 2013 **Rating** 91 **To** 2020 $17 CM ❂
Adelaide Hills Chardonnay 2013 **Rating** 91 **To** 2017 $24 CM
Ellen Street McLaren Vale Shiraz 2012 **Rating** 91 **To** 2026 $40 CM
Silver Hammer McLaren Vale Shiraz 2013 **Rating** 90 **To** 2019 $20 CM ❂
Eight Bells McLaren Vale Shiraz 2013 **Rating** 90 **To** 2018 $16 ❂
Little Demon Cabernet Merlot 2013 **Rating** 90 **To** 2020 $17 CM ❂

Mayer ★★★★★

66 Miller Road, Healesville, Vic 3777 **Region** Yarra Valley
T (03) 5967 3779 **www**.timomayer.com.au **Open** By appt
Winemaker Timo Mayer **Est.** 1999 **Dozens** 1000 **Vyds** 2.4ha
Timo Mayer, also winemaker at Gembrook Hill Vineyard, teamed with partner Rhonda Ferguson to establish Mayer on the slopes of Mt Toolebewong, 8km south of Healesville. The steepness of those slopes is presumably 'celebrated' in the name given to the wines (Bloody Hill). Pinot noir has the lion's share of the vineyard, with smaller amounts of shiraz and chardonnay – all high-density plantings. Mayer's winemaking credo is minimal interference and handling, and no filtration. Exports to the UK, Germany, Denmark, Singapore and Japan.

ŢŢŢŢŢ **Granite Upper Yarra Valley Pinot Noir 2013** It is probably autosuggestion, but the wine has a strong mineral and herbal streak; just when you think this may be too much for the fruit, resurgent dark cherry flavours come through emphatically on the back-palate and finish. Cellaring strongly recommended. Diam. 13.5% alc. **Rating** 96 **To** 2025 $55 ○
Close Planted Yarra Valley Pinot Noir 2013 The front label says nothing about the close-planted vines; the wine is tight, crisp and fresh, red fruits in abundance before a savoury, slightly herbal finish. Diam. 13.5% alc. **Rating** 95 **To** 2023 $55
Dr Mayer Yarra Valley Pinot Noir 2013 Good hue; has both textural and flavour complexity on the bouquet and palate; the palate gains intensity progressively through to the finish, ending with a flourish on the aftertaste. Great future. Diam. 13.5% alc. **Rating** 95 **To** 2025 $55
Bloody Hill Yarra Valley Pinot Noir 2013 Bright, clear crimson; has impeccable varietal expression on the bouquet and palate; the purity and balance can't be faulted, but it will gain more textural complexity if given the time it deserves. Diam. 13.5% alc. **Rating** 94 **To** 2023 $30 ○

ŢŢŢŢŢ **Big Betty Yarra Valley Shiraz 2013 Rating** 93 **To** 2027 $38

Mayfield Vineyard ★★★★

954 Icely Road, Orange, NSW 2800 **Region** Orange
T (02) 6365 9292 **www**.mayfieldvineyard.com **Open** W'ends 10–4
Winemaker Antonio D'Onise, Simon Gilbert **Est.** 1998 **Dozens** 12000 **Vyds** 20.3ha
The property – including the house in which owners Richard and Kathy Thomas now live – has a rich history as a leading Suffolk sheep stud, founded upon the vast fortune accumulated by the Crawford family via its biscuit business in the UK. The estate vineyard has 7.9ha of sauvignon blanc, 3.8ha of pinot noir, 3.4ha each of cabernet sauvignon and merlot, and slightly less than 1ha each of sangiovese and chardonnay. Only one wine was received for this edition, but the rating has been partially maintained. Exports to the UK and Asia.

ŢŢŢŢ **Single Vineyard Orange Cabernet Sauvignon 2012** The colour lacks depth, although the hue is acceptable; unambiguously light-bodied, it does have some choc-mint and cassis fruit, and should be consumed without delay. It seems rain has been a factor. Screwcap. 13.5% alc. **Rating** 88 **To** 2016 $28

Mayford Wines ★★★★☆

6815 Great Alpine Road, Porepunkah, Vic 3740 **Region** Alpine Valleys
T (03) 5756 2528 **www**.mayfordwines.com **Open** By appt
Winemaker Eleana Anderson **Est.** 1995 **Dozens** 650 **Vyds** 3ha
The roots of Mayford go back to 1995, when forester Brian Nicholson planted a small amount of shiraz, since extended to 0.8ha, chardonnay (1.6ha) and tempranillo (0.6ha). In their words, 'in-house winemaking commenced shortly after he selected his seasoned winemaker bride in '02. Wife and co-owner Eleana Anderson became a Flying Winemaker, working four vintages in Germany while completing her wine science degree at CSU (having much earlier obtained an arts degree). Vintages in Australia included one at Boynton's Feathertop (also at

Porepunkah), where she met her husband-to-be. Initially, she was unenthusiastic about the potential of tempranillo, which Brian had planted after consultation with Mark Walpole, Brown Brothers' viticulturist, but since making the first vintage in '06 she has been thoroughly enamoured of the variety. Eleana practises minimalist winemaking, declining to use enzymes, cultured yeasts, tannins and/or copper.

🍷🍷🍷🍷🍷 **Porepunkah Tempranillo 2013** A quantum leap forward for this winery and indeed for this variety in Australia. Fundamentally, this wine is built on structure more than on fruit, though there's plenty of body, plenty of licorice and red-cherried fruit, especially once it's been given a chance to breathe. The emphasis here though is on a ropey dryness, on savouriness, on spice and earth. This tiny vineyard has grown excellent tempranillo in the past, but this release is a shot at the stars. Screwcap. 14% alc. **Rating** 97 **To** 2026 $35 CM **○**

🍷🍷🍷🍷🍷 **Porepunkah Chardonnay 2013** Bright and frisky with edges of sophistication. It has drinkability down pat. Pear and citrus with mealy, smoky, spicy inputs. Excellent linger of flavour. Oak–fruit balance is better than previous releases, and the wine is all the better for it. Screwcap. 14% alc. **Rating** 94 **To** 2019 $35 CM

Maygars Hill Winery

53 Longwood–Mansfield Road, Longwood, Vic 3665 **Region** Strathbogie Ranges
T 0402 136 448 **www**.maygarshill.com.au **Open** By appt
Winemaker Contract **Est.** 1997 **Dozens** 900 **Vyds** 3.2ha
Jenny Houghton purchased this 8ha property in 1994, planting shiraz (1.9ha) and cabernet sauvignon (1.3ha). The name comes from Lieutenant Colonel Maygar, who fought with outstanding bravery in the Boer War in South Africa in 1901, and was awarded the Victoria Cross. In World War I he rose to command the 8th Light Horse Regiment, winning yet further medals for bravery. No wines were made in 2011 due to poor vintage conditions, but Maygar Hill returned triumphant in '12 and '13. Exports to Fiji.

🍷🍷🍷🍷🍷 **Shiraz 2013** This vineyard is incredibly consistent in fingerprinting the quality and the style of the fruit it produces. Brilliantly coloured, the flavours are at the midpoint between cool and warm, the medium-bodied palate with supple blackberry and satsuma plum fruit, precisely measured tannins, and a pinch of black pepper. Great value. Screwcap. 14% alc. **Rating** 95 **To** 2033 $25 **○**

Mayhem & Co

49 Collingrove Avenue, Broadview, SA 5083 **Region** Adelaide Hills
T 0468 384 817 **www**.mayhemandcowine.com.au **Open** Not
Winemaker Brendon Keys, Andrew Hill **Est.** 2009 **Dozens** 1400
Mayhem & Co. is a venture between Andrew Hill and Brendon Keys. Andrew and Brendon worked together many years ago at Wirra Wirra, and they have combined their skills in order to create the Mayhem & Co. brand. Brendon has made wine in Australia, NZ, the US and Argentina, and Andrew worked vintages at Wirra Wirra and Chapel Hill, before taking on senior sales and marketing roles with Koonara, Tomich Hill and Reschke Wines. The excellent wines are made from grapes purchased from various growers in the Adelaide Hills, Eden Valley and McLaren Vale. Exports to Hong Kong and China.

🍷🍷🍷🍷🍷 **Small Berries Blewitt Springs Shiraz 2013** Grown on a 40yo vineyard, now managed biodynamically. Wild yeast, whole berries, 30% new French oak. It takes time to unfurl in the glass, but the class and quality of this wine are undeniable. Tannin studs violets, meat, game and blackberry flavours to clovey, woody, peppery characters. It's dry and spicy but juicy and floral. There's an argument to say this has it all. Screwcap. 13.8% alc. **Rating** 96 **To** 2030 $40 CM **○**

🍷🍷🍷🍷🍷 **B&W Adelaide Hills Chardonnay 2013** **Rating** 93 **To** 2018 $40 CM

Mazza Wines

PO Box 480, Donnybrook, WA 6239 **Region** Geographe
T (08) 9201 1114 **www**.mazza.com.au **Open** Not
Winemaker Contract **Est.** 2002 **Dozens** 1000 **Vyds** 4ha
David and Anne Mazza were inspired by the great wines of Rioja and the Douro Valley, and continue a long-standing family tradition of making wine. They have planted the key varieties of those two regions: tempranillo, graciano, bastardo, souzao, tinta cao and touriga nacional. They believe they were the first Australian vineyard to present this collection of varieties on a single site, and I am reasonably certain they were correct in this belief. Whether it is still true is a matter of conjecture – it's a fast-moving scene in Australia these days. Exports to the UK.

♥♥♥♥♡ **Geographe Bastardo Rose 2014** Pale salmon-pink; the bouquet is filled with exotic spices, the palate bone dry, but with conviction to its tangy fruit; a bit of bite is welcome. 350 dozen made. Screwcap. 13.5% alc. **Rating** 92 **To** 2016 $18 ✪

Medhurst

24–26 Medhurst Road, Gruyere, Vic 3770 **Region** Yarra Valley
T (03) 5964 9022 **www**.medhurstwines.com.au **Open** Thurs–Mon & public hols 11–5
Winemaker Matt Steel **Est.** 2000 **Dozens** 5000 **Vyds** 15.2ha
The wheel has come full circle for Ross and Robyn Wilson. In the course of a very distinguished corporate career, Ross was CEO of Southcorp when it brought the Penfolds, Lindemans and Wynns businesses under the Southcorp banner. Robyn spent her childhood in the Yarra Valley, her parents living less than a kilometre away from Medhurst. The vineyard is planted to sauvignon blanc, chardonnay, pinot noir, cabernet sauvignon and shiraz, all running on a low-yield basis. A large winery was built in 2011; it focuses on small-batch production, and also provides contract winemaking services to others. The visual impact of the winery has been minimised by recessing the building into the slope of land and locating the barrel room underground. The winery was recognised for its architectural excellence at the Victorian Architecture Awards '12. Exports to Hong Kong and China.

♥♥♥♥♥ **Reserve Yarra Valley Shiraz 2012** Cool-climate Shiraz, dressed to kill. This is a wine of polish, complexity, sinewy tannin and serious persistence, all within an inherently savoury context. It tastes of walnuts, red and black cherries, smoky oak and sweet fresh herbs, the combination at once sophisticated and delicious. It's the first release of a Reserve Shiraz for Medhurst; the bar has been set at the top. Screwcap. 13% alc. **Rating** 96 **To** 2030 $60 CM ✪
Yarra Valley Chardonnay 2013 The bouquet and palate both have complexity, the bouquet with hints of funk, the palate with both depth and length to its stone fruit and citrus flavours, oak evident as much in the texture as in the nutty cashew notes. Screwcap. 13% alc. **Rating** 95 **To** 2023 $30 ✪
Reserve Yarra Valley Chardonnay 2012 Silken-textured and lengthy with ripe fruit flavour running seductively from start to finish. Textbook A Grade Chardonnay. Spicy oak is showy but complementary. The fruit here is like biting into a fleshy white peach, dripping with juice. Screwcap. 13.2% alc. **Rating** 95 **To** 2020 $60 CM
Steel's Hill Yarra Valley Pinot Noir 2013 Bright, clear crimson; the fresh and vibrant bouquet has a burst of red fruits and spices, moving to slightly darker fruits on the palate, providing an extra degree of complexity. Exceptional quality for an entry point Yarra Valley Pinot. Screwcap. 13% alc. **Rating** 95 **To** 2023 $24 ✪
Yarra Valley Pinot Noir 2013 Alive with bright cherried fruit but sordid and undergrowthy to boot. This wine will please a lot of folk. Spice and foresty notes pop their heads up too, but a gentle slide of creamy oak keeps all the components running smoothly. Screwcap. 13% alc. **Rating** 94 **To** 2022 $36 CM
Yarra Valley Pinot Noir 2012 The colour is notably light, the bouquet and palate all about clarity and purity courtesy of a hands-off regime in the winery; the balance is such that the wine will age well, but don't serve it to lovers of Barossa Shiraz. Screwcap. 13.2% alc. **Rating** 94 **To** 2020 $36

ŶŶŶŶŶ Reserve Yarra Valley Pinot Noir 2012 Rating 93 To 2021 $60 CM
Yarra Valley Sauvignon Blanc 2014 Rating 92 To 2015 $24 CM ✪
Steel's Hill Yarra Valley Chardonnay 2013 Rating 92 To 2020 $24 ✪
Reserve Cabernet Sauvignon 2012 Rating 92 To 2026 $60 CM

Meehan Vineyard   ★★★★

4536 McIvor Highway, Heathcote, Vic 3523 **Region** Heathcote
T 0407 058 432 **www**.meehanvineyard.com **Open** W'ends & public hols 10–5
Winemaker Phil Meehan **Est.** 2003 **Dozens** 1000 **Vyds** 2ha
In 1999, after their children had left the nest, Phil and Judy Meehan decided to return to the
country and grow grapes for sale to wineries. In that year they took the first step, planting a
small pinot noir vineyard at Bannockburn. It then took until April 2003 to find a near-perfect
site, just within the Heathcote town boundary, its northeast-facing gentle slope on the famous
Cambrian soil. Phil graduated with a Diploma of Winemaking and a Diploma of Viticulture
in '05, saying, 'After a mere six years of study I only learned, after all that time, just how much
more to winemaking there was to learn.' Exports to the UK.

ŶŶŶŶŶ Reserve Estate Shiraz 2013 Excellent colour; a richer, riper and more complex
wine than its varietal sibling, spice, oak and a pinch of pepper running through the
succulent fruit; ripe tannins build on the finish. Screwcap. 14.8% alc. **Rating** 94
To 2033 $45

ŶŶŶŶŶ Heathcote Shiraz 2012 Rating 93 To 2027 $35
Heathcote Shiraz 2013 Rating 92 To 2028 $25 ✪
Heathcote Cabernet Sauvignon 2012 Rating 90 To 2022 $35

Meerea Park   ★★★★★

Pavilion B, 2144 Broke Road, Pokolbin, NSW 2320 **Region** Hunter Valley
T (02) 4998 7474 **www**.meereapark.com.au **Open** 7 days 10–5
Winemaker Rhys Eather **Est.** 1991 **Dozens** 14 000
This is the project of Rhys and Garth Eather, whose great-great-grandfather, Alexander
Munro, established a famous vineyard in the 19th century, known as Bebeah. While the
range of wines chiefly focuses on semillon and shiraz, it extends to other varieties (including
chardonnay), and also into other regions. Meerea Park has moved its cellar door to the striking
Tempus Two winery now owned by the Roche family, situated on the corner of Broke Road/
McDonald Road. Other tenants of the building include the Smelly Cheese Shop, Oishi
Restaurant, Goldfish bar and cocktail lounge, The Barrel Room, and Tempus Two's own cellar
door. It hardly need be said that the quality of the wines, especially with 5 years' cellaring, is
outstanding. Exports to the UK, the US, Hong Kong, Singapore and China.

ŶŶŶŶŶ Aged Release Alexander Munro Individual Vineyard Hunter Valley
Semillon 2005 From the celebrated Braemore Vineyard planted in '69, and
still on an upwards trajectory. Bright green-straw; lime, honey, buttered toast
and acidity contribute equally to a great Hunter Valley Semillon, the length and
aftertaste prodigious. Screwcap. 11% alc. **Rating** 97 To 2035 $80 ✪

ŶŶŶŶŶ Alexander Munro Individual Vineyard Hunter Valley Semillon 2010
While still showing the life-giving acidity of Hunter Valley Semillon, this has an
extra layer to its panoply of lemon/citrus fruits, in turn elevating and driving
the impact of the finish and aftertaste. A very high-quality Semillon. Screwcap.
11.5% alc. **Rating** 96 To 2025 $45 ✪
Aged Release Alexander Munro Individual Vineyard Hunter Valley
Shiraz 2005 A full-bodied Shiraz with varietal and regional expression
contributing equally to the sombre black fruits, earth, leather and black olive
flavours. Still in its infancy, but has the balance to coast through the next two
decades, even then with more life ahead. Screwcap. 14.5% alc. **Rating** 96
To 2045 $120

Terracotta Individual Vineyard Hunter Valley Semillon 2010
Has confidently entered the second phase of its life, its bouquet fragrant, its palate with a wisp of honey joining the circus of citrus flavours. Keep this for as long as you like – or revel in it tonight. Screwcap. 11.5% alc. **Rating** 95 **To** 2025 $30 ✪
Hell Hole Individual Vineyard Hunter Valley Shiraz 2013 Rhys Eather obviously recognised the potential of the grapes early on in the piece when allocating the amount of new oak; you can see it, but it's tightly surrounded by the clasp of intense blackberry and earthy fruits; its tannins strengthen that clasp, but not brutally. Screwcap. 13.5% alc. **Rating** 95 **To** 2048 $60
Hell Hole Vineyard Semillon 2014 Rating 94 **To** 2024 $25 ✪

🍷🍷🍷🍷🍷 **Alexander Munro Chardonnay 2014** Rating 93 **To** 2024 $40
XYZ Hunter Valley Shiraz 2013 Rating 93 **To** 2022 $25 ✪
Indie Hunter Valley Shiraz Pinot 2013 Rating 93 **To** 2033 $40
Indie Hunter Valley Marsanne Roussanne 2014 Rating 92 **To** 2020 $30
Cabernet Merlot 2013 Rating 92 **To** 2020 $16 ✪

Merindoc Vintners   ★★★★★

2905 Lancefield–Tooborac Road, Tooborac, Vic 3522 **Region** Heathcote
T (03) 5433 5188 **www**.merindoc.com.au **Open** W'ends 10–4
Winemaker Steve Webber, Sergio Carlei, Bryan Martin **Est.** 1994 **Dozens** 2500
Vyds 60ha
Stephen Shelmerdine has been a major figure in the wine industry for over 25 years, like his family (who founded Mitchelton Winery) before him, and has been honoured for his many services to the industry. Substantial quantities of the grapes produced are sold to others; a small amount of high-quality wine is contract-made. The Merindoc and Willoughby Bridge wines are produced from the two eponymous estate vineyards in Heathcote. Exports to China.

🍷🍷🍷🍷🍷 **Merindoc Heathcote Riesling 2014** Challenges my hesitation about Heathcote Rieslings. It has classic lime/lemon fruit, which is a plus, but it's the soaring finish that seals the deal, with mouth-watering acidity. Screwcap. 12.5% alc. Rating 95 **To** 2029 $24 ✪
Willoughby Bridge Heathcote Rose 2014 Pale salmon-pink; the bouquet is full of scented roses, the palate opening with spicy red fruits, finishing unmistakably and pleasantly dry. The very model of a rose, Gilbert & Sullivan might sing. Screwcap. 14.4% alc. **Rating** 94 **To** 2016 $24 ✪
Willoughby Bridge Heathcote Syrah Grenache 2013 Clear, bright crimson-purple; a really enjoyable wine, both bouquet and palate demonstrating why some of the most astute winemakers are having a side bet on grenache in Heathcote; there isn't a scintilla of confection from the grenache, which follows in the footsteps of wines such as Chateau Rayas, and has a prosperous future. Screwcap. 14.5% alc. **Rating** 94 **To** 2033 $29 ✪

🍷🍷🍷🍷🍷 **Merindoc Vineyard Heathcote Shiraz 2012** Rating 92 **To** 2020 $45
Willoughby Bridge Heathcote Nebbiolo 2012 Rating 92 **To** 2019 $29
Heathcote Sparkling 2013 Rating 92 **To** 2016 $35 TS

Mermerus Vineyard   ★★★★

60 Soho Road, Drysdale, Vic 3222 **Region** Geelong
T (03) 5253 2718 **www**.mermerus.com.au **Open** Sun 11–4
Winemaker Paul Champion **Est.** 2000 **Dozens** 600 **Vyds** 2.5ha
Paul Champion has established pinot noir, chardonnay and riesling at Mermerus. The wines are made from the small but very neat winery on the property, with small-batch handling and wild yeast fermentation playing a major part in the winemaking, oak taking a back seat. Paul also acts as contract winemaker for small growers in the region.

🍷🍷🍷🍷🍷 **Bellarine Peninsula Riesling 2014** An attractive Riesling, not common in totally maritime climates such as the Bellarine Peninsula; fresh, bright and breezy, it has clear-cut lemony varietal character, aided and abetted by vibrant acidity on the close. Exceptional value. Screwcap. 12.5% alc. **Rating** 94 **To** 2024 $20 ✪

Bellarine Peninsula Chardonnay 2013 Fermented and matured in French barriques for 10 months. A most attractive cool-climate Chardonnay, with grapefruit to the fore, and ample white peach/stone fruit to back it up. Excellent value. Screwcap. 13.5% alc. **Rating** 94 **To** 2023 $25 ✪

Bellarine Peninsula Pinot Noir 2013 Very good colour, bright and clear; red and black cherries, liberally dusted with allspice, drive the bouquet and palate, the latter long and lifting invitingly on the finish and aftertaste. Screwcap. 14% alc. **Rating** 94 **To** 2023 $30 ✪

🍷🍷🍷🍷🍷 **Bellarine Peninsula Shiraz 2013 Rating** 91 **To** 2023 $25

Merricks Estate ★★★★★

Thompsons Lane, Merricks, Vic 3916 **Region** Mornington Peninsula
T (03) 5989 8416 **www**.merricksestate.com.au **Open** 1st w'end of month
Winemaker Paul Evans, Alex White **Est.** 1977 **Dozens** 2500 **Vyds** 4ha
Melbourne solicitor George Kefford, with wife Jacky, runs Merricks Estate as a weekend and holiday enterprise. It produces distinctive, spicy, cool-climate Shiraz, which has accumulated an impressive array of show trophies and gold medals. As the current tasting notes comprehensively demonstrate, the fully mature vineyard and skilled contract winemaking are producing top-class wines. Exports to Hong Kong.

🍷🍷🍷🍷🍷 **Mornington Peninsula Shiraz 2006** An exceptional bargain. It still retains a youthful hue, but has now arrived at the plateau of its drinking window, very likely to remain open for another 10 years; the spicy red berry fruits are vibrant, and the tannins have relaxed their grip, now friend, not foe. Diam. 14.2% alc. **Rating** 95 **To** 2026 $27 ✪

🍷🍷🍷🍷🍷 **Mornington Peninsula Chardonnay 2014 Rating** 92 **To** 2019 $32 CM
Mornington Peninsula Shiraz 2010 Rating 92 **To** 2021 $35 CM
Thompson's Lane Rose 2014 Rating 91 **To** 2016 $22 CM ✪

Merum Estate ★★★★☆

PO Box 840, Denmark, WA 6333 **Region** Pemberton
T (08) 9848 3443 **www**.merumestate.com.au **Open** Not
Winemaker Harewood Estate (James Kellie) **Est.** 1996 **Dozens** 4000 **Vyds** 10ha
Merum Estate stirred from slumber after morphing from grower and winemaker to pure grapegrowing after the 2006 vintage. Mike Melsom is the link with the past, for it was he and partner Julie Roberts who were responsible for the extremely good wines made in '05 and '06. The wines are released at three levels, headed by the Premium Reserve range.

🍷🍷🍷🍷🍷 **Premium Reserve Pemberton Sauvignon Blanc 2014** An object exercise in how to build structure and grip into young Sauvignon Blanc without breaking the freshness of the line and finish; oak joins hands with minerally acidity, but they agree to allow the fruit freedom to express both its herbal/vegetable and guava flavours. A Sauvignon Blanc with a future. Oxymoronic? Possibly, but so what? Screwcap. 12% alc. **Rating** 95 **To** 2019 $30 ✪

Premium Reserve Single Vineyard Pemberton Semillon 2013 Barrel fermentation is obvious on the toasty bouquet, and to a degree, on the palate; it retains a light-footed flavour profile, crisp and incipiently honeyed; it is constantly changing its persona, making it very interesting, but impossible to pin down. Screwcap. 13% alc. **Rating** 94 **To** 2030 $30 ✪

Premium Reserve Pemberton Shiraz 2012 An exuberant cool-climate Shiraz, a pocket rocket in terms of multi-spice red and black fruits, but only medium-bodied, offering a long window of opportunity; fine, powdery tannins seal the deal. Screwcap. 14.5% alc. **Rating** 94 **To** 2032 $30 ✪

ΨΨΨΨΨ Pemberton Sauvignon Blanc 2014 Rating 93 To 2016 $20 ✪
Pemberton Shiraz Viognier 2012 Rating 92 To 2017 $20 ✪

Miceli ★★★★

60 Main Creek Road, Arthurs Seat, Vic 3936 **Region** Mornington Peninsula
T (03) 5989 2755 **www**.miceli.com.au **Open** W'ends 12–5, public hols by appt
Winemaker Anthony Miceli **Est.** 1991 **Dozens** 3500 **Vyds** 5.5ha
This may be a part-time labour of love for general practitioner Dr Anthony Miceli, but that
hasn't prevented him taking the venture very seriously. He acquired the property in 1989
specifically to establish a vineyard, planting 1.8ha in '91. Subsequent plantings have brought it
to its present size, with pinot gris, chardonnay and pinot noir the varieties grown. Between '91
and '97 Dr Miceli completed the wine science course at CSU; he now manages both vineyard
and winery. One of the top producers of sparkling wine on the Peninsula.

ΨΨΨΨΨ Iolanda Mornington Peninsula Pinot Grigio 2012 Has more texture than
most Grigios, with a greater range of flavours from a month-long hand-picking,
even reaching into stone fruit. A point of difference with Pinot Grigio is always
valuable. I would have called this wine Gris, but so be it. Screwcap. 13.5% alc.
Rating 93 To 2016 $24 ✪
Olivia's Mornington Peninsula Chardonnay 2011 Gleaming straw-green;
has the slightly softer framework of many Mornington Peninsula Chardonnays,
although there's attractive, gentle stone fruit, and enough acidity; the oak has
wisely been kept in restraint. Screwcap. 13.5% alc. **Rating** 91 To 2020 $30
Lucy's Choice Mornington Peninsula Pinot Noir 2012 Deep colour; a
potent and complex Pinot in terms of both flavour and texture/structure; firmly in
the dark fruit/plum spectrum, with tannins to match. Has some juice been run off
for sparkling wine, I wonder? Regardless, patience needed; made for the long haul.
Screwcap. 13.5% alc. **Rating** 91 To 2027 $35

Michael Hall Wines ★★★★★

10 George Street, Tanunda, SA 5352 (postal) **Region** Mount Lofty Ranges Zone
T 0419 126 290 **www**.michaelhallwines.com **Open** Not
Winemaker Michael Hall **Est.** 2008 **Dozens** 1800
For reasons no longer relevant (however interesting), Michael Hall was once a jewellery
valuer for Sotheby's in Switzerland. He came to Australia in 2001 to pursue winemaking, a
lifelong interest, and undertook the wine science degree at CSU, graduating as dux in '05.
His vintage work in Australia and France is a veritable who's who: in Australia with Cullen,
Giaconda, Henschke, Shaw + Smith, Coldstream Hills and Veritas; in France with Domaine
Leflaive, Meo-Camuzet, Vieux Telegraphe and Trevallon. He is now involved full-time with
his eponymous brand, along with some teaching at the Nuriootpa TAFE. The wines are as
impressive as his CV suggests they should be. Exports to the UK.

ΨΨΨΨΨ Piccadilly Adelaide Hills Chardonnay 2013 Grown at altitude in the Adelaide
Hills. Shimmering quality. Restrained but doesn't leave you wanting. White peach,
spice, chalk through the finish, cucumber. Refreshing acidity but textural as a rule.
Will build further, given time. Screwcap. 12.9% alc. **Rating** 95 To 2020 $46 CM
Sang de Pigeon Adelaide Hills Pinot Noir 2013 Lightish colour but strong
personality. Sappy, sweet-sour notes dance through darker berry and cranberry
flavours. Lots of spice, with hints of charcuterie. Tannin is sewn throughout,
lending the wine a tight, disciplined impression. Finesse is but one of its fortes;
value but another. Screwcap. 13.1% alc. **Rating** 95 To 2021 $29 CM ✪
Flaxman's Valley Eden Valley Syrah 2012 Blueberry and baked plum flavours
get this wine up and running, abetted by green fennel and five spice, with jaunts
of both boysenberry and fresh, cedary oak sealing the deal. Bold but lively and,
perhaps most of all, meticulous. Screwcap. 13% alc. **Rating** 95 To 2025 $44 CM
Stonewell Valley Barossa Valley Shiraz 2012 Dressed to kill. Everything
about this wine comes across as polished and accomplished. Swish black-berried/

blue-berried fruit, bass notes of coal and dark earth, a shiny coat of smoky French oak and then pops of vibrant raspberry/boysenberry. Screwcap. 13.2% alc. **Rating** 95 **To** 2026 $44 CM

🍷🍷🍷🍷🍷 **Adelaide Hills Sauvignon Blanc 2014 Rating** 93 **To** 2016 $35 CM

Michelini Wines ★★★★

Great Alpine Road, Myrtleford, Vic 3737 **Region** Alpine Valleys
T (03) 5751 1990 **www**.micheliniwines.com.au **Open** 7 days 10–5
Winemaker Greg O'Keefe **Est.** 1982 **Dozens** 10 000 **Vyds** 34.5ha
The Michelini family are among the best-known grapegrowers in the Buckland Valley of Northeast Victoria. Having migrated from Italy in 1949, they originally grew tobacco, diversifying into vineyards in '82. The main vineyard (16.74ha), on terra rossa soil, is at an altitude of 300m, mostly with frontage to the Buckland River. The Devils Creek Vineyard (17.69ha) was planted in '91 on grafted rootstocks, merlot and chardonnay taking the lion's share. Exports to China.

🍷🍷🍷🍷🍷 **Alpine Valleys Marzemino 2012** Despite its light colour, it has a lively and long palate with an array of highly spiced red fruits, marzipan and orange skin-accented acidity. Offers more and more each time you return. Screwcap. 13.5% alc. **Rating** 91 **To** 2022 $22 ❂
Emo Selection Teroldego 2008 Still incredibly densely coloured, and chock full of sultry black fruits; a firm tannin finish. It's hard to visualise how the wine will develop, but whatever/wherever, it's a long way off. Screwcap. 13.5% alc. **Rating** 91 **To** 2030 $50

Mike Press Wines ★★★★★

PO Box 224, Lobethal, SA 5241 **Region** Adelaide Hills
T (08) 8389 5546 **www**.mikepresswines.com.au **Open** Not
Winemaker Mike Press **Est.** 1998 **Dozens** 12 000 **Vyds** 22.7ha
Mike and Judy Press established their Kenton Valley Vineyards in 1998, when they purchased 34ha of land in the Adelaide Hills at an elevation of 500m. They planted mainstream cool-climate varieties (merlot, shiraz, cabernet sauvignon, sauvignon blanc, chardonnay and pinot noir), intending to sell the grapes to other wine producers. Even an illustrious 43-year career in the wine industry did not prepare Mike for the downturn in grape prices that followed, and that led to the development of the Mike Press wine label. They produce high-quality Sauvignon Blanc, Chardonnay, Pinot Noir, Merlot, Shiraz, Cabernet Merlot and Cabernet Sauvignon, which are sold at mouth-wateringly low prices. Exports to Denmark.

🍷🍷🍷🍷🍷 **Single Vineyard Adelaide Hills Shiraz 2013** Good hue and depth; spicy/savoury nuances run through the black fruits of the bouquet, as befits the Adelaide Hills; the palate explores these themes in more detail (and depth), the tannins providing the framework for the examination. In the end, you are left to wonder how the wine is the bargain it is. Screwcap. 14.8% alc. **Rating** 95 **To** 2020 $14 ❂
Single Vineyard Adelaide Hills Cabernet Sauvignon 2013 Strong crimson hue; the estate-grown wine spent 12 months in French oak, emerging at the other end with the class and character one might expect to sell for $25 or more. It is perfectly sculpted, the varietal expression nigh-on perfect, the balance and length likewise. Fruit descriptors are essentially superfluous: if you like Cabernet, you will love this wine. Screwcap. 14.8% alc. **Rating** 95 **To** 2028 $14 ❂
Single Vineyard Adelaide Hills Merlot 2013 Matured in American and French oak for over 12 months. This is ridiculously priced, and should be a compulsory purchase (and consumption) by those who are fleeing the good ship Merlot. It opens confidently, but really brings home the bacon on the finish with a spice and black olive drive to the red fruits on the start of the palate. Screwcap. 14.6% alc. **Rating** 94 **To** 2023 $14 ❂

Single Vineyard Adelaide Hills Pinot Noir 2013 Rating 93 To 2020 $15 ○
MP One Single Vineyard Shiraz 2012 Rating 93 To 2022 $18 ○
Adelaide Hills Sauvignon Blanc 2014 Rating 92 To 2016 $13 ○
Single Vineyard Pinot Noir Rose 2014 Rating 91 To 2015 $13 ○

Miles from Nowhere

PO Box 197, Belmont, WA 6984 **Region** Margaret River
T (08) 9267 8555 **www.milesfromnowhere.com.au Open** Not
Winemaker Rory Clifton-Parks **Est.** 2007 **Dozens** 18 000 **Vyds** 46.9ha
Miles from Nowhere is one of the born-again wineries of Franklin (Frank) and Heather Tate; Frank was CEO of Evans & Tate for many years. The demise of Evans & Tate has been well chronicled, but has not prevented the Tates from doing what they know best. The plantings of petit verdot, chardonnay, shiraz, sauvignon blanc, semillon, viognier, cabernet sauvignon and merlot are scattered across the Margaret River region – miles from nowhere. Exports to the UK, Canada, Sweden and Thailand.

Margaret River Chardonnay 2014 Consistently with all the other wines under this label, a cut above most others at $18. The varietal expression is crystal clear, barrel-ferment oak subtle and integrated; the overall balance and elegance is admirable. Screwcap. 13.1% alc. **Rating** 93 To 2019 $18 ○
Margaret River Shiraz 2013 Good depth to the hue; an unambiguously good wine at this price, with bright and lively spicy red and black fruits, the tannin support just what the doctor ordered. Good now, but will hold for 5+ years. Screwcap. 14.4% alc. **Rating** 93 To 2020 $18 ○
Best Blocks Margaret River Shiraz 2013 Establishes its credentials quickly and then runs with them. Upfront flavours of mocha, olives, plums and toast give the wine both a darkness and a bit of grunt, before redcurrant and clove notes add brightness and a certain savouriness. Hand of oak is fractionally heavy but the overall effect is pleasing. Screwcap. 14.6% alc. **Rating** 93 To 2023 $32 CM
Margaret River Cabernet Merlot 2013 Mounts a charm offensive. Mid-weight flavours of blackcurrant, chocolate, gravel and mint come across as fresh and juicy and, more to the point, perfectly proportioned. Screwcap. 14.5% alc. **Rating** 93 To 2022 $18 CM ○
Best Blocks Margaret River Semillon Sauvignon Blanc 2014
10% fermented in oak, some of it new, the remainder in stainless steel. Pale colour, smoke and gravel accents to steely, pippy fruit, the finish then long and elegant. Zesty aftertaste. Almost too modest for its own good, but beautifully persistent. Screwcap. 12.8% alc. **Rating** 92 To 2016 $32 CM
Sauvignon Blanc Semillon 2014 Rating 91 To 2016 $18 CM ○
Best Blocks Chardonnay 2013 Rating 91 To 2017 $32 CM
Best Blocks Cabernet Sauvignon 2013 Rating 90 To 2022 $32 CM

Margaret River Sauvignon Blanc 2014 Rating 88 To 2015 $18 CM

Millbrook Winery

Old Chestnut Lane, Jarrahdale, WA 6124 **Region** Perth Hills
T (08) 9525 5796 **www.millbrookwinery.com.au Open** Wed–Sun 10–5
Winemaker Damian Hutton **Est.** 1996 **Dozens** 15 000 **Vyds** 7.8ha
The strikingly situated Millbrook Winery is owned by highly successful Perth-based entrepreneur Peter Fogarty and wife Lee. They also own Lake's Folly in the Hunter Valley and Deep Woods Estate in Margaret River. Millbrook draws on vineyards in the Perth Hills planted to sauvignon blanc, semillon, chardonnay, viognier, cabernet sauvignon, merlot, shiraz and petit verdot. The wines (Millbrook and Barking Owl) are of consistently high quality. Exports to Germany, Malaysia, Hong Kong, Singapore, China and Japan.

Pemberton Arneis 2014 This is a top-flight example of the variety so far tasted in Australia. There is what I can only describe as a grainy quality to the bouquet and palate, with a mix of pear skin, almond, green apple and lively lemony acidity. Screwcap. 13% alc. **Rating** 95 **To** 2017 $28 ✪

Barking Owl Shiraz 2012 An 'I've been everywhere' Shiraz from Margaret River, Geographe, Perth Hills and Great Southern, with 5% viognier co-fermented. Whether the multiple regions are just bits and pieces left over is irrelevant, for this is a truly delicious wine; its red and black fruits are set in a tapestry of spices and tannins, the oak perfectly pitched. Outstanding bargain. Screwcap. 14.5% alc. **Rating** 95 **To** 2022 $18 ✪

Estate Shiraz Viognier 2012 Hand-picked, destemmed for cold soak on top of 5% whole bunch viognier, open-fermented, hand-plunged twice daily, matured in French oak (30% new) for 20 months. Vivid crimson-purple; medium-bodied; it is small wonder it won the trophy for Best Shiraz at the Perth Hills Wine Show '14. Blackberry fruit is framed by abundant ripe tannins ex both oak and fruit. It deserves time, lots of it. Screwcap. 14.5% alc. **Rating** 95 **To** 2037 $35 ✪

Margaret River Sauvignon Blanc 2014 100% tank-fermented at 10–12°C for 4 weeks. Trophy for Best Sauvignon Blanc Perth Wine Show. This is a Sauvignon Blanc for all seasons and all audiences; it is impossible not to enjoy its friendly display of tropical fruits balanced by acidity. Great value. Screwcap. 13% alc. **Rating** 94 **To** 2016 $22 ✪

Barking Owl Margaret River Sauvignon Blanc Semillon 2014 An 80/20 blend. The bouquet is fresh, but doesn't prepare you for the drive of the palate, which snatches the full range of flavours from cut grass to snow pea and passionfruit. A gold medal at the Adelaide Wine Show '14 is no surprise. Screwcap. 12.5% alc. **Rating** 94 **To** 2017 $18 ✪

ⓉⓉⓉⓉⓉ LR Chardonnay 2013 **Rating** 93 **To** 2020 $45 CM
Mount Barker Riesling 2014 **Rating** 92 **To** 2025 $28
Margaret River Cabernet Sauvignon Malbec 2013 **Rating** 92 **To** 2028 $28
Pemberton Pinot Noir 2013 **Rating** 91 **To** 2019 $28
· Barking Owl Margaret River Chardonnay 2014 **Rating** 90 **To** 2017 $18 ✪

Milton Vineyard ★★★★★

14635 Tasman Highway, Cranbrook, Tas 7190 **Region** East Coast Tasmania
T (03) 6257 8298 **www**.miltonvineyard.com.au **Open** 7 days 10–5
Winemaker Winemaking Tasmania (Julian Alcorso) **Est.** 1992 **Dozens** 6000 **Vyds** 9.5ha
Michael and Kerry Dunbabin have one of the most historic properties in Tasmania, dating back to 1826. The property is 1800ha, meaning the vineyard (5ha of pinot noir, 1.45a each of riesling and pinot gris, 1.5ha each of chardonnay and gewurztraminer, plus 10 rows of shiraz) has plenty of room for expansion. A representative range of wines was not received for this edition, but the rating has been maintained. Exports to Japan.

ⓉⓉⓉⓉⓉ Pinot Noir 2013 Good colour and clarity; the bouquet and palate both have plenty of depth and energy; the centre of flavour on the palate is poached plum, with sundry spices. Screwcap. 13.4% alc. **Rating** 90 **To** 2021 $34

Ministry of Clouds ★★★★★

39a Wakefield Street, Kent Town, SA 5067 **Region** Various
T 0417 864 615 **www**.ministryofclouds.com.au **Open** Not
Winemaker Julian Forwood, Bernice Ong, Tim Geddes **Est.** 2012 **Dozens** 2500
Bernice Ong and Julian Forwood say, 'The name Ministry of Clouds symbolises the relinquishing of our past security and structure (ministry) for the beguiling freedom, independence and adventure (clouds) inherent in our own venture.' I doubt whether there are two partners in a new wine business with such extraordinary depth in sales and marketing of wine, stretching back well over 20 years. Trying to pick out highlights is futile, simply because there are so many of them. They bypassed owning vineyards or building wineries, instead headhunting key winemakers in the Clare Valley and Tasmania for riesling and chardonnay

respectively, and the assistance of Tim Geddes at his winery in McLaren Vale, where they make the red wines in conjunction with Tim. Exports to Singapore and Hong Kong.

🍷🍷🍷🍷🍷 **Single Vineyard Blewitt Springs Shiraz 2013** From the vineyard owned by the Patritti family, hand-picked, 4-day cold soak, whole berry ferment with 5–10% whole bunches, matured for 12 months in French barriques. This is a mighty wine, every step in the winemaking precisely calibrated to reflect the high quality of the fruit; this might well come from an even cooler climate than Blewitt Springs, itself the coolest part of McLaren Vale. Gloriously cadenced black fruits are the core, although French oak and tannins are also significant contributors. Screwcap. 14.5% alc. **Rating** 97 **To** 2043 $58 ❂

🍷🍷🍷🍷🍷 **Tasmania Chardonnay 2013** The grapes for this wine came from Michael Vischacki's Panorama Vineyard in the Huon Valley, and the Ellis family's Meadowbank Vineyard in the Derwent Valley; whole bunch-pressed direct to used French oak for wild yeast fermentation and maturation. Its delicacy and immaculate balance are deceptive, for the white peach and creamy/nutty fruit flavours have great length. Screwcap. 12.9% alc. **Rating** 96 **To** 2023 $48 ❂
McLaren Vale Shiraz 2013 Predominantly from the 66yo Patritti Vineyard; hand-picked and destemmed, open-fermented, 12 months in used French oak. Has a symphony of black fruits, licorice, bitter chocolate, finely structured savoury tannins adding to the texture, structure and length of a wine of great character and quality. Screwcap. 14% alc. **Rating** 96 **To** 2033 $29 ❂
McLaren Vale Tempranillo Grenache 2013 Both parcels separately hand-picked, open-fermented, hand-plunged, basket-pressed and matured in French oak, blended shortly prior to bottling. This is a seriously good (and delicious) wine with intensity and harmony to its full hand of royal red fruits, bejewelled with spices from the orient. Screwcap. 14.1% alc. **Rating** 95 **To** 2030 $29 ❂
McLaren Vale Mataro 2013 Hand-picked, whole berries, cold soak, open-fermented, basket-pressed to used French oak. A familiar recipe, but Ministry of Clouds uses it far better than many. The colour is excellent, and the supple red to purple berry flavours float on a cushion of superfine tannins. Screwcap. 14% alc. **Rating** 95 **To** 2033 $38
McLaren Vale Grenache 2013 Rating 94 **To** 2018 $38

🍷🍷🍷🍷🍷 **Clare Valley Riesling 2014 Rating** 91 **To** 2018 $29

Minko Wines   ★★★★

13 High Street, Willunga, SA 5172 **Region** Southern Fleurieu
T (08) 8556 4987 **www**.minkowines.com **Open** Wed–Fri, Sun 11–5, Sat 9.30–5
Winemaker James Hastwell, Linda Domas **Est.** 1997 **Dozens** 1800 **Vyds** 15.8ha
Mike Boerema (veterinarian) and Margo Kellet (ceramic artist) established the Minko vineyard on their cattle property at Mt Compass. The vineyard, which uses biodynamic methods, is planted to pinot noir, merlot, cabernet sauvignon, chardonnay, pinot gris and savagnin; 60ha of the 160ha property is heritage-listed. Exports to the UK.

🍷🍷🍷🍷🍷 **Pinot Grigio 2014** Straw-coloured; a well above average Grigio with vibrant pear, apple and a flash of pink grapefruit flavours, the finish long and compelling with its bright acidity. Bargain. Screwcap. 13% alc. **Rating** 94 **To** 2016 $19 ❂

🍷🍷🍷🍷🍷 **Fleurieu Peninsula Merlot 2012 Rating** 91 **To** 2032 $24

Minnow Creek   ★★★★☆

5 Hillside Road, Blackwood, SA 5051 (postal) **Region** McLaren Vale
T 0404 288 108 **www**.minnowcreekwines.com.au **Open** Not
Winemaker Tony Walker **Est.** 2005 **Dozens** 1800
Former Fox Creek winemaker Tony Walker has set up Minnow Creek in partnership with William Neubauer; the grapes are grown by Don Lopresti at vineyards just west of Willunga. The name of the venture reflects the intention of the partners to keep the business focused on

quality rather than quantity. Towards the end of 2014 a '13 Shiraz and '13 Reserve Cabernet Sauvignon were released. Tony Walker rates '13 cabernet sauvignon from across McLaren Vale as the best he has tasted in the past 10 years. Exports to the US, Canada and Germany.

🍷🍷🍷🍷🍷 **The Reserve McLaren Vale Cabernet Sauvignon Malbec 2013** Very good colour; matured for 20 months in French oak, it has a fragrant bouquet and a powerful palate; cassis and plum fruit are seamlessly joined together, and this union is in turn supported by tannins that are just a tad obvious at this stage, but are guaranteed to soften long before the fruit fades. A seriously good wine. Screwcap. 14% alc. **Rating** 95 **To** 2033 $52

🍷🍷🍷🍷🍷 **The Silver Minnow Sauvignon Blanc 2014 Rating** 91 **To** 2017 $20 ○

Mintaro Wines ★★★

Leasingham Road, Mintaro, SA 5415 **Region** Clare Valley
T (08) 8843 9150 **www**.mintarowines.com.au **Open** 7 days 10–4.30
Winemaker Peter Houldsworth **Est.** 1984 **Dozens** 2500 **Vyds** 10ha
Mintaro Wines' vineyards were planted in 1962, and were incorporated into a functioning winery complex in '85 by the present owner and winemaker, Peter Houldsworth. There are five vineyards in the Mintaro and Polish Hill districts of the Clare Valley, 4ha planted to riesling, and 3ha each of cabernet sauvignon and shiraz. Exports to Singapore.

🍷🍷🍷🍷 **Clare Valley Riesling 2013** Full-flavoured style, ready now if you wish, but has some further development potential. Screwcap. 12.5% alc. **Rating** 88 **To** 2019 $22
Clare Valley Cabernet Sauvignon Shiraz 2012 Rustic power, awash with black fruits; curious labelling seeking to downplay whatever shiraz is in the blend. Screwcap. 15% alc. **Rating** 88 **To** 2020 $23
Clare Valley Late Picked Riesling 2014 It is difficult to reconcile late-picked with 11% alcohol, notwithstanding its obvious residual sugar; finishes a bit rough, suggesting pressings. Screwcap. **Rating** 88 **To** 2019 $18

Mistletoe Wines ★★★★★

771 Hermitage Road, Pokolbin, NSW 2320 **Region** Hunter Valley
T (02) 4998 7770 **www**.mistletoewines.com.au **Open** 7 days 10–6
Winemaker Nick Paterson **Est.** 1989 **Dozens** 5000 **Vyds** 5.5ha
Mistletoe Wines, owned by Ken and Gwen Sloan, can trace its history back to 1909, when a vineyard was planted on what was then called Mistletoe Farm. The Mistletoe Farm brand made a brief appearance in the late '70s. The wines are made onsite by Nick Paterson, who has had significant experience in the Hunter Valley. The quality and consistency of these wines is irreproachable, as is their price.

🍷🍷🍷🍷🍷 **Reserve Hunter Valley Semillon 2014** Walks the fine line between youthful accessibility and all-out age-worthiness well. It tastes of lemon and straw with a whisper of grass, and extends confidently out through the finish. Screwcap. 12.2% alc. **Rating** 94 **To** 2021 $24 CM ○
Hunter Valley Shiraz 2013 Archetypal Hunter Valley Shiraz with black fruits, polished leather, warm spice and earth notes riding high on both bouquet and palate, yet coming together in a seamless whole. Has a long future. Screwcap. 13.5% alc. **Rating** 94 **To** 2038 $30 ○

🍷🍷🍷🍷🍷 **Hunter Valley Fiano 2014 Rating** 93 **To** 2015 $24 CM ○
Barrel Fermented Rose 2014 Rating 93 **To** 2016 $22 CM ○
Hilltops Shiraz 2013 Rating 92 **To** 2021 $24 CM ○
Hilltops Shiraz Viognier 2013 Rating 90 **To** 2020 $25 CM
Home Vineyard Semillon 2014 Rating 90 **To** 2017 $20 CM ○
Noble Viognier 2014 Rating 90 **To** 2017 $22 CM

Mitchell ★★★★★

Hughes Park Road, Sevenhill via Clare, SA 5453 **Region** Clare Valley
T (08) 8843 4258 **www**.mitchellwines.com **Open** 7 days 10–4
Winemaker Andrew Mitchell **Est.** 1975 **Dozens** 30000 **Vyds** 75ha
One of the stalwarts of the Clare Valley, established by Jane and Andrew Mitchell, producing long-lived Rieslings and Cabernet Sauvignons in classic regional style. The range now includes very creditable Semillon, Grenache and Shiraz. A lovely old stone apple shed provides the cellar door and upper section of the upgraded winery. Children Angus and Edwina are now working in the business, heralding generational changes. Over the years the Mitchells have established or acquired 75ha of vineyards on four excellent sites, some vines over 50 years old; all are managed organically, with the use of biodynamic composts for over a decade. Exports to the UK, the US, Canada, Singapore, Hong Kong, China and NZ.

ⵣⵣⵣⵣ **Clare Valley Semillon 2013** The bright, lemony acidity is the first thing that energises the palate, and from there on it's a stroll in the park, barrel ferment adding texture and structure, but in no way shrouding the varietal fruit. A delicious wine for Semillon lovers, looking to the style of Margaret River, not the Hunter Valley. Screwcap. 13.5% alc. **Rating** 95 **To** 2023 $22 ❂
Watervale Riesling 2014 Bred in the purple; the estate vineyards are 40yo, and the Mitchells have been on the case every year since then. They know how this wine will develop given a minimum of 5 years in bottle. It has the requisite length and balance, citrus and acid the engines to keep it accelerating for years. Screwcap. 13.5% alc. **Rating** 95 **To** 2024 $22 ❂
Peppertree Vineyard Clare Valley Shiraz 2012 Good colour; a very well balanced medium-bodied wine, content that the vintage, the variety and the place will all speak for themselves, with only mild assistance in the winery. The champion wines from '12 are now emerging, some towering over wines such as this, which is desperately unfair, but life wasn't meant to be easy, was it? Screwcap. 14.5% alc. **Rating** 94 **To** 2030 $28 ❂

ⵣⵣⵣⵣⵣ **McNicol Clare Valley Shiraz 2007 Rating** 91 **To** 2017 $40

Mitchell Harris Wines ★★★★★

38 Doveton Street North, Ballarat, Vic 3350 **Region** Pyrenees
T 0417 566 025 **www**.mitchellharris.com.au **Open** Sun–Tues 11–6, Wed 11–9, Thurs–Sat 11–11
Winemaker John Harris **Est.** 2008 **Dozens** 1800
Mitchell Harris Wines is a partnership between Alicia and Craig Mitchell and Shannyn and John Harris, the latter winemaker for this eponymous producer. John began his career at Mount Avoca, then spent eight years as winemaker at Domaine Chandon in the Yarra Valley, cramming in northern hemisphere vintages in California and Oregon. The Mitchells grew up in the Ballarat area, and have an affinity for the Macedon and Pyrenees districts. While the total make is not large, a lot of thought has gone into the creation of each of the wines. In 2012 a multipurpose space was created in an 1880s brick workshop and warehouse, the renovation providing a cellar door and education facility.

ⵣⵣⵣⵣⵣ **Pyrenees Cabernet Sauvignon 2013** Walks up to elegance and gives it a firm handshake. Dark-coloured but only medium-bodied, as a positive, with boysenberry and blackcurrant flavours matched perfectly to spicy/smoky/sawdusty oak and clove-like notes. Tannin spreads and builds through the wine like a wave, emphasising its ageability. Screwcap. 13.5% alc. **Rating** 96 **To** 2035 $28 CM ❂
Pyrenees Shiraz 2013 2% viognier. All French oak. Deep colour and flavour. Plums, cloves and blackberry with eucalypt and assorted dried spices. Impressive mouthfeel and length. Fine tannin. Elegant and supple but with real get up and go. A beauty. Screwcap. 13.8% alc. **Rating** 95 **To** 2030 $35 CM ❂
Pyrenees Sauvignon Blanc Fume 2014 When elegance met complexity. This offers all manner of goodness. Straightforward lemon, lime and nectarine flavours

swing into candle wax, lactose and mealy spice. It lilts, it drives, it swings, it sways. Quite delicious. Screwcap. 12% alc. **Rating** 94 **To** 2017 $25 CM ○

Pyrenees Mataro 2013 It doesn't look dark, and when you first pour it, it seems lightish, almost wishy-washy. But as it breathes it builds considerably, almost in a Nebbiolo-esque manner. Leather, plum, toast and coffee, with woody peppercorn notes adding edge. It's an intriguing wine, with a future. Screwcap. 13.8% alc. **Rating** 94 **To** 2025 $28 CM ○

♥♥♥♥♡ **Rose 2014 Rating** 91 **To** 2016 $22 CM ○

Mitchelton ★★★★★

Mitchellstown via Nagambie, Vic 3608 **Region** Nagambie Lakes
T (03) 5736 2222 **www**.mitchelton.com.au **Open** 7 days 10–5
Winemaker Travis Clydesdale **Est.** 1969 **Dozens** 12 000 **Vyds** 148ha
Mitchelton was founded by Ross Shelmerdine, who had a vision splendid for the striking winery, restaurant, observation tower and surrounding vineyards. The expected volume of tourism did not eventuate, and the business became embroiled in a long-running dispute. In 1994 it was acquired by Petaluma, but, once again, did not deliver the expected financial return, notwithstanding the long and faithful service of chief winemaker Don Lewis, or the quality of its best wines. In Aug 2012 a new chapter opened for Mitchelton, with the completion of an acquisition agreement by Gerry Ryan OAM, and son Andrew. Gerry founded caravan company Jayco in 1975, and as a consequence of the success of that company, has a virtually unlimited budget to take Mitchelton to the next level. Winemaker Travis Clydesdale has had a long association with Mitchelton, dating back 30 years to when he was a small boy and his father was cellar manager. Exports to all major markets.

♥♥♥♥♥ **Heathcote Shiraz 2013** Exceptionally well made, preserving all the vibrant black cherry fruit Heathcote can produce when the weather gods permit. In particular, there has been no attempt to over-ripen or over-extract the flavour or structure. Screwcap. 14% alc. **Rating** 96 **To** 2033 $40 ○

Blackwood Park Riesling 2013 This shares – indeed builds on – the promise of the '14, lime and apple anchored by a roll of steely acidity reaching down to the very roots of the wine. I fancy the chances of this wine over a long journey. Screwcap. 12% alc. **Rating** 94 **To** 2023 $19 ○

Print Shiraz 2013 A powerful, full-bodied Shiraz with black fruits of every description, and tannins to match. Demands time in the cellar, but has the length and balance to repay that time. Prior vintages lend support. Screwcap. 14% alc. **Rating** 94 **To** 2035 $70

Crescent Shiraz Grenache Mourvedre 2013 Bright crimson-purple; a most attractive, vibrant and juicy blend, with a shower of red fruits and sundry spices; it is supple and medium-bodied, with particularly good length and balance. Ready now, but will hold. Screwcap. 14% alc. **Rating** 94 **To** 2025 $28 ○

♥♥♥♥♡ **Blackwood Park Riesling 2014 Rating** 93 **To** 2024 $19 ○
Marsanne 2013 Rating 93 **To** 2025 $22 ○
Cabernet Sauvignon 2013 Rating 93 **To** 2028 $22 ○
Museum Release Blackwood Park Riesling 2005 Rating 92 **To** 2018 $28
Chardonnay 2014 Rating 92 **To** 2022 $22 ○

Mitolo Wines ★★★★★

PO Box 520, Virginia, SA 5120 **Region** McLaren Vale
T (08) 8282 9012 **www**.mitolowines.com.au **Open** Not
Winemaker Ben Glaetzer **Est.** 1999 **Dozens** 20 000
Mitolo had a meteoric rise once Frank Mitolo decided to turn a winemaking hobby into a business. In 2000 he took the plunge into the commercial end of the business, inviting Ben Glaetzer to make the wines. Split between the Jester range and single-vineyard wines, Mitolo is a red wine-dominant brand. Exports to all major markets.

🍷🍷🍷🍷🍷 **The Furies McLaren Vale Shiraz 2012** Screams its sense of place from the rooftops (a single vineyard on the Christies Beach soil formation near Willunga), plus its variety and vintage. This is a riveting wine of great quality, the black fruits cosseted by fine tannins and bright acidity. Great now or in 20+ years, or at any point along the way. Screwcap. 14.5% alc. **Rating** 97 **To** 2042 $58 ✪

🍷🍷🍷🍷🍷 **Angela McLaren Vale Shiraz 2013** Matured in mainly French oak (10% new) for 18 months. Very well made, speaking with equal clarity of its region and its variety; plum and black cherry fruits slide fluidly across the palate, oak a measured companion. Screwcap. 14.5% alc. **Rating** 95 **To** 2033 $35 ✪

Savitar McLaren Vale Shiraz 2012 Deep colour; a powerful, full-bodied Shiraz leaving not even a scintilla of doubt about its regional and varietal provenance, but does so secure in the knowledge of its balance and length; supple black fruits, licorice and dark chocolate are backed by quality oak and polished tannins on the long palate. Screwcap. 14.5% alc. **Rating** 95 **To** 2042 $80

7th Son 2013 65% grenache from Blewitt Springs; 32% shiraz and 3% sagrantino kept separate until blending. Destemmed, cool ferment, matured for 18 months in used French oak. An elegant, high-quality blend, the two major varieties playing off each other's strengths, with a full array of red and black fruits. Sure handling of extract and oak ties the knot. Screwcap. 15.5% alc. **Rating** 95 **To** 2028 $35 ✪

🍷🍷🍷🍷🍷 **Jester McLaren Vale Vermentino 2014** **Rating** 93 **To** 2016 $22 ✪
Jester McLaren Vale Sangiovese Rose 2014 **Rating** 93 **To** 2015 $22 ✪
Jester McLaren Vale Shiraz 2013 **Rating** 92 **To** 2030 $25 ✪
McLaren Vale Sagrantino 2012 **Rating** 92 **To** 2020 $25 ✪

Molly Morgan Vineyard ★★★★

496 Talga Road, Rothbury, NSW 2320 **Region** Hunter Valley
T (02) 4930 7695 **www**.mollymorgan.com **Open** Not
Winemaker Rhys Eather **Est.** 1963 **Dozens** 1200 **Vyds** 7.65ha
Molly Morgan has been acquired by Andrew and Hady Simon, who established the Camperdown Cellars Group, which became the largest retailer in Australia, in 1971, before moving on to other pursuits. They have been joined by Grant Breen, their former general manager at Camperdown Cellars. The property includes unirrigated semillon vines over 40 years old (used for the Old Vines Semillon), 2ha of chardonnay, 3.7ha shiraz and a few riesling vines.

🍷🍷🍷🍷🍷 **Hunter Valley Semillon 2014** Bright straw-green; has an abundant and moderately complex suite of aromas and flavours, lemon/lemongrass/lemon verbena tightly bound together by bright acidity. Will go the distance, and improve further. Screwcap. 11% alc. **Rating** 94 **To** 2026 $22 ✪

Molly's Cradle ★★★★

17/1 Jubilee Avenue, Warriewood, NSW 2102 **Region** Hunter Valley
T (02) 9979 1212 **www**.mollyscradle.com.au **Open** By appt
Winemaker Various Contract **Est.** 2002 **Dozens** 20 000 **Vyds** 9ha
Steve Skidmore and Deidre Broad created the Molly's Cradle brand concept in 1997, moving to reality with the first planting of estate vines in 2000, the first vintage following in '02. They have 2ha each of verdelho, chardonnay, merlot and shiraz, plus 1ha of petit verdot, but also look to other regions to supplement the estate-grown grapes. Exports to China.

🍷🍷🍷🍷🍷 **Vignerons Selection Cradle McLaren Vale Shiraz 2013** Deep, dense crimson-purple; flooded with blackberry, licorice and dark chocolate fruit on the bouquet and medium to full-bodied palate alike, aided and abetted by oak and fine-grained tannins; builds flavour even further on the finish and aftertaste. Screwcap. 14.8% alc. **Rating** 93 **To** 2033 $40

Vignerons Selection Cradle McLaren Vale Cabernet Sauvignon 2013 Blackcurrant and redcurrant with violet-like lift. No great show of oak and despite its density, remains bright and fresh as a result. Aniseedy aftertaste. All about fruit purity. Screwcap. 14.4% alc. **Rating** 92 **To** 2023 $30 CM

Adelaide Hills Sauvignon Blanc 2014 Crisp and fruit-driven with pippy passionfruit and slashed green grass characters. Middling concentration of flavours but with good extension through the finish. Screwcap. 11% alc. **Rating** 90 **To** 2015 $18 CM ○

Vintage Brut Methode Traditionnelle 2010 A vintage sparkling of elegance and restraint, with the mouthfeel, texture and earthy flavours of lees age supporting a fine acid line and subtle fruit characters of white citrus and red apple. A fine, creamy bead and well-integrated dosage complete a balanced blend of chardonnay, pinot noir and meunier. Diam. 12.3% alc. **Rating** 90 **To** 2015 $35 TS

♀♀♀♀ Molly May Pinot Grigio 2014 **Rating** 89 **To** 2015 $15 ○
McLaren Vale Shiraz 2012 **Rating** 89 **To** 2019 $18 CM ○

🍇 Mon Tout   ★★★★★

129 Brooks Road, Margaret River, WA 6285 **Region** Margaret River
T 0408 845 583 **www.**montout.com.au **Open** Not
Winemaker Richard Burch, Janice McDonald **Est.** 2014 **Dozens** NFP **Vyds** 28ha
This is the venture of second-generation vintner Richard Burch, son of Jeff and Amy Burch. Between 2003 and '12 he managed to spend two years at Curtin University studying viticulture and oenology, before deciding this wasn't his thing. He then had a gap year, travelling through Europe and Asia with friends, before homing pigeon-like returning to Perth to enrol in a three-degree wine marketing course at Edith Cowan University. Mon Tout is a small separate venture from his position of brand manager for the east coast of Australia for all Burch Family Wines. I have no doubt he has been involved in the selection of the grapes for and making of the Mon Tout wines, but the two biodynamic wines released from the '14 vintage reflect Janice McDonald's exceptional experience and skill in vinifying Margaret River wines.

♀♀♀♀♀ Biodynamic Shiraz 2014 Wild yeast-fermented and matured for 9 months in French oak. Vivid, deep crimson; a high-quality wine with a genesis of first-quality fruit well handled in the winery; it is full-bodied, yet polished and balanced, the tannins ripe, the oak already integrated. Has a great future. Screwcap. 13.5% alc. **Rating** 96 **To** 2039 $40 ○

Biodynamic Chardonnay 2014 Hand-picked, wild yeast-fermented and matured for 9 months in new French barriques. Margaret River to its bones, with that extra level of fruit inbuilt into the structure and flavour of the long, intense palate. A long life ahead. Screwcap. 13% alc. **Rating** 95 **To** 2027 $30 ○

🍇 Mons Rubra   ★★★★☆

Cheveley Road, Woodend North, Vic 3442 **Region** Macedon Ranges
T 0457 777 202 **www.**monsrubra.com **Open** Not
Winemaker Passing Clouds (Cameron Leith) **Est.** 2004 **Dozens** 400 **Vyds** 1ha
Mons Rubra has been developed by Max and Susan Haverfield. With a broad-based interest in wine, and after some research, they purchased their property in the Macedon Ranges; it is situated in the 600–700m elevation range, with friable volcanic soils. They settled on the most widely propagated clone of pinot noir in Australia, MV6, which seems to perform well wherever it is planted. Initially the wine was made by John Ellis at Hanging Rock (2004 to '10), but it is now being made by the Leith family at their Passing Clouds winery at Musk.

♀♀♀♀♀ Macedon Ranges Pinot Noir 2013 5-day cold soak, 10% whole bunches, 15 days on skins; 12 months in French oak (40% new). Bright, clear colour; skilled viticulture and viniculture have paid big dividends: a perfumed, red-fruited bouquet is reflected on the long palate, which surges on the finish and aftertaste; exquisite tannins and overall balance. Screwcap. 12.8% alc. **Rating** 96 **To** 2023 $31 ○

♀♀♀♀♀ Macedon Ranges Pinot Noir 2010 **Rating** 92 **To** 2017 $28

Montalto ★★★★★

33 Shoreham Road, Red Hill South, Vic 3937 **Region** Mornington Peninsula
T (03) 5989 8412 **www**.montalto.com.au **Open** 7 days 11–5
Winemaker Simon Black **Est.** 1998 **Dozens** 10 000 **Vyds** 23.3ha

John Mitchell and family established Montalto in 1998, but the core of the vineyard goes back to '86. There are 14.6ha of pinot noir, 4.1ha of chardonnay, 2.6ha of pinot gris, 1.2ha of shiraz and 0.8ha of sauvignon blanc. Intensive vineyard work opens up the canopy, with yields ranging between 3.7 and 6.1 tonnes per hectare. Wines are released in three ranges, the flagship Single Vineyard, Montalto and Pennon Hill. Montalto leases several vineyards that span the Peninsula, giving vastly greater diversity of pinot noir sources, and greater insurance against weather extremes. There is also a broad range of clones adding to that diversity. Montalto has hit new heights with its wines from these blocks. Exports to China

♀♀♀♀♀ **Single Vineyard Main Ridge Block Mornington Peninsula Pinot Noir 2013** Makes a stunning entrance and, excuse the hyperbole, leaves you breathless to the last sip. This is fundamentally undergrowthy and complex, and yet the plushness and purity of fruit does all the seducing. Oak gives the fruit a quick embrace and kiss and sends it on its way. Persistent? Yes, very. Screwcap. 13.7% alc. **Rating** 97 **To** 2026 $65 CM ✪

Pennon Hill Shiraz 2013 Superb crimson-purple; an exotically spiced cherry bouquet leads into a vibrant medium-bodied palate which faithfully follows the path of the bouquet; while intense, it allows freedom of movement in the mouth with ripples of spice, pepper, soused cherry and fine-grained tannins. The only surprise is that it didn't win a trophy to go with the gold medal Adelaide Wine Show '14. Screwcap. 14% alc. **Rating** 97 **To** 2033 $30 ✪

♀♀♀♀♀ **Estate Mornington Peninsula Chardonnay 2013** Announces itself in emphatic fashion. Strength, beauty, aroma and enduring length. Grapefruit, cashew, struck match and white peach. Volume of flavour, but cut and thrust too. Will cellar mid-term but absolutely no reason to wait. Screwcap. 13.2% alc. **Rating** 96 **To** 2019 $39 CM ✪

Single Vineyard The Eleven Chardonnay 2013 50% of the grapes underwent carbonic maceration, and the wine was wild yeast barrel-fermented in French puncheons with the inclusion of 4yo yeast lees; mlf adds a further dimension of texture. That this is an exceptionally intense and complex wine should come as no surprise; it follows the brilliant '12, but has caused some tasters to blink. 132 dozen made. Screwcap. 12.9% alc. **Rating** 96 **To** 2025 $55 ✪

Single Vineyard Tuerong Block Mornington Peninsula Pinot Noir 2013 It has excellent colour and generous plum and cherry fruit that doesn't stray from the boundaries of 100% correct varietal expression. A prime example of having one's cake and eating it – but delay the latter for as long as possible, allowing the wine to come into full flower. Screwcap. 13.8% alc. **Rating** 96 **To** 2028 $65 ✪

Estate Mornington Peninsula Pinot Gris 2013 Masterful and complex winemaking of 40 dozen bottles; whole bunch-pressed direct to barrel for wild yeast fermentation and mlf; yeast lees from prior vintages also added in conjunction with stirring, and 11 months in barrel with no SO_2 added until the conclusion of 75% mlf. The most complex Gris made in Australia, its mouthfeel beyond all others, fleshy and opulent. Screwcap. 13.5% alc. **Rating** 96 **To** 2018 $36

Pennon Hill Mornington Peninsula Rose 2014 A 70/25/5% blend of pinot noir, shiraz and gamay, the pinot and gamay given carbonic maceration before being wild-fermented in used barriques. Vivid crimson, it offers far more in flavour and texture than most roses; the bouquet and palate run the scales of cherry, raspberry and strawberry, the finish precise and emphatic. Food? Coming ready or not. Screwcap. 13.1% alc. **Rating** 95 **To** 2016 $25 ✪

Estate Mornington Peninsula Pinot Noir 2013 Beautiful. Swish. Has a sense of gravity about it without ever seeming heavy or dense. Refreshing boysenberry and redcurrant notes with strawberried brightness lifting through the finish. Spice notes. Undergrowth. Nutty bitterness. Screwcap. 13.7% alc. **Rating** 95 **To** 2021 $48 CM

Single Vineyard Merricks Block Mornington Peninsula Pinot Noir 2013
Cherries stewing in their own juice, clumps of earth, an assortment of dried spices and an encouraging pat of smoky, almost coffeed oak. A winning combination it certainly is. Ultra-fine tannin, shot with complex, undergrowthy flavour, almost feels like a bonus. Screwcap. 13.7% alc. **Rating** 95 **To** 2025 $65 CM

Pennon Hill Sauvignon Blanc 2014 Rating 94 **To** 2016 $25 ✪
Pennon Hill Chardonnay 2013 Rating 94 **To** 2019 $23 CM ✪
Pennon Hill Pinot Grigio 2014 Rating 94 **To** 2017 $25 ✪

Montara ★★★★★

76 Chalambar Road, Ararat, Vic 3377 **Region** Grampians
T (03) 5352 3868 **www**.montarawines.com.au **Open** Fri–Sun 11–4
Winemaker Leigh Clarnette **Est.** 1970 **Dozens** 3000 **Vyds** 19.2ha
Gained considerable attention for its Pinot Noirs during the 1980s, and continues to produce wines of distinctive style under the ownership of no less than six siblings of the Stapleton family. As I can attest from several visits over the years, the view from the cellar door is one of the best in the Grampians region. Exports to Canada, South Korea and China.

♟♟♟♟♟ **Gold Rush Riesling 2014** Immensely attractive, already with an abundance of varietal fruit on show in a grapefruit/lime spectrum, yet is so light on its feet that it's difficult to decide whether it is just fruit sweetness or whether there's a dab of residual sugar; the balance is such that endeavouring to decide is only of academic interest. Screwcap. 11.5% alc. **Rating** 95 **To** 2025 $23 ✪

Chardonnay 2013 Estate-grown and hand-picked; 9 months in French oak with regular lees stirring. Early picking has not deprived it of varietal fruit, indeed far from it; white peach, nectarine and grapefruit drive the long, crisp palate, balanced acidity freshening the finish. Screwcap. 12.5% alc. **Rating** 95 **To** 2020 $23 ✪

♟♟♟♟♟ **Grampians Pinot Noir 2013 Rating** 90 **To** 2020 $25

Montgomery's Hill ★★★★

South Coast Highway, Upper Kalgan, Albany, WA 6330 **Region** Albany
T (08) 9844 3715 **www**.montgomeryshill.com.au **Open** 7 days 11–5 (Jun–Aug 12–4)
Winemaker Plantagenet (Cath Oates), Castle Rock (Robert Diletti) **Est.** 1996
Dozens 6000
Montgomery's Hill is 16km northeast of Albany on a north-facing slope on the banks of the Kalgan River. Previously an apple orchard, it is a diversification for the third generation of the Montgomery family, Pamela and Murray. Chardonnay, cabernet sauvignon, cabernet franc, sauvignon blanc, shiraz and merlot were planted in 1996–97. The elegant wines are made with a gentle touch, and offer excellent value.

♟♟♟♟♟ **Albany Chardonnay 2012** Barrel-fermented and matured in French oak for 9 months. Gleaming straw-green; an attractive wine, managing to combine complexity with lively acidity, the oak evident, but not obtrusive; has good length and drive. Screwcap. 14% alc. **Rating** 94 **To** 2020 $25 ✪

♟♟♟♟ **Albany Sauvignon Blanc 2014 Rating** 89 **To** 2015 $20
Albany Unwooded Chardonnay 2014 Rating 89 **To** 2017 $20

Montoro Wines ★★★☆

PO Box 8016, Orange, NSW 2800 **Region** Orange
T (02) 6365 2442 **www**.montorowines.com.au **Open** Not
Winemaker Charlie Svenson, Will Rikard-Bell **Est.** 2009 **Dozens** 400 **Vyds** 3ha
Bob Derrick was a teacher at Mudgee TAFE when Gil Walquist asked him to teach aspects of the first viticulture course. Bob says that teaching the course was a two-way affair, where he

felt he learned just as much, if not more, from the local growers and winemakers who were his students. A chicken and egg affair if ever there was one. But it led to the next milestone, when he was invited by Brian Croser to enrol in the wine science course at Wagga Wagga, becoming the first student not directly employed in the wine industry at the time. Further down the track he and wife Jennifer arrived in Orange, in 1988, with sky-high interest rates making land acquisition impossible, and Bob had to be content with involvement in the newly formed Central Highlands Grapegrowers Association. When grapes were planted on the Montoro property over 1992–94, he thought all possibility of buying the Montoro land (which he had long admired) was lost. Karma meant that the property changed hands and the vineyard had been largely neglected. In 1999 Montoro was put on the market, and Bob and Jennifer were able to grab the opportunity. It took five years of hard work to rehabilitate the 3ha of shiraz, the ultimate reward coming in the Orange Wine Show '14, when their 2013 Pepper Shiraz won a gold medal. They produce five styles of Shiraz from the tiny vineyard: Pepper Shiraz, Dry Red, End of the Day Rose, Opal Eyes Sparkling Shiraz, Shiraz Blanc and Vintage Shiraz (fortified). I devoutly hope they remove Shiraz Blanc from the wine portfolio.

ΨΨΨΨΨ Pepper Shiraz 2013 Power of suggestion it may be, but there does seem to be a sprinkle of pepper here. Not too overt, but there. It's otherwise medium-bodied with cherry-plum flavours, emphasis on the cherry, and sweet oak. Generally well composed and certainly easy to drink, with spicy tannin just beginning to integrate. Screwcap. 14% alc. **Rating** 91 **To** 2023 $38 CM

ΨΨΨΨ End of the Day Orange Shiraz Rose 2014 Rating 89 **To** 2016 $14 ⭘

Montvalley   ★★★★

150 Mitchells Road, Mount View, NSW 2325 (postal) **Region** Hunter Valley
T (02) 4991 7993 **www**.montvalley.com.au **Open** Not
Winemaker Daniel Binet **Est.** 1998 **Dozens** 2000 **Vyds** 5.7ha
Having looked at dozens of properties over the previous decade, John and Deirdre Colvin purchased their 80ha property in 1998. They chose the name Montvalley in part because it reflects the beautiful valley in the Brokenback Ranges of which the property forms part, and in part because the name Colvin originates from France, 'col' meaning valley and 'vin' meaning vines. They have planted almost 6ha of vines, the lion's share to shiraz, with lesser amounts of chardonnay and semillon.

ΨΨΨΨΨ Semillon 2013 Well made Semillon in the heart of the expected style – tight, crisp and minerally, but with enough unsweetened lemon juice to sustain the wine as it grows with time in bottle. Screwcap. 10.5% alc. **Rating** 92 **To** 2028 $30
Chardonnay 2013 The wine spent 11 months in French oak; other pertinent facts obscured by scrawl all over the back label, including 'chardonnay'. It has considerable verve and drive, with grapefruit nuances alongside melon and stone fruit; one guesses the mlf has been prevented, the acidity very good. Screwcap. 14% alc. **Rating** 92 **To** 2019 $27
Shiraz 2013 Good colour; a supple and succulent Shiraz, estate-grown, hand-picked and matured in used French and American oak for 15 months; the oak is not over-intrusive, and the finish is bright and crisply juicy. Screwcap. 13.5% alc. **Rating** 92 **To** 2025 $25 ⭘

Moody's Wines   ★★★☆

'Fontenay', Stagecoach Road, Orange, NSW 2800 **Region** Orange
T (02) 6365 9117 **www**.moodyswines.com **Open** W'ends 10–5
Winemaker Madrez Wine Services (Chris Derrez) **Est.** 2000 **Dozens** 200 **Vyds** 2ha
Tony Moody's great-grandfather started a chain of retail shops in Merseyside, England, under the banner Moody's Wines, the business ultimately sold in 1965 to a brewery seeking to minimise competition. Tony planted 1ha of shiraz 'in a promising sheep paddock' in 2000, and has subsequently added 1ha of sauvignon blanc. Moody's is in the east of the Orange region, with lighter rainfall than the west, the soils clay rather than red earth.

ŸŸŸŸŸ **Sauvignon Blanc 2014** Frost followed by a hot, dry summer hasn't dampened the freshness or intensity of the wine, although the full range of tropical fruits is diminished; grassy/green pea notes join with pink grapefruit and ripe citrus flavours, acidity well balanced. Screwcap. 11.5% alc. **Rating** 91 **To** 2015 $20 **✪**

ŸŸŸŸ **Orange Shiraz 2014 Rating** 89 **To** 2017 $20

Moombaki Wines ★★★★★

341 Parker Road, Kentdale via Denmark, WA 6333 **Region** Denmark
T (08) 9840 8006 **www**.moombaki.com **Open** 7 days 11–5
Winemaker Harewood Estate (James Kellie) **Est.** 1997 **Dozens** 900 **Vyds** 2.4ha
David Britten and Melissa Boughey established vines on a north-facing gravel hillside with picturesque Kent River frontage. Not content with establishing the vineyard (cabernet sauvignon, shiraz, cabernet franc, malbec and chardonnay), they put in significant mixed tree plantings to increase wildlife habitats. They chose Moombaki as their vineyard name: it is a local Aboriginal word meaning 'where the river meets the sky'.

ŸŸŸŸŸ **Chardonnay 2013** Oak is immediately apparent. It announces the wine as a full style, worked, not likely to take prisoners. Perhaps even a little old-fashioned; or so it seems at first. Immediately after the impression of oak comes a pure, joyous, powerful hit of fruit, the length and texture of which sets you back on your heels. It won't go quietly but it has the ability to impress mightily. Screwcap. 13.5% alc. **Rating** 95 **To** 2019 $35 CM **✪**
Shiraz 2012 Not a big wine, but the proportions are excellent. It's like the difference between standard house design and architectural; most things are effectively the same but somehow everything just seems to fit/function better. Black cherry, peppercorn, slips of smoky oak, aged spicy meats. Refreshing acidity and savoury tannin. It all just works. Screwcap. 14.5% alc. **Rating** 95 **To** 2026 $39 CM

ŸŸŸŸŸ **Reserve 2011 Rating** 93 **To** 2024 $55 CM

Moondarra ★★★★☆

Browns Road, Moondarra via Erica, Vic 3825 (postal) **Region** Gippsland
T 0408 666 348 **www**.moondarra.com.au **Open** Not
Winemaker Neil Prentice **Est.** 1991 **Dozens** 3000 **Vyds** 10ha
Neil Prentice and family established their Moondarra Vineyard in Gippsland, eventually focusing on the 2ha of low-yielding pinot noir. Subsequently, they planted their Holly's Garden vineyard at Whitlands in the King Valley, where they have 8ha of pinot gris and pinot noir. It is from this vineyard that much of their wine comes. Exports to the US, Singapore, Hong Kong, the Philippines, South Korea and Japan.

ŸŸŸŸŸ **Holly's Garden Pinot Gris 2014** Intensity of fruit and a powerful finish. Arguably the best of this wine's line. Fennel, pear, lime and red apple with a perfumed, spicy finish. Makes an impression, but in any case is straight-out delicious. Screwcap. 12.5% alc. **Rating** 94 **To** 2015 $25 CM **✪**
Conception Gippsland Pinot Noir 2013 It's like stepping into a room full of fresh cranberry and red cherry fruit flavours, the walls hung with cold tea, undergrowth, game and a wealth of savoury spice notes. Bright acidity, almost into orange/blossom territory, does its part to foster a sense of distinctiveness. Moondarra often takes you on a journey; this wine maintains that tradition. Screwcap. 13% alc. **Rating** 94 **To** 2022 $60 CM
Conception Gippsland Pinot Noir 2012 Herbs, spices, earth and a parade of savoury courses before the main serve of fruit arrives. Dark cherries and beetroot with a foresty edge. It's a meal, and a high-class one, the emphasis on sophistication. Screwcap. 13% alc. **Rating** 94 **To** 2022 $60 CM
Paradise Garage Nebbiolo 2013 Exotically perfumed. Boysenberry, plum, roses and mandarin. It's almost hypnotising. The palate is juicy, jubey, pretty and well structured, though there's nothing excessively forceful about the tannin here;

it remains fluid and polished throughout. Moreish, to say the least. Screwcap. 12.5% alc. **Rating** 94 **To** 2021 $40 CM

ΨΨΨΨ♀ **Samba Side Gippsland Pinot Noir 2013** Rating 92 To 2022 $80 CM

Moores Hill Estate   ★★★★★

3343 West Tamar Highway, Sidmouth, Tas 7270 **Region** Northern Tasmania
T (03) 6394 7649 **www**.mooreshill.com.au **Open** 7 days 10–5
Winemaker Julian Allport **Est.** 1997 **Dozens** 4000 **Vyds** 4.5ha
The Moores Hill Estate vineyard (jointly owned by winemaker Julian Allport with Fiona and Lance Weller) consists of pinot noir, chardonnay and riesling, with a very small amount of cabernet sauvignon and merlot. The vines are located on a northeast-facing hillside, 5km from the Tamar River and 30km from Bass Strait.

ΨΨΨΨΨ **Riesling 2014** An ultra-fragrant bouquet opens the door to a Riesling with all the shimmering fruit and acidity that flits like a butterfly across and along the exceptionally pure palate. Screwcap. 11.2% alc. **Rating** 96 **To** 2029 $30 ✪
Pinot Noir 2013 Enticingly bright, clear crimson; the pure and fragrant red cherry/berry aromas of the bouquet lead onto an equally pure and vibrant palate. A beautifully elegant and detailed Pinot of the highest quality. Screwcap. 13.2% alc. **Rating** 96 **To** 2023 $34 ✪

ΨΨΨΨ♀ **Chardonnay 2013** Rating 90 To 2020 $35
Cabernet Merlot 2014 Rating 90 To 2018 $30

Moorilla Estate   ★★★★★

655 Main Road, Berriedale, Tas 7011 **Region** Southern Tasmania
T (03) 6277 9900 **www**.moorilla.com.au **Open** Wed–Mon 9.30–5
Winemaker Conor van der Reest **Est.** 1958 **Dozens** 9400 **Vyds** 15.36ha
Moorilla Estate was the second winery to be established in Tasmania in the 20th century, Jean Miguet's La Provence beating it to the punch by two years. However, through much of the history of Moorilla Estate, it was the most important winery in the state, if not in size but as the icon. Magnificently situated on a mini-isthmus reaching into the Derwent River, it has always been a must-visit for wine lovers and tourists. A new winery in 2010 saw a decrease of 80% from peak production to around 90 tonnes per year, sourced entirely from the vineyards around Moorilla and its St Matthias Vineyard (Tamar Valley). It's almost incidental that the new winery is part of an overall development said by observers (not Moorilla) to cost upwards of $150 million. Its raison d'être is the establishment of an art gallery (MONA) that has the highest atmospheric environment accreditation of any gallery in the southern hemisphere, housing both the extraordinary ancient and contemporary art collection assembled by Moorilla's owner, David Walsh, and visiting exhibitions from major art museums around the world. Exports to the UK and Hong Kong.

ΨΨΨΨΨ **Muse Riesling 2013** It is its own beast. Mandarin, apple, orange peel, lime and bath salt notes, all of which flavours seem flecked with spice through the finish. Subtle sweetness, subtle development, much chitter-chatter of flavour. Slashing acidity keeps the momentum going. Both impressive and delicious. Screwcap. 13.2% alc. **Rating** 95 **To** 2022 $30 CM ✪
Praxis Sauvignon Blanc 2014 Where has this Sauvignon Blanc been hiding? It is overflowing with luscious drink-me-quick fruit, more so than any Tasmanian Sauvignon Blanc I have ever tasted; the aftertaste is impacted by acidity, but in the best possible way, not imperilling the luscious fruit. Screwcap. 11.3% alc. **Rating** 95 **To** 2016 $25 ✪
Muse Sauvignon 2013 Variously fermented in stainless steel and barrel (wild yeast); after 2 months, the final blend returned to oak for 8 months' maturation. Radically different from the Praxis fruit bomb, with a smoky gun flint complexity to the bouquet, and contesting the ground on the palate with the still-evident richly luscious fruit. Screwcap. 13.5% alc. **Rating** 95 **To** 2017 $30 ✪

Praxis Pinot Noir 2013 The final blend came from 15 separate ferments using all the vinification methods known to man, largely wild yeast, the components matured in French oak (17% new). Bright crimson, it has an excellent juxtaposition of fragrant red fruits with fine, savoury bramble notes. Drink tonight or in 10 years, either will do. Screwcap. 13.6% alc. **Rating** 95 **To** 2025 $30 ◐
Cloth Label Red 2012 33/30/20/10/7% pinot noir, shiraz, cabernet sauvignon, cabernet franc and riesling, with an equally complicated fermentation and maturation regime, the components kept separate for the first 10 months before blending. The acid is only 6.4g/l, but tastes much higher; it's an awesome road to hoe for a mere 110 dozen made. Screwcap. 13.4% alc. **Rating** 95 **To** 2028 $110
Muse Chardonnay 2012 Rating 94 **To** 2021 $48 CM
Muse Pinot Gris 2013 Rating 94 **To** 2015 $30 CM ◐
Muse Cabernet Sauvignon Cabernet Franc 2012 Rating 94 **To** 2027 $40

🍷🍷🍷🍷🍷 **Praxis Chardonnay Musque 2014 Rating** 93 **To** 2020
Muse Pinot Noir 2012 Rating 93 **To** 2023 $48 CM
Muse St Matthias Vineyard Syrah 2012 Rating 93 **To** 2023 $48 CM

Moorooduc Estate ★★★★★

501 Derril Road, Moorooduc, Vic 3936 **Region** Mornington Peninsula
T (03) 5971 8506 **www.**moorooducestate.com.au **Open** 7 days 11–5
Winemaker Dr Richard McIntyre **Est.** 1983 **Dozens** 5000 **Vyds** 6.5ha
Richard McIntyre has taken Moorooduc Estate to new heights, having completely mastered the difficult art of gaining maximum results from wild yeast fermentations. Starting with the 2010 vintage, there has been a complete revamp of grape sources, and hence changes to the tiered structure of the releases. These changes were driven by the simple fact that the estate vineyards had no possibility of providing the 5000–6000 dozen bottles of wine sold each year. The entry point wines under the Devil Bend Creek label remain, as before, principally sourced from the Osborn Vineyard. The mid-priced Chardonnay and Pinot Noir are no longer single-estate vineyard wines, and are now simply labelled by vintage and variety. Next come the Robinson Vineyard Pinot Noir and Chardonnay, elevated to reserve wine status, priced a little below the ultimate 'Ducs' (Moorooduc Vineyard). Exports to the UK, the US, Canada, Hong Kong and Singapore.

🍷🍷🍷🍷🍷 **The Moorooduc McIntyre Pinot Noir 2013** Polish, class, length of flavour, X-factor. Cherries and darker berries/plums, infusions of assorted spice, fennel and chicory and orange peel. Tannin purrs from the mid-palate onwards. Exquisite. Screwcap. 14% alc. **Rating** 97 **To** 2024 $65 CM ◐

🍷🍷🍷🍷🍷 **The Moorooduc McIntyre Chardonnay 2013** Strap your hands to the engines, a wild ride is in store. Peach, hazelnut, matchsticks, bran, flint and roasted assorted stone fruits. It's not the flavours themselves, it's the combination, the run, the way the flavours ache on and on long after you've swallowed. Screwcap. 13.5% alc. **Rating** 96 **To** 2023 $65 CM ◐
Pinot Noir 2013 Balance is the key. It's a powerful release, dark of fruit and smouldering with spice, the mix of fruit sweetness and tangy acidity carried smoothly along by crackling spice and creamy oak. It pushes various buttons at just the right moments, keeping one eye on the future as it does so. Screwcap. 14% alc. **Rating** 95 **To** 2023 $38 CM
Robinson Pinot Noir 2013 Feels luscious and silken but then sturdy, almost gruff through the finish. Serious, but still up for a joke or two. Dark plums and cherries, wood spice aplenty, and gamey foresty notes. It all comes together quite beautifully. Screwcap. 14% alc. **Rating** 95 **To** 2023 $55 CM
McIntyre Shiraz 2013 Silken, spice-shot red with bright, perfumed, lively fruit to the fore. This puts a delicious spin on savoury, cool-climate Shiraz. Garden herbs, cherry-plum, cedary oak and ripples of spice. Harmonious, lengthy and most most especially, seductive. Screwcap. 13.5% alc. **Rating** 95 **To** 2028 $38 CM
Robinson Chardonnay 2013 Rating 94 **To** 2020 $55 CM

YYYY Chardonnay 2013 Rating 93 To 2019 $38 CM
Garden Vineyard Pinot Noir 2013 Rating 93 To 2021 $55 CM

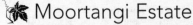

Moortangi Estate ★★★★

120 Wills Road, Dixons Creek, Vic 3775 **Region** Yarra Valley
T (03) 9600 4001 **www.**moortangiestate.com.au **Open** Not
Winemaker Sergio Carlei **Est.** 2002 **Dozens** NA **Vyds** 5.75ha
Paula and Pamela Hyland purchased a beautiful grazing property at Dixons Creek already
christened 'Moortangi'. They planted the north-facing paddocks with shiraz (4ha), cabernet
sauvignon (0.9ha), merlot (0.5ha) and viognier (0.35ha), but while waiting for the vines
to mature purchased shiraz from Heathcote for their first vintage. They have continued to
make the Old Vine Heathcote Shiraz from vines planted in the 1950s in grey loam soils, the
Cambrian Shiraz from red soils. By 2009 the vines were flourishing and they anticipated their
first vintage, but the Black Saturday bushfires devastated the property, destroying the majority
of their vines. In 2010 they saw shoots on their main planting of shiraz, and they have since
laboriously resurrected the vineyard on a vine-by-vine basis, and now oversee what they
regard as an exceptional vineyard. They say their love of wine brought them to this place, and
has been sorely tested, but ultimately fulfilled.

YYYY Cambrian Shiraz 2008 From vines grown in Heathcote, fermented in large
wooden vats, then matured in new and used French oak for 24 months. The
crimson-purple hue is exceptional for a 6yo wine, the flavours likewise; black
cherry and blackberry are framed by cedary oak and fine-grained tannins, the
finish long and balanced. Diam. 14% alc. **Rating** 93 **To** 2020 $35
Old Vine Heathcote Shiraz 2006 Obviously, a little more advanced than its '08
Cambrian sibling, and not having the same depth; nonetheless, open fermentation
and 24 months in new and used French oak have served this elegant, light to
medium-bodied wine well. Diam. 13.5% alc. **Rating** 90 **To** 2018 $55

YYYY Yarra Valley Chardonnay 2011 Rating 88 To 2015 $35

Moppity Vineyards ★★★★★

Moppity Road, Young, NSW 2594 (postal) **Region** Hilltops
T (02) 6382 6222 **www.**moppity.com.au **Open** Not
Winemaker Jason Brown **Est.** 1973 **Dozens** 30 000 **Vyds** 73ha
Jason Brown and wife Alecia, with backgrounds in fine wine retail and accounting, purchased
Moppity Vineyards in 2004 when it was already 31 years old. Initially they were content to
sell the grapes to other makers, but that changed with the release of the '06 Shiraz, which
won top gold in its class at the London International Wine & Spirit Competition. In Nov '09
the '08 Eden Road Long Road Hilltops Shiraz, made from Moppity Vineyards grapes, won
the Jimmy Watson Trophy. These awards are among a cascade of golds for its Shirazs, Riesling,
Tumbarumba Chardonnay and Cabernet Sauvignon. Production (and sales) have soared, and
all of the grapes from the estate are now used for the Moppity Vineyards brand. The Lock &
Key range provides exceptional value for money. Moppity has also established Coppabella, a
separate venture in Tumbarumba. Exports to the UK and China.

YYYYY Reserve Hilltops Shiraz 2013 Block 7. Hand-picked; 35% whole bunches;
5-day cold soak, cool ferment, matured 11 months in three French puncheons
(1 new). Winner Great Australian Shiraz Challenge '14, golds Melbourne and
NSW Small Makers. Has Moppity stamped all over the bouquet and palate;
intense black cherry, licorice, blackberry and spice fruit has engulfed the French
oak, and the tannins are gloriously fine and supple. 190 dozen made. Screwcap.
13.9% alc. **Rating** 97 **To** 2038 $70 **○**

YYYYY Lock & Key Single Vineyard Reserve Hilltops Shiraz 2013 An absurd
number of gold medals (5), even if one or two are from lesser competitions. An
exceptionally powerful intense and tightly focused wine, black fruits, licorice and
spice stitched together with tannins ex fruit and French oak. Will live for decades.
430 dozen made. Screwcap. 14% alc. **Rating** 96 **To** 2043 $25 **○**

Single Vineyard Hilltops Cabernet Sauvignon 2013 Block 1 Reynella clone; leaf-plucked, shoot-thinned, yield 5t/ha; hand-picked, 5-day cold soak, matured in French barriques (28% new) 13 months. A powerful, layered, but perfectly balanced and structured Cabernet, with persistent cool-grown cassis fruit supported by ripe tannins. Screwcap. 14% alc. **Rating** 96 **To** 2032 $30 ✪
Single Vineyard Hilltops Shiraz 2013 Block 8A; 4t/ha; hand-picked, 25% whole bunches, 5-day cold soak; matured for 11 months in French puncheons and hogsheads. More open-knit than its sibling, with spice, pepper and licorice to the fore, but no shortage of black cherry and blackberry fruit; very good tannin and oak support. Screwcap. 14% alc. **Rating** 95 **To** 2033 $30 ✪
Lock & Key Single Vineyard Hilltops Shiraz 2013 The entry point for four Moppity Shirazs, good enough to garner three gold medals in '14 and a 97 point gold at Melbourne Wine Awards. The texture and structure are outstanding, the cool-grown mix of red cherry, plum, spice and licorice ditto. Fantastic value. 1960 dozen made. Screwcap. 14% alc. **Rating** 95 **To** 2033 $20 ✪
Lock & Key Single Vineyard Hilltops Cabernet Sauvignon 2013 Block 17, yield 6.25t/ha, 4-day cold soak, cool ferment; matured in used French barriques for 13 months. Excellent crimson-purple; classic cassis varietal character is the driver, although tannins and oak lend carefully judged support. A really attractive wine. Screwcap. 13.9% alc. **Rating** 95 **To** 2028 $20 ✪
Lock & Key Single Vineyard Reserve Hilltops Cabernet Sauvignon 2013 Bright, clear crimson; the wine has a very fragrant bouquet, with cassis to the fore just as it is on the finely structured, juicy, palate. There is a subtext of cedary oak and some dried herbs that are strongly varietal. Screwcap. 14% alc. **Rating** 95 **To** 2028 $27

Morambro Creek Wines ★★★★★

PMB 98, Naracoorte, SA 5271 (postal) **Region** Padthaway
T (08) 8765 6043 **www**.morambrocreek.com.au **Open** Not
Winemaker Ben Riggs **Est.** 1994 **Dozens** 30 000 **Vyds** 178.5ha
The Bryson family has been involved in agriculture for more than a century, moving to Padthaway in 1955 as farmers and graziers. Since the '90s, they have progressively established large plantings of shiraz (88.5ha), cabernet sauvignon (47.5ha), chardonnay (34.5ha) and sauvignon blanc (8ha). The Morambro Creek and Mt Monster wines have been consistent winners of wine show medals, but the current releases take the wines onto a level not previously achieved. Exports to the UK, the US and other major markets.

♟♟♟♟♟ **Padthaway Chardonnay 2013** Individual parcels fermented, some wild yeast, then mlf and extended lees contact before 12 months in new and used French oak. A well-balanced wine, reflecting the careful vinification; stone fruit, grapefruit and fig all to be found working synergistically with nutty/creamy mlf influences. Screwcap. 13.5% alc. **Rating** 95 **To** 2020 $32 ✪
Padthaway Shiraz 2012 Good colour; an opulent, medium to full-bodied wine awash with black fruits, spices, fruitcake and well-integrated oak; the tannins, too, play a positive role in a wine with a long future. Screwcap. 14.5% alc. **Rating** 95 **To** 2032 $32 ✪

♟♟♟♟♟ **The Bryson Barrel Select 2012 Rating** 92 **To** 2025 $55
Padthaway Cabernet Sauvignon 2012 Rating 92 **To** 2027 $32

Morgan Simpson ★★★★

PO Box 39, Kensington Park, SA 5068 **Region** McLaren Vale
T 0417 843 118 **www**.morgansimpson.com.au **Open** Not
Winemaker Richard Simpson **Est.** 1998 **Dozens** 1500 **Vyds** 20.9ha
Morgan Simpson was founded by SA businessman George Morgan (since retired) and winemaker Richard Simpson, who is a graduate of CSU. The grapes are sourced from the Clos Robert Vineyard (where the wine is made), planted to shiraz (10.8ha), cabernet

sauvignon (3.8ha), mourvedre (3.5ha) and chardonnay (1.8ha), established by Robert Allen Simpson in 1972. Most of the grapes are sold, the remainder used to provide the reasonably priced, drinkable wines for which Morgan Simpson has become well known.

ŸŸŸŸŸ **Basket Press McLaren Vale Shiraz 2012** Open-fermented, matured in American oak hogsheads. Morgan Simpson says they don't use much oak, leaving the focus on the fruit and quintessential McLaren Vale expression thereof. Here it works to perfection, the wine as honest as the day is long, full of black fruits and dark chocolate, the tannins in balance and in need of no time to soften. Screwcap. 14.4% alc. **Rating** 94 **To** 2027 $22 ✪

ŸŸŸŸ **Basket Press McLaren Vale Shiraz 2011 Rating** 88 **To** 2016 $22

Morgan Vineyards ★★★★

30 Davross Court, Seville, Vic 3139 **Region** Yarra Valley
T 0422 396 356 **www.**morganvineyards.net.au **Open** Not
Winemaker Kate Goodman **Est.** 1971 **Dozens** 1000 **Vyds** 4.8ha
This business has had three owners since the first vines were planted in 1971 (cabernet sauvignon and pinot noir), extended in '89 (pinot noir), '91 (cabernet sauvignon and merlot), and '94 (chardonnay). Simon and Michele Gunther, the present owners, purchased the vineyard from Roger Morgan in 2010.

ŸŸŸŸŸ **Yarra Valley Chardonnay 2013** Has that imposing thumbprint of the Yarra Valley in the length of its palate and ascending aftertaste; the use of French oak has been cleverly restrained, allowing the grapefruit/white peach varietal aromas and flavours free play. Screwcap. 13.5% alc. **Rating** 94 **To** 2021 $35
Yarra Valley Merlot 2013 A high-quality example of a variety that so often fails to excite; cassis, plum and a touch of cedar inhabit the bouquet and palate alike; while no more than medium-bodied, its mouth-watering juicy fruit is very appealing. Screwcap. 13% alc. **Rating** 94 **To** 2023 $29 ✪

ŸŸŸŸŸ **Yarra Valley Pinot Noir 2013 Rating** 93 **To** 2023 $39

Morningside Vineyard ★★★★★

711 Middle Tea Tree Road, Tea Tree, Tas 7017 **Region** Southern Tasmania
T (03) 6268 1748 **Open** By appt
Winemaker Peter Bosworth **Est.** 1980 **Dozens** 500 **Vyds** 2.8ha
The name 'Morningside' was given to the old property on which the vineyard stands because it gets the morning sun first; the property on the other side of the valley was known as Eveningside. Consistent with the observation of the early settlers, the Morningside grapes achieve full maturity with good colour and varietal flavour. Production will increase as the vineyard matures, and as recent additions of clonally selected pinot noir (including 8104, 115 and 777) come into bearing. The Bosworth family, headed by Peter and wife Brenda, do all the vineyard and winery work, with conspicuous attention to detail.

ŸŸŸŸŸ **Pressings Pinot Noir 2012** The estate vineyard has 9 clones of pinot yielding 4t/ha; majority destemmed, 10–20% whole bunch; 4-day cold soak, then wild yeast-fermented; matured for 18 months in French oak (one-third new). Deep, dense colour signals a Pinot of exceptional depth and complexity, ripe plum and black cherry fruit having soaked up the new oak. Vinous Wagner. Screwcap. 13.5% alc. **Rating** 97 **To** 2027 $25 ✪

ŸŸŸŸŸ **Riesling 2014** From the 5-clone estate vineyard, fermented bone dry; the chalky, almost dusty, bouquet doesn't prepare you for the Bickford's lime juice flavours that fill every corner of the mouth; Tasmanian acidity seals the deal. Screwcap. 11.5% alc. **Rating** 95 **To** 2029 $25 ✪
Cabernets 2012 Five clones of cabernet sauvignon (80%), cabernet franc (15%) and petit verdot (5%); 24 months in French oak (30% new). The Richmond/

Coal River district is one of the best (only the Tamar River comes close) areas for cabernet in Tasmania. This is flavour-ripe, with good length and balance. Impressive. Diam. 13.7% alc. **Rating** 94 **To** 2027 $29 ○

♈♈♈♈♈ **Chardonnay 2013 Rating** 92 **To** 2018 $27

Morris ★★★★★

Mia Mia Road, Rutherglen, Vic 3685 **Region** Rutherglen
T (02) 6026 7303 **www**.morriswines.com.au **Open** Mon–Sat 9–5, Sun 10–5
Winemaker David Morris **Est.** 1859 **Dozens** 100 000 **Vyds** 96ha
One of the greatest of the fortified winemakers, ranking with Chambers Rosewood. Morris has changed the labelling system for its sublime fortified wines, with a higher-than-average entry point for the (Classic) Liqueur Muscat; Tokay and the ultra-premium wines are being released under the Old Premium Liqueur (Rare) label. The art of these wines lies in the blending of very old and much younger material. They have no equivalent in any other part of the world.

♈♈♈♈♈ **Old Premium Rare Liqueur Muscat NV** Deep olive-brown, coating the sides of the glass briefly when it is swirled; needless to say, is exceptionally rich and luscious, but – even more – complex, with a dense array of oriental sweet spices, dried raisins, and (for me) childhood memories of mother's Christmas pudding laced with brandy. And yes, this really does go with dark, bitter chocolate in any form. 500ml. Cork. 17.5% alc. **Rating** 98 **To** 2016 $75 ○
Old Premium Grand Rutherglen Muscat NV Deep olive-brown; dense spice, plum pudding and raisin aromas; utterly exceptional intensity and length; altogether in another dimension; while based upon some very old wine, is as fresh as a daisy. Cork. 17.5% alc. **Rating** 97 **To** 2016 $50 ○

♈♈♈♈♈ **Old Premium Rare Liqueur Tokay NV** Mahogany, with an olive rim; aromas of Christmas cake and tea; incredibly viscous and rich, with layer upon layer of flavours ranging through ginger snap, burnt butterscotch, and every imaginable spice, the length and depth of the palate as extraordinary as is that of the aftertaste. Released in tiny quantities each year to maintain the extreme average age of each release. 500ml. Screwcap. 18% alc. **Rating** 96 **To** 2016 $75 ○
Cellar One Classic Liqueur Rutherglen Topaque NV Orange grading to pale olive-brown on the rim; great Topaque and Muscat are made with the young wines as the starting point, and they have to be good. This wine is that and then some, with full-on butterscotch, tea leaf, cup cake and crème brûlée flavours, reaching a peak on the back-palate, before drying out nicely on the finish, leaving the mouth fresh and looking for the next sip. 500ml. Screwcap. 17.5% alc. **Rating** 94 **To** 2016 $35
Cellar One Classic Liqueur Rutherglen Muscat NV The colour has begun its shift to what will ultimately be dark brown with an olive-green rim; this is still in the light brown spectrum. The aromas simply lay a path for the palate, which is nothing more or less than liquid raisins, with rancio and cleansing fortifying spirit preventing the raisin flavours from cloying. The flavours of the two Cellar One wines are radically different, and those who do not know much about these wonderful wines should gather a few friends around to explore each of the wines and their inimitable difference. Screwcap. 17.5% alc. **Rating** 94 **To** 2015 $35

♈♈♈♈♈ **Rutherglen Durif 2010 Rating** 93 **To** 2040 $30
The Criollo Malbec 2012 Rating 92 **To** 2022 $25 ○
Blue Imperial Bin No. 80 Cinsault 2012 Rating 92 **To** 2021 $25 CM ○

Moss Wood ★★★★★

926 Metricup Road, Wilyabrup, WA 6284 **Region** Margaret River
T (08) 9755 6266 **www**.mosswood.com.au **Open** By appt
Winemaker Clare and Keith Mugford **Est.** 1969 **Dozens** 14 000 **Vyds** 18.14ha

Widely regarded as one of the best wineries in the region, producing glorious Chardonnay, power-laden Semillon and elegant Cabernet Sauvignon that lives for decades. Moss Wood also owns the Ribbon Vale Estate, the wines treated as vineyard-designated within the Moss Wood umbrella. The current releases are of exceptionally high quality. Exports to all major markets.

ŸŸŸŸŸ **Margaret River Chardonnay 2013** This very complex, very intense yet elegant Chardonnay has the best of all possible worlds, and so will you: it drinks well now, and will in 5, 10 and who knows how many more years out. The magic is in its balance and the fruit purity – white peach – achieved at relatively high alcohol, often an issue, here a virtue. Screwcap. 14% alc. **Rating** 96 **To** 2030 $65 **☼**
Ribbon Vale Vineyard Margaret River Merlot 2012 Good colour; arguably one of the best merlots in Australia at the present time; a beguiling blend of redcurrant, blackcurrant and plum ripe tannins precisely weighted, French oak integrated and balanced. Screwcap. 14% alc. **Rating** 96 **To** 2027 $60 **☼**
Ribbon Vale Vineyard Margaret River Cabernet Sauvignon Merlot 2012 Deep crimson-purple; a rich, complex, medium+-bodied wine, the bouquet and palate saturated with cassis, redcurrant and plum; exemplary tannin and oak management, better balanced (the tannins in particular) than the '11. Will develop superbly over many years to come. Screwcap. 14% alc. **Rating** 96 **To** 2032 $60 **☼**
Margaret River Semillon 2014 A wine unto itself, intense, deep and long; the vines are deep-rooted, and the grapes retain good acidity that provides both length and balance for the fruit expression of crushed lemon leaf, lemongrass and Meyer lemon. Screwcap. 13.5% alc. **Rating** 95 **To** 2034 $35 **☼**
Amy's 2013 A brightly coloured blend of cabernet, merlot and malbec; it is deliciously juicy and light on its feet, with cassis fruit centre stage; while the oak and tannins are not obvious, they do play a role in providing subtle support for the fruit. Screwcap. 14% alc. **Rating** 95 **To** 2033 $35 **☼**
Ribbon Vale Vineyard Margaret River Sauvignon Blanc Semillon 2014 **Rating** 94 **To** 2020 $32

ŸŸŸŸŸ **Amy's 2012** **Rating** 93 **To** 2022 $38

Mount Alexander Winery   ★★★★

410 Harcourt Road, Sutton Grange, Vic 3448 **Region** Bendigo
T (03) 5474 2567 **www**.mawine.com.au **Open** W'ends & public hols 10–5
Winemaker Bill Blamires **Est.** 2001 **Dozens** 2000 **Vyds** 7.4ha
Bill and Sandra Blamires acquired their property after a two-year search of the southern Bendigo area for what they considered an ideal location. They have firmly planted their faith in shiraz (5.9ha), with merlot, cabernet sauvignon, chardonnay and viognier contributing 1.5ha. The winery was previously called Blamires Butterfly Crossing (because of the butterfly population on Axe Creek, which runs through the property), but was changed due to confusion with Angove's Butterfly Ridge.

ŸŸŸŸŸ **Merlot 2012** A fresh and juicy bouquet and palate run in tandem, red berries riding high, no briar or earth notes to interrupt the flow. Good value, especially for its early-drinking style. Screwcap. 13.7% alc. **Rating** 92 **To** 2019 $20 **☼**
Mourvedre 2013 Light, bright colour; an attractive wine, with almost succulent red-berry fruits and fine tannins. Screwcap. 12.8% alc. **Rating** 92 **To** 2020 $24 **☼**

ŸŸŸŸ **Shiraz 2012** **Rating** 89 **To** 2020 $20

Mount Avoca   ★★★★★

Moates Lane, Avoca, Vic 3467 **Region** Pyrenees
T (03) 5465 3282 **www**.mountavoca.com **Open** 7 days 10–5
Winemaker William Talbot (Former) **Est.** 1970 **Dozens** 10 000 **Vyds** 23.46ha
A winery that has long been one of the stalwarts of the Pyrenees region, owned by Matthew and Lisa Barry. The estate vineyards (shiraz, sauvignon blanc, cabernet sauvignon, chardonnay,

merlot, cabernet franc and semillon) are organically managed, and provide the total intake of the winery. The wines are made in three ranges, starting with Moates Lane; the Growers Blend wines and Estate Range are the mainstay of the business. There are a handful of vineyard-designated wines that are quite outstanding. In the wake of William Talbot's resignation, a management gap seems to have been created, with only two wines submitted. In these circumstances the 5-star rating has been retained, but reduced from red to black. Exports to China.

🍷🍷🍷🍷🍷 **Moates Lane Shiraz 2012** This is a seriously good wine at its price. The colour is bright, and the flavours provide a juicy, lingering finish to the array of red and black cherry flavours; the tannins are fine, the oak barely perceptible. Drink whenever the mood takes you. Screwcap. 13.5% alc. **Rating** 90 **To** 2019 $11 ❍

🍷🍷🍷🍷 Jack Barry Pyrenees Sparkling Shiraz NV **Rating** 89 **To** 2015 $36 TS

Mount Burrumboot Estate ★★★☆

3332 Heathcote–Rochester Road, Colbinabbin, Vic 3559 **Region** Heathcote
T (03) 5432 9238 **www.**burrumboot.com **Open** W'ends & public hols 11–5
Winemaker Cathy Branson **Est.** 1999 **Dozens** 500 **Vyds** 16.5ha
To quote: 'Mount Burrumboot Estate was born in 1999, when Andrew and Cathy Branson planted vines on the Home Block of the Branson family farm, Donore, on the slopes of Mt Burrumboot, on the Mt Camel Range, above Colbinabbin. Originally the vineyard was just another diversification of an already diverse farming enterprise. However, the wine bug soon bit, and a winery was established. The first wine was contract-made in 2001 – however, '02 saw the first wine made by Cathy in the machinery shed, surrounded by headers and tractors. Very primitive, and the appearance of the new 50-tonne winery in '02 was greeted with great enthusiasm!' The original plantings of a little over 11ha of shiraz and merlot have since been expanded with lesser amounts of petit verdot, sangiovese, tempranillo, gamay, marsanne and viognier.

🍷🍷🍷🍷 **Heathcote Tempranillo 2010** Sweet/sour aromatics and indeed flavours but it's tangy and drinks easily enough. Cherries, sap, dried herbs and traces of tomato. Ready now. Screwcap. 13.7% alc. **Rating** 89 **To** 2017 $30 CM

Mount Camel Ridge Estate ★★★☆

473 Heathcote–Rochester Road, Heathcote, Vic 3523 **Region** Heathcote
T (03) 5433 2343 **www.**mountcamelridgeestate.com **Open** By appt
Winemaker Ian and Gwenda Langford **Est.** 1999 **Dozens** 350 **Vyds** 17ha
Ian and Gwenda Langford commenced planting their vineyard in 1999, the majority to shiraz (8.5ha), cabernet sauvignon (3.4ha) and merlot (3.4ha), with a little over 0.5ha each of petit verdot, viognier and mourvedre. The vineyard uses sustainable principles; the wines are made in open half-tonne vats, basket-pressed and matured in French oak with natural (wild) yeast fermentation. Exports to the US and China.

🍷🍷🍷🍷 **Heathcote Syrah 2012** Wild yeast-fermented, neither fined nor filtered. A light to medium-bodied wine with marked spice and pepper accents; gives the impression the grapes weren't completely ripe, sharpening the finish. Diam. 12.4% alc. **Rating** 88 **To** 2019 $65

Mount Cathedral Vineyards ★★★★☆

125 Knafl Road, Taggerty, Vic 3714 **Region** Upper Goulburn
T 0409 354 069 **www.**mtcathedralvineyards.com **Open** By appt
Winemaker Oscar Rosa, Nick Arena **Est.** 1995 **Dozens** 900 **Vyds** 5ha
The Rosa and Arena families established Mount Cathedral Vineyards in 1995, at an elevation of 300m on the north face of Mt Cathedral. The first plantings were of 1.2ha of merlot and 0.8ha of chardonnay, followed by 2.5ha of cabernet sauvignon and 0.5ha of cabernet franc in 1996. No pesticides or systemic chemicals are used in the vineyard. Oscar Rosa, chief

winemaker, has a Bachelor of Wine Science from CSU, and gained practical experience working at Yering Station in the late '90s.

ΨΨΨΨΨ **Cabernet Merlot 2012** Like the Merlot, spends 24 months in French oak, and is no less deeply coloured; the varietal expression is clarion clear, and the medium to full-bodied palate has more flesh, the tannins ripe and soft, yet persistent. Screwcap. 13% alc. **Rating** 95 **To** 2032 $24 **☻**

Chardonnay 2012 Hand-picked, whole bunch-pressed, fermented in French barriques, then 9 months stirring in barrel. Bright green-straw, it is particularly well balanced and structured; white peach, clingstone peach and melon fruit provide generous flavour. Screwcap. 12.8% alc. **Rating** 94 **To** 2017 $24 **☻**

Merlot 2012 Very deeply coloured; an extremely powerful wine, remarkable given its modest alcohol; cassis fruit has a veil of black olive and bramble, but the tannins are fine and balanced. A convincing follow-on from the impressive '10. A Merlot for real men. Screwcap. 13% alc. **Rating** 94 **To** 2027 $24 **☻**

ΨΨΨΨΨ **Reserve Cabernet Sauvignon 2012 Rating** 90 **To** 2020 $40

Mount Charlie Winery   ★★★☆

228 Mount Charlie Road, Riddells Creek, Vic 3431 **Region** Macedon Ranges
T (03) 5428 6946 **www**.mountcharlie.com.au **Open** Thurs–Sun 10–5
Winemaker Trefor Morgan **Est.** 1991 **Dozens** 600 **Vyds** 3ha
Mount Charlie's wines are sold principally by mail order and through selected restaurants. A futures program encourages mailing-list sales, with a substantial discount to the eventual release price. Owner/winemaker Trefor Morgan is perhaps better known as Professor of Physiology at Melbourne University. The vineyard is planted to 0.5ha each of chardonnay, sauvignon blanc, tempranillo, merlot, malbec and shiraz.

ΨΨΨΨ **Sauvignon Blanc 2014** A lot of people will love this. The flavour of sweet red apples, perhaps a slightly milkiness, with pear and honeysuckle notes juicing through the finish. Screwcap. 11.4% alc. **Rating** 88 **To** 2015 $18 CM

Mount Coghill Vineyard   ★★★☆

Cnr Pickfords Road/Coghills Creek Road, Coghills Creek, Vic 3364 **Region** Ballarat
T (03) 5343 4329 **www**.ballaratwineries.com/mtcoghill.htm **Open** W'ends 10–5
Winemaker Owen Latta **Est.** 1993 **Dozens** 300 **Vyds** 0.7ha
Ian and Margaret Pym began planting their tiny vineyard in 1995 with 1280 pinot noir rootlings, adding 450 chardonnay rootlings the next year. Since 2001 wine has been made and released under the Mount Coghill Vineyard label. Ian is an award-winning photographer, and his photographs are on display at the cellar door.

ΨΨΨΨ **Ballarat Chardonnay 2013** Tightly built from start to finish, reflecting the very cool climate with strong grapefruit accents; a touch of French oak works well. Screwcap. 12.5% alc. **Rating** 89 **To** 2019 $25

Mount Eyre Vineyards   ★★★★

173 Gillards Road, Pokolbin, NSW 2321 **Region** Hunter Valley
T 0438 683 973 **www**.mounteyre.com **Open** At Garden Cellars, Hunter Valley Gardens
Winemaker Andrew Spinaze, Mark Richardson **Est.** 1970 **Dozens** 5000 **Vyds** 45.5ha
This is the venture of two families whose involvement in wine extends in an unbroken line back several centuries: the Tsironis family in the Peleponnese, Greece, and the Iannuzzi family in Vallo della Lucania, Italy. Their vineyards are at Broke (the largest), with a smaller vineyard at Pokolbin. The three principal varieties planted are chardonnay, shiraz and semillon, with small amounts of merlot, viognier, chambourcin, verdelho, negro amaro, fiano and nero d'Avola. Exports to Canada, Hong Kong and China.

ΨΨΨΨΨ **Three Ponds Hunter Valley Semillon 2014** Lemony flavour, waxy texture, excellent length. Sits brightly in the glass. Drinks well young but time will be kind. Screwcap. 11% alc. **Rating** 93 **To** 2022 $20 CM **☻**

Three Ponds Fiano 2014 Refreshing, low-alc style but it's a white with grip, flavour and shape. Citrus and apple notes with a waxiness to both the mouthfeel and the flavour. Screwcap. 10.2% alc. **Rating** 91 **To** 2016 $20 CM ○

Mount Horrocks

The Old Railway Station, Curling Street, Auburn, SA 5451 **Region** Clare Valley
T (08) 8849 2243 **www**.mounthorrocks.com **Open** W'ends & public hols 10–5
Winemaker Stephanie Toole **Est.** 1982 **Dozens** 4500 **Vyds** 9.4ha
Owner/winemaker Stephanie Toole has never deviated from the pursuit of excellence in the vineyard and winery. She has three vineyard sites in the Clare Valley, each managed using natural farming and organic practices. The attention to detail and refusal to cut corners is obvious in all of her wines. The cellar door is in the old, renovated, Auburn railway station. Exports to the UK, the US and other major markets.

ΨΨΨΨΨ **Watervale Shiraz 2012** As usual, a portion (15%) was whole bunch foot-stamped in open fermenters, the balance in tanks with header boards; matured in French barriques (40% new) for 18 months. Marries power with finesse, its black fruits filling the medium to full-bodied palate, but does so with guile; it has outstanding line and length, and will be very long-lived, yet allow access at any point along the journey. Screwcap. 14% alc. **Rating** 96 **To** 2035 $39 ○
Watervale Riesling 2014 Bright straw-green; the vintage caused issues for riesling here and there in the Clare Valley, but not for this lovely wine; citrus blossom and crushed leaf aromas lead into a relatively full-flavoured palate, which doesn't lose focus on the finish, sustained by crisp minerally/citrussy acidity. Screwcap. 12.5% alc. **Rating** 95 **To** 2024 $32 ○
Clare Valley Cabernet Sauvignon 2012 Dispenses with the small amount of merlot included in prior vintages thanks to the balance of the cabernet from the low-yielding, organic vines. This is very near the top of Clare Valley Cabernet, with excellent varietal definition courtesy of a mix of cassis and savoury black olive offsets; the tannin and oak management are also admirable. A long and distinguished life ahead. Screwcap. 14% alc. **Rating** 95 **To** 2035 $39
Clare Valley Semillon 2013 In time-honoured fashion, 100% barrel-fermented, but the French oak is not the least overt, sinuously interwoven with ripe Meyer lemon and stone fruit flavours. A classic each-way proposition, now or much later. Screwcap. 13% alc. **Rating** 94 **To** 2025 $29 ○
Watervale Nero d'Avola 2012 It's a touch of class to say, as does Stephanie Toole, that a glass of Nero d'Avola in Cul de Sac (a wine bar in Rome) put her on the road to planting this variety. It is singularly intense, with spice, briar and rose hip tumbling around the palate, the intensity reflected in both the fruit and the cleansing acidity and finish. Screwcap. 14% alc. **Rating** 94 **To** 2020 $37
Cordon Cut Clare Valley Riesling 2014 Extremely rich and luscious; lime marmalade and preserved cumquat sweetness balanced by lemon sherbet acidity can't help but seduce – ideal by the glass (or half bottle) proposition for restaurants. 375ml. Screwcap. 11% alc. **Rating** 94 **To** 2018 $39

Mt Jagged Wines

Main Victor Harbor Road, Mt Jagged, SA 5211 **Region** Southern Fleurieu
T (08) 8554 9520 **www**.mtjaggedwines.com.au **Open** Thurs–Sun 10–5
Winemaker Simon Parker **Est.** 1989 **Dozens** 1000 **Vyds** 27.5ha
Mt Jagged's vineyard was established in 1989 by the White family, with close-planted semillon, chardonnay, merlot, cabernet sauvignon and shiraz. The vineyard sits at 350m above sea level on a diversity of soils, ranging from ironstone/clay for the red varieties to sandy loam/clay for the whites. The cool-climate vineyard (altitude and proximity to the ocean) produces fresh, crisp, zingy white wines and medium-bodied savoury reds of complexity and depth. In Jan '13 the property was purchased by Tod and Suzanne Warmer.

ŸŸŸŸ♀ **Knobby Club Cabernet Sauvignon 2013** Includes 5% merlot; matured for
18 months in new and used French and American oak. A fragrant and juicy light
to medium-bodied Cabernet, with hints of dried herb and bay leaf; good balance
and length. Screwcap. 14% alc. **Rating** 91 **To** 2028 $25

ŸŸŸŸ **Tangled Rope Shiraz 2013 Rating** 89 **To** 2030 $25
Bare Twig Semillon Sauvignon Blanc 2014 Rating 88 **To** 2018 $15 ○
Honey Myrtle Chardonnay 2014 Rating 88 **To** 2019 $20

Mount Langi Ghiran Vineyards   ★★★★★

Warrak Road, Buangor, Vic 3375 **Region** Grampians
T (03) 5354 3207 **www**.langi.com.au **Open** Mon–Fri 9–5, w'ends 10–5
Winemaker Ben Haines **Est.** 1969 **Dozens** 60 000 **Vyds** 86ha
A maker of outstanding cool-climate peppery Shiraz, crammed with flavour and vinosity,
and very good Cabernet Sauvignon. The Shiraz has long pointed the way for cool-climate
examples of the variety. The business was acquired by the Rathbone family group in 2002, and
the marketing integrated with the Yering Station and Xanadu Estate wines, a synergistic mix
with no overlap. Wine quality is exemplary. Exports to all major markets.

ŸŸŸŸŸ **Mast Grampians Shiraz 2012** A super-cuvee honouring the late Trevor Mast,
founder of Mount Langi Ghiran. Fastidious fruit selection and sophisticated
winemaking have paid big dividends. Cold-soaked, open-fermented, some whole
berries, 15–18 months in French oak. A glorious cascade of spice, pepper, licorice,
cherry and blueberry fruits on the medium-bodied palate is shaped by silky
tannins and perfectly integrated oak. Screwcap. 14.7% alc. **Rating** 98 **To** 2052
$50 ○
Mast Grampians Shiraz 2013 Big version of a Langi red; all its arms and legs
suggest that it has a long way to run. There's power here: fruit-driven and luscious,
with concentrated plum, cloves, freshly sawn cedar and black pepper flavours
careering through the palate to gorgeous effect. The finish is a wave, a series, a
long stretch of tannin with a rumble of fruit and spice flavours crashing through it.
It's as well prepared for the future as you could ever hope a wine to be. Screwcap.
14.6% alc. **Rating** 97 **To** 2040 $50 CM ○

ŸŸŸŸŸ **Langi Grampians Shiraz 2013** Ripe but medium-weight, impeccably well
balanced but with its character fully intact. Nothing is left to chance: it's expressive
of assorted spices, fruits, leathers and woods, but it's simultaneously neat, fresh and
finely stitched. Elegant, even. It doesn't just take a series of right steps; it doesn't
take any wrong or even questionable ones. The length and class of the finish
isn't just unsurprising, then; it feels, as you swallow, inevitable. It will continue to
impress for decades. Screwcap. 14.3% alc. **Rating** 96 **To** 2038 $120 CM
Cliff Edge Grampians Shiraz 2013 Good depth and hue; has that particular
array of spice, pepper and licorice seasoning to the black cherry and blackberry
fruits of Langi, the cleverly worked percentage of whole bunches in the ferment
adding another dimension; there is also a totally delicious envelope of juicy fruit
holding the wine together while lengthening the finish. Screwcap. 14.3% alc.
Rating 95 **To** 2028 $32 ○
Cliff Edge Riesling 2013 Slightly fuller style than usual but no less impressive.
Spice, pear and apple flavours shoot enthusiastically through the palate, though the
real drama is reserved for the finish, where the symbols come out and the flavours
ring loud and clear. Screwcap. 13% alc. **Rating** 94 **To** 2023 $25 CM ○
Cliff Edge Grampians Cabernet Sauvignon 2012 A strongly focused display
of cool-grown cabernet, the fragrant bouquet and powerful palate offering copious
cassis fruit offset by savoury/earthy/black olive notes and typical cabernet tannins.
In a different idiom from the '08 prior release, due to its higher alcohol. Screwcap.
15% alc. **Rating** 94 **To** 2027 $32

ŸŸŸŸ♀ **Cliff Edge Pinot Gris 2012 Rating** 93 **To** 2021 $25 CM ○

Mt Lofty Ranges Vineyard   ★★★★★

Harris Road, Lenswood, SA 5240 **Region** Adelaide Hills
T (08) 8389 8339 **www.**mtloftyrangesvineyard.com.au **Open** Fri–Sun & public hols 11–5
Winemaker Peter Leske, Taras Ochota **Est.** 1992 **Dozens** 3000 **Vyds** 4.6ha
Mt Lofty Ranges is owned and operated by Sharon Pearson and Garry Sweeney. Nestled high in the Lenswood subregion of the Adelaide Hills at an altitude of 500m, the very steep north-facing vineyard (pinot noir, sauvignon blanc, chardonnay and riesling) is hand-pruned and hand-picked. The soil is sandy clay loam with a rock base of white quartz and ironstone, and irrigation is kept to a minimum to allow the wines to display vintage characteristics.

ŶŶŶŶŶ Chardonnay 2013 Lenswood produces Chardonnays with an extra degree of power and intensity, the fruit flavours precisely stationed on the balance between citrus and stone fruit, taking the best from each, providing total fusion between white peach and grapefruit. Screwcap. 13% alc. **Rating** 95 To 2023 $30 ✪
Shiraz 2013 Right in the bullseye of the generously endowed style of Mt Lofty Ranges' red wines; sumptuous red and black cherry fruits have clear-cut spicy/pepper/licorice notes all underlining its cool-climate origins, sensitive winemaking doing the rest. Screwcap. 14% alc. **Rating** 95 To 2033 $30 ✪
Old Pump Shed Pinot Noir 2013 Very good crimson-purple; the very powerful structure is part of the DNA of Mt Lofty Ranges Pinot Noir; it is ultra-focused on its red and black cherry fruits, which are in turn bolstered by tannins and acidity, French oak somewhere close by. Has the breeding – and the need – for 3+ years in the cellar. Screwcap. 13.5% alc. **Rating** 94 To 2025 $30 ✪

ŶŶŶŶŶ Hand Picked Riesling 2014 **Rating** 93 To 2024 $27 ✪
Old Cherry Block Sauvignon Blanc 2014 **Rating** 91 To 2016 $20 ✪

Mount Majura Vineyard   ★★★★★

88 Lime Kiln Road, Majura, ACT 2609 **Region** Canberra District
T (02) 6262 3070 **www.**mountmajura.com.au **Open** Thurs–Mon 10–5
Winemaker Dr Frank van de Loo **Est.** 1988 **Dozens** 4000 **Vyds** 9.3ha
Vines were first planted in 1988 by Dinny Killen on a site on her family property that had been especially recommended by Dr Edgar Riek; its attractions were red soil of volcanic origin over limestone, with reasonably steep east and northeast slopes providing an element of frost protection. The tiny vineyard has been significantly expanded since it was purchased in '99. Blocks of pinot noir and chardonnay have been joined by pinot gris, shiraz, tempranillo, riesling, graciano, mondeuse, cabernet franc and touriga. In addition, there has been an active planting program for the pinot noir, introducing Dijon clones 114, 155 and 777. All the grapes used come from these estate plantings. One of the star performers in the Canberra District.

ŶŶŶŶŶ Canberra District Riesling 2014 Follows closely in the footsteps of the gold medal winning '13. The flowery bouquet leads into a palate of laser-like precision where lime, lemon and grapefruit are wound around a core of electric acidity, leaving the mouth fresh and thirsting for more. A special wine. Screwcap. 12.5% alc. **Rating** 97 To 2025 $27 ✪

ŶŶŶŶŶ Canberra District Pinot Noir 2013 Estate-grown MV6, 115 and 777 clones; 25% whole bunches; 6 days' cold soak, 7 days' wild ferment completed in French barriques (10% new). This is one of the best Pinots from the Canberra District. Savoury/sappy/spicy/whole bunch notes sit easily with red and black cherry fruits. 398 dozen made. Screwcap. 14% alc. **Rating** 95 To 2023 $27 ✪
Canberra District Shiraz 2013 Hand-picked; open-fermented, 25% whole bunches; matured in French barriques (26% new), bottled Jan '14. An intense and complex Shiraz that ticks each and every box; dark forest fruits, spice, pepper and licorice dance in the mouth, supported by savoury tannins. A long and distinguished life ahead. Screwcap. 15% alc. **Rating** 95 To 2043 $32 ✪

TSG Canberra District Tempranillo Shiraz Graciano 2013 A 60/27/13% blend. Has excellent colour; the red and black fruits of the bouquet spill through onto the medium-bodied palate, there joined and supported by fine-grained tannins, cedary oak also in the frame; the overall balance and mouthfeel are exceptional. Screwcap. 14.5% alc. **Rating** 95 **To** 2028 $32 ✪
Canberra District Tempranillo 2013 Hand-picked, 5 days' cold soak, wild yeast-fermented in open vats, then post-ferment maceration, 9 months' maturation in French oak (13% new). Good colour; predominantly black cherry fruit, some savoury tannin substrate; medium-bodied, with particularly good balance and length. Impossible to differentiate the points of four excellent Mount Majura '13 Tempranillos. Screwcap. 14.5% alc. **Rating** 95 **To** 2028 $42
Rock Black 2013 The original ('00) 0.36ha block of tempranillo, with an identical fermentation regime, but no new French oak. The expressive bouquet has a distinct perfume, the flavour spectrum with more spicy/savoury nuances to the core of lively black cherry fruit. Shares the length and balance of the other estate Tempranillos. 49 dozen made. Screwcap. 14.5% alc. **Rating** 95 **To** 2028 $45
Dry Spur 2013 From 0.95ha merlot grafted to tempranillo since '09; matured in French oak (14% new) for 8 months. The palate is distinctly juicy and supple, with red berry/cherry fruit offset by fine, meaty savoury tannins; has very good length and balance. 49 dozen made. Screwcap. 14.5% alc. **Rating** 95 **To** 2028 $45
Little Dam 2013 From a 0.52ha block originally planted to pinot noir, but grafted to tempranillo in '04. Made with the same fermentation regime, and 14% new oak. Here the flavours are more to plum and black cherry with hints of earth; the tannins are slightly rounder and deeper than those of its siblings. 48 dozen made. Screwcap. 14.5% alc. **Rating** 95 **To** 2028 $45
Canberra District Tempranillo 2013 **Rating** 95 **To** 2038 $42

🍷🍷🍷🍷🍷 **Canberra District Touriga 2013** **Rating** 93 **To** 2033 $27 ✪
Canberra District Graciano 2013 **Rating** 92 **To** 2020 $27

Mount Mary ★★★★★

Coldstream West Road, Lilydale, Vic 3140 **Region** Yarra Valley
T (03) 9739 1761 **www**.mountmary.com.au **Open** Not
Winemaker Sam Middleton **Est.** 1971 **Dozens** 4000 **Vyds** 12ha

Superbly refined, elegant and intense Cabernets and usually outstanding and long-lived Pinot Noirs fully justify Mount Mary's exalted reputation. The Triolet blend is very good; more recent vintages of Chardonnay are even better. Founder and long-term winemaker, the late Dr John Middleton, was one of the great, and truly original, figures in the Australian wine industry. He liked nothing more than to tilt at windmills, and would do so with passion. His annual newsletter grew longer as each year passed, although the paper size did not. The only change necessary was a reduction in font size, and ultimately very strong light or a magnifying glass (or both) was needed to fully appreciate the barbed wit and incisive mind of this great character. The determination of the family to continue the business is simply wonderful. Grandson Sam is protecting the Mount Mary legacy, and doing so with open-minded charm, not afraid to consider ways to make great wines even greater. Exports to the UK, the US, Denmark, Hong Kong, Singapore, South Korea and China.

🍷🍷🍷🍷🍷 **Yarra Valley Pinot Noir 2013** Let me put it upfront: corks don't come better than this. This was a great Pinot vintage, and everything about this patrician Pinot reflects this, and a great deal more. The colour is deep and bright, the bouquet with enough different aromas to cause the beagle to sit by the glass and refuse to move on, the palate with more of the same, no single fruit variety dominant, multi-spice waiting its turn, and the texture and structure of Grand Cru status. Get in the queue to buy this, don't worry about the price. 13% alc. **Rating** 98 **To** 2035 $120 ✪
Yarra Valley Chardonnay 2013 Has the power and intensity that positively ancient vines (in Yarra Valley terms) and a sacred site make almost inevitable, the vintage also chipping in. The special quality of Yarra Valley Chardonnay is length, on display here in all its glory, the fruit flavours precisely aligned between citrus

and stone fruit, the oak ex barrel fermentation and maturation now part of the fabric of the wine. Diam. 13.6% alc. **Rating** 97 **To** 2025 $95 **○**

TTTTT Yarra Valley Quintet 2013 Bright, clear colour; the fruit-filled, fragrant bouquet is followed by a classic Mount Mary palate: medium-bodied, and with a certain transparency akin to an orchestra with different instruments, the very essence thereof; near the flute are red fruits, the violin the black fruits, the bassoon tannins – all very different, but all in harmony, the sum of the parts greater than the whole. Cork. 12.9% alc. **Rating** 96 **To** 2035 $130

Yarra Valley Triolet 2013 Vertical tastings suggest this blend (75/13/12% sauvignon blanc, semillon, muscadelle) can outlive the Chardonnay, and that it needs more time to fully come out, as it were. There is a bracing zesty, almost crackling, array of flavours on the long palate, and it certainly invites the second, and the third, glass; the barrel-ferment oak is easily swallowed up by the fruit. Diam. 13% alc. **Rating** 95 **To** 2030 $85

Mount Monument Winery ★★★★☆

1399 Romsey Road, Romsey, Vic 3434 **Region** Macedon Ranges
T (03) 9261 1800 **www**.mountmonumentwines.com **Open** By appt
Winemaker Contract **Est.** 2008 **Dozens** 1000 **Vyds** 2.3ha
Prominent Melbourne architect Nonda Katsalidis acquired the vineyard in 2008, and embarked on major trellis redesign for the existing chardonnay, pinot noir and riesling, while undertaking major terracing works on a new site on the north face of Mt Monument, where 1ha of nebbiolo (with three clones) will be planted.

TTTTT Riesling 2014 Follows in the footsteps of Knight Granite Hills, with mouth-wateringly intense Bickford's (or Rose's) lime juice hitting the palate with the first sip, and continuing in an unbroken stream through to the finish. Delicious today, even more so in 5+ years. Screwcap. 12.5% alc. **Rating** 95 **To** 2029 $30 **○**

TTTTT Pinot Noir 2012 **Rating** 93 **To** 2022 $35
Chardonnay 2012 **Rating** 90 **To** 2017 $30

Mt Moriac Estate | Waurn Ponds Estate ★★★☆

580 Hendy Main Road, Mt Moriac, Vic 3240 **Region** Geelong
T (03) 5266 1116 **www**.kurabana.com **Open** Not
Winemaker Lee Evans **Est.** 1987 **Dozens** 9600 **Vyds** 35.3ha
The development of the quite extensive Kurabana Vineyard, west of Geelong in the foothills of Mt Moriac, began in 1987. Pinot noir (7.8ha) is the largest portion, followed by (in descending order) shiraz, chardonnay, sauvignon blanc, pinot gris and viognier. In 2009 there were a number of major changes: the name of the business was changed, and it purchased the Waurn Ponds Estate label and all current wine from Deakin University. It also leased the Waurn Ponds vineyard from Deakin, lifting the aggregate area to over 35ha. The two brands continue, but have a common headquarters and ownership.

TTTTT Mt Moriac Traditional Method 1 Blanc de Noirs 2006 At this price, this pretty sparkling Pinot Noir from mature estate vines in Geelong should have sold when it was first released 4 years ago; it's an elegantly mature style that retains impressive primary spice and red fruits amid its toasty brioche complexity. Value. Diam. 12.5% alc. **Rating** 91 **To** 2016 $25 TS

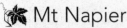 # Mt Napier ★★★★

PO Box 62, Tarrington, Vic 3301 **Region** Henty
T 0447 604 399 **Open** Not
Winemaker Christopher Ward **Est.** 1999 **Dozens** 300 **Vyds** 2ha
Christopher Ward says this is a weekend folly and passion rolled into 2ha of inspiration, exasperation, perspiration and occasionally exhilaration. Starting in 1999, he planted 1.2ha of shiraz with 4 clones, and 0.8ha of pinot noir (10 clones sourced from friends and neighbours,

Tarrington Vineyards) and a tiny quantity of viognier. The very close spacing of the vines was intended to control the predicted excessive vigour, and has worked well. The grapes are hand-picked by family and friends, and vinified in the small winery onsite by Chris. When he and his wife planted the small farm, the intention was to sell the grapes, but – in the same way as many others – purchasers started to evaporate in the early years of the new millennium, so he enrolled in a 2-year part-time viticulture/introductory winemaking course offered by the University of Melbourne at the Dookie campus. Tamara Irish was his winemaking mentor (emphasising quality over quantity) until she moved out of the area,

♀♀♀♀♀ **Tarrington Shiraz Viognier 2013** An elegant Shiraz Viognier from a very cool region, but not so cool that it prevented the grapes from achieving full phenological ripeness; it is a delightful example of the synergy of its blend, with a sheen to the flavours of red and black cherry and plum, the tannins fine, but ripe, the oak integrated. ProCork. 13.5% alc. **Rating** 94 **To** 2023 $25 ●

Mt Pilot Estate ★★★☆

208 Shannons Road, Byawatha, Vic 3678 **Region** North East Victoria Zone
T 0419 243 225 www.mtpilotestatewines.com.au **Open** By appt
Winemaker Marc Scalzo **Est.** 1996 **Dozens** 450 **Vyds** 13ha
Lachlan and Penny Campbell have planted shiraz (6ha), cabernet sauvignon (3ha), durif and viognier (2ha each). The vineyard has been planted on deep, well-drained granitic soils at an altitude of 250m near Eldorado, 20km from Wangaratta and 35km from Beechworth.

♀♀♀♀♀ **Cabernet Sauvignon 2013** Matured for 18 months in oak. The hue is good; the cabernet varietal expression rings true right through the palate; I'm in two minds about the oak, which by rights should have been better integrated by now. That said, the wine has considerable length, and time is on its side. Screwcap. 13.2% alc. **Rating** 90 **To** 2028 $30

Mount Pleasant ★★★★★

Marrowbone Road, Pokolbin, NSW 2320 **Region** Hunter Valley
T (02) 4998 7505 www.mountpleasantwines.com.au **Open** 7 days 10–5
Winemaker Jim Chatto, Scott McWilliam **Est.** 1921 **Dozens** NFP **Vyds** 88.2ha
McWilliam's Elizabeth and the glorious Lovedale Semillon are generally commercially available with four to five years of bottle age; they are treasures with a consistently superb show record. The individual vineyard wines, together with the Maurice O'Shea memorial wines, add to the lustre of this proud name. However, the appointment of Jim Chatto as group chief winemaker in 2013, and the '14 vintage, the best since 1965, has lifted the range and quality of the red wines back to the glory days of Maurice O'Shea in the 1930s and '40s. Henceforth will be known as Mount Pleasant, severing the (name) connection with McWilliam's. Exports to all major markets.

♀♀♀♀♀ **1946 Vines Rosehill Vineyard Hunter Valley Shiraz 2013** Charles King planted the Old Hill, but O'Shea recognised the same red volcanic soil on Rosehill; the impact of this wine is immediate and striking, its medium-bodied palate full of juicy red and black fruits which demand to be swallowed, not ejected. Rosehill wasn't given the care it deserved in prior decades, but better late than never. The 1880 Vines Old Hill is a cerebral wine, Rosehill goes straight to the heart. Screwcap. 13.5% alc. **Rating** 98 **To** 2063 $125 ●
Maurice O'Shea Shiraz 2013 Full, bright crimson-purple. One or two Maurice O'Shea releases since '87 have lacked drive and/or complexity; this is on the far extreme of high quality, pulsating with opulent, yet perfectly balanced and detailed red and black fruits; the silk and satin mouthfeel reflects the fruit on the one hand, a fine web of ripe tannins and grainy acidity on the other. Screwcap. 13.5% alc. **Rating** 98 **To** 2063 $130 ●
Mountain D Full Bodied Dry Red 2011 This Shiraz may be full-bodied, and would likely have been recognised as such by Maurice O'Shea. However, don't think it's full-bodied on a Barossa slide rule. It doesn't come from dense, ripe fruit;

rather it comes from the supple and velvety fruit, and its inbuilt tannins; red fruits, black fruits, spice, earth and cedar are all there. I fell head over heels in love with this wine as I matched it with food over several nights after the initial tasting. Screwcap. 13.5% alc. **Rating** 98 **To** 2051 $75 **○**

1946 Vines Lovedale Vineyard Hunter Valley Semillon 2014 The laser precision of this wine is a revelation; Lovedale is a large vineyard, not all planted in '46, and even the oldest planting has a section (this) that always outperforms the rest. This has a textbook range of every kind of lemon (grass, curd, juice) combined with talcy acidity to provide a palate of extreme length. It is all about 20 years hence, in the manner of a great young red wine – essential to put the price into perspective. Screwcap. 11.5% alc. **Rating** 97 **To** 2044 $75 **○**

1880 Vines Old Hill Vineyard Hunter Valley Shiraz 2013 Full crimson-purple; the immaculate balance of this medium-bodied Shiraz is the wellspring of its present and long-term future; it isn't flashy or oaky, the winemaking team confident that its sheer class will slowly reveal yet another facet as each decade rolls by; the black fruits and earthy Hunter Valley tannins invest the palate with fantastic length. Screwcap. 13.5% alc. **Rating** 97 **To** 2053 $125 **○**

Old Paddock & Old Hill Hunter Valley Shiraz 2013 Excellent hue; as with all the Mount Pleasant '13 Shiraz releases, the bouquet offers something new each time you return to it, this with gently warm earth and roast meat nuances; the palate is also Scarlet Pimpernel-like, at one moment with juicy red fruits, the next with savoury, bramble notes glued to fine tannins. Screwcap. 13.5% alc. **Rating** 97 **To** 2048 $49 **○**

Mountain A Medium Bodied Dry Red 2011 This tries to be a vinous tearjerker recreation of one of O'Shea's most celebrated wines, starting with an original label lookalike (this more à la mode). The bouquet is more pure, the mouth-watering palate more single-minded as it makes its assault on the taste buds. The grainy acidity of the Mount Pleasant releases is quite remarkable, extending the length like a magician's wand. Screwcap. 13.5% alc. **Rating** 97 **To** 2051 $75 **○**

ŶŶŶŶŶ   **Lovedale Single Vineyard Hunter Valley Semillon 2010** Still as fresh as a daisy, its freshness accentuated by a touch of CO_2 spritz deliberately left in the wine; the result is an unusual conjunction of delicacy and intensity, the explanation lying in its purity. It is truly difficult to visualise the end point of a Semillon such as this. Screwcap. 10% alc. **Rating** 96 **To** 2035 $70 **○**

Elizabeth Hunter Valley Semillon 2009 Cellar-aged. The price of this wine was checked twice with Mount Pleasant (aka McWilliam's), and is unbelievable. It is as fresh as a daisy; the colour is still pale, perhaps a touch greener than the '14 Elizabeth, the bouquet now speaking of variety and place, and the lemon/lemongrass flavours of the palate insistent and persistent, not heavy. Screwcap. 10.5% alc. **Rating** 96 **To** 2029 $19 **○**

Rosehill Vineyard Hunter Valley Shiraz 2013 Bright, clear crimson; gloriously fragrant, and a perfect example of the path that Hunter Valley Shiraz is pursuing with a single-minded obsession: flavour born of alcohol in the plus or minus 13% range that has freshness and effortless balance as its core belief, bringing with it a razor-sharp sense of place different from any other region in Australia. Screwcap. 13% alc. **Rating** 96 **To** 2043 $40 **○**

Eight Acres Semillon 2014 A particularly fine Semillon that has its parallels with Porongurup Riesling: both are deceptively light when young, and grow slowly, but with absolute certainty over 10–20 years. This wine starts with more mid-palate fruit than the bouquet suggests, the length and balance impeccable. Screwcap. 11.5% alc. **Rating** 95 **To** 2029 $27 **○**

Leontine Hunter Valley Chardonnay 2013 It was inevitable that Mount Pleasant would also raise the bar with its Chardonnay. It is as fresh as a cloudless spring day, slippery/catchy acidity probing and catching all corners of the mouth. One thing missing in action is overt oak, the one thing driving the wine is its acidity intermingled with white peach and apple fruit. Screwcap. 13% alc. **Rating** 95 **To** 2025 $35 **○**

B-Side CF14 Shiraz Montils 2014 Light, bright crimson-scarlet; the bouquet is highly fragrant, the palate a ravishingly juicy array of red fruits, tannins and oak barely making a mark; it is only light to medium-bodied, but don't be fooled: this will coast through many decades. Screwcap. 13% alc. **Rating** 95 **To** 2040 $40
Elizabeth Hunter Valley Semillon 2014 Rating 94 **To** 2025 $19 ✪

Mount Stapylton Wines ★★★★

14 Cleeve Court, Toorak, Vic 3142 (postal) **Region** Grampians
T 0425 713 044 **www**.mts-wines.com **Open** Not
Winemaker Don McRae, Caroline Mooney **Est.** 2002 **Dozens** 600 **Vyds** 2.2ha
Mount Stapylton Vineyard is planted on the historic Goonwinnow Homestead farming property at Laharum, on the northwest side of the Grampians in front of Mt Stapylton. In 2010 founders Howard and Samantha Staehr sold the homestead property, but leased back the vineyard. The Little Yarra Station Vineyard (1.2ha planted in '09) in the Yarra Valley provides the grapes for the Pamela Chardonnay and the Victoria Pinot Noir. The wines are listed with several iconic restaurants in Sydney and Melbourne.

🍷🍷🍷🍷🍷 **Jeffery Grampians Shiraz 2013** Matured in French and American oak. Deep, dense purple-crimson, its bouquet a thunderclap of black clouds, its palate the ensuing bolt of lightning. Tasting immediately after a 13% Hunter Valley Shiraz, at the opposite end of the Australian Shiraz style spectrum didn't help the cause of this wine, the alcohol chopping off the finish from the rest of the wine. Screwcap. 15% alc. **Rating** 90 **To** 2028 $65

Mount Terrible ★★★★★

289 Licola Road, Jamieson, Vic 3723 **Region** Central Victoria Zone
T (03) 5777 0703 **www**.mountterriblewines.com.au **Open** By appt
Winemaker John Eason **Est.** 2001 **Dozens** 350 **Vyds** 2ha
John Eason and wife Janene Ridley began the long, slow (and at times very painful) business of establishing their vineyard just north of Mt Terrible in 1992 – hence the choice of name. In 2001 they planted 2ha of pinot noir (MV6, 115, 114 and 777 clones) on a gently sloping, north-facing river terrace adjacent to the Jamieson River. DIY trials persuaded John to have the first commercial vintage in '06 contract-made, but he has since made the wines himself in a fireproof winery built on top of an underground wine cellar. John has a sense of humour second to none, but must wonder what he has done to provoke the weather gods, alternating fire, storm and tempest. The '12 and '13 vintages will be released in 2016. Exports to the UK.

🍷🍷🍷🍷🍷 **Jamieson Pinot Noir 2010** From clones 114, 115, 777 and MV6, cold-soaked (with 20% whole bunches) for 5 days before open fermentation, then 18 months in French oak. The colour is still youthful and bright, with no hint of bricking; the bouquet is building spicy perfume along with the still-primary fruit, the palate supple and fine, a hint of forest on the aftertaste adding to the palate. Still has years of life. Screwcap. 14% alc. **Rating** 95 **To** 2020 $42

🍷🍷🍷🍷🍷 **Jamieson Pinot Noir 2011 Rating** 90 **To** 2016 $21 ✪

Mount Towrong ★★★☆

10 Taylors Road, Mount Macedon, Vic 3441 **Region** Macedon Ranges
T 0419 542 630 **www**.mounttowrong.com.au **Open** W'ends & public hols 10–5
Winemaker Laura Sparrow **Est.** 1996 **Dozens** 500 **Vyds** 2ha
When George and Deirdre Cremasco commenced the establishment of their vineyard (chardonnay, nebbiolo and prosecco), they did so with the help of George's father and grandfather. Strongly influenced by their Italian heritage, the vineyard has been terraced, with Chardonnay the first wine produced, and some commendable Nebbiolo and Prosecco following in its footsteps.

ŦŦŦŦ   **Nebbiolo Rosa 2014** Clear, vivid crimson; cleverly made for those who
enjoy an off-dry style; poached cherries and spices are balanced by leafy acidity.
Screwcap. 11.5% alc. **Rating** 89 **To** 2015 $22
Vivace 2013 A hefty dose of 20% nebbiolo adds a full salmon hue and candied
strawberry flavours to 600m altitude Macedon Ranges chardonnay. It's young,
vivacious, extroverted and a little sweet on the finish. Disgorged Oct '14. Cork.
12% alc. **Rating** 88 **To** 2015 $25 TS

Mount Trio Vineyard   ★★★★☆

2534 Porongurup Road, Mount Barker WA 6324 **Region** Porongurup
T (08) 9853 1136 **www**.mounttriowines.com.au **Open** By appt
Winemaker Gavin Berry, Andrew Vesey, Caitlin Gazey **Est.** 1989 **Dozens** 3000 **Vyds** 8.8ha
Mount Trio was established by Gavin Berry and wife Gill Graham (plus partners) shortly after
they moved to the Mount Barker area in late 1988, Gavin to take up the position of chief
winemaker at Plantagenet, which he held until 2004, when he and partners acquired the now
very successful and much larger West Cape Howe. They have slowly built up the business,
increasing estate plantings with riesling (2.7ha), shiraz (2.4ha), sauvignon blanc (2ha) and pinot
noir (1.7ha). Exports to the UK, the US, Denmark and China.

ŦŦŦŦŦ   **Porongurup Shiraz 2013** Has the grace and elegance that the cool Porongurup
climate seems to bestow on all the varieties grown there – and that's all those
that matter (other than semillon). No more than medium-bodied, the wine has
intensity and length to its flavours of black fruit, black olive, multi-spice and oak;
its tannins are fine, closing the loop of a fine wine at a bargain price. Screwcap.
14.5% alc. **Rating** 95 **To** 2028 $21 ✪
Porongurup Riesling 2014 Right in the centre of Porongurup Riesling style,
almost painfully shy in its swaddling clothes, and a long way short of showing
its true nature, except, that is, for the precisely etched acidity that will provide
the foundation for its maturity 5–10 years down the track. Screwcap. 11.5% alc.
Rating 94 **To** 2029 $21 ✪

ŦŦŦŦŦ   **Porongurup Pinot Noir 2013** **Rating** 93 **To** 2020 $21 ✪
Great Southern Cabernet Merlot 2013 **Rating** 93 **To** 2021 $18 CM ✪

Mount View Estate   ★★★★★

Mount View Road, Mount View, NSW 2325 **Region** Hunter Valley
T (02) 4990 3307 **www**.mtviewestate.com.au **Open** Mon–Sat 10–5, Sun 10–4
Winemaker Scott Stephens **Est.** 1971 **Dozens** 3000 **Vyds** 16ha
Mount View Estate's vineyard was planted by the very knowledgeable Harry Tulloch almost
45 years ago; he recognised the quality of the red basalt volcanic soils of the very attractive
hillside vineyard. Owners John and Polly Burgess purchased the adjoining Limestone
Creek Vineyard in 2004 (planted in 1982), which fits seamlessly into Mount View Estate's
production. The quality of the wines is outstanding.

ŦŦŦŦŦ   **Reserve Hunter Valley Semillon 2014** Tasting next to '14 Rieslings simply
confirms the way modern Semillons have crept closer to Riesling in the last
decade or so. That said, the mix of lemongrass, wet stone and lime zest speaks of a
variety uniquely suited to the Hunter Valley. Five years will bring this towards its
ultimate destiny. Screwcap. 11.5% alc. **Rating** 95 **To** 2025 $35 ✪
Reserve Hunter Valley Shiraz 2013 Hunts in the same pack as Flagship,
bringing the same display of fruit, oak and tannin welded together in a potent, but
totally harmonious display of the synergy between the savoury/earthy underfelt
and the plum and blackberry fruits. Screwcap. 13.5% alc. **Rating** 95 **To** 2040 $40
Flagship Hunter Valley Shiraz 2013 A classic Hunter Valley Shiraz made for
the long haul; it is a barrel selection of the most intense fruit (and high-quality
oak) with the regional mix of spice, earth and polished leather as a substrate of the
savoury black fruits, optimal ripeness at a near-perfect level of alcohol. Deserves a
minimum of 10 years. Screwcap. 13.5% alc. **Rating** 95 **To** 2043 $55

Reserve Hunter Valley Chardonnay 2014 Hand-picked, crushed and destemmed, 20% straight to press, thence to barrel for wild yeast fermentation on full solids, 80% clear juice to tank and cultured yeast for initiation of fermentation, then to French oak for 6 months (20% new). Pretty close to a maximum result: to very complex, yet retaining grapefruit zest freshness and good length. Screwcap. 13% alc. **Rating** 94 **To** 2022 $35

ŸŸŸŸ **Hunter Valley Verdelho 2014 Rating** 89 **To** 2015 $20

Mountadam   ★★★★☆

High Eden Road, Eden Valley, SA 5235 **Region** Eden Valley
T (08) 8564 1900 **www**.mountadam.com.au **Open** By appt
Winemaker Natasha Mooney **Est.** 1972 **Dozens** 35 000 **Vyds** 80ha
Founded by the late David Wynn for the benefit of winemaker son Adam, Mountadam was (somewhat surprisingly) purchased by Cape Mentelle (doubtless under the direction of Möet Hennessy Wine Estates) in 2000. Rather less surprising was its sale in '05 to Adelaide businessman David Brown, who has extensive interests in the Padthaway region. Con Moshos (long-serving senior winemaker at Petaluma) made a significant impact in lifting the quality of the wines before returning to Brian Croser's Tapanappa Winery in the Adelaide Hills. Exports to the UK, France, Switzerland, Poland and Hong Kong.

ŸŸŸŸŸ **High Eden Estate Chardonnay 2013** Four selected clones, hand-picked, barrel-fermented in French barriques (45% new), and with encouragement ex stirring, went through full mlf. I would never have picked that, for the wine is as fresh as a new button, with great focus and length to its stone fruit, apple and grapefruit flavours. Screwcap. 13.5% alc. **Rating** 95 **To** 2023 $35 ✪
High Eden The Red 2012 A 52/48% blend of merlot and cabernet that spent 18 months in new French barriques. It is pleasant surprise that the oak doesn't dominate; it simply frames the fruit. This is a thoroughly enjoyable medium-bodied blend that will give pleasure whenever you tackle it. Screwcap. 14.5% alc. **Rating** 94 **To** 2032 $35

ŸŸŸŸŸ **Eden Valley Riesling 2014 Rating** 92 **To** 2024 $25 ✪
Patriarch High Eden Shiraz 2012 Rating 92 **To** 2022 $35
Eden Valley Pinot Gris 2014 Rating 90 **To** 2016 $25

Mr Mick   ★★★☆

7 Dominic Street, Clare, SA 5453 **Region** Clare Valley
T (08) 8842 2555 **www**.mrmick.com.au **Open** 7 days 10–5
Winemaker Tim Adams, Brett Schutz **Est.** 2011 **Dozens** 25 000
This is the venture of Tim Adams and wife Pam Goldsack, the name chosen to honour KH (Mick) Knappstein, a legend in the Clare Valley and the broader Australian wine community. Tim worked at Leasingham Wines with Mick between 1975 and '86, and knew him well. When Tim and Pam acquired the Leasingham winery in January 2011, together with its historic buildings, it brought the wheel full circle. Various commentators (including myself) have used Mick's great one-liner, 'There are only two types of people in the world: those who were born in Clare, and those who wish they had been.' Exports to China and NZ.

ŸŸŸŸ **Clare Valley Vermentino 2014** An immediately attractive juicy mix of lemon/ lime, apple and pink grapefruit; the finish half-suggests subliminal residual sugar. Could surprise with a year or two in bottle. Screwcap. 12% alc. **Rating** 89 **To** 2015 $17 ✪
Clare Valley Shiraz 2012 As befits Mr Mick, an honest wine that is fully reflective of the Clare Valley, its dark fruits basically left to speak for themselves, which they do well. Screwcap. 14% alc. **Rating** 88 **To** 2020 $17 ✪

Mr Riggs Wine Company ★★★★★

281 Main Road, McLaren Vale, SA 5171 **Region** McLaren Vale
T (08) 8383 2050 **www**.mrriggs.com.au **Open** 7 days 9–5
Winemaker Ben Riggs **Est.** 2001 **Dozens** 20000 **Vyds** 7.5ha
After a quarter of a century of winemaking experience, Ben Riggs is well established under his own banner. Ben sources the best fruit from individual vineyards in McLaren Vale, Clare Valley, Adelaide Hills, Langhorne Creek, Coonawarra, and from his own Piebald Gully Vineyard (shiraz and viognier). Each wine is intended to express the essence of not only the vineyard, but also the region's terroir. The vision of the Mr Riggs brand is unpretentious and personal: 'to make the wines I love to drink'. He drinks very well. Exports to the US, Canada, Denmark, Sweden, Germany, The Netherlands, Switzerland, China, Hong Kong, Singapore, Japan and NZ.

ΨΨΨΨΨ **Scarce Earth McLaren Vale Shiraz 2012** Good colour; a particularly well balanced and constructed Shiraz; the bouquet is full of character, the medium-bodied palate a seamless follow-on, with fruit, oak and tannins all singing harmoniously from the same page. Skilled winemaking. Diam. 14.5% alc. **Rating** 96 **To** 2032 $50 ✪
McLaren Vale Shiraz 2012 Spent 18 months in French and American oak. Opaque purple-crimson. The flavours are spread in layers across the densely packed, full-bodied palate, but are not hot or jammy; instead there is a display of savoury black fruits, licorice, earth and the regional anchor of dark chocolate, the tannins ripe and balanced. Diam. 14.5% alc. **Rating** 96 **To** 2032 $50 ✪
The Magnet McLaren Vale Grenache 2013 Beefy and substantial in a varietal context, though it's mostly packed with redcurrant and assorted red-berried fruit. The point is it has a rich ripeness to it. It also comes packed with dried spices and sandy tannin, and manages to simultaneously create a serious impression and be perfumed and frivolous. Screwcap. 14.5% alc. **Rating** 94 **To** 2021 $27 CM ✪
Yacca Paddock Adelaide Hills Tempranillo 2013 Silky smooth with just enough attitude to set it apart. Flavours are in the cherry-plum and cola realm, though notes of peppercorn and chocolate, as modest as they are, are important aspects of the wine's personality. Ultra fine-grained tannin, edges of mineral and finesse through the finish are all quality markers. Medium-weight but it has presence. Screwcap. 14.5% alc. **Rating** 94 **To** 2023 $27 CM ✪
Montepulciano d'Adelaide Hills 2013 The day savouriness walked into town was the day this wine said hallelujah. It's lively, perfumed and well fruited, but it has savoury spiciness oozing from its pores. White pepper, cured meats and firm, crushed clove notes adorn licorice, black cherry and assorted florals. It sounds delicious because it is. Screwcap. 14% alc. **Rating** 94 **To** 2024 $27 CM ✪

ΨΨΨΨΨ **Cold Chalk Adelaide Hills Chardonnay 2013** Rating 93 To 2020 $27 ✪
The Truant McLaren Vale Shiraz 2013 Rating 93 To 2023 $17 ✪
Outpost Coonawarra Cabernet 2013 Rating 93 To 2023 $24 CM ✪
Castro's Ligador Cabernet Malbec 2012 Rating 93 To 2022 $20 ✪
Castro's Ligador Shiraz Mataro 2012 Rating 91 To 2019 $20 ✪
Three Corner Jack McLaren Vale Shiraz Cabernet Merlot 2013 Rating 90 To 2019 $17 CM ✪

Mudgee Wines ★★★★

Henry Lawson Drive, Mudgee, NSW 2850 **Region** Mudgee
T (02) 6372 2244 **www**.mudgeewines.com.au **Open** 7 days 10–5
Winemaker Simon McMillan **Est.** 1963 **Dozens** 8000 **Vyds** 18ha
Things are very different at Mudgee Wines these days under the ownership of Bill Whalley and Jane McLean. The focus of the vineyard (and hence the wines) is on cabernet sauvignon, shiraz, durif, negro amaro and primitivo (including 1ha each of old bush-vine shiraz and cabernet sauvignon), the white wines Pinot Grigio, Verdelho and Chardonnay. Exports to Sweden, Finland, Hong Kong and China.

🍷🍷🍷🍷🍷 Linden Reserve Chardonnay 2013 This is a very well made wine by any standards; French oak has been put to best use, providing the stage for perfectly ripened chardonnay fruit to display its white stone fruit and melon flavours, acidity equally adroitly managed. Screwcap. 13% alc. **Rating** 94 **To** 2021 $25 ○

🍷🍷🍷🍷🍷 Cabernet VP 2011 Rating 92 To 2025 $20 ○
Pinot Grigio 2014 Rating 90 To 2016 $20 ○
Pinot Grigio 2013 Rating 90 To 2015 $25
Verdelho 2013 Rating 90 To 2018 $20 ○
Ruby NV Rating 90 To 2016 $20 ○

Munari Wines   ★★★★★

Ladys Creek Vineyard, 1129 Northern Highway, Heathcote, Vic 3523 **Region** Heathcote
T (03) 5433 3366 **www**.munariwines.com **Open** Tues–Sun 11–5
Winemaker Adrian Munari **Est.** 1993 **Dozens** 3000 **Vyds** 6.9ha
Established on one of the original Heathcote farming properties, Ladys Creek Vineyard is situated on the narrow Cambrian strip 11km north of the town. Adrian Munari has harnessed traditional winemaking practices with New World innovation to produce complex, fruit-driven wines that marry concentration and elegance. They are produced from estate plantings of shiraz, cabernet sauvignon, merlot, cabernet franc and malbec. The drought, followed by 2011 rain, has impacted greatly, but '12 saw a dramatic reversion to form. Exports to France, Denmark, Taiwan and China.

🍷🍷🍷🍷🍷 Black Lady Shiraz 2012 A blend of Munari's Lady Pass Heathcote Shiraz and Glen Eldon's Twisted Trunk Reserve Barossa Shiraz. Deep crimson-purple; this has complexity written all over it in big black letters, yet with a juicy, open-weave mouthfeel, the fruits purple and black, the medium-bodied palate with exceptional balance and length. The best of this unique blend so far made. Cork. 14.5% alc. **Rating** 97 **To** 2037 $110 ○

🍷🍷🍷🍷🍷 Ladys Pass Heathcote Shiraz 2012 Deep crimson-purple; spicy/peppery black fruit aromas accurately predict the textured medium to full-bodied palate; blackberry, anise and tar flavours are guarded by acidity, the tannins seamlessly woven through the finish. Screwcap. 14% alc. **Rating** 95 **To** 2032 $35 ○

🍷🍷🍷🍷🍷 The Beauregard Heathcote Shiraz 2012 Rating 93 To 2028 $25 ○
India Red Heathcote Cabernet Sauvignon 2012 Rating 93 To 2032 $30

Murdoch Hill   ★★★★★

260 Mappinga Road, Woodside, SA 5244 **Region** Adelaide Hills
T (08) 8389 7081 **www**.murdochhill.com.au **Open** By appt
Winemaker Michael Downer **Est.** 1998 **Dozens** 4000 **Vyds** 20.48ha
A little over 20ha of vines have been established on the undulating, gum-studded countryside of Charlie and Julie Downer's 60-year-old Erika property, 4km east of Oakbank. In descending order of importance, the varieties planted are sauvignon blanc, shiraz, cabernet sauvignon and chardonnay. Son Michael, with a Bachelor of Oenology degree from Adelaide University, is winemaker. Exports to the UK and China.

🍷🍷🍷🍷🍷 The Tilbury Single Vineyard Piccadilly Valley Adelaide Hills Chardonnay 2014 It prompts the word 'swoonworthy'. It combines deliciousness with beauty; it's sophisticated but not too clever for itself. It's beautifully pure in terms of fruit, carries creamy/almond-like oak lightly on its back, and rushes with fresh, succulent citrus and stone fruit out through the finish. Texture, class, zip and flavour; it does it all. Diam. 12.5% alc. **Rating** 96 **To** 2020 $40 CM ○
The Landau Single Vineyard Oakbank Adelaide Hills Syrah 2014
Crackerjack wine. Bursting with complex quality but moreish from the first sip to the last. Meat, violets, anise, sweet black cherry and cracks of pepper and assorted woody spice. It's fresh and lively but has volume aplenty. Indeed it fills the mouth,

reaching to all corners, leaving no stone unturned. Diam. 13% alc. **Rating** 96 To 2034 $46 CM ○

The Cronberry Adelaide Hills Shiraz 2013 Perfumed, peppery and nigh-on perfect expression of cool-climate shiraz. Bright serve of red and black berries, infusions of deli meats and both white and black pepper. Lacing of ultra-fine tannin. Inclusion of 25% whole bunches has proven entirely positive. Screwcap. 13.5% alc. **Rating** 96 To 2024 $28 CM ○

Adelaide Hills Chardonnay 2014 Flinty, stylish, flavoursome; you name it, this has it going on. Straw-coloured, with white peach, fennel and spicy oak flavours teaming to perfection. Full of life and flavour but dry and controlled to close. Screwcap. 12.5% alc. **Rating** 95 To 2019 $28 CM ○

The Phaeton Single Vineyard Piccadilly Valley Adelaide Hills Pinot Noir 2014 Pours on the charm. Not particularly deep in colour, but it produces a volume of flavour and scent. Spice box, swish cherries, a foresty element and woody spice. It's like a nature walk, complete with garden herbs and succulent berries aplenty. Satiny texture and firmish tannin the icing on a most delicious cake. Diam. 13% alc. **Rating** 95 To 2022 $46 CM

Adelaide Hills Pinot Noir 2014 20% whole bunches. Complex Pinot Noir with stem and spice notes roaring through fresh cherries and strawberries. Dry tannin seems at home in this environment. Attractive young but should mature well over the medium term. Screwcap. 13% alc. **Rating** 94 To 2021 $28 CM ○

♟♟♟♟♙ **Adelaide Hills Sauvignon Blanc 2014 Rating** 93 To 2015 $22 CM ○
The Surrey Single Vineyard Piccadilly Valley Adelaide Hills Pinot Meunier 2014 Rating 93 To 2020 $40 CM
Adelaide Hills Cabernet Sauvignon 2013 Rating 93 To 2024 $25 CM ○

Murray Street Vineyards ★★★★★

Murray Street, Greenock, SA 5360 **Region** Barossa Valley
T (08) 8562 8373 **www.**murraystreet.com.au **Open** 7 days 10–6
Winemaker Craig Viney **Est.** 2001 **Dozens** 20 000 **Vyds** 50ha
Andrew Seppelt and partner Bill Jahnke (the latter a successful investment banker) established Murray Street Vineyard in 2001. It very quickly established itself as a producer of exceptionally good wines. In '14, with the knowledge and consent of Bill Jahnke, Andrew began to establish a separate business, and in '15 Bill Jahnke assumed total ownership, appointing Craig Viney (who had worked alongside Andrew Seppelt for the previous eight years) as winemaker. Jahnke intends to upscale the production capability and distribution network. In future, the two brands of Murray Street and MSV will carry the flag.

♟♟♟♟♟ **Sophia 2012** Deep crimson-purple; a very richly endowed Shiraz with multiple layers of gently accented spicy licorice/black tea overtones to the well of blackberry fruits; beautifully balanced, and no more than medium to full-bodied. Moves with lightness and grace. Screwcap. 14% alc. **Rating** 97 To 2052 $75 ○

♟♟♟♟♟ **Gomersal 2012** Like all the Murray Street Vineyard '12 Shirazs, has excellent colour; sultry black fruits, licorice and spice on the bouquet and palate; despite the alcohol, the full-bodied wine steps lightly, leaving the mouth free for the next sip. Screwcap. 15% alc. **Rating** 96 To 2037 $55 ○

Greenock 2012 A complex, luscious and rich Shiraz, the bouquet with some oak influence, but not over the top; the palate is rich, velvety and complete. A great portrait of place in the context of an outstanding vintage. Screwcap. 14.7% alc. **Rating** 96 To 2047 $44 ○

Red Label Shiraz 2012 A complex bouquet with dark fruits and a background whisper of cold tea, along with an unexpected touch of cherry on the finish of the palate; the tannin extract has been expertly handled. Screwcap. 14.8% alc. **Rating** 95 To 2032 $35 ○

Benno 2012 A blend of shiraz and mataro. The colour is slightly lighter than its Shiraz siblings, providing a subtle indication of the different vectors in play, with hints of dark chocolate to the black fruits, and a slightly less compact structure.

All of this is achieved without the high alcohol threatening to blow up the finish.
Screwcap. 15.7% alc. Rating 95 To 2037 $75

White Label Barossa Shiraz 2012 Rating 94 To 2027 $25 ✪

♟♟♟♟♟ **Black Label Barossa Shiraz 2012** Rating 92 To 2022 $25 ✪
Black Label Barossa Semillon 2014 Rating 91 To 2024 $20 ✪
Black Label Barossa Grenache 2012 Rating 90 To 2016 $25

Murrindindi Vineyards

30 Cummins Lane, Murrindindi, Vic 3717 **Region** Upper Goulburn
T 0438 305 314 **www**.murrindindivineyards.com **Open** Not
Winemaker Hugh Cuthbertson **Est.** 1979 **Dozens** 6000 **Vyds** 16ha
This small winery is owned and run by Hugh Cuthbertson, established by parents Alan and
Jan (now retired) as a minor diversification from their cattle property. Hugh, himself with a
long and high-profile wine career, has overseen the marketing of the wines, including the
Family Reserve and Don't Tell Dad brands. Exports to the UK, the US, Finland and China.

♟♟♟♟♟ **Mr Hugh Coonawarra Cabernet Sauvignon 2013** Made from 'old vines',
though exactly or roughly how old is not explained. It's a taut, licoricey expression
of Coonawarra cabernet, strung tight with tannin, bold with blackcurrant and
lifted considerably by mint/eucalypt notes. It's medium-bodied but at the upper
end of the spectrum. Well cellared, a long life is guaranteed. Screwcap. 14.5% alc.
Rating 95 To 2035 $60 CM

♟♟♟♟♟ **Family Reserve Shiraz 2013** Rating 93 To 2024 $35 CM
Family Reserve Cabernet Sauvignon 2013 Rating 90 To 2028 $35 CM

Murrumbateman Winery ★★★☆

Cnr Barton Highway/McIntosh Circuit, Murrumbateman, NSW 2582
Region Canberra District
T (02) 6227 5584 **www**.murrumbateman-winery.com.au **Open** Fri–Sun 10–5
Winemaker Bobbie Makin **Est.** 1972 **Dozens** 1000 **Vyds** 4ha
Murrumbateman Winery draws upon 4ha of estate-grown sauvignon blanc and shiraz. It also
incorporates an à la carte restaurant and function room, together with picnic and barbecue areas.

♟♟♟♟♟ **Chardonnay 2014** Light straw-green; an attractive, fresh Chardonnay with
creative tension on the palate between white peach, citrus and pear, backed by
crisp acidity. Screwcap. 12.2% alc. Rating 90 To 2019 $25

♟♟♟♟ **Cabernet Sauvignon 2013** Rating 89 To 2028 $30
Shiraz 2013 Rating 88 To 2023 $30

MyattsField Vineyards ★★★★

Union Road, Carmel Valley, WA 6076 **Region** Perth Hills
T (08) 9293 5567 **www**.myattsfield.com.au **Open** Fri–Sun and public hols 11–5
Winemaker Josh and Rachael Davenport, Josh Uren **Est.** 2006 **Dozens** NA
MyattsField Vineyards is owned by Josh and Rachael Davenport, both with extensive
winemaking experience. Both have oenology degrees, and both have domestic and Flying
Winemaker experience, especially Rachael. In '06 they decided they would prefer to work for
themselves. They left their employment, building a winery in time for the '07 vintage. Their
vineyards include cabernet sauvignon, merlot, petit verdot, shiraz and chardonnay, and they
also take small parcels of grapes from regions as far away as Manjimup.

♟♟♟♟♟ **Shiraz Mourvedre Viognier 2013** The three varieties were co-fermented, not
easy to achieve with different ripening patterns. The authority of the black fruits
of the shiraz is not challenged, but the other two varieties add a dimension of red
fruit freshness to what is a very enjoyable and complete wine. Screwcap. 12.9% alc.
Rating 94 To 2025 $24 ✪

Joseph Myatt Reserve 2013 A 60/28/12% blend of cabernet, petit verdot and shiraz matured for 12 months in new American and French hogsheads. Given its warm region, this is a very creditable blend, with lively red and black juicy flavours supported by fine tannins and not unduly threatened by the oak, particularly given that it will recede over time. Screwcap. 15% alc. **Rating** 94 **To** 2033 $35

♀♀♀♀♀ **Dudley Durif 2013 Rating** 91 To 2020 $28

Myrtaceae   ★★★☆

53 Main Creek Road, Main Ridge, Vic 3928 **Region** Mornington Peninsula
T (03) 5989 2045 **www**.myrtaceae.com.au **Open** W'ends & public hols 12–5
Winemaker Julie Trueman **Est.** 1985 **Dozens** 300 **Vyds** 1ha
Owners John Trueman (viticulturist) and wife Julie (winemaker) began the planting of Myrtaceae in 1985, intending to make a Bordeaux-style red blend. It became evident that these late-ripening varieties were not well suited to the site, so the vineyard was converted to chardonnay (0.6ha) and pinot noir (0.4ha) in '98. Part of the property is devoted to the Land for Wildlife Scheme; the integrated Australian garden is a particular feature.

♀♀♀♀♀ **Mornington Peninsula Pinot Noir 2012** Ticks the boxes for colour, varietal expression, balance and length; still very youthful, and still needing the secondary foresty/spicy notes to ruffle the calm surface of the wine. Worth giving it more time. Screwcap. 13.5% alc. **Rating** 92 **To** 2022 $40

Naked Run Wines   ★★★★

36 Parawae Road, Salisbury Plain, SA 5109 (postal) **Region** Clare Valley/Barossa Valley
T 0408 807 655 **www**.nakedrunwines.com.au **Open** Not
Winemaker Steven Baraglia **Est.** 2005 **Dozens** 1200
Naked Run is the virtual winery of Jayme Wood, Bradley Currie and Steven Baraglia, their skills ranging from viticulture through to production, and also all-important sales and marketing (and not to be confused with Naked Wines). The riesling is sourced from Clare Valley, grenache from the Williamstown area of the Barossa Valley, and shiraz from Greenock. The price/quality ratio is utterly exceptional.

♀♀♀♀♀ **The First Clare Valley Riesling 2014** From a single high (475m) vineyard in the Sevenhill district. It is very fresh, with an attractive, chalky grip to the palate that bodes well for the future, balance and length not an issue; the citrus and green apple flavours are there, just waiting to do their thing. Screwcap. 12% alc. **Rating** 94 **To** 2029 $20
BWC Barossa Valley Shiraz 2013 From vineyards in Gomersal and Greenock; crushed, open-fermented, some wild ferment, 12 days on skins, matured in new and used French and American barriques for 20 months. Richly endowed with scrumptious red and black fruits wrapped within a coat of dark chocolate and ripe tannins. Like Street's Magnum ice cream, to be wolfed down. Screwcap. 14.5% alc. **Rating** 94 **To** 2028 $25 ⊙

♀♀♀♀♀ **The Aldo Old Vine Grenache Shiraz 2013 Rating** 93 To 2025 $20 ⊙
Hill 5 Clare Valley Shiraz Cabernet 2013 Rating 92 To 2028 $22 ⊙

Nannup Ridge Estate   ★★★★★

PO Box 2, Nannup, WA 6275 **Region** Blackwood Valley
T (08) 9756 2005 **www**.nannupridge.com.au **Open** Not
Winemaker Naturaliste Vintners (Bruce Dukes), Andries Mostert **Est.** 1998
Dozens 3500 **Vyds** 31ha
The business is owned by the Blizard and Fitzgerald families, who purchased the then unplanted property from the family that had farmed it since the early 1900s. Mark and Alison Blizard had in fact moved to the region in the early '90s and established a small vineyard on the banks of the beautiful Donnelly River. The partners established 31ha of mainstream varieties (and 1ha of tempranillo) backed by a (then) grape sale agreement with Constellation.

They still regard themselves as grapegrowers, but have successful wines skilfully contract-made from the estate production. Terrific value is par for the course. Exports to China.

🍷🍷🍷🍷 **Merlot 2013** Shows many others how it's done. Rich blackberry, choc-coffee and gravelly herb flavours. Minor bitterness, but not to a distracting extent. Substantial in all ways, yet balanced. Screwcap. 14.1% alc. **Rating** 93 **To** 2023 $30 CM
Cabernet Sauvignon 2013 Pure varietal character. Blackcurrant and dark olive with assorted leaves, mints and spices. Works up a head of steam through the front half, the power of pure fruit, then turns on a charm offensive through the back-palate. Needs a few years to soften but all is pointing in the right direction. Screwcap. 14.2% alc. **Rating** 93 **To** 2021 $30 CM
Firetower Sauvignon Blanc 2014 Bursting with fruit. Pulpy passionfruit and lemongrass. Loads it up and then lets you have it. Will please and impress a great many folk. Screwcap. 13.1% alc. **Rating** 92 **To** 2015 $21 CM ✪
Cabernet Merlot 2013 The charge of the blackberry brigade. Open the cap and it comes straight at you. There are dried herb notes, refreshing acidity and grainy tannin aspects here too, but the fruit takes all the focus. Screwcap. 14.2% alc. **Rating** 92 **To** 2024 $25 CM ✪
Senor Tempranillo 2013 Hearty. Hefty. Builds significant momentum via the delivery of blackberry, toast, dark chocolate and black earth flavour. Guts personified. Tannin has a rugged edge, but it's overlaid with velvet. Screwcap. 13.9% alc. **Rating** 92 **To** 2021 $25 CM ✪
Shiraz 2013 Creamy vanillan oak introduces a bold Shiraz, flush with blackberry, black earth and dry licorice flavours. Builds good momentum through the palate. Smooth throughout. Screwcap. 14.1% alc. **Rating** 91 **To** 2021 $30 CM

Narkoojee   ★★★★★

170 Francis Road, Glengarry, Vic 3854 **Region** Gippsland
T (03) 5192 4257 **www**.narkoojee.com **Open** 7 days 10.30–4.30
Winemaker Harry and Axel Friend **Est.** 1981 **Dozens** 6000 **Vyds** 10.3ha
Narkoojee Vineyard (originally a dairy farm owned by the Friend family) is near the old gold-mining town of Walhalla and looks out over the Strzelecki Ranges. The wines are produced from a little over 10ha of estate vineyards, with chardonnay accounting for half the total. Former lecturer in civil engineering and extremely successful amateur winemaker Harry Friend changed horses in 1994 to take joint control, with Axel Friend, of the family vineyard and winery, and hasn't missed a beat since; their skills show through with all the wines, none more so than the Chardonnay. Exports to Canada, Japan and China.

🍷🍷🍷🍷🍷 **Valerie Shiraz 2013** It's hard to stop yourself from tasting and drinking it; it has star factor. It's mid-weight, or a fraction heavier than that, and is surely splashed with spice and seductive oak. What really draws you in, though, is the way the cherry-plum fruit swings amiably through the palate before suddenly building a commanding presence through the finish. It almost provokes a double-take. It is bound to mature beautifully. Screwcap. **Rating** 96 **To** 2032 $60 CM ✪
Reserve Gippsland Pinot Noir 2013 Alive with scent; the palate follows on accordingly. Macerated cherries, flings of dry spice, stem notes and floral aspects. Undergrowthy complexity is here in abundance too. Oak is positive. Satiny texture. Positives abound. Screwcap. 14% alc. **Rating** 95 **To** 2024 $38 CM
Valerie Pinot Noir 2013 This wine sings. It's sour-sweet in some ways but it works quite beautifully. Cherries, plums, some stewy elements, more than a little spice. Oak adds texture as much as flavour, but it's the way the wine works as a whole that gets the heart racing. '13 was clearly a terrific season on the Narkoojee estate. Screwcap. 14% alc. **Rating** 95 **To** 2024 $60 CM
Reserve Maxwell Gippsland Cabernet Sauvignon 2013 Polished Cabernet boasting a heart of pure, ripe fruit and firm bones of tannin. Paints an impressive picture. All harmony and strength. Dark chocolate, blackcurrant, boysenberry and

minty, bay leaf notes. Firms and builds as it rests in the glass. Screwcap. 14% alc.
Rating 95 To 2028 $60 CM

🍷🍷🍷🍷🍷 **Lily Grace Gippsland Chardonnay 2014 Rating** 93 To 2020 $26 CM ❂
Valerie Chardonnay 2013 Rating 93 To 2018 $60 CM
Reserve Gippsland Chardonnay 2013 Rating 93 To 2020 $43 CM

Nashwauk   ★★★★☆

PO Box 852, Nuriootpa, SA 5355 **Region** McLaren Vale
T (08) 8562 4488 **www**.nashwaukvineyards.com.au **Open** Not
Winemaker Reid Bosward, Stephen Dew **Est.** 2005 **Dozens** 5000 **Vyds** 20ha
This is an estate-based venture, with 17ha of shiraz, 2ha of cabernet sauvignon and 1ha of
tempranillo, all except the tempranillo between 13 and 40+ years old. It is a stand-alone
business of the Kaesler family, and the first time it has extended beyond the Barossa Valley.
The striking label comes from satellite photos of the vineyard, showing the contour planting;
the name Nashwauk comes from Canada's Algonquin language, meaning 'land between'. The
property is situated in the (unofficial) Seaview subregion, with Kays, Chapel Hill and Coriole
as its neighbours; they all benefit from sea breezes and cooler nights. Exports to the US,
Singapore, Malaysia, Hong Kong and China.

🍷🍷🍷🍷🍷 **Wrecked McLaren Vale Shiraz 2010** Vines 20–40yo; matured in 2yo and 3yo
French oak for 24 months. Multiple forces are lined up here: the surprising impact
of the cedary oak, the strong overcoat of bitter chocolate, and the alcohol. The
latter loses the battle, leaving a palate of exceptional line and length, its savoury
nuances very enjoyable. Cork. 15% alc. **Rating** 95 To 2030 $70
McLaren Vale Shiraz 2012 The Nashwauk Vineyard has six soil types, the vines
30–40yo; matured in French oak (20% new). An unusually savoury and elegant
McLaren Vale Shiraz with a mix of red and black fruits, earth and fine tannins.
Screwcap. 14.5% alc. **Rating** 94 To 2027 $25 ❂
McLaren Vale Cabernet Sauvignon 2012 From 32yo contour plantings on a
south-facing hill; spent 10 days on skins, then pressed to French oak (30% new) for
2 years' maturation. You get a lot of Cabernet for your buck, built in a generous
mould that is hard to fault, particularly with the fine tannins on the finish.
Screwcap. 14.5% alc. **Rating** 94 To 2032 $25 ❂

🍷🍷🍷🍷🍷 **McLaren Vale Tempranillo 2012 Rating** 90 To 2027 $25

Nazaaray   ★★★★

266 Meakins Road, Flinders, Vic 3929 **Region** Mornington Peninsula
T (03) 5989 0126 **www**.nazaaray.com.au **Open** 1st w'end of month
Winemaker Paramdeep Ghumman **Est.** 1996 **Dozens** 800 **Vyds** 2.28ha
Paramdeep Ghumman is, as far as I am aware, the only Indian-born winery proprietor in
Australia. He and his wife purchased the Nazaaray vineyard property in 1991. An initial trial
planting of 400 vines in '96 was gradually expanded to the present level of 1.6ha of pinot
noir, 0.44ha of pinot gris and 0.12ha each of sauvignon blanc and shiraz. Notwithstanding the
micro size of the estate, all the wines are made and bottled onsite.

🍷🍷🍷🍷🍷 **Mornington Peninsula Chardonnay 2014** A lively and attractive wine,
looking much lower in alcohol than it is; grapefruit, nectarine and white peach are
the holy trinity of cool-grown Chardonnay, and that is exactly what you get here.
Screwcap. 14.5% alc. **Rating** 94 To 2022 $45

🍷🍷🍷🍷🍷 **Mornington Peninsula Pinot Gris 2013 Rating** 91 To 2017 $30

Nepenthe   ★★★★★

Jones Road, Balhannah, SA 5242 **Region** Adelaide Hills
T (08) 8398 8888 **www**.nepenthe.com.au **Open** 7 days 10–4
Winemaker Alex Trescowthick **Est.** 1994 **Dozens** 40 000 **Vyds** 108.68ha

Nepenthe quickly established its reputation as a producer of high-quality wines, but founder Ed Tweddell died unexpectedly in 2006, and the business was purchased by Australian Vintage Limited the following year. The winery was closed in '09, and winemaking operations transferred to McGuigan Wines (Barossa Valley). (The Nepenthe winery has since been purchased by Peter Leske and Mark Kozned, and provides contract winemaking services via their Revenir venture.) Nepenthe has over 100ha of close-planted vines spread over four vineyards in the Adelaide Hills, with an exotic array of varieties. Exports to the UK, the US and other major markets.

ŸŸŸŸŸ **Pinnacle Ithaca Adelaide Hills Chardonnay 2013** Barrel-fermented and matured on lees for 9 months in new and used French oak. This is a delicious wine in a riper, richer spectrum than many these days, its citrus-accented acidity giving the finish life and length. Screwcap. 13.5% alc. **Rating** 95 **To** 2025 $35 **❍**
Pinnacle Petraea Sauvignon Blanc 2014 Fermented and matured for 6 months in a 2500l French oak foudre. The bouquet has a hint of reduction that adds as much as it detracts; the tropical fruits are framed, if not highlighted, by the fermentation in oak. Screwcap. 12.5% alc. **Rating** 94 **To** 2016 $35
Pinnacle The Good Doctor Adelaide Hills Pinot Noir 2013 The best wine of vintage, matured for 10 months in French puncheons. Bigger, bolder and richer than its less expensive sibling, deserving (and needing) more time to relax and let light and shade give texture and air to the palate and finish. Screwcap. 13.5% alc. **Rating** 94 **To** 2028 $35
Adelaide Hills Tempranillo 2013 Takes a scoop of value and lays it on thick. Plush with raspberried, blueberried flavour, deliciously well matched to notes of dried herb, cola and mocha-like oak. Strung with tannin, juicy, sweet but savoury. Screwcap. 13.5% alc. **Rating** 94 **To** 2020 $20 CM **❍**

ŸŸŸŸŸ **Adelaide Hills Chardonnay 2013** **Rating** 92 **To** 2020 $20 **❍**
Adelaide Hills Pinot Gris 2014 **Rating** 92 **To** 2016 $20 **❍**
Adelaide Hills Pinot Noir 2013 **Rating** 92 **To** 2023 $20 **❍**
Adelaide Hills Sauvignon Blanc 2014 **Rating** 91 **To** 2015 $20 **❍**

New Era Vineyards   ★★★★

PO Box 391, Woodside SA 5244 **Region** Adelaide Hills
T 0413 544 246 **www**.neweravineyards.com.au **Open** Not
Winemaker Robert and Iain Baxter **Est.** 1988 **Dozens** 500 **Vyds** 13ha
The New Era vineyard is situated over a gold reef that was mined for 60 years until all recoverable gold had been extracted (mining ceased in 1940). The vineyard was originally planted to chardonnay, shiraz, cabernet sauvignon, merlot and sauvignon, mostly contracted to Foster's. Recently 2ha of cabernet sauvignon and 1.1ha of merlot have been grafted over to sauvignon blanc. Much of the production is sold to other winemakers in the region. The small amount of wine made has been the subject of favourable reviews.

ŸŸŸŸŸ **Basket Pressed Barrel Select Shiraz 2012** Aged for 24 months in all-French oak. It's a toasty, almost beefy expression of the Adelaide Hills, the oak influence no doubt overt but the wealth of fruit essentially up to the task. Black cherries and plums with clovey spice and mint. Substantial. Rumble of tannin takes no backward steps either. Screwcap. 13.5% alc. **Rating** 92 **To** 2022 $45 CM
Basket Pressed Shiraz 2012 Matured in French and American oak for between 18 and 24 months. Solid hit of flavour, smooth-skinned too, with blackberry, toast and malt flavours oozing confidently through the palate. Well flavoured, tidy and satisfying. Screwcap. 13.5% alc. **Rating** 91 **To** 2020 $22 CM **❍**
Winemaker's Selection Shiraz 2012 Seductive upfront, all blackberry and black cherry with a combination of saucy oak influence and woody, peppercorn-like spice. Clean and fruit-driven but with extras to enjoy. The finish is similarly effective, and is more or less satisfying, though the flavours stumble fractionally as they cross the line. Screwcap. 13.5% alc. **Rating** 90 **To** 2022 $30 CM

ŸŸŸŸ **Sauvignon Blanc 2014** **Rating** 89 **To** 2015 $20 CM

Newbridge Wines

18 Chelsea Street, Brighton, Vic 3186 (postal) **Region** Bendigo
T 0417 996 840 **www**.newbridgewines.com.au **Open** At Newbridge Hotel, Newbridge
Winemaker Mark Matthews (Contract), Andrew Simpson **Est.** 1996 **Dozens** 300
Vyds 1ha

The Newbridge property was purchased by Ian Simpson in 1979 partly for sentimental family history reasons, and partly because of the beauty of the property, situated on the banks of the Loddon River. It was not until 1996 that he decided to plant shiraz, and up to and including the 2002 vintage the grapes were sold to several local wineries. Ian retained the grapes and made wine in '03, and lived to see that and the following two vintages take shape before his death. The property is now run by his son Andrew, the wines contract-made by Mark Matthews, with enthusiastic support from Andrew. The foregoing covers the history, but not the vicissitudes of weather that have affected Newbridge and other wineries in the region: drought from '00–'10, then unprecedented floods in '11. Andrew was still scrambling to recover from the effect of the floods when the '12 vintage got underway; it repaid him for his tenacity and faith in the vineyard.

🍷🍷🍷🍷🍷 **Bendigo Shiraz 2012** It's been a tough few years for Newbridge, but the good times have returned with this vintage. Highly spiced, savoury black fruits have an unexpected slinky mouthfeel, which continues on to the aftertaste. An interesting future awaits. Screwcap. 14.5% alc. **Rating** 94 **To** 2027 $25 ●

Newtons Ridge Estate

1170 Cooriemungle Road, Timboon, Vic 3268 **Region** Geelong
T (03) 5598 7394 **www**.newtonsridgeestate.com.au **Open** Thurs–Mon 11–4 Oct–Easter
Winemaker David Falk **Est.** 1998 **Dozens** 850 **Vyds** 5ha

David and Carla Falk have operated a real estate and livestock agency in southwest Vic since 1989, the property 'just a couple of ridges away' from Newtons Ridge Estate. When they heard that founder David Newton had become ill and was contemplating pulling out the vines, they were able to purchase the vineyard, in 2012, completing a circle that began in the 1880s when Carla's family were among the first vignerons in Geelong – they produce wine in Switzerland to this day.

🍷🍷🍷🍷🍷 **Pinot Noir 2013** Good intensity to the colour; I don't have the faintest idea how the colour, bouquet and palate could have been achieved at this low level of alcohol; certainly there is a carpet of foresty notes, and some faint green herbal nuances to the palate, but it largely succeeds. It is possible the alcohol is in fact higher. A radical difference from the '12. Screwcap. 11.3% alc. **Rating** 91 **To** 2019 $35
Chardonnay 2013 Basket-pressed and matured in French barriques for 12 months. Some colour development signals a generously endowed wine, peach to the fore, citrus notes and oak providing some contrast. Screwcap. 12.3% alc. **Rating** 90 **To** 2018 $30
Summer Wine Rose 2013 Pinot noir and pinot meunier hand-picked by local community groups. Light pink, tinged with salmon; the bouquet has complex fruit aromas, the savoury palate likewise, but slightly compromised by a half-suggestion of sweetness, possibly ex the alcohol or low-level residual sugar. Screwcap. 13.5% alc. **Rating** 90 **To** 2016 $20 ●

Ngeringa

119 Williams Road, Mount Barker, SA 5251 **Region** Adelaide Hills
T (08) 8398 2867 **www**.ngeringa.com **Open** By appt
Winemaker Erinn Klein **Est.** 2001 **Dozens** 2500 **Vyds** 5ha

Erinn and Janet Klein say, 'As fervent practitioners of biodynamic wine growing, we respect biodynamics as a sensitivity to the rhythms of nature, the health of the soil and the connection between plant, animal and cosmos. It is a pragmatic solution to farming without the use of chemicals and a necessary acknowledgement that the farm unit is part of a great whole.' It is not an easy solution, and the Kleins have increased the immensity of the challenge by using ultra-close vine spacing of 1.5m × 1m, necessitating a large amount of hand-training of the vines plus a tiny crawler tractor. Lest it be thought they have stumbled onto biodynamic growing without understanding wine science, they teamed up while studying at Adelaide University in 2000 (Erinn – oenology, Janet – viticulture/wine marketing), and then spent time looking at the great viticultural regions of the Old World, with a particular emphasis on biodynamics. The JE label is used for the basic wines, Ngeringa only for the very best. Exports to the UK, the US, Canada, Austria, Sweden, Japan, Taiwan and China.

Adelaide Hills Pinot Noir 2012 Hand-picked; a small amount whole bunch-pressed (very unconventional), the remainder spending 28 days on skins, then 12 months in French oak (20% new). Has a fragrant, dark cherry bouquet, and an intense and long palate that sends all the right messages, the flavour and texture of the mouthfeel admirable. Screwcap. 13% alc. **Rating** 95 **To** 2022 $40
Adelaide Hills Chardonnay 2012 Luscious style for the most part until limey, tangy, steely flavour takes the reins through the finish. Significant serve of peach and meal-like flavours build an impressive attack. Straw-coloured. Piles on the seduction. Screwcap. 13.5% alc. **Rating** 94 **To** 2019 $40 CM
Rose 2013 95% shiraz, of which 70% was whole bunch-pressed direct to 9yo French barriques, 30% saignee from Ngeringa's best shiraz, drained off after 24 hours on skins, 11 months in barrel. Spicy red fruits run through the length of the very good palate. A seriously good rose, well worth the making. Screwcap. 12.5% alc. **Rating** 94 **To** 2016 $28 ✪
Sangiovese 2013 Lively fruit and yet sappy and spicy too. Almost Pinot-esque. Jubey cherries and boysenberries meet earth, pepper and twig-like notes. Finely tannic. For all its juiciness, every flavour here feels precisely placed. Screwcap. 13% alc. **Rating** 94 **To** 2020 $35 CM
Nebbiolo 2013 The Ngeringa wines go from strength to strength. This is a delicious Nebbiolo. It has power through the mid-palate but it's essentially tangy, juicy, elegant. Flavours of roasted nuts, dry cherries, herbs and assorted spices. Succulent-but-tannic finish. Screwcap. 13% alc. **Rating** 94 **To** 2023 $35 CM

Tempranillo 2013 Rating 92 **To** 2021 $35 CM
Viognier 2013 Rating 90 **To** 2015 $40 CM

Nicholson River   ★★★★☆

57 Liddells Road, Nicholson, Vic 3882 **Region** Gippsland
T (03) 5156 8241 **www.**nicholsonriverwinery.com.au **Open** 7 days 10–5 during hols
Winemaker Ken Eckersley **Est.** 1978 **Dozens** 1000 **Vyds** 8ha
Nicholson River's fierce commitment to quality in the face of the temperamental Gippsland climate and frustratingly small production has been handsomely repaid by some massive Chardonnays and impressive red wines (from estate plantings). Ken Eckersley refers to his Chardonnays not as white wines but as gold wines, and lists them accordingly in his newsletter.

Sangiovese 2013 This comes from the left field given its variety and region coupling, but it does so in impressive fashion. A mix of red and sour cherry fruit is given shape and length by fine-grained tannins. It all works really well: watch this space. 70 dozen made. Screwcap. 12.8% alc. **Rating** 95 **To** 2023 $45

Syrah Viognier 2013 Rating 88 **To** 2018 $45

Nick O'Leary Wines   ★★★★★

129 Donnelly Lane, Bungendore, NSW 2621 **Region** Canberra District
T (02) 6161 8739 **www.**nickolearywines.com.au **Open** By appt
Winemaker Nick O'Leary **Est.** 2007 **Dozens** 4500
At the ripe old age of 28, Nick O'Leary had been involved in the wine industry for over a decade, working variously in retail, wholesale, viticulture and winemaking. Two years earlier he had laid the foundation for Nick O'Leary Wines, purchasing shiraz from local vignerons

(commencing in 2006); riesling following in '08. His wines have had extraordinarily consistent success in local wine shows and competitions since the first vintages.

🍷🍷🍷🍷🍷 **Bolaro Shiraz 2013** From the Fischer Vineyard in the Murrumbateman area of the Canberra District. Trophies for Best Shiraz and Wine of the Year at the NSW Wine Awards plus gold medals at the Queensland and National Wine Show leave no room for argument. A picture-perfect confluence of varietal flavour and texture/structure give the wine a regal splendour more often associated with great Cabernet. Screwcap. 13.5% alc. **Rating** 97 **To** 2043 $55 ○

🍷🍷🍷🍷🍷 **Shiraz 2013** Three trophies at the Qld Wine Show '14, including Best Red Wine of Show, and thereby the Stodart Trophy. This success reflected the beautiful line, length and balance of this Canberra District Shiraz; the bouquet exudes a range of predominantly red fruits, the soft, but insistent tannins on the palate forming a guard of honour for those fruits. Oak? Yes, there's some, but you have to go looking for it. Fantastic value. Screwcap. 13.5% alc. **Rating** 96 **To** 2038 $30 ○
Riesling 2014 From Murrumbateman and Lake George vineyards. A superbly detailed Riesling with a floral bouquet and a delicate, but very long, lime/lemon palate, acidity precisely balanced. Screwcap. 12% alc. **Rating** 95 **To** 2029 $25 ○
Pyrenees Shiraz 2013 From the large, mature Malakoff Estate vineyard. The colour is vivid, the impact of the fruit like a roll of thunder as it enters the mouth, then relaxes its grip on the mid-palate; the back-palate borders on delicate. The savoury/earthy/peppery nuances of the black fruits add another dimension to the palate. Its best years are far into the future. Screwcap. 13.5% alc. **Rating** 95 **To** 2040 $35 ○

🍷🍷🍷🍷🍷 **Tempranillo 2013** **Rating** 92 **To** 2018 $32
Rose 2014 **Rating** 91 **To** 2016 $19 ○

Night Harvest ★★★★
PO Box 921, Busselton, WA 6280 **Region** Margaret River
T (08) 9755 1521 **www**.nightharvest.com.au **Open** Not
Winemaker Bruce Dukes **Est.** 2005 **Dozens** 40 000 **Vyds** 300ha
Andy and Mandy Ferreira arrived in Margaret River in 1986 as newly married young migrants. They soon became involved in the construction and establishment of new vineyards, as well as growing vegetables for the local and export markets. Their vineyard-contracting business expanded quickly when the region experienced its rapid growth in the late '90s, so the vegetable business was closed, and they put all their focus into wine. They were involved in the establishment of about 300ha of Margaret River vineyards, many of which they continue to manage today (Woodside Valley Estate and Chapman Grove are among the 16 estates that fall into this category.) As their fortunes grew, they purchased their own property and produced the first wines in 2005, employing contract winemakers Kevin McKay and Bruce Dukes. Harvesting is a key part of their business, and currently they harvest fruit from over 100 sites. Hence the Night Harvest brand was born, and Butler Crest was added as a premium label. Exports to the UK, the US, Thailand, Hong Kong and China.

🍷🍷🍷🍷🍷 **John George Cabernet Sauvignon 2013** Soft, almost pillowy Cabernet with a wealth of berried fruit flavour and sound, juicy, flowing length. Ticks boxes all along the way. Threads of bay leaves and assorted dried herbs run through fine-grained tannin. Will work equally well now or later. Screwcap. 13.5% alc. **Rating** 94 **To** 2025 $35 CM

🍷🍷🍷🍷 **John George Chardonnay 2014** **Rating** 93 **To** 2020 $27 CM ○

Nillumbik Estate ★★★★
195 Clintons Road, Smiths Gully, Vic 3760 **Region** Yarra Valley
T 0408 337 326 **www**.nillumbikestate.com.au **Open** Not
Winemaker John Tregambe **Est.** 2001 **Dozens** 1250 **Vyds** 2ha

In establishing Nillumbik Estate, John and Chanmali Tregambe won the multi-generational winemaking experience of John's parents, Italian immigrants who arrived in Australia in the 1950s. The estate plantings of pinot noir are supplemented by cabernet sauvignon, chardonnay, shiraz and nebbiolo purchased from Sunbury, Heathcote and the King Valley.

ŸŸŸŸŸ **Domenic's Paddock Yarra Valley Pinot Noir 2013** This is a high-quality Pinot built for the ages, although it isn't the rock of ages – it is certainly deeply flavoured and contoured, but there are no hard edges; black cherry, red cherry and plum (in that order of power) will see spicy notes develop over the next few years, underlining its potential. Screwcap. 13% alc. **Rating** 94 **To** 2021 $32

Old Earth Barrel Reserve Heathcote Shiraz 2012 From the 24ha estate vineyard, open-fermented for 7 days, matured for 18 months in French barriques (50% new). This is a serious Shiraz, with layer upon layer of rich black fruits, sandwiched between layers of quality French oak. The fruit has the power and balance to see the oak off the arena, but it won't happen overnight. Screwcap. 14% alc. **Rating** 94 **To** 2037 $48

ŸŸŸŸŸ **The Back Block King Valley Petit Verdot 2013 Rating** 91 **To** 2025 $28

916   ★★★★

916 Steels Creek Road, Steels Creek, Vic 3775 (postal) **Region** Yarra Valley
T (03) 5965 2124 **www**.916.com.au **Open** Not
Winemaker Ben Haines **Est.** 2008 **Dozens** 210 **Vyds** 2ha

916, established by John Brand and Erin-Marie O'Neill, is now one of three wineries in the *Wine Companion* using three digits as their name, others being 919 and 201. A year after they acquired their 8ha property, bushfires destroyed their home and all their possessions, but they have rebuilt their lives and home, reinvesting in wine and vineyard alike. Viticulturist John Evans, formerly at Yering Station and now at Rochford Wines, became involved with the vineyard in 1996. Having chosen their viticulturist well, they have a highly gifted winemaker in the form of Ben Haines. Exports to the US, China and Singapore.

ŸŸŸŸŸ **Yarra Valley Pinot Noir 2013** From MV6 clone vines planted in '96; 12 months' elevage. Strong, bright crimson-purple hue; a very expressive bouquet with a deep pinot and allspice aroma is replayed on the full, but well-balanced palate, plum, spice and positive oak all contributing. Sure to develop well. Diam. 13.5% alc. **Rating** 94 **To** 2023 $90

919 Wines   ★★★★

39 Hodges Road, Berri, SA 5343 **Region** Riverland
T (08) 8582 4436 **www**.919wines.com.au **Open** Wed–Sun & public hols 10–5
Winemaker Eric and Jenny Semmler **Est.** 2002 **Dozens** 1000 **Vyds** 17ha

Eric and Jenny Semmler have been involved in the wine industry since 1986, and have a special interest in fortified wines. Eric previously made fortified wines for Hardys at Berri Estates, and worked at Brown Brothers. Jenny has worked for Strathbogie Vineyards, Pennyweight Wines, St Huberts and Constellation. They have planted micro-quantities of varieties specifically for fortified wines: palomino, durif, tempranillo, muscat a petits grains, tinta cao, shiraz, tokay and touriga nacional. Notwithstanding their Riverland GI, they use minimal water application, deliberately reducing the crop levels, practising organic and biodynamic techniques. In 2011 they purchased the 12.3ha property at Loxton they now call 809 Vineyard. Eric Semmler was named Winemaker of the Year by *Winestate Magazine* in 2013.

ŸŸŸŸŸ **Pale Dry Apera NV** Has won a stack of accolades and medals. Is from a 3-year solera, but freshness (once bottled) is essential with Apera, and you don't know how long it has been in the bottle after it left 919 Wines. This green-straw wine has perfectly controlled nutty aldehyde aromas and a salty, fresh and dry finish. 500ml. Screwcap. 15.5% alc. **Rating** 94 **To** 2016 $30 ✪

ŸŸŸŸŸ **Shiraz 2014 Rating** 91 **To** 2034 $40
Limited Release Vintage (Red Fortified) 2013 Rating 91 **To** 2025 $50

Tempranillo 2012 Rating 90 To 2020 $42
Durif 2012 Rating 90 To 2032 $45
Classic Topaque NV Rating 90 To 2016 $40

Nintingbool ★★★★

56 Wongerer Lane, Smythes Creek, Vic 3351 (postal) **Region** Ballarat
T (03) 5342 4393 **www.**nintingbool.com **Open** Not
Winemaker Peter Bothe **Est.** 1998 **Dozens** 460 **Vyds** 2ha
Peter and Jill Bothe purchased the Nintingbool property in 1982 and built their home in '84,
using bluestone dating back to the goldrush period. They established an extensive Australian
native garden and home orchard, but in '98 diversified by planting pinot noir, a further
planting the following year lifting the total to 2ha. This is one of the coolest mainland regions,
and demands absolute attention to detail (and a warm growing season) for success.

ΨΨΨΨΨ **Smythes Creek Pinot Noir 2012** Hand-pruned and picked by family and
friends. Good depth to the colour; full, unambiguously ripe blood plum and
black cherry fruit, complexity arriving on the aftertaste thanks to a tickle of spice
and pepper reminding you of the very cool Ballarat climate. 350 dozen made.
Screwcap. 13.9% alc. **Rating** 94 **To** 2022 $33

ΨΨΨΨ **Smythes Creek Rose 2014** Rating 89 To 2016 $23

Noble Red ★★★★

18 Brennan Avenue, Upper Beaconsfield, Vic 3808 (postal) **Region** Heathcote
T 0400 594 440 **www.**nobleredwines.com **Open** Not
Winemaker Roman Sobiesiak **Est.** 2002 **Dozens** 500 **Vyds** 6ha
Noble Red is the venture of Roman and Margaret Sobiesiak, who acquired their property
in 2002. There was 0.25ha of shiraz planted in the 1970s, and since '02 a progressive planting
program has seen the area increase to 6ha, shiraz (3.6ha) accounting for the lion's share, the
remainder more or less equally split between tempranillo, mourvedre, merlot and cabernet
sauvignon. Roman and Margaret deliberately adopted a dry-grown approach, which meant
slow development during the prolonged drought, but their commitment remains undimmed.
Indeed, visiting many wine regions around the world and working within the industry locally
has simply increased their determination.

ΨΨΨΨΨ **Heathcote Durif 2012** Dense, inky purple; a monumental Durif, showing
no sign whatsoever of opening the door for business; just when it will do so is
anyone's guess; very much in the Noble Red house style, the influence of Adrian
Munari no less obvious. For lovers of huge red wines. Screwcap. 14.8% alc.
Rating 90 **To** 2032 $45

ΨΨΨΨ **Heathcote Shiraz 2013** Rating 89 To 2020 $28

Nocton Vineyard ★★★★☆

373 Colebrook Road, Richmond, Tas 7025 **Region** Southern Tasmania
T 0418 645 807 **Open** By appt
Winemaker Winemaking Tasmania (Julian Alcorso) **Est.** 1998 **Dozens** 10 000 **Vyds** 34ha
Nocton Vineyard is the reincarnation of Nocton Park. After years of inactivity (other than the
ongoing sale of the grapes from what is a first-class vineyard) it largely disappeared from sight.
It was ultimately acquired by a group of Sydney businessmen, together with a couple of expats
with interests in Hong Kong. Richard Meyman, who has had the carriage of developing and
marketing the new brand, is a small part of the ownership group. There are two labels: N1 for
the premium range, almost entirely made from estate-grown grapes, and the Coal River label
at a lower price. The quality across the two labels is very good.

ΨΨΨΨΨ **N1 Pinot Noir 2012** Full crimson-purple. Ticks all the boxes, and is still in
its primary phase, but with very good length and balance; red and black cherry

fruit has just the right amount of savoury tannins support to guarantee its future development in fine style. Screwcap. 13.8% alc. **Rating** 95 **To** 2023 $39

Coal River Valley Chardonnay 2011 Bright straw-green; a very attractive, fresh and vibrant fruit-driven Chardonnay, the varietal flavours of white peach, nectarine and grapefruit cushioned within a delicate filigree of nicely restrained acidity. Screwcap. 13.4% alc. **Rating** 94 **To** 2020 $25 ✪

Coal River Valley Pinot Noir 2013 Good hue and depth; the bouquet is highly expressive and perfumed; an emphatic and complex palate, with red fruits wreathed in bramble, suggesting whole bunches, but with overall flavour balance and excellent length. Screwcap. 13.1% alc. **Rating** 94 **To** 2022 $26 ✪

Limited Release Vineyard Reserve Noble Botrytis Semillon Sauvignon Blanc Chardonnay 2011 Yellow-orange; the full caboodle of cumquat, mandarin, walnut and spice flavours from total botrytis infection. 213g/l residual sugar; 375ml. Screwcap. 8.6% alc. **Rating** 94 **To** 2016 $23 ✪

N1 Chardonnay 2011 Rating 93 To 2018 $36
Coal River Valley Pinot Noir 2011 Rating 90 To 2020 $27
Coal River Valley Merlot 2012 Rating 90 To 2019 $26

Norfolk Rise Vineyard ★★★★

Limestone Coast Road, Mount Benson, SA 5265 **Region** Mount Benson
T (08) 8768 5080 **www**.norfolkrise.com.au **Open** Not
Winemaker Daniel Berrigan **Est.** 2000 **Dozens** 20 000 **Vyds** 130ha
This is by far the largest and most important development in the Mount Benson region. It is ultimately owned by a privately held Belgian company, G & C Kreglinger, established in 1797. In early 2002 Kreglinger acquired Pipers Brook Vineyard; it has maintained the separate brands of the two ventures. There are 46 blocks of sauvignon blanc, pinot gris, pinot noir, shiraz, merlot and cabernet sauvignon, allowing a range of options in making the six single-variety wines in the portfolio. The business has moved away from the export of bulk wine to bottled wine, with significantly better returns to the winery. Exports to Europe and Asia.

Mount Benson Pinot Grigio 2014 Tasty and tangy, and anything but white-on-white. This is pure, intense, strong with passionfruit and green apple flavour and then steely and lengthy through the finish. Gun wine, top value. Screwcap. 12.5% alc. **Rating** 93 **To** 2015 $16 CM ✪

Mount Benson Sauvignon Blanc 2014 If it ain't broke, don't fix it. This continues an excellent run for this label. Intense passionfruit and gunmetal with a grassy/lemongrassy side. Acid dangles fractionally ahead of the flavours on the finish but for purity and intensity of flavour this is the goods. Screwcap. 12% alc. **Rating** 92 **To** 2016 $16 CM ✪

Norton Estate ★★★★☆

758 Plush Hannans Road, Lower Norton, Vic 3401 **Region** Western Victoria Zone
T (03) 5384 8235 **www**.nortonestate.com.au **Open** Fri–Sun & public hols 11–4
Winemaker Best's Wines **Est.** 1997 **Dozens** 1300 **Vyds** 4.66ha
In 1996 the Spence family purchased a rundown farm at Lower Norton and, rather than farming the traditional wool, meat and wheat, trusted their instincts and planted vines on the elevated, frost-free, buckshot rises. The surprising vigour of the initial planting of shiraz prompted further plantings of shiraz, cabernet sauvignon and sauvignon blanc. The vineyard is halfway between the Grampians and Mt Arapiles, 6km northwest of the Grampians region, and has to be content with the Western Victoria Zone, but the wines show regional Grampians character and style.

Arapiles Run Shiraz 2013 Excellent hue and depth; the perfectly ripened fruit and sophisticated use of new French and some older American oak gives this wine real presence, yet not at the expense of elegance; satsuma plum, blackberry, licorice and a splash of bitter chocolate all coalesce on the long palate and aftertaste. Screwcap. 14% alc. **Rating** 95 **To** 2033 $37

🍷🍷🍷🍷🍷 Rockface Shiraz 2013 Rating 93 To 2028 $23 ✪
Cabernet Sauvignon 2013 Rating 93 To 2023 $23 ✪
Rockface Shiraz 2012 Rating 91 To 2025 $23 ✪
Sauvignon Blanc 2014 Rating 90 To 2015 $18 ✪

Norton Summit Vineyards ★★★☆

122B Nicholls Road, Norton Summit, SA 5136 **Region** Adelaide Hills
T (08) 8390 1986 **www**.nortonsummitvineyards.com **Open** By appt
Winemaker Kenn Fisher **Est.** 1998 **Dozens** 500 **Vyds** 1.5ha
Dr Kenn Fisher and partner Meredyth Taylor planted pinot noir and chardonnay in 1998.
The vineyard has five blocks, each with its own mesoclimate, orientation and soil type. To add
further complexity, four clones have been utilised. With additional vine age, the use of new
French oak has been increased to 30%. Kenn makes the wines using traditional methods of
open fermenters and a basket press.

🍷🍷🍷🍷🍷 Adelaide Hills Chardonnay 2009 Powering along nicely. Peach, honeysuckle
and toast flavours build a good head of steam before releasing/sliding out through
the finish. At the end of its run but good now. Screwcap. 13.5% alc. **Rating** 90
To 2016 $32 CM

🍷🍷🍷🍷 Adelaide Hills Chardonnay 2010 Rating 89 To 2016 $32 CM
Adelaide Hills Pinot Noir 2010 Rating 89 To 2020 $32 CM
Adelaide Hills Pinot Noir 2009 Rating 89 To 2017 $32 CM

Nova Vita Wines ★★★★

49 Peacock Road North, Lenswood, SA 5240 **Region** Adelaide Hills
T (08) 8356 0454 **www**.novavitawines.com.au **Open** Not
Winemaker Mark Kozned **Est.** 2005 **Dozens** 10 000 **Vyds** 46ha
Mark and Jo Kozned's 30ha Woodlands Ridge Vineyard is planted to chardonnay, sauvignon
blanc, pinot gris and shiraz. They have subsequently established the Tunnel Hill Vineyard, with
16ha planted to pinot noir, shiraz, cabernet sauvignon, sauvignon blanc, semillon, verdelho,
merlot and sangiovese. The name Nova Vita reflects the beginning of the Kozneds' new life,
the firebird on the label coming from their Russian ancestry. It is a Russian myth that only a
happy or lucky person may see the bird or hear its song. The increased vineyard resources have
led to the Mad Russian range, exclusive to Cellarmasters. The Kozneds have joined forces with
Peter Leske to form Revenir, a contract winemaking business that has purchased the former
Nepenthe winery. Exports to Singapore and China.

🍷🍷🍷🍷🍷 George Kozned Inheritance Crossed Sword Shiraz 2013 A medium to
full-bodied Shiraz that reveals its hand before the other players have arranged their
cards; plush black fruits, cedary oak and ripe tannins. So what you see in the first
sip is what you get with the last. Cork. 14% alc. **Rating** 93 **To** 2028 $25 ✪
Firebird Adelaide Hills Gruner Veltliner 2013 Gruner Veltliner is here to stay;
the white pepper is there, and this has really attractive mouthfeel, with a burst of
crisp acidity on the finish. Screwcap. 12% alc. **Rating** 92 **To** 2017 $25 ✪
Firebird Adelaide Hills S'Rose 2013 Hand-picked sangiovese, wild yeast-
fermented and matured in used French oak. Pale salmon-pink; crisp, fresh and dry,
with some fragrance on the bouquet; it has good length and persistence thanks to
breath-freshener acidity. Screwcap. 13% alc. **Rating** 92 **To** 2016 $20 ✪
Firebird Reserve Barossa Valley Shiraz 2011 Why would you leave the
Adelaide Hills and go to the Barossa Valley? In '11? And why make this a high-
priced Reserve release? There is the power of high-quality oak, but that's not
enough; yes, there's ripe shiraz fruit, too, and yes, it's a selection of the best
18 barrels. It came from the Pindarie Vineyard, which, according to Nova Vita is
the only patch of red clay over limestone in the Barossa Valley. Screwcap. 14% alc.
Rating 92 **To** 2031 $120

George Kozned Inheritance Shield Cabernet Merlot 2013 This has an SA appellation: how could that possibly be entered in the National Cool Climate Wine Show '14 (where it won a gold medal)? It has an abundance of cassis fruit, and a smack of tannins that need to settle down; ditto oak. Cork. 13.5% alc. **Rating** 91 **To** 2030 $25

Firebird Adelaide Hills Gruner Veltliner 2014 Matured in old oak barrels, so we are told, but not whether it was barrel-fermented. It looks to me like stainless steel-fermented, with its fresh, crisp fruit profile, apple, citrus and white pepper all waving a flag. Should develop like Riesling. Screwcap. 12% alc. **Rating** 90 **To** 2020 $25

Firebird Adelaide Hills S'Rose 2014 100% sangiovese, hand-picked, wild-fermented and then hands off. Pale salmon-pink, the wine repays the winemaking philosophy; forest fruits, notably fraises du bois, take hold of the palate, with a long, lingering, dry, but fruity, finish. Screwcap. 13% alc. **Rating** 90 **To** 2016 $20 ✪

Firebird Adelaide Hills Shiraz 2012 Matured in French oak for nearly 2 years. Deep crimson-purple; this is a powerful, medium to full-bodied wine, its flavour profile ripe and generous (to a fault?), the rhetorical question turning on some warm-climate nuances to the fruit; the tannins are ripe, the oak controlled. Screwcap. 14% alc. **Rating** 90 **To** 2022 $35

Firebird Cabernet Merlot 2012 There's a lot of flavour and activity going on here, much off the back of the vintage; ripe forest berry fruits engage with oak (which is obvious), and tannins to provide context and structure on the medium to full-bodied palate. Twin top. 13% alc. **Rating** 90 **To** 2027 $35

Nugan Estate   ★★★★★

Kidman Way, Wilbriggie, NSW 2680 **Region** Riverina
T (02) 9362 9993 **www.**nuganestate.com.au **Open** Mon–Fri 9–5
Winemaker Daren Owers **Est.** 1999 **Dozens** 500 000 **Vyds** 491ha
Nugan Estate arrived on the scene like a whirlwind. It is an offshoot of the Nugan Group headed by Michelle Nugan (until her retirement in Feb 2013), inter alia the recipient of an Export Hero Award in '00. In the mid-1990s the company began developing vineyards, and it is now a veritable giant, with five vineyards: Cookoothama (335ha), Manuka Grove (46ha) in the Riverina, Frasca's Lane (100ha) in the King Valley and McLaren Parish (10ha) in McLaren Vale. The wine business is now in the energetic hands of Matthew and Tiffany Nugan, Michelle's children. Exports to the UK, the US and other major markets.

ŸŸŸŸŸ **McLaren Parish Vineyard McLaren Vale Shiraz 2013** Finished its fermentation and matured for 16 months in new and 1yo French and American oak. Deep, dense colour; this is an opulent medium to full-bodied portrait of McLaren Vale, aided and abetted by confident use of oak; the fruit is luscious, briefly poached, and dipped in dark chocolate; the balance is such that 99% of the wine will be consumed long before its drink-to date. Screwcap. 14.5% alc. Rating 95 **To** 2038 $23 ✪

Frasca's Lane Vineyard King Valley Chardonnay 2013 An attractive Chardonnay, fermented in new and used French oak, and matured for 14 months. It has well above average intensity for King Valley Chardonnay, and likewise length; white peach and grapefruit flavours (not oak) do all the heavy lifting, and there's no need to rush the wine. Screwcap. 13.5% alc. **Rating** 94 **To** 2018 $20 ✪

Manuka Grove Vineyard Riverina Durif 2010 Excellent colour, still full, bright and deep; durif and the Riverina go hand in hand, the generous yields taming the tannins, but not dismembering the still luscious fruit. It all works so well. Screwcap. 14.5% alc. **Rating** 94 **To** 2020 $23 ✪

ŸŸŸŸŸ **Alfredo Dried Grape Shiraz 2013** Rating 93 **To** 2025 $23 ✪
Alcira Vineyard Cabernet Sauvignon 2012 Rating 92 **To** 2020 $23 ✪
Frasca's Lane Vineyard Pinot Grigio 2014 Rating 90 **To** 2016 $20 ✪
McLaren Parish Vineyard Shiraz 2012 Rating 90 **To** 2022 $23

O'Leary Walker Wines   ★★★★★

Horrocks Highway, Leasingham, SA 5452 **Region** Clare Valley
T (08) 8843 0022 **www**.olearywalkerwines.com **Open** Mon–Sat 10–4, Sun 11–4
Winemaker David O'Leary, Nick Walker **Est.** 2001 **Dozens** 20000 **Vyds** 35ha
David O'Leary and Nick Walker together had more than 30 years' experience as winemakers
working for some of the biggest Australian wine groups when they took the plunge in 2001
and backed themselves to establish their own winery and brand. Initially the principal focus
was on the Clare Valley, with 10ha of riesling, shiraz, cabernet sauvignon and semillon the
main plantings; thereafter attention swung to the Adelaide Hills, where they now have 25ha
of chardonnay, cabernet sauvignon, pinot noir, shiraz, sauvignon blanc and merlot. Exports to
the UK, Ireland and Asia.

ŶŶŶŶŶ   **Polish Hill River Riesling 2014** Bright straw-green; the fragrant, flowery citrus
blossom-filled bouquet accurately semaphores the totally delicious fruit of the
palate, lime juice to the fore, resting on a bed of exactly balanced minerally acidity.
Answers the challenge of WA's Porongurup/Great Southern in fine style. Screwcap.
12% alc. **Rating** 96 To 2029 $22 ◎
Wyebo Shiraz 2012 Flooded with spicy/peppery black fruits on the bouquet
and palate alike, licorice and polished leather also seeking an audience; the
medium-bodied palate sings like a bird, supple and juicy, lingering long after the
wine has left the mouth. Screwcap. 14.5% alc. **Rating** 96 To 2032 $35 ◎
Watervale Riesling 2014 Gleaming straw-green, a feature of a number of Clare
Valley Rieslings from '14. With over 50 years of combined experience, it's not
surprising David O'Leary and Nick Walker nailed this wine, with its zesty lemon
and lime fruit built on a bedrock of perfectly balanced acidity. Exceptional value.
Screwcap. 12% alc. **Rating** 94 To 2024 $18 ◎
Wyebo Adelaide Hills Sauvignon Blanc 2013 The bouquet is immediate in
its impact, with pine cone, wild herbs and flowers to the fore; the palate follows
on logically – and provocatively – with a barrage of flavours, citrus and green
capsicum. This is the polar opposite of the numerous anodyne Sauvignon Blancs.
Screwcap. 12% alc. **Rating** 94 To 2016 $19 ◎

ŶŶŶŶ͡Ŷ   **Adelaide Hills Sauvignon Blanc 2014** **Rating** 92 To 2016 $17 ◎
Adelaide Hills Chardonnay 2013 **Rating** 92 To 2021 $22 ◎
Last Cut Cane Cut Riesling 2014 **Rating** 92 To 2016 $35
Adelaide Hills Pinot Noir 2013 **Rating** 90 To 2020 $22

Oakdene   ★★★★★

255 Grubb Road, Wallington, Vic 3221 **Region** Geelong
T (03) 5256 3886 **www**.oakdene.com.au **Open** 7 days 10–4
Winemaker Robin Brockett, Marcus Holt **Est.** 2001 **Dozens** 6000 **Vyds** 12ha
Bernard and Elizabeth Hooley purchased Oakdene in 2001. Bernard focused on planting the
vineyard (shiraz, pinot gris, sauvignon blanc, pinot noir, chardonnay, merlot, cabernet franc
and cabernet sauvignon), while Elizabeth worked to restore the 1920s homestead. Much of
the wine is sold through the award-winning Oakdene Restaurant and cellar door. The quality
is exemplary, as is the consistency of that quality; Robin Brockett's skills are on full display.

ŶŶŶŶŶ   **William Single Vineyard Shiraz 2013** Wild yeast, small addition of whole
bunches, matured 16 months in new and used French barriques. This is as
powerful as cool-grown Shiraz can possibly be, full-bodied and taking no
prisoners, albeit nodding to the Rhône's Hill of Hermitage, its genetic ancestor.
Inky black fruits, excellent acidity and tannins all under the same star sign; will
outlive many of us. Screwcap. 13.9% alc. **Rating** 97 To 2063 $35 ◎

ŶŶŶŶŶ   **Liz's Single Vineyard Chardonnay 2013** Wild yeast-fermented and matured
for 11 months in new and used French barriques. Brings intensity, elegance and
length first up, leaving little more to be said other than a balanced display of

grapefruit, white peach and creamy/toasty oak. Screwcap. 13.2% alc. **Rating** 95 To 2020 $30 **✪**

Ly Ly Single Vineyard Pinot Gris 2013 100% barrel-fermented, plus 8 months' maturation in French barriques (15% new). Remarkably pure, crisp and vibrant given its vinification. The cost and effort have been handsomely repaid. This is a real wine. Screwcap. 13.7% alc. **Rating** 95 **To** 2018 $28 **✪**

Peta's Single Vineyard Pinot Noir 2013 Wild yeast, small addition of whole bunches; 11 months' maturation in new and used French barriques. An opulent Pinot Noir, very much in the style of Geelong and the Bellarine Peninsula; fleshy dark cherries, allied with lesser amounts of plum, will sustain the wine for years; the tannins are supportive and will help the wine into the prime of its life as the spice box opens. Screwcap. 13.6% alc. **Rating** 95 **To** 2025 $35 **✪**

Bernard's Single Vineyard Cabernets 2013 A crimson-purple 58/30/12% blend of merlot, cabernet franc and cabernet sauvignon, wild yeast-fermented and matured in new and used French barriques for 16 months. Yet another Oakdene '13 to over-deliver, flush with cassis, redcurrant and plum fruit given complexity by cedary oak and ripe tannins. Screwcap. 12.9% alc. **Rating** 95 **To** 2028 $28 **✪**

Single Vineyard Sauvignon Blanc 2014 **Rating** 94 **To** 2016 $21 **✪**
Jessica Single Vineyard Sauvignon 2014 **Rating** 94 **To** 2016 $28 **✪**

ŸŸŸŸŸ **Ly Ly Single Vineyard Pinot Gris 2014** **Rating** 93 **To** 2020 $28
Single Vineyard Pinot Grigio 2014 **Rating** 91 **To** 2016 $23 **✪**

Oakridge Wines   ★★★★★

864 Maroondah Highway, Coldstream, Vic 3770 **Region** Yarra Valley
T (03) 9738 9900 **www.**oakridgewines.com.au **Open** 7 days 10–5
Winemaker David Bicknell **Est.** 1978 **Dozens** 22 000 **Vyds** 9.8ha
Winemaker and CEO David Bicknell has proved his worth time and again as an extremely talented winemaker. At the top of the brand tier is 864, all Yarra Valley vineyard selections, and only released in the best years (Chardonnay, Shiraz, Cabernet Sauvignon, Riesling); next is the Oakridge Local Vineyard Series (the Chardonnay, Pinot Noir and Sauvignon Blanc come from the cooler Upper Yarra Valley; the Shiraz, Cabernet Sauvignon and Viognier from the Lower Yarra); and the Over the Shoulder range, drawn from all of the sources available to Oakridge (Sauvignon Blanc, Pinot Grigio, Pinot Noir, Shiraz Viognier, Cabernet Sauvignon). Exports to the UK, the US, Fiji, Papua New Guinea, Singapore, Hong Kong and China.

ŸŸŸŸŸ **864 Single Block Release Block A Lusatia Park Vineyard Yarra Valley Chardonnay 2013** Lusatia Park was planted in '85 with the very good P58 clone. Whole bunch-pressed direct to French oak (30% new) for wild yeast fermentation, 10 months in barrel. The bouquet has the touch of funk that is the hallmark of 864, the palate with a willowy, sinuous intensity, length and aftertaste. A seriously beautiful Chardonnay, greater than the sum of its parts. Screwcap. 13.3% alc. **Rating** 97 **To** 2028 $75 **✪**

864 Single Block Release Guerin Vineyard Block 4 Pinot Noir 2013 An impressive successor to the '12, made with whole-berry wild yeast fermentation with almost 4 weeks on skins, followed by 10 months on gross lees in barrel, then 6 months' settling in tank. It is hard to imagine a Pinot with greater complexity or structure, yet it is close to natural wine, having received only a single, light filtration. Demands time in bottle. Screwcap. 13.2% alc. **Rating** 97 **To** 2028 $75 **✪**

Local Vineyard Series Whitsend & Oakridge Vineyards Shiraz 2013 70% grown on the west-facing Whitsend and 30% on the north-facing Oakridge Vineyard; open-fermented with a mix of whole berries and whole bunches, then 14 months in French puncheons. Bright, vivid crimson; a prime example of the affinity between the Yarra Valley and shiraz: vibrant red fruits, spices, a pinch of pepper, and satin-smooth mouthfeel to a very long palate. Screwcap. 13.7% alc. **Rating** 97 **To** 2028 $38 **✪**

ΥΥΥΥΥ **Local Vineyard Series Guerin Vineyard Chardonnay 2013** Whole bunch-pressed straight to French puncheons for wild-yeast ferment on solids, then 11 months' maturation on lees. Has the Oakridge stamp all over it: a complex, slightly funky bouquet and great drive to the long, elegant, perfectly balanced palate, oak merely a vehicle. Screwcap. 13.4% alc. **Rating** 96 **To** 2023 $36 **○**

864 Single Block Release Drive Block Funder & Diamond Vineyard Yarra Valley Chardonnay 2013 To say you always know what to expect from the 864 Single Block series is to do it scant justice. Planted in '90 on the red volcanic soils of Wandin East, the bouquet is very complex, the palate with mouth-watering intensity that lifts it above the Barkala Ridge Chardonnay. Screwcap. 13.5% alc. **Rating** 96 **To** 2028 $75 **○**

Local Vineyard Series Guerin Vineyard Pinot Noir 2013 From the east-facing Guerin Vineyard in the Upper Yarra Valley; open-fermented whole-berry fermentation and maceration for 3 weeks, followed by 11 months' maturation in French oak. The flavours positively dance in the mouth, red fruits glistening in a superfine web of slinky tannins, oak a bit player. Lovely now, and in 5 years' time. Screwcap. 13.5% alc. **Rating** 96 **To** 2023 $36 **○**

864 Single Block Release Oakridge Vineyard Winery Block Yarra Valley Cabernet Sauvignon 2012 Hand-picked, destemmed, 4-day cold soak, wild yeast fermentation, 3-week post-fermentation maceration; 15 months in French oak. Sure handling and a high-quality vintage have presented a Cabernet of very high quality, its cassis fruit caressing every corner of the mouth, tannins in a micro-support role. Screwcap. 13.5% alc. **Rating** 96 **To** 2042 $75 **○**

Local Vineyard Series Guerin & Oakridge Fumare 2013 81% sauvignon blanc from the Upper Yarra and 19% semillon from the Lower Yarra; whole bunch-pressed to French puncheons for wild yeast fermentation and 9 months' maturation on lees. The bouquet is a little reticent, but the palate is a different kettle of fish, vibrantly alive, almost juicy, and with great length and balance, fruit (not oak) to the fore. Screwcap. 11.8% alc. **Rating** 95 **To** 2020 $32 **○**

Local Vineyard Series Willowlake Vineyard Yarra Valley Chardonnay 2013 Willowlake Vineyard is one of the oldest in the Upper Yarra, on the red soils of the Gladysdale district. While in the Local Vineyard Series camp, this has excellent grip and substance to its varietal expression of white peach and grapefruit. Screwcap. 12.7% alc. **Rating** 95 **To** 2028 $36

Local Vineyard Series Lusatia Park Vineyard Pinot Noir 2013 A simple, slightly scaled-back winemaking approach from that of the 864 series: whole berry, wild yeast, open fermentation for 3 weeks on skins, then 11 months' maturation in French oak. This is a totally delicious wine with glistening red berry fruits, and can be enjoyed tonight or in 5+ years. Screwcap. 13.3% alc. **Rating** 95 **To** 2023 $38

Semillon 2014 Rating 94 **To** 2024 $21 **○**

Barkala Ridge Vineyard Chardonnay 2013 Rating 94 **To** 2025 $36

Over the Shoulder Yarra Valley Pinot Noir 2013 Rating 94 **To** 2021 $22 **○**

864 Winery Block Syrah 2012 Rating 94 **To** 2027 $75

Oakvale ★★★★☆

1596 Broke Road, Pokolbin, NSW 2320 **Region** Hunter Valley
T (02) 4998 7088 **www**.oakvalewines.com.au **Open** 7 days 10–5
Winemaker James Becker **Est.** 1893 **Dozens** 5000 **Vyds** 29.4ha

For three-quarters of a century Oakvale was in the ownership of the founding Elliot family, whose original slab hut homestead is now a museum. In 2010 it was purchased by the Becker family, experienced grapegrowers and owners of the famed Steven's Vineyard. One of the must-see destinations in the Hunter, with vineyards now totalling almost 30ha.

ΥΥΥΥΥ **Ablington Vineyard Semillon 2014** Reflects the very good Hunter vintage. Refined, pure and elegant, it makes its point delicately but insistently; lime/lemon fruit is underwritten by crystalline acidity on the long, perfectly balanced palate. Has a great future. Screwcap. 10.5% alc. **Rating** 95 **To** 2029 $30 **○**

ŸŸŸŸŸ Shiraz 2013 Rating 93 To 2028 $25 ✪
Ablington Vineyard Chardonnay 2014 Rating 92 To 2018 $33 CM
Lustenberger Cabernet 2013 Rating 92 To 2023 $40 CM

Oakway Estate   ★★★☆

575 Farley Road, Donnybrook, WA 6239 **Region** Geographe
T (08) 9731 7141 **www.**oakwayestate.com.au **Open** W'ends & public hols 11–5
Winemaker Tony Davis **Est.** 1998 **Dozens** 1500 **Vyds** 2ha
Ria and Wayne Hammond run a vineyard, beef cattle and sustainable blue gum plantation
in undulating country on the Capel River in the southwest of WA. The grapes are grown
on light gravel and loam soils that provide good drainage giving even sun exposure to the
fruit and minimising the effects of frost. The vineyard is planted to shiraz, merlot, cabernet
sauvignon, muscat, sauvignon blanc and chardonnay, and the wines have won a number
of medals.

ŸŸŸŸ   Chardonnay 2014 Hand-picked, wild yeast-fermented in tank, no oak involved.
        What is present is attractive, but it's light-on. Very different from last year's wine.
        Screwcap. 13% alc. **Rating** 89 To 2016 $18 ✪
        Reserve Cabernet Sauvignon 2011 You really shouldn't use the word
        'charming' in describing Cabernet, but it fits this wine to a tee; it's all red fruits in
        a light to medium-bodied palate, and isn't bothered by tannins (or obvious oak).
        Screwcap. 14.5% alc. **Rating** 89 To 2020 $18 ✪

Occam's Razor   ★★★★

c/- Jasper Hill, Drummonds Lane, Heathcote, Vic 3523 **Region** Heathcote
T (03) 5433 2528 **www.**occamsrazorwines.com **Open** By appt
Winemaker Emily McNally **Est.** 2001 **Dozens** 300 **Vyds** 2.5ha
Emily McNally (née Laughton) decided to follow in her parents' footsteps after first seeing the
world and having a range of casual jobs. Having grown up at Jasper Hill, winemaking was far
from strange, but she decided to find her own way, buying the grapes from a small vineyard
owned by Jasper Hill employee Andrew Conforti and his wife Melissa. She then made the
wine 'with guidance and inspiration from my father'. The name comes from William of
Ockham (1285–1349), also spelt Occam, a theologian and philosopher responsible for many
sayings, including that appearing on the back label of the wine: 'what can be done with fewer
is done in vain with more'. Exports to the UK, the US, Canada and Singapore.

ŸŸŸŸ   Heathcote Shiraz 2013 Full crimson-purple; the complex bouquet has a
        strong line of polished leather and spice; the full-bodied palate takes no prisoners,
        brawling tannins grabbing the black fruits. Surely would have been far better at 14
        or 14.5% alcohol. Cork. 15% alc. **Rating** 89 To 2023 $48

Ocean Eight Vineyard & Winery   ★★★★☆

271 Tucks Road, Shoreham, Vic 3916 **Region** Mornington Peninsula
T (03) 5989 6471 **www.**oceaneight.com **Open** Thurs–Sun 12–5, 7 days Jan
Winemaker Michael Aylward **Est.** 2004 **Dozens** 5000 **Vyds** 16ha
Chris, Gail and Michael Aylward were involved in the establishment of the Kooyong vineyard
and winery, and after selling Kooyong in 2003, retained their 6ha pinot gris vineyard at
Shoreham. After careful investigation, they purchased another property, where they have now
planted 7ha of pinot noir and 3ha of chardonnay. A small winery has been set up, and the focus
will always be on estate-grown grapes. Exports to the UK and Canada.

ŸŸŸŸŸ   Pinot Noir 2013 Strong crimson-purple; a very rich, layered Pinot, with blood
        plum to the fore, then morello cherry; just when you think the fruit is a little one-
        dimensional, fine, savoury/foresty tannins on the finish haul it into line. Will be
        long-lived. Screwcap. 13.2% alc. **Rating** 95 To 2025 $50

ŸŸŸŸŸ   Verve Chardonnay 2013 Rating 91 To 2023 $50

Oceans Estate

290 Courtney Road, Karridale, WA 6288 (postal) **Region** Margaret River
T (08) 9758 2240 **www**.oceansestate.com.au **Open** Not
Winemaker Frank Kittler **Est.** 1999 **Dozens** 3000 **Vyds** 15ha
Oceans Estate was purchased by the Tomasi family (headed by Frank and Attilia) in 1995, and, between '99 and 2007, sauvignon blanc, semillon, chardonnay, merlot and pinot noir were planted. The wines are made onsite, the vineyards now in full bearing. Exports to Singapore.

 settings **Lashings Margaret River Semillon Sauvignon Blanc 2014** The semillon comes through loud and clear here, stamping the blend with drive and energy, yet allowing some passionfruit to come through on the finish. Screwcap. 12.5% alc. **Rating** 90 **To** 2016 $18 ✪

settings **Tomasi Margaret River Semillon 2014 Rating** 89 **To** 2018 $25
Lashings Margaret River Sauvignon Blanc 2014 Rating 89 **To** 2015 $20
Tomasi Margaret River Rose 2014 Rating 88 **To** 2015 $18

Ochota Barrels

Merchants Road, Basket Range, SA 5138 **Region** Adelaide Hills
T 0400 798 818 **www**.ochotabarrels.com **Open** Not
Winemaker Taras Ochota **Est.** 2008 **Dozens** 900 **Vyds** 0.5ha
Taras Ochota has had an incredibly varied career as a winemaker after completing his oenology degree at Adelaide University. He has not only made wine for top-end Australian producers, but has had a Flying Winemaker role in many parts of the world, most recently as consultant winemaker for one of Sweden's largest wine-importing companies, working on Italian wines from Puglia and Sicily made specifically for Oenoforos. Wife Amber has accompanied him to many places, working in a multiplicity of technical and marketing roles. Exports to the UK, the US, Canada, Denmark, Norway and Japan.

settings **Weird Berries in the Woods Gewurztraminer 2014** Instantaneously proclaims its varietal expression courtesy of spice, rose petal, lychee and a wisp of fresh ginger on the bouquet and palate alike; the depth of fruit is such that you wonder whether there is some residual sugar, where in fact there is none. 157 dozen made. Screwcap. 12.4% alc. **Rating** 96 **To** 2029 $35 ✪
Impeccable Disorder Pinot Noir 2014 Deeper colour than A Forest Pinot Noir, and has substantially greater fruit impact on the bouquet and mouthfeel; red and black cherry and plum fruits swell the aroma and occupy the centre of the palate; there are savoury spicy notes encircling those central flavours, but they do not dominate. 3–5 years should reveal a lovely wine with a stupid, in-house name a la D'Arenberg. Cork. 12.8% alc. **Rating** 95 **To** 2024 $80
Shellac Vineyard Syrah 2014 From Marananga in the Barossa Valley. Radically different, this the sun to I am the Owl's moon: opulent and fleshy, with savoury blackberry and plum fruit on a long, satisfying palate that has not been asked to carry a load of alcohol. Screwcap. 13.6% alc. **Rating** 95 **To** 2039 $60
The Slint Vineyard Chardonnay 2014 From the Adelaide Hills. You can sense the full bag of tricks: whole bunch-pressed, wild yeast-fermented, new oak barrels, (some) lees contact, mlf and anything else you care to name. Then there are the fruits: green apple, grapefruit, nashi pear and white peach. Screwcap. 12.4% alc. **Rating** 94 **To** 2024 $45
Surfer Rosa Garnacha 2014 Bright pink; a sculpted, highly focused palate with red berries and citrussy acidity engaged in a duel within a ring of minerally acidity, the finish dry and bright. Screwcap. 12.4% alc. **Rating** 94 **To** 2016 $25 ✪
I am the Owl Syrah 2014 From the Adelaide Hills, it has an expressive bouquet of cool-grown shiraz, spice, cracked pepper and black cherry fruits repeated on the medium-bodied palate, blackberry also joining the fray before a spicy farewell. Screwcap. 13.8% alc. **Rating** 94 **To** 2034 $40

ᵀᵀᵀᵀ♀ A Forest Pinot Noir 2014 Rating 93 To 2020 $45
The Fugazi Vineyard Grenache 2014 Rating 93 To 2016 $40
The Green Room Grenache Syrah 2014 Rating 91 To 2017 $35

Old Plains   ★★★★

71 High Street, Grange, SA 5023 (postal) **Region** Adelaide Plains
T 0407 605 601 **www**.oldplains.com **Open** Not
Winemaker Domenic Torzi, Tim Freeland **Est.** 2003 **Dozens** 4000 **Vyds** 14ha
Old Plains is a partnership between Tim Freeland and Domenic Torzi, who have acquired
small parcels of old vine shiraz (3ha), grenache (1ha) and cabernet sauvignon (4ha) in the
Adelaide Plains region. A portion of the wines, sold under the Old Plains and Longhop labels,
is exported to the US, Denmark, Hong Kong. Singapore and China.

ᵀᵀᵀᵀ♀ **Longhop Mount Lofty Ranges Shiraz 2013** It's a tidy wine all round. Mid-
weight serving of blackcurrant, leather, coffee grounds, boysenberry and mint
flavour, all well sustained through a mildly tannic but essentially fruit-filled finish.
Drinks well young but will cellar comfortably well mid-term. Screwcap. 14% alc.
Rating 91 To 2020 $18 CM ✪
Longhop Rose 2014 Rose made from old-vine grenache grown at 400m above
sea level in the Mount Lofty Ranges. Sweet perfume and flavour to the nose and
palate respectively but it finishes crisp and dry. Jellied strawberry notes. Easy to see
the appeal. Screwcap. 13.5% alc. **Rating** 90 To 2015 $18 CM ✪
Longhop Mount Lofty Ranges Cabernet Sauvignon 2013 Generous style
of red. Fills your mouth with blackcurrant and mulberry fruit flavour. Gum leaf
and dust-like notes add to the show. Well made, good value. Screwcap. 14% alc.
Rating 90 To 2020 $18 CM ✪
Mistura Touriga Amarela Cao 2014 You'd almost put this wine's flavours in
the 'acquired taste' basket. It's both sweet and sour, ashen, cherried, like sucking
on an old burnt stick, like a mix of dry tobacco and blackberry jubes. Yin and
yang. Fresh. Succulent. Intriguing. Best consumed young, it's imagined. Screwcap.
14% alc. **Rating** 90 To 2016 $18 CM ✪

ᵀᵀᵀᵀ **Longhop Mt Lofty Ranges Pinot Gris 2014** Rating 89 To 2015 $18 ✪

Olivers Taranga Vineyards   ★★★★★

246 Seaview Road, McLaren Vale, SA 5171 **Region** McLaren Vale
T (08) 8323 8498 **www**.oliverstaranga.com **Open** 7 days 10–4
Winemaker Corrina Wright **Est.** 1841 **Dozens** 8000 **Vyds** 85.42ha
William and Elizabeth Oliver arrived from Scotland in 1839 to settle at McLaren Vale. Six
generations later, members of the family are still living on the Whitehill and Taranga farms.
The Taranga property has 15 varieties planted (the lion's share shiraz and cabernet sauvignon,
with lesser quantities of chardonnay, chenin blanc, durif, fiano, grenache, mataro, merlot, petit
verdot, sagrantino, semillon, tempranillo, viognier and white frontignac). Corrina Wright (the
Oliver family's first winemaker) makes the wines and in 2011 the family celebrated 170 years
of grapegrowing. Exports to Canada, Hong Kong and China.

ᵀᵀᵀᵀ **M53 Shiraz 2010** Two hogsheads of new French oak (Mercurey and Remond)
the total make. Wow. The colour is inky deep, yet vibrant on the rim, and the
expressive bouquet is swamped by the tsunami of luscious blackberry fruit that
retains shape and balance against the odds, and has flourished with the aid of the
oak. The screwcap makes this a 50-year wine. 14.5% alc. **Rating** 96 To 2060 $180
McLaren Vale Shiraz 2013 From vines 7–70yo. The dense crimson-purple
colour accurately semaphores a plush, rich and complex full-bodied palate that
does not go over the top; dark fruits mesh perfectly with dark chocolate, the
tannins plentiful, but soft and round; the balance and length can't be faulted.
A long life ahead. Screwcap. 14.5% alc. **Rating** 95 To 2038 $30 ✪

Small Batch McLaren Vale Sagrantino 2012 Estate-grown, open-fermented, 50% extended 50-day maceration on skins, matured in used French hogsheads. The maceration has extracted the colour and masses of black cherry flavour, 70% cacao chocolate in the background, ripe tannins framing the flavours in fine style. Screwcap. 15% alc. **Rating** 95 **To** 2032 $40
YarnBomb by Corrina Wright Shiraz 2012 A Dan Murphy special release, and you can't cavil at either the clever label, or the quality of a palate flooded with supple, slurpy, chocolate-coated black fruits brought to order by well-managed tannins. Screwcap. 14.5% alc. **Rating** 94 **To** 2027 $23 ✪
Small Batch McLaren Vale Cabernet Sauvignon 2013 Batch 2402. Amarone-inspired. Keeps itself tidy and fresh as sweet, sinewy fruit flows through. Curranty, dusty, supple and yet firm. Balance, such an unsexy word, allows the fruit flavours to shine. The seduction creeps up on you but it certainly hits its mark. Screwcap. 14.5% alc. **Rating** 94 **To** 2024 $35 CM
Small Batch Vine Dried McLaren Vale Cabernet 2013 25% dried on the vine/on racks (or 50%, depending on whether you look at the PR material or the label), then blended and fermented with the normal pick (9 days later than the dried portion). Deeply coloured; all one can say is that the dried fruit (Amarone-like) component has married seamlessly with the conventionally picked portion, with a savoury twist on the finish. Screwcap. 14.5% alc. **Rating** 94 **To** 2033 $32

����� HJ Reserve McLaren Vale Shiraz 2011 **Rating** 93 **To** 2023 $55 CM
Small Batch McLaren Vale Grenache 2012 **Rating** 93 **To** 2042 $30
Small Batch McLaren Vale Tempranillo 2013 **Rating** 93 **To** 2020 $32 CM
Small Batch McLaren Vale Fiano 2014 **Rating** 92 **To** 2017 $24 ✪
Chica Small Batch Mencia Rose 2014 **Rating** 90 **To** 2015 $24

Olsen Wines Victoria ★★★

21 Carinish Road, Oakleigh South, Vic 3167 **Region** Port Phillip Zone/Yarra Valley
T (03) 9544 4033 **www**.vin888.com.au **Open** Mon–Fri 9.30–5
Winemaker Glenn Olsen **Est.** 1991 **Dozens** 65 000
Glenn Olsen, a science and engineering graduate of the University of Melbourne, has been involved in the wine industry since 1975, initially importing wines and spirits from Europe, then moving into retailing. In 1991, he and Angie Joson-Olsen started Olsen Wines, claiming to be Melbourne's first inner-suburban winery. Several others may dispute this claim, but that is perhaps neither here nor there. Most of the wines come from grapes grown either on the Murray River in Northeast Victoria (for the full-bodied Big Fella range), or in the Yarra Valley. Exports to the US, Canada, the Philippines, South Korea, Cambodia, Vietnam, Singapore, Hong Kong, Japan and China.

♗♗♗♗ **Barrel Aged Preservative Free Merlot 2013** Fresh berried flavours with a light coating of powdery milk chocolate. Gentle herbal notes too. Flows freely through the mouth. Screwcap. 13.8% alc. **Rating** 88 **To** 2015 $20 CM

🍇 One 4 One Estate ★★★

141 Killara Road, Gruyere, Vic 3770 **Region** Yarra Valley
T 0409 113 677 **Open** By appt
Winemaker Lisa Marino and consultants **Est.** 2010 **Dozens** 200 **Vyds** 3ha
Lisa and Joe Marino purchased the One 4 One Estate property in 2010 'after falling in love with the Yarra Valley views'. The land was part of the Yarraloch Estate, which was subdivided in the mid-1990s. 22ha of merlot had been planted in '07, and a little over 1ha of pinot noir was close-planted in '11 by the Marinos.

♗♗♗♗ **Limited Release Merlot 2013** Hand-picked and foot-stomped after a day in the fermenter; matured for 13 months in French barriques (50% new). Has red-berry fruit flavours, but with a nagging suspicion of some residual sweetness on the aftertaste. 87 dozen made. Screwcap. 12.8% alc. **Rating** 89 **To** 2023 $44

One Lonely Barrel

Bethany Road, Bethany, SA 5352 **Region** Barossa Valley
T 0413 271 241 **www**.onelonelybarrel.com.au **Open** Not
Winemaker John Samartzis **Est.** 2010 **Dozens** 250
John Samartzis made his first barrel of wine in 2002; he describes it as a disaster. Chastened,
he went looking for a 'how to' book, attending several winemaking courses, reading more
books, and with some help from a handful of friends, the '03 vintage was more successful.
The '05 and '06 vintages won Best in Class and Best in Show at the Amateur Winemakers
Competition in the Tanunda Show. In '12 his Personally Produced Barossa Shiraz became the
first commercial release, rather more than the one hogshead that he started with, the business
plan ultimately aiming for 1000 dozen, marketed to 250–300 wine lovers. He also produces
My Personally Selected wines, selling for less than the wine he makes.

♥♥♥♥♀ **Samartzis Personally Produced Barossa Shiraz 2013** A well made wine
that has a sense of both place and of the variety in the context of that place – the
same Barossa Valley vineyard and the same rows (hand-picked), matured in French
oak for 12 months. Needs time to soften and open up, but should do so. Screwcap.
14% alc. **Rating** 90 **To** 2028 $20 ✪
Samartzis Personally Produced Barossa Shiraz 2012 Has flourished in
the bottle, in keeping with the increase in price. Screwcap. 14.5% alc. **Rating** 90
To 2017 $25

Orange Mountain Wines

10 Radnedge Lane, Orange, NSW 2800 **Region** Orange
T (02) 6365 2626 **www**.orangemountain.com.au **Open** Wed–Fri 9–3, w'ends 9–5
Winemaker Terry Dolle **Est.** 1997 **Dozens** 3000 **Vyds** 1ha
Having established the business back in 1997, Terry Dolle made the decision to sell the
Manildra vineyard in 2009. He now makes wine from small parcels of hand-picked fruit, using
an old basket press and barrel maturation. These are all single-vineyard wines reflecting the
terroir of Orange. He has retained 1ha of chardonnay and pinot noir, which he manages along
with the winemaking. Exports to China.

♥♥♥♥♥ **1397 Shiraz Viognier 2012** Shiraz and viognier (7%) were co-fermented with
50% whole bunches. The wine spent 18 months in new French oak, and while
it is elegant and only medium-bodied at best, the fruit has integrated that oak,
simply leaving cedary notes to go with the spice and pepper underlying the cherry
fruit flavours. Lovely wine. Screwcap. 13.5% alc. **Rating** 95 **To** 2030 $42
Limited Release Riesling 2014 Hand-picked and sorted, important in this
vintage; cool-fermented, and made reductively (no oxygen impact). A power-
packed Riesling in the Orange Mountain style, citrus juice, pith, zest and crunchy
acidity tumbling all over each other. Demands Asian food, the spicier the better.
Screwcap. 12% alc. **Rating** 94 **To** 2025 $25 ✪
Limited Release Viognier 2013 The wine spent 12 months in oak. It is a
superior example of Viognier, with clear-cut varietal character in an apricot/
peach/musk spectrum; equally impressive are the texture and structure, sustained
by crunchy acidity. Screwcap. 13.5% alc. **Rating** 94 **To** 2016 $25 ✪

♥♥♥♥♀ **Limited Release Sauvignon Blanc 2014** **Rating** 92 **To** 2019 $22 ✪

Oranje Tractor

198 Link Road, Albany, WA 6330 **Region** Albany
T (08) 9842 5175 **www**.oranjetractor.com **Open** Sat–Mon 11–5 (Sat–Thurs school hols)
Winemaker Rob Diletti **Est.** 1998 **Dozens** 12 000 **Vyds** 2.9ha
The name celebrates the 1964 vintage, orange-coloured Fiat tractor, acquired when Murray
Gomm and Pamela Lincoln began the establishment of the vineyard. Murray was born next
door, but moved to Perth to work in physical education and health promotion. Here he met
nutritionist Pamela, who completed the wine science degree at CSU in 2000, before being

awarded a Churchill Fellowship to study organic grape and wine production in the US and Europe. When the partners established their vineyard, they went down the organic path.

ΨΨΨΨΨ **Albany Riesling 2014** Gin-clear colour; rather like young Semillon, it's as much about what it doesn't say as what it does; the crunchy acidity, the length, and the whisper of lime blossom coupled with elusive lime on the palate, absolutely guarantee that the wine will flower with a few years in bottle. Screwcap. 12% alc. **Rating** 94 **To** 2034 $26 ✪

ΨΨΨΨΨ **Albany Sauvignon Blanc 2014 Rating** 92 **To** 2017 $28

Orlando ★★★★

Barossa Valley Way, Rowland Flat, SA 5352 **Region** Barossa Valley
T (08) 8521 3111 **www**.pernod-ricard-winemakers.com **Open** Not
Winemaker Bernard Hickin **Est.** 1847 **Dozens** NFP **Vyds** 1600ha
Orlando is the parent who has been divorced by its child, Jacob's Creek (see separate entry). While Orlando is over 165 years old, Jacob's Creek is little more than 40 years old. For what are doubtless sound marketing reasons, Orlando aided and abetted the divorce, but the average consumer is unlikely to understand the logic, and – if truth be known – will care about it even less. The vineyard holding is for all brands (notably Jacob's Creek) and for all regions across SA, Vic and NSW; it will likely be less in coming years.

ΨΨΨΨΨ **Gramp's Shiraz 2011** Excellent result from the vintage. Sweet with blackberry, licorice, coal and clove flavours, ribbed with earthen tannin and flush with both fruit and toasty, resiny oak. It's true to the established style of the label, and the cooler vintage has helped balance it up a fraction; a semblance of elegance to a hearty show. Screwcap. 14.3% alc. **Rating** 92 **To** 2020 $22 CM ✪
Gramp's Botrytis Semillon 2011 It's not hard to imagine it being easy to find botrytis-affected grapes in the wet '11 season. This is deeply coloured, golden almost into brown, with apricot jam and marmalade swinging into sweet apple and honey. It has terrific intensity and some, but not a lot, of citrussy cut. Screwcap. 11.4% alc. **Rating** 90 **To** 2017 $22 CM

Ortus Wines ★★★★

22 Nile Street, Port Adelaide, SA 5015 (postal) **Region** South Australia
T 0408 496 155 **www**.ortuswines.com.au **Open** Not
Winemaker Tim Geddes **Est.** 2011 **Dozens** 5500
While Ortus was not established until September 2011, its family history dates back to 1848 and the arrival of Johann Gottlieb Bittner from Prussia; the owner of Ortus, Julie Cooper, is a descendant of Johann. She has more than 15 years' experience in the winery industry working for small through to large multinational companies in sales and marketing. Ortus purchases grapes from Tasmania, the Barossa Valley, Riverland, Coonawarra and McLaren Vale, producing three tiers of wines for both domestic and international markets. The wines are made in various wineries under the direction of Tim Geddes. Exports to Canada, Sweden, South Korea and China.

ΨΨΨΨΨ **Tasmania Pinot Noir 2012** Star-bright, clear crimson; the very fragrant, complex bouquet has berry fruits, spice and smoked meat aromas, and the energetic palate wastes no time in picking up the message of the bouquet; there is a thoroughly attractive array of harmonious flavours, fine, savoury tannins and French oak woven delicately through the fruit. Screwcap. 13% alc. **Rating** 94 **To** 2022 $30 ✪

ΨΨΨΨΨ **Tasmania Riesling 2012 Rating** 93 **To** 2027 $20 ✪

Ottelia

2280 V&A Lane, Coonawarra, SA 5263 **Region** Coonawarra
T 0409 836 298 **www.ottelia.com.au Open** By appt
Winemaker John Innes **Est.** 2001 **Dozens** 4000 **Vyds** 9ha
John and Melissa Innes moved to Coonawarra intending, in John's words, to 'stay a little while'. The first sign of a change of heart was the purchase of a property ringed by red gums, and with a natural wetland dotted with *Ottelia ovalifolia*, a native water lily. They still live in the house they built there, John having worked as winemaker at Rymill Coonawarra, while Melissa established a restaurant. After 20 years at Rymill, John left to focus on consultancy work throughout the Limestone Coast, and to establish and run Ottelia.

🍷🍷🍷🍷🍷 **Mount Gambier Sauvignon Blanc 2014** Excellent intensity. Shoots through the mouth and then drives out through the finish. Class act. Gunmetal, thistle, passionfruit and chalk. Boasts both elegance and impact. Screwcap. 11.8% alc. Rating 94 To 2016 $22 CM ✪

🍷🍷🍷🍷🍷 **Coonawarra Cabernet Sauvignon 2012** Rating 93 To 2024 $31 CM
Mount Benson Shiraz 2013 Rating 91 To 2022 $28 CM
Wrattonbully Pinot Gris 2014 Rating 90 To 2015 $22 CM

Ouse River Wines

PO Box 40, Ouse, Tas 7140 **Region** Southern Tasmania
T (03) 6287 1309 **www.ouseriverwines.com Open** Not
Winemaker Peter Dredge, David Calvert, Alain Rousseau (Contract) **Est.** 2002
Dozens 200 **Vyds** 8.3ha
Ouse River Wines is one of the most interesting developments in Tasmania. Bernard and Margaret Brain own a 1000ha property north of Ouse at the top end of the Derwent Valley on the edge of the central highlands. They run nine different enterprises on the property, the vineyard the most inland in Tasmania, with a continental climate, and diurnal temperature range during ripening of 7°C more than the areas surrounding Hobart. In the early 1990s Bernard and Margaret attended wine-tasting classes run by Phil Laing while he was a teacher at the local school, which prompted the planting of a trial area of six varieties to see whether they would ripen. In 2002 they approached Ray Guerin to see what he thought, the answer was a contract for 10 years with Hardys. The first planting of 1ha in late '02 was followed by an extra hectare planted each year until '06; a further 2ha was planted in '09, and 1.25ha in '11, with an end total of 4.7ha of pinot noir and 3.6ha of chardonnay. The pinot was incorporated in Arras from the second vintage, and in every vintage it has been made since. After the Hardys contract ended, 95% of the fruit was sold to five different purchasers, mainly for use in sparkling wine, but enough going to table wine to excite considerable interest. They asked the purchasers whether they would buy additional grapes, and the answer was 110 tonnes, which will drive substantial new plantings over the next two years, with ample suitable land.

🍷🍷🍷🍷🍷 **Pinot Noir 2013** Bright, clear crimson; a lively mix of fragrant red fruits and bramble on the bouquet; the palate has real elegance, with very good length and finish. Screwcap. 13.5% alc. Rating 92 To 2020 $25 ✪
Chardonnay 2013 A lively, fresh and crisp Chardonnay, framed on all sides by Tasmanian acidity, but in balance with the fruit; 3–5 years should do nicely, although it will live well beyond that. Screwcap. 13.4% alc. Rating 91 To 2022 $22 ✪

Out of Step

6 McKenzie Avenue, Healesville, Vic 3777 (postal) **Region** Yarra Valley
T 0424 644 693 **www.outofstepwineco.com Open** Not
Winemaker David Chatfield, Nathan Reeves **Est.** 2012 **Dozens** 1000
Out of Step is the micro virtual winery of David Chatfield and Nathan Reeves. David explains, 'I worked in the music industry for a long time promoting tours for international acts, so I'm very familiar with financial risk.' Nathan works full-time as a cellar hand at Sticks,

David works at the Lusatia Park Vineyard. Both are getting close to finishing their winemaking degrees, but are increasingly distracted by actually making the wines. Along the way they have variously chalked up experience at Stella Bella (Margaret River) and Vinify (California). Their initial foray with Sauvignon Blanc sourced from Lusatia Park was spectacular, and they have a Chardonnay from the vineyard that produces the Thousand Candles wines, and a Nebbiolo from the Malakoff Vineyard in the Pyrenees.

🍷🍷🍷🍷🍷 **Lone Star Creek Yarra Valley Sauvignon Blanc 2014** Hand-picked, pressed straight to barrel, wild yeast-fermented in French barriques (25% new), partial mlf. Full straw-green; this picks Yarra Valley sauvignon blanc up by the scruff of its neck and invests it with the character and structure so often missing in action. You actually want to drink this wine. Terrific value. 150 dozen made. Screwcap. 13% alc. **Rating** 95 **To** 2017 $24 **O**

Willoughby Bridge Heathcote GSM 2014 A 40/40/20% blend sourced from the Shelmerdine Willoughby Bridge Vineyard; some whole bunches used, but mainly destemmed, matured for 5 months in barrel (15% new). A surprise, packed with a seductive display of juicy satsuma plum and red-berry fruits offset by perfectly balanced savoury tannins. Screwcap. 14% alc. **Rating** 95 **To** 2024 $30 **O**

Outlook Hill Vineyard ★★★★

97 School Lane, Tarrawarra, Vic 3777 **Region** Yarra Valley
T (03) 5962 2890 **www**.outlookhill.com.au **Open** By appt
Winemaker Peter Snow, Al Fencaros **Est.** 2000 **Dozens** 500 **Vyds** 5.4ha
After several years overseas, former Melbourne professionals Peter and Lydia Snow returned to Australia in 1997 planning to open a wine tourism business in the Hunter Valley. However, they had second thoughts, and in 2000 moved to the Yarra Valley, where they have now established five B&B cottages, a vineyard, and a cellar door outlet, backed by a constant temperature wine storage cool room. Exports to China.

🍷🍷🍷🍷🍷 **Yarra Valley Cabernet Merlot 2013** Slinky smooth blend, polished by fine oak and smart with curranty fruit flavour. Brambly notes add complexity, as do woody spice notes. Tannin is ultra fine-grained. Game notes to the finish but it remains fluid and persistent. Screwcap. 13% alc. **Rating** 92 **To** 2023 $30 CM

🌿 Over the Edge Wines Tasmania ★★★☆

100–104 Mornington Road, Mornington, Tas 7018 **Region** Southern Tasmania
T 0457 587 713 **Open** Not
Winemaker Nick Johnston, Matthieu Bancal **Est.** 2013 **Dozens** 300
This brings together two Tasmanian restaurateurs and (apparently) self-taught winemakers, Nick Johnson and Matthieu Bancal. The aim is to grow climate-challenging varieties, such as petit verdot, cabernet franc, tempranillo and nebbiolo, which, for good reasons, have not been on the table in Tasmania. The usual micro-vinification techniques see hand-picking, wild yeast fermentation, basket-pressing and movement through gravity to oak for maturation.

🍷🍷🍷🍷🍷 **Cabernet 2013** Matured in used French oak for 9 months. Tries desperately hard to present a friendly face, but doesn't quite succeed; it is neutral, not unfriendly. All of which is probably too hard on the wine, for there is some sweet blackcurrant embedded in its heart. Screwcap. 13.2% alc. **Rating** 90 **To** 2023 $44

🍷🍷🍷🍷 **Cabernet Franc 2013 Rating** 88 **To** 2017 $44
Petit Verdot 2013 Rating 88 **To** 2018 $44

pacha mama ★★★★

PO Box 2208, Sunbury, Vic 3429 **Region** Various Vic
T 0432 021 668 **www**.pachamamawines.com.au **Open** Not
Winemaker Callie Jemmeson, Nina Stocker **Est.** 2010 **Dozens** 5000 **Vyds** 14ha
When David Jemmeson established pacha mama in 2010, he had already worked in the winery community for 30 years, his experience crossing the Tasman, and also businesses such

as Riedel. He also found time to travel to the Andean mountains, and says the liveliness, colour and vibrancy of South American culture was the inspiration for the brand (pacha mama is the Inca earth goddess). David also has a long history of interconnection with Don Lewis, dating back to their working together and developing the Mitchelton, Blackwood Park and Preece brands. The vineyard is planted to pinot gris, riesling and shiraz.

ᵀᵀᵀᵀᵀ **Heathcote Shiraz 2014** Leaps from the glass. It's the kind of wine that makes both the wine critic's job, and the drinker's task in choosing a wine, easy. It has a bit of spunk, a lot of blackberried fruit, complexing notes of sandalwood, clove and coffeed oak, and a good chatter of fresh, black-fruited flavour through the finish. It will work both now and later, but why wait? Screwcap. 14% alc. **Rating** 93 To 2021 $26 CM ○

Yarra Valley Chardonnay 2014 Modern, fresh, crisp Chardonnay with enough flavour to satisfy. Mid-intensity flavours of dry pear, apple, nectarine and fennel, with bacony oak and lactose notes whispering throughout. An easy wine to recommend. Screwcap. 13.3% alc. **Rating** 91 To 2017 $23 CM ○

Yarra Valley Chardonnay 2012 Easy-drinking pleasure with just enough funk notes to give it an impression of sophistication. Apple and pear flavours with chalk and struck match through the finish. Enough persistence to satisfy. Attractive offering all round. Screwcap. 12.8% alc. **Rating** 91 To 2020 $22 CM ○

ᵀᵀᵀᵀ **Riesling 2014 Rating** 89 To 2019 $20 CM
Central Victoria Pinot Gris 2014 Rating 89 To 2015 $20 CM
Yarra Valley Pinot Noir 2014 Rating 89 To 2019 $25 CM
Yarra Valley Pinot Noir 2012 Rating 89 To 2020 $25 CM

Pages Creek   ★★★★

624 Middle Teatree Road, Teatree, Tas 7017 **Region** Southern Tasmania
T (03) 6260 2311 **www.**pagescreekwine.com.au **Open** By appt
Winemaker Winemaking Tasmania (Julian Alcorso) **Est.** 1999 **Dozens** 1200 **Vyds** 4.5ha
In 1999 Peter and Sue Lowrie planted a vineyard on their 20ha Pages Creek property, named after the creek that runs through it. They have cabernet sauvignon, pinot noir, chardonnay and merlot. The tiny first vintage (2002) was consumed at their wedding.

ᵀᵀᵀᵀᵀ **Pinot Noir 2013** Good hue; opens with spiced plum aromas; a flamboyant style, with satsuma plum fruit, and a soft, easygoing mouthfeel. Screwcap. 13.5% alc. **Rating** 91 To 2020 $26

Palmer Wines   ★★★★★

1271 Caves Road, Dunsborough, WA 6281 **Region** Margaret River
T (08) 9756 7024 **www.**palmerwines.com.au **Open** 7 days 10–5
Winemaker Mark Warren, Bruce Jukes **Est.** 1977 **Dozens** 6000 **Vyds** 51.39ha
Steve and Helen Palmer have mature plantings of cabernet sauvignon, sauvignon blanc, shiraz, merlot, chardonnay and semillon, with smaller amounts of malbec and cabernet franc. Recent vintages have had major success in WA and national wine shows. Exports to Indonesia, Hong Kong and China.

ᵀᵀᵀᵀᵀ **Reserve Margaret River Chardonnay 2013** Deserves the Reserve tag. This is a Chardonnay of very considerable length, intensity and focus; pear, apple, grapefruit and white peach all present, but waiting for the next stage of development; the oak is integrated, the acidity balanced, so have no fear for its future. Screwcap. 13.2% alc. **Rating** 95 To 2023 $35 ○

Reserve Margaret River Shiraz 2013 French oak-matured. Deeply coloured, and bursting with ripe black fruits, this full-bodied Shiraz pushes the envelope of extract to the limit, but not beyond; the fruit, oak and tannins all sing from the same page. It just needs lots of time. Screwcap. 14.9% alc. **Rating** 95 To 2043 $45

Margaret River Reserve Cabernets The Grandee 2013 An estate-grown blend of cabernet, malbec, merlot and franc. It is effortlessly powerful and complex, with a cascade of blackcurrant fruit framed by quality oak and fine-grained, persistent tannins. Screwcap. 14% alc. **Rating** 95 **To** 2033 $35 ✪

Margaret River Shiraz 2013 Deep colour; if served blind, you might guess this came from SA or Vic, for it speaks of many things on its rich bouquet and full-bodied palate; the black fruits are intense, but not hot, the structure and texture keeping everything balanced. The one thing it needs is time. Screwcap. 14.9% alc. **Rating** 94 **To** 2038 $35

Margaret River Cabernet Sauvignon 2013 Again, picked at the absolute top end of ripeness, which crowds the finish, having opened proceedings with panache; there is cassis spilling out everywhere, and the tannin and oak management are good. Time may conceivably help, but Shiraz deals with elevated alcohol better than Cabernet. Screwcap. 14.8% alc. **Rating** 94 **To** 2038 $35

Margaret River Malbec 2013 Bright, full crimson-purple; an impressive rendition of Malbec, flush with varietal fruit in the usual dark plum spectrum; supple tannins and quality oak are neatly balanced and integrated. Screwcap. 14.2% alc. **Rating** 94 **To** 2025 $35

♟♟♟♟♟ **Margaret River Sauvignon Blanc 2014** Rating 93 To 2016 $25 ✪
Margaret River Cabernet Franc 2013 Rating 93 To 2028 $30
Margaret River Sauvignon Blanc Semillon 2014 Rating 92 To 2017 $25 ✪
Krackerjack Bin 2 2013 Rating 91 To 2023 $25
Krackerjack Bin 4 2013 Rating 90 To 2019 $25
Margaret River Merlot 2013 Rating 90 To 2030 $30

Pankhurst   ★★★☆

'Old Woodgrove', Woodgrove Road, Hall, NSW 2618 **Region** Canberra District
T (02) 6230 2592 **www**.pankhurstwines.com.au **Open** W'ends & public hols
Winemaker Brian Sinclair **Est.** 1986 **Dozens** 2000 **Vyds** 5ha
Agricultural scientist and consultant Allan Pankhurst and wife Christine (with a degree in pharmaceutical science) have established a split-canopy vineyard (pinot noir, chardonnay, cabernet sauvignon, merlot, sangiovese, tempranillo, semillon and sauvignon blanc). Pankhurst has had success with Pinot Noir, Chardonnay and, most recently, with its Cabernet Sauvignon and Sangiovese. Exports to China.

♟♟♟ **Dorothy May Canberra District Cabernet Sauvignon 2013** Matured for 10 months in French oak. It has moderate varietal character, with the flavours more towards plum than blackcurrant, but appropriate in the context of the light to medium-bodied palate. Top bronze rather than the silver medal it won at Cowra '14. Screwcap. 14.2% alc. **Rating** 89 **To** 2023 $30

Canberra District Sangiovese 2013 Matured for 10 months in French and Hungarian oak. Has some varietal character, with dusty sour cherry fruit, the savoury backdrop moving forward on the finish. Screwcap. 14% alc. **Rating** 88 **To** 2018 $30

Paracombe Wines   ★★★★

294b Paracombe Road, Paracombe, SA 5132 **Region** Adelaide Hills
T (08) 8380 5058 **www**.paracombewines.com **Open** By appt
Winemaker Paul Drogemuller, James Barry **Est.** 1983 **Dozens** 12500 **Vyds** 22.1ha
Paul and Kathy Drogemuller established Paracombe Wines in 1983 in the wake of the devastating Ash Wednesday bushfires. The winery is located high on a plateau at Paracombe, looking out over the Mount Lofty Ranges. The vineyard is run with minimal irrigation and hand-pruning, designed to keep yields low. The wines are made onsite, with every part of the production process through to distribution handled from there.

♟♟♟♟♟ **Adelaide Hills Cabernet Franc 2010** Paracombe has been a long-time leader in growing and making Cabernet Franc; its vineyard is mature, as is its expertise in handling the variety. The wine has a fragrance all of its own, spanning violets and fresh tobacco, the palate with sweet berries and spiced poached plum.

It has developed at a leisurely pace, and won't fall over any time soon. Screwcap. 14.5% alc. **Rating** 94 To 2025 $27 ⚫

🍷🍷🍷🍷♀ **Adelaide Hills Cabernet Sauvignon 2010** Rating 92 To 2022 $21 CM ⚫
Adelaide Hills Pinot Noir 2013 Rating 91 To 2022 $21 ⚫
Holland Creek Adelaide Hills Riesling 2014 Rating 90 To 2020 $20 CM ⚫
Adelaide Hills Shiraz 2010 Rating 90 To 2019 $21 CM ⚫
Adelaide Hills Pinot Noir Chardonnay NV Rating 90 To 2016 $35 CM

Paradigm Hill   ★★★★★

26 Merricks Road, Merricks, Vic 3916 **Region** Mornington Peninsula
T (03) 5989 9000 **www**.paradigmhill.com.au **Open** 1st w'end of month
Winemaker Dr George Mihaly **Est.** 1999 **Dozens** 1400 **Vyds** 4.2ha
Dr George Mihaly (with a background in medical research, biotechnology and pharmaceutical industries) and wife Ruth (a former chef and caterer) realised a 30-year dream of establishing their own vineyard and winery, abandoning their previous careers to do so. George had all the necessary scientific qualifications, and built on those by making the 2001 Merricks Creek wines, moving to home base at Paradigm Hill in '02, all along receiving guidance and advice from Nat White of Main Ridge Estate. The vineyard, under Ruth's control with advice from Shane Strange, is planted to 2.1ha of pinot noir, 0.9ha of shiraz, 0.82ha of riesling and 0.38ha of pinot gris. Exports to The Netherlands, Singapore and China.

🍷🍷🍷🍷🍷 **L'ami Sage Mornington Peninsula Pinot Noir 2013** The 19 separate facts on the back label include resveratrol (4.6mg/l) and (for example) pH and titratable acidity both at picking and at bottling, most relevant clones (MV6 and 115) and 18 months in oak (33% new). A pure and beautifully balanced Pinot, red and black cherry fruit gently framed by oak and fine-grained tannins. 658 dozen made. Screwcap. 13.5% alc. **Rating** 96 To 2025 $68 ⚫
Mornington Peninsula Pinot Gris 2014 Fermented in French oak (33% new, 67% 1yo). A distinct touch of pink; not for the first time, Paradigm Hill pulls a rabbit from the hat, leaving the nashi pear varietal flavour intact, but adding texture and complexity during the 6 months' maturation in oak; the finish is crisp and clean. Screwcap. 13.1% alc. **Rating** 95 To 2017 $56
Les Cinq Mornington Peninsula Pinot Noir 2013 Like L'ami Sage, 19 facts on the back label yet (curiously) no details of whole bunch/whole berry/crushed fruit. Not good enough, George. 115 clone, 18 months in French oak (33% new). Has greater elegance to its crisp red-cherry fruit, seemingly with higher acidity – but it has less (5.5g/l versus 5.9g/l). Very different texture and flavour profile. A purist's Pinot, needing time. Screwcap. 13.5% alc. **Rating** 95 To 2023 $80
Col's Block Mornington Peninsula Shiraz 2013 9-day cold soak, 5-day fermentation, 2 days' post-fermentation, 18 months in new and used French oak. Bright, clear colour; the bouquet is highly fragrant, the light to medium-bodied palate initially seeming light on, but builds on retasting, with bright red cherry fruit to the fore. Screwcap. 12.8% alc. **Rating** 94 To 2028 $50

🍷🍷🍷🍷♀ **Mornington Peninsula Riesling 2014** Rating 90 To 2025 $38

Paradise IV   ★★★★★

45 Dog Rocks Road, Batesford, Vic 3213 (postal) **Region** Geelong
T (03) 5276 1536 **www**.paradiseivwines.com.au **Open** Not
Winemaker Douglas Neal **Est.** 1988 **Dozens** 800 **Vyds** 3.1ha
The former Moorabool Estate has been renamed Paradise IV for the very good reason that it is the site of the original Paradise IV Vineyard, planted in 1848 by Swiss vigneron Jean-Henri Dardel. It is owned by Ruth and Graham Bonney. The winery has an underground barrel room, and the winemaking turns around wild yeast fermentation, natural mlf, gravity movement of the wine and so forth. Exports to China.

🍷🍷🍷🍷🍷 **The Dardel 2013** Deeply coloured Shiraz; lives up to its 19th and 21st century reputation, the highly expressive and fragrant bouquet with with red and black

fruits interleaved by touches of spice and licorice, leading into a medium-bodied patrician palate calmly waiting to proclaim its Joseph's coat of textured flavours. Screwcap. 13.5% alc. **Rating** 96 **To** 2033 $55 **⊙**
Chaumont 2013 85/7/5/3% estate-grown cabernet sauvignon, shiraz, cabernet franc and merlot provides a generous helping of cassis, cedar, spice and tobacco, the tannins fine and balanced. Ready whenever you are; sensitive winemaking on display. Screwcap. 13.5% alc. **Rating** 95 **To** 2028 $50

Paramoor Wines

439 Three Chain Road, Carlsruhe via Woodend, Vic 3442 **Region** Macedon Ranges
T (03) 5427 1057 **www.**paramoor.com.au **Open** Fri–Mon 10–5
Winemaker William Fraser **Est.** 2003 **Dozens** 1200 **Vyds** 1.5ha
Paramoor Wines is the retirement venture of Will Fraser, formerly Managing Director of Kodak Australasia. To be strictly correct, he is Dr William Fraser, armed with a PhD in chemistry from Adelaide University. Much later he added a diploma of wine technology from the University of Melbourne (Dookie campus). Paramoor is set on 17ha of beautiful country not far from Hanging Rock; it was originally a Clydesdale horse farm, with a magnificent heritage-style barn now used for cellar door sales and functions. Will has planted 0.5ha each of pinot noir, pinot gris and riesling, and leases 2.6ha of vines in the lower Goulburn Valley (shiraz, cabernet sauvignon, merlot). He also receives regular supplies of pinot noir and chardonnay from another Macedon Ranges vineyard owned by friends.

ΨΨΨΨΨ Kathleen Shiraz 2013 Matured for 12 months in American oak. Bright crimson; this is a very attractive medium to full-bodied wine with some Grampians-like spice, although it is of single-vineyard Heathcote origin; the palate picks up exactly where the bouquet leaves off, adding licorice to the blackberry fruits. Diam. 14.5% alc. **Rating** 94 **To** 2028 $28 **⊙**

ΨΨΨΨΨ Uncle Fred Heathcote Cabernet Sauvignon 2012 Rating 90 **To** 2022 $25

Paringa Estate

44 Paringa Road, Red Hill South, Vic 3937 **Region** Mornington Peninsula
T (03) 5989 2669 **www.**paringaestate.com.au **Open** 7 days 11–5
Winemaker Lindsay McCall **Est.** 1985 **Dozens** 15 000 **Vyds** 24.7ha
Schoolteacher-turned-winemaker Lindsay McCall has shown an absolutely exceptional gift for winemaking across a range of styles, but with immensely complex Pinot Noir and Shiraz leading the way. The wines have an unmatched level of success in the wine shows and competitions Paringa Estate is able to enter, the limitation being the relatively small production of the top wines in the portfolio. His skills are no less evident in contract winemaking for others. Exports to the UK, Canada, Denmark, Ukraine, Singapore, Hong Kong, China and Japan.

ΨΨΨΨΨ Estate Pinot Noir 2013 As ever, the colour is bright and deep, the bouquet a wonderland of red fruits, purple fruits and spices, the palate with inimitable Paringa Estate poise and drive, the mouth-watering array of black cherries and spices lifting and expanding on the finish in best peacock's tail fashion. Screwcap. 14.5% alc. **Rating** 96 **To** 2025 $60 **⊙**
The Paringa Single Vineyard Pinot Noir 2012 Surprisingly light colour, but crystal clear and bright; the intense bouquet sends a big come-on signal, both it and the palate with an almost ethereal display of pure red fruits. A lovely Pinot, but very different from the usual power of Paringa Estate. Screwcap. 13.5% alc. **Rating** 96 **To** 2025 $90
The Paringa Single Vineyard Shiraz 2012 Matured for 18 months in new and 1yo French barriques. Despite identical vinification to the Estate, this power-packed Shiraz is in blackberry and plum territory from the outset; licorice, cracked black pepper and full, ripe tannins provide complexity and depth of a high order. Screwcap. 14% alc. **Rating** 96 **To** 2042 $80

Estate Chardonnay 2013 Hand-picked, whole bunch-pressed straight to barrel, wild yeast-fermented in new and used French barriques, stirred, 11 months, no mlf. A beautifully structured and layered Chardonnay, varietal fruit expression its raison d'être, white peach, apricot and fig the centre of activity; the other adjuncts are there, doing their part as asked. Screwcap. 14% alc. **Rating** 95 **To** 2024 $35
Estate Shiraz 2012 Matured for 18 months in new and 1yo French barriques. Youthful, clear crimson; the fragrant bouquet verges on flowery; the light to medium-bodied palate relies on its deceptively silky mouthfeel, spicy bright fruit flavours and extreme length to make its point. Screwcap. 14% alc. **Rating** 95 **To** 2032 $50
The Paringa Single Vineyard Chardonnay 2013 **Rating** 94 **To** 2025 $50

ΨΨΨΨΨ Peninsula Chardonnay 2013 **Rating** 92 **To** 2020 $25
Estate Pinot Gris 2013 **Rating** 91 **To** 2017 $20

 # Paringa Wines | 3 Rings   ★★★
PO Box 486, Lonsdale DC, SA 5160 **Region** South Australia
T 0409 836 600 **www**.paringa.net **Open** Not
Winemaker Andrew Hercock **Est.** 1999 **Dozens** 80 000 **Vyds** 65ha
Not to be confused with the prestigious Paringa Estate of the Mornington Peninsula, this business nonetheless has blue blood in its wine veins. The Hickinbotham family has played a major role in the development of the wine industry in SA, Alan Robb Hickinbotham one of the people responsible for establishing the oenology course at Roseworthy Agricultural College (now part of the Adelaide Uni). He was a distinguished research scientist in his own right, and when Adelaide Uni constructed a new $3 million science laboratory, it was named the Hickinbotham Roseworthy Wine Science Laboratory. In 1971 Alan Hickinbotham and son David established the Clarendon Vineyard in the hills of the McLaren Vale region, closely followed by the establishment of the Paringa vineyard near Renmark in '74. Today the business is owned by David and Dena Hickinbotham, their son Alan Robb taking the christian names of his great-grandfather.

Parker Coonawarra Estate   ★★★★★
1568 Riddoch Highway, Penola, SA 5277 **Region** Coonawarra
T (08) 8737 3525 **www**.parkercoonawarraestate.com.au **Open** 7 days 10–4
Winemaker Phil Lehmann **Est.** 1985 **Dozens** 30 000 **Vyds** 20ha
Parker Coonawarra Estate is at the southern end of Coonawarra, on rich terra rossa soil over limestone. Cabernet sauvignon is the dominant variety (17.45ha), with minor plantings of merlot and petit verdot. It is now part of WD Wines Pty Ltd, which also owns Hesketh Wine Company and St John's Road in the Barossa Valley. Production has risen substantially since the change of ownership. Exports to all major markets.

ΨΨΨΨΨ 95 Block Cabernet Sauvignon 2012 The cabernet on the Abbey Vineyard is the highly rated Reynell clone, co-fermented with 5% petit verdot, spending 30 days on skins before maturation for 21 months in 100% new thick-staved French oak. It is richer, rounder and more flamboyant than the Terra Rossa Cabernet, with a splash of chocolate accompanying its cassis and mulberry fruit on the long palate. It is easy to see why it was not included in the more austere classicism of the yet-to-be-released First Growth. Screwcap. 14% alc. **Rating** 96 **To** 2037 $65
Terra Rossa Merlot 2012 Grown on a single clay pan over limestone patch on the Abbey Vineyard; the vines struggle, but give the fruit a unique resonance; 8% cabernet sauvignon is included for structure. After a short cold soak, the fermentation peaks at 28°C to 30°C, the wine spending 14 days on skins before maturation in 40% new French oak. It has a perfumed bouquet, heralding the red fruits, spice and a black olive savoury nuance; razor-sharp varietal character. Screwcap. 14% alc. **Rating** 95 **To** 2022 $35
Terra Rossa Cabernet Sauvignon 2012 No expense has been spared with the French 'Chateau' barrels that have extra thick staves, but the deep and powerful

cassis bouquet yields to the serious, autocratic stance of the cabernet tannins interwoven with blackcurrant, earth and a wisp of chocolate on the long palate. The legendary Reynella cabernet clone certainly makes its mark, the vines at full throttle as they approach their 30th birthday. Screwcap. 14% alc. **Rating** 95 To 2037 $35 ⊘

Chardonnay 2014 From two vineyards: mainly Williams, with less from another on V&A Lane, the Williams grapes barrel-fermented with wild and cultured yeasts, barrels stored at 2°C to extend fermentation time, then 6 months' lees contact; V&A Lane tank-fermented and matured. It is far more complex than most Coonawarra Chardonnays, with quite intense cool-grown fruit flavours and considerable length. Screwcap. 13% alc. **Rating** 94 To 2020 $24 ⊘

Shiraz 2013 Fermented in closed tanks for 10–12 days on skins, 50% aged in used French barriques and hogsheads for 9 months, the remainder in tank, plus a small percentage of Terra Rossa added at bottling. Very smart winemaking has kept the cost down and the quality up; the purple and black fruit flavours are given shape and context by just the right amount of oak. Screwcap. 14.5% alc. **Rating** 94 To 2028 $24 ⊘

Terra Rossa Shiraz 2012 Matured in French hogsheads, 66% new, it has a fragrant, elegant and expressive bouquet of small black fruits. The medium-bodied, supple palate shows more oak, but it is well integrated and will soon retreat into the background, giving way to the quality tannins on the finish. Finally, it carries its alcohol with ease. Screwcap. 14.5% alc. **Rating** 94 To 2032 $35

♟♟♟♟♟ **Cabernet Sauvignon 2013** Rating 93 To 2028 $24 ⊘

Parous ★★★★★

1 Gomersal Road, Tanunda, SA 5352 **Region** Barossa Valley
T 0437 159 858 **www**.parous.com.au **Open** Not
Winemaker Matt Head **Est.** 2010 **Dozens** 2500
Winemaker/proprietor Matt Head worked in the Hunter Valley, California and Margaret River for more than 15 years before making his home in the Barossa Valley and establishing Parous. It is focused on small-batch wines made from grapes sourced from the Barossa Valley and McLaren Vale. Exports to China.

♟♟♟♟♟ **Barossa Valley Shiraz 2012** Good depth and hue to the colour; although we are told nothing about the wine, the quality of the fruit is obvious, as is the skill of winemaker Matt Head; while it is medium-bodied, it also has flashes of full body on the black-fruited palate, and light body on the bright, long and cleansing finish. The oak? Positive and integrated. Screwcap. 14.5% alc. **Rating** 95 To 2037 $40

Passing Clouds ★★★★★

30 Roddas Lane, Musk, Vic 3461 **Region** Macedon Ranges
T (03) 5348 5550 **www**.passingclouds.com.au **Open** 7 days 11–5
Winemaker Cameron and Graeme Leith **Est.** 1974 **Dozens** 3500 **Vyds** 9.8ha
Graeme and son Cameron Leith have undertaken a monumental vine change. They have moved the entire operation that started way back in 1974 in Bendigo to its new location at Musk, near Daylesford. The vines at the original vineyard had been disabled by ongoing drought and all manner of pestilence, and it was no longer feasible to continue the business there. The emphasis has moved to elegant Pinot Noir and Chardonnay, with a foot still in Bendigo courtesy of their friends, the Adams at Riola. Exports to all major markets.

♟♟♟♟♟ **Graeme's Blend Shiraz Cabernet 2013** A 60/40% blend, matured in French oak. The bouquet and palate offer a complex array of purple and black fruits, licorice and a bramble note to the ripe, but persistent tannins that provide all-important structure and length. Bendigo. Screwcap. 14% alc. **Rating** 95 To 2035 $31 ⊘

The Angel 2013 The 23rd release of this predominantly cabernet sauvignon wine, matured for 18 months in French oak. Generously endowed with blackcurrant fruit on its bouquet, palate and aftertaste, telling you there's more than just fruit with its savoury twist. Screwcap. 14% alc. **Rating** 95 **To** 2038 $47

The Fools on the Hill Chardonnay 2013 The first release of a top-range Chardonnay; part wild yeast barrel-fermented with some solids, lees stirred, 100% mlf, matured in French oak (35% new) for 9 months. The result is a very complex and rich wine, but I can't help wondering if 50% mlf might have been a better approach. It's a tough call. Screwcap. 12.5% alc. **Rating** 94 **To** 2025 $47

Bendigo Shiraz 2013 Full crimson-purple; a very complex medium-bodied Shiraz in terms of flavour and texture; black and morello cherries have a star anise/forest floor edge, finely ground tannins adding to both flavour and texture. Screwcap. 14.3% alc. **Rating** 94 **To** 2033 $31

♀♀♀♀♀ **The Fools on the Hill Pinot Noir 2013 Rating** 92 **To** 2020 $47

Patina ★★★★★

109 Summerhill Lane, Orange, NSW 2800 **Region** Orange
T (02) 6362 8336 **www**.patinawines.com.au **Open** W'ends 11–5
Winemaker Gerald Naef **Est.** 1999 **Dozens** 3000 **Vyds** 3ha

Gerald Naef's home in Woodbridge in California was surrounded by the vast vineyard and winery operations of Gallo and Robert Mondavi. It would be hard to imagine a more different environment than that provided by Orange. Gerald and wife Angie left California in 1981, initially establishing an irrigation farm in the northwest of NSW; 20 years later they moved to Orange, and by 2006 Gerald was a final-year student of wine science at CSU. He set up a micro-winery at the Orange Cool Stores, and his first wine was a trophy-winning '03 Chardonnay.

♀♀♀♀♀ **Orange Chardonnay 2009** I like the energy and grip of this wine, and the balance between white peach/stone fruit and citrus/grapefruit; the flavours are seamless, and the wine is ageing slowly and with exceptional grace. Screwcap. 12.5% alc. **Rating** 96 **To** 2019 $30 ☻

Orange Riesling 2014 Some tropical fruit notes on the bouquet sound a warning, but the palate, while having a complex array of flavours, is fresh and vibrant, lime juice coming through strongly on the finish line. Very good cool-grown style. Screwcap. 12.1% alc. **Rating** 95 **To** 2024 $25 ☻

Reserve Orange Chardonnay 2010 Barrel-fermented and matured in new French oak for 12 months. The colour is still remarkably light and bright; it is a complex Chardonnay, with the fruit and oak arguing about their respective contributions, but on my count fruit comes out the clear winner; similar to the '11, but with more grip and intensity. Screwcap. 12% alc. **Rating** 95 **To** 2020 $45

Little Wood Orange Chardonnay 2011 Unusual approach: fermented at a low temperature in stainless steel and kept on lees for several months before 'a brief period in French oak'. I'm not sure I see much evidence of the oak, but the wine has excellent varietal flavour, drive and length; the aftertaste, in particular, is pure and fresh. Screwcap. 12.1% alc. **Rating** 94 **To** 2019 $25 ☻

Scandalous Riesling 2014 I don't know who created the name, but this is in fact a decorous Riesling, only barely off-dry, with crisp acidity rather than sweetness the key to the future. Screwcap. 12% alc. **Rating** 94 **To** 2029 $25 ☻

♀♀♀♀♀ **Orange Riesling 2013 Rating** 92 **To** 2023 $25 ☻
Orange Sauvignon Blanc 2014 Rating 91 **To** 2016 $25

Patrick of Coonawarra ★★★★★

Cnr Ravenswood Lane/Riddoch Highway, Coonawarra, SA 5263 **Region** Coonawarra
T (08) 8737 3687 **www**.patrickofcoonawarra.com.au **Open** 7 days 10–5
Winemaker Luke Tocaciu **Est.** 2004 **Dozens** 5000 **Vyds** 79.5ha

Patrick Tocaciu (who died in 2013) was a district veteran, with prior careers at Heathfield Ridge Winery and Hollick Wines. Wrattonbully plantings (41ha) cover all the major varieties, while the Coonawarra plantings (38.5ha) give rise to the Home Block Cabernet Sauvignon.

Patrick of Coonawarra also carries out contract winemaking for others. Son Luke, with a degree in oenology from Adelaide University and vintage experience in Australia and the US, has taken over in the winery.

ΨΨΨΨΨ **Estate Grown Shiraz 2010** From Wrattonbully; matured in new French and American oak. Still has excellent hue, and an aromatic red and black berry bouquet; the light to medium-bodied palate is as fresh as a daisy, and the fruit has absorbed the oak to an unexpected degree. Scores top points for its elegance, length and balance. Screwcap. 13.9% alc. **Rating** 95 **To** 2025 $29 **☉**

Grande Reserve Coonawarra Cabernet Sauvignon 2006 From 2ha of old vines; matured for 40 months in 100% new French oak, then held for 4 years in bottle before release: after Pat Tocaciu's death, but an appropriate testimonial. It is exceptionally long, and the oak – while obvious – has totally integrated into the cassis fruit. ProCork. 13.8% alc. **Rating** 95 **To** 2030 $125

Estate Grown Fume Blanc 2013 Given some skin contact, fermented on solids in 2yo French puncheons, then matured for 10 months in barrel with some lees contact. Early picking has highlighted the citrus component, although there are some tropical fruit nuances; an unqualified overall success, bright and juicy. 150 dozen made. Screwcap. 11.5% alc. **Rating** 94 **To** 2016 $25 **☉**

ΨΨΨΨ **Mother of Pearl Sauvignon Blanc 2014** **Rating** 89 **To** 2016 $19 **☉**

Patritti Wines ★★★★★

13–23 Clacton Road, Dover Gardens, SA 5048 **Region** Adelaide Zone
T (08) 8296 8261 **www**.patritti.com.au **Open** Mon–Sat 9–5 (7 days Dec)
Winemaker James Mungall, Ben Heide **Est.** 1926 **Dozens** 160 000 **Vyds** 16ha
A family-owned business offering wines at modest prices, but with impressive vineyard holdings of 10ha of shiraz in Blewitt Springs and 6ha of grenache at Aldinga North. The surging production points to success in export markets, and also to the utilisation of contract-grown grapes as well as estate-grown. Patritti is currently releasing wines of very high quality at enticing prices, and a range of lesser-quality wines at unfathomably low prices. The JPB Single Vineyard celebrates the arrival of Giovanni Patritti in Australia in 1925; he sold his wines under the 'John Patritti Brighton' label. Exports to the US and other major markets.

ΨΨΨΨΨ **JPB Shiraz 2013** Monumental fruit matched to a tremendous swagger of tannin. Saturated plum, blackberry, iodine, smoke and cloves, with creamy vanillan oak giving it all slippery smooth face. It builds such momentum that there is simply no stopping it through the finish; it's a long wave of flavour. 10, 20, 30 years; it will live as long as you desire. Cork. 14.5% alc. **Rating** 97 **To** 2045 $50 CM **☉**

ΨΨΨΨΨ **Sitadela McLaren Vale Shiraz Grenache 2012** Matured in large-format French oak over 20 months. The purity and power of the fruit is the thing; oak has slipped well away from the foreground, allowing cherry-plum, raspberry and earth notes to blossom. Tannin keeps everything tied down; everything about this wine speaks of high quality. Cork. 14.5% alc. **Rating** 96 **To** 2032 $80 CM

Marion Vineyard Limited Release Grenache Shiraz 2012 From the 100+yo Marion Vineyard (planted 1907) owned by the City of Marion, and leased to Patritti, the last operational winery in the district. Deep purple-crimson; a powerhouse, full-bodied wine with savoury, licorice, black fruits to the fore, yet retaining balance. The heavy bottle, the superb-quality cork, and the quality of the wine make the price unbelievable. 14.5% alc. **Rating** 96 **To** 2037 $24 **☉**

Lot Three Single Vineyard McLaren Vale Shiraz 2013 Deep colour and flavour. Burnt plums, blackberries, peppercorns and toasty vanillan, the latter happily married to the fruit. It all packs a quite significant punch, especially given the inclusion of serious revs of tannin. Long future ahead, cork permitting. 14% alc. **Rating** 94 **To** 2030 $30 CM **☉**

ΨΨΨΨΨ **Old Gate McLaren Vale Shire Shiraz 2013** **Rating** 93 **To** 2025 $20 CM **☉**

Paul Conti Wines

529 Wanneroo Road, Woodvale, WA 6026 **Region** Greater Perth Zone
T (08) 9409 9160 **www**.paulcontiwines.com.au **Open** Mon–Sat 10–5, Sun by appt
Winemaker Paul and Jason Conti **Est.** 1948 **Dozens** 4000 **Vyds** 14ha
Third-generation winemaker Jason Conti has assumed control of winemaking, although
father Paul (who succeeded his own father in 1968) remains involved in the business. Over
the years Paul challenged and redefined industry perceptions and standards; the challenge for
Jason is to achieve the same degree of success in a relentlessly and increasingly competitive
market environment, and he is doing just that. Plantings at the Carabooda Vineyard have
been expanded with tempranillo, petit verdot and viognier, and pinot noir and chardonnay
are purchased from Manjimup. In a further extension, a property has been acquired at
Cowaramup in Margaret River, with sauvignon blanc, shiraz, cabernet sauvignon, semillon,
muscat and malbec. Jason is a firm believer in organics, and the Swan Valley and Manjimup
vineyards will soon join the family's Cowaramup organic vineyard. The original 2ha vineyard
(shiraz) of the Mariginiup Vineyard remains the cornerstone. Exports to the UK, Malaysia,
China and Japan.

PPPPP Mariginiup Shiraz 2013 I have enjoyed this wine from as far back as 40 years
ago, but there hasn't been a better vintage than this one. Mature, indeed old, vines
give a sheen to the silky red and black fruits of the supple, medium-bodied palate,
oak barely evident, the tannins superfine. One of those dyed in the wool, now or
later, styles. Screwcap. 14.5% alc. Rating 95 To 2033 $28 ●

PPPPP Margaret River Cabernet Sauvignon 2013 Rating 93 To 2033 $20 ●
Margaret River Sauvignon Blanc 2014 Rating 92 To 2016 $18 ●
Margaret River Chardonnay 2013 Rating 90 To 2017 $20 ●

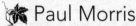 Paul Morris

3 Main Street, Minlaton, SA 5575 (postal) **Region** Clare Valley
T 0427 885 321 **www**.paulmorriswines.com.au **Open** Not
Winemaker Paul Morris **Est.** 2014 **Dozens** 500
Paul Morris has been in the broader wine business since 2002. Vineyard roles in McLaren Vale
and Lyndoch were followed by vintages in the Barossa Valley, Magill and Marlborough, NZ.
These periods of hands-on winery work were interspersed with sales and marketing positions,
broadening his experience. His main job at the present time is to raise funds for animal welfare
charities, but he plans to buy/create his own boutique winery if/when finances permit. Paul
has plans to expand the range in the future.

PPPPP Clare Valley Riesling 2014 Grapes crushed early and chilled to 4°C before
pressing, free-run juice fermented separately from the pressings. Some free SO_2
on the bouquet will disappear, and the already lovely juicy fruit will become even
more luscious. Terrific value. Screwcap. 12.2% alc. Rating 93 To 2025 $19 ●

PPPP Bush Vine Clare Valley Grenache 2014 Rating 89 To 2017 $19 ●

Paul Nelson Wines

11 Kemsley Place, Denmark, WA 6333 (postal) **Region** Great Southern
T 0406 495 066 **www**.paulnelsonwines.com.au **Open** Not
Winemaker Paul Nelson **Est.** 2009 **Dozens** 700
Paul Nelson started making wine with one foot in the Swan Valley, the other in the Great
Southern, while completing a bachelor's degree in viticulture and oenology at Curtin
University. He then worked successively at Houghton in the Swan Valley, Goundrey in
Mount Barker, Santa Ynez in California, South Africa (for four vintages), hemisphere hopping
to the Rheinhessen, three vintages in Cyprus, then moving to a large Indian winemaker in
Mumbai before returning to work for Houghton. He has since moved on from Houghton
and (in partnership with wife Bianca) makes small quantities of table wines.

ㅇㅇㅇㅇㅇ **Great Southern Fume Blanc 2014** Light colour but bold flavour. Beautiful integration of spicy oak, but slatey, minerally, stone fruit-like flavour is the dominating force. Sweet grassy notes add a moreishness as much as anything. The shape of this wine as it passes through your mouth is quite exquisite. Screwcap. 13% alc. **Rating** 94 **To** 2017 $32 CM

ㅇㅇㅇㅇㅇ **Maison Madeleine 2014 Rating** 93 **To** 2016 $32 CM
Riesling 2014 Rating 90 **To** 2020 $28 CM
Heathbank Meritage 2012 Rating 90 **To** 2020 $54 CM

Paul Osicka ★★★★★

Majors Creek Vineyard at Graytown, Vic 3608 **Region** Heathcote
T (03) 5794 9235 **Open** By appt
Winemaker Paul and Simon Osicka **Est.** 1955 **Dozens** NFP **Vyds** 13ha
The Osicka family arrived in Australia from Czechoslovakia in the early 1950s. Vignerons in their own country, their vineyard was the first new venture in Central and Southern Victoria for over half a century. With the return of Simon Osicka to the family business, there have been substantial changes. Simon had senior winemaking positions at Houghton, Leasingham, and as group red winemaker for Constellation Wines Australia, interleaved with vintages in Italy, Canada, Germany and France, working at the prestigious Domaine J.L. Chave in Hermitage for the '10 vintage. The fermentation of the red wines has been changed from static to open fermenters, and French oak has replaced American oak. 2015 marked the 60th anniversary of the planting of the vineyard. Exports to Denmark.

ㅇㅇㅇㅇㅇ **Moormbool Reserve Shiraz 2013** Selected from rows 30–58 of vines planted in '50, only made in the best vintages; open-fermented and macerated for a total of 4 weeks, matured in French hogsheads (30% new) for 18 months. This is very different from Majors Creek, with more intensity, focus and linear power, its extreme length underlining its demand for extended cellaring, its balance ensuring you won't be disappointed. Screwcap. 14.5% alc. **Rating** 97 **To** 2053 $48 ❂
Old Vines Majors Creek Vineyard Heathcote Cabernet Sauvignon 2013
A vineyard selection from vines planted in the '50s; open-fermented, 3 weeks on skins, matured in French oak (50% new) for 18 months. Primarily allocated to Majors Creek, 34 dozen left for this wine. The sheer power is awesome, and so is the purity of the focus, likewise the unfolding of the inevitably extreme length of the finish. Screwcap. 14.5% alc. **Rating** 97 **To** 2053 $42 ❂

ㅇㅇㅇㅇㅇ **Majors Creek Vineyard Shiraz 2013** Hand-picked in 11 parcels, 93% from vines planted in the '50s, some rows picked three times over 3 weeks; open-fermented with different treatments, some whole bunches in some ferments, all 3–4 weeks on skins, matured for 16 months in French hogsheads (25% new). A very distinguished wine, the complex bouquet setting the scene for the medium to full-bodied palate and its suave mix of black fruits, spice, pepper and licorice. Screwcap. 14.5% alc. **Rating** 96 **To** 2048 $35 ❂
Majors Creek Vineyard Cabernet Sauvignon 2013 Estate-grown, 90% from 30yo vines, 10% from vines planted in the '50s; open-fermented, 3 weeks on skins, matured in French oak (25% new) for 18 months. Deep purple-crimson; an exceptionally complex Cabernet of a style and quality rarely encountered in Australia; cassis/blackcurrant has dried herb and pepper/spice nuances alongside exemplary tannins. Screwcap. 14.5% alc. **Rating** 96 **To** 2048 $30 ❂

Paulett ★★★★★

Polish Hill Road, Polish Hill River, SA 5453 **Region** Clare Valley
T (08) 8843 4328 **www.**paulettwines.com.au **Open** 7 days 10–5
Winemaker Neil Paulett, Kelvin Budarick **Est.** 1983 **Dozens** 14000 **Vyds** 41.9ha
The Paulett story is a saga of Australian perseverance, commencing with the 1982 purchase of a property with 1ha of vines and a house, promptly destroyed by the terrible Ash Wednesday bushfires of the following year. Son Matthew joined Neil and Alison Paulett as a partner in

the business some years ago; he is responsible for viticulture on the property holding, much expanded following the purchase of a large vineyard at Watervale. The winery and cellar door have wonderful views over the Polish Hill River region, the memories of the bushfires long gone. Exports to the UK, the US, Denmark, Singapore, Malaysia, China and NZ.

ŸŸŸŸŸ **Polish Hill River Aged Release Riesling 2010** Has confidently entered what Dom Perignon's chief winemaker Richard Geoffroy would call its second plenitude, the richness of early maturity, honey and toast making their first appearance, with more to come. Screwcap. 12.5% alc. **Rating** 96 To 2025 $50 ✪
Polish Hill River Riesling 2014 Touch of class. Piercing and lime-riven but ribbed with slatey complexity. Burst of spice and lime rind to the aftertaste. Dry. Long. Screwcap. 12.5% alc. **Rating** 95 To 2026 $22 CM ✪
47/74 Hand Crafted Malbec Cabernet 2009 Neil Paulett was born in '47; Matthew Paulett in '74, hence the name. Poetry would suggest the blend should follow the same numbers, but alas it's a 60/40% blend. Regardless of numbers it's a big wine, heavy with earthen blackberry and vanillan oak and churning with robust tannin. It will have a long life, but it's already entering a seductive drinking zone. Screwcap. 14% alc. **Rating** 95 To 2028 $80 CM
Andreas Polish Hill River Shiraz 2010 Clare Shiraz in all its glory; kissed, but relatively unencumbered, by oak. Leather and mouth-watering blackberry, good density without being over the top, gum leaf and boysenberry. It's just starting to develop but still feels fresh. Tannin tucks neatly into the fruit. Immaculate. Screwcap. 14.5% alc. **Rating** 94 To 2026 $50 CM

ŸŸŸŸ♀ **Polish Hill River Shiraz 2010 Rating** 91 To 2021 $24 CM

Paxton ★★★★★

68 Wheaton Road, McLaren Vale, SA 5171 **Region** McLaren Vale
T (08) 8323 9131 www.paxtonvineyards.com **Open** 7 days 10–5
Winemaker Richard Freebairn **Est.** 1979 **Dozens** 20 000 **Vyds** 74.5ha
David Paxton is one of Australia's best-known viticulturists and consultants. He founded Paxton Vineyards in McLaren Vale with his family in 1979, and has since been involved in various capacities in the establishment and management of vineyards in several leading regions across the country. Son Michael, a former Flying Winemaker (with experience in Spain, South America, France and Australia), is responsible for making the wines. There are five vineyards: the Thomas Block (28ha), the Jones Block (22ha), Quandong Farm (19ha), Landcross Farm (2ha) and Maslin Vineyard (3.5ha). All five are certified biodynamic, making Paxton one of the largest biodynamic producers in Australia. A historic 1860s sheep farm on the site of the original village houses Paxton's tasting rooms and cellar door. Exports to the UK, the US, Canada, Denmark, Sweden, The Netherlands, Malaysia, Hong Kong, Taiwan and China.

ŸŸŸŸŸ **Jones Block Single Vineyard McLaren Vale Shiraz 2012** Three parcels open-fermented, one parcel finished fermentation in new American oak, the remainder with extended post-fermentation maceration; matured for 20 months in French barriques (75% new) and American barriques (45% new). The flavour pantechnicon rolls across the mouth like a deep ocean wave caused by a faraway storm, painting every surface of the mouth with a seamless display of black fruits and regional dark chocolate, quality oak a barely needed but welcome bonne bouche. Screwcap. 13.5% alc. **Rating** 97 To 2052 $37 ✪

ŸŸŸŸŸ **Quandong Farm Single Vineyard McLaren Vale Shiraz 2013** Biodynamically grown and wild yeast-fermented. While only medium-bodied, it has remarkable intensity and complex texture and structure to its array of predominantly black fruits and dark chocolate. Flavour achieved at this alcohol is its own reward. Screwcap. 13% alc. **Rating** 96 To 2028 $30 ✪
MV Biodynamic Shiraz 2013 The grapes come from four estate biodynamic vineyards, plus two contract biodynamic vineyards; separately fermented and matured in new and used American oak. Deep, dark crimson; essence of McLaren Vale shiraz, with waves of sultry black fruits and bitter chocolate, the

oak not blunting the delicious savoury nature of the wine. Exceptional value for biodynamic lovers. Screwcap. 14% alc. **Rating** 95 **To** 2028 $22 **⊙**
Elizabeth Jean 100 Year McLaren Vale Shiraz 2010 Serves to remind us that '10 was (also) a great vintage, and of the benefit of extended barrel and bottle maturation. Aromas of dark chocolate, pipe tobacco and quality oak lead into an unexpectedly focused, indeed elegant, palate with 'cool' black fruits to the fore. 30 years may well prove conservative. Screwcap. 15% alc. **Rating** 95 **To** 2040 $85
Thomas Block Single Vineyard McLaren Vale Chardonnay 2013 Whole bunch-pressed to French barriques (45% new), lees stirring post-fermentation, 12 months' maturation. Makes every post a winner, lifting the wine above most of its regional peers, with a complex offer of nectarine, melon and fig swathed in citrussy acidity and spicy oak. Screwcap. 13% alc. **Rating** 94 **To** 2023 $25 **⊙**
Cracker Barrels McLaren Vale Shiraz Cabernet 2011 67% old-vine shiraz and 33% cabernet sauvignon; small batch open-fermented and matured in French barriques. Excellent hue and depth for an '11; has exceptional presence and depth, a billboard advertisement for biodynamic vineyards; the blackcurrant and blackberry flavours duel with each other, the match drawn, the wet vintage ignored. Screwcap. 14.5% alc. **Rating** 94 **To** 2026 $49
The Vale Biodynamic McLaren Vale Cabernet Sauvignon 2012 Open-fermented with various methods including extended maceration; matured for 18 months in new and used French oak. The hue is good, not deep. A rare breed in the region, as it aspires to elegance, and largely achieves it; blackcurrant, black olive and dried herbs shut the door in the face of chocolate, the oak handling exemplary, and the tannins nicely weighted. Screwcap. 14% alc. **Rating** 94 **To** 2027 $25 **⊙**

ΥΥΥΥΥ **Biodynamic Single Vineyard McLaren Vale Pinot Gris 2014** Rating 93 **To** 2015 $20 CM **⊙**
Biodynamic Graciano 2013 Rating 93 **To** 2019 $30
Biodynamic Chardonnay 2012 Rating 92 **To** 2022 $37
Biodynamic Shiraz Rose 2014 Rating 90 **To** 2016 $19 **⊙**

Payne's Rise ★★★★

10 Paynes Road, Seville, Vic 3139 **Region** Yarra Valley
T (03) 5964 2504 **www**.paynesrise.com.au **Open** Thurs–Sun 11–5
Winemaker Franco D'Anna (Contract) **Est.** 1998 **Dozens** 1000 **Vyds** 5ha
Tim and Narelle Cullen have progressively established 5ha of cabernet sauvignon, shiraz, pinot noir, chardonnay and sauvignon blanc since 1998, new plantings continuing on a small scale, including several clones of chardonnay in 2014. They carry out all the vineyard work; Tim is also a viticulturist for a local agribusiness, and Narelle is responsible for sales and marketing. The contract-made wines have won several awards at the Victorian Wines Show.

ΥΥΥΥΥ **Yarra Valley Cabernet Sauvignon 2013** Good colour; an immediately attractive, juicy style redolent of cassis on the bouquet and palate alike, given even more flesh by well-handled French oak, tannins doing nothing to spoil the party. Screwcap. 13.5% alc. **Rating** 94 **To** 2028 $30 **⊙**

ΥΥΥΥΥ **Redlands Yarra Valley Shiraz 2013** Rating 90 **To** 2025 $35

Peccavi Wines ★★★★☆

1121 Wildwood Road, Yallingup Siding, WA 6282 **Region** Margaret River
T 0409 544 630 **www**.peccavi-wines.com **Open** By appt
Winemaker Brian Fletcher **Est.** 1996 **Dozens** 5000 **Vyds** 16ha
Jeremy Muller was introduced to the great wines of the world by his father when he was young, and says he spent years searching New and Old World wine regions (even looking at the sites of ancient Roman vineyards in England), but did not find what he was looking for until one holiday in Margaret River. There he found a vineyard in Yallingup that was available for sale, and he did not hesitate. He quickly put together an impressive contract

winemaking team, and appointed Colin Bell as viticulturist. The wines are released under two labels: Peccavi, for 100% estate-grown fruit (all hand-picked) and No Regrets, for wines with contract-grown grapes and estate material. The quality of the wines is very good, reflecting the skills and experience of Brian Fletcher. Exports to the UK, Germany, Denmark, Malaysia, Singapore, Indonesia, Hong Kong and China.

ΨΨΨΨΨ Margaret River Shiraz 2011 High-quality Shiraz. Perfumed, well fruited but generally savoury, with controlled tannin applying a sure tether to a beautifully persistent finish. Kirsch, cloves, assorted dry spice, dark chocolate and violet. Complex. Immaculate. Screwcap. 13.5% alc. **Rating** 95 **To** 2023 $45 CM
Margaret River Sauvignon Blanc Semillon 2012 Slashing style. Excellent intensity. Grapefruit, gravel, lemon rind and buoyant tropical fruits. Fills all corners of the mouth with flavour, then drills long through the finish. Screwcap. 12% alc. **Rating** 94 **To** 2015 $38 CM

ΨΨΨΨΨ **Margaret River Chardonnay 2012** Rating 93 To 2018 $52 CM
Margaret River Cabernet Sauvignon 2011 Rating 93 To 2024 $52 CM

Peel Estate ★★★★

290 Fletcher Road, Karnup, WA 6176 **Region** Peel
T (08) 9524 1221 **www**.peelwine.com.au **Open** 7 days 10–5
Winemaker Will Nairn, Mark Morton **Est.** 1974 **Dozens** 4000 **Vyds** 16ha
Peel's icon wine is the Shiraz, a wine of considerable finesse and with a remarkably consistent track record. Every year Will Nairn holds a Great Shiraz Tasting for six-year-old Australian Shirazs, and pits Peel Estate (in a blind tasting attended by 100 or so people) against Australia's best; it is never disgraced. The wood-matured Chenin Blanc is another winery specialty. Exports to the UK, Ireland, China and Japan.

ΨΨΨΨΨ **Old Vine Shiraz 2009** The vines in question were 36yo when this seriously good, and still exceptionally fresh, wine was made; medium-bodied, with a fragrant bouquet and silky red fruit palate, it also has good tannins; the oak has long since been absorbed by the fruit. Screwcap. 14% alc. **Rating** 94 **To** 2029 $40

ΨΨΨΨΨ **Wood Matured Chenin Blanc 2012** Rating 90 To 2020 $25

Penfolds ★★★★★

Tanunda Road, Nuriootpa, SA 5355 **Region** Barossa Valley
T (08) 8568 8408 **www**.penfolds.com **Open** 7 days 10–5
Winemaker Peter Gago **Est.** 1844 **Dozens** NFP
Penfolds is the star in the crown of Treasury Wine Estates (TWE), but its history predates the formation of TWE by close on 170 years. Its shape has changed both in terms of its vineyards, its management, its passing parade of great winemakers, and its wines. There is no other single winery brand in the New, or the Old, World with the depth and breadth of Penfolds. Retail prices range from less than $20 to $785 for Grange, which is the cornerstone, produced every year, albeit with the volume determined by the quality of the vintage, not by cash flow. There is now a range of regional wines with single varieties, and the Bin Range of wines that include both regional blends and (in some instances) varietal blends. Despite the very successful Yattarna and Reserve Bin A Chardonnays, and some impressive Rieslings, this remains a red wine producer at heart. Exports to all major markets.

ΨΨΨΨΨ Grange 2010 The core of this wine is Barossa Valley shiraz (85%), the remainder (and 4% cabernet sauvignon) from adjoining regions. It finished its fermentation in 100% new American oak hogsheads, where it spent the next 17 months. It has exceptional hue and depth to the colour; the smoky complexity to the black fruits (no red or blue) of the bouquet also offers licorice and earth aromas; only a great Burgundy could have more nuances defined each time you revert to the bouquet. You could lose yourself, Narcissus-like, looking endlessly into the reflection of the palate; for all its power, there is not a hair out of place, the tannins outstanding.

This will be one of the greatest Granges in the pantheon of '52, '55, '71, '96 and '06. Cork. 14.5% alc. **Rating** 99 **To** 2060 $785

RWT Barossa Valley Shiraz 2012 May explain why Kalimna Bin 28 is the least of the Bin series reds, for this wine takes the finest shiraz from the Barossa Valley once Grange has had its choice. This spends 16 months in French oak hogsheads (75% new), finishing its ferment in that oak, separating it at birth from Grange, which is in American oak. The bouquet abounds with black fruits, with sub-notes of dark chocolate, licorice and some charcuterie. The palate is drop-dead gorgeous, a curious description given its strongly savoury flavour range, but it achieves the unlikely. As with all these wines, the tannin structure is exceptional, the length prodigious. Screwcap. 14.5% alc. **Rating** 98 **To** 2040 $175 ✪

Bin 707 Cabernet Sauvignon 2012 Sourced from Coonawarra, Padthaway, Barossa Valley, Wrattonbully and the Adelaide Hills; the fermentation is completed and the wine spends 14 months in new American oak hogsheads. There is amazing depth to the purple-crimson colour. Its full-bodied colours are nailed to the mast immediately the wine enters the mouth; it's strange how the cabernet of this wine marries with the American oak, providing the ultimate Christmas cake of aromas and flavours; one of its great strengths is the tannin structure, which gives the wine its exceptional length (and mouthfeel along the way). Not made in '11. Cork. 14.5% alc. **Rating** 98 **To** 2040 $350

Yattarna Chardonnay 2012 Sourced from vineyards in the Derwent Valley and Coal Valley, Tasmania, Henty (Drumborg) and the Adelaide Hills. The wine was fermented in French oak barriques (45% new, 55% 1yo), and spent 8 months in those barriques in ultra-cool storage. The Tasmanian and Drumborg components really set the scene, as they are the two coolest regions/subregions of Australia. The palate has striking intensity, length and focus, dispensing equal amounts of pink grapefruit, white peach and minerally acidity, oak a mere conveyance, not an end in itself. Screwcap. 13.2% alc. **Rating** 97 **To** 2025 $150 ✪

Bin 389 Cabernet Shiraz 2012 Deep, dense crimson-purple; the profound bouquet offers every kind of black fruits imaginable, large and small, yet somehow leaves a space for more complex secondary characters to emerge given enough time. The palate takes all this, and adds to it with barrel-ferment characters introducing licorice and touches of wild herb. This fully lives up to the great expectations held of it (and of the vintage). Arguably the bargain of the '12s. Screwcap. 14.5% alc. **Rating** 97 **To** 2040 $80 ✪

Grandfather Rare Tawny NV Tawny brown hue; the very complex bouquet has gingerbread, spice and singed toffee aromas cut by the rancio that comes through on the long, intense, yet elegantly structured and balanced palate. A skilled blending of some younger wine has had the desired effect. Cork. 20% alc. **Rating** 97 **To** 2016 $100 ✪

🍷🍷🍷🍷🍷 **Bin 150 Marananga Barossa Valley Shiraz 2012** A relatively recent addition to the Bin range, one that has always appealed to me. Full crimson-purple; the fragrant bouquet sends multiple, if not downright mixed, messages of red berries, spices and smoky oak; the vibrant palate is led by juicy, sweet fruit, before spicy oak and superfine tannins add their weight to the length and finish. An altogether superior wine. Screwcap. 14.5% alc. **Rating** 96 **To** 2042 $80

Bin 51 Eden Valley Riesling 2014 The yield was significantly reduced by growing season conditions, but the quality did not suffer. The wine has a highly fragrant and flowery bouquet, lavender a good call; fully ripe citrus fruits of every kind ripple through the palate, minerally/stony acidity providing balance and length. Screwcap. 12.5% alc. **Rating** 95 **To** 2025 $30 ✪

Reserve Bin A Adelaide Hills Chardonnay 2013 Whole bunch-pressed, direct to barrel for wild yeast fermentation, 100% mlf; 9 months in French oak (40% new). The discreet bouquet has nectarine and peach aromas with some highly desirable funk; the palate is still to fully open up, but has excellent length, likewise control of oak ex the cold maturation. Trophy Best Wine of Show Adelaide Hills Wine Show '14. Screwcap. 13% alc. **Rating** 95 **To** 2022 $100

Cellar Reserve Adelaide Hills Chardonnay 2013 An example of Penfolds' mastery in making Chardonnay, the Adelaide Hills and Tasmania its killing fields when securing top-quality grapes. It has finesse, elegance and length, the fruit flavours perfectly modulated. Screwcap. 13% alc. **Rating** 95 **To** 2030 $34 ✪

Bin 407 Cabernet Sauvignon 2012 From Wrattonbully, Padthaway, McLaren Vale, Coonawarra and Langhorne Creek, partially barrel-fermented before spending 14 months in 22% French (100% new) and 68% American (19% new) oak hogsheads. An interesting wine; it's not until the finish of the palate and aftertaste that the leopard's spots become clear. You need to work backwards to find the bouquet, which has developed the cassis and plum fragrance it initially lacked, likewise the juicy fruit of the mid-palate. Screwcap. 14.5% alc. **Rating** 95 **To** 2032 $80

Cellar Reserve Barossa Valley Sangiovese 2012 Sangiovese as only Penfolds could make it: rich and full of ripe cherries – red, black, morello – with soft tannins doing no more than giving secondary support. The oak is not obtrusive, in case you wondered. Cork. 14% alc. **Rating** 95 **To** 2027 $50

Father Grand Tawny NV Rating 94 **To** 2016 $40

Penfolds Magill Estate   ★★★★★

78 Penfold Road, Magill, SA 5072 **Region** Adelaide Zone
T (08) 8301 5569 **Open** 7 days 10.30–5
Winemaker Peter Gago **Est.** 1844 **Dozens** NFP **Vyds** 5.2ha
This is the birthplace of Penfolds, established by Dr Christopher Rawson Penfold in 1844; his house is still part of the immaculately maintained property. It includes 5.2ha of precious shiraz used to make Magill Estate; the original and subsequent winery buildings, most still in operation or in museum condition; and the much-acclaimed Magill Restaurant, with panoramic views of the city, a great wine list and fine dining. All this is a 20-minute drive from Adelaide's CBD. Exports to the UK, the US and other major markets.

♟♟♟♟♟ **Magill Estate Shiraz 2012** Utterly exceptional colour, not normally one of Magill's strong points, opens proceedings. The bouquet adds a layer to the expectation engendered by the colour, with sweet leather à la the Hunter Valley, licorice, and a caravan of spices. The sheer finesse of the palate brings the wheel full circle; French oak adds to the cedary/savoury/spicy elements behind the blackberry and plum fruit. Joins the '06 as the best ever Magill Estate. Cork. 14.5% alc. **Rating** 97 **To** 2037 $130

Penley Estate   ★★★★★

McLeans Road, Coonawarra, SA 5263 **Region** Coonawarra
T (08) 8736 3211 www.penley.com.au **Open** Mon–Fri 10–4, w'ends 11–5
Winemaker Kym Tolley, Greg Foster **Est.** 1988 **Dozens** 35 000 **Vyds** 111ha
Owner Kym Tolley describes himself as a fifth-generation winemaker, the family tree involving both the Penfolds and the Tolleys. He worked in the industry for 17 years before establishing Penley Estate and has made every post a winner since, producing a succession of rich, complex wines, especially Cabernet Sauvignons with a degree of elegance. Exports to all major markets.

♟♟♟♟♟ **Steyning Coonawarra Cabernet Sauvignon 2012** Fermented in French hogsheads, matured in new French oak for 29 months. As with some of the other Penley wines, has a stained cork. Everything is written large with this wine – its label, its bottle, its fruit, oak and tannins. It is apparently trying to out-John Riddoch John Riddoch, but it's far too early to judge its success. 14.5% alc. **Rating** 96 **To** 2042 $120

Reserve Coonawarra Cabernet Sauvignon 2012 Submerged cap header boards, matured for 21 months in French oak. Cassis, earth, mint, oak and tannins all contribute in one way or another to this powerful expression of Coonawarra; has a good future. Cork. 14.5% alc. **Rating** 95 **To** 2037 $50

Special Select Coonawarra Shiraz 2012 Fermented with header boards 8–9 days, finished fermentation and matured in new French and American oak for 21 months. There is a forest of oak in the wine, even though the barrel fermentation helps integration. May ultimately escape from the forest, for the quality of the fruit is not in doubt. Cork. 14.5% alc. **Rating** 94 **To** 2032 $50

ΤΤΤΤΩ **Gryphon Coonawarra Merlot 2013 Rating** 92 **To** 2028 $20 ☺
Tolmer Cabernet Sauvignon 2012 Rating 92 **To** 2032 $32

Penmara   ★★★★

Unit 19, 75 Pacific Highway, Waitara, NSW 2077 (postal) **Region** Hunter Valley/Orange
T 0410 403 143 **www**.penmarawines.com.au **Open** Not
Winemaker John Hordern **Est.** 2000 **Dozens** 25 000 **Vyds** 120ha
Penmara, with its banner 'Five Families: One Vision', was formed when five family-owned vineyards joined together to create a new venture with a focus on export markets. Based in the Hunter Valley with vineyards also in Orange and other surrounding areas, Penmara has access to 120ha of shiraz, chardonnay, cabernet sauvignon, semillon, verdelho and merlot. Exports to the US, Canada, South Korea, Malaysia, Singapore and China.

ΤΤΤΤΩ **Family Select Hunter Valley Shiraz 2011** You would not pick it as a wine from a wet vintage. It tastes of blackberry, leather, fennel and toasty oak, and while it's not a blockbuster it still delivers plenty. It will last, but it's likely best consumed youngish. Cork. 14% alc. **Rating** 90 **To** 2021 $30 CM

Penna Lane Wines   ★★★★☆

Lot 51 Penna Lane, Penwortham via Clare, SA 5453 **Region** Clare Valley
T 0403 462 431 **www**.pennalanewines.com.au **Open** Fri–Sun 11–5
Winemaker Peter Treloar, Chris Proud **Est.** 1998 **Dozens** 4500 **Vyds** 4.37ha
Penna Lane is located in the beautiful Skilly Valley, approximately 10km south of Clare. The estate vineyard (shiraz, cabernet sauvignon and semillon), is planted at an elevation of approximately 450m, which allows a long, slow ripening period, usually resulting in wines with intense varietal fruit flavours. Exports to Hong Kong, South Korea, Fiji, Vietnam, Thailand, China and Japan.

ΤΤΤΤΤ **The Redemption Clare Valley Cabernet Sauvignon 2012** Deeply coloured, it has a compelling bouquet filled with blackcurrant fruit and balanced oak, the intense palate delivering more of the same in a measured and well-balanced framework. Its moderate alcohol is the joker in the pack. Screwcap. 13.5% alc. Rating 95 To 2032 $25 ☺
Skilly Valley Riesling 2014 Pale straw-green; a super-elegant and fine style, crisp, fresh and minerally; demands time to fulfil its undoubted future, for it has excellent length and balance, all suggesting 100% free-run juice. A nice contrast to the '14 Watervale, and vice versa. Screwcap. 12.5% alc. **Rating** 94 **To** 2029 $25 ☺

ΤΤΤΤΩ **Watervale Riesling 2014 Rating** 93 **To** 2024 $20 ☺

Penny's Hill   ★★★★★

281 Main Road, McLaren Vale, SA 5171 **Region** McLaren Vale
T (08) 8557 0800 **www**.pennyshill.com.au **Open** 7 days 10–5
Winemaker Alexia Roberts **Est.** 1988 **Dozens** 70 000 **Vyds** 44ha
Founded in 1988 by Tony and Susie Parkinson, Penny's Hill produces high-quality Shiraz (Footprint and The Skeleton Key) from its close-planted McLaren Vale estate, also the source of the Edwards Road Cabernet Sauvignon and The Experiment Grenache. Malpas Road and Goss Corner Vineyards complete the estate holdings, providing fruit for Cracking Black Shiraz and Malpas Road Merlot. White wines (The Agreement Sauvignon Blanc and The Handshake Chardonnay) are sourced from 'estates of mates' in the Adelaide Hills. All vineyards are under the tutelage of Mat Haaren. Penny's Hill cellars are located at the historic Ingleburne

Farm, which also houses the award-winning The Kitchen Door restaurant and Red Dot Gallery. Noted for its distinctive 'red dot' packaging. Exports to all major markets.

🍷🍷🍷🍷🍷 **Skeleton Key McLaren Vale Shiraz 2012** Open-fermented and matured in oak for 22 months. Deep crimson, still in the first flush of youth; a concentrated, no-holds-barred Shiraz shouting its region and variety from the rooftops; full of jet-black fruits, dripping with dark chocolate, it has remarkable balance thanks to its oak and tannin. Screwcap. 15% alc. **Rating** 96 **To** 2045 $35 ✪

The Agreement Adelaide Hills Sauvignon Blanc 2014 An altogether impressive Sauvignon Blanc with well above average intensity and drive to its prolific display of guava, kiwifruit, herb and all-encompassing grainy acidity that underpins the palate and finish. Screwcap. 12.5% alc. **Rating** 95 **To** 2016 $24 ✪

The Experiment McLaren Vale Grenache 2013 In 1996 century-old grenache bush vines were converted to a narrow-row trellis as an experiment. Open-fermented and matured for 18 months in barrel. I can visualise a top Rhône Valley vigneron itching to get his fingers on it. It has a supple, verging on velvety, mouthfeel, the flavours of cherry and satsuma plum on an airy bed of oak and tannins. Screwcap. 14.5% alc. **Rating** 95 **To** 2030 $35 ✪

Cracking Black McLaren Vale Shiraz 2013 A picture-perfect example of medium-bodied McLaren Vale Shiraz from an impressive vintage; blackberry, black cherry, dark chocolate and licorice engage the palate from the first sip; has very good length and balance. Screwcap. 14.5% alc. **Rating** 94 **To** 2035 $25 ✪

Edwards Road McLaren Vale Cabernet Sauvignon 2013 Matured in French oak for 18 months. Yet another Penny's Hill wine that has a personal stamp to it, making a triumvirate with region and variety. You know what you will get, in a totally positive way. Screwcap. 14.5% alc. **Rating** 94 **To** 2033 $25 ✪

🍷🍷🍷🍷♀ **The Specialized Shiraz Cabernet Merlot 2013 Rating** 92 **To** 2033 $25 ✪
Thomas Goss McLaren Vale Shiraz 2013 Rating 91 **To** 2023 $15 ✪
Thomas Goss Sauvignon Blanc 2014 Rating 90 **To** 2015 $15 ✪

Peos Estate   ★★★★☆

Graphite Road, Manjimup, WA 6258 **Region** Manjimup
T (08) 9772 1378 www.peosestate.com.au **Open** Not
Winemaker Forest Hill Vineyard, Rockcliffe **Est.** 1996 **Dozens** 8000 **Vyds** 36.8ha
The Peos family has farmed the West Manjimup district for over 50 years, the third generation of four brothers commencing the development of the vineyard in 1996. There is a little over 36ha of vines, including shiraz (10ha), merlot (6.8ha), chardonnay (6.7ha), cabernet sauvignon (4ha), sauvignon blanc (3ha), and pinot noir and verdelho (2ha each). Exports to Canada, Singapore and China.

🍷🍷🍷🍷♀ **Four Kings Single Vineyard Manjimup Shiraz 2013** Pushes the boundaries of ripeness, but its bold flavours of tar, blackberry, crushed gum leaves and hazelnut certainly pack a punch. Brighter notes of raspberry help ease the load. Plenty of stuffing. Screwcap. 14.5% alc. **Rating** 92 **To** 2025 $25 CM ✪

Four Aces Single Vineyard Manjimup Shiraz 2013 Strong flavours of bitumen, eucalypt and gravel; full marks for impact and weight though it's all quite blocky and unsubtle. Cork. 14.5% alc. **Rating** 92 **To** 2025 $35 CM

Four Kings Single Vineyard Manjimup Cabernet Merlot 2013 Firm structure, ripe fruit and sound length. This is fertile drinking territory. It's attractively mid-weight, offers dark cherry, bay leaf, kalamata and blackcurrant flavour; will drink well over the next decade. Screwcap. 14% alc. **Rating** 92 **To** 2024 $25 CM ✪

Four Aces Single Vineyard Manjimup Cabernet Sauvignon 2013 The flavour profile is pure cabernet. Dried tobacco, blackcurrant, dust and mulberry. It's mid-weight, adds (integrated) chocolatey oak to the show, and feels balanced and juicy to close. Screwcap. 14.5% alc. **Rating** 92 **To** 2023 $35 CM

Four Kings Single Vineyard Manjimup Pinot Noir 2014 Smoky and reductive and quite in-your-face about it. The merit of the underlying wine, though, withstands the barrage; sour plum and cherry notes are lifted by mint and assorted spice. But it's the line of acidity and the way the flavours flow in lockstep that have you barracking for it. Give it a good double-decant prior to serving. Screwcap. 14% alc. **Rating** 91 **To** 2021 $25 CM

ŶŶŶŶ   **Four Kings Cabernet Sauvignon 2013 Rating** 88 **To** 2022 $25 CM

Pepper Tree Wines   ★★★★★

Halls Road, Pokolbin, NSW 2321 **Region** Hunter Valley
T (02) 4909 7100 **www.**peppertreewines.com.au **Open** Mon–Fri 9–5, w'ends 9.30–5
Winemaker Scott Comyns **Est.** 1991 **Dozens** 50 000 **Vyds** 172,1ha
The Pepper Tree winery is part of a complex that also contains The Convent guest house and Roberts Restaurant. In 2002 it was acquired by a company controlled by Dr John Davis, who owns 50% of Briar Ridge. It sources the majority of its Hunter Valley fruit from its Tallavera Grove vineyard at Mt View, but also has premium vineyards at Orange, Coonawarra and Wrattonbully, which provide its Grand Reserve and Reserve (single-region) wines. Self-evidently, the wines are exceptional value for money. Following the departure of winemaker Jim Chatto in 2013, his understudy, Scott Comyns, has slipped easily into the chair of Chief Winemaker. Exports to Denmark, Singapore and China.

ŶŶŶŶŶ   **Single Vineyard Reserve Coquun Hunter Valley Shiraz 2013** The Tallawanta Vineyard vines are over 90yo, planted in '20, and for long owned by the Elliott family. It's hard to visualise – unless you taste it, of course – how such intensity, purity and length can be achieved by a wine that has such finesse and elegance to its well of blackberry, black cherry and spice fruit, tannins and oak judged to perfection. Screwcap. 14.5% alc. **Rating** 97 **To** 2048 $70 ◐

ŶŶŶŶŶ   **Single Vineyard Reserve Alluvius Hunter Valley Semillon 2014** The Braemore Vineyard, planted by Ken Bray at the end of the '60s, as the Hunter Valley was coming out of its deep sleep of the prior 80 years, is regarded as one of the best in the Valley. Despite its low alcohol, the wine fills every corner of the mouth with its layered lemongrass and lemon-citrus flavours, finely detailed acidity extending the present length and its future in the cellar. Screwcap. 10.5% alc. **Rating** 96 **To** 2039 $35 ◐
Single Vineyard Limited Release Rhodes Hunter Valley Semillon 2014 The grapes come from two nearby vineyards on Hermitage Road (despite 'Single Vineyard' on the label), both east–west oriented, both with sandy alluvial soils; the Trevena and Casuarina Vineyards are highly regarded, and Scott Comyns has captured all the grace and elegance of the fruit, allied with impeccable acidity and resultant length and balance. Screwcap. 11% alc. **Rating** 96 **To** 2034 $28 ◐
Single Vineyard Polly Fume Hunter Valley Orange Semillon Sauvignon 2014 'Single Vineyard' might be said to pick up from the bon mot of Polly Fume. It is barrel-fermented semillon from the Hunter Valley, sauvignon blanc from Orange, the sauvignon blanc coming over the top of the semillon in no uncertain fashion, but doing so with élan, providing a rich stream of tropical fruit, semillon's acidity striking back on the aftertaste. Screwcap. 12% alc. **Rating** 96 **To** 2017 $28 ◐
Single Vineyard Tallavera Hunter Valley Shiraz 2013 The Tallavera Vineyard is in the Mount View district, noted for its crumbly red soils over limestone. Here the intensity of the fruit of the bouquet and palate goes up several notches, black cherries joining the fray along with plum and mulberry; the tannins are scaled up proportionately, the finish similarly lengthened. A classic Hunter Shiraz of very high quality. Screwcap. 13.8% alc. **Rating** 96 **To** 2038 $45 ◐
Single Vineyard Reserve 8R Wrattonbully Merlot 2013 Clone 8R is the best of several promising new clones recently arrived from France, and resets the criteria and agenda for the variety with the precision and intensity of its fruit

structure. There are no woolly/plummy flavours, its sparkling red fruits, firmish tannins neatly presented on a platter of quality French oak. Its bottle development will be utterly fascinating. Screwcap. 14% alc. **Rating** 96 **To** 2038 $60 ✪

Single Vineyard Reserve Block 21A Wrattonbully Cabernet Sauvignon 2013 Cold-soaked for 5 days, fermentation 7 days, matured for 15 months in French oak. Deep crimson-purple; it is very intense, with layer upon layer of cassis fruit supported by ripe, fine-grained tannins and cedary oak; the balance and length are both impeccable. A long, lusty and productive life lies ahead. Screwcap. 14% alc. **Rating** 96 **To** 2040 $60 ✪

Single Vineyard Reserve Elderslee Road Wrattonbully Cabernet Sauvignon 2013 2-day cold soak, 7-day ferment, 18–20°C, matured in French oak for 15 months. Good hue; this is a high-quality Cabernet with very clear varietal expression, its deep blackcurrant fruit set in a pool of bay leaf, black olive and quality French oak, rimmed by appropriately firm tannins. Screwcap. 14.2% alc. **Rating** 96 **To** 2033 $42 ✪

Single Vineyard Reserve Calcare Coonawarra Cabernet Sauvignon 2013 From the best rows of Pepper Tree's small Coonawarra vineyard. A wine of breed, layered elegance and purity; it establishes its sense of place and variety with the first sip, and builds on that each time it is retasted; the fruit, oak, tannin and acid are in perfect harmony. Screwcap. 14.2% alc. **Rating** 96 **To** 2043 $42 ✪

Single Vineyard Limited Release Hunter Valley Shiraz 2013 Rating 95 To 2028 $35 ✪

Single Vineyard Limited Release Wrattonbully Classics 2013 Rating 95 To 2033 $25 ✪

Single Vineyard Reserve Strandlines Wrattonbully Cabernet Shiraz 2013 Rating 95 To 2038 $55

Limited Release Hunter Valley Semillon 2014 Rating 94 To 2024 $22 ✪

Single Vineyard Reserve The Gravels Wrattonbully Shiraz Viognier 2013 Rating 94 To 2033 $42

Pepperilly Estate Wines ★★★★

Suite 16, 18 Stirling Highway, Nedlands, WA 6009 (postal) **Region** Geographe
T 0401 860 891 **www.**pepperilly.com **Open** Not
Winemaker Damian Hutton **Est.** 1999 **Dozens** 2500 **Vyds** 11ha
Partners Geoff and Karyn Cross, and Warwick Lavis, planted their vineyard in 1991 with 2ha each of cabernet sauvignon, shiraz and sauvignon blanc, and 1ha each of semillon, viognier, chardonnay, mourvedre and grenache. The vineyard has views across the Ferguson Valley to the ocean, with sea breezes providing good ventilation.

🍷🍷🍷🍷🍷 **Ferguson Valley Shiraz 2013** Confidently over-delivers in terms of complexity; there is a wide range of spicy/savoury black fruits, licorice and spice on the bouquet and medium-bodied palate alike; the flavours build length, aided by savoury tannins. Terrific value. Screwcap. 14.5% alc. **Rating** 93 **To** 2025 $18 ✪

Purple Patch 2013 A 'best barrel' selection of 50/40/10% grenache, shiraz and mourvedre, the percentages varying from year to year. Geographe has a cooler climate than McLaren Vale, placing more emphasis on finesse and savoury fruit flavours, but the breeding of the wine is clear, and very different from the other Pepperilly Estate wines. Screwcap. 14.2% alc. **Rating** 91 **To** 2025 $24

Ferguson Valley Cabernet Malbec 2013 A 70/30% estate-grown blend. There is a slightly peppery (no pun intended) finish to the palate after the fragrant cassis and plum of the bouquet. Gives every indication that another year or two will calm things down nicely. Screwcap. 14% alc. **Rating** 91 **To** 2025 $24

Sauvignon Blanc Semillon 2014 No frills; sauvignon blanc does most of the work, with a full range of tropical fruits giving richness, the semillon contributing to the balance. Screwcap. 12% alc. **Rating** 90 **To** 2015 $18 ✪

🍷🍷🍷🍷 **Ferguson Valley Cabernet Shiraz 2013** Rating 89 To 2020 $18 ✪

Petaluma

254 Pfeiffer Road, Woodside, SA 5244 **Region** Adelaide Hills
T (08) 8339 9300 **www**.petaluma.com.au **Open** 7 days 10–5
Winemaker Andrew Hardy, Mike Mudge **Est.** 1976 **Dozens** 60 000 **Vyds** 240ha
The Petaluma range has been expanded beyond the core group of Croser Sparkling, Clare Valley Riesling, Piccadilly Chardonnay and Coonawarra (Cabernet Sauvignon/Merlot). Newer arrivals of note include Adelaide Hills Viognier and Adelaide Hills Shiraz. The SA plantings in the Clare Valley, Coonawarra and Adelaide Hills provide a more than sufficient source of estate-grown grapes for the wines. A new winery and cellar door were opened in 2015 on a greenfield site with views of Mount Lofty. Exports to all major markets.

ŶŶŶŶŶ **Tiers Piccadilly Valley Chardonnay 2012** This is a tiny portion of the Tiers Vineyard, separately bottled. Freed of the cork issues that bedevilled early vintages of Tiers, and with a vineyard that is now mature, this wine shows exceptional delicacy and purity that will take another 5–10 years to reach full maturity. Most remarkable is the way the oak is a mere conveyance, leaving the white peach fruit free play. Screwcap. 14% alc. **Rating** 97 **To** 2025 $115 **✪**

ŶŶŶŶŶ **Hanlin Hill Clare Valley Riesling 2014** Fragrant citrus blossom aromas are the segue for a palate with layers of lime and lemon fruit driving through to an emphatic finish and aftertaste, yet retaining finesse and elegance thanks to perfectly pitched acidity. Screwcap. 13% alc. **Rating** 96 **To** 2024 $28 **✪**
Piccadilly Valley Chardonnay 2013 The distinguished Piccadilly vineyard, and fermentation in Dargaud & Jaegle French oak imparting its typically restrained thumbprint, has produced a first-class wine, with a lineage second to none in SA. White peach, nectarine and a soft, creamy texture are offset by crisp acidity. Screwcap. 14% alc. **Rating** 96 **To** 2023 $40 **✪**
Adelaide Hills Shiraz 2012 From the B&V Vineyard on the eastern edge of the Adelaide Hills region, hand-picked together with some viognier, for a 14-day fermentation and maceration, then to French oak (60% new) for 17 months. Bright crimson-purple; a distinguished and notably complex wine, with an array of black fruits, licorice and pepper, tannins and oak playing a positive, complementary role. Screwcap. 14.5% alc. **Rating** 96 **To** 2042 $45 **✪**
Coonawarra Merlot 2010 Consistently one of the best and most authentic Merlots outside Margaret River; it is all about the balance between cassis and spicy black olive notes, not plum, and positive, yet fine tannin structure. Screwcap. 14% alc. **Rating** 95 **To** 2025 $50
White Adelaide Hills Sauvignon Blanc 2014 Rating 94 **To** 2016 $22 **✪**
White Adelaide Hills Pinot Noir 2013 Rating 94 **To** 2025 $26 **✪**
White Adelaide Hills Shiraz 2013 Rating 94 **To** 2030 $26 **✪**
Croser Rose NV Rating 94 **To** 2017 $25 **✪**

ŶŶŶŶŸ **White Adelaide Hills Chardonnay 2013 Rating** 93 **To** 2018 $22 **✪**
White Adelaide Hills Pinot Gris 2014 Rating 93 **To** 2017 $22 **✪**
White Adelaide Hills Shiraz 2012 Rating 93 **To** 2025 $25 **✪**
White Coonawarra Cabernet Sauvignon 2013 Rating 93 **To** 2028 $26 **✪**
Croser Late Disgorged Piccadilly Valley Pinot Noir Chardonnay 2002 Rating 92 **To** 2015 $55 TS

Peter Drayton Wines

Ironbark Hill Vineyard, 694 Hermitage Road, Pokolbin, NSW 2321 **Region** Hunter Valley
T (02) 6574 7085 **www**.pdwines.com.au **Open** 7 days 10–5
Winemaker Liz Jackson, Keith Tulloch **Est.** 2001 **Dozens** 10 000 **Vyds** 16.5ha
Owned by Peter and Leesa Drayton. Peter's father, Max Drayton, and brothers John and Greg, run Drayton's Family Wines. The estate plantings include shiraz, chardonnay, semillon, cabernet sauvignon, tempranillo, merlot, verdelho and tyrian. Peter is a commercial/industrial builder, so constructing the cellar door was a busman's holiday. The vineyard features an

atmospheric function venue and wedding chapel set among the vines, with events organised and catered for by Café Enzo. Exports to Vietnam, Hong Kong and China.

♥♥♥♥♥ **TJD Reserve Hunter Valley Semillon 2007** Vibrant straw-green; has hastened slowly and surely down its development path, still as fresh as a daisy, yet with an expansive citrus-filled back-palate and finish, acidity seen, but only just heard. Has a minimum of a further decade under its belt. Screwcap. 11% alc. **Rating** 97 To 2027 $54 ✪

♥♥♥♥♥ **Premium Release Semillon 2014** Fresh and singularly vibrant, clearly better than its Signature Reserve sibling; here there is pleasure to be had now, and more – a lot more – in the future as its minerally acidity and zesty/pithy lemon flavours build depth. Screwcap. 11% alc. **Rating** 95 To 2030 $25 ✪
Premium Release Shiraz 2013 Deep crimson-purple; this is at the top end of full-bodied Hunter Valley Shiraz, full of black fruits, a hint of leather and then unrolling a carpet of ripe tannins. In a way it is a retro style, but a very good one, with a great future in the way Hunter Valley Shiraz has. Screwcap. 13.5% alc. **Rating** 95 To 2043 $40

♥♥♥♥♡ **Signature Reserve Hunter Valley Semillon 2014 Rating** 91 To 2025 $25
Premium Release Hunter Valley Chardonnay 2014 Rating 90 To 2018 $25

Peter Lehmann   ★★★★★

Para Road, Tanunda, SA 5352 **Region** Barossa Valley
T (08) 8565 9555 **www**.peterlehmannwines.com **Open** Mon–Fri 9.30–5, w'ends & public hols 10.30–4.30
Winemaker Ian Hongell, Peter Kelly, Tim Dolan **Est.** 1979 **Dozens** 750 000
The seemingly indestructible Peter Lehmann (the person) died in June 2013, laying the seeds for what became the last step in the sale of the minority Lehmann family ownership in the company. The Hess Group of California had acquired control in '03 (leaving part of the capital with the Lehmann family), but a decade later it became apparent that Hess wished to quit its holding. Various suitors put their case forward, but Margaret Lehmann (Peter's widow) wanted ongoing family, not corporate, ownership. Casella thus was able to make the successful bid in November '14; its strategy for the future is still to become clear as at April '15.

♥♥♥♥♥ **Wigan Eden Valley Riesling 2010** Bright quartz-green; an immaculate wine with a track record second to none, and an example of top-class Eden Valley Riesling likewise. The first and foremost stage of cellaring has been done for you, but don't for a moment think the wine has run its course: its shape and balance are good for another decade. Screwcap. 12% alc. **Rating** 97 To 2025 $35 ✪
VSV Hongell Shiraz 2012 From a small block sustainably farmed by Ian and Daniela Hongell. Deeply coloured, it spent 10 days on skins before 12 months in French hogsheads; it is a black-fruited powerhouse that defies logic, with its calm elegance derived from skilled handling of its ripe tannins and subtle, cedary French oak. 750 dozen made. Screwcap. 14.5% alc. **Rating** 97 To 2042 $60 ✪

♥♥♥♥♥ **Moppa Shiraz 2013** Deeply coloured, its bouquet with some cool-grown nuances of dark chocolate, spice and licorice, the palate with multiple layers of black fruits making it medium to full-bodied, yet with supple, ripe tannins that simply add to, rather than detract from, its display of delicious dark fruits. Screwcap. 14.5% alc. **Rating** 96 To 2038 $30 ✪
VSV Blesing Shiraz 2012 The Blesing Vineyard is in the Southern Flinders Ranges, 400m above sea level; a relatively short 10-day fermentation was followed by 12 months in French oak. It is an exciting wine, with satsuma plum, licorice and spice notes embroidered by fine-grained tannins; emphatic length, yet elegant. 400 dozen made. Screwcap. 14.5% alc. **Rating** 96 To 2037 $60 ✪
Mentor Barossa Cabernet 2012 Finishes its fermentation and is matured in French hogsheads for 18 months. The varietal expression is faultless, redolent of black fruits corralled by some bramble and savoury tannins on the finish. A very

good vintage for Cabernet – indeed all red wines – in the Barossa Valley if the alcohol is controlled. Screwcap. 14.5% alc. **Rating** 96 **To** 2037 $45 ✪

VSV 1885 Shiraz 2013 Fermented for 10 days on skins, then 12 months' maturation in French oak. A distinguished, complex medium to full-bodied wine, with dried herb nuances threaded through the black fruits of the palate; just the right contribution from tannins and oak. Will prosper for decades. 330 dozen made. Screwcap. 14.5% alc. **Rating** 95 **To** 2043 $60

VSV Hearnden Eden Valley Shiraz 2013 From a single vineyard at 440m; 12 days on skins, matured for 12 months in French hogsheads. Interesting wine, marching to the beat of its own drum, spice and cedar joining the medium-bodied fruit, retrofitting it with a gently warm, savoury thrust before fruit returns in charge of the aftertaste. Screwcap. 14.5% alc. **Rating** 95 **To** 2038 $60

Lot #2 Stonewell Road Shiraz 2013 From the Hongell Vineyard. Deep, vivid crimson-purple; this is a wine of authority from the first whiff and first taste alike; potent black fruits are framed by firm, but fine, tannins that add length as well as balance. At once distinctly savoury yet juicy. Screwcap. 14.5% alc. **Rating** 95 **To** 2033 $30 ✪

Light Pass Shiraz 2013 Sourced from the Scholz Vineyard. Perfect depth and hue to the colour; the fragrant bouquet has blood plum fruit and a wreath of bitter chocolate, flavours repeated in fine detail on the medium-bodied palate. The wine has a nervous energy that makes it lighter on its feet, yet more intense on the long, lingering finish. Screwcap. 14.5% alc. **Rating** 95 **To** 2035 $30 ✪

8 Songs Barossa Shiraz 2012 This has a great track record, always with an edge of elegance that is very apparent here; with its seamless medium-bodied texture, there are even hints of spice and a whisper of licorice; plum and blackberry are the flavour vectors, couched in a supple embrace of ripe tannins and cedary oak. Screwcap. 14.5% alc. **Rating** 95 **To** 2042 $45

Black Queen Sparkling Shiraz 2010 Extracting the deep, brooding black fruits, dark chocolate, licorice and spice that epitomise the finest Barossa Shiraz, without firm tannins that threaten to topple a sparkling wine, is a precarious undertaking that calls for Jedi-like reflexes. The Lehmann team has pulled off a heroic stunt in the benchmark '10 season, with impeccably fine tannins, well-balanced dosage and beautifully creamy bead. The result is one of the finest Black Queens yet. Cork. 14% alc. **Rating** 95 **To** 2018 $45 TS

Ebenezer Road Shiraz 2013 Rating 94 **To** 2033 $30 ✪
Futures Barossa Shiraz 2012 Rating 94 **To** 2027 $26 ✪
Drawcard Barossa Shiraz 2012 Rating 94 **To** 2032 $28 ✪
Light Pass Cabernet Sauvignon 2013 Rating 94 **To** 2028 $30 ✪

Pewsey Vale ★★★★★

Eden Valley Road, Eden Valley, SA 5353 **Region** Eden Valley
T (08) 8561 3200 **www**.pewseyvale.com **Open** By appt
Winemaker Louisa Rose **Est.** 1847 **Dozens** 20 000 **Vyds** 65ha

Pewsey Vale was a famous vineyard established in 1847 by Joseph Gilbert, and it was appropriate that when the Hill-Smith family began the renaissance of the Eden Valley plantings in 1961, it should do so by purchasing Pewsey Vale and establishing 50ha of riesling. The Riesling also finally benefited from being the first wine to be bottled with a Stelvin screwcap, in '77. While public reaction forced the abandonment of the initiative for almost 20 years, Pewsey Vale never lost faith in the technical advantages of the closure. A quick taste (or better, a share of a bottle) of five to seven-year-old Contours Riesling will tell you why. Exports to all major markets.

🍷🍷🍷🍷🍷 **The Contours Museum Reserve Eden Valley Riesling 2010** The fragrant bouquet has notes of dried flowers and even a hint of spice/musk, the palate now on the development pathway with no obvious end in sight; you have to wait for the aftertaste to find all the wine has to offer so far, as citrus flavours ricochet around the mouth. Screwcap. 13% alc. **Rating** 95 **To** 2025 $34 ✪

The Contours Museum Reserve Eden Valley Riesling 2009 Bright green-gold; has just entered the early period of maturity, with gradual further development in store as it builds on the mix of lime, honey and toast already present. For the nerds, its low pH of 2.96, in conjunction with the screwcap, will underwrite its future. 12.5% alc. **Rating** 95 **To** 2029 $34 ✪

Prima Single Vineyard Eden Valley Riesling 2014 This really is a delicious wine; not as exotically lime-juicy as Mosel Riesling, but with perfect balance and length, and offering as much today as it will in 5 years. Screwcap. 9.5% alc. **Rating** 95 **To** 2029 $26 ✪

♥♥♥♥♀ **Single Vineyard Eden Valley Riesling 2014 Rating** 91 **To** 2024 $23 ✪

Pfeiffer Wines   ★★★★★

167 Distillery Road, Wahgunyah, Vic 3687 **Region** Rutherglen
T (02) 6033 2805 **www.**pfeifferwines.com.au **Open** Mon–Sat 9–5, Sun 10–5
Winemaker Chris and Jen Pfeiffer **Est.** 1984 **Dozens** 35 000 **Vyds** 32ha

Family-owned and run, Pfeiffer Wines occupies one of the historic wineries (built in 1880) that abound in Northeast Victoria, and which is worth a visit on this score alone. In 2012 Chris Pfeiffer was awarded an Order of Australia Medal (OAM) for his services to the wine industry. Both hitherto and into the future, Pfeiffer's Muscats, Topaques and other fortified wines are a key part of the business. The arrival of daughter Jen, by a somewhat circuitous and initially unplanned route, has dramatically lifted the quality of the table wines, led by the reds. Chris Pfeiffer celebrated his 40th vintage in '13, having well and truly set the scene for supremely gifted daughter Jen to assume the chief winemaking role in due course. Exports to the UK, the US, Canada, Belgium, Malaysia, Singapore and China.

♥♥♥♥♥ **Rare Rutherglen Muscat NV** Similar depth to the colour of the Grand, but more mahogany; significantly greater complexity, and the texture more viscous; the flavours include burnt toffee, raisin, Christmas pudding, spice and distinct rancio cleansing the finish. 500ml. Screwcap. 17.5% alc. **Rating** 98 **To** 2016 $123 ✪

Rare Rutherglen Topaque NV Clear burnt amber colour, grading to olive on the rim; is, comparatively speaking, lighter than most other Rutherglen Rare Topaques, but without sacrificing the full array of tea leaf, honey, cake and rich spices on the exceptionally long and well-balanced palate, with an amazing dry finish – dry in the best possible sense. 500ml. Screwcap. 17.5% alc. **Rating** 97 **To** 2016 $123 ✪

♥♥♥♥♥ **Grand Rutherglen Topaque NV** Mid-mahogany colour; a perfumed and rich bouquet, the lift of the rancio providing extra complexity and feeding through into the palate; here burnt toffee, Christmas cake and malt provide a luscious and complex, yet not heavy, finish. 500ml. Screwcap. 17.5% alc. **Rating** 96 **To** 2016 $84

Grand Rutherglen Muscat NV Deep colour; muscat to the back teeth; glorious Arabian spice and raisin interplay, touches of toffee and bitter chocolate, the length and balance perfect, as is the rancio. 500ml. Screwcap. 17.5% alc. **Rating** 96 **To** 2016 $84

Seriously Fine Pale Dry Apera NV Bright light green-gold; a very good example of a flor fino style, the flor not aggressive, giving the crisp apple fruit an almost silky texture. Screwcap. 16.5% alc. **Rating** 94 **To** 2015 $29 ✪

Seriously Nutty Medium Dry Apera NV Bright orange-gold; the rancio cut comes with nutty aromas and flavours, dried orange peel, and the clean finish of a spring day. Screwcap. 21.5% alc. **Rating** 94 **To** 2015 $50

Classic Rutherglen Topaque NV Bright gold-amber; has good varietal expression, with honeycomb, butterscotch and sweet cake flavours, balanced by the rancio, which also extends the finish. 500ml. Screwcap. 17.5% alc. **Rating** 94 **To** 2016 $29 ✪

Classic Rutherglen Muscat NV Very little difference in hue from the Rutherglen entry point wine, but greater focus and intensity to the raisin/plum pudding fruit; excellent rancio and cut to the long finish. 500ml. Screwcap. 17.5% alc. **Rating** 94 **To** 2016 $29 ✪

Carlyle Shiraz 2013 From Rutherglen, El Dorado, Heathcote and Alpine Valleys, all separately fermented then matured separately in French and American oak for 12–14 months. Bright colour; the oak is just a little too obvious, curate's egg-wise, but everything else about the wine shows the care and thought lavished on its predominantly red fruits and finely polished tannins. Screwcap. 14.5% alc. **Rating** 94 **To** 2033 $19 ❂

Carlyle Cabernet Merlot 2013 A 92//8% blend sourced from Rutherglen, Beechworth, Heathcote, King Valley and El Dorado; all with 2 days' cold soak, part finished fermentation in 1yo French hogsheads, all matured in barrel for 12 months. The strength of the cabernet provides a strong framework for the future; that said, its cassis fruit is welcoming now. Great value. Screwcap. 14% alc. **Rating** 94 **To** 2028 $19 ❂

Cabernet Sauvignon 2013 From Rutherglen, Heathcote and Beechworth; divided into four parcels: two cold-soaked 2–3 days then fermented in static fermenters, two fermented in an open vat, hand-plunged, pressed to new French hogsheads for completion of fermentation, all given lees contact for 9 months. All this work has paid handsome dividends at a near giveaway price, earthy cassis supported by fine fruit and oak tannins. Screwcap. 14.5% alc. **Rating** 94 **To** 2028 $25 ❂

Tempranillo 2013 Cold-soaked for 3 days; at 4° baume part of the wine was transferred to new American hogsheads to complete fermentation and 16 months' maturation, the remainder finished fermentation in tank, thence to used French oak. The breakout label design is in tune with the fruit, which pushes the Tempranillo envelope hard, grafting savoury depth onto black cherry fruit. Screwcap. 14.8% alc. **Rating** 94 **To** 2028 $24 ❂

Phaedrus Estate

220 Mornington–Tyabb Road, Moorooduc, Vic 3933 **Region** Mornington Peninsula **T** (03) 5978 8134 **www**.phaedrus.com.au **Open** W'ends & public hols 11–5 **Winemaker** Ewan Campbell, Maitena Zantvoort **Est.** 1997 **Dozens** 2000 **Vyds** 2.5ha Since Maitena Zantvoort and Ewan Campbell established Phaedrus Estate, they have gained a reputation for producing premium cool-climate wines. Their winemaking philosophy brings art and science together to produce wines showing regional and varietal character with minimal winemaking interference. The vineyard includes 1ha of pinot noir and 0.5ha each of pinot gris, chardonnay and shiraz. Exports to Hong Kong.

🍷🍷🍷🍷🍷 **Single Vineyard Reserve Mornington Peninsula Pinot Noir 2013** Foot-crushed, wild yeast-fermented, matured in 3 French hogsheads, 1 new, 2 1yo. Deeply coloured, this is a veritable powerhouse but isn't over-extractive, its plum and black cherry fruit mouth-coating, but in the best way. If you are after a full-bodied Pinot with a long future, this is it. Pinot is a broad church. Bottle no. 1091 of 1200. Screwcap. 13.9% alc. **Rating** 95 **To** 2028 $45

Mornington Peninsula Pinot Noir 2013 Foot-crushed, wild yeast-fermented, matured in French hogsheads (20% new). Very deep colour, even more than the Reserve; a rich, full-bodied Pinot that fills the mouth with its almost velvety fruit; just when you wonder about varietal character, the savoury lift on the finish says all is well. Screwcap. 13.7% alc. **Rating** 94 **To** 2025 $26 ❂

Single Vineyard Reserve Mornington Peninsula Shiraz 2013 From a special 8-row block; matured for 18 months in 2 French hogsheads, 1 new, 1 used. In typical Phaedrus style, built for eternity, with excellent colour, and a tightly structured, medium to full-bodied palate, black and purple fruits disputing centre stage, the tannins firm, the finish long. Bottle no. 410 of 800. Screwcap. 13.9% alc. **Rating** 94 **To** 2038 $45

PHI
★★★★★

Lusatia Park Vineyard, Owens Road, Woori Yallock, Vic 3139 **Region** Yarra Valley/Heathcote
T (03) 5964 6070 **www**.phiwines.com **Open** By appt
Winemaker Steve Webber **Est.** 2005 **Dozens** 1700 **Vyds** 15ha
This is a joint venture between two very influential wine families: De Bortoli and Shelmerdine.
The key executives are Stephen Shelmerdine and Steve Webber (and wives Kate and Leanne).
It rests upon the selection and management of specific blocks of vines without regard to cost.
The wines are made from the 7.5ha Lusatia Park Vineyard in the Yarra Valley, and the estate-
owned 7.5ha vineyard in Heathcote. The name, incidentally, is derived from the 21st letter of
the ancient Greek alphabet, symbolising perfect balance and harmony. It's courageous pricing,
but reflects the confidence the families have in the wines. Exports to the UK and China.

ŸŸŸŸŸ Single Vineyard Yarra Valley Pinot Noir 2013 It's not surprising that the
PHI and De Bortoli Pinot Noirs should have similarities: Steve Webber is the
winemaker of each, his guiding principle doing as little as possible in the winery.
This is a wine of real authority, with a mix of savoury red and black fruits backed
by savoury tannins. Screwcap. 13% alc. **Rating** 95 **To** 2023 $48
Heathcote Syrah Grenache Mourvedre 2012 Milks the sweet spot between
easy drinkability and posh complexity for all it's worth. It feels smooth and classy,
offers lively flavours of raspberry, blackberry and cloves, and throws earthen,
peppery characters aplenty through the finish. Tannin is fine, length is very good,
balance is to be marvelled at in itself. A wine to be sought out, snapped up, and
consumed with relish. Screwcap. 14% alc. **Rating** 95 **To** 2022 $25 CM ✪

ŸŸŸŸŸ Heathcote Rose 2014 **Rating** 93 **To** 2016 $24 CM ✪

Philip Shaw Wines
★★★★★

Koomooloo Vineyard, Caldwell Lane, Orange, NSW 2800 **Region** Orange
T (02) 6365 2334 **www**.philipshaw.com.au **Open** 7 days 11–5
Winemaker Philip and Daniel Shaw **Est.** 1989 **Dozens** 25 000 **Vyds** 47ha
Philip Shaw, former chief winemaker of Rosemount Estate and then Southcorp, first became
interested in the Orange region in 1985. In '88 he purchased the Koomooloo Vineyard and
began extensive plantings, the varieties including shiraz, merlot, pinot noir, sauvignon blanc,
cabernet franc, cabernet sauvignon and viognier. Son Daniel has joined Philip in the winery,
at a time when the quality of the portfolio of wines is going from strength to strength.
A representative range of wines was not received for this edition, but the rating has been
maintained. Exports to the UK, the US and other major markets.

ŸŸŸŸŸ No. 8 Orange Pinot Noir 2013 Given that Orange isn't exactly renowned for
its Pinot Noir, this could be construed as a rabbit out of a hat. It's fragrant and
delicate, fresh, is a far distance from anything dry-reddish, and yet feels confident
with flavour as it sets sail on the finish. Jellied fruits, sweet and sour, herbal/spice
inputs and a run of ribbed tannin. It would stand up in just about any company.
Screwcap. 13% alc. **Rating** 94 **To** 2021 $40 CM

Philippa Farr
★★★★★

PO Box 271, Wonthaggi, Vic 3995 **Region** Gippsland
T 0438 326 795 **www**.philippafarr.com.au **Open** Not
Winemaker Philippa Farr **Est.** 2012 **Dozens** 200 **Vyds** 0.5ha
This is take-three for the Farr family, father Gary and brother Nick having shown the way.
Growing up at Bannockburn, surrounded by vines and sheep, Philippa was exposed to
fine wine from an early age. In 2003 she undertook the vintage at Brokenwood, and after
completing the first year of a Bachelor of Wine Science degree, she returned to work at
Brokenwood full-time, studying part-time, until the completion of the '05 vintage. She says
that 'just to ensure her childhood upbringing on a sheep farm was not her true passion, she
followed a farming career in the following years in Gippsland'. She took time to complete

vintages at Bellvale, Domaine Dujac, By Farr and Purple Hen. After 4 years living in Gippsland, Philippa made her first Pinot Noir from half a hectare of high-density planted pinot.

♥♥♥♥♥ **Pinot Noir 2013** Wild yeast, 30% whole bunches, 3 weeks on skins, 30% new oak, unfiltered. It's a dark, brooding Pinot Noir, but most of all it's a seductive one. Dark cherry, sap, wood spice, a coating of smoky, cedary oak. From the first sip to the last, it has you hooked. Cork. 14% alc. **Rating** 95 **To** 2022 $45 CM

Pierrepoint Wines ★★★★☆

271 Pierrepoint Road, Tarrington, Vic 3300 **Region** Henty
T (03) 5572 5553 **www.**pierrepointwines.com.au **Open** Most days 11–6
Winemaker Scott Ireland (Contract) **Est.** 1998 **Dozens** 450 **Vyds** 5ha
Pierrepoint was established by Andrew and Jennifer Lacey on the foothills of Mt Pierrepoint between Hamilton and Tarrington at an altitude of 200m. The predominantly red buckshot soils of the vineyard are derived from ancient volcanic basalt, rich in minerals and free-draining. Two hectares each of pinot noir and pinot gris, and 1ha of chardonnay are planted on an ideal north-facing slope.

♥♥♥♥♥ **Alexandra Chardonnay 2013** The very cool Henty climate, low yields and high-quality winemaking join hands in producing a Chardonnay of exceptional intensity and length; yet it is light on its feet, with a fused mix of grapefruit and white peach. Screwcap. 12.5% alc. **Rating** 95 **To** 2023 $35 ✪
Pinot Noir 2012 Estate-grown with very low yield of 2.5t/ha; 12 months' maturation in French oak. Deeply coloured, its flavours are in the dark fruit spectrum, with black cherries and savoury plum flavours. A Pinot that will live and evolve for more than a decade. Screwcap. 13% alc. **Rating** 94 **To** 2025 $39

♥♥♥♥ **Nicks Pick Pinot Gris 2013 Rating** 89 **To** 2016 $29

Pierro ★★★★★

Caves Road, Wilyabrup via Cowaramup, WA 6284 **Region** Margaret River
T (08) 9755 6220 **www.**pierro.com.au **Open** 7 days 10–5
Winemaker Dr Michael Peterkin **Est.** 1979 **Dozens** 10 000 **Vyds** 7.85ha
Dr Michael Peterkin is another of the legion of Margaret River medical practitioners-vignerons; for good measure, he married into the Cullen family. Pierro is renowned for its stylish white wines, which often exhibit tremendous complexity; the Chardonnay can be monumental in its weight and texture. That said, its red wines from good vintages can be every bit as good. Exports to the UK, Denmark, Belgium, Russia, Malaysia, Indonesia, Hong Kong, Singapore and Japan.

♥♥♥♥♥ **Reserve Margaret River Cabernet Sauvignon Merlot 2011** The wine also includes cabernet franc, although the percentages are not specified. This is a distinguished and super-elegant Margaret River Cabernet Merlot, maturation in new French oak in no way obscuring the interplay of cassis, redcurrant and blueberry fruits, the tannins fine and supple, the length and aftertaste exemplary. Screwcap. 13.5% alc. **Rating** 96 **To** 2031 $77
Margaret River Chardonnay 2013 A classy Chardonnay providing a perfect take on Margaret River style, marrying depth and complexity with elegance and drive; white peach and a flick of citrussy acidity join with subtle French oak on the fresh, lingering finish. Screwcap. 14% alc. **Rating** 95 **To** 2023 $82
L.T.C. 2014 Semillon and sauvignon blanc, with a little touch of chardonnay. A complex bouquet with a touch of positive, funky reduction, thrust aside by the intensity and focus of the mineral, lemon citrus and apple palate; barrel fermentation has left only a memory on the finish. Screwcap. 13.5% alc. **Rating** 94 **To** 2016 $34

♥♥♥♥♡ **Cabernet Sauvignon Merlot L.T.Cf. 2012 Rating** 93 **To** 2022 $40

Pig in the House

Balcombe Road, Billimari, NSW 2804 **Region** Cowra
T 0427 443 598 **www**.piginthehouse.com.au **Open** Fri–Sun 11–5 by appt
Winemaker Antonio D'Onise **Est.** 2002 **Dozens** 1700 **Vyds** 25ha
Jason and Rebecca O'Dea established their vineyard (5ha each of merlot, shiraz and cabernet
sauvignon) on a block of land formerly used as home for 20 free-range pigs – making any
explanation about the name of the business totally unnecessary. Given its prior use, one would
imagine the vines would grow lustily, and it is no surprise that organic certification has been
given by Biological Farmers of Australia. The O'Deas have in fact taken the process several
steps further, using biodynamic preparations and significantly reducing all sprays. The wines
made are good advertisements for organic/biodynamic farming. Exports to Japan and China.

PPPPP **Certified Organic Cabernet Sauvignon 2012** Won the inaugural NASAA
Certified Organic Wine of the Year Award '14, competing with 100 wines from
around Aus. It is an elegant, medium-bodied wine, the overall balance very good;
the most remarkable feature is the clarity of its varietal expression given its Cowra
origin. Screwcap. 13.5% alc. **Rating** 91 **To** 2022 $25

PPPP **Certified Organic Shiraz 2013** **Rating** 89 **To** 2017 $25

Pike & Joyce

730 Mawson Road, Lenswood, SA 5240 **Region** Adelaide Hills
T (08) 8389 8102 **www**.pikeandjoyce.com.au **Open** Not
Winemaker Neil Pike, John Trotter, Steve Baraglia **Est.** 1998 **Dozens** 5000 **Vyds** 18.5ha
This is a partnership between the Pike family (of Clare Valley fame) and the Joyce family,
related to Andrew Pike's wife, Cathy. The Joyce family have been orchardists at Lenswood for
over 100 years, and also have extensive operations in the Riverland. Together with Andrew
they have established a vineyard planted to sauvignon blanc (5.9ha), pinot noir (5.73ha), pinot
gris (3.22ha), chardonnay (3.18ha) and semillon (0.47ha). The wines are made at the Pikes'
Clare Valley winery. Exports to the UK, China and other major markets.

PPPPP **Sirocco Adelaide Hills Chardonnay 2014** Its cool-climate elegance has
been achieved without any attenuation of the luscious white peach, grapefruit
and melon fruit, relaxing in its basket of fine, integrated French oak. Screwcap.
13.5% alc. **Rating** 95 **To** 2023 $35 ✪
Separe Adelaide Hills Gruner Veltliner 2014 A worthy addition to the
intrepid band of Gruner Veltliner explorers. The aromas are of pear, apple and
a hint of white pepper if you work on it, the palate building convincingly on
the trail left by the bouquet. This really is a very good wine, with great length.
Screwcap. 12% alc. **Rating** 95 **To** 2024 $28 ✪
Adelaide Hills Pinot Noir 2013 A blend of the best barrels (4 clones). Has
greater complexity and fruit weight than the Rapide, with nuances of black
cherry and plum, red fruits in the background. A barrel selection doesn't of itself
guarantee a high-quality wine, but it does here – a fine Adelaide Hills Pinot.
Screwcap. 14% alc. **Rating** 95 **To** 2023 $35 ✪
Descente Adelaide Hills Sauvignon Blanc 2014 The name stems from the
two steep slopes of sauvignon blanc directly in front of the cellar door. Quartz-
green; a mix of gooseberry, citrus and snow pea, the acidity fresh and bracing, the
length and balance good. Screwcap. 12% alc. **Rating** 94 **To** 2016 $24 ✪
Beurre Bosc Adelaide Hills Pinot Gris 2014 The name comes from the
Beurre Bosc variety of pear planted on what is now Block 1 (removed for the
pinot gris). A quiet bouquet gives way to a vividly flavoured palate, pear and
citrus (lime) engaged in a battle for supremacy. I could enjoy drinking this wine.
Screwcap. 13% alc. **Rating** 94 **To** 2016 $24 ✪

PPPPP **The Bleedings Pinot Noir Rose 2014** **Rating** 93 **To** 2015 $18 ✪
Rapide Adelaide Hills Pinot Noir 2013 **Rating** 93 **To** 2020 $22 ✪

Pikes ★★★★★

Polish Hill River Road, Sevenhill, SA 5453 **Region** Clare Valley
T (08) 8843 4370 **www**.pikeswines.com.au **Open** 7 days 10–4
Winemaker Neil Pike, Steve Baraglia **Est.** 1984 **Dozens** 35 000 **Vyds** 73ha
Owned by the Pike brothers: Andrew was for many years the senior viticulturist with Southcorp, Neil was a winemaker at Mitchell. Pikes now has its own winery, with Neil presiding. In most vintages its white wines, led by Riesling, are the most impressive. Planting of the vineyards has been an ongoing affair, with a panoply of varietals, new and traditional. The Merle is Pikes' limited-production flagship Riesling. Exports to the UK, the US and other major markets.

🍷🍷🍷🍷🍷 The Merle Clare Valley Riesling 2014 A single-block (Thicket) Riesling from the Polish Hill River district. Immediately takes hold of the palate with its powerful depth and length, the ripe fruit flavours balanced by the typical slatey acidity on the back-palate and finish. It has the grunt to evolve over decades to come. Screwcap. 12% alc. **Rating** 97 **To** 2044 $40 ✪

🍷🍷🍷🍷🍷 Traditionale Clare Valley Riesling 2014 Estate and contract-grown fruit from Polish Hill, Watervale and Sevenhill; this is the 30th consecutive release of this wine. Lemon leads the flavour charge, hotly pursued by lime, then vibrant acidity catching up on the finish, with a reprise of the lemon. Screwcap. 11% alc. **Rating** 95 **To** 2025 $26 ✪

The E.W.P. Clare Valley Shiraz 2012 A medium-bodied Shiraz, selected from two estate blocks, made to keep the emphasis on its origin; it has a spicy/savoury edge to its purple and black fruits, with oak and tannins carefully balanced. That drinking span starts tonight, and will cruise through the next 20 years before drawing breath. Screwcap. 13.5% alc. **Rating** 95 **To** 2037 $70

Hills & Valleys Clare Valley Riesling 2014 Green-quartz hue; an utterly delicious palate with abundant juicy lime and lemon fruit; its mouthfeel is particularly attractive, balance and length likewise. Screwcap. 10.5% alc. **Rating** 94 **To** 2025 $20 ✪

🍷🍷🍷🍷 Luccio Clare Valley Fiano 2014 **Rating** 93 **To** 2018 $18 ✪
Gill's Farm Clare Valley Mourvedre 2013 **Rating** 93 **To** 2025 $24 ✪
Valley's End Sauvignon Blanc Semillon 2014 **Rating** 91 **To** 2016 $22 ✪
Eastside Clare Valley Shiraz 2013 **Rating** 91 **To** 2023 $28
Olga Emmie Clare Valley Riesling 2014 **Rating** 91 **To** 2024 $20 ✪

Pimpernel Vineyards ★★★★★

6 Hill Road, Coldstream, Vic 3770 **Region** Yarra Valley
T 0457 326 436 **www**.pimpernelvineyards.com.au **Open** W'ends & public hols 11–5
Winemaker Damien Archibald, Mark Horrigan **Est.** 2001 **Dozens** 2000 **Vyds** 6ha
Lilydale-based cardiologist Mark Horrigan's love affair with wine started long before he had heard about either the Yarra Valley or his family's links, centuries ago, to Condrieu, France. He is a direct descendant of the Chapuis family, his ultimate ancestors buried in the Church of St Etienne in 1377. In a cosmopolitan twist, his father came from a Welsh mining village, but made his way to university and found many things to enjoy, not the least wine. When the family moved to Australia in 1959, wine remained part of everyday life and, as Mark grew up in the '70s, the obsession passed from father to son. In 2001 he and wife Fiona purchased a property in the Yarra Valley on which they have built a (second) house, planted a vineyard, and erected a capacious winery designed by WA architect Peter Moran. In the course of doing so they became good friends of near-neighbour the late Dr Bailey Carrodus; some of the delphic labelling of Pimpernel's wines is pure Carrodus.

🍷🍷🍷🍷🍷 Yarra Valley Pinot Noir Three 2013 From 0.25ha 'on a base of imported local limestone' added to the soil, clones 777 and MV6, wild and cultured yeasts, moderate stalks, moderate post-fermentation maceration with some stalks, 12 months in French oak (33% new). Is it the soil or the MV6 component that drives the very different fruit profile? Red fruits largely replace black on the evocative bouquet, and there is a finer, more lacy mouthfeel to the medium-bodied palate. Diam. 14.5% alc. **Rating** 96 **To** 2030 $75 ✪

GSM2 2013 A 43/35/22% blend of grenache, shiraz, mourvedre, with less than 1% of muscat of Alexandria; wild yeast-fermented, all components given 3–4 weeks' post-fermentation maceration, matured for 12 months in used oak. All ye who come here witness the generosity and perfect ripeness of this classic Rhône blend. Diam. 14.5% alc. **Rating** 96 **To** 2033 $45 ✪

Yarra Valley Viognier 2013 Believed to be a Grillet clone; made as per the Chardonnay: whole bunches are crushed, leaving the stalks with the fruit chilled and pressed to tank for fermentation, taken to used French barriques for completion, 100% mlf, some stirring. Works far better here than for Chardonnay; there is more obvious apricot/peach here than in most other Australian Viogniers. Diam. 14.2% alc. **Rating** 95 **To** 2019 $45

Yarra Valley Pinot Noir One 2013 Clones 777, 114 and 115, wild and cultured yeasts, open-fermented at a maximum of 30°C, minimal stalks, 12 months in French oak (20% new). Exudes serious intent from the first whiff through to the finish, its smoky/spicy aromas and flavours knitting together on the long, fleshy and seductive palate. Diam. 14.5% alc. **Rating** 95 **To** 2028 $45

Petit Grouch 2013 Shiraz co-fermented with 1–2% viognier, 14 months in French barriques (30% new). There's a tarry nuance on the bouquet that is hard to pin down, but ties in with the naked power of the full-bodied palate, black cherry and blackberry fruit supported by potent, ripe tannins and oak. Diam. 14.2% alc. **Rating** 95 **To** 2038 $50

Yarra Valley Marsanne Viognier 2013 A 50/50% blend made in the same way as the Viognier, employing 100% used oak. This is more about the future than the present, although there's a nice touch of juicy fruit before chalky acidity takes hold. Diam. 14.7% alc. **Rating** 94 **To** 2025 $40

ꙮꙮꙮꙮꙮ Yarra Valley Pinot Noir Two 2013 Rating 93 To 2023 $45
Yarra Valley Chardonnay 2013 Rating 90 To 2020 $45

Pindarie   ★★★★☆

946 Rosedale Road, Gomersal, SA 5352 **Region** Barossa Valley
T (08) 8524 9019 www.pindarie.com.au **Open** Mon–Fri 11–4, w'ends 11–5
Winemaker Peter Leske **Est.** 2005 **Dozens** 5000 **Vyds** 32.4ha
Owners Tony Brooks and Wendy Allan met at Roseworthy College in 1985. Tony was the sixth generation of farmers in SA and WA, and was studying agriculture; NZ-born Wendy was studying viticulture. On graduation Tony worked overseas managing sheep feedlots in Saudi Arabia, Turkey and Jordan, while Wendy worked for the next 12 years with Penfolds, commencing as a grower liaison officer and working her way up to become a senior viticulturist. She also found time to study viticulture in California, Israel, Italy, Germany, France, Portugal, Spain and Chile, working vintages and assessing vineyards for wine projects. In 2001 she completed a graduate diploma in wine business. The cellar door and café (which won a major tourism award in '12) has panoramic views. Exports to China.

ꙮꙮꙮꙮꙮ Black Hinge Reserve Barossa Valley Shiraz 2012 A single-vineyard, single-block, single-row selection, fermented in a small open fermenter, matured for 24 months in predominantly French oak. Deep crimson-purple; it is an immaculately balanced medium-bodied wine with black fruits, plus touches of licorice and tar, the tannins ripe, the oak in its due place. Cork. 14.5% alc. Rating 95 To 2032 $60

Eden Valley Riesling 2014 A perfumed bouquet with nuances of talc and lime blossom introduces a tangy, zesty palate where lemon, lime and minerally acidity take control on an extremely long finish. Will age very well. Screwcap. 11.5% alc. Rating 94 To 2029 $22 ✪

ꙮꙮꙮꙮꙮ Black Hinge Reserve Tempranillo 2013 Rating 91 To 2018 $50
T.S.S. Tempranillo Sangiovese Shiraz 2014 Rating 90 To 2020 $23

Pinelli Wines

30 Bennett Street, Caversham, WA 6055 **Region** Swan District
T (08) 9279 6818 **www**.pinelliwines.com.au **Open** Mon–Sat 9–5, Sun 10–5
Winemaker Robert and Daniel Pinelli **Est.** 1980 **Dozens** 17 000 **Vyds** 9.78ha
Domenic and Iolanda Pinelli emigrated from Italy in the mid-1950s, and it was not long
before Domenic was employed by Waldeck Wines, then one of the Swan Valley's more
important wineries. With the benefit of 20 years' experience gained with Waldeck, in '80 he
purchased a 2.8ha vineyard that had been established many years previously. It became the
site of the Pinelli family winery, cellar door and home vineyard, subsequently significantly
expanded, with cabernet sauvignon, colombard, merlot and shiraz. Son Robert graduated
with a degree in oenology from Roseworthy in 1987, and has been the winemaker at
Pinelli for over 20 years. His brother Daniel obtained a degree in civil engineering from the
University of WA in '94, but eventually the lure of the family winery became too strong, so he
joined his brother in '02, and obtained his oenology degree from CSU in '07. He graduated
with distinction, and was awarded the Domaine Chandon Sparkling Wine Award for best
sparkling wine production student.

Reserve Verdelho 2014 At face value, an odd Reserve nomenclature given the
price and variety, but not so surprising once the intensity of the stone fruit and
tropical fruit flavours surge through the mouth. No oak involved, just a subliminal
touch of sweetness. Will age well. Screwcap. 13% alc. **Rating** 91 **To** 2020 $17 ✪

Pipers Brook Vineyard

1216 Pipers Brook Road, Pipers Brook, Tas 7254 **Region** Northern Tasmania
T (03) 6382 7527 **www**.pipersbrook.com.au **Open** 7 days 10–5
Winemaker René Bezemer **Est.** 1974 **Dozens** 70 000 **Vyds** 194ha
The Pipers Brook Tasmanian empire has almost 200ha of vineyard supporting the Pipers
Brook and Ninth Island labels, with the major focus, of course, being on Pipers Brook.
Fastidious viticulture and winemaking, immaculate packaging and enterprising marketing
create a potent and effective blend. Pipers Brook operates two cellar door outlets, one at
headquarters, the other at Strathlyn. Pipers Brook is owned by Belgian-owned sheepskin
business Kreglinger, which has also established the large Norfolk Island winery and vineyard at
Mount Benson in SA (see separate entry). Exports to the UK, the US and other major markets.

Estate Riesling 2014 Flies straight into a storm of flavour. Scintillating. Lemon,
slate, mineral and steel. It hits and runs and doesn't let up. Screwcap. 13% alc.
Rating 96 **To** 2030 $34 CM ✪
Estate Gewurztraminer 2014 Characterised by its excellent length of
flavour. Spice, Turkish delight, crisp apple and lychee but not over the top or too
exaggerated; restraint and elegance are in vogue here, even as it delivers powerful
rounds of lingering flavour. Screwcap. 13% alc. **Rating** 95 **To** 2017 $34 CM ✪
Estate Pinot Noir 2012 The backgrounder detailing location, season, soil,
winemaking and lengthy tasting notes is identical for the '11 and '12, the wines
in fact radically different, this very good. Here the straightforward vinification and
maturation techniques have given rise to a wine with crystal clear and generous
varietal fruit expression. Screwcap. 13.5% alc. **Rating** 95 **To** 2023 $41
Kreglinger Vintage Brut Rose 2004 Making elegant, long-aged vintage rose
is challenging and René Bezemer has mastered it in this decade-old cuvee. To
achieve such a pretty, very pale salmon hue and such elegance from pinot noir
fully fermented in old oak barrels calls for nothing short of wizardry. Its maturity
gently draws spicy, secondary complexity and finely textured structure from wild
strawberry and red cherry fruit, closing linear, persistent, wonderfully understated,
yet resolutely confident. Disgorged Feb '14. Cork. 12.5% alc. **Rating** 95 **To** 2019
$65 TS
Estate Chardonnay 2013 Essentially delicious but with quality and class. Lime,
white peach and Granny Smith apple flavours come threaded with lanolin and oak
spice, but the juicy flavour sluicing through the palate is the main thrill. Screwcap.
13% alc. **Rating** 94 **To** 2020 $34 CM

ŢŢŢŢŢ Pirie Traditional Method NV Rating 93 To 2016 $32 TS
Estate Pinot Gris 2013 Rating 92 To 2016 $34 CM
Ninth Island Pinot Noir 2013 Rating 92 To 2019 $24 ◎
Kreglinger Vintage Brut 2006 Rating 92 To 2021 $55 TS
Sparkling 2008 Rating 91 To 2018 $37 TS
Ninth Island Sparkling NV Rating 91 To 2015 $30 TS

Pirramimma   ★★★★★

Johnston Road, McLaren Vale, SA 5171 **Region** McLaren Vale
T (08) 8323 8205 **www.**pirramimma.com.au **Open** Mon–Fri 10–4.30, w'ends &
public hols 10.30–5
Winemaker Geoff Johnston **Est.** 1892 **Dozens** 40 000 **Vyds** 91.5ha
A long-established family-owned company with outstanding vineyard resources. It is using
those resources to full effect, with a series of intense old-vine varietals including Semillon,
Sauvignon Blanc, Chardonnay, Shiraz, Grenache, Cabernet Sauvignon and Petit Verdot, all
fashioned without over-embellishment. Wines are released under several ranges: Pirramimma,
Stock's Hill, Pirra, Gilden Lily, Eight Carat, Wattle Park, Vineyard Select, Katunga and Lion's
Gate. Exports to the UK, the US and other major markets.

ŢŢŢŢŢ McLaren Vale Shiraz 2012 Full crimson-purple; crammed to the rafters on the
bouquet and palate alike; the fruit has some unexpected cherry and spice nuances
cohabiting with more conventional blackberry, bramble and dark chocolate;
the overall impact is very powerful and full-bodied, the aftertaste with some lift,
probably from the alcohol. Screwcap. 14.8% alc. **Rating** 95 **To** 2027 $30 ◎
ACJ 2010 A 42/31/20/7% blend of petit verdot, shiraz, cabernet and merlot. Still
deeply vividly coloured, this is full-on, full-bodied stuff, the deep wells of black
fruits encased in a shroud of tannin and oak. All the usual McLaren Vale bibs and
bobs, with licorice, allspice and dark chocolate. To be approached with caution and
respect around '25. Cork. 14.8% alc. **Rating** 95 **To** 2040 $70
Old Bush Vine McLaren Vale Grenache 2012 From two estate vineyards
planted in '44 and '68; hand-picked, open-fermented in old concrete vats, basket-
pressed and matured in used French barriques. It abounds with red fruits of every
description, with an overlay of spice and herb, finishing with superfine tannins.
Screwcap. 15% alc. **Rating** 94 **To** 2022 $30 ◎
Reserve Merlot 2012 Pirramimma's first Reserve Merlot, sourced from estate
vines plus those of 5 other growers; only 10% of the wine was matured in new
French barriques to keep the focus on varietal expression, the rest in tank. Its
savoury, black olive flavours gleaned a rare gold medal (for Merlot) from the
Sydney Wine Show '14. Screwcap. 14.8% alc. **Rating** 94 **To** 2027 $25 ◎

ŢŢŢŢŢ Wattle Park Adelaide Hills Shiraz 2010 Rating 93 To 2023 $30
McLaren Vale Grenache Shiraz 2012 Rating 93 To 2032 $30
War Horse Shiraz 2012 Rating 92 To 2042 $70
Stock's Hill Shiraz Petit Verdot 2010 Rating 92 To 2030 $20 ◎
Vineyard Select GTS 2012 Rating 90 To 2022 $20 ◎

Pizzini   ★★★★

175 King Valley Road, Whitfield, Vic 3768 **Region** King Valley
T (03) 5729 8278 **www.**pizzini.com.au **Open** 7 days 10–5
Winemaker Joel Pizzini **Est.** 1980 **Dozens** 37 000 **Vyds** 48.7ha
Fred and Katrina Pizzini have been grapegrowers in the King Valley for over 30 years, with
a substantial vineyard. Originally much of the grape production was sold, but today 80% is
retained for the Pizzini brand, and the focus is on winemaking, which has been particularly
successful. Their wines rank high among the many King Valley producers. It is not surprising
that their wines should span both Italian and traditional varieties, and I can personally vouch
for their Italian cooking skills. Katrina's A tavola! cooking school gives lessons in antipasti,
gnocchi, risotto, cakes and desserts, and of course, pasta. Exports to the UK and Japan.

ΨΨΨΨΨ **King Valley Riesling 2014** Excellent release. Combines flesh and flavour beautifully; this is a young Riesling of both intensity and body. It's textural, limey, floral and flush with ripe pear notes. It deserves to find many fans. Screwcap. 11.9% alc. **Rating** 94 **To** 2024 $18 CM ✪
Pietra Rossa King Valley Sangiovese 2013 The well-known Pizzini Sangiovese now has a new name; it will sit alongside a set of single-vineyard expressions/releases. It's a good vintage to launch a new name; the fruit juicy, fresh and beautifully inviting, the tannin dry and savoury but nestled safely in. Impressive persistence. Touch of class. Screwcap. 13.8% alc. **Rating** 94 **To** 2023 $28 CM ✪
Forza di Ferro Sangiovese 2013 Characterised by its dry, stringy, herbal tannin. Gamey. Nutty. Rose petals and red cherries, fragrant and appealing, before the dry savoury twists take over. Difficult wine to assess, and access. Serious and brooding. Needs lots of time. Looks to have a longish future ahead. Screwcap. 13.8% alc. **Rating** 94 **To** 2026 $55 CM

ΨΨΨΨΨ **King Valley Canaiolo 2013** Rating 93 **To** 2019 $24 CM ✪
Per gli Angeli 2007 Rating 93 **To** 2018 $65 CM
King Valley Friulano 2014 Rating 92 **To** 2015 $18 CM ✪
King Valley Rosetta 2014 Rating 92 **To** 2015 $19 CM ✪
King Valley Shiraz 2013 Rating 91 **To** 2020 $22 CM ✪
Lana Il Nostro Gallo Sangiovese 2012 Rating 91 **To** 2020 $24 CM
Coronamento King Valley Nebbiolo 2008 Rating 91 **To** 2019 $135 CM

Plan B   ★★★★

679 Calgardup Road, Forest Grove, WA 6286 **Region** Great Southern/Margaret River
T 0413 759 030 **www**.planbwines.com **Open** Not
Winemaker Bill Crappsley **Est.** 2005 **Dozens** 40000 **Vyds** 20ha
Plan B is a joint venture between Terry Chellappah, wine consultant, Bill Crappsley, a veteran winemaker/consultant and Andrew Blythe. The Shiraz is sourced from Bill's Calgardup Vineyard, the remaining wines from Arlewood, and all are single-vineyard releases. It has been a notably successful Plan B under Terry's management, with significant increases in production naturally following. In 2014 Bill Crappsley was awarded the Jack Mann Memorial Medal for significant services to the WA Wine Industry, coinciding with his 50 years in winemaking in WA. He had previously won the Di Cullen Award in '07, and the George Mulgrue Award in 1999, in each case recognising his services to the industry. Exports include the UK, Canada, China.

ΨΨΨΨΨ **TV Tempranillo 2013** 'TV' stands for tempranillo/viognier, the viognier only 2%. The tempranillo comes from a contract grower in Geographe, the viognier from Margaret River; spent 9 months in used French oak. The colour is vivid crimson, and tempranillo thumps the lectern as it announces its varietal make-up of multi-cherry personality, the viognier quite possibly having more effect than you might imagine in lifting the colour. More than just a piece of fun, although it will always be a hard decision whether to drink it now, or save some for later. Screwcap. 14% alc. **Rating** 94 **To** 2023 $25 ✪

ΨΨΨΨΨ **Margaret River Chardonnay 2014** Rating 93 **To** 2020 $27 ✪
OD Frankland River Riesling 2014 Rating 93 **To** 2020 $20 ✪
MB Frankland River Sauvignon Blanc 2014 Rating 90 **To** 2015 $20 ✪

Plantagenet   ★★★★★

Albany Highway, Mount Barker, WA 6324 **Region** Mount Barker
T (08) 9851 3111 **www**.plantagenetwines.com **Open** 7 days 10–4.30
Winemaker Chris Murtha **Est.** 1974 **Dozens** 60000 **Vyds** 130ha
Plantagenet was established by Tony Smith, who continues to be involved in its management 40 years later, notwithstanding that it has been owned by Lionel Samson & Son for many years. He established five vineyards: Bouverie in 1968, Wyjup in '71, Rocky Horror I in '88, Rocky Horror 2 in '97 and Rosetta in '99. These vineyards are the cornerstone of the

substantial production of the consistently high-quality wines that have always been the mark of Plantagenet: highly aromatic Riesling, tangy citrus-tinged Chardonnay, glorious Rhône-style Shiraz and ultra-stylish Cabernet Sauvignon. Exports to the UK, the US, Canada, China and Japan.

πππππ **Great Southern Chardonnay 2013** Estate-grown, wild yeast-fermented in French barriques with extended lees contact. Full of character and vitality; grapefruit and white peach figure skate with each other, the line perfect, the length admirable thanks in no small measure to minerally acidity. Screwcap. 13.6% alc. **Rating** 95 **To** 2023 $33 ✪

Great Southern Riesling 2014 The heart of this wine comes from 43yo vines on the estate Wyjup Vineyard in Mount Barker. It is a classic style, asking only one thing: patience. A superb wine with a further decade of life in front of it. Screwcap. 12% alc. **Rating** 95 **To** 2025 $26 ✪

πππππ **Omrah Sauvignon Blanc 2014** **Rating** 90 **To** 2015 $19 CM ✪

Poacher's Ridge Vineyard ★★★★★

1630 Spencer Road, Narrikup, WA 6326 **Region** Mount Barker
T (08) 9857 6066 **www**.poachersridge.com.au **Open** Fri–Sun 10–4
Winemaker Robert Diletti (Contract) **Est.** 2000 **Dozens** 1000 **Vyds** 6.9ha
Alex and Janet Taylor purchased the Poacher's Ridge property in 1999; before then it had been used for cattle grazing. The vineyard includes shiraz, cabernet sauvignon, merlot, riesling, marsanne and viognier. Winning the Tri Nations '07 merlot class against the might of Australia, NZ and South Africa with its '05 Louis' Block Great Southern Merlot was a dream come true. Nor was it a one-time success: Poacher's Ridge Merlot is always at, or near the top, of the tree.

πππππ **Louis' Block Great Southern Riesling 2014** Slashing-but-soft Riesling, sliced with lemony acidity but prettied up with orange blossom and lime leaf notes. Drinking well young, but will age. Screwcap. 12% alc. **Rating** 95 **To** 2024 $24 ✪

Sophie's Yard Great Southern Shiraz 2013 Even-tempered wine, but it doesn't leave anyone short-changed. Black cherry and blackberry with modest input from dry leaves and spice. Chocolatey oak plays a minor role. In short, it does the simple things well: flavour, length, balance, structure. All it needs is a couple of years to find its feet. Screwcap. 14% alc. **Rating** 95 **To** 2025 $28 ✪

πππππ **Louis' Block Cabernet Sauvignon 2013** **Rating** 92 **To** 2026 $28 CM
Louis' Block Marsanne 2013 **Rating** 90 **To** 2017 $20 CM ✪

Point Leo Road Vineyard ★★★★☆

PO Box 358, Red Hill South, Vic 3937 **Region** Mornington Peninsula
T 0406 610 815 **www**.pointleoroad.com.au **Open** Not
Winemaker Simon Black, Andrew Thomson **Est.** 1996 **Dozens** 650 **Vyds** 3.6ha
John Law and family planted 1.9ha of pinot noir and 1.5ha of chardonnay in 1996 as contract growers for several leading Mornington Peninsula wineries. Plantings were progressively expanded, including small amounts of pinot gris, lagrein and gewurztraminer. The vineyard was sold in late 2014, but the Point Leo Road brand will continue. They have two labels: Point Leo Road for premium wines, and Point Break the second label.

πππππ **Chardonnay 2013** Bright straw-green; has the silent power of the new breed of high-performance electric cars, but once stirred into action comes at you from every direction at once, and with no end in sight; remarkable grapefruit pith and zest held on rocky/gravelly acidity drives the long, sibilant palate. Screwcap. 12.9% alc. **Rating** 95 **To** 2028 $29 ✪

Pinot Noir 2013 Bright colour; the bouquet has an unusual but attractive, fragrant allspice character; the penetrating palate waltzes past the bouquet with polished cherry flavours that linger impressively on the finish and aftertaste. Has time on its side, and to spare. Screwcap. 13.9% alc. **Rating** 94 **To** 2022 $32

πππππ **Mornington Peninsula Lagrein 2011** **Rating** 92 **To** 2021 $25 ✪

Pokolbin Estate ★★★★★

McDonalds Road, Pokolbin, NSW 2321 **Region** Hunter Valley
T (02) 4998 7524 **www**.pokolbinestate.com.au **Open** 7 days 9–5
Winemaker Andrew Thomas (Contract) **Est.** 1980 **Dozens** 4000 **Vyds** 15.7ha
Pokolbin Estate has a very unusual, but very good, multi-varietal, multi-vintage array of wines available for sale at any one time. The Riesling is true Riesling, not misnamed Semillon, the latter being one of their best wines, and wines under screwcap going back six or seven vintages, and single-vineyard offerings to boot, are available.

🍷🍷🍷🍷🍷 **Phil Swannell Hunter Valley Semillon 2009** One of those Semillons that has made time stand (almost) still since first tasted Dec '09 (95 points). The colour is still pale, the bouquet and palate gloriously fresh and vibrant; its balance is exceptional, the lemon curd/lemongrass flavours with a supple mouthfeel not common with Semillon of this age, perhaps due to a subliminal touch of residual sugar. Unbeatable value. Screwcap. 11% alc. **Rating** 96 **To** 2029 $28 ❂

Phil Swannell Hunter Valley Semillon 2014 The skills of Andrew Thomas come through strongly on the bouquet and palate of this feisty citrus skin-charged wine, vibrant minerally acidity also helping the cause. Great value for a wine with a long future. Screwcap. 10.8% alc. **Rating** 95 **To** 2029 $25 ❂

Limited Release Reserve Hunter Valley Shiraz 2013 Exceptional colour; a supremely elegant medium-bodied Shiraz in mainstream Hunter Valley style, marrying red and black cherry and plum fruit with a gently savoury/earthy background; with 10+ years in bottle these characters will merge in a single, supple stream. Screwcap. 13.6% alc. **Rating** 95 **To** 2033 $50

Hunter Valley Riesling 2013 A freakish wine that has always over-delivered and confounded with its intense lemon citrus fruit bolstered by minerally acidity. In the bad old days of labelling Semillon as Hunter River Riesling, no one doubted it was Semillon, but truth is stranger than fiction. This has more depth to its flavour than young Semillon, but it's eerily similar; drink now or cellar. Screwcap. 10.8% alc. **Rating** 94 **To** 2023 $25 ❂

🍷🍷🍷🍷 **Phil Swannell Hunter Valley Semillon 2013** **Rating** 92 **To** 2018 $25 ❂
Belebula Limited Release Sangiovese 2013 **Rating** 91 **To** 2020 $25
Hunter Valley Riesling 2014 **Rating** 90 **To** 2020 $25
Phoenix Out of the Ashes Hunter Valley Semillon Sauvignon Blanc 2013 **Rating** 90 **To** 2016 $25

Polperro | Even Keel ★★★★☆

150 Red Hill Road, Red Hill, Vic 3937 **Region** Mornington Peninsula
T 0405 155 882 **www**.polperrowines.com.au **Open** Thurs–Mon 11–2
Winemaker Samuel Coverdale **Est.** 2006 **Dozens** 3000 **Vyds** 13ha
Sam Coverdale lives on the Mornington Peninsula, makes wine there full-time and surfs part-time. Before taking up residence on the Peninsula, he obtained his degree in oenology from CSU, and accumulated 10 years of winemaking experience in Australia, France, Spain and Italy. Polperro is his single-vineyard Mornington Peninsula range, and includes Pinot Noir, Chardonnay and Pinot Gris. Second label Even Keel uses grape varieties that best represent their region. Exports to Hong Kong.

🍷🍷🍷🍷🍷 **Even Keel Tumbarumba Chardonnay 2013** Beautifully packaged and presented. Core of white peach and green melon/nectarine with toast and chalk-like notes adding flavour and texture. Good power and length. Will drink and develop well over at least the next handful of years. Screwcap. 12.5% alc. **Rating** 92 **To** 2019 $35 CM

Pondalowie Vineyards ★★★★★

123 View Street, Bendigo, Vic 3550 **Region** Bendigo
T 0439 373 366 **www**.pondalowie.com.au **Open** W'ends 12–5
Winemaker Dominic Morris, Krystina Morris **Est.** 1997 **Dozens** 2500 **Vyds** 10ha

Dominic and Krystina Morris both have strong winemaking backgrounds gained in Australia, Portugal and France. Dominic worked alternate vintages in Australia and Portugal from 1995 to 2012, and Krystina has also worked at St Hallett and Boar's Rock. They have established 5.5ha of shiraz, 2ha each of tempranillo and cabernet sauvignon, and a little malbec. Incidentally, the illustration on the Pondalowie label is not a piece of barbed wire, but a very abstract representation of the winery kelpie dog. Exports to Hong Kong and Japan.

ＴＴＴＴＴ Shiraz 2013 Bright, expressive, attractive red wine. Clearly a wine of both value and quality. It tastes of cherry, cola, toast and violet, with malty notes simply adding to the seduction. House style brings tannin and pounds of flavour; this is in keeping with that style, but manages a soft, pretty face. Spot-on presentation of flavour. Screwcap. 14% alc. Rating 95 To 2028 $27 CM ❂

ＴＴＴＴＴ Vineyard Blend 2013 Rating 92 To 2022 $20 CM ❂
MT Tempranillo 2013 Rating 92 To 2025 $27 CM

Pooley Wines   ★★★★★

Belmont Vineyard, 1431 Richmond Road, Richmond, Tas 7025 **Region** Southern Tasmania
T (03) 6260 2895 **www**.pooleywines.com.au **Open** 7 days 10–5
Winemaker Anna Pooley **Est.** 1985 **Dozens** 6000 **Vyds** 16ha
Three generations of the Pooley family have been involved in the development of Pooley Wines, although the winery was previously known as Cooinda Vale. Plantings have now reached over 12ha in a region that is warmer and drier than most people realise. In 2003 the family planted pinot noir and pinot grigio (with more recent plantings of pinot noir and chardonnay) at Belmont Vineyard, a heritage property with an 1830s Georgian home and a second cellar door in the old sandstone barn and stables.

ＴＴＴＴＴ Pinot Grigio 2014 From the Coal River and East Coast; oxidative juice handling, then cool tank fermentation with inoculated yeast, fermented to dryness. This handling has resulted in a crystal clear colour devoid of hue; the palate is extraordinary, with all the intensity and drive of a young Riesling hitting you the moment you taste it, gripping the palate all the way through to the finish. Screwcap. 12.7% alc. Rating 96 To 2020 $27 ❂
Cooinda Vale Pinot Noir 2013 Hand-picked over 5 days, whole berry plus 5% whole bunches, matured for 9 months in French barriques (30% new). There is some colour development, the bouquet with a savoury/spicy edge to the dark cherry of the bouquet, the palate that of serious Pinot, powerful, layered and long. If 'imperious' is a word that can be used in the context of high-quality Pinot Noir, this wine is just that. Screwcap. 13.4% alc. Rating 95 To 2025 $50
Margaret Pooley Tribute Riesling 2014 Early-picked but fermented dry; demands extreme patience, a 20-year proposition if ever there was one; crackling acidity sends rapier thrusts through citrus fruits. Screwcap. 11.6% alc. Rating 94 To 2034 $50
Pinot Noir 2013 From the Coal River, Derwent and Tamar valleys; hand-picked between 19 Mar and 11 Apr; whole berries plus 10% whole bunches, matured for 8 months in French barriques (10% new). The wine is more linear than Cooinda Vale, driving through to the finish at high speed, leaving all and sundry in its wake; the tannins are fine; it is the flavours that have a Nebbiolo-like mix of red and sour cherries. Take to Piedmont for white truffle risotto. Screwcap. 13.4% alc. Rating 94 To 2023 $36

ＴＴＴＴＴ Coal River Riesling 2014 Rating 93 To 2024 $32
Matilda Pinot Noir Chardonnay 2010 Rating 91 To 2017 $45 TS

Poonawatta   ★★★★★

1227 Eden Valley Road, Flaxman Valley, SA 5235 **Region** Eden Valley
T (08) 8565 3248 **www**.poonawatta.com **Open** By appt
Winemaker Reid Bosward, Andrew Holt **Est.** 1880 **Dozens** 1500 **Vyds** 3.6ha

The Poonawatta story is complex, stemming from 0.8ha of shiraz planted in 1880. When Andrew Holt's parents purchased the Poonawatta property, the vineyard had suffered decades of neglect, and a slow process of restoration began. While that was underway, the strongest canes available from the winter pruning of the 1880 block were slowly and progressively dug into the stony soil of the site. It took seven years to establish the 0.8ha Cuttings block, and the yield is even lower than that of the 1880 block. Second label, Monties Block, sits underneath The Cuttings (from the 'new' vines) and, at the top, The 1880. The Riesling is produced from a single vineyard of 2ha hand-planted by the Holt family in the 1970s. Exports to France, Denmark, Hong Kong and China.

ＹＹＹＹＹ **Sub-Regional Collection Goodies Block Eden Valley Shiraz 2012** Some black cherry edges out the blackberry notes, leaving plum in place; it is as elegant as an Eden Valley Shiraz at this price can be, perfectly balanced, and has a similar mouthfeel to Bob's Block. 25 dozen made. Screwcap. 14.7% alc. **Rating** 96 To 2042 $50 **○**

Sub-Regional Collection Bob's Block Eden Valley Cabernet 2012 Excellent colour; the Eden Valley will almost always have the edge over the Barossa Valley with cabernet courtesy of intense cassis, bay leaf and black olive flavours; the tannins, too, are exemplary. Screwcap. 13.8% alc. **Rating** 96 To 2037 $50 **○**

The Eden Riesling 2014 Bright green-straw; shrieks Eden Valley, overflowing with its Meyer lemon and lime fruit filling all the senses, hiding much of the acidity that is in fact present, and which will carry the wine for years to come. 38 dozen made. Screwcap. 12% alc. **Rating** 95 To 2029 $26 **○**

Sub-Regional Collection Bob's Block Eden Valley Shiraz 2012 From 60+yo vines. A rich and intense wine, with multiple layers of predominantly blackberry and plum fruit, rests comfortably on a pillow of gentle tannins and significant oak. 25 dozen made. Screwcap. 14.4% alc. **Rating** 95 To 2042 $50

Regional Series The Four Corners of Eden Valley Shiraz 2012 A totally persuasive illustration of the Eden Valley. The fruit fragrance, flavour and mouthfeel have a distinctive edge of juicy freshness, doubtless due to the climate; it has great length, and a mouth-watering finish due to fine tannins, and in part to the red and black cherry fruit. Screwcap. 14.7% alc. **Rating** 95 To 2032 $35 **○**

Regional Series The Four Corners of Eden Valley Grenache Shiraz 2012 No percentage make-up is given, but it's relatively easy to see the red fruits of the grenache and the black fruits and fine-grained tannins of the shiraz. A very attractive fresh style, its best days still to come. Screwcap. 14.2% alc. **Rating** 94 To 2032 $35

Regional Series The Four Corners of Eden Valley Cabernet Shiraz 2012 A complex, supple medium to full-bodied blend with black fruits (berry, currant) doing the heavy lifting, the tannins ripe and well balanced. Going through the start of a long transition. Screwcap. 13.9% alc. **Rating** 94 To 2037 $35

Port Phillip Estate ★★★★★

263 Red Hill Road, Red Hill, Vic 3937 **Region** Mornington Peninsula
T (03) 5989 4444 **www**.portphillipestate.com.au **Open** 7 days 11–5
Winemaker Sandro Mosele **Est.** 1987 **Dozens** 2900 **Vyds** 9.3ha
Port Phillip Estate has been owned by Giorgio and Dianne Gjergja since 2000. The ability of the site (enhanced, it is true, by the skills of Sandro Mosele) to produce outstanding Syrah, Pinot Noir and Chardonnay, and very good Sauvignon Blanc, is something special. Whence climate change? Quite possibly the estate may have answers for decades to come. The futuristic, multimillion-dollar restaurant, cellar door and winery complex, designed by award-winning Wood/Marsh Architecture, overlooks the vineyards and Westernport Bay. Exports to the UK, Canada, Singapore and China.

ＹＹＹＹＹ **Single Vineyard Selection Serenne Shiraz 2013** Wild flashes of herbs, stalks, twigs and woodsmoke – it's like being caught in a windstorm – but with the volume of fruit to keep it luscious and drinker-friendly. This is a release and a half. Bright, pure, complex, fruit-filled and savoury; you name it, it has it in spades. Screwcap. 13.5% alc. **Rating** 96 **To** 2030 $50 CM ✪

Red Hill Chardonnay 2013 It creeps under your skin and quickly makes the experience of drinking it difficult to forget. It's one of those seamless wines where it's hard to tell how it does it: it just does. The simple fact is that is combines fruit, oak, acidity and texture to beautiful effect. Flint and struck-match complexity helps seal the deal. Screwcap. 13.5% alc. **Rating** 95 **To** 2021 $35 CM ✪

Red Hill Mornington Peninsula Pinot Noir 2013 Not too flashy but has both substance and poise. Macerated cherries, foresty notes, aged meats and dried spice. Seamless complexity. Tannin is firm but so fine it almost seems infused. Length is never in doubt. Great potential for the mid-term cellar. Screwcap. 14% alc. **Rating** 95 **To** 2023 $40 CM

Balnarring Mornington Peninsula Pinot Noir 2013 It cruises into town offering black cherry, plum, smoky oak and chicory, adds dried spice and foresty notes along the way, and finishes with a touch of (attractive) sourness. It seems in no hurry to leave; hence the flavours linger. The purr of quality. Screwcap. 13.5% alc. **Rating** 95 **To** 2021 $40 CM

Mornington Peninsula Sauvignon 2014 Wild yeast-fermented and mostly aged sur lie in concrete tanks; a small portion goes into barrel. It looks and tastes bright, all grapefruit, stone fruit, lemongrass and citrus, and boasts a dart of tangy acidity through the finish. It's perhaps most categorised, though, by the soft, pillowy texture to the mid-palate, followed by chalky, minerally grip. Top-notch release. Screwcap. 13.5% alc. **Rating** 94 **To** 2016 $26 CM ✪

🍷🍷🍷🍷🍷 **Salasso Mornington Peninsula Rose 2014 Rating** 93 **To** 2016 $24 CM ✪
Mornington Peninsula Shiraz 2013 Rating 93 **To** 2025 $38 CM

Portsea Estate ★★★★☆

PO Box 3148, Bellevue Hill, NSW 2023 **Region** Mornington Peninsula
T (02) 9328 6359 **www**.portseaestate.com **Open** By appt
Winemaker Tim Elphick **Est.** 2000 **Dozens** 1600 **Vyds** 3.14ha
Noted filmmaker Warwick Ross and sister (and silent partner) Caron Wilson-Hawley have moved fast and successfully since the first vintage in 2004. Having had the luxury of having their first seven vintages made at Paringa Estate by Lindsay McCall and his team, they have built an onsite winery, and hired winemaker Tim Elphick, who has impeccable cool-climate winemaking experience. Warwick's film *Red Obsession* (with Andrew Caillard MW playing a leading advisory role) has been completed and distributed through Village Roadshow. It took an inside look at Bordeaux, and was given high ratings by film critics around the world.

🍷🍷🍷🍷🍷 **Stonecutters Block Single Vineyard estate Chardonnay 2013** Only 1400 bottles made. Powerful but poised wine with grapefruit, white peach, flint and spicy/smoky oak notes aplenty. As delicious as it is impressive. Screwcap. 13.2% alc. **Rating** 94 **To** 2020 $55 CM

🍷🍷🍷🍷🍷 **Estate Chardonnay 2013 Rating** 90 **To** 2017 $28 CM

Possum Creek Vineyards ★★★★

PO Box 71, Tanunda, SA 5352 **Region** Barossa Valley
T (08) 8541 0800 **Open** Not
Winemaker Darren Heidenreich, Brad May **Est.** 1978 **Dozens** 360 **Vyds** 23.5ha
The Possum Creek Vineyards of today were planted by Murray and Lorraine Heidenreich in 1978. But the winery's history dates back to Murray's great-grandfather, Gottlieb Vorwerk, who was the first to plant vines on the property, in the 1860s. Those vines are no more, but the ownership of the property has remained in the family down the generations. Shiraz has the lion's share of the plantings with 11.4ha, followed by semillon (3.7ha), cabernet sauvignon (3.4ha), malbec and chardonnay (2ha each) and riesling (1ha).

ŶŶŶŶŶ **Barossa Valley Shiraz 2013** Impressive. The bouquet a symphony of dark fruits and an undertone of oak; the medium to full-bodied palate is deeply fruited with touches of dark chocolate, and just when you start to wonder whether it is one-dimensional, the fine, savoury tannins of the finish and aftertaste sweep all doubts away. Time is definitely on its side. Diam. 13.5% alc. **Rating** 94 **To** 2038 $45

ŶŶŶŶŶ **Barossa Valley Malbec 2013 Rating** 93 **To** 2033 $45
Barossa Valley Cabernet Sauvignon 2013 Rating 90 **To** 2023 $45

Possums Vineyard   ★★★★☆

88 Adams Road, Blewitt Springs, SA 5171 **Region** McLaren Vale
T (08) 8272 3406 **www**.possumswines.com.au **Open** By appt
Winemaker Pieter Breugem **Est.** 2000 **Dozens** 8000 **Vyds** 44.8ha
Possums Vineyard is owned by Dr John Possingham and Carol Summers. They have two vineyards in McLaren Vale – one at Blewitt Springs, the other at Willunga – covering shiraz (20a), cabernet sauvignon (16ha) and chardonnay (14ha), with lesser plantings of pinot gris, viognier and malbec. Winemaker Pieter Breugem has come from South Africa via the US and Constellation Wines. Exports to the UK, Denmark, Germany, Hong Kong and China.

ŶŶŶŶŶ **Dr John's Willunga Shiraz 2012** The region, viticulturist and winemaker all had their stars aligned for this utterly delicious, medium-bodied wine; black berries, blue berries and dark cherries dance across the mouth, showing a dab of spice and chocolate seasoning as they do so. The wine wants for nothing. Screwcap. 14.5% alc. **Rating** 95 **To** 2027 $30 ❂

ŶŶŶŶŶ **Possingham & Summers Malbec 2013 Rating** 92 **To** 2020 $18 ❂
Possingham & Summers Cabernet 2010 Rating 91 **To** 2017 $18 ❂

Poverty Hill Wines   ★★★★

PO Box 76, Springton, SA 5235 **Region** Eden Valley
T (08) 8568 2220 **www**.povertyhillwines.com.au **Open** Fri–Mon 10–5
Winemaker John Eckert **Est.** 2002 **Dozens** 5000 **Vyds** 29ha
I'm not sure whether there is a slight note of irony in the name, but Poverty Hill Wines brings together men who have had a long connection with the Eden Valley. Robert Buck owns a small vineyard on the ancient volcanic soils east of Springton, producing both shiraz and cabernet sauvignon. Next is Stuart Woodman, who owns the vineyard with the riesling that produced glorious wines in the early 1990s, and also has high-quality mature cabernet sauvignon. Finally there is John Eckert, who once worked at Saltram. He not only works as winemaker at Poverty Hill, but manages Rob Buck's vineyard and his own small block of young riesling in the highlands of Springton. Poverty Hill indeed. Exports to the US, Hong Kong and NZ.

ŶŶŶŶŶ **Eden Valley Riesling 2014** A flowery apple blossom bouquet leads into a user-friendly palate of lime, lemon and apple, each with equal billing, and a soft finish. Screwcap. 12.5% alc. **Rating** 90 **To** 2018 $20 ❂

Prancing Horse Estate   ★★★★★

39 Paringa Road, Red Hill South, Vic 3937 **Region** Mornington Peninsula
T (03) 5989 2602 **www**.prancinghorseestate.com **Open** Sat 12–5, Sun by appt
Winemaker Sergio Carlei **Est.** 1990 **Dozens** 1500 **Vyds** 6.5ha
Anthony and Catherine Hancy acquired the Lavender Bay Vineyard in early 2002, renaming it Prancing Horse Estate and embarking on increasing the estate vineyards, with 2ha each of chardonnay and pinot noir, and 0.5ha of pinot gris. The vineyard moved to organic farming in '03, progressing to biodynamic in '07. They appointed Sergio Carlei as winemaker, and the following year became joint owners with Sergio in Carlei Wines. An additional property 150m west of the existing vineyard was purchased, and 2ha of vines planted. Prancing Horse has become one of a small group of Australian wineries having wines made for them in Burgundy. Pascal Marchand makes an annual release of Morey-St-Denis Clos des Ormes

Premier Cru and Meursault Premier Cru Blagny, while Patrick Piuze makes four Chablis appellation wines. Exports to the UK, the US, France and Sweden.

ŶŶŶŶŶ Chardonnay 2012 Beautiful Chardonnay, hands down, fleshy with apple, white peach, lactose and nougat flavour and then cut with fine, fleshy, zesty citrus through the finish. Screwcap. 12.5% alc. **Rating** 95 **To** 2021 $55 CM

ŶŶŶŶ♀ The Pony Pinot Noir 2013 Rating 93 To 2021 $35 CM
Pinot Noir 2012 Rating 93 To 2021 $65 CM
The Pony Chardonnay 2013 Rating 91 To 2017 $30 CM

Pressing Matters

665 Middle Tea Tree Road, Tea Tree, Tas 7017 **Region** Southern Tasmania
T (03) 6268 1947 **www**.pressingmatters.com.au **Open** By appt 0408 126 668
Winemaker Paul Smart **Est.** 2002 **Dozens** 2000 **Vyds** 7.1ha
Greg Melick simultaneously wears more hats than most people manage in a lifetime. He is a top-level barrister (Senior Counsel), a Major General (the highest rank in the Australian Army Reserve) and has presided over a number of headline special commissions and enquiries into subjects as diverse as cricket match-fixing allegations against Mark Waugh and others and the Beaconsfield mine collapse. Yet, if asked, he would probably nominate wine as his major focus in life. Having built up an exceptional cellar of the great wines of Europe, he has turned his attention to grapegrowing and winemaking, planting 2.9ha of riesling at his vineyard in the Coal River Valley. It is a perfect north-facing slope, and the Mosel-style Rieslings are sweeping all before them. It is moderately certain that Greg is waiting impatiently for his multi-clone 4.2ha pinot noir block to perform in a similar manner. Exports to Singapore.

ŶŶŶŶŶ R9 Riesling 2014 Continues a remarkable track record of show success and deserved critical acclaim. The magic of the wine comes from its very low pH, high acidity and just under 9g/l of residual sugar. Coupled with its low alcohol, it makes this irresistible, and you don't realise the acidity has hidden the sugar. Screwcap. 10.9% alc. **Rating** 97 **To** 2034 $33 **O**

ŶŶŶŶŶ Pinot Noir 2012 The bouquet and palate have an arresting opulence of plum and black cherry fruit; in the manner of Tasmanian Pinots, has the strength and structure to sustain lengthy cellaring, and my guess is it will enter a prolonged plateau 5 years down the track. Screwcap. 13.9% alc. **Rating** 94 **To** 2025 $49

Preston Peak

31 Preston Peak Lane, Toowoomba, Qld 4352 **Region** Granite Belt
T (07) 4630 9499 **www**.prestonpeak.com **Open** Wed–Fri 11–3, w'ends 11–5
Winemaker Mike Hayes, Mark Ravenscroft **Est.** 1994 **Dozens** 1250 **Vyds** 11.8ha
Dentist owners Ashley Smith and Kym Thumpkin have a substantial wine and tourism business. The large, modern cellar door accommodates functions for up to 150 people, and is used for weddings and other events. It is situated less than 10 minutes from the Toowoomba city centre, with views of Table Top Mountain, the Lockyer Valley and the Darling Downs. The main estate vineyard is in the Granite Belt.

ŶŶŶŶŶ Hanging Rock Shiraz 2012 Dense colour and flavour. Ripe, sweet blackberry meets black pepper, cloves and smoky oak. It's both a seductive combination and a quality one. Screwcap. 14.2% alc. **Rating** 94 **To** 2024 $32 CM

ŶŶŶŶ♀ Single Vineyard Granite Belt Viognier 2014 Rating 93 To 2015 $28 CM

Preveli Wines

Prevelly Liquor Store, 99 Mitchell Drive, Prevelly, WA 6285 **Region** Margaret River
T (08) 9757 2374 **www**.preveliwines.com.au **Open** Mon–Fri 8.30–7, w'ends 10–7
Winemaker Fraser Gallop Estate **Est.** 1995 **Dozens** 4500 **Vyds** 5.5ha

While Preveli Wines is a relative newcomer, its owners, the Home family, have lived on the property for three generations. Vince and Greg Home also operate the Prevelly Park Beach Resort and Prevelly Liquor Store, where the wines are available for tasting. Fruit from the vineyard at Rosa Brook (semillon, sauvignon blanc, cabernet sauvignon, pinot noir and merlot) is supplemented by contracts with local growers.

ŢŢŢŢŢ **Margaret River Semillon Sauvignon Blanc 2014** Part of the semillon is fermented in French oak, the sauvignon blanc hand-picked and whole bunch-pressed. Every part of this wine is in its exact place, the flavours spanning passionfruit, guava and lychee through to a pleasantly grassy, yet fruity, finish. Screwcap. 13% alc. **Rating** 94 **To** 2019 $20 ◐

Wild Thing Margaret River Pinot Rose 2014 A parcel selected and hand-picked, cold-soaked for 48 hours, pressed, barrel-fermented in used French oak and briefly aged. Pale puce; pinot noir shines through brightly on both the bouquet and palate, and the fruit finish has been kept dry. Clever winemaking. Screwcap. 13.5% alc. **Rating** 94 **To** 2016 $23 ◐

ŢŢŢŢŢ **Wild Thing Sauvignon Blanc 2014 Rating** 92 **To** 2020 $23 ◐

Primo Estate

McMurtrie Road, McLaren Vale, SA 5171 **Region** McLaren Vale
T (08) 8323 6800 **www.**primoestate.com.au **Open** 7 days 11–4
Winemaker Joseph Grilli, Daniel Zuzolo **Est.** 1979 **Dozens** 30 000 **Vyds** 34ha
Joe Grilli has always produced innovative and excellent wines. The biennial release of the Joseph Sparkling Red (in its tall Italian glass bottle) is eagerly awaited, the wine immediately selling out. Also highly regarded are the vintage-dated extra-virgin olive oils. However, the core lies with the La Biondina, the Il Briccone Shiraz Sangiovese and the Joseph Moda Cabernet Merlot. The business has expanded to take in both McLaren Vale and Clarendon, with plantings of colombard, shiraz, cabernet sauvignon, riesling, merlot, sauvignon blanc, chardonnay, pinot gris, sangiovese, nebbiolo and merlot. Exports to all major markets.

ŢŢŢŢŢ **Il Briccone McLaren Vale Shiraz Sangiovese 2013** Deep purple-crimson; a tried and true blend for Primo Estate, matured in used oak to keep the emphasis on the luscious black fruits, more so here than in most prior vintages, marrying black cherry with satsuma plum and warm spices; the tannins have notes of wild herb to give the wine X-factor. Screwcap. 14.5% alc. **Rating** 95 **To** 2028 $25 ◐

Joseph Sparkling Red NV Aeons of maturity are bound up here, in shiraz from every vintage since the '80s, and a few before, and it shows in savoury, gamey, meaty complexity, set against unmistakable crushed ants. The character of McLaren Vale shiraz and cabernet shine through in black olives, black fruits, dark chocolate, pepper and mixed spice, lingering long on a finish supported by fine, soft, well-integrated tannins and a creamy bead. Disgorged July '14. Screwcap. 13.5% alc. **Rating** 94 **To** 2016 $80 TS

ŢŢŢŢŢ **La Biondina Colombard 2014 Rating** 93 **To** 2015 $16 ◐

Joseph d'Elena Adelaide Pinot Grigio 2014 Rating 91 **To** 2015 $30

Prince Albert

100 Lemins Road, Waurn Ponds, Vic 3216 **Region** Geelong
T 0412 531 191 **Open** By appt
Winemaker Fiona Purnell, David Yates **Est.** 1975 **Dozens** 350 **Vyds** 2ha
The original Prince Albert vineyard operated from 1857 to 1882, and was re-established on the same site by Bruce Hyett in 1975 (Bruce passed away in Feb 2013, aged 89). In '07 Dr David Yates, with a background based on a degree in chemistry, purchased the pinot noir-only venture. David is committed to retaining certified organic status for Prince Albert, and sees no reason to change the style of the wine, which he has always loved. Exports to the UK.

ΨΨΨΨΨ   **Geelong Pinot Noir 2012** Bright, clear crimson; a powerful rendition of site, vintage and variety; black and red cherry, blood plum and a swish of forest floor on the finish all contribute to a classy Pinot with a long future. Screwcap. 14.5% alc. **Rating** 94 **To** 2025 $43

ΨΨΨΨ   **Geelong Pinot Noir 2011 Rating** 88 **To** 2016 $42

Principia   ★★★★☆

139 Main Creek Road, Red Hill, Vic 3937 (postal) **Region** Mornington Peninsula
T (03) 5931 0010 **www**.principiawines.com.au **Open** By appt
Winemaker Darrin Gaffy **Est.** 1995 **Dozens** 600 **Vyds** 3.5ha
Darrin Gaffy's guiding philosophy for Principia is minimal interference, thus the vines (2.7ha of pinot noir and 0.8ha of chardonnay) are not irrigated, and yields are restricted to 3.75 tonnes per hectare or less, and all wine movements are by gravity or by gas pressure, which in turn means there is no filtration, and both primary and secondary fermentation are by wild yeast. 'Principia' comes from the word 'beginnings' in Latin: the *Principia* was Sir Isaac Newton's famous scientific work that incorporated his theory of gravitation and the laws of motion.

ΨΨΨΨΨ   **Chardonnay 2013** Barrel-fermented with wild yeast, 18 months' maturation and no use of pumps are the cornerstones of an elegant and flavoursome wine; white peach, nectarine, melon and creamy/figgy notes flow along the palate, oak simply a means to an end, the length excellent. Screwcap. 13.5% alc. **Rating** 95 **To** 2023 $40
Pinot Noir 2013 It has the same vinification as Altior, the same alcohol, from the same vineyard, so it's not surprising this is very similar in style; it has an even more obvious rectitude, and the reward of patience likely to materialise later. Screwcap. 13.7% alc. **Rating** 94 **To** 2023 $40
Altior Pinot Noir 2013 Wild yeast-fermented, matured for 18 months in French oak. Brightly hued, the bouquet inviting with its display of bright red berry fruit, spice and quality oak, the palate ramrod-straight, too proud to ask for the indulgence of 2–3 years' more bottle age. Screwcap. 13.7% alc. **Rating** 94 **To** 2025 $55

Printhie Wines   ★★★★★

489 Yuranigh Road, Molong, NSW 2866 **Region** Orange
T (02) 6366 8422 **www**.printhiewines.com.au **Open** Mon–Sat 10–4
Winemaker Drew Tuckwell **Est.** 1996 **Dozens** 20000 **Vyds** 33.1ha
Owned by the Swift family, Printhie has established itself at the forefront of quality viticulture and winemaking in Orange. The new generation at Printhie continues to make its mark with Ed Swift, former President of the Orange Region Vignerons Association and a participant of the Future Leaders Program. Winemaker Drew Tuckwell is a participant in the Wine Communicators of Australia Young Guns and Gurus program (as a young gun). The wine portfolio has been consolidated: the entry-level Mountain Range comprises six wines (three white, three red), the Mount Canobolas Collection (MCC) range is a quasi-reserve range, the Swift Family Heritage label is reserved for the best red wine of the vintage from estate-grown fruit with the Super Duper Chardonnay and Syrah the flagship releases. Exports to Canada and China.

ΨΨΨΨΨ   **Super Duper Orange Chardonnay 2012** A high-quality Chardonnay that ticks each and every box; pink grapefruit and white peach fruit bring cut and thrust to the palate, barrel-ferment inputs providing that magic touch of funk; great length and vitality. Screwcap. 12.9% alc. **Rating** 96 **To** 2022 $85
MCC Riesling 2014 Utterly delicious, already crammed with Bickford's lime juice flavours on the long, intense palate; while the acidity isn't obvious (thanks to the power of the fruit) it's certainly there, making this a high-quality each-way proposition: drink or keep. Screwcap. 11% alc. **Rating** 95 **To** 2029 $26

MCC Chardonnay 2013 Back label non-information is 'selectively picked from our estate vineyard and other Orange vineyards, then vinified with great care'. The wine is a fact worthy of more attention, with generous white peach, melon and pear fruit, the oak subtle and integrated. Screwcap. 13% alc. **Rating** 94 To 2020 $35

Mountain Range Merlot 2014 Wherefore art thou, Merlot? Well, it all depends on one's expectations: plummy or savoury, acknowledging its kinship with Cabernet or not. This splits the difference, but leans more to the latter, with an elegant, medium-bodied palate of purple fruits and spicy/savoury overtones, good length and good balance. Screwcap. 14.5% alc. **Rating** 94 To 2021 $20 ✪

 PPPP♀ **MCC Orange Shiraz 2013 Rating** 93 To 2028 $35
Swift Vintage Sparkling 2011 Rating 93 To 2019 $50 TS
Swift Cuvee Brut NV Rating 91 To 2016 $40 TS

PROJECT Forty Nine ★★★★
49 Ressom Lane, Beechworth, Vic 3747 **Region** Beechworth
T 0458 857 707 **www.**projectfortynine.com.au **Open** By appt
Winemaker Gary Mills, Rocco Esposito **Est.** 2012 **Dozens** 150
Rocco Esposito has had a long and distinguished career as a sommelier and wine director, formerly at Vue de Monde. He and wife Lisa Pidutti moved to Beechworth with the intention of growing a vineyard using biodynamic principles from the word go, with a total property size of just under 25ha. In the meantime, until the vines are in production, he is purchasing shiraz from the Warner Vineyard (opposite their property) and making it in the Yarra Valley with Gary Mills of Jamsheed. His daytime job is hospitality manager at All Saints Estate in Rutherglen, and he also provides consultancy services.

PPPP♀ **Beechworth Chardonnay 2013** Considerable yellow-gold colour development; a powerful wine from a challenging vintage; there is a mix of white peach and pink grapefruit held within a framework of rocky/grainy acidity. The question is whether the mid-palate will flesh out with more bottle age. Screwcap. 13.6% alc. **Rating** 93 To 2020 $44

Project Wine | Gotham Wines ★★★☆
PO Box 343, Mona Vale, NSW 1660 **Region** South Australia
T 0412 124 811 **www.**gothamwines.com.au **Open** Not
Winemaker Contract **Est.** 2004 **Dozens** 150000
Originally designed as a contract winemaking processing facility, Project Wine has now developed a sales and distribution arm that has rapidly developed markets, both domestically and overseas. The winery is located in the Langhorne Creek wine region and sources fruit from most key SA wine regions, including McLaren Vale, the Barossa Valley and Adelaide Hills. The diversity of grape sourcing allows the winery to produce a wide range of products, the most notable brands being Tail Spin, Three Pillars, Parson's Paddock and Bird's Eye View. It is also the home of Gotham Wines, which incorporates the Wine Men of Gotham, Gotham, Stalking Horse and Step by Step brands. Exports to the US, Canada, Denmark, Germany, Malaysia, Thailand, Indonesia, Japan and NZ.

PPPP **Project Wine Pioneer Road Eden Valley Riesling 2014** Single-vineyard, night-harvested. Does speak of the Eden Valley, although over-filling the bottle so it was impossible to pour without splashing it left, right and centre wasn't needed. It is a bundle of sweet citrus, ready to roll right now. Screwcap. 12.5% alc. **Rating** 89 To 2018 $18 ✪

Project Wine Parson's Paddock McLaren Vale Shiraz 2014 Uses a combination of fermentation techniques in conjunction with French oak. However made, this is a very useful McLaren Vale Shiraz, with the richness and dark fruit expected of the region. Screwcap. 14.5% alc. **Rating** 89 To 2018 $15 ✪

Gotham McLaren Vale Shiraz 2013 Various fermentation techniques, matured in American oak for 14 months. The colour is good, and the medium to full-bodied palate does have some black fruit complexity/sense of place. Screwcap. 14.5% alc. **Rating** 88 **To** 2017 $14 ✪

Provenance Wines ★★★★★

870 Steiglitz Road, Sutherlands Creek, Vic 3331 **Region** Geelong
T (03) 5281 2230 **www**.provenancewines.com.au **Open** By appt
Winemaker Scott Ireland, Sam Vogel **Est.** 1997 **Dozens** 2000 **Vyds** 5ha
Scott Ireland and partner Jen Lilburn established Provenance Wines in 1997 as a natural extension of Scott's years of winemaking experience, both here and abroad. Located in the Moorabool Valley, the winery team focuses on the classics in a cool-climate sense – Pinot Gris, Chardonnay and Pinot Noir in particular, as well as Shiraz. Fruit is sourced from both within the Geelong region and further afield (when the fruit warrants selection). They are also major players in contract making for the Geelong region.

🍷🍷🍷🍷🍷 **Golden Plains Chardonnay 2013** A 58/37/5% blend from Henty, Ballarat and Geelong. Whole bunch-pressed, fermented in used barriques and stainless steel, plus some '12 yeast lees, matured for 10 months. Its bouquet is complex, the palate has the drive and urgency that its cool birthplace would suggest, grapefruit firmly in command, but not the least bitter. Screwcap. 12.8% alc. **Rating** 95 **To** 2023 $28 ✪

Golden Plains Pinot Noir 2013 From three Geelong vineyards and two from Henty; various parcels with whole bunches 38% of the final blend, the remainder destemmed, 14 days on skins, matured in French barriques (26% new) for 10 months. Deeply coloured, it is equally deeply flavoured, with satsuma plum riding high on a substantial understorey of forest floor and fine tannins, the oak spot-on. A very long life ahead. Screwcap. 12.8% alc. **Rating** 95 **To** 2027 $30 ✪

Geelong Shiraz 2013 60% whole bunches, fermentation for 20 days on skins, roughly racked, 50% to concrete eggs and 50% to a second-use French demi muid (600l) vat for 10 months. Scott Ireland followed the same path last year, pushing conventional winemaking out of the window. The result is a complex, spicy bundle of red and black cherry fruits that is fresh and vibrant. Medium-bodied Shiraz in all its glory. Screwcap. 13.5% alc. **Rating** 95 **To** 2033 $32 ✪

Tarrington Pinot Gris 2013 Pale blush pink; Scott Ireland has wisely decided that the ultra-cool Henty region (and the skin contact involved in getting the grapes to Geelong) is all the wine needs, so intense and probing are its flavours, so long is the palate. Screwcap. 12.8% alc. **Rating** 94 **To** 2017 $26 ✪

Punch ★★★★★

2130 Kinglake Road, St Andrews, Vic 3761 (postal) **Region** Yarra Valley
T (03) 9710 1155 **www**.punched.com.au **Open** Not
Winemaker James Lance **Est.** 2004 **Dozens** 600 **Vyds** 3.45ha
In the wake of Graeme Rathbone taking over the brand (but not the real estate) of Diamond Valley, the Lances' son James and his wife Claire leased the vineyard and winery from David and Catherine Lance, including the 0.25ha block of close-planted pinot noir. In all, Punch has 2.25ha of pinot noir (including the close-planted), 0.8ha of chardonnay and 0.4ha of cabernet sauvignon. When the 2009 Black Saturday bushfires destroyed the crop, various grapegrowers wrote offering assistance, which led to the purchase of the grapes used for that dire year, and the beginning of the 'Friends of Punch' wines.

🍷🍷🍷🍷🍷 **Lance's Vineyard Yarra Valley Pinot Noir 2013** Estate-grown, all operations by hand, including picking. Very good hue and depth; a complex Pinot, great now, greater still in the future; black cherries, wafts of warm spices, and a hint of forest on the bouquet foretells an intense, yet finely boned, palate, balance and extreme length its hallmarks. Screwcap. 13.5% alc. **Rating** 97 **To** 2030 $55 ✪

Lance's Vineyard Close Planted Yarra Valley Pinot Noir 2013 Vines planted '80, 1.2 x 1m spacing. Light, but bright, hue; a highly scented and spicy bouquet, red fruits coming through strongly on the fine, elegantly structured palate, red cherry to the fore, the tannins gossamer-fine; literally caresses the mouth. Screwcap. 13% alc. **Rating** 97 **To** 2025 $90 **۞**

ȲȲȲȲȲ Lance's Vineyard Yarra Valley Chardonnay 2013 Vines planted '77 and '84. A notably complex and rich wine, yet not the least overblown; ripe stone fruit, fig, melon and creamy oak. It will hold, but will it ever be better? Screwcap. 13.5% alc. **Rating** 96 **To** 2020 $45 **۞**

Punt Road ★★★★★

10 St Huberts Road, Coldstream, Vic 3770 **Region** Yarra Valley
T (03) 9739 0666 **www.**puntroadwines.com.au **Open** 7 days 10–5
Winemaker Tim Shand **Est.** 2000 **Dozens** 20 000 **Vyds** 65.61ha
Punt Road is now under the sole ownership of the Napoleone family. All of the wines are produced from vineyards owned by the family; this has resulted in the introduction of the Airlie Bank range, a mostly sub-$20 Yarra Valley range made in a fruit-driven, lightly oaked style to complement the successful Punt Road range at the premium end of their offerings. There is also more focus on small-production single-vineyard wines under the Punt Road label. Exports to the US, Canada, Singapore, Hong Kong, Japan, China and other major markets.

ȲȲȲȲȲ Chemin Yarra Valley Syrah 2013 100% whole bunches, 12 days on skins, racked by gravity, bottled unfined and unfiltered. Star of a wine. Savoury, juicy, complex and with a resounding finish. Anise, black cherry, cloves, hazelnuts and cocoa. Autumnal notes aplenty, as you'd expect given the winemaking methods employed, but with numerous layers of texture and flavour, among them sweet, ripe fruit. Screwcap. 13% alc. **Rating** 96 **To** 2028 $45 CM **۞**
Chemin Yarra Valley Chardonnay 2013 It's straw-coloured and flinty, with both the box and most of the dice thrown at it, and yet purity of fruit remains the paramount play. Pear, lime, white peach, oatmeal and roasted nut characters tumble through the palate, dripping with delicious flavour. Long, spicy finish underlines the quality. Screwcap. 12.5% alc. **Rating** 95 **To** 2021 $45 CM
Napoleone Vineyard Yarra Valley Pinot Gris 2014 Outstanding value and quality. Clean, crunchy, powerful and yet dry and structural to close. Barley, lime, spiced red apples and a dry, almost minerally finish. Rock star Pinot Gris. Screwcap. 13% alc. **Rating** 95 **To** 2015 $22 CM **۞**
Napoleone Vineyard Yarra Valley Shiraz 2013 The spread of flavour as it first builds momentum and then uses it to effect through the finish establishes this wine as a class act. Punt Road has grown a leg in the past few years. Gorgeous, mid-weight cherry-plum fruit with boysenberry and violet as highlights. Integration of cedary oak. Fine-grained tannin. It's a wine of poise, polish and charm. Screwcap. 13% alc. **Rating** 95 **To** 2023 $29 CM **۞**
Chemin Yarra Valley Pinot Noir 2013 Wild yeast, 100% whole bunches. It's an elegant, complex display, all beetroot, crushed spice and dark cherry, with a sweep of cedary, clovey oak. Balance, texture, flavour and length: all are in excellent order. Screwcap. 13% alc. **Rating** 94 **To** 2022 $45 CM
Napoleone Vineyard Yarra Valley Pinot Noir 2013 In fine voice. Just that little bit extra in just the right places. Plush but refreshing flavours of boysenberry and dark cherry with a tangy, spice-flecked edge. Satiny mouthfeel. Pushes out confidently through the finish. The joy of well-set flavour, combined with an elegant disposition. Screwcap. 12.5% alc. **Rating** 94 **To** 2022 $29 CM **۞**
Coldstream Vineyards Yarra Valley Cabernet Sauvignon 2013 Clearly defined and seamless at once. Flavours of blackcurrant, bay leaf, briar bush and lead pencil direct this into classic Yarra Valley Cabernet territory. Makes it look easy. Screwcap. 13% alc. **Rating** 94 **To** 2025 $29 CM **۞**

ȲȲȲȲȲ Napoleone Vineyard Chardonnay 2013 **Rating** 93 **To** 2019 $25 CM **۞**
Napoleone Vineyard Yarra Valley Merlot 2013 **Rating** 93 **To** 2022 $29 CM
Napoleone Vineyard Pinot Noir 2014 **Rating** 92 **To** 2021 $29 CM
Airlie Bank Yarra Valley Shiraz 2013 **Rating** 92 **To** 2020 $18 CM **۞**

Purple Hands Wines

★★★★★

32 Brandreth Street, Tusmore, SA 5065 (postal) **Region** Barossa Valley
T 0401 988 185 **www**.purplehandswines.com.au **Open** Not
Winemaker Craig Stansborough **Est.** 2006 **Dozens** 2000 **Vyds** 13ha
This is a partnership between Craig Stansborough, who provides the winemaking know-how
and an 8ha vineyard of shiraz, northwest of Williamstown in a cooler corner of the southern
Barossa, and Mark Slade, who provides the passion. Don't ask me how this works – I don't
know, but I do know they are producing outstanding single-vineyard wines (the grenache is
contract-grown) of quite remarkable elegance. The wines are made at Grant Burge, where
Craig is chief winemaker. Exports to China.

♀♀♀♀♀ **Planta Circa Ancient Vine Barossa Valley Cabernet Sauvignon 2013**
Made from 468 vines planted circa 1880. Deep, vivid purple-crimson; a
remarkable wine from some of the oldest cabernet vines in the world, planted
around the same time as Penfolds Kalimna Vineyard; there is an intensity to the
fruit that is intangibly different, with a core of purity to the fountain of cassis fruit.
Sensitive winemaking has kept the role of oak to a minimum. 63 dozen made.
Diam. 14.5% alc. **Rating** 97 **To** 2053 $70 ○

♀♀♀♀♀ **Barossa Valley Shiraz 2013** Open-fermented, basket-pressed, matured for
18 months in French oak. One of a handful of Barossa Valley wineries able to
consistently make full-flavoured, varietally expressive wines at 13.5% to 14% alc.
Delicious purple and black fruits are crowned with spice and a hint of licorice, the
tannins ample to sustain the medium-bodied palate, but no more, the finish long
and uncluttered. Screwcap. 14% alc. **Rating** 96 **To** 2028 $30 ○
Old Vine Barossa Valley Grenache 2014 Hand-picked ex old bush vines,
30% whole bunches, hand-plunged 9 days, then matured for 9 months in used
puncheons. Light, bright crimson-purple, it continues Purple Hands' track record
with elegant Barossa Valley Grenache, filled with fresh red fruits and a pot pourri
of spices. Screwcap. 14% alc. **Rating** 95 **To** 2024 $30 ○
Barossa Valley Mataro Grenache Shiraz 2014 A 73/17/10% blend. If the
youthful colour is no surprise, the sheer complexity of the wine is a (pleasant)
surprise; dark fruits are interwoven with veins of ripe, dusty tannins, putting the
emphasis on structure and texture, doubtless ex the mataro. Give it time in the
cellar. Screwcap. 14% alc. **Rating** 95 **To** 2034 $30 ○

♀♀♀♀♀ **Adelaide Hills Pinot Gris 2014 Rating** 93 **To** 2016 $22 ○

Pyren Vineyard

★★★★☆

Glenlofty–Warrenmang Road, Warrenmang, Vic 3478 **Region** Pyrenees
T (03) 5467 2352 **www**.pyrenvineyard.com **Open** By appt
Winemaker Leighton Joy **Est.** 1999 **Dozens** 5000 **Vyds** 29ha
Brian and Kevyn Joy have planted 23ha of shiraz, 5ha of cabernet sauvignon and 1ha split
between malbec, cabernet franc and petit verdot on the slopes of the Warrenmang Valley near
Moonambel. Yield is restricted to between 3.7 and 6.1 tonnes per hectare. Exports to the UK,
the US, Canada, Vietnam and China.

♀♀♀♀♀ **Broken Quartz Rose 2014** Barrel-fermented saigneed shiraz cabernet,
8 months' lees contact in barrel. Pale salmon colour, frisky feel, cranberries and
spice, then juicy through the finish. So many of these wines are more acid than
flavour; this offers both – it's one of the better pale roses going around. Screwcap.
13% alc. **Rating** 92 **To** 2016 $20 CM ○

♀♀♀♀ **Broken Quartz Sauvignon Blanc 2014 Rating** 88 **To** 2016 $20 CM

Quarisa Wines

743 Slopes Road, Tharbogang, NSW 2680 (postal) **Region** South Australia
T (02) 6963 6222 **www**.quarisa.com.au **Open** Not
Winemaker John Quarisa **Est.** 2005 **Dozens** NFP

John Quarisa has had a distinguished career as a winemaker spanning over 20 years, working for some of Australia's largest wineries, including McWilliam's, Casella and Nugan Estate. He was also chiefly responsible in 2004 for winning the Jimmy Watson Trophy (Melbourne) and the Stodart Trophy (Adelaide). John and Josephine Quarisa have set up a very successful family business using grapes from various parts of NSW and SA, made in leased space. Production has risen in leaps and bounds, doubtless sustained by the exceptional value for money provided by the wines. Exports include the UK, Canada, Malaysia, Indonesia, Hong Kong and Japan.

ΨΨΨΨΨ **Johnny Q Shiraz Viognier 2013** From Coonawarra and Padthaway;
5% viognier co-fermented with the shiraz, part matured in oak, part in tank.
Has the expected bright colour, and a medium to full-bodied palate laden with predominantly black fruits. Ridiculously cheap, or exceptional winemaking, take your choice. Screwcap. 14.5% alc. **Rating** 91 **To** 2020 $12 ✪
Treasures Coonawarra Cabernet Sauvignon 2013 Standard Quarisa fermentation and maturation in new and used French and American oak for 16 months – amazing given the price of the wine. Vividly coloured, and has not only buckets of juicy varietal fruit to fill the glass with, but also some authentic Coonawarra cabernet structure. Screwcap. 14% alc. **Rating** 91 **To** 2020 $15 ✪
Treasures McLaren Vale Shiraz 2013 Machine-harvested at night; part fermented with header boards, part roto-fermented; 22°C fermentation, part pressed at 2° baume to finish fermentation in new oak, part fermented dry then to oak (new and used French and American) for 18 months. There's a strong licorice/choc-mint flavour train to hop aboard, and alight whenever you wish. Screwcap. 14.5% alc. **Rating** 90 **To** 2020 $15 ✪

ΨΨΨΨ **30 Mile Shiraz 2014** Rating 89 To 2020 $10 ✪
Johnny Q Shiraz 2013 Rating 89 To 2016 $12 ✪
Treasures Coonawarra Merlot 2013 Rating 89 To 2018 $15 ✪
30 Mile Cabernet Sauvignon 2014 Rating 88 To 2019 $10 ✪

Quealy Balnarring Vineyard ★★★★☆

62 Bittern–Dromana Road, Balnarring, Vic 3926 **Region** Mornington Peninsula
T (03) 5983 2483 **www**.quealy.com.au **Open** 7 days 11–5
Winemaker Kathleen Quealy, Kevin McCarthy **Est.** 1982 **Dozens** 8000 **Vyds** 8ha

Kathleen Quealy and husband Kevin McCarthy lost no time after T'Gallant was purchased from them by Foster's in 2003. While Kevin remained winemaker at T'Gallant, Kathleen established her eponymous brand, and in short order acquired Balnarring Estate winery (since significantly upgraded) and leased Earl's Ridge Vineyard near Flinders. In a move reminiscent of Janice McDonald at Stella Bella/Suckfizzle in Margaret River, she launched the winery with Pobblebonk (a white blend) and Rageous (a red blend), plus a Pinot Noir and a Pinot Gris as a passing nod to convention. The estate plantings are 2ha each of pinot noir, tocai friulano and pinot gris, and 1ha each of chardonnay and muscat giallo. Kathleen also leased the 10ha Tussie Mussie Vineyard (planted to pinot gris) in Merricks. Wines are also available at Merricks General Wine Store. She (with five children) is a human dynamo. In 2015 the stars came into alignment with Kevin McCarthy's return to full-time winemaking with Kathleen and their son Tom, who is specifically interested in the natural wine movement.

ΨΨΨΨΨ **Seventeen Rows Pinot Noir 2013** It pours on the velvet and along with it the seduction. This is a wine to settle in with. It's foresty, cherried, a touch meaty and has plenty of cedar-spice notes, but mostly it's about thick layers of satiny flavour, laced with fine threads of tannin. Effectively irresistible. Screwcap. 13.5% alc.
Rating 95 **To** 2023 $50 CM

ŸŸŸŸ♀ Tussie Mussie Pinot Gris 2014 Rating 93 To 2015 $30 CM
Pobblebonk Field Blend 2014 Rating 92 To 2015 $28 CM
Musk Creek Pinot Noir 2013 Rating 92 To 2020 $35 CM
Musk Creek Pinot Gris 2014 Rating 91 To 2015 $30 CM
Post Modern Clarity Turbul Friulano 2014 Rating 91 To 2018 $35 CM

Queens Pinch Vineyard

PO Box 144, Edgecliff, NSW 2027 **Region** Mudgee
T (02) 6372 7225 **www**.queenspinch.com **Open** Not
Winemaker Lisa Bray **Est.** 1995 **Dozens** 2000 **Vyds** 4ha
When Andrew Buchanan purchased the 4ha vineyard (planted to 3ha of cabernet sauvignon and 1ha of chardonnay), it had simply been a grapegrowing business, the grapes sold to other wineries in the region. He has turned that around, and while the cellar is not open, the wines are available from the website. Situated 10km from the centre of Mudgee, Andrew says, 'The story is that it was once Mudgee's brothel. As to whether this has anything to do with the naming of the area Queens Pinch is shrouded in the mysteries of time.'

ŸŸŸŸŸ Select Mudgee Cabernet Sauvignon 2009 An attractive Cabernet that has developed well, with supple blackcurrant, redcurrant and plum fruit; the oak and tannins are now well integrated on the harmonious, well-balanced palate. Screwcap. 13.5% alc. **Rating** 94 To 2024 $28 ♥

ŸŸŸŸ Mudgee Rose 2013 Rating 88 To 2016 $19
Mudgee Cabernet Sauvignon 2012 Rating 88 To 2017 $19

Quilty Wines

16 Inglis Street, Mudgee, NSW 2850 (postal) **Region** Mudgee
T 0419 936 233 **www**.quiltywines.com.au **Open** Not
Winemaker Des Quilty, Jacob Stein **Est.** 2008 **Dozens** 600
Owner Des Quilty grew up in the Hunter Valley and studied agriculture at the University of New England. To support himself while at university, he drifted into viticulture, his first job after graduation at Tyrrell's as assistant vineyard manager. He was soon promoted and formed part of the Tyrrell's management team in the first half of the 1990s. Over the latter half of the '90s he worked for a rural outlet supplying products to Hunter Valley grape and wine producers, before moving to Mudgee as a viticulturist around 2000. While his focus remains on that region, he has also been involved in vineyards in Orange and Young. He ventured into small-scale winemaking in '08, relying on the depth of his experience to secure small parcels of top-quality grapes to make top-quality wines.

ŸŸŸŸ Black Thimble Single Vineyard Coxs Crown Mudgee Shiraz 2012 From a cool vineyard site above Rylstone. Light colour; a light-bodied Shiraz grown in a cool, wet vintage; it's not surprising there is an edge to the red fruits slightly softened by oak. 159 dozen made. Screwcap. 13.5% alc. **Rating** 89 To 2020 $28
Silken Thread Single Vineyard Apple Tree Flat Mudgee Petit Verdot 2013 Grown in the right part of Mudgee for this late-ripening variety; has plenty of acidity backing the sultry black fruits and firm, but not dry, tannins. 119 dozen made. Screwcap. 14% alc. **Rating** 89 To 2018 $25

Raidis Estate

147 Church Street, Penola, SA 5277 **Region** Coonawarra
T (08) 8737 2966 **www**.raidis.com.au **Open** Thurs–Sun 12–6
Winemaker Steven Raidis **Est.** 2006 **Dozens** 4500 **Vyds** 24.29ha
The Raidis family has lived and worked in Coonawarra for over 40 years. Chris Raidis was only three years old when he arrived in Australia with his parents, who were market gardeners in Greece before coming here. In 1994 he planted just under 5ha of cabernet sauvignon; son Steven significantly expanded the vineyard in 2003 with sauvignon blanc, riesling, pinot gris,

merlot and shiraz. The cellar door was opened by then Deputy Prime Minister Julia Gillard in Nov '09, an impressive example of pulling power.

🍷🍷🍷🍷🍷 **Cheeky Goat Single Vineyard Coonawarra Pinot Gris 2014** Full-on pink from skin contact, but there is no phenolic pickup, rather the palate is crisp and fresh, with crunchy acidity to the pear and yellow peach fruit flavours (and even a hint of strawberry). Screwcap. 13.6% alc. **Rating** 90 **To** 2015 $20 ○

🍷🍷🍷🍷 **The Kid Single Vineyard Riesling 2014 Rating** 88 **To** 2017 $20
Wild Goat Single Vineyard Shiraz 2012 Rating 88 **To** 2020 $28

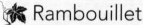

Rambouillet ★★★★

403 Stirling Road, Pemberton, WA 6260 **Region** Pemberton
T (08) 9776 0114 **www**.rambouillet.com.au **Open** 7 days 11–5
Winemaker Mike Garland **Est.** 2005 **Dozens** NFP **Vyds** 4.5ha
As so often happens, the husband and wife team of Alan and Leanne Rowe can't quite make up their mind about the year they established Rambouillet, the choice falling between 2003, when they acquired the 40ha property, and '05, when they planted the first vines. Their lack of capital, a common scenario, meant that Alan decided he would do all of the work in establishing the vineyard, complete with trellis and drip irrigation. 4.5ha may not seem much, but it was a major undertaking for one person, even though Leanne was always on hand to help where she could. They chose sauvignon blanc, chardonnay and shiraz, offering the Chardonnay in three versions: unwooded, lightly oaked and barrel-fermented, all under the aegis of contract winemaker Mike Garland. Even though the vineyard is remote, they live and work full-time on the property, with a de facto cellar door open 'most days'.

🍷🍷🍷🍷🍷 **Barrel Fermented Pemberton Chardonnay 2013** A silver medal at the Timber Town Wine Show '14 (the local derby) is a fair call; it's not so much the barrel fermentation and maturation as the nectarine and white peach at the heart of the palate that intrigues, heightened by citrussy acidity on the finish. Screwcap. 13.6% alc. **Rating** 91 **To** 2018 $25
Lightly Oaked Pemberton Chardonnay 2014 Allowing the grapes to become riper than is usual these days has worked well, investing the wine with citrus/grapefruit and melon flavours neatly supported by subtle oak. Has some future development prospects. Screwcap. 14.5% alc. **Rating** 90 **To** 2017 $20 ○

🍷🍷🍷🍷 **Aever Series Pemberton Shiraz 2011 Rating** 89 **To** 2026 $25
Pemberton Sauvignon Blanc 2014 Rating 88 **To** 2016 $20

Ravens Croft Wines ★★★★

274 Spring Creek Road, Stanthorpe, Qld 4380 **Region** Granite Belt
T (07) 4683 3252 **www**.ravenscroftwines.com.au **Open** Fri–Sun & public hols 10.30–4.30
Winemaker Mark Ravenscroft **Est.** 2002 **Dozens** 800 **Vyds** 1.2ha
Mark Ravenscroft was born in South Africa, and studied oenology there. He moved to Australia in the early 1990s, and in '94 became an Australian citizen. His wines come from estate plantings of verdelho and pinotage, supplemented by contract-grown grapes from other vineyards in the region. The wines are made onsite.

🍷🍷🍷🍷🍷 **The Waagee 2012** A 50/40/10% blend of cabernet, petit verdot and merlot from estate vineyards; matured in new and 1yo oak for 20 months. Solid colour; a powerfully structured wine with firm, savoury tannins to the fore, but enough black fruits to provide balance and encourage cellaring. Screwcap. 14% alc. **Rating** 93 **To** 2027 $50
Granite Belt Petit Verdot 2013 Built in heroic style, uncompromisingly full-bodied, with sombre black fruits and persistent, albeit fine-grained tannins. Match with heroic T-bone steak. Screwcap. 14.5% alc. **Rating** 90 **To** 2025 $35

🍷🍷🍷🍷 **Granite Belt Tempranillo 2014 Rating** 89 **To** 2017 $28
Granite Belt Pinotage 2013 Rating 89 **To** 2017 $40

Red Art | Rojomoma ★★★★☆

22 Julius Street, Tanunda, SA 5352 **Region** Barossa Valley
T 0421 272 336 **www.rojomoma.com.au** **Open** By appt
Winemaker Bernadette Kaeding **Est.** 2004 **Dozens** 400 **Vyds** 5.4ha

Bernadette Kaeding purchased the 5.4ha vineyard site in 1996, when it had 1.49ha of 80-year-old dry-grown grenache; over the next few years she planted the remaining 3.95ha with shiraz, cabernet sauvignon, petit verdot and tempranillo. Until 2004 the grapes from the old and new plantings were sold to Rockford, Chateau Tanunda, Spinifex and David Franz. In that year she decided to make a small batch of wine and continued to accumulate wine until '11, when she began selling the wines under the Red Art label. She has now reduced the buyers to two: Spinifex and David Franz. Bernadette says, 'My production and business continue to be small – and I like it that way.'

????? Red Art Single Vineyard Barossa Valley Cabernet Sauvignon 2012
A 10-day wild-yeast ferment was followed by 12 months in French oak (25% new). Bright purple-crimson; the fragrant cassis-accented bouquet leads into a fresh, medium-bodied palate, cassis and black olive/leaf supported by fine cabernet tannins. Impressive stuff. Screwcap. 13.5% alc. **Rating** 95 **To** 2037 $30 ❂

????? Red Art Barossa Valley Rose 2014 **Rating** 90 **To** 2016 $15 ❂
Red Art Barossa Valley Tempranillo 2013 **Rating** 90 **To** 2020 $25

Red Edge ★★★★☆

Golden Gully Road, Heathcote, Vic 3523 **Region** Heathcote
T 0407 422 067 **www.rededgewine.com.au** **Open** By appt
Winemaker Peter Dredge **Est.** 1971 **Dozens** 1500 **Vyds** 14ha

Red Edge's vineyard dates back to 1971 and the renaissance of the Victorian wine industry. In the early '80s it produced the wonderful wines of Flynn & Williams, and was rehabilitated by Peter and Judy Dredge, producing two quite lovely wines in their inaugural vintage and continuing that form in succeeding years. Exports to the US, Canada and China.

????? Heathcote Shiraz 2012 From the block planted in '71; hand-picked, 25% whole bunches, foot-trodden, the balance destemmed and wild yeast-fermented; matured for 21 months in new French oak. The juicy, medium-bodied palate overflows with satsuma plum, blackberry and black cherry fruit kept in check by the oak and fine-grained tannins. A lot of wine for the money. Screwcap. 14.6% alc. **Rating** 96 **To** 2042 $45 ❂

????? Heathcote Tempranillo 2011 **Rating** 91 **To** 2017 $28

 ## Red Feet Wines ★★★★☆

49 Cemetery Lane, King Valley, Vic 3678 **Region** King Valley
T (03) 5729 3535 **www.redfeet.com.au** **Open** Not
Winemaker Damien Star **Est.** 2010 **Dozens** 450 **Vyds** 1ha

Red Feet is the venture of 37-year-old Damien and his 30-year-old sister Megan Star, he the winemaker and viticulturist, she the business manager. Damien graduated with a wine science degree from CSU in 2001, and worked in the Riverina and Riverland before heading to Germany, Fingerlakes in the US, and finally Kamberra in the ACT. The most valuable three years of Damien's career were spent at Kamberra with Alex McKay (and indirectly the Hardys winemaking team, headed by Paul Lapsley); this came to an abrupt end when Constellation Wines (the then Hardys owner) mothballed the winery in 2006. Megan grew up on a farm with Damien, and understood the importance of quality and value-adding. She followed this lead by obtaining a Bachelor Degree in Agricultural Economics and a PhD in Natural Resource Management. Damien found his way to the King Valley, working on a short-term basis for several local wineries before he and Megan purchased a 33ha property in the King Valley, which had a house, a dilapidated vineyard and a farm shed. They replanted the vineyard with 1ha of sangiovese, nebbiolo, montepulciano and zinfandel. The shed, with its earth floor, became a de facto winery, its pride and joy a 300kg hand-operated basket press. The vineyard produced its first vintage in 2015.

ŸŸŸŸŸ **King Valley Syrah 2012** Some whole bunch included along with cold soak; open-fermented and hand-plunged. This is a distinctly superior King Valley Syrah, the colour bright and deep, the flavours of spiced plum and blackberry cushioned on expertly balanced and integrated tannins and oak. The finish, too, is excellent. Screwcap. 12.6% alc. **Rating** 95 To 2028 $35 ✪

ŸŸŸŸŸ **King Valley Pinot Gris 2014 Rating** 92 To 2016 $25 ✪
King Valley Sangiovese 2012 Rating 92 To 2018 $35
King Valley Riesling 2014 Rating 91 To 2024 $25
King Valley Gewurztraminer 2014 Rating 90 To 2020 $25
King Valley Rose 2014 Rating 90 To 2016 $15 ✪

Red Hill Estate ★★★★★

53 Shoreham Road, Red Hill South, Vic 3937 **Region** Mornington Peninsula
T (03) 5989 2838 **www**.redhillestate.com.au **Open** 7 days 11–5
Winemaker Barry Kooij **Est.** 1989 **Dozens** 25 000 **Vyds** 72.2ha
Red Hill Estate was established by Sir Peter Derham and family, and has three vineyard sites: Range Road, Red Hill Estate, and The Briars. Taken together, the three vineyards make Red Hill Estate one of the larger producers of Mornington Peninsula wines. The tasting room and restaurant have a superb view of Westernport Bay and Phillip Island. In 2007 it (surprisingly) merged with Arrowfield Estate in the Hunter Valley, both companies thereafter owned by the InWine Group until October '10, when InWine was acquired by Cheviot Bridge. Exports to the US, Canada, Ireland, Poland, Sweden, Singapore, Japan and Hong Kong.

ŸŸŸŸŸ **P&Q Mornington Peninsula Chardonnay 2012** The most complex of the '12 Red Hill Estate Chardonnays, yet still retains the finely strung elegance and balance that are the house style; here nectarine and white peach, with some creamy cashew nuances, part oak-derived, provide the core of the flavour. Screwcap. 14% alc. **Rating** 95 To 2025 $65
Mornington Peninsula Pinot Noir 2013 Bright and full colour; flooded with luscious cherry fruit on the bouquet and palate alike; latent spice will evolve as the wine develops over the next 5+ years, but there is plenty to enjoy here and now thanks to its balance and length. Screwcap. 13.5% alc. **Rating** 95 To 2023 $28 ✪
Merricks Grove Mornington Peninsula Pinot Noir 2012 Similar light, clear colour to its M&N sibling; both the fragrant bouquet and fresh red fruit palate are in very different style from M&N; here the emphasis is on supple, varietal fruit and less on structure. If the '13 premium releases are as good as the entry wine suggests, they will be worth waiting for. Screwcap. 14% alc. **Rating** 95 To 2022 $40
Mornington Peninsula Chardonnay 2012 Bright straw-green; has good mouthfeel and overall flavour, with white peach and grapefruit tightly woven together, acidity simply providing strength to the finish. Screwcap. 14% alc. **Rating** 94 To 2022 $28 ✪
Merricks Grove Mornington Peninsula Chardonnay 2012 Elegant wine, notable for the finely strung line of acidity running through the length of its palate; this, allied with the flavour falling more on the citrus/grapefruit side of the spectrum than stone fruit, will underwrite further development of the wine. Screwcap. 14% alc. **Rating** 94 To 2022 $40
M&N Mornington Peninsula Pinot Noir 2012 Light, clear colour; a complex pinot with pronounced foresty/savoury elements on the bouquet and palate, but enough fruit at present to carry those characters; which way the cat will jump as it develops in bottle is the question for what is Red Hill Estate's flagbearer. Screwcap. 14% alc. **Rating** 94 To 2023 $65

ŸŸŸŸŸ **Mornington Peninsula Chardonnay 2013 Rating** 92 To 2020 $19 ✪
Mornington Peninsula Pinot Grigio 2013 Rating 90 To 2015 $19 ✪
Mossolini Mornington Peninsula Shiraz 2012 Rating 90 To 2025 $65

Redbank

Whitfield Road, King Valley, Vic 3678 **Region** King Valley
T 0411 404 296 **www**.redbankwines.com **Open** Not
Winemaker Nick Dry **Est.** 2005 **Dozens** 33 000 **Vyds** 15ha
The Redbank brand was for decades the umbrella for Neill and Sally Robb's Sally's Paddock.
In 2005 Hill-Smith Family Vineyards acquired the Redbank brand from the Robbs, leaving
them with the winery, surrounding vineyard and the Sally's Paddock label. Redbank purchases
grapes from the King Valley, Whitlands, Beechworth and the Ovens Valley (among other
vineyard sources). Exports to all major markets.

Ellora Vintage Cuvee 2012 There's character and complexity here, with bottle
age lending medium straw hue and enticing nuances of toasted brioche and
nougat, while upholding the citrus and apple crunch of primary fruit. The accord
places it in a harmonious place for immediate drinking, structured with even acid
line and firm phenolic grip. Cork. 12% alc. **Rating** 90 **To** 2015 $25 TS

Sunday Morning King Valley Pinot Gris 2014 Rating 89 **To** 2016 $23
King Valley Fiano 2013 Rating 89 **To** 2017 $23
Ellora Vintage Cuvee 2013 Rating 89 **To** 2016 $25 TS
Emily Pinot Noir Chardonnay NV Rating 88 **To** 2015 $13 TS ✪

Redesdale Estate Wines

46 Gibbards Lane, Redesdale, Vic 3444 **Region** Heathcote
T (03) 5425 3236 **www**.redesdale.com **Open** By appt
Winemaker Tobias Ansted (Contract) **Est.** 1982 **Dozens** 800 **Vyds** 4ha
Planting of the Redesdale Estate vines began in 1982 on the northeast slopes of a 25ha
grazing property, fronting the Campaspe River on one side. The rocky quartz and granite soil
meant the vines had to struggle, and when Peter Williams and wife Suzanne Arnall-Williams
purchased the property in '88 the vineyard was in a state of disrepair. They have rejuvenated it,
planted an olive grove, and, more recently, erected a two-storey house surrounded by a garden
which is part of the Victorian Open Garden Scheme.

Heathcote Shiraz 2004 Re-release. First tasted 9 years ago, and the passage of
time has barely changed its colour, bouquet or black fruit flavours; if anything, it
has moved from medium-bodied to medium to full-bodied, the tannins keeping
pace with its black fruits. 92 points then and now. Screwcap. 15% alc. **Rating** 92
To 2022 $62

Heathcote Shiraz 2012 Rating 88 **To** 2027 $37

Redgate ★★★★★

659 Boodjidup Road, Margaret River, WA 6285 **Region** Margaret River
T (08) 9757 6488 **www**.redgatewines.com.au **Open** 7 days 10–4.30
Winemaker Joel Page **Est.** 1977 **Dozens** 6000 **Vyds** 18ha
Founder and owner of Redgate, the late Bill Ullinger, chose the name not simply because
of the nearby eponymous beach, but also because – so it is said – a local farmer (with a
prominent red gate at his property) had run an illegal spirit-still 100 or so years ago, and its
patrons would come to the property and ask whether there was any 'red gate' available. True
or not, Redgate was one of the early movers in the Margaret River, now with close to 20ha
of mature estate plantings (the majority to sauvignon blanc, semillon, cabernet sauvignon,
cabernet franc, shiraz and chardonnay, with smaller plantings of chenin blanc and merlot).
Exports to Denmark, Switzerland, Singapore, Japan and China.

Reserve Oak Matured Margaret River Sauvignon Blanc 2014 Flavour and
finesse. Killer combination. Indeed the balance of fruit, acid and oak is exemplary,
the (excellent) length of the finish then seeming like a fait accompli. Smoke, thistle,
gravel and citrus, passionfruit notes hidden beneath the bonnet. Ever so stylish.
Screwcap. 13.6% alc. **Rating** 95 **To** 2018 $29 CM ✪

WW Ullinger Reserve Margaret River Chardonnay 2013 Essence of chardonnay. White peach, grilled nuts, grapefruit and a sizzle of acidity. Oak plays an active role but in a seamless context. Seductive from the outset; generous through the mid-palate; lengthy and fine through the finish. Screwcap. 14% alc. Rating 95 To 2019 $65 CM

Margaret River Chardonnay 2013 Pale straw, tinge of green; peach and grapefruit, smoky/spicy oak. Sets the pitch and tunes it beautifully. Screwcap. 13.5% alc. Rating 94 To 2019 $35 CM

Margaret River Cabernet Sauvignon 2013 In excellent form. Power and length. Flavours of blackcurrant, bay leaves and dark olives come dressed in milk chocolate and tobacco. Firm, assertive tannin is as impressive as the fruit. A good drink and a statement in one. Screwcap. 14.3% alc. Rating 94 To 2025 $38 CM

Sauvignon Blanc Semillon 2014 Rating 92 To 2017 $23 CM ✪
Margaret River Shiraz 2013 Rating 92 To 2023 $33 CM
Margaret River Semillon 2014 Rating 90 To 2016 $25 CM
Margaret River Bin 588 2013 Rating 90 To 2023 $24 CM

Redheads Studios

733b Light Pass Road, Angaston, SA 5353 **Region** South Australia
T 0457 073 347 **Open** By appt
Winemaker Dan Graham **Est.** 2003 **Dozens** 10000
Redheads was established by Tony Laithwaite (of UK Cellarmaster fame) and wife Barbara in McLaren Vale. The aim was to allow young winemakers working under corporate banners to do some moonlighting, producing small-batch wines for Tony to sell throughout Australia and the world. Justin Lane, Adam Hooper, Nat McMurtie and Andrew Pieri were part of the early team; the winery evolved under the guidance of Steve Grimley, with some of the original members still involved in the making of the original wines, together with a fresh batch of younger, eager winemakers. A major change followed when the winery moved to Angaston, with Dan Graham heading the winemaking team, and now sourcing fruit from all over SA. While the scale of production has changed, the aim of making wines from new varieties and/ or with new styles continues.

Esule McLaren Vale Cabernet Sauvignon Cabernet Franc 2013 Very good crimson hue; an unusual left-field blend for McLaren Vale, but it works well; it is savoury and slightly earthy, but the fruit ripeness is perfect, the cassis, plum and chocolate holding each other in an embrace that no tongue shall put asunder, no matter how hard it may try. Cork. 14.5% alc. Rating 95 To 2028 $46

Barrel Monkeys McLaren Vale Shiraz 2013 Bright crimson; fairly and squarely expressive of place, variety and the style that has caught the attention of the world. It is joyously juicy, a flood of red (mostly) and black fruits, a dab of chocolate, and enough body to satisfy the most rusted-on carnivore. Screwcap. 14.5% alc. Rating 94 To 2028 $25 ✪

Dogs of the Barossa Shiraz 2012 Rating 88 To 2027 $50

Redman

Main Road, Coonawarra, SA 5263 **Region** Coonawarra
T (08) 8736 3331 www.redman.com.au **Open** Mon–Fri 9–5, w'ends 10–4
Winemaker Bruce, Malcolm and Daniel Redman **Est.** 1966 **Dozens** 18000 **Vyds** 34ha
In March 2008 the Redman family celebrated 100 years of winemaking in Coonawarra. The '08 vintage also marked the arrival of Daniel as a fourth-generation Redman winemaker. Daniel gained winemaking experience in Central Victoria, the Barossa Valley and the US before taking up his new position. It was felicitous timing, for the '04 Cabernet Sauvignon and '04 Cabernet Merlot were each awarded a gold medal from the national wine show circuit in '07, the first such accolades for a considerable time. A major vineyard rejuvenation program is underway, but there will be no change to the portfolio of wines. The quality has stabilised at a level in keeping with the long-term history of the winery and its mature vines.

♟♟♟♟♟ **Coonawarra Cabernet Sauvignon 2012** The grapes were mechanically harvested, crushed and destemmed in the vineyard, a technique developed by Redman decades ago; open-fermented, with 33% run off to new French hogsheads for completion of fermentation, the remainder to oak at the conclusion of fermentation. An elegant, medium-bodied Cabernet that shows Coonawarra in its best light. Cork. 13.7% alc. **Rating** 95 **To** 2032 $32 ✪

♟♟♟♟♟ **Coonawarra Cabernet Sauvignon Merlot 2009 Rating** 93 **To** 2025 $37

Reillys Wines   ★★★★★

Cnr Leasingham Road/Hill Street, Mintaro, SA 5415 **Region** Clare Valley
T (08) 8843 9013 www.reillyswines.com.au **Open** 7 days 10–4
Winemaker Justin Ardill **Est.** 1994 **Dozens** 25 000 **Vyds** 115ha
This has been a very successful venture for Adelaide cardiologist Justin Ardill and wife Julie, beginning as a hobby in 1994, but growing significantly over the intervening years. They now have vineyards at Watervale, Leasingham and Mintaro, growing riesling, cabernet sauvignon, shiraz, grenache, tempranillo and merlot. The cellar door and restaurant were built between 1856 and 1866 by Irish immigrant Hugh Reilly; 140 years later they were restored by the Ardills, distant relatives of Reilly, who have been making wines in the Clare Valley for a mere 20 years or so, selling them at yesteryear's prices. Exports to the US, Canada, Ireland, Malaysia, China and Singapore.

♟♟♟♟♟ **Watervale Riesling 2014** A very good Riesling in classic Watervale style, the vines grown on the red soil overlying limestone; balance is the key to a wine with a floral bouquet, and that fusion of lime and lemon flavours that is so attractive; its high acidity and low pH promise near-eternal life. Gold medal Adelaide Wine Show '14. Screwcap. 12.5% alc. **Rating** 95 **To** 2034 $22 ✪
Dry Land Clare Valley Fortified Shiraz 2013 Cold-soaked, open-fermented until fortification on skins, then spent 12 months in American hogsheads. Very powerful and complex, and the fermentation cut by fortification at exactly the right moment, with a luscious array of spiced black fruits running through the long, evenly balanced palate. Gold medal Clare Valley Wine Show '14. WAK screwcap. 19% alc. **Rating** 95 **To** 2030 $27 ✪

♟♟♟♟♟ **Ryder Watervale Riesling 2014 Rating** 93 **To** 2022 $14 ✪
Adelaide Hills Sauvignon Blanc 2014 Rating 91 **To** 2015 $19 ✪
Clare Valley Shiraz 2013 Rating 91 **To** 2033 $20 ✪
Clare Valley Cabernet Sauvignon 2012 Rating 91 **To** 2022 $20 ✪

Renards Folly   ★★★★

PO Box 499, McLaren Vale, SA 5171 **Region** McLaren Vale
T (08) 8556 2404 www.renardsfolly.com **Open** Not
Winemaker Tony Walker **Est.** 2005 **Dozens** 3000
The dancing foxes on the label, one with a red tail, give a subliminal hint that this is a virtual winery, owned by Linda Kemp. Aided by friend and winemaker Tony Walker, they source grapes from McLaren Vale, and allow the Vale to express itself without too much elaboration, the alcohol nicely controlled. Exports to the US, Canada, Germany and Singapore.

♟♟♟♟♟ **Fighting Fox McLaren Vale Shiraz 2013** Deep crimson-purple; a full-bodied wine, shouting its variety and region from the rooftops, black fruits, licorice and bitter chocolate to the fore; powerful tannins are in balance, the oak likewise. 20 years won't tire the wine. The label is attractive, reminiscent of a leading Rioja producer. Screwcap. 14% alc. **Rating** 94 **To** 2033 $30 ✪

♟♟♟♟♟ **McLaren Vale Sangiovese Cabernet 2012 Rating** 93 **To** 2020 $19 ✪
Fighting Fox Clare Valley Riesling 2014 Rating 92 **To** 2020 $18 ✪

Reschke Wines

Level 1, 183 Melbourne Street, North Adelaide, SA 5006 (postal) **Region** Coonawarra
T (08) 8239 0500 **www**.reschke.com.au **Open** Not
Winemaker Peter Douglas (Contract) **Est.** 1998 **Dozens** 15000 **Vyds** 155ha
The Reschke family has been a land owner in Coonawarra for 100 years, with a large holding
that is part terra rossa, part woodland. Cabernet sauvignon (with 120ha) takes the lion's share
of the plantings, with merlot, shiraz and petit verdot making up the balance. Exports to the
UK, Canada, Germany, Hong Kong and Japan.

Bull Trader Coonawarra Shiraz 2008 Has stood the test of time very well;
blackberry and plum flavours are infused with notes of cedar, new leather and
earth; the tannin and acid balance is excellent, the medium-bodied palate long and
satisfying. Ready now, but will hold. Screwcap. 14% alc. **Rating** 94 **To** 2023 $23 ○

Bull Trader Coonawarra Cabernet Merlot 2006 Rating 93 **To** 2021 $20 ○
Coonawarra Fume Sauvignon Blanc 2013 Rating 92 **To** 2016 $20 ○
Pierre De Ronsard Coonawarra Rose 2013 Rating 92 **To** 2015 $23 ○
Botrytis Late Picked Sauvignon Blanc 2010 Rating 91 **To** 2016 $26

Resolution Vineyard

4 Glen Street, South Hobart, Tas 7004 **Region** Southern Tasmania
T (03) 6224 9497 **www**.theresolutionvineyard.com **Open** By appt
Winemaker Frogmore Creek **Est.** 2003 **Dozens** 250 **Vyds** 0.8ha
Owners Charles and Alison Hewitt live in England and entrust the care of the property
and vineyard to Alison's father Peter Brown, with support from former Parks & Wildlife
ranger Val Dell. A love of red burgundy and fishing was sufficient for Charles to establish the
vineyard, planted to three clones of pinot noir, in Tasmania, where Alison had spent most of
her formative years. The vineyard is on a north-facing slope overlooking the D'Entrecasteaux
Channel. Exports to the UK.

Pinot Noir 2013 Bright, clear colour; a fragrant and fresh red berry bouquet is
precisely tracked by the crisp palate; elegance has been achieved at the expense of
fruit weight, but not to the extent of depriving the wine of enjoyment. Screwcap.
13.3% alc. **Rating** 90 **To** 2020 $30

Reynella

Reynell Road, Reynella, SA 5161 **Region** McLaren Vale/Fleurieu Peninsula
T 1800 088 711 **www**.exploreyourwine.com.au/reynella **Open** Mon–Tues 11–5,
Wed–Fri 10–5
Winemaker Paul Lapsley **Est.** 1838 **Dozens** NFP
John Reynell laid the foundations for Chateau Reynella in 1838; over the next 100 years the
stone buildings, winery and underground cellars, with attractive gardens, were constructed.
Thomas Hardy's first job in SA was with Reynella; he noted in his diary that he would be
able to better himself soon. He did just that, becoming by far the largest producer in SA by
the end of the 19th century; 150 or so years after Chateau Reynella's foundation CWA (now
Accolade Wines) completed the circle by acquiring it and making it corporate headquarters,
while preserving the integrity of the Reynella brand in no uncertain fashion. Exports to the
UK and Canada.

Basket Pressed McLaren Vale Shiraz 2012 Deep crimson-purple; open-
fermented and basket-pressed; shows that intense, full-bodied fruit flavours can be
achieved at a reasonable alcohol level; a wonderfully harmonious fusion of plum
and blackberry fruit flavours, quality oak and ripe tannins. A trophy-winning wine.
Screwcap. 14% alc. **Rating** 97 **To** 2042 $65 ○

Basket Pressed McLaren Vale Shiraz 2013 Small open fermenters, hydraulic-
plunged, basket-pressed, matured in French barriques for 16 months. The dense
colour attests to the quality of the fruit and the intelligent winemaking (in a state

of the art winery); it manages to combine richness with finesse, a gin-clear sense of place, and a lightness of foot aided by the controlled alcohol and superfine tannins. Screwcap. 14% alc. **Rating** 96 **To** 2035 $65 **۞**

Basket Pressed McLaren Vale Cabernet Sauvignon 2013 This is a distinguished Cabernet, but the colour isn't as compelling as it might be, perhaps warning that it won't be a cushy ride through to the finish; blackcurrant, herb, briar, bay leaf and slightly dusty tannins are all in action. I'm in two minds where it will head in the future. Screwcap. 14% alc. **Rating** 95 **To** 2033 $65

Rhythm Stick Wines ★★★★☆

89 Campbell Road, Penwortham, SA 5453 **Region** Clare Valley
T (08) 8843 4325 **www**.rhythmstickwines.com.au **Open** By appt
Winemaker Tim Adams **Est.** 2007 **Dozens** 1000 **Vyds** 1.62ha
Rhythm Stick has come a long way in a short time, and with a small vineyard. It is owned by Ron and Jeanette Ely, who in 1997 purchased a 3.2ha property at Penwortham. The couple had already decided that in the future they would plant a vineyard, and simply to obtain experience they planted 135 cabernet sauvignon cuttings from Waninga Vineyards in four short rows. They produced a few dozen bottles of Cabernet a year, sharing it with friends. In '02 they planted riesling, and the first harvest followed in '06, the grapes from this and the ensuing two vintages sold to Clare Valley winemakers. Prior to the '09 harvest they were advised that due to the GFC no grapes would be required, which advanced Ron's planned retirement after 40 years in electrical engineering consulting and management.

ΨΨΨΨΨ **Red Robin Reserve Single Vineyard Clare Valley Riesling 2014** In very different style from the '13, picked much riper, but does retain fresh and bright aromas and flavours; lime, mineral and apple speak of free-run juice, the acidity perfectly judged. Screwcap. 12.5% alc. **Rating** 94 **To** 2024 $25 **۞**

ΨΨΨΨ **Red Robin Clare Valley Riesling 2014** **Rating** 89 **To** 2017 $20

Richard Hamilton ★★★★★

Cnr Main Road/Johnston Road, McLaren Vale, SA 5171 **Region** McLaren Vale
T (08) 8323 8830 **www**.leconfieldwines.com **Open** Mon–Fri 10–5, w'ends 11–5
Winemaker Paul Gordon, Tim Bailey **Est.** 1972 **Dozens** 25 000 **Vyds** 71.6ha
Richard Hamilton has outstanding estate vineyards, some of great age, all fully mature. An experienced and skilled winemaking team has allowed the full potential of those vineyards to be realised. The quality, style and consistency of both red and white wines has reached a new level; being able to keep only the best parcels for the Richard Hamilton brand is an enormous advantage. Exports to the UK, the US, Canada, Denmark, Sweden, Germany, Belgium, Malaysia, Vietnam, Hong Kong, Singapore, Japan, China and NZ.

ΨΨΨΨΨ **Centurion McLaren Vale Shiraz 2013** From a single estate vineyard block planted in 1892, and with a great line of top vintages dating back to 1998, harmony and elegance always at the forefront. The use of French oak (rather than American) helps its cause, for the dark fruits easily exert their ascendancy over the tannin and oak, the latter two simply providing gentle structural framework, and lengthening the finish. Screwcap. 14.5% alc. **Rating** 96 **To** 2033 $75 **۞**

Watervale Riesling 2014 Sourced from an east-facing vineyard with an elevation of 500m. Has a very attractive mix of lime juice and lemon zest; has achieved depth of fruit without losing finesse, the decision of when to pick judged to perfection. Great value. Screwcap. 12.5% alc. **Rating** 94 **To** 2024 $20 **۞**

Burton's Vineyard Old Bush Vine McLaren Vale Grenache 2013 Sweet and pretty but still manages a deft touch in the exquisite balance and penetrating, spicy, sinewy length. Earth and raspberry, musk and fistfuls of dried, woody spice; delightful drinking. Screwcap. 14.5% alc. **Rating** 94 **To** 2025 $45 CM

ΨΨΨΨ⚑ **Adelaide Hills Sauvignon Blanc 2014** **Rating** 93 **To** 2018 $20 **۞**
Hut Block Cabernet Sauvignon 2013 **Rating** 92 **To** 2023 $20 **۞**

McLaren Vale Mr V 2014 Rating 90 To 2017 $16 CM ○
Colton's McLaren Vale G.S.M 2012 Rating 90 To 2019 $20 CM ○
Lot 148 McLaren Vale Merlot 2012 Rating 90 To 2021 $20 CM ○

Richard Meyman Wines ★★★★

PO Box 173, Franklin, Tas 7113 **Region** Southern Tasmania
T 0417 492 835 www.richardmeymanwines.com.au **Open** Not
Winemaker Winemaking Tasmania **Est.** 2010 **Dozens** 400
Richard Meyman had accumulated many years in the wine trade as grower, owner and
manager before returning to Tasmania to resurrect and run the important Nocton Park
vineyard in the Richmond/Coal River area. Few would dispute the primacy of pinot noir
as Tasmania's finest grape variety, and its multifaceted riesling is in the same quality league.
So it is that Richard has chosen those two varieties, and put them in the hands of Tasmania's
leading contract winemaker.

♟♟♟♟♟ **Waseca Riesling 2014** Bright green-yellow; Tasmanian acidity immediately puts
its stamp on the palate, providing structure and length for ripe citrus flavours. Now
or later. Screwcap. 12.6% alc. **Rating** 91 To 2024 $24

Richmond Grove ★★★★

Para Road, Tanunda, SA 5352 **Region** Barossa Valley
T (08) 8563 7303 www.richmondgrovewines.com **Open** Not
Winemaker Stephen Cook **Est.** 1983 **Dozens** NFP
Richmond Grove draws its grapes from diverse sources. The Richmond Grove Barossa Valley
and Watervale Rieslings, a legacy of master winemaker John Vickery, represent excellent value
for money year in, year out. The Coonawarra Cabernet Sauvignon is not as incongruous as it
may seem, for John Vickery was transferred to Coonawarra for a couple of years in the latter
stages of his career at Leo Buring, until sanity prevailed and he returned to the Barossa Valley
to continue making Riesling, thereafter moving to Richmond Grove prior to his retirement
in 2009.

♟♟♟♟♟ **Limited Release Watervale Vineyards Riesling 2013** A wine of elegant
length. Riven with lime, slate and spice, but the main game is the finish, where
it flourishes. A well-aimed dart. Pale straw-green and impeccably presented.
Screwcap. 12% alc. **Rating** 94 To 2025 $23 CM ○
Limited Release Coonawarra Vineyards Cabernet Sauvignon 2012
One part of the voluminous background material rings true, namely that
every barrel was tasted, all the lesser barrels excluded from the final blend. This
comprehensively over-delivers, with pure varietal fruit expression, excellent balance
and mouthfeel reflecting that fruit, oak and tannins are all perfectly weighted.
Screwcap. 14.4% alc. **Rating** 94 To 2030 $23 ○

♟♟♟♟♟ **Limited Release Watervale Riesling 2012** Rating 93 To 2027 $23 ○
Limited Release Barossa Shiraz 2012 Rating 92 To 2022 $23 CM ○

Ridgemill Estate ★★★★

218 Donges Road, Severnlea, Qld 4352 **Region** Granite Belt
T (07) 4683 5211 www.ridgemillestate.com **Open** Fri–Mon 10–5, Sun 10–3
Winemaker Martin Cooper, Peter McGlashan **Est.** 1998 **Dozens** 900 **Vyds** 2.1ha
Martin Cooper and Dianne Maddison acquired what was then known as Emerald Hill
Winery in 2004. In '05 they reshaped the vineyards, which now have plantings of chardonnay,
tempranillo, shiraz, merlot, cabernet sauvignon, saperavi, verdelho and viognier, setting a
course down the alternative variety road. The quite spectacular winery and cellar door facility
also operates self-contained cabins in the vineyard.

♟♟♟♟♟ **WYP Granite Belt Chardonnay 2013** Well made; good balance between oak
and the light-bodied array of white peach, melon and nectarine flavours. Trophy
Toowoomba Wine Show '14. Screwcap. 13.5% alc. **Rating** 92 To 2018 $35

Granite Belt Pinot G 2014 Nashi pear, apple and citrus flood the senses on the bouquet and palate alike; an impressive example of the variety, and a surprise packet. Screwcap. 13.5% alc. **Rating** 92 **To** 2016 $22 ✪

Granite Belt Shiraz Viognier 2012 A very savoury/spicy/brambly wine, the bouquet introducing a light to medium-bodied palate that initially looks a bit thin, but builds length impressively on retasting. Screwcap. 13.5% alc. **Rating** 90 **To** 2020 $30

🍷🍷🍷 **Granite Belt Jacquez 2012** Very good colour, deep and bright; a medium-bodied wine, with plum and blueberry fruits on the mid-palate. It doesn't push on through to the finish, the tannins not positive enough, a deficiency that most hybrids have to contend with. Brazil is the only country with significant plantings. Nonetheless, full of interest. **Rating** 89 **To** 2020 $30

RidgeView Wines ★★★★★

273 Sweetwater Road, Pokolbin, NSW 2320 **Region** Hunter Valley
T (02) 6574 7332 **www**.ridgeview.com.au **Open** Wed–Sun 10–5
Winemaker Darren Scott, Gary MacLean, Mark Woods **Est.** 2000 **Dozens** 5000 **Vyds** 9ha
Darren and Tracey Scott have transformed a 40ha timbered farm into a vineyard, together with self-contained accommodation and a cellar door. The lion's share of the plantings are 4.5ha of shiraz, with cabernet sauvignon, chambourcin, merlot, pinot gris, viognier and traminer making up a somewhat eclectic selection of other varieties. Exports to Japan.

🍷🍷🍷🍷🍷 **Aged Release Generations Reserve Hunter Valley Semillon 2011** Moving slowly but surely towards maturity another 4–5 years down the track. Sourced from Ken Bray's vineyards on sandy soil on Hermitage Road, made by Mark Woods. It is immaculately balanced, with lemongrass/Meyer lemon juice flavours and great line. Screwcap. 11.5% alc. **Rating** 95 **To** 2026 $30 ✪

Impressions Hunter Valley Chardonnay 2012 Picked before the rain from the Brokenback Vineyard and skilfully made by Mark Woods. Measured by any standards, including cool regions such as the Yarra Valley, this is an unambiguously good Chardonnay, with a balance of white peach, citrus and a nice touch of French oak on a notably long palate. Screwcap. 13% alc. **Rating** 95 **To** 2022 $30 ✪

Generations Reserve Hunter Valley Shiraz 2011 Grown on the estate Effen Hill Vineyard (what's in a name?); matured for 18 months in new and used oak, it is a classic – almost throwback – Hunter Valley style, with earth, polished leather and dark fruits superimposed on the depth and structure of the palate. A long future ahead – many decades. Screwcap. 13.7% alc. **Rating** 95 **To** 2045 $35 ✪

Generations Single Vineyard Reserve Hunter Valley Semillon 2014 From the old Brokenback Vineyard (ex Rothbury Estate), vines 35yo. Has all you could wish for in a young Semillon to be matured in your cellar for 5 years. Made by Mark Woods at Leogate. Screwcap. 11.3% alc. **Rating** 94 **To** 2024 $25 ✪

🍷🍷🍷🍷🍷 **Hunter Valley Viognier 2009 Rating** 90 **To** 2016 $25

Rieslingfreak ★★★★☆

8 Roenfeldt Drive, Tanunda, SA 5352 **Region** Clare Valley
T (08) 8563 3963 **www**.rieslingfreak.com **Open** By appt
Winemaker John Hughes **Est.** 2009 **Dozens** 4000 **Vyds** 35ha
The name of John Hughes' winery leaves no doubt about his long-term ambition: to explore every avenue of Riesling, whether bone-dry or sweet, coming from regions across the wine world, albeit with a strong focus on Australia. The wines made from his Clare Valley vineyard offer dry (No. 2, No. 3 and No. 4) and off-dry (No. 5 nd No. 8) styles. Exports to Canada, Hong Kong and NZ.

🍷🍷🍷🍷🍷 **No. 2 Riesling 2014** Polish Hill. Scintillating. Great intensity of fruit and of acid. It's so uncompromising that some will find the acidity over the top. Described by the winery as 'green lemon', and not wrong. There's more here than acid, though: the intensity of lime, apple blossom and slate flavour is substantial. Length looks after itself. Screwcap. 12% alc. **Rating** 96 **To** 2035 $35 CM ✪

No. 3 Riesling 2014 Clare Valley. Dry style but (orange) blossomy. Good intensity. Lime juice riddled with spice. Lifted and lively. Keeps the show going through the finish. Screwcap. 12.5% alc. **Rating** 94 **To** 2025 $23 CM ✪

♀♀♀♀♀ **No. 4 Riesling 2014 Rating** 93 **To** 2026 $23 CM ✪
No. 5 Riesling 2014 Rating 92 **To** 2021 $23 CM ✪
No. 8 Riesling 2014 Rating 91 **To** 2024 $35 CM

Rileys of Eden Valley ★★★★★

PO Box 71, Eden Valley, SA 5235 **Region** Eden Valley
T (08) 8564 1029 **www**.rileysofedenvalley.com.au **Open** Not
Winemaker Peter Riley, Jo Irvine (Consultant) **Est.** 2006 **Dozens** 900 **Vyds** 9.8ha
Rileys of Eden Valley is owned by parents Terry and Jan with son Peter Riley, who, way back in 1982, purchased 32ha of a grazing property that they believed had potential for quality grape production. The first vines were planted in that year and over the next 16 years plantings extended to 7.2ha. Minimal planting has occurred since, but in 2008 0.8ha of merlot was grafted to savagnin (in the belief that it was albarino). In '98 Terry retired from his position (Professor of Mechanical Engineering) at the University of SA, allowing him to concentrate on the vineyard, and, more recently, winemaking activities, but the whole family (including granddaughter Maddy) have been involved in the development of the property. It had always been intended that the grapes would be sold, but when not all the grapes were contracted in '06, the Rileys decided to produce some wine (even though they ended up with buyers for all of the production that year).

♀♀♀♀♀ **Jump Ship Shiraz 2012** Matured for 18 months in predominantly new French and used American and Hungarian oak. A very well balanced, medium-bodied wine, showing Eden Valley elegance to full effect, supple black fruits to the fore, touches of licorice and spice to the back and oak having the Jo Irvine-engendered integration ex the final stages of fermentation. Screwcap. 14% alc. **Rating** 95 **To** 2027 $25 ✪

Cabernet Sauvignon 2013 Estate-grown, matured for 18 months in used French oak. Deep crimson-purple; the totally delicious and harmonious wine showing just what a very good vintage in the Eden Valley can produce: a picture-perfect rendition of the variety, full of supple cassis and redcurrant fruit, the sidelight of dark chocolate replacing black olive. Terrific value. Screwcap. 13.5% alc. **Rating** 95 **To** 2038 $25 ✪

The Engineer Merlot 2012 Estate-grown, hand-picked, matured for 18 months in used French oak. The hue and depth of the colour are good, as is the bright, juicy cassis and plum fruit; the tannins are fine, and the oak is invisible in terms of flavour, but important for texture. Screwcap. 14% alc. **Rating** 94 **To** 2022 $25 ✪

♀♀♀♀♀ **Family Riesling 2014 Rating** 93 **To** 2024 $20 ✪

Ringer Reef Wines ★★★★

6835 Great Alpine Road, Porepunkah, Vic 3740 **Region** Alpine Valleys
T (03) 5756 2805 **www**.ringerreef.com.au **Open** Fri–Mon, school & public hols 12–5
Winemaker Bruce Holm **Est.** 2001 **Dozens** 1000 **Vyds** 4.1ha
This is the venture of Bruce and Annie Holm, Bruce having been involved in large-scale commercial wine production in Griffith and Mildura for 30 years before getting itchy feet. In 1996 he and Annie began searching for an appropriate property, and found an ideal 35ha property at Porepunkah. The first vines were planted in '98, and, except during vintage, Bruce travelled from Mildura every weekend to maintain the property. In 2000 they moved to Porepunkah, Bruce working first at Gapsted Wines, then with Sam Miranda Wines before 'retiring' in '08. In the meantime a winery and cellar door sales area had been built in '05, and they now have a Joseph's coat of chardonnay, merlot, montepulciano, moscato giallo, nebbiolo,

petit manseng, pinot noir, sangiovese and sauvignon blanc. A trip to Italy in August '11 led to further plantings of nebbiolo. All the wines are produced from estate-grown grapes.

♟♟♟♟♟ **Alpine Valleys Chardonnay 2012** The best of the Ringer Reef wines; barrel fermentation in French oak, and extended lees contact, has been well handled, leaving the stone fruit flavours freedom of expression. Screwcap. 12.8% alc. **Rating** 91 **To** 2018 $22 ⍟

Alpine Valleys Nebbiolo 2012 Very good colour for Nebbiolo, bright and clear; very much in the same house style as the other Ringer Reef red wines; well handled in the winery, but suggesting higher yields in the vineyard than perfection would require; the tannins are typical of Nebbiolo, but do not unbalance the palate. Screwcap. 14% alc. **Rating** 90 **To** 2020 $34

♟♟♟♟ **Alpine Valleys Montepulciano 2013 Rating** 89 **To** 2018 $28
Alpine Valleys Sangiovese 2012 Rating 88 **To** 2017 $24

Riposte   ★★★★★

PO Box 256, Lobethal, SA 5241 **Region** Adelaide Hills
T (08) 8389 8149 **www**.timknappstein.com.au **Open** Not
Winemaker Tim Knappstein **Est.** 2006 **Dozens** 10 500

It's never too late to teach an old dog new tricks when the old dog in question is Tim Knappstein. With 50+ years of winemaking and more than 500 wine show awards under his belt, Tim started yet another new wine life in 2006 with Riposte, a subtle response to the various vicissitudes he suffered over the years. While having no continuing financial interest in Lenswood Vineyards, established many years ago, Tim is able to source grapes from it and also from other prime sites in surrounding areas. The prices for almost all of the wines are astonishingly low. Exports to the UK, the US, Switzerland, Denmark, Indonesia and China.

♟♟♟♟♟ **The Dagger Adelaide Hills Pinot Noir 2014** Affordable Pinot Noir is rarely so scrumptious. Within the bounds of responsible serving and consumption of alcohol, this is a wine you just want to drink by the bucket load. It's immensely aromatic, complex, meaty and strewn with leaves, though its cherried/cranberried sweet-sour fruit is the motor to its moreishness. It's fabulous drinking at a fraction of what you'd expect to pay for such pleasure. Screwcap. 13.5% alc. **Rating** 95 **To** 2019 $20 CM ⍟

The Sabre Adelaide Hills Pinot Noir 2013 Small-batch open-fermented and 10 months in French oak (25% new). The bouquet sings of red and black cherry, allied with twists of raspberry and oak, the palate effortlessly carrying on with the refrain of the bouquet; has particularly good drive through to the finish and slightly savoury aftertaste. Screwcap. 13.5% alc. **Rating** 95 **To** 2023 $35 ⍟

The Scimitar Clare Valley Riesling 2014 Attacks upfront with lime, rind, red apple and spice and allows no time for breath; it keeps the show rollicking along all the way through to a lengthy/satisfying finish. Excellent. Screwcap. 11.5% alc. **Rating** 94 **To** 2022 $20 CM ⍟

♟♟♟♟♟ **The Foil Adelaide Hills Sauvignon Blanc 2014 Rating** 93 **To** 2016 $20 ⍟
The Halberd White Co-Ferment 2013 Rating 93 **To** 2017 $25 CM ⍟

Rise Vineyards   ★★★★☆

PO Box 7336, Adelaide, SA 5000 **Region** Clare Valley
T 0419 844 238 **www**.risevineyards.com.au **Open** Not
Winemaker Matthew McCulloch **Est.** 2009 **Dozens** 1500

Rise is very much a busman's holiday for owners Grant Norman and Matthew McCulloch. The two are a close-knit team, with Grant looking after the business and Matt the wine. Matt spent more than a decade in the UK wine trade. In 2006 Matt and wife Gina moved to the Clare Valley, where he was responsible for sales and marketing at Kirrihill Wines, of which Grant, an Australian wine industry veteran, was general manager. The move to Clare enabled Matt and Gina to realise a long-held dream of owning their own vineyard, growing the grapes and making the wine, with the help of Grant and his wife Alice. Having spent 11 years on the road working with more than 70 winemakers in 13 countries, Matt was convinced the focus of Rise should be on making small-scale, terroir-driven Riesling, Cabernet Sauvignon and Shiraz, reflecting the unique vineyard sites from which they come.

♟♟♟♟♟ Single Vineyard Watervale Riesling 2014 Free-run juice fermented separately at low temperatures with cultured yeasts. This is an exceptional young Riesling, already exposing its biceps and discouraging any criticism, bodybuilding following day by day, even if it is not strictly required. The lime juice of the palate is a wonder to behold. Screwcap. 11.5% alc. **Rating** 95 **To** 2029 $25 ✪

♟♟♟♟♀ Clare Valley Grenache 2013 Rating 91 **To** 2023 $25
Clare Valley Cabernet Sauvignon 2012 Rating 90 **To** 2022 $25

Rivergate Wines ★★★

580 Goornong Road, Axedale, Vic 3551 **Region** Bendigo
T (03) 5439 7367 www.rivergatewines.com.au **Open** By appt
Winemaker Greg Dedman, Geoff Kerr, Andrew Kutlarz **Est.** 1999 **Dozens** 550 **Vyds** 2.2ha
Rivergate Wines is the Kerr family business, producing intense-flavoured, full-bodied wines at Axedale, midway between Bendigo and Heathcote. They specialise in growing and producing Shiraz, from low-yielding, hand-tended estate vines. The wines are matured in French and American oak barriques for 12 months. When seasonal conditions permit, a small amount of Reserve Shiraz is made.

♟♟♟♟ Reserve Bendigo Shiraz 2007 Hand-picked, matured for 24 months in new and used American and French oak. Good depth to the colour; very full-bodied, at 8yo showing no sign of development, all guns roaring, alcohol first, tannins second, very ripe fruit third, and oak fourth. Screwcap. 14.8% alc. **Rating** 89 **To** 2037 $35

Riversdale Estate ★★★★☆

222 Denholms Road, Cambridge, Tas 7170 **Region** Southern Tasmania
T (03) 6248 5666 www.riversdaleestate.com.au **Open** At Zero Café, Hobart
Winemaker Nick Badrice **Est.** 1991 **Dozens** 9000 **Vyds** 37ha
Ian Roberts purchased the Riversdale property in 1980 while a university student, and says he paid a record price for the district. The unique feature of the property is its frontage to the Pittwater waterfront, which acts as a buffer against frost, and also moderates the climate during the ripening phase. It is a large property, with 37ha of vines, and one of the largest olive groves in Tasmania, producing 50 olive-based products. Five families live permanently on the estate, providing all the labour for the various operations, which also include four 5-star French Provincial cottages overlooking the vines. Wine quality is consistently good.

♟♟♟♟♟ Crater Chardonnay 2013 Pale quartz-green; the bouquet is fragrant, but it is the almost shocking power of the palate that creates the headlines for this hyper-intense Chardonnay. Grapefruit heads the roster of fruit, and also of the barrel-ferment oak, Tasmanian acidity the key to this power. Screwcap. 13% alc. Rating 95 To 2033 $50

♟♟♟♟♀ Centaurus Pinot Noir 2013 Rating 93 **To** 2025 $48
Pinot Noir 2013 Rating 91 **To** 2023 $26
Pinot Gris 2014 Rating 90 **To** 2016 $26

Rob Dolan Wines ★★★★★

21–23 Delaneys Road, South Warrandyte, Vic 3134 **Region** Yarra Valley
T (03) 9876 5885 www.robdolanwines.com.au **Open** By appt
Winemaker Rob Dolan, Mark Nikolich **Est.** 2010 **Dozens** 10 000 **Vyds** 20ha
Rob Dolan has been making wine in the Yarra Valley for over 20 years, and knows every nook and cranny there. In 2011 he was able to purchase the Hardys Yarra Burn winery at an enticing price. It is singularly well equipped, and as well as making the excellent Rob Dolan wines, he carries on an extensive contract winemaking business. Business is booming,

production having doubled, with exports driving much of the increase. Exports to the UK, Canada, Singapore, Hong Kong and China.

ŸŸŸŸŸ **Chardonnay 2014** Quality gear. Oak is taken up a notch from the True Colours range, which may or may not be a positive, but the general quality of the fruit and the extension of flavour through the finish firmly establishes its class. Grapefruit, pear, apple and oatmeal notes melt into spice and sweet sawdust. Both elegant and seductive. Screwcap. 13% alc. **Rating** 95 **To** 2021 $30 CM ✪
True Colours Chardonnay 2014 Beautiful balance and composure. Everything in its place, everything delivered at the right time. Peach, chalk, citrus and spicy oak, with lactose notes wafting throughout. Terrific value. Screwcap. 13% alc. **Rating** 95 **To** 2018 $24 CM ✪
Pinot Noir 2014 From the Upper Yarra Willowlake Vineyard, 15% whole bunches, the remainder whole berries, a warm ferment, hand-plunged, pressed to French oak (30% new) for 10 months. Bright colour, and a fragrant cherry and plum bouquet; the palate is long and insistent, with tangy bright red fruit flavours. Merits time in bottle, but no crime in drinking it tonight. Screwcap. 12.5% alc. **Rating** 94 **To** 2025 $35
Shiraz 2013 Black cherry, pepper and spice aromas lead directly into the fore-palate, which is no surprise; the tannins on the finish are, however, unexpected. The odds are they will soften well before the fruit fades, but the wine needs time. Screwcap. 13.5% alc. **Rating** 94 **To** 2025 $35 ✪
Yarra Valley Cabernet Sauvignon 2013 An elegant, medium-bodied Cabernet, reflecting its cool-grown origins with laid-back blackcurrant fruit, fine-grained tannins and a touch of black olive, oak in restraint. Drink whenever the mood takes you, cellaring not required. Screwcap. 13% alc. **Rating** 94 **To** 2025 $35

ŸŸŸŸŸ **True Colours Sauvignon Semillon 2014 Rating** 92 **To** 2016 $24 CM ✪
Pinot Noir 2013 Rating 92 **To** 2030 $35
Pinot Gris 2013 Rating 91 **To** 2015 $30 CM
Bon Blanc 2013 Rating 91 **To** 2016 $30
True Colours Yarra Valley Cabernet Shiraz Merlot 2013 Rating 90 **To** 2019 $24 CM

Rob Hall Wines   ★★★★☆

157 Pine Avenue, Healesville, Vic 3777 (postal) **Region** Yarra Valley
T 0448 224 003 **www.**robhallwine.com.au **Open** Not
Winemaker Rob Hall **Est.** 2013 **Dozens** 500 **Vyds** 3ha
Rob Hall has had considerable experience in making Yarra Valley chardonnay and pinot noir, previously at Mount Mary, and thereafter (and currently) at Kellybrook Winery. The 3ha vineyard (with equal amounts of pinot noir and chardonnay) has been established by his parents, and somewhere down the track Rob will have to decide whether he's going to go in at the deep end, find a way to plant more vines, and then be able to do his own thing full-time.

ŸŸŸŸŸ **Yarra Valley Chardonnay 2014** Light straw-green; a complex, pleasantly funky bouquet is a fitting overture to the equally complex palate, with white peach, nectarine and pink grapefruit framed by delicately toasty oak. Great value. Screwcap. 12.7% alc. **Rating** 95 **To** 2024 $25 ✪

ŸŸŸŸŸ **Yarra Valley Pinot Noir 2014 Rating** 90 **To** 2019 $25

Robert Channon Wines   ★★★★

32 Bradley Lane, Amiens, Qld 4352 **Region** Granite Belt
T (07) 4683 3260 **www.**robertchannonwines.com **Open** Mon, Tues & Fri 11–4, w'ends 10–5
Winemaker Paola Cabezas **Est.** 1998 **Dozens** 2000 **Vyds** 8ha

Peggy and Robert Channon have established verdelho, chardonnay, pinot gris, shiraz, cabernet sauvignon and pinot noir under permanent bird protection netting. The initial cost of installing permanent netting is high, but in the long term it is well worth it: it excludes birds and protects the grapes against hail damage. Also, there is no pressure to pick the grapes before they are fully ripe.

ϙϙϙϙϙ **Granite Belt Petit Verdot 2013** Demands attention for its impenetrable colour; matured in French and American oak; in full battle cruiser mode, but has that Petit Verdot ability to fold its tannins among the black fruits, and defies you to see through the looking glass. The development path for Petit Verdot is never easy to predict, this no exception. Screwcap. 14.5% alc. **Rating** 92 **To** 2028 $25 ✪

Granite Belt Chardonnay 2014 A very pleasant unwooded Chardonnay; it has clear varietal expression, white peach and rockmelon to the fore, but with a lively twist of grapefruit on the finish. Screwcap. 13.2% alc. **Rating** 90 **To** 2018 $20 ✪

Granite Belt Cabernet Sauvignon 2013 Matured in French and American oak for 12 months. The oak treatment for all the Robert Channon red wines is the same, but inflicting American oak on a medium-bodied Cabernet doesn't make sense, particularly given that this wine has/had the greatest potential. Screwcap. 14% alc. **Rating** 90 **To** 2023 $20 ✪

ϙϙϙϙ **Reserve Chardonnay 2014** **Rating** 89 **To** 2018 $35
Granite Belt Shiraz 2013 **Rating** 89 **To** 2020 $20
Granite Belt Shiraz Cabernet Sauvignon 2013 **Rating** 88 **To** 2020 $20

Robert Oatley Vineyards ★★★★★

Craigmoor Road, Mudgee, NSW 2850 **Region** Mudgee
T (02) 6372 2208 **www**.robertoatley.com.au **Open** 7 days 10–4
Winemaker Larry Cherubino, Marc Udy, Rob Merrick **Est.** 2006 **Dozens** NFP
Vyds 440ha
Robert Oatley Vineyards is the venture of the Oatley family, previously best known as the owners of Rosemount Estate, until it was sold to Southcorp. The chairman is Bob Oatley; the new venture is run by son Sandy, with considerable hitting power added by deputy executive chairman Chris Hancock. Wild Oats, as anyone with the remotest interest in yachting and the Sydney–Hobart Yacht Race will know, has been the name of Bob's racing yachts. The family has long owned vineyards in Mudgee, but the new business was rapidly expanded by the acquisition of the Montrose winery and the Craigmoor cellar door and restaurant. The recruitment of Larry Cherubino as a winemaker has been a major factor in the radical reshaping of the overall business, with all of the best wines now coming coming from WA. While there is a plethora of wines, the portfolio is easy to understand: at the bottom, Pocketwatch; next Wild Oats; Robert Oatley Signature Series; Robert Oatley Finisterre; and at the top, Robert Oatley The Pennant. Exports to the UK, the US and other major markets (including China).

ϙϙϙϙϙ **Robert Oatley Finisterre Margaret River Chardonnay 2014** Stunning wine in anyone's language. Power, texture, length and all-round X-factor. Grapefruit, peach, citrus and a seasoning of spice/toasty oak. Takes power and cuts it with elegance. Screwcap. **Rating** 96 **To** 2022 $37 CM ✪

Robert Oatley Finisterre Margaret River Cabernet Sauvignon 2012 Ultra-typical Margaret River Cabernet, with dusty/earthy nuances to the gently ripe blackcurrant and bay leaf varietal fruit; the tannin structure is particularly good, drawing out the complexity of the long, lingering finish. Screwcap. 14% alc. **Rating** 96 **To** 2027 $40 ✪

Robert Oatley Finisterre Porongurup Riesling 2014 Fresh Granny Smith apples, cut and dripping with juice. Squeezed with lime. Resting on slate. Tense, intense, and without pretence; pure, pristine quality. Screwcap. **Rating** 95 **To** 2025 $33 CM ✪

Robert Oatley Finisterre Coldstream Pinot Noir 2012 Keeps a cool head. Spice stitched intricately through attractively sour, cherried fruit. Delights along

the way but keeps the finish as the focus, where it fans impressively. Excellent now but should be better again later. Screwcap. 12.5% alc. **Rating** 95 **To** 2024 $37 CM
Robert Oatley Finisterre Gladysdale Pinot Noir 2012 In a very good place. Sweet, sour and savoury. Succulent too. Every foot in the right place. Apple, cherry, ground spice and stem. Both stewy and fresh. Excellent addition to the range. Screwcap. 13% alc. **Rating** 95 **To** 2025 $37 CM

Robert Oatley Margaret River Chardonnay 2014 Bright and sunny, with pear, apple and white peach flavours, before then raising more serious points. Said points come in the form of flint, matchstick and the grunt of grapefruit, all laced with smoky oak. Drinkability meets sophistication meets value. Screwcap. 12.5% alc. **Rating** 94 **To** 2019 $23 CM ✪

Robert Oatley McLaren Vale Shiraz 2013 Slips straight into seductive territory. Chocolate, coffee, blackberry and leather, with complex earthen notes capping things off nicely. A pretty wine without ever getting too cute. And a gutsy one, too. Screwcap. 14.5% alc. **Rating** 94 **To** 2021 $23 CM ✪

Robert Oatley McLaren Vale Grenache Shiraz Mourvedre 2014 Deliciousness well and truly in its sights. Cherry-plum, five-spice, ground coffee and sweet boysenberry. Combination works with aplomb. Fresh and eager. Super drinking. Screwcap. 13.5% alc. **Rating** 94 **To** 2020 $23 CM ✪

Robert Oatley Finisterre Great Southern Cabernet Sauvignon 2011 Pure, medium-weight, well-powered fruit bearing a coat of cedary, smoky, slinky oak. Balance feels off at first but as it rests in the glass it (relatively) quickly sets itself to rights. Bay leaf, peppercorn, blackcurrant and redcurrant. Long finish, complete with ultra-fine tannin. Screwcap. **Rating** 94 **To** 2026 $40 CM

Robert Oatley The Pennant Margaret River Cabernet Sauvignon 2011 Luscious style. Flooded with fruit and oak. Cassis, gravel, eucalypt, truffle and dried tobacco. Flushed with aroma, the flavour seemingly left with no option other than to gush forward. Tannin woven seamlessly into the spill of it all. Still a pup. Almost over-exuberant. But joyous good fun to drink; not something you often say of Cabernet. Screwcap. **Rating** 94 **To** 2036 $80 CM

🍷🍷🍷🍷🍸 **Robert Oatley Great Southern Riesling 2014** Rating 93 To 2024 $23 CM ✪
Robert Oatley Finisterre Pinot Noir 2012 Rating 92 To 2020 $37 CM
Four in Hand Barossa Shiraz 2013 Rating 92 To 2023 $27 CM
Wild Oats Mudgee Shiraz Viognier 2013 Rating 92 To 2020 $18 CM ✪
Robert Oatley Margaret River Cabernet Sauvignon 2013 Rating 91 To 2022 $23 CM ✪

Robert Stein Vineyard ★★★★★

Pipeclay Lane, Mudgee, NSW 2850 **Region** Mudgee
T (02) 6373 3991 **www**.robertstein.com.au **Open** 7 days 10–4.30
Winemaker Jacob Stein **Est.** 1976 **Dozens** 15000 **Vyds** 18.67ha
While three generations of the family have been involved since Robert (Bob) Stein began the establishment of the vineyard, the chain stretches even further back, going to Bob's great-great-grandfather, Johann Stein, who was brought to Australia by the Macarthur family to supervise the planting of the Camden Park vineyard. Bob's son Drew and grandson Jacob have now taken over winemaking responsibilities. Jacob worked vintages in Italy, Canada, Margaret River and Avoca, and, more particularly, in the Rheingau and Rheinhessen regions of Germany. Since his return one success has followed another. Exports to Germany, Hong Kong, Singapore and China.

🍷🍷🍷🍷🍷 **Reserve Mudgee Riesling 2014** Trophy for Best Wine of Show, Mudgee Wine Show '14. The wine is bone dry, but has excellent overall length and balance; classic restraint, and is built for the long haul; needs time to reveal all that is within. Screwcap. 12% alc. **Rating** 95 **To** 2029 $50
Mudgee Riesling 2014 Full of sweet, juicy lime fruit from the word go, and continuing through to the finish; the scale on the back label indicates the wine

is dry, but there may well be a few grams of residual sugar to balance the acidity. Ready when you are. Jacob Stein has rare skills with Riesling. Screwcap. 11.5% alc. Rating 95 To 2025 $35 ✪

Reserve Mudgee Chardonnay 2013 Wild yeast-fermented in French hogsheads, with a small portion taken through mlf. Gleaming straw-green; every decision at every step in the process was correct, and (remarkably) the early-picked fruit has prevailed with its grapefruit and melon flavours. Screwcap. 12.5% alc. Rating 95 To 2018 $40

Reserve Vintage Port 2013 Jacob Stein says he has been waiting for 5 years to make a Vintage Port style, and '13 provided him with the shiraz he needed. This is a particularly good wine, much drier and with more savoury complexity than most Australian Vintage Ports, very similar to Portuguese style though it shouldn't use the name. 375ml. Screwcap. 18% alc. Rating 95 To 2028 $30 ✪

Mudgee Semillon 2014 Semillon has always found that Mudgee provides a welcome environment. This is a prime example, its varietal expression of lemongrass, talc and mineral driving the long palate and airy aftertaste. Gold medal Mudgee Wine Show '14. Screwcap. 12% alc. Rating 94 To 2024 $25 ✪

🍷🍷🍷🍷🍷 **Mudgee Shiraz 2013** Rating 93 To 2025 $25 ✪
Reserve Mudgee Shiraz 2012 Rating 93 To 2027 $50
Reserve Mudgee Cabernet Sauvignon 2012 Rating 93 To 2025 $50
Harvest Gold 2013 Rating 93 To 2018 $30

Robertson of Clare   ★★★★☆

PO Box 149, Killara, NSW 2071 **Region** Clare Valley
T (02) 9499 6002 **www.**rocwines.com.au **Open** Not
Winemaker Leigh Eldredge, Biagio Famularo **Est.** 2004 **Dozens** NFP
This is the highly unusual venture of Bryan Robertson, initially producing a single wine: MAX V. The Bordeaux varieties that go to produce MAX V are all grown in the Clare Valley, and individual varietal parcels are matured in 19 variations of 100% new French oak barrels. The primary fermentation takes place in barrel using what is called 'vinification integrale'. MAX V has been joined by the Block 6 Shiraz. Exports to Singapore, Hong Kong and China.

🍷🍷🍷🍷🍷 **MAX V 2012** A 50/16/16/12/6% blend of cabernet sauvignon, cabernet franc, malbec and petit verdot, 33% fermented in new French 400l vinification integrale barrels, 67% fermented in open slate, 24 months' maturation in 19 variations of new French barriques. A wine that has long since decided on the rules of its own game, oak fetish the entry card; but in the manner of John Glaetzer and Wolf Blass, it flaunts it. Screwcap. 14.9% alc. Rating 95 To 2042 $75

🍷🍷🍷🍷🍷 **Block 6 Gentle Press Shiraz 2013** Rating 91 To 2028 $22 ✪

Rochford Wines   ★★★★★

878–880 Maroondah Highway, Coldstream, Vic 3770 **Region** Yarra Valley
T (03) 5962 2119 **www.**rochfordwines.com.au **Open** 7 days 9–5
Winemaker Marc Lunt **Est.** 1988 **Dozens** 9000 **Vyds** 23.2ha
This Yarra Valley property was purchased by Helmut Konecsny in 2002; he had already established a reputation for Pinot Noir and Chardonnay from the family-owned Romsey Park vineyard in the Macedon Ranges. Since '10, Helmut has focused on his Yarra Valley wineries and vineyards, with some grapes still sourced from small-parcel growers in the Macedon Ranges. Winemaker Marc Lunt had a stellar career as a Flying Winemaker over a six-year period in Bordeaux and Burgundy; in the latter region he worked at Armand Rousseau and Domaine de la Romanee-Conti. As well as a vineyard and winery, the property has a large restaurant and café, cellar door, retail shop, expansive natural amphitheatre and observation tower. It is a showpiece in the region, hosting a series of popular summer concerts. Exports to Norway, the Philippines, Singapore, Hong Kong and China.

ŸŸŸŸŸ **Chardonnay 2013** Crushed and pressed straight to barrel (25% new) with full solids, wild yeast-fermented, 12 months on lees in barrel, then 3 months on lees in tank. Very well made, ticking each and every box; its complexity lives hand in glove with its harmony and elegance; white peach, melon and citrus-tinged fruit have an admirable creamy texture. Screwcap. 13.9% alc. **Rating** 96 **To** 2023 $30 ✪

L'Enfant Unique Pinot Noir 2014 Hand-picked, destemmed, 80% whole bunches, open wild yeast-fermented, short cold soak, French oak (30% new) for 10 months. Notably bright and clear crimson, it has a perfumed bouquet, and a red fruits palate with elegance, intensity and length, the tangy aftertaste exactly as it should be. Screwcap. 13.5% alc. **Rating** 96 **To** 2024 $65 ✪

Pinot Noir 2014 Hand-picked, destemmed, 20% whole bunches, open wild yeast-fermented, 7-day cold soak, French oak (30% new) for 10 months. Fractionally deeper colour than L'Enfant Unique, with a glimmer of purple; significantly more powerful, with nuances of plum and bramble joining the cherry fruit; some spicy/earthy notes in the background. Will reward those with patience. Screwcap. 13.5% alc. **Rating** 95 **To** 2029 $36

Latitude Cabernet Merlot 2013 A 45/35/14/6% blend of cabernet sauvignon, merlot, shiraz and cabernet franc, wild yeast-fermented, 18 months in French oak (20% new). Deep but bright colour; this is not what you expect from a $20 wine, with intense cassis fruits nicely balanced by notes of bramble and unapologetic tannins to sustain it for years. Great bargain. Screwcap. 14% alc. **Rating** 95 **To** 2033 $20 ✪

la Droite Merlot Cabernet 2013 An 85/10/5% blend of merlot, cabernet sauvignon and cabernet franc, destemmed, wild yeast open-fermented, matured in French oak (20% new). Good colour; it has a fragrant bouquet of forest berries, then a long, medium to full-bodied palate with cassis, cedary/spicy tannins and a lingering, textured finish. Screwcap. 14.5% alc. **Rating** 95 **To** 2033 $30 ✪

Isabella's Vineyard Cabernet Sauvignon 2013 Destemmed, wild yeast open-fermented, 18 months in French oak (30% new). Good colour; a powerful, focused wine, its bouquet a fragrant mix of cassis, spice and cedar, the medium to full-bodied palate delivering precisely what is suggested by the bouquet, the surging finish better still. Screwcap. 14.5% alc. **Rating** 95 **To** 2038 $45

Latitude Yarra Valley Pinot Noir 2014 Hand-picked, destemmed, 20% whole bunches, open wild yeast-fermented, short cold soak, French oak (15% new) for 10 months. Bright, clear crimson; the fragrant red berry bouquet is pure pinot, signalling the mix of red and black cherry of the uncluttered and very well balanced palate, and reflecting the low yields of the vintage. Outrageous bargain. Screwcap. 13.5% alc. **Rating** 94 **To** 2023 $20 ✪

la Gauche Yarra Valley Cabernet 2013 A 90/8/2% blend of cabernet sauvignon, merlot and cabernet franc; wild yeast open-fermented, 18 months in French oak (20% new). Bright colour of medium depth; an attractive bouquet leads into a complex and proactive palate, with a mix of blackcurrant, ripe tannins, briar and oak. Should repay extended cellaring. Screwcap. 14.5% alc. **Rating** 94 **To** 2030 $30 ✪

ŸŸŸŸŸ **Cabernet Franc 2014 Rating** 93 **To** 2024 $30
Sauvignon Blanc 2014 Rating 91 **To** 2016 $27
Syrah 2013 Rating 91 **To** 2028 $30

RockBare   ★★★★☆

102 Main St, Hahndorf, SA 5245 **Region** McLaren Vale
T (08) 8388 7155 **www**.rockbare.com.au **Open** 7 days 11–5
Winemaker Marty O'Flaherty **Est.** 2000 **Dozens** 57 000 **Vyds** 47ha
RockBare Wines completed its first vintage in 2000. At the helm is winemaker Marty O'Flaherty, who was born and raised in the Western District of Victoria. He had a successful career as a chef, culminating in an award-winning term in charge at the acclaimed Stefano's in Mildura. Whilst there he had his vinous epiphany and duly headed off to Charles Sturt University on his winemaking odyssey, holding various winemaking positions before finally

landing at the helm of RockBare in 2009. The cellar door is located in the main street of Hahndorf. Exports to all major markets.

ŸŸŸŸŸ **Mojo Cabernet Sauvignon 2013** What a beautiful medium-bodied wine. It's all blackcurrant and mulberry, tobacco leaf and cedar wood. It's varietal, rounds all the bases well, is threaded with assertive tannin and lingers with complex flavour. Not a big wine by any stretch, with an ever-so-slight dip through the mid-palate, but everything is more or less spot on. A drop-dead bargain. Screwcap. 13.5% alc. **Rating** 94 **To** 2028 $19 CM ◐

ŸŸŸŸŸ **Mojo Shiraz 2013 Rating** 93 **To** 2021 $20 CM ◐
McLaren Vale Shiraz 2013 Rating 93 **To** 2026 $23 CM ◐
Tideway McLaren Vale Shiraz 2010 Rating 93 **To** 2026 $38 CM
Mojo Moscato 2014 Rating 90 **To** 2015 $17 CM ◐

Rockcliffe ★★★★★

18 Hamilton Road, Denmark, WA 6333 **Region** Denmark
T (08) 9848 2622 **www**.rockcliffe.com.au **Open** 7 days 11–5
Winemaker Coby Ladwig, Brenden Smith, Luke Eckersley **Est.** 1990 **Dozens** 1800
Vyds 10ha
The Rockcliffe winery and vineyard business, formerly known as Matilda's Estate, is owned by citizen of the world Steve Hall. As part of the name change of the business, the wine ranges echo local surf place names, headed by Rockcliffe itself, but extending to Third Reef, Forty Foot Drop and Quarram Rocks. One success has followed another, culminating in the trophy for Best Winery Under 300 Tonnes at the Perth Wine Show '12. Exports to Hong Kong and China.

ŸŸŸŸŸ **Single Site Frankland River Shiraz 2012** Vivid colour; a beautifully made cool-climate Shiraz, super-fragrant and pulsing with life on its endless medium-bodied palate; red and black fruits, allspice and finely etched tannins form a tapestry that draws you back again and again. Drink tonight or any time over the next 25 years. Screwcap. 13.8% alc. **Rating** 97 **To** 2037 $45 ◐

ŸŸŸŸŸ **Single Site Denmark Chardonnay 2013** The bouquet leaves no doubt about the quality of the wine; it is an immaculately balanced, utterly pure Chardonnay, the complex barrel-ferment aromas giving way to a seamless stream of nectarine, creamy cashew oak and grapefruit zest on the long palate, the finish faultless. Screwcap. 13.5% alc. **Rating** 96 **To** 2023 $28 ◐
Single Site Mount Barker Riesling 2014 A wine of unrelenting intensity. Stand aside, it's charging on through. Lime, tart apple, bath salts and a shatter of mineral. Penetrating length; indeed it builds as it flows. One for the cellar. Screwcap. 11.5% alc. **Rating** 95 **To** 2028 $28 CM ◐
Third Reef Great Southern Chardonnay 2013 The colour is still to develop (no harm in that), but there is no shortage of aroma, flavour or structure; grapefruit/grapefruit zest and pith and white stone fruit soar along the long, well-balanced palate; the oak has a support role, but isn't obvious. Screwcap. 13% alc. **Rating** 95 **To** 2023 $30 ◐
Third Reef Great Southern Cabernet Sauvignon 2013 A prime example of Great Southern Cabernet. It has layer upon layer of blackcurrant fruit, accompanied by savoury bay leaf/black olive notes, and a nod of French oak to the medium to full-bodied palate; the tannins are well balanced, but are unmistakably those of cabernet. Screwcap. 14% alc. **Rating** 95 **To** 2033 $30 ◐
Single Site Mount Barker Cabernet Sauvignon 2012 As expected, very well made, true to its region and variety; it has the varietal character of cool-grown cabernet, but the flavours are not the least green, and the positive use of oak has done its job well. It will cruise along for 20 years at least. Screwcap. 14% alc. **Rating** 95 **To** 2035 $45
Third Reef Great Southern Pinot Noir 2014 Excellent depth and hue; a powerful blood plum and cherry Pinot still in its infancy, the bouquet very

expressive; just when you think the fruit lacks shape on the palate, a savoury tang to the finish cracks the whip. This has 'cellar me' stamped on its forehead in large letters. Screwcap. 14% alc. **Rating** 94 **To** 2024 $30 ✪

Single Site Denmark Pinot Noir 2014 Good colour; the red cherry aroma and primary flavour of the palate are shipsafe, and just when you think that's it, the finish and aftertaste change the whole geometry of the wine, with a surge of spicy/foresty flavour still held within the overarching red cherry fruit. One to watch closely over the next few years. Screwcap. 14% alc. **Rating** 94 **To** 2024 $45

Third Reef Great Southern Shiraz 2013 Bright and clear colour; has all the brightness and sure-footed elegance of cool-grown shiraz, red and black cherry to the fore, spiked with notes of pepper, spice and licorice, the tannins gossamer-light. Screwcap. 14% alc. **Rating** 94 **To** 2028 $30 ✪

Quarram Rocks Great Southern Cabernet Shiraz 2012 Light, but healthy, colour; a lively, juicy wine, no more than medium-bodied, but with excellent mouthfeel thanks to silky tannins. Outstanding value for early drinking. Screwcap. 13.5% alc. **Rating** 94 **To** 2025 $20 ✪

🍷🍷🍷🍷🍷 **Third Reef Great Southern Riesling 2014 Rating** 93 **To** 2022 $22 CM ✪
Quarram Rocks Shiraz Cabernet 2013 Rating 92 **To** 2023 $21 ✪
Quarram Rocks Sauvignon Blanc Semillon 2014 Rating 91 **To** 2017 $20 ✪

Rockford   ★★★★★

131 Krondorf Road, Tanunda, SA 5352 **Region** Barossa Valley
T (08) 8563 2720 **www.**rockfordwines.com.au **Open** 7 days 11–5
Winemaker Robert O'Callaghan, Ben Radford **Est.** 1984 **Dozens** NFP
Rockford can only be described as an icon, no matter how overused that word may be. It has a devoted band of customers who buy most of the wine through the cellar door or mail order (Rocky O'Callaghan's entrancing annual newsletter is like no other). Some wine is sold through restaurants, and there are two retailers in Sydney, and one each in Melbourne, Brisbane and Perth. Whether they will have the Basket Press Shiraz available is another matter; it is as scarce as Henschke Hill of Grace (but less expensive). Ben Radford, whom I first met in South Africa some years ago, has been entrenched as Rocky's right-hand man, and is destined to take over responsibility for winemaking when the time comes for Rocky to step back from an active role. Exports to the UK, Canada, Switzerland, Russia, Vietnam, South Korea, Singapore, Japan, Hong Kong, China and NZ.

🍷🍷🍷🍷🍷 **Rifle Range Barossa Valley Cabernet Sauvignon 2012** Superb example of Barossa Cabernet. Balanced, ripe, generous and yet honed and persistent. Precision power. Flavours of blackberry, cassis, dust and dark chocolate build towards a twisting finale. It makes the asking price look cheap. Screwcap. 14.5% alc. **Rating** 97 **To** 2030 $41 CM ✪

🍷🍷🍷🍷🍷 **Basket Press Barossa Shiraz 2011** Difficult season, but it's not a difficult wine. Fans of the label with some already stashed in their cellar can breathe easy. It's fuller in body than the season might have predicted, but more elegant than is usual for this wine. Blackberry, raspberry, coffee grounds, toast and vanilla fill it out, with herbs and peppers whispering through the finish. Tannin is the key: it's ripe, fine, marked by its finesse and yet determined to get its point across. Perhaps not a long-termer, but no doubting either its merit or its drinking appeal. Cork. 14.2% alc. **Rating** 95 **To** 2023 $59 CM

Black Shiraz NV Loaded with complexity, first the primary Barossa Shiraz signatures of black plums, blackberries and black cherries, then dark chocolate, black olives and crushed ants, and finally notes of game and pan juices. Tannins are firm and fine, providing well-gauged grip and tension to a long and well-balanced finish, demanding time to soften and integrate. Don't drink it too cold, or too soon. Disgorged Sept '14. Cork. 13.5% alc. **Rating** 94 **To** 2024 $61 TS

🍷🍷🍷🍷🍷 **Local Growers Barossa Semillon 2011 Rating** 93 **To** 2019 $21 CM ✪
Moppa Springs G.M.S. 2010 Rating 93 **To** 2022 $27 CM ✪
Barossa Valley Alicante Bouchet 2014 Rating 90 **To** 2015 $20 CM ✪

Rockridge Estate

PO Box 374, Kent Town, SA 5071 **Region** Clare Valley
T (08) 8358 0480 **www**.rockridgewines.com.au **Open** Not
Winemaker Justin Ardill (red), Peter Leske (white) **Est.** 2007 **Dozens** 5000 **Vyds** 40ha
In the Vine Pull Scheme of the 1980s, the 120ha Leasingham Wines vineyard in the hills immediately above the hamlet of Leasingham was removed. Partially replanted in '99, this precious block of terra rossa over deep limestone is producing outstanding grapes, sold to Tim Adams, Kilikanoon, Reillys, Claymore, Old Station, Foster's and Yalumba. In 2007 owners Andrew Miller, Richard Yeend and Justin Ardill decided to retain a significant part of the crop to produce Riesling, Shiraz and Sparkling Riesling, purchasing sauvignon blanc from premium cool-climate regions.

 Clare Valley Shiraz 2013 Open-fermented for 10 days; 10 months' maturation in American and French oak. This artisan Shiraz partially answers the question posed by its Cellar Selection sibling, the fruit brighter; while more polish would have made a better wine, this gives you plenty for your dollar. Screwcap. 14.5% alc. **Rating** 89 **To** 2018 $15 ✪
Watervale Riesling 2014 I'm not convinced that detectable residual sugar suits Watervale, however successful the great Riesling maker John Vickery was in the '70s with the style; nonetheless, this will please those hunting in the $15 or below price range. Screwcap. 12.5% alc. **Rating** 88 **To** 2020 $15 ✪
Cellar Selection Clare Valley Shiraz 2013 Estate-grown from the Watervale vineyard, open-fermented, matured in French hogsheads. You get a lot, if not too much, for your dollar; the full-bodied palate is full of ripe fruits and brash tannins; you have to ask why 15%, not 14%, thus avoiding the dead fruit characters. Screwcap. 15% alc. **Rating** 88 **To** 2019 $20

Rocky Passes Estate ★★★★☆

1590 Highlands Road, Whiteheads Creek, Vic 3660 **Region** Upper Goulburn
T (03) 5796 9366 **www**.rockypasses.com.au **Open** Sun 11–5
Winemaker Vitto Oles **Est.** 2000 **Dozens** 350 **Vyds** 2ha
Vitto Oles and Candi Westney run this tiny, cool-climate, carbon-neutral, venture situated at the southern end of the Strathbogie Ranges, which in fact falls in the Upper Goulburn region. They have planted 1.8ha of shiraz and 0.2ha of viognier, growing the vines with minimal irrigation and preferring organic and biodynamic soil treatments. Vitto is also a fine furniture designer and maker, with a studio at Rocky Passes.

Syrah Viognier 2013 Typical deep, bright colour; there is a complex tapestry of flavours on the medium to full-bodied palate, with cherries (red, black and sour) joining with cool-grown notes of spice and pepper. Neither oak nor tannins are overtly assertive, but the tannins do provide texture for the finish, Screwcap. 14.5% alc. **Rating** 94 **To** 2028 $20 ✪

Rohrlach Family Wines ★★★★

PO Box 864, Nuriootpa, SA 5355 **Region** Barossa Valley
T (08) 8562 4121 **www**.rohrlachfamilywines.com.au **Open** Not
Winemaker Peter Schell (Contract) **Est.** 2000 **Dozens** 1000 **Vyds** 160.6ha
Brothers Kevin, Graham and Wayne Rohrlach, with wives Lyn, Lynette and Kaylene, are third-generation owners of prime vineyard land, the first plantings made back in 1930 by their paternal grandfather. Until 2000 the grapes were sold to two leading Barossa wineries, but (in a familiar story) in that year some of the grapes were retained to make the first vintage of what became Rohrlach Family Wines.

 Mum's Block Barossa Valley Shiraz 2012 Exceptional vivid and deep colour for a 3yo wine; it is filled with luscious plum and blackberry fruit, but is yet to connect the line from the mid-palate through to the finish. I guess it will do so, but it won't happen overnight. Screwcap. 14.5% alc. **Rating** 92 **To** 2032 $42

Rolf Binder

Cnr Seppeltsfield Road/Stelzer Road, Tanunda, SA 5352 **Region** Barossa Valley
T (08) 8562 3300 **www.**rolfbinder.com **Open** Mon–Sat 10–4.30, Sun on long weekends
Winemaker Rolf Binder, Christa Deans **Est.** 1955 **Dozens** 39 500 **Vyds** 110ha
Rolf Binder, formerly known as Veritas, was established in the Barossa Valley in 1955 by
Rolf Heinrich Binder. Today second-generation winemakers Rolf Binder and Christa Deans
produce an extensive range of highly acclaimed wines from the estate and premium Barossa
and Eden Valley vineyards. The Hahn family were among the original Barossa Valley settlers,
and were heavily involved with grapegrowing from 1845. The JJ Hahn brand was created in
1997 as a joint venture between sixth-generation Barossans James and Jacqui Hahn and Rolf
Binder. Since their retirement, Rolf has assumed ownership of the brand.

Hanisch Barossa Valley Shiraz 2012 The vineyard was planted in 1972 by
Rolf Binder and his father; it became apparent that a small 12-row part of the
vineyard consistently produced superior grapes, and in good vintages this is
vinified separately. A supremely elegant medium-bodied Shiraz that effortlessly
stamps its blackberry and plum fruit on the palate, with exactly proportioned
gently savoury tannins. Cork. 14% alc. **Rating** 97 **To** 2035 $110 ◐

JJ Hahn Western Ridge 1975 Planting Shiraz 2012 Matured in American
and French oak. Full crimson-purple; there is a juicy freshness at the heart of
the wine, the flavours of the medium-bodied palate more or less equally divided
between red and black fruits; silky tannins and fully integrated oak provide a
confident finish. Screwcap. 14% alc. **Rating** 95 **To** 2032 $35 ◐
Eden Valley Montepulciano 2012 Good depth to the colour; this is the
labrador of the grape world, ever generous, but with its breed always evident;
has great depth to its mix of sensual dark cherry and spiced plum fruit, and the
unexpected flash of light on the finish and aftertaste adds even further to its allure.
WAK screwcap. 14% alc. **Rating** 95 **To** 2027 $30 ◐
Eden Valley Riesling 2014 Eden Valley to its bootstraps; the lime and lemon
blossom aromas (almost) say it all, the zesty palate picking up the cue without
missing a beat, the floral characters mirrored in the crisp acidity and finish.
Screwcap. 12.5% alc. **Rating** 94 **To** 2029 $25 ◐
Heysen Barossa Valley Shiraz 2012 An elegant, spicy/savoury wine, with
red fruits walking in lockstep with fine-grained tannins and integrated oak. Will
continue on the same path for years to come, but I'd like to see a touch more
fruit – Socratean dissatisfaction at work. WAK screwcap. 14% alc. **Rating** 94
To 2027 $70
Heinrich Barossa Valley Shiraz Mataro Grenache 2012 Medium red-
purple; no more than medium-bodied, but has a brightness to the blend over and
above many such from the Barossa Valley; juicy red fruits and balanced acidity draw
saliva from the mouth, and lengthen the finish. A very good wine. WAK screwcap.
14% alc. **Rating** 94 **To** 2025 $35

Halliwell Barossa Valley Shiraz Grenache 2012 **Rating** 93 **To** 2022 $22 ◐
Hales Barossa Valley Shiraz 2013 **Rating** 92 **To** 2027 $18 ◐
JJ Hahn Stelzer Road Merlot 2013 **Rating** 92 **To** 2020 $22 ◐
Barossa Valley Shiraz 2013 **Rating** 91 **To** 2025 $18 ◐
JJ Hahn Shiraz Cabernet 2011 **Rating** 91 **To** 2020 $22 CM ◐
JJ Hahn Homestead Cabernet 2012 **Rating** 91 **To** 2020 $22 CM ◐
Veritas Limited Release Petite Sirah 2012 **Rating** 91 **To** 2025 $25

Romney Park Wines

116 Johnsons Road, Balhannah, SA 5242 **Region** Adelaide Hills
T (08) 8398 0698 **www.**romneyparkwines.com.au **Open** By appt
Winemaker Rod and Rachel Short **Est.** 1997 **Dozens** 1000 **Vyds** 3ha
Rod and Rachel Short planted chardonnay, shiraz and pinot noir in 1997. The first vintage was
in 2002, made from 100% estate-grown grapes. Yields are limited to 3.7–5 tonnes per hectare

for the red wines, and 2–3 tonnes for the Chardonnay. The vineyard is managed organically, with guinea fowl cleaning up the insects, all vines hand-picked and hand-pruned. In every way (including the wines) has the beauty of a hand-painted miniature. Exports to China.

�♙♙♙♙ Adelaide Hills Fume Blanc 2013 Wild yeast, 100% mlf, all matured in older oak. Brilliant result. Excellent intensity of flavour. Lime, passionfruit, sweet pea and gravelly, smoky notes. Emphasis is on lively fruit but there's a plushness to the texture. It all concludes satisfyingly, if not excitingly. Screwcap. 13% alc. **Rating** 95 **To** 2018 $28 CM ✪

Gloria Adelaide Hills Chardonnay 2013 A mouthful of flavour but elegance remains its friend. Tangy lime and white peach flavours lead into creamy/spicy oak and the bite of grapefruit. It feels as if its questions are behind it; all queries are resolved. Time to relax and enjoy. Diam. 13.5% alc. **Rating** 95 **To** 2020 $50 CM

Methode Traditonnelle Adelaide Hills Sparkling Shiraz 2008 After 6 years on lees, this estate Shiraz admirably upholds the fragrant spice and pepper of Adelaide Hills shiraz in a style of impressively luscious, deep black plum, black cherry, dark chocolate and licorice. Fine, peppery tannins linger long on a finish upheld by bright acidity and fruit of great integrity. Disgorged Dec '14. Cork. 14% alc. **Rating** 94 **To** 2023 $45 TS

♙♙♙♙♙ Adelaide Hills Shiraz 2012 **Rating** 93 **To** 2027 $45
Reserve Adelaide Hills Pinot Noir 2012 **Rating** 92 **To** 2020 $55

Ros Ritchie Wines   ★★★★☆

1974 Long Lane, Barwite, Vic 3722 **Region** Upper Goulburn
T 0448 900 541 **www**.rosritchiewines.com **Open** By appt
Winemaker Ros Ritchie **Est.** 2008 **Dozens** 2000 **Vyds** 5ha
Ros Ritchie was winemaker at the Ritchie family's Delatite winery from 1981 to 2006, but moved on to establish her own winery with husband John in '08. They lease a vineyard (merlot and cabernet sauvignon) close to Mansfield and source their white wines from growers who work in tandem with them to provide high-quality grapes. Foremost are Gumbleton, Retief and Baxendale Vineyards, the last planted by the very experienced viticulturist Jim Baxendale (and wife Ruth) high above the King River Valley. All the vineyards are managed with minimal spray regimes. Exports to Hong Kong and China.

♙♙♙♙♙ Dead Man's Hill Vineyard Gewurztraminer 2014 Ros Ritchie is a long-term practitioner in the arcane art of persuading Australian gewurztraminer to deliver anything resembling that which comes from Alsace. This is a very well balanced wine with some rose petal and lychee, but it's not that as much as the layered and long finish that is so beguiling and satisfying. Screwcap. 13% alc. **Rating** 94 **To** 2027 $25 ✪

♙♙♙♙♙ Barwite Vineyards Riesling 2014 **Rating** 90 **To** 2020 $25

Rosabrook Margaret River Wine   ★★★★☆

Yungarra Estate, Lot 68 Yungarra Drive, Quedjinup, WA 6281 **Region** Margaret River
T (08) 9368 4555 **www**.rosabrook.com.au **Open** Not
Winemaker Brian Fletcher **Est.** 1980 **Dozens** 12 000 **Vyds** 25ha
Mike and Sally Calneggia have been at the forefront of vineyard development in Margaret River over the past decade, and also have various winemaking interests. The original Rosabrook estate vineyards were established between 1984 and '96. In 2007 Rosabrook relocated its vineyard to the northwestern end of the Margaret River wine region, overlooking Geographe Bay and the Indian Ocean. The warm days and cool nights, influenced by the ocean, result in slow, mild-ripening conditions. Exports to Dubai, Hong Kong and China.

♙♙♙♙♙ Single Vineyard Estate Cabernet Sauvignon 2012 Cabernet Sauvignon can be off-putting with its autocratic stance, but here it is, quite simply, delicious, awash with supple, lively, redcurrant and cassis fruit framed by new French oak and fine

tannins; balance and length are equally impressive. Screwcap. 14.5% alc. **Rating** 96
To 2042 $45 ⚫

ΨΨΨΨ♀ **Shiraz 2013 Rating** 92 To 2021 $25 CM ⚫
Cabernet Sauvignon 2013 Rating 91 To 2022 $25 CM
Cabernet Merlot 2013 Rating 90 To 2018 $17 ⚫

Rosemount Estate ★★★★★

114 Chaffeys Road, McLaren Vale, SA 5171 **Region** McLaren Vale
T (08) 8323 6220 **www.**rosemountestate.com.au **Open** Mon–Sat 10–5, Sun 11–5
Winemaker Matt Koch **Est.** 1888 **Dozens** NFP **Vyds** 441ha
Rosemount Estate has vineyards in McLaren Vale, Fleurieu, Coonawarra and Robe that are
the anchor for its top-of-the-range wines. It also has access to other TWE estate-grown grapes,
but the major part of its intake for the Diamond Label wines is supplied by contract growers
across SA, NSW, Vic and WA. As the tasting notes show, the quality and range of the wines
has greatly improved over the past few years as Rosemount Estate endeavours to undo the
damage done to the brand around the new millennium. Ironically, the large onsite winery was
closed in November 2014, winemaking transferred to other major wineries owned by TWE.
Exports to all major markets.

ΨΨΨΨΨ **Balmoral McLaren Vale Syrah 2013** Perfect for the cellar. Power of inky plum
and blackberry fruit with meaty ribs of earthen tannin. Bold, beautiful and a touch
brutal. Smoky vanillan oak is in plentiful but appropriate supply. Top of its game.
Screwcap. **Rating** 96 To 2040 $75 CM ⚫
Nursery Project Grenache 2012 Beautiful expression of grenache. Momentum
of sweet fruit, a power of savoury spice and taut strings of tannin. Bright but
composed. Not overly complex now, but if you can bear not to lap it up now, it
will be in time. Screwcap. 13.5% alc. **Rating** 95 To 2022 $30 CM ⚫
Gillets Block Single Vineyard McLaren Vale Dry Red Cabernet
Sauvignon 2013 Balance is a beautiful but underrated thing; in wine as much
as in art, sport, life. This sets an even, harmonious pitch and holds it like a long
extended note. Blackcurrant, saltbush, olive, musk and sweet dry leaf, threaded
through with finely spun tannin. It helps give the 'single vineyard' push a good
name. Screwcap. **Rating** 95 To 2033 $50 CM
MV Collection Cabernet Sauvignon 2012 Gold and trophy winner Decanter
World Wine Awards '14 for Aus Bordeaux varietals over £15, and is indeed an
elegant and well-balanced Cabernet, cassis and briar notes on both the bouquet
and medium-bodied palate; tannins and a subtle hint of oak complete the picture.
Screwcap. 14% alc. **Rating** 94 To 2022 $25 ⚫

ΨΨΨΨ♀ **District Release McLaren Vale Shiraz 2013 Rating** 93 To 2021 $20 CM ⚫
McLaren Vale G.S.M. 2013 Rating 93 To 2022 $40 CM
District Release Traditional 2012 Rating 93 To 2023 $20 CM ⚫
MV Collection Shiraz 2013 Rating 92 To 2022 $25 CM ⚫
Little Berry Shiraz 2012 Rating 92 To 2020 $30 CM
District Release Robe Chardonnay 2013 Rating 91 To 2017 $20 CM ⚫
MV Collection Shiraz 2012 Rating 90 To 2022 $25
MV Collection G.S.M. 2013 Rating 90 To 2016 $25

Rosenthal Wines ★★★★★

24 Rockford Street, Denmark, WA 6333 **Region** Great Southern
T 0417 940 851 **www.**rosenthalwines.com.au **Open** Not
Winemaker Luke Eckersley, Coby Ladwig **Est.** 2001 **Dozens** 4000 **Vyds** 4ha
Rosenthal Wines is a small part of the much larger 180ha Springfield Park cattle stud situated
between Bridgetown and Manjimup. Dr John Rosenthal acquired the property from Gerald
and Marjorie Richings, who in 1997 had planted a small vineyard as a minor diversification.
The Rosenthals extended the vineyard, which is equally divided between shiraz and cabernet

sauvignon. The wines have had significant show success, chiefly in WA-based shows. Rosenthal Wines is now owned by Luke Eckersley (winemaker at Willoughby Park). Exports to China.

ŢŢŢŢŢ **The Marker Manjimup Southern Forest Cabernet Shiraz 2012** Standard vinification, matured for 16 months in French oak (40% new). Still has a vivid primary hue, and vivid cassis and blackberry fruits with exceptional energy, tension and drive; the great length of the palate and aftertaste is an inevitable reflection of the amazing fruit. Screwcap. 14.5% alc. **Rating** 96 **To** 2042 $28 ✪

The Marker Pemberton Pinot Noir 2014 Hand-picked, crushed into small open fermenters for cold soak, then warm-fermented (peak 25°C), 9 months' maturation in French oak (40% new). Vivid hue; a garden of red flower scents on the bouquet, the palate echoing the bouquet, although not all the buds are open; the way the wine finishes is a sure sign of what is around the corner; just a little patience required. Screwcap. 14.5% alc. **Rating** 95 **To** 2024 $28 ✪

The Marker Great Southern Riesling 2014 Hand-picked, whole bunch-pressed, cold-fermented with natural yeast. Quartz-white; has the authority and drive that are the markers of the region, fruit and minerally acidity intertwined, lime and grapefruit at its heart. Screwcap. 12% alc. **Rating** 94 **To** 2029 $28 ✪

Richings Great Southern Chardonnay 2014 Hand-picked fruit chilled and whole bunch-pressed direct to French oak for wild-yeast ferment in a temperature-controlled room for slow fermentation, lees-stirred weekly until balanced, 9 months' maturation. A super-elegant wine, still needing to build a little more flesh over the next year. Screwcap. 13.5% alc. **Rating** 94 **To** 2024 $38

Garten Series Cabernet Sauvignon 2013 Standard Rosenthal vinification/oak maturation (18 months French oak, 30% new). Impressive depth to its crimson-purple colour; blackcurrant, bay leaf, dark chocolate and a touch of plum march across the medium to full-bodied palate. An unbeatable proposition for cellaring. Screwcap. 14.5% alc. **Rating** 94 **To** 2033 $22 ✪

ŢŢŢŢŢ **The Marker Southern Forest Shiraz 2013 Rating** 93 **To** 2025 $28
Garten Series Merlot 2013 Rating 92 **To** 2028 $22 ✪

Rosenvale Wines ★★★★☆

467 Research Road, Nuriootpa, SA 5355 **Region** Barossa Valley
T 0407 390 788 **www.**rosenvale.com.au **Open** By appt
Winemaker James Rosenzweig, Philip Leggett **Est.** 1999 **Dozens** 3000 **Vyds** 105ha
The Rosenzweig family vineyards, some old and some new, are planted to riesling, semillon, chardonnay, grenache, shiraz, merlot and cabernet sauvignon. Most of the grapes are sold to other producers, but some are retained and vinified for release under the Rosenvale label.

ŢŢŢŢŢ **Old Vines Reserve Barossa Valley Semillon 2014** From vines planted in '40, fully barrel-fermented in used oak, with no overlay on the clear-cut varietal character; this comes at the top of the tree for this style of Barossa Valley Semillon, leaving the most attractive herb and lemon fruit to strut its stuff. Screwcap. 12.5% alc. **Rating** 95 **To** 2029 $39

Barossa Rose 2014 Rosenvale planted tinto cao, tinta molle and graciano specifically to make rose; picked and fermented together once pressed. Bright pink, with a flowery bouquet. The red berry-filled palate has a real sense of style, long and dry, yet supple and fruity. Screwcap. 12.5% alc. **Rating** 94 **To** 2017 $24 ✪

Old Vines Reserve Cabernet Sauvignon 2012 Matured for 2 years in French oak. This wine breaks the rules: the cabernet expression hasn't been compromised by the alcohol; it certainly is ripe, with some Ribena notes, but the tannins and oak both work well in taming the tiger. Diam. 15% alc. **Rating** 94 **To** 2032 $39

ŢŢŢŢŢ **Estate Barossa Shiraz 2013 Rating** 91 **To** 2028 $24

Rosily Vineyard

871 Yelverton Road, Wilyabrup, WA 6284 **Region** Margaret River
T (08) 9755 6336 **www**.rosily.com.au **Open** 7 days Dec–Jan 11–5
Winemaker Mike Lemmes, Mike Scott **Est.** 1994 **Dozens** 5500 **Vyds** 12.28ha
The partnership of Mike and Barb Scott and Ken and Dot Allan acquired the Rosily Vineyard site in 1994, and the vineyard was planted over three years to sauvignon blanc, semillon, chardonnay, cabernet sauvignon, merlot, shiraz, grenache and cabernet franc. The first crops were sold to other makers in the region, but by '99 Rosily had built a 120-tonne capacity winery. It has gone from strength to strength, all of its estate-grown grapes being vinified under the Rosily Vineyard label, substantially over-delivering for their prices. Exports to China.

ŸŸŸŸŸ **Margaret River Sauvignon Blanc 2014** From the Wilyabrup district, a good start, the promise fulfilled by a full suite of lemongrass, herb and gooseberry flavours, augmented by a touch of oak that fits like a glove. Screwcap. 13% alc. **Rating** 94 **To** 2017 $19 ✪
Other Side of the Moon 2011 Estate-grown and made, this 75/25% grenache shiraz blend is (surprisingly) Rosily's second label. It spent 16 months in French oak (25% new), and the crimson hue is star-bright; the bouquet and palate continue the surprise with delicious cherry and raspberry fruit supported by a trio of acidity, fine tannins and integrated oak. Exceptional, unexpected bargain. Screwcap. 14% alc. **Rating** 94 **To** 2021 $17 ✪
Margaret River Cabernet Sauvignon 2012 Estate-grown; matured for 16 months in French oak (40% new). An elegant Margaret River Cabernet with bell-clear varietal expression on its bouquet and supple palate; cassis and savoury black olive components create positive tension and complexity, cedary oak the peacekeeper. 630 dozen made. Screwcap. 14% alc. **Rating** 94 **To** 2025 $25 ✪
The Cartographer 2010 49/27/21/3% cabernet sauvignon, cabernet franc, merlot and petit verdot. Distinctly savoury, but none the worse for that, because the mouthfeel and balance are very good, and there are plum, cassis and black cherry fruits within the carapace provided by earthy tannins and French oak. 650 dozen made. Screwcap. 14% alc. **Rating** 94 **To** 2025 $23 ✪

ŸŸŸŸŸ **Margaret River Semillon 2014** **Rating** 93 **To** 2018 $19 ✪
Margaret River Semillon Sauvignon Blanc 2014 **Rating** 93 **To** 2017 $20 ✪
Margaret River Shiraz 2009 **Rating** 93 **To** 2019 $23 ✪

Ross Hill Wines

134 Wallace Lane, Orange, NSW 2800 **Region** Orange
T (02) 6365 3223 **www**.rosshillwines.com.au **Open** 7 days 10.30–5
Winemaker Phil Kerney **Est.** 1994 **Dozens** 25 000 **Vyds** 18.2ha
Peter and Terri Robson planted chardonnay, merlot, sauvignon blanc, cabernet franc, shiraz and pinot noir on north-facing slopes of the Griffen Road vineyard in 1994. In 2007, their son James and his wife Chrissy joined the business, and the Wallace Lane vineyard (pinot noir, sauvignon blanc and pinot gris) was planted next to the fruit packing shed which is now the winery. No insecticides are used in the vineyard, the grapes are hand-picked and the vines are hand-pruned. With the Wallace Lane vineyard now in full bearing, production has increased from 15 000 to 25 000 dozen. Exports to Singapore, Bali, Hong Kong and China.

ŸŸŸŸŸ **Pinnacle Series Orange Sauvignon Blanc 2014** Whole bunch-pressed, wild yeast-fermented. Quartz-green hue; this is Orange Sauvignon Blanc at its best, with vibrant fruit and chalky acidity on the finish; the mid-palate has tropical fruits and a squeeze of lemon to tone down the more flamboyant flavours, making it more food-friendly. Screwcap. 12.6% alc. **Rating** 95 **To** 2016 $30 ✪
Pinnacle Series Orange Cabernet Sauvignon 2013 Hand-picked, wild yeast open-fermented, matured in French barriques for 18 months. A lively wine with a strong minty undertone to the cassis fruit; the tannins are fine and balanced, the oak evident, but not too assertive; the overall balance and length get it over the line. Screwcap. 14.5% alc. **Rating** 95 **To** 2028 $40

Tom & Harry Orange Cabernet Sauvignon 2012 Bright, clear crimson; there is clear-cut varietal fruit expression on the bouquet and palate, cassis to the fore, with cabernet tannins on the finish, which have softened and integrated markedly over the 12 months since the wine was first tasted. Trophy Orange Wine Show '14 a justified award. Screwcap. 13.5% alc. **Rating** 95 **To** 2027 $25 ○

Pinnacle Series Orange Chardonnay 2014 Hand-picked, whole bunch-pressed, wild yeast-fermented and matured in French oak. A particularly fine, elegant, tightly structured and focused Chardonnay that has entirely absorbed the oak; it has a long and lively finish. Screwcap. 13% alc. **Rating** 94 **To** 2025 $35

Pinnacle Series Orange Chardonnay 2013 Whole bunch-pressed direct to French oak for wild yeast fermentation. Intense and complex, with an array of aromas and flavours spanning the full gamut of citrus and stone fruit, and a few exotic touches, including fresh ginger, and honey on the finish – or is there a subliminal touch of sweetness? Screwcap. 12.5% alc. **Rating** 94 **To** 2023 $35

Pinnacle Series Orange Pinot Gris 2014 Hand-picked, whole bunch-pressed, wild yeast-fermented. Has more grip and presence than the majority of Pinot Gris, nashi pear and apricot kernel aromas and flavours, the palate long, the finish lingering. Screwcap. 13.2% alc. **Rating** 94 **To** 2017 $30 ○

Pinnacle Series Orange Shiraz 2013 Wild yeast open-fermented, matured in French barriques for 18 months. Clear, bright colour; the medium-bodied palate is very savoury, spicy and peppery, emphatically underlining its cool-grown origin. A love it or leave it style. Screwcap. 14.5% alc. **Rating** 94 **To** 2028 $40

Pinnacle Series Orange Cabernet Franc 2013 Hand-picked, wild yeast-fermented, matured in French oak for 18 months. The bouquet is fragrant, clearly detailing its mix of tobacco leaf and red fruits, the palate with the same dichotomy, tobacco/savoury elements with their noses in front of the red fruits, but only just. Screwcap. 14.5% alc. **Rating** 94 **To** 2023 $40

Route du Van ★★★★

PO Box 1465, Warrnambool, Vic 3280 **Region** Various Vic
T (03) 5561 7422 **www**.routeduvan.com **Open** Not
Winemaker Tod Dexter **Est.** 2010 **Dozens** 8000
The Dexter (Tod and Debbie) and Bird (Ian and Ruth, David and Marie) families have been making or selling wine for 30 years. They were holidaying in the picturesque vineyards and ancient Bastide villages of southwest France when they decided to do something new that was all about fun: fun for them, and fun for the consumers who bought their wines, which would have a distinctive southern French feel to them. The prices are also friendly, at $15–20 a bottle, bistros one of the target markets. The business is obviously enjoying great success, production up from 3500 dozen to its present level off the back of expanded export markets. Exports to the UK, the US, Norway, Sweden and Poland.

Yarra Valley Sauvignon Blanc Semillon 2013 A 72/24% blend, with 4% vermentino; fermented in stainless steel and barrel. Has obvious complexity, citrussy acidity giving a sure-footed foundation for this flavour depth, the accent as much savoury as fruity. Screwcap. 12% alc. **Rating** 93 **To** 2016 $20 ○

Yarra Valley Pinot Noir 2013 Part machine, part hand (for whole bunches) picked; part cold-soaked prior to fermentation. Light, but bright colour, with a fragrant red fruit bouquet and a light to medium-bodied palate. A pretty Pinot, ready when you are. Screwcap. 13% alc. **Rating** 91 **To** 2020 $20 ○

Heathcote Shiraz 2013 Destemmed into open and rotary fermenters with a portion of whole berries; 14 days on skins, then 35% in used oak for 6 months, the remainder held in stainless steel. A full-bodied Heathcote style, replete with blackberry and plum fruit; the stainless steel has retained freshness, but the tannins need to mellow over the next few years – and they will do just that if given the chance. Screwcap. 13.9% alc. **Rating** 91 **To** 2028 $20 ○

Yarra Valley Chardonnay 2012 Rating 89 **To** 2016 $20
Street Art White 2013 Rating 88 **To** 2016 $15 ○
Street Art Red 2013 Rating 88 **To** 2016 $15 ○

Rowanston on the Track

2710 Burke & Wills Track, Glenhope, Vic 3444 **Region** Macedon Ranges
T (03) 5425 5492 **www**.rowanston.com **Open** 7 days 10–5
Winemaker Laura Sparrow, John Frederiksen **Est.** 2003 **Dozens** 5000 **Vyds** 9.3ha
John and Marilyn Frederiksen are no strangers to grapegrowing and winemaking in the
Macedon Ranges. They founded Metcalfe Valley Vineyard in 1995, planting 5.6ha of shiraz
and going on to win gold medals at local wine shows. They sold the vineyard in early 2003
and moved to their new property, which now has over 9ha of vines (shiraz, riesling, sauvignon
blanc, merlot and pinot noir). The heavy red soils and basalt ridges hold moisture, which
allows watering to be kept to a minimum. Rowanston has joined the Wine Export Initiative
(WEXI), a co-operative of 36 small wineries across Australia that has recently opened two
retail outlets in Singapore. Exports to Hong Kong, Singapore and China.

ΨΨΨΨΨ **Macedon Ranges Shiraz 2012** Has retained good colour; the bouquet is
   particularly complex, with nuances of spice and coffee to the blood plum aromas,
   raspberry and blackberry joining in on the palate; fine-grained tannins complete
   the picture of a fine, cool-climate Shiraz that may surprise with its longevity.
   Screwcap. 14.1% alc. **Rating** 94 **To** 2032 $25 ✪

ΨΨΨΨΨ **Macedon Ranges Riesling 2014 Rating** 91 **To** 2025 $20 ✪

Rowlee Wines

19 Lake Canobolas Road, Orange, NSW 2800 **Region** Orange
T 0438 059 108 **www**.rowleewines.com.au **Open** By appt
Winemaker PJ Charteris (Consultant) **Est.** 2000 **Dozens** 1600 **Vyds** 7.8ha
Rowlee first evolved as a grazing property of 2000 acres in the 1850s. It is now 80 acres, but
still with the original homestead built circa 1880. The property has retired from its grazing
days and is now home to 20 acres of vineyards first planted in 2000 by the Samodol family.
Varieties include pinot noir, pinot gris, nebbiolo, arneis, chardonnay, riesling and sauvignon
blanc. The Rowlee Vineyard is situated on the sloping northerly aspect of an extinct volcano,
Mount Canobolas, and at 920m is rich in basalt soils. The site's aspect and airflow have the
potential to provide high-quality fruit. With single-vineyard wine production, commercial
quantities first commenced in 2013, in partnership with viticulturist Tim Esson and family.

ΨΨΨΨΨ **Orange Chardonnay 2013** A particularly well made wine, hand-picked, wild
   yeast-fermented, 50% mlf, and 8 months in French oak (15% new). The balance
   between the bright white peach and citrus fruit, oak and zesty acidity could
   not be improved on, the 50% mlf a bold throw, but totally successful. Screwcap.
   13% alc. **Rating** 94 **To** 2018 $35
   Orange Pinot Noir 2013 Grown at 900m; 10% whole bunches in the ferment.
   An impressively generous Pinot, yet doesn't go over the top; plum fruit has both
   dimension and length, and will sustain the wine as it develops spicy secondary
   characters over the years. Screwcap. 13.5% alc. **Rating** 94 **To** 2023 $35

Rudderless

Victory Hotel, Main South Road, Sellicks Beach, SA 5174 **Region** McLaren Vale
T (08) 8556 3083 **www**.victoryhotel.com.au **Open** 7 days
Winemaker Pete Fraser (Contract) **Est.** 2004 **Dozens** 450 **Vyds** 2ha
It's a long story how Doug Govan, owner of the Victory Hotel (circa 1858), came to choose
the name Rudderless for his vineyard. The vineyard, divided among shiraz, graciano, grenache,
malbec, mataro and viognier, surrounds the hotel, which is situated in the foothills of the
Southern Willunga Escarpment as it falls into the sea. The wines are mostly sold through the
Victory Hotel, where the laid-back Doug Govan keeps a low profile.

ΨΨΨΨΨ **Sellicks Hill McLaren Vale Graciano Malbec 2012** The vivid purple-crimson
   colour heralds a wine with astonishing depth to its luscious black fruits, anything

but rudderless: it's akin to a melody that is replayed again and again in the brain. Screwcap. 14% alc. **Rating** 96 **To** 2032 $35 ❍

Sellicks Hill McLaren Vale Grenache 2012 Brightly coloured, this is the epitome of McLaren Vale Grenache, with its fresh cornucopia of bright red fruits and firm finish that has no need of structural assistance from shiraz, and has no confection fruit. Screwcap. 14.5% alc. **Rating** 95 **To** 2025 $35 ❍

Sellicks Hill McLaren Vale Mataro 2012 Has good colour, and a savoury/ spicy web spun around red fruits on the palate, superfine tannins throwing their lot in with the web; then the chameleon strikes as the last taste has burst through the web shouting about its fruit. Screwcap. 14% alc. **Rating** 95 **To** 2027 $35 ❍

Rumbalara

137 Fletcher Road, Fletcher, Qld 4381 **Region** Granite Belt
T (07) 4684 1206 www.rumbalarawines.com.au **Open** 7 days 10–5
Winemaker Stephen Oliver **Est.** 1974 **Dozens** 3000 **Vyds** 3.25ha
The property now known as Rumbalara was first surveyed before 1908. Part of the land occupied by early owners was a mining lease containing a silver-bearing quartz intrusion discovered during the construction of the railway linking Brisbane and Sydney. The land was originally used as an orchard, with the first grapes planted in '28. Bob and Una Gray purchased the property in '74 and planted and grafted (onto existing rootstock) classic wine grape varieties including semillon and cabernet sauvignon. Rumbalara was purchased by Mike and Bobbi Cragg in 2002, Mike making the wines until '11.

ΨΨΨΨΨ **Merlot 2013** 'Barrel aged' is the cryptic information; well, what oak and for how long doesn't matter, for it's all come out well, with bright red fruits on the light to medium-bodied palate, and a gently savoury twist on the finish. Well priced. Screwcap. 13% alc. **Rating** 92 **To** 2018 $20 ❍

ΨΨΨΨ **Cabernet Sauvignon 2013 Rating** 88 **To** 2017 $20

🍂 Running Horse Wines

1133 Milbrodale Road, Broke, NSW 2330 (postal) **Region** Hunter Valley
T 0474 156 786 www.runninghorsewines.com.au **Open** Not
Winemaker Nick Patterson **Est.** 2000 **Dozens** 500 **Vyds** 7ha
David Fromberg, the founding owner of Running Horse Wines, completed his jockey's apprenticeship in 1997, weight issues ending that career, but leading to Running Horse Wines. (I know at least two jockeys who had successful professional careers before turning to professional wine life, both very successful, both good friends.) The first plantings were in 2000 (5ha), with another 2ha of shiraz planted in '01, taking the total of that variety to 5.5ha. When the cellar door opens later this year, there will be six vintages of Shiraz, two of Semillon, and a number of other wines with one or more vintages on sale.

ΨΨΨΨ **Classic Aged Hunter Valley Shiraz 2006** The impact of 30% new and 30% 1yo French oak (the remainder older) is too obvious, even after 8 years. Definitely a wine for oak lovers, for there is some fruit under the oak overcoat. Screwcap. 14% alc. **Rating** 88 **To** 2021 $25

Rusty Mutt

26 Columbia Avenue, Clapham, SA 5062 (postal) **Region** McLaren Vale
T 0402 050 820 www.rustymutt.com.au **Open** Not
Winemaker Scott Heidrich **Est.** 2009 **Dozens** 800
Scott Heidrich has lived under the shadow of Geoff Merrill for 20 years, but has partially emerged into the sunlight with his virtual micro-winery. Back in 2006 close friends and family (Nicole and Alan Francis, Stuart Evans, David Lipman and Phil Cole) persuaded Scott to take advantage of the wonderful quality of the grapes that year and make a small batch of Shiraz. The wines are made at a friend's micro-winery in McLaren Flat. The name Rusty Mutt comes from Scott's interest in Chinese astrology, and feng shui; Scott was born in the year of the dog, with the dominant element being metal, hence Rusty Mutt. What the ownership

group doesn't drink is sold through fine wine retailers and selected restaurants, with a small amount exported to the UK, Singapore and China.

🍷🍷🍷🍷 Shiraz 2012 The Confucian stars are in alignment with this wine, place, variety and vintage all working maximum magic, yet each leaving airspace so that elegance comes to the fore. It's a fair guess the bottle will be empty long before you realise what has happened. Screwcap. 14.5% alc. **Rating** 96 **To** 2027 $28 ☺

🍷🍷🍷 Catnip 2014 **Rating** 89 **To** 2015 $24

Rutherglen Estates ★★★★

Cnr Great Northern Road/Murray Valley Highway, Rutherglen, Vic 3685
Region Rutherglen
T (02) 6032 7999 **www**.rutherglenestates.com.au **Open** At Tuileries Complex, Rutherglen 7 days 10–5.30
Winemaker Marc Scalzo **Est.** 1997 **Dozens** 10 000 **Vyds** 26.5ha
Rutherglen Estates is one of the larger growers in the region. The focus of the business has changed by reducing its own fruit intake while maintaining its contract processing. Production has turned to table wine made from parcels of fruit hand-selected from five Rutherglen vineyard sites. Rhône and Mediterranean varieties such as durif, viognier, shiraz and sangiovese are a move away from traditional varieties, as are alternative varieties including zinfandel, fiano and savagnin. Exports to the UK, the US, Canada, Thailand and China.

🍷🍷🍷🍷 Single Vineyard Fiano 2013 Barrel-fermented in French oak; small wonder Rutherglen Estates is pleased with the result, and the potential for the variety; it has a core of citrus surrounded by nutty dried herb nuances, giving both flavour and textural complexity. Screwcap. 12.5% alc. **Rating** 94 **To** 2020 $24 ☺

🍷🍷🍷🍷 Single Vineyard Sangiovese 2013 **Rating** 91 **To** 2017 $22 CM ☺
Single Vineyard Viognier 2013 **Rating** 90 **To** 2015 $22 CM
Viognier Roussanne Marsanne 2013 **Rating** 90 **To** 2016 $32 CM
Red Shiraz Durif 2013 **Rating** 90 **To** 2020 $15 ☺
Single Vineyard Durif 2013 **Rating** 90 **To** 2021 $24 CM

Rymill Coonawarra ★★★★☆

Riddoch Highway, Coonawarra, SA 5263 **Region** Coonawarra
T (08) 8736 5001 **www**.rymill.com.au **Open** 7 days 10–5
Winemaker Sandrine Gimon **Est.** 1974 **Dozens** 35 000 **Vyds** 144ha
The Rymills are descendants of John Riddoch and have long owned some of the finest Coonawarra soil, upon which they have grown grapes since 1970. The promotion of Champagne-trained Sandrine Gimon to chief winemaker (after three years as winemaker at Rymill) is interesting. Sandrine is a European version of a Flying Winemaker, having managed a winery in Bordeaux, and made wine in Champagne, Languedoc, Romania and WA. Sandrine became an Australian citizen in 2011. The winery building also houses the cellar door and art exhibitions, which, together with viewing platforms of the winery, make it a must-see destination for tourists. Exports to all major markets.

🍷🍷🍷🍷 Cabernet Sauvignon 2012 Estate-grown, and spent 12 months in French oak. A powerful but pure evocation of the variety that Coonawarra should be providing more frequently than it does; firm blackcurrant fruit is framed by equally firm tannins and cedary oak; its balance assures its development in bottle over many years to come. Diam. 14% alc. **Rating** 95 **To** 2037 $33 ☺

🍷🍷🍷🍷 The Dark Horse Cabernet Sauvignon 2013 **Rating** 92 **To** 2025 $24 ☺
The Yearling Cabernet Sauvignon 2013 **Rating** 92 **To** 2018 $16 ☺
The Yearling Sauvignon Blanc 2014 **Rating** 90 **To** 2015 $16 ☺

Saddler's Creek ★★★★☆

Marrowbone Road, Pokolbin, NSW 2320 **Region** Hunter Valley
T (02) 4991 1770 **www.**saddlerscreek.com **Open** 7 days 10–5
Winemaker Brett Woodward **Est.** 1989 **Dozens** 6000 **Vyds** 10ha
Saddler's Creek is a boutique winery that is little known outside of the Hunter Valley but has built a loyal following of dedicated supporters. It came onto the scene over 25 years ago with some rich, bold wines, and maintains this style today. Fruit is sourced from the Hunter Valley and Langhorne Creek, with occasional forays into McLaren Vale, Wrattonbully and other premium fruit-growing regions. Exports to the Cook Islands.

🍷🍷🍷🍷🍷 **Ryan's Reserve Semillon 2014** Ryan is the former long-serving Mount Pleasant winemaker Phil Ryan. The intensity of the '11 vintage shines through, as do the intense layers of citrus fruit, here reaching into the far realms of grapefruit; the finish is long and fresh, characters the wine will have for many years ahead. Screwcap. 11% alc. **Rating** 95 **To** 2034 $32 ○

Reserve Riesling 2014 Aromas of steel wool introduce a wine of considerable intensity and structure, the flavours of lime, apple and lemon all precisely lined up on a palate promising much for the future. Screwcap. 11.5% alc. **Rating** 94 **To** 2034 $32

Classic Hunter Semillon 2014 Its name is appropriate enough, although there's no common usage as such; lemongrass, lemon drops – you name it. There is also the essential shaft of pure acidity. Screwcap. 11% alc. **Rating** 94 **To** 2029 $26 ○

Saddler's Shiraz Viognier 2013 A brightly coloured blend, 5% viognier seemingly co-fermented. High-toned flavours of blackcurrant and blackberry are given structure by the fruit itself and by a coupling of tannins and oak. Screwcap. 13.9% alc. **Rating** 94 **To** 2033 $36

Bluegrass Langhorne Creek Cabernet Sauvignon 2013 A rich wine in every way. The deep colour, the cassis fruit, soft tannins and chewy oak all come together on the palate. A good example of the Baroque style, as Wolf Blass discovered 40+ years ago. Screwcap. 13.5% alc. **Rating** 94 **To** 2038 $38

Reserve Langhorne Cabernet 2012 A lively, fresh and clearly varietal wine that has used some sort of pea and thimble trick to keep attention away from maturation in American barriques for 22 months. The cassis fruit has good cabernet tannins, and is guaranteed a long life. 200 dozen made. Screwcap. 14.5% alc. **Rating** 94 **To** 2032 $65

Ryan's Reserve Cabernet Shiraz 2013 Lighter colour than Bluegrass The Blend, but is far more focused, elegant and long; selection of oak has been one of the factors involved, fruit quality another; there are juicy streams of blackcurrant and blackberry, held neatly in check by fine tannins. Screwcap. 14.5% alc. **Rating** 94 **To** 2030 $48

🍷🍷🍷🍷🍷 **Reserve Semillon 2010** Rating 92 **To** 2020 $32
Botrytis Supreme 2013 Rating 92 **To** 2015 $36
Ryan's Reserve Stephanie's Vineyard Chardonnay 2014 Rating 90 **To** 2017 $36

St Anne's Vineyards ★★★☆

64 Garrards Road, Myrniong, Vic 3341 **Region** Perricoota
T (03) 5480 0099 **www.**stanneswinery.com.au **Open** 7 days 9–5
Winemaker Richard McLean **Est.** 1972 **Dozens** 80 000 **Vyds** 182ha
The McLean family has a multi-pronged grapegrowing and winemaking business, with 182ha of vines on the Murray River. All of the mainstream varieties are grown, the lion's share to chardonnay, shiraz, cabernet sauvignon and merlot, with lesser quantities of semillon, sauvignon blanc, durif and petit verdot. There is also a very small planting at Myrniong in the Pentland Hills, a 50-minute drive from the heart of Melbourne, where the main cellar door is situated. There are three other cellar doors: Moama (Cnr 24 Lane and Perricoota Road), Lorne (150 Mount Joy Parade) and Echuca (53 Murray Esplanade). Exports to China.

ΫΫΫΫΫ **Heathcote Shiraz 2013** Beefy, extractive style with peppercorn, musky vanillan and blackberry flavour in abundance. Tannin pulls the wine slightly out of whack but served alongside steak it would come into its own. Screwcap. 14% alc. **Rating** 90 **To** 2026 $28 CM

ΫΫΫΫ **Chardonnay 2013 Rating** 88 **To** 2016 $16 CM ✪
Liqueur Muscat NV Rating 88 **To** 2015 $28 CM

St Hallett   ★★★★★

St Hallett Road, Tanunda, SA 5352 **Region** Barossa
T (08) 8563 7000 **www**.sthallett.com.au **Open** 7 days 10–5
Winemaker Stuart Blackwell, Toby Barlow, Shelley Cox **Est.** 1944 **Dozens** 210 000
St Hallett sources all grapes from within the Barossa GI, and is synonymous with the region's icon variety, shiraz. Old Block is the ultra-premium leader of the band (using old-vine grapes from Lyndoch and Eden Valley), supported by Blackwell (Greenock, Ebenezer and Seppeltsfield). Stuart Blackwell and Toby Barlow continue to explore the geographical, geological and climatic diversity of the Barossa, manifested through individual processing of all vineyards and single-vineyard releases. Exports to all major markets.

ΫΫΫΫΫ **Old Block Barossa Shiraz 2012** The average age of the vines is 88 years, and are both Barossa Valley and Eden Valley; standard static fermentation approach with pump-overs, but varied for each parcel, matured in a mix of new and used French oak. The colour is perfect, the medium-bodied palate exquisitely balanced and proportioned, red and black fruits both on parade; it has an almost airy grace to the way it moves along the palate to a lingering finish. WAK screwcap. 13.8% alc. **Rating** 98 **To** 2047 $100 ✪
Single Vineyard Release Mattschoss Eden Valley Shiraz 2013 Standard fermentation, matured for 10 months in French oak (13% new, 40% 1yo, 47% 2–3yo). There is an instantaneous recognition of the Eden Valley on the palate, the fruit profile with a luminous polish and a freshness. It's deceptive, for it has great drive and purity, poetry in motion. Screwcap. 13.5% alc. **Rating** 97 **To** 2038 $50 ✪

ΫΫΫΫΫ **Single Vineyard Release Materne Barossa Valley Shiraz 2013** Matured for 9 months in French hogsheads (30% new). The interplay between these single-vineyard wines is ever-fascinating, particularly given the relatively narrow parameters of the handling of the fruit in the winery. The juicy red fruits could make you think this lovely wine is from the Eden Valley. WAK screwcap. 14.5% alc. **Rating** 96 **To** 2038 $50 ✪
Garden of Eden Barossa Shiraz 2013 Various parcels separately fermented for 10 days, matured in French oak. It has a brighter and finer fruit spectrum, along with spice and pepper, which sets it apart from most of its Barossa Valley cohort. How much is due to the chemical composition or its Eden Valley origins is an academic exercise, the easy answer to say a bit of each, easier still to taste the four St Hallett individual vineyard wines. Screwcap. 13.5% alc. **Rating** 95 **To** 2033 $25 ✪
Single Vineyard Release Dawkins Eden Valley Shiraz 2013 9-day fermentation, matured for 8 months in French oak (20% new). The fragrance of the bouquet changes gear on the palate into a deep well of dark fruits, licorice and spice, with ample tannins providing a firm structure. The decision to only use 20% new oak was right on the money, as was the slightly shorter maturation time. Screwcap. 14% alc. **Rating** 95 **To** 2043 $50
Blackwell Barossa Shiraz 2013 Fermented for 6–8 days, matured for 18 months in new and used American oak, plus 6 months in bottle. Deep crimson-purple and full-bodied, sultry dark fruits guard the door, prised ajar on the finish by pleasingly edgy tannins and a twist of oak. Diam. 14.5% alc. **Rating** 95 **To** 2038 $38

Single Vineyard Release Scholz Estate Barossa Valley Shiraz 2013
Matured for 11 months in American oak (25% new). The American oak is magnetically drawn to (or by) blackberry, plum and earthy fruit. WAK screwcap. 14.5% alc. **Rating** 95 **To** 2038 $50
Faith Barossa Shiraz 2013 Rating 94 **To** 2022 $19 CM ❂
The Reward Barossa Cabernet Sauvignon 2012 Rating 94 **To** 2027 $30 ❂
Barossa Mataro 2013 Rating 94 **To** 2030 $25 ❂
Barossa Touriga Nacional 2013 Rating 94 **To** 2023 $25 ❂

St Huberts ★★★★★

Cnr Maroondah Highway/St Huberts Road, Coldstream, Vic 3770 **Region** Yarra Valley
T (03) 5960 7096 www.sthuberts.com.au **Open** 7 days 10–5
Winemaker Greg Jarratt **Est.** 1966 **Dozens** NFP **Vyds** 20.49ha
The St Huberts of today has a rich 19th century history, not least in its success at the 1881 Melbourne International Exhibition, which featured every type of agricultural and industrial product. The wine section alone attracted 711 entries. The Emperor of Germany offered a Grand Prize, a silver gilt epergne, for the most meritorious exhibit in the show. A St Huberts wine won the wine section, then competed against objects as diverse as felt hats and steam engines to wine the Emperor's Prize, featured on its label for decades thereafter. Like other Yarra Valley wineries, it dropped from sight at the start of the 20th century, was reborn in 1966, and after several changes of ownership, became part of what today is TWE. The wines are made at Coldstream Hills, but have their own, very different, focus. Whereas Coldstream Hills is driven by Chardonnay and Pinot Noir, St Huberts is dominated by Cabernet and the single-vineyard Roussanne. Its grapes come from warmer sites, particularly the valley floor, and are part owned and part under contract. Coldstream Hills' vines are on hillside slopes, with significant amounts coming from the estate vineyards in the Upper Yarra Valley. Oak use, too is different, albeit 100% French. Chardonnay and Viognier are also made, but are peripheral to the main business.

🍷🍷🍷🍷🍷 **Yarra Valley Cabernet Sauvignon 2013** Deep colour; a high-quality Cabernet with exemplary varietal character from the first whiff through to the finish and aftertaste; blackcurrant fruit is at the core of the wine, complexed by 16 months in French barriques (30% new) and fine, ripe cabernet tannins on the long finish. Screwcap. 13% alc. **Rating** 96 **To** 2035 $35 ❂
Yarra Valley Roussanne 2014 Hand-picked, whole bunch-pressed and fermented in new and used French oak. The tightly packed aromas and citrus/pear flavours underline the capacity roussanne has when grown in the Yarra Valley to develop slowly and gracefully over many years, the small yield adding to that potential. Screwcap. 14% alc. **Rating** 95 **To** 2027 $30 ❂
Yarra Valley Chardonnay 2013 No skimping on the volume of flavour. Has an opulence to it. Sweet, ripe peach, citrus, toast and struck match notes. Not without clear signs of oak, but the fruit is bell clear, refreshingly so, as it rings out through the finish. Will improve in the bottle over the next year or two. Screwcap. 13% alc. **Rating** 94 **To** 2020 $27 CM ❂

🍷🍷🍷🍷🍸 **Yarra Valley Late Harvest Viognier 2014 Rating** 91 **To** 2018 $30 CM

St John's Road ★★★★☆

Kapunda–Truro Road, St Kitts, SA, 5356 **Region** Barossa Valley
T (08) 8362 8622 www.stjohnsroad.com **Open** Not
Winemaker Phil Lehmann **Est.** 2002 **Dozens** 20 000 **Vyds** 20ha
St John's Road is now part of WD Wines Pty Ltd, which also owns Hesketh Wine Company and Parker Coonawarra Estate. After drifting for a while following the death of founder Martin Rawlinson, St John's Road is now back in the game, the vineyards increased to 20ha, production and quality also rising. Exports to the UK, Canada and Europe.

🍷🍷🍷🍷🍷 **Peace of Eden Riesling 2014** While cold-settling of free-run juice followed by a cool ferment in stainless steel is standard stuff, titratable acidity of 7.6g/l set against 5.4g/l of residual sugar isn't common in temperate regions such as the Eden Valley. Pale, gleaming green-straw; miraculously, the acidity is more than balanced by luscious Bickford's lime juice flavours. Classic drink now or later. Screwcap. 12% alc. **Rating** 95 **To** 2029 $22 ✪

🍷🍷🍷🍷🍷 **Blood & Courage Barossa Shiraz 2013 Rating** 93 **To** 2028 $22 ✪
Workhorse Shiraz Cabernet 2013 Rating 93 **To** 2027 $22 ✪
Motley Bunch GSM 2013 Rating 92 **To** 2021 $22 CM ✪

St Leonards Vineyard ★★★☆

St Leonards Road, Wahgunyah, Vic 3687 **Region** Rutherglen
T 1800 021 621 **www**.stleonardswine.com.au **Open** Thurs–Mon 10–5
Winemaker Dan Crane, Nick Brown **Est.** 1860 **Dozens** 10 000 **Vyds** 8ha
An old favourite, relaunched in late 1997 with a range of premium wines cleverly marketed through an attractive cellar door and bistro at the historic winery on the banks of the Murray. It is essentially a satellite operation of All Saints, under the same ownership and management. Exports to the UK and the US.

🍷🍷🍷🍷 **Shiraz 2012** Wild yeast-fermented for 2 weeks, pressed in a 120yo press, matured in used French barriques. Has an unexpected swish of spice, possibly ex the oak, but not obviously so; the medium-bodied palate is well balanced and structured, the wine ready now, but will hold. Screwcap. 14% alc. **Rating** 89 **To** 2018 $27

Saint Regis ★★★★

35 Waurn Ponds Drive, Waurn Ponds, Vic 3216 **Region** Geelong
T (03) 5241 8406 **www**.saintregis.com.au **Open** 7 days 11–5
Winemaker Peter Nicol **Est.** 1997 **Dozens** 500 **Vyds** 1ha
Saint Regis is a family-run boutique winery focusing on estate-grown shiraz, and locally sourced chardonnay and pinot noir. Each year the harvest is hand-picked by members of the family and friends, with Peter Nicol (assisted by wife Viv) the executive onsite winemaker. Peter, with a technical background in horticulture, is a self-taught winemaker, and has taught himself well, also making wines for others.

🍷🍷🍷🍷🍷 **White Wombat Chardonnay 2013** Bright straw-green; a tightly scripted Chardonnay, with controlled barrel-ferment inputs to the grapefruit and white peach fruit, thence to minerally acidity on the finish. Time is on its side. Screwcap. 13% alc. **Rating** 92 **To** 2020 $25 ✪
The Reg Shiraz 2013 Full crimson-purple; rich, deep, cool-grown style; blackberry, black cherry, licorice and tar all have their say. Given the alcohol, the slightly tart finish comes as a surprise. Screwcap. 14.8% alc. **Rating** 90 **To** 2023 $25

🍷🍷🍷🍷 **Wild Reserve Geelong Pinot Noir 2013 Rating** 88 **To** 2017 $25

Salitage ★★★★

14429 Vasse Highway, Pemberton, WA 6260 **Region** Pemberton
T (08) 9776 1771 **www**.salitage.com.au **Open** Fri–Tues 10–4
Winemaker Patrick Coutts **Est.** 1989 **Dozens** 10 000 **Vyds** 21.4ha
Owned and operated by John and Jenny Horgan, Salitage is a showpiece of Pemberton. John had worked and studied under the guidance of Robert Mondavi in California, and also acquired a share in the famous Burgundy winery, La Pousse d'Or (with other Aussie investors, all of whom have since sold out). Exports to Indonesia, Singapore, Taiwan, Japan and China.

🍷🍷🍷🍷🍷 **Unwooded Chardonnay 2013** An attractive unwooded take on the variety; the Pemberton climate allows the development of both grapefruit and white peach flavours at an appropriate level of alcohol and retention of acidity – and no hint of Sauvignon Blanc characters. Screwcap. 13.5% alc. **Rating** 91 **To** 2016 $20 ✪
Chardonnay 2013 There is what I assume to be a deliberate touch of funky reduction on the bouquet, amplified by the underlying grapefruit nuances of both

that bouquet and palate; the finish, too, is likely to polarise opinions: is it, or is it not, bitter? Screwcap. 13.5% alc. **Rating** 90 **To** 2020 $35

Salomon Estate ★★★★★

17 High Street, Willunga, SA 5171 **Region** Southern Fleurieu
T 0412 442 228 **www**.salomonwines.com **Open** Not
Winemaker Bert Salomon, Mike Farmilo **Est.** 1997 **Dozens** 6500 **Vyds** 12.1ha
Bert Salomon is an Austrian winemaker with a long-established family winery in the Kremstal region, not far from Vienna. He became acquainted with Australia during his time with import company Schlumberger in Vienna; he was the first to import Australian wines (Penfolds) into Austria, in the mid-1980s, and later became head of the Austrian Wine Bureau. He was so taken by Adelaide that he moved his family there for the first few months each year, sending his young children to school and setting in place an Australian red winemaking venture. He retired from the Bureau and is now a full-time travelling winemaker, running the family winery in the northern hemisphere vintage, and overseeing the making of the Salomon Estate wines at Chapel Hill. Salomon Estate now shares a cellar door with Hither & Yon, just a few steps away from the Saturday farmers' market in Willunga. Exports to the UK, the US, and other major markets.

99999 **Alttus Shiraz 2009** Excellent retention of colour; savoury, earthy black fruits and notes of bitter chocolate are held in a tight embrace of quality oak and ripe tannins; a high-quality medium to full-bodied Shiraz with a long life ahead. Cork. 14.5% alc. **Rating** 96 **To** 2039 $110
Finniss River Shiraz 2012 The expressive bouquet of black fruits, earth, licorice and dark chocolate plays out to perfection on the medium-bodied palate, which has impeccable line, length and balance; the tannins and oak provide a fully integrated framework for the fruit. Cork. 14.5% alc. **Rating** 95 **To** 2032 $40
Fleurieu Peninsula Syrah V 2013 Shiraz was co-fermented with a small amount of viognier. This often results in some softening of the palate, but this wine retains power, concentration and texture, savoury tannins carrying the back-palate and finish to a long conclusion. Screwcap. 14.5% alc. **Rating** 94 **To** 2033 $30 ✪
The Verve Free Red 2013 Spent 42 days on skins before maturation in used oak for 12 months; lees and tannins were relied on until bottling, at which stage minimal SO$_2$ was added. It is plush, rich and decidedly powerful, black fruits, licorice and tannins to the fore until a bright finish provides freshness and balance. Shiraz/Mourvedre. Screwcap. 14.5% alc. **Rating** 94 **To** 2023 $32
Norwood Shiraz Cabernet 2013 Matured for 12 months in mostly used barriques. Has neatly tailored savoury black fruits, with nips of licorice, bitter chocolate and a touch of herb; the oak and tannins have both been well handled, and both contribute to the length and depth of the palate. Screwcap. 14.5% alc. **Rating** 94 **To** 2033 $25 ✪
Finniss River Cabernet Sauvignon 2012 A savoury edge to the blackcurrant fruit of the bouquet sets the scene for the medium-bodied palate, where fine-grained tannins also come into play, but in neither case throwing the wine out of balance, simply establishing its pleasantly earthy style, sure to welcome food. Cork. 14.5% alc. **Rating** 94 **To** 2027 $35

Saltram ★★★★★

Murray Street, Angaston, SA 5353 **Region** Barossa Valley
T (08) 8561 0200 **www**.saltramwines.com.au **Open** 7 days 10–5
Winemaker Shavaughn Wells, Richard Mattner **Est.** 1859 **Dozens** 150 000
There is no doubt that Saltram has taken strides towards regaining the reputation it held 30 or so years ago. Grape sourcing has come back to the Barossa Valley for the flagship wines. The red wines, in particular, have enjoyed great show success over the past decade, with No. 1 Shiraz and Mamre Brook leading the charge. Some of the brand management/label initiatives might lead some to lose sight of the quality of some of its best wines. Exports to all major markets.

ŸŸŸŸŸ Marble Quarry Barossa Valley Shiraz 2012 From a single vineyard on Marble Quarry Road in the Barossa. Matured in seasoned vats of unknown origin. It's a rich, ripe style but it's not overdone and it's no stranger to finesse. Saturated plum, peppercorn and blueberry fruit flavour with a dark, earthen character running beneath. Satiny texture and firm but integrated tannin; it is a beautifully tailored red wine. Screwcap. 14% alc. **Rating** 96 **To** 2032 $95 CM

No. 1 Barossa Shiraz 2010 Follows prior releases in maturing old-vine shiraz in a mix of French oak and smaller barrels. It has freakish colour, still a deep, vivid crimson-purple; black fruits of every description, licorice and polished leather illuminate the bouquet and palate, tannins adding to both the present and the long-term future of the wine. Screwcap. 14.5% alc. **Rating** 96 **To** 2045 $100

The Journal Barossa Valley Shiraz 2010 Broodier than a mother hen. Coal, damp earth, reduced blackberry and sweet boysenberry flavours sulk and seduce in equal measure. Grainy tannin moves slowly but inexorably through the mouth. Hurry? Not on your nelly. This has a long road ahead and it'll perform in its own sweet time. Screwcap. 14.5% alc. **Rating** 96 **To** 2040 $175 CM

Pepperjack Scotch Fillet Graded McLaren Vale Shiraz 2013 The firm hand of high-grade Australian shiraz. A steak wine par excellence. Rich blackberry and smoky oak, a wealth of savoury/grainy tannin, shoots of fennel and blackberry jam. For all its plain, black fruit flavour, the wine's strong, grainy tannin holds a commanding position in the wine, and should both a) see it team beautifully with char-grilled protein, and b) help ensure its longevity in the cellar. Screwcap. 14.5% alc. **Rating** 96 **To** 2035 $50 CM ✪

Mamre Brook Eden Valley Riesling 2014 The floral, citrus blossom bouquet promises much, and the palate does not disappoint; it has luscious lime and lemon juice flavours framed by crisp acidity on the long finish. Drink now or in a decade or more. Screwcap. 12% alc. **Rating** 95 **To** 2029 $23 ✪

Winemakers Selection Cabernet Sauvignon 2012 The Barossa Valley and cabernet don't always speak from the same page, but they do so here with a vengeance; the bouquet sets the scene with its precocious display of blackcurrant and violets, the juicy heart of the palate adding dark cherry before tightly controlled cabernet tannins complete the story. Screwcap. 14% alc. **Rating** 95 **To** 2042 $50

Mr Pickwick's Limited Release Particular Tawny NV Crushing intensity and length. Sour and nutty with slick, sweet, fresh toffee, dried fruits, rancio and coffee notes. Dances out through the finish. Irrepressible. Cork. 19.5% alc. **Rating** 95 **To** 2016 $75 CM

Mamre Brook Barossa Shiraz 2012 **Rating** 94 **To** 2037 $38
Mamre Brook Barossa Cabernet 2012 **Rating** 94 **To** 2026 $38 CM

ŸŸŸŸŸ Pepperjack Barossa Shiraz Cabernet 2013 **Rating** 93 **To** 2022 $30 CM
Limited Release Winemaker's Selection Semillon 2014 **Rating** 92 **To** 2019 $25 CM ✪
Pepperjack Barossa Shiraz 2013 **Rating** 92 **To** 2021 $30 CM
1859 Barossa Shiraz 2013 **Rating** 91 **To** 2020 $21 CM ✪

Sam Miranda of King Valley ★★★★☆

1019 Snow Road, Oxley, Vic 3678 **Region** King Valley
T (03) 5727 3888 **www.**sammiranda.com.au **Open** 7 days 10–5
Winemaker Sam Miranda **Est.** 2004 **Dozens** 20 000 **Vyds** 15ha
Sam Miranda, grandson of Francesco Miranda, joined the family business in 1991, striking out on his own in 2004 after Miranda Wines was purchased by McGuigan Simeon. The High Plains Vineyard is in the Upper King Valley at an altitude of 450m; estate plantings are supplemented by some purchased grapes. The cellar door and restaurant designed by leading Sydney architect Alex Popov provide both wine, and wine and food, opportunities. Exports to the UK and Fiji.

🍷🍷🍷🍷🍷 Estate Vineyard Sangiovese 2013 A selection of 8 rows were hand-picked and fermented in new 700l French oak rotating barrels, then 8 weeks on skins, pressed and fed back to the same barrels for 12 months' maturation. You might have expected the oak to overwhelm the fruit, but it doesn't; nor has there been any excessive extraction of tannins. All up, a really enjoyable cherry-filled Sangiovese. Screwcap. 13.1% alc. **Rating** 95 To 2023 $35 ❂

TNT Tempranillo Nebbiolo Tannat 2011 Excellent colour; a clever name; how on earth so much red fruit came out of '11 is a miracle; it is crammed full of juicy red fruits, silky tannins adding to the appeal. Screwcap. 13.1% alc. **Rating** 94 To 2025 $35

🍷🍷🍷🍷🍷 **Super King Sangiovese Cabernet 2013** Rating 93 To 2023 $30
Single Vineyard Glenrowan Durif 2013 Rating 93 To 2025 $35
Estate Vineyard Barbera 2013 Rating 92 To 2020 $35
Single Vineyard Tempranillo 2013 Rating 91 To 2019 $35
Single Vineyard Pinot Grigio 2014 Rating 90 To 2016 $22

Samuel's Gorge ★★★★★
193 Chaffeys Road, McLaren, SA 5171 **Region** McLaren Vale
T (08) 8323 8651 **www.**gorge.com.au **Open** 7 days 11–5
Winemaker Justin McNamee **Est.** 2003 **Dozens** 3500 **Vyds** 10ha
After a wandering winemaking career in various parts of the world, Justin McNamee became a winemaker at Tatachilla in 1996, where he remained until 2003, leaving to found Samuel's Gorge. He has established his winery in a barn built in 1853, part of the old Seaview Homestead. The historic property was owned by Sir Samuel Way, variously Chief Justice of the South Australian Supreme Court and Lieutenant Governor of the state. The grapes come from small contract growers spread across the ever-changing (unofficial) subregions of McLaren Vale, and are basket-pressed and fermented in old open slate fermenters lined with beeswax. Exports to the US, Canada, Hong Kong and NZ.

🍷🍷🍷🍷🍷 McLaren Vale Shiraz 2013 Good colour; has focus and intensity from the first whiff through to the finish of the medium to full-bodied palate; the impact of 70% cacao dark chocolate and licorice seems to shrink, not increase, the alcohol, giving the wine the architecture and balance for a long life. Definitely food-friendly, even now, more again down the track. Cork. 14.5% alc. **Rating** 95 To 2033 $40

McLaren Vale Shiraz 2012 Deep, but bright hue; McLaren Vale is prone to emphasise its terroir at the best of times, but seldom more trenchantly than here; whether the bitter dark chocolate surrounds the black fruits or vice versa doesn't really matter, for there is no untangling of either flavour; it is dismissively full-bodied, with an autocratic character usually found with Cabernet. Cork. 14.5% alc. Rating 95 To 2037 $40

🍷🍷🍷🍷🍷 **McLaren Vale Grenache 2013** Rating 91 To 2020 $40
McLaren Vale Tempranillo 2013 Rating 90 To 2043 $40
McLaren Vale Mourvedre 2013 Rating 90 To 2033 $40

Sandalford ★★★★★
3210 West Swan Road, Caversham, WA 6055 **Region** Margaret River
T (08) 9374 9374 **www.**sandalford.com **Open** 7 days 9–5
Winemaker Hope Metcalf **Est.** 1840 **Dozens** 60 000 **Vyds** 105ha
Sandalford is one of Australia's oldest and largest privately owned wineries. In 1970 it moved beyond its original Swan Valley base, purchasing a substantial property in Margaret River that is now the main source of its premium grapes. Wines are released under the Element, Winemakers, Margaret River and Estate Reserve ranges, with Prendiville Reserve at the top. Exports to all major markets.

🍷🍷🍷🍷🍷 Prendiville Reserve Margaret River Shiraz 2013 Fermentation starts in stainless steel, the juice run to new French barriques to finish fermentation, then

12 months' maturation in barrel. The sheer power and quality of the fruit, and the shorter time in barrel, minimises the impact of the new oak, allowing the focus to remain on the black fruits and berry flavours; the tannin management is also of the highest calibre. Screwcap. 14.5% alc. **Rating** 96 **To** 2032 $90

Estate Reserve Margaret River Chardonnay 2013 Very much in the elegant mode of Sandalford's Estate Reserve style, the fruit having made short order of the new French oak in which it was barrel-fermented, and matured on lees. The primary flavours are of grapefruit and white-fleshed stone fruits, succoured by crisp, natural acidity. Screwcap. 13.5% alc. **Rating** 95 **To** 2023 $35 ✪

Estate Reserve Margaret River Shiraz 2012 Estate-grown grapes commenced fermentation in small static fermenters, the must transferred to new and 1yo French barriques to finish fermentation, then 18 months in those barrels. This is the epitome of elegant, medium-bodied Shiraz, with red and black cherry, blackberry and spicy fruit flavours; while the barrel-ferment oak characters are obvious, I like them. Screwcap. 14.5% alc. **Rating** 95 **To** 2025 $35 ✪

Prendiville Reserve Margaret River Shiraz 2012 Power and persuasion. It climbs straight into its work with plum, blackberry and bay leaf notes of great concentration, polished to a high lustre with the assistance of smoky, resiny, creamy oak. It's a hand-in-glove combination, with muscular tannin then pulling it all tight. Immaculate force. Screwcap. 14.5% alc. **Rating** 95 **To** 2035 $90 CM

♛♛♛♛♕ **Estate Reserve Sauvignon Semillon 2014** **Rating** 93 **To** 2017 $25 ✪
Classic Dry White Semillon Sauvignon 2014 **Rating** 93 **To** 2015 $20 ✪

Sandhurst Ridge   ★★★★☆

156 Forest Drive, Marong, Vic 3515 **Region** Bendigo
T (03) 5435 2534 **www**.sandhurstridge.com.au **Open** 7 days 11–5
Winemaker Paul Greblo **Est.** 1990 **Dozens** 3000 **Vyds** 7.3ha
The Greblo brothers (Paul is the winemaker, George the viticulturist), with combined experience in business, agriculture, science and construction and development, began the establishment of Sandhurst Ridge in 1990, planting the first 2ha of shiraz and cabernet sauvignon. Plantings have increased to over 7ha, principally cabernet and shiraz, but also a little merlot, nebbiolo and sauvignon blanc. As the business has grown, the Greblos have supplemented their crush with grapes grown in the region. Exports to Norway, Malaysia, Taiwan, Hong Kong, Japan and China.

♛♛♛♛♛ **Reserve Bendigo Shiraz 2012** Hand-picked, open-fermented, basket-pressed to French barriques for 19 months. Deep, bright purple; the vintage (and possibly the extra year in bottle) has produced the most elegant Sandhurst Ridge wine to date, spicy plum and blackberry fruit complexed by fine, persistent tannins and good oak handling. Diam. 14% alc. **Rating** 95 **To** 2032 $42

Fringe Bendigo Shiraz 2013 The grapes are grown on nearby vineyards, the winemaking identical to the estate wine; the bouquet is fragrant, the palate with more spicy/savoury nuances than its sibling, adding interest. Screwcap. 15.4% alc. **Rating** 94 **To** 2030 $24 ✪

Bendigo Shiraz 2013 Hand-picked estate fruit; open-fermented, basket-pressed, matured in French and American barriques for 18 months. Deeply coloured, very well balanced and structured; luscious fruits are supported by deft oak handling, and the tannins are ripe. Screwcap. 14.7% alc. **Rating** 94 **To** 2038 $32

♛♛♛♛♕ **Fringe Bendigo Cabernet Sauvignon 2013** **Rating** 90 **To** 2023 $24

Sanguine Estate   ★★★★★

77 Shurans Lane, Heathcote, Vic 3523 **Region** Heathcote
T (03) 5433 3111 **www**.sanguinewines.com.au **Open** W'ends & public hols 10–5
Winemaker Mark Hunter **Est.** 1997 **Dozens** 3500 **Vyds** 21.57ha
The Hunter family – parents Linda and Tony at the head, and their children Mark and Jodi, with their respective partners Melissa and Brett – began establishing the vineyard in 1997. It

has grown to 21ha of shiraz, with token plantings of chardonnay, viognier, merlot, tempranillo, petit verdot, cabernet sauvignon and cabernet franc. Low-yielding vines and the magic of the Heathcote region have produced Shiraz of exceptional intensity, which has received rave reviews in the US, and led to the 'sold out' sign being posted almost immediately upon release. With the ever-expanding vineyard, Mark has become full-time vigneron, and Jodi full-time general manager and business developer. Exports to Singapore and China.

ŸŸŸŸŸ **Inception Heathcote Shiraz 2013** Almost ridiculously good from all angles. Profound blackberry and plum fruit flavour, saucy/spicy/smoky input from oak, and sandalwood and earth-like grain/flavour. It hits, explodes, ripples and runs. There's quite a deal of tannin but it's so well folded into the fruit, and generally so well balanced, that the wine can be enjoyed effectively at any stage of its development. Screwcap. 14.8% alc. **Rating** 96 **To** 2032 $40 CM ❂

D'Orsa Heathcote Shiraz 2012 Two years in large-format French oak, 60% of it new. A portion of the wine sees extended skin contact. It's deeply fruited, still quite reticent and backward in its development, full of asphalt, blackberry and chocolatey oak flavour, lightly sprinkled with eucalypt and dry leaf matter. Flavour piled upon flavour. Indeed it's a wine best suited to those who value fruit density above almost all else. Cork. 14.8% alc. **Rating** 95 **To** 2028 $60 CM

Wine Club Heathcote Shiraz 2013 The names of the 'wine club' members involved in the blending of this wine are listed on the back label. A nice touch. It's a rich, generous wine with a firm kick of tannin. Blackberry, vanilla, licorice and five-spice notes do all the talking. It sits on the heroic or muscular side of medium weight but its strength is not without discipline. Impressive. Screwcap. 14.8% alc. **Rating** 94 **To** 2026 $35 CM

Robo's Mob Heathcote Shiraz Cabernet 2013 Strong-armed wine. Big tannin, big flavour. Bursting with bold, black-berried fruit married to mint and cedar wood notes. Waves of tannin crash through the finish. Plenty of grunt, but with polish to match. Screwcap. 14.8% alc. **Rating** 94 **To** 2028 $35 CM

ŸŸŸŸ♀ **Music Festival Heathcote Shiraz 2013** **Rating** 93 **To** 2024 $30 CM
Heathcote Tempranillo 2013 **Rating** 93 **To** 2022 $30 CM
Progeny Heathcote Shiraz 2013 **Rating** 92 **To** 2021 $25 CM ❂

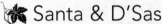
🌺 Santa & D'Sas ★★★★

2 Pincott Street, Newtown, Vic 3220 **Region** Various
T 0417 384 272 **www**.santadsas.com.au **Open** Not
Winemaker Andrew Santarossa, Matthew Di Sciascio **Est.** 2014 **Dozens** 1500
Santa and D'Sas brings together two winemakers who met while studying for their Bachelor of Applied Science (Wine Science) degrees. Their first collaboration was to make a student wine as part of their formal studies. Thereafter they went their separate ways, Andrew Santarossa as far afield as Houghton, then returning to the Yarra Valley working for Giant Steps and Domaine Chandon. Currently he is winemaker for his own Fratelli Wines, and consults to Mandala Wines. Matthew Di Sciascio, with dual degrees in wine science and viticulture, was one of the proprietors, winemaker and viticulturist at Bellbrae Estate in Geelong (2000–'10) as well as winemaker at Otway Estate ('08–'09). Since '11 he has been a vintage winemaker at Galli Estate, consultant winemaker at Clyde Park and has developed DiSciascio Family Wines. Late in '12 Andrew and Matthew decided they should make another wine together, and one thing has led to another in quick succession.

ŸŸŸŸŸ **Graal Geelong Pinot Noir 2013** Bright crimson-purple; a fragrant bouquet and a slippery, juicy palate built on red and black cherry fruit; a feeling of guilt for executing a magnum on the tasting table, but hurriedly topped up and recapped, the aftertaste lingering in the mouth. Definitely worth jumping onto a rarely seen magnum of good-quality Pinot Noir with many years to go. No. 63 of 210 magnums made. Screwcap. 13.1% alc. **Rating** 94 **To** 2030 $98

Geelong Pinot Noir 2013 Good depth of colour; a very well made Pinot with a supple, rich, red and black cherry mid-palate reflecting the bouquet, then

a mouth-watering savoury finish giving the wine closure. Screwcap. 13.1% alc.
Rating 94 To 2025 $29 ○

ϮϮϮϮ King & Yarra Valleys Pinot Gris 2014 Rating 89 To 2016 $22
Yarra Valley Pinot Noir 2013 Rating 89 To 2020 $30
King Valley Prosecco NV Rating 88 To 2015 $22 TS

Santolin Wines ★★★★☆

c/- 21–23 Delaneys Road, South Warrandyte, Vic 3136 **Region** Yarra Valley
T 0402 278 464 **www**.santolinwines.com.au **Open** Not
Winemaker Adrian Santolin **Est.** 2012 **Dozens** 500
Adrian Santolin grew up in Griffith, NSW, and has worked in the wine industry since he was
15. He moved to the Yarra Valley in '07 with wife Rebecca, who has worked in marketing
roles at various wineries. Adrian's love of Pinot Noir led him to work at wineries such as
Wedgetail Estate, Rochford, De Bortoli, Sticks and Rob Dolan Wines. In '12 his dream came
true when he was able to buy 2 tonnes of pinot noir from the Syme-on-Yarra Vineyard,
increasing production in '13 to 4 tonnes, split between chardonnay and pinot noir, the
chardonnay sourced from Yarraland Vineyard at Chirnside Park. The Boy Meets Girl wines are
sold through www.nakedwines.com.au Exports to the UK and the US.

ϮϮϮϮϮ Individual Vineyard Yarra Valley Pinot Noir 2014 50% whole bunches,
50% whole berries, matured in French oak (30% new). Full of bright fruit
energy. Tasted 10 months prior to release (Jan '16), it should flourish by that time,
however good it is now. Screwcap. 13% alc. Rating 94 To 2025 $45

ϮϮϮϮϙ Individual Vineyard Yarra Valley Sauvignon 2014 Rating 93 To 2017 $28
A&R Reserve Boy Meets Girl Shiraz Viognier 2013 Rating 93 To 2016
$19 ○
Family Reserve Chardonnay 2014 Rating 92 To 2024 $23 ○
Family Reserve Syrah 2014 Rating 92 To 2020 $22 ○
Boy Meets Girl Shiraz Cabernet 2013 Rating 90 To 2016 $13 ○

Saracen Estates ★★★★

Level 10, 225 St Georges Terrace, Perth, WA 6000 **Region** Margaret River
T (08) 9486 9410 **www**.saracenestates.com.au **Open** Mon–Fri 9–5
Winemaker Bob Cartwright (Consultant) **Est.** 1998 **Dozens** 5000
The sale of the Saracen Estate property has left a cloud of uncertainty over how the business
intends to operate into the future. Maree Saraceni and her brother Dennis Parker are running
a virtual winery operation in 2014 and '15 through their Perth office, employing contract
winemaker Bob Cartwright, who is buying Margaret River harvest and making wine at
Thompson's Estate. They advise us to 'watch this space'.

ϮϮϮϮϮ Margaret River Sauvignon Blanc Semillon 2014 Bursts into life with
Margaret River banners flying; equal space is given to the sauvignon blanc and the
semillon, and no suggestion of oak; passionfruit and guava are topped and tailed
by live-wire lemony acidity powering through to the finish. Screwcap. 13.2% alc.
Rating 94 To 2017 $22 ○

Sarsfield Estate ★★★☆

345 Duncan Road, Sarsfield, Vic 3875 **Region** Gippsland
T (03) 5156 8962 **www**.sarsfieldestate.com.au **Open** By appt
Winemaker Dr Suzanne Rutschmann **Est.** 1995 **Dozens** 1000 **Vyds** 2ha
Owned by Suzanne Rutschmann, who has a PhD in chemistry, a Diploma in Horticulture
and a BSc (Wine Science) from CSU, and Swiss-born Peter Albrecht, a civil and structural
engineer who has also undertaken various courses in agriculture and viticulture. For a part-
time occupation, these are exceptionally impressive credentials. Their vineyard (pinot noir,
cabernet, shiraz, cabernet franc and merlot) was planted between 1991 and '98. Sarsfield Pinot
Noir has enjoyed success in both domestic and international wine shows. No insecticides

are used in the vineyard; the winery runs on solar and wind energy and relies entirely on rainwater.

🍷🍷🍷🍷⭒ **Pinot Noir 2012** It's all sinew and spice but it runs long through the finish and has just enough flesh to impose itself. A prime example of autumnal style: more about length than breadth, but at no point do you feel short-changed. Over the mid-term at least it should develop well. Screwcap sealed, thankfully. 12.7% alc. **Rating** 93 **To** 2023 $26 CM ✪

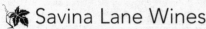

Savina Lane Wines ★★★★

90 Savina Lane, Severnlea, Qld 4380 **Region** Granite Belt
T (07) 4683 5377 **www.**savinalanewines.com.au **Open** Wed–Sat 10–5
Winemaker Mike Hayes **Est.** 2012 **Dozens** 800 **Vyds** 3.5ha
Brad and Cheryl Hutchings spent 30 years on the Sunshine Coast, with a number of successful businesses including Underwater World, advertising agency Lucas de Malliac, and Brad's career as an agriculture consultant to the region. In March 2012 they moved from Buderim to the vineyard to live, throwing themselves in at the deep end, but secure in the knowledge they had secured the services of one of the very best contract winemakers in the region, Mike Hayes. Vines have been grown on the Savina Lane property for 40 years, and they inherited fiano, viognier, tempranillo and graciano as well as some 40-year-old dry-grown shiraz. They knew they had made the right decision when their 2012 Old Vine Shiraz won two trophies for Queensland wines at the Australian Small Winemakers Show '14, failing to win the National Trophy by half a point. If this were not enough, their 2013 Fiano Classico and 2012 Reserve Graciano won gold medals at the following Australian Alternative Varieties Wine Show in Mildura. The existing vineyard occupies 3.5ha of a 21ha property, and they are planting petit manseng and montepulciano, which should come into bearing in the 2018 vintage.

🍷🍷🍷🍷🍷 **Reserve Granite Belt Millenium Shiraz 2012** Clings closely to its Reserve Millenium sibling, but does have an added dimension to the mid-palate fruit of dark cherry and plum, without losing freshness; fine-grained, savoury tannins lengthen the finish. Screwcap. 14% alc. **Rating** 94 **To** 2027 $42

🍷🍷🍷🍷⭒ **Granite Belt Fiano Classico 2013 Rating** 93 **To** 2019 $35
Reserve Granite Belt Tempranillo 2012 Rating 93 **To** 2022 $38
Reserve Granite Belt Old Vine Shiraz 2012 Rating 92 **To** 2025 $65
Granite Belt Wild Yeast Viognier 2013 Rating 90 **To** 2016 $35

SC Pannell ★★★★★

60 Olivers Road, McLaren Vale, SA 5171 **Region** McLaren Vale
T (08) 8271 7118 **www.**scpannell.com.au **Open** 7 days 11–5
Winemaker Stephen Pannell **Est.** 2004 **Dozens** 15 000 **Vyds** 22ha
The only surprising piece of background is that it took (an admittedly still reasonably youthful) Stephen (Steve) Pannell (and wife Fiona) so long to cut the painter from Constellation/ Hardys and establish their own winemaking and consulting business. Steve radiates intensity, and extended experience has resulted in wines of the highest quality right from the first vintage. The Pannells have purchased two vineyards in McLaren Vale, the first planted in 1891 with a precious patch of 3.6ha of shiraz. A second property was purchased in 2014, lifting the estate vineyards to a total of 22ha. '14 also saw the establishment (technically the acquisition) of a cellar door, now fully renovated. Steve manages the vineyard with the aim of generating full flavour ripeness as close to 13% as possible. The future for the Pannells is limitless, the icon status of the label already established. Exports to the UK.

🍷🍷🍷🍷🍷 **Adelaide Hills Syrah 2013** Winner of the Jimmy Watson Trophy '14. Seductive from the first drop to the last. Spice-shot berries, black and red, a coating of nuts and cream giving the flavours a sheen. Amaro-like infusions. Sophisticated and yet generally accessible. Beautiful, grainy, peppery length, seamed by ultra-fine tannin. Poster child of savoury-accented Australian red wine. Screwcap. 14% alc. **Rating** 97 **To** 2030 $30 CM ✪

ΨΨΨΨΨ **Adelaide Hills Sauvignon Blanc 2014** Hand-picked, free-run juice, some wild-ferment to add texture, which you meet in the entrance lobby before going through to the dining room with guava, passionfruit and sliced lemon piled on platters yea high. Having had your fill, leaving through the lobby brings forth a savoury farewell. Screwcap. 13% alc. **Rating** 95 **To** 2016 $25 ✪

Koomilya DC Block Shiraz 2013 The ultimate 'look, no hands' approach: crush and press the grapes into a 5yo 2700l vat, leave it strictly alone for 17 months, then bottle it. Deeply coloured, this is 100% full-bodied, with multiple layers of black fruits and ripe tannins blotting out everything except bitter dark chocolate. Will be prodigiously long-lived. Screwcap. 14% alc. **Rating** 95 **To** 2048

Field Street McLaren Vale Shiraz 2013 This estate vineyard, planted in '70, was acquired in '14; matured in French oak (20% new). Wow. This isn't the trendy SC Pannell with aspirations to make light to medium-bodied reds for connoisseurs of fine things, but a throwback to Steve Pannell's days with Hardys (there is an explanation, but no space). It is opulently rich, medium to full-bodied, with fruit and oak in unison, and the punters will just love it to death. And they won't look foolish. Screwcap. 14% alc. **Rating** 95 **To** 2043 $25 ✪

By SCP McLaren Vale Tempranillo 2014 Includes 10% tinto cao; matured in used French puncheons for 8 months. Has the same gravitas that is unique to McLaren Vale Grenache, immediately establishing this is a real red wine, not a raspberry milkshake. You don't even have to go past the bouquet to know its cred; dark fruits as much as red, and good tannins to boot. Screwcap. 14% alc. **Rating** 95 **To** 2024 $25 ✪

McLaren Vale Grenache Shiraz Touriga 2013 Rating 94 **To** 2023 $28 ✪
Tempranillo Touriga 2013 Rating 94 **To** 2023 $28 ✪

ΨΨΨΨΨ **Tempranillo Touriga 2014** Rating 93 **To** 2027 $30
Adelaide Hills Pinot Grigio 2014 Rating 92 **To** 2016 $25 ✪
By SCP Adelaide Hills Nebbiolo 2012 Rating 92 **To** 2024 $28

Scarpantoni Estate   ★★★★☆

Scarpantoni Drive, McLaren Flat, SA 5171 **Region** McLaren Vale
T (08) 8383 0186 **www.**scarpantoniwines.com **Open** Mon–Fri 9–5, w'ends 11.30–4.30
Winemaker Michael and Filippo Scarpantoni **Est.** 1979 **Dozens** 37 000 **Vyds** 40ha
Scarpantoni has come a long way since Domenico Scarpantoni purchased his first vineyard in 1958. He worked for Thomas Hardy at its Tintara winery, then as vineyard manager for Seaview Wines, and soon became one of the largest private grapegrowers in the region. The winery was built in '79 with help from sons Michael and Filippo, who continue to manage the company. Michael and Filippo grew up on part of Oxenberry Farm, originally settled in 1840, and in 1998 were able to purchase part of the property. The Oxenberry wines are made in a different style from that of Scarpantoni, and are available only from its cellar door at 24–26 Kangarilla Road, McLaren Flat. Exports to the UK and other major markets.

ΨΨΨΨΨ **Riserva Shiraz Cabernet 2012** Spent 21 months in oak, appropriate given the weight of the black fruits of the bouquet and palate; there is an added layer of licorice, spice and dark chocolate on the palate, which finishes with élan, paying no attention to the alcohol. Screwcap. 15% alc. **Rating** 95 **To** 2032 $65

ΨΨΨΨΨ **Pinot Noir 2013** Rating 93 **To** 2023 $25 ✪
Oxenberry Two Tribes 2013 Rating 92 **To** 2020 $20 ✪
Durif 2013 Rating 91 **To** 2025 $25

Schild Estate Wines   ★★★★☆

Cnr Barossa Valley Way/Lyndoch Valley Road, Lyndoch, SA 5351 **Region** Barossa Valley
T (08) 8524 5560 **www.**schildestate.com.au **Open** 7 days 10–5
Winemaker Scott Hazeldine **Est.** 1998 **Dozens** 40 000 **Vyds** 163ha
Ed Schild is a Barossa Valley grapegrower who first planted a small vineyard at Rowland Flat in 1952, steadily increasing his vineyard holdings over the next 50 years to their present level.

The flagship wine is made from 150-year-old shiraz vines on the Moorooroo Block. The cellar door is in the old ANZ Bank at Lyndoch, and provides the sort of ambience that can only be found in the Barossa Valley. Exports to all major markets.

🍷🍷🍷🍷🍷 **Moorooroo Limited Release Barossa Valley Shiraz 2010** Four rows of vines, sufficient to make 200 dozen, were planted by Johann and William Jacob in 1847. Deep, healthy colour, exceptional in a wine nearing 5yo; made in new and used French hogsheads, this is still a wine in an early stage of a very long life; it is extremely concentrated, but has immaculate balance to its blackberry, anise and plum fruit. A bargain for 167 years of liquid history. Cork. 14.5% alc. **Rating** 97 To 2040 $90 ✪

🍷🍷🍷🍷🍷 **Ben Schild Reserve Single Vineyard Barossa Valley Shiraz 2010** From a vineyard above Lyndoch; open-fermented, matured for 24 months in new and used French, American and Hungarian oak. It has a complex array of blackberry, blueberry, plum and mocha flavours; earthy acidity provides freshness and lift on the finish. Screwcap. 14.5% alc. **Rating** 94 To 2025 $35
Barossa Valley Grenache Mourvedre Shiraz 2013 A 47/27/26% blend. The vivid crimson colour sends a message of the equally bright palate with its synergistic and unusually harmonious blend, the gamut of red fruits retaining brightness and shape (and no confection). Exceptional value — one of the bargains of the year. Screwcap. 14.5% alc. **Rating** 94 To 2023 $15 ✪

🍷🍷🍷🍷 **Barossa Valley Shiraz 2013** Rating 89 To 2023 $20
Barossa Valley Cabernet Sauvignon 2012 Rating 89 To 2020 $20
Barossa Valley Shiraz 2012 Rating 88 To 2019 $20

Schubert Estate   ★★★★★

Roennfeldt Road, Marananga, SA 5355 **Region** Barossa Valley
T (08) 8562 3375 **www**.schubertestate.com **Open** By appt
Winemaker Steve Schubert **Est.** 2000 **Dozens** 1100 **Vyds** 14ha
Steve and Cecilia Schubert are primarily grapegrowers, with 12ha of shiraz and 2ha of viognier. They purchased the 25ha property in 1986, when it was in such a derelict state that there was no point trying to save the old vines. Both were working in other areas, so it was some years before they began replanting, at a little under 2ha per year. Almost all the production is sold to Torbreck. In 2000 they decided to keep enough grapes to make a barrique of wine for their own (and friends') consumption. They were sufficiently encouraged by the outcome to venture into the dizzy heights of two hogsheads a year (since increased to four or so). The wine is made with wild yeast, open fermentation, basket-pressing and bottling without filtration. Exports to Germany, Malaysia, Hong Kong and China.

🍷🍷🍷🍷🍷 **The Lone Goose Barossa Valley Shiraz 2010** Estate-grown, the shiraz co-fermented with 3–4% viognier. Has retained excellent hue, and a full flush of luscious and fresh fruit, the viognier no doubt playing a role in this; it is medium-bodied, but rollicks around the mouth with its mix of satsuma plum, mocha and vestiges of licorice, the finish long and well balanced. Drink now or in the distant future. Screwcap. 14.5% alc. **Rating** 95 To 2030 $26 ✪
The Sentinel Barossa Valley Shiraz 2010 A limited production from the estate Goose-yard Block; spent 24 months in French oak. It is full of plum, blackberry, chocolate, mocha and fruitcake; ripe, fine-grained tannins tie the parcel together very well. Screwcap. 14.5% alc. **Rating** 95 To 2030 $32 ✪
Goose-yard Block Barossa Valley Shiraz 2012 Estate-grown, open-fermented, basket-pressed and matured in oak for 22 months. Powerful and potent, it seems to have borrowed some McLaren Vale dark chocolate to run alongside its foresty black fruits before a warm finish and aftertaste. Cork. 15% alc. **Rating** 94 To 2027 $60

🍷🍷🍷🍷🍷 **The Gosling Barossa Valley Shiraz 2011** Rating 92 To 2021 $20 ✪

Schwarz Wine Company ★★★★★

Biscay Road, Tanunda, SA 5352 **Region** Barossa Valley
T 0417 881 923 **www**.schwarzwineco.com.au **Open** At Artisans of Barossa
Winemaker Jason Schwarz **Est.** 2001 **Dozens** 2500

The economical name is appropriate for a business that started with 1 tonne of grapes making two hogsheads of wine in 2001. The shiraz was purchased from Jason Schwarz's parents' vineyard in Bethany, the vines planted in 1968; the following year half a tonne of grenache was added, once again purchased from the parents. Production remained static until '05, when the grape sale agreements to another (larger) winery were terminated, freeing up 1.8ha of shiraz and 0.8ha of grenache. From this point on things moved more quickly: in '06 Jason, while working with Peter Schell of Spinifex, formed a partnership (Biscay Road Vintners) with Peter giving each total control over production. Exports to the US, Canada, France, Singapore, Hong Kong and China.

🍷🍷🍷🍷🍷 The Schiller Barossa Valley Shiraz 2013 Made from 400 shiraz vines planted by Carl August Otto Schiller in the 1880s. It's Barossa shiraz in all its glory. Ripe, black-berried, aniseed fruit meets smoke, iced coffee and ground spice. It has more than a little 'come hither' about it yet it's also sophisticated and complex. In short, it's a slashing wine. Screwcap. 14.5% alc. Rating 96 To 2030 $70 CM ✪
Nitschke Block Barossa Valley Shiraz 2013 A wealth of dark fruit flavour is thickly but firmly applied. Raspberry, jubey blackberry, woodsmoke and licorice, a slide of spicy oak continuing the seductive impression. Fruit quality here is sensational. Screwcap. 14.3% alc. Rating 95 To 2027 $40 CM

🍷🍷🍷🍷🍷 Meta Barossa Shiraz 2013 Rating 93 To 2027 $35 CM
Barossa Valley Shiraz Mataro 2013 Rating 93 To 2025 $30 CM
Meta Barossa Valley Grenache 2014 Rating 93 To 2021 $35 CM
Barossa Valley GSM 2013 Rating 93 To 2022 $28 CM
Meta Barossa Valley Mataro 2013 Rating 92 To 2021 $35 CM

Scion Vineyard & Winery ★★★★

74 Slaughterhouse Road, Rutherglen, Vic 3685 **Region** Rutherglen
T (02) 6032 8844 **www**.scionvineyard.com **Open** 7 days 10–5
Winemaker Rowly Milhinch **Est.** 2002 **Dozens** 1650 **Vyds** 3.2ha

Scion Vineyard was established by retired audiologist Jan Milhinch, who is a great-great-granddaughter of GF Morris, founder of the most famous Rutherglen wine family. Jan has now handed the baton on to son Rowland (Rowly), who continues to manage the vineyard, planted on a quartz-laden red clay slope to durif, viognier, brown muscat and orange muscat, and make the wines.

🍷🍷🍷🍷🍷 Rutherglen Durif 2013 Fermented in open concrete vats; matured 16 months in French hogsheads (40% new). Deep purple-crimson; even by the standards of Durif, this is notably full-bodied and concentrated, but all the components are in remarkable balance. I would cellar it for a minimum of 10 years, but could share a glass tonight without concern. Screwcap. 13.2% alc. Rating 94 To 2028 $35

🍷🍷🍷🍷🍷 Rutherglen Viognier 2013 Rating 92 To 2016 $25 ✪
After Dark 2013 Rating 92 To 2023 $29
Rutherglen Viognier 2014 Rating 90 To 2017 $25
Rutherglen Rose 2014 Rating 90 To 2016 $25
Muscat Nouveau 2013 Rating 90 To 2016 $29
Grand Muscat NV Rating 90 To 2016 $59

Scorpo Wines ★★★★★

23 Old Bittern–Dromana Road, Merricks North, Vic 3926 **Region** Mornington Peninsula
T (03) 5989 7697 **www**.scorpowines.com.au **Open** By appt
Winemaker Paul Scorpo, Sandro Mosele (Contract) **Est.** 1997 **Dozens** 3500 **Vyds** 9.64ha

Paul Scorpo has a background as a horticulturist/landscape architect, working on major projects ranging from private gardens to golf courses in Australia, Europe and Asia. His family has a love of food, wine and gardens, all of which led to them buying a derelict apple and cherry orchard on gentle rolling hills between Port Phillip and Westernport bays. They have established pinot gris (4.8ha), pinot noir (2.8ha), chardonnay (1ha) and shiraz (1ha). Exports to Singapore and Hong Kong.

🍷🍷🍷🍷🍷 **Mornington Peninsula Chardonnay 2011** Searing chardonnay. Straw-green colour; white peach, apple, citrus and oatmeal, with spicy oak playing a positive role. Flavour upfront but persistence plus. Quite beautiful. Screwcap. 13% alc. Rating 96 To 2021 $41 CM ☑

Mornington Peninsula Pinot Noir 2013 A standout release. Generosity of perfume and fruit is exemplary, though there is no lack of acid or tannin structure. Foresty dark cherries, plum, spices, meaty oak, perhaps even fennel. The overall effect is thoroughly gorgeous. Screwcap. 13.5% alc. Rating 96 To 2024 $49 CM ☑

Mornington Peninsula Pinot Gris 2014 Terrific intensity of flavour. If it must be Pinot Gris then there's an argument to say that it must be this. Pear drop, slate, spice and mineral characters soar through the palate, impressing and delighting in equal measure. Screwcap. 13.5% alc. Rating 95 To 2016 $35 CM ☑

Mornington Peninsula Shiraz 2010 In excellent form, as is the entire Scorpo range. White pepper melts into black cherry-plum and woodsmoke. Offers a good burst of ripe fruit but it's characterised by its pepperiness. Spicy tannin spins through the finish. I can't recall a better Scorpo Shiraz. Screwcap. 13% alc. Rating 95 To 2022 $35 CM ☑

Aubaine Mornington Peninsula Chardonnay 2014 Light straw colour. Tastes delicious. Pear, lime and spice with highlights of red apple. Swings both effortlessly and juicily through the palate, dripping flavour as it goes. Screwcap. 13% alc. Rating 94 To 2019 $31 CM

Noirien Mornington Peninsula Pinot Noir 2014 It only sees 5% new oak but it feels polished and plush, with satiny cherry-plum flavours leading into more savoury, foresty elements. It's a pretty wine, but it also has substance; it's charming. Screwcap. 13% alc. Rating 94 To 2020 $31 CM

Scotchmans Hill ★★★★★

190 Scotchmans Road, Drysdale, Vic 3222 **Region** Geelong
T (03) 5251 3176 **www**.scotchmans.com.au **Open** 7 days 10.30–4.30
Winemaker Robin Brockett, Marcus Holt **Est.** 1982 **Dozens** 50000
The change of ownership and management of Scotchmans Hill, now owned by a group of Melbourne investors, in no way reflected any shortcoming in the consistency and quality of the wines produced by long-serving winemaker Robin Brockett, assisted by Marcus Holt. Exports to Asia and other major markets.

🍷🍷🍷🍷🍷 **Cornelius Single Vineyard Pinot Noir 2012** Destemmed, cold soak and more new oak than the standard '13. The colour is still vivid; it has more texture and significantly more drive and length, with fraises du bois in a wreath of fine-grained, but persistent tannins on the long finish. Seriously good Pinot. Screwcap. 13% alc. Rating 96 To 2022 $55 ☑

Bellarine Peninsula Shiraz 2013 Destemmed, 5-day cold soak, wild yeast-fermented for 7 days at 28°C, matured in new and used French barriques for 16 months. The deep, intense colour hoists the battle colours of an extremely powerful Shiraz that nonetheless is not extractive, nor has dead fruit; blackberry compote, licorice, tar, spice and pepper are all on parade on the full-bodied palate. The longer you give it, the better it will be. Screwcap. 14.5% alc. Rating 96 To 2043 $30 ☑

Cornelius Single Vineyard Syrah 2012 Has all the suppleness and elegance in the world, given Rolls-Royce treatment in the winery. It has utterly delicious red fruits at its heart, with a garland of gently spicy/savoury tannins and French oak. Lovely now or in 20 years. Screwcap. 14% alc. **Rating** 96 **To** 2035 $65 **○**

Cornelius Single Vineyard Sauvignon 2013 Makes the point in capital letters that it's possible to have elegant Sauvignon Blanc that doesn't have a wheelbarrowful of tropical fruits; here it's a tap-tap of flavours, not a big bass drum; there are flecks of citrus zest, apple and gooseberry, and the illusion of a touch of oak. Screwcap. 13% alc. **Rating** 95 **To** 2020 $46

Cornelius Single Vineyard Bellarine Peninsula Chardonnay 2012 The bouquet has complexity, the palate energy and drive to its fresh display of nectarine and grapefruit flavours; barrel-ferment oak inputs have been precisely measured. Screwcap. 13.5% alc. **Rating** 95 **To** 2022 $55

Estella Single Vineyard Adelaide Hills Sauvignon Blanc 2013 Rating 94 **To** 2016 $23 **○**

Bellarine Peninsula Pinot Noir 2013 Rating 94 **To** 2023 $30 **○**

ŸŸŸŸŸ **Bellarine Peninsula Sauvignon Blanc 2014 Rating** 93 **To** 2016 $21 **○**
Cornelius Norfolk Vineyard Pinot Noir 2012 Rating 92 **To** 2020 $55
Bellarine Peninsula Chardonnay 2013 Rating 91 **To** 2020 $28

Scott   ★★★★★

102 Main Street, Hahndorf, SA 5245 **Region** Adelaide Hills
T (08) 8388 7330 **www**.scottwines.com.au **Open** W'ends 11–5
Winemaker Sam Scott **Est.** 2009 **Dozens** 3000

Sam Scott's great-grandfather worked in the cellar for Max Schubert, and passed his knowledge on to Sam's grandfather. It was he who gave Scott his early education. Sam enrolled in business at university, continuing the casual retailing he had started while at school with Booze Brothers, picking up the trail with Baily & Baily. Next came wine wholesale experience with David Ridge, selling iconic Australian and Italian wines to the trade. This then led to a job with Michael Fragos at Tatachilla in 2000, and since then he has been the 'I've been everywhere man', working all over Australia, and in California. He moved to Bird in Hand winery at the end of '06, where Andrew Nugent indicated that it was about time he took the plunge on his own account, and this he has done. Scott is a star in the making. Best Cellar Door, Adelaide Hills Wine Show '14. Exports to the UK.

ŸŸŸŸŸ **Adelaide Hills Chardonnay 2013** From a south-facing slope planted in '83 in the Piccadilly Valley; hand-picked, chilled whole bunches pressed to new and used French oak for a wild-yeast ferment. A seriously delicious wine, the fruit at optimum ripeness, the oak perfectly balanced, the acidity refreshing the finish. 60 dozen made. Screwcap. 13.5% alc. **Rating** 96 **To** 2025 $40 **○**

Adelaide Hills Shiraz 2012 From an ultra-low yield of less than 2.5 tonnes per hectare in a warmer Adelaide Hills site. The bouquet offers black cherry and satsuma plum, but in no way prepares you for the explosive power and concentration of the black-fruited palate, beyond anything you might normally expect from the Adelaide Hills; the wine has balance, so the essential cellaring will pay rewards. Screwcap. 14% alc. **Rating** 95 **To** 2037 $40

Adelaide Hills Fiano 2014 Pale straw-green; shows fiano's varietal character to advantage; it has excellent structure and mouthfeel, the flavours of ripe citrus and other lesser assorted tree fruits, the length and finish also impressive. Screwcap. 13.5% alc. **Rating** 94 **To** 2017 $26 **○**

Lo Zingaro 2013 An exotic 68/19/13% blend of shiraz, sangiovese and lagrein. The colour is deep and bright, the bouquet a fragrant burst of red and black cherries allied with notes of spice, the medium to full-bodied palate adding licorice, but needing a few years to soften and open up. Lots in store for the patient. Screwcap. 14% alc. **Rating** 94 **To** 2027 $26 **○**

La Prova Barossa Valley Nero d'Avola 2013 A variety still finding its way in Aus, but far from alone, and this perfectly made example should encourage others to follow. It is supple, medium-bodied, with both red and black currants on display, a few nudges from pistachio and spice adding to the allure. The nero d'Avola was grafted onto 20yo semillon vines. Screwcap. 14% alc. **Rating** 94 **To** 2020 $23 **○**

🍷🍷🍷🍷🍷 La Prova Adelaide Hills Aglianico Rosato 2014 Rating 93 To 2016 $23 ✪
La Prova Barossa Valley Lagrein 2012 Rating 93 To 2027 $23 ✪
La Prova Adelaide Hills Pinot Grigio 2014 Rating 92 To 2016 $23 ✪
La Prova Sangiovese 2013 Rating 92 To 2019 $23 ✪

Seabrook Wines ★★★★☆

1122 Light Pass Road, Tanunda, SA 5352 **Region** Barossa Valley
T 0427 224 353 **www.**seabrookwines.com.au **Open** By appt
Winemaker Hamish Seabrook **Est.** 2004 **Dozens** 1200 **Vyds** 10ha
Hamish Seabrook is the youngest generation of a proud Melbourne wine family once involved in wholesale and retail distribution, and as leading show judges of their respective generations. Hamish, too, is a wine show judge, but was the first to venture into winemaking, working with Best's and Brown Brothers in Vic before moving to SA with wife Joanne. In 2008 Hamish set up his own winery, on the family property in Vine Vale, having previously made the wines at Dorrien Estate and elsewhere. Here they have shiraz (4.4ha), cabernet sauvignon (3.9ha), and mataro (1.8ha), and also continue to source small amounts of shiraz from the Barossa and Pyrenees. Exports to Hong Kong and China.

🍷🍷🍷🍷🍷 **The Chairman Great Western Shiraz 2012** A cascade of spicy, savoury, peppery black fruits runs through the long, medium-bodied palate, the tannins and oak both on the money. Great Western produces Shiraz of great class. Screwcap. 14.5% alc. Rating 95 To 2032 $28 ✪

🍷🍷🍷🍷🍷 **The Merchant Barossa Valley Shiraz 2012** Rating 92 To 2027 $28
The Judge Eden Valley Riesling 2014 Rating 91 To 2021 $22 CM ✪

Sedona Estate ★★★★★

182 Shannons Road, Murrindindi, Vic 3717 **Region** Upper Goulburn
T (03) 9730 2883 **www.**sedonaestate.com.au **Open** Wed–Sun & public hols 11–5
Winemaker Paul Evans **Est.** 1998 **Dozens** 2600 **Vyds** 4ha
Sedona Estate, established by Paul Evans and Sonja Herges, is located in the picturesque Yea Valley, gateway to Victoria's high country. The unique combination of abundant sunshine, cool nights and low rainfall in this elevated wine region provides a true cool climate for growing premium-quality fruit.

🍷🍷🍷🍷🍷 **Yea Valley Sangiovese 2013** Matured for 18 months in French oak. This variety is Sedona's ace in the hole, and it has increased its plantings by 25%, taking cuttings from its vines. A clear, brilliant crimson, the bouquet of cherry blossom, the palate with all of the seduction of a young, high-quality Pinot Noir; red cherries sit in a silken web, tannins well off to one side. A truly lovely Sangiovese. Screwcap. 13% alc. Rating 96 To 2028 $25 ✪
Reserve Yea Valley Shiraz 2013 Bright crimson-purple; a very well made wine picked at precisely the right moment; both the bouquet and palate are very complex, with black fruits at the core surrounded by notes of iodine, spice, pepper and licorice strap; the tannins are exemplary, as is the length. Screwcap. 13.5% alc. Rating 95 To 2038 $34 ✪
Limited Reserve Yea Valley Cabernet Sauvignon 2013 A medium to full-bodied Cabernet, with cassis, bay leaf and dried herb and black olive all in the fruit mix, cedary oak and savoury tannins filling the profile. Diam. 13.5% alc. Rating 94 To 2033 $34

🍷🍷🍷🍷🍷 **Reserve Yea Valley Merlot 2013** Rating 93 To 2028 $34
Yea Valley Sauvignon Blanc 2014 Rating 90 To 2017 $18 ✪
Yea Valley Cabernet Merlot 2013 Rating 90 To 2025 $22

Semprevino ★★★★

1 Waverly Drive, Willunga, SA 5171 **Region** McLaren Vale
T 0417 142 110 **www**.semprevino.com.au **Open** Not
Winemaker Russell Schroder **Est.** 2006 **Dozens** 700
Semprevino is the venture of three men who became close friends while studying at Monash University in early 1990s – Russell Schroder (mechanical engineering), Simon Doak and David Bruce (both science) – although all three branched in different directions after graduating in 1993. The prime mover is Russell, who, after working for CRA/Rio Tinto for five years, left on a four-month trip to Western Europe and became captivated with the life of a vigneron. Returning to Australia, he enrolled in part-time wine science at CSU, spending the next six years working for BlueScope Steel, obtaining his wine science degree in 2005. Between '03 and '06 he worked vintages in Italy and Vic, coming under the wing of Stephen Pannell at Tinlins (where the Semprevino wines are made) in '06.

ŢŢŢŢŢ **McLaren Vale Shiraz 2013** Right in the groove. Hearty blackberry, licorice and milk chocolate flavours ooze through the palate, aided by a general creaminess of texture, with clove/peppercorn-like notes brightening up the finish. Oomph wrapped in silken robes. Screwcap. 14.5% alc. **Rating** 93 **To** 2024 $28 CM
McLaren Vale Pinot Gris 2014 Rich, spicy style. Stone fruit and ginger aplenty. Dry to the point of chalkiness through the finish. Accomplished. Screwcap. 13.1% alc. **Rating** 90 **To** 2015 $18 CM ✪

Seppelt ★★★★★

36 Cemetery Road, Great Western, Vic 3377 **Region** Grampians
T (03) 5361 2239 **www**.seppelt.com.au **Open** 7 days 10–5
Winemaker Adam Carnaby, Melanie Chester **Est.** 1865 **Dozens** NFP **Vyds** 500ha
Seppelt once had dual, very different, claims to fame. The first was as Australia's foremost producer of both white and red sparkling wine, the former led by Salinger, the latter by Show Sparkling, and Original Sparkling Shiraz. The second claim, even more relevant to the Seppelt of today, was based on the small volume, superb red wines made by Colin Preece from the 1930s through to the early '60s. These were ostensibly Great Western-sourced, but – as the laws of the time allowed – were often region, variety and vintage blends, assembled by Preece at the time of bottling. Two of his commercial labels (also of high quality) were Moyston and Chalambar, the latter recently revived. Preece would have been a child in a lolly shop if he'd had today's viticultural resources to draw on, and would be quick to recognise the commitment of the winemakers and viticulturists to the supreme quality of today's portfolio. Exports to the UK, Europe and NZ.

ŢŢŢŢŢ **Drumborg Vineyard Riesling 2014** The '14 vintage is the 50th anniversary of the establishment of the vineyard, and this glorious Riesling is a fitting testament. It has spectacular intensity, drive and length to its lemon, lime and slate flavours and texture. The 7.8g/l of residual sugar is perfectly balanced by 8.5g/l of acidity. Screwcap. 11.5% alc. **Rating** 97 **To** 2050 $40 ✪
St Peters Grampians Shiraz 2013 Small-batch open-fermented, hand-plunged, matured for 14 months in small and large-format French oak. Deep crimson; a wine bred in the purple; there is an operatic chorus of purple and black fruits with highlights of spice, gentle, yet persistent tannins, oak the final movement. Screwcap. 13.5% alc. **Rating** 97 **To** 2048 $80 ✪
Mount Ida Heathcote Shiraz 2013 Small batch fermentation with extended post-fermentation maceration, matured in new and used French barriques. Deep, verging on inky, colour foretells a mysterious bouquet, travelling in a nether-world of black fruits, exotic spices and copious amounts of dark matter defying description; the palate eases up to a degree, not confronting, its balance and length quietly calming you, but still promising an ever-interesting path in coming decades. Screwcap. 14.5% alc. **Rating** 97 **To** 2053 $55 ✪

ŢŢŢŢŢ **Drumborg Vineyard Henty Chardonnay 2013** Bright straw-green; picked at precisely the right moment, the fruit quality vigilantly protected in the winery thereafter; white peach, grapefruit and a hint of passionfruit drive the bouquet and palate alike, the barrel-ferment inputs a key part of the support of the long palate. Screwcap. 13% alc. **Rating** 96 **To** 2028 $40 ✪

Drumborg Vineyard Pinot Noir 2013 Bright, clear crimson; this is a beautiful Pinot, with its mouthfeel, balance and length amazing given its lowish alcohol; spiced plum and cherry aromas are mirrored on the supple, silky finish and lingering aftertaste. Screwcap. 12.5% alc. **Rating** 96 **To** 2023 $45 ✪

Chalambar Grampians Heathcote Shiraz 2013 High-quality grapes and skilful winemaking create a vividly coloured Chalambar that would have greatly pleased its creator, Colin Preece, whose great wines were usually blends of varieties and/or regions. The spicy, fragrant black fruits of the Grampians provide the elegance and intensity, Heathcote adding mid-palate flesh. This will age superbly, and is a great bargain. Screwcap. 14.5% alc. **Rating** 96 **To** 2038 $27 ✪

Great Western Riesling 2014 The bouquet is still reticent, but the palate makes up for that in no uncertain fashion, with a veritable ocean of sweet lime and Meyer lemon fruit, underpinned by good acidity. Seductive now, likewise in a decade or more. Screwcap. 10.5% alc. **Rating** 95 **To** 2034 $27 ✪

Jaluka Henty Chardonnay 2013 **Rating** 94 **To** 2023 $27 ✪

♥♥♥♥♡ **Original Sparkling Shiraz 2012** **Rating** 93 **To** 2026 $27 TS ✪
Salinger Vintage Cuvee 2011 **Rating** 93 **To** 2017 $30

Seppeltsfield ★★★★★

Seppeltsfield Road, Seppeltsfield via Nuriootpa, SA 5355 **Region** Barossa Valley
T (08) 8568 6200 **www**.seppeltsfield.com.au **Open** 7 days 10.30–5
Winemaker Fiona Donald **Est.** 1851 **Dozens** 10 000 **Vyds** 100ha
This historic Seppelt property and its treasure trove of fortified wines dating back to 1878 was purchased by Janet Holmes à Court, Greg Paramor and Kilikanoon Wines in 2007, from Foster's Wine Estates (now Treasury Wine Estates). Foster's kept the Seppelt brand for table and sparkling wines, mostly produced at Great Western, Vic (see separate entry). In '09 Warren Randall (ex sparkling winemaker for Seppelt at Great Western in the 1980s) acquired 50% of Seppeltsfield and became Managing Director. In February '13, Randall increased his shareholding in Seppeltsfield to over 90%. The change also marks a further commitment to the making of table wine as well as more focused marketing of the treasure trove of fortified wines. Exports to Hong Kong and China.

♥♥♥♥♥ **100 Year Old Para Liqueur 1915** There is no other wine in the world with as much explosive power as this; 100ml is the equivalent of 1500ml of conventional wine, or 500ml of Rare Rutherglen Tokay or Muscat. The first micro-sip sends all the senses of taste into a frenzy, with burnt toffee, treacle and molasses magically balanced and freshened by rancio and, even more, acidity. The aroma of the wine will stay in the empty glass for an hour or more, as will its viscosity stain the glass dark mahogany. 100ml. Cork. 21.6% alc. **Rating** 100 **To** 2016 $500

Paramount Collection DP 273 Museum Reserve Rich Rare Apera NV Glowing orange-brown; more sweet, spicy fruit than DP 898 woven through the rancio of the bouquet; has amazing texture and structure, fuller-bodied, but still moving with a fairy's touch along and across the palate; is sweet and fruity one moment, dry the next. The more I taste this wine, the more its extreme length and finesse impresses. 500ml. Cork. 22.8% alc. **Rating** 99 **To** 2016 $499

Paramount Collection DP 62 Museum Reserve Muscat NV Olive-brown, not as dark as DP 64, but every bit as viscous when being poured; raisins, raisins, raisins, Christmas pudding, hints of licorice, the most bitter of chocolate; the palate is absurd – how can it be so complex and electrifying when it first enters the mouth, then chimera-like, transform itself into a gloriously pure, fine and impossibly long back-palate and finish? 500ml. Cork. 17% alc. **Rating** 99 **To** 2016 $699

Paramount Collection DP 64 Museum Reserve Tokay NV Dark umber-brown grading to dark olive-green on the rim; pours as thickly as any rare

Northeast Victoria fortified, and similarly stains the glass; burnt toffee, celestial wild honey, Christmas cake, way beyond tea leaf/cold tea; explodes in the mouth, the tsunami of flavours almost painful, but constantly changing, a vinous equivalent of computer laser-colouring of buildings. 500ml. Cork. 17% alc. **Rating** 99 To 2016 $699

Paramount Collection DP 898 Museum Reserve Aged Flor Apera NV Bright russet-gold; intense rancio aromas, dried orange peel piercing and long, momentarily off-dry on entry to the mouth, thence to a bracingly dry finish that lingers on and on. 500ml. Cork. 23.7% alc. **Rating** 98 To 2016 $499

♀♀♀♀♀ **Über Barossa Valley Shiraz 2012** Deep crimson colour; an object exercise in how full-bodied Shiraz flavours can be presented in such a balanced framework that the alcohol is not a factor; blackberry, satsuma plum, blackcurrant and French oak are so seamlessly stitched together that their respective contributions are not easily analysed; the palate is no more than medium-bodied, the tannins polished and supple, the oak barely visible. Available only through the cellar door/website, the packaging an eloquent rear vision view of the 19th century. Screwcap. 14.7% alc. **Rating** 95 To 2037 $150

Tempranillo 2013 Fiona Donald doesn't want to make a fruit bomb, nor allow the grapes to become overripe. It is fermented and taken through mlf in tank, then transferred to used barriques for maturation. An elegant, savoury wine with sour cherry fruit; texture is its strongest point, with a cross-cut of grain one way, satin the other. Only available at cellar door. Screwcap. 14% alc. **Rating** 95 To 2018 $30

Serafino Wines   ★★★★★

Kangarilla Road, McLaren Vale, SA 5171 **Region** McLaren Vale
T (08) 8323 0157 **www.**serafinowines.com.au **Open** Mon–Fri 10–4.30, w'ends & public hols 10–4.30
Winemaker Charles Whish **Est.** 2000 **Dozens** 30 000 **Vyds** 100ha
After the sale of Maglieri Wines to Beringer Blass in 1998, Maglieri founder Serafino (Steve) Maglieri acquired the McLarens on the Lake complex originally established by Andrew Garrett. The operation draws upon 40ha each of shiraz and cabernet sauvignon, 7ha of chardonnay, 2ha each of merlot, semillon, barbera, nebbiolo and sangiovese, and 1ha of grenache. Part of the grape production is sold. Between 1997 and 2007, Serafino Wines won a succession of major trophies in Australia and the UK. The Cabernet Sauvignon has been particularly successful. Exports to the UK, the US, Canada, Hong Kong, Malaysia and NZ.

♀♀♀♀♀ **Terremoto Single Vineyard McLaren Vale Syrah 2012** Hosanna, a producer using a screwcap on its best wine, quality cork on its second best. A beautifully balanced Syrah that caresses the mouth with deceptive power – no sledgehammer here, just shiraz of remarkable purity to its blue and black fruits, supported by some oak and supple tannins. Screwcap. 14% alc. **Rating** 97 To 2042 $150 ❂

♀♀♀♀♀ **Sharktooth McLaren Vale Shiraz 2012** Estate-grown from some of the best blocks; spent 18 months in French and American oak (50% new). A wholly distinguished and elegant medium-bodied wine, with focus, length and perfect balance to its array of dark fruits and gently savoury tannins. Cork. 14% alc. **Rating** 96 To 2032 $80

McLaren Vale Shiraz 2013 Deeply coloured; the bouquet is very complex, with black fruits, leather, earth, licorice and dark chocolate leading into a supple medium to full-bodied palate; here structure and texture give precisely measured support to the strongly varietal expression. The sense of place is also clear. Screwcap. 14% alc. **Rating** 95 To 2028 $26 ❂

Reserve McLaren Vale Grenache 2013 Excellent colour; is a model for McLaren Vale Grenache with its seamless marriage of red fruits, spice and fine-grained, but persistent, tannins extending the length of the finish and aftertaste. Screwcap. 14.5% alc. **Rating** 95 To 2027 $40

Reserve McLaren Vale Grenache 2012 Is holding onto the bright hue of youth very well; a great example of a wine with a massive drinking window: from now until 20 years from vintage; the balance of its structure and flavour is impeccable, its silky display of intense red and black fruits mesmerising, the tannins equally fine but persistent. Screwcap. 14.5% alc. **Rating** 95 To 2032 $35 ❂

Sharktooth Wild Ferment Chardonnay 2013 Rating 94 To 2023 $40
GSM Grenache Shiraz Mataro 2013 Rating 94 To 2028 $26 ❂
McLaren Vale Cabernet Sauvignon 2013 Rating 94 To 2033 $26 ❂
BDX McLaren Vale Cabernet Sauvignon Merlot Carmenere Cabernet Franc 2013 Rating 94 To 2023 $26 ❂

🍷🍷🍷🍷🍷 **McLaren Vale Chardonnay 2013 Rating** 92 To 2018 $22 ❂
Bellissimo Fiano 2014 Rating 91 To 2015 $20 CM ❂
Bellissimo Tempranillo 2013 Rating 91 To 2018 $20 CM ❂
Bellissimo Montepulciano 2014 Rating 91 To 2017 $20 ❂

Serrat   ★★★★★

PO Box 478, Yarra Glen, Vic 3775 **Region** Yarra Valley
T (03) 9730 1439 **www.**serrat.com.au **Open** Not
Winemaker Tom Carson **Est.** 2001 **Dozens** 300 **Vyds** 2.04ha
Serrat is the family business of Tom Carson (after a 12-year reign at Yering Station, now running Yabby Lake and Heathcote Estate for the Kirby family) and wife Nadege Suné. They have close-planted (at 8800 vines per hectare) 0.8ha each of pinot noir and chardonnay, 0.4ha of shiraz, and a sprinkling of viognier. Serrat was devastated by the Black Saturday bushfires in February 2009, the entire vintage destroyed. That is now a nightmare of the past, viticulture and winemaking hitting new heights with the '14 Yarra Valley Shiraz Viognier named 2016 *Wine Companion* Wine of the Year (from a field of 8863 wines).

🍷🍷🍷🍷🍷 **Yarra Valley Shiraz Viognier 2014** If anyone thinks Shiraz Viognier can't attain fully ripe flavour development at 13% they should move heaven and earth to get hold of a bottle of this wine. Gloriously coloured, it has a Joseph's coat of forest berry fruits, flashing red and black flavours, spice and cracked pepper, quality oak also contributing. The most remarkable feature is the way it refuses to let its flavours leave the mouth after you have swallowed it, introducing another level to the concept of palate length and aftertaste. It also proves the greatest wines are perfect from the first moment they are bottled, the future revealing different facets, but not impinging on their quality. Screwcap. 13% alc. **Rating** 99 To 2044 $40 ❂

🍷🍷🍷🍷🍷 **Yarra Valley Chardonnay 2014** A super-elegant Chardonnay, perfectly capturing the line and extreme length that is the mark of the region; grapefruit leads the flavours, followed by white peach and minerally acidity; oak plays an important role in building on the structure provided by the acidity. All good, as they say, but more again in due course. Screwcap. 13% alc. **Rating** 96 To 2029 $40 ❂

Yarra Valley Pinot Noir 2014 Bright, clear crimson; the fragrance of the bouquet sends an unequivocal message of a complex web of red fruits, spice and a perfectly presented touch of forest floor. Elegance and length are the key words for a Pinot with a long and prosperous journey ahead. Screwcap. 13% alc. **Rating** 96 To 2029 $40 ❂

Yarra Valley Grenache Noir 2014 This takes Grenache into Alice in Wonderland territory, its brilliant clarity and perfumed bouquet taking you through the looking glass into a panorama of juicy red berries of every description; tannins and acidity are there, but seemingly always on the other side of the looking glass no matter how quickly you jump back and forth. Screwcap. 13% alc. **Rating** 96 To 2029 $40 ❂

Sevenhill Cellars

111c College Road, Sevenhill, SA 5453 **Region** Clare Valley
T (08) 8843 4222 **www**.sevenhill.com.au **Open** 7 days 10–5
Winemaker Liz Heidenreich, Brother John May **Est.** 1851 **Dozens** 25 000 **Vyds** 95.8ha
One of the historical treasures of Australia; the oft-photographed stone wine cellars are the
oldest in the Clare Valley, and winemaking remains an enterprise within the Jesuit Province
of Australia. Value for money is excellent, particularly for the powerful Shiraz and Riesling;
all the wines reflect the estate-grown grapes from old vines. Notwithstanding the difficult
economic times, Sevenhill Cellars has increased its vineyard holdings from 74 to 95ha, and
naturally, production has risen. Exports to the UK, Switzerland, Indonesia, Malaysia, Vietnam,
Japan, Hong Kong and China.

🍷🍷🍷🍷🍷 **Inigo Clare Valley Shiraz 2012** Three blocks of vines, 150, 70 and 38yo; open-
fermented in slate vats, basket pressed and matured in French oak (25% new).
I can't begin to understand how it has avoided the dead fruit characters that
usually haunt 15.5% alcohol wines; the deep, savoury, brooding black fruits,
quality oak and very good tannin structure and texture all hit the mark. Screwcap.
Rating 95 To 2042 $25 ✪

St Francis Xavier Single Vineyard 2014 From the 0.85ha Weikert Vineyard,
one of five vineyards owned by Sevenhill. A tightly focused Riesling with excellent
squeaky acidity and a long, fine palate; elegance and balance are the key words.
Screwcap. 12% alc. **Rating** 94 To 2029 $35

Inigo Clare Valley Shiraz 2013 The vines are more than 70yo; 100yo slate
open fermenters, hand-plunged, basket-pressed, matured in 25% new French and
75% used French and American oak. Dense, inky purple-crimson, this is a vinous
black hole in space, fruit, oak and tannins implacably welded together, not allowing
the alcohol to make a mark. Screwcap. 15.2% alc. **Rating** 94 To 2038 $28 ✪

Inigo Clare Valley Cabernet Sauvignon 2013 An awesomely powerful wine
despite its modest alcohol; layer upon layer of midnight black fruits, black olive
and gnarly tannins lay the foundation for a life as long as that of Brother John May.
Screwcap. 14% alc. **Rating** 94 To 2043 $28 ✪

🍷🍷🍷🍷🍷 **Museum Release St Francis Xavier Riesling 2010** Rating 93 To 2020 $40
Inigo Clare Valley Grenache 2013 Rating 93 To 2028 $28
St Ignatius 2012 Rating 91 To 2021 $40
Classic Topaque NV Rating 91 To 2016 $25
Clare Valley Fine Old Tawny NV Rating 90 To 2016 $25

Seville Estate

65 Linwood Road, Seville, Vic 3139 **Region** Yarra Valley
T (03) 5964 2622 **www**.sevilleestate.com.au **Open** 7 days 10–5
Winemaker Dylan McMahon **Est.** 1972 **Dozens** 60 100 **Vyds** 8.08ha
Dr Peter McMahon and wife Margaret commenced planting Seville Estate in 1972, part of
the resurgence of the Yarra Valley. Peter and Margaret retired in '97, selling to Brokenwood.
Graham and Margaret Van Der Meulen acquired the property in 2005, bringing it back into
family ownership. Graham and Margaret are hands-on in the vineyard and winery, working
closely with winemaker Dylan McMahon, who is the grandson of Peter and Margaret. The
philosophy is to capture the fruit expression of the vineyard in styles that reflect the cool
climate. Peter McMahon, having survived wife Margaret, died peacefully, aged 88, in Oct '13.
Exports to the US, Fiji, Taiwan and China.

🍷🍷🍷🍷🍷 **Reserve Chardonnay 2013** Scintillating style, flavour and execution. This grabs
you by the shirt and refuses to let go. A power of white peach, grapefruit, wheat
and struck match flavours, all in harmony and all full of running from the start to
the long finish. Screwcap. 13% alc. **Rating** 96 To 2020 $70 CM ✪

Old Vine Reserve Shiraz 2013 Exquisite fruit and tannin profile. Age-
worthiness is emblazoned across its chest and yet seamlessness is already its middle
name. Dark cherry and chocolate with pepper and woodsmoke notes; it's fruity

and spicy, yet sturdy, the generosity of the fruit runs along strict rails. Screwcap. 13.5% alc. Rating 96 To 2033 $70 CM ⊙

Chardonnay 2014 In pristine shape. Perfectly presented and flavoured. Lemon, white peach and grapefruit with complexing notes of oatmeal, toasty oak and flint. Rings clear and convincing through the finish. Screwcap. 13% alc. **Rating** 94 To 2020 $36 CM

Reserve Chardonnay 2014 A wine of elegant power, still resolving itself but clearly of high quality. Lemon curd, white peach, spicy-sweet oak and chalk, with a pure burst of refreshing flavour reaching out through the finish. Its best days are a few years away. Screwcap. 13% alc. **Rating** 94 To 2021 $70 CM

 Yarra Valley Riesling 2014 Rating 93 To 2020 $36 CM
Yarra Valley Shiraz 2013 Rating 93 To 2024 $36 CM
The Barber Yarra Valley Chardonnay 2014 Rating 92 To 2018 $24 CM ⊙
The Barber Yarra Valley Rose 2014 Rating 91 To 2015 $24 CM
Yarra Valley Pinot Noir 2014 Rating 91 To 2020 $36 CM
Yarra Valley Cabernet Merlot 2013 Rating 91 To 2020 $24 CM

Seville Hill ★★★★

8 Paynes Road, Seville, Vic 3139 **Region** Yarra Valley
T (03) 5964 3284 **www**.sevillehill.com.au **Open** 7 days 10–6
Winemaker Dominic Bucci, John D'Aloisio **Est.** 1991 **Dozens** 3000 **Vyds** 6ha
John and Josie D'Aloisio have had a long-term involvement in the agricultural industry, which ultimately led to the establishment of the Seville Hill vineyard in 1991. Plantings of cabernet sauvignon replaced the old apple and cherry orchard on the site. A small winery was established on the property, with long-term friend Dominic Bucci and John D'Aloisio making the wines. In 2011 1ha of the original 6ha was grafted over to nebbiolo, barbera, sangiovese and tempranillo. John and Josie's sons Christopher, Jason and Charles are also involved in all aspects of the business.

 Yarra Valley Merlot 2010 Has retained freshness, and belies its alcohol; blackcurrant, plum and a trace of black olive are complemented by fine-grained tannins and integrated French oak. A good Merlot – a rare beast. Cork. 14.5% alc. Rating 93 To 2025 $30
Yarra Valley Sauvignon Blanc 2014 Has more presence and varietal character than many Yarra Valley Sauvignon Blancs; here gooseberry, snow pea, lime and zesty acidity provide both length and depth. Ready now. Screwcap. 13.5% alc. Rating 90 To 2015 $27
Yarra Valley Pinot Noir 2013 Good colour; a potent and complex Pinot all about flavour and structure; not so much about finesse. Needs time to smooth the wrinkles, and should repay cellaring. Cork. 13.8% alc. Rating 90 To 2023 $30

 Yarra Valley Cabernet Sauvignon 2010 Rating 89 To 2020 $30

Sew & Sew Wines ★★★★

PO Box 1924, McLaren Flat, SA 5171 **Region** Adelaide Hills
T 0419 804 345 **www**.sewandsewwines.com.au **Open** Not
Winemaker Jodie Armstrong **Est.** 2004 **Dozens** 200
Owner and winemaker Jodie Armstrong works as a viticulturist by day, consulting to vineyards in the Adelaide Hills and McLaren Vale, at night making small amounts of wine. The grapes are chosen from small sections of three of the vineyards that Jodie manages, making the wines in garagiste facilities in the Adelaide Hills and McLaren Vale with the support of local oenological talent.

 Adelaide Hills Syrah 2012 Single clone (1654), hand-picked, open-fermented, hand-plunged for 14 days, matured in used French (66%) and new American (34%) oak. Deep purple-crimson, it revels in its cool-climate origin, spice and pepper liberally sprinkled on its red and black cherry fruits, the open-weave tannin

structure supporting the fruit and its faintly herbal finish. Screwcap. 13.5% alc.
Rating 94 **To** 2027 $35

ŦŦŦŦŦ **Adelaide Hills Chardonnay 2013** Rating 92 To 2020 $35

Shadowfax   ★★★★★

K Road, Werribee, Vic 3030 **Region** Geelong
T (03) 9731 4420 **www.**shadowfax.com.au **Open** 7 days 11–5
Winemaker Matt Harrop **Est.** 2000 **Dozens** 15 000
Shadowfax is part of an awesome development at Werribee Park, a mere 20 minutes from
Melbourne. The truly striking winery, designed by Wood Marsh Architects and built in 2000,
is adjacent to the extraordinary private home built in the 1880s by the Chirnside family and
known as The Mansion. It was then the centrepiece of a 40 000ha pastoral empire, and the
appropriately magnificent gardens were part of the reason for the property being acquired by
Parks Victoria in the early 1970s. The Mansion is now The Mansion Hotel, with 92 rooms
and suites. Exports to the UK, Japan, NZ and Singapore.

ŦŦŦŦŦ **Waterson Road Macedon Ranges Pinot Noir 2013** Light colour, strong
personality. Dark cherry, ground spice, mint and cloves with fragrant green herbs
swaying in the background. A wine of poise, unbroken lines and fresh, satiny
length. Tannin has been judged to perfection. Screwcap. 13% alc. **Rating** 96
To 2025 $50 CM ✪
Midhill Chardonnay 2013 20yo vineyard at 530m. Wild yeast-fermented. Straw
colour, excellence sense of both presence and power, grapefruit and white peach
notes with inflections of chalk, spice and toast. A little more time in bottle will do
it no harm. Screwcap. 13% alc. **Rating** 95 **To** 2020 $50 CM
Macedon Ranges Chardonnay 2013 Grown on three separate vineyards, all
Macedon Ranges. It's an exemplary wine, neat and tidy but oozing substance.
Peach, bacon, oatmeal and cool lines of acidity. Textural finish. Not a big wine, but
it sits on the right side of the modern equation; it's certainly not too lean, with
plenty of flavour to grab onto. Screwcap. 13% alc. **Rating** 95 **To** 2020 $32 CM ✪
Werribee Rose 2014 Made from estate-grown cinsaut, mondeuse and pinot
noir; given a short maceration on skins, then pressed to used French barriques.
Deep, clear, blueish crimson; liqueur cherries, strawberries and exotic spices fill
the long, fruity, but bone-dry palate. A rose with abundant attitude. Screwcap.
12.5% alc. **Rating** 95 **To** 2017 $22 ✪
Macedon Ranges Pinot Noir 2013 In varietal terms the value here is not to
be sniffed at. It's polished, charming, has enough power and more than enough
length. It tastes of dark cherry, forest, graphite and cloves, though it's the wine's
pretty, rose-petal notes that attract the most attention. Quite beautiful all round.
Screwcap. 13% alc. **Rating** 94 **To** 2020 $32 CM
Port Phillip Heathcote Shiraz 2012 From the winery vineyard at Werribee
and from Heathcote. A super-elegant, light to medium-bodied wine, tripping
lightly along the palate with its profusion of spices, red fruits and plums; the
tannins are a silken gauze, the oak surprisingly well integrated. Ready now or
soonish. Screwcap. 13.5% alc. **Rating** 94 **To** 2022 $24 ✪

Sharmans   ★★★★

175 Glenwood Road, Relbia, Tas 7258 **Region** Northern Tasmania
T (03) 6343 0773 **www.**sharmanswines.com.au **Open** W'ends 11–5 Mar–May & Sept,
7 days Dec–Feb
Winemaker Jeremy Dineen, Ockie Myburgh, Stewart Bryne **Est.** 1986 **Dozens** 2200
Vyds 7ha
When Mike Sharman planted the first vines at Relbia in 1986, he was the pioneer of the
region, and he did so in the face of widespread belief that it was too far inland, and frost-prone.
He proved the doomsayers wrong, helped by the slope of the vineyard draining cold air away
from the vines. In 2012 the property was acquired by Dr Ian and Melissa Murrell and Matt

and Miranda Creak. Both Mike and his viticulturist, Bill Rayner, continue to help with the management of the vineyard, with direction from Matt. In '13 an additional 3.5ha of vines were planted, taking the total to 7ha, the larger plantings being 2.3ha of pinot noir and 1ha each of chardonnay and pinot gris; the balance is made up of smaller plantings of riesling, sauvignon blanc, cabernet sauvignon, merlot, shiraz, muscat, saperavi and dornfelder – a mixed grill if ever there was one.

ΨΨΨΨΨ **Sauvignon Blanc 2014** Has a ghetto blast of multiple flavours, and the attitude that so mysteriously escapes most Tasmanian Sauvignon Blancs. For once, flights of fancy are all on the table: melon rind, cosmetic spices, passionfruit, banana, guava and ripe capsicum. Serve fully chilled with any dish on a hot day. Screwcap. 12% alc. **Rating** 94 **To** 2017 $28 ◯

Pinot Noir 2013 Good colour; the clever use of oak is one part of the complexity of the wine, its excellent length another; the spicy/savoury, yet fine, palate suggests some whole-bunch inclusions, but it's not always easy to decide with Tasmanian Pinot. Screwcap. 14% alc. **Rating** 94 **To** 2021 $35

ΨΨΨΨႳ **Chardonnay 2013 Rating** 93 **To** 2020 $30
Riesling 2014 Rating 92 **To** 2024 $28

Shaw + Smith ★★★★★

136 Jones Road, Balhannah, SA 5242 **Region** Adelaide Hills
T (08) 8398 0500 **www**.shawandsmith.com **Open** 7 days 11–5
Winemaker Martin Shaw, Adam Wadewitz **Est.** 1989 **Dozens** NFP **Vyds** 80.9ha
Cousins Martin Shaw and Michael Hill Smith MW already had unbeatable experience when they founded Shaw + Smith as a virtual winery in 1989. The brand was firmly established as a leading producer of Sauvignon Blanc by the time they acquired a 42ha property at Woodside known as the M3 Vineyard (as it is owned by Michael and Matthew Hill Smith and Martin Shaw). In '99 Martin and Michael purchased the 36ha Balhannah property, building the superbly designed winery in 2000 and planting more sauvignon blanc, shiraz, pinot noir and riesling. It is here that visitors can taste the wines in appropriately beautiful surroundings. In '13 the partners acquired the long-established and distinguished Tolpuddle Vineyard in the Coal River/Richmond area of southern Tasmania (see separate entry); they market those wines (Chardonnay and Pinot Noir) separately. Exports to all major markets.

ΨΨΨΨΨ **Adelaide Hills Shiraz 2013** Vivid crimson; the fragrant array of black cherry, blackberry, spice and cracked pepper aromas feed into the beautifully textured and proportioned palate, where silky tannins provide perfect support and mouthfeel. A top-notch successor to the acclaimed '12. Screwcap. 14% alc. **Rating** 97 **To** 2035 $44 ◯

ΨΨΨΨΨ **Adelaide Hills Riesling 2014** Half whole bunch-pressed, half crushed and pressed. An attractive, if left-field, parade of citrus, Granny Smith apples and tropical fruits provides a juicy coating for the tongue before neatly coiled acidity opens, lengthens and balances the finish. Screwcap. 11% alc. **Rating** 95 **To** 2029 $30 ◯

Adelaide Hills Sauvignon Blanc 2014 The run of quality continues, but the vibrancy of this release sets it apart. This glistens both in the glass and on the palate. Vibrant tropical fruit with nuances of cut grass and chalk. Bounces with flavour from the attack all the way through to a lengthy finish. Reeks of fruit and confidence. Screwcap. 12% alc. **Rating** 95 **To** 2016 $25 CM ◯

Adelaide Hills Pinot Noir 2013 From the winery block, and from Shaw + Smith's recently purchased Lenswood vineyard (higher and cooler); a hand-plunged mix of whole berry and whole bunches, with a pre-ferment cold soak and post-ferment maceration; matured in French barriques. A caboodle of every type of cherry fruit flavour, round and satisfying, long and well balanced. Needs time. Screwcap. 12.5% alc. **Rating** 94 **To** 2023 $45

Shaw Family Vintners

Myrtle Grove Road, Currency Creek, SA 5214 **Region** Currency Creek/McLaren Vale
T (08) 8555 4215 **www**.shawfamilyvintners.com **Open** 7 days 10–5
Winemaker John Loxton **Est.** 2001 **Dozens** 100 000 **Vyds** 461ha
Richard and Marie Shaw ventured into the wine industry by planting shiraz in the early 1970s
at McLaren Flat. They still have the original vineyards, and during the Vine Pull Scheme of
the '80s saved several neighbours' valuable old shiraz and grenache. Their three sons are also
involved in the family business. Extensive vineyards are now held in McLaren Vale (64ha)
and Currency Creek (350ha), with a modern winery in Currency Creek. There are now six
price tiers: Icon (The Encounter Cabernet Sauvignon, The Ballaster Cabernet Sauvignon and
The Figurehead Shiraz), Emetior and RMS, Single Vineyard, Ballast Stone, Stonemason and
Steeple Jack. RMS is the flagship release, named in honour of founder Richard Morton Shaw.
Shaw Family has a second cellar door and café at Signal Point, Goolwa. Underwent a name
change from Ballast Stone Estate to Shaw Family Vintners in 2014. Exports to the UK, the
US, Canada, Fiji, NZ and China.

🍷🍷🍷🍷🍷 **The Ballaster McLaren Vale Cabernet Sauvignon 2010** From 65yo
vines, matured in French puncheons for 2 years. A light year removed from
the raw power of The Encounter, here elegance is the theme, with cassis and
cedar interwoven, tannins at a modest boil; the line, length and balance are all
exceptional. Cork. 14% alc. **Rating** 96 **To** 2025 $80
The Encounter Currency Creek Cabernet Sauvignon 2012 Hand-selected
bunches are dried for 2 weeks then placed in small fermenters for carbonic
maceration for 10 days, then crushed and fermented for 10 days; 12 months'
maturation in French oak. Dense colour; I don't understand how or why, but
the alcohol doesn't come over the top of the blackcurrant fruit, the fine tannins
providing the finish, not alcohol. Cork. 16% alc. **Rating** 95 **To** 2032 $80
Emetior Limited Release McLaren Vale Shiraz 2012 Heaven forbid that
anyone should try to pick up a dozen bottles of this wine: how can glass be so
heavy? It is an allegory for the wine, yet it manages to carry the alcohol with its
vibrant array of red and black fruits, anise and dark chocolate; the silky tannins are,
I suspect, the answer. Cork. 15% alc. **Rating** 94 **To** 2032 $60

🍷🍷🍷🍷🍷 **Stonemason Cabernet Sauvignon 2013** **Rating** 90 **To** 2018 $15 ✪
Ballast Stone Monster Pitch McLaren Vale Cabernet Sauvignon 2013
Rating 90 **To** 2025 $25

Shaw Vineyard Estate ★★★★☆

34 Isabel Drive, Murrumbateman, NSW 2582 **Region** Canberra District
T (02) 6227 5827 **www**.shawvineyards.com.au **Open** Wed–Sun & public hols 10–5
Winemaker Graeme Shaw, Tony Steffania **Est.** 1999 **Dozens** 12 000 **Vyds** 33ha
Graeme and Ann Shaw established their vineyard (cabernet sauvignon, merlot, shiraz, semillon
and riesling) in 1998 on a 280ha fine wool-producing property established in the mid-1800s
and known as Olleyville. It is one of the largest privately owned vineyard holdings in the
Canberra area. Their children are fully employed in the family business, Michael as viticulturist
and Tanya as cellar door manager. The cellar door offers a wide range of local produce, as
well as handmade ceramics from Deruta in Italy. Shaw Vineyard Estate operates a 'wine shop'
cellar door in conjunction with Suntay Wines in Hainan Island, China, with plans for further
cellar doors in Shi Jia Zuang and Changzhi. Exports to Canada, The Netherlands, Vietnam,
Singapore, Thailand, the Philippines and China.

🍷🍷🍷🍷🍷 **Isabella Reserve Canberra District Riesling 2014** Terrific intensity. Limey
flavour attacks from the word go and continues all the way through to a thrilling
finish. Musk, various florals and spice notes play an active role. Sweetness adds to
the volume of flavour, but it's that sizzling acidity that sets the wine aloft. Screwcap.
11.5% alc. **Rating** 95 **To** 2026 $30 CM ✪

🍷🍷🍷🍷🍷 **Semillon Sauvignon Blanc 2014** **Rating** 91 **To** 2016 $22 CM ✪
Winemakers Selection Riesling 2014 **Rating** 90 **To** 2018 $16 CM ✪
Winemakers Selection Shiraz 2013 **Rating** 90 **To** 2019 $16 CM ✪

She-Oak Hill Vineyard

82 Hope Street, South Yarra, Vic 3141 (postal) **Region** Heathcote
T (03) 9866 7890 **www**.sheoakhill.com.au **Open** Not
Winemaker Sanguine Estate (Mark Hunter) **Est.** 1995 **Dozens** 550 **Vyds** 5ha
This is the venture of Judith Firkin and Gordon and Julian Leckie, who between 1975 and '95 planted shiraz (4.5ha) and chardonnay (0.5ha). The vineyard is located on the southern and eastern slopes of She Oak Hill, 6km north of Heathcote. It lies between Jasper Hill's Emily's Paddock and Mt Ida vineyards, and thus has the same type of porous, deep red Cambrian soil. The decision to opt for dry-grown vines has meant low yields.

Aurelio's Heathcote Shiraz 2013 From 38yo estate vines, matured in French barriques. Good colour; a powerful, full-bodied Shiraz with layers of plum fruit; seems to miss a step on the finish; not easy to tell what is going on, and where it will go. Given the benefit of the doubt given its breeding. Screwcap. 14.5% alc. **Rating** 90 **To** 2023 $25

Shepherd's Hut

PO Box 194, Darlington, WA 6070 **Region** Porongurup
T (08) 9299 6700 **www**.shepherdshutwines.com **Open** Not
Winemaker Rob Diletti (Contract) **Est.** 1996 **Dozens** 2000 **Vyds** 15.5ha
The shepherd's hut that appears on the wine label was one of four stone huts used in the 1850s to house shepherds tending large flocks of sheep. When WA pathologist Dr Michael Wishart (and family) purchased the property in 1996, the hut was in a state of extreme disrepair. It has since been restored, still featuring the honey-coloured Mount Barker stone. Riesling, chardonnay, sauvignon blanc, shiraz and cabernet sauvignon have been established. The business is now owned by son Philip and wife Cathy, who also run a large farm of mainly cattle. Most of the grapes are sold to other makers in the region, but those retained make high-quality wine at mouth-watering prices thanks to the skill of winemaker Rob Diletti.

Pinot Noir 2013 It leads with its jaw in the prettiest of ways. It's all upfront and perfumed with a crush of spices barrelling in behind. Jubey black cherry flavours are the mainstay, but there are many floral and spice influences here; it's better described as a tag team effort. Screwcap. 13.3% alc. **Rating** 92 **To** 2020 $21 CM ✪

Porongurup Shiraz 2010 Rating 88 **To** 2017 $22 CM

Shingleback

3 Stump Hill Road, McLaren Vale, SA 5171 **Region** McLaren Vale
T (08) 8323 7388 **www**.shingleback.com.au **Open** 7 days 10–5
Winemaker John Davey, Dan Hills **Est.** 1995 **Dozens** 120 000 **Vyds** 110ha
Brothers Kym and John Davey planted and nurture their family-owned and sustainably managed vineyard on land purchased by their grandfather in the 1950s. Shingleback has been a success story since its establishment. Its 110ha of estate vineyards are one of the keys to that success, winning the Jimmy Watson Trophy '06 for the '05 D Block Cabernet Sauvignon. The well made wines are rich and full-flavoured, but not overripe (and, hence, not excessively alcoholic). Exports to the UK, the US, Canada, Switzerland, Germany, Indonesia, Vietnam, China and NZ.

Unedited McLaren Vale Shiraz 2013 Full crimson-purple; singularly full-bodied and intense, the flavours pulsating throughout the long carry in the mouth; a very complex and distinguished wine that, despite all of its intensity, remains light-footed, inviting you back repeatedly to experience its many facets. Cork. 14.5% alc. **Rating** 97 **To** 2043 $80 ✪

The Gate McLaren Vale Shiraz 2013 Full crimson-purple; a richly upholstered full-bodied wine, with a savoury/tarry/dark chocolate framework for the blackberry fruit, tannins adding their voice to the finish of the palate. This has the depth and balance to live and develop for decades to come. Cork. 14.5% alc. Rating 96 To 2043 $35 ✪

D Block Reserve McLaren Vale Shiraz 2012 Bright, full crimson-purple; a selection from French and American oak barrels; the sense of place and varietal expression combine synergistically, the oak absorbed by the power of the fruit, the tannins ripe and balanced. Cork. 14.5% alc. Rating 96 To 2042 $55 ✪

Davey Estate Reserve McLaren Vale Shiraz 2013 Small-batch open-fermented, 14 months' maturation in American and French oak. Deep purple-crimson; a totally convincing step up the quality ladder from Davey Brothers, with greater depth to its bouquet and medium to full-bodied palate alike, the theme of black fruits, dark chocolate and balanced tannins providing a seriously good wine at the price. Screwcap. 14.5% alc. Rating 94 To 2033 $23 ✪

ᵠᵠᵠᵠᵠ Davey Estate Reserve Cabernet 2013 Rating 93 To 2028 $23 ✪
Red Knot McLaren Vale Shiraz 2014 Rating 92 To 2025 $15 ✪
Davey Brothers McLaren Vale Shiraz 2013 Rating 92 To 2025 $18 ✪
Haycutters McLaren Vale Shiraz 2013 Rating 91 To 2023 $17 ✪
Haycutters Salmon McLaren Vale Rose 2014 Rating 90 To 2015 $16 ✪
Davey Brothers McLaren Vale Shiraz 2012 Rating 90 To 2022 $18 ✪
Red Knot Cabernet Sauvignon 2014 Rating 90 To 2024 $15 ✪

Shirvington   ★★★★★

PO Box 220, McLaren Vale, SA 5171 **Region** McLaren Vale
T (08) 8323 7649 **www**.shirvington.com **Open** Not
Winemaker Kim Jackson **Est.** 1996 **Dozens** 800 **Vyds** 23.8ha
The Shirvington family began the development of their McLaren Vale vineyards in 1996 under the direction of viticulturist Peter Bolte, and now have almost 24ha under vine, the majority to shiraz and cabernet sauvignon, with small additional plantings of mataro and grenache. A substantial part of the production is sold as grapes, the best reserved for the Shirvington wines as exemplified by the '11 vintage. Exports to the UK and the US.

ᵠᵠᵠᵠᵠ The Redwind McLaren Vale Shiraz 2011 Has the same superb, deep colour as its siblings. Finished its fermentation in two French puncheons, one new, the other 1yo. One of the best McLaren Vale Shirazs to come from this vintage, it has exceptional medium-bodied mouthfeel from fruit and oak tannins, flavours of black fruits and (I promise you) the burnt caramel and freshly ground coffee described by the Shirvingtons. Cork. 14.5% alc. Rating 96 To 2031 $75 ✪

Scarce Earth Block 9 McLaren Vale Shiraz 2011 Matured in a 2yo French hogshead for 15 months. A complete wine that shows just how well the vineyard coped with the weather. Strong and deeply coloured, it has copious black fruits, plum and dark chocolate fruit flavours supported by velvety tannins. 31 dozen made. Cork. 14.8% alc. Rating 95 To 2031 $45

The Redwind McLaren Vale Cabernet Sauvignon 2011 100% finished barrel ferment in and matured for 19 months in 90% French, 10% American oak (100% new). Given that only 30 dozen bottles were made, the 90/10% split is impossible unless it refers to mixed staves in a barrel. This to one side, it has great depth and generosity to the fruit, which is strongly varietal, and does carry the new oak. Cork. 14.5% alc. Rating 95 To 2036 $70

ᵠᵠᵠᵠᵠ McLaren Vale Shiraz 2011 Rating 91 To 2026 $38
McLaren Vale Cabernet Sauvignon 2011 Rating 90 To 2018 $35

Shoofly | Frisk   ★★★

PO Box 119, Mooroolbark, Vic 3138 **Region** Various
T 0405 631 557 **www**.shooflywines.com **Open** Not
Winemaker Ben Riggs, Behn Payton, Garry Wall **Est.** 2003 **Dozens** 39 000
This is a far-flung, export-oriented, business. It purchases a little over 620 tonnes of grapes each vintage, the lion's share (surprisingly) riesling (250 tonnes), followed by shiraz (200 tonnes)

and chardonnay (50 tonnes); the remainder is made up of pinot noir, gewurztraminer, merlot, dolcetto and muscat gordo blanco. Ben Riggs makes Shoofly Shiraz and Chardonnay at Vintners McLaren Vale; Shoofly Pinot Noir is made by Behn Payton at Punt Road in the Yarra Valley; Frisk Riesling is made by Garry Wall at King Valley Wines. The bulk of exports go to the US, Canada and Ireland.

ŶŶŶŶ **Frisk Prickly Riesling 2014** A fun, party-ready, off-dry Riesling with a light fizz. It tastes of baked apple, lime zest and honey; clean, fruity and appealing. It's well made and priced right. Give it a very stern chill and drink it like Moscato. Screwcap. 9.5% alc. **Rating** 88 **To** 2015 $10 TS ❁

Shottesbrooke   ★★★★☆

Bagshaws Road, McLaren Flat, SA 5171 **Region** McLaren Vale
T (08) 8383 0002 **www.**shottesbrooke.com.au **Open** Mon–Fri 10–4.30, w'ends 11–5
Winemaker Hamish Maguire, Duncan Kennedy **Est.** 1984 **Dozens** 12000 **Vyds** 30.64ha
Founded by Nick Holmes, who has since passed the winemaking baton on to stepson Hamish Maguire, Shottesbrooke these days is a very different business from that of the 1980s and '90s. As well as the great advantage of over 30ha of mature vines in McLaren Vale, it has ongoing access to sauvignon blanc from the Adelaide Hills. Exports to all major markets.

ŶŶŶŶŶ **McLaren Vale Cabernet Sauvignon 2012** The region and the variety share front stage, the former contributing some bitter chocolate, the latter blackcurrant and balanced tannins; there is a good volume of fruit here for a wine with a clear future. Screwcap. 14.5% alc. **Rating** 93 **To** 2022 $20 ❁
Single Vineyard Jenkin's Vineyard McLaren Vale Shiraz 2013 Grapes grown on the Lazy Ballerina trellis; 9 months in French oak. The trellis was developed for cool regions needing maximum exposure of the grapes to sunlight; it's hard to pin down, but there is something missing on the mid to back-palate. 500 dozen made. Screwcap. 14.5% alc. **Rating** 90 **To** 2023 $40
McLaren Vale Shiraz 2012 From 30+yo estate vines. Shrieks of its region, with chocolate augmented by vanillan/mocha oak and soft tannins. Carnivore heaven at the right price. Screwcap. 14.5% alc. **Rating** 90 **To** 2020 $20 ❁

ŶŶŶŶ **Estate Series Sauvignon Blanc 2014 Rating** 89 **To** 2015 $20
Estate Series Cabernet Sauvignon 2012 Rating 89 **To** 2019 $20
Estate Series GSM 2013 Rating 88 **To** 2016 $20

Shut the Gate Wines   ★★★★

2 Main North Road, Watervale, SA 5452 **Region** Clare Valley
T 0488 243 200 **Open** 7 days 10–4.30
Winemaker Contract **Est.** 2013 **Dozens** 5000
Shut the Gate is the venture of Richard Woods and Rasa Fabian, which took shape after five years' involvement in the rebranding of Crabtree Watervale Wines, followed by 18 months of juggling consultancy roles. During this time Richard and Rasa set the foundations for Shut the Gate, with striking and imaginative labels (and parables) catching the eye. The engine room of the business is the Clare Valley, where the wines are contract-made and the grapes for many of the two ranges of wines are sourced. They have chosen their grape sources and contract winemakers with considerable care. Exports to Canada and Hong Kong.

ŶŶŶŶŶ **For Freedom Polish Hill River Riesling 2014** Purity, power and finesse. Clean lime and slate flavours pick up the pace quickly and then hold through a lengthy finish. It will cellar, but it's a delight to drink as a youngster. Screwcap. 12% alc. **Rating** 94 **To** 2025 $25 CM ❁
For Hunger Single Site Clare Valley Pinot Noir 2012 Complex texture and flavour. Fresh and stewed cherries, eucalypt, undergrowth, meat and a gentle rub of spicy oak. A scented wine. An engaging one with more than a little presence. Screwcap. 14% alc. **Rating** 94 **To** 2022 $28 CM ❁

Ripple Iron Clare Valley Sangiovese 2012 Shut the Gate comes up with a left-field winner here; there is a plethora of sultry red and black cherry fruit on the bouquet and palate, but it is the wonderfully fresh and juicy aftertaste that gives this wine its special quality. Screwcap. 14.5% alc. **Rating** 94 **To** 2020 $20 ✪

ŢŢŢŢŢ **For Hunger Clare Valley Grenache 2012 Rating** 93 **To** 2021 $25 CM ✪
For Love Watervale Riesling 2014 Rating 91 **To** 2021 $25 CM
For Freedom Sauvignon Blanc 2014 Rating 91 **To** 2016 $28
The Forager Clare Valley Shiraz 2010 Rating 91 **To** 2020 $20 CM ✪

Sidewood Estate   ★★★★★

92 Mappinga Road, Oakbank, SA 5243 **Region** Adelaide Hills
T (08) 8389 9234 **www**.sidewood.com.au **Open** Wed–Sun 11–5
Winemaker Darryl Catlin, Natasha Mooney **Est.** 2000 **Dozens** 20 000 **Vyds** 67ha
Sidewood Estate is part-vineyard and part-horse stables and racehorse training. Owned by Owen and Cassandra Inglis since 2004, both aspects of the business are flourishing. Sidewood Estate lies in the Onkaparinga Valley, with the vines weathering the coolest climate in the Adelaide Hills. In recent times it has undergone a substantial planting regeneration program, the vineyard growing to almost 70ha, and extensive investment in modern viticulture equipment has resulted in improved yields. Wines are released under the Sidewood Estate, Stable Hill and Mappinga labels; Mappinga is the new premier range, named after the road on which Sidewood resides. The cellar door is at Maximilian's Restaurant, 15 Onkaparinga Valley Road, Verdun. Exports to the UK, the US, Canada, Belgium, Norway, Malaysia, Hong Kong, Singapore, Thailand and China.

ŢŢŢŢŢ **Mappinga Shiraz 2013** 100% Adelaide Hills, 4 clones separately picked and wild yeast-fermented, 20% whole-bunch carbonic maceration, matured for 22 months in new and used French oak. Deep, vivid crimson-purple; the bouquet is attractive, but it is the length and balance of the intense, medium-bodied palate that sends the taste buds into overdrive with spice, pepper and sage underlying the majestic array of black cherry, blood plum and blackberry fruits; the tannin and oak balance is immaculate. Screwcap. 14.5% alc. **Rating** 97 **To** 2043 $55 ✪

ŢŢŢŢŢ **Adelaide Hills Shiraz 2013** Multiple clones from the estate Oakbank Vineyard; co-fermented with 25% whole bunches, finished in French barriques (30% new) and 12 months' maturation. Gold medals Melbourne and Adelaide Wine Shows '14. A great example of the synergy between the Adelaide Hills and shiraz, producing an unequivocally cool-grown style, yet with a thoroughly engaging richness to its strongly spiced black fruits and ripe tannins. Screwcap. 14% alc. **Rating** 96 **To** 2043 $25 ✪
Mappinga Reserve Adelaide Hills Chardonnay 2012 Hand-picked, whole bunch-pressed, chilled 1–2 days, partially wild yeast-fermented in tank, then to French barriques (60% new), 7 months', 35% mlf. I am mystified by the huge price differential between this and its '13 vintage counterpart; certainly this wine has both restraint and simultaneous complexity, only plus its incremental increase in length. Screwcap. 13.5% alc. **Rating** 95 **To** 2022 $35 ✪
Adelaide Hills Pinot Noir 2013 Clones 113, 144, 777 and MV6; partial fermentation in open pots, then finished fermentation in French barriques (15% new), followed by 18 months' maturation. A very well made and expressive Pinot that ticks all the boxes; the mouthfeel has that X-factor from partial barrel ferment, the oak perfectly integrated and providing context for the spiced plum fruit. Exceptional value. Screwcap. 13.5% alc. **Rating** 95 **To** 2025 $25 ✪
Adelaide Hills Sauvignon Blanc 2014 Hand-picked over a number of days for complexity, chilled overnight before whole bunch pressing and cool fermentation in stainless steel. An unusually elegant wine with ripe citrus and gooseberry fruit to the fore. Screwcap. 13% alc. **Rating** 94 **To** 2016 $20 ✪
The Owen Adelaide Hills Chardonnay 2014 Hand-picked, Dijon clones 76 and 91, whole bunch-pressed after 48 hours' chilling, one new French

puncheon and two 1yo barriques, partial mlf, 10 months in oak. Punctilious attention to detail is obvious from the outset, but I obstinately wonder whether the mlf added to rather than detracted from the palate; there's much to like, regardless of the question. Screwcap. 13% alc. **Rating** 94 **To** 2023 $55
Adelaide Hills Chardonnay 2013 60% whole bunch-pressed and wild yeast-fermented, 40% with cultured yeasts, 30% barrel-fermented in French barriques, 10% in tank. $20? You have to be joking. This is a complex, yet welcoming Chardonnay, packed to the rafters with varietal fruit at the tipping point between stone fruit and citrus, the latter winning on the finish and aftertaste, the former up to the mid-palate. Screwcap. 13.5% alc. **Rating** 94 **To** 2023 $20

ŸŸŸŸŸ **Mappinga Adelaide Hills Sauvignon Blanc 2013** Rating 93 To 2018 $35
Chloe Cuvee 2012 Rating 93 To 2016 $30 TS
Adelaide Hills Isabella Rose 2012 Rating 93 To 2015 $25 TS
Adelaide Hills Pinot Gris 2014 Rating 92 To 2015 $20
Stable Hill Mustang Shiraz 2013 Rating 91 To 2028 $18
Stable Hill The Little Villager Pinot Noir 2013 Rating 90 To 2017 $18

Sieber Road Wines ★★★★

Sieber Road, Tanunda, SA 5352 **Region** Barossa Valley
T (08) 8562 8038 **www.**sieberwines.com **Open** 7 days 11–4
Winemaker Tony Carapetis **Est.** 1999 **Dozens** 4500 **Vyds** 18ha
Richard and Val Sieber are the third generation to run Redlands, the family property, traditionally a cropping/grazing farm. They have diversified into viticulture with shiraz (14ha) the lion's share, the remainder viognier, grenache and mourvedre. Son Ben Sieber is the viticulturist. Exports to Canada and China.

ŸŸŸŸŸ **Barossa Valley Shiraz Grenache 2012** A 71/29% blend; 7-day ferment, matured for 15 months in 2yo French oak. Gold medal/trophy Marananga Wine Show '14. The blackberry and plum fruit of the shiraz obviously dominates proceedings, but the red berry/raspberry flavours of the grenache have no confection notes and slide seamlessly alongside the shiraz. A very attractive, well-made wine. Screwcap. 14.3% alc. **Rating** 94 **To** 2032 $20

ŸŸŸŸŸ **Shiraz Mataro 2012** Rating 92 To 2017 $20
Grenache Shiraz Mourvedre 2012 Rating 92 To 2022 $20
Douceur Viognier 2014 Rating 90 To 2015 $20

Silent Way ★★★★★

PO Box 630, Lancefield, Vic 3435 **Region** Macedon Ranges
T 0409 159 577 **www.**silentway.com.au **Open** Not
Winemaker Matt Harrop **Est.** 2009 **Dozens** 1000 **Vyds** 1.2ha
This is a busman's holiday for partners Matt Harrop and Tamara Grischy (and their three children, Jai, Ivy and Sofia), who purchased their small property in 2007, 10 years after they were married. They have planted 1.2ha of chardonnay, and buy semillon and pinot noir from the Quarry Ridge Vineyard at Kilmore. The name comes from a Miles Davis record made in February '69, regarded as a masterpiece and one of the most inventive recordings of all time. The labels feature artwork originally created by friend Daniel Wallace for their wedding, turned into labels by friend Mel Nightingale. Earthworms, birds, snakes, friendship and love are the symbols for Silent Way.

ŸŸŸŸŸ **Macedon Ranges Chardonnay 2013** The Macedon Ranges welcomes warm vintages, the very cool nights slowing the ripening and retaining acid levels. This is a vibrantly fresh and lively wine, wild yeast-fermented in French oak (10% new), leaving the delicious nectarine and citrus fruit firmly in command, braced by natural acidity. Screwcap. 13% alc. **Rating** 95 **To** 2023 $35
Pinot Noir 2014 From the Quarry Ridge Vineyard at Kilmore; hand-picked, wild yeast-fermented with 40% whole bunches, 22 days on skins, French oak-matured. Great crimson colour, a bouquet stacked with satsuma plum fruit, a

palate with exceptional weight and concentration. Vinocide not to give the wine a minimum of 3 years' maturation. Screwcap. 13% alc. **Rating** 95 **To** 2024 $25 ⚫

♟♟♟♟♙ **Serpens Semillon & Friends 2014 Rating** 93 **To** 2025 $25 ⚫

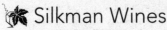 ## Silkman Wines   ★★★★★

c/- The Small Winemakers Centre, McDonalds Road, Pokolbin, NSW 2320
Region Hunter Valley
T 0414 800 256 **www.**silkmanwines.com.au **Open** 7 days 10–5
Winemaker Shaun and Liz Silkman **Est.** 2013 **Dozens** 1000

Winemaking couple Shaun and Liz Silkman (nee Jackson) (Liz was one-time dux of the Len Evans Tutorial), were both born and raised in the Hunter Valley, and worked many vintages (both in Australia and abroad) before joining forces at First Creek Wines, where Liz is senior winemaker. This gives them the opportunity to make small quantities of the three classic varieties of the Hunter Valley: Semillon, Chardonnay and Shiraz. Unsurprisingly, the wines so far released have been of outstanding quality, the 2014 Reserve Semillon winning trophies/recognition as Best Young Semillon at the NSW Wine Awards '14, ditto at the Winewise Small Vignerons Awards '14, and a gold medal at Sydney Wine Show '15.

♟♟♟♟♟ **Reserve Hunter Valley Semillon 2014** Occasionally a star is born and you get to watch; Silkman is one such. This wine is tight but lengthy, something of a contradiction, but rules are for lesser mortals. It's effortless, and yet tension is everywhere. It tastes of wax and citrus with various complexities whispered but not yet spoken. You could call it a sketch of the great wine it will become, except that that would do the pleasure of drinking it young, in all its fragrant fancy, a disservice. Screwcap. 11% alc. **Rating** 96 **To** 2032 $30 CM ⚫
Reserve Chardonnay 2014 Complex but generous. This is another beauty. Grapefruit, bran, white peach and struck match notes fly about the palate, causing trouble as they go, in the most positive of senses. Stony, flinty length tops things off perfectly. Screwcap. 13% alc. **Rating** 96 **To** 2019 $40 CM ⚫
Hunter Valley Shiraz Pinot Noir 2013 The two varieties blended in equal proportion. Produced from 'an extremely small parcel of exceptional fruit, grown in the heart of Pokolbin'. It's savoury and spicy and then fruity, and it wants for nothing. It's satiny on the tongue, medium–bodied, and as insistent as it is persistent; just when you think it's done, the flavours keep pushing on, as champion wines tend to do. Balance is perfect; so too integration of oak. A thing of beauty. Screwcap. 13.1% alc. **Rating** 96 **To** 2032 $40 CM ⚫
Blackberry Hunter Valley Semillon 2014 Pale straw–green. Flavours of snow pea, lemon curd, fennel and pure citrus. Slight spritz. It marshals and unfolds and then bursts through the finish, a young talent showing its wares, putting its hand up. It's almost impossible not to be swept along. Screwcap. 11% alc. **Rating** 95 **To** 2026 $30 CM ⚫
Hunter Valley Shiraz 2013 Bright in the glass; fresh-faced flavours of cherry-plum, licorice, earth and dried spice; elegant but powerful, with beautifully judged oak. Linger of smoky minerality to the aftertaste elevates it further. Screwcap. 13% alc. **Rating** 94 **To** 2030 $35 CM

Silkwood Wines   ★★★★

5204/9649 Channybearup Road, Pemberton, WA 6260 **Region** Pemberton
T (08) 9776 1584 **www.**silkwoodwines.com.au **Open** Fri–Mon & public hols 10–4
Winemaker Blair Meiklejohn **Est.** 1998 **Dozens** 8000 **Vyds** 23.5ha

Silkwood Wines has been owned by the Bowman family since 2004. The vineyard is patrolled by a large flock of guinea fowl, eliminating most insect pests and reducing the use of chemicals. In '05 the adjoining vineyard was purchased, lifting the estate plantings to 23.5ha; plantings include shiraz (5.4ha), cabernet sauvignon (4.3ha) and merlot (3.5ha), with smaller amounts of sauvignon blanc, chardonnay, pinot noir, riesling and zinfandel. The cellar door, restaurant and four luxury chalets overlook the large lake on the property. Exports to Malaysia, Singapore and China.

ΨΨΨΨΨ **Pemberton Dry Riesling 2014** This is radically better than the Leaf Range Riesling; just for starters is its bone-dry minerally drive, then the flavours of apple skin, lemon zest and a dusting of talc; it has the length and balance to develop exponentially. Screwcap. 10.9% alc. **Rating** 94 To 2029 $25 ○

ΨΨΨΨΨ **Pemberton Pinot Noir 2013** Rating 93 To 2023 $28
Pemberton Chardonnay 2013 Rating 91 To 2023 $25
Pemberton Shiraz 2013 Rating 91 To 2025 $26
Leaf Range Premium Red 2011 Rating 91 To 2026 $22 ○
Leaf Range Pemberton Verdelho 2014 Rating 90 To 2017 $22

Silver Spoon ★★★★☆

503 Heathcote–Rochester Road, Mount Camel, Vic 3523 **Region** Heathcote
T 0412 868 236 **www.**silverspoonestate.com.au **Open** By appt
Winemaker Peter Young **Est.** 2008 **Dozens** 250 **Vyds** 22ha
When Peter and Tracie Young purchased an existing shiraz vineyard on the top of the Mt Camel range in 2008, they did not waste any time. They immediately planted a second vineyard, constructed a small winery, and in '13 acquired a neighbouring vineyard. The name comes from the Silver Spoon fault line that delineates the Cambrian volcanic rock, and the old silver mines on the property. Peter became familiar with vineyards when working as a geologist in the 1970s in the Hunter Valley, and more recently completed the Master of Wine Technology and Viticulture degree at Melbourne University.

ΨΨΨΨΨ **Heathcote Shiraz Viognier 2013** Always hard to resist a pretty face. This is perfumed, well integrated, amply flavoured and balanced. As they say in the classics: we have a live one here. Plums, cherries, violets and modest rounds of black pepper and crushed dry spice. Ultra fine-grained tannin. Screwcap. 14.6% alc. **Rating** 95 To 2022 $28 CM ○

ΨΨΨΨΨ **Heathcote Shiraz 2013** Rating 93 To 2026 $28 CM
Heathcote Viognier 2014 Rating 91 To 2016 $25 CM

Silver Wings Winemaking ★★★★

28 Munster Terrace, North Melbourne, Vic 3051 **Region** Central Victoria Zone
T (03) 9329 8161 **www.**silverwingswines.com **Open** By appt
Winemaker Keith Brien **Est.** 2003 **Dozens** 600 **Vyds** 2.5ha
This is the venture of Keith Brien, formerly of Cleveland. He offers contract winemaking and export consulting, as well as making the Silver Wings wines from contract-grown grapes (3ha of mourvedre and 1ha of shiraz) from 50-year-old vines, and 2.5ha of riesling at Whitlands. The cellar door, which also runs wine education programs and social events, is in North Melbourne.

ΨΨΨΨΨ **Central Victoria Old Vines Mataro 2008** Includes 9% shiraz, vinification and maturation the same as the Shiraz. A totally improbable wine, but also totally successful and appealing, flush with still-lively plummy fruit, its tannins long since resolved during its lengthy elevage. Diam. 13.5% alc. **Rating** 93 To 2023 $24 ○
Late Disgorged Grand Reserve Brut XO 1996 Quite likely the latest release sparkling in the country, it shows the full effect of 18 years on lees, infusing exotic, sweet pipe smoke nuances and madeirised burnt orange notes that suggest it might have been happier 5 years ago. XO Cognac liqueur only serves to heighten this effect, and it may well have benefited from a fresh, young liqueur. Tense, heightened acidity seems like it may never be tamed. Nonetheless, a fascinating curio of 75% chardonnay and 25% pinot noir. Cork. 12% alc. **Rating** 91 To 2015 $55 TS
Central Victoria Old Vines Shiraz 2008 An 85/15% blend of shiraz and mataro planted in the early '60s at Shepparton, components aged in a mix of

new and used French, American and Hungarian hogsheads and barriques for 33 months before blending and bottling. This is certainly out of left field, but has succeeded in living through the prolonged oak ageing, emerging as a balanced medium-bodied Shiraz with sweet black cherry fruit and integrated oak. Diam. 13.5% alc. **Rating** 90 **To** 2020 $24

Simon Whitlam & Co

PO Box 1108, Woollahra, NSW 1350 **Region** Hunter Valley
T (02) 9007 5331 **Open** Not
Winemaker Edgar Vales (Contract) **Est.** 1979 **Dozens** 2800
My association with the owners of Simon Whitlam – Andrew and Hady Simon, Nicholas and Judy Whitlam, and Grant Breen – dates back to the late 1970s, at which time I was a consultant to the Simons' leading wine retail shop in Sydney, Camperdown Cellars. The association continued for a time after I moved to Melbourne in '83, but ceased altogether in '87 when Camperdown Cellars was sold, thereafter merged with Arrowfield Wines. The Simon Whitlam label was part of the deal, and it passed through a number of corporate owners until 20 years later, when the original partners regained control of the business.

Hunter Valley Semillon Sauvignon Blanc 2014 Not in a bad place. Developing steadily; not for ageing, but attractive notes of lemon, wax and tropical fruit make for good drinking now. Texture is a highlight too. Screwcap. 11.7% alc. **Rating** 89 **To** 2016 $23 CM
Hunter Valley Chardonnay 2014 Solid flavour throughout with a bit of zip and zest through the finish. Lime and nectarine with an element of toasty/spicy oak. Puts on a friendly face. Screwcap. 13.3% alc. **Rating** 89 **To** 2016 $23 CM

Sinapius Vineyard

4232 Bridport Road, Pipers Brook, Tas 7254 **Region** Northern Tasmania
T 0417 341 764 www.sinapius.com.au **Open** Thur–Mon 11–4
Winemaker Vaughn Dell **Est.** 2005 **Dozens** 800 **Vyds** 3ha
Vaughn Dell and Linda Morice purchased the former Golders Vineyard in 2005 (originally planted in 1994). More recent vineyard plantings include 13 clones of pinot noir and eight clones of chardonnay, as well as a small amount of gruner veltliner. The new vineyard is close-planted, ranging from 5100 vines per hectare for the gruner veltliner to 10 250 vines per hectare for the pinot noir and chardonnay. The wines are made with a minimalist approach: natural ferments, basket-pressing, extended lees ageing and minimal fining and filtration.

Home Vineyard Pinot Noir 2013 75% from 20yo estate vines, 25% from the newer, ultra close-planted vineyard (12 clones); 60% whole bunch, 40% destemmed, wild yeast-fermented for 21 days on skins, 12 months in French oak (30% new). The fragrant and complex forest berry and spice bouquet is a foreplay of the intense palate, with its plum and berry fruit laced with spice and supported by excellent tannins. Sinapius' best Pinot so far, with a great future. Screwcap. 13.5% alc. **Rating** 96 **To** 2023 $48 ○
Home Vineyard Chardonnay 2013 75% from 20yo vines, 25% new vines, hand-picked, whole bunch-pressed, wild yeast fermentation, lees stirring, 12 months in French oak (50% new, 50% 1yo). This has excellent focus, length and drive to its finely articulated white peach palate, finished with balanced acidity; it has totally absorbed its oak. Screwcap. 13% alc. **Rating** 95 **To** 2025 $48
Tamar Valley Riesling et al 2014 An 85/10/5% co-fermented blend of riesling, gruner veltliner and pinot gris, very low yields leading to concentration of flavour; whole bunch-pressed, two-thirds fermented and matured in used puncheons, the remainder in stainless steel, on lees for 7 months, partial mlf, 150 dozen made. Bright straw-green; the wine has a distinguished and interesting palate, its texture and structure all-important, even if its riesling origins are still evident. Could blow the house down in 10 years. Screwcap. 12.7% alc. **Rating** 95 **To** 2029 $34 ○

Pipers Brook Chardonnay 2013 Hand-picked from a single 20yo vineyard, whole bunch-pressed, wild yeast, 10 months' maturation in French puncheons (65% new, 35% 1yo), 220 dozen made. Elegant, (and inevitably) fresh, Tasmania being what it is; if anything, gains intensity as it passes along the palate. Screwcap. 13% alc. **Rating** 94 **To** 2023 $38

Sinclair's Gully ★★★★

288 Colonial Drive, Norton Summit, SA 5136 **Region** Adelaide Hills
T (08) 8390 1995 **www.**sinclairsgully.com **Open** W'ends & public hols 12–4 (Aug–June), Fri 5–9 (Jan–Mar)
Winemaker Contract **Est.** 1998 **Dozens** 1000 **Vyds** 1ha
Sue and Sean Delaney purchased their property at Norton Summit in 1997. The property had a significant stand of remnant native vegetation, with a State Conservation Rating, and much energy has been spent in restoring 8ha of pristine bushland, home to 130 species of native plants and 66 species of native birds, some recorded as threatened or rare. The adoption of biodynamic viticulture has coincided with numerous awards for the protection of the natural environment and, more recently, eco-tourism; they operate the only eco-certified cellar door in the Adelaide Hills, and have won innumerable ecological and general tourism awards. Sparkling wine disgorgement demonstrations are a particular attraction.

♆♆♆♆♆ **Chardonnay 2013** Estate fruit was barrel-fermented and matured in French barriques. Builds intensity as it travels along the palate, although the end point is still on the delicate side. Screwcap. 13.5% alc. **Rating** 92 **To** 2019 $30

Singlefile Wines ★★★★★

90 Walter Road, Denmark, WA 6333 **Region** Great Southern
T (08) 9840 9749 **www.**singlefilewines.com **Open** 7 days 11–5
Winemaker Mike Garland, Coby Ladwig (Contract) **Est.** 2007 **Dozens** 6000 **Vyds** 3.75ha
In 1986 geologists Phil and Viv Snowden moved from South Africa to Perth, where they developed their their successful multinational mining and resource services company, Snowden Resources. Following the sale of the company in 2004, they decided to turn their attention to their long-held desire to make and enjoy fine wine. Their research of the principal wine regions of Australia confirmed their desire to settle where cool-climate wines of outstanding quality could be produced. In '07 they bought an established vineyard (planted in '89) in the beautiful Denmark subregion. They pulled out the old shiraz and merlot vines, kept and planted more chardonnay, and retained Larry Cherubino to set up partnerships with established vineyards in Frankland River, Porongurup, Denmark, Pemberton and Margaret River to make the rest of the wines in the distinguished Singlefile portfolio. The cellar door, tasting room and restaurant are strongly recommended. The consistency of the quality of the Singlefile wines is outstanding, as is their value for money. Exports to the US, Japan and China.

♆♆♆♆♆ **Family Reserve Denmark Chardonnay 2013** Estate-grown, from vines planted in '89, whole bunch-pressed and fermented in French barriques (40% new, 60% used), matured for 7 months, with lees stirring and 15% mlf. A wine of exceptional intensity and length, the power of fruit such that it has absorbed the oak with ease; grapefruit, white peach and nectarine are the flavour drivers, barrel-ferment and mlf adding texture and structure. Screwcap. 13.9% alc. **Rating** 97 **To** 2025 $50

♆♆♆♆♆ **The Vivienne Denmark Chardonnay 2013** Hand-picked 24 Feb, 9 and 24 Mar, chilled, whole bunch-pressed, wild yeast-fermented with full solids in new and used French barriques, on lees for 8 months. Only made in exceptional vintages. Elegance, not flamboyance, is the cornerstone of this beautifully expressed Chardonnay, with the full scale of flavours from a remarkable month-long picking schedule. 132 dozen made. Screwcap. 12.7% alc. **Rating** 96 **To** 2033 $80
Frankland River Cabernet Sauvignon 2013 Hand-picked and sorted, 12-day cold soak, matured for 16 months in French barriques (40% new). Deep crimson, this has all the hallmarks of Frankland Cabernet: full-bodied yet perfectly balanced

blackcurrant fruit with hand-stitched bespoke tannin. Has a very long life ahead. Screwcap. 14% alc. **Rating** 96 **To** 2048 $37 ✪

The Philip Adrian Frankland River Cabernet Sauvignon 2012 From the Riversdale Vineyard, matured in high-quality cedary French oak. A remarkable fusion of intense varietal character, and an almost airy, open-weave texture and structure courtesy of sensitive winemaking extracting just enough fine-grained tannin to provide a complete wine. Screwcap. 14.5% alc. **Rating** 96 **To** 2035 $80

Pemberton Fume Blanc 2014 Wild yeast-fermented in stainless steel, then 60% transferred for maturation in French barriques (half new, half 1yo). A strikingly rich, complex and powerful wine, its sauvignon blanc fruit base almost irrelevant. European in its feel. Screwcap. 13.7% alc. **Rating** 95 **To** 2018 $30 ✪

Denmark Chardonnay 2014 Estate-grown, chilled overnight, whole bunch-pressed to barriques (30% new, 70% 1yo), matured for 6 months. The fruit must have been of very high quality, for it has responded very well to the winemaking thumbprints, mlf increasing its complexity, but not diminishing the drive or freshness of the palate. Screwcap. 14.1% alc. **Rating** 95 **To** 2025 $30 ✪

Frankland River Shiraz 2013 From the high-quality Riversdale Vineyard; hand-picked and sorted, open-fermented for 20 days, matured in low-toast French barriques for 7 months. Deep crimson-purple; demonstrates that opulence and finesse can create synergy; the black fruits have touches of licorice, pepper and forest floor, the tannins are fine, the finish clear and long. Screwcap. 14% alc. **Rating** 95 **To** 2038 $37

Clement V 2013 Mataro, shiraz and grenache from the Riversdale Vineyard, each batch kept separate and cold-soaked for 10 days; matured for 9 months in new (30%) and used barriques. The vivid colour heralds a striking wine with a cascade of red and black fruits, licorice, spice and pepper all in play, the tannins savoury but fine, the overall impact medium-bodied. A new arrival in Great Southern. Screwcap. 14.5% alc. **Rating** 95 **To** 2028 $30 ✪

Mount Barker Riesling 2014 The slide rule on the back label puts the wine in the drier half of the medium-sweet category and rightly so – indeed the lack of any mention of sweetness on the front label is entirely understandable, for it is the fruit and minerally acidity that define the wine, which will transform itself over the next decade or so. Screwcap. 10.7% alc. **Rating** 95 **To** 2025 $25 ✪

Porongurup Riesling 2014 Rating 94 **To** 2034 $25 ✪
Denmark Semillon Sauvignon Blanc 2014 Rating 94 **To** 2018 $25 ✪
Denmark Pinot Noir 2014 Rating 94 **To** 2025 $33

Sirromet Wines   ★★★★☆

850–938 Mount Cotton Road, Mount Cotton, Qld 4165 **Region** Granite Belt
T (07) 3206 2999 **www**.sirromet.com **Open** 7 days 9–4.30
Winemaker Adam Chapman, Jessica Ferguson **Est.** 1998 **Dozens** 50 000 **Vyds** 98.7ha
This ambitious venture has succeeded in its aim of creating Qld's premier winery. The founding Morris family retained a leading architect to design the striking state-of-the-art winery; the state's foremost viticultural consultant to plant three major vineyards (in the Granite Belt); and the most skilled winemaker practising in Qld, Adam Chapman, to make the wine. It has a 200-seat restaurant, a wine club, and is firmly aimed at the tourist market, taking advantage of its situation, halfway between Brisbane and the Gold Coast. Exports to Sweden, South Korea, Papua New Guinea, Hong Kong, China and Japan.

🍷🍷🍷🍷🍷 **Wild Granite Belt Chardonnay 2013** 7% crushed and wild yeast-fermented on skins plus 4 months in a ceramic egg and 100% mlf, hand-pressed to new French oak for 11 months; 14% wild solids-fermented plus mlf in new French oak; 79% wild yeast-fermented in new French oak (no mlf) for 12 months. Whatever black magic has overtaken Sirromet's red wines hasn't affected this wine: even though the vinification is far out in left field, it also works to provide a wine with all the precision and length expected of high-quality Chardonnay. 340 dozen made. Screwcap. 13.3% alc. **Rating** 95 **To** 2023 $89

Vineyard Selection Granite Belt Pinot Gris 2014 The colour is the salmon-pink of a flashy rose, beyond anything I have ever seen from a Pinot Gris, the flavour appropriately imposing. The back label suggests a tiny touch of oak, but not the where or the how, although some fermentation on skins may be an answer to all the questions posed. What I can't understand is the price. Screwcap. 13.5% alc. Rating 94 To 2017 $21 ○

Signature Collection Terry Morris Merlot 2013 Matured for 15 months in American oak. Has the fragrance and freshness that eludes most regions/makers outside WA; cassis and plum fruit has a nice touch of cedar and cigar box, the tannins fine, the finish fresh. Screwcap. 14% alc. **Rating** 94 To 2028 $35

�♥♥♥ **Terry Morris Shiraz Viognier 2013** Rating 93 To 2028 $35
Terry Morris Chardonnay 2012 Rating 91 To 2017 $35

Sister's Run   ★★★★

PO Box 382, Tanunda, SA 5352 **Region** Barossa
T (08) 8563 1400 **www**.sistersrun.com.au **Open** Not
Winemaker Elena Brooks **Est.** 2001 **Dozens** NFP
Sister's Run is owned by noted Barossa Valley vignerons Carl and Peggy Lindner (owners of Langmeil), directly employing the skills of Elena Brooks as winemaker, and, indirectly, the marketing know-how of husband Zar Brooks. The Stiletto and Boot are those of Elena, and the motto 'The truth is in the vineyard, but the proof is in the glass' is, I would guess, the work of Zar Brooks. Exports to all major markets.

♥♥♥♥♥ **Epiphany McLaren Vale Shiraz 2013** The grapes were grown by Tony Parkinson. The colour is good, although not quite as bright as Calvary Hill; whatever room for discussion on that score is not available on the bouquet and palate, where bitter chocolate is woven through powerful black fruits, tannins balanced and integrated. Scores for its balance. Screwcap. 14.5% alc. **Rating** 90 To 2028 $18 ○

♥♥♥♥ **Calvary Hill Lyndoch Shiraz 2013** Rating 89 To 2025 $18 ○
Bethlehem Block Gomersal Cabernet 2012 Rating 88 To 2020 $18

Sittella Wines   ★★★★☆

100 Barrett Street, Herne Hill, WA 6056 **Region** Swan Valley
T (08) 9296 2600 **www**.sittella.com.au **Open** Tues–Sun & public hols 11–5
Winemaker Colby Quirk **Est.** 1998 **Dozens** 8000 **Vyds** 10ha
Perth couple Simon and Maaike Berns acquired a 7ha block (with 5ha of vines) at Herne Hill, making the first wine in 1998 and opening a most attractive cellar door facility later in the year. They also own the Wildberry Springs Estate vineyard in Margaret River. Consistent and significant wine show success has brought well-deserved recognition for the wines. Exports to the US, Japan and China.

♥♥♥♥♥ **Reserve Margaret River Chardonnay 2014** It walks out on the tightrope, doesn't put a foot wrong, and even has time/poise enough to throw in a few tricks. It's hard not to be struck by this wine. It's built on acid and has a steely stare in its eye, but white peach, sweetly spiced oak and an undercurrent of grapefruit are all integral to the performance. There's a touch of smoky reduction, in the most positive of ways, but the thrill really is in the succulent length of it. Screwcap. 13.5% alc. Rating 95 To 2021 $29 CM ○

♥♥♥♥♥ **Shiraz Grenache Tempranillo 2014** Rating 93 To 2019 $17 CM ○
Berns Reserve 2013 Rating 93 To 2028 $44 CM
Verdelho 2014 Rating 91 To 2017 $19 CM ○
Berns and Walsh Pinot Noir 2014 Rating 91 To 2020 $22 CM ○
Petit Verdot 2013 Rating 91 To 2022 $24 CM
Sauvignon Blanc Semillon 2014 Rating 90 To 2016 $22 CM
Swan Valley Shiraz 2013 Rating 90 To 2019 $24 CM
Show Reserve Liqueur Muscat NV Rating 90 To 2015 $32 CM

Six Acres

20 Ferndale Road, Silvan, Vic 3795 **Region** Yarra Valley
T 0408 991 741 **www**.sixacres.com.au **Open** W'ends 10–4
Winemaker Aaron and Ralph Zuccaro **Est.** 1999 **Dozens** 470 **Vyds** 1.64ha
Six Acres is the family business of Ralph and Lesley Zuccaro, who have a successful optical dispensing business, and decided to plant a vineyard in 1999 with pinot noir (0.82ha), cabernet sauvignon (0.62ha) and merlot (0.2ha). Son Aaron, a biochemist, grew restless in the confines of a laboratory, and started his winemaking career in 2007, thereafter enrolling in CSU's bachelor of wine science course, graduating in '12. During his time at CSU he worked at Chandon Australia, and is now assistant winemaker at Innocent Bystander. The small size of the property means that all of the work is carried out by the family.

ΨΨΨΨΩ **Yarra Valley Pinot Noir 2013** Good colour; a strongly constructed Pinot Noir, with black cherries and a gentle suggestion of forest floor; has the length and balance to kick on over the next 5+ years. Screwcap. 13.3% alc. **Rating** 90 To 2023 $24

Skillogalee

Trevarrick Road, Sevenhill via Clare, SA 5453 **Region** Clare Valley
T (08) 8843 4311 **www**.skillogalee.com.au **Open** 7 days 10–5
Winemaker Dave Palmer **Est.** 1970 **Dozens** 15 000 **Vyds** 50.3ha
David and Diana Palmer purchased the small hillside stone winery from the George family at the end of the 1980s and have fully capitalised on the exceptional fruit quality of the Skillogalee vineyards. All the wines are generous and full-flavoured, particularly the reds. In 2002 the Palmers purchased next-door neighbour Waninga Vineyards, with 30ha of 30-year-old vines, allowing an increase in production without any change in quality or style. Exports to the UK, Canada, Switzerland, Malaysia and Singapore.

ΨΨΨΨΨ **Trevarrick Single Contour Clare Valley Shiraz 2012** Deep, dense crimson-purple; estate-grown, from the hillside vines planted in '70. A wine of great class and elegance, with a seductive array of red and black cherry fruits, spice and pepper on its bouquet, precisely repeated on the supple, juicy, silky medium-bodied palate. So easy to enjoy now, most will be long since consumed prior to its notional best-by date. Screwcap. 13.5% alc. **Rating** 97 To 2047 $73 ◑

ΨΨΨΨΨ **Trevarrick Single Contour Clare Valley Cabernet Franc 2012** Dense in the context of the variety. Fresh, lively, grassy flavour on raisiny, curranty fruit. Has a spirited personality, a joie de vivre. Tannin is fine. Finish is enduring. Decision to bottle this as a varietal wine was fully warranted. Screwcap. 14.5% alc. **Rating** 94 To 2025 $75 CM

ΨΨΨΨΩ **Clare Valley Riesling 2014** Rating 93 To 2022 $24 CM ◑
Basket Pressed Clare Valley The Cabernets 2012 Rating 93 To 2027 $32
Basket Pressed Clare Valley Shiraz 2012 Rating 92 To 2023 $32 CM
Take Two Shiraz Cabernet 2012 Rating 92 To 2022 $24 CM ◑
Malbec Cabernet Rose 2014 Rating 91 To 2016 $22 CM ◑

Skimstone

1307 Castlereagh Highway, Apple Tree Flat, Mudgee, NSW 2850 **Region** Mudgee
T (02) 6373 1220 **www**.skimstone.com.au **Open** Thurs–Mon & public hols 11–5
Winemaker Joshua Clementson **Est.** 2009 **Dozens** 3000 **Vyds** 15ha
This is a joint venture between Josh and Kate Clementson and Michael and Anne-Marie Horton; the Clementsons live on and run the estate and cellar door. Josh had previously worked for Orlando (one year), then Peter Logan (five years), and is vineyard manager at Huntington Estate. The partners were thus able to see the potential of the rundown Apple Tree Flat vineyard in 2007, and have since worked hard to bring the vineyard back to full health.

♀♀♀♀♀ **Mudgee Sangiovese Rose 2014** Salmon-pink; a fragrant rose petal and spice bouquet is followed by a well-textured palate, with a reprise of the aromas of the bouquet, the finish soft, but dry. Screwcap. 12.5% alc. **Rating** 91 **To** 2016 $22 ○
Mudgee Barbera 2013 Cold-soaked, wild yeast-fermented and basket-pressed. Barbera was brought to Mudgee at the behest of the late Italian-born and trained winemaker Carlo Corino, one of nature's gentlemen. He'd be pretty happy with this wine, its natural acidity acting as a counterbalance to its alcohol and berry fruit. Screwcap. 15% alc. **Rating** 91 **To** 2028 $28

Smallfry Wines   ★★★★★

13 Murray Street, Angaston, SA 5353 **Region** Barossa Valley
T (08) 8564 2182 **www**.smallfrywines.com.au **Open** By appt tel 0412 153 243
Winemaker Wayne Ahrens **Est.** 2005 **Dozens** 1500 **Vyds** 27ha
The engagingly named Smallfry Wines is the venture of Wayne Ahrens and partner Suzi Hilder. Wayne is from a fifth-generation Barossa family; Suzi is the daughter of well-known Upper Hunter viticulturist Richard Hilder and wife Del, partners in Pyramid Hill Wines. Both have degrees from CSU, and both have extensive experience – Suzi as a senior viticulturist for TWE, and Wayne's track record including seven vintages as a cellar hand at Orlando Wyndham and other smaller Barossa wineries. Their vineyards in the Eden Valley (led by cabernet sauvignon and riesling) and the Vine Vale area of the Barossa Valley (shiraz, grenache, semillon, mourvedre, cabernet sauvignon and riesling) are certified biodynamic/organic. Exports to the UK, the US, the Philippines, Singapore, Hong Kong, Japan and China.

♀♀♀♀♀ **Aged Release Eden Valley Riesling 2009** Bright straw-green; redolent with lime and lemon aromas, together with a hint of toast on the bouquet; the juicy palate takes the whole flavour impact up to another dimension, fruit and acidity in immaculate balance. Screwcap. 11.5% alc. **Rating** 95 **To** 2020 $30 ○
Eden Valley Cabernet Sauvignon 2012 The '12 vintage and the Eden Valley have joined forces to produce high-quality cabernet grapes that have then been handled sensitively in the winery, oak and tannins adding their weight to the blackcurrant fruit, but not going over the top. Screwcap. 14.5% alc. **Rating** 95 **To** 2032 $32 ○
Barossa Valley Shiraz Muscadelle 2011 Doubtless co-fermented, bringing back the Peter Lehmann/Saltram blends of the '60s. A wholly remarkable outcome from '11, with no green notes whatsoever, instead a plush array of plum and black cherry fruit backed by very good tannins and oak. Screwcap. 14% alc. **Rating** 94 **To** 2026 $48

♀♀♀♀♀ **Eden Valley Riesling 2014 Rating** 93 **To** 2024 $25 ○
Joven Barossa Tempranillo Garnacha 2014 Rating 93 **To** 2015 $25 ○
Barossa Valley Shiraz 2012 Rating 92 **To** 2037 $32

Smidge Wines   ★★★★★

62 Austral Terrace, Malvern, SA 5061 (postal) **Region** South Eastern Australia
T (08) 8272 0369 **www**.smidgewines.com **Open** Not
Winemaker Matt Wenk **Est.** 2004 **Dozens** 1000
The business is owned by Matt Wenk and wife Trish Callaghan, and was for many years an out-of-hours occupation for Matt; his day job was as winemaker for Two Hands Wines (and Sandow's End). In 2013 he retired from Two Hands, and plans to increase production of Smidge to 8000 dozen over the next few years. His retirement meant the Smidge wines could no longer be made at Two Hands, and the winemaking operations have been moved to McLaren Vale, where Smidge is currently leasing a small winery. Smidge owns the vineyard in Willunga which provides the grapes for all of the Cabernet Sauvignon releases and some of the McLaren Vale Shiraz. The vision is to build a modern customised facility on the Willunga property in the not-too-distant future. Production of shiraz and mourvedre from the Barossa Valley, and whites from the Adelaide Hills, will continue, supplemented by Eden Valley shiraz and Blewitt Springs shiraz. Exports to the UK and the US.

ŸŸŸŸŸ **Magic Dirt Eden Valley Shiraz 2012** Matured in a 3yo barrel for 20 months. The oak best allows the site to express itself. This is a seriously good Shiraz, with a gently spicy/smoky overtone to the black fruits of the bouquet and palate; good though the fruit is, it is the sheer poise and shape of the mouthfeel that is so impressive. Cork. 14.5% alc. **Rating** 96 **To** 2037 $65 ✪

Magic Dirt Greenock Barossa Valley Shiraz 2012 Matured for 20 months in a single 4yo French barrique. Deeply coloured, this is as far removed from its Eden Valley counterpart as the moon is from the sun; it is sumptuously rich and velvety, the impact of ripe, fresh fruit, not dead fruit, the alcohol merely a number. Cork. 15% alc. **Rating** 96 **To** 2043 $100

S Barossa Valley Shiraz 2012 A best barrels blend, most sourced from a south-facing slope in Greenock; a barrel classification tasting in Nov chose the barrels to be blended, then returned to used French oak for 20 months. There is an elegance to the wine that partially stems from 13% Eden Valley fruit, liquid poetry in the balance of this wine. Cork. 14.8% alc. **Rating** 96 **To** 2040 $65 ✪

The GruVe Adelaide Hills Gruner Veltliner 2014 From a manicured vineyard high in the Adelaide Hills at Verdun; picked at dawn, whole bunch-pressed, clear juice warmed to 16°C until wild yeast fermentation commenced, then cooled to 12°C until the last stage of fermentation. This is brilliantly, vibrantly fresh, with crisp citrus foremost, but with enough of the white pepper of gruner veltliner to convince. Screwcap. 12.5% alc. **Rating** 95 **To** 2029 $20 ✪

La Grenouille McLaren Vale Cabernet Sauvignon 2013 40yo vines; fermentation 12 days, post-fermentation 9 days, matured in used French puncheons for 13 months. Deep, inky purple-crimson, it has super-intense cassis fruit driving the bouquet and medium to full-bodied palate alike; it's at the upper end of the ripeness scale, but it works. Screwcap. 14.5% alc. **Rating** 94 **To** 2033 $30 ✪

ŸŸŸŸŸ **Houdini McLaren Vale Shiraz 2013 Rating** 93 **To** 2028 $20 ✪
Houdini Adelaide Hills Sauvignon Blanc 2014 Rating 91 **To** 2015 $20 ✪

Smith & Hooper ★★★★

Caves Edward Road, Naracoorte, SA 5271 **Region** Wrattonbully
T 0412 847 383 **www**.smithandhooper.com **Open** By appt
Winemaker Peter Gambetta **Est.** 1994 **Dozens** 15 000 **Vyds** 62ha
On one view of the matter, Smith & Hooper is simply one of many brands within various of the Hill-Smith family financial/corporate structures. However, it is estate-based, with cabernet sauvignon and merlot planted on the Hooper Vineyard in 1994, and cabernet sauvignon and merlot planted on the Smith Vineyard in '98. Spread across both vineyards are 9ha of trial varieties. Exports to all major markets.

ŸŸŸŸŸ **Reserve Merlot 2013** Has far greater intensity and length than its lesser sibling, setting the pace with the expressive bouquet and long, persistent palate, where cassis meets an unexpected twist of chocolate before savoury tannins take command on the finish. Cork. 14% alc. **Rating** 94 **To** 2028 $27 ✪

ŸŸŸŸŸ **Cabernet Sauvignon Merlot 2010 Rating** 91 **To** 2020 $21 CM ✪
Sauvignon Blanc Semillon 2013 Rating 90 **To** 2016 $19 ✪
Pinot Grigio 2014 Rating 90 **To** 2016 $18 ✪
Cabernet Sauvignon Merlot 2012 Rating 90 **To** 2027 $20 ✪

Smithbrook ★★★☆

Smithbrook Road, Pemberton, WA 6260 **Region** Pemberton
T (08) 9772 3557 **www**.smithbrookwines.com.au **Open** By appt
Winemaker Ashley Lewkowski **Est.** 1988 **Dozens** 10 000 **Vyds** 93ha
Smithbrook is a major player in the Pemberton region. In 2009 the Lion Nathan wine group sold the vineyard to the Fogarty Wine Group that also owns Lake's Folly in the Hunter Valley, Deep Woods Estate in the Margaret River and Millbrook Winery in the Perth Hills. Lion

Nathan has retained the Smithbrook brand and trademarks, and will continue to market the range of wines under the Smithbrook and Yilgarn labels; the Fogarty Wine Group will sell bulk wine made from grapes grown at the Smithbrook Vineyard to Lion Nathan under a long-term bulk wine supply agreement.

🍷🍷🍷🍷🍷 **Yilgarn Rouge 2011** An elegant, but remarkably intense, blend of merlot and cabernet sauvignon reflecting (in part) finishing its fermentation in new and used French oak; the tannins thus obtained add a special mouthfeel to the lively display of cassis fruit. Screwcap. 14.5% alc. **Rating** 93 **To** 2021 $35

Snake + Herring   ★★★★★

PO Box 918, Dunsborough, WA 6281 **Region** South West Australia Zone
T 0419 487 427 **www**.snakeandherring.com.au **Open** Not
Winemaker Tony Davis **Est.** 2010 **Dozens** 7000
This is the venture of Tony (Snake) Davis and Redmond (Herring) Sweeny. Both started university degrees before finding that they were utterly unsuited to their respective courses. Having stumbled across Margaret River, Tony's life changed forever; he enrolled at Adelaide University's Roseworthy Campus, thereafter doing vintages in the Eden Valley, Oregon, Beaujolais and Tasmania, before three years at Plantagenet, next Brown Brothers, then a senior winemaking role at Yalumba, a six-year stint designing Millbrook Winery in the Perth Hills, and four years with Howard Park in Margaret River. Redmond's circuitous course included a chartered accounting degree and employment with an international accounting firm in Busselton, and the subsequent establishment of Forester Estate in 2001, in partnership with Kevin McKay. Back on home turf he is the marketing and financial controller of Snake + Herring. Exports to China.

🍷🍷🍷🍷🍷 **High + Dry Porongurup Riesling 2014** Quartz-white; this and its Mount Barker sibling are a perfect illustration of the differences between the two subregions; this is almost painfully shy, lime/citrus only breaking free of the electric acidity at the last moment. It's only prior experience with Porongurup Rieslings that allows you to be totally confident about the future. Screwcap. 12% alc. **Rating** 95 **To** 2030 $28 ✪

Hallelujah Porongurups Chardonnay 2013 Pale straw-green, this has no colour tricks up its sleeve, but it does surprise with its greater verve and intensity than its Corduroy sibling, grapefruit in the vanguard, but plenty of nectarine and white peach, zesty acidity and good oak management. Porongurup strikes again. Screwcap. 12.5% alc. **Rating** 95 **To** 2035 $38

Business Time Mount Barker Shiraz 2013 Mount Barker has a special flavour base reminiscent of the Grampians. It is a black fruit picture gilded with red decorations, the tannins like built-in cupboards, simply functional, but more than useful. This wine is barely medium-bodied, and certainly elegant, the line, length and balance all correct. Screwcap. 13.5% alc. **Rating** 95 **To** 2033 $38

The Distance Higher Ground Porongurup Cabernet Sauvignon 2012 This is in best Snake + Herring style, a very different proposition from its The Distance Karridale sibling; it is medium-bodied, and secure in its elegant clothing, with cassis and superfine tannins taking it in turns to push their claims to be heard, although no more than that. Screwcap. 14% alc. **Rating** 95 **To** 2027 $58

Teardrop Mt Barker Riesling 2014 Quartz-white; this side of the divide between between Mount Barker and Porongurup is more relaxed, citrus and apple joining hands with the acidity right from the word go, albeit gaining power on the finish. This will always be several years in front of High + Dry. Screwcap. 12% alc. **Rating** 94 **To** 2028 $28 ✪

Corduroy Karridale Chardonnay 2013 A super-elegant Chardonnay that could only realistically come from the cool climate of Karridale, a light year away from (say) Wilyabrup, let alone further north. The pale colour plays tricks, gin-clear one moment, with colour the next; the judges at the Qantas Wine Show of WA '14 had no problems, rewarding the white peach fruit, subtle oak and perfectly pitched acidity with a gold medal. Screwcap. 13% alc. **Rating** 94 **To** 2025 $38

Cannonball Margaret River Cabernet Sauvignon Merlot Petit Verdot 2012 A truly seductive semi-Bordeaux blend, semi both in terms of numbers of varieties and in the joyous richness of the fruit, with cassis, blackberry, redcurrant and plum framed by ripe tannins and a dash of quality French oak. Screwcap. 14% alc. **Rating** 94 **To** 2032 $38

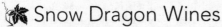 **Dirty Boots Cabernet Sauvignon 2013** Rating 93 To 2033 $23 ○
The Distance Gigantic Karridale Margaret River Cabernet Sauvignon 2012 Rating 93 To 2032 $58
Tough Love Chardonnay 2013 Rating 92 To 2020 $23 ○
Calypso Margaret River Merlot Cabernet Franc Cabernet Sauvignon 2012 Rating 92 To 2021 $23 CM ○
The Hard Road Porongurups Pinot Noir 2013 Rating 91 To 2018 $35
Wide Open Road Pinot Noir 2014 Rating 90 To 2020 $23

🍁 Snow Dragon Wines ★★★★☆

1318 North Coast Road, Wisanger, SA 5223 **Region** Kangaroo Island
T 0417 788 499 **www**.snowdragonwines.com.au **Open** Not
Winemaker Michael Sykes **Est.** 1994 **Dozens** NFP **Vyds** 3ha
You might wonder how a 6ha vineyard on the secluded north coast of Kangaroo Island has been named Snow Dragon, particularly given that the vineyard was previously known as Cape D'Estaing. In 2009, Andrew and Sue Bigwood purchased the vineyard from the founding quartet who, after 14 years of highly successful operation, decided to go their separate ways. Sue grew up on Kangaroo Island, and says, 'The swell of the ocean runs through my veins.' Her snowboarding husband Andrew now lives and works (as a General Practitioner) on the Island with their sons, Kai and Shalin, together with dragon dogs Rafiki and Ruby. Sue retired from an amazing zoo vet career, to be house-mother and manage the vineyard and marketing. Both Sue and Andrew were involved in grape to bottle activities in another winery, and have translated their skills to Snow Dragon, the major change being going biodynamic. And their holidays? The snow fields of NSW.

🍷🍷🍷🍷🍷 **Kangaroo Island Shiraz 2013** Deep, but vivid purple; a lusciously layered medium to full-bodied wine with blackberry, poached plum star anise and licorice all in play on the velvety, rich palate, the tannins soft, yet penetrating. Screwcap. 14.8% alc. **Rating** 95 **To** 2033 $42
Kangaroo Island Cabernet Sauvignon 2013 The deep crimson-purple colour announces a densely packed, full-bodied palate with a deep well of savoury blackcurrant fruit, high-quality oak and tannins playing their part in the overall picture. Screwcap. 14.4% alc. **Rating** 94 **To** 2033 $42

🍁 Soho Road Vineyard NR

c/- 600 Banks Road, Marcus Hill, Vic 3222 **Region** Geelong
T 0418 171 661 **Open** Not
Winemaker William Derham **Est.** 2012 **Dozens** 500 **Vyds** 2.5ha
Soho Road Vineyard was planted by Ian and Wendy Coghill in 1978, and is believed to be the oldest vineyard on the Bellarine Peninsula. The site on Soho Road, Drysdale overlooks Swan Bay and Port Phillip Heads. The vineyard (split equally between chardonnay and pinot noir) is run organically: sheep graze in the vineyard in autumn and winter, providing fertiliser, reducing weeds and the need for the use of chemicals. Now a 50/50% joint venture between owners Malcolm and Jan Hastings and Will Derham, owner of Banks Road Vineyard, the wines are made at Banks Road.

Solitaire Estate ★★★★

PO Box 486, Echunga, SA 5153 **Region** Adelaide Hills
T 0432 787 041 **www**.solitaireestate.com.au **Open** Not
Winemaker Linda Domas **Est.** 2007 **Dozens** 2000 **Vyds** 18.6ha

The Solitaire Estate vineyard has a rich history. It was once part of a much larger property originally owned by one of SA's viticultural pioneers, John Barton Hack. He grew grapes on his Echunga property in the 1840s, and even sent a sample of his 'Hock' to Queen Victoria, following in the footsteps of Walter Duffield, who had earlier sent Queen Victoria a case of 1844 white, and was promptly prosecuted for making wine without the requisite licence. Re-establishment of the vineyard began in 1999 (by former owner Jock Calder and family), with sauvignon blanc, shiraz and riesling planted. The vineyard was purchased by Paul Freer and Dennis Clift in 2007; they have increased the plantings. The current releases represent excellent value.

ŸŸŸŸŸ **Adelaide Hills Cabernet Sauvignon 2011** Astonishing colour and purity of varietal expression on the bouquet and palate alike given the vintage and the price; masses of cassis, no hint of green or mint, just superfine tannins to support the fruit. Bargain+++. Screwcap. 14.5% alc. **Rating** 93 **To** 2021 $16 ✪
Adelaide Hills Sauvignon Blanc 2014 Good grief: hand-picked and grown in the Adelaide Hills — and $13. Moreover, there is a full house of tropical fruits (any of the usual descriptors could be validly used) and there is enough acidity to sustain that fruit. No further comment on the value required. Screwcap. 13.1% alc. **Rating** 90 **To** 2015 $13 ✪

ŸŸŸŸ **Adelaide Hills Riesling 2014 Rating** 89 **To** 2020 $13 ✪
Adelaide Hills Chardonnay 2014 Rating 88 **To** 2017 $13 ✪

Sons & Brothers Vineyard ★★★★★

Spring Terrace Road, Millthorpe, NSW 2798 **Region** Orange
T (02) 6366 5117 **www.sonsandbrothers.com.au Open** Not
Winemaker Dr Chris Bourke **Est.** 1978 **Dozens** 300 **Vyds** 2ha
Chris and Kathryn Bourke do not pull their punches when they say, 'Our vineyard has had a chequered history, because in 1978 we were trying to establish ourselves in a non-existent wine region with no local knowledge and limited personal knowledge of grapegrowing and winemaking. It took us about 15 years of hit and miss before we started producing regular supplies of appropriate grape varieties at appropriate ripeness levels for sales to other NSW wineries.' Chris has published two fascinating papers on the origins of savagnin in Europe, and also traced its movements in Australia after it was one of the varieties collected by James Busby — and moved just in time to save the last plantings in NSW of Busby's importation.

ŸŸŸŸŸ **Cabernet of Millthorpe 2013** Sons & Brothers made no wines from their cool, high-altitude vineyard in Orange in either the '11 (wet) or '12 (cold) vintages. This is a lovely comeback, with 8% savagnin co-fermented, heightening the cassis and redcurrant fruit of the finely structured, long medium-bodied palate. Will age with certainty. Crown seal. 13.8% alc. **Rating** 95 **To** 2025 $25 ✪

Sons of Eden ★★★★★

Penrice Road, Angaston, SA 5353 **Region** Barossa
T (08) 8564 2363 **www.sonsofeden.com Open** 7 days 11–6
Winemaker Corey Ryan, Simon Cowham **Est.** 2000 **Dozens** 7000 **Vyds** 60ha
Sons of Eden is the venture of winemaker Corey Ryan and viticulturist Simon Cowham, who both learnt and refined their skills in the vineyards and cellars of Eden Valley. Corey is a trained oenologist with over 20 vintages under his belt, having cut his teeth as a winemaker at Henschke. Thereafter he worked for Rouge Homme and Penfolds in Coonawarra, backed up with winemaking stints in the Rhône Valley, and in 2002 took the opportunity to work in NZ for Villa Maria Estates. In '07 he won the Institute of Masters of Wine scholarship. Simon has had a similarly international career, covering such diverse organisations as Oddbins, UK and the Winemakers' Federation of Australia. Switching from the business side to grapegrowing when he qualified as a viticulturist, he worked for Yalumba as technical manager of the Heggies and Pewsey Vale vineyards. With this background, it comes as no surprise to find that the estate-grown wines are of outstanding quality. Exports to the US, Hong Kong, the Philippines, Taiwan and China.

♀♀♀♀♀ Freya Eden Valley Riesling 2014 Elegance is its middle name, but there's still a good core of limey fruit. It's a dry, structural style, but its moreishness is right up there. Apple blossom and talc flavours aid this impression, as does a line of mouth-watering acidity. It's built to age, arguably, but as a young wine it's delicious. Screwcap. 12% alc. **Rating** 95 **To** 2024 $25 CM ✪

Zephyrus Barossa Valley Shiraz 2013 Luscious Shiraz at the riper end of the spectrum. Some alcohol heat but generally loaded with asphalt, blackberry and dark, earthen flavour, the latter notes running the show from the mid-palate onwards. Tremendous concentration of flavour and fine, melted tannin to match. Screwcap. 14.5% alc. **Rating** 94 **To** 2030 $45 CM

Kennedy Barossa Valley Grenache Shiraz Mourvedre 2013 Rip of grainy tannin here gives the tide of leathery, plummy flavour a sense of sure footing. Brighter notes of raspberry and fennel add life and lift. You'd have to be pretty hard to please not to thoroughly enjoy this wine. Screwcap. 14.5% alc. **Rating** 94 **To** 2024 $29 CM ✪

Eurus Eden Valley Cabernet Sauvignon 2012 Fluid, sensuous expression of cabernet with mint, blueberry and blackcurrant flavours sliding effortlessly through the palate. Light sprays of dried herbs and smoky oak give an effect of light/shade. Tannin is fine and earthen/dusty. Medium-bodied, and exemplary. Screwcap. 14.5% alc. **Rating** 94 **To** 2027 $60 CM

♀♀♀♀♀ Pumpa Cabernet Sauvignon Shiraz 2012 Rating 93 **To** 2022 $29 CM
Selene Barossa Valley Tempranillo 2012 Rating 92 **To** 2021 $45 CM

Sorrenberg   ★★★★★

Alma Road, Beechworth, Vic 3747 **Region** Beechworth
T (03) 5728 2278 **www.**sorrenberg.com **Open** By appt
Winemaker Barry and Jan Morey **Est.** 1986 **Dozens** 1600 **Vyds** 4.8ha
Barry and Jan Morey keep a low profile, but the wines from their vineyard at Beechworth have a cult following not far removed from that of Giaconda; chardonnay, sauvignon blanc, semillon, pinot noir, merlot, cabernet franc, cabernet sauvignon and gamay are the principal varieties planted on the north-facing, granitic slopes. Gamay and Chardonnay are the winery specialties. Exports to Japan.

♀♀♀♀♀ Beechworth Sauvignon Blanc Semillon 2013 80/20% blend. Wild yeast, 8 hours' skin contact, 100% barrel ferment in (mostly) large-format oak. It's open for business in a flavour sense but it's so smoky and taut through the finish that you'd have to think there's more to be revealed, given an ounce of time. Dry grass, melon and lanolin notes coo gently in the background. Cracking wine. Cork. 13.5% alc. **Rating** 95 **To** 2019 $30 CM ✪

Gamay 2013 Fermented with a portion of whole bunches and a small addition of pinot. This release sees the wine at the peak of its powers. Bright, elegant, perfumed and long. Medium-bodied at its most intense point, but full of chewy, dry, spice-laden character throughout. Floral. Insistent of tannin. Savoury. Excellent from all angles. Cork. 13.2% alc. **Rating** 95 **To** 2023 $42 CM

Beechworth Chardonnay 2013 Barrel-fermented (wild yeast) and 100% goes through mlf. Complex hard cheese and lees notes to the nose lead into a powerful palate of grapefruit, nectarine, almonds and fennel. There's a textural lusciousness to this wine, but limey acidity keeps it feeling vibrant and fresh. Real sense of presence. Cork. 13.4% alc. **Rating** 94 **To** 2020 $50 CM

Soul Growers   ★★★★

187 Barritt Road, Lyndoch, SA 5351 **Region** Barossa Valley
T 0439 026 727 **www.**soulgrowers.com **Open** Fri 11–4
Winemaker Paul Heinicke **Est.** 1998 **Dozens** 4500 **Vyds** 6.8ha
In January 2014 Paul Heinicke (one of the four founders of the business) purchased the shares previously held by David Cruickshank and James and Paul Lindner. The vineyards remain the same, but Soul Growers has also moved into its own winery at Lyndoch. Its estate vineyards

are mainly on hillside country in the Seppeltsfield area, with shiraz, cabernet sauvignon, grenache and chardonnay the most important, and lesser plantings of mataro and black muscat; there are then pocket-handkerchief blocks of shiraz at Tanunda, mataro at Nuriootpa and a 1.2ha planting of grenache at Krondorf. Exports to the US, Canada, Singapore, Hong Kong and China.

🍷🍷🍷🍷🍷 **Slow Grown Barossa Shiraz 2013** Musky vanillan oak makes a clear appearance but it's married well to dark, slinky, vigorous fruit. Plums, cloves, aniseed and boysenberry. Ultra-fine tannin. Freshness, spunk, general balance and tannin management: all ticks. Cork. 15% alc. **Rating** 94 **To** 2026 $50 CM

🍷🍷🍷🍷🍷 **Cellar Dweller Cabernet Sauvignon 2012** Rating 91 To 2025 $50 CM
Provident Barossa Valley Shiraz 2012 Rating 90 To 2021 $25 CM

Soumah ★★★★☆

18 Hexham Road, Gruyere, Vic 3770 **Region** Yarra Valley
T (03) 5962 4716 **www.**soumah.com.au **Open** 7 days 10–5
Winemaker Scott McCarthy **Est.** 1997 **Dozens** 10 000 **Vyds** 19.5ha
Unravelling the story behind the exotically named Soumah, and its strikingly labelled Savarro (reminiscent of 19th-century baroque design), was a voyage of discovery up and down a series of minor dead-end roads. Soumah is in fact an acronym meaning South of Maroondah (Highway), while Savarro is an alternative name for savagnin. This is the venture of Brett Butcher, who has international experience in the hospitality industry as CEO of the Langham Group, and a long involvement in retailing wines to restaurants in many countries. Tim Brown is viticultural director. The many varieties planted have been clonally selected and grafted onto rootstock with the long-term future in mind, although some of the sauvignon blanc is already being grafted over to bracchetto. Exports to Canada, South Korea, Singapore, Hong Kong, Japan and China.

🍷🍷🍷🍷🍷 **Single Vineyard Yarra Valley Chardonnay 2014** Estate-grown, wild yeast barrel-fermented (25% new), matured on lees for 8 months, some barrels allowed mlf. An altogether serious Chardonnay, all the winemaker cards played at the right time and in the right way; the creamy/figgy nuances from the partial mlf are held in place by white peach fruit, gently toasty oak and grapefruity acidity on the finish. Trophy Sydney Wine Show '14. 400 dozen made. Screwcap. 13.1% alc. Rating 96 To 2022 $35 ✪

🍷🍷🍷🍷🍷 **Single Vineyard Yarra Valley Pinot Noir 2014** Rating 93 To 2029 $32
Equilibrio Yarra Valley Pinot Noir 2014 Rating 92 To 2029 $68
Single Vineyard Yarra Valley Savarro 2014 Rating 91 To 2016 $26 CM
Single Vineyard Ai Fiori Rose 2014 Rating 91 To 2015 $24 CM
Single Vineyard Sauvignon Blanc 2014 Rating 90 To 2015 $25
Skye Blox Yarra Valley Chardonnay 2014 Rating 90 To 2017 $21 CM ✪
Single Vineyard Brachetto d'Soumah 2014 Rating 90 To 2016 $24

Spence ★★★

760 Burnside Road, Murgheboluc, Vic 3221 **Region** Geelong
T (03) 5265 1181 **www.**spencewines.com.au **Open** 1st Sun each month
Winemaker Peter Spence **Est.** 1997 **Dozens** 400 **Vyds** 3.2ha
Peter and Anne Spence were sufficiently inspired by an extended European holiday, which included living on a family vineyard in Provence, to purchase a small property specifically for the purpose of establishing a vineyard and winery. It remains a part-time occupation; Peter is an engineering manager at the Ford product development plant in Geelong, Anne a teacher. They have planted 3.2ha on a north-facing slope in a valley 7km south of Bannockburn; the lion's share to three clones of shiraz (1.83ha), the remainder to chardonnay, pinot noir and fast-diminishing cabernet sauvignon (it is being grafted over to viognier for use in the Shiraz). The vineyard attained full organic status in 2008, since then using complete biodynamic practices. The well-priced wines have been made with the sure hand of the fast-learning Peter.

♥♥♥♥ Geelong Pinot Noir 2013 Light, bright colour; red and black cherry fruits are surrounded by a palisade of savoury/herbaceous tannins. Work in progress in both the vineyard and the winery. Screwcap. 13.5% alc. **Rating** 88 **To** 2018 $30

Spinifex   ★★★★★

PO Box 511, Nuriootpa, SA 5355 **Region** Barossa Valley
T (08) 8564 2059 **www.**spinifexwines.com.au **Open** At Artisans of Barossa
Winemaker Peter Schell **Est.** 2001 **Dozens** 6000
Peter Schell and Magali Gely are a husband and wife team from NZ who came to Australia in the early 1990s to study oenology and marketing at Roseworthy College. They have spent four vintages making wine in France, mainly in the south, where Magali's family were vignerons for generations near Montpellier. The focus at Spinifex is the red varieties that dominate in the south of France: mataro (more correctly mourvedre), grenache, shiraz and cinsaut. The wine is made in open fermenters, basket-pressed, with partial wild (indigenous) fermentations, and relatively long post-ferment maceration. This is a very old approach, but nowadays à la mode. Exports to the UK, Canada, Belgium, Singapore, Hong Kong, China and NZ.

♥♥♥♥♥ Miette Barossa Valley Shiraz 2013 Pete Schell does not have to be lectured about alcohol levels one way or the other. He is interested in balanced flavour ripeness, here achieved without apparent effort. Red fruits certainly play the main theme, but there are also some darker fruit notes linked to the ripe tannins that make up the whole. Bargain. Screwcap. 14% alc. **Rating** 95 **To** 2028 $22 ✪

 Spring Mountain Wines   ★★★★☆

Oakley Lane, Broke, NSW 2330 **Region** Hunter Valley
T (02) 6572 2753 **www.**springmountainwines.com.au **Open** Not
Winemaker Various **Est.** 2009 **Dozens** 3000 **Vyds** 28ha
The 28ha of semillon, chardonnay (10ha each) and verdelho and sauvignon blanc (4ha each) were planted in the early 1980s. It was strictly a grape producer, but went through various changes of ownership until acquired by AGL Energy as part of its exploration for natural gas and coal seams in the Hunter Valley. Obviously very conscious of the negatives of its business, AGL launched its Wine Excellence Scholarship, open to Hunter Valley winemakers using Hunter Valley white grapes, the winner electing whether to take a trip to a recognised international wine growing region, or defray the employment of a trainee in their winery. The well-known and highly credentialled winemaker Daniel Binet was awarded the first scholarship, in 2012.

♥♥♥♥♥ Hunter Valley Semillon 2014 Pale straw-green; herb and crushed lemon leaf aromas, then an intense and incisive palate that drives at high speed through to the mouth-watering finish and aftertaste. Great bargain. Screwcap. 11% alc. **Rating** 95 **To** 2030 $19 ✪
Hunter Valley Semillon 2013 Light straw-green; has abundant personality and drive, and while not quite as intense as the freakish '14, has delicious flavours in the full citrus spectrum; the length and balance will underwrite its future development. Screwcap. 11.9% alc. **Rating** 94 **To** 2023 $19 ✪

♥♥♥♥♀ Hunter Valley Semillon 2012 Rating 92 **To** 2020 $19 ✪
Hunter Valley Chardonnay 2013 Rating 90 **To** 2015 $19 ✪

Spring Vale Vineyards   ★★★★☆

130 Spring Vale Road, Cranbrook, Tas 7190 **Region** East Coast Tasmania
T (03) 6257 8208 **www.**springvalewines.com **Open** 7 days 11–4
Winemaker Matt Wood **Est.** 1986 **Dozens** 8000 **Vyds** 17.6ha
Rodney Lyne has progressively established pinot noir (6.5ha), chardonnay (2ha), gewurztraminer (1.6ha), pinot gris and sauvignon blanc (1ha each). Spring Vale also owns the Melrose Vineyard, which is planted to pinot noir (3ha), sauvignon blanc and riesling (1ha each) and chardonnay (0.5ha). Exports to Singapore and Hong Kong.

ŸŸŸŸŸ Pinot Noir 2013 Light colour but complex and powerful. It's not to be taken lightly. Stewed cherries, spice, foresty notes, sweet black tea and crushed dry leaves. It draws you in. It establishes its flavours quickly and then teases all the way through to a long finish. Screwcap. 13.5% alc. Rating 95 To 2022 $45 CM

ŸŸŸŸŸ Gewurztraminer 2013 Rating 92 To 2015 $28 CM
Reserve Chardonnay 2013 Rating 92 To 2020 $45 CM
Melrose Pinot Noir 2013 Rating 92 To 2019 $25 CM ○
Chardonnay 2013 Rating 91 To 2020 $25 CM

Springton Hills Wines ★★★☆

41 Burnbank Grove, Athelstone, SA 5076 (postal) **Region** Eden Valley
T (08) 8337 7905 **www**.springtonhillswines.com.au **Open** Not
Winemaker John Ciccocioppo **Est.** 2001 **Dozens** 2000 **Vyds** 6.5ha
The Ciccocioppo family migrated from central Italy in the 1950s; as is so often the case, wine was in their veins. In 2001, second-generation John and wife Connie purchased a grazing property at Springton, and began the planting of shiraz and riesling. Each year they increased the shiraz and riesling blocks, but also added smaller amounts of cabernet sauvignon, grenache and a smaller amount still of montepulciano. The wines are available for tasting at the Barossa Small Winemakers Centre at Chateau Tanunda. Good label design and packaging.

ŸŸŸŸ Eliza's Eden Valley Riesling 2014 Some colour development; a generous wine, with ripe citrus fruit, moderate acidity and good length. Ready now or soonish. Screwcap. 12% alc. Rating 89 To 2018 $19 ○
Rock Ridge Eden Valley Shiraz 2012 Hand-picked, crushed, fermented, basket-pressed, matured 24 months in oak. Has no shortage of rustic power, the finish a little phenolic. Screwcap. 14.3% alc. Rating 89 To 2022 $22

Squitchy Lane Vineyard ★★★★☆

Medhurst Road, Coldstream, Vic 3770 **Region** Yarra Valley
T (03) 5964 9114 **www**.squitchylane.com.au **Open** W'ends 11–5
Winemaker Robert Paul **Est.** 1982 **Dozens** 2000 **Vyds** 5.75ha
Owner Mike Fitzpatrick acquired his taste for fine wine while a Rhodes scholar at Oxford University in the 1970s. Returning to Australia he guided Carlton Football Club to two premierships as captain, then established Melbourne-based finance company Squitchy Lane Holdings. The wines of Mount Mary inspired him to look for his own vineyard, and in '96 he found a vineyard of sauvignon blanc, chardonnay, pinot noir, merlot, cabernet franc and cabernet sauvignon planted in '82 just around the corner from Coldstream Hills and Yarra Yering. The wines are made at Medhurst.

ŸŸŸŸŸ Peter's Block Yarra Valley Pinot Noir 2013 Selected as the best Pinot of the vintage, honouring Peter Sykes, who inspired Mike Fitzpatrick (as did Mount Mary). Good colour, the bouquet with none of the question marks of its lesser varietal sibling, the palate with black cherry and plum fruit sweeping serenely along from the opening chord through to the last note. Screwcap. 13.5% alc. Rating 95 To 2025 $55
Yarra Valley Cabernet Merlot 2013 An attractive, synergistic (as it should be) blend with blackcurrant/cassis rippling along the supple, almost juicy, palate; you know the tannins are there, but they are relegated to second place. Screwcap. 13% alc. Rating 94 To 2028 $26 ○
Yarra Valley Cabernet Franc 2013 An interesting contrast to Wantirna Estate Hannah Cabernet Franc Merlot. It is sheer misfortune for this wine to come up in the same tasting, for the comparison (unfairly) makes this wine look slightly lead-footed. But if you want a 20-year development bet, I'll back this wine. Screwcap. 13.5% alc. Rating 94 To 2033 $55

 Stage Door Wine Co

22 Whibley Street, Henley Beach, SA 5022 **Region** Eden Valley
T 0400 991 968 **Open** Not
Winemaker Graeme Thredgold **Est.** 2013 **Dozens** 500

It took a long time for Graeme Thredgold to establish this still-embryonic wine business. Having been a successful professional musician for 15 years during the 1980s and '90s, working six nights a week, he developed vocal nodules in the early '90s, putting an end to his musical career. Having spent so much time working in hotels and nightclubs, a new occupation stared him in the face: the liquor industry. In '92 he began working for Lion Nathan as a sales representative, then five years with SA Brewing, in '98 venturing into the world of wine as national sales manager for Andrew Garrett before moving on to the more fertile pasture of Tucker Seabrook as state sales manager for SA around 2000. Further roles with Barossa Valley Estate and general manager of Chain of Ponds Wines added to an impressive career in sales and marketing, before he made his final move as general manager of Eden Hall Wines, which just happens to be owned by his sister and brother-in-law, David and Mardi Hall. It is they who have given him the opportunity to source some high-quality grapes and contract winemaking of his Eden Valley Shiraz and Cabernet Sauvignon.

ŶŶŶŶŶ **Eden Valley Shiraz 2013** Deep, dense colour, bright rim; the colour inspires confidence, the bouquet building on that, and the medium to full-bodied palate duly delivers a wine of real class; it is supple and rich, with satsuma plum, blackberry, pepper and a touch of black licorice fruit on a lattice work of ripe tannins and integrated oak. Screwcap. 14% alc. **Rating** 96 **To** 2043 $50 ✪
Eden Valley Cabernet Sauvignon 2013 Good colour; the bouquet and medium to full-bodied palate sing from the same page, blackcurrant encircled by nuances of black olive, bitter chocolate and cedary oak. It all adds up to a wine with a long life ahead. Screwcap. 14% alc. **Rating** 94 **To** 2038 $50

Staindl Wines

63 Shoreham Road, Red Hill South, Vic 3937 (postal) **Region** Mornington Peninsula
T 0419 553 299 **www**.staindlwines.com.au **Open** By appt
Winemaker Rollo Crittenden (Contract) **Est.** 1982 **Dozens** 400 **Vyds** 3.1ha

As often happens, the establishment date for a wine producer can mean many things. In this instance it harks back to the planting of the vineyard by the Ayton family, and the establishment of what was thereafter called St Neots. Juliet and Paul Staindl acquired the property in 2002, and, with the guidance of Phillip Jones, have extended the plantings to 2.6ha of pinot noir, 0.4ha of chardonnay and 0.1ha of riesling, the vineyard run biodynamically. Ironically, all the 30-year-old chardonnay vines have been removed (and replanted) due to eutypa, a die-back disease that decimates the crop, and is an increasing problem in many parts of Victoria and SA.

ŶŶŶŶŶ **Mornington Peninsula Pinot Noir 2013** Seductive for both its fruit and its oak. It's a foresty Pinot Noir with stewy dark cherry and spicy oak combining to create a wine of both power and gravity. It's succulent, it flows, it has sweet tips of fruit-filled flavour but enough savouriness and tannin to underline its seriousness. Now or later. Screwcap. 13% alc. **Rating** 93 **To** 2021 $50 CM

Staniford Wine Co

20 Jackson Street, Mount Barker, WA 6324 **Region** Great Southern
T 0405 157 687 **www**.stanifordwineco.com.au **Open** By appt
Winemaker Michael Staniford **Est.** 2010 **Dozens** 600

Michael Staniford has been making wine in the Great Southern since 1995, principally as senior winemaker for Alkoomi at Frankland River, with additional experience as a contract maker for other wineries. The business is built around single-vineyard wines; a Chardonnay from a 20-year-old vineyard in Albany and a Cabernet Sauvignon from a 15-year-old vineyard in Mount Barker. The quality of these two wines is every bit as one would expect. Michael plans to introduce a Riesling and Shiraz with a similar individual-vineyard origin, quality being the first requirement.

TTTTT **Great Southern Reserve Cabernet Sauvignon 2012** From the Denbarker district; a blend of cabernet with small amounts of merlot and petit verdot, matured for 18 months in French oak. Very complex, earthy fruits immediately lock horns with robust tannins, but you can sense there will be an opening not too far down the track. Strange though it may seem, there's a certain degree of elegance here. Screwcap. 13.5% alc. **Rating** 95 **To** 2032 $38

Stanton & Killeen Wines   ★★★★★

440 Jacks Road, Murray Valley Highway, Rutherglen, Vic 3685 **Region** Rutherglen
T (02) 6032 9457 **www.**stantonandkilleenwines.com.au **Open** Mon–Sat 9–5, Sun 10–5
Winemaker Andrew Drumm **Est.** 1875 **Dozens** 15 000 **Vyds** 38ha
In '15 Stanton & Killeen celebrated its 140th anniversary, with a number of changes throughout the business. Andrew Drumm, formerly the CSU winemaker, was in place for his first vintage at Stanton & Killeen. He joined Ruston Prescott, who had been appointed vineyard manager in December '13. The business is owned by Wendy Killeen and her two children, Simon and Natasha. Wendy had embraced the role of CEO in July '11, using skills learnt working in the business community in Northeast Victoria. Natasha manages the website, newsletter production and all consumer-focused communications. Simon has chosen to broaden his winemaking knowledge and skills by working outside the company. Exports to the UK, Switzerland and Hong Kong.

TTTTT **Rare Rutherglen Topaque NV** Deep olive-brown; very complex, with strong rancio acting to cleave the burnt caramel/toffee, Christmas cake, honey and grilled nut flavours, the age obvious from the viscosity of the wine. A new and impressive addition to the portfolio. 375ml. Screwcap. 18.5% alc. **Rating** 97 **To** 2016 $100 ✪
Rare Rutherglen Muscat NV All hints of red have gone, leaving a brown centre grading to hints of olive on the rim; this is the final step up the ladder of lusciousness, incredibly rich, the rancio sufficient to do its job of balancing the wine, but no more; there is a cornucopia of flavours and spices; it has huge length and intensity, and wherever your imagination takes you, it will be found in the glass. 375ml. Screwcap. 18.5% alc. **Rating** 97 **To** 2016 $100 ✪

TTTTT **Grand Rutherglen Muscat NV** The rim colour is olive-brown; the bouquet is very complex and powerful, the palate with multiple layers of flavour and brilliant texture; the art here has been to keep the wine fresh despite its age. Has a glorious finish, long and sustained. 500ml. Screwcap. 18.5% alc. **Rating** 96 **To** 2016 $80
Classic Rutherglen Topaque NV Radically deeper in colour than the standard Rutherglen Topaque – golden brown. With an average age of 12 years, strong tea leaf, malt and toffee characters come through, the clever use of some younger material providing cut and freshness; is light on its feet, and has great length. 500ml. Screwcap. 18% alc. **Rating** 95 **To** 2016 $34 ✪
Classic Rutherglen Muscat NV Deep golden brown; the striking bouquet is full of perfumed, spicy raisin aromas; the palate has exceptionally rich mouthfeel and texture in the classic context; raisin fruit and rancio play tag with each other on the layered flavours of the palate, the average age of 12 years obvious; has a very long and satisfying finish. 500ml. Screwcap. 18% alc. **Rating** 95 **To** 2016 $34 ✪
Moodemere Rutherglen Shiraz 2013 Rating 94 **To** 2025 $22 ✪
The Prince Reserva 2013 Rating 94 **To** 2028 $45
Classic Rutherglen Tawny NV Rating 94 **To** 2016 $34

TTTTT **Rutherglen Durif 2013 Rating** 93 **To** 2033 $35
Rutherglen Topaque NV Rating 93 **To** 2016 $20 ✪
Rutherglen Muscat NV Rating 93 **To** 2016 $20 ✪
Rutherglen Shiraz Durif 2013 Rating 92 **To** 2028 $22 ✪

Stargazer Wine ★★★★★

161 Broke Road, Pokolbin, NSW, 2320 **Region** Tasmania
T 0408 173 335 **www**.stargazerwine.com.au **Open** Not
Winemaker Samantha Connew **Est.** 2012 **Dozens** 1000

Samantha (Sam) Connew has racked up a series of exceptional achievements, commencing with Bachelor of Law and Bachelor of Arts degrees, majoring in political science and English literature, from the University of Canterbury, Christchurch, NZ, but showing her future direction by obtaining a postgraduate diploma of oenology and viticulture from Lincoln University, Canterbury, NZ. Sam moved to Australia, undertaking the advanced wine assessment course at the Australian Wine Research Institute in 2000, being chosen as a scholar at the 2002 Len Evans Tutorial, winning the George Mackey Award for the best wine exported from Australia in '04; and in '07 was made International Red Winemaker of the Year at the International Wine Challenge, London. After a highly successful and lengthy position as chief winemaker at Wirra Wirra, Sam moved to the Hunter Valley, albeit with frequent forays to Tasmania to make the first wines for her own business, something she said she would never do. The emotive name (and label) is in part a tribute to Abel Tasman, the first European to sight Tasmania before proceeding to the South Island of NZ, navigating by the stars. Unsurprisingly, she believes her ultimate destiny will be in Tasmania.

TTTTT **Derwent Valley Riesling 2014** Light quartz-green; a super-elegant wine with lime and Tasmanian apple flavours providing a duet, bright acidity a regional hallmark, but nonetheless balanced and already acting to draw out the finish. Screwcap. 12.5% alc. **Rating** 95 **To** 2029 $30 ✪
Huon Valley Pinot Noir 2013 Light, bright crimson; the perfumed, spicy lavender and red fruit aromas of the bouquet lead into a silky and supple palate; Abel Tasman's 'right pointing compass' would instantly fix onto this delicious wine. Screwcap. 13.5% alc. **Rating** 95 **To** 2023 $50

Steels Creek Estate ★★★★☆

1 Sewell Road, Steels Creek, Vic 3775 **Region** Yarra Valley
T (03) 5965 2448 **www**.steelsckestate.com.au **Open** W'ends & public hols 10–6
Winemaker Simon Peirce **Est.** 1981 **Dozens** 400 **Vyds** 1.7ha

The Steels Creek vineyard (chardonnay, shiraz, cabernet sauvignon, cabernet franc and colombard), family-operated since 1981, is located in the picturesque Steels Creek Valley with views towards the Kinglake National Park. All the wines are made onsite by winemaker owner Simon Peirce, following renovations to the winery. Exports to China.

TTTTT **Yarra Valley Shiraz 2013** Deep, dense colour, bright rim; the colour inspires confidence, the bouquet builds on that, and the medium to full-bodied palate duly delivers a wine of real class; it is supple and rich, with satsuma plum, blackberry, pepper and a touch of black licorice built on a latticework of ripe tannins and integrated oak. Diam. 13.4% alc. **Rating** 96 **To** 2043 $35 ✪
Single Vineyard Yarra Valley Cabernet Franc 2013 Vibrant crimson-purple; cabernet franc is not an easy variety to tame, but this has done it, even if the oak contribution is obvious; there are vibrant red fruits, and if you look really carefully, you may find a hint of unlit cigar. Diam. 13% alc. **Rating** 94 **To** 2028 $32

TTTT **Single Vineyard Yarra Valley Colombard 2013 Rating** 89 **To** 2020 $22

Steels Gate ★★★★

227 Greenwoods Lane, Steels Creek, Vic 3775 **Region** Yarra Valley
T 0413 949 948 **www**.steelsgate.com.au **Open** Not
Winemaker Han Lau **Est.** 2010 **Dozens** 160 **Vyds** 2ha

Brad Atkins and Matthew Davis acquired a 2ha vineyard of 25 to 30-year-old dry-grown chardonnay and pinot noir in 2009. For reasons unexplained, the owners have a particular love of gates, and as the property is at the end of Steels Creek, the choice of Steels Gate was obvious. The next step was to engage French designer Cecile Darcy to create what is known today as the Steels Gate logo.

ΨΨΨΨΩ **Yarra Valley Pinot Noir 2013** Estate-grown; 10% whole bunches 'and a few other secret, left field techniques'. The colour is relatively light, but bright; the mouthfeel is immediately reassuring, but both the fragrant bouquet and palate have an exotic array of characters, with distinct nuances of orange peel on the bouquet, and savoury/charcuterie notes underneath the plum of the palate. Keeps you guessing to the end. Screwcap. 13.5% alc. **Rating** 93 **To** 2020 $25 ⚫

Stefani Estate ★★★★★

122 Long Gully Road, Healesville, Vic 3777 **Region** Yarra Valley/Heathcote
T (03) 9570 8750 **www.**stefaniestatewines.com.au **Open** By appt
Winemaker Peter Mackey **Est.** 1998 **Dozens** 3300 **Vyds** 28.5ha
Stefano Stefani came to Australia in 1985. Business success has allowed Stefano and wife Rina to follow in the footsteps of Stefano's grandfather, who had a vineyard and was an avid wine collector. The first property they acquired was at Long Gully Road in the Yarra Valley, planted to pinot grigio, cabernet sauvignon, chardonnay and pinot noir. The next was in Heathcote, where they acquired a property adjoining that of Mario Marson (ex Mount Mary), built a winery and established 14.4ha of vineyard, planted to shiraz, cabernet sauvignon, merlot, cabernet franc, malbec and petit verdot. In 2003 a second Yarra Valley property, named The View, reflecting its high altitude, was acquired and Dijon clones of chardonnay and pinot noir were planted. In addition, 1.6ha of sangiovese, mammolo bianco, malvasia, aleatico, trebbiano and crepolino bianco have been established, using scion material from the original Stefani vineyard in Tuscany. Since '13 all wines have been made in the Yarra Valley, with Peter Mackey taking over winemaking from Mario Marson. The transition has been seamless, with wine quality exceptionally good. Exports to China.

ΨΨΨΨΨ **Boccalupo Yarra Valley Sangiovese 2013** The vines come from cuttings from the vineyard owned by the Stefani family's grandfather in Tuscany; matured for 12 months in French barriques (20% new). It is full of beautifully juicy red cherry fruit, the tannins silky smooth, the balance excellent. First-class Sangiovese. Screwcap. 13% alc. **Rating** 96 **To** 2025 $35 ⚫

The View Yarra Valley Pinot Noir 2013 The vineyard has an altitude of 300m, not common in the Yarra Valley; hand-picked, bunch-sorted, open-fermented, matured in new and used French oak for 12 months. Excellent colour; a refined, disciplined Pinot full of dark cherry and plum fruit on the bouquet and supple palate. Exudes confidence, knowing it will develop into something quite special. Diam. 14% alc. **Rating** 95 **To** 2025 $45

The Gate Yarra Valley Shiraz 2013 Hand-picked; open-fermented, with a month-long post-ferment maceration, matured in new and used French oak for 12 months. Good colour; a highly fragrant bouquet with red fruits and spice populating the silky, medium-bodied palate; has very good line, length and balance, reflecting the outstanding vintage. Diam. 14% alc. **Rating** 95 **To** 2035 $45

Heathcote Vineyard Shiraz 2013 Bunch-sorted, and the usual Stefani vinification. Deeply coloured, with a rich bouquet and palate of blackberry, licorice and spice; since the grapes were picked at the same time (as the Barrel Selection) and the vinification is similar, it is not surprising that the two wines have so many things in common. Diam. 14% alc. **Rating** 95 **To** 2043 $45

Heathcote Vineyard Shiraz 2012 Open-fermented and hand-plunged, matured for 18 months in French barriques (25% new). The oak is evident on the bouquet, less so on the medium-bodied palate with its juicy fruits, predominantly red; the tannins provide exactly measured structure. Diam. 13% alc. **Rating** 95 **To** 2032 $45

Barrel Selection Heathcote Shiraz 2013 Hand-picked from the estate's 'single vineyard' in Heathcote; bunch-sorted, open-fermented, hand-plunged, matured for 12 months in new and used French oak. The barrel selection focused on texture; the black fruits do indeed have an extra layer of texture, but the wine is still medium-bodied, and is supple. Diam. 14% alc. **Rating** 94 **To** 2033 $35

Heathcote Merlot 2013 Made using the standard Stefani approach, book-ended by hand sorting, and maturation in new and used French oak for 12 months. It's a pretty snappy Merlot, with cassis and plum welded together by fine tannins and a whip of oak. Diam. 13.5% alc. **Rating** 94 **To** 2028 $45

The Gate Yarra Valley Cabernet Sauvignon 2012 Matured for 15 months in French barriques. Has a fragrant red-berry bouquet and juicy medium-bodied palate reflecting the moderate alcohol, but without any penalty of green or minty fruit; the finish is particularly enjoyable, the fruit making light work of the tannins. Diam. 13% alc. **Rating** 94 **To** 2032 $45

ҬҬҬҬҬ **The View Yarra Valley Vineyard Chardonnay 2012 Rating** 93 **To** 2022 $45

Stefano de Pieri   ★★★★

27 Deakin Avenue, Mildura, Vic 3502 **Region** Murray Darling
T (03) 5021 3627 **www**.stefano.com.au **Open** Mon–Fri 8–6; w'ends 8–2
Winemaker Sally Blackwell, Stefano de Pieri **Est.** 2005 **Dozens** 25 000
Stefano de Pieri decided to have his own range of wines that reflect his Italian spirit and the region he lives in. Mostly hand-picked, the fruit comes from a variety of Mildura vineyards, including the highly respected Chalmers Nursery vineyard. They are intended to be fresh and zesty, deliberately aiming at lower alcohol, to retain as much natural acidity as possible, designed to go with food, and inexpensive and easy to enjoy, reflecting Stefano's philosophy of generosity and warmth. The emphasis is on the Italian varieties, from arneis to aglianico, including a frizzante pinot grigio and the innovative blend of moscato gialla, garganega and greco, while retaining some of the local workhorses such as cabernet and chardonnay.

ҬҬҬҬҬ **L'Unico 2012** Expensive screen-printed bottle; a blend of sangiovese and cabernet that ticks the boxes; it's certainly savoury, but no more than it should be, blackcurrant and black cherry each hard at work, and you don't have to worry about distracting tannins. Screwcap. 13.5% alc. **Rating** 92 **To** 2020 $24 ❂

Primitivo di qualita 2013 From the Barossa Valley. Primitivo, aka Zinfandel, is easy to enjoy, its plum and chocolate flavours usually – as here – with balancing acidity. I particularly like this modestly priced version. Screwcap. 14% alc. **Rating** 90 **To** 2017 $19 ❂

ҬҬҬҬ **Arneis di qualita 2014 Rating** 89 **To** 2016 $19 ❂
Sangiovese di qualita 2013 Rating 89 **To** 2016 $20
Tre Viti 2014 Rating 88 **To** 2016 $18

Stefano Lubiana   ★★★★★

60 Rowbottoms Road, Granton, Tas 7030 **Region** Southern Tasmania
T (03) 6263 7457 **www**.slw.com.au **Open** Thurs–Mon 11–4 (closed Jul)
Winemaker Steve Lubiana **Est.** 1990 **Dozens** NFP **Vyds** 25ha
Monique and Steve Lubiana left Riverland grapegrowing and winemaking in 1990, and purchased a greenfield site at Granton. In '91 they planted the first 2.5ha of their current 25ha vineyard. The first Pinot Chardonnay sparkling and Pinot Noir and Chardonnay table wines were made in '93. Five years later they began total organic vineyard management, evolving into a program of biodynamic management. Exports to the UK, Singapore, Indonesia, Japan, Hong Kong and China.

ҬҬҬҬҬ **Collina Chardonnay 2011** Exquisite. A wine of length, grace and power. Grapefruit, lemon rind, lactose, cedar wood and white peach flavours burst through the palate and continue long after you've swallowed. Chardonnay dreams are made of stuff like this. Tight, flinty, almost granular finish caps a stunning experience. Screwcap. 13% alc. **Rating** 97 **To** 2021 $90 CM ❂

Sasso Pinot Noir 2012 Deeply flavoured and tannic and yet pretty and perfumed. Plum and cherry, dried Italian herbs, wood spice and anise. It's an immensely pleasing wine, even though the content is serious. It's a wine of light and shade, drama and detail. As well as it performs now, it's impossible to drink it without yearning to see what its future holds. Screwcap. 13.5% alc. **Rating** 97 **To** 2025 $110 CM ❂

ŸŸŸŸŸ **Estate Pinot Noir 2013** Looks bright in the glass and offers an array of fruit/ spice perfumes, but its worth is anything but superficial. This is sitting in a beautiful place. Cherry-plum, twigs, forest and spice, smoky oak and some bound, reductive forces. Tannin is simultaneously long, sinewy and wrapped in velvet; it twists strongly through the wine but the effect remains soft. Wines such as this make you marvel at what Australian Pinot Noir has become. Screwcap. 14% alc. **Rating** 95 To 2022 $48 CM

Vintage Brut 2005 Impressively youthful at almost a decade of age, proclaiming the endurance of Tasmanian chardonnay (60%, the balance pinot noir), sustaining the lively crunch of lemon zest and pear, polished by 8 years of lees maturity into a silky, soft style of well-integrated acidity, invisible dosage and understated complexity of brioche, candied citrus rind and lemon butter. Finishing long and seamless, this is an impressive Lubiana, with the energy to live for some time yet. Disgorged Sept '13. Cork. 12.5% alc. **Rating** 94 To 2020 $53 TS

Collina Chardonnay 2012 Emerging slowly from its shell. You never want to be in a hurry with top-flight Tasmanian whites. Straw-green colour, some milk-like notes, honeysuckle and citrus with green apple and white peach. It's highly textural, layered and lengthy, but various song-sheets are being read from; time will get them all onto one, and then the fun will begin. Screwcap. 13% alc. **Rating** 94 To 2022 $90 CM

Estate Chardonnay 2012 Ripe and generous with oodles of length. Sweet cedar, peach and citrus, uncompromisingly bold, with toasty oak detailing the finish. There's more oak than you'd usually want to accommodate, but there's an explanation: fruit power. Screwcap. 14% alc. **Rating** 94 To 2021 $48 CM

ŸŸŸŸ♀ **Riesling 2013** Rating 93 To 2021 $32 CM
Sauvignon Blanc 2014 Rating 93 To 2016 $30 CM
Primavera Chardonnay 2013 Rating 93 To 2020 $30 CM
Pinot Gris 2013 Rating 93 To 2016 $30 CM
Blue Label Riesling 2013 Rating 92 To 2021 $28 CM
Primavera Pinot Noir 2013 Rating 92 To 2022 $32 CM

Steinborner Family Vineyards ★★★☆

91 Siegersdorf Road, Tanunda, SA 5352 **Region** Barossa Valley
T 0414 474 708 **www**.sfvineyards.com.au **Open** By appt
Winemaker David Reynolds **Est.** 2003 **Dozens** 2000 **Vyds** 12ha
Steinborner Family Vineyards is owned and operated by David and Rebecca Reynolds and Rebecca's father, Michael Steinborner. Their Ancestry Vineyards are located on the floor of the Barossa Valley in Vine Vale. Shiraz (some over 80 years old) accounts for two-thirds of the total plantings, with equal quantities of marsanne, viognier, durif and semillon making up the rest. Exports to Indonesia, Hong Kong, Singapore, Malaysia and China.

ŸŸŸŸ♀ **Barossa Deutsche Shiraz 2010** Estate-grown; matured for 3 years in French oak of unspecified age. The deep crimson-purple colour is exceptional for its age, although the long time in oak has played a role in this. If you enjoy Barossa Shiraz not overburdened by alcohol, this is a must-buy proposition with its powerful display of poached plum, blackberry and spice; there is a slight lift to the wine that may cause the technocrats to blink. Cork. 14% alc. **Rating** 92 To 2025 $16 ✪

ŸŸŸŸ **Caroliene Barossa Valley Semillon 2014** Rating 89 To 2024 $15 ✪
Barossa Ancestry Shiraz Marsanne 2009 Rating 89 To 2019 $28

Stella Bella Wines ★★★★★

205 Rosabrook Road, Margaret River, WA 6285 **Region** Margaret River
T (08) 9758 8611 **www**.stellabella.com.au **Open** 7 days 10–5
Winemaker Luke Jolliffe, Ross Dawkins, Stuart Pym (Consultant) **Est.** 1997
Dozens 50 000 **Vyds** 87.9ha

This enormously successful winemaking business produces wines of true regional expression, with fruit sourced from the central and southern parts of Margaret River. The company owns and operates five vineyards, and also purchases fruit from 7–10 small contract growers. Substantial quantities of wines covering all styles and price points make this an important producer for Margaret River. Exports of Stella Bella, Suckfizzle and Skuttlebutt labels to all major markets.

ΨΨΨΨΨ Serie Luminosa Margaret River Cabernet Sauvignon 2011 A wine to provoke a hushed silence. It's a sensation. It's built for the long haul, is beautifully balanced and powered, rushes blackcurrant, dried herbs, red berries, cedar wood and peanut shell flavours through the mouth, and leaves a deep impression as it bursts out through the finish. It almost goes without saying that this is a wine to both savour and cellar. Screwcap. 14% alc. **Rating** 97 **To** 2035 $75 CM ✪

ΨΨΨΨΨ Suckfizzle Margaret River Sauvignon Blanc Semillon 2011 The philosophical connection between this wine and Flowstone's Sauvignon Blanc (and White Bordeaux) is obvious: barrel fermentation in French oak, followed by extended maturation. The result is a complete fusion of flavour and texture, a mellow richness in which varietal expression is of secondary importance. Screwcap. 13.5% alc. **Rating** 96 **To** 2021 $45 ✪
Serie Luminosa Margaret River Chardonnay 2012 Succulent with fennel, lime, pear and grapefruit, the array of fruit matched perfectly to spicy, sawdusty oak and chalk-like nuances. It's beautiful until the finish, where it takes things up a notch. Screwcap. 12.5% alc. **Rating** 96 **To** 2022 $65 CM ✪
Serie Luminosa Margaret River Cabernet Sauvignon 2012 Stern discipline is rarely so enjoyable; or not in polite company, anyway. This is both a sure, firm hand and a wealth of supple fruit, the two sides of the coin combining to produce a statuesque wine of magnificent quality. Screwcap. 13.5% alc. **Rating** 96 **To** 2035 $75 CM ✪
Margaret River Cabernet Sauvignon 2011 Vivid crimson–purple colour points to a long future; beautifully pitched in terms of ripeness, it balances cassis and redcurrant fruit against firm cabernet tannins, cedary oak the glue to hold the parts together. A distinguished wine. Screwcap. 14% alc. **Rating** 95 **To** 2031 $32 ✪
Margaret River Chardonnay 2012 **Rating** 94 **To** 2019 $32 CM
Serie Luminosa Margaret River Chardonnay 2011 **Rating** 94 **To** 2019 $65
Margaret River Cabernet Sauvignon 2012 **Rating** 94 **To** 2030 $32 CM
Suckfizzle Margaret River Cabernet Sauvignon 2010 **Rating** 94 **To** 2030 $55

ΨΨΨΨΩ Margaret River Sauvignon Blanc 2014 **Rating** 93 **To** 2016 $24 CM ✪
Margaret River Tempranillo 2012 **Rating** 93 **To** 2027 $30
Semillon Sauvignon Blanc 2014 **Rating** 92 **To** 2016 $21 CM ✪
Margaret River Pink Moscato 2014 **Rating** 92 **To** 2015 $19 CM ✪
Skuttlebutt Sauvignon Blanc Semillon 2014 **Rating** 91 **To** 2016 $18 CM ✪
Skuttlebutt Margaret River Rose 2014 **Rating** 91 **To** 2016 $18 ✪
Cabernet Sauvignon Merlot 2012 **Rating** 91 **To** 2023 $24 CM

Steve Wiblin's Erin Eyes   ★★★★★

58 Old Road, Leasingham, SA 5452 **Region** Clare Valley
T (08) 8843 0023 **www.**erineyes.com.au **Open** Not
Winemaker Steve Wiblin **Est.** 2009 **Dozens** 1700
Having sold his share of Neagles Rock Vineyards, Steve Wiblin has struck out on his own with Erin Eyes. He explains the name thus: 'In 1842 my English convict forebear John Wiblin gazed into a pair of Erin eyes. That gaze changed our family make-up and history forever. In the Irish-influenced Clare Valley, what else would I call my wines but Erin Eyes?' While focusing on Shiraz, Cabernet Sauvignon and Riesling, he is venturing into Grenache (often very difficult in the Clare Valley) and Sangiovese, putting serious health issues behind him.

♥♥♥♥♥ **Clare Valley Riesling 2014** Bright straw-green; a striking wine with varietal flavour, texture and grainy acidity running throughout, combining harmoniously; juicy lemon and green apple flavours boost the long palate and its crisp, lingering finish. Screwcap. 11.6% alc. **Rating** 95 **To** 2024 $22 ✪

Clare Valley Shiraz 2013 One of those wines where you're happy to be taken prisoner. It's dense and luscious but well disciplined, with strict rules of tannin and lines of acid maintaining order amid the riot of black berried fruit. Cedary oak has melted straight down into the wine's inky depths. Great value, all things considered. Screwcap. 14.5% alc. **Rating** 95 **To** 2035 $28 CM ✪

The 75 Barossa Valley Grenache Shiraz 2013 '75' refers to the age of the grenache vines, not the composition of the blend. A wine of considerable stature, full of raspberry, spice and black cherry; supporting tannins have a savoury ring to them, giving both flavour and structure balance. Screwcap. 14.9% alc. **Rating** 95 **To** 2025 $40

Clare Valley Cabernet Sauvignon 2013 The power and the glory. This is lusciously fruited and sternly tannic at once. Blackcurrant, cloves, eucalypt and a wash of smooth-skinned oak. No query over its length. Impressive Clare Valley Cabernet. Screwcap. 14.5% alc. **Rating** 94 **To** 2028 $28 CM ✪

♥♥♥♥♡ **Clare Valley Merlot 2013 Rating** 91 **To** 2021 $28 CM
Clare Valley Sangiovese 2013 Rating 90 **To** 2018 $28 CM

Sticks Yarra Valley   ★★★★★

259 Unley Road, Malvern, SA 5061 **Region** Yarra Valley
T (08) 8271 4321 **www**.sticks.com.au **Open** Not
Winemaker Travis Bush, Tom Belford **Est.** 2000 **Dozens** 30 000
Sticks acquired the former Yarra Ridge 3000-tonne capacity winery in 2005, and 24ha of estate vineyards, mainly planted in 1983. The estate production is significantly supplemented by contract-grown grapes sourced elsewhere in the Yarra Valley and surrounding regions. Sticks also provides substantial contract-making facilities for wineries throughout the Yarra Valley. Exports to the UK, the US, Hong Kong and China.

♥♥♥♥♥ **Vineyard Select Willowlake A8 Block Pinot Noir 2013** Vines planted in '79; open fermentation of whole berries, cold soak, fermented dry, transferred to tank then new and used hogsheads, matured on lees for 16 months. Very good hue, full and bright; the bouquet resonates with plum, the palate picking up the theme, and adding a touch of black cherry for emphasis. Very good now, will be even better in a few years. Screwcap. 12.5% alc. **Rating** 95 **To** 2023 $45

Vineyard Select Sticks Estate A1 Block Cabernet Sauvignon 2013 Open-fermented at 26–28°C for 9 days, pressed to new and used French hogsheads for 15 months' maturation. A totally convincing portrait of Yarra Valley cabernet, its cassis fruit with a juicy, juicy character, pulling redcurrants into the picture, neatly framed by fine tannins. Screwcap. 12.5% alc. **Rating** 95 **To** 2038 $40

Vineyard Select Upper Ngumby K Block Chardonnay 2014 Hand-picked, whole bunch-pressed to French hogsheads (28% new) for fermentation and maturation on lees for 8 months. Gleaming straw-green, it is power-packed, but not heavy; white peach, melon and grapefruit are seamlessly welded, the oak integrated and balanced. Screwcap. 13% alc. **Rating** 94 **To** 2021 $35

♥♥♥♥♡ **Sauvignon Blanc 2014 Rating** 92 **To** 2016 $18 ✪
Chardonnay 2013 Rating 92 **To** 2020 $18 ✪
Sparkling 2011 Rating 92 **To** 2019 $35 TS

Stockman's Ridge Wines   ★★★★

21 Boree Lane, Lidster, NSW 2800 **Region** Orange
T (02) 6365 6512 **www**.stockmansridge.com.au **Open** Thurs–Mon 1105
Winemaker Jonathan Hambrook **Est.** 2002 **Dozens** 2500 **Vyds** 3ha

Stockman's Ridge Wines, founded and owned by Jonathan Hambrook, started its wine life in Bathurst, before relocating to its present vineyard on the northwest slopes of Mount Canobolas, at an elevation of 800m. The 3ha of vines are planted to merlot, shiraz, pinot gris and sauvignon blanc, but Jonathan also has an interest in producing savagnin, zinfandel and gruner veltliner.

ϙϙϙϙϙ **Rider Central Ranges Pinot Gris 2013** The bright pale green colour sets the scene for a fresh pear, apple and citrus-flavoured palate, the finish fresh and crunchy. More Grigio than Gris, perhaps, but undoubtedly refreshing. Screwcap. 12.4% alc. **Rating** 90 **To** 2016 $23

Campfire Central Ranges Late Harvest Semillon 2013 Is clean and pure, late harvest/cane-cut, not botrytis; the fermentation has been stopped at the right point to leave the sweetened lemon juice flavours free play. At its best with fresh fruit. 500ml. Screwcap. 9.9% alc. **Rating** 90 **To** 2017 $35

Stone Bridge Wines   ★★★★☆

Section 113 Gillentown Road, Clare, SA 5453 **Region** Clare Valley
T (08) 8843 4143 **www**.stonebridgewines.com.au **Open** Thurs–Mon 10–4
Winemaker Craig Thomson, Angela Meaney **Est.** 2005 **Dozens** 6000 **Vyds** 29ha
Stone Bridge Wines started out as a hobby but has turned into a commercial enterprise for its owners, Craig and Lisa Thomson. They say that Craig's 16 years as a baker have assisted in the art of winemaking: 'It's all about the mix.' Their own patch of shiraz provides part of the annual crush; riesling, pinot gris, cabernet sauvignon and malbec are purchased from local growers. The cellar door is a rammed-earth and iron building with picturesque surrounds, where on Sundays Sept–May (weather permitting), visitors can relax and enjoy a gourmet wood-oven pizza. Exports to Canada, Denmark, Singapore and China.

ϙϙϙϙϙ **Clare Valley Cabernet Malbec 2012** A complex blend, almost trademarked by Wendouree, but with Leasingham also contributing decades ago, and now Stone Bridge. It really does work, with dark berry forest fruits, a hint of bitter chocolate and a whistle stop of plum, the tannins ripe. Great value. Screwcap. 14.5% alc. Rating 95 To 2037 $24 ✪

ϙϙϙϙϙ **Clare Valley Grenache Mataro 2013** Rating 93 To 2023 $26 ✪
Clare Valley Riesling 2014 Rating 92 To 2024 $22 ✪
Bowerbird Old Tawny NV Rating 91 To 2016 $30

Stonefish   ★★★★★

24 Kangarilla Road, McLaren Vale, SA 5171 **Region** Various
T (02) 9668 9930 **www**.stonefishwines.com.au **Open** Not
Winemaker Contract, Peter Papanikitas **Est.** 2000 **Dozens** 10 000
Founder and owner Peter Papanikitas has been involved in various facets of the wine industry for the past 30 years. Initially his contact was with companies that included Penfolds, Lindemans and Leo Buring, then he spent five years working for Cinzano, gaining experience in worldwide sales and marketing. In 2000 he established Stonefish, a virtual winery operation, in partnership with the various grapegrowers and winemakers, principally in the Barossa Valley and Margaret River, who provide the wines. The value for money has never been in doubt, but Stonefish moved to another level with its '12 Icon and Reserve Barossa Shirazs. Exports to China, Thailand, Vietnam, Hong Kong, Indonesia, the Philippines, the Maldives, Singapore and Fiji.

ϙϙϙϙϙ **Icon Barossa Valley Shiraz 2012** Hand-picked, open-fermented, matured in new and used French oak. Vivid crimson-purple colour heralds a high-quality wine and expensive package, the cork the best money can buy; there is a perfect symbiosis between the blackberry fruits and exactly judged and integrated French oak. This is a giant leap forward for the Stonefish brand. In a bottle weighing several kg. 14.5% alc. **Rating** 97 **To** 2042 $90 ✪

ΨΨΨΨ **Reserve Barossa Shiraz 2012** This is a very smart Barossa Shiraz, immediately ticking all the boxes; there is an energy to the purple fruits that lifts the finish into a fresh, juicy mouthfeel; soft, ripe tannins and integrated oak add a dimension to the well-balanced plummy finish. Cork. 14.5% alc. **Rating** 95 **To** 2028 $26 ✪

ΨΨΨ **Margaret River Shiraz 2013 Rating** 88 **To** 2016 $18
Blackwood Valley Merlot 2012 Rating 88 **To** 2017 $18

Stoney Rise ★★★★★

Hendersons Lane, Gravelly Beach, Tas 7276 **Region** Northern Tasmania
T (03) 6394 3678 **www**.stoneyrise.com **Open** By appt
Winemaker Joe Holyman **Est.** 2000 **Dozens** 2000 **Vyds** 7.2ha
This is the venture of Joe and Lou Holyman. The Holyman family had been involved in vineyards in Tasmania for 20 years, but Joe's career in the wine industry, first as a sales rep, then as a wine buyer, and more recently working in wineries in NZ, Portugal, France, Mount Benson and Coonawarra, gave him an exceptionally broad-based understanding of wine. In 2004 Joe and Lou purchased the former Rotherhythe vineyard, which had been established in 1986, and set about restoring the vineyard to its former glory. There are two ranges: the Stoney Rise wines, focusing on fruit and early drinkability, and the Holyman wines, with more structure, more new oak and the best grapes, here the focus on length and potential longevity. Exports to the UK, The Netherlands and Japan.

ΨΨΨΨ **Holyman Project X Pinot Noir 2013** Glorious colour; here the bouquet is even more fragrant than the Holyman, and the palate has a juicy quality that doesn't need to ram the point home; the tannins are superfine, and the finish speaks as much of the purity of the fruit as of the undoubtedly good structure. Screwcap. 13% alc. **Rating** 96 **To** 2028 $90
Holyman Chardonnay 2013 Bright straw-green; a complex rendition of Tasmanian Chardonnay, with barrel-ferment influences to the fore on both the bouquet and palate on first acquaintance, grapefruit, almond and crunchy acidity asserting themselves on the long finish and aftertaste. A prosperous future lies ahead. Screwcap. 13.5% alc. **Rating** 95 **To** 2025 $45
Pinot Noir 2013 Bright, clear crimson-purple; the ultra-fragrant small red fruits of the bouquet do not prepare you for the power of the palate, with foresty/ stemmy tannins woven through the abundant red berry/cherry fruits, providing texture as well as a flavour counterpart to the juicy red fruits on the long finish. Screwcap. 13.5% alc. **Rating** 95 **To** 2023 $29 ✪
Pinot Noir 2014 Matured in French oak. Vibrant, clear, deep crimson-purple; this may be tailored as an early-release style, but there is an awful lot to enjoy, with its cherry and satsuma plum pulling out all the stops. Treat it as an each-way proposition if you will, but do keep a few bottles for another day. Screwcap. 13% alc. **Rating** 94 **To** 2024 $29 ✪

ΨΨΨΨ **Holyman Pinot Noir 2013 Rating** 92 **To** 2025 $50

Stonier Wines ★★★★★

Cnr Thompson's Lane/Frankston–Flinders Road, Merricks, Vic 3916
Region Mornington Peninsula
T (03) 5989 8300 **www**.stonier.com.au **Open** 7 days 11–5
Winemaker Michael Symons, Will Byron **Est.** 1978 **Dozens** 30 000 **Vyds** 17.6ha
This may be one of the most senior wineries on the Mornington Peninsula, but that does not stop it moving with the times. It has embarked on a serious sustainability program that touches on all aspects of its operations. It is one of the few wineries in Australia to measure its carbon footprint in detail, using the officially recognised system of WFA; it is steadily reducing its consumption of electricity; it uses rainwater, collected from the winery roof, for rinsing and washing in the winery, as well as supplying the winery in general; it has created a balanced ecosystem in the vineyard by strategic planting of cover crops and reduction of sprays; and has reduced its need to irrigate. All the Stonier wines are estate-grown and made

with a mix of wild yeast (from initiation of fermentation), and cultured yeast (added towards the end of fermentation to ensure no residual sugar remains), and almost all are destemmed to open fermenters; all have a two-stage maturation, always French oak and variable use of barriques and puncheons for the first stage. Exports to Europe, Canada, Malaysia, Vietnam, Hong Kong and China.

ΥΥΥΥΥ **W-WB Mornington Peninsula Pinot Noir 2013** Departs from the usual Stonier vinification process, with 100% whole bunches, 13 months in barriques. The whole-bunch approach can reduce the colour density, but not so here; I fell in love with whole-bunch Pinot 40 years ago (DRC, Dujac) and this has that wild (sauvage) character; there is a trade-off between stem tannins and skin tannins, but it's an exceptional wine. Screwcap. 14.4% alc. **Rating** 97 **To** 2025 $85 ✪

ΥΥΥΥΥ **Thompson Vineyard Mornington Peninsula Chardonnay 2013** From the original vineyard planted in '78 next to Brian Stonier's house; fermented in two 1yo puncheons for 10 months, no mlf. The most elegant and refined of the Stonier Chardonnays, going about its business quietly, but not allowing the finesse, nor the balance between fruit/oak/acidity, to escape your notice; great finish. Screwcap. 13% alc. **Rating** 96 **To** 2025 $55 ✪

Jack's Ridge Vineyard Mornington Peninsula Chardonnay 2012 A small selection from the 1.18ha vineyard, now 15+yo; only 44 dozen made. whole bunch-pressed, barrel-fermented, 20% new French oak, 13 months; 40% mlf. Has significantly more stone fruit flesh than the standard (multi-vineyard) wine, and masterly mouthfeel. Screwcap. 13% alc. **Rating** 96 **To** 2025 $40 ✪

KBS Vineyard Mornington Peninsula Pinot Noir 2013 Old vines, lyre trellis, yielding little more than 2.5t/ha matured for 8 months in 43% new oak, then blended for 5 months in used oak. Has some savoury elements to both the bouquet and fine-boned palate, part oak, part fruit-derived; a deceptively powerful finish. Screwcap. 14% alc. **Rating** 96 **To** 2025 $75 ✪

Lyncroft Vineyard Mornington Peninsula Pinot Noir 2013 A variation on the normal making, with extended maceration on skins for 20 days, French barrique and puncheon maturation (67% new) for standard two-stage maturation. The cool site has thoroughly justified these vinification elaborations, for it remains unruffled, the bouquet fragrant, the juicy red fruit flavours just that, oak and tannins not the least extractive. Screwcap. 13.5% alc. **Rating** 96 **To** 2023 $55 ✪

Stonier Family Vineyard Mornington Peninsula Pinot Noir 2013 The vineyard was planted in '82, and was originally the base of the first Reserve, still part used there, most (72 dozen) for this wine. 50% new barriques. The colour is excellent, the bouquet with a special fragrance and lift, the palate vital, yet with a polish to the red and black cherry fruits running through to the exceptionally long finish. Screwcap. 13.5% alc. **Rating** 96 **To** 2025 $85

Reserve Mornington Peninsula Pinot Noir 2013 From six vineyards; the blend is put together shortly prior to the transfer of the six vineyards to second maturation (5 months in barriques). There is unquestionable synergy here, with cadences rising and falling on the supple palate. Screwcap. 13.5% alc. **Rating** 96 **To** 2025 $60 ✪

Merron's Vineyard Mornington Peninsula Pinot Noir 2012 122 dozen bottles made from a tiny crop on the 1.7ha vineyard; open-fermented, with 23 days on skins, matured for 8 months in 60% new French oak, 5 months in older oak. Supremely elegant, with a perfumed red fruit bouquet, and a long palate making its most emphatic statement on the finish and aftertaste. Screwcap. 13.5% alc. **Rating** 96 **To** 2020 $55 ✪

Cuvee Rose 2008 Pale salmon pink; an elegant, fine and very long palate, with fraises du bois (forest strawberry) flavours allied with spicy brioche characters. Remarkable wine. Screwcap. 13% alc. **Rating** 96 **To** 2018 $45 ✪

Mornington Peninsula Chardonnay 2013 Rating 95 **To** 2023 $25 ✪
Lyncroft Vineyard Mornington Peninsula Chardonnay 2013 Rating 95 **To** 2023 $45

KBS Vineyard Mornington Peninsula Chardonnay 2013 Rating 95
To 2025 $55
Thompson Vineyard Mornington Peninsula Chardonnay 2012 Rating 95
To 2022 $55
Mornington Peninsula Pinot Noir 2013 Rating 95 To 2023 $28
Jack's Ridge Vineyard Mornington Peninsula Pinot Noir 2013 Rating 95
To 2023 $50
Windmill Vineyard Mornington Peninsula Pinot Noir 2013 Rating 95
To 2025 $65
Jack's Ridge Vineyard Mornington Peninsula Pinot Noir 2012 Rating 95
To 2019 $50

Stormflower Vineyard ★★★★

3503 Caves Road, Wilyabrup, WA 6280 **Region** Margaret River
T (08) 9755 6211 **www.**stormflower.com.au **Open** 7 days 11–5
Winemaker Stuart Pym, Ian Bell **Est.** 2007 **Dozens** 1800 **Vyds** 9ha
The Stormflower Vineyard was bought in 2007 by David Martin, Howard Cearns and Nic
Trimboli, three friends better known as co-founders of the Little Creatures Brewery in
Fremantle. They thought the location of the property (and the vineyard on it that had been
planted in the mid-'90s) was ideal for producing high-quality wines. Whether they knew that
storms hit the property on a regular basis, with hail and wind impacting the crop in most
seasons, isn't known. What is known is the investment they have made in the vineyard by
pulling out one-third of the vines planted in the wrong way, in the wrong place, leaving the
present 9ha of cabernet sauvignon, shiraz, chardonnay, sauvignon blanc, semillon and chenin
blanc in place. The driving force in the vineyard is David Martin, with a family background
in agriculture. During the first few years of their ownership, they moved the management
focus towards organic compost and natural soil biology, in '13 starting the process of gaining
organic certification.

ΨΨΨΨΨ **Dry Red Margaret River Cabernet Shiraz 2009** Free flow of eucalypt and
blackcurrant flavours before a firm hand of tannin reins them in. Fresh, fruit-
driven and remarkably lively given its age. Good now but has many more years of
development up its sleeve. Screwcap. 14.5% alc. **Rating** 93 **To** 2025 $40 CM
Margaret River Shiraz 2013 Upper end of mid-weight, plums edging into
blackberry, clovey oak with traces of spice. Straight lines of flavour but generous
within them. Not unimpressive. Screwcap. 14.5% alc. **Rating** 92 **To** 2024 $30 CM
Margaret River Sauvignon Blanc 2014 Pungent tropical fruit flavour with a
cuddly softness to its mouthfeel. Barley sugar note to the mid-palate is attractively
offset by lime and gravel notes. Entirely enjoyable. Screwcap. 13% alc. **Rating** 91
To 2015 $20 CM

Studley Park Vineyard ★★★★

5 Garden Terrace, Kew, Vic 3101 (postal) **Region** Port Phillip Zone
T (03) 9254 2777 **www.**studleypark.com **Open** Not
Winemaker Llew Knight (Contract) **Est.** 1994 **Dozens** 250 **Vyds** 0.5ha
Geoff Pryor's Studley Park Vineyard is one of Melbourne's best-kept secrets. It is on a bend
of the Yarra River barely 4km from the Melbourne CBD, on a 0.5ha block once planted to
vines, but for a century used for market gardening, then replanted with cabernet sauvignon.
A spectacular aerial photograph shows that immediately across the river, and looking directly
to the CBD, is the epicentre of Melbourne's light industrial development, while on the
northern and eastern boundaries are suburban residential blocks.

ΨΨΨΨΨ **Cabernet Sauvignon 2008** Open-fermented, hand-plunged, French and
American oak. Quite remarkable retention of crimson-purple hue; equally
remarkable and delicious retention of super-fresh cassis fruit; the oak isn't intrusive,
likely largely used, not new, the tannins falling neatly into line without protest.
Screwcap. 14% alc. **Rating** 94 **To** 2023 $25

ΨΨΨΨΨ **Rose 2014 Rating** 90 **To** 2017 $15

Stumpy Gully

1247 Stumpy Gully Road, Moorooduc, Vic 3933 **Region** Mornington Peninsula
T 1800 STUMPY (788679) **www**.stumpygully.com.au **Open** Fri–Sun 11–5
Winemaker Wendy, Frank and Michael Zantvoort **Est.** 1988 **Dozens** 6800 **Vyds** 40ha
Frank and Wendy Zantvoort began planting their first vineyard in 1988; Wendy, having enrolled in the oenology course at CSU, subsequently graduated with a B.App.Sc. (Oenology). In addition to the original vineyard, they have deliberately gone against prevailing thinking with their Moorooduc vineyard, planting it solely to red varieties, predominantly cabernet sauvignon, merlot and shiraz. They believe they have one of the warmest sites on the Peninsula, and that ripening should present no problems to late-ripening varieties such as shiraz and sangiovese. Exports to all major markets.

ΨΨΨΨΨ **Magic Black Zantvoort Reserve Mornington Peninsula Pinot Noir 2013** Strong girders of tannin hold up ample serves of fruit and oak. The word 'substantial' springs to mind. Black cherry, spicy oak, mint and rich, stewy plums. A force to be reckoned with, in need of time. Screwcap. 14% alc. **Rating** 93 **To** 2025 $48 CM

Crooked Post Zantvoort Reserve Mornington Peninsula Shiraz 2013 Dusty nose, almost muted, not sure the seal has done the wine any favours, but there is a core of dark, brooding black-berried fruit on clear show. Indeed the depth of flavour here is impressive, with dry licorice and dark cherry notes pushing through a fine slick of coffeed oak. Stringy herb notes lie far beneath. Not your standard Mornington Shiraz by any stretch. Diam. 14.1% alc. **Rating** 91 **To** 2023 $48 CM

Mornington Peninsula Riesling 2014 Fresh and clean. Apple and bath salts with a track of spice. Mid-intensity and ready to rip now. Screwcap. 12.1% alc. **Rating** 90 **To** 2019 $25 CM

Peninsula Panorama Pinot Noir 2014 Loads the flavours upfront and there's enough volume to carry the momentum all the way (just) to the finish. Made to drink well in its youth. Red and black cherries, some smoky spice. Job well done in general. Screwcap. 12.9% alc. **Rating** 90 **To** 2017 $20 CM ✪

Mornington Peninsula Sangiovese 2013 Mid-weight, savoury-accented, all cherry and earth with creamy input from oak. Builds flavour and presence as it breathes in the glass. Screwcap. 13.8% alc. **Rating** 90 **To** 2021 $25 CM

ΨΨΨΨ **Mornington Peninsula Pinot Noir 2014** Rating 89 To 2021 $30 CM
Mornington Peninsula Sauvignon Blanc 2014 Rating 88 To 2015 $20 CM
Shark Point Pinot Gris 2014 Rating 88 To 2016 $30 CM

🍇 Suffoir Vineyard   NR

144 Mount Eccles Road, Macarthur, Vic 3286 **Region** Henty
T 0430 284 554 **Open** By appt
Winemaker Pieter Badenhorst **Est.** 2012 **Dozens** 200 **Vyds** 1ha
Pieter and Michelle Badenhorst are both expatriate South Africans, who came separately to Australia with very different agendas. Pieter has a Masters degree in molecular genetics from Stellenbosch University, leading to a research career in molecular plant breeding, and after five years, he applied for a job offered by the Department of Environment and Primary Industries in Hamilton. The job interview was conducted over the phone, and he left South Africa two weeks later. Michelle came for a year of backpacking her way around Australia, and her cousin introduced the two, suggesting Michelle call in to stay with Pieter on her travels. End of story. They have planted 1ha of pinot noir on two very different soil types, giving rise to the possibility of making two Pinots each year. It has to be said that in 2013 the grapes simply did not achieve phenolic ripeness, but hopefully the experience will not be lost.

Summerfield ★★★★★

5967 Stawell–Avoca Road, Moonambel, Vic 3478 **Region** Pyrenees
T (03) 5467 2264 **www**.summerfieldwines.com **Open** 7 days 10–5
Winemaker Mark Summerfield **Est.** 1979 **Dozens** 7000 **Vyds** 40.5ha
Founder Ian Summerfield handed over the winemaker reins to son Mark several years ago.
Mark has significantly refined the style of the wines with the introduction of French oak, and
by reducing the alcohol without compromising the intensity and concentration of the wines.
If anything, the longevity of the wines produced by Mark will be even greater than that of the
American-oaked wines of bygone years. Exports are now directed solely to China.

ㅜㅜㅜㅜㅜ **R2 Shiraz 2012** Hand-picked from a single block, open-fermented, 30% whole
bunches, matured for 22 months in American oak (30% new), 150 dozen made.
A no-holds-barred, powerful full-bodied Shiraz, but has the focus and balance to
its array of plum, blackberry, licorice, tannins and oak to make light work of that
power. Cork. 14% alc. **Rating** 96 To 2037 $70 ✪
Sahsah Shiraz 2013 Hand-picked from vines planted in '70, open-fermented,
30% whole bunches, fermentation finished in French oak (30% new). 150 dozen
made. Has a vibrancy and sense of purpose to its red and black fruits, and a fresh
juicy finish. A really attractive wine, the sheer length of the palate admirable.
Screwcap. 13.8% alc. **Rating** 95 To 2033 $50
Tradition 2013 A 46/25/21/8% blend of merlot, shiraz, cabernet and franc.
A luscious blend that really comes into its own at this level of alcohol; there is no
pinching of flavour by green tannins, nor the slightest hint of any blowsy fruit.
Excels itself. Screwcap. 13.3% alc. **Rating** 95 To 2033 $35 ✪
Jo Cabernet 2012 From the same block as the Reserve, but the best; 150 dozen
made. The fruit selection comes from years of experience, so it's not surprising
that the line, length and balance are all very good. The cassis/blackcurrant fruit has
positive touches of bay leaf and dried herbs, the tannins ripe, underpinning the
structure. Screwcap. 14% alc. **Rating** 95 To 2032 $80
Saieh Shiraz 2013 Rating 94 To 2028 $50
Reserve Shiraz 2013 Rating 94 To 2030 $55
Merlot 2013 Rating 94 To 2028 $35
Reserve Cabernet Sauvignon 2013 Rating 94 To 2033 $55

ㅜㅜㅜㅜㅜ **Shiraz 2013 Rating** 92 To 2028 $35
Cabernet Sauvignon 2013 Rating 92 To 2028 $35

Sunset Winery ★★★★☆

4564 Hog Bay Road, Penneshaw, SA 5222 **Region** Kangaroo Island
T (08) 8553 1378 **www**.sunset-wines.com.au **Open** 7 days 11–5
Winemaker Colin Hopkins **Est.** 2003 **Dozens** 3300
This boutique winery is owned and run by friends and business partners Colin Hopkins and
Athalie and David Martin. The winery and cellar door have elevated sea views overlooking
Eastern Cove and beyond, surrounded by 14ha of native bushland. Sunset Winery was the
first dedicated cellar door on Kangaroo Island, and offers a range of products to accompany
the Sauvignon Blanc, Chardonnay, Cabernet Sauvignon, Shiraz and Sparkling Shiraz sourced
from local growers. A representative range of wines was not received for this edition, but the
rating has been maintained.

Surveyor's Hill Vineyards ★★★☆

215 Brooklands Road, Wallaroo, NSW 2618 **Region** Canberra District
T (02) 6230 2046 **www**.survhill.com.au **Open** W'ends & public hols
Winemaker Brindabella Hills (Dr Roger Harris), Greg Gallagher (sparkling) **Est.** 1986
Dozens 1000 **Vyds** 10ha
Surveyor's Hill vineyard is on the slopes of the eponymous hill, at 550–680m above sea level. It
is an ancient volcano, producing granite-derived, coarse-structured (and hence well-drained)
sandy soils of low fertility. This has to be the ultimate patchwork-quilt vineyard, with 1ha each

of chardonnay, shiraz and viognier; 0.5ha each of roussanne, marsanne, aglianico, nero d'Avola, mourvedre, grenache, muscadelle, moscato giallo, cabernet franc, riesling, semillon, sauvignon blanc, touriga nacional and cabernet sauvignon.

🍷🍷🍷🍷🍷 **Hills of Hall Tinto 2013** The fragrant red berry bouquet leads into a bright spicy/savoury light to medium-bodied palate that provides a reprise of the bouquet, adding a fine web of tannins to underpin both the structure and length. Screwcap. 13.3% alc. **Rating** 92 **To** 2023 $22 ✪

Sutherland Estate ★★★★★

2010 Melba Highway, Dixons Creek, Vic 3775 **Region** Yarra Valley
T 0402 052 287 **www.**sutherlandestate.com.au **Open** W'ends & public hols 10–5
Winemaker Cathy Phelan, Angus Ridley, Rob Hall **Est.** 2000 **Dozens** 1500 **Vyds** 4ha
The Phelan family established Sutherland Estate in 2000 when they purchased a mature 2ha vineyard at Dixons Creek. Further plantings followed: the plantings now consist of 1ha each of chardonnay and pinot noir, and 0.5ha each of gewurztraminer, cabernet sauvignon, tempranillo and shiraz. Ron Phelan designed and built the cellar door, which enjoys stunning views over the Yarra Valley, while daughter Cathy studied Wine Science at CSU. The sparkling wines are made by Phil Kelly, the reds by Cathy and partner Angus Ridley (who has been at Coldstream Hills for the last nine years), and the Chardonnay by Rob Hall.

🍷🍷🍷🍷🍷 **Daniel's Hill Vineyards Yarra Valley Shiraz 2014** Picked in two parcels 8 days apart, the first destemmed and wild yeast-fermented to dryness, the second with 15% whole bunches, both with a cold soak, both hand-plunged; the second parcel (with cultured yeast over-seeded) caught up, and both parcels were free-run direct to new and used French barriques. A lovely, vibrantly juicy Shiraz with all boxes ticked: balance, integration of oak, fine tannins and a wanton display of spicy red and black fruit on the long palate. Screwcap. 13.2% alc. **Rating** 96 **To** 2029 $30 ✪
Daniel's Hill Vineyard Yarra Valley Chardonnay 2014 Hand-picked, whole bunch-pressed, fermented in French barriques (20% new) with 60% cultured yeast, 40% wild yeast, no mlf. A brisk, bright wine, described as being at the crossover point between stone fruits and citrus, and I wouldn't quarrel with that; the natural acidity gives the palate great energy and drive, oak providing such framework as the wine needed. Screwcap. 12.7% alc. **Rating** 95 **To** 2026 $30 ✪
Daniel's Hill Vineyards Pinot Noir 2014 Part free-run to new and used French barriques, the pressings released at 1.5° baume of sugar ex whole berries, with fermentation completed in used barriques. The clear, bright crimson colour foreshadows an elegant and vibrant light to medium-bodied wine; red cherry and touches of forest strawberries are the theme of a neatly orchestrated Pinot. Screwcap. 12.9% alc. **Rating** 94 **To** 2020 $30 ✪

🍷🍷🍷🍷🍷 **Daniel's Hill Vineyard Tempranillo 2014** **Rating** 90 **To** 2020 $30

Sutton Grange Winery ★★★★

Carnochans Road, Sutton Grange, Vic 3448 **Region** Bendigo
T (03) 8672 1478 **www.**suttongrange.com.au **Open** Sun 12–4
Winemaker Gilles Lapalus **Est.** 1998 **Dozens** 5000 **Vyds** 12ha
The 400ha Sutton Grange property is a horse training facility acquired in 1996 by Peter Sidwell, a Melbourne businessman with horse racing and breeding interests. A lunch visit to the property by long-term friends Alec Epis and Stuart Anderson led to the decision to plant shiraz, merlot, cabernet sauvignon, viognier and sangiovese, and to the recruitment of French winemaker Gilles Lapalus, who just happens to be the partner of Stuart's daughter. The winery is built from WA limestone. Exports to the UK, Canada, Switzerland and Malaysia.

🍷🍷🍷🍷🍷 **Estate Viognier 2013** Gleaming straw-green; a very good rendition of this challenging variety, providing convincing varietal character in a peach/apricot spectrum, but keeping the finish fresh and well balanced. Screwcap. 14% alc. **Rating** 93 **To** 2017 $45

Estate Syrah 2010 Care is needed with this wine: if the finish and aftertaste are to your liking, go for it, for there's a lot on offer before you get to the aftertaste. I'm happy to do that, but I can see technical judges giving it a hard time. Screwcap. 14% alc. **Rating** 92 **To** 2030 $50

Fairbank Ancestral Sparkling Rose 2014 Textural, savoury and enticing, this is a sparkling rose made only with grapes. No added acid makes it soft, no dosage keeps it refreshingly dry and no preservative means it needs to be drunk right away. It's a blend of syrah, cabernet, merlot and viognier that tastes like tamarillos, guavas and pomegranate, with softly textured palate grip. Disgorged Dec '14. Cork. 12% alc. **Rating** 91 **To** 2015 $30 TS

Estate Ram's Horn Block Syrah 2010 Deep colour; the light to medium-bodied palate has a mix of spicy black fruits, oak, spice and a fleck of mint; there are savoury notes, but within reason. Screwcap. 14% alc. **Rating** 90 **To** 2020 $60

🍷🍷🍷🍷 **Fairbank Viognier 2014** **Rating** 89 **To** 2018 $30
Fairbank Rouge 2012 **Rating** 89 **To** 2018 $22
Fairbank Rose 2014 **Rating** 88 **To** 2016 $22
Estate Rose 2013 **Rating** 88 **To** 2016 $32

Swan Valley Wines ★★★☆

261 Haddrill Road, Baskerville, WA 6065 **Region** Swan Valley
T (08) 9296 1501 **www**.swanvalleywines.com.au **Open** Thurs–Sun & public hols 10–5
Winemaker Paul Hoffman **Est.** 1999 **Dozens** 1500 **Vyds** 6ha

Peter and Paula Hoffman, with sons Paul and Thomas, acquired their property in 1989. It had a long history of grapegrowing, the prior owner having registered the name Swan Valley Wines in '83. The decision to release three Chenin Blancs – Sec, Demi Sec and Moelleux – is a precise (completely legitimate) copy of some of the best Loire Valley producers of Chenin Blanc, the most notable being Marc Bredif. Those wines have cellaring capacity of 70 years or more if kept in the cool chalk caves on the banks of the Loire Valley. The Australian climate will not permit that, but it will be interesting to see how the three wines develop.

🍷🍷🍷🍷½ **Sec Chenin Blanc 2010** Re-release. The good acidity obvious when first tasted 4 years ago is still there, as is the juicy lemony fruit. A convincing example of Chenin Blanc's ability to age, even if not to the extent of Loire Valley Chenin (100 years or more). Screwcap. 12.2% alc. **Rating** 92 **To** 2025 $25 ✪

🍷🍷🍷🍷 **Extent Tempranillo Garnacha Monastrell 2014** **Rating** 89 **To** 2017 $25
Extent Semillon Chenin Blanc 2014 **Rating** 88 **To** 2017 $17 ✪

Swinging Bridge ★★★★★

33 Gaskill Street, Canowindra, NSW 2804 **Region** Central Ranges Zone
T 0409 246 609 **www**.swingingbridge.com.au **Open** Fri–Sun 11–6
Winemaker Tom Ward **Est.** 1995 **Dozens** 4000 **Vyds** 14ha

Swinging Bridge was founded by Mark Ward, who immigrated to Australia in 1965 from the UK with an honours degree in agricultural science from Cambridge University. He has been succeeded by Tom and Georgie Ward. The vineyard is part of a farming property, Gayton, 10km from Canowindra. The name comes from a suspension walking bridge that crosses the Belubula River at the foot of the vineyard. Swinging Bridge has had considerable wine show success. In Oct 2013 Tom Ward, in partnership with Vines to Venues' Nick Bacon, purchased Orange's best known and regarded wine bar, The Union Bank, having previously added a vineyard in Orange (at 900m) to join their Canowindra vineyard.

🍷🍷🍷🍷🍷 **Reserve Orange Chardonnay 2013** Elegance and power. Flavour and length. This is in exceptionally fine form. Grapefruit, toast, white peach and spice notes build and hone and stretch. Combines high pleasure with thrilling persistence. Screwcap. 12.5% alc. **Rating** 96 **To** 2021 $38 CM ✪

Single Vineyard Series Mrs Payten Orange Chardonnay 2013 Trophy Orange Wine Show '14. Lengthy style with plenty of flesh. Peach, pear, wheat and bacony, almost malty oak, the various aspects combined making for a most seductive package. Velvety as it rolls along the tongue but then chalky through the finish. No doubting its excellence. Screwcap. 13% alc. **Rating** 95 **To** 2020 $32 CM ○

○○○○○ **Museum Release Canowindra Shiraz 2009 Rating** 93 **To** 2019 $45 CM
Single Vineyard Series M.A.W. Pinot Noir 2013 Rating 92 **To** 2022 $38 CM
Reserve Canowindra Shiraz 2013 Rating 92 **To** 2026 $45 CM
Canowindra Shiraz 2013 Rating 91 **To** 2021 $23 CM ○
Canowindra Chardonnay 2013 Rating 90 **To** 2017 $20 CM ○

Swings & Roundabouts ★★★★☆

2807 Caves Road, Yallingup, WA 6232 **Region** Margaret River
T (08) 9756 6640 **www**.swings.com.au **Open** 7 days 10–5
Winemaker Brian Fletcher **Est.** 2004 **Dozens** 20 000 **Vyds** 5.86ha
The Swings & Roundabouts name comes from the expression used to encapsulate the eternal balancing act between the various aspects of grape and wine production. Swings aims to balance the serious side with a touch of fun. There are four ranges: Kiss Chasey, Life of Riley, Swings & Roundabouts and the Backyard Stories. Exports to the US and China.

○○○○○ Backyard Stories Margaret River Cabernet Sauvignon 2013 Bright crimson; a very elegant wine, cassis first up on the bouquet and palate, with a supporting chorus of black olive, dried herbs and a sympathetic waft of French oak; the tannins are fine and persistent. Screwcap. 14% alc. **Rating** 95 **To** 2030 $39

○○○○○ **Backyard Stories Chenin Blanc 2012 Rating** 93 **To** 2020 $29
Margaret River Shiraz 2013 Rating 93 **To** 2028 $22 ○
Margaret River Rose 2014 Rating 92 **To** 2016 $22 ○
Margaret River Cabernet Merlot 2013 Rating 91 **To** 2020 $22 ○
Margaret River Sauvignon Blanc Semillon 2014 Rating 90 **To** 2016 $22
Margaret River Chenin Blanc 2014 Rating 90 **To** 2016 $20 ○

Swinney Vineyards ★★★★★

325 Frankland–Kojonup Road, Frankland River, WA 6396 **Region** Frankland River
T (08) 9200 4483 **www**.swinneyvineyards.com.au **Open** Not
Winemaker Cherubino Consulting **Est.** 1998 **Dozens** 1500 **Vyds** 111.2ha
The Swinney family (parents Graham and Kaye, and son and daughter Matt and Janelle) has been resident on their 2500ha property since settled by George Swinney in 1922. In the '90s they decided to diversify, and have since planted a very substantial, high-quality vineyard on undulating ironstone gravel and loam soils, home to jarrah and red gums. The lion's share of the plantings go to shiraz (45ha) and cabernet sauvignon (37ha), followed by semillon (5ha) and chardonnay (5ha), and they lease 1ha of riesling. They also pushed the envelope by establishing grenache (3.5ha), tempranillo (4ha) and mourvedre (1.6ha) as bush vines, a rarity in this part of the world. With Larry Cherubino making the wines, it is not surprising that they are as good as they are. Exports to the UK.

○○○○○ Ingenue Riesling 2014 This is Frankland River Riesling at its best, imperious in its diamond-cut flavours, crushed lime leaf on the way through the bouquet to the palate; unsweetened lime and lemon flavours are enhanced by glittering acidity. Screwcap. 12.8% alc. **Rating** 95 **To** 2029 $32 ○
Ingenue Shiraz 2013 The striking label and gold Luxe screwcap have a siren allure; this vintage is very different from the (very good) black-fruited '12; the fragrant bouquet sets a red fruit agenda for an elegant and harmonious red cherry play, fine tannins and integrated oak sealing the deal. Screwcap. 13% alc. **Rating** 95 **To** 2033 $35 ○

○○○○○ **Ingenue Tirra Lirra White 2014 Rating** 90 **To** 2020 $30

Swooping Magpie

860 Commonage Road, Yallingup, WA 6282 **Region** Margaret River
T (08) 9756 6227 **www**.swoopingmagpie.com.au **Open** Mon–Fri 10–4, w'ends 10–5
Winemaker Ian Bell, Mark Thompson (Contract) **Est.** 1997 **Dozens** 2000 **Vyds** 4.5ha
Neil and Leann Tuffield's vineyard is situated in the hills behind the coastal town of Yallingup.
The name 'was inspired by a family of magpies who consider the property part of their
territory'. Vineyard plantings (shiraz, semillon, chenin blanc, verdelho, cabernet franc, cabernet
sauvignon and muscat a petit grains) are supplemented by purchased sauvignon blanc, chenin
blanc, shiraz, cabernet sauvignon and merlot. Exports to Vietnam, Singapore and Thailand.

Margaret River Semillon Sauvignon Blanc 2014 Straw-green colour;
attractive delivery of citrus, gooseberry and snow pea flavours; good mouthfeel.
Much to recommend it, just needs a little more length. Screwcap. 13.2% alc.
Rating 88 **To** 2015 $20 CM

Sylvan Springs

40 Blythmans Road, Blewitt Springs, SA 5171 (postal) **Region** McLaren Vale
T 0447 744 755 **www**.sylvansprings.com.au **Open** Not
Winemaker Brian Light (Consultant) **Est.** 1974 **Dozens** 3400 **Vyds** 35.34ha
The Pridmore family was involved in grapegrowing and winemaking in McLaren Vale for
four generations, spanning over 100 years. Cyril Pridmore established The Wattles Winery in
1896, and purchased Sylvan Park, one of the original homesteads in the area, in 1901. The
original family land in the township of McLaren Vale was sold in '78, but not before third-
generation Digby Pridmore had established vineyards (in '74) near Blewitt Springs. When he
retired in '90, his son David purchased the vineyard (planted to nine varieties). Sylvan Springs
is now owned by Tony Yew. Exports to the US, Canada, Denmark and China.

Hard Yards McLaren Vale Shiraz 2012 Fermentation finished in barrel gives
that textural and flavour lift which can't be achieved in any other way; there are
equal amounts of spice, cedar and dark chocolate framing and intersecting with
the ripe, not overripe, black fruits and rounded tannins. Bargain from a great
vintage. Screwcap. 14.5% alc. **Rating** 92 **To** 2025 $19 ○

Hard Yards Sauvignon Blanc Semillon 2012 Rating 88 **To** 2016 $15 ○

Symphonia Wines

1699 Boggy Creek Road, Myrrhee, Vic 3732 **Region** King Valley
T (03) 5729 7641 **www**.symphoniafinewines.com.au **Open** By appt
Winemaker Lilian Carter **Est.** 1998 **Dozens** 1500 **Vyds** 28ha
Peter Read and his family are veterans of the King Valley, commencing the development of
their vineyard in 1981. As a result of extensive trips to both Western and Eastern Europe,
Peter embarked on an ambitious project to trial a series of grape varieties little known in this
country. Current owners Peter and Suzanne Evans are committed to continuing Peter Read's
pioneering legacy, making Arneis, Petit Manseng, Pinot Grigio, Savagnin, Tannat, Tempranillo
and Saperavi.

King Valley Petit Manseng 2013 Full of racy acidity, as expected of the variety,
but a chalkiness to the texture adds a (welcome) extra element. The development
of this wine over the next few years will be an interesting journey. Crystallised
lemon and understated stone fruit notes with a dry, piercing finish. Screwcap.
13% alc. **Rating** 90 **To** 2019 $24 CM

King Valley Arneis 2014 Rating 89 **To** 2020 $24

Symphony Hill Wines

2017 Eukey Road, Ballandean, Qld 4382 **Region** Granite Belt
T (07) 4684 1388 **www**.symphonyhill.com.au **Open** 7 days 10–4
Winemaker Mike Hayes **Est.** 1999 **Dozens** 6000 **Vyds** 3.5ha

Ewen Macpherson purchased what was then an old table grape and orchard property in 1996. A partnership with his parents, Bob and Jill Macpherson led to development of the vineyard, while Ewen completed his Bachelor of Applied Science in viticulture (2003). The vineyard (now much expanded) was established using state-of-the-art technology; vineyard manager/winemaker Mike Hayes is a third-generation viticulturist in the Granite Belt region, and became an equal co-owner of Symphony Hill in '14. He also has impressive academic achievements, with a degree in viticulture, followed by a Masters in Professional Studies – Viticulture, and was awarded a Churchill Fellowship (in '12) to study alternative wine grape varieties in Europe. Symphony Hill has firmly established its reputation as one of the Granite Belt's foremost wineries. Exports to China and Japan.

ŢŢŢŢŢ **Gewurztraminer 2014** All about texture, although not derived from any interposition of oak; there are typically elusive aromas of rose petal and spice on the bouquet, lychee and fleeting citrus on the palate; good balance and length, made without resort to residual sugar. Screwcap. 12.6% alc. **Rating** 93 To 2017 $35

Pinot Gris 2014 Exceptionally tidy and well presented. Bright flavours of pear, dry and sweet, with crunchy apple and spice notes maintaining the vigour. Very good. Screwcap. 12.6% alc. **Rating** 93 To 2015 $30 CM

Granite Belt Fiano 2014 Excellent intensity, fresh and crisp, with melon, nashi pear and apple notes aplenty. This works, and then some. Length and texture are on song too. Screwcap. 12.6% alc. **Rating** 93 To 2016 $30 CM

Reserve Lagrein 2013 The modest alcohol is at the heart of the complex messages delivered by this wine, which, while notably low in tannins, has a glittering array of ever-changing dark fruits and flushes of red fruits. Food and contemplation required. Screwcap. 12.5% alc. **Rating** 93 To 2020 $65

Barrel Fermented Gewurztraminer 2014 More sizzle than an Australia Day BBQ. This is alive with scent and flavour, mostly of the Turkish delight and lychee variety, but also with sweet orange and mandarin notes. Screwcap. 13.9% alc. **Rating** 92 To 2016 $45 CM

Reserve Granite Belt Shiraz 2013 Tangy style with chocolatey oak soaked through cherry and cranberry-flavoured fruit. Attractively perfumed and with a sour-sweet, savoury appeal. Completely non-traditional in Australian Shiraz terms but it's well structured and has an insistence through the finish. Screwcap. 14.2% alc. **Rating** 92 To 2024 $60 CM

Reserve Petit Verdot 2012 Rosemary Hill Vineyard. Mid-weight flavours of tar, violet, blackberry and reductive, rubbery aspects. It's not a heavy wine, but it doesn't lack flavour, tannin or length. Responds well to air: should be decanted if consumed now, and should perform well given a few years in a cool, dark place. Screwcap. 14.5% alc. **Rating** 92 To 2021 $65 CM

Reserve Sauvignon Blanc 2014 Rating 91 To 2016 $25 CM
Family Reserve Granite Belt Verdelho 2014 Rating 91 To 2017 $25 CM
Viognier 2014 Rating 91 To 2015 $30 CM
Granite Belt Petit Manseng 2014 Rating 91 To 2019 $30 CM
Reserve Pinot Noir 2012 Rating 91 To 2020 $45 CM
Granite Belt Shiraz Viognier 2013 Rating 90 To 2021 $45 CM

ŢŢŢŢ **Granite Belt Shiraz 2013 Rating** 89 To 2020 $25 CM
Danying Cabernets 2012 Rating 89 To 2021 $25 CM
Pinot Noir Chardonnay 2011 Rating 88 To 2016 $30 TS

Syrahmi ★★★★☆

PO Box 438, Heathcote, Vic 3523 **Region** Heathcote
T 0407 057 471 **www.**syrahmi.com.au **Open** Not
Winemaker Adam Foster **Est.** 2004 **Dozens** 1500
Adam Foster worked as a chef in Vic and London before moving to the front of house and becoming increasingly interested in wine. He then worked as a cellar hand with a who's who in Australia and France, including Torbreck, Chapoutier, Mitchelton, Domaine Ogier, Heathcote Winery, Jasper Hill and Domaine Pierre Gaillard. He became convinced that the Cambrian soils of Heathcote could produce the best possible Shiraz, and since 2004 has purchased grapes from the region, using the full bag of winemaking techniques. Exports to the US and Japan.

ŸŸŸŸŸ La La Shiraz 2010 From the Greenstone Vineyard, 40% whole bunches, 100% new French oak for 42 months; due for release late '15. This has all the attitude and style expected of a wine with such a pedigree, but won't appeal to everyone. I think Adam Foster has pushed the envelope to its limits, but the spicy, peppery black fruits have the concentration and energy to justify the extreme survivor challenge set for it. Screwcap. 13.2% alc. **Rating** 96 **To** 2040 $120
Mourvedre 2013 The equable climate of Heathcote suits many red varieties, and it doesn't break ranks with this elegant and expressive purple and red-berried wine, its tannins fine and balanced. Screwcap. 14.2% alc. **Rating** 94 **To** 2025 $42

ŸŸŸŸŸ Dreams Heathcote Shiraz 2012 **Rating** 92 **To** 2032 $55
Demi Heathcote Shiraz 2014 **Rating** 91 **To** 2020 $25

T'Gallant ★★★★☆

1385 Mornington–Flinders Road, Main Ridge, Vic 3928 **Region** Mornington Peninsula
T (03) 5931 1300 **www.**tgallant.com.au **Open** 7 days 9–5
Winemaker Kevin McCarthy **Est.** 1990 **Dozens** NFP **Vyds** 8ha
Husband and wife consultant winemakers Kevin McCarthy and Kathleen Quealy carved out such an important niche market for the T'Gallant label that in 2003, after protracted negotiations, it was acquired by Beringer Blass (now part of TWE). The acquisition of a 15ha property and the planting of 8ha of pinot gris gave the business a firm geographic base, as well as providing increased resources for its signature wine. In April '15 TWE announced its intention to sell the business.

ŸŸŸŸŸ Tribute Pinot Noir 2013 Excellent, deep, bright crimson-purple; packed full with red cherry, black cherry and plum on both its bouquet and powerful palate, spice and forest nuances waiting in the wings for their chance to come onto centre stage and join the fruit chorus. MV6 clone strikes again. Screwcap. 13% alc. **Rating** 95 **To** 2025 $40
Juno Mornington Vineyard Pinot Noir 2013 A strikingly complex Pinot, with foresty, earthy nuances running through the predominantly red fruits from go to whoa; at this stage of its development, a work in progress, asking for (and deserving) more time for its mysteries to be revealed. Screwcap. 13% alc. **Rating** 94 **To** 2025 $100
Cyrano Pinot Noir 2013 A good Pinot Noir wasting no time in ticking all the boxes, its fragrant plum and cherry seamlessly migrating from the bouquet to the palate; here the type of extract – mainly tannins – is exactly right, for it doesn't block out the beams of sunlight. Screwcap. 13% alc. **Rating** 94 **To** 2023 $28 ○

ŸŸŸŸŸ Grace Pinot Grigio 2014 **Rating** 93 **To** 2016 $25 ○
Tribute Pinot Gris 2013 **Rating** 93 **To** 2016 $34
Odysseus Nebbiolo 2012 **Rating** 92 **To** 2025 $45

Tahbilk ★★★★★

254 O'Neils Road, Tabilk, Vic 3608 **Region** Nagambie Lakes
T (03) 5794 2555 **www.**tahbilk.com.au **Open** Mon–Sat 9–5, Sun 11–5
Winemaker Alister Purbrick, Neil Larson, Alan George **Est.** 1860 **Dozens** 100 000
Vyds 221.5ha

A winery steeped in tradition (with National Trust classification), which should be visited at least once by every wine-conscious Australian, and which makes wines – particularly red wines – utterly in keeping with that tradition. The essence of that heritage comes in the form of the tiny quantities of Shiraz made from vines planted in 1860. Serendipitous, perhaps, but the current release wines are absolutely outstanding. A founding member of Australia's First Families of Wine. 2016 *Wine Companion* Winery of the Year. Exports to all major markets.

ΨΨΨΨΨ **1860 Vines Shiraz 2009** Has retained excellent hue; this is truly liquid history, as every one of the vines was planted in 1860, with no replants – just ever-increasing gaps where vines have died. This is a super-elegant, perfectly balanced, medium-bodied wine, the flavours encompassing black cherry, plum and dried herb, fine tannins and high-quality French oak providing the gently savoury finish. Screwcap. 12.5% alc. **Rating** 98 **To** 2050 $290
Eric Stevens Purbrick Shiraz 2009 From vines with an average age of 35 years, matured in a mix of French and American oak. Here the aromas and flavours are very complex, with blackberry somewhere in the centre of a globe spinning around in an exotic mix of spices, licorice and herbs; the magic lies in the fresh, almost juicy, finish. Screwcap. 13.5% alc. **Rating** 97 **To** 2050 $70 ◐

ΨΨΨΨΨ **1927 Vines Marsanne 2006** An exceptional wine from 79yo estate vines, the colour still pale quartz-green, the bouquet fragrant, and the palate as fresh as a daisy; crunchy acidity underlies the classic varietal mix of honeysuckle and unsweetened lemon juice. Screwcap. 10.5% alc. **Rating** 96 **To** 2036 $45 ◐
1927 Vines Marsanne 2005 Has a necklace of 8 gold medals (and a trophy) on the front label, similar to Tyrrell's Museum Semillons, with which it shares many features. Most obviously, the dancing ballerina feet of the acidity establishing both the structure and flavour melody behind that acidity. This has further to go than the '09 Museum Marsanne released at the same time. Screwcap. 10.5% alc. **Rating** 96 **To** 2025 $45 ◐
Old Vines Cabernet Shiraz 2012 The colour, the bouquet and the palate all attest to the youth of the wine, yet it has all the hallmarks of the old vines; blackcurrant, blackberry and cherry fruit are the drivers of the bouquet and palate alike. The most remarkable aspect is the fine, supple tannins, making it a classic two-way proposition. Screwcap. 14% alc. **Rating** 96 **To** 2027 $45 ◐
Museum Release Marsanne 2009 Museum? I don't think so. This is still an adolescent, with years to travel before it reaches full maturity, let alone retirement to an old wines' home. On the one hand, there is vibrant citrussy acidity, on the other a distinct edge of honeyed flavour build-up. That said, there are lots of reasons to enjoy it right now. Screwcap. 13.1% alc. **Rating** 95 **To** 2020 $24 ◐
Eric Stevens Purbrick Cabernet Sauvignon 2009 Has retained excellent colour; very much in the tradition of long-lived Cabernets ex Tahbilk, now with the added certainty (and longevity) of the screwcap; foresty blackcurrant fruit has a finely worked tannin structure for long-term cellaring. Screwcap. 13.5% alc. **Rating** 95 **To** 2034 $70
Roussanne Marsanne Viognier 2013 Rating 94 **To** 2018 $25 CM ◐
Grenache Shiraz Mourvedre 2013 Rating 94 **To** 2023 $25 CM ◐
Cabernet Sauvignon 2012 Rating 94 **To** 2025 $20 ◐

ΨΨΨΨΨ **Viognier 2014 Rating** 93 **To** 2016 $20 ◐
Marsanne 2014 Rating 92 **To** 2029 $18 ◐
Shiraz 2012 Rating 92 **To** 2022 $20 ◐

Talbots Block Wines   ★★★★

PO Box 1211, Clare, SA 5453 **Region** Clare Valley
T 0402 649 979 **www.talbotsblock.com.au Open** Not
Winemaker Contract **Est.** 2011 **Dozens** 800 **Vyds** 5ha
Thanks to careers in government and the oil industry, Alex and Bill Talbot started their journey to wine in 1997 while working and living at Woomera in the SA desert. They purchased land in the Sevenhill area of the Clare Valley, having fallen in love with the place,

and dreamed of some day making wine for their friends. They then moved to various places in Asia, including Kuala Lumpur, Jakarta and Singapore, their minds always returning to their Sevenhill vineyard. They now live in the house they built high on the block, giving views across the vineyard, and have the opportunity to tend the vines whenever they please. Initially the grapes were sold, but in 2012 they kept enough of the production to have 500 dozen made across their two distinctly different Shiraz styles. The labels are striking and evocative.

ŸŸŸŸŸ **The Prince Clare Valley Shiraz 2013** From the low-yielding (3.2t/h) Talbot's Block vineyard at Sevenhill; open-fermented with pump-overs, and matured for 12 months in 1yo American oak. A richly robed, mouth-filling style, all the focus on blackberry and plum fruit; the tannins are soft, the wine ready to go. Screwcap. 14.7% alc. **Rating** 92 **To** 2023 $25 ⦿

Talijancich   ★★★★★

26 Hyem Road, Herne Hill, WA 6056 **Region** Swan Valley
T (08) 9296 4289 **www**.taliwine.com.au **Open** Sun–Fri 11–5
Winemaker James Talijancich **Est.** 1932 **Dozens** 10 000
A former fortified wine specialist (with old Liqueur Tokay) now making a select range of table wines, with particular emphasis on Verdelho – each year there is a tasting of fine 3yo Verdelho from both Australia and overseas. James Talijancich is an energetic and effective ambassador for the Swan Valley as a whole. The rating is solely for his fortified wines. Exports to China, Japan and Hong Kong.

ŸŸŸŸŸ Aged 30 Years Rare Tawny NV Massively powerful and concentrated, full-on liqueur style; uniquely Swan Valley, extraordinarily luscious, heading to Seppeltsfield 100 Year Old Para in weight (although not flavour). Cork. 20% alc. Rating 95 To 2016 $80

Talisman Wines   ★★★★

PO Box 354, Cottesloe, WA 6911 **Region** Geographe
T 0401 559 266 **www**.talismanwines.com.au **Open** Not
Winemaker Peter Stanlake **Est.** 2009 **Dozens** 2500 **Vyds** 9ha
Kim Robinson (and wife Jenny) began the development of their vineyard in 2000, and now have cabernet, shiraz, malbec, zinfandel, chardonnay, riesling and sauvignon blanc. Kim says that 'after eight frustrating years of selling grapes to Evans & Tate and Wolf Blass, we decided to optimise the vineyard and attempt to make quality wines'. The measure of their success has been consistent gold medal (and some trophies) performance at the Geographe Wine Show. They say this could not have been achieved without the assistance of vineyard manager Victor Bertola, and winemaker Peter Stanlake.

ŸŸŸŸŸ **Ferguson Valley Sauvignon Blanc 2014** A bright, lively and juicy Sauvignon Blanc with well above average depth of fruit flavour without losing focus; green pineapple, guava and a touch of passionfruit are at once lengthened, yet tightly framed, by citrussy acidity. Screwcap. 12.8% alc. **Rating** 93 **To** 2016 $18 ⦿
Barrique Ferguson Valley Sauvignon Blanc Fume 2014 Barrel fermentation in used oak has increased the dimension and texture of the palate, but shaded the vibrant fruit of its unwooded sibling. Swings and roundabouts. Screwcap. 12.8% alc. **Rating** 93 **To** 2016 $25 ⦿
Gabrielle Ferguson Valley Chardonnay 2013 Wild yeast-fermented in new and 1yo French barriques. A complex wine, the slightly smoky bouquet leading to a bright, crisp finish, with grapefruit, apple and pear encountered at various points along the way. Screwcap. 14% alc. **Rating** 92 **To** 2020 $32
Ferguson Valley Shiraz 2012 Bright, although relatively light, colour; a fragrant, lively wine with red cherry, raspberry and strawberry flavours enhanced by a soft oak and tannin combination. Screwcap. 13.5% alc. **Rating** 90 **To** 2027 $30

ŸŸŸŸ Ferguson Valley Cabernet Malbec 2011 Rating 89 To 2017 $20
Ferguson Valley Riesling 2014 Rating 88 To 2020 $20

Tallavera Grove | Carillion

749 Mount View Road, Mount View, NSW 2325 **Region** Hunter Valley
T (02) 4990 7535 **www.**tallaveragrove.com.au **Open** Thurs–Mon 10–5
Winemaker Gwyn Olsen **Est.** 2000 **Dozens** 2500 **Vyds** 188ha
Tallavera Grove is one of the many wine interests of Dr John Davis and family. The family
is a 50% owner of Briar Ridge, and also owns a 12ha vineyard in Coonawarra, the 100ha
Stonefields Vineyard at Wrattonbully and a 36ha vineyard at Orange (the Carillion wines are
sourced from this vineyard). The 40ha Hunter Valley vineyards are planted to chardonnay,
shiraz, semillon, verdelho, cabernet sauvignon and viognier.

ΨΨΨΨΨ **Tallavera Grove Fenestella Hunter Valley Shiraz 2013** Deep, clear crimson-
purple; twice the price of its sibling, and quite literally, twice as good; it has the
sumptuous polish of top-quality Hunter Shiraz, with red and black fruits taking
equal space on the bouquet and palate, sustained by superbly honed tannins and
integrated oak. Screwcap. 13.5% alc. **Rating** 96 To 2043 $50 ○
Carillion Orange Riesling 2014 Gold medal Orange Wine Show '14. Crisp,
clean flavour, excellent drive of citrus running the length of the palate, and then
a flourish to the finish. Textbook in the most positive of ways. Cutting acidity
and prominent spice/chalk notes, but drinking well young. Screwcap. 11.5% alc.
Rating 95 To 2023 $25 CM ○
Tallavera Grove Hunter Valley Semillon 2014 Top-quality now or later style;
the bouquet is distinctly floral, the palate alive with juicy Meyer lemon fruit given
length, balance and structure by its backbone of minerally acidity. It will remain
inviolate as the citrus notes acquire a honeyed edge first, followed by toast later.
Screwcap. 12% alc. **Rating** 95 To 2034 $25 ○
Carillion Estate Grown Orange Verduzzo 2014 Crammed to the gills
with all sorts of spices and flavours; brown spices, biscuits and dried fruits on the
bouquet are joined by musk, more dried fruits and some all-important acidity
on the finish. This is quite a wine: tell me more. Screwcap. 13.5% alc. **Rating** 94
To 2017 $22 ○

ΨΨΨΨΨ **Carillion Orange Sauvignon Blanc 2014** Rating 93 To 2016 $22 ○
Carillion Orange Pinot Gris 2014 Rating 91 To 2017 $22 ○
Tallavera Grove Hunter Valley Verdelho 2014 Rating 91 To 2018 $20 ○
Tallavera Grove Hunter Valley Shiraz 2013 Rating 91 To 2025 $25
Carillion The Feldspars Orange Shiraz 2013 Rating 90 To 2023 $38
Carillion Orange Cabernet Merlot 2013 Rating 90 To 2025 $22
**Davis Premium Vineyards Rogue Series Foot Stomped Hunter Valley
Sagrantino 2013** Rating 90 To 2020 $30

Taltarni

339 Taltarni Road, Moonambel, Vic 3478 **Region** Pyrenees
T (03) 5459 7900 **www.**taltarni.com.au **Open** 7 days 10–5
Winemaker Robert Heywood, Peter Warr **Est.** 1972 **Dozens** 80 000 **Vyds** 78.5ha
The American owner and founder of Clos du Val (Napa Valley), Taltarni and Clover Hill
(see separate entry) has brought the management of these three businesses and Domaine de
Nizas (Languedoc) under the one roof, the group known as Goelet Wine Estates. Taltarni is
the largest of the Australian ventures, its estate vineyards of great value and underpinning the
substantial annual production. In Nov 2014, Taltarni's viticulturist, Matthew Bailey, received
the prestigious Viticulturist of the Year Award from the Australian Society of Viticulture
and Oenology. During his tenure at Taltarni he has established what he calls 'insectariums',
continuing, 'These are like insect holiday resorts. The good insects eat the bad insects that
eat the vines.' The insectariums are established in permanent vegetation corridors, each
containing around 2000 native plants, that provide a pollen and nectar source for the beneficial
insects, reducing the need for chemicals and other controls of the vineyards. Exports to all
major markets.

ŸŸŸŸŸ **Estate Pyrenees Shiraz 2012** An 88/6/5/1% blend of shiraz, mourvedre, cabernet and viognier matured in new and used French oak. The bouquet has elusive hints of sandalwood and polished black leather, the medium to full-bodied palate bringing a complex array of fruit flavours onto centre stage, blackberry foremost, but with a swirl of activity behind it. Top vintage, top result. Screwcap. 14.5% alc. **Rating** 95 **To** 2037 $40

Estate Pyrenees Cabernet Sauvignon 2012 Includes 10% shiraz, both varieties estate-grown and matured in new and used French barriques. A full-bodied Cabernet speaking loudly of its place (and variety); blackcurrant fruit is offset by bay leaf/dried herbs, firm tannins and cedary French oak. Screwcap. 14.5% alc. **Rating** 95 **To** 2037 $40

Tache Chardonnay Pinot Noir Pinot Meunier 2011 An engaging interplay between the wonderfully tangy notes of morello cherries, wild strawberries and pink grapefruit and the gently silky, softening influence of a few years of yeast age. The result is seamless, having attained that magical moment in its evolution where vivacity and grace find comfortable union. It has texture, persistence and wonderful acid line. Still one of the best value roses on the shelves. Diam. 11.7% alc. **Rating** 94 **To** 2016 $26 TS ✪

Fume Blanc 2013 From the Pyrenees (62%) and Tasmania (38%); fermented and matured in French oak for 12 months, with lees stirring for the first 6 months. The regional blend has been totally synergistic; the flavours range through snow pea, kiwifruit/tropical fruits and minerally acidity. A very good Sauvignon Blanc. Screwcap. 13.5% alc. **Rating** 94 **To** 2017 $25 ✪

Reserve Pyrenees Shiraz Cabernet 2008 Made during a prolonged drought, and in a hot vintage, and has to be admired for surmounting that dual challenge. It has retained depth to its good colour; black fruits, savoury tannins, and a contrasting mix of cedar and mocha, make for a very complex wine. Cork. 14.5% alc. **Rating** 94 **To** 2033 $65

Petit Verdot 2013 Matured in French oak barriques. Has the typical deep colour of Petit Verdot, and the four square black fruits, licorice and bitter chocolate, all without the penalty of excessive tannins. A gentle giant. Screwcap. 14.5% alc. **Rating** 94 **To** 2028 $25 ✪

ŸŸŸŸ♀ **Shiraz Viognier 2013** **Rating** 92 **To** 2025 $25 ✪
Brut 2011 **Rating** 92 **To** 2016 $26 TS

Tamar Ridge | Pirie ★★★★★

1a Waldhorn Drive, Rosevears, Tas 7277 **Region** Northern Tasmania
T (03) 6330 0300 **www**.brownbrothers.com.au **Open** 7 days 10–5
Winemaker Tom Wallace **Est.** 1994 **Dozens** 14000 **Vyds** 120ha
In August 2010 Brown Brothers purchased Tamar Ridge from Gunns Limited for $32.5 million. While Dr Andrew Pirie has retired from his former position of CEO and chief winemaker, he points out that the end of his five-year tenure happened to coincide with the acquisition. Tasmania is the one region of Australia with demand for grapes and wine exceeding supply. Tamar Ridge was well managed during the seven years it was owned by Gunns, avoiding the financial meltdown of Gunns. Exports to all major markets.

ŸŸŸŸŸ **Tamar Ridge Riesling 2014** Piercing flavour. Orange, lime and barley. Gets itself sorted and slings through the palate at a rate of knots. Flavour and length. Screwcap. 12.5% alc. **Rating** 95 **To** 2028 $24 CM ✪

Tamar Ridge Pinot Gris 2014 Gold Tas Wine Show '15. Has exceptional line, length and integrity; superb acidity within the context of a freakishly good class in the show. This will go the distance in the cellar. Screwcap. **Rating** 95 **To** 2019 $26 ✪

Pirie NV Speaks loud and clear of its Tasmanian origin, although nothing is specified about its varietal base, whether bottle-fermented or not (probably is) and how long it spent on lees; it certainly will flourish with time in bottle. Trophy Qld Wine Show '13. Cork. 12.5% alc. **Rating** 95 **To** 2019 $30 ✪

ᵀᵀᵀᵀ⸮ Tamar Ridge Reserve Pinot Noir 2013 Rating 93 To 2022 $50 CM
Pirie Sparkling Rose 2009 Rating 92 To 2016 $50 TS
Tamar Ridge Botrytis Riesling 2013 Rating 92 To 2019 $25 CM ✪
Tamar Ridge Sauvignon Blanc 2014 Rating 91 To 2015 $24 CM
Tamar Ridge Pinot Noir 2013 Rating 91 To 2020 $30 CM

Tambo Estate

96 Pages Road, Tambo Upper, Vic 3885 **Region** Gippsland
T (03) 5156 4921 **Open** By appt
Winemaker Alastair Butt **Est.** 1994 **Dozens** 800 **Vyds** 5.11ha
Bill and Pam Williams returned to Australia in the early 1990s after seven years overseas, and began the search for a property which met the specific requirements for high-quality table wines established by Dr John Gladstones in his masterwork *Viticulture and Environment*. They chose a property in the foothills of the Victorian Alps on the inland side of the Gippsland Lakes, with predominantly sheltered, north-facing slopes. They planted a little over 5ha of chardonnay (the lion's share of the plantings, with 3.4ha), sauvignon blanc, pinot noir, cabernet sauvignon and a splash of merlot. They are mightily pleased to have secured the services of Alastair Butt (one-time maker at Seville Estate).

ᵀᵀᵀᵀᵀ Gippsland Lakes Pinot Noir 2013 Very good colour, bright and deep, mirrored by the bouquet and palate with deliciously deep, rounded fruit and supple tannins throughout. Can be enjoyed tonight, but there is even more in store down the track. Screwcap. 13.8% alc. **Rating** 95 To 2023 $27 ✪
Gippsland Lakes Sauvignon Blanc 2014 Hand-picked, whole bunch-pressed, wild yeast-fermented in used French barriques, 5 months' maturation on lees. A splendidly generous and complex wine, with tropical fruits neatly balanced by green pea/herbal nuances. Screwcap. 13.4% alc. **Rating** 94 To 2016 $24 ✪
Gippsland Lakes Chardonnay 2013 Whole bunch-pressed, wild yeast barrique-fermented, some stirring, 10 months in barrel. Has that combination of pure varietal expression and intensity of flavour that permeates all Tambo wines. Screwcap. 13.9% alc. **Rating** 94 To 2020 $25 ✪

Tamburlaine

358 McDonalds Road, Pokolbin, NSW 2321 **Region** Hunter Valley
T (02) 4998 4200 **www**.mywinery.com **Open** 7 days 9.30–5
Winemaker Mark Davidson, Ashley Horner **Est.** 1966 **Dozens** 60 000 **Vyds** 125ha
A thriving business that (until exports started to grow significantly) sold over 90% of its wine through the cellar door and by mailing list (with an active tasting club members' cellar program). The maturing of the estate-owned Orange vineyard led to the introduction of reserve varietals across the range. Both the Hunter Valley and Orange vineyards are now certified organic. Exports to Malaysia, South Korea, Nepal, Japan and China.

ᵀᵀᵀᵀᵀ Reserve Hunter Valley Semillon 2014 Has all the attributes of high-quality modern Semillon, the combination of quality grapes, protective winemaking and a screwcap all locking in every skerrick of aroma and flavour, thereby cross-dressing with riesling, the fruit accented on lemongrass/lemon to be sure, rather than lime (which can lurk in the background); riveting acidity makes up the balance. Screwcap. 10.2% alc. **Rating** 95 To 2029 $33 ✪
Reserve Orange Sauvignon Blanc 2014 Part wild yeast-fermented in Hungarian oak, part whole bunch-pressed and open-fermented, all given extended lees contact. A bold approach that has paid off; the complex flavours, headed by citrus, lime and orange peel, green pineapple and snow pea, linger long on the finish. Screwcap. 11.9% alc. **Rating** 95 To 2016 $33 ✪
Reserve Orange Chardonnay 2014 The back label says 'ripe nectarine and melon, shortbread and toasted almond with some star anise and ginger notes'. I would subtract the star anise and ginger, accept the rest, and add grapefruit zest. It's a livewire wine. Screwcap. 12.8% alc. **Rating** 94 To 2020 $33

Reserve Hunter Valley Syrah 2013 Matured in French and American oak. Bright, clear crimson, it has an expressive and inviting bouquet, the elegant medium-bodied palate with more red fruits than usual for the Hunter Valley, but none the worse for that; the only blemish is acidity, which may turn into a virtue down the track. Screwcap. 12.8% alc. **Rating** 94 **To** 2028 $44

ⓎⓎⓎⓎⓎ **Reserve Orange Syrah 2013 Rating** 90 **To** 2020 $44

Taminick Cellars   ★★★★

339 Booth Road, Taminick via Glenrowan, Vic 3675 **Region** Glenrowan
T (03) 5766 2282 **www**.taminickcellars.com.au **Open** Mon–Sat 9–5, Sun 10–5
Winemaker James Booth **Est.** 1904 **Dozens** 2000 **Vyds** 19.7ha
Peter Booth is a third-generation member of the Booth family, who have owned this winery since Esca Booth purchased the property in 1904. James Booth, fourth generation and current winemaker, completed his wine science degree at CSU in 2008. The red wines are massively flavoured and very long-lived, notably those from the 9ha of shiraz planted in 1919. Trebbiano and alicante bouschet were also planted in '19; the much newer arrivals include nero d'Avola.

ⓎⓎⓎⓎⓎ **Botrytis 2012** Botrytis Trebbiano. Taminick has a reputation for 'massive' wines and this is massively sweet and intense. It's golden in colour, massed with sweet apricot jam and honey notes, and cut (crucially) with limey acidity. It's too sweet and too much, but credit where credit is undoubtedly due; Australian dessert wines rarely attain this kind of intensity. A decade or so ago this would have been a candidate for 'cult' status. Drinkers are advised to enter at their own risk. 375ml. Screwcap. 10.5% alc. **Rating** 94 **To** 2019 $25 CM ❂

ⓎⓎⓎⓎⓎ **Durif Shiraz 2013 Rating** 92 **To** 2022 $16 CM ❂

Tapanappa   ★★★★★

15 Spring Gully Road, Piccadilly, SA 5151 **Region** South Australia
T (08) 7324 5301 **www**.tapanappawines.com.au **Open** Thurs–Mon 11–4
Winemaker Brian Croser **Est.** 2002 **Dozens** 2500 **Vyds** 16.7ha
Tapanappa has come home in many ways in 2015. It has the original Petaluma winery back, and a cellar door open at the picturesque Tiers Vineyard. Equally importantly, it is now wholly own by Brian and Ann Croser, albeit with the involvement of daughter and son-in-law Lucy and Xavier Bizot. The business as usual components are the Whalebone Vineyard at Wrattonbully (planted to cabernet sauvignon, shiraz and merlot over 30 years ago), the Tiers Vineyard (chardonnay) at Piccadilly in the Adelaide Hills, and the Foggy Hill Vineyard on the southern tip of the Fleurieu Peninsula (pinot noir).

ⓎⓎⓎⓎⓎ **Whalebone Vineyard Wrattonbully Merlot Cabernet Franc 2012** Still has excellent crimson-purple colour; has spent close on 3 years making its way into bottle, an especially long time for a blend such as this, but it clearly needed it; there is a complex interplay between cedar, cigar box, blackcurrant, dried herbs and a persistent tattoo of fine-grained tannins on the very long palate. Cork. 14.6% alc. **Rating** 96 **To** 2037 $80

Foggy Hill Vineyard Fleurieu Peninsula Pinot Noir 2013 Light colour, but with a bright hue; the flowery bouquet of spice, rose petals and small red fruits is followed by a light, perfectly balanced palate, the promised red fruits duly delivered; the finish is long and in lockstep with all that has preceded it. Cork. 13.9% alc. **Rating** 95 **To** 2023 $49

Whalebone Vineyard Wrattonbully Cabernet Shiraz 2012 An unusual style for Tapanappa, opulent, ripe and juicy blackberry, blackcurrant and mulberry fruits in total command; oak and tannins are presently shaded by the fruit. By all rights, should settle down with time. Cork. 15.1% alc. **Rating** 95 **To** 2032 $50

Tiers Vineyard Piccadilly Valley Chardonnay 2013 An extremely intense and focused wine; the fruit is a blend of citrus, stone fruit and apple; the barrel-ferment inputs and oak maturation have been swallowed by the fruit. Needs several years to relax and open for business. Screwcap. 13.8% alc. **Rating** 94 **To** 2028 $80

Tar & Roses

61 Vickers Lane, Nagambie, Vic 3608 (postal) **Region** Central Victoria Zone
T (03) 5794 1811 **www**.tarandroses.com.au **Open** Not
Winemaker Don Lewis, Narelle King **Est.** 2004 **Dozens** 18 000 **Vyds** 5ha
While Don Lewis and Narelle King have made and marketed the Tar & Roses wines for
some years, the business is owned by Tar & Roses Pty Ltd, a company in which neither has a
financial interest. It's all rather complicated, but life wasn't meant to be simple.

Tar & Roses Heathcote Shiraz 2013 Rich and ripe, but schmick. Flavours of
blackberry, dark chocolate and warm asphalt flood the palate with sweet, hearty
flavour, but it doesn't forget its manners and at all points seems breathy in its
eagerness to please. Screwcap. 14.9% alc. **Rating** 94 **To** 2022 $22 CM ○
Tar & Roses Tempranillo 2013 Substantial Tempranillo and an excellent one.
This is alive with dark-hearted flavour, is perfectly well structured and clips meaty
oak to its lapel, just to complete the look. Black cherry, chicory, chocolate and
plum flavours hold sway for the most part. Value, needless to say, is right up there.
Screwcap. 14.5% alc. **Rating** 94 **To** 2022 $24 CM ○

Tar & Roses Heathcote Sangiovese 2013 **Rating** 93 **To** 2021 $24 CM ○
Tar & Roses Lewis Riesling 2014 **Rating** 91 **To** 2020 $24 CM
Tar & Roses Pinot Grigio 2014 **Rating** 91 **To** 2015 $19 CM ○

Tarrahill.

340 Old Healesville Road, Yarra Glen, Vic 3775 **Region** Yarra Valley
T (03) 9730 1152 **www**.tarrahill.com **Open** By appt
Winemaker Jonathan Hamer, Geof Fethers **Est.** 1992 **Dozens** 700 **Vyds** 6.5ha
Owned by former Mallesons Lawyers partner Jonathan Hamer and wife Andrea, a former
doctor and daughter of Ian Hanson, who made wine for many years under the Hanson-
Tarrahill label. Ian had a 0.8ha vineyard at Lower Plenty, but needed 2ha to obtain a
vigneron's licence. In 1990 the Hamers purchased a property in the Yarra Valley and planted
the requisite vines (pinot noir – ultimately destroyed by the 2009 bushfires). In '92 Jonathan
planted a further 2ha, and spent all his weekends looking after the vineyard. This became
increasingly difficult, so the Hamers planted yet more vines to justify the employment of a
vineyard manager. Nonetheless, he and company director friend Geof Fethers continued to
work weekends in the vineyard, and in '04 decided that they would undertake a wine science
degree (at CSU); they graduated in '11. In '12 Jonathan retired from law and planted more
vineyards (cabernet sauvignon, cabernet franc, merlot, malbec and petit verdot, to make a
Bordeaux blend), and Ian (aged 86) retired from winemaking. Andrea has also contributed,
with a second degree (horticulture); she is a biodynamics advocate.

Le Batard 2012 Blend of (mostly) pinot noir with input from shiraz and
cabernet sauvignon. The input from the latter two makes the pinot noir almost
seem like a distant memory. This is meaty but plush, floral but awash with dark
berried fruit. Toasty, cedary oak is on the march too, its spicier notes forming an
enchanting double-act with the wine's meatier notes. We have both a wine and a
producer here of real character and, potentially, of great note. Screwcap. 14.4% alc.
Rating 96 **To** 2030 $30 CM ○
Chardonnay 2011 Abandon all preconceptions and allow yourself to enter its
world. One sniff/taste and it's abundantly clear that something different and all-
encompassing is at hand. It tastes of chalk, lactose, lemon and white peach and has
floral overtones. Creamy oak is here too; it makes you wonder whether a wine
can be lean and rich at once. Struck match complexity too? Do you need to ask?
Screwcap. 12.4% alc. **Rating** 95 **To** 2022 $30 CM ○

Cabernet Sauvignon 2011 **Rating** 90 **To** 2023 $45 CM

TarraWarra Estate

311 Healesville–Yarra Glen Road, Yarra Glen, Vic 3775 **Region** Yarra Valley
T (03) 5962 3311 **www**.tarrawarra.com.au **Open** Tues–Sun 11–5
Winemaker Clare Halloran **Est.** 1983 **Dozens** 15000 **Vyds** 28.98ha

TarraWarra is, and always has been, one of the top-tier wineries in the Yarra Valley. Founded by Marc Besen AO and wife Eva, it has operated on the basis that quality is paramount, cost a secondary concern. The creation of the TarraWarra Museum of Art (twma.com.au) in a purpose-built building provides another reason to visit; indeed, many visitors come specifically to look at the ever-changing displays in the Museum. Changes in the vineyard include the planting of shiraz and merlot, and in the winery, the creation of a four-tier range: a deluxe MDB label made in tiny quantities and only when the vintage permits; the single-vineyard range; a Reserve range; and the 100% estate-grown varietal range. Exports to France, the Maldives, Vietnam, Singapore Hong Kong and China.

Reserve Yarra Valley Chardonnay 2013 From the '83 planting; whole bunch-pressed to French oak (25% new) for wild yeast fermentation, 10 months' maturation. The bouquet has some toasty complexity, but the very long palate is an exercise in purity and focus, the flavours of white peach and a touch of cream. Screwcap. 12.8% alc. **Rating** 95 **To** 2023 $50

Yarra Valley Chardonnay 2013 There's a fine line between pleasure and pain and this is squarely in the former camp. It shows a wealth of oak, in some ways, and yet it pulls it off with flair. It tastes of oatmeal, peach, grapefruit and cedar spice; it's slippery smooth; it lingers terrifically. Chardonnay drinkers far and wide will adore this. Screwcap. 13% alc. **Rating** 95 **To** 2020 $28 CM ✪

Reserve Yarra Valley Pinot Noir 2013 Bright, clear crimson-purple; an elegant, sophisticated Pinot Noir embracing the full spectrum of Yarra Valley pinot aromas and flavours on its highly fragrant bouquet and palate; the juicy red and black cherry fruits are framed by fine, but persistent, savoury tannins on the lingering finish. Screwcap. 13.5% alc. **Rating** 95 **To** 2025 $70

Yarra Valley Pinot Noir 2013 Good colour and a particularly expressive bouquet are followed by an impressively articulated palate; spiced plum aromas and flavours are in perfect sync with the restrained, but evident, oak and finely honed tannins. Screwcap. 13.5% alc. **Rating** 95 **To** 2022 $28 ✪

Late Disgorged Blanc de Blancs 2010 Rating 91 **To** 2020 $60 TS

Tatachilla

151 Main Road, McLaren Vale, SA 5171 **Region** McLaren Vale
T (08) 8563 7000 **www**.tatachillawines.com.au **Open** Not
Winemaker Jeremy Ottawa **Est.** 1903 **Dozens** 43000 **Vyds** 12.4ha

Tatachilla was reborn in 1995 but has had a tumultuous history going back to 1903. Between then and '61 the winery was owned by Penfolds; it was closed in '61 and reopened in '65 as the Southern Vales Co-operative. In the late '80s it was purchased and renamed The Vales but did not flourish; in '93 it was purchased by local grower Vic Zerella and former Kaiser Stuhl chief executive Keith Smith. After extensive renovations, the winery was officially reopened in '95 and won a number of tourist awards and accolades. It became part of Banksia Wines in 2001, in turn acquired by Lion Nathan in '02. Exports to all major markets.

Foundation McLaren Vale Shiraz 2012 The great vintage and the elevation of the Tatachilla vineyard in the Clarendon district come together with sensitive winemaking to produce this elegant, medium-bodied wine; black forest berry fruit, with that bitter chocolate centre so much the regional mark of McLaren Vale in close attendance; fine-grained tannins and quality oak complete a perfect rendition of place and variety. Screwcap. 14.5% alc. **Rating** 96 **To** 2037 $60 ✪

McLaren Vale Shiraz 2013 Rating 92 **To** 2033 $16 ✪
McLaren Vale Cabernet Sauvignon 2013 Rating 90 **To** 2020 $19 ✪

Tatler Wines

477 Lovedale Road, Lovedale, NSW 2321 **Region** Hunter Valley
T (02) 4930 9139 **www**.tatlerwines.com **Open** 7 days 10–5
Winemaker Daniel Binet **Est.** 1998 **Dozens** 6000 **Vyds** 15ha

Tatler Wines is a family-owned company headed by Sydney hoteliers, brothers Theo and Spiro Isak (Isakidis). The name comes from the Tatler Hotel on George Street, Sydney, which was purchased by father James (Dimitri) Isak in 1974 and operated by the family until its closure in '86. In '98 the Tatler name was reborn with the purchase of a 40ha property in Lovedale. The vineyard is planted to 7ha of chardonnay and 4ha each of semillon and shiraz, and the wines are made onsite in the recently renovated winery. Exports to the US.

ŸŸŸŸŸ **Nigel's Hunter Valley Semillon 2012** Bright green-quartz; from the Lovedale district, it is a super-powerful semillon still in the making, but already flooded with citrus fruit running into lime juice – most unusual, and totally hedonistic. Great each-way bet. Screwcap. 9.5% alc. **Rating** 95 **To** 2027 $25
The Nonpariel Hunter Valley McLaren Vale Shiraz 2010 Exceptional colour; the new French oak in which it spent 18 months is still evident, but sits well in the context of the powerful dark chocolate inputs from McLaren Vale; I don't think the wine is anywhere near its peak, and the overall balance and mouthfeel should steer it safely for another 15 years of development, and a long plateau thereafter. Screwcap. 14% alc. **Rating** 94 **To** 2035 $45
The Filibuster Canberra Shiraz 2010 Since last tasted, 3 years ago, has developed well, much as expected; earthy/leathery Hunter Valley regional notes are now in play alongside black fruits; the excellent colour retention is also a good indicator. Screwcap. 14% alc. **Rating** 94 **To** 2025 $35

ŸŸŸŸ **Dimitri's Paddock Chardonnay 2013** **Rating** 89 **To** 2017 $25

Taylor Ferguson ★★★

Level 1, 62 Albert Street, Preston, Vic 3072 (postal) **Region** South Eastern Australia
T (03) 9487 2599 **www**.alepat.com.au **Open** Not
Winemaker Norman Lever **Est.** 1996 **Dozens** 40 000

Taylor Ferguson is the much-altered descendant of a business of that name established in Melbourne in 1898. A connecting web joins it with Alexander & Paterson (1892) and the much more recent distribution business of Alepat Taylor, formed in 1996. The development of the Taylor Ferguson wines has been directed by winemaker Norman Lever, using grapes sourced from various regions, mainly from Coonawarra, Langhorne Creek and the Riverina. Exports to Germany, Iraq, Singapore, Malaysia, Vietnam, Taiwan and China.

ŸŸŸŸ **Fernando The First Shiraz 2011** Grown on 80yo vines. Syrupy flavours, dark chocolate, tar and blackberry, with threads of acid and alcohol dangling from the finish. It's not harmonious, but there is a lot of flavour here. Cork. 13.515% alc. **Rating** 88 **To** 2020 $40 CM

Taylors

Taylors Road, Auburn, SA 5451 **Region** Clare Valley
T (08) 8849 1111 **www**.taylorswines.com.au **Open** Mon–Fri 9–5, w'ends 10–4
Winemaker Adam Eggins, Phillip Reschke **Est.** 1969 **Dozens** 250 000 **Vyds** 400ha

The family-founded and owned Taylors continues to flourish and expand – its vineyards are now by far the largest holding in the Clare Valley. There have also been changes in terms of the winemaking team and the wine style and quality, particularly through the outstanding St Andrews range. With each passing vintage, Taylors is managing to do the same for the Clare Valley as Peter Lehmann did for the Barossa Valley. Recent entries in international wine shows have resulted in a rich haul of trophies and gold medals for wines at all price points. A founding member of Australia's First Families of Wine. Exports (under the Wakefield brand due to trademark reasons) to all major markets.

𝖸𝖸𝖸𝖸𝖸 **St Andrews Single Vineyard Release Clare Valley Riesling 2014** Often held back for release with 5 years' bottle age, but this already has such finesse and balance that part is on the market, a decision validated by the trophy for Best Riesling, Melbourne Wine Awards '14; lemon, lime and apple blossom tell of the flavours to follow. Screwcap. 11% alc. **Rating** 96 **To** 2034 $35 ✪

St Andrews Single Vineyard Release Clare Valley Shiraz 2012 It's very clear this has been made from an exceptional parcel of estate fruit, for it has an elegance and length not commonly found in the Clare Valley; likewise, its range of spicy red fruits merging with gently savoury/earthy nuances is exceptional. Screwcap. 14.5% alc. **Rating** 96 **To** 2032 $60 ✪

The Visionary Exceptional Parcel Limited Release Cabernet Sauvignon 2012 Front and back label extended panegyric for patriarch Bill Taylor. It strongly suggests extended maturation in new French oak, possibly the conclusion of fermentation in that oak. The structure and balance of this excellent wine are very different from that of St Andrews, and it will be open for business sooner. Screwcap. 14% alc. **Rating** 96 **To** 2032 $180

St Andrews Single Vineyard Release Clare Valley Cabernet Sauvignon 2012 Trophy Clare Valley Wine Show '14, plus three international gold medals. This is the power and the glory of cabernet, arms akimbo with a defiant snarl on its face, black olive, earth, briar, bramble and the clasp of a patch of wild blackberries if you stumble into it. Screwcap. 14.5% alc. **Rating** 95 **To** 2042 $75

The Visionary Exceptional Parcel Limited Release Cabernet Sauvignon 2010 Presented in a super-heavyweight tall bottle with expensive labelling, this certainly looks the part, however heavy its carbon footprint must be. The wine opens with sweet cassis fruit, then cedary oak begins its song, powdery tannins providing the drumbeat. Difficult to achieve more in the Clare Valley with cabernet. Screwcap. 14% alc. **Rating** 95 **To** 2030 $150

Jaraman Cabernet Sauvignon 2013 Rating 94 **To** 2030 $30 ✪

TWP Taylors Winemaker's Project Cabernet Sauvignon Merlot Malbec Cabernet Franc 2013 Rating 94 **To** 2023 $32

𝖸𝖸𝖸𝖸𝖸 **Clare Valley Riesling 2014 Rating** 93 **To** 2020 $19 ✪

Jaraman Clare Valley McLaren Vale Shiraz 2013 Rating 93 **To** 2025 $30

Reserve Parcel Cabernet Sauvignon 2013 Rating 93 **To** 2028 $25 ✪

Clare Valley Cabernet Sauvignon 2013 Rating 92 **To** 2023 $19 ✪

The Pioneer Clare Valley Shiraz 2012 Rating 91 **To** 2026 $200

Clare Valley Tempranillo 2014 Rating 91 **To** 2017 $19 ✪

TeAro Estate   ★★★☆

20 Queen Street, Williamstown, SA 5351 **Region** Barossa Valley
T (08) 8524 6860 **www.**tearoestate.com **Open** Fri–Mon 10–5
Winemaker Todd Rowett, Russell Johnson **Est.** 2001 **Dozens** 2000 **Vyds** 58.2ha
TeAro Estate is a family-owned and operated wine business located in the southern Barossa Valley. In 1919 great-grandfather Charlie Fromm married Minnie Kappler, who named their home block TeAro. They planted shiraz and semillon, their only equipment a single crowbar (and their bare hands). Under the guidance of second and third-generation Ron and Trevor, the vineyard has grown to just over 58ha. Until 2001 the grapes were sold, but in that year Trevor decided to have a tonne of shiraz made for the local football club. It has been the fourth generation, including vigneron Ryan Fromm and brother-in-law Todd Rowett, that has been responsible for the proliferation of varieties. The vineyards are planted (in descending size) to shiraz, cabernet sauvignon, semillon, chardonnay, pinot noir, riesling, viognier, sauvignon blanc, pinot gris, tempranillo, merlot, mourvedre and grenache. Exports to China.

𝖸𝖸𝖸𝖸𝖸 **The Charred Door Shiraz 2013** There's some bulk to the fruit here but it remains fresh and spotlessly well polished. This is a lovely release. Pure, dark-berried fruits, charry oak, ground spice/mocha notes and throughout, an attractive smokiness. It has a sheen to it. Screwcap. 14.8% alc. **Rating** 94 **To** 2026 $30 CM ✪

𝖸𝖸𝖸𝖸𝖸 **Jokers Grin 2014 Rating** 90 **To** 2019 $24 CM

Telera

PO Box 3114, Prahran East, Vic 3181 **Region** Mornington Peninsula
T 0407 041 719 **www**.telera.com.au **Open** Not
Winemaker Michael Telera **Est.** 2007 **Dozens** 40 **Vyds** 0.4ha
The claim to have the smallest commercial winemaking business in Australia is frequently made, but I would put my money on this being the smallest, just under half a hectare (an acre) of sauvignon blanc and pinot noir sufficient to produce 40 dozen bottles a year. It was established by Michael and Susanne (Lew) Wynne-Hughes, who planted the vines in 2000, naming the venture MLF Wines. In '11 Michael Telera leased the vineyard, and, following the death of Michael Wynne-Hughes in that year, the name was changed to Telera. He has learnt the trade through 6 vintages as a cellar hand/assistant winemaker at Dr George Mihaly's Paradigm Hill winery, and it's not surprising he is making high-quality wines (presumably at Paradigm Hill). He produces shiraz sourced from other growers on the Peninsula, and plans to plant 12 rows of pinot noir on the leased property, making the total 20 rows of pinot noir and 9 rows of sauvignon blanc.

🍷🍷🍷🍷🍷 **Mornington Peninsula Fume Sauvignon Blanc 2013** A blood brother of the '14, with many, many things in common, first and foremost the subtlety of the use of barrel fermentation; it may simply be a reflection of the positive way this wine has developed in bottle, but there is a glimmer of kiwi/tropical fruit. All up, two distinguished Sauvignon Blancs. Screwcap. 12.3% alc. **Rating** 95 **To** 2019 $25 ❂
Mornington Peninsula Fume Sauvignon Blanc 2014 Barrel-fermented and matured on lees for 6 months. Has excellent drive, intensity and precision, stemming from early picking, unsweetened grapefruit likewise. It's such a finely balanced decision, and here it was a few days (out of 180) too early. Screwcap. 12.3% alc. **Rating** 94 **To** 2020 $25 ❂

🍷🍷🍷🍷🍷 **Mornington Peninsula Pinot Noir 2013 Rating** 91 **To** 2018 $55
Mornington Peninsula Shiraz 2012 Rating 90 **To** 2022 $39

Tellurian ★★★★★

408 Tranter Road, Toolleen, Vic 3551 **Region** Heathcote
T 0431 004 766 **www**.tellurianwines.com.au **Open** By appt
Winemaker Tobias Ansted **Est.** 2002 **Dozens** 3000 **Vyds** 21.87ha
The vineyard is situated on the western side of Mt Camel at Toolleen, on the red Cambrian soil that has made Heathcote one of the foremost regions in Australia for the production of Shiraz (Tellurian means 'of the earth'). Viticultural consultant Tim Brown not only supervises the Tellurian estate plantings, but also works closely with the growers of grapes purchased under contract for Tellurian. Further Rhône red and white varieties were planted on the Tellurian property in 2011. Exports to the UK and China.

🍷🍷🍷🍷🍷 **Block 3 TLR Heathcote Shiraz 2013** Similar vinification to Pastiche, except 18 months in a new French puncheon and 2 used barriques. Still medium to full-bodied, but marginally more rounded and supple than its siblings. The flavours are every bit as complex, the earthy tannins equally important in framing the palate. Screwcap. 14.8% alc. **Rating** 95 **To** 2038 $39
Pastiche Heathcote Shiraz 2013 Destemmed, open fermenters for 14–30 days, matured for 10 months in large-format French vats (50%), smaller French (40%) and American (10%), 10% new. This has the most expressive bouquet of the '13 Tellurian Shirazs, red fruits as well as black on display; there is an almost juicy quality to the medium-bodied palate, the finish long and balanced, the aftertaste striking. Great value. Screwcap. 13.8% alc. **Rating** 95 **To** 2029 $27 ❂
Block 3 SR Heathcote Shiraz 2013 Destemmed, 9 days' fermentation, matured for 18 months in a new French 500l puncheon and a 600l demi-muid. A supple, complex Shiraz with a mix of plum and black fruits in a cocoon of cedary, spicy oak and superfine tannins. Screwcap. 14.8% alc. **Rating** 94 **To** 2035 $39

Tranter Heathcote Shiraz 2013 Destemmed, not crushed, short cold soak, fermented in a French vat, open fermenter and concrete, pressed to 90% French and 10% American barriques (50% new) for 14 months then 4 months in 5000l oak vats. An insistently complex medium to full-bodied wine, with sultry black fruits, cracked black pepper, bitter chocolate and savoury tannins. Screwcap. 14.8% alc. **Rating** 94 **To** 2035 $39

Heathcote Grenache Shiraz Mourvedre 2013 **Rating** 91 **To** 2020 $34

Temple Bruer ★★★★

689 Milang Road, Angas Plains, SA 5255 **Region** Langhorne Creek
T (08) 8537 0203 **www.**templebruer.com.au **Open** Mon–Fri 9.30–4.30
Winemaker David Bruer, Vanessa Altmann **Est.** 1980 **Dozens** 18 000 **Vyds** 56ha
Temple Bruer was in the vanguard of the organic movement in Australia and was the focal point for the formation of Organic Vignerons Australia. Part of the production from its estate vineyards is used for its own label, part sold. Winemaker-owner David Bruer also has a vine propagation nursery, likewise run on an organic basis. Exports to the UK, the US, Canada, Sweden, Japan and China.

TB 621 Preservative Free Organic Mataro Shiraz Grenache 2014 A 36/34/30% blend sourced from the Riverland, Eden Valley and Langhorne Creek. Healthy colour; it has sufficient brightness and freshness to stay the course with the benefit of its screwcap. A good example of preservative-free wine for those with allergic reactions to SO_2. 14% alc. **Rating** 90 **To** 2016 $20 ○
Organic Langhorne Creek Autumn Harvest Riesling 2011 Neatly balanced sweetness and acidity a good starting point; to be enjoyed before the meal, during it, or at the finish with a fruit/cake (not cream)-based dessert; there are flavours of lime leaf, lemon, green pineapple and fennel that come and go, the acidity spot on. Screwcap. 12% alc. **Rating** 90 **To** 2017 $18 ○

Loxton White Frontignac #2 2014 **Rating** 88 **To** 2015 $25

Tempus Two Wines ★★★★☆

Broke Road, Pokolbin, NSW 2321 **Region** Hunter Valley
T (02) 4993 3999 **www.**tempustwo.com.au **Open** 7 days 10–5
Winemaker Andrew Duff **Est.** 1997 **Dozens** 55 000
Tempus Two is a mix of Latin (Tempus means time) and English. It has been a major success story, production growing from 6000 dozen in 1997 to 55 000 dozen today. Its cellar door, restaurant complex (including the Oishii Japanese restaurant) and small convention facilities are situated in a striking building. The design polarises opinion; I like it. Exports to all major markets.

Uno Hunter Valley Shiraz 2013 From 25yo vines on the St Albans Vineyard in the Upper Hunter. It doesn't put a foot wrong though its best days are far ahead of it. Mid-weight cherry-plum and earth flavours are set with firm, assertive tannin, the lot splashed with creamy/cedary/bacony oak. Will be a beauty once it's had time to mature. Diam. 13.5% alc. **Rating** 95 **To** 2035 $75 CM

Pewter Hunter Valley Chardonnay 2014 **Rating** 93 **To** 2019 $30 CM
Copper Series Sauvignon Blanc 2014 **Rating** 92 **To** 2015 $20 CM ○
Pewter Cabernet Sauvignon 2013 **Rating** 92 **To** 2024 $30 CM
Verdelho 2014 **Rating** 90 **To** 2016 $17 CM ○

Ten Minutes by Tractor ★★★★★

1333 Mornington–Flinders Road, Main Ridge, Vic 3928 **Region** Mornington Peninsula
T (03) 5989 6455 **www.**tenminutesbytractor.com.au **Open** 7 days 11–5
Winemaker Richard McIntyre, Martin Spedding, Jeremy Magyar **Est.** 1999
Dozens 7000 **Vyds** 34.4ha

The energy, drive and vision of Martin Spedding have transformed Ten Minutes by Tractor since he acquired the business in early 2004. In mid-'06 Ten Minutes By Tractor purchased the McCutcheon Vineyard; it also has long-term leases on the other two original home vineyards (Judd and Wallis), thus having complete control over grape production. Three new vineyards have been added in recent years: the one at the cellar door and restaurant site is organically certified and is used to trial organic viticultural practices that are progressively being employed across all the vineyards; the others are in the north of the Peninsula. There are now three ranges: Single Vineyard, from the home Judd, McCutcheon and Wallace Vineyards; Estate, the best blend of pinot and of chardonnay from the home vineyards; and finally 10X, from the other estate-owned Mornington Peninsula vineyards. The restaurant has one of the best wine lists to be found at any winery. Exports to the UK, Canada, Sweden and Switzerland.

ΨΨΨΨΨ **Judd Vineyard Chardonnay 2013** From vines planted in '94. It lays it on upfront but then there's a serious amount of sizzle through the finish. One sip and strike, it's on, hold on for your life. Figs, smoke, grapefruit, flint and toasted, roasted spices. Worthy of the word 'sensational'. Screwcap. 13.6% alc. **Rating** 97 **To** 2021 $65 CM ✪

ΨΨΨΨΨ **McCutcheon Mornington Peninsula Chardonnay 2013** The nonchalance here is sensational. It's fleshy, flavoursome and easygoing and yet, when it finishes, it's brilliantly persistent. Not lean, but searing. Not fat, but loaded with oatmeal, yellow stone fruit and sweet, creamy, cedary oak. It's generous for the most part but savvy enough to stash away a few tricks for a later date; despite the flesh, it's taut. Screwcap. 13.6% alc. **Rating** 96 **To** 2021 $65 CM ✪

Wallis Vineyard Pinot Noir 2013 Satiny and delicious, with brilliant extension of flavour. Style and substance. Sweet-sour berries, crushed dry spices, woodsmoke and undergrowthy/foresty notes. It starts well and gets better and better. Screwcap. 13.8% alc. **Rating** 96 **To** 2022 $75 CM ✪

McCutcheon Mornington Peninsula Pinot Noir 2013 Lightish colour, but there ends the ambivalence. This is three parts savoury, one part pretty, the combined effect irresistible. It tastes mostly of crushed dry leaves, woody spices, smoky oak and foresty notes, though a sweet, strawberried exuberance keeps the mood chipper. It's satiny, sweet and savoury at once; the glory of pinot noir. Screwcap. 13.8% alc. **Rating** 95 **To** 2022 $75 CM

Wallis Chardonnay 2013 Deep colour and flavour with peach, cashew, fig and grapefruit notes flooding the mouth. It doesn't leave too much to the imagination though it's still reasonably taut, and strings a fine line of succulent flavour out through the finish. Screwcap. 13.6% alc. **Rating** 94 **To** 2020 $65 CM

Coolart Road Pinot Noir 2013 Moody, broody, deep-flavoured wine. Stewed black cherries, leafy spices and smoke-like notes pull the curtain tight against brighter, strawberried notes. Tannin accordingly is firm; it's not the easiest wine to fathom but it generally looks the goods for future development. Screwcap. 13.8% alc. **Rating** 94 **To** 2021 $75 CM

Estate Mornington Peninsula Pinot Noir 2013 Deeply flavoured, predominantly savoury release with tobacco, sap, woodsmoke and foresty characters threading strands of intricate flavour through black cherry, almost olivey fruit. No shortage of length, complexity or beauty. Screwcap. 13.8% alc. **Rating** 94 **To** 2022 $46 CM

ΨΨΨΨΨ **Estate Chardonnay 2013** **Rating** 93 **To** 2019 $42 CM

10X Mornington Peninsula Pinot Noir 2013 **Rating** 93 **To** 2019 $32 CM

10X Sauvignon Blanc 2013 **Rating** 92 **To** 2016 $28 CM

10X Mornington Peninsula Chardonnay 2013 **Rating** 92 **To** 2019 $30 CM

10X Mornington Peninsula Rose 2013 **Rating** 92 **To** 2016 $24 CM ✪

Blanc de Blancs 2010 **Rating** 92 **To** 2020 $65 TS

Tenafeate Creek Wines

1071 Gawler–One Tree Hill Road, One Tree Hill, SA 5114 **Region** Adelaide Zone
T (08) 8280 7715 **www**.tcw.com.au **Open** Fri–Sun & public hols 11–5
Winemaker Larry and Michael Costa **Est.** 2002 **Dozens** 2000 **Vyds** 1ha
Long-term friends Larry Costa, a former hairdresser, and Dominic Rinaldi, an accountant,
embarked on winemaking as a hobby in 2002. The property, with its 1ha of shiraz, cabernet
sauvignon and merlot, is situated on the rolling countryside of One Tree Hill in the Mount
Lofty Ranges. The business has grown rapidly, with grenache, nebbiolo, sangiovese, petit
verdot, chardonnay, semillon and sauvignon blanc purchased to supplement the estate-grown
grapes. Michael Costa, Larry's son, has 14 vintages under his belt, mainly in the Barossa Valley,
with Flying Winemaker stints to southern Italy and Provence. The red wines have won many
medals over the years.

Basket Press Grenache 2012 Hand-picked from a 28yo single vineyard at
One Tree Hill, fermented in old temperature-controlled milk vats and basket-
pressed; matured in used French hogsheads for 18 months. Full of delicious red
fruits that give no hint of excessive alcohol, and linger on the finish and aftertaste.
Deserves its two gold medals. Drink sooner rather than later for maximum
enjoyment. Screwcap. 15% alc. **Rating** 95 **To** 2018 $25 ✪

Basket Press Merlot 2012 Rating 90 **To** 2022 $25

Terindah Estate

★★★★★

90 McAdams Lane, Bellarine, Vic 3223 **Region** Geelong
T (03) 5251 5536 **www**.terindahestate.com **Open** 7 days 10–4
Winemaker Chris Sargeant **Est.** 2003 **Dozens** 2500 **Vyds** 5.6ha
Retired quantity surveyor Peter Slattery bought the 48ha property in 2001, intending to plant
the vineyard, make wine and develop a restaurant. He has achieved all of this (with help from
others, of course), planting shiraz, pinot noir, pinot gris, picolit, chardonnay and zinfandel.
Picolit is most interesting: it is a highly regarded grape in northern Italy, where it makes small
quantities of high-quality sweet wine. It has proved to be very temperamental here, as in Italy,
with very unreliable fruit set. In the meantime, he makes classic wines of very high quality
from classic grape varieties – not wines for sommeliers to drool over because they're hip.

Single Vineyard Pinot Noir 2013 Clones MV6 and 114, destemmed, whole
berry (70%), whole bunches (30%), wild yeast matured for 14 months in new
French oak. This is the glass full, not half full; there is that finely spun backdrop of
tannins à la Burgundy, and a delicious counterpoint between cherry and savoury/
oak notes. Screwcap. 13% alc. **Rating** 95 **To** 2023 $35 ✪
Single Vineyard Shiraz 2013 Destemmed, wild yeast open-fermented, 14
months in French hogsheads. Has excellent depth to the colour, and an expressive,
complex bouquet of black fruits and charcuterie; the plush palate has an expansive
palette of flavours feeding off the bouquet, ripe tannins the foundation for a long
future. Screwcap. 13.5% alc. **Rating** 95 **To** 2038 $65
Single Vineyard Chardonnay 2013 Whole bunch-pressed, wild yeast barrel-
fermented in French oak (33% new), aged on lees for 8 months with weekly
stirring. This amount of stirring is uncommon these days, but it has worked
well here, helping build the texture of the palate without taking away from the
freshness of the varietal fruit profile. Screwcap. 14% alc. **Rating** 95 **To** 2020 $35 ✪
McAdam's Lane Bellarine Peninsula Sauvignon Blanc 2013 66% tank-
fermented (inoculated), 12–14% aged on lees (no stirring), 34% wild yeast-
fermented in used barrels at 18–20°C on lees with stirring for 8 months. Astute
winemaking has maximised the potential of the grapes, lively fresh fruit flavours
given texture and context by the barrel-ferment component. Screwcap. 12.5% alc.
Rating 94 **To** 2016 $25 ✪
McAdam's Lane Bellarine Peninsula Shiraz Viognier 2013 8% whole-
bunch viognier co-fermented, the shiraz destemmed and crushed; wild yeast open-
fermented; 14 months in used French oak. The colour is bright crimson-purple,

the bouquet fragrant, the palate spicy and vibrant, its blood plum fruit with a garland of gently savoury tannins. Screwcap. 14.5% alc. **Rating** 94 **To** 2028 $30 ○

🍷🍷🍷🍷♀ **Single Vineyard Rose 2013** Rating 91 To 2016 $25
Single Vineyard Pinot Gris 2013 Rating 90 To 2016 $30
Single Vineyard Zinfandel 2013 Rating 90 To 2018 $45

Terra Felix   ★★★★

52 Paringa Road, Red Hill South, Vic 3937 (postal) **Region** Central Victoria Zone
T 0419 539 108 **www**.terrafelix.com.au **Open** Not
Winemaker Ben Haines **Est.** 2001 **Dozens** 12 000 **Vyds** 7ha
Long-term industry stalwarts Peter Simon and John Nicholson, with an involvement going back well over 30 years, have built on the estate plantings of pinot noir (5ha) and chardonnay (2ha) through purchases from Coonawarra, McLaren Vale, Barossa Valley, Langhorne Creek, Yarra Valley and Strathbogie Ranges. Terra Felix exports 70% of its production to China.

🍷🍷🍷🍷🍷 **Yarra Valley Shiraz 2013** 97% shiraz and 3% viognier from a single vineyard at Coldstream, matured in new and used French oak for 18 months. Bright, full crimson, with very good texture and structure; the only question is the amount of oak. Well worthy of time in the bottle to sort things out. Diam. 14% alc. Rating 94 To 2025 $45

🍷🍷🍷🍷 **Chardonnay 2012** Rating 89 To 2017 $18 ○

Terramoré Wines   ★★★★

Box 1, Coonawarra, SA 5263 **Region** Coonawarra
T (08) 8736 5139 **www**.terramorewines.com.au **Open** Not
Winemaker Ben Wurst **Est.** 2009 **Dozens** 4000 **Vyds** 38ha
The Gartner family (parents Phil and Mandy, and children Taylor, Abbi and Cooper) has been involved in grapegrowing in Coonawarra for 20 or so years, and also runs a company managing 300ha of vineyards in Coonawarra and Padthaway. With the downwards pressure on grape prices, in 2009 they decided to keep part of the crop from their estate vineyards (20ha of cabernet sauvignon, 14ha shiraz and 4ha of sauvignon blanc) and venture into the wine market. They chose Barbara Harkness, the Adelaide designer famous for creating the yellow tail label, to come up with a name and a label design. The Gartners say, 'Terramoré is a play on words: "Terra" of course being the terroir for which Coonawarra is renowned, and "amoré" meaning love, creating the perfect word for those connoisseurs who truly understand great terroir and love wine.'

🍷🍷🍷🍷♀ **Coonawarra Shiraz 2012** Well made, speaking eloquently of its variety and place; supple and smooth, the medium-bodied palate primarily driven by black cherry and blackberry fruit, vanillan oak and fine-grained tannins playing a pure support role, but nonetheless adding to the overall appeal. Screwcap. 14.5% alc. Rating 93 To 2025 $23 ○
Coonawarra Cabernet Sauvignon 2012 An attractive, well-balanced, medium-bodied cabernet showing Coonawarra at its best in this price range. Cassis, spice, coffee and a touch of mulberry all come together well, tannin and oak in support. WAK screwcap. 14% alc. Rating 93 To 2027 $23 ○

Terre à Terre   ★★★★★

PO Box 3128, Unley, SA 5061 **Region** Wrattonbully
T 0400 700 447 **www**.terreaterre.com.au **Open** At Tapanappa
Winemaker Xavier Bizot **Est.** 2008 **Dozens** 1000 **Vyds** 8ha
It would be hard to imagine two better-credentialled owners than Xavier Bizot (son of the late Christian Bizot of Bollinger fame) and wife Lucy Croser (daughter of Brian and Ann Croser). 'Terre à terre', incidentally, is a French expression meaning down-to-earth. The close-planted vineyard is on a limestone ridge, adjacent to Tapanappa's Whalebone Vineyard. The

vineyard area has increased (3ha each of cabernet sauvignon and sauvignon blanc and 1ha each of cabernet franc and shiraz), leading to increased production. Wines are released under the Terre à Terre, Down to Earth, Sacrebleu and Daosa labels. Exports to Taiwan and Hong Kong.

🍷🍷🍷🍷🍷 **Single Vineyard Wrattonbully Sauvignon Blanc 2014** Fermented in a mix of 14 used French barriques and 10 600l demi-muids, left on lees for 1 month, racked, SO_2 added and returned to one 2000l foudre and 10 demi-muids. Xavier Bizot has well and truly mastered the impossible: given tremendous texture and structure by the oak handling, yet simultaneously highlighting the intense stream of pure citrus, stone fruit and snow pea flavours. Will not die in its tracks either. Screwcap. 12% alc. **Rating** 97 **To** 2017 $35 ✪

🍷🍷🍷🍷🍷 **Single Vineyard Wrattonbully Cabernet Sauvignon 2013** Matured in a new 4000l French foudre for 12 months, then to a used 4000l foudre for a final 10 months, 5% cabernet franc added. A thoroughly elegant and poised cabernet, opening with cassis/blackcurrant, then a matrix of oak, cedar, dried herb and savoury tannins taking the wine through to a powerful conclusion. Cork. 14.4% alc. **Rating** 96 **To** 2033 $35 ✪

🍷🍷🍷🍷🍷 **Down to Earth Sauvignon Blanc 2014 Rating** 93 **To** 2017 $24 ✪
Down to Earth Cabernets Shiraz 2013 Rating 91 **To** 2023 $24

Tertini Wines   ★★★★★

Kells Creek Road, Mittagong, NSW 2575 **Region** Southern Highlands
T (02) 4878 5213 **www.**tertiniwines.com.au **Open** Thurs–Mon 10–5
Winemaker Jonathan Holgate **Est.** 2000 **Dozens** 3000 **Vyds** 7.9ha
When Julian Tertini began the development of Tertini Wines in 2000, he followed in the footsteps of Joseph Vogt 145 years earlier. History does not relate the degree of success that Joseph had, but the site he chose then was, as it is now, a good one. Tertini has pinot noir and riesling (1.8ha each), cabernet sauvignon and chardonnay (1ha each), arneis (0.9ha), pinot gris (0.8ha), merlot (0.4ha) and lagrein (0.2ha). Winemaker Jonathan Holgate, who is responsible for the outstanding results achieved at Tertini, presides over High Range Vintners, a contract winemaking business also owned by Julian Tertini. Exports to Asia.

🍷🍷🍷🍷🍷 **Private Cellar Collection Southern Highlands Riesling 2013** Trophy for Best Riesling Sydney Wine Show '14. It's a high price for a young Riesling, but it's a seriously good wine, flooded with lime juice fruit intermeshed with probing acidity, the palate with great length and balance. 65 dozen made. Screwcap. 11.1% alc. **Rating** 97 **To** 2025 $50 ✪

🍷🍷🍷🍷🍷 **Southern Highlands Riesling 2013** Tertini was able to take the best riesling for its Private Cellar wine without stripping this wine of some delicious lime and lemon fruit; the line, length and balance are very good, the aftertaste especially convincing. Screwcap. 11.2% alc. **Rating** 95 **To** 2023 $30 ✪
Southern Highlands Pinot Noir 2012 Whole-bunch inclusion and 9 months in French oak were the genesis of this wine. Holding onto its youthful hue very well; ticks the boxes with its dark fruit aromas and flavours, and strong splash of forest floor. Three trophies Australian Highlands Wine Show '14. Screwcap. 13.8% alc. **Rating** 94 **To** 2020 $45

🍷🍷🍷🍷🍷 **Private Cellar Collection Lagrein 2013 Rating** 92 **To** 2020 $40
Hilltops Shiraz 2013 Rating 91 **To** 2020 $28
Orange Pinot Gris 2014 Rating 90 **To** 2016 $26
Southern Highlands Rose 2014 Rating 90 **To** 2015 $20 ✪

Teusner   ★★★★★

29 Jane Place, Tanunda, SA 5352 (postal) **Region** Barossa Valley
T (08) 8562 4147 **www.**teusner.com.au **Open** At Artisans of Barossa
Winemaker Kym Teusner, Matt Reynolds **Est.** 2001 **Dozens** 15 000

Teusner is a partnership between former Torbreck winemaker Kym Teusner and brother-in-law Michael Page, and is typical of the new wave of winemakers determined to protect very old, low-yielding, dry-grown Barossa vines. The winery approach is based on lees-ageing, little racking, no fining or filtration, and no new American oak. As each year passes, the consistency, quality (and range) of the wines increases; there must be an end point, but it's not easy to guess when, or even if, it will be reached. Exports to the UK, the US, Canada, The Netherlands, Malaysia, Singapore and Japan.

ŸŸŸŸŸ **The Riebke Barossa Valley Shiraz 2013** Deeply coloured; resplendently mouth-filling. Plum, blackberry and licorice tumble around each other on the medium to full-bodied palate; all this is good, but the quality of the tannins and acidity on the savoury finish is even better. Great value. Screwcap. 14.5% alc. **Rating** 95 **To** 2033 $26 ❂

The Wark Family Shiraz 2013 Vivid crimson-purple colour announces a wine aflame with energy – befitting the Wark family (daughter Marnie painted the emblematic label); the intensity and focus of the wine are excellent, with sultry black fruits, wisps of olive, earth and pickled plum sustained by finely detailed tannins. Screwcap. 14.5% alc. **Rating** 95 **To** 2028 $26 ❂

Albert 2012 The brute has class. Blue, black and red berry notes join to form a powerful chorus of flavour. You feel the power from the first sip and yet it comes across as seamless, soft, moreish. Mint, sawdust, ground spice and violet notes add both complexity and a veneer of prettiness; Marlon Brando petting a dove. Vigorous length of flavour and firm tannins are key assets. Screwcap. 14.5% alc. **Rating** 95 **To** 2025 $55 CM

Avatar 2013 Well named; the Barossa Valley origin of its grenache mataro shiraz blend would not be easy to differentiate from top-end McLaren Vale examples. Spiced plum, blackberry, and a contrasting nuance of savoury/earthy notes from the mataro provide backbone; all come together perfectly. Screwcap. 14.5% alc. **Rating** 95 **To** 2030 $38

The Independent Barossa Valley Shiraz Mataro 2013 There is no question that mataro adds a colour to the artist's palette, and to the consumer's palate, with an elusive graphite edge to the blackberry and plum fruit aromas and flavours. A wine that may not need food, but will smile broadly if given some. Screwcap. 14.5% alc. **Rating** 94 **To** 2025 $25 ❂

The Gentleman Eden Valley Cabernet Sauvignon 2013 Grown on one of the highest vineyards in the Eden Valley. Deep, but bright crimson-purple, it is literally flooded with blackcurrant/cassis fruit, the tannins ripe but fine, and entirely appropriate – indeed indispensable – for Cabernet, the oak eaten by the fruit. Screwcap. 14.5% alc. **Rating** 94 **To** 2028 $26 ❂

ŸŸŸŸ♀ **Woodside Sauvignon Blanc 2014 Rating** 93 **To** 2016 $23 CM ❂
Joshua 2014 Rating 93 **To** 2020 $32 CM
Salsa Barossa Valley Rose 2014 Rating 92 **To** 2016 $22 ❂

The Bridge Vineyard ★★★★★

Shurans Lane, Heathcote, Vic 3552 **Region** Heathcote
T (03) 5441 5429 **www**.thebridgevineyard.com.au **Open** Select w'ends
Winemaker Lindsay Ross **Est.** 1997 **Dozens** 1000 **Vyds** 4.75ha
This venture of former Balgownie winemaker Lindsay Ross and wife Noeline is part of a broader business known as Winedrops, which acts as a wine production and distribution network for the Bendigo wine industry. The wines are sourced from long-established vineyards, providing shiraz (4ha), malbec (0.5ha) and viognier (0.25ha). The viticultural accent is on low-cropping, and thus concentrated flavours, the winemaking emphasis on finesse and varietal expression.

ŸŸŸŸŸ **Shurans Lane Heathcote Shiraz 2012** A hand-corker must have been a nightmare – it takes enormous pressure to distort a Diam as much as that in this bottle, the same issue as that of the '10. The wine in the bottle shows no ill effects now, and may never do so; it has a fragrant, polished bouquet with licorice and spice to the fore, the well-balanced, medium to full-bodied palate full of deliciously spicy/juicy black fruits. Lindsay Ross nailed this one. 14% alc. **Rating** 96 **To** 2037 $50 **⊙**

Shurans Lane Heathcote Shiraz Malbec 2012 Deep crimson-purple; the malbec is an interesting component, bringing satsuma plum onto the table from the word go, adding a bracelet of spicy richness to the black fruits of the shiraz; the texture of the medium to full-bodied palate clinches the deal for a hedonistic wine with a long future. Diam. 13.5% alc. **Rating** 95 **To** 2037 $40

The Grapes of Ross ★★★★

PO Box 14, Lyndoch, SA 5351 **Region** Barossa Valley
T (08) 8524 4214 **www.grapesofross.com.au Open** Not
Winemaker Ross Virgara **Est.** 2006 **Dozens** 2000
Ross Virgara spent much of his life in the broader food and wine industry, taking the plunge into commercial winemaking in 2006. The grapes come from a fourth-generation family property in the Lyndoch Valley, and the aim is to make fruit-driven styles of quality wine. His fondness for frontignac led to the first release of Moscato, followed in due course by Rose, Shiraz, Sparkling Shiraz, Grenache Shiraz and The Charmer Sangiovese Merlot Cabernet Sauvignon. Exports to China.

ㅏㅏㅏㅏㅏ **Old Vine Barossa Valley Shiraz 2012** Dark and inky but tangy and fresh. It puts on a good spread. Boysenberry, licorice, tar and blackberry, with a fine slick of creamy oak. Hard to fault; easy to admire. Cork. 14.6% alc. **Rating** 94 **To** 2028 $65 CM

ㅏㅏㅏㅏㅏ **Black Rose Barossa Valley Shiraz 2013 Rating** 91 **To** 2023 $34 CM

The Hairy Arm ★★★★☆

18 Plant Street, Northcote, Vic 3070 (postal) **Region** Sunbury/Heathcote
T 0409 110 462 **www.hairyarm.com Open** Not
Winemaker Steven Worley **Est.** 2004 **Dozens** 500
Steven Worley graduated as an exploration geologist, then added a Master of Geology degree, followed by a postgraduate Diploma in Oenology and Viticulture. Until December 2009 he was general manager of Galli Estate Winery, The Hairy Arm having started as a university project in '04. It has grown from a labour of love to a commercial undertaking, focusing exclusively on shiraz grown variously in the Heathcote, Sunbury, Upper Goulburn Valley and Yarra Valley regions. The hairy arm, incidentally, is Steven's. Exports to Canada.

ㅏㅏㅏㅏㅏ **Sunbury Shiraz 2013** Wild yeast-fermented with 30% whole bunches in small open fermenters; matured in Remond (Burgundy) oak. Bright crimson; this is a wine buzzing with excitement in its bouquet and palate alike; fruit and oak spices are embedded in the satsuma plum and poached cherry flavours of the elegant, but very long, palate. Screwcap. 14% alc. **Rating** 95 **To** 2028 $30 **⊙**

Heathcote Nebbiolo 2012 Wild yeast-fermented in small pots (1.5 tonnes) with 15% whole bunches, then 2 years in very good used oak. The promised 'serious tannins' were no doubt there early in its life, but are now positively gentlemanly (or, to avoid sexism, ladylike), a necessary adjunct to the dark red berry fruits and cedar of the long, medium-bodied palate. Screwcap. 13.5% alc. **Rating** 94 **To** 2025 $45

The Islander Estate Vineyards ★★★★★

PO Box 868, Kingscote, SA 5223 **Region** Kangaroo Island
T (08) 8553 9008 **www.iev.com.au Open** By appt
Winemaker Jacques Lurton **Est.** 2000 **Dozens** 6500 **Vyds** 10ha
Established by one of the most famous Flying Winemakers in the world, Bordeaux-born and trained and part-time Australian resident Jacques Lurton. He has established a close-planted

vineyard; the principal varieties are cabernet franc, shiraz and sangiovese, with lesser amounts of grenache, malbec, semillon and viognier. The wines are made and bottled at the onsite winery in true estate style. After several vintages experimenting with a blend of sangiovese and cabernet franc, Jacques has settled on cabernet franc as the varietal base of the signature wine, The Investigator. Exports to the UK, Canada, France, Germany, Denmark, The Netherlands, Finland, Poland, the United Arab Emirates, New Caledonia, Hong Kong, Macau, China and NZ.

ȚȚȚȚȚ **Old Rowley Kangaroo Island Shiraz Grenache 2013** A 65/35% blend; part carbonic maceration at 30°C for 10 days in a closed vat saturated with CO_2; after 30 days the grapes are pressed and the rest of the fermentation is of clear juice alone; the remainder is normally fermented, and the parcels separately matured for 2 years in 630l barrels. The colour is excellent, the wine gloriously fresh and extremely complex, with vibrant plum and black cherry fruits, the tannins superfine. Cork. 14% alc. **Rating** 96 **To** 2033 $35 **☉**
Bark Hut Road 2013 A blend of cabernet franc and shiraz, each variety fermented separately with wild yeast, fermented and macerated for 5–6 weeks, undergoing mlf in tank, matured in new and used French barrels for 18 months, the best barrels selected for this wine. Bright crimson-purple; this is a complex wine with a blend of sour and morello cherry, cedar/cigar box notes, and persistent, fine tannins. Cork. 13.5% alc. **Rating** 95 **To** 2025 $25 **☉**

ȚȚȚȚȚ **Shiraz 2013 Rating** 92 **To** 2028 $25 **☉**

The Lake House Denmark ★★★★★

106 Turner Road, Denmark, WA 6333 **Region** Denmark
T (08) 9848 2444 **www**.lakehousedenmark.com.au **Open** 7 days 10–5
Winemaker Harewood Estate (James Kellie) **Est.** 1995 **Dozens** 8000 **Vyds** 5.2ha
Garry Capelli and Leanne Rogers purchased the property in 2005 and have restructured the vineyard to grow varieties suited to the climate – chardonnay, pinot noir, semillon and sauvignon blanc – incorporating biodynamic principles. They also control a couple of small family-owned vineyards in Frankland River and Mount Barker, with a similar ethos. Wines are released in three tiers: the flagship Premium Reserve range, the Premium Block range, and the quirky He Said, She Said easy-drinking wines. The combined cellar door, restaurant and gourmet food emporium is a popular destination.

ȚȚȚȚȚ **Premium Reserve Single Vineyard Semillon Sauvignon Blanc 2014**
Semillon is the deal maker in this wine, however seamless it may be; a lemon-accented vibrancy runs through the full length of the palate and aftertaste. No frills, but a thoroughly impressive outcome, and will offer a different – but good – face down the track. Screwcap. 12% alc. **Rating** 95 **To** 2020 $35 **☉**
Premium Reserve Single Vineyard Frankland River Shiraz 2012 Marches to the beat of its own drum, a singular purity to its red and black cherry fruit draped over an array of spice, pepper, licorice and dark chocolate flavours; no more than medium-bodied, but has a great deal going for it. Screwcap. 14.5% alc. **Rating** 95 **To** 2030 $45
Premium Reserve Premium Selection Riesling 2014 Gleaming, light straw-green; a deliciously flavoured and balanced wine with lime and apple aromas and flavours; drives in the safety lane, but will it take a risk and accelerate as it warms to the task with time? Screwcap. 12% alc. **Rating** 94 **To** 2025 $40
Premium Block Selection Great Southern Semillon Sauvignon Blanc 2014 Winemaker Garry Capelli sees pea, hay, asparagus, white peach, cut grass, melon, grapefruit, quince, passionfruit, lemon and lime, a deconstruction way beyond my powers. But I do see well above average concentration and length, tropical fruits in the ascendant, the finish bringing the needed citrussy acidity into play. Screwcap. 12.5% alc. **Rating** 94 **To** 2017 $25 **☉**
Premium Reserve Premium Selection Frankland River Mount Barker Shiraz 2012 Has had an extended period of over 2 years in mainly used French oak; whether the two components were blended early or late doesn't really

matter, for there is a seamless fusion; an elegant medium-bodied palate, with spice, mocha, pepper and cedar woven through black cherry and plum fruit. Screwcap. 14.5% alc. **Rating** 94 **To** 2028 $40

ŸŸŸŸŸ **Single Vineyard Selection Sauvignon 2014 Rating** 93 **To** 2016 $25 ✪
Premium Block Selection Riesling 2014 Rating 92 **To** 2024 $25 ✪
Museum Release Premium Reserve Single Vineyard Frankland Shiraz 2008 Rating 92 **To** 2018 $70
Premium Block Selection Merlot 2013 Rating 92 **To** 2028 $25 ✪
Methode Traditionnelle Brut Cuvee 2009 Rating 92 **To** 2019 $40 TS

The Lane Vineyard ★★★★★

Ravenswood Lane, Hahndorf, SA 5245 **Region** Adelaide Hills
T (08) 8388 1250 **www**.thelane.com.au **Open** 7 days 10–4.30
Winemaker Michael Schreurs, John Edwards **Est.** 1993 **Dozens** 25 000 **Vyds** 75ha
After 15 years at The Lane Vineyard, Helen and John Edwards, and sons Marty and Ben, took an important step towards realising their long-held dream – to grow, make and sell estate-based wines that have a true sense of place. In 2005, at the end of the (now discontinued) Starvedog Lane joint venture with Hardys, they commissioned a state-of-the-art 500-tonne winery, bistro and cellar door overlooking their vineyards on picturesque Ravenswood Lane. Having previously invested in Delatite, and much earlier established Coombe Farm in the Yarra Valley, the Vestey Group (UK), headed by Lord Samuel Vestey and the Right Honourable Mark Vestey, have acquired a significant shareholding in The Lane Vineyard. Exports to the UK, the US, Canada, The Netherlands, Belgium, Hong Kong and China.

ŸŸŸŸŸ **Reunion Single Vineyard Adelaide Hills Shiraz 2012** Fine expression of cool-climate shiraz. Indeed it's immaculate in all respects. It tastes of black cherry, smoky oak, bacon fat, and a delicious array of fragrant, green/dry herbs. Tannin is peppery and assertive but carefully folded into the flavour. It's just starting out on its life journey but it has packed its bags thoughtfully. Screwcap. 13.5% alc. **Rating** 96 **To** 2032 $65 CM ✪
Reginald Germein Single Vineyard Adelaide Hills Chardonnay 2013 Vinified class. Smells, feels and tastes delicious, and lingers beautifully on the tongue. Grapefruit, white peach and spicy, creamy oak. Appreciably complex aftertaste. Screwcap. 13% alc. **Rating** 95 **To** 2021 $100 CM
Beginning Single Vineyard Adelaide Hills Chardonnay 2013 Composed entirely of Dijon clone 95, one of the very best. Fermented and matured in used (70%) and new (30%) French oak. It is a very pure and intense wine, with the distinctive clone 95 grapefruit-nuanced mouthfeel and grip; has unlimited development potential. Screwcap. 13% alc. **Rating** 95 **To** 2023 $39
Block 14 Single Vineyard Basket Press Adelaide Hills Shiraz 2013 Obviously enough, the wine was basket-pressed, and matured in a mix of new used French oak. Deep crimson-purple in colour; the bouquet has that distinctive perfume of cool-grown Shiraz, the highly spiced/peppery black cherry fruit of the mid-palate laced with a filigree of fine tannins driving through to the finish. Screwcap. 13.5% alc. **Rating** 95 **To** 2033 $39
Gathering Adelaide Hills Sauvignon Blanc Semillon 2013 A 70/30% blend, separately fermented and matured in a complex amalgam of stainless steel, new and used French oak. It offers a totally delicious, seamless marriage of fruit and oak, and is a very smart entry point wine, with a track record of maturing gracefully over 5+ years. Screwcap. 13% alc. **Rating** 94 **To** 2017 $35
Block 5 Single Vineyard Adelaide Hills Shiraz 2013 Takes a bit to come around but given time to breathe this really impresses. It's a smoky, twiggy, reductive wine with cherry-plum flavoured fruit cooking up a world of savoury-sweet deliciousness. Tannin takes no backward steps; it's firm but fair. A fine future awaits. Screwcap. 13.5% alc. **Rating** 94 **To** 2026 $30 CM ✪

🍷🍷🍷🍷🍷 Block 1A Chardonnay 2013 Rating 92 To 2018 $20 CM
Single Vineyard John Crighton Adelaide Hills Shiraz Cabernet
Sauvignon 2012 Rating 92 To 2032 $110 CM
19th Meeting Cabernet Sauvignon 2012 Rating 92 To 2028 $65 CM
Block 2 Pinot Gris 2014 Rating 91 To 2015 $25 CM
Cuvee Helen Blanc de Blancs 2008 Rating 91 To 2016 $55 TS

The Ninth Mile   ★★★

PO Box 254, Beechworth, Vic 3747 **Region** Beechworth
T (03) 5728 3052 **www**.theninthmile.com **Open** Not
Winemaker Adrian Kearton **Est.** 2003 **Dozens** 200 **Vyds** 1ha
Adrian and Conna Kearton have established part of their vineyard on what was once the
Mayday Hills 'lunatic asylum' vegetable garden, and part in the township of Stanley, 9km
southeast of Beechworth at an elevation of 750m. It is hardly surprising that the Keartons say
their wines are handmade.

🍷🍷🍷🍷 **Beechworth Viognier 2013** Direct style. Juicy fruit. Lime, sweet nectarine, pear
and spice. Sherry notes on the nose. Interesting. Screwcap. 12.1% alc. **Rating** 89
To 2015 $24 CM

The Old Faithful Estate   ★★★★★

281 Tatachilla Road, McLaren Vale, SA 5171 **Region** McLaren Vale
T 0419 383 907 **www**.adelaidewinemakers.com.au **Open** By appt
Winemaker Nick Haselgrove, Warren Randall **Est.** 2005 **Dozens** 1000 **Vyds** 5ha
This is a 50/50 joint venture between American John Larchet and Adelaide Winemakers (see
separate entry). John has long had a leading role as a specialist importer of Australian wines
into the US, and guarantees the business whatever sales it needs there. Its shiraz, grenache and
mourvedre come from old, single-site blocks in McLaren Vale. Exports to the US, Canada,
Switzerland, Russia, Hong Kong and China.

🍷🍷🍷🍷🍷 **Top of the Hill McLaren Vale Shiraz 2012** Dense red with black fruit
churning through a field of grainy tannin. One for the long haul. It tastes of
blackberry, saltbush, sweet tobacco and milk chocolate, though fruit rather than
oak is on serve. Diam. 14.5% alc. **Rating** 95 To 2032 $50 CM

🍷🍷🍷🍷🍷 Cafe Block McLaren Vale Shiraz 2011 Rating 91 To 2021 $50 CM

The Overflow Estate 1895   ★★★

21 Sykes Street, Ascot, Brisbane, Qld 4007 (postal) **Region** Queensland Zone
T 0402 793 889 **www**.theoverflowestate1895.com.au **Open** Not
Winemaker Mike Hayes **Est.** 2011 **Dozens** 150 **Vyds** 1.6ha
The story of the estate is almost as long as Tolstoy's *War and Peace*. Suffice it to say that after
100 years of ownership by various branches of the Joyce family, this property was sold to the
families of David Morgan and Philip Usher in July 2008. Those families (and friends) planted
the vineyard in '10, a venture dwarfed by the 500 breeding cattle, a sand-mining operation,
the so-called Hill of Stone continuously mined for sandstone blocks since '00, and 480ha
of eucalypt forest. All of this is overlooked by a massive, historic house. Exports to the UK
and NZ.

The Pawn Wine Co.   ★★★★☆

10 Banksia Road, Macclesfield, SA 5153 **Region** Adelaide Hills
T 0438 373 247 **www**.thepawn.com.au **Open** Not
Winemaker Tom Keelan **Est.** 2002 **Dozens** 5000 **Vyds** 54.92ha
This is a partnership between Tom and Rebecca Keelan and David and Vanessa Blows. Tom
was for some time manager of Longview Vineyards at Macclesfield in the Adelaide Hills,
and consulted to the neighbouring vineyard, owned by David and Vanessa. In 2004 Tom and

David decided to make some small batches of Petit Verdot and Tempranillo at the Bremerton winery, where Tom is now vineyard manager. The wines are sourced from grapes grown on their Macclesfield vineyards; the remainder of the grapes supply brands such as Shaw + Smith, Penfolds, Orlando and Scott Winemaking.

ΥΥΥΥΥ **The Austrian Attack Adelaide Hills Gruner Veltliner 2014** A delicious Gruner Veltliner showing just why the variety and riesling grow next to each other in Austria. Granny Smith apple, white pepper and lemon are fused together in a slinky stream across the long, fresh palate. Will cellar well, and grow in doing so. Screwcap. 11.5% alc. **Rating** 95 **To** 2024 $28 **✪**

ΥΥΥΥΥ **Jeu de Fin Reserve Release Shiraz 2012 Rating** 93 **To** 2032 $32
The Gambit Adelaide Hills Sangiovese 2013 Rating 93 **To** 2020 $24 **✪**

The Roy Kidman Wine Co ★★★

Comaum School Road, Coonawarra, SA 5263 **Region** Coonawarra
T 0417 878 933 www.roykidman.com.au **Open** Not
Winemaker Peter Douglas (Contract) **Est.** 2003 **Dozens** 5000 **Vyds** 55.9ha
Branches of the Kidman family have been part of Coonawarra viticulture since 1970, and long before that one of the great names in the Australian cattle industry. Tim, Philip and Mardi Kidman (brothers and sister) run a separate business from that of cousin Sid Kidman, with 40.2ha of cabernet sauvignon and 15.7ha of shiraz, planting the first 2ha of shiraz in 1970, and moving into wine production in 2003, albeit still selling the major part of the grape production. Roy the Cattleman (Cabernet Sauvignon) is a tribute to their paternal grandfather, who worked as a stockman for his uncle Sir Sidney Kidman. Exports to Sweden, Hong Kong, Singapore, Malaysia, Thailand and China.

ΥΥΥΥ **Bar Over Box Sauvignon Blanc 2014** Quartz-white; while in the light brigade, what it has to offer has some attractive tropical fruits anchored by a near-invisible strand of acidity. Screwcap. 11.3% alc. **Rating** 89 **To** 2015 $17 **✪**

The Story Wines ★★★★★

1/407 Wattletree Road, Malvern East, Vic 3145 (postal) **Region** Grampians
T 0411 697 912 www.thestory.com.au **Open** Not
Winemaker Rory Lane **Est.** 2004 **Dozens** 2500
Over the years I have come across winemakers with degrees in atomic science, doctors with specialties spanning every human condition, town planners, sculptors and painters, and Rory Lane adds yet another to the list: a degree in ancient Greek literature. He says that after completing his degree, and 'desperately wanting to delay an entry into the real world, I stumbled across and enrolled in a postgraduate wine technology and marketing course at Monash University, where I soon became hooked on ... the wondrous connection between land, human and liquid'. Vintages in Australia and Oregon germinated the seed, and he zeroed in on the Grampians, where he purchases small parcels of high-quality grapes for his Shirazs, making the wines in a small factory where he has assembled a basket press, a few open fermenters, a mono pump and some decent French oak.

ΥΥΥΥΥ **Westgate Vineyard Shiraz 2013** Bright crimson-purple; the initial impression is of elegance, and it doesn't take long before red and purple fruits start to sing on the long, medium-bodied palate; the texture and balance are of finesse and undoubted complexity. Screwcap. 14% alc. **Rating** 95 **To** 2033 $55
Grampians Shiraz 2013 Impressive colour and equally impressive depth to its medium to full-bodied palate; black fruits, licorice strap and an inbuilt framework of savoury tannins all join hands. A long and prosperous future ahead. 800 dozen made. Screwcap. 13.8% alc. **Rating** 95 **To** 2033 $28 **✪**

ΥΥΥΥΥ **Westgate Vineyard Grampians Blanc Marsanne Roussanne Viognier 2013 Rating** 93 **To** 2017 $28 CM
Henty Pinot Noir 2013 Rating 92 **To** 2020 $28
Heathcote Grenache 2014 Rating 91 **To** 2018 $28

The Trades ★★★★

13/30 Peel Road, O'Connor, WA 6163 (postal) **Region** Margaret River
T (08) 9331 2188 **www**.terrawines.com.au **Open** Not
Winemaker Brad Wehr (Contract) **Est.** 2006 **Dozens** 700
Thierry Ruault and Rachel Taylor have run a wholesale wine business in Perth since 1993, representing a group of top-end Australian and foreign producers. By definition, the wines they offered to their clientele were well above $20 per bottle, and they decided to fill the gap with a contract-made Shiraz and Sauvignon Blanc from Margaret River.

ŸŸŸŸŸ Grasscutters Margaret River Sauvignon Blanc 2014 The back label is full of Brad Wehr witticisms, culminating with the Lot number, OMG/WTF/LOL. The wine is more serious: 20% barrel-fermented, adding mouthfeel to the citrus, green pea and white peach fruit flavours. You get the humour for free, or the wine: your choice. Screwcap. 13% alc. **Rating** 92 **To** 2016 $18

The Wanderer ★★★★★

2850 Launching Place Road, Gembrook, Vic 3783 **Region** Yarra Valley
T 0415 529 639 **www**.wandererwines.com **Open** By appt
Winemaker Andrew Marks **Est.** 2005 **Dozens** 500
Andrew Marks is the son of Ian and June Marks, owners of Gembrook Hill, and after graduating from Adelaide University with a degree in oenology he joined Southcorp, working for six years at Penfolds (Barossa Valley) and Seppelt (Great Western), as well as undertaking vintages in Coonawarra and France. He has since worked in the Hunter Valley, Great Southern, Sonoma County in the US and Costa Brava in Spain – hence the name of his business.

ŸŸŸŸŸ Yarra Valley Shiraz 2013 A vividly coloured wine entirely at peace with itself, fruit, tannins and oak all doing their own thing within a supple, smooth and seamless framework, the aftertaste with a burst of perfectly ripened small red fruits. Screwcap. 13% alc. **Rating** 96 **To** 2030 $38
Upper Yarra Valley Pinot Noir 2013 Light, bright and clear colour; a wine of considerable purity, cherry and plum seamlessly woven together, the palate supple, the finish very long. The whole bunches have undoubtedly contributed, but it's not obvious. Diam. 13.5% alc. **Rating** 95 **To** 2025 $55

ŸŸŸŸŸ Yarra Valley Pinot Noir 2013 Rating 93 **To** 2023 $38

The Willows Vineyard ★★★★

Light Pass Road, Light Pass, Barossa Valley, SA 5355 **Region** Barossa Valley
T (08) 8562 1080 **www**.thewillowsvineyard.com.au **Open** Wed–Mon 10.30–4.30
Winemaker Peter and Michael Scholz **Est.** 1989 **Dozens** 6500 **Vyds** 42.74ha
The Scholz family have been grapegrowers for generations and have over 40ha of vineyards, selling part of the crop. Current-generation winemakers Peter and Michael Scholz make rich, ripe, velvety wines under their own label, some marketed with some bottle age. Exports to the UK, Canada, Switzerland, China and NZ.

ŸŸŸŸŸ Bonesetter Barossa Shiraz 2012 Intense with blackberry, asphalt, mint and saltbush flavour. It's not a fresh style but it's cakey and dense. You don't have a conversation with it; it lectures you. Raspberry and fennel root notes lift out of the wine given time to breathe; a much-needed glimmer. Points for sheer concentration. Cork. 14.9% alc. **Rating** 93 **To** 2025 $60 CM
Seven G Grenache Shiraz 2013 Spearmint runs through a velvety serve of dark/red berry and mocha. Lively, especially given its high alcohol. Finishes warm, but it's hard to turn away from the flavours themselves. Screwcap. 15.2% alc. **Rating** 91 **To** 2019 $26 CM
Barossa Valley Riesling 2014 Attractive mix of sweet lime and spice with talc through the finish. Fruit flesh and acidity aren't quite working in harmony at this early stage but they will do given time to settle. Hit of limey flavour upfront is deliciously varietal. Screwcap. 10.5% alc. **Rating** 90 **To** 2020 $17 CM

ŶŶŶŶ Barossa Valley Shiraz 2012 Rating 89 To 2021 $28 CM
       Barossa Valley Semillon 2014 Rating 88 To 2020 $17 CM ✪

Thick as Thieves Wines   ★★★★★

355 Healesville–Kooweerup Road, Badger Creek, Vic 3777 **Region** Yarra Valley
T 0417 184 690 **www.tatwines.com.au Open** By appt
Winemaker Syd Bradford **Est.** 2009 **Dozens** 1100 **Vyds** 1ha

Syd Bradford is living proof that small can be beautiful, and, equally, that an old dog can learn new tricks. A growing interest in good food and wine might have come to nothing had it not been for Pfeiffer Wines giving him a vintage job in '03. In that year he enrolled in the wine science course at CSU, moving to the Yarra Valley in '05. He gained experience at Coldstream Hills (vintage cellar hand), Rochford (assistant winemaker), Domaine Chandon (cellar hand) and Giant Steps/Innocent Bystander (assistant winemaker). In '06 Syd achieved the Dean's Award of Academic Excellence at CSU and in '07 was the sole recipient of the A&G Engineering Scholarship. Aged 35, he was desperate to have a go at crafting his own 'babies', and in '09 came across a small parcel of arneis from the Hoddles Creek area, and Thick as Thieves was born. In '10 he purchased small parcels of arneis, chardonnay, pinot noir and nebbiolo, making his wine in a home away from home. The techniques used to make his babies could only come from someone who has spent a long time observing and thinking about what he might do if he were calling the shots. Exports to Japan and Singapore.

ŶŶŶŶŶ Another Bloody Yarra Valley Chardonnay 2014 Whole bunch-pressed direct
       to French oak puncheons (40% new), 60% mlf and some lees stirring. Generosity
       is the name of the game, and you have to unpick that generosity to reveal the
       structure and citrussy acidity within; the low yield of the vines shines through.
       Screwcap. 12.5% alc. Rating 95 To 2024 $35 ✪
       Driftwood Yarra King Valley Pinot Gamay 2014 A 60/40% blend: MV6
       Yarra pinot, 4-day cold soak; King Valley gamay 100% whole bunch-fermented; all
       100% wild yeast, some barrel fermentation. Plan A worked like a dream, the colour
       good, the palate vibrant and lively, with red cherry, wild strawberries, a pinch of
       spice and a long, fresh finish. Screwcap. 12.5% alc. Rating 95 To 2020 $30 ✪
       The Aloof Alpaca Yarra Valley Arneis 2014 Whole bunch foot-stomped
       for 24 hours, then pressed straight to used barriques for warm (22°C) wild yeast
       fermentation; no mlf, 4 months in barrel with minimal lees stirring. The result is a
       wine with almost velvety mouthfeel, and dried orange flavours. Impossible to pick
       it in a blind tasting. Screwcap. 13.5% alc. Rating 94 To 2020 $25 ✪

ŶŶŶŶŶ The Show Pony Sauvignon Blanc 2014 Rating 92 To 2016 $30
       The Love Letter King Valley Sylvaner 2014 Rating 90 To 2016 $25

Third Child   ★★★★

134 Mt Rumney Road, Mt Rumney, Tas 7170 (postal) **Region** Southern Tasmania
T 0419 132 184 **www.thirdchildvineyard.com.au Open** Not
Winemaker John Skinner, Rob Drew **Est.** 2000 **Dozens** 800 **Vyds** 3ha

John and Marcia Skinner planted 2.5ha of pinot noir and 0.5ha of riesling in 2000. It is very much a hands-on operation, the only concession being the enlistment of Rob Drew (from an adjoining property) to help John with the winemaking. When the first vintage ('04) was reaching the stage of being bottled and labelled, the Skinners could not come up with a name and asked their daughter Claire. 'Easy,' she said. 'You've got two kids already; considering the care taken and time spent at the farm, it's your third child.'

ŶŶŶŶŶ Ella Mae Riesling 2014 Trademark Tassie acidity, but there's a plushness
       to this. Full-bodied lime, spice and sweet apple notes flood the palate with
       delicious flavour. Pale colour but mouth-filling. Great advertisement for the high
       drinkability of Riesling. Screwcap. 11% alc. Rating 93 To 2023 $22 CM ✪
       Benjamin's Reserve Pinot Noir 2013 The winery's top-tier Pinot Noir. It
       offers more of everything. More mocha-like oak, greater depth of flavour, and
       more tannin through the finish. It's a big wine in Pinot Noir terms, all plum and

dark cherry, with spice, dried herb and twig-like notes dancing from the mid-palate onwards. Screwcap. 13.5% alc. **Rating** 93 **To** 2021 $44 CM

Jack Ryan Pinot Noir 2013 Accessible and highly likeable but not with complexity. This is keen value. Undergrowth, dark cherry-tipping-into-plum, chicory and a decent serving of spice. Dangerous drinkability. Screwcap. 13.5% alc. **Rating** 92 **To** 2019 $22 CM ✪

Thomas Nicholas Pinot Noir 2013 Depth of fruit and oak, with a tanginess, an undergrowthy aspect. There's a good deal of flavour and a true Pinot Noir experience on offer here for a reasonably modest price. Coffeed oak is a clear player, but it feels generally well balanced, adeptly tannic, and well measured through the finish. Screwcap. 13.5% alc. **Rating** 92 **To** 2020 $28 CM

❦ Thistledown Wines

c/- Revenir, Peacock Road North/Vickers Road, Lenswood, SA 5240 **Region** South Australia
T +44 7778 003 959 **www.**thistledownwines.com **Open** Not
Winemaker Peter Leske, Giles Cook MW, Fergal Tynan MW **Est.** 2010 **Dozens** 4000
Giles Cook MW and Fergal Tynan MW are based in Scotland, and have a collective 40 years' experience of buying and selling Australian wines. They have been friends since 1998, when they met over a pint of beer on the evening before the first Master of Wine course they were about to embark on. In 2006 they established Alliance Wine Australia, which purchases Australian wines for distribution in the UK, and took the process one step further when Alliance began the Thistledown Wines venture. This is owned and directed by the partners from the ground up, focusing on Barossa Valley Shiraz, McLaren Vale Grenache, and smaller amounts of custom-made wine from the Adelaide Hills and Langhorne Creek. The wines are made under Peter Leske's direction at his Revenir small-batch winery in the Adelaide Hills. Giles says he has particular affection for grenache, and is precisely right (in my view) when he says, 'McLaren Vale grenache is world class, and it best expresses itself when made in the mould of Pinot Noir.' Small wonder, then, that they are moving to 500-litre puncheons, looking for attractive, aromatic styles with elegance and energy rather than dense dry red character. Exports to the UK, the US and NZ.

🍷🍷🍷🍷🍷 **The Basket Case Old Vine Barossa Valley Shiraz 2013** Good hue; there's plenty happening on the medium to full-bodied palate, which has some dark chocolate nuances (more commonly found in McLaren Vale) that give the wine a certain gravitas; the savoury fruits of the medium-bodied palate have ample length and good balance. Screwcap. 14.5% alc. **Rating** 91 **To** 2023 $37

The Basket Case Old Vine Barossa Valley Shiraz 2012 Points for smoothness. And for integration of fruit and oak. It tastes of dark, toasty plums, licorice and choc mint, though what you notice most, perhaps, is the smoothness of the ride. Screwcap. 14% alc. **Rating** 91 **To** 2022 $35 CM

🍷🍷🍷🍷 **The Vagabond Grenache 2013** **Rating** 89 **To** 2018 $30
The Cunning Plan Langhorne Creek Shiraz 2013 **Rating** 88 **To** 2018 $26

Thomas Wines

c/- The Small Winemakers Centre, McDonalds Road, Pokolbin, NSW 2320
Region Hunter Valley
T 0418 456 853 **www.**thomaswines.com.au **Open** 7 days 10–5
Winemaker Andrew Thomas, Richard Done **Est.** 1997 **Dozens** 8000 **Vyds** 3ha
Andrew Thomas came to the Hunter Valley from McLaren Vale to join the winemaking team at Tyrrell's. After 13 years, he left to undertake contract work and to continue the development of his own label. He makes individual-vineyard wines, underlining the subtle differences between the various subregions of the Hunter. Plans for the construction of an estate winery have been abandoned for the time being, and for the foreseeable future he will continue to lease the James Estate winery on Hermitage Road, while the cellar door will continue at the Small Winemakers Centre. The major part of the production comes from long-term arrangements with growers of semillon (15ha) and shiraz (25ha); an additional 3ha of shiraz is

leased. The quality of the wines and the reputation of Andrew Thomas have never been higher. Exports to the US and Japan.

ΨΨΨΨΨ Braemore Hunter Valley Semillon 2014 Hand-picked with 'fishing headlamps' between 2am and 9am, enabling whole bunch pressing of cool fruit. Herb, grass, lime and lemon aromas and flavours whirl through the bouquet and superbly balanced palate, with lemon zest acidity cleansing and lengthening the finish and aftertaste. Screwcap. 10.8% alc. **Rating** 97 **To** 2034 $30 ○

Cellar Reserve Braemore Hunter Valley Semillon 2009 Glowing yellow-green; sheer perfection, with a shimmering array of lemon, lemongrass and lemon zest leading the charge, tantalising hints of honey and toast around the corner; phenomenal length and intensity. Figuratively, will live forever. Screwcap. 11.2% alc. **Rating** 97 **To** 2034 $50 ○

Kiss Limited Release Hunter Valley Shiraz 2013 Great colour; unalloyed black fruits illuminate the bouquet and the uncompromisingly full-bodied palate. Here tannins frame everything that follows yet it has the balance that is the hallmark of the Thomas Shirazs. Recalls the story of Professor George Saintsbury, the great English wine author of a century ago, who, when confronted with an 1846 Hermitage, commented it was 'the manliest wine' he had ever tasted. Screwcap. 13.6% alc. **Rating** 97 **To** 2053 $65 ○

ΨΨΨΨΨ The O.C. Hunter Valley Semillon 2014 I cannot recall a 6 month-old (or a 12 month-old) Semillon with as much flavour on offer as this wine, thus fully justifying Andrew Thomas's suggestion of great early drinking without compromising its long-term potential; potent lemongrass and lime aromas and flavours have thrilling acidity, providing both structure and balance. Screwcap. 11.7% alc. **Rating** 96 **To** 2029 $23 ○

Elenay Barrel Selection Hunter Valley Shiraz 2013 'Lips and arseholes' says the back label, and I'll say no more. Deep, but bright crimson-purple; the bouquet is inviting, and the wine roars into exuberant life on the multifaceted, medium to full-bodied, and beautifully structured, palate; here satsuma plum, an airbrush of twigs, and a juicy, lingering finish will keep you interested for decades to come. Screwcap. 13.5% alc. **Rating** 96 **To** 2043 $45 ○

Sweetwater Hunter Valley Shiraz 2013 Deep red volcanic soil over limestone. Excellent depth and hue to the colour; it has black cherry, plum and some smoky bacon oak on the bouquet, the palate with equal proportions of depth and length, all in a dark berry spectrum, supple tannins present and correct. Screwcap. 14% alc. **Rating** 95 **To** 2038 $35 ○

DJV Vineyard Selection Hunter Valley Shiraz 2013 Déjà vu old vines – get the pun? Vibrant clear crimson colour; there's a lot happening on the bouquet and ultra-fresh, light to medium-bodied, red-fruited palate; delicate and fresh, it needs no patience whatsoever, but the balance will hold it if you insist. Screwcap. 12.8% alc. **Rating** 95 **To** 2023 $30 ○

Synergy Vineyard Selection Shiraz 2013. **Rating** 94 **To** 2025 $23 ○
Two of a Kind Shiraz 2013 **Rating** 94 **To** 2028 $24 ○

ΨΨΨΨϘ Six Degrees Vineyard Selection Semillon 2014 **Rating** 92 **To** 2020 $23 ○
Two of a Kind Semillon Sauvignon Blanc 2014 **Rating** 91 **To** 2015 $20 ○

Thompson Estate   ★★★★★

299 Tom Cullity Drive, Wilyabrup, WA 6284 **Region** Margaret River
T (08) 9755 6406 **www**.thompsonestate.com **Open** Tues–Sun 11–5
Winemaker Bob Cartwright, Paul Dixon **Est.** 1994 **Dozens** 10000 **Vyds** 28.63ha
Cardiologist Peter Thompson planted the first vines at Thompson Estate in 1997, inspired by his and his family's shareholdings in the Pierro and Fire Gully vineyards, and by visits to many of the world's premium wine regions. The vineyard is planted to cabernet sauvignon, cabernet franc, merlot, chardonnay, sauvignon blanc, semillon, pinot noir and malbec. Thompson Estate wines are made by Bob Cartwright (former Leeuwin Estate winemaker) at its state-of-the-art winery. Exports to Canada, Singapore, Hong Kong and China.

ΨΨΨΨΨ **Margaret River Chardonnay 2013** Night machine-harvested, pressed and cold-settled to star brightness, cold-fermented, inoculated with a pure culture, in 100% new French oak. The long experience of Bob Cartwright at Leeuwin Estate shines through: the intensity of the fruit has absorbed the impact of the oak without breaking into a sweat, and the 8g/l of acidity will help underwrite its very long future. Screwcap. 13.5% alc. **Rating** 96 **To** 2028 $50 ✪

SSB Margaret River Semillon Sauvignon Blanc 2014 A 60/40% estate blend, pressed and cold-fermented in tank after brief skin contact; part of the sauvignon blanc barrel-fermented and matured in used French oak. The depth and complexity of the wine emanates from the vineyard, with a parade of tropical fruits grafted onto the citrus and mineral of the semillon and its life-giving acidity. A really nice wine. Screwcap. 12.5% alc. **Rating** 95 **To** 2020 $35 ✪

Margaret River Cabernet Sauvignon 2012 An 87.5/7.2/5.3% blend of cabernet, merlot and franc open-fermented, plunged, with 7 days' post-ferment maceration, 18 months in French oak. It has exceptional drive and intensity to its mix of savoury blackcurrant, redcurrant and earthy fruit. Demands respect. Screwcap. 14% alc. **Rating** 95 **To** 2042 $45

Four Chambers Sauvignon Blanc Semillon 2014 A 63/37% blend given a few hours' skin contact, then cold-fermented in tank, a small amount barrel-fermented. A very good example of a Margaret River specialty, with both depth and length to its array of juicy gooseberry, stone fruit and lemon flavours. Hard to expect more at this price. Screwcap. 12% alc. **Rating** 94 **To** 2017 $22 ✪

Cabernet Merlot 2012 A 78/12/10% blend of estate-grown cabernet, merlot and franc, with 18 months in used French oak. It is an exercise in harmony between blackcurrant/cassis, a dash of black olive and ripe tannins, oak underpinning the texture/structure, rather than the flavour. Screwcap. 14% alc. **Rating** 94 **To** 2032 $35

ΨΨΨΨΩ **Four Chambers Margaret River Shiraz 2013 Rating** 93 **To** 2025 $22 ✪

Thorn-Clarke Wines   ★★★★★

Milton Park, 266 Gawler Park Road, Angaston, SA 5353 **Region** Barossa Valley
T (08) 8564 3036 **www.**thornclarkewines.com.au **Open** Mon–Fri 9–5, Sat 11–4
Winemaker Helen McCarthy **Est.** 1987 **Dozens** 80000 **Vyds** 268ha
Established by David and Cheryl Clarke (née Thorn), and son Sam, Thorn-Clarke is one of the largest family-owned estate-based businesses in the Barossa. Their winery is close to the border between the Barossa and Eden valleys, and three of their four vineyards are in the Eden Valley: the Mt Crawford Vineyard is at the southern end of the Eden Valley, while the Milton Park and Sandpiper vineyards are further north in the Eden Valley. The fourth vineyard is at St Kitts, in the northern end of the Barossa Ranges, established when no other vignerons had ventured onto what was hitherto considered unsuitable soil. In all four vineyards careful soil mapping has resulted in matching of variety and site, with all of the major varieties represented. The quality of grapes retained for the Thorn-Clarke label has resulted in a succession of trophy and gold medal winning wines at very competitive prices. Exports to all major markets.

ΨΨΨΨΨ **Ron Thorn Barossa Shiraz 2012** Substantial wine in all respects. The Incredible Hulk in a glass, though a lot classier. Deep blackberry, boysenberry and coffee-cream flavour, a deep river of tannin, an aspect of brood but no lack of brightness either. It's a heavy hitter, but it's not just that: it's neat, it exercises its power both responsibly and with a form of precision, and it flies boldly through the finish as if there's not a shadow of a doubt that the future is a place where it belongs. Cork. 14.8% alc. **Rating** 97 **To** 2040 $95 CM ✪

William Randell Eden Valley Cabernet Sauvignon 2012 Eden Valley, cabernet sauvignon and '12 is a potent combination, with guaranteed success, but it excels itself in this wine, with its joyous display of cassis, superfine tannins and all-encompassing freshness. Screwcap. 14.5% alc. **Rating** 97 **To** 2037 $60 ✪

ΨΨΨΨΨ **Eden Trail Riesling 2014** Elegant but piercing. Lime, bath salts, slate and floral aromas/flavours. Slight spritz but this is a ripping wine: it knows exactly what it's about and how to get there. Direct line from start to finish, gathers momentum fast and drives out through the finish. Screwcap. 12% alc. **Rating** 96 To 2028 $24 CM ☻

Shotfire Barossa Shiraz 2013 Champing at the bit to show off its sweet, jubey fruit, but chains of herb-shot tannin keep the class in order. There is no doubting this is a beautiful wine to drink. It sits on the cusp of jamminess, all jellied and blackberried, its hints of raspberry and mint simply ramping the deliciousness higher. Value, what value. Screwcap. 14.5% alc. **Rating** 95 To 2028 $25 CM ☻

Shotfire Barossa Quartage 2012 A blend of cabernet sauvignon, cabernet franc, petit verdot and merlot. Comes from a distinguished line of wines that have over-delivered, and this wine is up there with the best. While much of its quality comes from the vineyard, it has also been very well made; its blackcurrant, redcurrant, cherry and spice flavours flow in a seamless stream across the palate and aftertaste. Screwcap. 14.5% alc. **Rating** 95 To 2027 $28 ☻

Barossa Valley Graciano 2013 Rating 94 To 2024 $30 CM ☻

ΨΨΨΨ♀ **William Randell Barossa Shiraz 2012 Rating** 93 To 2037 $60
Eden Trail Shiraz 2012 Rating 93 To 2023 $28 CM
Shotfire Barossa Quartage 2013 Rating 93 To 2028 $25 CM ☻
Shotfire Cabernet Shiraz 2012 Rating 92 To 2021 $25 CM ☻

Thousand Candles
★★★★☆

PO Box 148, Seville, Vic 3139 **Region** Yarra Valley
T 0400 654 512 **www**.thousandcandles.com.au **Open** Not
Winemaker William Downie **Est.** 2010 **Dozens** 1000 **Vyds** 37ha
What is now called the Thousand Candles vineyard was originally known as Killara Estate, which was planted in 1997. The Thousand Candles name comes from a 19th century account harking back to its indigenous occupiers. A ceremony granting free passage to the lands around the property was witnessed by a European who, referring to the tribesmen dramatically holding aloft their firesticks, remarked, 'It's as if the twilight of the evening had been interrupted by a thousand candles.' And indeed the property is a dramatic one, plunging from a height of several hundred metres above the Yarra River down to its flood plains. The east-facing upper level flat land and the upper part of the slopes were planted to 37ha of vines. Another level of drama was added when the first wine under the new ownership (itself shrouded in mystery) came from the wet vintage of '11, and was a highly unusual blend of shiraz with a dash of pinot noir and a drop of sauvignon blanc. The price was a mind-bending $100 a bottle, but I should add that it was well reviewed by those who had the opportunity to taste it. The '12 is a less challenging – and better – wine, but the Ouija board varietal guessing game may have to be resolved somewhere down the track.

ΨΨΨΨ♀ **Yarra Valley 2013** This release is highly polished and beautifully tannic, its curls of dryness adding gravity to fruit flavours of boysenberry, licorice, beetroot and violet. Dry spice and hay-like characters add savouriness to the show. Variety isn't the name of the game (it's all about site) but the use of shiraz, pinot and sauvignon blanc here give the wine an architectural vibe; the materials aren't stock standard, but everything feels thought-out and precisely placed. Diam. 13.5% alc. **Rating** 93 To 2025 $110 CM

Three Dark Horses
★★★★☆

49 Fraser Avenue, Happy Valley, SA 5159 **Region** McLaren Vale
T 0405 294 500 **www**.3dhcom.au **Open** Not
Winemaker Matt Broomhead **Est.** 2009 **Dozens** 1500
Three Dark Horses is the new project for former Coriole winemaker Matt Broomhead. After vintages in southern Italy and the Rhône Valley he returned to McLaren Vale in 2009 and, with his father Alan, runs this business buying quality grapes thanks to the long experience they both have in the region. The third dark horse is Matt's 89-year-old grandfather, a vintage regular. Exports to China.

ŶŶŶŶŶ **McLaren Vale Shiraz 2013** 70yo vines; wild yeast-fermented, and matured in new (40%) and used French oak. Deeply coloured, it takes you on a ride through an ever-changing parade of black cherry, plum, spice and tasty licorice; really shines on the back-palate and finish, the flavours soaring, yet is no more than medium-bodied. Screwcap. 14.5% alc. **Rating** 95 **To** 2028 $25 ✪

MC Adelaide Hills Chardonnay 2014 Carbonic maceration for 7 days, basket-pressed to used oak for full solids fermentation, lees stirred, unfined and unfiltered. This is a wine with attitude, and will entrance devotees of natural wine, and even those who aren't; acidity provides the spine for a complex, tightly wound palate and aftertaste. Screwcap. 12.5% alc. **Rating** 94 **To** 2020 $25 ✪

GT McLaren Vale Grenache Touriga 2014 A 75/25% blend co-fermented with wild yeast, unoaked/fined/filtered. The colour is good, the bouquet fragrant, and the palate is positively alive with a chorus of red fruits, the acidity perfectly pitched. It will develop and change character in the manner of grenache blends from the southern Rhône. Screwcap. 14% alc. **Rating** 94 **To** 2024 $25 ✪

ŶŶŶŶŶ **McLaren Vale Grenache 2013** **Rating** 92 **To** 2020 $25 ✪

3 Drops   ★★★★☆

PO Box 1828, Applecross, WA 6953 **Region** Mount Barker
T (08) 9315 4721 **www.3drops.com Open** Not
Winemaker Robert Diletti (Contract) **Est.** 1998 **Dozens** 5000 **Vyds** 21.5ha

The three drops are not the three founders (John Bradbury, Joanne Bradbury and, formerly, Nicola Wallich), but wine, olive oil and water, all of which come from the substantial property at Mount Barker. The plantings are riesling, sauvignon blanc, semillon, chardonnay, cabernet sauvignon, merlot, shiraz and cabernet franc, irrigated – like the olive trees – by a large wetland on the property. 3 Drops also owns the 14.7ha Patterson's Vineyard. Exports to Canada, Singapore, Malaysia, Hong Kong and China.

ŶŶŶŶŶ **Great Southern Riesling 2014** Further evidence of the supreme quality of Great Southern riesling is not really needed, but this glorious wine supplies it nonetheless. The combination of purity and intensity, of lime juice, lime leaf and sparkling, crystalline acidity says it all; the length is prodigious. Screwcap. 12% alc. **Rating** 96 **To** 2029 $26 ✪

ŶŶŶŶŶ **Great Southern Sauvignon Blanc 2014** **Rating** 93 **To** 2015 $22 ✪

3 Oceans Wine Company   ★★★★☆

Cnr Boundary Road/Bussell Highway, Cowaramup, WA 6284 **Region** Margaret River
T (08) 9756 5656 **www.3oceans.com.au Open** 7 days 10–5
Winemaker Ben Roodhouse, Jonathan Mettam **Est.** 1999 **Dozens** 160 000

After a period of spectacular growth and marketing activity, Palandri went into voluntary administration in February 2008. In June of that year the Ma family, through their 3 Oceans Wine Company Pty Ltd, acquired the Margaret River winery, the 30-year-old Margaret River vineyard and 347ha of Frankland River vineyards. In October '08 it also acquired the Palandri and Baldivis Estate brands. There is a strong focus on the emerging markets of the Asia Pacific region, but no neglecting of the domestic market. Given the size of production, the quality of the wines is very impressive. Exports to the UK and Asia.

ŶŶŶŶŶ **The Explorers Margaret River Sauvignon Blanc Semillon 2013** Estate-grown and wild yeast barrel-fermented in French oak. A powerful wine, fruit dominating the oak, not vice versa, which is – of course – a good thing. It has the structure to develop well for a few years, the flavours poised between tropical and grassy. Screwcap. 12.9% alc. **Rating** 94 **To** 2017 $32

The Explorers Margaret River Chardonnay 2012 Wild yeast fermentation in French oak, then lees stirring for 8 months have resulted in a superior wine with intense grapefruit and white peach flavours cradled by positive texture and structure. Early picking doesn't always work, but does here. Screwcap. 12.5% alc. **Rating** 94 **To** 2021 $32

Palandri The Chairman Shiraz 2009 This is a complex wine with exceptional colour for its age, and spicy black fruits typical of Frankland River coupled with savoury tannins and a generous supply of oak. Presumably earmarked for export. A screwcap would guarantee its future over many decades. Cork. 14% alc. Rating 94 To 2029 $250

Palandri The Chairman Shiraz 2008 Rating 93 To 2025 $240 CM
The Explorers Frankland River Shiraz 2012 Rating 92 To 2025 $32
The Explorers Cabernet Sauvignon 2012 Rating 92 To 2027 $32
The Rivers White Classic 2014 Rating 91 To 2016 $16 CM ◎
The Explorers Frankland River Shiraz 2013 Rating 91 To 2022 $36 CM
The Estates Frankland River Margaret River Sauvignon Blanc Semillon 2013 Rating 90 To 2016 $21 ◎

Three Willows Vineyard ★★★☆

46 Montana Road, Red Hills, Tas 7304 **Region** Northern Tasmania
T 0438 507 069 **www**.threewillowsvineyard.com.au **Open** Most days 10.30–5 (summer), 11–4.30 (winter)
Winemaker Philip Parés **Est.** 2002 **Dozens** 270 **Vyds** 1.8ha
Philip Parés and Lyn Prove have planted a micro-vineyard with pinot noir, pinot gris and baco noir (a hybrid). It is 50km west of Launceston, near Deloraine, on a gentle north-facing slope at an elevation of 220–250m.

Pinot Gris 2013 Quite delicious. Clear notes of red apple, lime and rosewater. Compact and textural. Well weighted and balanced. Screwcap. 13% alc. Rating 91 To 2016 $26 CM

Pinot Rose 2013 Rating 88 To 2016 $22 CM
Genevieve Pinot Noir 2013 Rating 88 To 2019 $32 CM

Tidswell Wines ★★★★☆

14 Sydenham Road, Norwood, SA 5067 **Region** Limestone Coast Zone
T (08) 8363 5800 **www**.tidswellwines.com.au **Open** By appt
Winemaker Ben Tidswell, Wine Wise Consultancy **Est.** 1994 **Dozens** 3000 **Vyds** 136.4ha
The Tidswell family (now in the shape of Andrea and Ben Tidswell) has two large vineyards in the Limestone Coast Zone near Bool Lagoon; the lion's share is planted to cabernet sauvignon and shiraz, with smaller plantings of merlot, sauvignon blanc, petit verdot, vermentino and pinot gris. Tidswell is a fully certified member of WFA's environmental sustainability program. Wines are released under the Jennifer, Heathfield Ridge and Caves Road labels. Exports to Canada, Denmark, Germany, Singapore, Japan and China.

Jennifer Limited Release Cabernet Sauvignon 2012 If only Tidswell had graced its best wine with a screwcap, consigning the cork to its lesser-priced sibling ... This is a more powerful and dense wine, all the components of fruit, tannins and oak upscaled, yet retaining the lush softness of that sibling; cassis and plum ooze from every pore. 14.5% alc. Rating 96 To 2032 $65 ◎
Wild Violet Limestone Coast Sauvignon Blanc 2014 A surprise packet, with the full suite of tropical fruit flavours on the bouquet and palate; a suggestion of residual sugar on the finish is balanced (if it be there) by crisp acidity. Enjoy this wine without delay. Screwcap. 12% alc. Rating 94 To 2017 $18 ◎

Heathfield Cabernet Sauvignon 2012 Rating 93 To 2032 $28
Heathfield Shiraz 2012 Rating 92 To 2025 $28

Tilbrook Estate ★★★★☆

17/1 Adelaide Lobethal Road, Lobethal, SA 5241 **Region** Adelaide Hills
T (08) 8389 5318 **www**.tilbrookestate.com.au **Open** Fri–Sun & public hols 11–5
Winemaker James Tilbrook **Est.** 1999 **Dozens** 1500 **Vyds** 3.97ha

James and Annabelle Tilbrook have almost 5ha of multi-clone chardonnay and pinot noir, plus sauvignon blanc and pinot gris, at Lenswood. The winery and cellar door are in the old Onkaparinga Woollen Mills building in Lobethal; this not only provides an atmospheric home, but also helps meet the very strict environmental requirements of the Adelaide Hills in dealing with winery waste water. English-born James came to Australia in 1986, aged 22, but a car accident led to his return to England. Working for Oddbins and passing the WSET diploma set his future course. He returned to Australia, met Annabelle, purchased the vineyard and began planting it in '99. Finding the best combination of variety and site is a work in progress. Exports to the UK.

ŢŢŢŢŢ **Reserve Lenswood Vineyard Adelaide Hills Chardonnay 2012** Fresh flavours of flint, fennel, figs and citrus lead logically to a finish flush with toasty, chalky notes. A more modern style than the estate is perhaps known for and all the better for it. There's power and persistence here but it's the way the wine stands tall and firm that really signals its quality. Screwcap. 13.5% alc. **Rating** 95 **To** 2020 $40 CM

ŢŢŢŢŢ **Adelaide Hills Shiraz 2012 Rating** 91 **To** 2021 $22 CM ◐

Tim Adams   ★★★★★

Warenda Road, Clare, SA 5453 **Region** Clare Valley
T (08) 8842 2429 **www**.timadamswines.com.au **Open** Mon–Fri 10.30–5, w'ends 11–5
Winemaker Tim Adams, Brett Schutz **Est.** 1986 **Dozens** 60 000 **Vyds** 145ha
Tim Adams and partner Pam Goldsack preside over a highly successful business. Having expanded the range of estate plantings with tempranillo, pinot gris and viognier, in 2009 the business took a giant step forward with the acquisition of the 80ha Leasingham Rogers Vineyard from CWA for a reported price of $850 000, followed in '11 by the purchase of the Leasingham winery and winemaking equipment (for less than replacement cost). The winery is now a major contract winemaking facility for the region.

ŢŢŢŢŢ **Clare Valley Riesling 2014** Sourced from a number of vineyards, this year gaining two new components: the Skilly Ridge Vineyard and a high vineyard at Penwortham. Bright, crisp and with the hallmark Clare Valley length; lemon blossom and lemon flavour is the fulcrum for both present and future enjoyment, the zesty finish another plus. Screwcap. 11.5% alc. **Rating** 95 **To** 2024 $22 ◐
Clare Valley Cabernet Malbec 2010 A blend of 65% estate-grown cabernet and 35% malbec grown by neighbour Richard Hughes. This isn't Wendouree, but it's a very good example of the synergy of cabernet and malbec in the Clare Valley, the juicy plum fruit of the malbec contentedly nestling in the arms of the cabernet. Still full of life, and won't tire for many years. Screwcap. 14.5% alc. **Rating** 94 **To** 2025 $25 ◐

ŢŢŢŢŢ **The Fergus 2012 Rating** 92 **To** 2020 $24 ◐
Clare Valley Pinot Gris 2014 Rating 90 **To** 2016 $22 CM

Tim Gramp   ★★★★

Mintaro/Leasingham Road, Watervale, SA 5452 **Region** Clare Valley
T (08) 8344 4079 **www**.timgrampwines.com.au **Open** W'ends 12–4
Winemaker Tim Gramp **Est.** 1990 **Dozens** 6000 **Vyds** 16ha
Tim Gramp has quietly built up a very successful business, and by keeping overheads to a minimum provides good wines at modest prices. Over the years the estate vineyards (shiraz, riesling, cabernet sauvignon and grenache) have been expanded significantly. Exports to Malaysia, Taiwan and China.

ŢŢŢŢŢ **Watervale Cabernet Sauvignon 2013** It's become such a lively wine, not thick or overdone in any way; it's boysenberried and curranty with slips of sweet mint, the elegance and juiciness of it entirely easy to take. Well-structured and substantial enough, so no one will be left unsatisfied, but it keeps freshness and life to forefront. Screwcap. 14.5% alc. **Rating** 93 **To** 2022 $22 CM ◐

Watervale Tempranillo 2013 Tempranillo looks to have a future in the Clare Valley. This first release of a Watervale Tempranillo from Tim Gramp ably shows why: it's fleshy, mid-weight, chewy, carries a semblance of cherry-cola fruit sweetness, looks dark but bright in the glass, and shows flashes of graphite through the finish. Not a bad show. Screwcap. 14.5% alc. **Rating** 91 **To** 2017 $21 CM ✪
Watervale Riesling 2014 Generous serve of melon and lime with edges of rind and spice. Drinking very well in its youth, suggesting there's no better time to hook in than right now. Screwcap. 12% alc. **Rating** 90 **To** 2019 $20 CM ✪

Tim McNeil Wines ★★★★

71 Springvale Road, Watervale, SA 5452 **Region** Clare Valley
T (08) 8843 0040 **www.**timmcneilwines.com.au **Open** Fri–Sun & public hols 11–5
Winemaker Tim McNeil **Est.** 2004 **Dozens** 1500 **Vyds** 2ha
When Tim and Cass McNeil established Tim McNeil Wines, Tim had long since given up his teaching career, graduating with a degree in oenology from Adelaide University in 1999. He then spent 11 years honing his craft at important wineries in the Barossa and Clare valleys. In Aug 2010 Tim McNeil Wines became his full-time job. The McNeils' 16ha property at Watervale includes mature dry-grown riesling. The cellar door overlooks the riesling vineyard, with panoramic views of Watervale and beyond. Exports to Canada.

🍷🍷🍷🍷🍷 **Shiraz 2012** A mouth-filling, dense and opulent wine with an attractive tarry/earthy balance to the density of the varietal fruit, the oak adding another strand to the storyline. All it needs is as much time as you can possibly give it, for it will develop superbly. Screwcap. 14.5% alc. **Rating** 94 **To** 2032 $34

🍷🍷🍷🍷🍷 **Reserve Watervale Riesling 2014 Rating** 93 **To** 2021 $32
On the Wing Shiraz 2012 Rating 92 **To** 2032 $20 ✪

Tim Smith Wines ★★★★★

PO Box 446, Tanunda, SA 5352 **Region** Barossa Valley
T 0416 396 730 **www.**timsmithwines.com.au **Open** Not
Winemaker Tim Smith **Est.** 2002 **Dozens** 4000 **Vyds** 1ha
With a talent for sourcing exceptional old vine fruit from the Barossa floor, Tim Smith has created a small but credible portfolio of wines, currently including Mataro, Grenache, Shiraz, Viognier, and more recently Eden Valley Riesling. Tim left his full-time winemaking role with a large Barossa brand in 2011, allowing him to concentrate 100% of his energy on his own brand. In '12 Tim joined forces with the team from First Drop (see separate entry), and has moved winemaking operations to a brand-new winery fondly named 'Home of the Brave', in Nuriootpa. Exports to the UK, the US, Canada, Denmark, Taiwan and Singapore.

🍷🍷🍷🍷🍷 **Barossa Shiraz 2013** Sourced from 10 vineyards, the oldest 130yo; part Barossa Valley, part Eden Valley. Made with great skill, matured on fine yeast lees in mostly French oak. This is a seriously good wine, awash with black fruits, licorice and fine, brambly tannins; the balance and length are perfect, the oak fully integrated. Screwcap. 14.5% alc. **Rating** 96 **To** 2043 $36 ✪
Barossa Mataro 2013 A delicious wine in every respect; an ultra-supple and smooth medium-bodied palate rolls smoothly over hill and dale with its array of plum and black cherry garnished with the full array of sweet spices, finishing with velvety tannins. Screwcap. 14.5% alc. **Rating** 96 **To** 2028 $36 ✪
Eden Valley Riesling 2014 From a single vineyard at an elevation of 450m. Pale quartz-green, the fragrant citrus blossom bouquet sets the scene for a palate that ticks all the boxes; lime juice flavours, crisp steely acidity, and a long, cleansing finish. Screwcap. 12% alc. **Rating** 95 **To** 2027 $25 ✪
Barossa Mataro Grenache Shiraz 2013 Tim Smith has this blend working far in his (and therefore drinkers') favour. It's become a house specialty. This is a rich, generous release, chock-a-block with ripe black berries, chocolatey oak, cracked pepper and assorted roasted nut flavours. It's dense but bright and spicy; it lifts from

the glass but then sinks deep into all corners of the mouth. A standout. Screwcap. 14.5% alc. Rating 95 To 2024 $28 CM ❂

Eden Valley Viognier 2014 Wild yeast-fermented in new and used oak, then lees-contacted and stirred. Has excellent, mouth-filling texture and an abundance of varietal fruit achieved without phenolic coarseness; yellow peach, ginger and incipient honey all contribute. Screwcap. 13% alc. **Rating** 94 **To** 2018 $28 ❂

Bugalugs Barossa Valley Shiraz 2013 This may be only medium-bodied, but it pulls no punches; energetic plum and dark forest berries, plus splashes of spice, tar and earth give it length and purpose; the colour and overall structure are other adjuncts of a great-value wine. Screwcap. 14.5% alc. **Rating** 94 **To** 2028 $22 ❂

🍷🍷🍷🍷 Bugalugs Barossa Grenache 2013 Rating 89 To 2018 $22

Tinklers Vineyard   ★★★★★

Pokolbin Mountains Road, Pokolbin, NSW 2320 **Region** Hunter Valley
T (02) 4998 7435 **www.**tinklers.com.au **Open** 7 days 10–5
Winemaker Usher Tinkler **Est.** 1946 **Dozens** 5000 **Vyds** 41ha
Three generations of the Tinkler family have been involved with the property since 1942. Originally a beef and dairy farm, vines have been both pulled out and replanted at various stages, and part of the adjoining 80-year-old Ben Ean Vineyard has been acquired. Plantings include semillon (14ha), shiraz (11.5ha), chardonnay (6.5ha) and smaller areas of merlot, muscat and viognier. The majority of the grape production continues to be sold to McWilliam's and Tyrrell's. Usher has resigned his roles as chief winemaker at Poole's Rock and Cockfighter's Ghost to take on full-time responsibility at Tinklers, and production has been increased to meet demand. Exports to Sweden, Singapore and China.

🍷🍷🍷🍷🍷 **U and I Hunter Valley Shiraz 2013** Open-fermented, hand-plunged, basket-pressed, new French oak. Deeply coloured; the bouquet has more black fruits than red, and perfectly balanced tannins are hand-stitched through the plum and blackberry fruit. The palate is medium to full-bodied, long and complete. Will outlive many who read these words. Screwcap. 14% alc. **Rating** 96 **To** 2053 $45 ❂

Reserve Hunter Valley Semillon 2014 Estate-grown, hand-picked and whole bunch-pressed. Quartz-white; it has the particular, not common, acidity I call squeaky, as the tongue is momentarily caught on the gums as the wine is savoured; lemon, lemon verbena and lemongrass are all accentuated by its acidity. Screwcap. 11.5% alc. **Rating** 95 **To** 2034 $35 ❂

Old Vines Hunter Valley Shiraz 2013 Estate vines planted in '48, open-fermented, basket-pressed, 10 months in French oak. Bright, clear, crimson colour; the bouquet is fragrant and filled with red fruits, the medium-bodied palate juicy, fine and long, full of red fruits with splashes of licorice and sweet earth; the tannins are superfine. Screwcap. 13.5% alc. **Rating** 95 **To** 2033 $35 ❂

Hunter Valley Shiraz Viognier 2013 Old-vine shiraz co-fermented with 8% viognier, matured in new French oak. Bright crimson colour introduces a fresh, perfumed bouquet and a relaxed, but expressive, palate with bright red fruits and just a whisper of Hunter earth reminding you of its place. Screwcap. 13.5% alc. **Rating** 95 **To** 2028 $25 ❂

School Block Hunter Valley Semillon 2010 Pale, bright, straw-green; calmly and slowly moving towards full maturity somewhere in the current decade, but will live much longer; lemon/lemongrass and crisp acidity are still the drivers, toast yet to appear. The only possibly criticism is the acidity, but that's a small bone of contention. Screwcap. 11.9% alc. **Rating** 94 **To** 2020 $25 ❂

Poppys Hunter Valley Chardonnay 2014 Poppy's Vineyard is on deep sandy loam, ideal for white wines. It is very elegant, and equally well balanced, with melon, citrus and stone fruit all in play, the acidity a bastion for the future. Screwcap. 13% alc. **Rating** 94 **To** 2021 $25 ❂

🍷🍷🍷🍷🍷 PMR Merlot 2014 Rating 93 To 2020 $25 ❂
Hunter Valley Viognier 2014 Rating 92 To 2016 $22 ❂
Lucerne Paddock Verdelho 2014 Rating 91 To 2016 $18 ❂

Tintara ★★★★★

202 Main Road, McLaren Vale, SA 5171 **Region** McLaren Vale
T (08) 8329 4124 **www.**tintara.com.au **Open** 7 days 10–4.30
Winemaker Paul Carpenter **Est.** 1876 **Dozens** NFP
Tintara was the third of the three substantial winery and vineyard enterprises in the early days of McLaren Vale. It was established by Dr Alexander Kelly, who purchased 280ha of land in 1861 and planted the first vines in '63. It grew rapidly – indeed too rapidly, because it ran into financial difficulties and was acquired by Thomas Hardy in '76. He recovered his purchase price with wine sales over the following year. It has been – and continues to be – a brand owned by Hardys, albeit with a semi-autonomous existence; its wines all come from the best McLaren Vale vineyards owned by, or contracted to, Hardys, and the deliberately limited production ensures its wines are always good. Exports to the US, Canada, Europe and the Pacific Islands.

🍷🍷🍷🍷🍷 **McLaren Vale Shiraz 2013** Deeply coloured and perfectly proportioned, it declares its region, its variety, its open-fermented and basket-pressed upbringing right from the first whiff and sip. Well-handled oak is another plus. Because it is so balanced, most will be drunk before its glory days 30 years away. Screwcap. 14.5% alc. **Rating** 95 **To** 2045 $28 ✪
McLaren Vale Cabernet Sauvignon 2012 Elegance and McLaren Vale are not incompatible, or an oxymoron. Savoury/cedary/earthy blackcurrant fruit is the driver of this wine on the bouquet and palate alike, the tannins finely honed, the oak restrained. Open fermentation and basket-pressing have played a role in this, but so has the sheer quality of a beautiful Cabernet. Screwcap. 14% alc. **Rating** 95 **To** 2027 $28 ✪
McLaren Vale Cabernet Sauvignon 2013 Has an elegant medium to full-bodied palate with ultra-clear varietal expression largely free of McLaren Vale chocolate, leaving cedary tannins and a touch of cedary earth to provide complexity. Screwcap. 14% alc. **Rating** 94 **To** 2028 $28 ✪

Tintilla Wines ★★★★★

725 Hermitage Road, Pokolbin, NSW 2320 **Region** Hunter Valley
T (02) 6574 7093 **www.**tintilla.com.au **Open** 7 days 10.30–6
Winemaker James and Robert Lusby **Est.** 1993 **Dozens** 4000 **Vyds** 6.52ha
The Lusby family has established shiraz (2.2ha), sangiovese (1.6ha), merlot (1.3ha), semillon (1.2ha) and cabernet sauvignon (0.2ha) on a northeast-facing slope with red clay and limestone soil. Tintilla was the first winery to plant sangiovese in the Hunter Valley (in 1995). The family has also planted an olive grove producing four different types of olives, which are cured and sold from the estate.

🍷🍷🍷🍷🍷 **Patriarch Hunter Valley Syrah 2011** Night-harvested fruit was cold-stabilised (a technique used with white wine juice or wine, but seldom prior to fermentation of red must). Weird. However, 18 months in French and American oak has resulted in a supple, medium-bodied Shiraz showing the quality of the '11 vintage in all its glory; graceful and perfectly balanced, the red and black fruits have finely spun fruit and oak tannins in convincing support. Screwcap. 14% alc. **Rating** 96 **To** 2031 $60 ✪
Museum Release Angus Hunter Semillon 2007 Gleaming straw-green; still remarkably fresh, full of unsweetened lemon, lemongrass and minerally acidity; poised for another decade of development; great length and persistence. Screwcap. 10.5% alc. **Rating** 95 **To** 2025 $40
Pebbles Brief Hunter Valley Chardonnay 2013 The modern face of Hunter Valley Chardonnay, producing impressive varietal character; has abundant texture and structure to the array of grapefruit, white peach and melon fruit; the impact of barrel fermentation and maturation in French barriques is minimal. Screwcap. 13% alc. **Rating** 95 **To** 2020 $30 ✪

Reserve Hunter Valley Shiraz 2011 Has an identical nonsensical back label to its Patriarch sibling, and is very nearly as good. This is Hunter Valley Shiraz at its classic best, with a glorious display of faintly earthy/spicy red and black fruits, the texture exceptionally good, as are the length, line and overall balance. Screwcap. 14% alc. **Rating** 95 **To** 2031 $40

Angus Semillon 2013 Taut and focused; grown on red soil (unusual for semillon), but the '07 Angus Museum Release underlines the almost unlimited development potential; the one caveat is the unsweetened lemon juice acidity that may challenge some. Screwcap. 11.5% alc. **Rating** 94 **To** 2018 $30 ✪

Tobin Wines

34 Ricca Road, Ballandean, Qld 4382 **Region** Granite Belt
T (07) 4684 1235 **www.**tobinwines.com.au **Open** 7 days 10–5
Winemaker Adrian Tobin **Est.** 1964 **Dozens** 1500 **Vyds** 5.9ha

In the early 1960s the Ricca family planted table grapes, followed by shiraz and semillon in '64–66, which are said to be the oldest vinifera vines in the Granite Belt region. The Tobin family (headed by Adrian and Frances) purchased the vineyard in 2000 and has increased the plantings, which now consist of shiraz, cabernet sauvignon, merlot, tempranillo, semillon, verdelho, chardonnay, muscat and sauvignon blanc, with some remaining rows of table grapes. The emphasis has changed towards quality bottled wines, with considerable success, as the tasting notes show.

🍷🍷🍷🍷🍷 **Isabella Aged Semillon 2009** Almost no colour development; a remarkable wine, like the '14 Isabella – tasted in distinguished Hunter Valley company, and yielded nothing. Lemon zest, dried herbs and bracing acidity give it personality and length, soaring on the finish and aftertaste. Deserves its price. Screwcap. 11% alc. **Rating** 95 **To** 2024 $50

Isabella Semillon 2014 Tasted alongside some very good '14 Hunter Valley Semillons, this wine stood up remarkably well. It has clearly defined varietal character in a lemongrass and garden herb spectrum, the acidity exactly as it should be. This will cruise through the rest of the decade. Screwcap. 11.7% alc. **Rating** 94 **To** 2024 $28 ✪

Charlotte Sauvignon Blanc 2014 Barrel-fermented in what would appear to be used French oak, the wine has a presence and depth of flavour that belies its low alcohol; the faintly smoky aromas are backed up by snow pea, fresh-cut herbs and lemon zest flavours; the length and finish are also impressive. Screwcap. 11.6% alc. **Rating** 94 **To** 2015 $45

Elliot Merlot 2013 An interesting wine, with an unexpected depth and structure, blackcurrant and black olive setting the tone, tannins in support. Very well made, and I can see where the price comes from. Merits time in the cellar. Bottle no. 262 of 2700. Screwcap. 13.9% alc. **Rating** 94 **To** 2025 $45

🍷🍷🍷🍷🍷 **Max Shiraz Block Two 2013 Rating** 91 **To** 2023 $45
Max Shiraz Block One 2013 Rating 90 **To** 2020 $45

Tokar Estate

6 Maddens Lane, Coldstream, Vic 3770 **Region** Yarra Valley
T (03) 5964 9585 **www.**tokarestate.com.au **Open** 7 days 10.30–5
Winemaker Martin Siebert **Est.** 1996 **Dozens** 4000 **Vyds** 14ha

Leon Tokar established 14ha of now mature chardonnay, pinot noir, shiraz, cabernet sauvignon and tempranillo at Tokar Estate, one of many vineyards on Maddens Lane. All the wines have performed well in regional shows, with early success (and continued) for the Tempranillo, and very distinguished Cabernet Sauvignon.

🍷🍷🍷🍷🍷 **Yarra Valley Cabernet Sauvignon 2013** Trophy and gold medal winner on the Victorian show circuit, following in the footsteps of the highly successful '12. Picture-perfect example of Yarra Valley Cabernet. Olives and blackcurrant, green herbs and pencilly oak. Steadily approaching full-bodied. An impressive wine to say the least. Screwcap. 14.5% alc. **Rating** 96 **To** 2035 $33 CM ⊙

The Aria Tempranillo 2013 1600 bottles produced. Given a long maceration on skins before being matured for 15 months in all French, all new oak. It's a substantial, commanding wine, thick with berry and choc flavour and showing large bones of tannin. Floral aspects lend a prettiness to a wine that shows no signs of compromise. Screwcap. 14.5% alc. **Rating** 96 **To** 2028 $80 CM

Yarra Valley Chardonnay 2013 Exemplary. Similar to the '12, but with a greater level of complexity, mostly of the funk/struck match variety. Pear, grapefruit and bacon fat notes lead to a steely, minerally finish. Elegance and complexity but no shortage of raw power. Screwcap. 13.2% alc. **Rating** 95 **To** 2021 $33 CM ⊙

Yarra Valley Pinot Noir 2013 Gold medal Yarra Valley Wine Show '14. Fluid style, middle of the road, has some heft but not to any exaggerated degree, and generates appreciable perfume. Crushed leaves and cherry-plum flavours before a tangy finish. Rises to the occasion given the chance to breathe in the glass. Screwcap. 13.8% alc. **Rating** 94 **To** 2022 $28 CM ⊙

♀♀♀♀♀ **Yarra Valley Shiraz 2013** **Rating** 93 **To** 2025 $28 CM
Yarra Valley Rose 2014 **Rating** 90 **To** 2015 $25 CM
Yarra Valley Shiraz Cabernet 2013 **Rating** 90 **To** 2023 $28 CM

Tolpuddle Vineyard ★★★★★

37 Back Tea Tree Road, Richmond, Tas, 7025 **Region** Southern Tasmania
T (08) 8398 0500 **www.**tolpuddlevineyard.com **Open** At Shaw + Smith
Winemaker Martin Shaw, Adam Wadewitz **Est.** 1988 **Dozens** 1800 **Vyds** 20ha
If ever a new winery was born with blue blood in its veins, Tolpuddle would have to be it. The vineyard was established in 1988 on a magnificent continuous downhill slope facing northeast, and in '06 won the inaugural Tasmanian Vineyard of the Year Award. Michael Hill Smith MW and Martin Shaw are joint managing directors, with Matthew Hill Smith the third shareholder. David LeMire looks after sales and marketing; Adam Wadewitz, one of Australia's brightest winemaking talents, is senior winemaker; and Ray Guerin, one of Australia's most experienced viticulturists, with specialist expertise in cool-climate vineyards, is group viticulturist. Vineyard manager Carlos Souris loses nothing in comparison, with over 30 years of grapegrowing in Tasmania under his belt, and an absolutely fearless approach to making a great vineyard even greater. Exports to the US, the UK, Canada, Denmark, China, Japan and Singapore.

♀♀♀♀♀ **Chardonnay 2013** This label is certain to grace some of the greatest Aus Pinots and Chardonnays in the years ahead, the vineyard (planted in '88) a Tasmanian jewel. The most remarkable part of this wine is its combination of finesse, length and intensity of varietal fruit flavour, in turn based on the laser etching of Tasmanian acidity. Screwcap. 12.5% alc. **Rating** 97 **To** 2025 $65 ⊙

Pinot Noir 2013 Bright, clear crimson; the bouquet is at once powerful, yet eloquently varietal in precisely the same fashion as the palate; black cherry and plum lead the way, red fruits bringing up the rear; it has exceptional intensity and drive, with fine tannins reminiscent of those of top-flight Burgundy. Screwcap. 12.5% alc. **Rating** 97 **To** 2025 $75 ⊙

Tomboy Hill ★★★★★

204 Sim Street, Ballarat, Vic 3350 (postal) **Region** Ballarat
T (03) 5331 3785 **Open** Not
Winemaker Scott Ireland (Contract) **Est.** 1984 **Dozens** 700 **Vyds** 3.6ha
Former schoolteacher Ian Watson seems to be following the same path as Lindsay McCall of Paringa Estate (also a former schoolteacher) in extracting greater quality and style than any other winemaker in his region. Since 1984 Ian has slowly and patiently built up a patchwork quilt of small plantings of chardonnay and pinot noir. In the better years, single-vineyard

Chardonnay and/or Pinot Noir are released; Rebellion Chardonnay and Pinot Noir are multi-vineyard blends, but all 100% Ballarat. After difficult vintages in '11 and '12, Tomboy Hill returns in top form with the '13 wines, and Ian is equally happy with his '14s.

ΨΨΨΨΨ **William's Picking Ballarat Pinot Noir 2013** Not all that dark in colour but the palate certainly makes an impact. This is a Pinot Noir with flavours and textures flying everywhere. Meat, game, cherry-plum, sap and spearmint. Dry, spicy tannin draws back through the wine, almost forcing the flavours to linger. Firm, velvety and complex. It works very well now, but will be better again given a few years' sleep. Screwcap. 13% alc. **Rating** 95 **To** 2022 $75 CM

Rebellion Ballarat Goldfields Pinot Noir 2013 In excellent form. Maintains its shape beautifully as it rolls along your tongue. Tangy cherry and plum with foresty, spicy, meaty inputs. Both complex and acidic, but not in your face about either. Tannin is firm and confident, as is the wine as a whole. Screwcap. 12.8% alc. **Rating** 95 **To** 2021 $30 CM ✪

Rebellion Ballarat Goldfields Chardonnay 2013 High acidity but abundant perfume and flavour. Hits up with custard apple and lactose aroma before pouring a stream of spice, chalk, flowery apple, barley and lime through the palate. Smoulders through the finish; the motor of flavour keeps running long after you swallow. Screwcap. 12.5% alc. **Rating** 94 **To** 2019 $30 CM ✪

Tomfoolery   ★★★★★

517 Stockwell Road, Light Pass, SA 5355 **Region** Barossa
T 0447 947 782 **www.**tomfoolerywines.com.au **Open** By appt
Winemaker Ben Chipman **Est.** 2004 **Dozens** 6000 **Vyds** 6.5ha
The name of Ben Chipman and Toby Yap's business should not be taken at face value; the quality of the packaging is a better guide to the serious intent – and skills – of the partners. Each has a real job outside Tomfoolery, but not to the extent of preventing a serious approach to the making of the wines. All the right boxes are ticked for marketing to China and the US. Having commenced with 1 tonne of shiraz from the 2004 harvest, the range has now been extended to include Sauvignon Blanc, Pinot Gris, Cabernet Sauvignon, Cabernet Franc, Mataro, Tempranillo and Pinot Noir. Exports to the US and China.

ΨΨΨΨΨ **Black & Blue Barossa Shiraz 2013** Open-fermented, basket-pressed, and matured for 12 months in French barriques. A full-bodied, full-blooded single-vineyard Shiraz with luscious red and black fruits convincingly contrasted with fine-grained tannins; the overall balance and length are faultless. Screwcap. 14.5% alc. **Rating** 95 **To** 2038 $40

Son of a Gun Barossa Cabernet Sauvignon Shiraz 2013 The relative success of Cabernet Shiraz versus Bordeaux blends is largely due to the inadequacy of the merlot and cabernet franc, etc rather than the cabernet itself. This underlines the issue in bold letters: the luscious shiraz effortlessly joins the cabernet (itself no slouch) to provide a wine that ticks all the boxes. Screwcap. 14.5% alc. **Rating** 95 **To** 2033 $25 ✪

Burla Negra Barossa Tempranillo 2013 Deeply coloured and richly plumed, it pushes the alcohol envelope to just short of breaking point, which is very fortunate, because this is pure hedonism, its red cape looking for a bull to fight, or better still, eat. Screwcap. 14.8% alc. **Rating** 95 **To** 2028 $25 ✪

ΨΨΨΨΨ **Skullduggery Barossa Mataro Shiraz 2013** **Rating** 90 **To** 2030 $30

Tomich Wines   ★★★★☆

87 King William Road, Unley, SA 5061 **Region** Adelaide Hills
T (08) 8299 7500 **www.**tomichhill.com.au **Open** By appt
Winemaker John and Randal Tomich, Ben Riggs **Est.** 2002 **Dozens** 30 000 **Vyds** 130ha
Patriarch John Tomich was born on a vineyard near Mildura, where he learnt firsthand the skills and knowledge required for premium grapegrowing. He went on to become a well-known Adelaide ear, nose and throat specialist. Taking the wheel full circle, he completed

postgraduate studies in winemaking at the University of Adelaide in 2002, and embarked on the Master of Wine revision course from the Institute of Masters of Wine. His son Randal is a cutting from the old vine (metaphorically speaking), having invented new equipment and techniques for tending the family's vineyard in the Adelaide Hills, resulting in a 60% saving in time and fuel costs. Exports to the US, Europe, Hong Kong, Singapore and China.

ŶŶŶŶŶ **Woodside Vineyard Adelaide Hills Sauvignon Blanc 2014** A particularly engaging Sauvignon Blanc, with a rainbow of gently sweet tropical and stone fruit aromas and flavours, keeping the palate fresh, juicy and lively. Hard to resist a wine like this. Screwcap. 12.5% alc. **Rating** 95 **To** 2016 $25 ✪

Woodside Vineyard Adelaide Hills Gruner Veltliner 2014 If you repeatedly swirl the glass for the bouquet, white pepper appears there as well as on the ultra-fresh, crisp and lively palate; it has a delicacy that also translates as an urgency, and the wine will mature every bit as well as a Riesling. Screwcap. 12.5% alc. **Rating** 94 **To** 2020 $25 ✪

Woodside Park Vineyards Adelaide Hills Gruner Veltliner 2013 Nearly identical to Tomich Woodside Vineyard Gruner Veltliner, except that this has greater weight and richness, reflecting its slightly higher alcohol. I'm not sure this doesn't work even better with its juicy fruit, but it's a line call. Screwcap. 13% alc. **Rating** 94 **To** 2020 $20 ✪

ŶŶŶŶŶ **Wing and a Prayer Sauvignon Blanc 2014 Rating** 93 **To** 2015 $20 ✪
Rhyme and Reason Pinot Grigio 2014 Rating 91 **To** 2015 $20 ✪
Woodside Vineyard Pinot Grigio 2014 Rating 90 **To** 2015 $25
Up & Away Adelaide Hills Rose 2014 Rating 90 **To** 2015 $20 ✪
Woodside Park Vineyards Adelaide Hills Chardonnay Pinot Noir NV Rating 90 **To** 2018 $20 ✪

Toolangi Vineyards   ★★★★★

PO Box 9431, South Yarra, Vic 3141 **Region** Yarra Valley
T (03) 9827 9977 **www**.toolangi.com **Open** By appt
Winemaker Various contract **Est.** 1995 **Dozens** 8000 **Vyds** 12.2ha
Garry and Julie Hounsell acquired their property in the Dixons Creek area of the Yarra Valley, adjoining the Toolangi State Forest, in 1995. The primary accent is on pinot noir and chardonnay, accounting for all but 2.7ha, which is predominantly shiraz and a little viognier. Winemaking is by Yering Station (Willy Lunn), Giaconda (Rick Kinzbrunner), Hoddles Creek Estate (Franco D'Anna) and Oakridge (David Bicknell), as impressive a quartet of winemakers as one could wish for. Exports to the UK, Hong Kong, Singapore, Japan and China.

ŶŶŶŶŶ **Pauls Lane Yarra Valley Pinot Noir 2013** Estate-grown, hand-picked, and made at Hoddles Creek Estate; matured in French oak barriques for 10 months. Exemplary colour; the fragrant, lightly spiced bouquet leads into a palate that has what the French call nervosity, an almost three-dimensional combination of tactile and flavour characters that are woven together to provide exceptional energy and length. Screwcap. 13.5% alc. **Rating** 97 **To** 2028 $42 ✪

ŶŶŶŶŶ **Estate Yarra Valley Chardonnay 2013** Estate-grown, made at Oakridge Estate, and matured in French oak for 11 months; fine and elegant, the wine has the length and finesse that comes in large measure from the vineyard, but also has the unmistakable thumbprint of David Bicknell in the guise of the complex bouquet. Screwcap. 13.5% alc. **Rating** 96 **To** 2028 $38 ✪

Yarra Valley Chardonnay 2013 Estate-grown; made at Yering Station and matured in French oak for 11 months. Classic Yarra Valley Chardonnay, with great length and depth; white peach and nectarine fruit fill the mouth, but the acidity cuts short any tendency to go over the top, the oak also contributing to the structure. Screwcap. 13.8% alc. **Rating** 95 **To** 2025 $26 ✪

Estate Yarra Valley Pinot Noir 2013 From low-cropped estate vines; made at Oakridge Estate by David Bicknell, it was matured in French oak for 11 months; it creeps up on you, elegantly insistent each time it is smelt and tasted, every part of the fruit, oak and tannins precisely locked in step with each other. Screwcap. 14% alc. **Rating** 95 **To** 2023 $38

Yarra Valley Pinot Noir 2013 Part estate-grown, part from a vineyard in Yarra Glen. Made at Yering Station, and matured in French oak for 12 months. Has excellent colour, clear and deep; silky and supple, its varietal expression is flawless, as are its balance and length. Screwcap. 13.5% alc. **Rating** 95 **To** 2023 $26 ✪

Pauls Lane Yarra Valley Shiraz 2013 Made at Coldstream Hills and at Hoddles Creek Estate, where it was blended and bottled after 18 months in French oak; the colour is deep, the palate with considerable presence and complexity, its savoury assemblage of red and black cherry fruits and supporting tannins providing a mouth-watering finish and aftertaste. Screwcap. 13.8% alc. **Rating** 95 **To** 2038 $38

Toorak Winery ★★★☆

Vineyard 279 Toorak Road, Leeton, NSW 2705 **Region** Riverina
T (02) 6953 2333 **www**.toorakwines.com.au **Open** Mon–Fri 10–5, w'ends by appt
Winemaker Robert Bruno **Est.** 1965 **Dozens** 200000 **Vyds** 145ha

A traditional, long-established Riverina producer with a strong Italian-based clientele around Australia. Production has increased significantly, utilising substantial estate plantings and grapes purchased from other growers in the Riverina and elsewhere. Wines are released under the Toorak Estate, Willandra Estate, Amesbury Estate and Wirrabilla Estate labels. While in absolute terms the quality is not great, the low-priced wines in fact over-deliver in many instances. Exports to the US, Norway, Russia, Nigeria, India, Singapore, Guam, Papua New Guinea, the Philippines, Japan and China.

🍷🍷🍷🍷🍷 **Willandra Estate Reserve Langhorne Creek Shiraz 2013** Rich, loose, easy-access flavour. The tracksuit pants of wine: comfortable, no pretension, for everyday use. Blackberries and black jelly beans. A semblance of shape to the finish. Pretty well done, in its style. Screwcap. 14% alc. **Rating** 90 **To** 2019 $25 CM

Top Note ★★★★

546 Peters Creek Road, Kuitpo, SA 5172 **Region** Adelaide Hills
T 0406 291 136 **www**.topnote.com.au **Open** By appt
Winemaker Nick Foskett **Est.** 2011 **Dozens** 200 **Vyds** 17ha

Computer chip designer Nick and opera singer Cate Foskett were looking for a lifestyle property in the Adelaide Hills after full-on careers in their very different occupations. By chance they came across a 24ha property planted to five varieties, all mainstream except for 0.5ha of a rare mutation of semillon turning the skin red. They say, 'Despite the small hurdles of our not knowing much about anything and none of the grapes being under contract, we sold our city house, enrolled in postgraduate viticulture and winemaking at the Waite Campus, University of Adelaide, and became grapegrowers.' Two years on, Cate became possibly the only qualified operatic viticulturist in the world, and still works as a singer between harvests, managing the vineyard and sales. Nick has continued winemaking studies and they will be expanding the make to five wines; currently they produce a rose from the rare red semillon and a Pinot Noir. Further down the rainbow is an idea to build a micro-winery onsite, convert their cottage to a cellar door, and hold music and food functions.

🍷🍷🍷🍷🍷 **Adelaide Hills Pinot Noir 2013** Clones G8V3, MV6 and D4V2; destemmed to open fermenters for a 2-day cold soak, then 8 days' fermentation and post-ferment maceration; matured 10 months in French oak (40% new). Deep crimson-purple, this is (in Pinot terms) a medium to full-bodied wine, with plum and black cherry fruit staying within the bounds of varietal expression. Smart packaging is a plus. Screwcap. 13% alc. **Rating** 91 **To** 2020 $35

Topper's Mountain Wines ★★★★

5km Guyra Road, Tingha, NSW 2369 **Region** New England
T 0411 880 580 **www**.toppers.com.au **Open** By appt
Winemaker Mike Hayes **Est.** 2000 **Dozens** 1700 **Vyds** 9.79ha

Following a partnership dissolution, Topper's Mountain is now solely owned by Mark Kirkby. Planting began in the spring of 2000, with the ultimate fruit salad trial of 15 rows each of innumerable varieties and clones. The total area planted was made up of 28 separate plantings, many of these with only 200 vines in a block. As varieties proved unsuited, they were grafted over to those that held the most promise. Thus far, Gewurztraminer and Sauvignon Blanc hold most promise among the white wines, the Mediterranean reds doing better than their French cousins. The original 28 varieties are now down to 16; chardonnay, gewurztraminer, sauvignon blanc, tempranillo, shiraz and merlot are the commercial varieties, the remainder in the fruit salad block still under evaluation. Integrated pest management has been successfully adopted throughout the vineyard.

New England Gewurztraminer 2014 All the flavour and aroma and yet remarkably elegant. The rosewater and musk notes here are almost lollied, though lychee and talc notes do their best to create a more restrained, or textural impression. Nothing gathers or tugs; everything is ironed and pristine here. Screwcap. 12.6% alc. **Rating** 92 **To** 2016 $35 CM

Barrel Ferment New England Gewurztraminer 2014 The oak works, but whether or not it was necessary is another thing. It makes for a heavier wine, arguably with another dimension of flavour but with slightly less elegant presentation. Musk, lychee, oak-spice and rosewater. It's very well made and very good, though the non-wood version is better drinking. Screwcap. 12.7% alc. **Rating** 92 **To** 2016 $35 CM

Barrel Ferment New England Sauvignon Blanc 2014 Fruit intensity is impressive, texture has been softened by the influence of oak, and the finish has a convincing ring. This is in a good place, and will keep most drinkers entertained. Screwcap. 11.9% alc. **Rating** 92 **To** 2017 $35 CM

Red Earth Child 2012 This year's blend is made up of tempranillo, tannat, nebbiolo and barbera. It's one of those wines that builds power beyond its weight; the flavours gather speed and force without seeming to pedal all that hard. Juicy acidity, a variety of berry flavours, floral inputs and both smoky, reductive notes and spice. Many different forces produce a single delicious impression. Screwcap. 13.9% alc. **Rating** 92 **To** 2021 $38 CM

Bricolage Blanc 2014 It's a white wine with plenty of attitude. Turkish delight notes flood both the nose and the palate, with rose petals, honeysuckle and pear flavours fleshing things out from there. The alcohol is low but the flavours are heady. Searing acidity shoots out through the finish. It won't go quietly, that's for sure. Screwcap. 12.9% alc. **Rating** 90 **To** 2016 $35 CM

Wild Ferment New England Barbera 2012 **Rating** 89 **To** 2019 $32 CM
New England Nebbiolo 2012 **Rating** 88 **To** 2022 $38 CM
New England Tannat 2012 **Rating** 88 **To** 2020 $32 CM

Torbreck Vintners   ★★★★★

Roennfeldt Road, Marananga, SA 5352 **Region** Barossa Valley
T (08) 8562 4155 **www.torbreck.com** **Open** 7 days 10–6
Winemaker Craig Isbel, Scott McDonald **Est.** 1994 **Dozens** 70 000 **Vyds** 86ha
Torbreck Vintners was already one of Australia's best-known high-quality red wine makers when, in Sept 2013, it gained further headlines for all of the wrong reasons. Although it had not been widely known, wealthy Californian entrepreneur and vintner Peter Kight (of Quivira Vineyards) had acquired 100% ownership of the Torbreck business. There was a highly acrimonious and public parting of the ways between Torbreck founder David Powell and Peter Kight. It serves no useful purpose to detail the accusations and counteraccusations, most of which in any event bore no relevance to the quality of the wines. The winemaking team headed by Craig Isbel, supported by Scott McDonald and Russell Burns, all in place for some years, will continue to make the wines. The brand structure remains as before: the top quartet led by The Laird (single-vineyard Shiraz), RunRig (Shiraz/Viognier), The Factor (Shiraz) and Descendant (Shiraz/Viognier); next The Struie (Shiraz) and The Steading (Grenache/Mataro/Shiraz). Exports to all major markets.

ŸŸŸŸŸ **The Loon 2013** A Rhône-inspired blend of shiraz and roussanne, but no indication whether co-fermented. There is plenty of energy and drive to the mix of black fruits and licorice flavours; no issues with the alcohol. Screwcap. 15% alc. **Rating** 95 **To** 2028 $30 ✪

Cuvee Juveniles 2013 Despite the name, this is a blend of old-vine grapes (grenache, shiraz and mataro). Bright crimson-purple; the palate is full-bodied, but supple and smooth, plum, blackberry, cherry, spice and licorice all in the frame provided by the tannins. Screwcap. 15% alc. **Rating** 95 **To** 2028 $25 ✪

Woodcutter's Barossa Valley Shiraz 2013 Part estate, part contract-grown. Strongly coloured, this has more grunt and depth than some of its predecessors, with savoury black fruits occupying centre stage, ripe tannins stationed in the wings to block any escape. Screwcap. 15% alc. **Rating** 94 **To** 2028 $25 ✪

The Factor 2012 Matured for 2 years in predominantly older oak. Torbreck is one of the arch high priests of the thunderous alcohol school. This is nothing to do with the departure of former winemaker David Powell, and doesn't reflect my personal opinion of the style, which has its adherents; within its idiom it is imposing. Shiraz. Cork. 15.5% alc. **Rating** 94 **To** 2032 $125

Les Amis 2012 A sprawling giant of a Grenache, the density of the fruit reflecting low-yielding old vines and an extractive approach in the winery. Very difficult to give points for a polarising wine such as this – my points are devoid of personal preference. Cork. 15.5% alc. **Rating** 94 **To** 2032 $188

The Steading 2013 A blend of renache, mataro and shiraz. Predictably complex and mouth-filling; the grenache has been overwhelmed by the impact of the mataro and shiraz, licorice, tar and earth coming to the fore, coupled with tannins and alcohol. Give it time. Screwcap. 15.5% alc. **Rating** 94 **To** 2033 $38

ŸŸŸŸŸ **The Steading Blanc 2013 Rating** 91 **To** 2019 $38
Descendant 2012 Rating 90 **To** 2025 $125

Torzi Matthews Vintners ★★★★

Cnr Eden Valley Road/Sugarloaf Hill Road, Mt McKenzie, SA 5353 **Region** Eden Valley **T** 0412 323 486 **www.torzimatthews.com.au Open** By appt
Winemaker Domenic Torzi **Est.** 1996 **Dozens** 3000 **Vyds** 10ha

Domenic Torzi and Tracy Matthews, former Adelaide Plains residents, searched for a number of years before finding a block at Mt McKenzie in the Eden Valley. The block they chose is in a hollow; the soil is meagre, and they were in no way deterred by the knowledge that it would be frost-prone. The result is predictably low yields, concentrated further by drying the grapes on rack, thus reducing the weight by around 30% (the Appassimento method is used in Italy to produce Amarone-style wines). Newer plantings of sangiovese and negro amaro, and an extension of the original plantings of shiraz and riesling, have seen the wine range increase. Exports to the UK and Denmark.

ŸŸŸŸŸ **1903 Single Vineyard of Domenico Martino Shiraz Grenache Mourvedre 2012** From a vineyard planted in 1903 on Moppa Hill. Tidy price in that context. It tastes as much of smoke and mineral as it does of cherry, fennel and dark, spicy blackberry. Oak plays a secondary role at most. Earthen savouriness rises appreciably through the finish. Much to appreciate here. Screwcap. 14.2% alc. **Rating** 94 **To** 2023 $35 CM

ŸŸŸŸŸ **Schist Rock Eden Valley Shiraz 2013 Rating** 92 **To** 2022 $20 CM ✪

Totino Estate ★★★★

982 Port Road, Albert Park, SA 5014 (postal) **Region** Adelaide Hills
T (08) 8349 1200 **www.totinowines.com.au Open** Not
Winemaker Damien Harris **Est.** 1992 **Dozens** 15 000 **Vyds** 29ha

Don Totino migrated from Italy in 1968, and at the age of 18 became the youngest barber in Australia. He soon moved on, into general food and importing and distribution. Festival City, as the business is known, has been highly successful, recognised by a recent significant award from the Italian government. In 1998 he purchased a rundown vineyard at Paracombe in the Adelaide Hills, since extending the plantings to 29ha of chardonnay, pinot grigio, sauvignon blanc, sangiovese and shiraz. Various family members, including daughter Linda, are involved in the business. Exports to Italy and China.

ŶŶŶŶŶ **Adelaide Hills Pinot Grigio 2014** Chalky texture, apple-like flavour, hints of spice and a textural, satisfying finish. Everything is in excellent order here. Screwcap. 12% alc. **Rating** 93 **To** 2015 $19 CM ✪

SSC Adelaide Hills Sangiovese Shiraz Cabernet 2012 Savoury-accented, but there's plenty of fruit to tuck into here. Beautifully balanced all round. Black cherry, fresh leather, peppercorns and black pepper itself. Light to mid-weight but succulent. It almost demands that you pour yourself another glass. Screwcap. 13% alc. **Rating** 92 **To** 2019 $20 CM ✪

Sangiovese Rose 2013 Chewy aspect is a clear positive. This has the lunch/dining table written all over it. Red cherries, raspberries and ample savoury spice. Smells and tastes delicious. Screwcap. 12% alc. **Rating** 91 **To** 2016 $18 CM ✪

Adelaide Hills Shiraz 2013 Gets it pretty right. Full-bodied, more so than you might expect of Adelaide Hills Shiraz, with bitumen, black cherry and ripe, sweet plum flavours swooping through the palate. Woody spice is here in good measure too, as is a clip of clovey oak. Tannin is firm but it's drinking well already. Screwcap. 14% alc. **Rating** 91 **To** 2020 $22 CM ✪

Sauvignon Blanc 2014 Clean as a whistle. Fresh, crisp and flavoursome enough. Passionfruit and sweet pea notes. Mid-weight but gets the job done in uncomplicated fashion. Screwcap. 12% alc. **Rating** 90 **To** 2015 $19 CM ✪

Reserve Adelaide Hills Shiraz 2012 Balls with ripe, plummy, toasty flavour. A 'more is better' kind of wine. It has general appeal because of its exaggerated serving size of fruit, but the diamond has been left largely uncut/unpolished here. Cork. 14.5% alc. **Rating** 90 **To** 2020 $30 CM

ŶŶŶŶ **Alexia Sparkling Blush Cuvee NV** **Rating** 89 **To** 2016 $19 TS ✪

Towerhill Estate ★★★★☆

RMB 501 Albany Highway, Kojonup, WA 6395 (postal) **Region** Mount Barker
T (08) 9831 0693 **www.towerhillwine.com.au** **Open** Not
Winemaker Mike Garland **Est.** 1993 **Dozens** 420 **Vyds** 5ha
Towerhill Estate was established in 1993 by the Williams family, who began the planting of the (now) 5ha vineyard of cabernet sauvignon, merlot, riesling and chardonnay. The venture was acquired by former sheep farmer Julian Hanna in 2007; he runs the estate vineyard in partnership with Leith Schmidt. The first vintage was in '08, its Riesling from that year winning the Best Riesling trophy at the Perth Wine Show '12, yet another testament to the skills of Robert Diletti at Castle Rock Estate. Since then winemaking has shifted to the nearer Mount Shadforth contract winemaking facility run by Mike Garland and Andrew Hoadley. A somewhat unusual policy sees their wines held back for release when mature. Exports to Singapore.

ŶŶŶŶŶ **Dry Riesling 2012** Some colour development, but it's a good straw-green hue; the flavours are in the same arc, the citrus with greater depth than the younger wines – again, as it should be. Screwcap. 13% alc. **Rating** 95 **To** 2022 $29 ✪

Dry Riesling 2013 Significantly tighter, crisper and finer than the '14 Riesling Royale, with a stony minerality underpinning the citrus and apple fruit flavours on the long palate. Screwcap. 12% alc. **Rating** 94 **To** 2023 $27 ✪

Dry Riesling 2010 Bright straw-green; at 5yo has reached the edge of the plateau ahead, full to the brim with ripe citrus fruits, plus a touch of honey; the acidity operates as a minor brake on the tumultuous fruit. Screwcap. 12.9% alc. **Rating** 94 **To** 2020 $35

ŶŶŶŶŶ **Mount Barker Cabernet Merlot 2012** **Rating** 92 **To** 2032 $37
Mount Barker Riesling Royale 2014 **Rating** 91 **To** 2017 $27

Tractorless Vineyard ★★★

12587 Hume Highway, Sutton Forest, NSW 2577 **Region** Southern Highlands
T (02) 4858 1788 **www**.tractorlessvineyard.com.au **Open** 7 days 10–4
Winemaker Jeff Aston, Mark Bourne **Est.** 2013 **Dozens** NFP **Vyds** 12ha
The winery name puts the philosophy of winemakers and owners Jeff Aston and Mark Bourne in high relief. All of the vineyard work is now done in accordance with biodynamic practices (but, it would seem, without certification so far), in particular involving the integration of intensive cell grazing of sheep in the growing season. This means the elimination of weed control and mid-row grass management, at the same time producing 100% grass-fed lamb. It has to be said that the Southern Highlands' temperamental summer weather will provide challenges for biodynamic management in wet vintages.

ŸŸŸŸ **Riesling 2013** Although the label simply says 'Wine of Australia', it in fact comes from the Southern Highlands of NSW; it has enjoyable lime juice flavours before wandering a little on the finish. Screwcap. 12.5% alc. **Rating** 89 **To** 2018 $30
Pinot Gris 2013 Offers some gris complexity with its full-flavoured palate, raising the question of possible oak use somewhere in the mix; lees and even mlf are other possibilities. Screwcap. 13.5% alc. **Rating** 89 **To** 2015 $30

Train Trak ★★★★

957 Healesville–Yarra Glen Road, Yarra Glen, Vic 3775 **Region** Yarra Valley
T (03) 9730 1314 **www**.traintrak.com.au **Open** Wed–Sun 10–5
Winemaker Robert Paul (Contract) **Est.** 1995 **Dozens** 1800 **Vyds** 16ha
The unusual name comes from the Yarra Glen to Healesville railway, which was built in 1889 and abandoned in 1980 – part of it passes by the Train Trak vineyard. The vineyard is planted (in descending order) to pinot noir, cabernet sauvignon, chardonnay and shiraz. Zonzo's restaurant makes exceptional pizzas in a wood-fired oven. Exports to Canada, the Pacific Islands, China and Japan.

ŸŸŸŸ⧸ **Yarra Valley Pinot Noir 2013** Dry and spicy with smoky cherry-plum flavours fleshing out the palate. High tension, and not much comic relief; all the components are pedalling furiously. It should drink well given a year or two to mellow. Screwcap. 13% alc. **Rating** 90 **To** 2020 $30 CM

Trapeze ★★★★☆

2130 Kinglake Road, St Andrews, Vic 3761 (postal) **Region** Yarra Valley
T (03) 9710 1155 **Open** Not
Winemaker James Lance, Brian Conway **Est.** 2011 **Dozens** 900
This is the venture of friends James Lance (Punch) and Brian Conway (Izway Wines). While James is firmly attached to the Yarra Valley, Brian divides his time between the Barossa Valley and Melbourne, having made wine from the Rhône varietals for many years. He wanted to tackle the Burgundy varieties but realised this was not going to happen just because he felt the need; thus the partnership came about, extended with Chardonnay from 2013.

ŸŸŸŸŸ **Yarra Valley Pinot Noir 2013** Hand-picked, wild yeast-fermented, not fined or filtered. Bright, full purple-crimson; a picture of the richness of pinot noir in '13, improbably enough a better vintage than '12, and certain to be longer-lived; engorged with dark cherry and plum, yet retains balance and finesse; the tannins are likewise present, but perfectly pitched, oak having done its job. Screwcap. 13.5% alc. Rating 96 **To** 2025 $32 **○**
Chardonnay 2013 It's a wine that seems to wake and slowly stretch itself out as it rests in the glass. It's not in any hurry. Slatey, spicy, spliced with flavours of pear and citrus, given gravitas by grapefruit and toasty oak. Will be better in a couple of years, but an impeccable release. Screwcap. 13.5% alc. **Rating** 94 **To** 2020 $28 CM **○**

Travertine Wines

78 Old North Road, Pokolbin, NSW 2320 **Region** Hunter Valley
T (02) 6574 7329 **www**.travertinewines.com.au **Open** Wed–Sun 10–4
Winemaker Liz Jackson **Est.** 1988 **Dozens** 3000 **Vyds** 10.73ha
This is the reincarnation of Pendarves Estate, originally planted by medico-cum-wine historian-cum-wine health activist Dr Phillip Norrie. It was purchased by Graham Burns in January 2008, and vineyard manager Chris Dibley, who had previously worked in the vineyard, was brought back to 'get the place back up to scratch'. There is a Joseph's coat of plantings including pinot noir (2.35ha), verdelho (2.25ha), chardonnay (1.25ha) and chambourcin (1.7ha), and lesser plantings of tannat, semillon, shiraz and merlot.

ŶŶŶŶŶ **Hunter Valley Fiano 2014** Matured on lees in old oak. Soft-centred but remains fruit-driven. Pineapple, apple and pear notes, crisp and clean, with a wash of musk through the finish. Screwcap. 13.3% alc. **Rating** 90 **To** 2015 $25 CM

ŶŶŶŶ **Hunter Valley Sauvignon Blanc 2014** **Rating** 89 **To** 2015 $20 CM
Hunter Valley Chardonnay 2013 **Rating** 89 **To** 2017 $25 CM

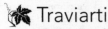Traviarti

39 Elgin Road, Beechworth, Vic 3747 **Region** Beechworth
T 0439 994 075 **www**.traviarti.com **Open** By appt
Winemaker Daniel Balzer, Simon Grant **Est.** 2011 **Dozens** 400 **Vyds** 0.43ha
After 15 years in the wine trade, first as a buyer in retail, followed by sales and marketing roles for producers, Simon Grant and partner Helen Murray spent several years looking for the right place to grow nebbiolo, the wine which had the greatest appeal for them. When they moved to Beechworth to run a grapegrowers' co-operative, they found the site and planted both nebbiolo and tempranillo in 2011. At around 600m on the red decomposed shale and mudstone soils just above the town of Beechworth, they have planted multiple clones on a combination of rootstocks and their own roots. In the meantime, and until these vines come into bearing, they have sourced cabernet sauvignon from Mark Walpole's Beechworth vineyard.

ŶŶŶŶŶ **Beechworth Cabernet Sauvignon 2013** First commercial release. Grown on the Fighting Gully Vineyard. It's a polished wine with no lack of flavour. Peanut and blackcurrant with the succulence of black cherry. Swings refreshingly through the palate, confident but at ease. A drinking Cabernet, almost luncheon in style. Screwcap. 13.8% alc. **Rating** 93 **To** 2024 $30 CM

Trellis ★★★★★

Valley Farm Road, Healesville, Vic 3777 **Region** Yarra Valley
T (03) 5962 5723 **www**.trelliswines.com.au **Open** By appt
Winemaker Luke Houlihan **Est.** 2007 **Dozens** 1000 **Vyds** 3.2ha
This is the venture of winemaker Luke Houlihan and viticulturist Greg Dunnett. Luke was formerly winemaker at Yarra Ridge and Long Gully Estate, and Greg owns Valley Farm Vineyard. The pinot noir has had several distinguished purchasers over the years, and there has never been any doubt about the quality of the fruit, which is from the dry-grown vines.

ŶŶŶŶŶ **Yarra Valley Chardonnay 2013** The Upper Yarra Valley has a special relationship with chardonnay, magnifying (in the best sense) the character of most (not all) Lower Yarra chardonnay; here the difference is the higher natural acidity giving a breath of mineral, and an extra dimension of high notes to the bouquet, and pure-bred white peach fruit. Screwcap. 12.8% alc. **Rating** 95 **To** 2023 $35 ✪

ŶŶŶŶŶ **Yarra Valley Chardonnay 2014** **Rating** 92 **To** 2020 $35
Yarra Valley Pinot Noir 2013 **Rating** 91 **To** 2020 $35
Heathcote Syrah 2014 **Rating** 90 **To** 2024 $35

Trentham Estate

Sturt Highway, Trentham Cliffs, NSW 2738 **Region** Murray Darling
T (03) 5024 8888 **www.**trenthamestate.com.au **Open** 7 days 9.30–5
Winemaker Anthony Murphy, Shane Kerr **Est.** 1988 **Dozens** 70000 **Vyds** 49.9ha
Remarkably consistent tasting notes across all wine styles from all vintages attest to the expertise of ex-Mildara winemaker Tony Murphy, a well-known and highly regarded producer, with estate vineyards on the Murray–Darling. With an eye to the future, but also to broadening the range of the wines on offer, Trentham Estate is selectively buying grapes from other regions with a track record for the chosen varieties. The value for money is unfailingly excellent. Exports to the UK, China and other major markets.

ΨΨΨΨΨ **Family Reserve Tasmania Pinot Noir 2013** That Tony Murphy magic is on full display here: first, finding the grapes; second, handling them with such skill; and third, managing to sell the wine at this price. The fragrant bouquet is flooded with red fruits, the supple and satisfying palate finishing with a trumpet of darker fruit, integrated French oak, and perfectly weighted spicy acidity. Screwcap. 13.5% alc. Rating 95 To 2023 $26 ✪

Family Reserve Chardonnay 2013 Another seriously good wine from Trentham, joining the Family Reserve Tasmania Pinot Noir. This is equally sensitively made, with perfect balance between acidity (can be an issue in Tas) and beautifully defined white peach and nectarine fruit, barrel-ferment oak kept in appropriate restraint. Excellent value. Screwcap. 13% alc. **Rating** 94 **To** 2020 $26 ✪

La Famiglia Sangiovese Rose 2014 Rose hips/petals light the bouquet; the palate is a rarely encountered essay in purity: dry, yet definitely – if delicately – fruity. This is one way to perfection (in rose terms), the other way is barrel fermentation, which is radically different and more expensive and, of course, more complex. Screwcap. 11.5% alc. **Rating** 94 **To** 2016 $15 ✪

ΨΨΨΨΩ **Estate Verdejo 2014 Rating** 90 **To** 2015 $16 CM ✪
Estate Shiraz 2013 Rating 90 **To** 2018 $16 CM ✪

Trevelen Farm

506 Weir Road, Cranbrook, WA 6321 **Region** Great Southern
T (08) 9826 1052 **www.**trevelenfarm.com.au **Open** By appt
Winemaker Harewood Estate (James Kellie) **Est.** 1993 **Dozens** 3000 **Vyds** 6.5ha
In 2008 John and Katie Sprigg decided to pass ownership of their 1300ha wool, meat and grain-producing farm to son Ben and wife Louise. However, they have kept control of the 6.5ha of sauvignon blanc, riesling, chardonnay, cabernet sauvignon and merlot planted in 1993. When demand requires, they increase production by purchasing grapes from growers in the Frankland River subregion. Riesling will remain the centrepiece of the range. Exports to the US, Japan and China.

ΨΨΨΨΨ **Riesling 2014** Bright, gleaming quartz-green, it throws down the gauntlet to SA; while it is awash with fused lime/lemon/apple flavours, there is a steely backbone of finely detailed acidity that will hold the wine together for 20 years or more. Screwcap. 12% alc. **Rating** 96 **To** 2034 $25 ✪

Frankland Reserve Merlot 2011 This is from the big end of town, full-bodied and with layers of blackcurrant fruit wreathed in tannins. It is nowhere near ready for drinking, but given 5+ years it could spring a major surprise, and continue doing so thereafter. Screwcap. 14.5% alc. **Rating** 94 **To** 2031 $23 ✪

The Tunney Cabernet Sauvignon 2011 An unusual Cabernet, with spice, mocha, chocolate and blackcurrant whirling dervishes on the bouquet and palate; yet all up it is no more than medium-bodied; the cassis that comes through on the finish gets a major tick. Screwcap. 14.5% alc. **Rating** 94 **To** 2029 $25 ✪

ΨΨΨΨΩ **Katie's Kiss Riesling 2014 Rating** 92 **To** 2024 $16 ✪
Sauvignon Blanc Semillon 2014 Rating 90 **To** 2016 $16 ✪

Trevor Jones Fine Wines ★★★★☆

173 Jollytown Road, Lyndoch, SA 5351 **Region** Barossa Valley
T 0417 869 981 **www**.trevorjonesfinewines.com.au **Open** By appt
Winemaker Trevor Jones **Est.** 1998 **Dozens** 4000 **Vyds** 5ha
The Trevor Jones and Kellermeister brands were for many years linked by family ties. Up to 2010 Trevor Jones (the person) was winemaker and production manager for Kellermeister, but he has left to concentrate on the eponymous business owned by himself and wife Mandy. With 35 years' winemaking experience, he is also providing consultancy advice to wineries in the Barossa. In April '15 he was charged by police with wilful damage to Kellermeister's wines then in tank by opening the valves, thus emptying the contents into drains leading from the winery. The prosecution presented CCTV footage showing Jones in the act. A tragedy for all concerned. The winery rating simply reflects the tasting notes made before the event. Exports to the US, Switzerland and Japan.

♥♥♥♥♥ **Belle-Terroir Sorciere Sauvage 2012** Sorciere Sauvage is the single vineyard from which Trevor Jones has been buying fruit for 20 years. Prolonged fermentation and maceration on skins was followed by 2 years in new French hogsheads. The sheer intensity and length of the flavour is awesome. Counterintuitively, it is not impacted by the alcohol, or, for that matter, the oak; instead there is the most delicious mouth-filling array of silky, supple shiraz fruit flavours. WAK screwcap. 15% alc. **Rating** 97 **To** 2042 $60 ❂

♥♥♥♥♥ **Epernay Vineyard Dry Grown Shiraz 2013** Heart of darkness. Intense, inky, slinky smooth fruit, slightly jammy but lively with raspberry, tar, black jelly bean and blackberry flavour, and coated with a seductive slide of spicy, coffeed oak. It sounds over the top but it isn't; it works, and it's fundamentally delicious. Screwcap. 15% alc. **Rating** 94 **To** 2030 $25 CM ❂
Epernay Vineyard Dry Grown GSM 2013 The power, the flesh, the sweet ooze of flavour. This wine will leave no one in two minds. It's intense with raspberry and jubey blackberry, the veneer of sawdusty, resiny oak giving it a high-gloss feel. Alcohol is accommodated more or less easily. This is a wine for both lovers of this blend and for GSM-doubters. Screwcap. 15.5% alc. **Rating** 94 **To** 2030 $20 CM ❂

♥♥♥♥♡ **Eriksen's Reserve Shiraz 2013 Rating** 92 **To** 2028 $55 CM
Dry Grown Shiraz Cabernet 2012 Rating 92 **To** 2021 $20 CM ❂
Celestial Riesling 2014 Rating 90 **To** 2020 $20 CM ❂

Truffle & Wine Co ★★★★☆

Seven Day Road, Manjimup, WA 6248 **Region** Pemberton
T (08) 9777 2474 **www**.truffleandwine.com.au **Open** 7 days 10–4
Winemaker Mark Aitken, Ben Haines **Est.** 1997 **Dozens** 4700 **Vyds** 10ha
Owned by a group of investors from various parts of Australia who have successfully achieved their vision of producing fine wines and black truffles. The winemaking side is under the care of Mark Aitken, who, having graduated as dux of his class in applied science at Curtin University in 2000, joined Chestnut Grove as winemaker in '02. The truffle side of the business is run under the direction of Harry Eslick, with 13000 truffle-inoculated hazelnut and oak trees on the property. Truffle Hill is now the premium label for a range of wines that is sold domestically; the Truffle & Wine Co. label is the ultra-premium label, the best from the Yarra Valley, with 50% of this range exported to international restaurant clients through the exclusive distributors of the truffles. Exports to all major markets.

♥♥♥♥♥ **Yarra Valley Margaret River Chardonnay 2013** 75% from Yering in the Yarra Valley; 25% from Stevens Road in Margaret River. Wild yeast-fermented in barrel. The result is complex, steely, struck by flint notes and severely acidic through the finish. Don't let that put you off. Flavours of grapefruit and green apple power through the palate. It's a tight, long, engrossing wine; it just desperately needs extra time in the bottle. Screwcap. 12.8% alc. **Rating** 96 **To** 2021 $45 CM ❂

Yarra Valley Pinot Noir 2013 From two Yarra Valley vineyards, one at Coldstream and one at Yering. Boysenberry, snapped twigs, peppers and sour cherries. It's ripped with spice and tannin and acidity; a whirl of sensations lingers well after you've swallowed, like a wind current. It's hard to imagine this doing anything other than ageing very well. Screwcap. 13.8% alc. **Rating** 94 **To** 2024 $50 CM

TWC Cabernets 2012 Cabernet sauvignon, merlot, cabernet franc and petit verdot blend. It's a dense display of curranty, gravelly fruit, the integration of oak quite faultless, as is the extension of flavour through the finish. Everything about this wine suggests that it will be long-lived, and that patience will be rewarded. Diam. 13.9% alc. **Rating** 94 **To** 2032 $60 CM

⟡⟡⟡⟡⟡ **Pemberton Riesling 2014** Rating 92 To 2027 $26 CM
Truffle Hill Sauvignon Blanc Semillon 2014 Rating 92 To 2016 $22 CM ✪
Truffle Hill Reserve Cane-cut Riesling 2014 Rating 92 To 2017 $35 CM
Truffle Hill Pemberton Merlot 2012 Rating 91 To 2020 $24 CM

Trust Wines

PO Box 8015, Seymour, Vic 3660 **Region** Central Victoria Zone
T (03) 5794 1811 **www.trustwines.com.au Open** Not
Winemaker Don Lewis, Narelle King **Est.** 2004 **Dozens** 800 **Vyds** 5ha
Partners Don Lewis and Narelle King had been making wine together for many years at Mitchelton, and Priorat, Spain. Don came from a grapegrowing family in Red Cliffs, near Mildura, and in his youth was press-ganged into working in the vineyard. When he left home he swore never to be involved in vineyards again, but in 1973 found himself accepting the position of assistant winemaker to Colin Preece at Mitchelton, where he remained until his retirement 32 years later. Narelle, having qualified as a chartered accountant, set off to travel, and while in South America met a young Australian winemaker who had just completed vintage in Argentina, and who lived in France. The lifestyle appealed greatly, so on her return to Australia she obtained her winemaking degree from CSU and was offered work by Mitchelton as a bookkeeper and cellar hand. The estate-base wines are a reflection of Central Victorian style. They also make the Tar & Roses wines, but have no beneficial interest in that business.

⟡⟡⟡⟡⟡ **Crystal Hill White 2014** Gewurztraminer, savagnin, riesling and viognier. Hedonistic aroma and flavour. Ginger, melon, honeysuckle, nectarine and assorted other fireworks. Crackle of quartz to the finish. Excellent intensity. Holds nothing back. Screwcap. 13.5% alc. **Rating** 92 **To** 2016 $18 CM

Shiraz 2012 Glowing purple; fleshy plum, clove and mint flavours build a strong case for both quality and drinkability. Chewy tannin gives it a lipsmacking, where's-the-pizza quality. Convincing from go to whoa. Screwcap. 14.2% alc. **Rating** 92 **To** 2022 $27 CM

Tscharke

376 Seppeltsfield Road, Marananga, SA 5360 **Region** Barossa Valley
T 0438 628 178 **www.tscharke.com.au Open** Thurs–Mon 10–5
Winemaker Damien Tscharke **Est.** 2001 **Dozens** 5000 **Vyds** 28ha
Damien Tscharke grew up in the Barossa Valley among the vineyards at Seppeltsfield and Marananga. In 2001 he began the production of Glaymond, four estate-grown wines based on what he calls the classic varieties (following the trend of having catchy, snappy names), followed by wines under the Tscharke brand using the alternative varieties of tempranillo, graciano, zinfandel, montepulciano and savagnin. Like the Glaymond wines, these are estate-grown, albeit in limited quantities. Exports to the US, Canada, Denmark, Belgium, Germany, Israel, Indonesia, Singapore and China.

⟡⟡⟡⟡⟡ **Tscharke The Master Marananga Montepulciano 2012** Bright crimson-purple; the fragrant, perfumed bouquet is followed by a delicious red-fruited palate; this is one of several examples that suggest a real future in Aus, even if it is in retreat in Italy. Screwcap. 14% alc. **Rating** 94 **To** 2023 $25 **☻**

ŦŦŦŦŦ **Barossa Valley Shiraz Shiraz Shiraz 2012** Rating 93 To 2020 $20 **☻**
Red Hair Marananga Graciano 2013 Rating 92 To 2023 $25 **☻**
Tscharke Matching Socks Touriga 2013 Rating 90 To 2018 $20 **☻**

Tuck's Ridge
★★★★★

37 Shoreham Road, Red Hill South, Vic 3937 **Region** Mornington Peninsula
T (03) 5989 8660 **www**.tucksridge.com.au **Open** 7 days 11–5
Winemaker Michael Kyberd, Matthew Bisogni **Est.** 1985 **Dozens** 6000 **Vyds** 3.4ha
Tuck's Ridge has changed focus significantly since selling its large Red Hill vineyard. It retained the Buckle Vineyards of chardonnay and pinot noir that consistently provide outstanding grapes (and wine). The major part of the production is purchased from the Turramurra Vineyard. Exports to the US and Hong Kong.

ŦŦŦŦŦ **Buckle Pinot Noir 2013** Hand-picked, crushed/pressed, matured in French oak (30% new). Perfect hue and depth to its colour is no surprise, and leaves no doubt about the sheer class of the bouquet and palate; cherry and plum are interleaved with delicate nuances of savoury, but superfine, tannins running through to an incredibly long, lingering finish. Grand Cru? You betcha. Screwcap. 13.9% alc. Rating 97 To 2025 $100 **☻**

ŦŦŦŦŦ **Buckle Chardonnay 2013** Hand-picked, whole bunch-pressed, fermented in French oak (30% new), and matured for 9 months. The extra depth that the Penfolds 58 clone has wherever it is grown shines through strongly, perfectly displayed by precisely judged winemaking. Screwcap. 13.8% alc. Rating 96 To 2028 $50 **☻**
Turramurra Chardonnay 2013 The main chardonnay clone in Southeastern Australian is I10V1, a tried and true performer; the wine is very expressive and lively, with juicy white peach and grapefruit in tandem, the French oak well balanced and integrated. Screwcap. 13.8% alc. Rating 95 To 2021 $40
Mornington Peninsula Pinot Noir 2013 Bright and clear colour heralds a finely groomed Pinot with effortless communication of its fragrant, ever so clearly varietal, base; red summer fruits wreathed in a fine web of spice and invisible-but-real tannins. Screwcap. 13.9% alc. Rating 95 To 2023 $39
Mornington Peninsula Shiraz 2013 A prime example of cool-climate shiraz grown at the edge of comfort, akin to pinot in Burgundy, cabernet in Bordeaux. Here the weather gods have smiled, leaving the wine with an urgency and drive to its multiplicity of red fruits, spices and pepper; ultimately drawn together by the excellent balance the wine has on the back-palate and finish. Screwcap. 14.2% alc. Rating 95 To 2025 $35 **☻**
Mornington Peninsula Tempranillo 2013 Good colour; as lively on its feet as you could wish, with a pot pourri of cherries, red and black, poached and fresh; a dainty garland of tannins completes a delicious wine. Screwcap. 15.1% alc. Rating 95 To 2020 $35 **☻**
Mornington Peninsula Sauvignon Blanc 2014 Rating 94 To 2015 $24 **☻**
Mornington Peninsula Chardonnay 2013 Rating 94 To 2019 $29 **☻**
Mornington Peninsula Pinot Gris 2014 Rating 94 To 2016 $29 **☻**

Tulloch
★★★★★

Glen Elgin, 638 De Beyers Road, Pokolbin, NSW 2321 **Region** Hunter Valley
T (02) 4998 7580 **www**.tullochwines.com.au **Open** 7 days 10–5
Winemaker Jay Tulloch, First Creek **Est.** 1895 **Dozens** 35 000 **Vyds** 80ha
The Tulloch brand continues to build success on success. Its primary grape source is estate vines owned by part-shareholder Inglewood Vineyard in the Upper Hunter Valley. It also owns the JYT Vineyard established by Jay Tulloch in the mid-1980s at the foot of the Brokenback Range in the heart of Pokolbin. The third source is contract-grown fruit from other growers

in the Hunter Valley and further afield. Skilled winemaking by First Creek Winemaking Services has put the icing on the winemaking cake, and Christina Tulloch is a livewire marketer. By way of postscript, 2013 marked Jay Tulloch's 50th Hunter Valley vintage, 2015 Tulloch's 120th anniversary. Exports to Belgium, the Philippines, Singapore, Hong Kong, Malaysia, Thailand, Japan and China.

ɸɸɸɸɸ **Private Bin Dry Red Shiraz 2013** A commemorative release marking the 50th vintage for Jay Tulloch (and a history full of twists and turns). This is a wine with effortless power, quintessential Hunter Valley Shiraz with fresh earth/leather wound through the bright, clear blackberry and cherry fruit; oak and tannins provide a balanced support role. Screwcap. 12.5% alc. **Rating** 96 **To** 2033 $50 ✪
Pokolbin Dry Red Shiraz 2013 Clear crimson-purple; juicy, slurpy red fruits drive the long and elegant medium-bodied palate; a convincing demonstration of the purity Hunter Shiraz can provide at modest alcohol levels without losing its strong sense of place. Screwcap. 12.3% alc. **Rating** 95 **To** 2028 $25 ✪
Limited Release G3 Shiraz 2013 Creamy, slippery oak does its best to conceal what is an exceptionally pure, and typical, regional expression of shiraz. It's mid-weight tending towards light, but its grainy, earthen tannin carves a fine swathe, and the complexity of flavour it takes with it is entirely what you would hope for. It almost goes without saying that it needs time, not so much to soften, but to reveal itself in its best light. Screwcap. 12.5% alc. **Rating** 95 **To** 2035 $100 CM

ɸɸɸɸɸ **Limited Release Julia Semillon 2014** **Rating** 93 **To** 2022 $30 CM
JYT Selection 2013 **Rating** 92 **To** 2028 $40
Hunter River White Semillon 2014 **Rating** 91 **To** 2024 $25

Turkey Flat   ★★★★★

Bethany Road, Tanunda, SA 5352 **Region** Barossa Valley
T (08) 8563 2851 **www**.turkeyflat.com.au **Open** 7 days 11–5
Winemaker Mark Bulman **Est.** 1990 **Dozens** 20 000 **Vyds** 47.83ha
The establishment date of Turkey Flat is given as 1990 but it might equally have been 1870 (or thereabouts), when the Schulz family purchased the Turkey Flat vineyard, or 1847, when the vineyard was first planted to the very old shiraz that still grows there today alongside 8ha of equally old grenache. Plantings have since expanded significantly, now comprising shiraz (24ha), grenache (10.5ha), cabernet sauvignon (5.9ha), mourvedre (3.7ha), and smaller plantings of marsanne, viognier and dolcetto. The business is run by sole proprietor Christie Schulz. Exports to the UK, the US and other major markets.

ɸɸɸɸɸ **The Ancestor Barossa Valley Shiraz 2012** The first release of a wine made entirely from the estate's 1847 shiraz planting. It is all about finesse, length and balance, not naked power; it is supple, medium-bodied and nonchalantly carries the full array of black fruits and finely spun savoury tannins of the ancient vines; oak is no more than a vehicle. Screwcap. 14.5% alc. **Rating** 96 **To** 2037 $150
Barossa Valley Rose 2014 A specifically grown and tailored blend. Small wonder it is one of the best selling roses on the market, its upgraded label print and branded clear glass bottle drawing the eye; it is supremely elegant, fresh and balanced, its red fruits sparkling like stars on a clear night – there is no static or distraction from its message. Screwcap. 13.5% alc. **Rating** 95 **To** 2015 $18 ✪
Barossa Valley Shiraz 2013 Turkey Flat has long established a distinguished, yet seemingly effortless, medium-bodied style that doesn't have to carry the burden of high alcohol; the flavours cover the full range of red, purple and black fruits, with a juicy core given texture and shape by precisely managed oak and tannins. Its overarching balance guarantees a long life. Screwcap. 14.3% alc. **Rating** 95 **To** 2038 $47
The Last Straw 2013 Partially dried marsanne grapes were fermented in new French oak and then bottle-matured for 15 months. Bright green-gold. It is extremely complex, the sweetness balanced by savoury spicy flavours; prolonged cellaring might see an exceptional wine develop. 375ml. Screwcap. 15.5% alc. **Rating** 95 **To** 2028 $35 ✪

Butchers Block White 2014 49% marsanne, 35% viognier, 16% roussanne. Excellent power and intensity of flavour. Toast, nougat, stone fruit and lemon butter. Rich but zesty. Spicy too. Thoroughly prosecutes its case. Screwcap. 13% alc. **Rating** 94 **To** 2018 $23 CM **○**
Butchers Block Red 2013 A 48/28/24% estate-grown blend of shiraz, grenache and mataro. It has the gravitas more often encountered in McLaren Vale than the Barossa Valley in its display of predominantly black fruits and absence of confection; it is only medium-bodied, but has immaculate fruit/tannin/oak balance and integration. Screwcap. 14.5% alc. **Rating** 94 **To** 2029 $19 **○**

ŸŸŸŸŸ **Barossa Valley Mataro 2014 Rating** 93 **To** 2024 $32
Barossa Valley Grenache 2013 Rating 92 **To** 2023 $29
5 Month Skin Contact Roussanne 2014 Rating 90 **To** 2015 $28 CM

Turner's Crossing Vineyard ★★★★★

747 Old Bridgewater–Serpentine Road, Serpentine, Vic 3517 **Region** Bendigo
T 0427 843 528 **www**.turnerscrossingwine.com **Open** By appt
Winemaker Sergio Carlei **Est.** 1998 **Dozens** 6000 **Vyds** 42ha
The name of this outstanding vineyard comes from local farmers crossing the Loddon River in the mid to late 1800s on their way to the nearest town. The vineyard was planted in 1999 by former corporate executive and lecturer in the business school at La Trobe University, Paul Jenkins. However, Paul's experience as a self-taught viticulturist dates back to '85, when he established his first vineyard, at Prospect Hill, planting all the vines himself. The grapes from both vineyards have gone to a who's who of winemakers in Central Victoria, but an increasing amount is being made into wines of exceptional quality for Turner's Crossing. Phil Bennett and winemaker Sergio Carlei have joined Paul as co-owners of the vineyard, with Sergio putting his money where his winemaking mouth is. Exports to the UK, the US, Canada, Taiwan, Singapore and China.

ŸŸŸŸŸ **Bendigo Shiraz Viognier 2012** Wild yeast co-fermented in open wooden vats, then aged in used French barriques for 16 months. The bouquet and palate are extremely complex, with a wonderful array of spicy, savoury, peppery overtones to the blackberry and plum fruit; despite the complexity and intensity the wine possesses, it is also very elegant and carefully detailed, the open-vat fermentation and maturation in used oak responsible for the texture and length, rather than the flavour, of the wine. This will always be a great wine with food. Top value, too. Screwcap. 14.5% alc. **Rating** 96 **To** 2037 $27 **○**

ŸŸŸŸŸ **Limited Edition Bendigo Picolit 2013 Rating** 90 **To** 2018 $25

Twisted Gum Wines ★★★★

2253 Eukey Road, Ballandean, Qld 4382 **Region** Granite Belt
T (07) 4684 1282 **www**.twistedgum.com.au **Open** W'ends 10–4
Winemaker Andy Williams (Contract) **Est.** 2007 **Dozens** 700 **Vyds** 2.8ha
Tim and Michelle Coelli bring diverse and interesting backgrounds to this venture. During his university days in the early 1980s Tim began reading weekly wine columns of a certain journalist and bought recommended red wines from Wynns and Peter Lehmann, liked the wines, and with wife Michelle 'bought dozens and dozens ...' Tim became a research economist, and during periods of living and working in Europe, he and Michelle became well acquainted with the wines of France, Spain and Italy. Michelle has a degree in agricultural science which, she says, 'has not been well utilised because four children came along'. When they found a beautiful 40ha bush property on a ridge near Ballandean (at an altitude of 900m) with dry-grown vines already planted, they did not hesitate.

ŸŸŸŸŸ **Single Vineyard Granite Belt Chardonnay 2013** Despite its low alcohol, the flavours are ripe and clearly varietal, with white peach, melon and fig in the lead. Unwooded, and justifiably proud of it. Screwcap. 12% alc. **Rating** 90 **To** 2016 $25

ŸŸŸŸ **Single Vineyard Granite Belt Shiraz 2013 Rating** 89 **To** 2020 $35

Two Hands Wines ★★★★★

273 Neldner Road, Marananga, SA 5355 **Region** Barossa Valley
T (08) 8562 4566 **www**.twohandswines.com **Open** 7 days 10–5
Winemaker Ben Perkins **Est.** 2000 **Dozens** 50 000 **Vyds** 15ha

The 'hands' in question are those of SA businessmen Michael Twelftree and Richard Mintz, Michael in particular having extensive experience in marketing Australian wine in the US (for other producers). On the principle that if big is good, bigger is better, the style of the wines has been aimed squarely at the palate of Robert Parker Jr and *Wine Spectator*'s Harvey Steiman. Grapes are sourced from the Barossa Valley (where the business has 15ha of shiraz), McLaren Vale, Clare Valley, Langhorne Creek and Padthaway. The emphasis of the wines is on sweet fruit and soft tannin structure, all signifying the precise marketing strategy of what is a very successful business. Exports to the US and other major markets.

ŸŸŸŸŸ **The Boy Eden Valley Riesling 2014** From 100yo vines. Light, bright straw-green, it is a Riesling of exceptional delicacy that catches hold of you the moment you look into its eyes, without a word spoken; its balance and length are perfect; it needs no hoity-toity words to get its message across. Screwcap. 11.5% alc. Rating 96 To 2029 $25 ✪

Yacca Block Single Vineyard Menglers Hill Eden Valley Shiraz 2012 This is quite different from the other wines in the Single Vineyard series, the Eden Valley providing a cooler-climate style; it is more open in its weave and texture, with delicious spicy elements to its red and black fruits, the mouthfeel graceful, the finish fine and balanced. Cork. 14.5% alc. Rating 96 To 2032 $100

Twelftree Schuller Blewitt Springs Grenache 2013 85yo vines, 14 days on skins, French oak and stainless steel puncheons, 161 dozen made. Exceptional bright, clear colour; a full array of red fruits, the tannins particularly fine and supple; has more savoury nuances than its siblings, but at the same time has purity above and beyond the others. Screwcap. 14% alc. Rating 96 To 2028 $45 ✪

Gnarly Dudes Barossa Valley Shiraz 2013 Deep, dense crimson-purple; fills the senses from the get-go, its expressive, dark-fruited bouquet seamlessly leading into a palate that offers an almost mesmerising interplay between perfectly ripe black fruits on the one hand, and savoury, finely grained tannins on the other. Screwcap. 14.8% alc. Rating 95 To 2033 $27 ✪

Angels' Share McLaren Vale Shiraz 2013 Two Hands' wines are always perfectly groomed, and abounding with all things nice, yet not to the extent of obscuring the sense of place; here delicious black cherry/plum/blackberry fruit is wrapped in a coat of high-quality dark chocolate, tannins and oak almost incidental. Screwcap. 14.8% alc. Rating 95 To 2028 $27 ✪

Windmill Block Single Vineyard Stonewell Barossa Valley Shiraz 2012 Bright crimson-purple; counterintuitively, doesn't leap out in the context of its vintage siblings with its much lower alcohol; the colour is superb, but so is that of its siblings; it has a complex, layered palate with a range of licorice, bitter chocolate and sour cherry fruits, and a powerful finish, the overall balance very good. Cork. 13.5% alc. Rating 95 To 2027 $100

Twelftree Copperview Onkaparinga Gorge McLaren Vale Grenache 2013 A broader range of flavours, and an even more powerful thrust ex the alcohol. At the end of the day, the two wines can't be split on quality, just style – and even there they are closer than I could have imagined would be possible. Screwcap. 15% alc. Rating 95 To 2025 $45

Twelftree Churinga Watervale Clare Valley Grenache 2013 Particularly good colour; a powerful wine with McLaren Vale allusions. Of course it is in fact what it purports to be, a top-quality Grenache that will outlive your patience. Screwcap. 14.5% alc. Rating 95 To 2025 $45

Twelftree Moritz Blewitt Springs Grenache 2013 Yet another dimension and intensity of power courtesy of Blewitt Springs; red and black cherry fruits; excellent length and balance. Screwcap. 15% alc. Rating 95 To 2025 $45

Sexy Beast McLaren Vale Cabernet Sauvignon 2013 Deep, dense crimson-purple; flooded with the swirls of cassis and dark chocolate/choc-mint flavours of

McLaren Vale, alcohol no problem; oak and tannins are largely observers of what is going on around them. Screwcap. 14.5% alc. **Rating** 95 **To** 2028 $27 ○

The Wolf Clare Valley Riesling 2014 Rating 94 **To** 2025 $25 ○
Fields of Joy Clare Valley Shiraz 2013 Rating 94 **To** 2033 $27 ○
Secret Block Shiraz 2012 Rating 94 **To** 2027 $100
Twelftree Grenache Mataro 2013 Rating 94 **To** 2033 $35
Brave Faces GSM 2013 Rating 94 **To** 2025 $27 ○

2 Mates   ★★★★☆

Cnr Kangarilla Road/Foggo Road, McLaren Vale, SA 5171 **Region** McLaren Vale
T 0411 111 198 **www.2mates.com.au Open** 7 days 11–5
Winemaker Matt Rechner, Mark Venable, David Minear **Est.** 2003 **Dozens** 500
The two mates are Mark Venable and David Minear, who say, 'Over a big drink in a small bar in Italy a few years back, we talked about making "our perfect Australian Shiraz". When we got back, we decided to have a go.' The wine ('05) was duly made, and won a silver medal at the *Decanter Magazine* World Wine Awards in London, in some exalted company. Exports to the UK and China.

🍷🍷🍷🍷🍷 **McLaren Vale Shiraz 2012** From vineyards of various ages, some up to 140yo. Full crimson-purple. The black fruits come leaping out of the glass with the first swirl, and likewise fill the mouth with the first sip, their flanks with a shield of French oak, the tannins bordering on luscious (not a description I have ever used before); the wine oozes potential from every pore (where did that licorice come from?), and begs for a decade to allow it to breathe. Not $130, but $30. Still available. Screwcap. 15.1% alc. **Rating** 96 **To** 2052 $30 ○

🍷🍷🍷🍷 **Adelaide Hills Sauvignon Blanc 2013 Rating** 89 **To** 2015 $15 CM ○

Two Rivers   ★★★★

2 Yarrawa Road, Denman, NSW 2328 **Region** Hunter Valley
T (02) 6547 2556 **www.tworiverswines.com.au Open** 7 days 11–4
Winemaker Liz Silkman **Est.** 1988 **Dozens** 10 000 **Vyds** 67.5ha
A significant part of the viticultural scene in the Upper Hunter Valley, with almost 70ha of vineyards, involving an investment of several million dollars. Part of the fruit is sold under long-term contracts, and part is made for the expanding winemaking and marketing operations of Two Rivers, the chief brand of Inglewood Vineyards. The emphasis is on Chardonnay and Semillon, and the wines have been medal winners at the Hunter Valley Wine Show. It is also a partner in the Tulloch business, together with the Tulloch and Angove families, and supplies much of the grapes for the Tulloch label. A contemporary cellar door adds significantly to the appeal of the Upper Hunter Valley as a wine-tourist destination.

🍷🍷🍷🍷🍷 **Stones Throw Hunter Valley Semillon 2014** Clean lines and flavour and acidity. Pure and crisp. Lemon and slate with an edge of fennel. Playing its cards close to its chest, for now. Screwcap. 10.6% alc. **Rating** 92 **To** 2022 $16 CM ○

Reserve Hunter Valley Chardonnay 2014 Pale straw-green. Elegant flavour profile with apple, peach and creamy oak, all in modest but satisfying volume. Not especially lengthy, but harmonious and appealing. Screwcap. 13.6% alc. **Rating** 90 **To** 2016 $24 CM

Reserve Hunter Valley Shiraz 2013 Both elegant and smooth-skinned, with cherry-plum flavours aided by trademark Hunter leather/earth. Travels through the mouth nicely. Screwcap. 12.5% alc. **Rating** 90 **To** 2019 $28 CM

🍷🍷🍷🍷 **Hidden Hive Hunter Valley Verdelho 2014 Rating** 89 **To** 2017 $16 CM ○

Twofold   ★★★★★

142 Beulah Road, Norwood, SA 5067 (postal) **Region** Various
T (02) 9572 7285 **Open** Not
Winemaker Tim Stock, Nick Stock, Neil Pike (Contract) **Est.** 2002 **Dozens** 500

This is the venture of brothers Nick and Tim Stock, both of whom have had a varied background in the wine industry (primarily at the marketing end, whether as sommeliers or in wholesale) and both of whom have excellent palates. Their contacts have allowed them to source single-vineyard Rieslings from Sevenhill in the Clare and Eden valleys, a single-vineyard Shiraz from Heathcote, and an Eden Vineyard Riesling.

🍷🍷🍷🍷🍷 **Clare Valley Riesling 2012** Now 2 years down the track from its birth, the wine is starting to take the shape of an adult; it still has years in front of it, but the way the fruit flavour intensifies on the back-palate and finish guarantees prosperity. Screwcap. 12% alc. **Rating** 94 **To** 2025 $23 ◐

Heathcote Shiraz 2009 A complex, opulent and rich wine, oak playing a significant role in shaping the bouquet and palate; licorice, spice and earth join with the dark plum fruit (and oak) on the mid to back-palate. Screwcap. 13.5% alc. **Rating** 94 **To** 2020 $37

🍷🍷🍷🍷 **Perdu Heathcote Shiraz 2011 Rating** 89 **To** 2018 $26

Tynan Wines

PO Box 164, Wickham, NSW 2293 **Region** Various
T 0402 442 614 **www**.tynanwines.com.au **Open** Not
Winemaker Mark Tynan **Est.** 2009 **Dozens** 500
Mark Tynan, founder and owner of this eponymous business, is currently studying for a master of viticulture and oenology degree at CSU. He is sharing winemaking facilities with a couple of Hunter Valley winemakers, and is preparing to establish his own winery. There he will make varietal wines sourced from various parts of NSW.

🍷🍷🍷🍷🍷 **Hunter Valley Pinot Gris 2014** Well put together. Attractive combination of flavours. Pears, chalk, spice and nectarine. Has a dry sense of purpose but also out-and-out fruitiness. No lack of character either. Screwcap. 12% alc. **Rating** 92 **To** 2015 $25 CM ◐

🍷🍷🍷🍷 **Orange Sauvignon Blanc 2013 Rating** 89 **To** 2015 $25 CM
Mudgee Shiraz 2013 Rating 88 **To** 2022 $50 CM

Tyrrell's

Broke Road, Pokolbin, NSW 2321 **Region** Hunter Valley
T (02) 4993 7000 **www**.tyrrells.com.au **Open** Mon–Sat 8.30–5, Sun 10–4
Winemaker Andrew Spinaze, Mark Richardson **Est.** 1858 **Dozens** 200 000
Vyds 158.22ha
One of the most successful family wineries, a humble operation for the first 110 years of its life that has grown out of all recognition over the past 40 years. Vat 1 Semillon is one of the most dominant wines in the Australian show system, and Vat 47 Chardonnay is one of the pacesetters for this variety. It has an awesome portfolio of single-vineyard Semillons released when 5–6 years old. Its estate plantings are over 116ha in the Hunter Valley, 15ha in the Limestone Coast and 26ha in Heathcote. A founding member of Australia's First Families of Wine. Exports to all major markets.

🍷🍷🍷🍷🍷 **Vat 1 Hunter Semillon 2014** Only available to Wine Club members now, the main release 5 years down the track. Made from the estate's Short Flat Vineyard, the blocks dating back to 1923, this is destined to add yet more trophies to the Tyrrell's warehouse of such tributes. Its balance and mouthfeel are remarkable, supple and juicy, yet cleansed by gently insistent acidity. Screwcap. 11.5% alc. **Rating** 97 **To** 2039 $48 ◐

Johnno's Semillon 2014 From a single estate vineyard planted in 1908 on the alluvial sandy flats below the winery, wild yeast-fermented cloudy juice the starting point. How much of its character comes from the 100+yo vines, how much from the winemaking is immaterial: this wine, of which only 250 dozen bottles were made, has an extra level of flavour, texture and structure, zesty lemony acidity providing its farewell call. Screwcap. 11.5% alc. **Rating** 97 **To** 2040 $46 ◐

Old Patch Hunter Valley Shiraz 2013 This block (on Neil Stephens' vineyard) was planted in 1869, the oldest in the Hunter Valley; hand-picked, open-fermented, matured in a new 2700l French cask. This is a wine that shows its breed and ancestry, the bouquet fragrant, the medium-bodied palate a seamless brocade of intricately detailed red fruits and silky tannins. 297 dozen made. Why only $60? Screwcap. 13% alc. **Rating** 97 **To** 2043 $60 ✪

ɥɥɥɥɥ **Vat 47 Hunter Chardonnay 2011** The brilliant straw-green colour introduces a wine that traces its lineage back to '71, the skill involved oozing from every pore and facet, not the least in the tangy citrus/grapefruit farewell. Screwcap. 13.5% alc. **Rating** 96 **To** 2021 $80

Vat 9 Hunter Shiraz 2013 Very much in a style Tyrrell's has made its own in the last decade or more, with a super-fresh, savoury medium-bodied palate of excellent length. It goes without saying that it will repay extended cellaring. Screwcap. 13% alc. **Rating** 96 **To** 2038 $67 ✪

Museum Release Vat 1 Hunter Semillon 2010 From two dry-grown blocks with an average age of 60 years. Five years have passed since the wine was made, but it's oh so young and fresh, with years of life in front of it; its balance and length are faultless, so its future is gold-plated, but I must point it as it is today. Screwcap. 11.5% alc. **Rating** 95 **To** 2040 $85

Single Vineyard Stevens Hunter Semillon 2010 Gleaming straw-green; the bouquet immediately tells you this has reached the first level of maturity – the first plenitude, as Richard Geoffroy, Dom Perignon winemaker, would say. The palate is in lockstep with the bouquet, honey and lightly browned toast making an appearance, acidity an ever-present reminder that there is no need to rush. Screwcap. 11% alc. **Rating** 95 **To** 2025 $35 ✪

Johnno's Hunter Valley Shiraz 2013 The colour is relatively light, the wine elegant rather than powerful. It needs to build on the foundations that are already there and, given its antecedents, I think it will (and surprise doubting Thomases). Screwcap. 12.8% alc. **Rating** 95 **To** 2033 $60

Single Vineyard HVD Hunter Semillon 2010 The HVD vineyard was planted in 1908. Despite a touch of spritz, this has started down its development path with the first hint of honey joining the lively, tangy, lemon/lemongrass flavours, the acidity crisp and reassuring. Screwcap. 11% alc. **Rating** 95 **To** 2030 $35 ✪

Brookdale Hunter Valley Semillon 2013 **Rating** 94 **To** 2019 $19 ✪
Single Vineyard Belford Hunter Chardonnay 2013 **Rating** 94 **To** 2020 $35
HVD & The Hill Hunter Valley Pinot Noir 2013 **Rating** 94 **To** 2028 $30 ✪
Single Vineyard Stevens Hunter Shiraz 2013 **Rating** 94 **To** 2028 $40

ɥɥɥɥɥ **Hunter Valley Semillon 2014** **Rating** 93 **To** 2027 $23 ✪
Lost Block Heathcote Shiraz 2013 **Rating** 92 **To** 2020 $18 ✪
Lost Block Orange Sauvignon Blanc 2014 **Rating** 91 **To** 2015 $18 CM ✪

Ulithorne   ★★★★☆

The Mill at Middleton, 29 Mill Terrace, Middleton, SA 5213 **Region** McLaren Vale
T 0419 040 670 **www.**ulithorne.com.au **Open** W'ends & public hols 10–4
Winemaker Rose Kentish, Brian Light **Est.** 1971 **Dozens** 2500 **Vyds** 7.2ha
Ulithorne produces small quantities of red wines from selected parcels of grapes from a vineyard in McLaren Vale planted by Rose Kentish's father-in-law, Frank Harrison, over 40 years ago. Rose's dream of making small-batch, high-quality wines from exceptional grapegrowing regions around the world has taken her to France, where she has made a Vermentinu on the island of Corsica and a Rose in Provence under the Ulithorne label. In 2013 Sam Harrison and Rose Kentish purchased an old vineyard in the heart of McLaren Vale, with 4ha of shiraz and 3.2ha of grenache dating back to 1945. They expect to have a winery and cellar door built on their Kay's Road Vineyard by late '16. Exports to the UK, Canada, The Netherlands, Malaysia and China.

ɥɥɥɥɥ **Dona McLaren Vale Grenache Shiraz Mourvedre 2013** A 60/30/10% blend, cold-soaked and cool-fermented for 10 days, each component separately matured in used French oak for 12 months, then blended and matured for a further 3 months. Rose Kentish's 4 vintages in France show in this very good wine, with a generous supply of red and black fruits sewn together by exactly measured tannins. Screwcap. 14% alc. **Rating** 95 **To** 2028 $24 ✪

Frux Frugis McLaren Vale Shiraz 2012 Matured for 24 months in French oak (20% new). An elegant, medium-bodied wine with a strong overlay of sundry spicy/savoury influences on its predominantly black fruit flavours; balance and length are the strong points of the medium-bodied palate. Cork. 14.5% alc. **Rating** 94 **To** 2037 $80

Chi McLaren Vale Grenache Shiraz 2013 Old bush vines, 80/20% blend, separately vinified, both parcels matured in used oak for 14 months. Provides that elusive combination of rich fruits and spicy, bright mouthfeel and aftertaste. Cork. 15% alc. **Rating** 94 **To** 2028 $38

🍇 Ulupna Winery ★★★

Suite 107, 620 St Kilda Road, Melbourne, Vic 3006 (postal) **Region** Goulburn Valley
T (03) 9533 8831 **www**.ulupnawinery.com.au **Open** Not
Winemaker Daniele Ferrari, Vio Buga **Est.** 1999 **Dozens** NFP **Vyds** 22ha

Ulupna is the venture of the Bogdan and Ferrari families, which started out as a retirement activity for Nick and Kathy Bogdan, conceived by daughter Viviana Ferrari. Since 2000, the family has planted 22ha of vines on the banks of the Murray River: shiraz (50%), cabernet sauvignon (30%) and chardonnay (20%). The vineyard has been planned to allow for expansion in the years ahead. The multi-talented Viviana is responsible for the marketing of the wines, which until 2012 was largely directed to China, followed by South Korea and Hong Kong. These plans have been expanded with local distribution and sales, with the Americas and Europe also in contemplation. The wines are made under the direction of Vio Buga, who also designed and planted the vineyard.

♟♟♟♟ Cellar Reserve Shiraz Cabernet 2013 70/30%. Medium-weight fruit profile. Loose-knit. Boysenberry, spice, dates and licorice. Some volatility. Some black pepper. Keeps itself on the positive side of the equation. Screwcap. 14.8% alc. **Rating** 89 **To** 2023 $33 CM

Phoenix Royal Shiraz 2010 Just starting to develop but still plenty of beef. Strong flavours of blackberry jam, asphalt and earth, slipped with toasty oak. Shows its alcohol keenly; was picked too late. Price seems ambitious. Screwcap. 15.2% alc. **Rating** 88 **To** 2020 $50 CM

Umamu Estate ★★★★★

PO Box 1269, Margaret River, WA 6285 **Region** Margaret River
T (08) 9757 5058 **www**.umamuestate.com **Open** Not
Winemaker Bruce Dukes (Contract) **Est.** 2005 **Dozens** 5000 **Vyds** 16.5ha

Chief executive Charmaine Saw explains, 'My life has been a journey towards Umamu. An upbringing in both eastern and western cultures, graduating in natural science, training as a chef, combined with a passion for the arts and experience as a management consultant have all contributed to my building the business creatively yet professionally.' The palindrome Umamu, says Charmaine, is inspired by balance and contentment. In practical terms this means an organic approach to viticulture and a deep respect for the terroir. In 1997, Charmaine's parents fell in love with the property and its plantings, dating back to '78, of cabernet sauvignon (6ha), chardonnay (3.5ha), shiraz (1.7ha), semillon (2.2ha), sauvignon blanc (1.5ha), merlot (0.9ha) and cabernet franc (0.7ha); the maiden vintage under the Umamu label followed in 2005. Exports to the UK, Hong Kong, Malaysia, Indonesia and Singapore.

♟♟♟♟♟ Margaret River Chardonnay 2012 Light straw-green; a distinguished wine, calmly moving along its journey to full maturity a couple of years hence; it is in the understated, yet totally convincing, style Umamu seeks, white peach, melon and lemony acidity sewn together by an invisible thread of oak. Screwcap. 12.8% alc. **Rating** 95 **To** 2032 $50

Ann's Cabernet Sauvignon 2011 In very different style from the '12 standard version, here with more obvious ripeness to the cassis-accented fruit, albeit kept in check by ultra fine-grained tannins and quality French oak. Screwcap. 13.5% alc. Rating 95 To 2031 $48

🍷🍷🍷🍷 **Margaret River Cabernet Sauvignon 2012** Rating 92 To 2027 $58
MacAnn Cane Cut Sauvignon Blanc 2014 Rating 92 To 2017 $69

Underground Winemakers ★★★★★

1282 Nepean Highway, Mt Eliza, Vic 3931 **Region** Mornington Peninsula
T (03) 9775 4185 **www**.ugwine.com.au **Open** 7 days 10–5
Winemaker Peter Stebbing **Est.** 2004 **Dozens** 10000 **Vyds** 12ha
Owned by Adrian Hennessy, Jonathon Stevens and Peter Stebbing. Each has made wine in Alsace, Burgundy, Northern Italy and Swan Hill. Each has extensive experience in the vineyards and wineries of the Mornington Peninsula. Their first step in 2004 was to lease a small winery at Mt Eliza that had closed years earlier, but still had a vineyard with some of the oldest plantings of pinot noir, pinot gris and chardonnay on the Peninsula. Their portfolio is nothing if not eclectic: Pinot Gris, Pinot Noir and Chardonnay from the Mornington Peninsula, and Durif, Moscato, Cabernet Merlot and Shiraz from Northern and Central Victoria.

🍷🍷🍷🍷 **Mornington Peninsula Pinot Noir 2013** Two clones from two Mornington Peninsula vineyards; extended maceration, matured in used French oak. Excellent crimson hue; overflows with black cherry and plum fruit, but has the undercarriage to make light of its depth of flavour, which is strongly varietal; mouthfeel/texture and length are also very good. An outrageous bargain. Screwcap. 13.5% alc. Rating 95 To 2025 $18 ❂
San Pietro Pinot Noir 2012 Grown on 'our' Mornington Peninsula vineyard, clones MV6 (60%) and 115 (40%), matured in French barriques (15% new) for 15 months. Has held onto its youthful hue; an altogether impressive Pinot, swiftly ticking all the boxes, cruising through the mid-palate before opening its peacock tail on the long finish and aftertaste. Screwcap. 13% alc. Rating 95 To 2022 $22 ❂

🍷🍷🍷🍷 **Dr Durif 2012** Rating 91 To 2018 $28

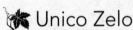 Unico Zelo ★★★★

24 Victoria Street, Gumeracha, SA 5233 **Region** Adelaide Hills
T 0415 660 990 **www**.unicozelo.com.au **Open** By appt
Winemaker Brendan and Laura Carter **Est.** 2012 **Dozens** 3000
Brendan and Laura Carter have strung their star to fiano, nebbiolo and nero d'Avola, purchasing these varieties from the Adelaide Hills, Polish Hill River and Riverland. In 2012 they were able to retro-fit their Adelaide Hills winery into an old, disused apple cool store in Gumeracha; the economy of doing this, and sourcing the grape varieties as they have, allows them to achieve their aim of making approachable wines for reasonable prices with a philosophy of minimal intervention along the way. The venture into orange wine via its '14 Esoterico was (in my view) a failure.

🍷🍷🍷🍷 **The River Riverland Nero d'Avola 2014** Hand-picked. Ancient soils! Wild yeast-fermented, 30% whole bunches, 160 dozen made. Distinctly juicy fruit with plum and cherry waltzing insouciantly across the palate before a delicately savoury finish. Diam. 13% alc. Rating 93 To 2024 $23 ❂
Adelaide Hills Pinot Noir 2014 100% whole bunches; wild yeast-fermented with a long maceration, then matured in a single used French barrel, 25 dozen 'orchestrated'. Given a single barrel straitjacket, this is a promising start, with contrasting sweet and savoury fruit flavours in search of structure. Screwcap. 13% alc. Rating 90 To 2019 $35

🍷🍷🍷 **Adelaide Hills Grenache 2014** Rating 89 To 2016 $35
Cherry Fields Adelaide Hills Dolcetto 2014 Rating 88 To 2017 $23

Upper Reach

77 Memorial Avenue, Baskerville, WA 6056 **Region** Swan Valley
T (08) 9296 0078 **www**.upperreach.com.au **Open** 7 days 11–5
Winemaker Derek Pearse **Est.** 1996 **Dozens** 4000 **Vyds** 8.45ha

This 10ha property on the banks of the upper reaches of the Swan River was purchased by Laura Rowe and Derek Pearse in 1996. The original 4ha vineyard was expanded, and plantings now include chardonnay, shiraz, cabernet sauvignon, verdelho, semillon, merlot, petit verdot and muscat. All wines are estate-grown. Several years ago they leased the restaurant area to Anthony and Annalis Broad, who now run Broads Restaurant at Upper Reach, encased by full-length glass doors and surrounded by a deck overlooking the vineyard. They have integrated the cellar door with the restaurant, the glass walls bringing vineyard views into the cellar door, where wines are tasted in Riedel glasses. Next they constructed a deck where visitors can relax and enjoy a glass or two, resulting in *Gourmet Traveller: Wine* choosing Upper Reach as the Star Cellar Door in the Swan Valley.

ΨΨΨΨΨ **Reserve Swan Valley Shiraz 2011** Still on a journey. It needs to be retasted several times for it to be given justice; the gold medal at the Swan Valley Wine Show '14 is entirely appropriate in the context of a regional wine show, and the wine has an assured future. Screwcap. 14% alc. **Rating** 94 **To** 2026 $38
The Gig Shiraz Grenache 2012 The blend comes together well; black fruits and tannins from the shiraz are given life and movement by the red fruits and spices of the grenache; the synergy provided is the essence of the wine. Screwcap. 14% alc. **Rating** 94 **To** 2027 $25 ❂
Frankland River Cabernet Sauvignon 2012 Matured in French oak, which certainly adds a dimension to the naturally intense cassis and bramble fruit that opens on the bouquet and progressively gains power through to the ascending finish. Should be very long-lived. Screwcap. 14% alc. **Rating** 94 **To** 2037 $45

ΨΨΨΨΨ **Swan Valley Petit Verdot 2012 Rating** 93 **To** 2027 $45
Reserve Cabernet Sauvignon 2013 Rating 91 **To** 2025 $30

Valhalla Wines

163 All Saints Road, Wahgunyah, Vic 3687 **Region** Rutherglen
T (02) 6033 1438 **www**.valhallawines.com.au **Open** 7 days 10–4
Winemaker Anton Therkildsen **Est.** 2001 **Dozens** 1400 **Vyds** 2.5ha

Anton Therkildsen and wife Antoinette Del Popolo planted their vineyard in 2002 (shiraz and durif), and purchase viognier, marsanne, grenache and mourvedre from local growers, reflecting their interest in the wines of the Rhône Valley. Anton uses traditional winemaking methods, making and cellaring the wines in their straw-bale winery. Sustainable viticulture practices are used, with minimal use of sprays and annual planting of cover crops between the rows. Rainwater harvesting, recycled packaging, a worm farm and the composting of grape skins and stalks complete the picture.

ΨΨΨΨΨ **Rutherglen Durif 2012** Yet further proof that Anton Therkildsen has really got his head around the challenges and opportunities of the Rutherglen climate. Still brilliantly deep in colour, the structure and mouthfeel a revelation, with predominantly black fruits anchored as much by acidity as by tannins. A Durif of uncommon quality. Screwcap. 14.2% alc. **Rating** 96 **To** 2032 $34 ❂

ΨΨΨΨΨ **Rutherglen Marsanne 2013 Rating** 91 **To** 2017 $25 CM
Rutherglen Grenache Shiraz Mourvedre 2013 Rating 91 **To** 2020 $25
The Goat 2013 Rating 90 **To** 2020 $20 ❂
Rutherglen Shiraz 2013 Rating 90 **To** 2020 $28

Vasarelli Wines

164 Main Road, McLaren Vale, SA 5171 **Region** McLaren Vale
T (08) 8323 7980 **Open** 7 days 8–5
Winemaker Nigel Dolan (Contract) **Est.** 1995 **Dozens** 18 000 **Vyds** 33ha

Pasquale (Pat) and Vittoria (Vicky) Vasarelli moved with their parents from Melbourne to McLaren Vale in 1976. They began the establishment of their vineyard, and over the succeeding years increased the area under vine to its present size, planted to semillon, sauvignon blanc, chardonnay, pinot gris, vermentino, shiraz, cabernet sauvignon and merlot. Until '95 the grapes were sold to other producers, but in that year they joined Cellarmaster Wines and the Vasarelli label was born. In a reverse play of the usual pattern, they opened a cellar door in 2009 on a small property they had purchased in '92.

PPPPP **McLaren Vale Cabernet Franc 2013** Plenty of attitude. Grass, herbs, dust and powdered chocolate characters splash over ripe, curranty fruit. Not your standard fare, but it works. No reason why it won't develop well in the medium term either. Screwcap. 15% alc. **Rating** 90 **To** 2020 $21 CM **○**

PPPP **Family Reserve Chardonnay 2013** **Rating** 88 **To** 2016 $21 CM
Family Reserve McLaren Vale Merlot 2013 **Rating** 88 **To** 2018 $21 CM

Vasse Felix   ★★★★★

Cnr Tom Cullity Drive/Caves Road, Cowaramup, WA 6284 **Region** Margaret River
T (08) 9756 5000 **www**.vassefelix.com.au **Open** 7 days 10–5
Winemaker Virginia Willcock **Est.** 1967 **Dozens** 150 000 **Vyds** 232ha
Vasse Felix was the first winery to be built in the Margaret River. Owned and operated by the Holmes à Court family since 1987, Vasse Felix has undergone extensive changes and expansion. Chief winemaker Virginia Willcock energised the winemaking and viticultural team with her no-nonsense approach and fierce commitment to quality. The estate vineyards contribute all but a small part of the annual production, and are scrupulously managed, quality the sole driver. Wines include top of the range Heytesbury (a Cabernet blend) and Heytesbury Chardonnay; the Estate range of varietal wines; Classic Dry White and Dry Red; Filius Chardonnay and Cabernet Merlot; and Theatre White and Red. Limited quantities of specialty wines include Cane Cut Semillon, Viognier and Tempranillo. Exports to all major markets.

PPPPP **Heytesbury Margaret River Chardonnay 2013** Spent 9.5 months in French oak (73% new, 27% 1–2yo). The track record of this great Chardonnay label speaks for itself: it is all about breed and disciplined power; the grapes were picked at exactly the right moment, the fruit–oak balance calculated down to the finest imaginable degree, the length beyond any doubt or discussion. Screwcap. 13% alc. **Rating** 97 **To** 2025 $70 **○**

PPPPP **Margaret River Chardonnay 2013** Estate-grown, hand-picked, whole bunch-pressed, wild yeast-fermented cloudy juice; 9 months in French oak (55% new). This is an altogether different idiom from its sister Chardonnays, its purity and intensity cutting through the palate like a surgeon's scalpel, the length and aftertaste prodigious. Screwcap. 13% alc. **Rating** 96 **To** 2025 $37 **○**
Filius Chardonnay 2013 The wine spent 9 months in French oak, 28% new; it leaps out of the glass with a great burst of energy, an awesome entry point Margaret River Chardonnay from one of the region's truly great producers; white peach on entry morphs to pink grapefruit on the vibrantly fresh finish. Screwcap. 13% alc. **Rating** 95 **To** 2019 $27 **○**
Filius Cabernet Merlot 2013 A 60/30/10% blend of cabernet, merlot and malbec matured in French oak. The super-fragrant bouquet heralds an elegant, light to medium-bodied wine that engages your attention through its seamless, silky and harmonious palate of red and black small-berry fruits. Superb drink now/soon style. Screwcap. 14.5% alc. **Rating** 95 **To** 2020 $27 **○**
Margaret River Cabernet Sauvignon 2012 Bright, clear crimson-purple; the bouquet sets the scene with its pristine display of redcurrant and blackcurrant fruit, with the barest hint of cedar, the silky medium-bodied palate unhurriedly imposing itself on the way through to the lingering finish. Classic restraint. Screwcap. 14.5% alc. **Rating** 95 **To** 2032 $42
Margaret River Sauvignon Blanc Semillon 2014 **Rating** 94 **To** 2016 $24 **○**

Classic Dry White SSB 2014 Rating 94 To 2017 $19 ○
Margaret River Shiraz 2012 Rating 94 To 2027 $37

♀♀♀♀♀ Classic Dry Red Shiraz Cabernet 2013 Rating 91 To 2023 $19 ○

Velo Wines ★★★★★

755 West Tamar Highway, Legana, Tas 7277 **Region** Northern Tasmania
T (03) 6330 3677 **www**.velowines.com.au **Open** 7 days 10–5
Winemaker Micheal Wilson, Winemaking Tasmania **Est.** 1966 **Dozens** 3000
The story behind Velo Wines is fascinating, wheels within wheels. The 0.9ha of cabernet
sauvignon and 0.5ha of pinot noir of the Legana Vineyard were planted in 1966 by Graham
Wiltshire, legitimately described as one of the three great pioneers of the Tasmanian wine
industry. Micheal and Mary Wilson returned to Tasmania in '91 after living in Italy and France
for a decade. Micheal had been an Olympic cyclist and joined the professional ranks, racing
in all the major European events. Imbued with a love of wine and food, they spent 'seven
long hard years in the restaurant game'. Somehow, Micheal found time to become a qualified
viticulturist, and was vineyard manager for Moorilla Estate, based at St Matthias; Mary spent
five years working in wine wholesaling for leading distributors. In 2001 they purchased the
Legana Vineyard, planted so long ago, and they have since painstakingly rehabilitated the
almost 50-year-old vines. They have also built a small winery where Micheal makes the red
wines; Winemaking Tasmania makes the white wines. A representative range of wines was not
received for this edition, but the rating has been maintained.

♀♀♀♀♀ Pinot Noir 2013 Bright, clear and full colour; the palate is full of complex black
fruits and round tannins. Built for the long haul, and should handsomely repay
patience. Screwcap. 13.5% alc. **Rating** 90 To 2025 $32

Verdun Park Wines ★★★★

14 Sandow Road, Verdun, SA 5245 **Region** Adelaide Hills
T (08) 8388 7357 **www**.verdunparkwines.com.au **Open** Fourth w'end each month 12–5
Winemaker Michael Sykes **Est.** 2009 **Dozens** 500 **Vyds** 2ha
Verdun Park is owned by Sandy and Bob Voumard (with backgrounds in education and
accountancy) and run with the assistance of their daughter Danielle and son-in-law Shaun
McBeath (viticulturist). The initial release, 2009 Lyla Sauvignon Blanc, was made from
specifically selected contract-grown grapes, and went on to win a gold medal at the fiercely
contested (for sauvignon blanc) Adelaide Hills Wine Show '09.

♀♀♀♀♀ Albert Arthur Adelaide Hills Shiraz 2010 Deep colour, slight spritz, ample
flavours of licorice and wood spice with dark cherry in enthusiastic support.
Prominent gum leaf overtones. Looks very young even as a 5yo; it's easy to think
this has many years left ahead of it. Juicy, fruit-filled finish. Screwcap. 14% alc.
Rating 92 To 2024 $37 CM
Adelaide Hills Ruby Rose 2014 Made from shiraz. Bright crimson-salmon
colour. Lively aromatics and mid-palate before turning dry as you swallow.
Buoyant with raspberry and strawberry, fresh and raring to go. Screwcap. 12.5% alc.
Rating 90 To 2015 $20 CM ○

Vickery Wines ★★★★★

28 The Parade, Norwood, SA 5067 **Region** Clare Valley/Eden Valley
T (08) 8362 8622 **www**.vickerywines.com.au **Open** Not
Winemaker John Vickery, Phil Lehmann **Est.** 2014 **Dozens** 2000 **Vyds** 12ha
It must be a strange feeling for John Vickery to begin at the beginning again, 60 years after his
first vintage in 1951. His interest in, love of, and exceptional skills with Riesling began with
Leo Buring in 1955 at Chateau Leonay. Over the intervening years he became the uncrowned
but absolute monarch of Riesling makers in Australia until, in his semi-retirement, he passed
the mantle on to Jeffrey Grosset. Along the way he had (unsurprisingly) won the Wolf Blass
Riesling Award at the Canberra International Riesling Challenge 2007, and had been judged

by his peers as Australia's Greatest Living Winemaker in a survey conducted by *The Age Epicure* in '03. His new venture has been undertaken in conjunction with Phil Lehmann, with 12ha of Clare and Eden Valley riesling involved, and wine marketer Jonathon Hesketh moving largely invisibly in the background. As one might hope and expect, the first release under the Vickery label is a beautifully groomed and proportioned Riesling of the highest quality.

ΨΨΨΨΨ **WVR 192 CB Watervale Riesling 2014** There is nothing extravagant about this wine; on the contrary, it is beautifully groomed and proportioned from its citrus blossom bouquet through to its deceptively intense lime and lemon palate. A fitting tribute indeed. Screwcap. 11.5% alc. **Rating** 95 **To** 2034 $23 ✪

Victory Point Wines   ★★★★★

4 Holben Road, Cowaramup, WA 6284 **Region** Margaret River
T 0417 954 6555 **www.**victorypointwines.com **Open** By appt
Winemaker Mark Messenger (Contract) **Est.** 1997 **Dozens** 2500 **Vyds** 13ha
Judith and Gary Berson (the latter a partner in the Perth office of a national law firm) have set their aims high. They established their vineyard without irrigation, emulating those of the Margaret River pioneers (including Moss Wood). The fully mature plantings comprise 4.2ha chardonnay and 0.5ha of pinot noir, the remainder Bordeaux varieties, with cabernet sauvignon (6.2ha), cabernet franc (0.5ha), malbec (0.8ha) and petit verdot (0.7ha).

ΨΨΨΨΨ **Margaret River Cabernet Sauvignon 2010** Incorporates 2% each of petit verdot and cabernet franc, matured for 19 months in French oak (50% new). Has retained a youthful line, and a youthful grip to the medium to full-bodied palate, resulting in an exceptionally long finish; the flavours are all in a sombre/black spectrum, but the tannins are fine and ripe, the oak totally integrated. Screwcap. 14% alc. **Rating** 96 **To** 2035 $40 ✪
The Mallee Root Cabernet Franc Malbec Cabernet Sauvignon 2012 An estate 40/31/23/6% blend, also including petit verdot; matured in French oak (50% new) for 19 months. An altogether elegant style, medium-bodied and perfectly balanced; cassis, redcurrant and spice are garnished by cedary oak and supple, silky tannins. Screwcap. 14% alc. **Rating** 95 **To** 2032 $30 ✪
Margaret River Malbec 2012 A once-off wine prompted by the sheer quality of the fruit; it has remarkable elegance for a variety not noted for this character; quality French oak and skilled winemaking have also coaxed mid-palate fruit to provide balance, courtesy of plum and black berry flavours. Screwcap. 14% alc. **Rating** 95 **To** 2032 $40

ΨΨΨΨΨ **Margaret River Rose 2014 Rating** 92 **To** 2015 $20 ✪

View Road Wines   ★★★★

Peacocks Road, Lenswood, SA 5240 **Region** Adelaide Hills
T 0402 180 383 **www.**viewroadwines.com.au **Open** Not
Winemaker Josh Tuckfield **Est.** 2011 **Dozens** 700
View Road Wines sources prosecco, arneis, chardonnay, sangiovese, merlot, sagrantino and syrah from Adelaide Hills vineyards; shiraz, aglianico and sagrantino for McLaren Vale vineyards; and nero d'Avola and fiano from the Riverland. All of the wines are wild yeast-fermented, and are matured in used oak.

ΨΨΨΨΨ **McLaren Vale Shiraz 2013** Richly flavoured and well composed. On song. Blackberry, peppercorn and milk chocolate, smooth to the touch and generous to a fault. Laced with fine-grained, smoky/spicy tannin. Excellent. Screwcap. 14.5% alc. **Rating** 94 **To** 2025 $37 CM

ΨΨΨΨΨ **Picked by my Wife Arneis 2014 Rating** 92 **To** 2016 $22 CM ✪
Picked by my Wife Tempranillo 2013 Rating 90 **To** 2019 $27 CM

Vigna Bottin

Lot 2 Plains Road, Sellicks Hill, McLaren Vale, SA 5171 **Region** McLaren Vale
T 0414 562 956 **www**.vignabottin.com.au **Open** Not
Winemaker Paolo Bottin **Est.** 2006 **Dozens** 750 **Vyds** 16ha

The Bottin family migrated to Australia in 1954 from Treviso in northern Italy, where they were grapegrowers. The family began growing grapes in McLaren Vale in 1970, focusing on mainstream varieties for sale to wineries in the region. When son Paolo and wife Maria made a trip back to Italy in '98, they were inspired to do more, and, says Paolo, 'My love for barbera and sangiovese was sealed during a vintage in Pavia. I came straight home to plant both varieties in our family plot. My father was finally happy!' They now trade under the catchy phrase 'Italian Vines, Australian Wines'.

McLaren Vale Barbera 2013 The acidity of barbera comes in useful in McLaren Vale, keeping the polished red apple and plum flavours bright and fresh on the medium-bodied palate. Screwcap. 13.5% alc. **Rating** 90 **To** 2018 $28

McLaren Vale Sangiovese Rosato 2014 Rating 89 **To** 2016 $24
McLaren Vale Sangiovese 2013 Rating 89 **To** 2017 $28
McLaren Vale Vermentino 2014 Rating 88 **To** 2016 $24

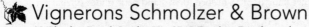 Vignerons Schmolzer & Brown

39 Thorley Road, Stanley, Vic 3747 **Region** Beechworth
T 0411 053 487 **www**.vsandb.com.au **Open** By appt
Winemaker Tessa Brown **Est.** 2014 **Dozens** 500 **Vyds** 2ha

Winemaker/viticulturist Tessa Brown graduated from CSU with a degree in viticulture in the late 1990s, and undertook postgraduate winemaking studies at Adelaide Uni in the mid-2000s. Her self-description of being 'reasonably peripatetic' covers her winemaking in Orange in '99, Canberra, SA, Rioja, Strathbogie Ranges and Central Otago before joining Kooyong and Port Phillip Estate in '08. She and architect partner Jeremy Schmolzer have kept an eye on Northeast Victoria for a number of years, and in '09 Mark Walpole showed them a property that he described as 'the jewel in the crown of the GI'. When it came onto the market unexpectedly in '12, they were in a position to jump. The property (named Thorley) was a 20ha cleared property; they began planting chardonnay and shiraz in Oct '14, and plan to plant riesling and nebbiolo in the spring of '15. By sheer chance, just across the road from Thorley was a tiny vineyard, a bit over 0.4 hectares, with dry-grown pinot and chardonnay around 20 years old. When they realised it was not being managed for production, they struck up a working relationship with the owners, getting the vineyard into shape, and made their first (very good) wines in '14.

Brunnen Chardonnay 2014 Grown at Stanley in the upper reaches of the Beechworth region. It's tempting to call it a wine of line and length due to its thrilling line of fresh acidity, but it has so much flavour draped from it that such talk could easily give the wrong impression. In short, it's both exquisite and seductive. Screwcap. 13% alc. **Rating** 95 **To** 2022 $39 CM

Pret-A-Rose Rose 2014 Rating 93 **To** 2016 $26 CM ○

Vinaceous Wines

49 Bennett Street, East Perth, WA 6004 (postal) **Region** Various
T (08) 9221 4666 **www**.vinaceous.com.au **Open** Not
Winemaker Gavin Berry, Michael Kerrigan **Est.** 2007 **Dozens** 25 000

This is the somewhat quirky venture of wine marketer Nick Stacy (West Cape Howe), Michael Kerrigan (winemaker/partner Hay Shed Hill) and Gavin Berry (winemaker/partner West Cape Howe). The brand is primarily directed at the US market, which took 90% of the four wines in the first release, the remaining 10% shared among all other markets. The wines are not primarily sourced from WA, as one might expect, but variously from McLaren Vale, Barossa Valley and the Limestone Coast, with a Verdelho, and the possibility of a Reserve

Shiraz, from WA. The Right Reverend V wines are sourced from the premium regions of WA. Divine Light Verdelho, Snake Charmer Shiraz, Red Right Hand Shiraz Grenache Tempranillo and Raconteur Cabernet Sauvignon, coupled with ornate, turn-of-the-19th-century labels, suggest the flavour of the wines and their export focus. Exports to the UK, the US, Canada, South America, Denmark, Indonesia, the Philippines, Thailand, Singapore and Hong Kong.

ΨΨΨΨΨ **Raconteur Margaret River Cabernet Sauvignon 2013** Hand-picked, open-fermented, 10% whole bunches, basket-pressed into French and American barriques (25% new) to finish fermentation, 14–16 months' maturation in those barriques. A medium to full-bodied Cabernet in the best traditions of Margaret River, loaded with blackcurrant fruit, ripe tannins and integrated, yet positive, oak. And the price is right. Screwcap. 14.5% alc. **Rating** 95 **To** 2033 $25 ✪
Voodoo Moon Margaret River Malbec 2013 Identical vinification and maturation to the other Vinaceous red wines. Deep crimson-purple, it is exotically plush and rich, with a mix of fresh blackberries and blackberry and plum jam – yet it's not jammy, per se, and is studded with oriental spices. Screwcap. 14% alc. **Rating** 95 **To** 2025 $25 ✪
Snake Charmer McLaren Vale Shiraz 2013 Hand-picked, open-fermented, 10% whole bunches; finished fermentation and 15 months' maturation in French and American barriques (25% new). Finishing the ferment in barrel isn't widely used, notwithstanding the example of Grange and top-level Penfolds red wines; this wine certainly shows that the oak is well integrated, simply part of a wider canvas of elegant black fruits, licorice and dark chocolate, all with a lilt to their flavour and mouthfeel. Screwcap. 14.5% alc. **Rating** 94 **To** 2033 $25 ✪
Red Right Hand Margaret River Shiraz Grenache Tempranillo 2013 Vividly coloured, it is a left-field Margaret River blend, unsurprisingly bright and lively in the mouth, with spicy red fruit running amok on the long, medium-bodied palate. This has all the makings of an exceptional wine in the future; great value. Screwcap. 14.5% alc. **Rating** 94 **To** 2038 $25 ✪
Right Reverend V Patientia Cabernet Sauvignon 2013 From two Mount Barker vineyards, matured in French barriques (25% new). This is tailor-made for those intimidated by the tannic power of austere Cabernets in classic mode; here ripe cassis/blackcurrant is warmed by good French oak, and balanced by ripe, not austere, tannins. Screwcap. 14.5% alc. **Rating** 94 **To** 2028 $24 ✪

ΨΨΨΨΨ **Right Reverend V Temperantia Riesling 2014** **Rating** 93 **To** 2029 $24 ✪
Right Reverend V Industria Chardonnay 2014 **Rating** 92 **To** 2021 $24 ✪
Right Reverend V Caritas Rose 2014 **Rating** 92 **To** 2016 $24 ✪
Right Reverend V Benevolentia Syrah 2013 **Rating** 92 **To** 2033 $24 ✪

Vinden Estate ★★★★

17 Gillards Road, Pokolbin, NSW 2320 **Region** Hunter Valley
T (02) 4998 7410 **www.**vindenestate.com.au **Open** Wed–Sun 10–5
Winemaker Guy Vinden, John Baruzzi **Est.** 1998 **Dozens** 1000 **Vyds** 6.5ha
Sandra and Guy Vinden have a beautiful home and cellar door, landscaped gardens and a vineyard that includes shiraz (2.5ha), merlot and alicante bouschet (2ha each), with the Brokenback mountain range in the distance. The wines are made onsite, using estate-grown red grapes; semillon and chardonnay are purchased from other growers. The reds are open-fermented, hand-plunged and basket-pressed.

ΨΨΨΨΨ **Back Block Shiraz 2009** The colour is still deep, the high-quality cork still virginal; there is a velvety richness to the fruit, still to show any earthy/leathery regional markers, but its sheer opulence promises decades of life for that to emerge. A very interesting full-bodied wine. 14.5% alc. **Rating** 93 **To** 2034 $40
Hunter Valley Semillon 2013 Well made, satisfying all the criteria for cellaring, but with sufficient flavour on offer to drink it now – or whenever. Screwcap. 10.5% alc. **Rating** 91 **To** 2023 $25

Basket Press Hunter Valley Shiraz 2012 How on earth Vinden Estate managed to save the wine from the rain that caused many Hunter Valley makers to abandon their shiraz as not worth picking I have no idea; it's ripe in both flavour and alcohol terms. It would be perfectly legal to blend in 15% top-quality McLaren Vale or Barossa Valley Shiraz, plenty of which was available at the time, but we have no way of knowing. Screwcap. 14% alc. **Rating** 91 **To** 2027 $32

ŸŸŸŸ **Hunter Valley Chardonnay 2013** Rating 89 To 2017 $26

Vinifera Wines ★★★☆

194 Henry Lawson Drive, Mudgee, NSW 2850 **Region** Mudgee
T (02) 6372 2461 **www**.viniferawines.com.au **Open** Mon–Sat 10–5, Sun 10–4
Winemaker Jacob Stein **Est.** 1997 **Dozens** 1200 **Vyds** 12ha
Having lived in Mudgee for 15 years, Tony McKendry (a regional medical superintendent) and wife Debbie succumbed to the lure; they planted their small (1.5ha) vineyard in 1995. In Debbie's words, 'Tony, in his spare two minutes per day, also decided to start Wine Science at CSU in 1992.' She continues, 'His trying to live 27 hours per day (plus our four kids!) fell to pieces when he was involved in a severe car smash in 1997. Two months in hospital stopped full-time medical work, and the winery dreams became inevitable.' Financial compensation finally came through and the small winery was built. The now-expanded vineyard includes chardonnay, cabernet sauvignon (3ha each), semillon, tempranillo, grenache (1.5ha each) and smaller plantings of graciano and monastrell.

ŸŸŸŸŸ **Organic Mudgee Graciano 2013** Very good colour; Graciano isn't a wine that was meant to be easy, but this has more friendly than unfriendly notes, savoury red and black fruits, its tannins fine-grained and (relatively) ripe. Screwcap. 14.5% alc. **Rating** 91 **To** 2018 $36

Vinrock ★★★★☆

23 George Street, Thebarton, SA 5031 (postal) **Region** McLaren Vale
T (08) 8408 8900 **www**.vinrock.com **Open** Not
Winemaker Michael Fragos (Consultant) **Est.** 1998 **Dozens** 18 000 **Vyds** 30ha
Owners Don Luca, Marco Iannetti and Anthony De Pizzol all have backgrounds in the wine industry, none more than Don, a former board member of Tatachilla. He also planted the Luca Vineyard in 1998 (20ha of shiraz, 5ha each of grenache and cabernet sauvignon). The majority of the grapes are sold, but steadily increasing quantities of wine have been made from the best blocks in the vineyard, many at tempting prices. Exports to Canada, Hong Kong, China and NZ.

ŸŸŸŸŸ **Block 18 McLaren Vale Shiraz 2013** Ah yes; deeply imprinted with varietal and regional DNA; black fruits, dark chocolate, fulsome ripe tannins and no dead fruit; indeed there is a spicy savoury twist on the finish that gives a lift of outright freshness. 130 dozen made. Screwcap. 14.5% alc. **Rating** 95 **To** 2030 $45

ŸŸŸŸŸ **McLaren Vale Grenache 2013** Rating 93 To 2024 $23
McLaren Vale Grenache Shiraz Mataro 2013 Rating 93 To 2023 $23 ✪
McLaren Vale Shiraz 2013 Rating 92 To 2023 $23 ✪
Terra Mia Grenache Shiraz Mataro 2013 Rating 90 To 2017 $17 ✪
McLaren Vale Cabernet Sauvignon 2013 Rating 90 To 2020 $23

Vinteloper Wines ★★★★

PO Box 2601, Kent Town, SA 5071 **Region** Various
T 0415 297 787 **www**.vinteloper.com.au **Open** Not
Winemaker David Bowley **Est.** 2008 **Dozens** 1500
Raised in the Adelaide foothills, vineyards and wineries had permeated David Bowley's mind before he left school. It was inevitable that he would obtain his agricultural science (oenology) degree at Adelaide University (in 2002); he worked at wineries and overseas over the next two

years. A career in basketball meant a conventional day job was needed, and he worked for the Australian Wine & Brandy Corporation for six years, squeezing in a single-vineyard McLaren Vale Shiraz during the last two years. He then took the plunge, and moved into full-time winemaking, seeking to match variety and region. He has also experimented with art versus science, making Watervale Riesling in two very different ways.

ŸŸŸŸŸ **Adelaide Hills Pinot Noir 2013** Feels composed at every turn. Cherries and plums stewed in their own juices, rhubarb and ground spice. Stalk notes have soaked straight down into the wine; fruit is the dominant player. Perfumed start and finish. Screwcap. 13.5% alc. **Rating** 92 **To** 2020 $38 CM

Vintners Ridge Estate ★★★★

Lot 18 Veraison Place, Yallingup, Margaret River, WA 6285 **Region** Margaret River
T 0417 956 943 **www**.vintnersridge.com.au **Open** By appt
Winemaker Flying Fish Cove (Simon Ding) **Est.** 2001 **Dozens** 500 **Vyds** 2.1ha
When Maree and Robin Adair purchased the Vintners Ridge vineyard in 2006 (cabernet sauvignon), it had already produced three crops, having been planted in Nov '01 (which is a perfectly permissible establishment date). The vineyard overlooks the picturesque Geographe Bay.

ŸŸŸŸŸ **Margaret River Cabernet Sauvignon 2013** Matured in new and used French oak for 16 months. Crimson-purple; a finely wrought Cabernet with a mix of cassis and bay leaf on both the bouquet and very long, well-balanced palate; the oak and tannin management has been its own reward. Screwcap. 13.8% alc. **Rating** 94 **To** 2028 $30 ✪

Virgara Wines ★★★★

Lot 11 Heaslip Road, Angle Vale, SA 5117 **Region** Adelaide Plains
T (08) 8284 7688 **www**.virgarawines.com.au **Open** Mon–Fri 9–5, w'ends 11–4
Winemaker Tony Carapetis **Est.** 2001 **Dozens** 45 000 **Vyds** 118ha
In 1962 the Virgara family – father Michael, mother Maria and 10 children – migrated to Australia from southern Italy. Through the hard work so typical of many such families, in due course they became market gardeners on land purchased at Angle Vale ('67), and in the early '90s acquired an existing vineyard in Angle Vale. The plantings have since expanded to almost 120ha of shiraz, cabernet sauvignon, grenache, malbec, merlot, riesling, sangiovese, sauvignon blanc, pinot grigio and alicante. In 2001 the Virgara brothers purchased the former Barossa Valley Estates winery, but used it only for storage and maturation. The death of Domenic Virgara in a road accident led to the employment of former (and, before that, Tahbilk) Palandri winemaker Tony Carapetis, and the full re-commissioning of the winery. Exports to the US, Canada, China, Thailand, Malaysia and Japan.

ŸŸŸŸŸ **Gran Reserve Adelaide Shiraz 2013** Oak plays a leading role, but it marries well to fresh, cranberried, beefy fruit flavour. Smoke, dried herbs and floral elements play a role too. This is a world away from the '12. Fine-grained tannin is the finishing touch to a quality release. Diam. 14.7% alc. **Rating** 94 **To** 2025 $30 CM ✪

ŸŸŸŸŸ **Gran Reserve Cabernet Sauvignon 2013 Rating** 91 **To** 2025 $30 CM
Gran Reserve Merlot Cabernet Sauvignon Malbec 2012 Rating 90 **To** 2021 $50 CM

Voyager Estate ★★★★★

Lot 1 Stevens Road, Margaret River, WA 6285 **Region** Margaret River
T (08) 9757 6354 **www**.voyagerestate.com.au **Open** 7 days 10–5
Winemaker Steve James, Travis Lemm **Est.** 1978 **Dozens** 36 000 **Vyds** 110ha
The late mining magnate Michael Wright pursued several avenues of business and agriculture before setting his sights on owning a vineyard and winery. It was thus an easy decision when

he was able to buy what was then called Freycinet Estate from founder and leading viticulturist Peter Gherardi in 1991. Peter had established the vineyard in '78, and it was significantly expanded by Michael over the ensuing years. Apart from the Cape Dutch-style tasting room and vast rose garden, the signpost for the estate is the massive Australian flag pole – after Parliament House in Canberra, the largest flag pole in Australia. Michael's daughter, Alexandra Burt, has been at the helm of Voyager Estate for many years, supported by general manager Chris Furtado and a long-serving and committed staff. Michael will be remembered as a larger than life character, more at home in his favourite work pants and boots than a suit, and never happier than when trundling around the estate on a four-wheeler or fixing a piece of machinery. Exports to the UK, the US, Canada, Singapore, Japan, Hong Kong and China.

ŸŸŸŸŸ **Tom Price Margaret River Semillon Sauvignon Blanc 2012** A 67/33% blend, hand-picked, whole bunch-pressed semillon fermentation in French oak (50% new), the sauvignon blanc pressed direct to barrel, lees-stirred, 8 months in barrel. A lavish and complex wine, with waves of tropical fruits interleaved with minerally/lemony acidity. Its length and persistence are remarkable. Screwcap. 13.2% alc. **Rating** 96 **To** 2022 $85

Project 95 Margaret River Chardonnay 2012 The project is to present clone 95, here with a juicy make-up to its predominantly stone fruit mid-palate before switching to a more pithy/minerally mode on the finish, with grapefruit in the ascendancy. Screwcap. 12.4% alc. **Rating** 96 **To** 2022 $55 ○

Margaret River Chardonnay 2012 Slight colour development is not surprising; the choice of oak for the barrel fermentation was spot on, allowing the fine varietal fruit expression free rein, riding high on its minerally acidity; the overall balance and elegance are exceptional. Screwcap. 13% alc. **Rating** 96 **To** 2022 $45 ○

Project Gin Gin Margaret River Chardonnay 2012 The Gin Gin clone has always been recognised for the generosity of its flavour, here with a mix of white peach and nectarine to the fore, grapefruit occupying the back-palate; the oak use and overall handling have produced a wine of considerable elegance. Screwcap. 13.2% alc. **Rating** 95 **To** 2020 $55

Margaret River Shiraz 2013 Bright crimson colour heralds a wine full of vitality; red berry flavours surge through the mouth, gauzy tannins in the background adding to the exuberant mouthfeel and length. Screwcap. 14% alc. **Rating** 95 **To** 2028 $38

Margaret River Cabernet Sauvignon Merlot 2011 A complete wine from the opening stanza through to the encore, singing with great clarity about its varietal make-up and its sense of place; cassis/blackcurrant fruit is given complexity by dusty tannins and integrated French oak, the overall balance impeccable. Screwcap. 14% alc. **Rating** 95 **To** 2031 $70

Project U12 North Block Margaret River Cabernet Sauvignon 2011 Deep colour; it is a rich and full-bodied Cabernet with layers of blackcurrant and earth to the fore; well-balanced and integrated tannins and oak complete a Cabernet full of vitality and style. Screwcap. 14% alc. **Rating** 95 **To** 2041 $90

Margaret River Sauvignon Blanc Semillon 2014 Rating 94 **To** 2017 $24 ○
Project V9 Old Block Cabernet Sauvignon 2011 Rating 94 **To** 2026 $90
Tom Price Cabernet 2010 Rating 94 **To** 2036 $150

Walter Clappis Wine Co   ★★★★☆

Rifle Range Road, McLaren Vale, SA 5171 **Region** McLaren Vale
T (08) 8323 8818 **www**.hedonistwines.com.au **Open** Not
Winemaker Walter and Kimberley Clappis **Est.** 1982 **Dozens** 12 000 **Vyds** 35ha
Walter Clappis (once known as Bill) has been a stalwart of the McLaren Vale wine scene for decades. The estate plantings of shiraz (14ha), cabernet sauvignon (10ha), merlot (9ha) and tempranillo (2ha) are the cornerstone of his business, which also provides the home for the Amicus wines. Exports include the UK, the US, Canada and China.

ŸŸŸŸŸ **Amicus Reserve Shiraz 2010** Arms loaded with chocolatey goodness wrap themselves around a trunk of smoky, blackberried, earthen fruit. It's dense but not dull, super-ripe but not baked or dead; there's vigour to be found here. Tannin spreads in filigreed form, and while there's a good deal of oak on display, the push of fruit through the finish exudes confidence. Screwcap. 14.5% alc. **Rating** 96 To 2028 $75 CM ✪

Down The Rabbit Hole Shiraz 2013 All about smoothness of texture and density. Dark chocolate, rich blackberry, toasty oak and lots of all three. A meal in itself, and a satisfying one. Screwcap. 14% alc. **Rating** 94 To 2025 $30 CM ✪

The Hedonist Shiraz 2013 Even-tempered and well presented. Rests in a comfortable place. Offers blackberry, coffee-cream and red cherry flavours before exiting with a juicy fruit-led flourish. Ever so enjoyable. Screwcap. 13.5% alc. **Rating** 94 To 2023 $25 CM ✪

ᵀᵀᵀᵀ♀ **The Hedonist Cabernet 2012** Rating 92 To 2022 $25 CM ✪

Wangolina Station ★★★★☆

Cnr Southern Ports Highway/Limestone Coast Road, Kingston SE, SA 5275
Region Mount Benson
T (08) 8768 6187 **www**.wangolina.com.au **Open** 7 days 10–5
Winemaker Anita Goode **Est.** 2001 **Dozens** 5000 **Vyds** 11ha
Four generations of the Goode family have been graziers at Wangolina Station, but now Anita Goode has broken with tradition by becoming a vigneron. She has planted sauvignon blanc, shiraz, cabernet sauvignon, semillon and pinot gris. Exports to the UK.

ᵀᵀᵀᵀᵀ **Spectrum Mount Benson Syrah 2012** The wine is an eye-opener. Perfectly well balanced, integrated and structured, delicate but with enough power to impress, filigreed through the finish. It's a modern style and a quality one. Dark cherries, flings of dry spice, a slip of saucy oak and pretty, floral notes. The antithesis of the 'blood and thunder' style. It will cellar, but already it's hard to stop yourself from diving back for more. Screwcap. 14% alc. **Rating** 95 To 2025 $50 CM

ᵀᵀᵀᵀ♀ **Limestone Coast Pinot Gris 2014** Rating 90 To 2015 $20 CM ✪
Single Vineyard Mount Benson Syrah 2012 Rating 90 To 2022 $35 CM
Limestone Coast Shiraz Cabernet 2012 Rating 90 To 2018 $20 CM ✪

Wanted Man ★★★★

School House Lane, Heathcote, Vic 3523 **Region** Heathcote
T (03) 9654 4664 **www**.wantedman.com.au **Open** Not
Winemaker Matt Harrop, Simon Osicka **Est.** 1996 **Dozens** 2000 **Vyds** 9.3ha
The Wanted Man vineyard was planted in 1996, and has been managed by Andrew Clarke since 2000, producing Jinks Creek's Heathcote Shiraz. That wine was sufficiently impressive to lead Andrew and partner Peter Bartholomew (a Melbourne restaurateur) to purchase the vineyard in 2006, and give it its own identity. The vineyard is planted to shiraz (4ha), marsanne, viognier, grenache, roussanne and mourvedre. The quirky Ned Kelly label is the work of Mark Knight, cartoonist for the *Herald Sun*. Exports to the UK, Canada, Denmark, France and Hong Kong.

ᵀᵀᵀᵀᵀ **Single Vineyard Heathcote Marsanne Viognier 2012** Maturation in oak has proven an astute step. Mid-palate fruit richness, lactose and spice notes, citrus and smoke-like through the finish. It works beautifully. Screwcap. 13% alc. **Rating** 94 To 2017 $25 CM ✪

ᵀᵀᵀᵀ♀ **Single Vineyard Heathcote Shiraz 2012** Rating 93 To 2024 $35 CM
Single Vineyard Heathcote Mataro 2013 Rating 93 To 2022 $35 CM

Wantirna Estate ★★★★★

10 Bushy Park Lane, Wantirna South, Vic 3152 **Region** Yarra Valley
T (03) 9801 2367 **www**.wantirnaestate.com.au **Open** Not
Winemaker Maryann and Reg Egan **Est.** 1963 **Dozens** 830 **Vyds** 4.2ha

Reg and Tina Egan were among the early movers in the rebirth of the Yarra Valley. The vineyard surrounds the house in which they live, which also incorporates the winery. These days Reg describes himself as the interfering winemaker, but in the early years he did everything, dashing from his legal practice to the winery to check on the ferments. Today much of the winemaking responsibility has been transferred to daughter Maryann, who has a degree in wine science from CSU. Both have honed their practical skills among the small domaines and chateaux of Burgundy and Bordeaux, inspired by single-vineyard, terroir-driven wines. Maryann was also a winemaker for many years in Domaine Chandon's infancy. Tina keeps the mailing list and accounts under control, as well as having that all-important role of looking after the pickers during vintage. Exports to Hong Kong, Singapore and Japan.

🍷🍷🍷🍷🍷 **Isabella Yarra Valley Chardonnay 2013** Five barrels only. Pale colour. Fresh, racy pear, peach and citrus, woodsmoke and cedar spice. Picture perfect. Powerful but elegant. Simply beautiful. Screwcap. 13.5% alc. **Rating** 95 **To** 2020 $60 CM
Lily Yarra Valley Pinot Noir 2013 Sinewy. Smoky. Dry cherries. Sap. Beautiful lines of refreshing acidity. Has a juiciness but is built on acid more than it is on volume of fruit. Tannin draws impressively throughout. Diam. 13% alc. **Rating** 95 **To** 2024 $66 CM
Hannah Yarra Valley Cabernet Franc Merlot 2012 Bright crimson-purple; a supremely elegant and finely tuned blend; light-bodied it may be, but it has surprising length and intensity to its ever-so-pretty display of small red fruits. Blends such as this are rare outside Margaret River, and even there they are far from common. Diam. 13% alc. **Rating** 95 **To** 2022 $115
Amelia Yarra Valley Cabernet Sauvignon Merlot 2012 It's a pure, balanced, effortless wine. Fresh blackcurrant/boysenberry and lead pencil, integrated choc-coffee notes, black olives, violet and dried herbs. It's all done with such easy style, or so it seems in the glass. Diam. 12.5% alc. **Rating** 94 **To** 2028 $66 CM

Warner Glen Estate   ★★★★★

PO Box 218, Melville, WA 6956 **Region** Margaret River
T (08) 9337 4601 **www.**warnerglenestate.com.au **Open** Not
Winemaker Bruce Dukes, Amanda Kramer (Contract) **Est.** 1993 **Dozens** 12500
Vyds 30.8ha
Father and son John and Travis French purchased a 100ha property abutting the Chapman Brook and Blackwood National Park in the southern part of Margaret River in 1992. Says Travis, 'We then realised that we had to do something with it, so the thing at the time to be done with rural land was to plant vines, and so we did.' Sauvignon blanc and semillon constitute the lion's share, but there are significant plantings of chardonnay, cabernet sauvignon, shiraz and merlot. Until 2006 they were content to sell their grapes to Cape Mentelle, but in that year they decided to have wine contract-made by the highly experienced Bruce Dukes and Amanda Kramer. Given the maturity of the vineyards, it is not surprising that the wines are of such high quality.

🍷🍷🍷🍷🍷 **P.B.F. Margaret River Sauvignon Blanc Semillon 2012** A 60/40% blend fermented in a mix of used French barriques and puncheons. The approach has worked to perfection, the drive of the fruit in no way diminished by the complexity derived from the barrel ferment. A really classy wine, still firing on all cylinders, with time to go. Screwcap. 13.2% alc. **Rating** 96 **To** 2017 $30 ❂
P.B.F. Margaret River Sauvignon Blanc Semillon 2013 A 60/40% blend, barrel-fermented and matured in 50% French puncheons and 50% French barriques. It seems clear that most of the oak used was not new, for the winemaking has resulted in a complex mix of passionfruit and lemon verbena laced together by acidity and oak (the oak evident as much in mouthfeel as in flavour). Screwcap. 13.2% alc. **Rating** 95 **To** 2020 $30 ❂
The Pick Reserve Margaret River Chardonnay 2012 While the back label 'passionately crafted' sets my teeth on edge, this elegant and intense Chardonnay is of undoubtedly high quality, with tension between its grapefruit/white peach

fruit and French oak/acidity drawing out the long palate and aftertaste. Screwcap. 13.6% alc. **Rating** 95 **To** 2022 $45

Margaret River Cabernet Sauvignon 2013 Matured for 15 months in barriques from the centre of France. A striking wine with a precocious display of cassis, black olive, bay leaf, licorice and spice on the bouquet and firm, medium-bodied palate alike; the savoury, mouth-watering tannins empower the long finish, oak in a reprise role. Screwcap. 13.9% alc. **Rating** 95 **To** 2033 $30 ✪

Margaret River Cabernet Sauvignon 2012 Includes 8% merlot; the cabernet was fermented for 12 days, the merlot for 10, before being taken to French barriques for 15 months' maturation. A perfectly weighted and structured wine, driven by pure cassis fruit framed by cedary oak and fine-grained tannins. Screwcap. 13.9% alc. **Rating** 95 **To** 2025 $30 ✪

Margaret River Shiraz 2013 Rating 94 **To** 2025 $30 ✪

Frog Belly Cabernet Sauvignon 2013 Rating 94 **To** 2023 $20 ✪

Warner Vineyard

PO Box 344, Beechworth, Vic 3747 **Region** Beechworth
T 0438 331 768 **www.**warnervineyard.com.au **Open** Not
Winemaker Gary Mills **Est.** 1996 **Dozens** 400 **Vyds** 4.48ha
The Warner family – Graeme, Gwen, Stuart and Katie – planted their vineyard in 1996, astutely choosing shiraz (2.3ha) and chardonnay (1.4ha) as their main game, with 0.8ha of roussanne and marsanne as a side bet. As the vines began to move to maturity, it became clear that their choice of the decomposed granitic soils was 100% correct, and the grapes were much in demand, Giaconda taking the shiraz and Jamsheed the chardonnay. In the lead-up to the '12 vintage, the family decided to keep enough grapes to have Gary Mills (Jamsheed) make around 200 dozen of each wine.

🍷🍷🍷🍷🍷 **The Rest Beechworth Roussanne 2013** Bunch-sorted, then whole bunch-pressed to French oak of various ages (some new) for wild yeast fermentation, and kept on lees in that oak until bottled in Feb '14. Bright straw-green, it is a potent and savoury wine, with some bitter aloe/almond kernel nuances. Will build even more with time. Screwcap. 13.5% alc. **Rating** 92 **To** 2018 $33

Warrabilla

6152 Murray Valley Highway, Rutherglen, Vic 3685 **Region** Rutherglen
T (02) 6035 7242 **www.**warrabillawines.com.au **Open** 7 days 10–5
Winemaker Andrew Sutherland Smith **Est.** 1990 **Dozens** 10000 **Vyds** 20.4ha
Andrew Sutherland Smith and wife Carol have built a formidable reputation for their wines, headed by the Reserve trio of Durif, Cabernet Sauvignon and Shiraz, quintessential examples of Rutherglen red table wine at its most opulent. Their vineyard has been extended by the planting of riesling and zinfandel. Andrew spent 15 years with All Saints, McWilliam's, Yellowglen, Fairfield and Chambers before setting up Warrabilla, and his experience shines through in the wines. You either accept or regret the alcohol; no half measures.

🍷🍷🍷🍷🍷 **Parola's Limited Release Shiraz 2013** Yes, Warrabilla has a yeast strain that is not suffocated by the alcohol, and yes, it is 100% new American oak. Andrew Sutherland Smith stands defiant: he has a sufficient loyal clientele to buy all the wine he makes, and he doesn't spring surprises. The curious thing about his wines is the relative lack of tannin structure; it may well be precisely this that his customers appreciate. Diam. 17% alc. **Rating** 94 **To** 2025 $35

Reserve Shiraz 2013 Impenetrably dense and deep colour; another curiosity: the alcohol seems more obvious, but ignites a greater range of flavours. And it must be said that if you like the style, and don't have to drive anywhere after dinner, they represent good value. The low litres per tonne figure a significant part of the production cost. Diam. 16.5% alc. **Rating** 94 **To** 2028 $25 ✪

Parola's Limited Release Durif 2013 Impenetrable colour; how the super-heroic yeasts complete fermentation is one of life's sweet mysteries; I doubt there is another table wine in the world with alcohol to match this. The weird thing is that there are flavours of spiced black fruits and licorice encased in dark chocolate, lots of vanilla from 100% new American oak, yet little or no heat from the alcohol, and no kick from the tannins. Diam. 17.5% alc. **Rating** 94 **To** 2033 $37

🍷🍷🍷🍷🍷 **Reserve Durif 2013 Rating** 91 **To** 2023 $27

Warramate ★★★★

27 Maddens Lane, Gruyere, Vic 3770 **Region** Yarra Valley
T (03) 5964 9219 **www**.warramatewines.com.au **Open** Not
Winemaker Sarah Crowe **Est.** 1970 **Dozens** 3000 **Vyds** 6.6ha
A long-established and perfectly situated winery reaping the full benefits of its 40-year-old vines; recent plantings have increased production. All the wines are well made, the Shiraz providing further proof (if such be needed) of the suitability of the variety to the region. In 2011 was purchased by the partnership that owns the adjoining Yarra Yering; the Warramate Vineyard and brand have been kept as a separate operation, using the existing vineyards. Exports to Malaysia, Singapore, Hong Kong and China.

🍷🍷🍷🍷🍷 **White Label Yarra Valley Pinot Noir 2012** From four clones planted on the estate vineyard, matured in French oak (30% new) for 18 months. Its perfumed bouquet morphs into an elegant, spice-laden palate with forest fruits (including fraises du bois) to the fore. Screwcap. 13.5% alc. **Rating** 94 **To** 2022 $28

🍇 Warramunda Estate ★★★★★

860 Maroondah Highway, Coldstream, Vic 3770 **Region** Yarra Valley
T 0412 694 394 **www**.warramundaestate.com.au **Open** Fri–Sun 10–6
Winemaker Ben Haines **Est.** 1998 **Dozens** 1200 **Vyds** 19.2ha
In 1998 long-term owners the Vogt family began planting vines on their property, which has a substantial frontage to the Maroondah Highway at Coldstream. Over the next 8 years they established 19.2ha of cabernet sauvignon, pinot noir, marsanne, viognier, and shiraz. All of the grapes were purchased by Yering Station under an ongoing contract. In 2007 the situation changed, when the Magdziarz family – Robert, Irene, and daughter Olivia – bought the property. Both their parents survived the odds of concentration camps in World War II, and separately were able to make their way to Australia. Robert started as a butcher, which led to cooking and hospitality, thence to front of house, and ultimately management. All this before he was appointed, at the age of 25, to be general manager of the Moonee Valley Racing Club. Irene had started in hospitality, but changed her career to the police force, becoming a senior detective. When she felt the need to go back to where she had begun, hospitality, she met Robert. She introduced him to wine, and it so engulfed them that they completed diplomas in viticulture in the mid-1990s, and bought land at Kyneton to plant their first vineyard. Nothing succeeds like experience, and they realised the difficulties, selling the vineyard in 2003, but never giving up their dream of becoming successful vignerons. In 2007 they were on hand when the Vogts decided to sell, and the rest is history.

🍷🍷🍷🍷🍷 **Marsanne 2014** The (apparent) decision not to use oak will pay dividends as the wine matures and grows in bottle – simply look at Yeringberg and Tahbilk. All the balance needed is there in spades. Screwcap. 13% alc. **Rating** 95 **To** 2029 $35
Syrah 2013 Has an overall abundance of flavours ranging from red through to predominantly black fruits, and a complex counterpoint between spicy/peppery/savoury notes on the one hand, varietal fruit on the other; the balance and length are beyond criticism. Diam. 13.8% alc. **Rating** 95 **To** 2028 $35

🍷🍷🍷🍷🍷 **Yarra Valley Pinot Noir 2013 Rating** 90 **To** 2020 $40
Yarra Valley Cabernet Sauvignon 2013 Rating 90 **To** 2025 $48

Warrenmang Vineyard & Resort   ★★★★☆

Mountain Creek Road, Moonambel, Vic 3478 **Region** Pyrenees
T (03) 5467 2233 **www**.warrenmang.com.au **Open** 7 days 10–5
Winemaker Sean Schwager **Est.** 1974 **Dozens** 15000 **Vyds** 32.1ha
Luigi and Athalie Bazzani continue to watch over Warrenmang; a new, partially underground barrel room with earthen walls has been completed, wine quality remains high, and the accommodation for over 80 guests, plus a restaurant, underpin the business. Over the 40 years that Luigi and Athalie have been at Warrenmang, a very loyal clientele has been built up. The business is quietly on the market, Luigi and Athalie having long since earned their retirement. However, they have taken one step to reduce their workload: employing the highly experienced Sean and Cathy Dunn to manage the resort. Exports to Denmark, The Netherlands, Poland, Taiwan, Singapore, Malaysia and China.

♙♙♙♙♙ **Black Puma Pyrenees Shiraz 2009** Hand-picked, open-fermented, basket-pressed and matured for 24 months in French oak. An appropriately full-bodied wine, with multiple layers of black fruits, the French oak also contributing; a touch of volatile acidity does not justify down-pointing it. Cork. 14.5% alc. **Rating** 95 To 2024 $80

♙♙♙♙♙ **Pyrenees Sauvignon Blanc 2013 Rating** 90 To 2015 $25

Warwick Billings   ★★★★☆

c/- Post Office, Lenswood, SA 5240 (postal) **Region** Adelaide Hills
T 0405 437 864 **www**.wowique.com.au **Open** Not
Winemaker Warwick Billings **Est.** 2009 **Dozens** 250
This is the venture of Warwick Billings and partner Rose Kemp. Warwick was a cider maker in the UK who came to study at Roseworthy, and got diverted into the wine world. He completed postgraduate oenology at Adelaide University in 1995, and worked for Miranda Wine, Orlando and Angove Family Winemakers from 2002 to '08, along the way moonlighting in France and Spain for 12 vintages. Warwick's approach to his eponymous label is self-deprecating, beginning with the name Wowique, and saying, 'Occasionally a vineyard sings to the winemaker. [We] have taken one of these songs and put it into a bottle.' The vineyard in question is an unusual clone of chardonnay nurtured on a sloping hilltop site in Mt Torrens. Warwick's final word on all of this is, 'The winemaking is unashamedly inspired by Burgundy, but care is taken to acknowledge that the soil is different, the clones are often different, the climate is definitely different, and the end consumer is usually different.'

♙♙♙♙♙ **Wowique Single Vineyard Adelaide Hills Chardonnay 2013** Amazingly, the colour is still gin-clear at 2yo, giving advance warning of a super-elegant wine yet to show all its wares; the obvious question is whether this will be a Peter Pan fizzer, and my answer to that is no. Screwcap. 12.5% alc. **Rating** 93 To 2023 $32
Wowique Single Vineyard Adelaide Hills Pinot Noir 2013 Very good, clear colour; a well-balanced and structured Pinot, with plum fruit and hints of spice; on the light-bodied side, and doesn't need cellaring for more than a few years at the outside. Screwcap. 13.5% alc. **Rating** 90 To 2018 $38

Water Wheel   ★★★★☆

Bridgewater-on-Loddon, Bridgewater, Vic 3516 **Region** Bendigo
T (03) 5437 3060 **www**.waterwheelwine.com **Open** Mon–Fri 9–5, w'ends 12–3
Winemaker Peter Cumming, Bill Trevaskis **Est.** 1972 **Dozens** 30000 **Vyds** 136ha
Peter Cumming, with more than two decades of winemaking under his belt, has quietly built on the reputation of Water Wheel year by year. The winery is owned by the Cumming family, which has farmed in the Bendigo region for 50+ years, with horticulture and viticulture special areas of interest. Over half the vineyard area is planted to shiraz (75ha), followed by chardonnay, sauvignon blanc (15ha each), cabernet sauvignon, malbec (10ha each), and smaller plantings of petit verdot, semillon, roussanne and grenache. Water Wheel continues to make wines that over-deliver at their modest prices. Exports to the UK, the US, Canada, Switzerland, Denmark and NZ.

** TTTTT Bendigo Shiraz 2013** Good colour; combines generosity with complexity, the fruit offering blackberry and plum flavours, with hints of charcuterie in the backdrop, the tannins fine and supple, then a savoury aftertaste. Screwcap. 14.8% alc. **Rating** 93 **To** 2023 $18 ✪

Baringhup Bendigo Shiraz 2013 For the most part the alcohol keeps itself remarkably well hidden, sitting in behind dense blackberry and asphalt-like fruit. It's intense, mouth-coating and chocolatey, the generosity of flavour seeing no point in stopping just because you've swallowed. Screwcap. 15.5% alc. **Rating** 91 **To** 2022 $20 CM ✪

TTTT Bendigo Malbec 2013 Rating 89 **To** 2021 $18 CM ✪

Watershed Premium Wines ★★★★★

Cnr Bussell Highway/Darch Road, Margaret River, WA 6285 **Region** Margaret River
T (08) 9758 8633 **www**.watershedwines.com.au **Open** 7 days 10–5
Winemaker Severine Logan, Conrad Tritt **Est.** 2002 **Dozens** 130000 **Vyds** 187ha
Watershed Wines has been set up by a syndicate of investors, with no expense spared in establishing the substantial vineyard and striking cellar door, with a 200-seat café and restaurant. Situated towards the southern end of the Margaret River region, its neighbours include Voyager Estate and Leeuwin Estate. Exports to Germany, Indonesia, Fiji, Thailand, Papua New Guinea, Singapore, Hong Kong and China.

TTTTT Senses Margaret River Sauvignon Blanc 2014 Half fermented in French oak, half in stainless steel. The oak is evident on the bouquet, but the tsunami of intense fruit on the palate sweeps all else away; opens with snow pea and lemon, then moves into passionfruit, finishing with crystalline acidity. Screwcap. 13% alc. **Rating** 95 **To** 2016 $30 ✪

Awakening Single Block A1 Margaret River Chardonnay 2013 Wild yeast barrel-fermented in new and 1yo French oak. Pale, but bright, straw-green; the wine is exceptionally tight and fiercely focused on its grapefruit and white peach fruit, floating on a base of big, potent, crisp acidity and nutty oak. Good now, but its best years are before it. Screwcap. 13.5% alc. **Rating** 95 **To** 2023 $45

Senses Margaret River Shiraz 2012 Matured for 18 months in French and American oak. Bright crimson-purple; a vibrant and fresh Shiraz, red fruits, black fruits, fine spice and even finer tannins dancing with abandon in the mouth. Didn't need its gold medal at the Cowra Wine Show '14 to push its claims – just lovely stuff. Screwcap. 14.5% alc. **Rating** 95 **To** 2027 $30 ✪

Senses Margaret River Cabernet Merlot 2012 An 84/16% blend matured for 18 months in French oak. Cabernet is certainly the senior partner in every way; blackcurrant, black olive, cedar, and even licorice, are framed by brambly tannins on the long palate. A purist style, plum absent. Screwcap. 14.5% alc. **Rating** 95 **To** 2027 $30 ✪

Awakening Margaret River Cabernet Sauvignon 2012 Matured for 18 months in French barriques. Cassis rides high, wide and handsome in this vibrantly juicy and fresh wine, and while it will live, there is every reason to jump in and enjoy it for what it is today. Continues the line of the wine's history. Screwcap. 14% alc. **Rating** 95 **To** 2027 $65

Shades Sauvignon Semillon 2014 Rating 94 **To** 2016 $19 ✪

TTTTT Shades Unoaked Chardonnay 2014 Rating 93 **To** 2020 $19 ✪

Waterton Vineyards ★★★★★

PO Box 125, Beaconsfield, Tas 7270 **Region** Northern Tasmania
T (03) 6394 7214 **www**.watertonhall.com.au **Open** Not
Winemaker Winemaking Tasmania (Julian Alcorso) **Est.** 2006 **Dozens** 450 **Vyds** 2ha
Jennifer Baird and Peter Cameron purchased this remarkable property in 2002. Waterton Hall was built in the 1850s and modified extensively by well-known neo-gothic architect Alexander North in 1910. The property was owned by the Catholic church from '49–'96,

variously used as a school, a boys' home and a retreat. Following its sale the new owners planted 1ha of riesling at the end of the '90s. Jennifer and Peter extended the vineyard with 1ha of shiraz, electing to sell the riesling until 2006, when part was first made under the Waterton label.

🍷🍷🍷🍷🍷 **Riesling 2013** Bright and clear colour; this has more flesh and weight than most of its vintage peers, tied together by firm acidity on the finish, with a farewell twist of citrus pith. Backed up its top-gold medal Tas Wine Show '14 with a gold in '15, having barely moved: still incredibly youthful, fresh and vibrant. Screwcap. 11.6% alc. **Rating** 96 **To** 2023 $29 ☉
Riesling 2012 Shows the first real sign of colour development; the palate is exceptionally fresh and tight; the long, intense and chiselled finish guarantees an exceptionally long future. Gold Tas Wine Show '15. Screwcap. **Rating** 96 **To** 2027

WayWood Wines ★★★★★

67 Kays Road, McLaren Vale, SA 5171 **Region** McLaren Vale
T (08) 8323 8468 **www.**waywoodwines.com **Open** Fri–Mon 11–5
Winemaker Andrew Wood **Est.** 2005 **Dozens** 1500
This is the culmination of Andrew Wood and Lisa Robertson's wayward odyssey. Andrew left his career as a sommelier in London, and retrained as a winemaker, working in Portugal, the UK, Italy and the Granite Belt (an eclectic selection), settling in McLaren Vale in early 2004. Working with Kangarilla Road winery for the next six years, while making small quantities of Shiraz, Cabernets and Tempranillo from purchased grapes, led them to Nebbiolo, Montepulciano and Shiraz. Andrew and Lisa opened a new cellar door in '15, Lisa's business, Luscious Red, offering food at the cellar door.

🍷🍷🍷🍷🍷 **McLaren Vale Shiraz 2012** The region shrieks loudly from the first whiff, with blackberry, earth, spice, bitter chocolate and polished leather all seeking to be heard; the perfectly balanced medium-bodied palate facilitates this, but doesn't play favourites. Screwcap. 14.4% alc. **Rating** 95 **To** 2027 $24 ☉
McLaren Vale Cabernet Sauvignon 2012 Very bright colour; all the WayWood wines proclaim their McLaren Vale origin first, their varietal make-up close behind; here the synergy is in full swing. This isn't Margaret River or Coonawarra Cabernet, it is McLaren Vale, and vive la différence. Screwcap. 14.5% alc. **Rating** 95 **To** 2032 $28 ☉
McLaren Vale Tempranillo 2013 Bright colour and depth; has good varietal expression from go to whoa; sour, morello and red cherries are all to be had, and the tannins are buried in the fabric of the wine. Deserves a high-quality piece of char-grilled steak. Screwcap. 13.9% alc. **Rating** 95 **To** 2030 $35 ☉
McLaren Vale Montepulciano 2013 Deep crimson-purple; there are plenty of good things going on here: a vivid colour, a chorus of satsuma and blood plum with a high note of red fruit, and a bass line of ripe, yet savoury tannins. Impressive stuff. Screwcap. 13.5% alc. **Rating** 94 **To** 2033 $35

🍷🍷🍷🍷♀ **Fluzi Quattro 2014** Rating 93 To 2017 $20 ☉
McLaren Vale Cabernet Sangiovese 2012 Rating 93 To 2020 $28
Quattro Vini 2013 Rating 92 To 2020 $24 ☉

Wendouree ★★★★★

Wendouree Road, Clare, SA 5453 **Region** Clare Valley
T (08) 8842 2896 **Open** Not
Winemaker Tony Brady **Est.** 1895 **Dozens** 2000 **Vyds** 12ha
An iron fist in a velvet glove best describes these extraordinary wines. They are fashioned with commitment from the very old vineyard (shiraz, cabernet sauvignon, malbec, mataro and muscat of alexandria), with its unique terroir, by Tony and Lita Brady, who rightly see themselves as custodians of a priceless treasure. The 100-year-old stone winery is virtually unchanged from the day it was built; this is in every sense a treasure beyond price. Wendouree has never made any comment about its wines, but the subtle shift from the lighter end of

full-bodied to the fuller end of medium-bodied seems to be a permanent one (always subject to the dictates of the vintage). The best news of all is that I will drink some of the Wendourees I have bought over the past 10 years before I die, and not have to rely on my few remaining bottles from the 1970s (and rather more from the '80s and '90s).

🍷🍷🍷🍷🍷 **Shiraz 2013** A perfect rendition of medium-bodied Shiraz, burdened neither by massive alcohol nor oak, allowing the black fruits, led by blackberry and supported by hints of licorice and earth, free play. The overall texture is exceptional, the tannins smooth and supple. Screwcap. 14% alc. **Rating** 98 **To** 2048 $55
Cabernet Sauvignon 2013 Full purple-crimson hue. An elegant Wendouree Cabernet Sauvignon, only 2yo? Oxymoron? Believe me, this is the epitome of elegance in Cabernet terms, with a fluid line and mouthfeel, cassis and a hint of mint to the fore, fine-grained tannins as much on the aftertaste as the finish. A wine that progressively reveals its latent power as it is retasted again and again. Screwcap. 13.8% alc. **Rating** 97 **To** 2048 $55

🍷🍷🍷🍷🍷 **Shiraz Malbec 2013** A strikingly lively palate, with juicy berry fruits to the fore. There is real synergy to be had here, lifting the flavours and the mouthfeel, and building layers of flavour which grow and grow each time you come back to it. Screwcap. 14% alc. **Rating** 96 **To** 2043 $45
Shiraz Mataro 2013 The mataro is very evident in the structure and texture of the wine, adding a savoury/spicy/earthy element. Once again, the overall balance is exemplary – as is the length. Its charms are less immediately obvious, but the end impression is of a totally delicious wine. Screwcap. 13.7% alc. **Rating** 96 **To** 2043 $45
Cabernet Malbec 2013 Has a degree of impact and presence that caught me by surprise the first time I tasted it, no surprise from retasting other than the affirmation of its power. This is a wine of royal bloodlines, both of its predecessors and the 1971 Stanley Leasingham Bin 56 Cabernet Malbec adding a further testimonial. Screwcap. 13.8% alc. **Rating** 96 **To** 2045 $55

West Cape Howe Wines   ★★★★★

Lot 14923 Muir Highway, Mount Barker, WA 6324 **Region** Mount Barker
T (08) 9892 1444 **www.**westcapehowewines.com.au **Open** 7 days (various hours)
Winemaker Gavin Berry, Andrew Vasey **Est.** 1997 **Dozens** 60 000 **Vyds** 310ha
West Cape Howe is owned by a partnership of four West Australian families, including winemaker/managing partner Gavin Berry (27 vintages in the Great Southern) and viticulturist/partner Rob Quenby. Grapes are sourced from estate vineyards in Mount Barker and Frankland River. The Langton Vineyard (Mount Barker) has 100ha planted to cabernet sauvignon, shiraz, riesling, sauvignon blanc, chardonnay and semillon, and the Russell Road Vineyard (Frankland River) has 210ha planted. West Cape Howe also sources select parcels of fruit from valued contract growers. Best Value Winery 2016 *Wine Companion*. Exports to the UK, the US, Denmark, Singapore, Japan, Hong Kong, Taiwan and China.

🍷🍷🍷🍷🍷 **Mount Barker Riesling 2014** Sourced from Block 6 of the Langton Vineyard, picked over a period of weeks. Everything about the wine screams quality, and puts beyond doubt the ability of Great Southern to produce superb Riesling when made with the skill evident here; intense varietal citrus blossom aromas and flavours, the acidity a strand of stainless steel wire running through and providing the structure for the endless finish. Screwcap. 12% alc. **Rating** 96 **To** 2029 $19 ✪
Two Steps Mount Barker Shiraz 2012 The Langton Vineyard provides high-quality shiraz, this wine coming from the best parcels. Deep crimson-purple, its bouquet sets the scene with its precocious display of black fruits, spice, pepper and cedary French oak all in tune; the mouthfeel is satin smooth and precise, yet also sees touches of licorice adding to the flavour profile. Screwcap. 14.5% alc. **Rating** 96 **To** 2032 $30 ✪
Book Ends Mount Barker Cabernet Sauvignon 2012 Made from the best and oldest blocks on the estate Langton Vineyard. It has a gloriously fragrant

bouquet and a wonderfully pure expression of cool-climate cabernet on the long, medium-bodied palate; the oak and tannins lend support, but not intrusively so. Screwcap. 14.5% alc. **Rating** 96 **To** 2032 $30 ●

Styx Gully Mount Barker Chardonnay 2014 The best chardonnay grapes are barrel-fermented/matured in French oak. A vibrant and expressive Chardonnay with grapefruit and white peach neatly balanced by each other, and likewise with the oak; the finish is long and fresh. Screwcap. 12.5% alc. **Rating** 95 **To** 2025 $28 ●

Perth Hills Frankland Tempranillo 2013 The bright crimson-purple colour introduces a thoroughly left-field regional blend; it succeeds brilliantly, the earthy black cherry notes of the Perth Hills encased in a juicy, spicy envelope provided by the Frankland River component, the net result a palate of great length and balance. Screwcap. 14.5% alc. **Rating** 95 **To** 2023 $22 ●

Mount Barker Sauvignon Blanc 2014 Rating 94 To 2015 $22 ●
Cabernet Merlot 2013 Rating 94 To 2025 $17 ●

Tempranillo Rose 2014 Rating 92 To 2016 $17 ●
Hannah's Hill Cabernet Merlot 2013 Rating 92 To 2025 $20 ●
Two Peeps Sauvignon Blanc Semillon 2014 Rating 91 To 2016 $20 ●
Semillon Sauvignon Blanc 2014 Rating 91 To 2016 $17 ●
Chardonnay 2013 Rating 91 To 2018 $17 ●
Shiraz 2013 Rating 91 To 2023 $17 ●

Westlake Vineyards ★★★★★

Diagonal Road, Koonunga, SA 5355 **Region** Barossa Valley
T 0428 656 208 **www**.westlakevineyards.com.au **Open** By appt
Winemaker Darren Westlake **Est.** 1999 **Dozens** 300 **Vyds** 36.2ha
Darren and Suzanne Westlake tend 22ha of shiraz, 6.5ha of cabernet sauvignon, 2ha of viognier, and smaller plantings of petit verdot, durif, mataro, grenache and graciano planted on two properties in the Koonunga area of the Barossa Valley. They do all the vineyard work personally, and have a long list of high-profile winemakers queued up to buy the grapes, leaving only a small amount for production under the Westlake label. Suzanne is a sixth-generation descendant of Johann George Kalleske, who came to SA from Prussia in 1838; the 717 Convicts label draws on the history of Darren's ancestor Edward Westlake, who was transported to Australia in 1788.

Albert's Block Shiraz 2013 Establishes its class from the outset and never allows any doubts to set in. Inky fruit oozes through the palate, all licorice and blackberry and peppercorn, putting on the kind of satiny parade that will have people sitting up straighter to take notice. Sweet, supple finish. Super-ripe but super-good. Drink any time from now. Diam. 15% alc. **Rating** 95 **To** 2026 $30 CM ●

Eleazar Shiraz 2013 A striking wine in all respects. Violets, peppercorns and mint paint a pretty image but then dark licorice, cola, chocolate and saturated plum flavours thrust inkily forward. It's sweet and ultra-ripe but it's buffed to a great lustre and issues layer after layer of flavour. A warm, slightly porty finish is the only query. Diam. 15% alc. **Rating** 94 **To** 2026 $60 CM

Whicher Ridge ★★★★★

200 Chapman Hill East Road, Busselton, WA 6280 **Region** Geographe
T (08) 9753 1394 **www**.whicherridge.com.au **Open** Thurs–Mon 10–5
Winemaker Cathy Howard **Est.** 2004 **Dozens** 1000 **Vyds** 5ha
It is hard to imagine a founding husband-and-wife team with such an ideal blend of viticultural and winemaking experience accumulated over a combined 40-plus years. Cathy Howard (née Spratt) was a winemaker for 16 years at Orlando and St Hallett in the Barossa Valley, and at Watershed Wines in Margaret River. She now has her own winemaking consulting business covering the southwest regions of WA, as well as making the Whicher Ridge wines. Neil Howard's career as a viticulturist spans more than 25 years, beginning in the Pyrenees region with Taltarni Vineyards and Blue Pyrenees Estate, before moving to

Mount Avoca as vineyard manager for 12 years. When he moved to the west, he managed the Sandalford Wines vineyard in Margaret River for several years, then developed and managed a number of smaller vineyards throughout the region. Whicher Ridge's Odyssey Creek Vineyard at Chapman Hill has sauvignon blanc, cabernet sauvignon and viognier. The Howards have chosen the Frankland River subregion of the Great Southern to supply shiraz and riesling, and also buy grapes from Margaret River.

ΨΨΨΨΨ **Elevation Cabernet Sauvignon 2011** Whicher Ridge's flagship wine. The fruit is very expressive, and has not been overwhelmed by the oak; there is a finesse to the way the tight-knit flavours of cassis, blackberry and spice impress themselves on the palate, for the tannins are fine and relaxed. Most attractive wine. Screwcap. 13.5% alc. **Rating** 96 **To** 2036 $36 ✪
Frankland River Riesling 2013 Sourced from the mature Justin Vineyard halfway between the towns of Frankland and Rocky Gully. Tank-pressed, mainly free-run, but with some solids added back to balance the 7.18g/l acidity. A hint of reduction promptly gives way to the expansive citrus and green apple fruit of the textured palate. Screwcap. 12% alc. **Rating** 95 **To** 2029 $28 ✪
Sauvignon Blanc 2013 From the estate Odyssey Creek Vineyard; 30% fermented in new and 1yo French oak, the remainder in tank, each with a different cultured yeast; matured for 12–14 months. Very complex and powerful with a European accent, fruit, oak and minerally acidity all bound together on a very long and focused palate. Screwcap. 12% alc. **Rating** 95 **To** 2016 $25 ✪

ΨΨΨΨΨ **Margaret River Chardonnay 2013 Rating** 90 **To** 2020 $33
Geographe Viognier 2013 Rating 90 **To** 2017 $29

Whispering Brook   ★★★★

Hill Street, Broke, NSW 2330 **Region** Hunter Valley
T (02) 9818 4126 **www**.whispering-brook.com **Open** W'ends 11–5, Fri by appt
Winemaker Susan Frazier, Adam Bell **Est.** 2000 **Dozens** 2000 **Vyds** 3ha
It took some time for partners Susan Frazier and Adam Bell to find the property on which they established their vineyard 15 years ago. It has a combination of terra rossa loam soils on which the reds are planted, and sandy flats for the white grapes. The partners have also established an olive grove and accommodation for 10–18 guests in the large house set in the vineyard. Exports to Canada and Japan.

ΨΨΨΨΨ **Basket Pressed Hunter Valley Touriga Nacional 2014** Musky, vanillan oak obscures the 'difference' of the fruit, though in a way it also makes it more accessible. Volume of flavour here is certainly impressive, and attractive. It tastes of earth, tangy cherry and mineral, with a buoyant mix of both sweetness and savouriness running freely through the finish. Screwcap. 14% alc. **Rating** 91 **To** 2021 $35 CM
Limited Release Chardonnay 2014 Ripe stone fruit and sweet, sawdusty, almost bubblegum oak flavours lay down the ground rules for this amiable white. It starts big but finishes elegant; rarely a bad road for a wine to travel. Acidity tidies it all up, but there is plenty to hold onto here. Screwcap. 13.5% alc. **Rating** 90 **To** 2017 $28 CM

Whispering Hills   ★★★☆

580 Warburton Highway, Seville, Vic 3139 **Region** Yarra Valley
T (03) 5964 2822 **www**.whisperinghills.com.au **Open** 7 days 10–6
Winemaker Murray and Darcy Lyons **Est.** 1985 **Dozens** 800 **Vyds** 5ha
Whispering Hills is owned and operated by the Lyons family (Murray, Audrey and Darcy Lyons). Murray and Darcy are responsible for the winemaking, while Audrey takes care of the cellar door and distribution. The vineyard was established in 1985 with further plantings in '96 and some grafting in 2003, and now consists of cabernet sauvignon (2ha), riesling, chardonnay and pinot noir (1ha each). Exports to Sweden and Japan.

ŸŸŸŸŸ Seville Yarra Valley Cabernet Sauvignon 2013 A very savoury style that just makes its way over the herbal threshold, helped by optimum use of well-integrated oak and balanced tannin extract. Screwcap. 13% alc. **Rating** 93 **To** 2023 $24 ⊙

Whistle Post ★★★★☆

PO Box 340, Coonawarra, SA 5263 **Region** Coonawarra
T 0408 708 093 **www**.whistlepost.com.au **Open** Not
Winemaker John Innes **Est.** 2012 **Dozens** 4000 **Vyds** 63ha
This is the venture of Brian and Jennifer Smibert, together with their son Angus. The establishment date is correct, but there is in fact a quarter of a century of Smibert grapegrowing: 32ha of cabernet sauvignon, 22ha of chardonnay, 8ha of merlot and 1ha of sauvignon blanc. The grapes were the subject of a 25-year contract to supply Hardys, and when that finished, the Whistle Post brand began in serious production. The family had put its toe into the water in 2010, with a small amount of wine made on an experimental basis. Part of the annual grape production is sold to others, and one would expect this arrangement to continue into the future.

ŸŸŸŸŸ Reserve Cabernet Sauvignon 2012 It takes a millisecond to understand the use of 'Reserve' for this wine compared to its much cheaper brethren. It is complex, with skilled use of quality oak and control of tannins; blackcurrant is the raison d'être of the wine, but it allows a little Coonawarra mint and earth to add to its complexity and texture. Screwcap. 14% alc. **Rating** 95 **To** 2032 $40

ŸŸŸŸŸ Cabernet Sauvignon 2012 **Rating** 92 **To** 2022 $20 ⊙

Whistler Wines ★★★★★

Seppeltsfield Road, Marananga, SA 5355 **Region** Barossa Valley
T (08) 8562 4942 **www**.whistlerwines.com **Open** 7 days 10.30–5
Winemaker Josh Pfeiffer **Est.** 1999 **Dozens** 5000 **Vyds** 14.5ha
Four generations of Pfeiffers, spanning 80 years, have been growing grapes in SA. Third-generation brothers Chris and Martin established Whistler Wines in 1999, and in 2013 'retired' (their word and quotation marks) from managing the business, inviting children Matt (finance and distribution), Mel (cellar door, one year later winning the peer-judged Best Cellar Door in the Barossa Region) and Josh (winemaking and viticulture) to 'step up'.

ŸŸŸŸŸ Barossa Shiraz 2012 Shows the '12 vintage face very well; a fragrant bouquet of gently spiced red and black fruits, then a supple, medium-bodied palate, fruit, oak and tannins all in harmony; the length is admirable. Screwcap. 14.5% alc. **Rating** 95 **To** 2027 $40
Get in my Belly Barossa Valley Grenache 2014 20% whole bunches, wild yeast-fermented, foot-stomped, 21 days on skins, 6 months' maturation in used oak. Good colour; has generous depth, texture and structure, even by the standards of McLaren Vale; purple-red fruits show no confection at all. A distinguished wine. Cork. 14% alc. **Rating** 95 **To** 2024 $35 ⊙
The Reserve Barossa Shiraz 2012 Deep colour; while its Barossa sibling relies on elegance to make its point, this relies on concentration and power, black fruits and tannins allied with tar and licorice. A case of chacun à son goût. 250 dozen made. Screwcap. 14.5% alc. **Rating** 94 **To** 2032 $70

ŸŸŸŸŸ Barossa Merlot 2012 **Rating** 92 **To** 2020 $27
Barossa Cabernet Sauvignon 2012 **Rating** 92 **To** 2025 $30

White Rock Vineyard ★★★★

1171 Railton Road, Kimberley, Tas 7304 (postal) **Region** Northern Tasmania
T 0407 972 156 **www**.whiterockwine.com.au **Open** At Lake Barrington Estate
Winemaker Winemaking Tasmania, Frogmore Creek **Est.** 1992 **Dozens** 400 **Vyds** 3ha
Phil and Robin Dolan have established White Rock Vineyard in the northwest region of Tasmania, which, while having 13 wineries and vineyards, is one of the least-known parts

of the island. Kimberley is 25km south of Devonport, in the sheltered valley of the Mersey River. The Dolans have planted pinot noir, chardonnay, riesling, pinot gris and dornfelder, the lion's share going to the first two varieties. It has been a low-profile operation partly because of its location. The wines are sold online and through local restaurants and the cellar door at Lake Barrington Estate.

🍷🍷🍷🍷🍷 **Riesling 2013** Opens proceedings with a highly fragrant bouquet of citrus and passionfruit carrying through to the palate; has good line and length; the result is a thoroughly attractive wine. Screwcap. 11.2% alc. **Rating** 92 **To** 2023 $23 ✪
Dawn Red Dornfelder 2013 Very good structure/texture on the mid-palate, the only problem the lack of tannin depth on the back-palate. Dornfelder is a German cross. Jancis Robinson describes it as the most successful of red grape crosses, making dark, velvety wines. Screwcap. **Rating** 92 **To** 2018 $33

Wicks Estate Wines   ★★★★☆

21 Franklin Street, Adelaide, SA 5000 (postal) **Region** Adelaide Hills
T (08) 8212 0004 **www.**wicksestate.com.au **Open** Not
Winemaker Leigh Ratzmer **Est.** 2000 **Dozens** 20 000 **Vyds** 38.1ha
Tim and Simon Wicks had a long-term involvement with orchard and nursery operations at Highbury in the Adelaide Hills prior to purchasing their 54ha property at Woodside in 1999. They planted fractionally less than 40ha of chardonnay, riesling, sauvignon blanc, shiraz, merlot and cabernet sauvignon, following this with the construction of a winery in 2004. Wicks Estate has won more than its fair share of wine show medals over the years, the wines priced well below their full worth. Exports to The Netherlands, Singapore, Hong Kong and China.

🍷🍷🍷🍷🍷 **Eminence Adelaide Hills Shiraz Cabernet 2012** A 55/45% blend matured for 12 months in new French oak. Typical '12 colour, it was born of a desire to produce a first-class wine in a first-class vintage, and the palate delivers just that, the blackcurrant and blackberry fruit combination very synergistic, the texture, weight and structure exemplary. Screwcap. 14.5% alc. **Rating** 95 **To** 2032 $60
Adelaide Hills Shiraz 2013 The bouquet is inviting, but doesn't prepare you for the explosion of exceptionally intense flavour as the wine enters the mouth; it is almost inevitable that it should back off somewhat on the back-palate, but this is still a very good wine, and a steal at the price. Screwcap. 14.5% alc. **Rating** 94 **To** 2035 $20 ✪

🍷🍷🍷🍷🍷 **Adelaide Hills Cabernet Sauvignon 2013** **Rating** 92 **To** 2033 $20 ✪
Adelaide Hills Riesling 2014 **Rating** 90 **To** 2020 $18 CM ✪
Adelaide Hills Sauvignon Blanc 2014 **Rating** 90 **To** 2015 $18 CM ✪
Adelaide Hills Chardonnay 2014 **Rating** 90 **To** 2020 $18 ✪

wightwick   ★★★★

323 Slatey Creek Road North, Invermay, Vic 3352 **Region** Ballarat
T (03) 5332 4443 **www.**wightwick.com.au **Open** By appt
Winemaker Simon Wightwick **Est.** 1996 **Dozens** 180 **Vyds** 0.4ha
wightwick might be described as an angel on a pinhead exercise. Keith and Ann Wightwick planted the tiny estate vineyard to 0.15ha of chardonnay and 0.25ha of pinot noir in 1996. Son Simon works as a viticulturist and winemaker in the Yarra Valley, and looks after the vineyards on weekends (using organic principles) and the micro-winemaking during vintage. The Pinot Noir is hand-plunged and basket-pressed, with racking via gravity and minimal fining.

🍷🍷🍷🍷🍷 **Ballarat Pinot Noir 2012** Excellent release. Spicy and sappy, but well fruited. Tangy acidity, but not at the expense of flavour. Modest tannin, but it manages to curl into the fruit and curry favour with the wine as a whole. Pretty aromatics, but a serious palate. Screwcap. 12.8% alc. **Rating** 94 **To** 2021 $35 CM

Wignalls Wines

448 Chester Pass Road (Highway 1), Albany, WA 6330 **Region** Albany
T (08) 9841 2848 **www**.wignallswines.com.au **Open** 7 days 11–4
Winemaker Rob Wignall, Michael Perkins **Est.** 1982 **Dozens** 7000 **Vyds** 18.5ha
While the estate vineyards have a diverse range of sauvignon blanc, semillon, chardonnay, pinot noir, merlot, shiraz, cabernet franc and cabernet sauvignon, founder Bill Wignall was one of the early movers with pinot noir, producing wines that, by the standards of their time, were well in front of anything else coming out of WA (and up with the then limited amounts being made in Vic and Tas). The establishment of an onsite winery, and the assumption of the winemaking role by son Rob, with significant input by Michael Perkins, has seen the quality and range of wines increase. Exports to Denmark, Japan, Singapore and China.

Great Southern Shiraz 2013 A totally seductive wine reflecting its very cool climate, yet with a cascade of supple red and purple fruits threaded through with warm spices and black pepper, the tannins superfine, but sufficient to give the palate balance and character. Good now, good – perhaps even better – in 5+ years' time. Screwcap. 13.8% alc. **Rating** 95 **To** 2028 $25 ✪
Single Vineyard Albany Pinot Noir 2013 Crushed and destemmed, 2-day cold soak, numerous small ferments, 'various yeast strains to extract as much flavour from individual rows', French oak for 10 months on lees. Crystal-clear colour; it has a highly expressive and fragrant bouquet, then a fresh, supple palate, its dancing red fruits the driving force, oak and tannins in a pure support role. Screwcap. 14.2% alc. **Rating** 94 **To** 2023 $35

Premium Albany Chardonnay 2013 Rating 92 **To** 2023 $35

Wild Dog Winery

Warragul–Korumburra Road, Warragul, Vic 3820 **Region** Gippsland
T (03) 5623 1117 **www**.wilddogwinery.com **Open** 7 days 11–5
Winemaker Folkert Janssen **Est.** 1982 **Dozens** 4000 **Vyds** 10.1ha
Wild Dog is a family-owned business operated by Gary and Judy Surman. Since acquiring the business in 2005 much work has been done in the vineyard (planted in 1982) with grafting, replanting and retrellising, and winery expansion (all wines are now made onsite). They have also built a restaurant overlooking the vineyard. Now one of the larger wineries in Gippsland, and one of the more consistent producers of good-quality wines.

Gippsland Shiraz 2013 A 90/10% blend of shiraz and viognier, matured in French oak (10% new) and tank for 18 months. Bright crimson-purple; this is a very smart cool-grown Shiraz, picked at the right moment, giving it vibrancy and perfume, yet not depriving it of structure and depth; morello cherry, spice and a sprinkle of black pepper provide a perfectly balanced palate needing no patience, but it will wait if need be. Screwcap. 13.5% alc. **Rating** 95 **To** 2033 $27 ✪
Reserve Gippsland Shiraz 2013 A 90/10% blend of shiraz and viognier, matured in French oak (50% new) for 18 months. Excellent colour introduces a complex medium-bodied wine; red cherry, black cherry and plum are intertwined with French oak and a skein of soft tannins. It will go the distance, and reveal more still as it ages. Screwcap. 13% alc. **Rating** 95 **To** 2038 $45
Gippsland Cabernet Sauvignon 2013 An 85/10/5% blend of cabernet, merlot and franc, 80% matured in oak (10% new) and 20% in tank. Bright crimson-purple hue; it has clear-cut, zesty cassis and bay leaf/dried herb flavours, the tannins fine and well balanced. The winemaking approach has worked a treat. Screwcap. 13% alc. **Rating** 94 **To** 2025 $23 ✪

Wild Ice Gippsland Ice Riesling 2011 Rating 93 **To** 2020 $30
Gippsland Wild Rose 2014 Rating 90 **To** 2015 $19 ✪

Wild Duck Creek Estate ★★★★

764 Spring Flat Road, Heathcote, Vic 3523 **Region** Heathcote
T (03) 5433 3133 **www**.wildduckcreekestate.com **Open** By appt
Winemaker David and Liam Anderson **Est.** 1980 **Dozens** 3500 **Vyds** 15ha
The first release of Wild Duck Creek Estate from the 1991 vintage marked the end of 12 years
of effort by David and Diana Anderson. They began planting the 4.5ha vineyard in 1980, made
their first tiny quantities of wine in '86, the first commercial quantities of wine in '91, and built
their winery and cellar door facility in '93. Son Liam has joined this idiosyncratic, but very
successful, business and says 'If I can see my fingers through the wine, Dad's done something
wrong.' He is also part of the team steering the vineyard to biodynamic status. Exports to the
US (where Duck Muck has become a cult wine), the UK and other major markets.

ΨΨΨΨΨ **Springflat Heathcote Shiraz 2010** The '10 vintage allowed the heroic style of
Wild Duck Creek free rein; there are multiple layers of black fruits, licorice and
mocha/fruitcake flavours on the mid-palate, but curiously, the wine backs off on
the back-palate and finish. Screwcap. 15.5% alc. **Rating** 93 **To** 2025 $55
Springflat Heathcote Shiraz 2011 The grapes come from 8 sites spread across
Heathcote; matured for 22 months in 40% new French and American hogsheads.
Deeply and brightly coloured, it shows none of the dilution of most of the red
wines of the vintage, although not everyone will be pleased by the alcohol. An
excellent outcome, reflecting endless work in the vineyard and careful sorting of
the fruit. Screwcap. 15% alc. **Rating** 92 **To** 2025 $55

ΨΨΨΨ **Yellow Hammer Hill 2011 Rating** 89 **To** 2020 $29
Ducks & Drakes Cabernet Sauvignon 2011 Rating 89 **To** 2020 $40

Will Taylor Wines ★★★★

1B Victoria Avenue, Unley Park, SA 5061 **Region** Various
T (08) 8271 6122 **www**.willtaylor.com.au **Open** By appt
Winemaker Various contract **Est.** 1997 **Dozens** 300
Will Taylor is a partner in the leading Adelaide law firm Finlaysons, and specialises in wine
law. He and Suzanne Taylor have established a classic negociant wine business, having wines
contract-made to their specifications. Moreover, they choose what they consider the best
regions for each variety; thus Clare Valley Riesling, Adelaide Hills Sauvignon Blanc, Hunter
Valley Semillon, Coonawarra Cabernet Sauvignon and Yarra Valley Pinot Noir. Exports
to China.

ΨΨΨΨΨ **Coonawarra Cabernet Sauvignon 2009** From a different Coonawarra
vineyard from that previously used, and blended with Coonawarra malbec from
this vineyard, inspired by a visit to Mendoza. The structure of the wine is its strong
point, with typical Coonawarra earth tannins a convincing subtext to blackcurrant
and mulberry fruit. Diam. 14.5% alc. **Rating** 94 **To** 2030 $40

Willem Kurt Wines ★★★★

Croom Lane, Beechworth, Vic 3747 **Region** Beechworth
T 0428 400 522 **www**.willemkurtwines.com.au **Open** Not
Winemaker Daniel Balzer **Est.** 2014 **Dozens** 300 **Vyds** 1ha
This is the venture of Daniel and Marije Balzer, he with a German background, she Dutch.
The name of the winery is drawn from the middle names of their two children: Willem
(Dutch) and Kurt (German), in each instance reflecting long usage in the two families. Daniel
moved into the wine industry in 1998, having already obtained a science degree, working first
at Yarra Ridge (including a vintage in Germany) before moving to Gapsted Wines in 2003,
then completing his Bachelor of Wine Science at CSU the following year. The past 7 years
have been given over to contract winemaking for smaller producers, and it was inevitable
that sooner or later they would start making wine for their own brand. They currently lease a
vineyard in Beechworth, and buy select parcels of fruit. Beechworth is the region they know
and love best, the plan being to buy land and establish their own vineyard and winery. The
quality of the wines made to date suggests it should succeed.

♟♟♟♟♀ **Beechworth Chardonnay 2013** Beautifully balanced and seamless in all
respects. Pure varietal character/flavour with spicy oak and ginger notes in the
background. Nectarine, grapefruit and oatmeal. Open for business now. Screwcap.
13.3% alc. **Rating** 92 **To** 2017 $34 CM
Alpine Valleys Vermentino 2014 Plenty of texture and flavour. This new
producer really seems to know what it's about. Apple, dry pear, powdered milk
and spice flavours with an undercurrent of dried herbs. The wine's mouthfeel is
arguably the real highlight. Screwcap. 12% alc. **Rating** 92 **To** 2015 $25 CM ✪
Beechworth Shiraz 2012 Beechworth, Alpine Valleys and King Valley shiraz.
Beautifully integrated. Pepper and spice backed by a healthy but elegant serve of
dark cherry and licorice flavour. Well honed. Kiss of oak polishes things off nicely.
Screwcap. 13.8% alc. **Rating** 92 **To** 2021 $32 CM

Willespie

555 Harmans Mill Road, Wilyabrup via Cowaramup, WA 6284 **Region** Margaret River
T (08) 9755 6248 **www**.willespie.com.au **Open** 7 days 10.30–5
Winemaker Loren Brown **Est.** 1976 **Dozens** 3000 **Vyds** 17.53ha
Willespie has produced many attractive white wines over the years, typically in brisk,
herbaceous Margaret River style; all are fruit rather than oak-driven. The business has been
on the market for some time, and part of the vineyards has been sold. Exports to the UK,
Malaysia and Japan.

♟♟♟♟♀ **Old School Margaret River Cabernet Franc 2010** Cabernet franc, cabernet
sauvignon and merlot 86/9.5/4.5%. French oak for 3 years. 255 dozen. Charming,
soft, fluent fruit and oak before a temper of grunty, assertive tannin takes hold.
Musk, mint, violets, blackberry and toast flavours/scents. Leafy notes too. Lots to
sink your teeth into. Diam. 14.5% alc. **Rating** 92 **To** 2022 $28 CM
Old School Barrel Fermented Margaret River Semillon 2010 Glowing
yellow. Kaffir lime and honeysuckle, nettle and ripe tropical fruit. Full-bodied.
Over the top in many ways yet it sizzles through the finish. Still going strong as a
5yo. Screwcap. 13.5% alc. **Rating** 91 **To** 2018 $28 CM
Margaret River Red 2010 Cabernet, shiraz, merlot. 3 years in barrel. Not
your average easy/early drinker. Delivers fruit and tannin in hearty measure.
Blackcurrant, tar and gravel with raspberry and vanilla. Ready to drink now, but
won't fall over in a hurry. Screwcap. 15% alc. **Rating** 91 **To** 2019 $20 CM ✪
Basket Pressed Margaret River Cabernet Sauvignon 2006 Fully mature
and drinking well, if not quite at its absolute best. Leather and tobacco leaves,
assorted spice and sweet, curranty, violet-accented fruit. Provides a pleasurable aged
wine experience. Diam. 13.5% alc. **Rating** 90 **To** 2018 $45 CM

♟♟♟♟ **Margaret River Riesling 2014** Rating 89 **To** 2020 $23 CM
Old School Chardonnay 2012 Rating 88 **To** 2017 $30 CM

Willoughby Park

678 South Coast Highway, Denmark, WA 6333 **Region** Great Southern
T (08) 9848 1555 **www**.willoughbypark.com.au **Open** 7 days 10–5
Winemaker Luke Eckersley **Est.** 2010 **Dozens** 13000 **Vyds** 19ha
Bob Fowler, who comes from a rural background and had always hankered after a farming
life, stumbled across the opportunity to achieve this in early 2010. Together with wife
Marilyn, he purchased the former West Cape Howe winery and surrounding vineyard that
became available when West Cape Howe moved into the far larger Goundrey winery. In '11
Willoughby Park purchased the Kalgan River vineyard and business name, and winemaking
operations have been transferred to Willoughby Park. There are now three labels: Willoughby
Park, the Great Southern premium brand for estate and purchased grapes; Kalgan River
single-vineyard range; and Jamie & Charli, a sub-$20 Great Southern range of wines. Exports
to Norway and China.

ŸŸŸŸŸ **Kalgan Ironrock Riesling 2014** Made in two batches, the first approximately 80%, whole bunch-pressed to tanks, cold-settled, racked and wild yeast-fermented at 13–14°C; the second batch crushed, on skins in the press for 12 hours, then drained to French oak for wild yeast fermentation. The moment you taste it you can sense this is going to be a long journey, as the exceptionally complex texture and structure become progressively more potent as you traverse all that unfolds in the mouth. Screwcap. 12.5% alc. **Rating** 97 **To** 2030 $35 ✪

ŸŸŸŸŸ **Kalgan Ironrock Albany Chardonnay 2013** Bright colour, showing the first stage of development; this is a seriously good Chardonnay, rippling with waves of flavour on the long palate before the cleansing finish; obviously barrel-fermented with significant new oak, wild yeast and the works, the end result a wine of power and harmony. Screwcap. 13.5% alc. **Rating** 96 **To** 2025 $40 ✪

Kalgan Ironrock Shiraz 2012 Hand-picked, small-batch open-fermented, hand-plunged, 18 months in French and American oak. There is a lacy mouthfeel that allows the simultaneous transmission of spice, red and black cherry fruits, anise, pepper and tannins, yet all with a breezy freshness. Screwcap. 13% alc. **Rating** 96 **To** 2032 $55 ✪

Kalgan River Riesling 2014 Much expected, and much delivered; beautifully structured and detailed, with an exceptional degree of purity to its blossom aromas and delicately precise palate of citrus and green apple flavours. Its balance will ensure its future, and – in the manner of young high-quality Semillon – there is more left in the kit bag than has so far been taken out. Screwcap. 12.5% alc. **Rating** 95 **To** 2029 $27 ✪

Kalgan River Shiraz 2012 Less cerebral than Ironrock, but with many of its best features; its brilliant colour reflects 30 months' elevage, mainly in used French oak; it has an expressive array of plum, cherry and raspberry flavours, fine tannins and a background of oriental spices. Wants to keep the conversation going for as long as you have time to spare. Screwcap. 13% alc. **Rating** 95 **To** 2027 $30 ✪

Kalgan River Cabernet Sauvignon 2012 Doesn't have the elegance of its Ironrock sibling, but has more depth and structure without going over the top; abounds with cassis fruit tempered by hints of bay leaf and black olive, the tannins posing no threat to the fruit, but sufficient to support it. Screwcap. 13.5% alc. **Rating** 95 **To** 2032 $30 ✪

Kalgan River Albany Chardonnay 2013 **Rating** 94 **To** 2023 $30 ✪
Kalgan Ironrock Albany Cabernet Sauvignon 2012 **Rating** 94 **To** 2027 $55

ŸŸŸŸŸ **Great Southern Sauvignon Blanc 2014** **Rating** 91 **To** 2016 $22 ✪
Shiraz 2011 **Rating** 91 **To** 2023 $22 ✪

Willow Bridge Estate   ★★★★★
178 Gardin Court Drive, Dardanup, WA 6236 **Region** Geographe
T (08) 9728 0055 **www**.willowbridge.com.au **Open** 7 days 11–5
Winemaker Kim Horton **Est.** 1997 **Dozens** 20 000 **Vyds** 59ha
Jeff and Vicky Dewar have followed a fast track in developing Willow Bridge Estate since acquiring the spectacular 180ha hillside property in the Ferguson Valley: chardonnay, semillon, sauvignon blanc, shiraz and cabernet sauvignon were planted, with merlot, tempranillo, chenin blanc and viognier following. Many of its wines offer exceptional value for money. On 22 March 2015, Willow Bridge's 44-year-old senior winemaker, Simon Burnell, died in a windsurfing accident off the coast of Margaret River. It revived memories of the death of Craggy Range winemaker Doug Wiser in Hawke's Bay in '04 while kite-surfing. Kim Horton, with extensive experience in WA, most recently as Senior Winemaker at Ferngrove, has been appointed to take Simon's place. Exports to the UK, China and other major markets.

ŸŸŸŸŸ **Dragonfly Geographe Sauvignon Blanc Semillon 2014** A cut above almost all other sub-$20 SBS blends, it has intense, piercing flavours reaching out to citrus/grass on one hand, tropical on the other, but also given an extra measure of texture and structure by a portion of barrel fermentation. Screwcap. 12.3% alc. **Rating** 95 **To** 2016 $20 ✪

G1-10 Geographe Chardonnay 2014 Glides effortlessly across the palate. It's complex but it demands nothing of the drinker. Pear, apple, cashew and grapefruit. Succulent midsection and a long, fleshy finish. Screwcap. 12.5% alc. **Rating** 95 **To** 2019 $30 CM ✪

Gravel Pit Geographe Shiraz 2013 The vines are grown on the remnants of a gravel pit, reducing the yield and concentrating the flavour profile of plum and blackberry fruit, complexity further aided by the inclusion of small amounts of grenache and mataro. The wine is complete in every way. Screwcap. 13.4% alc. **Rating** 95 **To** 2033 $30 ✪

Dragonfly Geographe Shiraz 2013 Bright crimson; the fragrant, verging on flowery, bouquet has red berries, spice and a dusting of cooking chocolate, the supple medium-bodied palate spanning a similar range, starting with sweet fruit and finishing with fine, cedary tannins reflecting maturation in new and used French oak. Screwcap. 13.1% alc. **Rating** 94 **To** 2023 $20 ✪

Coat of Arms Geographe Cabernet Merlot 2013 Seductive blackcurrant, black olive and lead pencil notes lead into dark chocolate and mint. Calm and composed for the most part though the finish is serious with tannin. Still finding its feet, but over the mid-term and longer it will drink and mature well. Screwcap. 13.4% alc. **Rating** 94 **To** 2027 $30 CM ✪

Solana Geographe Tempranillo 2013 A full-bodied and complex rendition of Tempranillo; black cherry, anise, earth, spice and tannin all thump the drum of this wine. Great with a flame-grilled slab of beef Spanish style. Screwcap. 13.3% alc. **Rating** 94 **To** 2023 $28 ✪

🍷🍷🍷🍷🍷 **Rosa de Solana Tempranillo Rose 2014 Rating** 93 **To** 2016 $25 CM ✪
Dragonfly Geographe Chardonnay 2014 Rating 90 **To** 2016 $20 ✪

Willow Creek Vineyard ★★★★★

166 Balnarring Road, Merricks North, Vic 3926 **Region** Mornington Peninsula
T (03) 5989 7448 **www**.willow-creek.com.au **Open** 7 days 11–5
Winemaker Geraldine McFaul **Est.** 1989 **Dozens** 5000 **Vyds** 18ha
Significant changes have transformed Willow Creek over the past 7 years. In 2008, winemaker Geraldine McFaul, with many years of winemaking in the Mornington Peninsula under her belt, was appointed, and worked with viticulturist Robbie O'Leary to focus on minimal intervention in the winery; in other words, to produce grapes in perfect condition. In '13 the Li family arrived from China and expanded its portfolio of hotel and resort properties in Australia by purchasing Willow Creek, with plans to develop a luxury 39-room boutique hotel on the site. This will be the 7th in the Li hotel group.

🍷🍷🍷🍷🍷 **Mornington Peninsula Pinot Noir 2013** Intense, clear purple-crimson; the evocative bouquet has blanched black cherry and cherry pip aromas, the palate delivering in spades all the promise of the bouquet; it has great length, line and balance, the dark cherry flavours coating the mouth, yet doing so without effort (or extraction). Screwcap. 13.8% alc. **Rating** 96 **To** 2028 $40 ✪

Mornington Peninsula Chardonnay 2012 Particularly fine Chardonnay. Characterised by its length but awash with flavour. Builds and builds in the glass; always an excellent sign. Citrus, pear, grapefruit and a range of cedar wood and spice notes. Flinty. Feels good on the tongue, and has excellent cut and drive. Screwcap. 13% alc. **Rating** 95 **To** 2020 $40 CM

Mornington Peninsula Rose 2014 Destemmed and crushed, then chilled and macerated on skins for 24 hours to extract colour; barrel-fermented to dryness in used barrels. Pale crimson; fragrant red cherry/strawberry aromas; a very attractive rose with precision and life to its red fruits, the finish crisp and dry. Screwcap. 13% alc. **Rating** 95 **To** 2016 $28 ✪

Mornington Peninsula Brut 2008 50/50% traditional method chardonnay and pinot noir; spent 5 years on lees before being disgorged Nov '13. While its long time on lees has built complexity, it retains elegance and freshness, the finish particularly long and satisfying. Cork. 12.5% alc. **Rating** 95 **To** 2018 $40

ŸŸŸŸŸ Mornington Peninsula Sauvignon Blanc 2014 Rating 93 To 2015 $35
Mornington Peninsula Pinot Gris 2014 Rating 93 To 2016 $35
Mornington Peninsula Chardonnay 2013 Rating 91 To 2016 $40
Mornington Peninsula Pinot Noir 2012 Rating 91 To 2018 $40

Wills Domain ★★★★★

Cnr Brash Road/Abbey Farm Road, Yallingup, WA 6281 **Region** Margaret River
T (08) 9755 2327 **www**.willsdomain.com.au **Open** 7 days 10–5
Winemaker Naturaliste Vintners (Bruce Dukes) **Est.** 1985 **Dozens** 12500 **Vyds** 20.8ha
When the Haunold family purchased the original Wills Domain vineyard in 2000, they were
adding another chapter to a family history of winemaking stretching back to 1383 in what is
now Austria. Remarkable though that may be, more remarkable is that Darren, who lost the
use of his legs in an accident in 1989, runs the estate (including part of the pruning) from his
wheelchair. The vineyard is planted to shiraz, semillon, cabernet sauvignon, sauvignon blanc,
chardonnay, merlot, petit verdot, malbec, cabernet franc and viognier. Exports to Canada,
Indonesia, Hong Kong and China.

ŸŸŸŸŸ Block 2 Semillon 2014 An impressive Semillon that marches strictly to the beat
of its own drum. The mouthfeel and complexity of the full suite of lemon, citrus
pith and zest, and a delicious hint of white peach, half suggest some oak has been
used. Whether or not that is the case is irrelevant because of the coherence of the
wine. Screwcap. 13.5% alc. **Rating** 96 To 2029 $27 ❂
Cuvee d'Elevage Chardonnay 2013 'Judiciously fermenting, evolving and
maturing the wine for up to 24 months in only the finest selection of French oak
barriques,' explains the back label. And indeed, this is a Chardonnay of considerable
intensity and complexity, only the colour giving an indication of its long sojourn
in oak; ripe white peach fruit is lengthened by citrussy acidity, the oak simply
adding emphasis. Screwcap. 14% alc. **Rating** 95 To 2023 $65
Cuvee d'Elevage Shiraz 2013 Matured for 24 months in French barriques.
Has a fragrant bouquet with spicy red fruits to the fore, the silky medium-bodied
palate given extra length by the combination of fruit and oak tannins. Impressive
in its own niche style. Screwcap. 14% alc. **Rating** 95 To 2028 $80
Cuvee d'Elevage Cabernet Sauvignon 2012 When you find the back label
explaining the winemaking approach is identical for chardonnay and cabernet
sauvignon, you start to wonder. This is a medium-bodied wine, but with several
streams of flavour, one cassis, the other cedar and dried herb, running through
the palate and its lingering finish. It is the aftertaste that gets it across the line.
Screwcap. 14% alc. **Rating** 95 To 2032 $90
Block 8 Chardonnay 2013 Light straw-green; an elegant and vital wine with
gin-clear varietal fruit expression on the bouquet and palate alike; white peach and
nectarine lead the pink grapefruit notes, the French oak fully integrated; excellent
length. Screwcap. 13.5% alc. **Rating** 94 To 2021 $30 ❂
Cabernet Merlot 2013 Shares the purity of virtually all of the Wills Domain
wines, and the drive this purity engenders. Blackcurrant/cassis fruit has a backdrop
of bramble and bay leaf; while the flavour is robust, the line continues unbroken
through to the long finish. Screwcap. 14.5% alc. **Rating** 94 To 2028 $20 ❂

ŸŸŸŸŸ Margaret River Semillon Sauvignon Blanc 2014 Rating 93 To 2016 $20 ❂
Block 5 Margaret River Shiraz 2013 Rating 92 To 2020 $30
Block 9 Margaret River Scheurebe 2014 Rating 91 To 2017 $28

Willunga 100 Wines ★★★★☆

c/- Tintara, 202 Main Road, McLaren Vale, SA 5171 (postal) **Region** McLaren Vale
T 0427 271 280 **www**.willunga100.com **Open** Not
Winemaker Tim James, Kate Day **Est.** 2005 **Dozens** 15000
Willunga 100 is solely owned by Liberty Wines UK, sourcing its grapes from McLaren Vale
and from Adelaide Hills (pinot gris and a portion of its viognier). Tim James has come on

board as consultant winemaker, Kate Day continuing in the executive role. Exports to the UK, the US, Canada, Singapore, Hong Kong, Japan and China.

🍷🍷🍷🍷🍷 **McLaren Vale Cabernet Shiraz 2013** Plenty of beef on the bones. Dark, brooding blackcurrant and asphalt flavours with gum leaf in support. Iron chains of tannin threaded through the fruit. Uncompromising style. Will be very long-lived. Price is almost ridiculous. Screwcap. 14% alc. **Rating** 95 **To** 2033 $22 CM ✪

🍷🍷🍷🍷🍷 **McLaren Vale Grenache 2013 Rating** 93 **To** 2021 $22 CM ✪
Grenache Rose 2014 Rating 92 **To** 2016 $22 CM ✪
McLaren Vale Shiraz Viognier 2013 Rating 92 **To** 2021 $22 CM ✪
The Hundred Grenache 2013 Rating 90 **To** 2018 $30 CM

Wilson Vineyard   ★★★★★
Polish Hill River, Sevenhill via Clare, SA 5453 **Region** Clare Valley
T (08) 8843 4310 **Open** W'ends 10–4
Winemaker Daniel Wilson **Est.** 1974 **Dozens** 3000 **Vyds** 11.9ha
In 2009 the winery and general operations were passed on to son Daniel Wilson, the second generation. Daniel, a graduate of CSU, spent three years in the Barossa with some of Australia's largest winemakers before returning to Clare in '03. Parents John and Pat Wilson still contribute in a limited way, content to watch developments in the business they created. Daniel continues to follow John's beliefs about keeping quality high, often at the expense of volume, and rather than talk about it, believes the proof is in the bottle. At Daniel's side are wife Tamara and daughters Poppy and Isabelle.

🍷🍷🍷🍷🍷 **Polish Hill River Riesling 2014** Chilled bunches were whole bunch-pressed to retain maximum varietal fruit flavour; the fragrant blossom-filled bouquet leads into an elegant, but intense, and perfectly balanced, palate; pure citrus juice and rind flavours run seamlessly through to the finish and aftertaste. Screwcap. 12% alc. **Rating** 95 **To** 2034 $29 ✪
Handplunge Clare Valley Shiraz 2010 Very good colour for its age; a full-bodied Shiraz that fills every corner of the mouth, yet does so with a surprisingly gentle, velvety touch; the bouquet is very fragrant and complex, Swiss chocolate and touches of licorice following on the palate, the tannins ripe and plush, oak simply doing its job. Screwcap. 14.7% alc. **Rating** 95 **To** 2030 $38
DJW Clare Valley Riesling 2014 From a small block in the Polish Hill River district planted in '97. Manages to combine generosity with freshness and clear cut lime and extreme length; lime and lemon positively sizzle on the palate in a sherbet-like display of fruit. Screwcap. 12% alc. **Rating** 94 **To** 2029 $24 ✪
408 Old Vines Clare Valley Zinfandel 2012 The grapes were hand-picked and rack-dried before fermentation in tiny 1-tonne open fermenters. It's strange how this Amarone-style treatment lifts the alcohol without making the finish hot; here red and black cherries, raspberry and spices flow through to the medium-bodied finish with rare style. Screwcap. 15.5% alc. **Rating** 94 **To** 2022 $38

🍷🍷🍷🍷🍷 **Watervale Riesling 2014 Rating** 93 **To** 2020 $19 ✪
Inquisicion Clare Valley Tempranillo 2012 Rating 90 **To** 2020 $38

Wimbaliri Wines   ★★★☆
3180 Barton Highway, Murrumbateman, NSW 2582 **Region** Canberra District
T (02) 6227 5921 **www.**wimbaliri.com.au **Open** W'ends 10–5
Winemaker Scott Gledhill **Est.** 1988 **Dozens** 600 **Vyds** 2.2ha
John and Margaret Andersen moved to the Canberra District in 1987, establishing their vineyard at Murrumbateman in '88, bordering Clonakilla. The vineyard is close-planted with chardonnay, pinot noir, shiraz, cabernet sauvignon and merlot (plus a few vines of cabernet franc). In 2009 the winery was purchased by Scott and Sarah Gledhill. Scott, born in Wallsend (NSW), is a sixth-generation descendant of German vine dressers who emigrated to the

Hunter Valley in the 1850s; Sarah draws upon her science background to assist in the vineyard and winemaking.

⚲⚲⚲⚲⚲ **35th Parallel Murrumbateman Chardonnay 2013** Hand-picked, whole-bunch basket-pressed into French oak, lees-stirred for 9 months, then further time in barrel (bottled Oct '14). The approach has worked well, investing the wine with complexity, but leaving rockmelon, nectarine and fig fruit with a gentle touch of citrussy acidity. Diam. 13% alc. **Rating** 90 **To** 2017 $20 ○

⚲⚲⚲⚲ **Murrumbateman Shiraz Viognier 2013 Rating** 88 **To** 2023 $40

Windance Wines   ★★★★

2764 Caves Road, Yallingup, WA 6282 **Region** Margaret River
T (08) 9755 2293 **www.**windance.com.au **Open** 7 days 10–5
Winemaker Tyke Wheatley **Est.** 1998 **Dozens** 4000 **Vyds** 7.25ha
Drew and Rosemary Brent-White own this family business, situated 5km south of Yallingup. Cabernet sauvignon, shiraz, sauvignon blanc, semillon and merlot have been established, incorporating sustainable land management and organic farming practices where possible. The wines are exclusively estate-grown. Daughter Billie and husband Tyke Wheatley now run operations: Billie, a qualified accountant, was raised at Windance, and manages the business and the cellar door, and Tyke (with winemaking experience at Picardy, Happs and Burgundy) has taken over the winemaking and manages the vineyard.

⚲⚲⚲⚲⚲ **Margaret River Unoaked Chardonnay 2014** An impressive example, the fruit with the varietal integrity and intensity often conspicuous by its absence; white peach, melon and grapefruit are all in balance. Made to be enjoyed now, but will be with us for several years yet. Screwcap. 12.5% alc. **Rating** 94 **To** 2016 $20 ○

⚲⚲⚲⚲⚲ **Margaret River Merlot 2013 Rating** 92 **To** 2020 $22 ○
Margaret River Cabernet Merlot 2013 Rating 92 **To** 2025 $22 ○
Reserve Margaret River Shiraz 2013 Rating 90 **To** 2025 $30

Windowrie Estate   ★★★☆

Windowrie Road, Canowindra, NSW 2804 **Region** Cowra
T (02) 6344 3234 **www.**windowrie.com.au **Open** At The Mill, Cowra
Winemaker Antonio D'Onise **Est.** 1988 **Dozens** 30 000 **Vyds** 240ha
Windowrie Estate was established by the O'Dea family in 1988 on a substantial grazing property at Canowindra, 30km north of Cowra. A portion of the grapes is sold to other makers, but increasing quantities are being made for the Windowrie Estate and The Mill labels. The cellar door is in a flour mill – built in 1861 from local granite – that ceased operations in 1905 and lay unoccupied for 91 years until restored by the O'Dea family. Exports to Canada, China, Japan and Singapore

⚲⚲⚲⚲ **The Mill Hilltops Cabernet Merlot 2013** An 85/15% blend, the cabernet from Hilltops, the merlot from Orange, separately fermented and matured in French and American oak for 12 months prior to blending. A well-conceived wine, flooded with flavour and slight sweetness on the finish. Screwcap. 14.5% alc. **Rating** 88 **To** 2018 $18

Windows Estate   ★★★★★

4 Quininup Road, Yallingup, WA 6282 **Region** Margaret River
T (08) 9756 6655 **www.**windowsestate.com **Open** 7 days 10–5
Winemaker Chris Davies **Est.** 1996 **Dozens** 3500 **Vyds** 6.3ha
Chris Davies planted the Windows Estate vineyard (cabernet sauvignon, shiraz, chenin blanc, chardonnay, semillon, sauvignon blanc and merlot) in 1996, at the age of 19, and has tended the vines ever since. Initially selling the grapes, Chris moved into winemaking in 2006 and has had considerable show success for the consistently outstanding wines. Exports to Germany, Singapore and Taiwan.

🍷🍷🍷🍷🍷 Single Vineyard Margaret River Semillon Sauvignon 2014 A 65/35% blend from two dry-grown estate blocks, with 25% barrel fermentation in new French barriques. The oak is totally integrated, allowing the intense fruit flavours – ranging from Meyer lemon to a flash of white peach, then on to tropical fruits – free play. Exceptional value. Screwcap. 12% alc. **Rating** 96 **To** 2020 $24 ✪
Basket Pressed Margaret River Cabernet Sauvignon 2012 Open-fermented, basket-pressed and matured in French barriques for 18 months. What can only be described as classic Cabernet, with layers of interleaved cassis and fine-grained tannins in symbiotic union; the balance of the palate guarantees an indefinitely long life. Screwcap. 14.5% alc. **Rating** 96 **To** 2035 $35 ✪
Single Vineyard Margaret River Sauvignon Blanc 2014 Intensity is the key. Flavour hits, runs, then bursts out through the finish. Passionfruit, lime, gravel and dried grass. Precision in a glass. Screwcap. 12% alc. **Rating** 95 **To** 2017 $22 CM ✪
Margaret River Chardonnay 2013 Full style but firm and well mannered. Grapefruit, lemon pith and peach build an impressive main course of flavours before spice and cream notes bring in the after dinners. Chalky, toasty length. Top notch. Screwcap. 14% alc. **Rating** 95 **To** 2020 $39 CM

🍷🍷🍷🍷🍷 **Margaret River Shiraz 2012** **Rating** 93 **To** 2025 $30 CM
Margaret River Cabernet Merlot 2012 **Rating** 93 **To** 2025 $30 CM

Wine x Sam   ★★★★☆

1896 Tarcombe Road, Avenel, Vic 3664 (postal) **Region** Strathbogie Ranges
T 0408 587 702 **www**.winebysam.com.au **Open** Not
Winemaker Sam Plunkett, Arran Murphy **Est.** 2013 **Dozens** 30 000 **Vyds** 10.2ha
There are more twists and turns behind the story of Wine x Sam than in an episode of *Australian Story*. Fully detailed, they extend to two tightly typed A4 pages, so I will have to content myself with milepost explanations. In 1991 Sam Plunkett returned home to the family farm with an economics degree and a Melbourne rock band experience. Grapes were planted, and the family made the mudbrick winery using materials from the site. They made a manual 1-tonne rotofermenter, the first crusher and the tanks. A decade or so later they set up a new winery in the township of Avenel, and once again did it all themselves on a very much larger scale. In 2004 they were able to buy a large neighbouring winery (Dominion Wines), and this brought forth a partnership with the Fowles family. In '11, Fowles bought the Plunkett family's shareholding, leaving part of the vineyard (7ha of shiraz and 3.2ha of chardonnay). Whatever temptation to build a third winery (and equipment) by hand was dispelled when the opportunity came to set up winemaking at the Taresch family's Elgo Estate winery. Less than two years later the Plunkett interests had leased the entire Elgo winery, and now have the responsibility for making the Elgo wines as well as their own brands. A large contract make for Naked Wines will see 20 000 dozen go to this destination alone, but with plenty of flesh left on the bone for Wine x Sam. Exports to the UK, the US and China.

🍷🍷🍷🍷🍷 **The Victorian Strathbogie Ranges Shiraz 2013** From the family Whitegate Vineyard, 80% matured in 1yo French puncheons, 10% in new French and 10% in new American puncheons, one barrel of lagrein added. 3 gold medals in '14, including the Great Australian Shiraz Challenge. Another wine to over-deliver in spades; perfectly ripened shiraz is awash with satsuma plum fruit, with a remarkably long and juicy finish. Screwcap. 14.3% alc. **Rating** 95 **To** 2023 $20 ✪
Elgo Vineyard Strathbogie Ranges Cabernet Sauvignon 2013 The fragrant bouquet has nuances of eucalypt and herb within its cassis mainframe; it is only medium-bodied, and the tannins are not an issue of any description, yet 80% of the wine was matured in new French hogsheads; the cigar box needs more time to settle down, but should do so. Screwcap. 14% alc. **Rating** 94 **To** 2030 $40
Whitegate Vineyard Strathbogie Ranges Cabernet Sauvignon 2013 The back label has ominous descriptions of drying and of velvety tannins (an odd conjunction) and the contribution of a young Californian winemaker who spent the vintage with the Plunketts. I expected tannin gridlock, but there is no such thing, just a swell of cassis and redcurrant fruit, tannins doing exactly what they should. Screwcap. 14.8% alc. **Rating** 94 **To** 2030 $40

♟♟♟♟♟ Box Grove Vineyard Nagambie Lakes Shiraz 2013 Rating 91 To 2033 $40
The Victorian Pinot Gris 2014 Rating 90 To 2015 $20 ✪
The Butterfly Effect Shiraz 2013 Rating 90 To 2018 $14 ✪

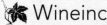 Wineinc ★★★☆

38 Willows Road, Gresford, NSW 2311 **Region** Various
T (02) 4938 9444 **www**.wineinc.com.au **Open** Not
Winemaker Bruce Glugston **Est.** 2004 **Dozens** 20000
Until Bruce Clugston and Fiona White sold their Gotham and Wine Men of Gotham brands, Wineinc was simply a holding company for their interests. They have started again, and we learn that in his younger years, Bruce was a mathematician – thus the nod to the work of Benoit Mandelbrot, through whom mathematic algorithms became art, hence Fractal art and the Fractal label. This is the label for regional and varietal links, thus Barossa Valley shiraz, Coonawarra cabernet sauvignon, Yarra Valley chardonnay and Adelaide Hills sauvignon blanc. The Abstraction label is limited to SA shiraz and chardonnay, both targeted at the seemingly impossible $5 per bottle market. Oh, and there is the Mastermind brand that was left over from the sale of Gotham.

♟♟♟♟♟ Fractal Coonawarra Cabernet Sauvignon 2012 Don't read the back label if
you treasure the English language, but its gushing about the quality of this wine –
at a give-away price – has an element of truth. By some distance, it is the best
of the Fractal range, with good varietal character, length and balance. Screwcap.
13.9% alc. **Rating** 90 To 2020 $13 ✪

Wines by Geoff Hardy ★★★★★

327 Hunt Road, McLaren Vale, SA 5171 **Region** South Australia
T (08) 8323 2700 **www**.winesbygeoffhardy.com.au **Open** 7 days 11–5
Winemaker Geoff Hardy, Shane Harris **Est.** 1980 **Dozens** 58000 **Vyds** 3.4ha
Geoff Hardy's great-great-grandfather, the original Thomas Hardy, first planted grapes in SA in the 1850s and was one of the founding fathers of the Australian wine industry. In 1980, Geoff left the then family company, Thomas Hardy & Sons, to make his own way in all sectors of the Australian wine business, together with wife Fiona. Wines by Geoff Hardy is made up of three ventures/brands founded by Geoff: Pertaringa in McLaren Vale, K1 by Geoff Hardy in the Adelaide Hills (Tunan Rd, Kuitpo) and Hand Crafted by Geoff Hardy sourced from a variety of premium regions across SA. Geoff opened a third cellar door for his Hand Crafted brand on the main street of Hahndorf in 2014. Exports to Canada, the UK, Sweden, Finland, Malaysia, South Korea, Indonesia, Japan, Hong Kong and China.

♟♟♟♟♟ Pertaringa Rifle & Hunt Adelaide Cabernet Sauvignon 2012 A full-bodied
Cabernet that really gets its act together from the get-go: cassis and cedar on the
bouquet and supple, flavour-stacked palate alike; has excellent depth and balance,
and a long, pleasure-filled palate. Diam. 14.5% alc. **Rating** 96 To 2032 $40 ✪
Pertaringa The Yeoman 2013 My ancient bones creak and protest when I
pick up a bottle as heavy as this – picking up a 6-bottle case would be seriously
difficult, 12 bottles needing a block and tackle. The colour is dense, the bouquet
a black hole in space, the full-bodied palate in proportion to the bottle. Its inky
black fruits blot out daylight and starlight alike; the fruit is so profound it negates
any discussion of alcohol, oak or tannins. Diam. 15% alc. **Rating** 95 To 2053 $195
Pertaringa Over The Top McLaren Vale Shiraz 2012 Deep but vivid
crimson-purple; the bouquet and palate are as rich and focused as the colour
suggests, and the alcohol is not OTT; it has a riot of black fruits, cracked black
pepper, licorice and allspice framed by fine tannins, oak struggling to make its
presence felt. Will outlive many who buy it (Diam permitting). 15% alc. **Rating** 95
To 2047 $40
K1 Adelaide Hills Shiraz 2012 Deep crimson-purple; the complex, rich
bouquet is replete with black fruits, licorice, tar and spice, oak also part of the
landscape; the medium to full-bodied palate fulfils the promise of the bouquet:

layered and intense, but reflecting its cool climate. Excellent future. Screwcap. 14% alc. **Rating** 95 **To** 2032 $35 ⊘

K1 Adelaide Hills Cabernet Sauvignon 2012 A classy example of the variety, trimming its cassis fruit with a touch of black olive/earthy austerity feeding into the fine-grained tannins running through the length of the palate. Will breeze through the years ahead. Screwcap. 14.5% alc. **Rating** 95 **To** 2030 $35 ⊘

Hand Crafted GSM 2013 A 70/22/18% blend from McLaren Vale, eerily close to the '10 version, loudly but melodiously proclaiming its Rhône blend and its McLaren Vale origin: a parade of fragrant red fruits, splashes of chocolate, ripe, fine tannins and overall balance in a medium-bodied framework. Delicious stuff. Screwcap. 14.5% alc. **Rating** 95 **To** 2023 $30 ⊘

Pertaringa Rifle & Hunt Adelaide Cabernet Sauvignon 2013 Deeply coloured; a particularly juicy and vibrant Cabernet with none of the pain the variety can inflict; oak and tannins are the essential counterpoints to the fruit, providing structure and (if you like) discipline; has excellent length and balance. Diam. 14.5% alc. **Rating** 95 **To** 2033 $40

K1 Adelaide Hills Chardonnay 2014 Rating 94 **To** 2025 $35
Pertaringa Over The Top Shiraz 2013 Rating 94 **To** 2043 $40
Pertaringa Understudy Cabernet 2013 Rating 94 **To** 2028 $22 ⊘
Hand Crafted Langhorne Creek Graciano 2013 Rating 94 **To** 2027 $30 ⊘

ŢŢŢŢŢ **Hand Crafted Riesling 2014 Rating** 93 **To** 2024 $25 ⊘
Pertaringa Stage Left Adelaide Merlot 2013 Rating 93 **To** 2022 $22 ⊘
Geoff Hardy GMH Pinot Noir 2013 Rating 92 **To** 2020 $20 ⊘
Pertaringa Undercover Shiraz 2013 Rating 92 **To** 2023 $22 ⊘
Pertaringa Two Gentlemen's GSM 2013 Rating 92 **To** 2025 $22 ⊘

Wines by KT ★★★★★

Main North Road, Watervale, SA 5452 **Region** Clare Valley
T 0419 855 500 **www.**winesbykt.com **Open** By appt
Winemaker Kerri Thompson **Est.** 2006 **Dozens** 1400
KT is winemaker Kerri Thompson. Kerri graduated with a degree in oenology from Roseworthy Agricultural College in 1993, and thereafter made wine in McLaren Vale, Tuscany, Beaujolais and the Clare Valley, becoming well known as the Leasingham winemaker in the Clare Valley. She resigned from Leasingham in 2006 after seven years at the helm, and after a short break became winemaker at Crabtree. Here she is also able to make Wines by KT, sourcing the grapes from two local vineyards, one biodynamic, the other farmed with sulphur and copper sprays only. Exports to the UK.

ŢŢŢŢŢ **Churinga Vineyard Watervale Riesling 2014** The Churinga Vineyard riesling was planted 60 years ago, Made in the core KT fashion, this wine is ablaze with intense citrus (verging on white peach) fruit on entry to the palate, energetically moving to glorious, mouth-watering acidity on the lingering finish and aftertaste. Screwcap. 12.5% alc. **Rating** 97 **To** 2032 $33 ⊘

ŢŢŢŢŢ **5452 Riesling 2014** From the Peglidis and Churinga Vineyards, both in Watervale (with a postcode of 5452). Organic/biodynamic from vineyard to bottle, the wine has a fragrant, flowery (citrus blossom) bouquet and a fresh, crisp palate of considerable purity, built on a foundation of minerally acidity; awesome length. 450 dozen made. Screwcap. 12% alc. **Rating** 96 **To** 2027 $22 ⊘

Peglidis Vineyard Watervale Riesling 2014 Bunch-sorted; wild yeast-fermented (as are all KT Rieslings), with distinct floral/talc spice aromas leading into an utterly seductive palate of lime, lemon and orange flavours in a jeweller's setting of perfect acidity. Screwcap. 12% alc. **Rating** 96 **To** 2032 $35 ⊘

Melva Wild Fermented Riesling 2014 The bouquet instantly signals a different key to the song of riesling, the complex, multifaceted aromas as much spicy as they are fruity; the palate, too, has a distinctive mouthfeel, momentarily fleshy before slatey acidity kicks in on the back-palate and finish. Screwcap. 12% alc. **Rating** 95 **To** 2030 $33 ⊘

Churinga Vineyard Watervale Shiraz 2012 Only 5 barriques (110 dozen) of
this wine were made. It is no more than medium-bodied, but has very complex
texture and structure, spice and cedar threaded through the blue and black
fruit spectrum, fine, ripe tannins underlining its texture as much as its structure.
Screwcap. 14% alc. **Rating** 95 To 2032 $42
Churinga Cabernet Sauvignon 2012 Rating 94 To 2027 $42
Tinta by KT Tempranillo 2012 Rating 94 To 2017 $21 ○

5452 Shiraz Grenache Tempranillo Mataro 2012 Rating 92 To 2022 $26

Wines for Joanie   ★★★★

163 Glendale Road, Sidmouth, Tas 7270 **Region** Northern Tasmania
T (03) 6394 7005 **www**.winesforjoanie.com.au **Open** Fri–Mon 10–5
Winemaker Contract **Est.** 2013 **Dozens** 250 **Vyds** 5ha
Andrew (Rew) and Prue O'Shanesy lived on a small cattle and cropping farm in Queensland,
but they realised it wasn't a viable stand-alone business. They sold it, and had no idea what to
do next. Northern Territory? A coffee plantation at Byron Bay? Then someone mentioned a
vineyard was for sale in northern Tasmania. Look no further: Rew is a viticulturist and both
love drinking wine. In the blink of an eye they were heading across Bass Strait 'with the ute,
two cattle dogs, a horse and a prissy cat'. They started working on a budget for a vineyard,
trying to make the budget tell them what they wanted to hear. They eventually tore up the
budget, took the plunge and bought Glendale, the little farm they now call home. They
now have three dogs, two horses, the prissy cat, a couple of chooks, some sheep, a few cows
and a baby boy called Angus. Joanie was Rew's mother, an inspiring, vivacious, creative and
strong woman.

Chardonnay 2013 The integrity and quality of the varietal fruit expression are
mouth-watering, easily taming the Tasmanian acidity, which simply assumes a
support role; the flavour wheel takes in pink grapefruit, white peach and Granny
Smith apple, oak almost invisible. Screwcap. 13.5% alc. **Rating** 93 To 2025 $48
Sparkling NV Fresh, lively and full of juicy fruits, strawberry and white peach
to the fore; while flavourful, Tasmanian acidity comes through on a white charger.
Time on cork will be more than useful. Diam. 12.5% alc. **Rating** 92 To 2020 $35

Pinot Noir 2013 Rating 89 To 2020 $48

Winetrust Estates   ★★★☆

Murray Valley Highway, Swan Hill, Vic 3585 **Region** Swan Hill
T (02) 9949 9250 **www**.winetrustestates.com **Open** Not
Winemaker Callum Peace, Marion Peligri **Est.** 1999 **Dozens** 57 000 **Vyds** 88.9ha
Mark Arnold is the man behind Winetrust Estates, drawing on a lifetime of experience in
all aspects of the wine industry. Production of the wines from all vineyards in the group is
centralised at the Garacama Winery at Swan Hill, the origin of the grapes either self-grown,
contract-grown or produced under a joint venture across five regions in Vic, SA and WA. The
top-of-the-range Picarus red wines come from the Limestone Coast; the Ocean Grove and
Firebox Ridge ranges cover all the major varietal wines plus a few newcomers. Exports to the
UK, the US, Canada, China, Japan, Singapore, Hong Kong and Thailand.

Picarus Wrattonbully Cabernet Sauvignon 2013 Fresh fruit laced with
chocolatey oak and set by firmish tannin. All is in good order here. Blackcurrant,
redcurrant and gum leaf flavours do the bulk of the talking; you feel in sure hands
all along the way. Screwcap. 14% alc. **Rating** 91 To 2020 $23 CM ○

Picarus Clare Valley Riesling 2014 Rating 89 To 2019 $19 CM ○
Argon Bay Reserve Chardonnay 2013 Rating 89 To 2015 $17 ○
Picarus Victoria Pinot Gris 2014 Rating 89 To 2015 $16 CM ○
Alazarane Swan Hill Shiraz 2013 Rating 88 To 2015 $29 CM
Picarus Wrattonbully Shiraz 2013 Rating 88 To 2019 $23 CM

Winstead

75 Winstead Road, Bagdad, Tas 7030 **Region** Southern Tasmania
T (03) 6268 6417 **Open** By appt
Winemaker Neil Snare **Est.** 1989 **Dozens** 350 **Vyds** 1.2ha
The good news about Winstead is the outstanding quality of its extremely generous and rich Pinot Noirs, rivalling those of Freycinet for the abundance of their fruit flavour without any sacrifice of varietal character. The bad news is that production is so limited, with only 0.8ha of pinot noir and 0.4ha riesling being tended by fly fishing devotee Neil Snare and wife Julieanne.

🍷🍷🍷🍷🍷 **Lot 7 Pinot Noir 2012** A welcome return for Winstead with this deeply coloured, ripe, rich, powerful, but not over the top, Pinot. Will be long-lived. Screwcap. **Rating** 94 **To** 2025

Wirra Wirra

McMurtrie Road, McLaren Vale, SA 5171 **Region** McLaren Vale
T (08) 8323 8414 **www**.wirrawirra.com **Open** Mon–Sat 10–5, Sun & public hols 11–5
Winemaker Paul Smith, Paul Carpenter **Est.** 1894 **Dozens** 180 000 **Vyds** 51.31ha
Long respected for the consistency of its white wines, Wirra Wirra has now established an equally formidable reputation for its reds. The wines are of exemplary character, quality and style, The Angelus Cabernet Sauvignon and RWS Shiraz battling each other for supremacy, with The Absconder Grenache one to watch. Long may the battle continue under the direction of managing director Andrew Kay and the winemaking team of Paul Smith, Paul Carpenter and Tom Ravech, who forge along the path of excellence first trod by the late (and much loved) Greg Trott, the pioneering founder of modern-day Wirra Wirra. Its acquisition of Ashton Hills in April 2015 adds a major string to its top-quality bow. Exports to all major markets.

🍷🍷🍷🍷🍷 **The Angelus McLaren Vale Cabernet Sauvignon 2013** From the coolest districts of McLaren Vale; matured for 18 months in French barriques (20% new), usual rack and returns. This is a beautifully weighted and structured, medium-bodied Cabernet, showing how much synergy can be generated between place and variety; pure cassis fruit has the finest line of tannin support imaginable, the length perfect. Screwcap. 14% alc. **Rating** 97 **To** 2043 $70 ✪

🍷🍷🍷🍷🍷 **Patritti Single Vineyard Shiraz 2013** Open-fermented and basket-pressed, racked at 4-month intervals over 18 months after mlf, matured in French puncheons, egg white-fined. This must have had mind-boggling power in the wake of fermentation, and is still power-packed. Anyone who drinks this before '23 will be guilty of vinocide, anyone thereafter will be inordinately pleased with themselves – and the wine. Screwcap. 14.5% alc. **Rating** 96 **To** 2050 $132

Scarce Earth Whaite Block Shiraz 2012 The cool Blewitt Springs climate makes its statement more clearly than the geology. Wirra Wirra says it selected the best single-vineyard parcels to make 45 dozen (2 barriques). It is very elegant, supple and bordering juicy, oak evident, but not OTT, the tannins superfine. Great now, but will hold. Screwcap. 14.5% alc. **Rating** 96 **To** 2027 $130

The Absconder McLaren Vale Grenache 2013 Hand-picked from 95yo vines; crushed (80%) to small open fermenters, 20% whole bunches, matured in used French puncheons for 9 months. McLaren Vale Grenache at its elegant best, with ultra-fragrant red berry aromas, the palate a juicy/spicy extension of the bouquet. Screwcap. 14.5% alc. **Rating** 96 **To** 2028 $70 ✪

Woodhenge McLaren Vale Shiraz 2013 Maturation in French and American oak of various sizes (35% new) for 17 months with rack and return every 4 months might seem a lot, but it's part of the standard procedure at Wirra Wirra, and you can't argue with the result, for this is of Stonehenge/Woodhenge dimensions. It is only because of the balance between its components that the wine can be enjoyed soonish, but it needs more than a decade to come into full flower. Screwcap. 14.5% alc. **Rating** 95 **To** 2033 $35 ✪

RSW McLaren Vale Shiraz 2013 Three parcels from Blewitt Springs, McLaren Flat and Seaview (average age of vines 40 years) kept separate for the first 14 months' maturation in French oak (20% new), then a barrel selection blended for the last 3 months. It is unashamedly full-bodied, with liqueur cherry, poached plum and blackberry jam fruit given the appropriate discipline of tar, and ripe but substantial tannins to bring it into balance. Screwcap. 14.5% alc. **Rating** 95 To 2043 $70

The 12th Man Adelaide Hills Chardonnay 2014 Rating 94 To 2022 $31
Catapult McLaren Vale Shiraz 2013 Rating 94 To 2028 $24 ✪
Church Block McLaren Vale Cabernet Sauvignon Shiraz Merlot 2013 Rating 94 To 2025 $23 ✪

🍷🍷🍷🍷♀ **The Lost Watch Riesling 2014** Rating 93 To 2026 $22 CM ✪
Hiding Champion Sauvignon Blanc 2014 Rating 93 To 2015 $24 CM ✪
Mrs Wigley Grenache Rose 2014 Rating 93 To 2015 $18 CM ✪

🌿 Wirrega Vineyards   ★★★★

PO Box 94, Mundulla, SA 5270 **Region** Limestone Coast
T (08) 8743 4167 **www**.wirregavineyards.com **Open** Not
Winemaker Trevor Roether **Est.** 1993 **Dozens** 300 **Vyds** 163ha
This is the venture of what might kindly be called wine village elders, or, less kindly, likely suspects, as they have an awesome amount of knowledge about every aspect of the wine industry. In 1993 they formed a partnership to develop this large vineyard which, until 2013, was content to stick to its knitting of supplying grapes for some of the partners' own enterprises, and to businesses as large as Pernod-Ricard. For the record, the partners are Scott Collett, Rocco Melino, Roger Oakeshott, Grant Tilbrook, John Younger and Guido Zuccoli. The Lilliputian production will skyrocket if the partners so wish, for the quality is obvious.

🍷🍷🍷🍷🍷 **Sfera Shiraz 2013** Full colour; a flamboyantly voluptuous wine that teeters on the edge of alcohol-induced warmth, but stays on the right side with its carefree display of red fruits, black fruits and ripe tannins, oak almost incidental. Screwcap. 14.9% alc. **Rating** 94 To 2030 $40

Wise Wine   ★★★★★

237 Eagle Bay Road, Eagle Bay, WA 6281 **Region** Margaret River
T (08) 9750 3100 **www**.wisewine.com.au **Open** 7 days 11–5
Winemaker Andrew Siddell, Matt Buchan, Larry Cherubino (Consultant) **Est.** 1986
Dozens 20 000 **Vyds** 6ha
Wise Wine, headed by Perth entrepreneur Ron Wise, has been a remarkably consistent producer of high-quality wine. The vineyard adjacent to the winery in the Margaret River is supplemented by contract-grown grapes from Pemberton, Manjimup and Frankland River. The estate plantings are (in descending order of size) cabernet sauvignon, shiraz and zinfandel. The value for money of many of the wines is extraordinarily good. Exports to the UK and Singapore.

🍷🍷🍷🍷🍷 **Single Vineyard Karridale Chardonnay 2013** Beautifully integrated and harmonious. Pear and white peach with chalk and sweet, toasty oak. In fine fettle. Flavours ring out through the finish. Screwcap. 13% alc. **Rating** 95 To 2019 $45 CM

Single Vineyard Wilyabrup Cabernet Sauvignon 2012 Everything in its place, and in good order. Packed and ready for the long journey ahead. Neat flavours of tar, cassis, chocolate and bay leaves, its oak almost completely consumed by the depth of dark fruit. Tannin is firm, fine and not to be messed with, though again the fruit keeps its influence discreet. Screwcap. 14.5% alc. **Rating** 95 To 2035 $50 CM

Lot 80 Margaret River Cabernet Sauvignon 2012 Burly, beefy and substantial. Sets its course and there's no swaying it. A wealth of black-berried fruit, gravelly notes, mint, liquid dark chocolate and churns of earth. Tannin is a low, throaty grumble throughout. Cellar beckons. Screwcap. 14.5% alc. **Rating** 94 To 2032 $35 CM

ΥΥΥΥΥ **Margaret River Cabernet Merlot 2013** Rating 91 To 2021 $20 CM ✪
Margaret River Pinot Grigio 2014 Rating 90 To 2015 $28 CM

Witches Falls Winery ★★★★★

79 Main Western Road, North Tamborine, Qld 4272 **Region** Queensland Zone
T (07) 5545 2609 **www.**witchesfalls.com.au **Open** Mon–Fri 10–4, w'ends 10–5
Winemaker Jon Heslop **Est.** 2004 **Dozens** 12000 **Vyds** 0.4ha
Witches Falls is the venture of Jon and Kim Heslop. Jon has a deep interest in experimenting with progressive vinification methods in order to achieve exceptional and interesting results. He has a degree in applied science (oenology) from CSU, and experience working in the Barossa and Hunter valleys as well as at Domaine Chantel Lescure, Burgundy, and a Napa-based wine grower. Witches Falls grapes are sourced from the Granite Belt, and it is one of the consistently good performers in that context. Exports to Malaysia, South Korea, Japan and China.

ΥΥΥΥΥ **Wild Ferment Granite Belt Sauvignon Blanc 2013** Pressed to French barriques for a wild yeast fermentation, left on lees for 2 months, then racked and returned to barrel for a further 8 months. The result is an unambiguously good Sauvignon Blanc with considerable complexity, yet a pure line of fruit drives through to the finish and aftertaste in a citrus/yellow fruit spectrum. Screwcap. 12% alc. **Rating** 95 To 2017 $32 ✪
Wild Ferment Granite Belt Viognier 2013 By chance, tasted alongside another barrel-fermented Viognier at a slightly higher price, and emerged the clear winner, here with an elegance and freshness, and also the apricot/peach flavours of the variety. Top marks for such a challenge. Screwcap. 12.4% alc. **Rating** 95 To 2017 $32 ✪
Prophecy Syrah 2012 This is an impressive medium to full-bodied Shiraz, attesting to the continued evolution of the Granite Belt. Black fruits, warm spices, pepper and anise dance along the bouquet and palate, finishing with perfectly balanced tannins. Screwcap. 14.3% alc. **Rating** 95 To 2030 $51
Prophecy Granite Belt Cabernet Sauvignon 2012 Matured in new and used oak. An energetic wine, the fruit flavours changing rapidly on the palate, flitting through the full echelon of black fruits allied with dusty/savoury tannins and oak. Screwcap. 14.4% alc. **Rating** 94 To 2027 $51

ΥΥΥΥΥ **Co-Inoculated Sauvignon Blanc 2014** Rating 93 To 2015 $24 ✪
Wild Ferment Granite Belt Chardonnay 2013 Rating 93 To 2019 $32
Wild Ferment Granite Belt Verdelho 2013 Rating 93 To 2016 $32
Granite Belt Merlot 2011 Rating 92 To 2021 $28
Wild Ferment Granite Belt Cabernet Franc 2013 Rating 91 To 2020 $32

Wolf Blass ★★★★★

97 Sturt Highway, Nuriootpa, SA 5355 **Region** Barossa Valley
T (08) 8568 7311 **www.**wolfblasswines.com.au **Open** Mon–Fri 9–5, w'ends 10–5
Winemaker Chris Hatcher (Chief), Matt O'Leary, Marie Clay **Est.** 1966 **Dozens** NFP
Although merged with Mildara and now under the giant umbrella of TWE, the brands (as expected) have been left largely intact. The Wolf Blass wines are made at all price points, ranging through Red, Yellow, Gold, Brown, Grey, Black, White and Platinum labels, at one price point or another covering every one of the main varietals. The pre-eminent quality of the red wines over the white wines has reasserted itself, but without in any way diminishing the attraction the latter have. All of this has occurred under the leadership of Chris Hatcher, who has harnessed the talents of the winemaking team and encouraged the changes in style. Exports to all major markets.

⍓⍓⍓⍓⍓ **The Master Pasquin Vineyard Langhorne Creek Cabernet Shiraz 2012**
The Pasquin Vineyard, planted for Wolf Blass Wines in '94–'95 by Wolf's first and only chief winemaker, John Glaetzer, and Langhorne Creek legend Bill Potts. A 61/39% blend, it spent 18 months in new and used French and American oak barrels; it is a seriously lovely wine, the sheer intensity (and harmony) of the lush black fruits giving the palate energy and life from the start to the finish. A tribute to the man and the vintage. Screwcap. 14.5% alc. **Rating** 97 **To** 2037 $350

Black Label Cabernet Sauvignon Shiraz 2012 Deep crimson-purple; whereas the '11 had to fight every inch of the way, this wine displays almost contemptuous ease in the way it has marshalled the layers of black fruits and ripe tannins that soak up the new oak inputs. This will be one of the long-lived, great Black Labels. Screwcap. 14.7% alc. **Rating** 97 **To** 2042 $130 ✪

Black Label Cabernet Sauvignon Shiraz 2010 A 51/49% blend that spent 22 months in 61% new French, 19% new American, and 20% 1yo French oak. It is exceptionally fresh, the secret its very high (for red wine) 8g/l of acidity and low pH (3.34). I believe it passes the test of balance (the alcohol of 15% is needed given the acid level), which means it will live for many decades under its screwcap. All the expected flavours – blackberry, blackcurrant, plum, bitter chocolate and cedar – are there in abundance. 15% alc. **Rating** 97 **To** 2050 $140 ✪

⍓⍓⍓⍓⍓ **Sapphire Label Lyndoch 5351 Barossa Shiraz 2012** A most attractive collage of black cherry, licorice and spice, all characters associated with cool-climate shiraz, as is the almost feline grace of the mouthfeel. Screwcap. 14.5% alc. **Rating** 96 **To** 2033 $90

Sapphire Label St John's Ebenezer Road 5355 Barossa Shiraz 2012 The juicy mouthfeel of this wine, with its delicious display of peppery blackcurrant fruits, puts it in a category all of its own. Screwcap. 14.5% alc. **Rating** 96 **To** 2033 $90

White Label Robe Mount Benson Shiraz Cabernet 2012 Must have Wolf Blass (the man) grinding his teeth, never a Limestone Coast supporter; even Coonawarra was for long excluded from his red wines, Robe and Mount Benson must be the final indignity. But perhaps he will be as enthralled by the supple, yet complex rainbow of fruit aromas and flavours the wine has; its balance and length are every bit as good. Screwcap. 14.5% alc. **Rating** 96 **To** 2042 $50 ✪

Brown Label Classic Shiraz 2012 A sentimental return to mark Wolf Blass's 80th birthday after being discontinued after '01; a blend from McLaren Vale (58%), Langhorne Creek (22%) and the Barossa Valley (20%), matured in new French (95%) and American oak. It's clear top-quality parcels of fruit have been used, for it has tremendous drive and persistence to its black fruits; tannins and oak are mere adjuncts. Screwcap. 14.5% alc. **Rating** 96 **To** 2042 $50 ✪

Platinum Label Medlands Vineyard Barossa Valley Shiraz 2012 A very well made wine, elegance written large across its face, off to one side of the normal Wolf Blass top-end wines, spicy notes on the bouquet and palate an amalgam of fruit and oak; it is only medium-bodied, and has exceptional line, length and balance. If this is to be the future style of Wolf Blass top reds, we will be in for a treat. Time will tell whether it's a one-off from the great '12 vintage. Screwcap. 14% alc. **Rating** 96 **To** 2035 $200

White Label Eden Valley Riesling 2013 A striking wine, its airy lightness and flavour spectrum consistent with its low alcohol; the sherbet mouthfeel and lemon flavours are likewise part of the same story. Has a Germanic touch to it. Screwcap. 11% alc. **Rating** 95 **To** 2028 $34 ✪

Sapphire Label Dorrien 5352 Barossa Shiraz 2012 The fruit expression is distinctly intense, with blackberry, blueberry and a waft of bitter chocolate. Screwcap. 14.5% alc. **Rating** 95 **To** 2027 $90

White Label Adelaide Hills Cabernet Sauvignon 2012 Deep, bright colour; cool-grown blackcurrant/cassis fruit brooks no argument about its central role, oak in perfect balance, tannins fine and ripe. Screwcap. 14.5% alc. **Rating** 95 **To** 2032 $50

Grey Label Langhorne Creek Cabernet Shiraz 2013 Completed fermentation in new and used French and American oak followed by 18 months' maturation in those barrels, the percentages of the varieties not disclosed. A powerhouse, full-bodied and complex, with a deep well of black fruits, licorice, oak and a farewell touch of dark chocolate borrowed from McLaren Vale. Screwcap. 14.5% alc. **Rating** 95 **To** 2043 $45

Grey Label Langhorne Creek Cabernet Shiraz 2012 A 77/33% blend, with each of the components separately matured in a mix of new and used French and American oak for 18 months. A high-quality wine by any standards, reflecting the vintage conditions: perfect throughout. Vibrant blackberry and plum fruit lead the way on the bouquet and palate, the oak under control at all points along the way, the tannins ripe and soft. Screwcap. 14.5% alc. **Rating** 95 **To** 2032 $45

Black Label Cabernet Sauvignon Shiraz 2011 Exceptional colour for the vintage, deep and healthy; self-evidently, the result of the most disciplined fruit selection; it is only medium-bodied, but has focus, length and balance to the blackcurrant/blackberry fruit amalgam; it is only on the finish and aftertaste that a hint of the wet vintage is evident. Screwcap. 14% alc. **Rating** 95 **To** 2031 $130

White Label Piccadilly Valley Chardonnay 2013 Rating 94 **To** 2025 $34
Grey Label McLaren Vale Shiraz 2013 Rating 94 **To** 2040 $45
Sapphire Label Moculta 5353 Barossa Shiraz 2012 Rating 94 **To** 2035 $90
Grey Label McLaren Vale Shiraz 2012 Rating 94 **To** 2033 $45
Gold Label Coonawarra Cabernet Sauvignon 2013 Rating 94 **To** 2028 $28 ○

Wood Block Wines ★★★☆

PO Box 318, Coonawarra, SA 5263 **Region** Coonawarra
T 0417 878 933 **www.**woodblockwines.com.au **Open** Not
Winemaker Peter Douglas (Contract) **Est.** 2009 **Dozens** 3500 **Vyds** 34.45ha
Wood Block is the venture of Tim and Sarah Kidman, a family name that resonates in Coonawarra and in the minds of those who know the history of the eponymous cattle-grazing family. Tim was only three years old when his maternal grandfather, Grant Wood, first planted shiraz on the terra rossa soil. He and wife Sarah are now the third generation to care for the vineyard, which now comprises cabernet sauvignon, shiraz and viognier. Only a small part of the production is vinified under the Wood Block Wines label, by the infinitely experienced Peter Douglas.

♟♟♟♟♟ **Single Vineyard Coonawarra Shiraz 2013** Deep, dense colour; Coonawarra doesn't produce many Shirazs with the weight and density of this wine, a throwback to the era when fruit and tannins, not oak, did the talking. Will surely be very long-lived, and will improve markedly over the years in front of it. Screwcap. 14.2% alc. **Rating** 93 **To** 2043 $30

Wood Park ★★★★★

263 Kneebones Gap Road, Markwood, Vic 3678 **Region** King Valley
T (03) 5727 3778 **www.**woodparkwines.com.au **Open** At Milawa Cheese Factory
Winemaker John Stokes, Richard Trevillian **Est.** 1989 **Dozens** 7000 **Vyds** 16ha
John Stokes planted the first vines at Wood Park in 1989 as part of a diversification program for his property at Bobinawarrah, in the hills of the Lower King Valley, east of Milawa. The vineyard is managed with minimal chemical use, winemaking a mix of modern and traditional techniques (what wine isn't?). The reach of Wood Park has been expanded with Beechworth Pinot Noir, and a mix of mainstream and alternative varieties, all well made. It also has a cellar door in Ford St, Beechworth. Exports to Taiwan, Singapore, Hong Kong and China.

♟♟♟♟♟ **Beechworth Pinot Noir 2013** Beechworth forever teases with its Pinots, but for once decides to be serious, with a wine that ticks all the boxes: complex, but pleasing, aromas and a long palate that could have travelled from Burgundy; there is a seductive forest floor flavour foundation that is at once savoury and wild-fruited. Surprise, surprise. Screwcap. 13% alc. **Rating** 95 **To** 2023 $26 ○

Reserve King Valley Cabernet Sauvignon 2013 A very neatly composed Cabernet with perfectly ripened fruit; blackcurrant/cassis is the frontrunner, but olive and bay leaf aren't far behind, and cabernet tannins have surreptitiously gained a foothold right from the start of the palate, but are content with that role; the oak, too, is well integrated. Screwcap. 13.5% alc. **Rating** 95 **To** 2033 $40
Reserve King Valley Shiraz 2013 Deep colour; a rich, full-bodied Shiraz wreathed with succulent plum, black cherry and blackberry fruit, a dab of licorice and spice also in the frame; the tannins are supple, the oak integrated. Screwcap. 14% alc. **Rating** 94 **To** 2033 $40
Reserve King Valley Zinfandel 2013 Has a fresh-crushed raspberry aroma, then a red-fruit palate; the texture is fine, the mouthfeel supple, the finish juicy. Only medium-bodied, it already sings for its supper. Screwcap. 15% alc. **Rating** 94 **To** 2025 $50

TTTTT **Roussanne 2012** **Rating** 93 **To** 2018 $28
Monument Lane Cabernet Shiraz 2013 **Rating** 93 **To** 2028 $24 ○

Woodgate Wines ★★★★

43 Hind Road, Manjimup, WA 6258 **Region** Manjimup
T (08) 9772 4288 **www**.woodgatewines.com.au **Open** Thurs–Sat 10–4.30, Sun 12.30–4.30
Winemaker Mark Aitken **Est.** 2006 **Dozens** 2500 **Vyds** 7.9ha
This is the family-owned business of Mark and wife Tracey Aitken, Tracey's mother Jeannette Smith, and her brother Robert and his wife Linda Hatton. Mark became a mature-age student at Curtin University, obtaining his oenology degree in 2001 as Dux, earning a trip to Bordeaux to undertake vintage, returning to work at Manjimup's Chestnut Grove winery from '02. In '05 he and Tracey began their own contract winemaking business, as well as making wine for their Woodgate brand. Most of the grapes come from the estate plantings of cabernet sauvignon, chardonnay, sauvignon blanc, pinot noir and merlot, supplemented by grapes from a leased vineyard. The name of the sparkling wine, Bojangles, reflects the family's musical heritage, which stretches back three generations and includes vocalists, guitarists, pianists, a trumpeter, a saxophonist, two drummers and a double bass player.

TTTTT **Pemberton Sauvignon Blanc Semillon 2014** Pristine example of the style. Cut grass, chalk and passionfruit flavours. Is generous enough but keeps an even head. Finishes confidently. Screwcap. 12.5% alc. **Rating** 93 **To** 2015 $18 CM ○
Pemberton Pinot Gris 2014 Textural style. Shows the addition of gewurztraminer pretty keenly. Floral Turkish delight, melon and citrus notes. Smoky in a complexing way. Rich and spicy. Tending towards hedonism. Screwcap. 13.6% alc. **Rating** 91 **To** 2015 $22 CM ○
Reserve Two Tribes Merlot Cabernet Malbec 2013 52% Pemberton merlot, 44% Frankland cabernet, 4% Frankland malbec. Generally supple, with a slight kink through the finish. It delivers medium-weight flavours of blackberry, mulberry and earth before a wealth of briary tannin takes the reins. Drinks well now but should be at its best in the mid-term. Screwcap. 14% alc. **Rating** 91 **To** 2023 $30 CM
Manjimup Merlot 2013 Enough flavour, but not a lot of give. It's like sitting on a lounge-chair sans cushion. In its favour is a solid framework of tannin and acid, the flavours of dark olive, bay leaf, dry licorice and mulberry kept sturdy and strict at all times. It should improve over the coming few years and beyond. Screwcap. 13.5% alc. **Rating** 90 **To** 2020 $22 CM

TTTT **Reserve Liqueur Carnelian 2009** **Rating** 88 **To** 2016 $35 CM

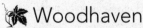 Woodhaven ★★★★

87 Main Creek Road, Red Hill, Vic 3937 **Region** Mornington Peninsula
T 0421 612 178 **www**.woodhavenvineyard.com.au **Open** By appt
Winemaker Lee and Neil Ward **Est.** 2003 **Dozens** 150 **Vyds** 1.6ha

Woodhaven is the venture of Lee and Neil Ward, both qualified accountants for 30 years in Melbourne, albeit working in different fields. They then spent two years looking for a suitable site on the Mornington Peninsula, and ultimately found one high on Red Hill. Bringing the venture through to the point of production has been a slow and, at times, frustrating business. They decided from the outset to be personally responsible for all aspects of growing the grapes and making the wines, relying on the advice readily given to them by George and Ruth Mihaly of Paradigm, David and (the late) Wendy Lloyd of Eldridge, and John and Julie Trueman of Myrtacae. They also decided to grow the vines organically and biodynamically, and it took 8 years until they produced their first two barrels of wine, in 2010. In '13 the vines finally produced more than one barrel of each wine from the 0.8ha each of pinot noir and chardonnay. These blocks had both been planted over a period of time, and they expect the later plantings to be in production by '16, with a consequent increase in production.

ΨΨΨΨ Pinot Noir 2013 Estate-grown, hand-picked, cold soak plus fermentation 18 days on skins, French oak (50% new) maturation for 18 months. Clear crimson-purple; the razor sharp varietal definition on the bouquet is mirrored in the palate, with black cherry and plum fruit framed by French oak that is yet to fully integrate, but will surely do so. Screwcap. 13.5% alc. **Rating** 93 **To** 2023 $50

Woodlands

3948 Caves Road, Wilyabrup, WA 6284 **Region** Margaret River
T (08) 9755 6226 **www.**woodlandswines.com **Open** 7 days 10–5
Winemaker Stuart and Andrew Watson **Est.** 1973 **Dozens** 15 000 **Vyds** 22.12ha
Founder David Watson had spectacular success with the Cabernets he made in 1979 and the early '80s. Commuting from Perth on weekends and holidays, as well as raising a family, became all too much, and for some years the grapes from Woodlands were sold to other Margaret River producers. With the advent of sons Stuart and Andrew (Stuart primarily responsible for winemaking), the estate has bounced back to pre-eminence. The wines come in four price bands, the bulk of the production under the Chardonnay and Cabernet Merlot varietals, then a series of Reserve and Special Reserves, then Reserve de la Cave, and finally Cabernet Sauvignon. The top-end wines primarily come from the original Woodlands Vineyard, where the vines are over 40 years old. Exports to Indonesia, Malaysia, Singapore, Japan and China.

ΨΨΨΨΨ Thomas Margaret River Cabernet Sauvignon 2012 Cabernet plus 3% malbec and 1% cabernet franc is matured for 21 months in 100% new French oak. Bright crimson; the wine nearly escapes under the radar, until it starts accelerating on the mid-palate and hurtles through the finish and aftertaste, drawing saliva as the intensity of cassis, earth, black olive and cedar spear through the mouth. Screwcap. 13.5% alc. **Rating** 97 **To** 2047 $130 ✪

ΨΨΨΨΨ Chloe 2013 Fermented and matured in French oak for 12 months. Absolutely in the midst of the most complex Margaret River Chardonnays, with stone fruit, melon and fig lined up against pink/white grapefruit, oak acting as a referee. These classy wines brook no argument. Screwcap. 13.5% alc. **Rating** 96 **To** 2025 $75 ✪
Margaret 2013 A 78/11/11% blend of cabernet, merlot and malbec matured in French oak for 18 months. A Margaret River classic, albeit with a niche all of its own given by the juicy freshness of the palate, and by its effortless length and finish. Simply beautiful. Screwcap. 13.5% alc. **Rating** 96 **To** 2033 $45 ✪
Margaret River Chardonnay 2014 Very pale straw-green; a medley – and melody – of white peach, melon and grapefruit interwoven with barrel-ferment characters and discreet French oak, all in the mainstream of elegant Margaret River Chardonnay, acidity carrying the fruit well into the aftertaste. Screwcap. 13.5% alc. **Rating** 95 **To** 2024 $25 ✪
Reserve de la Cave Margaret River Cabernet Franc 2013 Consistently among the best Cabernet Francs in Australia, admittedly from a small field, and only 25 dozen made. The question must be asked whether this is Dr Samuel's dog preaching, the answer being it's more than that, with a haunting floral bouquet and

a finely detailed and structured red-berry palate. Screwcap. 13.5% alc. **Rating** 95
To 2033 $75

Reserve de la Cave Margaret River Malbec 2013 Poised like a ballet dancer,
unlikely for a Malbec, but this is no ordinary example, its plum fruit with a sheen
of silky tannins; French oak is also particularly well integrated, adding to the
length. Bottle no. 299 of 300. Screwcap. 13.5% alc. **Rating** 95 To 2028 $75

Margaret River Cabernet Merlot 2013 Rating 94 To 2033 $25 ◐

Emily 2013 Rating 94 To 2028 $39

Woods Crampton ★★★★★

PO Box 417, Hamilton, NSW 2303 **Region** Barossa Valley
T 0417 670 655 **www**.woods-crampton.com.au **Open** Not
Winemaker Nicholas Crampton, Aaron Woods **Est.** 2010 **Dozens** 10 000
This is one of the most impressive ventures of Nicholas Crampton (his association with
McWilliam's is on a consultancy basis) and winemaking friend Aaron Woods. The two make
the wines at the Sons of Eden winery with input advice from Igor Kucic. The quality of the
wines, and the enticing prices, has seen production soar from 1500 to 10 000 dozen, with
every expectation of continued success around the corner.

🍷🍷🍷🍷🍷 **Old Vine Eden Valley Shiraz 2013** Hand-picked, destemmed, some
whole bunches, 5-day cold soak, some wild fermentation, temperature-cooled
fermentation, matured in new and used French hogsheads for 18 months, not
racked or stirred. This is such good fruit sourcing/winemaking and marketing; it is
a super-elegant wine with an intense peacock's tail display of red, purple and black
fruits, and a burst of spice/pepper usually found in super-cool regions. It's the cat's
pyjamas. Screwcap. 14% alc. **Rating** 96 To 2033 $26 ◐

Barossa Valley Mataro Rose 2014 94/3/3% shiraz, grenache and shiraz, wild
yeast-fermented in used puncheons, 6 months on lees. Bright puce; the bouquet is
so fragrant it borders on perfume, the palate bone dry on the finish, juicy on the
journey through; a savoury element helps the texture. A lovely rose at any price.
367 dozen made. Screwcap. 13.5% alc. **Rating** 95 To 2016 $20 ◐

High Eden Riesling 2014 Single vineyard, hand-picked; chilled overnight, then
whole bunch-pressed. Good Riesling from start to finish, its varietal expression
unimpeachable, its length and balance likewise. Its best years are in front of it.
Screwcap. 12.5% alc. **Rating** 94 To 2024 $25 ◐

Old Vine Barossa Valley Mataro 2013 Hand-picked from a single 80yo
vineyard; open-fermented, 25% whole bunches, cool ferment, hand-plunged,
matured for 15 months in large used barrels. Very well made, as always. Black fruits
rule the roost, with earthy tannins in close attendance, but there's no bitterness
whatsoever, and the balance will ensure that the wine matures with grace.
440 dozen made. Screwcap. 14.5% alc. **Rating** 94 To 2028 $26 ◐

🍷🍷🍷🍷🍷 **The Primrose Path McLaren Vale Shiraz 2013** Rating 93 To 2018 $17 ◐
The Big Show 2013 Rating 93 To 2021 $22 CM ◐
Bonvedro 2013 Rating 93 To 2021 $26 CM ◐
Barossa Valley Pedro 2014 Rating 92 To 2016 $22 CM ◐

Woodsoak Wines ★★★★

38 Smillie Street, Robe, SA 5276 **Region** Robe
T 0437 681 919 **www**.woodsoakwines.com.au **Open** 7 days 10–9
Winemaker Duane Coates, Peta Baverstock **Est.** 2010 **Dozens** 800 **Vyds** 22ha
The Woodsoak farming property has been in the Legoe family for over 60 years, grazing cattle
and sheep. In 1998 Will and Sonia Legoe diversified into grapegrowing, followed (inevitably)
by a small batch of wine made in 2006 for family and friends; and finally the commercial
establishment of Woodsoak Wines in '10. The vineyard includes cabernet sauvignon, shiraz,
merlot and pinot noir; the Cabernet, Shiraz and Rose are named after their three children,
the Pyaar Pinot Noir after the Hindi word for love. The Legoes say, 'We ran out of children,
and there was no call for more.'

ȲȲȲȲ   **Raj Robe Shiraz 2010** Volume of flavour, mostly in the blackcurrant, mint and saltbush spectrum, followed in by gritty tannin and a sizeable push of leathery, creamy blackberry. It delivers a lot of flavour for the price. Screwcap. 13.5% alc. **Rating** 89 **To** 2025 $18 CM ○

Vijay Robe Cabernet Sauvignon 2012 Clearly varietal, all mulberry, dust and blackcurrant with briary, bushy edges. Some bitterness to the aftertaste, but not to an alarming degree. Will drink better in another few years than it does now. Screwcap. 14% alc. **Rating** 89 **To** 2024 $18 CM ○

Woodstock ★★★★★

215 Douglas Gully Road, McLaren Flat, SA 5171 **Region** McLaren Vale
T (08) 8383 0156 **www**.woodstockwine.com.au **Open** 7 days 10–5
Winemaker Ben Glaetzer **Est.** 1905 **Dozens** 25 000 **Vyds** 18.44ha
The Collett family is among the best known in McLaren Vale, the late Doug Collett AM for his World War II exploits flying Spitfires and Hurricanes with the RAF and RAAF, returning to study oenology at Roseworthy Agricultural College, and rapidly promoted to take charge of SA's largest winery, Berri Co-operative. In 1973 he purchased the Woodstock Estate, built a winery, and crushed its first vintage in '74. Son Scott Collett, once noted for his fearless exploits in cars and on motorcycles, became winemaker in '82, and won numerous accolades; equally importantly, he purchased an adjoining shiraz vineyard planted circa 1900 (now the source of The Stocks Shiraz) and a bush-vine grenache vineyard planted in '30. In '99, he joined forces with Ben Glaetzer; Scott passed responsibility for winemaking to Ben, but retained the responsibility for the estate vineyards. Exports to most major markets.

ȲȲȲȲȲ   **Collett Lane Cabernet Sauvignon 2012** Bright colour; is (unsurprisingly) very similar to the '13, this more savoury/earthy (with marked acidity), but with ample cassis fruit to carry those characters. This provides potent proof of the ability of McLaren Vale to provide cabernet of high quality. Screwcap. 14.3% alc. **Rating** 96 **To** 2037 $45 ○

The Stocks Single Vineyard McLaren Vale Shiraz 2013 From 31 rows of carefully tended south-facing vines planted in 1900. Has excellent colour, and manages to carry its alcohol without complaint, a heroic effort. Black fruits have a wrapping of dark chocolate proclaiming the region, oak and tannins providing structure, balance and longevity. Screwcap. 15.4% alc. **Rating** 95 **To** 2043 $80

Collett Lane Cabernet Sauvignon 2013 Deep colour; tasted 15 months prior to its release in Apr '16. It is a very good Cabernet in the making, all its components in balance: potent cassis fruit, firm, but not dry, tannins, and good oak. No hesitation in giving it gold medal points, for its balance and freshness ensure its long-term future. Screwcap. 14.4% alc. **Rating** 95 **To** 2038 $45

McLaren Vale Botrytis Semillon 2013 Gleaming green-gold; a wine largely made in the vineyard, the quality of the botrytis mould all-important (no black or grey rot); the wine is unequivocally sweet, but has more freshness to its stone fruit flavours and better balanced acidity than many of its peers. Enjoy now. Screwcap. 10.5% alc. **Rating** 95 **To** 2015 $20 ○

McLaren Vale Shiraz 2013 12 months' maturation in small oak. Deep crimson-purple. It has an utterly seductive display of luscious black fruits, dark chocolate, licorice and ripe tannins all singing from the same line on the same page. Screwcap. 14.8% alc. **Rating** 94 **To** 2030 $25 ○

McLaren Vale Cabernet Sauvignon 2013 A rich and potent mouth-filling style, abounding with blackcurrant and Swiss chocolate flavours, the tannins plentiful but round and ripe. It doesn't need any patience, but will fly high for many years to come. Screwcap. 14.8% alc. **Rating** 94 **To** 2033 $25 ○

ȲȲȲȲȲ   **Naughty Monte Montepulciano 2013** Rating 93 To 2025 $30
McLaren Vale Very Old Fortified NV Rating 93 To 2016 $45
Mary McTaggart McLaren Vale Riesling 2013 Rating 90 To 2022 $28
Single Vineyard Chardonnay 2013 Rating 90 To 2018 $20 ○

Woody Nook

506 Metricup Road, Wilyabrup, WA 6280 **Region** Margaret River
T (08) 9755 7547 **www**.woodynook.com.au **Open** 7 days 10–4.30
Winemaker Neil Gallagher, Michael Brophy **Est.** 1982 **Dozens** 7500 **Vyds** 14.23ha
Woody Nook, with a backdrop of 18ha of majestic marri and jarrah forest, doesn't have the
high profile of the biggest names in Margaret River, but has had major success in wine shows
over the years. It was purchased by Peter and Jane Bailey in 2000, and major renovations have
transformed Woody Nook, with a new winery, a gallery tasting room for larger groups and
an alfresco dining area by the pond. A link with the past is Neil Gallagher's continuing role
as winemaker, viticulturist and minority shareholder. Exports to the UK, the US, Canada,
Bermuda, Hong Kong and China.

ŸŸŸŸŸ **Single Vineyard Margaret River Chardonnay 2013** Has a complex web
of flavours extending from melon to peach to apple, underwritten by gently
citrussy acidity, toasty oak well integrated and balanced. Still on an upwards track.
Screwcap. 14% alc. **Rating** 95 **To** 2023 $32 ✪
Gallagher's Choice Margaret River Cabernet Sauvignon 2013 From vines
planted in '82. A full-bodied, but very well structured and balanced Cabernet,
anchored with sturdy blackcurrant fruit and ripe tannins. At the very start of what
will be a long journey, but with little or nothing to rattle the cage on the way to
full maturity. Diam. 14% alc. **Rating** 95 **To** 2043 $50
Single Vineyard Margaret River Shiraz 2012 2 years in American oak has
curiously had relatively little impact on the flavour profile of the palate, its savoury,
albeit fine, black fruits remaining in control – a near-identical play of the '11
vintage wine. Diam. 14.5% alc. **Rating** 94 **To** 2027 $32
Single Vineyard Margaret River Cabernet Merlot 2013 The hue is bright,
although not particularly deep; cassis, redcurrant and slightly savoury/black olive
twist are framed by oak and tannins; all the components are in balance, but need
some years to knit. Diam. 14% alc. **Rating** 94 **To** 2028 $32

ŸŸŸŸŸ **Kelly's Farewell Semillon Sauvignon 2014** **Rating** 93 **To** 2018 $22 ✪
Killdog Creek Margaret River Tempranillo 2013 **Rating** 93 **To** 2020 $22 ✪

Wykari Wines

PO Box 905, Clare, SA 5453 **Region** Clare Valley
T (08) 8842 1841 **www**.wykariwines.com.au **Open** Not
Winemaker Neil Paulett **Est.** 2006 **Dozens** 1200 **Vyds** 20ha
Local Clare families Rob and Mandy Knight and Peter and Robyn Shearer own two
vineyards, one to the north, the other to the south of Clare. The vineyards were first planted in
1974, and are dry-grown and hand-pruned. In all there is shiraz, riesling, cabernet sauvignon
and chardonnay.

ŸŸŸŸŸ **Single Vineyard Clare Valley Riesling 2014** Although the same alcohol
as Naughty Boy, this has an extra dimension at every point along the way, yet
without any exaggeration; lime/lemon blossom on the bouquet translates directly
onto the palate, with a distinctive slippery acidity lengthening the finish. Screwcap.
11.6% alc. **Rating** 94 **To** 2030 $22 ✪
Single Vineyard Clare Valley Shiraz 2013 Deep crimson-purple; the fragrant
black fruits and cracked pepper of the bouquet lead into a medium-bodied palate
that gives equal space to the gently luscious black fruits and the structure and
texture ex oak and tannins. A prosperous future. Screwcap. 14.6% alc. **Rating** 94
To 2033 $26 ✪

ŸŸŸŸŸ **Naughty Girl Clare Valley Shiraz 2013** **Rating** 91 **To** 2023 $18 ✪
Clare Valley Cabernet Sauvignon 2012 **Rating** 91 **To** 2022 $24
Naughty Boy Clare Valley Riesling 2014 **Rating** 90 **To** 2022 $18 ✪

Wyndham Estate

700 Dalwood Road, Dalwood, NSW 2335 **Region** Hunter Valley
T (02) 4938 3444 **www**.wyndhamestate.com **Open** 7 days 9.30–4.30
Winemaker Steve Meyer **Est.** 1828 **Dozens** 800 000 **Vyds** 87ha
This historic property is now merely a shopfront for the Wyndham Estate label. The Bin
wines often surprise with their quality, representing excellent value; the Show Reserve wines,
likewise, can be very good. The wines come from various parts of South Eastern Australia,
sometimes specified, sometimes not. Exports to Canada, Europe and Asia.

ΨΨΨΨΩ **George Wyndham Founder's Reserve Barossa McLaren Vale Cabernet
Merlot 2011** Firm, curranty red with leaf, mint and fruit notes working more or
less in harmony. Redcurrant notes add some lift, if not life. Can't argue with this,
especially given the vintage. Screwcap. 13.7% alc. **Rating** 90 **To** 2019 $22 CM

ΨΨΨΨ **Bin 777 Semillon Sauvignon Blanc 2013 Rating** 88 **To** 2016 $16 CM **○**
Bin 555 Shiraz 2013 Rating 88 **To** 2019 $16 CM **○**

Wynns Coonawarra Estate ★★★★★

Memorial Drive, Coonawarra, SA 5263 **Region** Coonawarra
T (08) 8736 2225 **www**.wynns.com.au **Open** 7 days 10–5
Winemaker Sue Hodder, Luke Skeer, Sarah Pidgeon **Est.** 1897 **Dozens** NFP
Large-scale production has not prevented Wynns (an important part of TWE) from producing
excellent wines covering the full price spectrum, from the bargain-basement Riesling and
Shiraz through to the deluxe John Riddoch Cabernet Sauvignon and Michael Shiraz. Even
with steady price increases, Wynns offers extraordinary value for money. Large investments
since 2000 in rejuvenating and replanting key blocks under the direction of Allen Jenkins, and
skilled winemaking by Sue Hodder, have resulted in wines of far greater finesse and elegance
than most of their predecessors. Exports to the UK, the US, Canada and Asia.

ΨΨΨΨΨ **Michael Limited Release Shiraz 2012** Marries elegance with depth and
power, elegance controlling the union. Whereas oak is often very obvious in young
Michael releases, here it is just a veneer for the supple plum, black cherry and
blackberry fruits, the tannins likewise perfectly pitched. Coonawarra didn't miss
out on the great '12 vintage. Screwcap. 13.5% alc. **Rating** 97 **To** 2052 $150 **○**
John Riddoch Limited Release Cabernet Sauvignon 2012 Has great
depth to its strong purple-crimson hue, telegraphing an ultra-powerful wine in
the tradition of John Riddoch, needing a minimum of 10 years to relax. In wine
terms, the case to delay its release to coincide with that of Grange is obvious, but
in marketing and/or financial terms it simply won't happen. A great John Riddoch
in the making. Screwcap. 13.5% alc. **Rating** 97 **To** 2052 $150 **○**

ΨΨΨΨΨ **Black Label Shiraz 2013** Excellent depth to the colour heralds a wine replete
with an abundance of purple and black fruits seamlessly woven together on the
medium to full-bodied palate; oak and tannins provide the framework for a wine
with a very long life ahead. Screwcap. 13.5% alc. **Rating** 96 **To** 2048 $45 **○**
Black Label Cabernet Sauvignon 2013 Investment in the vineyards and in
the winery is paying big dividends, viticulturist Alan Jenkins and winemakers
Sue Hodder and Sarah Pigeon with total control. The colour and sheer power
of the varietal expression achieved at this level of alcohol is totally admirable;
blackcurrant, blackberry and black olive are welded together with powdery tannins
and perfectly judged oak. Screwcap. 13.5% alc. **Rating** 96 **To** 2048 $45 **○**
Childs Single Vineyard Cabernet Sauvignon 2012 The vineyard was planted
in '69, and the vines were cut back and reworked in '09, giving what was always
a very good vineyard a new lease of life, appropriate given the tannin structure
of the wine, a foundation for its fresh, bright fruit profile. Screwcap. 13.5% alc.
Rating 96 **To** 2037 $80
Alex 88 Single Vineyard Cabernet Sauvignon 2012 Planted by Wynns in
'88, and right from the outset has produced exceptional cabernet, often included

in John Riddoch or Black Label. The exceptional quality of '12 has facilitated the release of enough fruit to make this wine, which is an exemplary medium-bodied Cabernet, its black fruits held in a fine web of ripe tannins and French oak. Screwcap. 13.5% alc. **Rating** 95 **To** 2037 $80

Shiraz 2013 Rating 94 **To** 2028 $25 CM ✪
V&A Lane Selected Vineyards Shiraz 2013 Rating 94 **To** 2028 $60
The Siding Cabernet Sauvignon 2013 Rating 94 **To** 2028 $25 ✪
V&A Lane Cabernet Shiraz 2013 Rating 94 **To** 2028 $60

♟♟♟♟♟ **Chardonnay 2014 Rating** 92 **To** 2017 $25 ✪
Cabernet Shiraz Merlot 2012 Rating 92 **To** 2022 $25 ✪
Limited Release The Gables Cabernet Shiraz 2012 Rating 92 **To** 2025 $30

Wynwood Estate   ★★★★☆

310 Oakey Creek Road, Pokolbin, NSW 2320 **Region** Hunter Valley
T (02) 4998 7885 **www**.wynwoodestate.com.au **Open** 7 days 10–5
Winemaker Peter Lane **Est.** 2011 **Dozens** 7000 **Vyds** 28ha

Wynwood Estate is owned by Winston Wine Pty Ltd, the Australian arm of what is described as one of the largest and fastest-growing wine distributors in China, with 100 wine stores established across the country. Wynwood has almost 30ha of low-yielding vineyards, including shiraz (8ha), merlot (5ha), chardonnay (4ha), verdelho (3ha) and muscat (1ha). It has some dry-grown 95-year-old shiraz vines that only produce an average of 0.75 tonnes of fruit each vintage. Plantings were extended in 2014 with durif (3ha), malbec and roussanne (1ha each). Wynwood also sources cabernet, franc, grenache and merlot from company-owned vineyards in the Barossa Valley. Winemaker Peter Lane has had a long career in the Hunter Valley, beginning at Mount Pleasant for six years, moving to Tulloch in the early 1990s, then Tyrrell's until 2012.

♟♟♟♟♟ **Reserve Hunter Valley Semillon 2014** The grapes were grown on the alluvial
      soils so suited to semillon; hand-picked and basket-pressed, with only the free-
      run juice used, a very low extraction rate given the limitations of the basket
      press in the first instance. The wine is super-elegant and lemony-juicy, its acidity
      particularly refreshing, but in balance. Screwcap. 11% alc. **Rating** 95 **To** 2029 $45
      Reserve Hunter Valley Shiraz 2013 From the same 70yo vineyard on
      red volcanic soils as the Capercaillie Shirazs. The wine has a complex array of
      contrasting dark-berry sweetness and earthy/savoury/leather notes that are strongly
      regional; has largely absorbed its French oak, and is elegant. Screwcap. 13.1% alc.
      Rating 94 **To** 2028 $70
      Grey Gum Hunter Valley Shiraz 2013 Estate-grown, hand-picked, open-
      fermented, 14 months in French hogsheads (30% new). A bright and lively wine
      with very good colour, and that poised elegance that marks Hunter Valley's '13
      vintage Shirazs. It is on the light side of medium-bodied, but doesn't want for red
      berry flavours or length. Screwcap. 13% alc. **Rating** 94 **To** 2030 $28 ✪

♟♟♟♟♟ **Grey Gum Cabernet Sauvignon 2012 Rating** 90 **To** 2025 $40

Xabregas   ★★★★★

Spencer Road, Mount Barker, WA 6324 **Region** Mount Barker
T (08) 6389 1382 **www**.xabregas.com.au **Open** Not
Winemaker Mike Garland, Andrew Hoadley **Est.** 1996 **Dozens** 10000 **Vyds** 80ha

Owners of Xabregas, the Hogan family, have five generations of WA history and family interests in sheep grazing and forestry in the Great Southern, dating back to the 1860s. Terry Hogan, founding chairman, felt the Mount Barker region was 'far too good dirt to waste on blue gums', and vines were planted in 1996. The Hogan family concentrates on the region's strengths – Shiraz and Riesling. The tasting notes for the wines which follow were made for and published in the 2015 *Wine Companion*, but are still the only wines on release, other than the '14 Mount Barker Riesling. Exports to the US, Singapore, Japan, China and NZ.

🍷🍷🍷🍷🍷 **X by Xabregas Spencer Syrah 2011** Spencer Vineyard contains the sandstone and granite soil type that is unique to the region. Similar intensity to Figtree, but with a slightly different and broader spread of aromas and flavours bringing up more exotic Asian spices, including garam masala, clove and black pepper. Screwcap. 14.3% alc. **Rating** 96 **To** 2041 $55 ✪

X by Xabregas Figtree Syrah 2011 Figtree Vineyard is planted on a north-facing slope with good elevation, on raw ironstone gravel (known locally as coffee rock). Densely flavoured, with intense black fruits, licorice, anise, briar, quality oak and ripe tannins; intensely savoury, yet the black fruits continue at the helm of the palate. Screwcap. 13.8% alc. **Rating** 96 **To** 2041 $55 ✪

Mount Barker Shiraz 2011 Deeply coloured, it is a potent and imposing entry-point wine, way below its single-vineyard siblings' prices, yet crammed to the gills with black fruits, anise, licorice, pepper and spice; the flavours continue to ricochet well into the aftertaste. Screwcap. 14.2% alc. **Rating** 95 **To** 2031 $25 ✪

Mount Barker Riesling 2014 Fully dry; this has the rectitude of young Porongurup Riesling, desperately trying to hide its light under a bushel. Without pontificating, you have to taste Great Southern Riesling over a period of years to be able to pierce the veil with confidence and see the promise which is as yet far from obvious. In racing parlance, follow the breeding, not the last race form. Screwcap. 12.7% alc. **Rating** 94 **To** 2034 $22 ✪

🍷🍷🍷🍷🍷 **Mount Barker Cabernet Sauvignon 2011** **Rating** 92 **To** 2022 $22 ✪

Xanadu Wines ★★★★★

Boodjidup Road, Margaret River, WA 6285 **Region** Margaret River
T (08) 9758 9500 **www**.xanaduwines.com **Open** 7 days 10–5
Winemaker Glenn Goodall **Est.** 1977 **Dozens** 70 000 **Vyds** 109.5ha
Xanadu Wines was established in 1977 by Dr John Lagan. In 2005 it was purchased by the Rathbone family, and together with Glenn Goodall's winemaking team they have significantly improved the quality of the wines. The vineyard has been revamped via soil profiling, precision viticulture, improved drainage and reduced yields, with production bolstered through the acquisition of the Stevens Road Vineyard in '08. The winemaking has undergone finetuning with selective French oak and natural fermentation playing an important role in the Xanadu wine styles. Exports to most major markets.

🍷🍷🍷🍷🍷 **Reserve Margaret River Cabernet Sauvignon 2012** Includes 5% each of malbec and petit verdot; destemmed and crushed, hand-plunged and pump-overs; extended post-fermentation maceration for 28 days, matured in French barriques (50% new) for 14 months before final barrel selection, then blended and matured for 2 months in used French oak. A very powerful exposition of cabernet with a cavalcade of flavours of cassis/blackcurrant, mulberry and even a hint of plum, all enhanced by quality oak and ripe tannins. Screwcap. 14.5% alc. **Rating** 98 **To** 2047 $85 ✪

Stevens Road Margaret River Cabernet Sauvignon 2012 From Block 3, crushed/destemmed to open fermenters, hand-plunged for 7 days, matured in French barriques (40% new) for 14 months, final blend assembled, then 2 more months in used French oak. Has that X-factor of Stevens Road, with a fragrance, purity and clarity of varietal fruit that needs no elaboration in the winery beyond that which it receives. Screwcap. 14% alc. **Rating** 97 **To** 2037 $65 ✪

Reserve Margaret River Chardonnay 2013 From the Lagan Vineyard, Gin Gin clone, hand-picked, whole bunch-pressed, wild yeast-fermented in French oak (35% new), lees-stirred during 9-month maturation, no mlf; a selection of the best barrels. This is the most complex of the '13 Xanadu Chardonnays, yet retains the hallmark precision and elegance of its siblings. Indeed, it half-succeeds in hiding its light under a bushel, for its extreme length can be missed if you rush from one to the other. Screwcap. 13.5% alc. **Rating** 97 **To** 2030 $85 ✪

ΨΨΨΨΨ **Stevens Road Margaret River Chardonnay 2013** From Block 2, hand-picked, whole bunch-pressed, wild yeast-fermented in French barriques (30% new), no mlf, a selection of the best barrels. A gloriously elegant and poised wine, effortlessly filling the mouth with grapefruit and minerally acidity. Don't think this is going to need time to tame that acidity; on the contrary, you will be searching for the next glass. Screwcap. 13% alc. **Rating** 96 **To** 2028 $65 ✪

Stevens Road Margaret River Shiraz 2013 Destemmed and crushed with open rollers to stainless steel for fermentation a 26°C for 5–7 days, 60% pressed early and finished fermentation in mainly new French oak, the batches combined for maturation in French barriques (35% new). Bright crimson, and equally bright fruit on the bouquet and medium-bodied palate, the fruit foremost, framed by supple tannins and integrated oak. Screwcap. 14% alc. **Rating** 96 **To** 2033 $65 ✪

Margaret River Cabernet Sauvignon 2012 89/6/5% cabernet sauvignon, malbec and petit verdot, small batch-fermented with 4 weeks on skins, then 14 months in French barriques (40% new). As expected of Xanadu, a distinguished Cabernet with excellent varietal expression portrayed with finesse; the tannin management ex the time on skins has paid major dividends. Screwcap. 14% alc. **Rating** 96 **To** 2035 $35 ✪

DJL Sauvignon Semillon 2014 A 63/25% blend plus 2% muscadelle; the sauvignon blanc was whole bunch-pressed and wild yeast-fermented in French oak, likewise the muscadelle; the semillon was crushed, free-run juice fermented in stainless steel with cultured yeast; barrels (10% new). The bouquet is a little reticent, the vigorous and vibrant palate most assuredly not; it has a mouth-filling suite of tropical and herbal/citrus flavours that gain maximum impact on the finish and aftertaste. Screwcap. 12.5% alc. **Rating** 95 **To** 2017 $24 ✪

DJL Margaret River Chardonnay 2013 Whole bunch-pressed, and 100% barrel-fermented; French oak (20% new); lees-stirred for 9 months; no mlf; 70% from Lagan Estate and Stevens Road Vineyards, 30% from Karridale. Exceptional value at this price given its breeding, but even more the rapier intensity to the white peach and cashew flavours; grapefruity acidity to close. Screwcap. 13.5% alc. **Rating** 95 **To** 2020 $24 ✪

Margaret River Chardonnay 2013 Gin Gin clone, hand-picked, whole bunch-pressed, wild yeast-fermented in French oak (25% new), lees-stirred during 9-month maturation, no mlf. It might be seen as a high-priced entry point for Xanadu, but the quality of this precisely articulated, intense and long wine is fully justified. All three '13 Xanadu Chardonnays have a marvellous fusion of white peach and pink grapefruit. Screwcap. 13.5% alc. **Rating** 95 **To** 2023 $35 ✪

DJL Margaret River Cabernet Sauvignon 2012 Includes 4% each of malbec and petit verdot, and 2% cabernet franc; fermented 5–7 days, a significant amount of post-fermentation maceration, 14 months in French barriques (20% new). Brightly hued, it has lively cassis fruit married to almost spicy tannins and sympathetic oak. Screwcap. 14% alc. **Rating** 95 **To** 2032 $24 ✪

Stevens Road Margaret River Graciano 2013 Destemmed and chilled for a 4-day cold soak, cultured yeast fermentation in small open fermenters for 4 days, pressed at 8° baume and taken to used barriques for completion of fermentation and 16 months' maturation in 1–2yo barriques. Vibrantly fresh and spicy, with a mix of sour and black cherry fruit, plus a garnish of fine, savoury tannins. Screwcap. 14% alc. **Rating** 95 **To** 2030 $65

Next of Kin Margaret River Chardonnay 2013 **Rating** 94 **To** 2020 $18 ✪
DJL Margaret River Shiraz 2012 **Rating** 94 **To** 2027 $24 ✪
Next of Kin Cabernet Sauvignon 2012 **Rating** 94 **To** 2025 $18 ✪
Margaret River Petit Verdot 2011 **Rating** 94 **To** 2031 $65

Yabby Lake Vineyard   ★★★★★

86–112 Tuerong Road, Tuerong, Vic 3937 **Region** Mornington Peninsula
T (03) 5974 3729 **www**.yabbylake.com **Open** 7 days 10–5
Winemaker Tom Carson, Chris Forge **Est.** 1998 **Dozens** 3350 **Vyds** 50.8ha

This high-profile wine business was established by Robert and Mem Kirby (of Village Roadshow), who had been landowners in the Mornington Peninsula for decades. In 1998 they established Yabby Lake Vineyard, under the direction of vineyard manager Keith Harris; the vineyard is on a north-facing slope, capturing maximum sunshine while also receiving sea breezes. The main focus is the 25ha of pinot noir, 14ha of chardonnay and 8ha of pinot gris; 3h of shiraz, merlot and sauvignon blanc take a back seat. The arrival of the hugely talented Tom Carson as Group Winemaker has added lustre to the winery and its wines, making the first Jimmy Watson Trophy for a Pinot Noir in 2014, and continuing to blitz the Australian wine show circuit with Single Block Pinots. Exports to the UK, Canada, Sweden, Singapore, Hong Kong and China.

ΨΨΨΨΨ **Single Block Release Block 6 Mornington Peninsula Chardonnay 2013**
Mendoza clone grapes are hand-picked, pressed directly into French puncheons for a wild-yeast ferment and maturation (without mlf) for 10 months. It is an exquisitely balanced wine, grapefruit and almond kernel to the fore, the finish of great length. Screwcap. 12% alc. **Rating** 97 **To** 2025 $95 ©
Single Block Release Block 1 Mornington Peninsula Pinot Noir 2013
Cold-soaked in small open pots; 14 days on skins; matured in French puncheons for 10 months. Bright crimson; the bouquet is highly floral and scented with intriguing Asian spices shot through its bevy of red and black cherry fruits, the palate combining all of the characters of the bouquet with a nuanced savoury twist. Screwcap. 13.5% alc. **Rating** 97 **To** 2025 $95 ©
Single Block Release Block 2 Mornington Peninsula Pinot Noir 2013
Made in the same fashion as Block 1. Spicy, savoury notes run through the intensely focused red fruits of the bouquet and very long palate; silky tannins are a feature, oak simply in the background; its length is admirable, and will repay cellaring many times over. Screwcap. 13.5% alc. **Rating** 97 **To** 2025 $95 ©

ΨΨΨΨΨ **Single Vineyard Mornington Peninsula Chardonnay 2013** An epitome of modern Australian Chardonnay, fruit, oak and natural acidity seamlessly woven together into a wine that will always have an element of restrained delicacy, but will flourish mightily with 5 years in bottle, and live much longer. Screwcap. 12.5% alc. **Rating** 96 **To** 2023 $45 ©
Single Vineyard Mornington Peninsula Pinot Noir 2013 Assured winemaking builds on the clarion-clear varietal expression of the fruit, red berries doing much of the heavy lifting; the fragrant, scented bouquet, with a wreath of spice, leads into a supple, perfectly balanced and proportioned palate, the silky superfine tannins providing a 10-year future. Screwcap. 13.5% alc. **Rating** 96 **To** 2024 $60 ©
Single Vineyard Mornington Peninsula Pinot Gris 2014 **Rating** 94 **To** 2016 $30 ©
Pink Claw Grenache Rose 2014 **Rating** 94 **To** 2016 $24 CM ©
Single Vineyard Mornington Peninsula Syrah 2013 **Rating** 94 **To** 2025 $30 ©

ΨΨΨΨΨ **Red Claw Pinot Noir 2014** **Rating** 92 **To** 2020 $24 CM ©
Red Claw Chardonnay 2014 **Rating** 91 **To** 2017 $24 CM
Red Claw Pinot Gris 2014 **Rating** 91 **To** 2015 $24 CM

Yal Yal Estate   ★★★★☆

15 Wynnstay Road, Prahran, Vic 3181 (postal) **Region** Mornington Peninsula
T 0416 112 703 **www**.yalyal.com.au **Open** Not
Winemaker Sandro Mosele **Est.** 1997 **Dozens** 1000 **Vyds** 2.63ha
In 2008 Liz and Simon Gillies acquired a vineyard planted in 1997 to 1.6ha of chardonnay and a little over 1ha of pinot noir. Since 2000 the wines have been made by Sandro Mosele (under the watchful eyes of the Gillies).

ΨΨΨΨΨ **Yal Yal Rd Mornington Peninsula Chardonnay 2013** A superfine and elegant style, bred to stay. White peach, apple and melon fruit is cosseted in subtle French

oak, the acidity fresh but balanced, the finish long and fine. Screwcap. 13.5% alc.
Rating 95 To 2021 $30 ✪

ΨΨΨΨΫ Yal Yal Rd Mornington Peninsula Pinot Gris 2013 Rating 92 To 2015 $30
Yal Yal Rd Mornington Peninsula Pinot Noir 2013 Rating 91 To 2023 $30

Yalumba   ★★★★★

40 Eden Valley Road, Angaston, SA 5353 **Region** Eden Valley
T (08) 8561 3200 **www**.yalumba.com **Open** 7 days 10–5
Winemaker Louisa Rose (Chief), Peter Gambetta, Kevin Glastonbury **Est.** 1849
Dozens 930 000 **Vyds** 180ha
Family-owned and run by Robert Hill-Smith, Yalumba has a long commitment to quality
and great vision in its selection of vineyard sites, new varieties and brands. It has always been
a serious player at the top end of full-bodied (and full-blooded) Australian reds, and was a
pioneer in the use of screwcaps. While its estate vineyards are largely planted to mainstream
varieties, it has taken marketing ownership of viognier. However, these days its own brands
revolve around the Y Series and a number of stand-alone brands across the length and breadth
of SA. A founding member of Australia's First Families of Wine. Celebrated 165 years in
November 2014. Exports to all major markets.

ΨΨΨΨΨ The Virgilius Eden Valley Viognier 2013 It's hard to imagine anyone being
disappointed by this. Its complexity isn't a challenge; it brings you along with it.
It's redolent of wheat and stone fruits, smoke and spice. It tastes simultaneously
interesting, different and comforting. It is, in short, quite brilliant. Screwcap.
13.5% alc. **Rating** 96 To 2018 $46 CM ✪
Paradox Northern Barossa Valley Shiraz 2012 Dense crimson-purple hue,
still 100% youthful; this is a mighty wine, with awesome concentration and power;
as always, a handwritten sticker lab label says nothing whatsoever about the wine –
extremely frustrating when it is as good as this. Black fruits, licorice and almost
velvety tannins fill the mouth with contentment, frustration to one side. Cork.
13.5% alc. **Rating** 96 To 2037 $45 ✪
Eden Valley Roussanne 2013 This only underlines the point: if Yalumba had
dedicated itself to roussanne, not viognier, the results would have been momentous.
A first release from young vines, this hits the jackpot; it is vital with what the
French call 'nervosity', the long palate with real drive ex citrus zest, the bouquet
with blossom and biscotti aromas. Screwcap. 12.5% alc. **Rating** 95 To 2023 $24 ✪
The Octavius Old Vine Barossa Shiraz 2009 Syrupy and luscious with dark,
coffeed flavour saturating its heart. It's a big, sweet wine but in many ways it shows
how such a style can and should be done. Licorice and jellied blackberry flood the
palate and extend out through the finish. It's sweet and full but it's not hot or dead;
it maintains a keen liveliness. Oak plays a leading role but fresh, dark fruit stands
right up to it. Cork. 13.9% alc. **Rating** 95 To 2030 $112 CM
Single Site Tri-Centenary Vineyard Vine Vale Grenache 2012 Deep, bright
crimson-purple; this is a thoroughly satisfying full-bodied Grenache, different from
prior releases, its texture and structure akin to that of old-vine Shiraz; black fruits
are on equal terms with red, and the tannins are firm, but balanced; the cork is
satisfactory. 13.5% alc. **Rating** 95 To 2027 $60
FDR1A 2012 I imagine the blend records for this wine, first made in '74, have
changed little over the intervening years. It's a very interesting wine, a blend of
73% cabernet, 27% shiraz, all from the Eden Valley; its combination of blackcurrant,
blackberry and plum all speak of quality. Cork. 13.5% alc. **Rating** 95 To 2035 $45
The Steeple Shiraz 2010 Rating 95 To 2032 $68
FSW8B Wrattonbully Botrytis Viognier 2014 Rating 94 To 2018 $29 ✪

ΨΨΨΨΫ Eden Valley Shiraz + Viognier 2012 Rating 93 To 2023 $34 CM
Tri-Centenary Vineyard Grenache 2011 Rating 93 To 2022 $60 CM
Eden Valley Viognier 2013 Rating 92 To 2017 $24 ✪
The Guardian Eden Valley Shiraz Viognier 2012 Rating 92 To 2027 $24 ✪

Old Bush Vine Barossa Grenache 2014 Rating 92 To 2016 $20 ✪
Running With Bulls Tempranillo 2013 Rating 92 To 2018 $24 CM ✪
Patchwork Barossa Shiraz 2013 Rating 91 To 2025 $22 ✪

Yangarra Estate Vineyard ★★★★★

809 McLaren Flat Road, Kangarilla SA 5171 **Region** McLaren Vale
T (08) 8383 7459 **www.**yangarra.com.au **Open** 7 days 10–5
Winemaker Peter Fraser, Shelley Torresan, Charlie Seppelt, Chris Carpenter **Est.** 2000
Dozens 15 000 **Vyds** 89.3ha
This is the Australian operation of Jackson Family Wines, one of the leading premium wine producers in California, which in 2000 acquired the 172ha Eringa Park vineyard from Normans Wines (the oldest vines dated back to 1923). The renamed Yangarra Estate Vineyard is the estate base for the operation, which built a state-of-the-art premium red wine facility in '10, and is moving to certified organic status with its vineyards. In '12 Jackson Family Wines purchased the historic Clarendon Vineyard from the Hickinbotham family. The Hickinbotham Clarendon Vineyard wines are made by Charlie Seppelt and Chris Carpenter. Peter Fraser is in charge of the Yangarra brand, and has taken Yangarra Estate to another level altogether with his innovative winemaking and desire to explore all of the possibilities of the Rhône Valley red and white styles. Thus you will find grenache, mourvedre, tempranillo, cinsaut, carignan, graciano, counoise and muscardin all planted by the end of '15; picpoul noir, terret noir and vaccarese are around the corner. The white varieties span roussanne, grenache blanc, bourboulenc and picpoul blanc, the latter three likewise due to be planted by the end of '15. Then you see ceramic eggs being used in parallel with conventional fermenters. In '15 he was named Winemaker of the Year at the launch of the 2016 *Wine Companion*.

🍷🍷🍷🍷🍷 Ironheart McLaren Vale Shiraz 2012 Hand-picked, open-fermented, hand-plunged, 25% whole bunches, 75% whole berry, wild yeast fermentation, 15 months on lees in French oak (40% new). Full, deep crimson-purple; this is a Shiraz with some of the accoutrements of Cabernet Sauvignon, but without any loss of its core identity; black fruits have great depth and tannin structure, the depth not greater than the length. Power with balance, and an unqualifiedly long future. 372 dozen made. Screwcap. 14.5% alc. **Rating** 97 To 2052 $100 ✪
High Sands McLaren Vale Grenache 2012 From the highest section (210m) of the '46 bush-vine grenache, hand-picked, mechanically sorted, cold soak, open-fermented, hand-plunged, wild yeast-fermented, on lees in used French oak for 12 months. Deep, bright colour; the complex dark fruits of the bouquet lead into a palate of exceptional depth and dimension, not least the firm tannins more often encountered in Cabernet than Shiraz, and almost never in Grenache. Amazing. 160 dozen made. Screwcap. 14% alc. **Rating** 97 To 2042 $125 ✪

🍷🍷🍷🍷🍷 Roux Beaute Roussanne 2013 50% fills a 675l ceramic egg, foot-trodden and fermented on skins, remaining there for 120 days before pressing; the other 50% is pressed into a second ceramic egg and fermented off skins. The fresh varietal fruit is held in a distinct chalky/pithy embrace, the length and balance faultless. The fascinating question is how long it will live. 68 dozen made Screwcap. 13.5% alc. **Rating** 96 To 2025 $65 ✪
McLaren Vale Shiraz 2013 12 vineyard blocks; 50% whole berries, 20% whole bunches, open-fermented. Deep, but bright, crimson-purple; this is full-bodied McLaren Vale Shiraz at its very best, not the least extractive or clumsy, simply complex, the result of top-quality fruit and highly intelligent winemaking. Screwcap. 14.5% alc. **Rating** 96 To 2038 $25 ✪
Small Pot Whole Bunch McLaren Vale Shiraz 2013 Open-fermented, hand-plunged, 25% whole bunches, cold soak, wild yeast, on lees 15 months in French oak (15% new), barrel selection. Bright colour introduces a wine that skips along a sunlit path, the black cherry fruit with flashes of chocolate, oak and tannins coming and going, here one moment, gone the next, then back again. 297 dozen made. Screwcap. 14% alc. **Rating** 96 To 2033 $45 ✪

Small Pot Ceramic Egg McLaren Vale Grenache 2013 Destemmed and mechanically berry-sorted, 50% crushed, tipped into two 675l ceramic eggs. Fermentation occurs in the eggs; remains on skins for 120 days post-fermentation, the pressings not used. The colour is clear and bright; a perfumed bouquet, then a palate brimming with bright red fruits supported by a spider web of ultra-fine tannins. It is the perfume that is so extraordinary. 94 dozen made. Screwcap. 14.5% alc. **Rating** 96 **To** 2023 $45 ✪

McLaren Vale Viognier 2014 Hand-picked from the 1.4ha estate block, whole bunch basket-pressed, predominantly tank-fermented, then used French oak for 4 months, lees-stirred. In typical Yangarra fashion, it has captured the best bits of Viognier, impressive to say the least, especially its fruit lift on the finish. 362 dozen made. Screwcap. 12% alc. **Rating** 95 **To** 2020 $25 ✪

Old Vine McLaren Vale Grenache 2013 From bush vines planted in '46 in Blewitt Springs' sandy soils; hand-picked, mechanically sorted, 50% whole berries, cold soak, open-fermented, wild yeast, on lees in used French oak for 9 months. Bright crimson; a Grenache with serious intent, its tightly focused and structured palate way above the norm, the pure core of bright red fruits precisely delineated and very long. A Grenache for the long haul. Screwcap. 14.5% alc. **Rating** 95 **To** 2038 $32 ✪

GSM McLaren Vale Grenache Shiraz Mourvedre 2013 A 49/29/22% blend of grenache, shiraz and mourvedre. Hand-picked, mechanically sorted, 50% whole berries, cold soak, open fermenters, plunged, wild yeast-fermented, kept on lees in 100% used French oak for 9 months. Brilliant hue; the wine effortlessly communicates its distinguished breeding, the medium-bodied palate with a silken line of fruit, then a thin coat of fine, savoury tannins. Screwcap. 14% alc. **Rating** 95 **To** 2028 $28 ✪

McLaren Vale Roussanne 2014 **Rating** 94 **To** 2025 $32

Yarra Burn ★★★★

4/19 Geddes Street, Mulgrave, Vic 3170 **Region** Yarra Valley
T 1800 088 711 **www**.yarraburn.com.au **Open** Not
Winemaker Ed Carr **Est.** 1975 **Dozens** NFP
At least in terms of name, this is the focal point of Accolade's Yarra Valley operations. However, the winery was sold, and the wines are now made elsewhere. The Upper Yarra vineyard largely remains. The lack of interest in the brand and its quality is as sad as it is obvious. Exports to the US, Indonesia, Malaysia, the Pacific Islands, China and Japan.

♀♀♀♀♀ Pinot Noir Chardonnay Rose 2007 8yo Yarra Valley rose should not sell for such a measly price, particularly when it presents such graceful, creamy, silky structure, pretty medium salmon hue, subtle mature complexity and secondary red fruit accuracy, revelling in its pinot noir core (a little more than two-thirds, the balance mostly chardonnay, with a dribble of meunier). It's intricately assembled and elegantly appealing, one of the best sparkling wines on the shelves under $20 this year. Cork. **Rating** 94 **To** 2016 $20 TS ✪

♀♀♀♀♀ Premium Cuvee Rose NV Rating 93 **To** 2016 $19 TS ✪
Premium Cuvee Brut NV Rating 91 **To** 2016 $17 TS ✪

Yarra Yering ★★★★★

Briarty Road, Coldstream, Vic 3770 **Region** Yarra Valley
T (03) 5964 9267 **www**.yarrayering.com **Open** 7 days 10–5
Winemaker Sarah Crowe **Est.** 1969 **Dozens** 3000 **Vyds** 26.37ha
In September 2008, founder Bailey Carrodus died, and in April '09 Yarra Yering was on the market. It was Bailey Carrodus's clear wish and expectation that any purchaser would continue to manage the vineyard and winery, and hence the wine style, in much the same way as he had done for the previous 40 years. Its acquisition in June '09 by a small group of investment bankers seems to have fulfilled that wish. The low-yielding, unirrigated vineyards have always

produced wines of extraordinary depth and intensity. Dry Red No. 1 is a cabernet blend; Dry Red No. 2 is a shiraz blend; Dry Red No. 3 is a blend of touriga, tinta cao, tinta amarela, tinta roriz and souzao; Pinot Noir and Chardonnay are not hidden behind delphic numbers; Underhill Shiraz is from an adjacent vineyard purchased by Yarra Yering over a decade ago; and Potsorts is an extraordinary vintage port style made from the same varieties as Dry Red No. 3. Sarah Crowe, who had carved a remarkable reputation as a winemaker in the Hunter Valley in a relatively short time, was appointed winemaker in the wake of Paul Bridgeman's departure to Levantine Hill after the '13 vintage. Exports to the UK, the US, The Netherlands, Malaysia, Singapore, Hong Kong and China.

ΨΨΨΨΨ **Carrodus Cabernet Sauvignon 2013** A selection from the topmost corner of the '69 plantings. Deep purple-crimson; the most striking feature of this striking wine is its purity. Add in its glorious varietal integrity, with cassis fruit wrapped around 100% new French oak, and the silky, supple tannins so rarely found with Cabernet, and you start to glimpse the future of a 35-year wine. Cork. 13% alc. **Rating** 97 **To** 2048 $250

Dry Red No. 1 2013 A 70/15/10/5% blend of cabernet sauvignon, merlot, malbec and petit verdot planted in '69, matured for 20 months in 100% new French barriques. Deep crimson-purple, it proclaims its regal birth with the first whiff of the bouquet, the first sip of the palate. Always great, this medium to full-bodied wine pushes past previous vintages with the sheer perfection of its flavour profile, mouthfeel, and, above all else, its balance. Screwcap. 13.5% alc. **Rating** 97 **To** 2053 $92 ✪

ΨΨΨΨΨ **Carrodus Pinot Noir 2013** Built on the best two barrels from the '69 and '81 plantings. Has great fragrance to the bouquet, and a silky texture to the extremely long and well-balanced palate; the latent power and depth of the palate attests to the dry-grown old vines on what is an exceptionally distinguished site. Cork. 13.5% alc. **Rating** 96 **To** 2030 $250

Dry Red No. 2 2013 A blend of 96% shiraz, 2% viognier and 1% each of marsanne and mataro co-fermented on frozen viognier skins. Based on '73 plantings, the first Côte Rôtie style made in Australia. A highly perfumed bouquet; its medium-bodied palate has more red-berry notes than that of the adjoining Underhill block; calmly elegant until the expansion and power of the finish. Screwcap. 13.5% alc. **Rating** 96 **To** 2043 $92

Chardonnay 2013 Basket-pressed with skin contact, fermented and matured in French barriques; despite mlf has crisp, natural acidity underneath multiple layers of stone fruit, fig and melon. Heroic, countercultural style. Screwcap. 13.5% alc. **Rating** 95 **To** 2025 $86

Dry White No. 1 2013 A 90/10% blend of semillon and chardonnay; crushed, with skin contact prior to pressing, fermented in used French barriques, 100% mlf. Bright straw-green; a complex bouquet with some smoky/funky characters notwithstanding the mlf, the palate built on a foundation of crisp acidity; the lemon/lemongrass fruit of semillon will grow and expand with honey and toast over the next 5+ years. Screwcap. 12.5% alc. **Rating** 95 **To** 2028 $86

Pinot Noir 2013 From estate vines; open-fermented in original 0.6 tonne fermenters; some stalk return; 11 months in French oak (40% new). Good depth and hue; the bouquet and medium-bodied palate are filled with plum and cherry fruit, spice and French oak providing texture and context. Has prodigious length, with a long and assured future. Screwcap. 13.5% alc. **Rating** 95 **To** 2030 $92

Underhill 2013 From the 3.2ha block of shiraz planted in '73 fronting Maddens Lane, purchased by Bailey Carrodus in the '90s, and long since given the same care as Yarra Yering's original plantings. Bright crimson-purple; a profound and rich Shiraz, with black fruits, licorice and savoury spices, the tannins fine and long. Screwcap. 13.5% alc. **Rating** 95 **To** 2038 $92

Carrodus Viognier 2013 Rating 94 **To** 2018 $160
Dry Red No. 3 2013 Rating 94 **To** 2028 $86

Yarrabank

38 Melba Highway, Yarra Glen, Vic 3775 **Region** Yarra Valley
T (03) 9730 0100 **www**.yering.com **Open** 7 days 10–5
Winemaker Michel Parisot, Willy Lunn **Est.** 1993 **Dozens** 5000 **Vyds** 4ha

Yarrabank is a highly successful joint venture between the French Champagne house Devaux and Yering Station, established in 1993. Until '97 the Yarrabank Cuvee Brut was made under Claude Thibaut's direction at Domaine Chandon, but thereafter the entire operation has been conducted at Yarrabank. There are 4ha of dedicated 'estate' vineyards at Yering Station (planted to pinot noir and chardonnay); the balance of the intake comes from growers in the Yarra Valley and southern Vic. Wine quality has consistently been outstanding, frequently with an unmatched finesse and delicacy. A representative range of wines was not received for this edition, but the rating has been maintained. Exports to all major markets.

♥♥♥♥ **Late Disgorged 2007** Extended time on lees has built a full straw-yellow hue, almond meal character, hints of woodsmoke, struck flint reductive notes and a chewy mouthfeel. It finishes dry and firm, with some bitter almond skin texture. A lesser vintage for this great label. Diam. **Rating** 89 **To** 2015 $55 TS

YarraLoch

Studio 308, 15–87 Gladstone Street, South Melbourne, Vic 3205 **Region** Yarra Valley
T (03) 9696 1604 **www**.yarraloch.com.au **Open** By appt
Winemaker David Bicknell **Est.** 1998 **Dozens** 3000 **Vyds** 12ha

This is the ambitious project of successful investment banker Stephen Wood. He has taken the best possible advice, and has not hesitated to provide appropriate financial resources to a venture that has no exact parallel in the Yarra Valley or anywhere else in Australia. Twelve hectares of vineyards may not seem so unusual, but in fact he has assembled three entirely different sites, 70km apart, each matched to the needs of the variety/varieties planted on that site. Pinot noir (4.4ha) is planted on the Steep Hill Vineyard, with a northeast orientation, and a shaley rock and ironstone soil. Cabernet sauvignon (4ha) has been planted at Kangaroo Ground, with a dry, steep northwest-facing site and abundant sun exposure in the warmest part of the day, ensuring full ripeness. Just over 3.5ha of merlot, shiraz, chardonnay and viognier are planted at the Upper Plenty Vineyard, 50km from Kangaroo Ground. This has an average temperature 2°C cooler and a ripening period 2–3 weeks later than the warmest parts of the Yarra Valley. Add skilled winemaking and some sophisticated (and beautiful) packaging, and you have a 5-star recipe for success. Exports to Hong Kong, Malaysia and China.

♥♥♥♥♥ **Stephanie's Dream Single Vineyard Chardonnay 2013** P58 (82%) and Mendoza clones. The Yarra Valley and the skill of contract maker David Bicknell have (unsurprisingly) produced a Chardonnay of very high quality (I wonder why only one gold at the Melbourne Wine Show '14, and a silver at the National Wine Show), with a gloriously racy and long palate that sets all the taste buds jumping with its matrix of citrus and stone fruits, oak a mere conveyance. Screwcap. 13% alc. **Rating** 96 **To** 2025 $50

♥♥♥♥♀ **Single Vineyard Pinot Noir 2013** **Rating** 93 **To** 2023 $30
Stephanie's Dream Pinot Noir 2012 **Rating** 92 **To** 2017 $50
Stephanie's Dream Cabernet Sauvignon 2012 **Rating** 91 **To** 2022 $40

Yarrambat Estate
★★★

45 Laurie Street, Yarrambat, Vic 3091 (postal) **Region** Yarra Valley
T (03) 9717 3710 **www**.yarrambatestate.com.au **Open** By appt
Winemaker Rob Ellis (Contract) **Est.** 1995 **Dozens** 1350 **Vyds** 2.6ha

Ivan McQuilkin has pinot noir, cabernet sauvignon, chardonnay and merlot in his vineyard in the northwestern corner of the Yarra Valley, not far from the Plenty River. It is very much an alternative occupation for Ivan, whose principal activity is as an international taxation consultant to expatriate employees. While the decision to make wine was at least in part triggered by falling grape prices, hindsight proves it to have been a good one. Exports to Singapore and China.

TTTT **Cabernet Merlot 2012** Bright colour; there are sharply etched flavours that are just too confronting now; one hopes that time will soften the profile of the wine. Screwcap. 14% alc. **Rating** 88 **To** 2020 $23

Yarran Wines ★★★★☆

178 Myall Park Road, Yenda, NSW 2681 **Region** Riverina
T (02) 6968 1125 **www.**yarranwines.com.au **Open** Mon–Sat 10–5
Winemaker Sam Brewer **Est.** 2000 **Dozens** 7000 **Vyds** 30ha
Lorraine Brewer (and late husband John) were grapegrowers for over 30 years, and when son Sam completed a degree in wine science at CSU, they celebrated his graduation by crushing 1 tonne of shiraz, fermenting the grapes in a milk vat. The majority of the grapes from the estate plantings are sold, but each year a little more has been made under the Yarran banner; along the way a winery with a crush capacity of 150 tonnes has been built. Sam worked for Southcorp and De Bortoli in Australia, and overseas (in the US and China), but after 10 years (in 2009) decided to take the plunge and concentrate on the family winery, with his parents. The majority of the grapes come from the family vineyard, but some parcels are sourced from growers, including Lake Cooper Estate in the Heathcote region. It is intended that the portfolio of regions will be gradually increased, and Sam has demonstrated his ability to make silk purses out of sow's ears, and sell them for the price of the latter. Exports to China.

TTTTT **Leopardwood Limited Release Yenda Petit Verdot 2013** Petit verdot thrives in warm climates, notwithstanding its home in Bordeaux. First, it retains excellent colour; second, it retains some black olive austerity along with its blackcurrant fruits; third, its tannins are auto-trimmed; fourth, it responds well to new oak. All of these characters are lifted to the highest level in this wine. Screwcap. 14.2% alc. **Rating** 95 **To** 2028 $20 ◗
Leopardwood Limited Release Heathcote Shiraz 2013 Dancing shoes of toasty vanillan oak but it's all business from there. Stern blackberry, clove and blackcurrant flavours move inexorably towards a grunty, substantial finish. Steal at the price. Screwcap. 14.5% alc. **Rating** 94 **To** 2025 $20 CM ◗

TTTTT **Shiraz 2013** Rating 93 To 2025 $12 ◗
Leopardwood Limited Release Durif 2013 Rating 92 To 2021 $22 CM ◗
Sauvignon Blanc 2014 Rating 91 To 2015 $12 ◗
Shiraz 2014 Rating 91 To 2019 $12 CM ◗
Heathcote Cabernet Sauvignon 2013 Rating 91 To 2019 $12 ◗

Yarrawood Estate ★★★★

1275 Melba Highway, Yarra Glen, Vic 3775 **Region** Yarra Valley
T (03) 9730 2003 **www.**yarrawood.com.au **Open** Mon–Fri 10–5, w'ends 8–5
Winemaker Contract **Est.** 1996 **Dozens** 25 000 **Vyds** 40.6ha
Yarrawood Estate has pinot noir (10.6ha), cabernet sauvignon (7.9ha), chardonnay (7.2ha), merlot (5.3ha), shiraz (4.5ha) and lesser amounts of sauvignon blanc, riesling and verdelho. The Tall Tales wines are contract-made from the estate-grown grapes. The cellar door and café are located on the Melba Highway, 3km north of Yarra Glen, overlooking the vineyard. Exports to Singapore, Japan and China.

TTTTT **Tall Tales Pinot Noir 2013** Bright, clear crimson-purple hue; has brightness, purity and drive to its display of small red and forest fruits; its length and balance underwrite its future and the appearance of spice and perfume. Set fair to sail. Screwcap. 13% alc. **Rating** 94 **To** 2023 $26 ◗

TTTTT **Tall Tales Shiraz 2013** Rating 91 To 2028 $26
Tall Tales Botrytis Riesling 2013 Rating 90 To 2018 $24

🍇 Yeates Wines   ★★★★

138 Craigmoor Road, Mudgee, NSW 2850 **Region** Mudgee
T 0427 791 264 **www**.yeateswines.com.au **Open** By appt
Winemaker Jacob Stein **Est.** 2010 **Dozens** 200 **Vyds** 16ha

In 2010 Alexander (Sandy) and Victoria Yeates purchased the vineyard known as Mountain
Blue under the aegis of Rosemount Estate. Part of the condition of sale imposed by vendor
Foster's was that the vineyard name remain the property of Foster's, the last Mountain Blue
vintage being '06. By '10 the vineyard was very rundown, with no continuity of vineyard
management, the vines riddled with trunk disease. A program of bringing the vines back to
full health is underway, but it is clear that this is going to take some time. Most of the grapes
are sold, 3–5 tonnes a year retained for the Yeates wine brand.

🍷🍷🍷🍷🍷 **The Gatekeeper Mudgee Shiraz 2013** Matured in new and 1yo French and
American hogsheads for 16 months. Good hue; it is a pleasant, light to medium-
bodied Shiraz, the accent on red fruits, and the oak helping to build flavour and
interest. Screwcap. 13.5% alc. **Rating** 90 **To** 2020 $25

The Gatekeeper Mudgee Cabernet 2012 Matured for 15 months in new
and 1yo French oak, which certainly makes its mark on the bouquet and palate
alike; it is only light to medium-bodied, but has good texture and structure, with
cedar, olive and spice nuances underpinning the cassis-accented fruit. Screwcap.
13.5% alc. **Rating** 90 **To** 2019 $25

🍷🍷🍷🍷 **The Gatekeeper Mudgee Cabernet 2013 Rating** 88 **To** 2018 $25

Yelland & Papps   ★★★★★

Lot 501 Nuraip Road, Nuriootpa, SA 5355 **Region** Barossa Valley
T (08) 8562 3510 **www**.yellandandpapps.com **Open** Mon–Sat 10–4
Winemaker Michael Papps **Est.** 2005 **Dozens** 4000 **Vyds** 1ha

Michael and Susan Papps (née Yelland) set up this venture after their marriage in 2005. It is
easy for them to regard the Barossa Valley as their home, for Michael has lived and worked in
the wine industry in the Barossa Valley for more than 20 years. He has a rare touch, the wines
consistently excellent, but also pushing the envelope; as well as using a sustainable approach to
winemaking with minimal inputs, he has not hesitated to challenge orthodox approaches to
a number of aspects of conventional fermentation methods.

🍷🍷🍷🍷🍷 **Divine Barossa Valley Grenache 2012** From vines planted in the early 1920s;
wild yeast open-fermented, basket-pressed, 24 months in French oak (25% new).
Quintessential high-quality Grenache; medium-bodied, it has a fragrant red fruit
bouquet and electrifying intensity and energy to the palate. Surely this and Second
Take put paid to the argument that Grenache has to have alcohol of 15+% to
succeed. This is so bloody delicious it very nearly brings tears to the eyes; do
I have to spit it out?! Screwcap. 14% alc. **Rating** 97 **To** 2032 $75 ✪

🍷🍷🍷🍷🍷 **Devote Greenock Barossa Valley Shiraz 2013** From 30yo vines planted by
the Materne family, 4th generation grapegrowers; wild yeast-fermented in an open
fermenter for 17 days, basket-pressed and matured in new and used French and
American oak for 20 months. It is an elegant, medium-bodied Shiraz, with the red
fruit drive that comes from this alcohol level, the silky palate drawing you back
again and again, the fine tannins an integral part of its indisputable high quality.
Screwcap. 13.6% alc. **Rating** 96 **To** 2038 $35 ✪

Divine Barossa Valley Shiraz 2012 Selected in the vineyard as the best parcels
of the vintage from 50yo vines planted by the Materne family; hand-picked, wild
yeast open-fermented, basket-pressed, matured in French oak (60% new) for
24 months. Still has a vivid, full crimson-purple hue; this comes at you from every
angle, luscious black fruits, ripe tannins and lots of quality oak. The components
are so perfectly balanced there is no feeling of weight, just utterly seductive
ambrosia. Screwcap. 13.1% alc. **Rating** 96 **To** 2042 $75 ✪

Second Take Barossa Valley Grenache 2014 52% whole bunches, 48% crushed, wild yeast-fermented, 28 days on skins, matured for 7 months in French oak (34% new). Light, bright, clear crimson; a super-fresh, vibrant and juicy red cherry, raspberry and almost citrussy, light to medium-bodied palate. This is unalloyed hedonism – there are no secret messages hidden within, just a single 'have me tonight' invitation. Screwcap. 13.4% alc. **Rating** 95 **To** 2024 $40
Barossa Valley Vermentino 2014 Has considerable presence on the bouquet and palate alike; citrus blossom and citrus zest drive the expressive, aromatic bouquet, happily picked up by the long and satisfying palate, grainy acidity at ease with the fruit flavours. Screwcap. 11.5% alc. **Rating** 94 **To** 2016 $22

Second Take Adelaide Hills Pinot Noir 2014 Rating 93 To 2024 $40
Devote Barossa Valley Shiraz Roussanne 2013 Rating 93 To 2023 $35
Barossa Valley Barbera Rose 2014 Rating 92 To 2016 $22 ☺
Vin de Soif 2013 Rating 92 To 2018 $25 ☺
Barossa Valley Pinot Blanc Pinot Gris 2014 Rating 91 To 2016 $22 ☺

Yellowglen ★★★★

The Atrium, 58 Queensbridge Street, Southbank, Vic 3006 **Region** South Eastern Australia
T 1300 651 650 **www**.yellowglen.com **Open** Not
Winemaker Trina Smith **Est.** 1971 **Dozens** NFP
Yellowglen is not only the leading producer of sparkling wine in the TWE group, but the largest producer of sparkling wine in Australia. In 2012 it announced a major restructuring of its product range, adding single-vineyard traditional-method wines under the Exceptional Vintage XV label. Trina Smith is a highly accomplished winemaker. Exports to the UK, the US, Canada, Japan and NZ.

Vintage Pinot Noir Chardonnay 2013 There's flesh here, both in succulent white nectarine fruit and in suggestions of the honeyed complexity of a couple of years of maturity, contrasting neatly with the crunch and zest of fresh citrus fruit. A primary, young and fruity style that finishes more sophisticated than one might expect for this price, with lingering acid line the highlight, and dosage appropriately subdued. Cork. 11.5% alc. **Rating** 91 **To** 2016 $19 TS ☺

Peacock Lane by Samantha Wills Cuvee NV Rating 88 To 2015 $23 TS

Yering Station ★★★★★

38 Melba Highway, Yarra Glen, Vic 3775 **Region** Yarra Valley
T (03) 9730 0100 **www**.yering.com **Open** 7 days 10–5
Winemaker Willy Lunn, Darren Rathbone **Est.** 1988 **Dozens** 60 000 **Vyds** 112ha
The historic Yering Station (or at least the portion of the property on which the cellar door sales and vineyard are established) was purchased by the Rathbone family in 1996 and is also the site of the Yarrabank joint venture with French Champagne house Devaux (see separate entry). A spectacular and very large winery was built, handling the Yarrabank sparkling and the Yering Station table wines, immediately becoming one of the focal points of the Yarra Valley, particularly as the historic Chateau Yering, where luxury accommodation and fine dining are available, is next door. Willy Lunn, a graduate of Adelaide University, has more than 25 years' cool-climate winemaking experience around the world, including at Petaluma, Shaw + Smith and Argyle Winery (Oregon). Exports to all major markets.

Reserve Yarra Valley Shiraz Viognier 2013 It has developed a distinguished pedigree over the past decade, but even in that context, this is a peak release. Form, flavour, flow and overall structure are all at the top of their game. So too the integration of viognier. Swish, concentrated plum and white pepper, anise, smoky oak and peppercorns. Everything works as a team. Tannin churns through much of the wine, though complex fruit flavour holds sway. One for the ages. Screwcap. 14.5% alc. **Rating** 98 **To** 2040 $90 CM ☺

Scarlett Pinot Noir 2013 Hand-picked, crushed, 5-day cold soak, 3 weeks' fermentation and maceration, matured in used French oak for 10 months. Bright, clear colour; an extremely complex Pinot with a seamless coupling of texture, structure and perfectly ripened pinot fruit. At the end of the day it is the silky cherry fruit, steering a middle course between strawberry and plum, that makes this wine what it is. Honours the memory of viticulturist Nathan Scarlett, who died in '13, aged in his 30s. Screwcap. 13% alc. **Rating** 97 **To** 2028 $200

🍷🍷🍷🍷🍷 **Reserve Yarra Valley Chardonnay 2013** It has that extra sweep, that certain something. It's almost enough to send a tingle down your spine. This builds enough and promises plenty. It sings with grapefruit, flint, spicy/smoky oak and white peach, all these flavours presenting as a unified whole. The finish is then persistence personified. Screwcap. 13.5% alc. **Rating** 96 **To** 2021 $90 CM
Reserve Yarra Valley Pinot Noir 2013 Some of the best wines are an acquired taste; others would appeal to just about anyone. This is one of the latter. Its quality would impress the keenest of enthusiasts and likewise seduce the novice. It's perfumed, seamless, neat as a pin and yet worthy of getting a little excited over. It essentially tastes of cherry-plum shot with spice, but the slip of oak and satiny texture, not to mention sinewy persistence, helps elevate it to another level. Screwcap. **Rating** 96 **To** 2022 $90 CM
Yarra Valley Shiraz Viognier 2012 The calling card of Yering Station, the style established by Tom Carson during his time as chief winemaker. The viognier is co-fermented, and the wine is matured in French barriques, part new. The fragrant bouquet and supple, elegant palate is charged with spicy/peppery red fruits, the tannins fine and silky. Long-term development is assured. Screwcap. 13% alc. **Rating** 95 **To** 2032 $38
Yarra Valley Chardonnay 2013 Rating 94 **To** 2019 $38 CM
Yarra Valley Pinot Noir 2013 Rating 94 **To** 2020 $38 CM
Village Yarra Valley Cabernet Sauvignon 2012 Rating 94 **To** 2032 $24 ✪

🍷🍷🍷🍷🍷 **Village Yarra Valley Marsanne 2013 Rating** 93 **To** 2018 $25 CM ✪
Little Yering Yarra Valley Chardonnay 2013 Rating 92 **To** 2016 $18 ✪
Little Yering Yarra Valley Pinot Noir 2013 Rating 92 **To** 2017 $18 ✪

Yeringberg   ★★★★★

Maroondah Highway, Coldstream, Vic 3770 **Region** Yarra Valley
T (03) 9739 0240 **www.**yeringberg.com **Open** By appt
Winemaker Guill and Sandra de Pury **Est.** 1863 **Dozens** 1500 **Vyds** 3.66ha
Guill de Pury and daughter Sandra, with Guill's wife Katherine in the background, make wines for the new millennium from the low-yielding vines re-established in the heart of what was one of the most famous (and infinitely larger) vineyards of the 19th century. In the riper years, the red wines have a velvety generosity of flavour rarely encountered, while never losing varietal character; the long-lived Marsanne Roussanne takes students of history back to Yeringberg's fame in the 19th century. Exports to the US, Switzerland, Hong Kong and China.

🍷🍷🍷🍷🍷 **Yeringberg 2012** Deep, but clear crimson-purple; a true field blend, with cabernet sauvignon, cabernet franc, merlot, malbec and petit verdot all included once any bunch sorting has been completed, cabernet sauvignon contributing the lion's share; will stand out in the decades to come as one of the greatest, its glorious array of red and black fruits folded within a silky tannin fabric, French oak totally integrated. Screwcap. 12.5% alc. **Rating** 98 **To** 2052 $75 ✪

🍷🍷🍷🍷🍷 **Yarra Valley Chardonnay 2013** Full-bodied attack, but it becomes more elegant as it drives through the palate. Complexity it certainly does not lack. Peach, bacon, spice and nectarine at first, but increasingly wheaty and dry pear-like from the mid-palate onwards. Wonderful length. Stunning wine. Screwcap. 13% alc. **Rating** 96 **To** 2024 $50 CM ✪
Yarra Valley Shiraz 2012 Seductively textured and fruited but its smoky, bacony, bunchy flourishes are the real heart starters. This has cellarability written all over it.

Dark cherry, plum and roasted nut flavours talk a pretty good game in themselves. Gorgeous blend of fruitiness and herb/spice notes. Screwcap. 12.5% alc. **Rating** 96 To 2037 $60 CM ✪

Yarra Valley Pinot Noir 2012 Bright, clear crimson-purple; perfect poise and balance to a wine with complex red and black berry fruit, 100% destemmed; 7 days on skins; 22 months in barrel (40% new oak). Spicy, savoury fruit flavours. Screwcap. 13.5% alc. **Rating** 95 To 2020 $75

Yarra Valley Viognier 2013 Looks bright in the glass and is alive with scent. Ginger, apricot and hay-like aroma/flavour. Balanced and textural. Bursts with flavour through the finish. Makes deliciousness look easy; no mean feat for this variety. Screwcap. 14% alc. **Rating** 94 To 2016 $35 CM

Yarra Valley Marsanne Roussanne 2013 58% marsanne, 42% roussanne. 50 dozen made. Soft, textural style with honeysuckle, peach and citrus flavours aplenty. No shortage of flavour but it finishes with daring acidity. Continues an outstanding run. Screwcap. 13% alc. **Rating** 94 To 2022 $50 CM

Yes said the Seal

1251–1269 Bellarine Highway, Wallington, Vic 3221 **Region** Geelong
T (03) 5250 6577 **www**.yessaidtheseal.com.au **Open** 7 days 10–5
Winemaker Darren Burke **Est.** 2014 **Dozens** 1000 **Vyds** 2ha
This is a new venture for David and Lyndsay Sharp, long-term vintners on Geelong's Bellarine Peninsula. It is situated onsite at the Flying Brick Cider Co's Cider House in Wallington. The 2ha of estate vineyard were planted to shiraz in 2010; the remaining varieties are purchased from growers on the Bellarine Peninsula. One of the ten best new wineries in the 2016 *Wine Companion*.

🍷🍷🍷🍷🍷 The Bellarine Chardonnay 2014 Matured in French oak, minimal stirring, partial mlf. Thoughtful winemaking has, it seems to me, had the right result; the wine is elegant and at peace with itself; the varietal flavours are perfectly modulated, stone fruit and grapefruit equally balanced, the freshness preserved by the quasi-Chablis decision to limit stirring but facilitate some mlf influence. Screwcap. 13% alc. **Rating** 95 To 2021 $35 ✪
The Bellarine Shiraz 2014 Whole-berry fermentation, moderate fermentation temperatures, French oak. Bright, deep crimson; has been allowed to fully ripen, and this has paid dividends, the intensity of the spicy/peppery black fruits of the bouquet and palate held neatly in check by fine, ripe tannins and good oak handling. A long life ahead. Screwcap. 14.5% alc. **Rating** 95 To 2034 $35 ✪

🍷🍷🍷🍷🍷 The Bellarine Pinot Noir 2014 **Rating** 92 To 2050 $35

Yilgarnia

1847 Redmond West Road, Redmond, WA 6327 **Region** Denmark
T (08) 9845 3031 **www**.yilgarnia.com.au **Open** W'ends & school hols 11–5 Oct–Apr
Winemaker Peter and Anthony Buxton, Michael Staniford (Consultant) **Est.** 1997
Dozens 4000 **Vyds** 13.5ha
Melbourne-educated Peter Buxton travelled across the Nullarbor over 40 years ago and settled on a bush block of 163ha on the Hay River, 6km north of Wilson Inlet. For the first 10 years Peter worked for the Department of Agriculture in Albany, surveying several of the early vineyards in WA; he recognised the potential of his family's property. The vineyard (chardonnay, sauvignon blanc, shiraz, cabernet sauvignon, semillon and merlot) is planted on north-facing blocks, the geological history of which stretches back 2 billion years. Exports to Singapore.

🍷🍷🍷🍷🍷 Denmark Semillon Sauvignon Blanc 2014 A glorious, generously flavoured and built wine, the bouquet opening with lemongrass likely ex the semillon, then moving on to allow the sauvignon blanc to send its flavour forces into play with gooseberry, sweet capsicum and Meyer lemon, the acidity a given. Value personified. Screwcap. 13.5% alc. **Rating** 94 To 2020 $17 ✪

ŶŶŶŶŶ **Denmark Semillon 2013** Rating 92 To 2023 $19 ✪
       Denmark Sauvignon Blanc 2014 Rating 92 To 2016 $19 ✪

Z Wine   ★★★★★

PO Box 135, Lyndoch, SA 5351 **Region** Barossa Valley
T 0422 802 220 **www**.zwine.com.au **Open** By appt
Winemaker Janelle Zerk **Est.** 1999 **Dozens** 5500 **Vyds** 1ha
Sisters Janelle and Kristen Zerk are the dynamic duo behind Z Wine. The Zerk family has been growing grapes in the Barossa Valley since 1846, but fifth-generation Janelle is the first family member to pursue a winemaking career, and has made wine in Tuscany, Burgundy (Puligny Montrachet) and Sonoma, California. Kirsten has a wine marketing degree from Adelaide University. Grapes are sourced from the family's Lyndoch vineyard. The Rustica wines are sold exclusively through Dan Murphy. Exports to China.

ŶŶŶŶŶ **Julius Barossa Valley Shiraz 2013** From 20yo vines planted by Janelle and Kristen Zerk, their father and grandfather. A supremely honest and generous Barossa Valley Shiraz, but by no means a sledgehammer; the bouquet is expressive, the medium-bodied palate very well structured and balanced, with ripe blackberry fruit neatly balanced by fine, ripe tannins and well-judged oak. Screwcap. 14.5% alc. **Rating** 95 **To** 2033 $45
       Museum Release Barossa Valley Shiraz 2006 A very complex wine with a multitude of aromas and flavours: briar, spiced black fruits, anise and bitter chocolate; it is medium-bodied, and has good length. Above all else, this yearns for a slow-cooked game casserole. Screwcap. 14% alc. **Rating** 95 **To** 2021 $50
       Aveline Barossa Valley Rose 2014 Hand-picked 70yo grenache, 30 hours on skins, then pressed and fermented with some solids. The highly aromatic bouquet and palate have toffee apple aromas and flavours in abundance, yet don't cloy, the finish bright and dry. Screwcap. 12.5% alc. **Rating** 94 **To** 2016 $20 ✪
       Section 3146 Barossa Valley Shiraz 2013 Good colour; the bouquet has intriguing cinnamon/coffee aromas, which continue as part of a broader matrix of plum and blackberry fruit; the tannin and oak contributions are in balance, and are positive. Screwcap. 14.5% alc. **Rating** 94 **To** 2028 $35
       Roman Barossa Valley Grenache Shiraz Mataro 2013 A 72/16/12% hand-picked blend. Plenty of depth to the colour, and even more to the aroma and flavour span; red and black fruits, smoked meat and cinnamon spice all gambol on the bouquet and medium-bodied palate. Doesn't take a backwards step. Screwcap. 14.5% alc. **Rating** 94 **To** 2020 $28 ✪

ŶŶŶŶŶ **Eden Valley Riesling 2014** Rating 93 To 2024 $22 ✪
       Rustica Barossa Valley Shiraz 2012 Rating 90 To 2018 $15 ✪
       Rustica Reserve Barossa Valley Shiraz 2012 Rating 90 To 2018 $30

Zarephath Wines   ★★★☆

424 Moorialup Road, East Porongurup, WA 6324 **Region** Porongurup
T (08) 9853 1152 **www**.zarephathwines.com **Open** Mon–Sat 10–5, Sun 10–4
Winemaker Robert Diletti **Est.** 1994 **Dozens** 1500 **Vyds** 8.9ha
The Zarephath vineyard was owned and operated by Brothers and Sisters of The Christ Circle, a Benedictine community. In 2014 they sold the property to Rosie Singer and her partner Ian Barrett-Lennard, who live on the spot full-time and undertake all the vineyard work. The cellar door incorporates a rustic café serving homemade lunches and platters. Ian's son Andrew has recently graduated as a winemaker and is working at Woodlands winery in Margaret River, but with no onsite winery, Zarephath will continue to have its wines made by Rob Diletti.

ŶŶŶŶŶ **Porongurup Riesling 2013** Has already developed a rich, fruit-filled palate with tropical overtones – enjoyable, but outside the usual Porongurup style, made to be enjoyed tonight. Screwcap. 12.5% alc. **Rating** 90 **To** 2018 $30

ŶŶŶŶ   **Porongurup Pinot Noir 2013** Rating 88 To 2017 $30

Zema Estate ★★★★★

14944 Riddoch Highway, Coonawarra, SA 5263 **Region** Coonawarra
T (08) 8736 3219 **www**.zema.com.au **Open** Mon–Fri 9–5, w'ends & public hols 10–4
Winemaker Greg Clayfield **Est.** 1982 **Dozens** 20000 **Vyds** 61ha
Zema is one of the last outposts of hand-pruning in Coonawarra, with members of the Zema
family tending the vineyard set in the heart of Coonawarra's terra rossa soil. Winemaking
practices are straightforward; if ever there was an example of great wines being made in the
vineyard, this is it. The extremely popular and equally talented former Lindemans winemaker
Greg Clayfield has joined the team, replacing long-term winemaker Tom Simons. Exports to
the UK, Vietnam, Hong Kong, Japan, Singapore and China.

🍷🍷🍷🍷🍷 **Family Selection Coonawarra Cabernet Sauvignon 2010** Matured for
22 months in new and 1yo French hogsheads. The pick of the Zema '10 wines,
and a fine example of Coonawarra Cabernet. Blackcurrant/cassis fruit is juicy and
intense, cascading through the palate and finish, sweeping the oak and tannins to
one side. Screwcap. 14% alc. **Rating** 96 **To** 2040 $46 ✪
Family Selection Coonawarra Shiraz 2010 Matured for 22 months in
American and French hogsheads. It has retained bright red colour, with no
change evident; the medium to full-bodied palate has a seamless display of black
berries, plum, mocha and supple tannins providing very good length and balance.
Screwcap. 14.5% alc. **Rating** 95 **To** 2032 $46
Coonawarra Shiraz 2012 Matured for 14 months in French and American oak.
The vintage was excellent, the vines are over 30yo, and the winemaking has been
content to allow the wine to speak for itself without elaboration; it is fresh, supple
and perfectly balanced, a style that often flies under the radar. Screwcap. 14.5% alc.
Rating 94 **To** 2032 $25 ✪

🍷🍷🍷🍷🍷 **Cluny Coonawarra Cabernet Merlot 2012 Rating** 93 **To** 2030 $25 ✪

Zig Zag Road ★★★

201 Zig Zag Road, Drummond, Vic 3446 **Region** Macedon Ranges
T (03) 5423 9390 **www**.zigzagwines.com.au **Open** Thurs–Mon 10–5
Winemaker Eric Bellchambers, Llew Knight **Est.** 1972 **Dozens** 600 **Vyds** 4.5ha
Zig Zag Road's dry-grown vines produce relatively low yields, and until 1996 the grapes
were sold to Hanging Rock Winery. In 2002 Eric and Anne Bellchambers became the third
owners of this vineyard, planted by Roger Aldridge in '72. The Bellchambers have extended
the plantings with riesling and merlot, supplementing the older plantings of shiraz, cabernet
sauvignon and pinot noir.

🍷🍷🍷🍷 **Macedon Ranges Shiraz 2011** Lightweight, cherried, spicy Shiraz with a
kick of juicy acidity. Dry tannin adds shape. Light but good. Screwcap. 12.5% alc.
Rating 88 **To** 2019 $25 CM

Zilzie Wines ★★★★

544 Kulkyne Way, Karadoc, Vic 3496 **Region** Murray Darling
T (03) 5025 8100 **www**.zilziewines.com **Open** Not
Winemaker Hayden Donohue **Est.** 1999 **Dozens** 200000 **Vyds** 572ha
The Forbes family has been farming since the early 1990s; Zilzie is currently run by Ian and
Ros Forbes, with sons Steven and Andrew, and the diverse range of farming activities now
includes grapegrowing from substantial vineyards. Having established a dominant position as
a supplier of grapes to Southcorp, Zilzie formed a wine company in '99 and built a winery
in 2000, expanding it in '06 to its current capacity of 45000 tonnes. The wines consistently
far exceed expectations, given their prices, that consistency driving the production volume
to 200000 dozen – this in an extremely competitive market. The business includes contract
processing, winemaking and storage, its own wines enticingly priced. Exports to the UK,
Canada, Hong Kong and China.

ŶŶŶŶŶ **Regional Collection Barossa Shiraz 2013** From various vineyards; cool-fermented 7–10 days, mlf in tank, matured for 12 months in French barriques. This is a surprise packet, notably fragrant and fresh on its expressive bouquet and lively medium-bodied palate. Now try to tell me you can't get character under 15% alcohol. Top value. Screwcap. 13.5% alc. **Rating** 92 **To** 2020 $18 ○
Regional Collection Yarra Valley Chardonnay 2014 Barrel-fermented in French barriques and lees-stirred. An absolutely authentic Yarra Valley Chardonnay, with the intensity and length the Valley provides with Chardonnay; the oak wasn't new, and it's a fair bet the wine was early-bottled, but at this price there's no cause for complaint. Screwcap. 12.5% alc. **Rating** 90 **To** 2018 $18 ○
Selection 23 Shiraz 2014 Parcels fermented in temperature-controlled stainless steel for 7–10 days, pressed to American and French oak for mlf, then blended. There's a staggering amount of wine – stylish wine – for the price. It has length, it has structure, it has complexity, all delivered in a light-bodied, drink-me-quick frock. Screwcap. 13.5% alc. **Rating** 90 **To** 2016 $11 ○

ŶŶŶŶ **Selection 23 Chardonnay 2014** Rating 89 To 2016 $11 ○
Adelaide Hills Pinot Gris 2014 Rating 89 To 2015 $18 ○
Selection 23 Rose 2014 Rating 89 To 2016 $11 ○
Adelaide Hills Pinot Noir 2014 Rating 89 To 2017 $18 ○
King Valley Prosecco 2014 Rating 89 To 2015 $23 TS

Zitta Wines   ★★★★☆

3 Union Street, Dulwich, SA 5065 (postal) **Region** Barossa Valley
T 0419 819 414 **www**.zitta.com.au **Open** Not
Winemaker Angelo De Fazio **Est.** 2004 **Dozens** 2000 **Vyds** 26.3ha
Owner Angelo De Fazio says that all he knows about viticulture and winemaking came from his father (and generations before him). It is partly this influence that has shaped the label and brand name: Zitta is Italian for 'quiet', and the seeming reflection of the letters of the name Zitta on the bottle is in fact nothing of the kind; turn the bottle upside down, and you will see it is the word Quiet. The vineyard dates back to 1864, with a few vines remaining from that time, and a block planted with cuttings taken from those vines. Shiraz dominates the plantings (22ha), the balance made up of chardonnay, grenache and a few mourvedre vines; only a small amount of the production is retained for the Zitta label. The property has two branches of Greenock Creek running through it, and the soils reflect the ancient geological history of the site, in part with a subsoil of river pebbles reflecting the course of a long-gone river. Exports to China.

ŶŶŶŶŶ **Single Vineyard Greenock Barossa Valley Shiraz 2012** Fleshy, ripe, strung with tannin, and remarkably vibrant and fresh given its high alcohol. Raspberry and blackberry notes with input from sawdusty cedar and clove. Well balanced and appealing. Screwcap. 14.9% alc. **Rating** 91 **To** 2024 $50 CM
Single Vineyard Bernardo Barossa Valley Shiraz 2012 Spends 24 months in French and American oak. Vibrant plum, raspberry and squishy blackberry flavour make for enjoyable drinking. At the sweeter end of the spectrum, but maintains an easygoing, fresh appeal. Screwcap. 14.7% alc. **Rating** 90 **To** 2019 $31 CM
Union Street Single Vineyard Barossa Valley Shiraz 2012 Makes a clear impression. Blackberry and mocha flavour with a gun smoke-like edge. Integrated, earthen tannin. Well balanced. Ample serve of juicy, dark-berried fruit. Screwcap. 14.5% alc. **Rating** 90 **To** 2019 $19 CM ○

ŶŶŶŶ **Grenache Shiraz Mourvedre 2012** Rating 88 To 2018 $33 CM

Zonte's Footstep   ★★★★☆

PO Box 2424, McLaren Vale, SA 5171 **Region** McLaren Vale
T (08) 8383 2083 **www**.zontesfootstep.com.au **Open** Not
Winemaker Ben Riggs **Est.** 1997 **Dozens** 20 000 **Vyds** 214.72ha

Zonte's Footstep has been very successful since a group of long-standing friends, collectively with deep knowledge of every aspect of the wine business, decided it was time to do something together. Along the way there has been some shuffling of the deck chairs, all achieved without any ill feeling from those who moved sideways or backwards. The major change has been a broadening of the regions (Langhorne Creek, McLaren Vale, the Barossa and Clare valleys and elsewhere) from which the grapes are sourced. Even here, however, most of the vineyards supplying grapes are owned by members of the Zonte's Footstep partnership. Exports to the UK, Belgium, Sweden, The Netherlands, South Korea, Thailand, Singapore and China.

ŸŸŸŸŸ **Chocolate Factory Single Site McLaren Vale Shiraz 2013** A gold medal at the San Francisco International Wine Competition and a silver medal at the San Diego Critics International Wine Competition says much about marketing horizons. It is distinctly fragrant, only just medium-bodied, with savoury elegance more than power its aim – counterintuitive for this reason, and making it an odd man out. Screwcap. 14.5% alc. **Rating** 94 **To** 2023 $25 ✪

Lake Doctor Single Site Langhorne Creek Shiraz 2013 One of three identically labelled regional wines, the others McLaren Vale and Barossa Valley, the making virtually identical, focused on the rich fruit each wine has, but tempered by the dictates of the region. Here there is the essential soft mid-palate fruit of Langhorne Creek, but it also has an admirable degree of finesse. Screwcap. 14.5% alc. **Rating** 94 **To** 2023 $25 ✪

Baron Von Nemesis Single Site Barossa Valley Shiraz 2013 Deep crimson-purple; a mix of satsuma and blood plum floods the bouquet with a spicy and meaty undertone; the generous medium to full-bodied palate picks up those characters seamlessly, adding ripe, powdery tannins. More powerful than its siblings. Screwcap. 14.5% alc. **Rating** 94 **To** 2028 $25 ✪

Z-Force 2012 The inky colour reflects the single-vineyard blend of shiraz and durif (aka petite syrah). It's all about raw power or, if you prefer, Z-Force. (Z-Force was a specialist allied forces unit that operated behind enemy lines in World War II, specialising in guerrilla warfare.) Sombre black fruits, licorice and earth are the drivers, tannins present, of course, but not the least aggressive; the curious outcome is a full-bodied wine that, with the right food, is approachable now. Screwcap. 14.5% alc. **Rating** 94 **To** 2032 $50

ŸŸŸŸŸ **Scarlet Ladybird Rose 2014** **Rating** 92 **To** 2016 $18 ✪
Avalon Tree Cabernet 2012 **Rating** 91 **To** 2020 $25
Violet Beauregard Malbec 2013 **Rating** 91 **To** 2023 $22 ✪

Index

♀	**Cellar door sales**
¶¶	**Food:** lunch platters to à la carte restaurants
⊢	**Accommodation:** B&B cottages to luxury vineyard apartments
⚬	**Music events:** monthly jazz in the vineyard to spectacular yearly concerts

Mornington Peninsula (Vic)